APA Handbook of

Industrial and Organizational Psychology

American Psychological Association • Handbooks in Psychology

APA Handbook of

Industrial and Organizational Psychology

VOLUME 2

Selecting and Developing Members for the Organization

Sheldon Zedeck
Editor-in-Chief

American Psychological Association • Washington, DC

Published by
American Psychological Association
750 First Street, NE
Washington, DC 20002-4242
www.apa.org

To order
APA Order Department
P.O. Box 92984
Washington, DC 20090-2984
Tel: (800) 374-2721; Direct: (202) 336-5510
Fax: (202) 336-5502; TDD/TTY: (202) 336-6123
Online: www.apa.org/books/
E-mail: order@apa.org

In the U.K., Europe, Africa, and the Middle East, copies may be ordered from
American Psychological Association
3 Henrietta Street
Covent Garden, London
WC2E 8LU England

Typeset in Berkeley by Circle Graphics, Inc., Columbia, MD

Printer: Edwards Brothers, Ann Arbor, MI
Cover Designer: Naylor Design, Washington, DC

Library of Congress Cataloging-in-Publication Data

APA handbook of industrial and organizational psychology / Sheldon Zedeck, editor-in-chief. — 1st ed.
p. cm. — APA Handbooks in psychology)
Includes bibliographical references and index.
ISBN-13: 978-1-4338-0727-5
ISBN-10: 1-4338-0727-0
ISBN-13: 978-1-4338-0732-9 (vol. 1)
ISBN-10: 1-4338-0732-7 (vol. 1)
[etc.]
1. Psychology, Industrial. 2. Organizational behavior. I. Zedeck, Sheldon. II. American Psychological Association. III. Title: Handbook of industrial and organizational psychology.

HF5548.8.A684 2011
158.7—dc22

2009048439

British Library Cataloguing-in-Publication Data
A CIP record is available from the British Library.

Printed in the United States of America
First Edition

Contents

Volume 2: Selecting and Developing Members for the Organization

Editorial Board

Part I

FOUNDATIONS OF SELECTION AND DEVELOPMENT

CHAPTER 1

WORK ANALYSIS: FROM TECHNIQUE TO THEORY

Frederick P. Morgeson and Erich C. Dierdorff

Work analysis is ubiquitous in organizational settings. As is often noted, work analysis serves as the foundation for virtually every human resource (HR) activity, including job description, classification, and evaluation; selection system development; job and team design; performance management programs; training program development; compensation program development; career management systems; workforce planning; and legal compliance (Brannick, Levine, & Morgeson, 2007). In short, work analysis is an essential HR tool. Given this plethora of uses, it is likely that work analysis data are the most widely collected type of HR data in both large and small organizations.

Traditionally, the analysis of work has been viewed as a process of collecting information about jobs (McCormick, 1979). As a consequence, research has tended to focus on a variety of technical and procedural issues, such as what, how, when, and from whom to collect data. More recently, however, scholars have begun exploring a range of theoretically driven issues associated with the collection of work-related information (Dierdorff & Rubin, 2007; Morgeson & Campion, 1997, 2000; Sanchez & Levine, 2000). One outcome of this expanded focus has been the suggestion that the term *job analysis* be replaced with the broader term *work analysis* (Sanchez, 1994; Sanchez & Levine, 1999, 2001). Given the recent focus on the broader world of work, coupled with our desire to move from a focus on job analysis techniques to a focus on work analysis theory, we use the term *work analysis* throughout this chapter. This encompasses traditional job analysis topics as well as more recent innovations in work analysis.

We seek to achieve two primary goals in this chapter. First, we offer some historical background and review of past work analysis research. This provides a sense of what research has been conducted in this area. However, we want to move beyond a simple summarization of past research. Thus, our second goal is to draw from the considerable body of work analysis research to discuss recent innovations and map out a strategy for moving work analysis research forward. Quite frankly, we want to shake things up a bit and try to stimulate some new thinking in the work analysis domain. We feel not only that work analysis is foundational to any understanding of individual and organizational performance, but also that there are still many important and interesting research questions to be answered. Thus, our goal in this chapter is to be a little provocative and approach work analysis in a slightly different way than it has been approached in the past, all in the hopes of moving this area of research forward.

To do this, we first provide an extended definition of work analysis. Our goal is to define work analysis in such a way as to not only incorporate past conceptualizations but also create a more flexible and inclusive definition that helps us advance future research. Second, we briefly review the history of

We thank Mike Brannick, Wally Borman, Ed Levine, Paul Sackett, Juan Sanchez, and Olga Smit-Voskuijl for their comments on an earlier version of this chapter. We really tried to incorporate your great ideas.

work analysis. Such a review enables us to understand the evolution of work analysis by identifying where we have been and what is still left to be done. Third, we discuss the range of practical choices that need to be made when analyzing work. A number of considerations go into making these choices, and we discuss the pros and cons of these choices. Fourth, we then discuss the Occupational Information Network (O*NET), which is the biggest innovation in work analysis in recent years. Fifth, we discuss a recent stream of research that has sought to explore how different factors can influence the quality of work analysis information. Sixth, we then highlight a range of potential future research directions for work analysis. Finally, we conclude with a discussion of how we can take a more theoretical view of work analysis as research proceeds into the 21st century. (See also Vol. 1, chap. 13, this handbook.)

DEFINING WORK ANALYSIS

Work analysis can be defined as the systematic investigation of (a) work role requirements and (b) the broader context within which work roles are enacted. Because this definition differs somewhat from past definitions, further explanation is warranted. We use the term *work role requirement* as a short-hand way of describing both work and worker requirements. Work requirements would include such things as the tasks performed and the general responsibilities (or work activities) of those performing the work. Worker requirements would include the different types of knowledge, skill, ability, and other characteristics that are needed to perform the work (see also Dierdorff & Morgeson, 2007). Such a distinction between work and worker requirements is consistent with the "two worlds of human behavioral taxonomies" identified by Dunnette (1976) and the "activity" and "attribute" distinction more recently articulated by Sackett and Laczo (2003).

In addition, we have deliberately chosen to focus on roles rather than the traditional focus on jobs for five reasons. First, as an expected pattern or set of behaviors interrelated with the behaviors of others (Biddle, 1979; Katz & Kahn, 1978; Stewart, Fulmer, & Barrick, 2005), a role subsumes the traditional work requirements of both tasks and responsibilities and thus helps integrate across work requirements. This offers a more flexible language with which to describe and discuss work. Second, a focus on roles enables the explicit acknowledgment of connections to and among other role holders, as well as the embeddedness of roles in the broader work context. Although often touched on in traditional definitions, this has tended to be neglected in practice. Third, one of the traditional criticisms of work analysis is that it tends to view jobs as static entities (Guion, 1993). By focusing on roles, we move away from a more static conceptualization of jobs to a more flexible roles orientation. Thus, work analysis could consider not only prescribed or established task elements, but also discretionary or emergent task elements (Ilgen & Hollenbeck, 1991; Morgeson & Humphrey, 2008). Fourth, focusing on jobs tends to place an emphasis on work activities, leading some to conceptualize work analysis in a narrow fashion (Harvey, 1991). However, it is clear that work analysis includes the study of both work activities and worker attributes (Sackett & Laczo, 2003; Sanchez & Levine, 2001). Considering roles and role enactment leads more naturally to a consideration of worker attributes.

Fifth, focusing on jobs places an emphasis on individual job incumbents. Although this is often justified given the uses of work analysis data, it tends to ignore the fact that jobs are situated in a larger team and organizational context. One problem with focusing primarily on individual jobs is that there is an insufficient link to an organization's business goals and strategies (Schippmann et al., 2000), prompting many to pursue a quasi-work analytic approach like competency modeling. The role concept, in contrast, is implicitly multilevel. For example, a role can be described in terms of individual role holder work activities, the combination of roles that exist within a team that produces interdependent collective action, and the structure of organizations as a system of roles (Katz & Kahn, 1978). Thus, in conducting a work analysis, a focus on roles could alert the analyst to consider how individual roles connect to the broader system of roles within the organization and the implications of these connections for the specific role under consideration.

HISTORY OF WORK ANALYSIS

Collecting work-related information has long been important to large-scale human endeavors. For example, Mitchell, Bennett, and Strickland (1999) pointed out that the first effort to document information about work could be seen over 3,000 years ago in the Imperial Court of China (circa 1115 B.C.). During the more recent times of the past century, Münsterberg (1913) pioneered systematic methods for estimating job requirements for personnel selection purposes and job design. The first history of work analysis was compiled by Uhrbrock (1922), in which he emphasized using job analysis for setting performance standards and introduced the need to identify personal attributes associated with successful job performance (Wilson, 2006). Perhaps in a bit of historical irony, Frederick Taylor actually used the term *work analysis* in the early 1900s (Cunningham, 2000), despite our modern day depiction of scientific management as having an exclusive emphasis on reductionism to the most molecular of behavioral elements!

Even with these rich historical linkages, what we have come to currently recognize as the field of work analysis has its firmest roots in research conducted after the 1940s. Because there have been several excellent reviews of this period (e.g., Mitchell, 1988; Mitchell & Driskill, 1996; Primoff & Fine, 1988), we do not discuss these historical developments in detail. Instead, we focus on trends in work analysis research over the last 50 years. Although published work analysis research certainly predates 1960, we felt that a nearly half-century snapshot would be sufficient for depicting any important trends. We searched PsycINFO for work analysis research published since 1960 using keywords such as *job analysis, work analysis, job specification,* and so forth. We restricted our search to only research published in peer-reviewed journals, thus excluding dissertations, technical reports, and books. Finally, an article's primary focus had to be work analysis to be included. Thus, articles that simply presented the results of work analysis (e.g., job description of a nursing occupation) and tangentially related articles not specifically focused on work analysis (e.g., job redesign, synthetic validity) were excluded.

Figure 1.1 displays the frequency of work analysis publications across the 48-year time period. In total, the search produced 193 work analysis journal articles that have been published in peer-reviewed journals. When examined by each decade, close to one third (30%) of the articles were published during the 1980s alone. Approximately 7% of the publications were during the 1960s, and 17% were during the 1970s. The publication percentages for articles in the 1990s and 2000–2008 were nearly equivalent

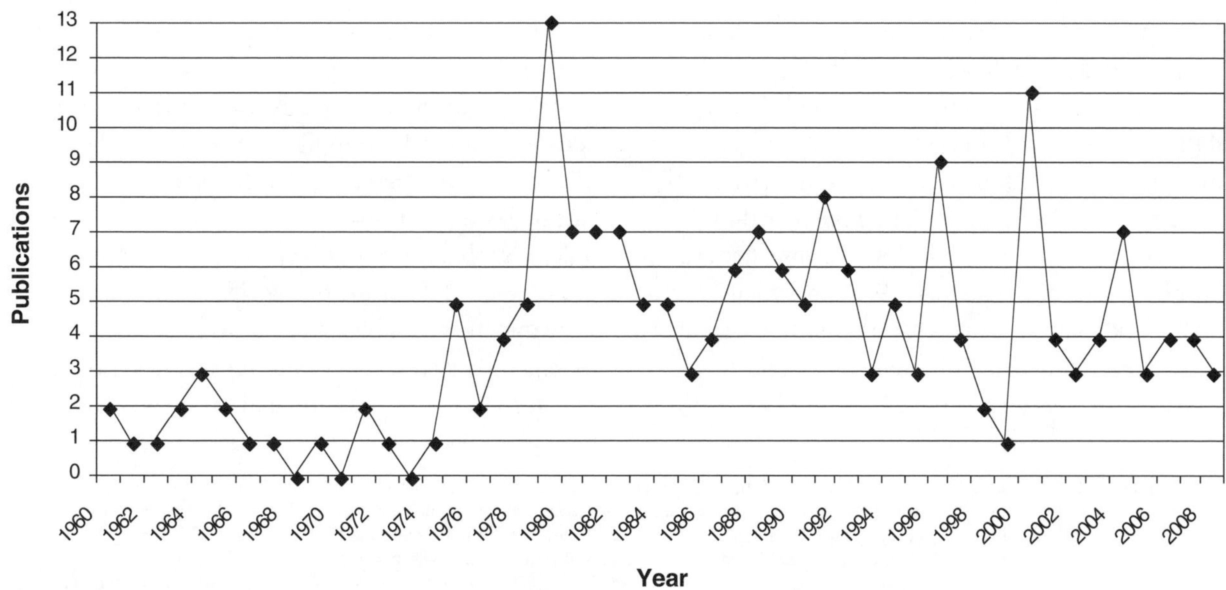

FIGURE 1.1. Frequency of work analysis publications from 1960–2008.

(about 23%). Thus, with respect to pure volume, it appears that almost as many work analysis articles have been published before and after 1990 (54% compared with 46%). The pattern of publications after this date also appears to display greater variability, as represented by the larger peaks and valleys in the figure. Additionally, around this time, it was widely discussed among work analysis scholars that work analysis research was not garnering much respect (i.e., being published) in industrial–organizational (I/O) and management journals (Cunningham, 1989). However, a more nuanced examination of previous work analysis articles reveals trends that may shed light on this historical concern.

The data in Figure 1.1 clearly show that work analysis research is alive and well and is being published in peer-reviewed journals, albeit with slightly more variability in volume in recent years. Note, however, that this conclusion is in an absolute sense (i.e., exclusively focusing on work analysis research). Cascio and Aguinis (2008) recently found in their content analysis of *Journal of Applied Psychology* and *Personnel Psychology* that research within the work analysis domain has waned relative to other research domains within I/O psychology. With this in mind, we examined what journals have published work analysis articles and how the publishing outlets may have changed over time. To accomplish this, we categorized the collected work analysis articles into two broad groupings: (a) those published in one of the "top seven" journals (as identified by Podsakoff, MacKenzie, Bachrach, & Podsakoff, 2005) and (b) those published in any other journal. The results of this analysis are displayed in Figure 1.2.[1] These findings show a striking trend toward proportionally fewer work analysis articles being published in the top seven journals across the 48-year time period. For example, from 1960 to 1979, approximately 77% of all work analysis articles were published in one of the top seven journals. Although this proportion decreased to 58% during the 1980s, the overall number of work analysis articles in top seven journals still increased from the previous decade. The most noticeable decrease began in the 1990s, where only about 28% of work analysis articles were published in top seven journals, and this downward trend continues today (e.g., 27% since 2000). Collectively, these results suggest that work analysis research is increasingly absent from the most influential journals.

Such a decrease is unfortunate, in part because of the influence the top journals have on shaping the field. For example, one might wonder whether the substantial volume of research concerning the Position Analysis Questionnaire (PAQ; McCormick, Jeanneret, & Mecham, 1972) would have been conducted (and subsequently published) if the original research had not appeared in a monograph within *Journal of Applied Psychology,* one of the top applied psychology journals. Or, as another example, whether there would have been such widespread acceptance and ensuing use of the critical-incident technique had it not been published in *Psychological Bulletin* (Flanagan, 1954), a top psychology journal.

To get a better sense of publication trends over time, we qualitatively reviewed the work analysis articles to see if we could further discern any patterns in the type of research being published over the last 50 years. This examination produced 10 broad categories shown in Table 1.1. This table also provides the percentages of articles falling into each category. These data show that, with the exception of research examining rater training and rating scales, work analysis research has a relatively even distribution across the topical groupings (ranging from 8% to 15%). However, percentage differences for some categories were apparent with respect to the nearly 5 decades that the research spans. For example, all of the research focusing on specific work analysis instruments was published prior to 1990, as well as the majority of research (75%) regarding various analytic techniques (e.g., factor analysis). The majority of

[1] Podsakoff et al. (2005) divided management-related journals, which includes top I/O psychology journals, into quartiles on the basis of the journal's impact (as assessed by citations per article). The top quartile consisted of the *Academy of Management Journal, Academy of Management Review, Administrative Science Quarterly, Journal of Applied Psychology, Organizational Behavior and Human Decision Processes, Personnel Psychology,* and *Strategic Management Journal.* These "top seven" journals accounted for almost 61% of all citations between 1981 and 1999. Moreover, the top seven journals "averaged almost six times more citations per paper (23.93 vs. 4.54) from 1981 to 1999 than the seven bottom journals" (Podsakoff et al., 2005, p. 481). Although some of these journals do not necessarily publish work analysis articles, many of them do. These journals are, however, highly influential and thus represent a good way to examine the prominence of work analysis research in the field of psychology.

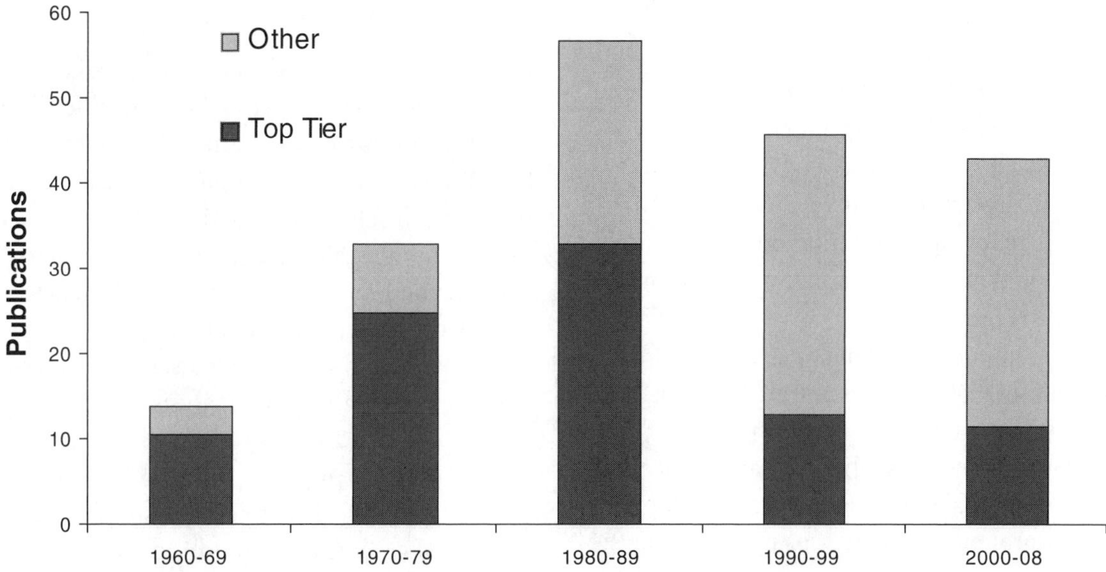

FIGURE 1.2. **Work analysis publications in the top seven journals (top tier) and all other journals.**

research on job classification and clustering occurred during the 1970s and 1980s (70%). In comparison, articles published on three of the topics (development of instruments, procedures, or taxonomies; uses for work analysis information or results; and general or topical reviews) were rather evenly spread throughout the 5 decades. Finally, research in the area of reliability and validity and in the area of factors influencing ratings was primarily conducted since 1990 (74% and 57%, respectively).

This qualitative investigation yields two key insights. First, there are notable omissions in past work analysis research. For example, Sackett and Laczo (2003) previously described several important changes in work analysis practice that had taken place by the time of their review of the field. These changes included personality-oriented work analysis, competency modeling, cognitive task analysis, strategic job analysis, and issues of accuracy in work analysis. However, published research on most of these changes remains largely absent. That is, the empirical work analysis literature offers little evidence regarding a host of questions surrounding the ramifications of these changes (e.g., issues of utility, reliability, validity, legality, acceptance).

Furthermore, Sackett and Laczo (2003) noted this same empirical paucity over 5 years ago. For example, from our literature search, since 2003, only a single published article examined the use of strategic job analysis (e.g., Siddique, 2004), and this was merely an indirect examination. The same situation was found for personality-oriented work analysis as well (e.g., Cucina, Vasilopoulos, & Sehgal, 2005). Two exceptions to this scarcity trend are in the areas of competency modeling and issues of accuracy. Since 2003, at least four articles have included examinations related to competency modeling (e.g., Goffin & Woycheshin, 2006; Lievens & Sanchez, 2007; Lievens, Sanchez, & De Corte, 2004; Morgeson, Delaney-Klinger, Mayfield, Ferrara, &

TABLE 1.1

Work Analysis Topics Studied

Category	Percent
Development of instruments, procedures, or taxonomies	13.47
Reliability and validity	13.99
Instrument-specific research	10.36
Uses for job analysis information–results	13.47
General or topical review	12.95
Job classification and clustering	8.81
Rater training	2.59
Factors influencing ratings	14.51
Rating scales	1.04
Other analytic techniques	8.29

Campion, 2004) and five articles have focused on factors related to accuracy (e.g., Dierdorff & Rubin, 2007; Dierdorff & Wilson, 2003; K. Prien, Prien, & Wooten, 2003; Van Iddekinge, Putka, Raymark, & Eidson, 2005; Wang, 2003). Thus, it appears that work analysis research needs to begin to focus research attention on some of the techniques and changes that have occurred in work analysis practice.

A second implication of our analysis is that the topical focus of work analysis research has not changed all that much over the past 50 years. This is especially true for work analysis research concerned with more technical questions, such as developing new procedures or taxonomies, using work analysis data for different purposes (e.g., content-related validity for test creation), and so forth. Thus, it appears that considerable work analysis research continues to focus on technical issues rather than theoretical issues. Perhaps this can explain the relative decrease in work analysis research in the top journals. As the field of I/O psychology has matured, empirical research is expected to make stronger theoretical contributions. To the extent that work analysis research is unable to contribute theoretically, it will likely be shut out from the top journals in the field.

However, there does appear to be some hope, as there has been a recent increase in the amount of work analysis research going beyond these traditional areas. One common thread among this research is the focus on a theory-driven understanding of the various nonjob factors that influence work analysis judgments. For example, this research has been conceptually driven using cognitive (schema) theory (e.g., Lievens & Sanchez, 2007), role theory (e.g., Dierdorff & Morgeson, 2007; Dierdorff & Rubin, 2007), and impression management (self-presentation) theory (e.g., Morgeson et al., 2004). Important to work analysis research, this recent trend may indicate that a reinvigoration of the topics examined in work analysis, as well as a grounding of such research in relevant psychological theory, is both fruitful and necessary. We return to these points in greater detail within ensuing sections of this chapter.

WORK ANALYSIS CHOICES

Conducting a work analysis involves making numerous choices. These choices reflect the different ways a work analysis can be conducted in practice. We first discuss the range of choices that can be made, including the choice of descriptor, the methods to use, the rating scales to use (if using the questionnaire method), and the sources of work analysis data. Because these choices are driven by the purpose of the work analysis, we then discuss the intersection of the purposes and work analysis choices.

Descriptor Type

Broadly speaking, descriptors are simply the various features of work examined during a work analysis (Brannick et al., 2007). There are three major types of descriptors that can be used in work analysis. The first concerns the requirements of the work itself and involves the activities performed by workers (Sackett & Laczo, 2003). The two most commonly discussed work requirements are the specific tasks performed and more general work responsibilities. Tasks are collections of specific work elements and include actions, the object of the action, and the purpose or results of the action (Fine & Getkate, 1995) as individuals fulfill their work roles. Of importance, tasks are typically specific to a particular work role. For example, the tasks for an industrial machinery mechanic would include such things as disassembling machinery and equipment to remove parts and make repairs and repairing and replacing broken or malfunctioning components of machinery and equipment.

Responsibilities are collections of related tasks that represent a set of generic behaviors applicable across a wide variety of work roles (Cunningham, 1996). As such, responsibilities are broad activity or behavior statements that are aggregates of several highly related behaviors used in accomplishing major work goals (Jeanneret, Borman, Kubisiak, & Hanson, 1999). Continuing our example, responsibilities for an industrial machinery mechanic would include repairing and maintaining equipment and inspecting equipment, structures, or material.

The second major type of descriptor concerns worker requirements and involves a consideration of the worker characteristics needed to successfully perform the work (Sackett & Laczo, 2003). Four commonly discussed worker requirements include knowledge, skill, ability, and other characteristics. Knowledge can be defined as collections of discrete but related facts and information about a given domain, such as biology, mathematics, or medicine (Costanza, Fleishman, & Marshall-Mies, 1999). A further distinction is often made between declarative (knowledge of what) and procedural (knowledge of how) knowledge (Campbell, McCloy, Oppler, & Sager, 1993).

Skills reflect the level of proficiency or competency to perform a task or learned activity (Peterson et al., 2001). Skills can be divided into basic and cross-functional categories. Basic skills are thought to facilitate learning or knowledge acquisition and include such things as writing or critical thinking skills. For their part, cross-functional skills are developed capabilities that foster performance across job contexts and include such things as problem solving and negotiation skills. Skills are commonly thought to improve with training and experience on a particular task.

Abilities are relatively enduring basic capacities for performing a range of different activities (Fleishman, Costanza, & Marshall-Mies, 1999). This would include cognitive (e.g., verbal, quantitative), psychomotor (e.g., reaction time, manual dexterity), physical (e.g., strength, endurance), and sensory–perceptual (e.g., visual, auditory) abilities. Relative to knowledge and skill, abilities are thought to be more stable over time.

Other characteristics is a catch-all category designed to encompass all other potentially relevant factors that might be important for successful performance. Other characteristics that are commonly discussed include personality and motivational traits (e.g., conscientiousness, leadership, initiative), specific forms of work and educational experience, and licensure and certification that may be required in certain fields (e.g., registered nurses, certified public accountant).

The third major type of descriptor concerns the work context within which work is performed (and roles are enacted). Work context can be broadly defined as "situational opportunities and constraints that affect the occurrence and meaning of organizational behavior as well as functional relationships between variables" (Johns, 2006, p. 386) and consists of task, social, and physical aspects (Hattrup & Jackson, 1996; Johns, 2006; Strong, Jeanneret, McPhail, Blakley, & D'Egidio, 1999). The task context reflects the structural and informational conditions under which work roles are enacted and includes such things as the amount of autonomy and task clarity, the consequence of error inherent in the work, level of accountability, and the resources available to perform the task. The social context reflects the nature of role relationships and interpersonal contingencies that exist among workers and includes such things as social density, different forms of communication, the extent and type of interdependence with others, and the degree of interpersonal conflict present in the work environment. The physical context reflects elements of the material space or built environment within which work roles are enacted and includes general environmental conditions (e.g., noise, lighting, temperature, air quality), presence of hazardous work conditions (e.g., radiation, high places, disease exposure), and overall physiological job demands (e.g., sitting, standing, walking, climbing). Although the nature of the context is not often explicitly taken into account when conducting work analysis, recent research has shown it can have a pronounced effect on work role requirements (Dierdorff & Morgeson, 2007).

Method

Once a decision is made on the type of descriptor(s), the next choice involves the method to use to collect data on those descriptors. There are many different methods to use (see Ash, 1988; Brannick et al., 2007, for comprehensive lists), but some of the most common include observation, individual interviews, group meetings, and questionnaires. Note that there is very little research that compares the relative effectiveness of these different work analysis methods (see Ash & Levine, 1980, for a framework for evaluating work analysis methods). A general rule of thumb, however, would be to use multiple methods that could permit subsequent triangulation of collected information, as well as the opportunity to capture different perspectives of the target work roles under examination. Of course, time requirements, cost effectiveness, and, most importantly, the intended purpose of the information (discussed later in this section) must be considered when choosing work analysis methods.

Observation can take several forms, but the most often used method involves direct observation, whereby someone not directly involved in the task performance (e.g., a supervisor, job analyst) observes workers as they complete their tasks. Generally, an observer would record (via notes, checklists, or questionnaires) the what, why, and how of various aspects of the work. Other forms of observation include having supervisors record or recall particularly effective or ineffective worker behaviors (i.e., critical incidents) or video recording worker task performance for later analysis. Although time consuming, an advantage of observation is that it is not subject to problems of selective recall or other reporting biases on the part of workers (but there is potential bias in terms of what is recalled). However, for some jobs it may not be possible to observe key aspects of the job, particularly for work that has a large mental or knowledge component (i.e., most work processes occurs in the head of the worker).

Individual interviews involve conducting interviews with respondents one at a time. Typically, interviews are conducted with multiple different types of respondents (e.g., workers, supervisors) who are asked similar types of questions about the work. Interviews enable the acquisition of detailed information, in part because the interviewer can prompt the interviewee for additional details and check or otherwise question the validity of the information being transmitted. A major challenge of interviews is that some individuals might not be able to describe what they do or what the work requires in sufficient detail. This is particularly likely to occur if an individual has been working in the role for an extended period of time and has routinized the performance of major tasks. Another potential limitation is interviewer bias in terms of faulty recording or recall of the content of the interview itself.

Group meetings (also called "subject matter expert" [SME] meetings) involve getting a number of workers, supervisors, or technical experts together to discuss various aspects of the work. Typically, one would conduct separate meetings for workers, supervisors, and technical experts, in part because one would likely focus on different aspects of the work with the different groups. Such meetings are usually facilitated by a job analyst and are a more efficient way to collect information than the individual interview. Common activities in group meetings include brainstorming or generating lists of activities or attributes or evaluating data that have been previously gathered. An advantage of group meetings is the possibility of consensus, which is often needed for implementation of a work analysis product. However, group meetings can be subject to numerous dysfunctional group processes, including a lack of participation by some group members and conformity to a dominant group member. Such social processes are discussed in greater detail later.

Questionnaires are structured surveys (either paper and pencil or computer based) used to collect information on any of the work role requirements discussed previously. There has been a tremendous amount of research on the questionnaire method (somewhat in contrast to the other methods). The bulk of this research has focused on the presentation and evaluation of particular work analysis methods or questionnaires (although recognize that the use of custom, organization-specific work analysis questionnaires is widespread). Some examples of the questionnaire approach include the task inventory approach (e.g., Gael, 1983), the PAQ (McCormick et al., 1972), and the O*NET (Peterson et al., 2001). The evaluation of each of these questionnaire methodologies is beyond the scope of this chapter, but one advantage of this method is its ability to systematically gather a large amount of work-related information that can be quantitatively summarized. These strengths, however, should be balanced against some potential weaknesses. Questionnaire respondents can be overwhelmed by the task (some questionnaires can be several hundred questions long and involve numerous rating scales) and subsequently provide responses that are unreliable and inaccurate.

Type of Rating Scale

As noted, the questionnaire method has received a great deal of attention. One of the key decisions to be made when using the questionnaire methodology is which kind of rating scale to use. In this section, we discuss some of the rating scales that have been used in the past. Although many of these scales have been used to collect task-related information, they can also be used to collect other work and worker requirement data. Table 1.2 provides examples of some of the most commonly used scales.

It is often helpful to obtain estimates about how often particular tasks are performed. To do so, researchers have used different types of frequency scales. At least two different options are possible when measuring frequency. In the first, a frequency estimate is made using highly specific time-based estimates (e.g., from "about once per year" to "about once each hour or more often"). In the second, a less specific estimate is provided (e.g., from "never" to "very often"). We are not aware of any research that has directly compared these two different types of frequency scales, but we have used both in our research with good results. We have found that sometimes respondents have difficulty making the highly specific frequency estimates. In some ways, it is almost too precise, given the way workers often view their job. We have more to say about the complexity of the judgments often made in work analysis a little bit later.

One frequency scale that seems to have fallen somewhat out of favor is the relative time-spent scale. This could be due, in part, to the criticisms leveled against this kind of scaling by Harvey (1991), who suggested that such a "within-job relative" rating scale (e.g., the time spent on a particular task

TABLE 1.2

Commonly Used Job Analysis Rating Scales

Type of rating scale	Anchors
Frequency	
"I perform this task . . ." (Gael, 1983)	1 = *about once per year,* 2 = *about once every six months or less,* 3 = *about once each month,* 4 = *about once each week,* 5 = *about every other day,* 6 = *about every day or more often (not each hour),* and 7 = *about once each hour or more often*
"I perform this task . . ." (Drauden, 1988)	0 = *never,* 1 = *rarely,* 2 = *occasionally,* 3 = *sometimes,* 4 = *often,* and 5 = *very often*
Importance	
"How important is this task to the performance of your present job?"	1 = *not important,* 2 = *somewhat important,* 3 = *important,* 4 = *very important,* and 5 = *extremely important*
Criticality–consequence of error	
"Indicate the degree to which an incorrect performance would result in negative consequences." (Brannick, Levine, & Morgeson, 2007)	1 = *consequences of error are not at all important,* 2 = *consequences of error are of little importance,* 3 = *consequences are of some importance,* 4 = *consequences are moderately important,* 5 = *consequences are important,* 6 = *consequences are very important,* and 7 = *consequences are extremely important*
Task difficulty	
"Indicate the difficulty in doing a task correctly relative to all other tasks within a single job." (Brannick et al., 2007)	1 = *one of the easiest of all tasks,* 2 = *considerably easier than most tasks,* 3 = *easier than most tasks performed,* 4 = *approximately ½ tasks are more difficult, ½ less,* and 5 = *harder than most tasks performed*
Required on entry	
"Review each task statement and ask yourself the following question: 'When is a new employee expected to be able to possess this knowledge or skill?' "	1 = *not expected to possess immediately, but after formal training is provided,* 2 = *not expected to possess immediately, but can be quickly learned on the job,* and 3 = *should be able to possess immediately*

compared with the time spent on other tasks) makes cross-job comparisons problematic. It is interesting to note that research has found that relative time spent and both absolute and relative frequency scales provide largely the same information (Friedman, 1990, 1991; Manson, Levine, & Brannick, 2000). Although this does not speak to making cross-job comparisons, it does suggest that within a job, any of these frequency scales are likely equivalent.

In addition to frequency, it is often useful to obtain estimates about the importance of particular tasks to the overall work role. At least two different strategies have been used in past research. In the first, judgments of criticality or consequences of error (the extent to which the incorrect performance of a task would result in negative consequences) and difficulty (how hard it is to perform a task correctly) are combined into an overall index of importance (Sanchez & Levine, 1989). In the second, the importance of a task is directly estimated by simply asking how important the task is to performance on the job. Research has shown that direct estimates are as reliable as composites of difficulty and criticality (Sanchez & Fraser, 1992).

Although the preceding rating scales have typically been used in the context of task questionnaires (and more generally in activity-based work analysis), attribute-oriented work analysis efforts have also used the questionnaire method. Of the rating scales described above, only minor modifications would be needed to adapt them for use with attribute descriptors. For example, instead of referencing the frequency of task performance, the rating scale could reference the frequency with which knowledge or skills are needed on the job. A similar adjustment can be made for importance. In fact, importance rating scales have been used in both the PAQ and O*NET.

There are, however, some rating scales that take on particular relevance in attribute questionnaires. For example, a key question when conducting work analysis for the purposes of developing a selection system is the extent to which a particular attribute is needed at the point of entry (hiring) or whether it can be learned (trained) on the job. This can provide input into which attributes to focus on during selection assessments (but also note the same question could be asked about when a worker is expected to be able to perform tasks) and which to include in formal training programs.

The final rating scale we discuss is not included in Table 1.2 but is particularly salient to attribute-oriented questionnaires. This is the level of the attribute that is required by the job. Originally developed for use in Fleishman's Ability Requirements Scales (Fleishman, 1992), its use has been extended to multiple domains in O*NET. The basic idea is that any work role has a particular amount or level of ability or skill needed for effective performance. In practice, level rating scales range from low to high but typically use behavioral anchors that are illustrative of different levels of the attribute. For example, the ability of "reaction time" (defined as the ability to quickly respond [with the hand, finger, or foot] to a signal [sound, light, picture] when it appears) could have anchors for low, moderate, and high levels of ability as follows: "start to slow down the car when a traffic light turns yellow," "throw a switch when a red warning light goes off," and "hit the brake when a pedestrian steps in front of the car," respectively.

Despite the distinctions that are made among these different rating scales, there is evidence that many of these distinctions are often lost on the workers who complete work analysis questionnaires. For example, although level and importance rating scales are quite different conceptually, in the initial pilot test of O*NET (Peterson, Mumford, Borman, Jeanneret, & Fleishman, 1999), level and importance scales were often highly correlated (in the low .90s). The rating scales of importance and criticality have also shown high overlap (rs > .80), whereas correlations between difficulty to learn ratings and importance and criticality ratings have ranged from moderate to high (rs from .37 to .77; Manson et al., 2000; Sanchez & Fraser, 1992; Sanchez & Levine, 1989). Finally, a meta-analysis by Dierdorff and Wilson (2003) showed variability in interrater reliability estimates of ratings using importance ($r = .71$), frequency ($r = .69$), difficulty ($r = .63$), and time-spent ($r = .67$) scales, but the 80% confidence intervals for these estimates were overlapping, indicating a lack of significant differences. In total, this evidence suggests that despite their conceptual independence, respondents who complete work analysis surveys are not always able to make the same sort of fine distinctions that are prompted by different rating scales. This suggests that if multiple response scales are to be used, then they should be chosen so as to minimize redundancy and ensure alignment with the intended purposes of the work analysis.

Source

Once a method is determined, the next choice involves deciding the source of the work analysis information. Common sources include written documentation, role incumbents, technical experts, supervisors, clients, and job analysts. A wide variety of written documentation can be used to support a work analysis effort. This would include such things as existing job descriptions, previous work analyses, published information about the work role (e.g., from publicly available databases, such as O*NET), training manuals or other documents used to prepare workers for the role, and checklists or operating guides for any of the equipment, tools, or other work aids. Collecting this kind of documentation is typically the first step in the work analysis, as one seeks to compile all the known information about the work role. One benefit of this source of information is that its collection can be very cost efficient. However, the work analysis practitioner must be aware that existing documentation could be outdated or may lack sufficient depth or breadth to be useful for the intended purpose of the work analysis.

Role incumbents are another useful source of work analysis information. Incumbents are a useful source of information because of their familiarity with the role and specific knowledge about what is done on a day to day basis. However, some incumbents may not be able to effectively articulate exactly what they do, either because of a lack of verbal ability or a lack of motivation to provide accurate and reliable information. Technical experts are individuals who do not perform the role but have some sort of specialized expertise with the work that is performed. Examples might include engineers who design a manufacturing process, chemists who study the effects of drug interactions, lawyers who write and approve contracts, or professors who are experts in the discipline that underlies the work being studied. Such experts are likely to provide an important perspective on the technical aspects of the work, particularly in terms of ideal system functioning.

Supervisors (either the immediate supervisor or a higher level manager) can also provide a useful perspective on the work role requirements. Supervisors may have a higher level of verbal ability than incumbents and thus might be able to provide work role information that incumbents are unable to articulate effectively. In addition, supervisors are probably less motivated to distort or otherwise bias the information they provide. Finally, given their hierarchical position, they are likely to have a broader perspective with respect to differences among the work roles and the attributes needed for successful role performance. Despite these positive features, however, one major problem with supervisors as a source is that they may have less detailed and nuanced information about the work role because they do not actually perform the work (and may not even know how to perform the work).

Work analysts are another source of information. These can be either HR professionals inside the organization who have expertise and training in work analysis methods or outside consultants or experts. In a typical work analysis, work analysts serve an integrative role by designing and implementing the variety of methods discussed earlier. Some advantages of work analysts are that they tend to produce highly reliable ratings, have no (or little) motivation to bias the results, and are able to integrate the large amounts of information that typically result from a thorough work analysis. However, unless they accumulate enough information about the work, work analysts may lack adequate information to make good decisions. Finally, because experienced work analysts often have prior exposure to similar work roles, they may be subject to preexisting stereotypes about the work. Unless they are careful, their decisions may be influenced by their stereotypes instead of the actual work itself.

Although one could choose to use only one (or a subset) of these sources when conducting a work analysis, in practice, a comprehensive work analysis would entail using all sources to varying degrees. In addition to capturing different perspectives of the work role under examination, using multiple sources may have the added benefit of producing higher quality work analysis information, as some research has shown differences across different data sources (e.g., Dierdorff & Wilson, 2003). A process commonly used in practice is to begin by reviewing existing written documentation. This documentation then informs subsequent data collection from role incumbents and technical experts. Supervisors then check and augment the data collected from incumbents and experts. Analysts then compile all the information (and likely were intimately involved in collecting the data) and draw relevant conclusions. Such an approach is often highly effective because it provides a more accurate description of the work and worker requirements. In addition, by gathering input from the relevant stakeholders, it can enhance acceptance of any HR system that is built from the findings of the work analysis.

Purpose of Work Analysis

As noted at the beginning of this section (and implicitly throughout), the choices made when designing and conducting a work analysis depend on the reason or purpose of the work analysis. There are numerous reasons why one might conduct a work analysis, including selection system development, job and team design, performance management system design, training system development, compensation system development, and career management systems. Because a comprehensive review of these purposes is beyond the scope of this chapter (see Ash, 1988; Brannick et al., 2007; McCormick, 1979, for complete lists), we have chosen to focus on what goes into making such choices and providing some selective examples.

Perhaps the most important consideration when making work analysis choices is how the information will be used. For example, conducting a work analysis to determine what kinds of selection tools to use would place a priority on identifying the attributes (e.g., knowledge, skill, ability, other characteristics) needed to effectively perform the work and the extent to which certain attributes (e.g., skills) are needed immediately on the job and others can be learned once on the job. Conducting a work analysis for developing a new training program, however, would place a premium on the activities performed, in part because the activities form the core of the training program content. If the intention is to carry out a work analysis to produce information for job descriptions–specifications, then emphasis would be on a full breadth of descriptors (activities, attributes, and context), with attention paid to ascertaining the importance of these descriptors to role performance. As these examples illustrate, the ultimate use of the work analysis information plays a major part in any decisions that are made.

Beyond the use of the information, several other ancillary considerations deserve mention, including quality, cost, acceptability, and legal defensibility. Although one would always like to obtain as high a quality of information as possible, quality considerations often must be balanced against cost considerations. All else being equal, the highest quality work analysis information will be the most costly. Organizations often have to make pragmatic decisions about when a work analysis is good enough. We return to issues of quality in more detail in a subsequent section. Acceptability is another important consideration, particularly if the work analysis has major implications for current workers. For example, if a work analysis is being conducted to redesign jobs or determine pay levels, then choices should be made to include the interested parties wherever possible. Interested parties can include incumbents whose jobs are being redesigned or whose pay is being affected and labor unions who represent job incumbents. A final consideration would be legal defensibility. If one were conducting a work analysis in an environment where the resulting HR system might be subject to legal challenge, fully documenting a detailed and thorough (i.e., high quality) work analysis would be advised. For example, if a work analysis is being conducted to revise a performance management system where there have been allegations of gender discrimination, then a complete and thorough work analysis would need to be carefully documented.

O*NET

Arguably the most significant innovation in work analysis of the past several decades has been the development of O*NET by the U.S. Department of Labor. Although other occupational classification systems exist both in North America (e.g., Canada's National Occupation Classification) and in Europe (e.g., International Standard of Occupational Classification and EurOccupations), O*NET encompasses the broadest scope of work information ranging from labor market data and wages to important knowledge, skills, and required tasks. As such, O*NET is a comprehensive system of occupational information designed to replace the *Dictionary of Occupational Titles* (*DOT*), which was first published in 1939. There were numerous reasons why the *DOT* was in need of replacement (Dunnette, 1999). Most salient among these reasons were (a) the lack of information to allow cross-job comparisons, which permit classification and determination of similarities and differences across a variety of work roles; (b) the primary focus on task information to the exclusion of other important work role requirements, such as knowledge, skills, abilities, and traits; (c) the limited description of the conditions under which work is performed (e.g., the *DOT* mainly described aspects of the physical context); and (d) the numerous difficulties of maintaining the currency of the information in a rapidly changing world of work. A special panel was commissioned by the federal government (Advisory Panel for the Dictionary of Occupational Titles, or APDOT) to review these issues surrounding the *DOT* and to offer recommendations for improvement and alternative approaches. As a result, APDOT released a final report (APDOT, 1993) that outlined a roadmap toward creating what would later become O*NET. For more details regarding how this process unfolded, readers are encouraged to consult Dunnette (1999) and Dye and Silver (1999).

At the heart of O*NET is its content model, which theoretically organizes the wide variety of information that can be used to describe the world of work. The content model is shown in Figure 1.3 and comprises six major areas: worker characteristics, worker requirements, experience requirements, occupation requirements, workforce characteristics, and occupation-specific information (Mumford & Peterson, 1999; Peterson et al., 2001). Of importance, this structure enables a focus on areas that describe important attributes and characteristics of both workers and the work itself. Table 1.3 displays the types of descriptors that fall within each domain of the content model. Also shown in the table are the conceptual categories of these descriptors and the sources from which data are collected. More specific information may be found in Peterson et al. (2001) or at O*NET OnLine (see http://online.onetcenter.org).

With regard to the field of work analysis, several features of the content model are especially noteworthy. First, the model represents a comprehensive way to conceptualize virtually all of the types of work-related data that are of interest to both individuals and organizations. For example, the model subsumes

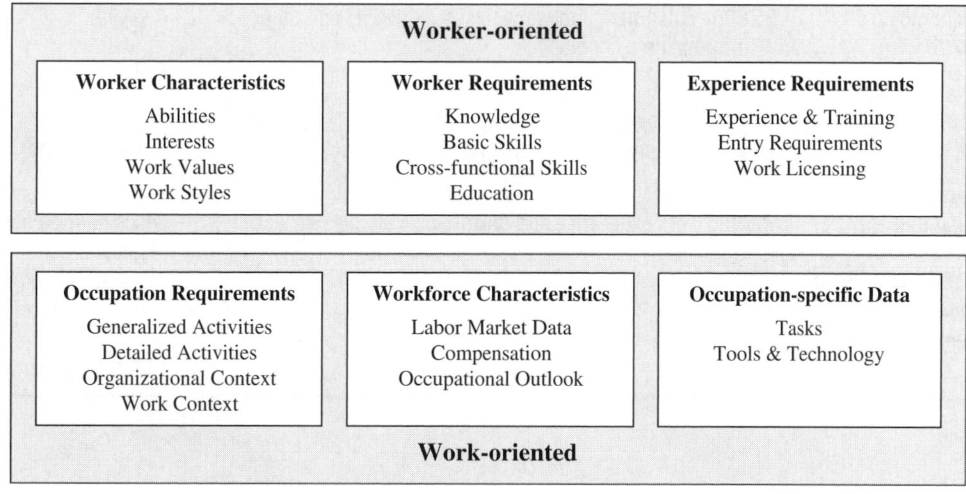

FIGURE 1.3. Content model for the Occupational Information Network.

TABLE 1.3

Content Model Descriptor Types and Categories

Domain and descriptor type	Descriptor categories or details	Data source
Occupation requirements		
Generalized work activities	Information input, mental processes, work output, and interacting with others	Role incumbents
Detailed work activities	2,165 activities (e.g., administer medications or treatments, analyze psychological testing data, prepare records of customer charges)	Analysts
Work context	Interpersonal relationships, physical work conditions, and structural job characteristics	Role incumbents
Organizational context	Organizational structure, human resources systems and practices, goals, roles at work, culture, and role of supervisors	Not currently collected
Worker requirements		
Basic skills	Content skills and process skills	Role incumbents
Cross-functional skills	Social skills, complex problem-solving skills, technical skills, systems skills, and resource management skills	Role incumbents, analysts
Knowledge	Business and management, manufacturing and production, engineering and technology, mathematics and science, health services, education and training, arts and humanities, law and public safety, communications, and transportation	Role incumbents, analysts
Education	Required level of education, instructional program required, and educational level in specific subjects	Bureau of Labor Statistics and Department of Education (third category not collected)
Worker characteristics		
Abilities	Cognitive abilities, psychomotor abilities, physical abilities, and sensory abilities	Analysts
Work styles	Achievement orientation, social influence, interpersonal orientation, adjustment, conscientiousness, independence, and practical intelligence	Role incumbents
Occupational interests	Realistic, investigative, artistic, social, enterprising, and conventional	Analysts
Occupational values	Achievement, working conditions, recognition, relationships, support, and independence	Analysts
Occupation-specific information		
Tasks	25–30 tasks per occupation	Role incumbents
Tools and technology	25,000+ equipment, tools, machines, software, and other information technology	Analysts
Workforce characteristics		
Labor market information	Wages, employment statistics, and so forth	Bureau of Labor Statistics
Occupational outlook	Employment projections (e.g., growth, shrinkage)	Bureau of Labor Statistics
Experience requirements		
Experience and training	Related work experience and on-the-job training	Office of Apprenticeship and role incumbents
Basic skill entry requirements		Not currently collected
Cross-functional skill entry requirements		Not currently collected
Licensing		Office of Apprenticeship

labor market data, wages, and occupational forecasts, as well as the attribute and activity requirements necessary for occupational performance. Second, the model posits a taxonomic structure for most of its domains. For instance, the worker characteristic domain of abilities is grouped into four broad categories, with more specific abilities contained within each grouping. This taxonomic approach is beneficial primarily because it directly incorporates multiple levels of data specificity. This is valuable because it allows one to choose between various levels of specificity in a particular domain, depending on the intended use of the information.

Third, the model establishes a common language with which to describe the world of work. Using standardized descriptors is essential for cross-occupation comparisons that seek to identify similarities or differences between occupations. The benefits of a common language are numerous, in part because it can serve as a unifying force that eliminates the potential confusion that is created when a host of similar descriptors are used to capture work role requirements.

Finally, the model also allows for occupation-specific information, such as detailed task information, wage information, and so forth. Such occupation-specific data were central to the original *DOT*. Of importance, the incorporation of this type of information ensures that, in addition to more molar cross-occupational comparisons, more molecular within-occupation descriptions are possible. Further, occupation-specific data are necessary for a number of HR purposes, such as developing training programs or generating position descriptions (Sager, Mumford, Baughman, & Childs, 1999).

Using O*NET in Practice

In addition to characteristics of the content model described above, the information contained within the O*NET database holds particular value for the HR practitioner. First, the information is nationally representative of the U.S. workforce and is "fresh" in the sense that it has been collected in the past 7 years, with nearly three quarters of the occupations updated since 2005. Second, the data available in the O*NET system are more descriptive than information typically found in the products of many work analyses in practice (e.g., job descriptions and specifications). As an example, consider the ambiguity and widely variant levels of specificity of the descriptors commonly found in online job postings. O*NET provides descriptors that are clearly defined and theoretically based.

As we discussed earlier, a single right way to conduct work analysis does not exist, but, rather, the chosen approach must be congruent with the ultimate uses of the collected information. Likewise, it would be a mistake to suggest that there is only one way to effectively use O*NET in practice. With that said, we believe O*NET can make a substantial contribution to improving the effectiveness of work analysis in practice. This is probably best accomplished by utilizing O*NET as a starting point for work analysis efforts. The O*NET database would then serve as a foundation upon which to undertake one's own work analysis, regardless of the ultimate purpose. Following this logic, a practitioner would first consult O*NET to locate the relevant occupation(s) matching the focal role(s) of his or her work analysis, as well as the desired descriptors most relevant to the intended purpose (e.g., tasks and/or skills for designing training programs, skills and/or traits for choosing selection instruments). Then, the practitioner would use these data to inform their own in-house data collection efforts, whether these efforts are as simple as SME or incumbent verification of existing O*NET information (through ratings, rankings) or as complex as customized initiatives that seek to generate more company-specific information to augment O*NET data (e.g., knowledge germane to particular software systems, responsibilities or activities described in the language of a particular business function or department, etc.). In this sense, O*NET can provide generalizable data to help ground and facilitate local work analysis projects. Considering that work analysis results are frequently the key components to establishing content-related validity evidence, coupling local work analysis results with information from the nationally representative O*NET database may bolster the defensibility of decisions based on such evidence.

Recent O*NET Developments

Since its initial pilot testing and development (see Peterson et al., 1999, 2001, for greater details), O*NET has undergone a number of important revisions, updates, and additions. First, the occupational coding scheme for O*NET has been aligned with the Bureau of Labor Statistics's Standard Occupational Classification system (available from http://www.bls.gov/SOC) to ensure compliance with the requirements of all federal statistical agencies reporting occupational data (Levine, Nottingham, Paige, & Lewis, 2000). These coding changes have adjusted the total number of occupations in the O*NET system to 949, of which 812 were included in data collection efforts as of 2006. This represents a significant departure from the roughly 12,000 titles in the *DOT* and the 1,120 titles in the early versions of the O*NET database.

Second, the original O*NET database was populated with analyst ratings. Several domains in the O*NET database have subsequently been updated on a semiannual basis with ratings collected from role incumbents, as noted in the previous section. Publication of these data derived from incumbents began in 2003 and continues today. Thus far, the vast majority (96%) of the 812 data-level occupations have been updated with incumbent data.

Third, new data pertaining to the variety of tools and technology needed for occupational performance have been recently added to the O*NET database (Brendle, Rivkin, & Lewis, 2008). Currently, tools and technology information have been generated for 327 occupations, with 427 occupations (53%) slated for completion by 2008. Over 25,000 tools and technology objects have been collected thus far, making this portion of the O*NET database the largest in terms of sheer volume. The number of objects per occupation range from 12 to 300. In general, "tools" refer to machine, equipment, and tools, whereas "technology" refers to software. Table 1.4 shows examples of tools and technology for several occupa-

TABLE 1.4

Examples of O*NET Tools and Technology

Tools and technology objects	UNSPSC classification
Surveying technicians	
Electrotapes, measuring chains, tellurometers	Distance meters
Echosounders, fathometers	Sonars
Total stations, Tribrach level bubble adjusting blocks, Tribrach optical plummet adjusting cylinders	Theodolities
MicroSurvey FieldGenius, Survey Starnet Software	Database reporting software
ESRI ArcView, Geomechanical design analysis GDA software	Map creation software
Anesthesiologists	
Intra-arterial catheters, Swan Ganz artery catheters	Arterial line catheters
Precordial stethoscopes, pretracheal stethoscopes	Electronic stethoscopes or accessories
AetherPalm InfusiCalc, Skyscape 5-Minute Clinical Consult	Medical software
EDImis Anesthesia Manager, Healthpac Computer Systems H2000 Anesthesia Billing Software	Accounting software
Marketing managers	
ClickTracks software, online advertising reporting software	Analytical or scientific software
Atlas OnePoint GO TOAST, Microsoft Project	Project management software
Accountants	
Best MIP Fund Accounting, Intuit QuickBooks, Sage CPAPractice Manager	Accounting software
ACCUCert software, Intrax ProcedureNet, tax compliance property tax management software	Compliance software
AuditWare software, Cartesis Magnitude iAnalysis, fixed-assets depreciation software	Financial analysis software

Note. Classifications are from the lowest level of the United Nations Standard Products and Services Code (UNSPSC) taxonomy (available at http://www.unspsc.org). O*NET = Occupational Information Network.

tions. Because of the substantial number of objects, as well as the hierarchical structure that underlies O*NET data, a critical need is to organize the tools and technology information. Currently, the tools and technology data are classified according to an existing and established taxonomy entitled the United Nations Standard Products and Services Code (available from www.unspsc.org). Of importance, the use of this taxonomy allows for cross-occupational comparisons and further promotes the common language approach inherent in the O*NET content model.

A final recent O*NET development is interesting to note. To reiterate, one of the key recommendations in the aforementioned APDOT report was the need to maintain currency in occupational information. To accomplish this, efforts have been made to identify what are termed "new and emerging" occupations (Dierdorff, Cantwell, & Nottingham, 2008). Such occupations (a) involve significantly different work than that performed by incumbents of other preexisting occupations and (b) are not adequately reflected in the current O*NET system. Efforts to identify new and emerging occupations are focused on specific industries or sectors that have been deemed as "high growth" by the Department of Labor's Employment and Training Administration. High-growth industries are those sectors projected to add substantial numbers of new jobs or affect the growth of other industries or that have existing or emerging businesses that are being transformed by technology and innovation, requiring new skill sets (Dierdorff et al., 2008). Table 1.5 shows examples of these high-growth industries as well as examples of new and emerging occupations that have been identified for inclusion in the O*NET database. As of 2008, 102 new and emerging occupations have been generated. For work analysis in general, these efforts focused on identifying and describing new and emerging occupations highlight the value of attending to more molar forces at the labor market and economic levels that shape the way work is performed but are rarely addressed in work analysis practice.

O*NET: Some Remaining Questions

The O*NET system represents the most significant theoretical development in work analysis in recent history and reflects the cumulative expertise of over 50 years of work analysis research (Campion, Morgeson, & Mayfield, 1999). The developments described in the previous section also suggest that efforts to improve, update, and extend O*NET appear promising. Nonetheless, certain areas are in need of further attention. We highlight a few of these in the next several paragraphs.

Although the core of the O*NET system grew out of an extensive pilot study that sought to offer reliability, validity, and other evaluative evidence for the domains covered by the content model (Peterson et al., 1999), there has been little published empirical research in the more than 10 years since this developmental research was undertaken. For example, much of the basic research conducted in the pilot study has yet to be replicated (and extended) on the current database. This research includes examinations of reliability, discriminability, and underlying factor structures of the present O*NET database, which now has several domains based on role incumbent ratings as well as analyst ratings. Such research is essential to the broader field of work analysis, considering that O*NET represents our state-of-the-art practices. The little research that has been conducted has focused on applications of O*NET data or uses of O*NET data in other non-work-analysis investigations.

One example of application-oriented research is a study by Jeanneret and Strong (2003) that examined the utility of using select generalized work activities from O*NET for estimating job component validity. These authors showed positive evidence that O*NET descriptors were significantly predictive of general cognitive ability (via General Aptitude Test Battery and Wonderlic test scores). LaPolice, Carter, and Johnson (2008) described another study using a job component validity approach, which is a validation technique where relationships between quantitative work analysis data (e.g., levels of skills required by the job) and test scores of role incumbents are assessed across various jobs. This research supported the usefulness of O*NET knowledge, skill, ability, and generalized work activity data in predicting adult literacy test scores. A third example of O*NET application research is a study conducted by Converse, Oswald, Gillespie, Field, and Bizot (2004), in which they

TABLE 1.5

O*NET New and Emerging Occupations

High-growth industry	New and emerging occupation	Definition
Advanced manufacturing	Mechatronics engineers	Apply knowledge of mechanical, electrical, and computer engineering theory and methods to the design of automation, intelligent systems, smart devices, or industrial systems control.
Automotive	Fuel cell engineers	Design, evaluate, modify, and construct fuel cell components and systems for transportation, stationary, or portable applications.
Biotechnology	Geneticists	Research and study the inheritance of traits at the molecular, organism, or population level. May evaluate or treat patients with genetic disorders.
Construction	Nondestructive testing specialists	Test the safety of structures, vehicles, or vessels using radiograph (X-ray), ultrasound, fiber optic, or related equipment.
Energy	Energy auditors	Conduct energy audits of buildings, building systems, and process systems. May also conduct investment grade audits of buildings or systems.
Financial services	Risk management specialists	Analyze company balance sheets and apply mathematical models to calculate risk associated with trading or credit transactions.
Geospatial technology	Geodetic surveyors	Measure large areas of the Earth's surface using satellite observations, global positioning systems, light detection and ranging, or related sources.
Health care	Cytotechnologists	Stain, mount, and study cells to detect evidence of cancer, hormonal abnormalities, and other pathological conditions following established standards and practices.
Homeland security	Intelligence analysts	Gather, analyze, and evaluate information from a variety of sources, such as law enforcement databases, surveillance, intelligence networks, and geographic information systems. Use data to anticipate and prevent organized crime activities, such as terrorism.
Hospitality	Spa managers	Plan, direct, or coordinate activities of a spa facility. Coordinate programs, schedule and direct staff, and oversee financial activities.
Nanotechnology	Nanosystems engineers	Design, develop, and supervise the production of materials, devices, and systems of unique molecular or macromolecular composition, applying principles of nanoscale physics and electrical, chemical, and biological engineering.
Retail trade	Loss prevention managers	Plan and direct policies, procedures, or systems to prevent the loss of assets. Determine risk exposure or potential liability and develop risk control measures.
Transportation	Logistics engineers	Design and analyze operational solutions for projects such as transportation optimization, network modeling, process and methods analysis, cost containment, capacity enhancement, routing and shipment optimization, and information management.

Note. High-growth industries identified by the U.S. Department of Labor's Employment and Training Administration. O*NET = Occupational Information Network.

outlined and evaluated a process for career guidance that matched individuals to occupations using O*NET abilities. Finally, Reiter-Palmon, Brown, Sandall, Buboltz, and Nimps (2006) described research that used O*NET data in the development and implementation of a Web-based work analysis process.

In terms of research that centrally focuses on O*NET itself, rather than its applications, even fewer studies have been conducted. One example is research conducted by Hadden, Kravets, and Muntaner (2004), who used exploratory factor analysis to examine a version of the O*NET database populated with analyst ratings. The authors found evidence that this database possessed a factor structure that was comparable with the *DOT*. Because this study was conducted with the older, analyst-version of the O*NET database, no conclusions can be made regarding the factor structure of the current incumbent-populated database. Another study by Eggerth, Bowles, Tunick, and Andrew (2005) examined the convergent validity of O*NET occupational interests (also analyst derived) as compared with the *DOT* Holland codes and the Strong Interest Inventory. These authors found varying levels of agreement in the scores produced across the three instruments, with the highest agreement levels between O*NET and the *DOT* and Strong Interest Inventory scores.

Finally, Dierdorff and Morgeson (2009) provided the only study to date that directly investigates incumbent ratings from the O*NET database. These authors used variance component analysis and meta-analysis to examine sources of variance and interrater reliability of ratings on O*NET tasks, generalized work activities, knowledge, skills, and work styles (traits). Variance component analysis was used to partition rating variance into two sources: (a) variance due to the item (i.e., "true" differences) and (b) variance due to the rater (i.e., idiosyncratic differences). Using data collected from job incumbents across 309 occupations ($N = 41{,}137$), Dierdorff and Morgeson found that larger proportions of variance (more than twice the amount) were generally attributable to items rather than to raters. The one exception to this general trend was for rating of work styles, where the opposite finding was evident (i.e., twice as much variance was due to the rater). Meta-analysis showed similar results, with lower interrater reliability for work style ratings, suggesting that incumbents are likely to show lower consensus when rating the traits that are important to performing their roles. Taken collectively, the results of this study offer generally favorable results for incumbent ratings of O*NET tasks, generalized work activities, knowledge, and skills.

Broadly speaking, the O*NET-related research evidence accumulated thus far appears to support the quality and viability of the data. However, we believe there are at least three key areas that still require directed treatment. First, the need for additional evaluative research cannot be overstated. Brannick et al. (2007) raised an interesting point of comparison with regard to the predecessor of O*NET when they stated, "despite its limitations, the DOT benefited from many years of research conducted on it" (p. 122). Research investigating topics such as the factor structure underlying O*NET data, relationships between analyst and incumbent ratings, and the uniqueness or redundancy in types of ratings (importance vs. level ratings) are broad examples of such empirical needs. Second, more work is necessary to further explicate the efficacy of applying O*NET data to the wide variety of HR systems (e.g., selection, compensation). With over 3.5 million page views per month of the O*NET OnLine website (Brendle et al., 2008), it would appear that O*NET information is being widely used. In addition, O*NET data are often used by governmental agencies to form various workforce strategy initiatives, such as focused training investments (Dierdorff & Cox, 2008).

However, to our knowledge, there exists no direct evidence of how extensive and for what purposes O*NET is used by organizations. It also is important to note that application-oriented research should focus less on documenting a particular process or describing case studies and instead turn attention to more useful criteria, such as the validity, utility, acceptance, and effectiveness of the systems using O*NET information. Third, it is unclear whether some content model areas for which information is not currently available will be the beneficiaries of future data collection efforts. For example, the organizational context descriptors (e.g., high performance work practices, culture) developed for O*NET would be particularly valuable not only to work analysis research, but also to many other areas of I/O psychology and management (Campion et al., 1999).

THE QUALITY OF WORK ANALYSIS INFORMATION

Because of its centrality to so many HR systems, considerable research has been focused on ensuring that work analysis data are of high quality. This has been reflected, in part, by research that has focused on the interrater reliability of work analysis data. Moreover, as one might expect, when properly conducted, work analysis data are highly reliable (see Dierdorff & Wilson, 2003, for a meta-analytic summary). However, reliability is only one component of data quality. A bigger issue is the validity and accuracy of work analysis data. In this section, we first discuss how accuracy has been conceptualized in work analysis. Next, we discuss the range of potential influences on work analysis data. Finally, we close with a discussion of the kinds of inferences that are made in work analysis and the resulting inferential leap that is often made when conducting work analysis.

Accuracy in Work Analysis

The issue of the accuracy of work analysis data is a difficult one. In many respects, work is a social construction (as our focus on role enactment emphasizes). As such, it is not clear what is meant by work analysis accuracy. Part of the problem is that most work analysis research has relied on the principles of classical test theory (Campion et al., 1999; Harvey, 1991). Classical test theory would suggest that there is a "true score" for a given work role, that true scores are stable across time, and that measurement variation is error that can be eliminated by aggregating across sources and time (Nunnally & Bernstein, 1994). This has led researchers to aggregate data across sources (e.g., incumbents) to determine the true score for a given role. In this view, work analysis data quality is indexed by estimating interrater reliability.

However, there is considerable reason to believe that the assumptions of classical test theory are inappropriate, in part because there are potentially numerous influences on the quality of work analysis data (Morgeson & Campion, 1997). This has led some to advocate and use a generalizability theory perspective (Sanchez & Levine, 2000; Van Iddekinge et al., 2005). An advantage of generalizability theory is that it enables one to simultaneously estimate multiple sources of measurement error. Despite its advantages (i.e., it allows one to model multiple sources of variance in work analysis data), generalizability theory is also predicated on the notion of a stable true score.

Other work analysis researchers have attempted to assess accuracy more directly by taking steps to identify those who might not be answering correctly. Most of these methods involve the inclusion of specific items or indices to detect such individuals (e.g., carelessness index, Green & Stutzman, 1986; infrequency index, Green & Veres, 1990; veracity items, McCormick, 1960; false reporting index, Pine, 1995). Such indices generally include two types of items: (a) veracity items considered to be requisite and thus performed by all incumbents in a given work role and (b) distractor or "bogus" items considered to be unrelated to the job and never performed by incumbents. Another approach has been to repeat particular items in a rate–rerate approach so as to assess intrarater consistency (Wilson, Harvey, & Macy, 1990). In general, such approaches to assessing accuracy are best suited for collecting work analysis information using the questionnaire method. Although offering the benefit of direct estimation of accuracy (i.e., they represent an unambiguous index of accuracy), these approaches do have some associated costs, such as increasing the overall length of the survey and reducing the face validity of the survey (e.g., respondents may wonder why bogus items are being presented or why items are being "unnecessarily" repeated).

Another perspective on the issue of accuracy in work analysis data was forwarded by Morgeson and Campion (1997). They suggested that instead of focusing on any particular single true score estimate, one could simply index the accuracy of work analysis data in multiple ways, in part because different sources of inaccuracy have different effects on work analysis data. The implications of this are that only by taking a multidimensional view of accuracy could one begin to understand the quality of the data. They identified six aspects of work analysis data quality. First was interrater reliability, which is the most commonly used measure of data quality in the work analysis domain (Dierdorff & Wilson, 2003). Interrater reliability reflects consistency across raters and indexes rater covariation (Shrout & Fleiss, 1979). Second was interrater agreement, which reflects the absolute level of agreement across raters and thus indexes the degree to which different raters make similar ratings (Kozlowski & Hattrup, 1992). Third was discriminability between jobs, which reflects between-job variance and the ability to distinguish between different jobs. Fourth was dimensionality of factor structures, which reflects the extent to which factor structures are complex or multidimensional. Fifth was mean ratings, which reflects inappropriately elevated or depressed ratings. Sixth was completeness, which reflects the extent to which the work analysis data are complete or comprehensive. Thus, one way to evaluate the accuracy of work analysis data is to focus on a broader set of criteria.

Sources of Variance in Work Analysis Data

Although considerable energy has been devoted to developing work analysis methods that generate reliable and valid data, the bulk of this research rests on the implicit assumption that any error is essentially random in nature. Proceeding from this assumption, most work analysis research has sought to eliminate such error through traditional means, such as using sophisticated sampling strategies and standardizing work analysis materials. However, there is reason to believe that work analysis data are subject to systematic (and predictable) sources of variance. If this is the case, then the traditional ways of controlling error will be ineffective and resulting work analysis data will be inaccurate. We now turn to a brief review of factors that may impact work analysis data. Prior to this discussion, however, it is important to acknowledge that although some of the issues we highlight have been supported in past work analysis research, other issues are more speculative, based on suggestive evidence, and thus require additional research.

Rater influences. Researchers have long acknowledged that certain rater characteristics may influence work analysis outcomes. For example, Madden (1962, 1963) explored the role of job familiarity and E. P. Prien and Saleh (1963) explored the role of job tenure. As Harvey (1991, p. 115) noted, "one cannot simply assume that job analysis ratings will be unaffected by characteristics of the rater." Supporting this conclusion, recent research has demonstrated that a considerable amount of variance in work analysis outcomes is indeed due to rater characteristics. For example, Van Iddekinge et al. (2005) found that 21.6% and 29.1% of the error variance in single-rater reliabilities of knowledge, skill, ability, and other characteristics importance ratings and needed-at-entry ratings (respectively) were attributable to rater idiosyncrasies. As such, it is important to explore how attributes of the raters (or source) can impact work analysis information.

First, general cognitive ability may impact work analysis information in a number of ways. Within the same job, individuals of higher cognitive ability might be able to provide more accurate and complete work analysis information because of their superior job knowledge (Hunter, 1986) of the focal role than those of lower cognitive ability. Cornelius and Lyness (1980) offered additional reasons why cognitive ability might influence the quality of work analysis judgments. In work analysis, respondents are often asked to make inferences or abstract judgments about aspects of the work, or they may be asked to integrate a large amount of information. Because of the cognitive demands of these judgments, those high in cognitive ability have an advantage because of their additional mental resources. These integrative judgments can be viewed as controlled processes (W. Schneider & Shiffrin, 1977), and cognitive ability is highly predictive of success in such processes (Ackerman & Humphreys, 1990). Greater cognitive ability may also result in more accurate work information, because many questionnaires require a high reading level (Ash & Edgell, 1975; Harvey, Friedman, Hakel, & Cornelius, 1988), and cognitive ability is related to education level. Research has supported the relationship between educational level and reliability or other differences in work analysis data (Cornelius & Lyness, 1980; Fried & Ferris, 1986; Green & Veres, 1990; Landy & Vasey, 1991).

Two caveats should be considered regarding cognitive ability. First, incumbents with noticeably higher cognitive ability may create extraneous information that could lead analysts or supervisors to rate the job requirements higher for these individuals, even though the underlying work is the same. Second, incumbents with higher cognitive ability may have qualitatively different experiences in the work setting because they are assigned (or take on) additional or different (e.g., higher level or more complex) tasks. This could influence the tasks and knowledge, skills, abilities, and other characteristics they generate, as well as ratings of importance and time spent. In support of this, Morgeson, Delaney-Klinger, and Hemingway (2005) recently found that cognitive ability was positively related to the number of tasks performed. These differences may be more pronounced on jobs where there is increased autonomy or opportunity for discretionary behavior.

Second, different personality characteristics may influence work analysis responding in a variety of ways. For example, individuals high in conscientiousness may be more careful and diligent in their responding, resulting in more reliable and accurate responses. Or, individuals high in extraversion may incorporate more socially oriented work elements into their focal role, thereby changing the nature of the work they perform, compared with less extraverted coworkers who are in the same role. Although there have been attempts to systematically measure the personality requirements of work (e.g., Raymark, Schmit, & Guion, 1997), there have been few attempts to explore how different personality characteristics are related to work analysis data. Future research should address this gap.

Another important attribute is work experience. More experienced incumbents may provide more accurate information because they may have greater information and insight into the job. The research evidence is mixed, however, with some studies showing differences (Borman, Dorsey, & Ackerman, 1992; Landy & Vasey, 1991; Sanchez & Fraser, 1992) and others not (Mullins & Kimbrough, 1988; Schmitt & Cohen, 1989; Silverman, Wexley, & Johnson, 1984). Furthermore, some of the differences in work analysis information may be due to differences in the jobs performed by more experienced incumbents.

For example, Borman et al. (1992) found significant differences in 9 of 12 time-spent scores between more and less experienced stockbrokers. It appears that as stockbrokers advance in their careers, they are involved in distinctly different activities, with a relationship-building phase early and a relationship-maintenance phase later. Landy and Vasey (1991) found similar differences for more and less experienced police officers. Finally, Sanchez and Fraser (1992) found that when rating task importance, individuals differentially weight time spent and difficulty of learning as a function of their job experience. However, Mullins and Kimbrough (1988) found no such experience differences for police officers in the generation of critical incidents, although groups were divided into very narrow bands of experience (e.g., each group constituted an increment of only 1 year of experience). Another view of work experience and work analysis has been provided by Richman and Quiñones (1996). They found that less experience with an experimental task was related to more accurate estimates of the frequency with which individual task elements had been performed and correct identification of tasks performed. They suggested that individuals have more difficulty recalling the frequency of specific events if similar events occurred frequently.

Given these mixed findings, understanding the role of work experience in work analysis judgments is an important area of future research. In investigating this issue, however, it would be important to adopt a multidimensional view of work experience. Tesluk and Jacobs (1998) developed a model of work experience that specifies measurement modes of work experience (i.e., amount, time, density, timing, type) and levels of specification (i.e., task, job, work group, organization, career–occupation). Any research on experience should seek to measure multiple aspects of experience, as some (e.g., task, job) may be more logically connected to work analysis than others (e.g., organization, occupation). Future research should also explore different rating scales, as differences in experience may also depend on the rating scale used. For example, all incumbents may identify the same tasks as critical, regardless of experience, but the amount of time they spend on different tasks may vary with experience. Also, differences with experience may be more pronounced if the jobs have some autonomy or opportunity for discretion in terms of which tasks to perform or the relative emphasis tasks are given.

A final rater attribute that might be important is the performance level of workers. As with the other rater influences, empirical results have been mixed. For instance, Borman et al. (1992) found significant relationships between time-spent ratings and performance of stockbrokers. Mullins and Kimbrough (1988) also found significant differences between low- and high-performing patrolpersons in their importance ratings. In contrast, Wexley and Silverman (1978) found no performance differences in importance and time-spent ratings in a sample of retail store managers. Conley and Sackett (1987) also found no differences in terms of either task generation or ratings of knowledge, skill, and ability between high- and low-performing juvenile officers. Finally, Aamodt, Kimbrough, Keller, and Crawford (1982) found no performance-related differences in the type of critical incident categories generated by residence hall workers.

As with the other attributes, differences in work analysis responses may be due to genuine differences in the jobs performed by higher performing employees. Better employees may be assigned additional or different tasks because they are more able to handle the extra work or as a reward for their high performance. In addition, low performers could be more likely to leave the organization (on a voluntary basis or by being terminated), which would introduce issues of range restriction that might affect relationships between experience and work analysis ratings.

Social and cognitive influences. Although rater attributes have been previously identified as a potential influence on work analysis information, it is only more recently that other potential influences have been identified. In fact, Morgeson and Campion (1997) identified 16 distinct potential social and cognitive sources of inaccuracy. The social sources "are created by normative pressures from the social environment and reflect the fact that individuals act and reside in a social context," whereas the cognitive sources "reflect problems that primarily result from the person as an information processor with distinct limitations" (p. 628). Given the in-depth discussion of these processes in past research (Morgeson & Campion, 1997), we only provide an overview and selected examples. The reader is referred to the original article for a more extended discussion.

Social sources are divided into social influence and self-presentation processes. Social influence processes include three distinct processes that occur when judgments are made in group settings. The first is conformity pressures, which reflects the fact that a group can exert quite a bit of normative influence to reach consensus. For example, in an SME group meeting, there are often strong pressures from a majority of group members to reach a certain conclusion (e.g., a particular aspect of the work is essential). Even if another group member disagrees, it is likely that they will go along because of the pressure for conformity that will exist. The second is extremity shifts (also called "group polarization"), which refers to the tendency for group member opinions to become more extreme following group discussion. The third is motivation loss, which reflects the tendency for individuals to exert less effort when in a group as compared with an individual setting. This can have the unfortunate result of not obtaining all the input of group members, resulting in deficient work analysis information.

Self-presentation processes included three processes that reflect an individual's attempt to present him- or herself in a particular light. The first is impression management, which reflects attempts to present oneself in such a way as to "create and maintain desired perceptions of themselves" (Gardner & Martinko, 1988, p. 321). Incumbents are likely to "inflate" the value of their job, particularly when the outcome of the work analysis might potentially benefit them (e.g., such as when a compensation system is being redesigned). The second is social desirability, which reflects "a need for social approval and acceptance and the belief that this can be attained by means of culturally acceptable and appropriate behaviors" (Marlowe & Crowne, 1961, p. 109). For example, Smith and Hakel (1979) found that incumbents and supervisors displayed considerable response inflation on socially desirable work analysis items compared with analyst ratings. The third is demand effects, which reflects the tendency of individuals to play the "good subject" role and respond in such a way as to validate external expectations. One might imagine a situation where a work analyst conveys to role holders that a certain set of skills are particularly important, and the role holders subsequently validate this expectation by rating them as highly important.

Cognitive sources are divided into limitations in information-processing systems and biases in information-processing systems. Limitations in information-processing systems include three different processes. The first is information overload, which reflects the fact that human information processing has limits when attempting to process complex or large quantities of information. For example, when confronting numerous, detailed activity and attribute statements in a work analysis questionnaire, respondents may simply be unable to effectively process all the information. The second is heuristics, which reflects the fact that individuals often rely on simplifying heuristics (such as representativeness and availability) when making judgments (Tversky & Kahneman, 1974). Because these heuristics imperfectly mirror reality, they tend to result in inaccurate judgments. The third is categorization, which reflects the fact that individuals tend to organize their experiences into distinct categories. Once categorized, subsequent inferences about the experience are made with respect to the category and not the specific experiences. Thus, if a role holder has concluded that "my work is highly complex," then he or she is likely to make subsequent inferences consistent with this conclusion.

Biases in information-processing systems include seven processes. The first is carelessness, which reflects response distortion due to inattention. For example, work analysis respondents often do not read questionnaire items closely (e.g., they do not realize that an item is reverse coded) or carefully (e.g., they indicate they perform tasks that they could not possibly perform) enough. The second is extraneous information, which can create inaccuracy when information not relevant to the work analysis is somehow included or considered. For example, in a work analysis conducted for the purpose of determining pay levels, knowledge of current pay levels can influence the resulting work analysis information. The third is inadequate information, which refers to situations where raters have incomplete job information. This can occur if inexperienced (or naive) raters are used or if analysts have not conducted a systematic analysis of the work. The fourth is order and contrast effects, which involves the influence of contextual ratings effects, such as order (primacy and recency) and contrast effects. Primacy effects refer to the influence of initial information (e.g., the first interviews conducted by an analyst), whereas recency effects refer to the influence of recent information (e.g., how recently performed tasks might be overly salient). Contrast effects reflect distortions caused by differences between stimuli. For example, if a work analyst had been rating a number of low-level roles, he or she might give inappropriately high ratings to an average-level job because of the implicit contrast between jobs.

The fifth is halo, which occurs when ratings are assigned on the basis of global impressions rather than a systematic consideration of differences among separate categories. One way that halo might affect work analysis is that if the task domain or work behavior is not sampled adequately enough, then there is likely to be more of a reliance on global impressions. The sixth is leniency and severity, which reflects a general response tendency to give consistently high (leniency) or low (severity) ratings. Leniency is more likely in work analysis, in part because of a general reluctance to be overly critical when making work analysis judgments. The seventh is method effects, which reflects the fact that when data are collected through a single method, there can be spurious covariation among responses. This is likely to be an issue in work analyses when the questionnaire method is used and all the data are collected from a single source at a single point in time.

Contextual influences. Another category of factors that may influence work analysis information stems from the context within which work roles are performed. As discussed earlier, aspects of work context are one of the descriptor types that work analysis seeks to understand. Thus, features of work context can be a type of information directly collected during work analysis, such as when elements of the task, social, and physical environments in which roles are enacted are assessed. In addition, it is important to recognize that contextual forces are also likely to shape how work roles are perceived and ultimately enacted. Katz and Kahn (1978, p. 195) explained this relationship by stating that role enactment "does not occur in isolation; it is itself shaped by additional or contextual factors." In this sense, work context not only shapes how a work role is enacted, but also may serve as a systematic source of variance in work analysis data.

Contextual influences on work analysis information can be examined using an omnibus approach or a discrete approach. Discrete descriptions of work context focus on more specific classes of variables, such as those described earlier (i.e., delineating task, social, and physical elements). In contrast, an omnibus approach entails a broader consideration of contextual influences and "refers to an entity that comprises many features or particulars" (Johns, 2006, p. 391). That is, an omnibus approach accounts for contextual effects using more molar boundary conditions. For instance, one useful entity for studying omnibus context is that of occupation. In relation to how work context may influence variance in work analysis data, a discrete approach might focus on the effects of social context (e.g., role interdependence) on work analysis ratings, whereas an omnibus approach might focus on the organizational effects on ratings (e.g., ratings of similar roles in different companies).

Work analysis research has used both approaches to studying contextual effects. With regard to omnibus context effects, Van Iddekinge et al. (2005) examined whether the error variance in knowledge, skill, ability, and other characteristics ratings were impacted by the organization in which raters worked (these effects were not significant). Another study by Taylor, Li, Shi, and Borman (2008) showed that mean ratings and rank ordering of items from several O*NET domains were quite similar across four different countries. With regard to discrete context effects, Lindell, Claus, Brandt, and Landis (1998) found discrete features of organizations (e.g., size, formalized structure, technology) were correlated with time-spent ratings on tasks (average $r = .32$) but not importance ratings. Finally, Dierdorff, Rubin, and Morgeson (2009) examined both omnibus and discrete context effects on managerial work role requirements. These authors found evidence of omnibus context effects, as the type of managerial occupation (e.g., financial manager, HR manager) accounted for 4% to 39% of the total variability ($p < .01$) in importance ratings on 18 work role requirements spanning responsibility, skills, knowledge, and trait domains. Further, discrete elements from the task, social, and physical contexts (e.g., autonomy, interdependence, hazardous work conditions) accounted for additional variance in these ratings (roughly 18% of between-occupation variance across dimensions of discrete context).

From the accuracy of work analysis data to the quality of work analysis inferences. As the preceding discussion highlights, there are numerous potential influences on work analysis data. In addition to questions about the prevalence of such influences, another question centers around the extent to which any observed variability of work analysis data reflects meaningful differences in role enactment as opposed to error or inaccuracy. Because individuals often enact similar roles in slightly different ways (Biddle, 1979; Graen, 1976; Katz & Kahn, 1978), not all observed differences necessarily reflect inaccuracy. The possibility that some variance in work analysis data may be due to legitimate differences in role enactment introduces another key challenge in understanding work analysis accuracy, leading some to suggest that because work is a social construction, there is no gold standard of accuracy in work analysis (Sanchez & Levine, 2000).

A potential resolution of the dilemma, however, is to shift the focus from the accuracy of work analysis data (which has been the traditional conceptualization) to a focus on the quality of work analysis inferences (Morgeson & Campion, 2000). This is a potentially useful shift for two reasons. First, it is difficult to establish the stability or objectivity of work analysis data. As such, we can only begin to approximate (via some of the criteria discussed above) the accuracy of the data. Second, work analysis data are often completely based on human judgment (Goldstein, Zedeck, & Schneider, 1993). Put another way, "The making of job ratings can be conceptualized as an inferential decision" (Sanchez & Levine, 1994, p. 48), where the process of inductive inference involves drawing general conclusions from specific examples (Hempel, 1965). Thus, one could begin to describe the different kinds of inferences that are made in work analysis and then develop some means for estimating the quality of the inferences made. Instead of evaluating the quality of work analysis data, one would evaluate the quality of the inferences one is making on the basis of the work analysis data.

The first step in such an endeavor would be to describe the different types of inferences made in work analysis. Morgeson and Campion (2000) developed an integrative framework that identifies three key inferences that specifically occur in work analysis (see Figure 1.4). First, the work descriptive inference involves the extent to which a description of work activities (i.e., tasks and responsibilities) faithfully represents the physical and mental activities underlying role performance. Second, the work specification inference involves the extent to which a specification of worker attributes (i.e., knowledge, skill, ability, and other characteristics) reflects the psychological constructs underlying role-related aptitudes. Third, the operational inference involves the extent to which the identified worker attributes are needed to perform identified work activities.[2] The quality of these inferences could then be evaluated by "deriving theory-based expectations about how scores should behave under various conditions and assessing the extent to which these expectations receive support" (see Aguinis, Mazurkiewicz, & Heggestad, 2009, p. 433).

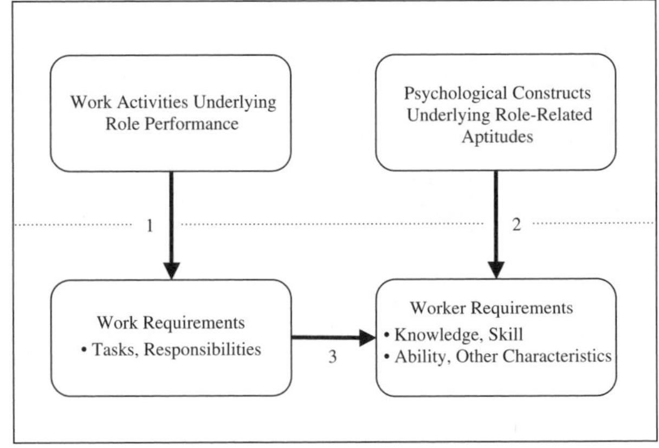

FIGURE 1.4. Key inferences that occur in work analysis. From "Accuracy in Job Analysis: Toward an Inference-Based Model," by F. P. Morgeson and M. A. Campion, 2000, *Journal of Organizational Behavior, 21,* p. 823. Copyright 2000 by John Wiley & Sons, Ltd. Adapted with permission.

One implication of this model is that some inferences require a greater inferential leap than other inferences, where the inferential leap in work analysis can be defined as the complexity of the evaluative judgments made about various work role requirements. This complexity is reflected in leaping from observations of work activities to inferences about role requirements. All types of work analysis judgments require some sort of inferential leap, in part because even the most observable aspects of a role (e.g., the performance of very specific tasks) usually require one to move from observable behavior to judgments about such behavior (e.g., frequency of performance, importance to the role). Such a view has been recently recognized and supported in the work analysis literature (e.g., Lievens & Sanchez, 2007; Lievens et al., 2004; Morgeson et al., 2004; Voskuijl & van Sliedregt, 2002).

Recent research by Dierdorff and colleagues (Dierdorff & Morgeson, 2007, 2009; Dierdorff & Rubin, 2007; Dierdorff & Wilson, 2003) has provided some indirect evidence of the inferential leap required by work analysis ratings. This research has shown rating differences attributable to the work descriptor being judged, such as the variation in levels of reliability, carelessness, consensus, and discriminability of work analysis ratings. Broadly speaking, this research suggests that ratings of less specific and directly observable descriptors (e.g., traits) require a larger inferential leap than more molecular and visible descriptors (e.g., tasks). This research also suggests that the inferential leap may systematically vary because of the source (analysts vs. role incumbent) as well as work context (e.g., amount of discretion in one's role).

[2] The operational inference is similar to what Gatewood and Feild (2001) called the "work–worker attribute leap." In addition, Gatewood and Feild described three other types of inferential leaps pertinent to HR activities in general (see also Sanchez & Levine, 2000): (a) the worker attribute–organizational intervention leap, (b) the work–performance measure leap, and (c) the organizational intervention–performance measure leap. Because these latter three types of inferential leaps do not directly deal with the collection of work analysis data but instead refer to the development HR systems (e.g., selection systems), we do not discuss them further.

Understanding the nature of the inferential leap in work analysis is important for at least two reasons. First, as we discussed, work analysis judgments have been typically treated as free from systematic error. However, we now understand that work analysis judgments are subject to various systematic sources of error and inaccuracy (Morgeson et al., 2004; Van Iddekinge et al., 2005). Focusing on work analysis inferences helps us better estimate the quality of our work analyses as well as helps us make appropriate inferences about the data that are collected. Second, the popularity of competency modeling approaches to work analysis (Lucia & Lepsinger, 1999; Schippmann, 1999) has resulted in an increased emphasis on abstract, holistic work descriptors (Schippmann et al., 2000). Focusing on the nature of the inferences made when collecting this type of information helps us better understand the potential limitations that attend the use of such descriptors. For the work analysis practitioner, a better understanding of the types of inferences required and the consequences of these inferences (e.g., changes in levels of consensus and carelessness) can allow for better work analysis design decisions. For example, evidence suggests that incumbents are likely to show lower consensus when rating traits than when rating duties or skills (Dierdorff & Morgeson, 2009). Thus, using analysts to rate trait descriptors, or using multiple types of respondents (incumbents, supervisors, trainers), would be beneficial when capturing judgments about these abstract descriptors.

LOOKING AHEAD: FUTURE AVENUES OF RESEARCH

In this section, we offer a number of potentially fruitful areas for future work analysis researchers to pursue. These suggestions are by no means exhaustive but are intended to address some more traditional areas of work analysis research and to stimulate new thinking in areas not conventionally falling under the purview of work analysis. To accomplish this, we propose topics we believe are potentially fruitful avenues for future research, most of which would be viewed as germane to the field of work analysis. We then discuss several other areas that hold the potential to meaningfully extend work analysis research into other theoretical domains. To the extent possible, we present illustrative research questions throughout the ensuing discussion.

Variance in Work Analysis Ratings

Accumulating empirical evidence shows that considerable variance in work analysis ratings is attributable to idiosyncratic sources as compared with the dimension upon which a work role is being judged (e.g., skills).[3] From a practical standpoint, idiosyncratic variance is generally viewed as undesirable because these rating differences are not due to consensus differences in the target work role and, if large enough, make aggregation of work analysis ratings problematic. Fortunately, recent research has shown that rater training (frame-of-reference training) can be an effective way to decrease idiosyncratic variance in attribute descriptor ratings provided by analysts (Lievens & Sanchez, 2007) and incumbents (Aguinis et al., 2009). These results are promising and suggest that additional research is warranted. Other forms of rater training shown to be effective in the performance appraisal literature, such as rater error training or performance dimension training (see Woehr & Huffcutt, 1994), should also be investigated. In addition, rater training could be applied to other common work analysis inferences, such as judgments about the linkages between tasks and knowledge, skill, ability, and other characteristics for purposes of identifying selection instruments. Of importance, future research should include not only traditional work analysis criteria (e.g., reliability, accuracy), but also criteria relevant to training interventions (e.g., affective outcomes, cost effectiveness).

A second way to approach the idiosyncratic variance found in work analysis ratings is to search for variables that can account for this variation. Future work analysis research could use Morgeson and Campion's (1997) framework discussed earlier to guide such investigations. For example, these authors offer over a dozen specific research propositions, many of which have yet to be subjected to empirical testing. In fact, to date, only two studies have applied

[3] Although, as we discussed earlier, some of the variance is likely to be systematic and explainable.

this conceptual framework to examine potential sources of inaccuracy in work analysis ratings, and both have shown meaningful results (Dierdorff & Rubin, 2007; Morgeson et al., 2004). Beyond these two studies, however, there is substantial research that remains to be conducted using this framework.

A third way to explore variance in work analysis ratings would be to draw from the broader I/O literature to understand some of the factors that might be related to differences in role enactment. This includes work attitudes (e.g., job satisfaction, commitment, fairness perceptions; Conte, Dean, Ringenbach, Moran, & Landy, 2005), the relationship between workers and their immediate supervisors (Hofmann, Morgeson, & Gerras, 2003), the amount of autonomy present in the work (Morgeson, Delaney-Klinger, & Hemingway, 2005), work experience (Borman et al., 1992), and ability (Morgeson, Delaney-Klinger, & Hemingway, 2005). A fuller understanding of how these (and other) factors relate to work analysis ratings would help us better understand the meaning of rating differences and whether differences reflect inaccuracy or meaningful differences in role enactment.

Exploring Relationships Among Different Work Role Requirements

Another avenue for future research is an examination of the relationships among the different work role requirements. Such cross-domain research would include exploring the linkages between attributes and activities. Indeed, fundamental to the majority of theory in I/O psychology (and most fields of psychology) has been the notion that person attributes are antecedent to work behaviors. In this sense, cross-domain research offers valuable information regarding such relationships. Further, the pursuit of a unified theory of performance, which necessarily includes cross-domain specifications, has long been a part of the work analysis tradition (e.g., Fleishman, 1975). An example of this pursuit can be seen in the well-accepted "data–people–things" descriptive framework adopted in the *DOT*. One interesting question is whether this framework still holds in the contemporary world of work. Some empirical evidence indicates that additional factors (e.g., organizational structure) might be required to adequately describe variance in work role requirements (Hadden et al., 2004).

Research that explicates precisely how cross-domain relationships vary across different types of work roles (e.g., occupations) would also be beneficial. Such research not only would increase our theoretical understanding of how attributes link to activities, but also holds promise to improve the practices built from work analysis information. For example, cross-domain specifications are central to job component validity approaches, which seek to analyze the relationship between work analysis data and validity data across various work roles (Jeanneret, 1992). In addition, a better understanding of how cross-domain relationships vary across work roles provides valuable information pertaining to validity generalization (Schmidt & Hunter, 1977), which has long recognized the effects of different occupations on validity estimates (see Ghiselli, 1966). Here, instead of treating occupation as simply a nondifferentiated moderator of validity variability to be subsequently controlled as an artifact, one could extend work analysis information for use in meta-analyses to more meaningfully examine what particular features of occupations are exerting influence (e.g., work context, occupational complexity).

Theory and research falling under the rubric of interactional psychology is a final area that cross-domain work analysis research could inform. In the interactional psychology literature, the importance of considering both the individual and the situation as joint determinants of work behavior has long been encouraged (Block & Block, 1981; Bowers, 1973; Magnussen & Endler, 1977; Terborg, 1981). Because the primary goal of work analysis is to systematically discover work role requirements and the context in which these requirements are enacted, work analysis research is particularly relevant for interactional psychology.

One area to which work analysis research could contribute is a more thorough understanding of how concepts such as situation strength (Mischel, 1977), trait relevance (Tett & Burnett, 2003), and context effects (Johns, 2006) theoretically and empirically operate to shape work behavior. For example, the notion of situation strength has been criticized for being overly broad and lacking emphasis on important qualitative aspects of context that make a given attribute relevant to role enactment. At the same time, however, both situation strength and trait relevance are necessary for understanding attribute and activity relationships (Tett & Burnett, 2003; Tett & Guterman, 2000). One way future research could empirically examine how these theoretical concepts function is to use work analysis to examine pertinent cross-domain linkages. Here, features of the work context (e.g., facets of task, social, or physical context) would represent varying levels of situation strength, whereas trait relevance could be systematically varied by testing the relationships between relevant–irrelevant attributes and work behavior.

For example, research could investigate how the strength of social context shapes the relationships between socially relevant attributes (e.g., extraversion, conflict negotiation skills) or irrelevant attributes (e.g., conscientiousness, critical thinking skills) and role behaviors of an interpersonal nature (e.g., helping coworkers, teaching others). Presumably, the efficacy of simultaneously using both the situation strength and trait relevance concepts would be evident if a strong social context exerts greater influence on the relationships between socially relevant attributes (e.g., social orientation) and interpersonal role behaviors (e.g., helping others) when compared with the associations between socially irrelevant attributes and these behaviors.

Models of Role Performance

The above discussion alludes to what we believe may be the most fruitful area into which work analysis theory and research could be extended, namely, how work analytic data can be used to better understand role performance. Although this is not necessarily a new connection when one considers that general theories of performance have been directly based on empirical results from work analyses (e.g., Campbell et al., 1993), nonetheless, there exists today very little cross-fertilization of theory and research between the work analysis and job performance domains. Such connections would be valuable for a number of reasons. First, work analysis is sometimes characterized as simply an atheoretical, descriptive process that is necessitated primarily because of legal codifications (e.g., *Albemarle Paper Co. v. Moody,* 1975) and professional standards (e.g., *Principles for the Validation and Use of Personnel Selection Procedures;* Society for Industrial and Organizational Psychology, 2003). Of course, we believe there are many other reasons why work analysis is crucial to organizations, not the least of which is to improve the decisions made in various HR practices. However, this does suggest that one way to increase value perceptions of work analysis research is to demonstrate how such data relate to individual effectiveness. As authors of work analysis research who have, on numerous occasions, dealt with the "so what" question about our field of study, further justification of why work analysis matters has a certain appeal.

However, there is another reason for extending work analysis theory and research into the performance domain that is perhaps more fundamental than addressing criticisms of work analysis relevance. When research is focused on the definition, measurement, or prediction of performance, it is essentially concerned with the manner with which work role requirements are fulfilled. This notion is consistent, for example, with the contrast between work analysis as identifying requisite role behaviors and performance appraisal as identifying which of these behaviors are to be subject to evaluation (i.e., deemed valuable by the organization or its agents). The key idea here is that work analytic data, which are purposefully derived to discover the requirements of work role enactment, can therefore be meaningfully brought to bear within any related research that examines the nature of job performance or attempts to account for performance differences across individuals. Furthermore, there are several ways to link work analysis data to performance data at the multiple levels that are typically of interest to organizational researchers (i.e., individual, team, and organizational). Cognitive task analysis approaches could also be potentially useful, as they focus on discovering differences between experts and novices, which is another way to conceptualize antecedents to superior performance.

Work Analysis and Organizational Performance

At the organizational or firm level, future research could examine how work analysis contributes to so-called high-performance work practices (HPWP). Such practices have included different recruitment strategies, systematic personnel selection, strategic training, performance management systems, a variety of different compensation systems, use of teams, and HR planning (Huselid, 1995; Pfeffer, 1998), all of which are purported to increase individuals' knowledge, skills, and motivation for the benefit of the organization (Becker & Huselid, 1998). Several studies have provided supportive empirical evidence that HPWP are associated with organizational performance, including reduced turnover and increased sales, profits, and market value (Delaney & Huselid, 1996; Huselid, 1995; Huselid, Jackson, & Schuler, 1997).

The role of work analysis as an element of HPWP, however, has been uneven. In some of the seminal research in the area, work analysis was an explicit dimension of "employee skills and organizational structures" (Huselid, 1995, p. 646). In particular, organizations were assessed in terms of "the proportion of the workforce whose job has been subjected to a formal job analysis" (Huselid, 1995, p. 646). In addition, Delery and Doty (1996, p. 834) focused on the nature of job descriptions in use at the organization (e.g., "the duties of this job are clearly defined," "this job has an up-to-date job description," "the job description for this job contains all of the duties performed by individual employees"), which is one fundamental aspect of work analysis. Finally, in more recent research, Toh, Morgeson, and Campion (2008) explored how individual HR practices could be described in terms of coherent bundles of HR practices. In terms of work analysis, these HR practices included the number of selection systems in place that were based on formal work analyses and the number of training programs used that incorporated a careful, systematic training needs analysis.

In other HPWP research, however, the role of work analysis has been neglected. From our standpoint, this is an unfortunate omission for two reasons. First, as past research has shown, work analysis is an important component of HPWP. Second, as this chapter has shown, work analysis underlies all of these HPWP, as it provides the vital data required to effectively create and maintain such systems. Thus, an important opportunity is missed in some HPWP research, namely, the chance to move beyond merely capturing whether these practices are used and instead ascertaining how these practices are built (i.e., on what information they are based).

An additional point regarding work analysis and HPWP research is that this line of future inquiry would be congruent with previous calls for empirical investigation of strategic work analysis (see Sackett & Laczo, 2003). The ultimate goal of strategic work analysis is to forecast work role requirements of new roles that are expected to exist in the future or current roles that are expected to substantially change (Cronshaw, 1998; B. Schneider & Konz, 1989). This more predictive purpose of strategic work analysis holds particular salience to activities surrounding HR planning, which also involves forecasting various human capital needs. Further, recent research indicates that of the variety of specific practices designated as HPWP, HR planning has the largest effects on organizational performance (Combs, Liu, Hall, & Ketchen, 2006). Thus, future work analysis research that examines topics exclusive to strategic work analysis, as well as how this approach relates to effective HR planning, would be quite valuable.

Extending Work Analysis to the Team Level

Virtually all of the past work analysis research has focused on the individual level of analysis. Thus, another potential opportunity exists in extending work analysis research to the team level. In this respect, there are at least three areas of future research. First, work analysis research could pursue the development of a taxonomy of the work role requirements necessary for enacted roles within teams. Although several scholars have identified various requirements needed for team performance (e.g., Campion, Medsker, & Higgs, 1993), these have been primarily concerned with designing teams and determining what characteristics separate effective from ineffective teams. In addition, some attention has been devoted to conducting team task analyses, with a particular emphasis on the importance of interdependence within a team (Arthur, Edwards, Bell, Villado, & Bennett, 2005). Thus, the opportunity exists for more systematic and comprehensive work analysis efforts seeking to identify those work role requirements germane to working in teams.

Second, work analysis research could examine the validity and generalizability of existing models of team role requirements. For example, Stevens and Campion (1994) outlined 14 different worker requirements (knowledge, skills, abilities) pertinent to teamwork organized into five groupings: (a) conflict resolution, (b) collaborative problem solving, (c) communication, (d) goal setting and performance management, and (e) planning and task coordination. Although this conceptual model was based on an extensive literature review, empirical research examining or using this model remains scarce. However, there is some evidence suggesting these worker requirements do contribute to performance in team settings (Morgeson, Reider, & Campion, 2005; Stevens & Campion, 1994). From a work analysis perspective, it would be interesting to empirically investigate how well this conceptual model actually functions across various work roles that should differ with respect to teamwork characteristics. In other words, one could test whether the model can meaningfully and systematically discriminate between work roles that are embedded in team contexts versus those that are not. For example, one could examine how relationships among the worker requirements specified by the model vary in relation to enacting work roles in more team-oriented contexts (i.e., those with high interdependence, shared goals, etc.). Presumably, the worker requirements specified in the models should be more salient to enacting work roles in more team-oriented contexts.

A third topic for future work analysis research to address is how consensus among individual role holders regarding important work role requirements might impact group or unit effectiveness. Role theorists use the term *consensus* to denote sharedness or agreement among the expectations held by various role holders (Biddle, 1986). At more molar levels, consensus has been thought to lead to more effective integration of social systems (Biddle, 1979) because roles serve the important function of coordinating and integrating the behavior of individuals (Katz & Kahn, 1978). This has led some work analysis researchers to wonder whether greater consensus could result in overall increases in cross-role-holder effectiveness (Dierdorff & Morgeson, 2007). At the same time, some costs might be associated with too much consensus among individual role holders, such as less innovation and creativity. Future research is needed to examine the potential consequences of consensus, or disagreement, for the effective functioning of units or groups.

The Implications of Role Expectations

Conceptualizing work analysis judgments made by role incumbents as representing important expectations regarding how they enact their work roles allows the field of work analysis to expand considerably into other theoretical areas. Role expectations are simply beliefs about what a given role entails (Ilgen & Hollenbeck, 1991) and are important antecedents to role enactment. With regard to work analysis, the content of role expectations is reflected in judgments of various work role requirements (Dierdorff & Morgeson, 2007). Role expectations are important to a number of individual-level outcomes. For example, clarity with regard to one's work role has substantial positive ramifications for job performance, satisfaction, and organizational commitment (Abramis, 1994; Tubre & Collins, 2000). In addition, the breadth with which individuals define their work roles has been shown to impact job performance (Morgeson, Delaney-Klinger, & Hemingway, 2005). The above findings suggest that examining role expectations in particular is a fruitful avenue for future work analysis research.

One area of research in which role expectations are especially relevant is the recent work focused on the effects of role definitions on the performance of organizational citizenship behavior (OCB). Despite its early definition of being extra-role work behavior (Organ, 1988; Organ, Podsakoff, & MacKenzie, 2006), studies have shown that individuals frequently view OCB as falling within the requirements of their work roles (Haworth & Levy, 2001; Hui, Lam, & Law, 2000; Morrison, 1994). As a result, OCB researchers have begun to investigate how OCB role definitions impact whether individuals will engage in OCB (Kamdar, McAllister, & Turban, 2006; McAllister, Kamdar, Morrison, & Turban, 2007).

Work analysis research could meaningfully contribute to this area of inquiry for at least two reasons. First, from its early descriptions, OCB has always been conceptualized as generic work behavior, applicable to a wide variety of work roles (Borman & Penner, 2001). This suggests that such behavior could easily fall within the work role requirements commonly captured in work analysis. For work analysis research, the implication is that OCB research can be meaningfully informed by results from the study of work role requirements. It is interesting to note that the premise that OCB is indeed widely applicable across work roles has yet to be empirically substantiated, which is a question that can be directly addressed by future work analysis research.

Second, OCB role definitions in the extant research are typically operationalized by administering to role incumbents the same measurement scale (or with very slight variation) used to capture subsequent performance of OCB. Such operationalizations of role perceptions seek to ascertain whether employees view OCB as part of their work roles and what consequences this role definition may have on ensuing OCB performance. However, these operationalizations do increase the risk of common method bias, as the same scales are used as antecedents and criteria. An alternative way for work analysis research to study whether role perceptions influence the performance of OCB would be to examine how role expectations affect the enactment of OCB. Here, role expectations could better depict how individuals construe the entirety of their work roles (vs. only if OCB is role related) and could expand to capture role perceptions of both activity and attribute requirements. For example, role expectations regarding activities and attributes that are interpersonal in nature could be examined to determine if they predict whether role incumbents engage in OCB as part of their role enactment.

This approach to focusing on broader role expectations is also consistent with recent suggestions that an individual's orientation toward his or her work role is an encompassing concept that can include various facets, such as passive, strategic, and collective orientations (Parker, 2007). The latter role orientation has particular salience to OCB performance because it pertains to how individuals construe their roles with regard to working with others toward goal attainment. Important to note is that one's orientation and expectations toward one's work role are known to be shaped by features of the work context, such as autonomy and interdependence (Dierdorff & Morgeson, 2007; Parker, 2007). As mentioned earlier, work context descriptors clearly fall within the scope of work analysis. Thus, future work analysis research could test whether features of the work context moderate the potential relationships between role orientations, role expectations, and OCB.

The Role of Context

In addition to the research topics discussed above within different levels of analysis, there are a number of cross-level questions that work analysis research could address. Many of these possible contributions stem from the fact that work analysis research provides a systematic way of describing contextual variables (Dierdorff, 2008). Indeed, several authors have pointed to the difficulties surrounding exactly how to delineate the major elements that comprise context as a major reason for the lack of context-oriented research in I/O psychology and organizational behavior (Hattrup & Jackson, 1996; Johns, 2006). One example of using work analytic data to examine contextual effects can be seen in a recent study by Dierdorff and Ellington (2008). These authors integrated work context information from O*NET into examinations of how the nature of occupational roles shapes whether individuals experience work–family conflict. Other potential areas that could similarly benefit from work analysis research include person–environment fit (e.g., demands–abilities approach; Kristof, 1996) and work design (e.g., moderators of the design characteristics–satisfaction relationship; Morgeson & Humphrey, 2008).

In addition to work context, future work analysis research could examine other broader contextual factors, such as the impact of national culture. Findings from recent research have been equivocal on the influence of national culture. For example, one study found very small effects, suggesting that work analysis data are transportable across cultures (Taylor et al., 2008), whereas another study found national culture to be related to the frequency with which certain kinds of work behaviors were performed (Shin, Morgeson, & Campion, 2007). These mixed results suggest more research is warranted. In addition to national culture, aspects of organizational culture (e.g., values) would be an example of other broader contextual effects that could be investigated.

Finally, it may be interesting to examine how larger changes that are occurring in the broader world of work might shape the outcomes of work analysis. The impact of globalization, prevalence of interorganizational relationships, use of outsourcing, and reliance on information technology for communication are all examples of shifts in the world of work. Such forces are perhaps unlikely to change the primary goal of work analysis—systematically uncovering activities and attributes and the work context in which roles are performed—but rather these forces could very well impact the salience of the various outcomes of work analysis. For example, the products of work analysis may become even more important for HR planning, where an emphasis is placed on assessing current and forecasting future human capital needs. In addition, practitioners of work analysis may need to be aware of broader forces not normally considered related to work analysis concerns (e.g., changes in industry practices, meta-technology [geospatial, biotechnology, etc.], labor economics) to contextualize their findings for use in organizational strategy and HR management decisions.

CONCLUSION: TOWARD A MORE THEORETICAL VIEW OF WORK ANALYSIS

As we hope this chapter has made clear, work analysis not only has a long history in I/O psychology, but also has a promising future. Our goal was to not only review past research, but also point to numerous opportunities for future research, particularly in areas often not traditionally considered to be the purview of work analysis research. We recognize that many researchers conduct work analysis but may not consider themselves work analysis scholars. In a practical sense, then, future work analysis research would be well-served if those involved in substantive research that relies on work analysis data (e.g., selection researchers) were attuned to the opportunities to incorporate research questions about work analysis in the course of their ongoing efforts.

Perhaps the most pressing issue for future work analysis research, however, is to adopt a more theoretically grounded approach, such that research not only makes a contribution to the practice of work analysis, but also advances theory. Of course, there is considerable historical precedent in work analysis research for such a theoretical grounding. Functional job analysis was based in the data–people–things framework, and the PAQ drew from the stimulus–organism–response paradigm that underlies behaviorism. However, as science has progressed, reliance on such overarching frameworks has decreased in favor of more middle-range theories (Merton, 1949). We feel that middle-range theories hold the most promise for advancing work analysis research. Thus, instead of attempting to develop a theory of work analysis, we advocate that work analysis researchers begin to draw from the numerous theoretical frameworks discussed earlier (e.g., role theory, social and cognitive psychological theory) in their future research efforts. Such an approach is certain to reenergize the field of work analysis.

References

Aamodt, M. G., Kimbrough, W. W., Keller, R. J., & Crawford, K. J. (1982). Relationship between sex, race, and job performance level and the generation of critical incidents. *Educational and Psychological Research, 2,* 227–234.

Abramis, D. J. (1994). Work role ambiguity, job satisfaction, and job performance: Meta-analyses and review. *Psychological Reports, 75,* 1411–1433.

Ackerman, P. L., & Humphreys, L. G. (1990). Individual differences theory in industrial and organizational psychology. In M. D. Dunnette & L. M. Hough (Eds.), *Handbook of industrial and organizational psychology* (Vol. 1, 2nd ed., pp. 223–282). Palo Alto, CA: Consulting Psychologists Press.

Advisory Panel for the Dictionary of Occupational Titles. (1993). *The new DOT: A database of occupational titles for the twenty-first century (final report).* Washington, DC: U.S. Employment Service, U.S. Department of Labor Employment and Training Administration.

Aguinis, H., Mazurkiewicz, M. D., & Heggestad, E. D. (2009). Using Web-based frame-of-reference training to decrease biases in personality-based job analysis: An experimental field study. *Personnel Psychology, 62,* 405–438.

Albemarle Paper Co. v. Moody, 422 U.S. 405 (1975).

Arthur, W., Jr., Edwards, B. D., Bell, S. T., Villado, A. J., & Bennett, W. (2005). Team task analysis: Identifying tasks and jobs that are team based. *Human Factors, 47,* 654–669.

Ash, R. A. (1988). Job analysis in the world of work. In S. Gael (Ed.), *The job analysis handbook for business, industry and government* (Vol. 1, pp. 3–13). New York: Wiley.

Ash, R. A., & Edgell, S. L. (1975). A note on the readability of the position analysis questionnaire. *Journal of Applied Psychology, 60,* 765–766.

Ash, R. A., & Levine, E. L. (1980). A framework for evaluating job analysis methods. *Personnel, 57,* 53–59.

Becker, B. E., & Huselid, M. A. (1998). High performance work systems and firm performance: A synthesis of research and managerial implications. *Research in Personnel and Human Resources Journal, 16,* 53–101.

Biddle, B. J. (1979). *Role theory: Expectations, identities, and behavior.* New York: Academic Press.

Biddle, B. J. (1986). Recent developments in role theory. *Annual Review of Sociology, 12,* 67–92.

Block, J., & Block, J. H. (1981). Studying situational dimensions: A grand perspective and some limited empiricism. In D. Magnusson (Ed.), *Toward a psychology of situations: An interactional perspective* (pp. 85–103). Hillsdale, NJ: Erlbaum.

Borman, W. C., Dorsey, D., & Ackerman, L. (1992). Time-spent responses as time allocation strategies: Relations with sales performance in a stockbroker sample. *Personnel Psychology, 45,* 763–777.

Borman, W. C., & Penner, L. A. (2001). Citizenship performance: Its nature, antecedents, and motives. In B. W. Roberts & R. Hogan (Eds.), *Personality psychology in the workplace* (pp. 45–61). Washington, DC: American Psychological Association.

Bowers, K. S. (1973). Situationalism in psychology: An analysis and critique. *Psychological Review, 80,* 307–336.

Brannick, M. T., Levine, E. L., & Morgeson, F. P. (2007). *Job analysis: Methods, research, and applications for human resource management* (2nd ed.). Thousand Oaks, CA: Sage.

Brendle, M., Rivkin, D. W., & Lewis, P. M. (2008, April). Developing O*NET tools and technology: Information for a changing workplace. In E. Dierdorff & S. Cox (Chairs), *Meeting the challenges of occupational analysis in a rapidly changing workplace: Implications for the O*NET system.* Symposium conducted at the 23rd annual meeting of the Society for Industrial and Organizational Psychology, San Francisco.

Campbell, J. P., McCloy, R. A., Oppler, S. H., & Sager, C. E. (1993). A theory of performance. In N. Schmitt & W. Borman (Eds.), *Personnel selection in organizations* (pp. 35–70). San Francisco: Jossey-Bass.

Campion, M. A., Medsker, G. J., & Higgs, A. C. (1993). Relations between work group characteristics and effectiveness: Implications for designing effective work groups. *Personnel Psychology, 46,* 823–850.

Campion, M. A., Morgeson, F. P., & Mayfield, M. (1999). O*NET's theoretical contributions to job analysis research. In N. G. Peterson, W. C. Borman, M. D. Mumford, P. R. Jeanneret, & E. A. Fleishman (Eds.), *An occupational information system for the 21st century: The development of O*NET* (pp. 297–304). Washington, DC: American Psychological Association.

Cascio, W. F., & Aguinis, H. (2008). Research in industrial and organizational psychology from 1963 to 2007: Changes, choices, and trends. *Journal of Applied Psychology, 93,* 1062–1081.

Combs, J. G., Liu, Y., Hall, A. T., & Ketchen, D. J. (2006). How much do high performance work practices matter? A meta-analysis of their effects on organizational performance. *Personnel Psychology, 59,* 501–528.

Conley, P. R., & Sackett, P. R. (1987). Effects of using high- versus low-performing job incumbents as sources of job-analysis information. *Journal of Applied Psychology, 72,* 434–437.

Conte, J. M., Dean, M. A., Ringenbach, K. L., Moran, S. K., & Landy, F. L. (2005). The relationship between work attitudes and job analysis ratings: Do task rating scale type and task discretion matter? *Human Performance, 18,* 1–21.

Converse, P. D., Oswald, F. L., Gillespie, M. A., Field, K. A., & Bizot, E. B. (2004). Matching individuals to occupations using aptitudes and the O*NET: Issues and an application in career guidance. *Personnel Psychology, 57,* 451–487.

Cornelius, E. T., & Lyness, K. S. (1980). A comparison of holistic and decomposed judgment strategies in job analysis by job incumbents. *Journal of Applied Psychology, 65,* 155–163.

Costanza, D. P., Fleishman, E. A., & Marshall-Mies, J. C. (1999). Knowledge. In N. G. Peterson, M. D. Mumford, W. C. Borman, P. R. Jeanneret, & E. A. Fleishman (Eds.), *An occupational information system for the 21st century: The development of O*NET* (pp. 71–90). Washington, DC: American Psychological Association.

Cronshaw, S. (1998). Job analysis: Changing nature of work. *Canadian Psychology, 39,* 5–13.

Cucina, J. M., Vasilopoulos, N. L., & Sehgal, K. (2005). Personality-based job analysis and the self-serving bias. *Journal of Business and Psychology, 20,* 275–290.

Cunningham, J. W. (1989, August). Discussion. In R. J. Harvey (Chair), *Applied measurement issues in job analysis.* Symposium presented at the annual meeting of the American Psychological Association, New Orleans, LA.

Cunningham, J. W. (1996). Generic descriptors: A likely direction in occupational analysis. *Military Psychology, 8,* 247–262.

Cunningham, J. W. (2000). Introduction to a new journal. *Ergometrika, 1,* 1–23.

Delaney, J. T., & Huselid, M. A. (1996). The impact of human resource management practices on performance in for-profit and nonprofit organizations. *Academy of Management Journal, 39,* 949–969.

Delery, J. E., & Doty, D. H. (1996). Modes of theorizing in strategic human resource management: Tests of universalistic, contingency, and configurational performance predictions. *Academy of Management Journal, 39,* 802–835.

Dierdorff, E. C. (2008, April). *Illuminating the "murky ground": Linking context theory to empirical research.* Symposium presented at the 23rd annual meeting of the Society for Industrial and Organizational Psychology, San Francisco.

Dierdorff, E. C., Cantwell, A. R., & Nottingham, J. (2008, April). *Capturing and defining new and emerging occupations in high-growth sectors.* Symposium presented at the 23rd annual meeting of the Society for Industrial and Organizational Psychology, San Francisco.

Dierdorff, E. C., & Cox, S. P. (2008, April). *Meeting the challenges of occupational analysis in a rapidly changing workplace: Implications for the O*NET system.* Symposium presented at the 23rd annual meeting of the Society for Industrial and Organizational Psychology, San Francisco.

Dierdorff, E. C., & Ellington, J. K. (2008). It's the nature of work: Examining behavior-based sources of work–family conflict across occupations. *Journal of Applied Psychology, 93,* 883–892.

Dierdorff, E. C., & Morgeson, F. P. (2007). Consensus in work role requirements: The influence of discrete occupational context on role expectations. *Journal of Applied Psychology, 92,* 1228–1241.

Dierdorff, E. C., & Morgeson, F. P. (2009). Effects of descriptor specificity and observability on incumbent work analysis ratings. *Personnel Psychology, 62,* 601–628.

Dierdorff, E. C., & Rubin, R. S. (2007). Carelessness and discriminability in work role requirement judgments: Influences of role ambiguity and cognitive complexity. *Personnel Psychology, 60,* 597–625.

Dierdorff, E. C., Rubin, R. S., & Morgeson, F. P. (2009). The milieu of managerial work: integrative framework linking context to role requirements. *Journal of Applied Psychology, 94,* 972–988.

Dierdorff, E. C., & Wilson, M. A. (2003). A meta-analysis of job analysis reliability. *Journal of Applied Psychology, 88,* 635–646.

Drauden, G. M. (1988). Task inventory analysis in industry and the public sector. In S. Gael (Ed.), *The job analysis handbook for business, industry, and government* (Vol. 2, pp. 1051–1071). New York: John Wiley & Sons.

Dunnette, M. D. (1976). Aptitudes, abilities, and skills. In M. D. Dunnette (Ed.), *Handbook of industrial and organizational psychology* (pp. 473–520). Chicago: Rand McNally.

Dunnette, M. D. (1999). Introduction. In N. G. Peterson, M. D. Mumford, W. C. Borman, P. R. Jeanneret, & E. A. Fleishman (Eds.), *An occupational information system for the 21st century: The development of O*NET* (pp. 3–7). Washington, DC: American Psychological Association.

Dye, D., & Silver, M. (1999). The origins of O*NET. In N. G. Peterson, M. D. Mumford, W. C. Borman, P. R. Jeanneret, & E. A. Fleishman (Eds.), *An occupational information system for the 21st century: The development of O*NET* (pp. 9–19). Washington, DC: American Psychological Association.

Eggerth, D. E., Bowles, S. M., Tunick, R. H., & Andrew, M. E. (2005). Convergent validity of O*NET Holland code classifications. *Journal of Career Assessment, 13,* 150–168.

Fine, S. A., & Getkate, M. (1995). *Benchmark tasks for job analysis: A guide for functional job analysis (FJA) scales.* Mahwah, NJ: Erlbaum.

Flanagan, J. C. (1954). The critical incident technique. *Psychological Bulletin, 51,* 327–358.

Fleishman, E. A. (1975). Toward a taxonomy of human performance. *American Psychologist, 30,* 1127–1149.

Fleishman, E. A. (1992). *Fleishman-Job Analysis Survey (F-JAS).* Potomac, MD: Management Research Institute.

Fleishman, E. A., Costanza, D. P., & Marshall-Mies, J. (1999). Abilities. In N. G. Peterson, M. D. Mumford, W. C. Borman, P. R. Jeanneret, & E. A. Fleishman (Eds.), *An occupational information system for the 21st century: The development of O*NET* (pp. 175–196). Washington, DC: American Psychological Association.

Fried, Y., & Ferris, G. R. (1986). The dimensionality of job characteristics: Some neglected issues. *Journal of Applied Psychology, 71,* 419–426.

Friedman, L. (1990). Degree of redundancy between time, importance, and frequency task ratings. *Journal of Applied Psychology, 75,* 748–752.

Freidman, L. (1991). Correction to Friedman (1990). *Journal of Applied Psychology, 76,* 366.

Gael, S. (1983). *Job analysis: A guide to assessing work activities.* San Francisco: Jossey-Bass.

Gardner, W. L., & Martinko, M. J. (1988). Impression management in organizations. *Journal of Management, 14,* 321–338.

Gatewood, R. D., & Feild, H. S. (2001). *Human resource selection.* Orlando, FL: Harcourt Brace.

Ghiselli, E. (1966). *The validity of occupational aptitude tests.* New York: Wiley.

Goffin, R. D., & Woycheshin, D. E. (2006). An empirical method of determining employee competencies/ KSAOs from task-based job analysis. *Military Psychology, 18,* 121–130.

Goldstein, I. L., Zedeck, S., & Schneider, B. (1993). An exploration of the job analysis–content validity process. In N. Schmitt & W. C. Borman (Eds.), *Personnel selection in organizations* (pp. 3–34). San Francisco: Jossey-Bass.

Graen, G. B. (1976). Role making processes within complex organizations. In M. D. Dunnette (Ed.), *Handbook of industrial and organizational psychology* (pp. 1201–1245). Chicago: Rand McNally.

Green, S. B., & Stutzman, T. (1986). An evaluation of methods to select respondents to structured job-analysis questionnaires. *Personnel Psychology, 39,* 543–564.

Green, S. B., & Veres, J. G. (1990). Evaluation of an index to detect inaccurate respondents to a task analysis inventory. *Journal of Business and Psychology, 5,* 47–61.

Guion, R. (1993). The need for change: Six persistent themes. In N. Schmitt & W. Borman (Eds.), *Personnel selection in organizations* (pp. 481–497). San Francisco: Jossey-Bass.

Hadden, W. C., Kravets, N., & Muntaner, C. (2004). Descriptive dimensions of US occupations with data from the O*NET. *Social Science Research, 33,* 64–78.

Harvey, R. J. (1991). Job analysis. In M. D. Dunnette & L. M. Hough (Eds.), *Handbook of industrial and organizational psychology* (Vol. 2, 2nd ed., pp. 71–163). Palo Alto, CA: Consulting Psychologists Press.

Harvey, R. J., Friedman, L., Hakel, M. D., & Cornelius, E. T. (1988). Dimensionality of the job element inventory, a simplified worker-oriented job analysis questionnaire. *Journal of Applied Psychology, 73,* 639–646.

Hattrup, K., & Jackson, S. E. (1996). Learning about individual differences by taking situations seriously. In K. R. Murphy (Ed.), *Individual differences and behavior in organizations* (pp. 507–547). San Francisco: Jossey-Bass.

Haworth, C. L., & Levy, P. E. (2001). The importance of instrumentality beliefs in the prediction of organizational citizenship behaviors. *Journal of Vocational Behavior, 59,* 64–75.

Hempel, C. G. (1965). *Aspects of scientific explanation and other essays in the philosophy of science.* New York: The Free Press.

Hofmann, D. A., Morgeson, F. P., & Gerras, S. (2003). Climate as a moderator of the relationship between LMX and content specific citizenship: Safety climate as an exemplar. *Journal of Applied Psychology, 88,* 170–178.

Hui, C., Lam, S. S. K., & Law, K. K. S. (2000). Instrumental values of organizational citizenship behavior for promotion: A field quasi-experiment. *Journal of Applied Psychology, 85,* 822–828.

Hunter, J. E. (1986). Cognitive ability, cognitive aptitudes, job knowledge, and job performance. *Journal of Vocational Behavior, 29,* 340–362.

Huselid, M. A. (1995). The impact of human resource management practices on turnover, productivity, and corporate financial performance. *Academy of Management Journal, 38,* 635–672.

Huselid, M. A., Jackson, S. E., & Schuler, R. S. (1997). Technical and strategic human resource management effectiveness as determinants of firm performance. *Academy of Management Journal, 40,* 171–188.

Ilgen, D. R., & Hollenbeck, J. R. (1991). The structure of work: Job design and roles. In M. D. Dunnette & L. M. Hough (Eds.), *Handbook of industrial and organizational psychology* (Vol. 2, 2nd ed., pp. 165–207). Palo Alto, CA: Consulting Psychologists Press.

Jeanneret, P. R. (1992). Applications of job component/ synthetic validity to construct validity. *Human Performance, 5,* 81–96.

Jeanneret, P. R., Borman, W. C., Kubisiak, U. C., & Hanson, M. A. (1999). Generalized work activities. In N. G. Peterson, M. D. Mumford, W. C. Borman, P. R. Jeanneret, & E. A. Fleishman (Eds.), *An occupational information system for the 21st century: The development of O*NET* (pp. 49–69). Washington, DC: American Psychological Association.

Jeanneret, P. R., & Strong, M. H. (2003). Linking O*NET job analysis information to job requirement predictors: An O*NET application. *Personnel Psychology, 56,* 423–429.

Johns, G. (2006). The essential impact of context on organizational behavior. *Academy of Management Review, 31,* 386–408.

Katz, D., & Kahn, R. L. (1978). *The social psychology of organizations* (2nd ed.). New York: Wiley.

Kamdar, D., McAllister, D. M., & Turban, D. B. (2006). "All in a day's work": How follower individual differences and justice perceptions predict OCB role definitions and behavior. *Journal of Applied Psychology, 91,* 841–855.

Kozlowski, S. W. J., & Hattrup, K. (1992). A disagreement about within-group agreement: Disentangling issues of consistency versus consensus. *Journal of Applied Psychology, 77,* 161–167.

Kristof, A. L. (1996). Person–organization fit: An integrative review of its conceptualizations, measurement, and implications. *Personnel Psychology, 49,* 1–49.

Landy, F. J., & Vasey, J. (1991). Job analysis: The composition of SME samples. *Personnel Psychology, 44,* 27–50.

LaPolice, C. C., Carter, G. W., & Johnson, J. J. (2008). Linking O*NET descriptors to occupational literacy requirements using job component validation. *Personnel Psychology, 61,* 405–441.

Levine, J., Nottingham, J., Paige, B., & Lewis, P. (2000). *Transitioning O*NET to the Standard Occupational Classification.* Raleigh, NC: National Center for O*NET Development.

Lievens, F., & Sanchez, J. I. (2007). Can training improve the quality of inferences made by raters in competency modeling? A quasi-experiment. *Journal of Applied Psychology, 92,* 812–819.

Lievens, F., Sanchez, J. I., & De Corte, W. (2004). Easing the inferential leap in competency modeling: The effects of task-related information and subject matter expertise. *Personnel Psychology, 57,* 881–904.

Lindell, M. K., Clause, C. S., Brandt, C. J., & Landis, R. S. (1998). Relationship between organizational context and job analysis task ratings. *Journal of Applied Psychology, 83,* 769–776.

Lucia, A., & Lepsinger, R. (1999). *The art and science of competency models: Pinpointing critical success factors in organizations.* San Francisco: Jossey-Bass.

Madden, J. M. (1962). The effect of varying the degree of rater familiarity in job evaluation. *Personnel Administrator, 25,* 42–46.

Madden, J. M. (1963). A further note on the familiarity effect in job evaluation. *Personnel Administrator, 26,* 52–54.

Magnussen, D., & Endler, N. S. (1977). *Personality at the crossroads: Current issues in interactional psychology.* Hillsdale, NJ: Erlbaum.

Manson, T. M., Levine, E. L., & Brannick, M. T. (2000). The construct validity of task inventory ratings: A multitrait–multimethod analysis. *Human Performance, 13,* 1–22.

Marlowe, D., & Crowne, D. P. (1961). Social desirability and response to perceived situational demands. *Journal of Consulting Psychology, 25,* 109–115.

McAllister, D. M., Kamdar, D., Morrison, E. W., & Turban, D. B. (2007). Disentangling role perceptions: How perceived role breadth, discretion, instrumentality and efficacy relate to helping and taking charge. *Journal of Applied Psychology, 92,* 1200–1211.

McCormick, E. J. (1960). *Effect of amount of job information required on reliability of incumbents' check-list reports* (WADD-TN-60-142). Lackland Air Force Base, TX: Personnel Research Laboratory, Wright Air Development Division.

McCormick, E. J. (1979). *Job analysis: Methods and applications.* New York: ANACOM.

McCormick, E. J., Jeanneret, P. R., & Mecham, R. C. (1972). A study of job characteristics and job dimensions as based on the Position Analysis Questionnaire (PAQ) [Monograph]. *Journal of Applied Psychology, 56,* 347–368.

Merton, R. K. (1949). *Social theory and social structure: Toward the codification of theory and research.* Glencoe, IL: Free Press.

Mischel, W. (1977). The interaction of person and situation. In D. Magnusson & N. S. Endler (Eds.), *Personality at the crossroads: Current issues in interactional psychology* (pp. 333–352). Hillsdale, NJ: Erlbaum.

Mitchell, J. L. (1988). History of job analysis in military organizations. In S. Gael (Ed.), *The job analysis handbook for business, industry, and government* (pp. 30–36). New York: Wiley.

Mitchell, J. L., Bennett, W., & Strickland, W. J. (1999, May). *Current and future trends in job analysis systems and technologies: Studying the world of work in AD 2000 and beyond.* Symposium sponsored by the Institute for Job and Occupational Analysis, the U.S. Air Force Research Laboratory, and the Human Resources Research Organization, San Antonio, TX.

Mitchell, J. L., & Driskill, W. E. (1996). Military job analysis: A historical perspective. *Military Psychology, 8,* 119–142.

Morgeson, F. P., & Campion, M. A. (1997). Social and cognitive sources of potential inaccuracy in job analysis. *Journal of Applied Psychology, 82,* 627–655.

Morgeson, F. P., & Campion, M. A. (2000). Accuracy in job analysis: Toward an inference-based model. *Journal of Organizational Behavior, 21,* 819–827.

Morgeson, F. P., Delaney-Klinger, K. A., & Hemingway, M. A. (2005). The importance of job autonomy, cognitive ability, and job-related skill for predicting role breadth and job performance. *Journal of Applied Psychology, 90,* 399–406.

Morgeson, F. P., Delaney-Klinger, K. A., Mayfield, M. S., Ferrara, P., & Campion, M. A. (2004). Self-presentation processes in job analysis: A field experiment investigating inflation in abilities, tasks, and competencies. *Journal of Applied Psychology, 89,* 674–686.

Morgeson, F. P., & Humphrey, S. E. (2008). Job and team design: Toward a more integrative conceptualization of work design. In J. Martocchio (Ed.), *Research in personnel and human resource management* (Vol. 27, pp. 39–92). Bingley, United Kingdom: Emerald Group Publishing.

Morgeson, F. P., Reider, M. H., & Campion, M. A. (2005). Selecting individuals in team settings: The importance of social skills, personality characteristics, and teamwork knowledge. *Personnel Psychology, 58,* 583–611.

Morrison, E. W. (1994). Role definitions and organizational citizenship behavior: The importance of the employee's perspective. *Academy of Management Journal, 37,* 1543–1567.

Mullins, W. C., & Kimbrough, W. W. (1988). Group composition as a determinant of job analysis outcomes. *Journal of Applied Psychology, 73,* 657–664.

Mumford, M. D., & Peterson, N. G. (1999). The O*NET content model: Structural considerations in designing jobs. In N. G. Peterson, M. D. Mumford, W. C. Borman, P. R. Jeanneret, & E. A. Fleishman (Eds.), *An occupational information system for the 21st century: The development of O*NET* (pp. 21–30). Washington, DC: American Psychological Association.

Münsterberg, H. (1913). *Psychology and industrial efficiency*. Boston: Houghton Mifflin.

Nunnally, J. C., & Bernstein, I. H. (1994). *Psychometric theory* (3rd ed.). New York: McGraw-Hill.

Organ, D. W. (1988). *Organizational citizenship behavior: The good soldier syndrome*. Lexington, MA: Lexington Books.

Organ, D. W., Podsakoff, P. M., & MacKenzie, S. B. (2006). *Organizational citizenship behavior: Its nature, antecedents and consequences*. Beverly Hills, CA: Sage.

Parker, S. K. (2007). "That is my job": How employees' role orientation affects their job performance. *Human Relations, 60,* 403–434.

Peterson, N. G., Mumford, M. D., Borman, W. C., Jeanneret, P. R., & Fleishman, E. A. (1999). *An occupational information system for the 21st century: The development of O*NET*. Washington, DC: American Psychological Association.

Peterson, N. G., Mumford, M. D., Borman, W. C., Jeanneret, P. R., Fleishman, E. A., Campion, M. A., et al. (2001). Understanding work using the occupational information network (O*NET): Implications for practice and research. *Personnel Psychology, 54,* 451–492.

Pfeffer, J. (1998). Seven practices of successful organizations. *California Management Review, 40,* 96–124.

Pine, D. E. (1995). Assessing the validity of job ratings: An empirical study of false reporting in task inventories. *Public Personnel Management, 24,* 451–459.

Podsakoff, P. M., MacKenzie, S. M., Bachrach, D. G., & Podsakoff, N. P. (2005). The influence of management journals in the 1980's and 1990's. *Strategic Management Journal, 26,* 473–488.

Prien, E. P., & Saleh, S. D. (1963). A study of bias in job analysis and evaluation. *Journal of Industrial Psychology, 1,* 113–117.

Prien, K., Prien, E., & Wooten, W. (2003). Interrater reliability in job analysis: Differences in strategy and perspective. *Public Personnel Management, 32,* 125–141.

Primoff, E. S., & Fine, S. A. (1988). A history of job analysis. In S. Gael (Ed.), *The job analysis handbook for business, industry, and government* (pp. 14–29). New York: Wiley.

Raymark, P. H., Schmit, M. J., & Guion, R. M. (1997). Identifying potentially useful personality constructs for employee selection. *Personnel Psychology, 50,* 723–736.

Reiter-Palmon, R., Brown, M., Sandall, D. L., Buboltz, C., & Nimps, T. (2006). Development of an O*NET web-based job analysis and its implementation in the U.S. Navy: Lessons learned. *Human Resource Management Review, 16,* 294–309.

Richman, W. L., & Quiñones, M. A. (1996). Task frequency rating accuracy: The effect of task engagement and experience. *Journal of Applied Psychology, 81,* 512–524.

Sackett, P. R., & Laczo, R. M. (2003). Job and work analysis. In W. C. Borman, D. R. Ilgen, & R. J. Klimoski (Eds.), *Comprehensive handbook of psychology: Industrial and organizational psychology* (Vol. 12, pp. 21–37). New York: John Wiley & Sons.

Sager, C. E., Mumford, M. D., Baughman, W. A., & Childs, R. A. (1999). Occupation-specific descriptors: Approaches, procedures, and findings. In N. G. Peterson, M. D. Mumford, W. C. Borman, P. R. Jeanneret, & E. A. Fleishman (Eds.), *An occupational information system for the 21st century: The development of O*NET* (pp. 227–236). Washington, DC: American Psychological Association.

Sanchez, J. I. (1994). From documentation to innovation: Reshaping job analysis to meet emerging business needs. *Human Resource Management Review, 4,* 51–74.

Sanchez, J. I., & Fraser, S. L. (1992). On the choice of scales for task analysis. *Journal of Applied Psychology, 77,* 545–553.

Sanchez, J. I., & Levine, E. L. (1989). Determining important tasks within jobs: A policy-capturing approach. *Journal of Applied Psychology, 74,* 336–342.

Sanchez, J. I., & Levine, E. L. (1994). The impact of rater's cognition on judgment accuracy: An extension into the job analysis domain. *Journal of Business and Psychology, 9,* 47–57.

Sanchez, J. I., & Levine, E. L. (1999). Is job analysis dead, misunderstood, or both? New forms of work analysis and design. In A. Kraut & A. Korman (Eds.), *Evolving practices in human resource management* (pp. 43–68). San Francisco: Jossey-Bass.

Sanchez, J. I., & Levine, E. L. (2000). Accuracy or consequential validity: Which is the better standard for job analysis data? *Journal of Organizational Behavior, 21,* 809–818.

Sanchez, J. I., & Levine, E. L. (2001). The analysis of work in the 20th & 21st centuries. In N. Anderson, D. S. Ones, H. K. Sinangil, & C. Viswesvaran (Eds.), *Handbook of industrial, work and organizational psychology* (Vol. 1, pp. 71–89). Thousand Oaks, CA: Sage.

Schippmann, J. S. (1999). *Strategic job modeling: Working at the core of integrated human resources*. Mahwah, NJ: Erlbaum.

Schippmann, J. S., Ash, R. A., Battista, M., Carr, L., Eyde, L. D., Hesketh, B., et al. (2000). The practice of competency modeling. *Personnel Psychology, 53,* 703–740.

Schmidt, F. L., & Hunter, J. E. (1977). Development of a general solution to the problem of validity generalization. *Journal of Applied Psychology, 62,* 529–540.

Schmitt, N., & Cohen, S. A. (1989). Internal analyses of task ratings by job incumbents. *Journal of Applied Psychology, 74,* 96–104.

Schneider, B., & Konz, A. M. (1989). Strategic job analysis. *Human Resource Management, 28,* 51–63.

Schneider, W., & Shiffrin, R. M. (1977). Controlled and automatic human information processing: I. Detection, search and attention. *Psychological Review, 84,* 1–66.

Shin, S. J., Morgeson, F. P., & Campion, M. A. (2007). What you do depends on where you are: Understanding how domestic and expatriate work requirements depend upon the cultural context. *Journal of International Business Studies, 38,* 64–83.

Shrout, P. E., & Fleiss, J. L. (1979). Intraclass correlations: Uses in assessing rater reliability. *Psychological Bulletin, 86,* 420–428.

Siddique, C. M. (2004). Job analysis: A strategic human resource management practice. *International Journal of Human Resource Management, 15,* 219–244.

Silverman, S. B., Wexley, K. N., & Johnson, J. C. (1984). The effects of age and job experience on employee responses to a structured job analysis questionnaire. *Public Personnel Management, 13,* 355–359.

Smith, J. E., & Hakel, M. D. (1979). Convergence among data sources, response bias, and reliability and validity of a structured job analysis questionnaire. *Personnel Psychology, 32,* 677–692.

Society for Industrial and Organizational Psychology. (2003). *Principles for the validation and use of personnel selection procedures* (4th ed.). Bowling Green, OH: Author.

Stevens, M. J., & Campion, M. A. (1994). The knowledge, skill, and ability requirements for teamwork: Implications for human resource management. *Journal of Management, 20,* 503–530.

Stewart, G. L., Fulmer, I. S., & Barrick, M. R. (2005). An exploration of member roles as a multilevel linking mechanism for individual traits and team outcomes. *Personnel Psychology, 58,* 343–365.

Strong, M. H., Jeanneret, P. R., McPhail, S. M., Blakley, B. R., & D'Egidio, E. L. (1999). Work context: Taxonomy and measurement of the work environment. In N. G. Peterson, M. D. Mumford, W. C. Borman, P. R. Jeanneret, & E. A. Fleishman (Eds.), *An occupational information system for the 21st century: The development of O*NET* (pp. 127–145). Washington, DC: American Psychological Association.

Taylor, P. J., Li, W., Shi, K., & Borman, W. C. (2008). The transportability of job information across countries. *Personnel Psychology, 61,* 69–111.

Terborg, J. R. (1981). Interactional psychology and research on human behavior in organizations. *Academy of Management Review, 6,* 569–576.

Tesluk, P. E., & Jacobs, R. R. (1998). Toward an integrated model of work experience. *Personnel Psychology, 51,* 321–355.

Tett, R. P., & Burnett, D. D. (2003). A personality trait-based interactionist model of job performance. *Journal of Applied Psychology, 88,* 500–517.

Tett, R. P., & Guterman, H. A. (2000). Situation trait relevance, trait expression, and cross-situational consistency: Testing a principle of trait activation. *Journal of Research in Personality, 34,* 397–423.

Toh, S. M., Morgeson, F. P., & Campion, M. A. (2008). Human resource configurations: Investigating fit with the organizational context. *Journal of Applied Psychology, 93,* 864–882.

Tubre, T. C., & Collins, J. M. (2000). Jackson and Schuler (1985) revisited: A meta-analysis of the relationships between role ambiguity, role conflict, and job performance. *Journal of Management, 26,* 155–169.

Tversky, A., & Kahneman, D. (1974, September 27). Judgment under uncertainty: Heuristics and biases. *Science, 185*(4157), 1124–1131.

Uhrbrock, R. S. (1922). The history of job analysis. *Administration, 3,* 164–168.

Van Iddekinge, C. H., Putka, D. J., Raymark, P. H., & Eidson, C. E. (2005). Modeling error variance in job specification ratings: The influence of rater, job, and organization-level factors. *Journal of Applied Psychology, 90,* 323–334.

Voskuijl, O. F., & van Sliedregt, T. (2002). Determinants of interrater reliability of job analysis: A meta-analysis. *European Journal of Psychological Assessment, 18,* 52–62.

Wang, N. (2003). Examining reliability and validity of job analysis survey data. *Journal of Applied Measurement, 4,* 358–369.

Wexley, K. N., & Silverman, S. B. (1978). An examination of differences between managerial effectiveness and response patterns on a structured job analysis questionnaire. *Journal of Applied Psychology, 63,* 646–649.

Wilson, M. A. (2006). A history of job analysis. In L. Koppes (Ed.), *Historical perspectives in industrial and organizational psychology* (pp. 219–242). Mahwah, NJ: Erlbaum.

Wilson, M. A., Harvey, R. J., & Macy, B. A. (1990). Repeating items to estimate the test–retest reliability of task inventory ratings. *Journal of Applied Psychology, 75,* 158–163.

Woehr, D. J., & Huffcutt, A. I. (1994). Rater training for performance appraisal: A quantitative review. *Journal of Occupational and Organizational Psychology, 67,* 189–205.

CHAPTER 2

RECRUITMENT: A REVIEW OF RESEARCH AND EMERGING DIRECTIONS

Brian R. Dineen and Scott M. Soltis

As the first decade of the 21st century comes to a close, companies are challenged as never before to attain the necessary human and social capital to develop, maintain, and increase their competitive advantage. Although organizations continue to wage the "war for talent," as it has popularly been phrased (e.g., Lavelle, 2003), this contest has increased both in scope and complexity, with recruiters claiming difficulty in finding good workers and acquiring talent (see Ployhart, 2006). The result is a fascinating yet multiplex environment that holds great research potential. For example, the poaching of employees has become a more public phenomenon, especially in the technology sector, as start-ups frequently court employees at established firms such as Google and Microsoft (Delaney, 2007; see also Gardner, 2005). Even more apparent is the recent boom of social networking sites designed for domestic and international job seekers such as linkedin.com and doostang.com (McConnon, 2007). Recruiters interested in poaching passive job candidates might use these sites by first developing relationships with candidates before luring them away from competitors (Cappelli, 2001; Lievens & Harris, 2003). Thus Web technology and the increased pace of recruitment activities have leveled the information playing field and have gained importance recently as intriguing research topics.

This chapter is devoted to reviewing the research that might inform this challenging landscape and also proposes new areas of research spawned by new developments and related anecdotal reports (e.g., Billsberry, 2007). Specifically, our goals are to (a) present a detailed model of the recruitment process; (b) provide a selective review of recent research pertaining to the context, strategies, and processes associated with the stages depicted; and (c) suggest several future avenues for recruitment research. We view recruitment as a process (Rynes, 1991; Rynes & Cable, 2003) and thus define it as the actions organizations take to generate applicant pools, maintain viable applicants, and encourage desired candidates to join those organizations.

This chapter is intended to complement reviews of the recruitment literature, both previous (Barber, 1998; Ehrhart & Ziegert, 2005; Rynes & Cable, 2003) and recent (Breaugh, 2008; Breaugh, Macan, & Grambow, 2008). A general theme of these reviews has been to recommend a more comprehensive examination of recruitment. Specifically, Barber (1998) and Rynes and Cable (2003) called for more integration of the context in which recruitment occurs. Breaugh et al. downplayed contextual issues and suggested exploring recruitment stages integratively, while also calling for more nuanced approaches to the study of certain topics. Viewing these excellent reviews as a foundation, we add our unique insights, cover additional studies, and call attention to new or expanded research areas. We focus mainly on research that has occurred since Rynes and Cable's review and present their conclusions in Exhibit 2.1 as a means of placing our review in the context of previous research findings. As will become evident, these previous findings are organized thematically in

Exhibit 2.1
Summary of Findings Reported by Rynes and Cable (2003)

Environmental and Contextual Considerations

Firm

- Location, size, and organizational image are important factors in job seekers' application decisions.
- Organizational reputation or image is highly correlated with organizational familiarity and moderately correlated with profitability and industry.
- The most likely routes to improving organizational image are to improve familiarity and to increase the amount of information available to applicants.
- Organizational image appears to be important to applicant decisions both because it sends signals about more specific job attributes and because it influences expected pride from membership (i.e., social identity).
- Other organizational-level characteristics, particularly size and industry, are used to make inferences about more specific vacancy characteristics.
- Some of the main determinants of perceived person–organization fit are the same as factors influencing perceived organizational image.
- Applicants' preinterview beliefs about organizations affect their interview performance and impressions. Applicants with positive preinterview exhibit more positive impression management behaviors, ask more positive confirmatory questions, and perceive recruiter behaviors more positively.
- In general, affirmative action policies are perceived positively by those who might benefit from them and negatively by white males.
- Negative reactions to affirmative action can be minimized by placing a strong emphasis on merit (e.g., affirmative action as tiebreaker policies) and explaining the reasons behind the policy.
- Although there are some organizational characteristics that are widely favored by most job seekers (e.g., fairness, high pay), the strength—and sometimes direction—of preferences varies according to individual differences in values, personality, or beliefs.

Vacancy

- Pay and benefits are of at least moderate importance in job choice. However, importance varies across individuals and market characteristics.
- In general, college students prefer high pay levels, pay raises based on individual rather than team performance, fixed rather than variable pay, and flexible rather than fixed benefits.
- Job challenge and interesting work appear to be particularly important to students who have exhibited high academic and social achievement.
- High pay levels, strong promotion opportunities, and performance-based pay are relatively more important to students with high levels of social achievement (e.g., extracurricular activity, offices).
- High academic achievers (i.e., those with high GPA and test scores) are more attracted by commitment-based employment philosophies than are high social achievers.
- Organizations appear to modify vacancy characteristics in reactive rather than strategic fashion, thus limiting potential recruitment effectiveness.

Labor Market

- High-quality applicants (i.e., as assessed by grades and number of job offers) generally appear to be more critical of recruiting practices (e.g., recruiters, recruiting delays). However, those with greater work experience may be slightly more forgiving.

Generating Viable Candidates

Targeting Strategies

- White males still have better access than other groups to informal sources of referral.
- Social referrals are still unequal by race and gender, and they have effects on employment outcomes.
- Job seekers' social networks explain variance in job choices over and above general preferences and specific academic preparation.

Messaging Strategies

- Results regarding recruitment source effects are inconsistent across studies. Even the strongest conclusion from research conducted before 1991—that informal sources are superior to formal ones in terms of posthire outcomes—appears to be open to question.
- Sources differ in terms of the types of applicants they produce and the amount of information they appear to provide. However, the precise nature of these differences varies across studies.

Exhibit 2.1 (*Continued*)

- Individuals often use more than one source in locating and applying for jobs. The typical practice of coding only one source is problematic and can have a substantial effect on study results.
- The same source (e.g., the Internet) can be used in different ways by different employers. Thus, the types of applicants attracted and the amount of information associated with the same source can also vary dramatically across employers.
- Realistic job previews (RJPs) are associated with consistent, but small, increases in employee retention.
- RJPs do not appear to cause greater applicant self-selection out of the applicant process. The issue of whether different types of employees self-select as a result of RJPs remains unexamined.
- Applicants appear to go through two phases of job search, as follows: (a) a broad, exploratory phase in which general information is sought mostly through formal sources and (b) a more focused stage in which informal sources are increasingly used to gain detailed information about a small subset of identified alternatives.

Maintaining Status of Viable Applicants

Screening Considerations

- Applicant reactions to selection procedures can be explained largely in terms of perceived fairness or justice.
- In general, applicants appear to accept the use of cognitive ability tests in selection.
- Although there are sometimes differences in perceived test fairness across demographic groups, there is little evidence that the use of testing causes job seekers to drop out of applicant pools.
- In campus recruiting contexts, delays between recruitment phases can cause significant dropout from applicant pools. Dropout will probably be most severe among applicants with the most opportunities.
- In other types of labor markets, dropout due to delays may be heaviest among those who need immediate employment.

Interactions With Organizational Agents

- Recruiters can make a difference to applicants' job choices, particularly at the extremes of recruiter effectiveness. However, recruiter effects are typically overshadowed by job and organizational attributes.
- Line recruiters and representatives met on site visits are more influential (in either direction) than staff recruiters and representatives met on campus.
- Applicants regard trained recruiters as somewhat more effective than untrained ones, although the effects on job choices are probably not large.
- Trained recruiters are more likely to follow a standardized protocol in interviews and to ask more screening-related questions. Thus, they are probably likely to produce more valid selection decisions.
- Although applicants like recruiters who spend more time recruiting than selecting, attraction to the job itself may suffer if recruitment is overemphasized relative to selection.
- Recruiter characteristics are often used to make inferences about organizational and job characteristics and likelihood of receiving an offer.
- Recruiters and other organizational representatives are often mentioned as sources of applicant beliefs about person–organization fit.
- Recruiter behaviors (particularly warmth) have a clear effect on applicant interview performance. Applicant behaviors have much less effect on recruiter behaviors, suggesting that recruiters have much more control over interview processes and outcomes than do applicants.

Note. From *Handbook of Psychology: Industrial and Organizational Psychology* (Vol. 12, p. 69), by W. C. Borman, D. R. Ilgen, and R. J. Klimoski (Eds.), 2003, Hoboken, NJ: Wiley. Copyright 2003 by Wiley. Adapted with permission.

Exhibit 2.1 according to the recruitment process framework we introduce next.

FRAMEWORK OF THE RECRUITMENT PROCESS

Keeping previous conclusions in mind, we present the framework shown in Figure 2.1 as a guide to the current review. Figure 2.1 integrates Barber's (1998) and Breaugh et al.'s (2008) sequential stage models and also integrates Rynes and Cable's (2003) more explicit consideration of environmental and contextual issues as well as key process issues. Specifically, Figure 2.1 illustrates three primary recruitment stages: generating viable candidates, maintaining the status of viable candidates, and achieving closure in terms of encouraging desired candidates to accept job offers and join the organization. Two key decision points demarcate

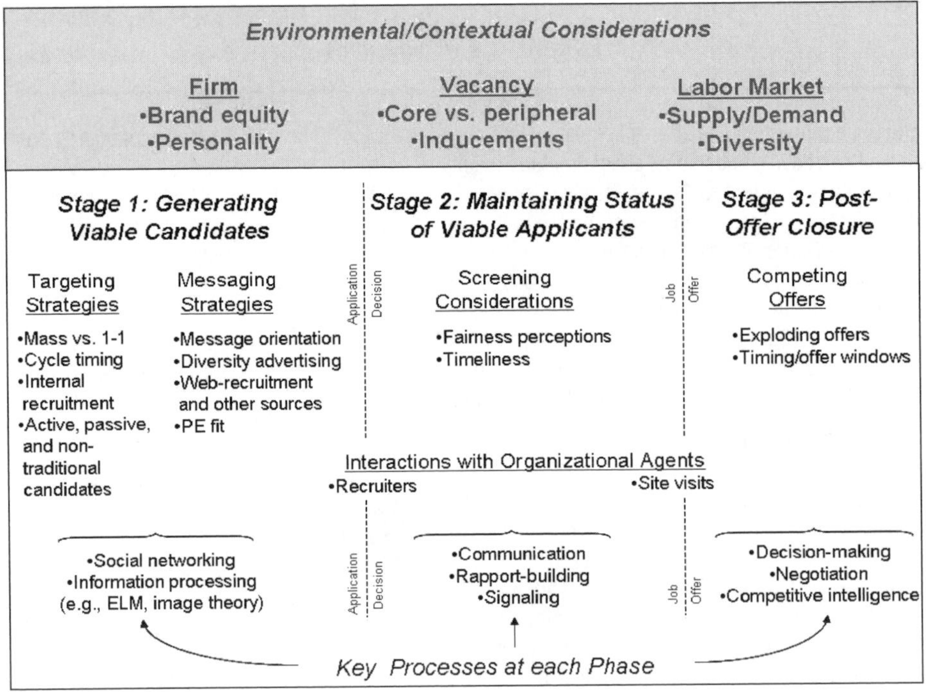

FIGURE 2.1. Framework of the recruitment process. PE = person–environment; ELM = elaboration likelihood model.

these three stages: the job seeker's decision to formally enter the selection process (i.e., application decision) and the organization's decision to formally invite the applicant to join the company (i.e., job offer).

Specifically, Figure 2.1 shows that before job seekers decide to apply, organizations work to generate viable job candidates (Stage 1). Figure 2.1 suggests various targeting strategies related to timing and types of candidates to target, as well as messaging strategies such as diversity advertising and use of various recruitment sources such as the Web. Exhibit 2.1 shows research that had occurred within this stage as of the Rynes and Cable (2003) review, including limited work on targeting and messaging strategies that yielded little in the way of consistent results.

Once job seekers actually apply, organizations must then focus on maintaining the status of the most viable applicants (Stage 2). At this stage, timeliness and perceived fairness of the selection process become important considerations, as do interactions with organizational agents such as recruiters (which can also occur before the job seeker applies, as indicated in Figure 2.1) and site visits (which can also occur after the job offer). Here, previous research (Exhibit 2.1) indicates notable progress in assessing recruiter effects and somewhat limited progress in terms of the recruitment effects related to applicant screening processes.

After organizations formally offer positions, they must persuade candidates to join the organization (Stage 3). For example, timing issues again become important in terms of windows of opportunity for persuading job seekers who have competing offers. Virtually no work had occurred within this stage at the time of Rynes and Cable's (2003) review, as reflected in Exhibit 2.1.

The bottom of Figure 2.1 also portrays key process variables that are particularly relevant at each stage. For example, at Stage 1, recruiters' social networking might help identify viable candidates to target, and job seekers' information processing determines how well various messaging strategies might work. At Stage 2, communication and signaling become more important as job seekers learn more details about the position. At Stage 3, processes such as job choice decision making and negotiation are likely to be key.

Finally, overlaid across the entire recruitment process are environmental and contextual considerations, as illustrated at the top of Figure 2.1. Specifically, we view certain firm-level characteristics as well as vacancy and labor market characteristics as potentially influencing core considerations at any of the three stages. For example, the labor market, firm brand equity, or the nature of the vacancy (e.g., whether an organization considers it to be core or peripheral to their mission) may drive the use of targeting or messaging strategies or exploding offers (i.e., job offers that are rescinded if not accepted within a predetermined time period). A fair amount of work had occurred in the area of environmental and contextual characteristics at the time of Rynes and Cable's (2003) review (Exhibit 2.1), especially in terms of firm and specific vacancy characteristics. However, these scholars indicated the need for continued work along these lines.

We recognize that not all of the categories in Figure 2.1 have necessarily received sufficient research attention either prior to or during the time covered in our review to draw definitive conclusions. In those cases we discuss the issue (e.g., recruiting older candidates) and discuss directions in which we would like to see the research move. In other areas that have received more attention (e.g., firm reputation, recruiter interactions), we selectively review pertinent findings to update the literature. We begin by reviewing the literature pertaining to key environmental and contextual considerations that potentially affect all three recruitment stages.

ENVIRONMENTAL AND CONTEXTUAL CONSIDERATIONS

Nearly 20 years ago, Rynes and Barber (1990) called for more focus on contingencies in the recruitment process, but progress has only recently been evident. As Figure 2.1 shows, we posit that recruitment activities are contingent on characteristics of the recruiting firm, the specific vacancy, and the prevailing labor market. Each potentially plays an important role throughout the stages of recruitment, and we discuss them in turn.

Firm Characteristics

Following earlier work attempting to link the recruitment and marketing literatures (Maurer, Howe, & Lee, 1992), studies in recent years have increasingly examined firm characteristics in the context of recruitment. Specifically, characteristics receiving attention have been brand image (Collins & Stevens, 2002), organizational image (Chapman, Uggerslev, Carroll, Piasentin, & Jones, 2005), reputation (Turban & Cable, 2003), firm personality (Slaughter, Zickar, Highhouse, & Mohr, 2004), and firm knowledge (Cable & Turban, 2001). Although earlier work reflected in Exhibit 2.1 also examined some of these characteristics, researchers have begun to take a more nuanced perspective on these topics by integrating marketing concepts to a greater degree.

For example, Turban and Cable (2003), after controlling for industry, number of recruiters available to interview, and interview date, found links between firm reputation and applicant pool outcomes including increased numbers of applicants generated ($\Delta R^2 = .02$, a 5% increase above control variables) and higher-quality applicants and interviewees produced (in terms of grade point average; $\Delta R^2 = .03$, a 14% increase for applicants; and $\Delta R^2 = .06$, a 30% increase for interviewees). Cable and Turban (2003) found that job seekers recalled significantly more information about familiar firms ($\beta = .20$). They also found that applicants' perceptions that a company had a favorable reputation increased the pride they anticipated from joining the organization ($\beta = .28$), which translated into lower salary requirements to work for higher-reputation firms ($\beta = -.19$). Collins and Stevens (2002) found applicant pool size and quality to be influenced by brand equity generated through sponsorships, word-of-mouth, publicity, and general recruitment advertising (and combinations thereof). Collins and Han (2004) found that all but sponsorship influenced brand image via general attitudes toward a company or perceived job attributes. More specifically, Collins and Han focused on differences in effects of low-involvement recruitment strategies (i.e., requiring little or no search and processing effort; e.g., visual stimuli, sponsorships of sporting events) versus high-involvement strategies (i.e., greater cognitive processing effort; e.g., detailed description of job-organization characteristics). They found that low-involvement strategies are beneficial primarily in terms of applicant pool size and quality when a firm has not already invested in corporate advertising or does not already have a good reputation. Conversely, a firm that uses high-involvement practices must have already established awareness in the minds of job seekers, either through a priori advertising or reputation-building efforts (Δ adjusted R^2 interaction effects ranged from .09 to .13 for advertising and reputation, representing increases of between 24% and 37% over main effects and industry and company size control variables).

Complementing these studies and once again moving beyond previous findings in Exhibit 2.1, Collins (2007) found that product awareness moderates the influence of high- or low-involvement recruitment practices, such that low-involvement practices enhance application intentions and actual application decisions but are more effective when product awareness is low. When product awareness is high, high-involvement practices are more effective in influencing these outcomes (ΔR^2 for the block of interactions = .22 for application intentions, representing a 76% increase over main effects and control variables; Δ Cox and Snell R^2 = .12 for application decisions, representing a 55% increase).

Vacancy Characteristics

The nature of the vacancy itself also continues to be an important contextual factor (Rynes & Barber, 1990). Chapman et al. (2005) provided meta-analytic evidence that job-organizational factors were among the stronger predictors of recruitment outcomes, including particularly strong effects of type of work on pursuit intentions ($\rho = .53$). They also noted that pay ($\rho = .15$) and the combination of compensation and advancement ($\rho = .14$) predict pursuit intentions to a much lesser degree than many other vacancy characteristics. However, earlier work (Williams & Dreher, 1992) suggested that although pay does not influence the number of applicants, it could influence job acceptance rates. This importance is underscored by the increased effect pay has on acceptance intentions ($\rho = .28$; Chapman et al., 2005).

Studies also have begun to consider the role of specific non-pay inducements such as work–life benefits, flexible work, and career paths on job pursuit intentions and perceptions of the organization. Casper and Buffardi (2004) examined work–life benefits and flexible work schedules using a wide sample of job seekers and new hires recently starting a job. The authors found that flexible work schedules and dependent care assistance influenced both job pursuit intentions ($\beta = .27$, $\beta = .21$) and perceived organizational support ($\beta = .28$, $\beta = .43$). Carless and Wintle (2007) found that flexible ($M = 4.07$) or dual career paths ($M = 3.69$) were significantly more attractive than traditional career paths ($M = 2.83$, all on a 5-point scale). Rau and Hyland (2002) drew on boundary theory (Ashforth, Kreiner, & Fugate, 2000) and found that individuals with higher role conflict found flexible work schedules relatively more attractive, likely because they reduce the cost of role transitions and thus ease role conflict. However, those with lower role conflict found telecommuting relatively more attractive, likely because it increases boundary flexibility and reduces transition costs across role boundaries, whereas those experiencing greater role conflict found such blurring of roles to be unattractive. These findings challenge the assumption that job seekers universally desire telecommuting and flexible work arrangements.

Several studies span the firm and vacancy contextual categories identified in Figure 2.1. Lievens and Highhouse (2003) and Slaughter et al. (2004) compared traditional *instrumental* factors related to the vacancy (e.g., pay, benefits) with *symbolic* characteristics (e.g., "personality") of firms. In studies of students and bank employees, Lievens and Highhouse found that organization trait inferences predicted attraction above job-organizational factors ($\Delta R^2 = .09$, a 22% increase, and $\Delta R^2 = .18$, a 53% increase, in these respective samples). They also found more differentiation among organizations based on trait inferences (i.e., vs. job-organizational attributes), suggesting room for competitive advantage based on symbolic factors such as brand image. Slaughter et al. validated a five-dimensional measure of organizational personality (e.g., style, thrift, boy scout, dominance, innovativeness), finding all but the dominance factor to relate to attraction ($R^2 = .32$ with thrift negatively related) when modeled simultaneously.

That organizations are better able to distinguish themselves in terms of symbolic factors compared with more instrumental vacancy-based factors makes sense considering the increased transparency of instrumental factors such as pay via sources such as the Web (e.g., http://www.salary.com). Indeed, researchers have suggested that the Web levels the playing field for job seekers and lowers costs of searching for comparative information about instrumental vacancy characteristics (Lievens & Harris, 2003; Rynes & Cable, 2003). In general, the tension between symbolic and instrumental factors highlights that recruitment research should incorporate multiple predictors as a way of gaining a more realistic picture of the overall process.

In terms of specifically examining the impact of symbolic factors, considerable work remains. For example, much research has focused on comparing firms that have positive images with firms that have no discernable images but has failed to account for temporal effects related to image. Thus, research is needed that examines the short- and long-term effects of a negative image or reputation or the mechanisms that might explain changes in image or reputation perceptions over time. As an exception, Brooks, Highhouse, Russell, and Mohr (2003) showed that familiar companies engender more polarized reactions (in either positive or negative directions) than do unfamiliar companies, thus calling into question the overall relationship between familiarity and reputation or attraction past work has suggested (Barber, 1998).

A pragmatic reason for researchers to focus on firms with low images or reputations is that such firms have greater need for prescriptive recruitment advice, whereas high-reputation firms often enjoy a steady stream of candidates, making selection rather than recruitment key to overall staffing utility. In general, research is needed regarding how to affect or leverage a firm's reputation or image. For example, the research presented earlier might have implications for small firms' recruitment strategies (Williamson, Cable, & Aldrich, 2002). A useful starting point might be Cable and Turban's (2001) flow diagram for leveraging various levels of image, familiarity, and reputation. The diagram prescribes actions (e.g., maintain low profile, modify or correct employer image using experiential information sources) based on firm familiarity, reputation, and accuracy of understanding of employer image.

Overall, progress is evident over the past few years in examining vacancy characteristics and characteristics that span firm and vacancy categories, compared with the prior piecemeal conclusions shown in Exhibit 2.1. The Chapman et al. (2005) meta-analysis provided a much-needed synthesis of prior findings in these areas, and the recent consideration of flexible work and holistic examinations of symbolic and instrumental characteristics are encouraging yet still leave open the need for continued research attention.

Labor Market Characteristics

Consistent with Rynes and Barber (1990), we believe the literature would benefit if researchers more extensively embraced labor market characteristics as a key contextual aspect of recruitment (Billsberry, 2007) that is likely to affect relationships across stages. Cappelli (2005) concluded that businesses cannot know whether a labor shortage is likely someday, but they certainly cannot expect a labor surplus in the foreseeable future. However, this prediction, combined with recent unemployment levels and fluctuations in the global job market, implies the need to reconsider and better customize general recruitment strategies to match labor's current supply and demand. For example, levels of internal demand and external supply of candidates might dramatically alter recruitment strategies; job seekers who perceive that they have more or fewer choices are likely to react differently to recruitment stimuli. Also, the nature of the labor market has shifted toward what has been termed a *free agent* market (Rynes & Cable, 2003). This raises the interesting question of just how much effort people put into their job search when they expect that their tenure may be short. Finally, labor supply diversity has the potential to dramatically alter recruitment strategies and approaches in the United States (e.g., an aging workforce, more Hispanic workers). As was the case at the time of Rynes and Cable's review (Exhibit 2.1), there continues to be gaps in our understanding in this area.

Keeping these critical firm, vacancy, and labor market contextual factors in mind, we turn to a discussion of the three primary recruitment stages. We present key processes and outcomes that we believe are most relevant to each stage while acknowledging that these processes and outcomes are not necessarily exhaustive or bound solely to a particular stage.

GENERATING VIABLE CANDIDATES

The generation of viable job candidates (Stage 1 in Figure 2.1) greatly determines the potential utility of the remainder of the staffing process (Barber, 1998). As will be seen as the remainder of our review unfolds, this stage of the recruitment process has received the greatest research attention. In accordance with Figure 2.1, we explore general targeting strategies (i.e., whom and when to target) and the messages embedded in recruitment (i.e., where and how to target). Key processes within this stage include social networking between recruiters and potential applicants and the type of information processing in which job seekers engage. Important outcomes at this stage should include high-quality and/or diverse applicant pools (Carlson, Connerley, & Mecham, 2002), along with building relationships with potential candidates. Thus, the ratio of viable candidates to total applicants is critical, as are other yield ratios (e.g., number of candidates ultimately hired to number of applicants).

However, much previous and current research has focused on attraction as the key mechanism for generating an applicant pool. For example, Chapman et al. (2005) identified six antecedent categories that have been related to attraction in varying degrees (job and organizational attributes, $\rho = .39$; recruiter characteristics, $\rho = .29$; perceptions of the recruitment process, $\rho = .42$; perceived fit, $\rho = .45$; perceived alternatives, $\rho = .16$; and hiring expectancies, $\rho = .33$). Although this key outcome has not changed dramatically, research into what makes an organization attractive has begun to reflect contemporary trends by examining antecedents such as organizational ecological reputation (Aiman-Smith, Bauer, & Cable, 2001) and work–life benefits (Carless & Wintle, 2007). As discussed earlier, Carless and Wintle found a significant link between various work–life benefits and organizational attraction. Aiman-Smith et al. found that ecological rating more strongly affected attractiveness ($\beta = .34$) than did pay ($\beta = .28$), promotion opportunity ($\beta = .23$), or layoff policy ($\beta = .29$).

An outcome closely aligned yet distinct from attraction, job pursuit intentions captures the extent to which an individual will actively strive to join the organization. For the job seeker, attraction is more passive, but pursuit intentions indicate a more active mind-set with regard to vying for a position. Job seekers might be attracted to a company but may perceive that they are underqualified for the advertised position and decide not to pursue it. The Chapman et al. (2005) meta-analysis also suggested that most of the antecedents of attraction have received various levels of research attention and are also important for affecting job pursuit intentions (job and organizational attributes, $\rho = .38$; recruiter characteristics, $\rho = .36$; perceptions of the recruitment process, $\rho = .27$; perceived fit, $\rho = .55$; and hiring expectancies, $\rho = .33$). The previously cited studies of ecological reputation (Aiman-Smith et al., 2001) and work–life benefits (Casper & Buffardi, 2004) found significant (though generally weaker) effects on pursuit intentions in addition to attraction. In terms of the importance of diversity in organizations, Brown, Cober, Keeping, and Levy (2006) found that participants who were high in racial tolerance were more likely to pursue employment at organizations that emphasize diversity values ($\Delta R^2 = .08$, or a 40% increase over racial tolerance and diversity values condition main effects).

Targeting Strategies

After organizations identify their desired outcomes but before they craft recruitment communications or choose a medium to disseminate messages, they must identify target audiences they wish to recruit. The potential is great for interplay between contextual considerations and targeting strategies identified in Figure 2.1. For example, whether the company considers the vacancy to be a core or peripheral position may drive their targeting or messaging strategies. Also, the number of vacancies for a given position relative to forecasted labor supply might affect the relative importance of applicant pool quality versus quantity outcomes, which in turn may influence strategies. Despite prior work in this area, research is lacking on many fronts.

Broader targeting decisions. Previous work has focused on the targeting of various demographic groups. For example, Rynes, Orlitzky, and Bretz (1997) found that experienced hires were evaluated more highly than new graduates on several skill-based characteristics, although new graduates were rated more highly on open-mindedness and willingness to learn. Use of experienced hires was also related to organizational growth but less dynamic business environments. However, companies also make broader decisions about their overall targeting strategies. Efforts might consist of person-to-person (i.e., one-to-one) communication, whereby a recruiter initiates contact with specifically qualified people, or an employee refers friends or acquaintances. Relational approaches might include maintaining contact with groups of former employees. The *boomerang effect*, typical of companies such as P&G (e.g., Horovitz, 2003), describes the recruitment of former employees. A more traditional approach is to recruit en masse by disseminating messages with broad appeal that do not target any single individual.

Companies with exemplary reputations may choose not to recruit but rather to allow candidates to proactively approach them. Social identity theory suggests that organizational membership partly shapes self-concept (Ashforth & Mael, 1989). Thus, to enhance self-esteem and personal prominence, job seekers are likely to be attracted to firms that enjoy favorable reputations. Such firms may expect larger applicant pools (Turban & Cable, 2003).

Scholars have recently raised the related issue of the firm as celebrity. It takes longer for a firm to build contextual factors such as reputation, brand image, or product awareness, but certain system shocks might bring windfalls to organizations in terms of recruitment. Rindova, Pollock, and Hayward (2006) described this as the *celebrity effect*, manifested when the mass media dramatizes an event related to a firm, and suddenly the general public views that firm as more attractive, regardless of actual performance metrics or longer-term proof of quality. For example, the *Flutie effect* is the "phenomenon of having a successful college sports team increase the exposure and prominence of a university" ("Flutie Effect," 2008) and refers to Boston College's 16% spike in applications for undergraduate admissions the year after the school's quarterback, Doug Flutie, beat an archrival opponent with a miraculous touchdown pass in the final seconds of a key football game. Although the duration of such an effect is unknown, the finding is generally consistent with Rindova, Williamson, Petkova, and Sever's (2005) finding that the prominence dimension of reputation, and not the perceived product quality dimension, predicted price premiums organizations enjoyed. From a recruitment perspective, firms might try to capitalize on this phenomenon by strategically using the mass media to publicize their programs or accomplishments. Of course, as with firm reputation, a negative system shock might work against a firm. Also, the long-term sustainability of this approach is open to investigation.

Timing issues. Another key targeting decision identified in Figure 2.1 involves when an organization should engage in recruitment activities (Rynes & Cable, 2003). For example, some job seekers (e.g., college graduates) and some jobs (e.g., holiday retail) operate in distinct cycles. When companies consider these cycles, questions arise: When in our particular recruitment cycle should we move? Can we be too early? Should we try to preempt the market? For example, the authors' university basketball program recently made the national news when its former head coach offered a scholarship to an eighth grader. Soelberg's (1967) implicit favorite model suggests possible benefits to firms that enter the recruitment market early. However, given that the practice is salient, unfortunately little research has been done in cycle timing since Rynes (1991) addressed it in her review.

Internal recruitment. Also largely falling outside the realm of prior research and prior recruitment reviews (e.g., Breaugh et al., 2008; Taylor & Collins, 2000) is *internal recruitment*. We view this as a vital missing link (see also Billsberry, 2007). First, global staffing and expatriate assignments are receiving more attention, given the globalization of business in general. Gong (2003b) presented a model of the mix of parent-country nationals, host-country nationals, and third-country nationals optimal for global staffing purposes. This model informs the recruitment strategy of parent companies when trying to fill positions in foreign subsidiaries. Gong (2003a) found that when cultural distance is greater and companies use parent-company expatriates for staffing top management jobs, they increase their subsidiary labor productivity.

Second, internal recruitment processes potentially produce turf wars over valued human capital. For example, Ling and Dineen (2005) used agency and stewardship theories to suggest that managers may either hinder or encourage efforts of valued employees to transfer internally. Specifically, agency theory predicts that managers will act in self-interest and tend to hinder transfers of valued employees. Stewardship theory predicts that managers will maximize firm and employee interests by encouraging deserving employees to transfer internally, even if such transfers will be detrimental to the manager. The authors suggested that success of these efforts depends on managers' levels of social capital within the firm. Discovering ways to hinder managers' hoarding behavior and encourage career building of valued employees (e.g., through incentives or other governance mechanisms) therefore seems important if companies are to use internal recruitment (see also SHRM, 2008). Somaya, Williamson, and Lorinkova (2008) recently offered a related and intriguing perspective: "letting go" of valued human capital, although seemingly detrimental, may actually be beneficial from the standpoint of creating social network ties to new areas of the business where transferees move (or in Somaya et al.'s case, to competitors). Finally, Ostroff and Clark (2001) found that various antecedent demographics (e.g., education, gender, children under the age of 15), job-related variables (e.g., information, attitudes, future employment), and community- and family-related variables predicted various internal mobility opportunities (e.g., lateral promotions, with or without relocation). Among the myriad of results this study offered was that lateral moves involving a career change were less appealing to those with smaller children, ostensibly because moving involved a greater potential disruption in family dynamics. Conversely, only moving concerns were related to willingness to accept promotions without corresponding career changes.

Recruiting passive job candidates. One of the more interesting issues covered over the last few years has been the recruiting of *passive* job candidates—employed individuals not actively searching for jobs but willing to consider outside opportunities. Termed *poaching* or *talent raiding,* this targeting strategy has become increasingly prevalent (Cappelli, 1999). For example, Rao and Drazin (2002) found that young or poorly connected mutual fund firms were more likely to recruit from competitors to increase innovation. In general, newer or less connected firms use poaching to gain entry into product markets when resources are more highly constrained. Poaching also allows newer firms to integrate more quickly to industry norms and avoid the mistakes that experienced employees of older firms have already learned. By contrast, well-connected firms do not appear to gain as much from poaching, possibly because they gain only redundant talent exposure and may even be constrained by their level of connectedness.

Of course, an unresolved issue is the threshold at which a valued employee will submit to poaching overtures and move to a lesser-connected, newer firm, and thus higher-risk career position. Related to this question is where firms should go to try to recruit passive job seekers. Dunford, Boudreau, and Boswell (2005) found that executives were more apt to search for jobs when their stock options had a market value below their exercise price ($\beta = .13$), a situation called *underwater*. Dunford, Oler, and Boudreau (2008) found that executives—especially CEOs—were more likely to turn over when faced with underwater options. This suggests a potential strategy of targeting employees of poorly performing firms; thus, the labor market generally seems to have direct implications for poaching strategies. The extensive job search literature also might offer recruiters insight into who might be more likely to be searching for new jobs (e.g., Kanfer, Wanberg, & Kantrowitz, 2001).

Yet another factor associated with poaching is the competitive responses that poached firms might use. Gardner (2005) examined this issue among software industry competitors. He posited that poached firms may ignore the poaching or they may respond defensively (e.g., raising their inducement levels, requiring remaining employees to sign non-compete agreements) or retaliatorily/defensively (e.g., poaching talent from the firm that initiated the poaching, severing business relationships). As the value of poached human capital increases, retaliatory/defensive responses become more likely in comparison with purely defensive responses, and this effect is further enhanced as transferability of human capital increases. In general, these results suggest that firms losing human capital through poaching will retaliate if they see that the poaching is damaging their interests or heightening the competitiveness of the poaching firm. Finally, poaching may be a network-driven phenomenon. Williamson and Cable (2003), for example, found that firms were more likely to hire top management team members from organizations with which they had board of director interlocks ($\beta = .59$, $SE = .23$).

Targeting nontraditional candidates. Rynes and Barber (1990) claimed that firms should increase their focus on nontraditional applicants to redress projected labor shortages. Very little work has considered the recruitment strategies that might be optimal for older workers, although it has been well documented that the working population is aging and a large percentage of older workers expect to continue working past retirement age (cf. Adams & Rau, 2004). Indeed, with some sources claiming considerable differences in work preferences of "Generation Y" versus baby-boomer generation workers (Armour, 2005) and some suggesting far fewer differences (e.g., Deal, 2007), rigorous research is needed in this area.

Some work has begun to address predictors of bridge employment among older workers (i.e., employment between retirement from a full-time position and full retirement; e.g., Adams & Rau, 2004; Davis, 2003), and this may be a fruitful area in which to begin. Davis identified several key factors that lead retirees to participate in bridge employment (e.g., career pull opportunities, entrepreneurial orientations) or to avoid such employment (e.g., age, organizational tenure, clear retirement plans). Adams and Rau also found traditional constraints (e.g., inadequate transportation, poor health) to relate negatively to job seeking (incident rate ratio = .77, where the incident rate ratio refers to an increase [if the value is greater than one] or decrease [if less than one] in the rate of job seeking activity expected with a one-unit change in a predictor). Surprisingly, older-worker constraints (e.g., perceived stereotypes against older workers) related positively to older-worker job search behavior (incident rate ratio = 1.41), although the authors surmised that older-worker constraint perceptions could be heightened because of job search experiences or experiences with rejection. To the extent that recruitment efforts can alleviate concerns over these constraints (e.g., Walmart's image as an age-friendly workplace), companies may gain an advantage in attracting older workers.

To recruit older workers, firms might also look to factors that engage older employees. Avery, McKay, and Wilson (2007) found that older workers are more engaged when they are satisfied with both younger and older coworkers ($\Delta R^2 = .07$, or a 39% increase over several other demographic controls). Thus, communications aimed at recruiting older workers might highlight how well potential older workers will likely fit with coworkers (i.e., person–group fit) rather than focusing solely on how well their abilities will fit the job demands or how their values will match the organization's values. Rau and Adams (2005) also discovered that targeted equal employment opportunity statements, in combination with the opportunity to transfer knowledge through mentoring and flexible schedules, had more influence than any of these policies alone (partial $\eta^2 = .04$). Beyond targeting older workers, other nontraditional applicant populations deserve research attention, and we review work related to diversity advertising in the following section.

Thus, targeting strategy research progress has been less in terms of building on prior findings (which, as shown in Exhibit 2.1, were already limited) but more in terms of beginning to explore newer critical areas such as internal recruitment, poaching, and the recruitment of older workers. Although encouraging, researching a greater breadth of targeting strategies will need to be matched by attempts to provide richer, more in-depth investigations in these areas.

Messaging Strategies

Figure 2.1 indicates that once a company determines its targeting strategy, it must develop and disseminate recruitment messages. Although potential messaging strategies have great breadth, we selectively review research related to message orientation and diversity messaging and some recent sourcing research. We further recognize that messages designed to influence person–environment fit are another crucial element of the applicant generation stage and we refer readers to Volume 3, chapter 1, this handbook, and Kristof-Brown, Zimmerman, and Johnson (2005) for detailed overviews of that literature.

Message orientation. A key consideration in crafting a recruitment message is the message orientation (Frase-Blunt, 2003). Here, work has addressed the use of screening, recruiting, or dual-purpose orientations. For example, Williamson, Lepak, and King (2003) found that recruiting-oriented Web sites (i.e., those that try to "sell" the company to a recruit) influenced content usefulness perceptions to a greater extent than screening-oriented Web sites (i.e., those that provide information to allow job seekers to withdraw if they are a poor fit; $\beta = .20$). Usefulness perceptions then led to attraction ($\beta = .41$). Dual-purpose orientations exhibited a slightly lower but nonsignificant difference from recruiting orientation in terms of attraction. However, as noted more than 20 years ago (Rynes & Boudreau, 1986), we know little about how these strategic recruitment decisions are made. Dineen and Williamson (2008) provided preliminary evidence suggesting that recruiter compensation characteristics (i.e., whether a recruiter was compensated based on applicant pool quality rather than quantity; $\gamma = .34$) and higher firm reputation ($\gamma = .22$) influenced recruiter use of a screening orientation and that a screening orientation was linked to applicant pool quality ($\beta = .19$). Another key unresolved issue is when in the recruitment process an organization should provide recruitment-oriented messages and when it should provide screening-oriented messages.

Considering once again contextual factors such as firms with negative reputations or particularly undesirable job features, it is interesting to consider messaging strategies that these firms might use. Ashforth, Kreiner, Clark, and Fugate (2007) provided a framework of approaches to avoid negative employee reactions to "dirty work" (i.e., undesirable work offered to sanitation workers or tobacco company employees). Using an exploratory, semistructured interview format, these authors found that such companies used tactics such as the formation of occupational ideologies (e.g., "This work is valuable to society despite its negatives") or social buffers (e.g., a pest-exterminator company might include exterminators' testimonials about the satisfaction they have given their customers). Other possibilities are the use of humor and defensive tactics such as social comparison with others who are relatively worse off (e.g., one tobacco company comparing itself with another that has a worse public relations record). It would be interesting to see how these approaches could be applied to a recruitment context.

Finally, we recognize that screening- versus recruiting-oriented approaches build on the well-documented realistic job preview (RJP) tradition (e.g., Phillips, 1998; Wanous, 1992). Although we do not replicate Breaugh's (2008) recent extensive review of the RJP literature, we reiterate a key point from that review in response to concerns about potential adverse self-selection effects (e.g., Bretz & Judge, 1998). That is, even if negative information leads highly qualified job seekers to drop out of a selection process, that result still seems better than having them become disillusioned after the recruitment process and quit soon after starting the job.

Diversity advertising. Recent attention has been given to the way recruitment communications portray diversity. For example, it is increasingly recognized that to recruit minorities and women, firms must impress on these groups that the company values diversity (Avery & McKay, 2006) by signaling fairness and inclusion. Avery and McKay presented a framework of impression management techniques organizations can use to convey diversity images to potential minority applicants. They posited that firms could use *ingratiation* by portraying highly diverse ads, recruiting at traditional minority institutions, or placing recruiting ads in targeted media (e.g., traditional women's magazines). An organization might also use *promotion* by presenting evidence of successful diversity management or *exemplification* by sponsoring minority events. Such efforts are thought to depend in part on (a) an organization's broader reputation for diversity (e.g., a defensive strategy might be optimal for a poor-reputation firm, whereas an assertive strategy might benefit a high-reputation firm) and (b) the available pool of diverse applicants. These ideas should also be studied in the context of other diverse populations such as older or disabled workers and should be directly compared with other factors (e.g., what happens when a less-diverse-friendly firm offers superior inducements).

Given this general backdrop, two means of promoting a diversity image have been studied: the demographics of recruiters (not shown to have as much impact; $\rho = -.05$ to .03; Chapman et al., 2005) and recruitment advertisement diversity. In general, advertisements depicting diversity and Equal Employment Opportunity statements tend to be more attractive. For example, Avery, Hernandez, and Hebl (2004) found that Black and Hispanic participants were more attracted to companies when their recruitment advertisements used a Black or Hispanic representative instead of a Caucasian representative ($d = 1.07$ for Black participants, $d = .78$ for Hispanics). It is worth noting that the representative's race did not affect Caucasian participants. The authors concluded that Black and Hispanic applicants were attracted because of a similarity mechanism, not because they perceived that the organization valued diversity. Cropanzano, Slaughter, and Bachiochi (2005) found that job seekers generally found preferential treatment plans to be unappealing, which suggests that minority applicants want to be perceived as having been treated fairly and not as receiving preferential treatment.

Regarding the shaping of perceptions of organizational diversity, Kim and Gelfand (2003) examined the role that race and ethnic identity play in forming organizational inferences from diversity initiatives that are included in recruitment brochures. Ethnic identity and diversity initiative significantly affect socioemotional inferences, such as treatment of employees and relationships among employees. A recruitment brochure that included a diversity initiative also increased the likelihood that those who were high in ethnic identity would take the job offer, although this effect was small ($\Delta R^2 = .01$). Race did not exhibit a significant main effect on inferences or job offer acceptance. Martins and Parsons (2007) corroborated this finding by demonstrating that individuals' attitudes and beliefs about gender-related issues (e.g., gender identity, attitudes toward affirmative action) moderated the impact of gender diversity initiatives in recruitment literature on attraction. Finally, Avery (2003) found that openness to racial diversity moderated the effectiveness of diversity portrayals in recruitment advertisements and that such portrayals were useful only for supervisory positions. This further suggests that restricting diversity portrayals to lower-level employees may do more harm than good by raising cynicism among minority job seekers. Taken together, it seems important for firms to try to understand the mindset of their target audience and to use diversity material carefully.

Recent recruitment source research. Companies must somehow disseminate the messaging strategies described earlier. In Figure 2.1 we note that Web recruitment and other sources play a crucial role in executing messaging strategies. We review the recruitment source literature and the critiques associated with it in less depth, given previous efforts (see Exhibit 2.1 and Breaugh, 2008). We do, however, note recent developments in three areas: social networks, word-of-mouth, and Web-based recruitment.

First, studies have long implied that social networks have a role in recruitment either as conduits to job information (Granovetter, 1973) or as resources that shape individual decisions (Kilduff, 1990). More recently, Leung (2003) explicitly examined the use of social and business networks in the staffing of entrepreneurial ventures. This exploratory study suggested that social ties were used heavily to fill human resource needs in the start-up phase of a company with a shift toward business network ties in the growth phase. In addition, in a finding somewhat contrary to Granovetter's famous strength of weak ties argument, Leung provided preliminary evidence that companies used strong, direct ties in both the start-up and growth phases when selecting new employees. Although this finding may be an artifact of the nature of the sample (i.e., entrepreneurial ventures often lack legitimacy and thus require a great deal of trust on behalf of new employees) and sample size (i.e., four organizations), it is important nonetheless in helping understand the role of networks as a recruiting source. The previously discussed work by Williamson and Cable (2003) also took a networks approach in examining the role of board interlocks in hiring decisions (see also Somaya et al., 2008).

Recent work has also examined word-of-mouth communication that takes place within informal networks. For example, Van Hoye and Lievens (2007a) found that word-of-mouth (i.e., informal Web-based communication about companies) was viewed as more credible (partial $\eta^2 = .19$) and associated with higher organizational attractiveness (partial $\eta^2 = .08$) than Web-based testimonials. Van Hoye and Lievens (2007b) further discovered that negative word-of-mouth information could interfere with the effect of recruitment advertising. In general, nonrecruitment-related word-of-mouth communications might be perceived as more credible and lead to more accurate culture perceptions (Cable, Aiman-Smith, Mulvey, & Edwards, 2000) than recruitment-related communications (Kanar, Collins, & Bell, 2006), probably because, being from an external source, it is not perceived as trying to sell the organization (Fisher, Ilgen, & Hoyer, 1979). This is consistent with other work that has found that social network contacts influence job seekers (Kilduff, 1990). Word-of-mouth information from potential coworkers may be viewed as more credible because they are expected to have heightened expertise (Cable & Turban, 2001).

Another recruitment source that has, not surprisingly, seen tremendous growth over the last decade is the World Wide Web; Ployhart (2006) described this growth as "nothing short of radical" (p. 875). Research has suggested that the Web is a powerful tool for sending messages to potential applicants, and scholars have suggested that the Web makes it easier for job seekers to find information about companies and apply for jobs (Lievens & Harris, 2003). However, the popular press has reported that the Web has increased extraneous application traffic from unqualified job seekers (Frase-Blunt, 2003; "Internet misuse," 2003).

Cober, Brown, Keeping, and Levy (2004) presented a model of the relationships between organizational Web sites and recruitment outcomes. In general, they proposed that Web site façade relates to job seekers' reactions but less strongly when job seekers have favorable prior attitudes toward the organization. These attitudes then influence job seekers' perceptions of usability, Web site attitude, and actual search behavior, which in turn influence image, familiarity, and applicant attraction. One of Cober et al.'s more interesting propositions suggested that simply browsing a company's Web site could alter organizational image.

Building on Cober et al.'s (2004) work, Allen, Mahto, and Otondo (2007) examined objective factors (e.g., job-organization attributes), subjective factors (e.g., brand image and fit), and critical contact factors (e.g., nature of Web-site medium) on applicant attraction. Using a large sample mostly comprising job seekers browsing actual job ads, Allen et al. found that organizational image, but not mere familiarity, related to attitudes toward the organization ($\beta = .32$). They suggested that media richness perceptions also affected credibility and satisfaction, which related to attitudes toward the organization. Cable and Yu (2006) also found that, in general, richer and more credible mediums enhanced the correspondence between pre- and postviewing organizational image beliefs, even if such beliefs were already overestimated. Job seekers tended to hold underestimated perceptions of organizational images prior to exposure to career fair or Web-based sources (i.e., a Web page or electronic bulletin board).

The aforementioned research further suggested that smaller or unfamiliar firms might be able to overcome barriers related to being unknown if they can first direct job seekers to their Web site. This renders the process of driving job seekers to a company Web site an important and overlooked research topic. Returning to the work of Collins and colleagues (e.g., Collins & Han, 2004), once a viewer is on a Web site, high- versus low-involvement recruitment strategies might be optimal depending on a firm's brand image or reputation.

Whereas Web-based recruitment research thus far has tended to be recruitment-oriented (i.e., attracting a maximum number of job seekers as the goal), some research has also examined the quality of applicants that might be generated by using features such as interactivity that are mostly available only on the Web. Dineen and colleagues (Dineen, Ash, & Noe, 2002: Dineen, Ling, Ash, & DelVecchio, 2007; Dineen, & Noe, 2009) have shown that providing job seekers with customized information might encourage them to consider the information more carefully by making it more experiential or personally relevant (Cable & Turban, 2001), which might lead to better outcomes (e.g., well-fitting job seekers may be more attracted; poorly fitting job seekers might be less attracted). Specifically, Dineen and Noe found that customization is better at encouraging poorly fitting job seekers to eliminate themselves than at encouraging well-fitting job seekers to apply (odds ratios = 1.64 for person–organization fit and 2.13 for demands–abilities fit). Such a finding is consistent with image (Ordonez, Benson, & Beach, 1999) and prospect (Kahneman & Tversky, 1979) theories, which suggest that job seekers tend to screen-out poor options more than they screen-in good options. Furthermore, when a company narrows the initial pool of applicants, it decreases its legal liabilities because it must later reject fewer applicants. Related to Cober et al. (2004) and Allen et al. (2007), good aesthetic features may be necessary to trigger the benefits of customization (Dineen et al., 2007) and may be even more important for firms that have low familiarity (Collins & Han, 2004), such as the fictitious companies used in Dineen and colleagues' research.

Foundational to these findings is the notion of job seeker processing motivation (Breaugh & Starke, 2000). Specifically, it is likely that applicant pool quality is tied at least partly to the degree to which job seekers are willing and able to carefully scrutinize recruitment information. Recent work has begun to draw on the elaboration likelihood model (ELM) to address these issues (e.g., Cable & Turban, 2001; Dineen & Noe, 2009; Jones, Schultz, & Chapman, 2006; Roberson, Collins, & Oreg, 2005). Developed by Petty and Cacioppo (1986), the ELM suggests that people can be persuaded through a central route of high elaboration where information is given careful attention or through a more peripheral route where information is more passively processed without careful thought. For example, Jones et al. found that those exposed to a condition that encouraged peripheral processing of information chose ads containing non-job-related features such as attractive fonts rather than those containing higher-quality arguments. In general, understanding prior job seeker cognitions and how they influence recruitment information processing at different recruitment stages is important in understanding this information's impact on job seeker decision making.

Finally, limited work has differentiated between various subsources in Web-based recruitment. For example, Jattuso and Sinar (2003) found that generalized job boards such as monster.com or careerbuilder.com attracted lower-quality applicants (in terms of educational qualifications, $d = .67$; and skills, $d = .13$) and applicants with a lesser degree of fit ($d = 1.68$) than industry/position specific job boards such as tvjobs.com or salesjobs.com. A replication of this study may be useful given that many of the more general job boards now have specialized subcomponents (e.g., engineering.careerbuilder.com). Future Web-based recruitment research should continue to address job seeker reactions to these different subsources in terms of usefulness and privacy concerns (Lievens & Harris, 2003). Investigations might also address the types of Web-based recruitment information that are used at different recruitment stages (e.g., job board information in the applicant generation phase, electronic bulletin boards that offer neutral testimonials about company culture in the post-offer stage), and the use of third-party recruitment firms as intermediaries between companies and job seekers.

Even though considerable work remains, progress has been evident in the area of messaging strategies, relative to the prior work outlined in Exhibit 2.1. We are encouraged by the move away from attempts to examine general source effects to more nuanced investigations of specific sources such as the Web or word-of-mouth communications. Also, recent work has continued to draw on the RJP tradition but has expanded that concept to look at overall firm characteristics (e.g., negative reputations) and message frames (e.g., screening, dual-purpose). Finally, diversity advertising has received attention that has previously been largely absent.

Organizations experience relative levels of success in generating viable candidates for their vacancies. Once an applicant pool is generated, organizations must turn their attention to maintaining the status of their most viable applicants.

MAINTAINING THE STATUS OF VIABLE APPLICANTS

The second stage of the recruitment process comprises organizational efforts to ensure that viable, higher-quality applicants maintain interest in being considered for vacancies. As organizations form applicant pools or court candidates individually, screening considerations often take center stage in terms of workforce planning, but they also likely transfer to recruitment considerations, as shown in Figure 2.1. Indeed, often overlooked is the continuing need for effective, ongoing recruitment of candidates at this stage to maintain their status as potential employees until the company can tender job offers. As indicated in Figure 2.1, several processes are vital to this stage, including communication and rapport building as job applicants continue to interact with organization agents. Specifically, it is primarily at this stage that recruiters and those involved in site visits build rapport with applicants and signal organizational intentions. Indeed, as shown in Figure 2.1, interactions with organizational agents take place across all three stages, but are most prominent during applicant maintenance. Key outcomes at this stage include remaining competitive with other firms seeking similar job candidates and tendering offers in a timely manner to maximize the chances of employing valued applicants. Thus a parallel topic in this stage is the way in which applicants screen out companies and withdraw from the pool.

Several chapters in this handbook address issues related to screening and selection and are not covered here (see in particular chap. 13, this volume). For an overview of one key recruitment consideration—selection process fairness perceptions—we refer the reader to chapter 12 of this volume. Another key consideration is selection process timeliness. Yet, since Rynes, Bretz, and Gerhart (1991) found that delays in the selection process can lead to attrition from that process, especially among more qualified applicants, little has been accomplished from a research perspective to build on these findings. Thus, for purposes of our review, we specifically address two primary issues: recruiter interactions and site visits. As will become apparent by the shorter length of this section (and the next) in relation to previous sections of this chapter, opportunities for research are plentiful.

Although, as with other topics, researchers have recently reviewed recruiter interactions (Breaugh, 2008), we address some key issues. Chapman et al. (2005) concluded that recruiter personableness exhibits a fairly strong relationship with pursuit intentions ($\rho = .50$). However, its effects are weaker for more distal outcomes such as job choice, and it is likely that applicants rely less on recruiter signals as more information about job and organizational characteristics becomes salient. Alternatively, recruitment initiatives such as recruiter behaviors likely signal job-organizational characteristics, and research has generally shown that job-organization factors mediate the effects of attraction on recruitment (Turban, 2001). Indeed, it appears that later in the process when job seekers decide whether to accept the job, they focus more on what their work environment will be like rather than on particular aspects of the recruitment process such as recruiter interactions, and earlier longitudinal work showed this to be true from the application phase through the job choice decision stage (Taylor & Bergmann, 1987).

Some researchers have attempted to ground the role of recruiters in psychological theory. For example, Larsen and Phillips (2002) laid out a series of propositions regarding the propensity for recruiters to influence applicants based on the ELM. Specifically, they proposed that recruiter demographics and friendliness exert less influence on job applicant attraction when those applicants engage in central processing of organizational and job attributes. Job applicants' use of central processing is more likely, for example, when they possess lower stress levels, or greater job and company knowledge, interview experience, financial need, or self-esteem. Alternatively, Chapman and Webster (2006) used expectancy theory and concepts of procedural justice and signaling to unpack the mechanisms underlying recruiter–applicant interactions. The authors found that recruiter friendliness was related to applicant perceptions of procedural justice of the process, post-interview organizational attractiveness, and expectancy of receiving an offer (βs = .60, .21, and .26, respectively). Rynes et al. (1991) found, however, that signaling more greatly affected less-experienced job seekers. Despite these recent studies, progress has generally been limited in the area of recruiter interactions since the Rynes and Cable (2003) review (Exhibit 2.1). However, rather than indicating a need for additional work, we do not view recruiter interactions as having as high of a priority going forward as other topics covered in this review.

Conversely, as reviewed by Breaugh et al. (2008) and indicated in Exhibit 6.1, researchers have generally neglected on-site visits, although job applicants often decide about organizations during those times. Previous work has shown that site-visit perceptions relate to job choice ($R^2 = .05$; Turban, Campion, & Eyring, 1995). More recently, McKay and Avery (2006) provided a comprehensive model of the site-visit process in terms of racioethnic issues. They suggest that minority site visitors perceive a stronger link between organizational/community diversity, vertical integration, and diversity climate perceptions, as well as between quality of site-visit/community interactions and diversity climate perceptions. Diversity climate relates to acceptance intentions and even more so when job opportunities are perceived to be high. This model, if verified, might have important implications for firms looking to move diverse candidates from job application to job choice. It seems especially important given that site visits likely provide a truer picture of a company's diversity climate than applicants might glean from initial recruiting communications and failure to uphold those first communications might not only lead minority candidates to drop out but might also lead them to translate these misunderstood communications to other minority job seekers. Future research should address this issue as well as extend McKay and Avery's propositions to older job seekers or other nontraditional populations.

After organizations complete their selection processes, and assuming they have successfully retained viable applicants, they typically extend job offers to chosen candidates. From here, organizations must use closure processes to ensure that the candidates accept the offers. We now turn to this stage.

POSTOFFER CLOSURE

After firms tender job offers to desired candidates, much work remains from a recruitment standpoint. Indeed, *postoffer closure* is often overlooked but can be a vital tipping point between a valued job applicant accepting an offer or going elsewhere, often to a competitor. Key processes likely to occur at this stage include the applicant's decision making, offer negotiation, and the organization's ability to recognize competitors' overtures toward the candidate in terms of inducements and offer timing.

Job choice continues to receive attention as a critical outcome at this stage. For example, in terms of the postoffer/prehire time period, Breaugh, Greising, Taggart, and Chen (2003) studied the effects of recruiting sources on the propensity to hire, finding that direct applicants (8.1%) and employee referrals (12.4%) were hired at greater rates than those recruited through newspapers (1.1%), colleges (1.3%), or job fairs (4.8%). Boswell, Roehling, LePine, and Moynihan (2003) longitudinally examined over several recruitment phases how 14 job and organization factors related to offer acceptance or rejection. They found that the most-mentioned factors influencing acceptance decisions were nature of work (37.6%), location (37.6%), company culture (36.5%), and advancement opportunities (25.8%). As shown in Figure 6.1, ongoing interactions with firm agents likely carry over in terms of importance in this final stage. In the study conducted by Boswell et al. (2003), respondents indicated that meeting with multiple constituents while on a site visit positively affected job choice decisions as did follow-up contacts from the company.

The aforementioned studies represent the most proximal postoffer outcomes (e.g., hiring rate, acceptance intentions), yet continued attention is needed to additional distal outcomes such as turnover, performance, and satisfaction of new hires (Hoffman & Woehr, 2006; Meglino, Ravlin, & DeNisi, 2000). More subtle outcomes might include negotiated changes in salary level (i.e., How much does a company need to concede to secure the employment of a job candidate?) or maintenance of internal equity among job incumbents. The issue of external competitiveness (Milkovich & Newman,

2008) suggests that companies are pressured to extend lucrative offers. However, they risk upsetting the balance or equity perceptions of current employees who hold similar positions within the organization. Although studied extensively under the umbrella of *wage compression* in the labor and economics literatures (e.g., Heyman, 2008), little research has been done regarding how potential wage compression issues might affect an organization's approach to postoffer recruitment.

Among the recruitment issues relevant at this stage, investigations of multiple and/or competing offers seem critical. The most valued recruits are also the most likely to have several job offers. This makes processes such as negotiation vital to recruitment all the way to the point of job acceptance. Furthermore, the issues of job choice timing and exploding offers seem crucial (Rynes & Cable, 2003; Schwab, Rynes, & Aldag, 1987). Yet, little research has been done on job choice timing, and the scant research that has been conducted on exploding offers has found no significant effects on job choice outcomes (Boswell et al., 2003). Schwab et al. addressed the issue of multiple offers using marginal utilities (i.e., by assessing the marginal utility of continuing to pursue additional offers vs. taking the current offer without knowing the value of potential offers). They also addressed simultaneous versus sequential evaluation of alternatives, which returns to the need for research investigations to include multiple jobs to enhance external validity. Horvath and Millard (2008) recently provided preliminary evidence suggesting that attraction–intention relationships varied in a nonlinear fashion across recruitment stages (e.g., pre/postoffer) but also as a function of other vacancies simultaneously being considered. For example, the relationship between attraction and applicant intentions partially depended on where the candidate was with other companies (e.g., postoffer). However, it is important to note that the Chapman et al. (2005) meta-analysis did not find very strong effects for perceived alternatives on acceptance intentions ($\rho = -.06$) or actual job choice ($\rho = .07$), suggesting that simultaneous offers might be less important than at first glance. Chapman et al. speculated that quality rather than quantity of competing offers may be influential.

Other interesting issues might surface at this stage and deserve research attention. Given demographic shifts in nontraditional family arrangements (e.g., Conlin, 2003), work and family issues such as transferability to a new location and care for an elderly parent often occur on a case-by-case basis, making job offer and subsequent negotiation processes more challenging and complex. Another interesting issue is whether prior contextual characteristics such as brand equity and vacancy characteristics matter as much at this stage. Finally, a key process at this stage might be a firm's engagement in *competitive intelligence,* or knowledge of competitors' actions or likely actions. For example, knowing the window of opportunity competing offers have given job seekers would be valuable during salary negotiations, as would knowledge of specific packages competitors have offered. Network ties within an industry might help firms gain advantage here. In general, given the dearth of prior work in the postoffer closure area (as reflected in Exhibit 2.1), we view this is a new area ripe for fresh perspectives and rigorous work.

FUTURE DIRECTIONS AND CONCLUSION

With this review of the recruitment literature come recommendations for future research. In closing, we suggest several areas beyond those mentioned. First, we have identified several studies that examined key outcomes within specific phases. However, researchers have tried to build on earlier studies (e.g., Cable & Judge, 1996; Taylor & Bergmann, 1987) through longitudinal research capturing multiple phases. For example, Carless (2005) studied the effects of perceived person–job and person–organization fit over time on attraction and likelihood of accepting a job offer. Chapman and Webster (2006) collected data at multiple times to observe recruiter effects on placement, attraction, job choice, and job choice intentions.

Chapman et al.'s (2005) meta-analytic evidence highlighted the importance of continuing to study recruitment relationships over multiple stages by suggesting that attraction is not directly related to job choice but rather is at least partially mediated by pursuit and acceptance intentions. It is also important to note that at later recruitment stages restriction in range on predictors may be at issue. Chapman et al. noted that person–environment fit and job choice relationships might be restricted because poorly fitting individuals have already eliminated themselves at earlier stages (see Cable & Judge, 1996, for a discussion of this issue). Indeed, in Chapman et al., job choice was the weakest predicted outcome.

Second, although little work has addressed unit- or firm-level outcomes, it is incumbent on researchers to approach investigations in this way (e.g., firm-level financial outcomes, unit-level turnover; e.g., Ployhart, 2006; Rynes & Cable, 2003; Taylor & Collins, 2000). This may require cross-level research designs spanning several companies. Ployhart provided a diagram outlining a process of linking micro and macro levels of analysis. Taylor and Collins encouraged researchers to assess recruitment issues within the purview of the resource-based view of the firm (Barney, 1991). Specifically, they encouraged researchers and recruitment specialists to evaluate recruitment efforts according to how valuable, rare, and/or inimitable they are, and thus assess their potential to provide a source of sustainable competitive advantage. Also important are continued assessments of applicant pool size and quality. It is encouraging that these are starting to receive attention from scholars (e.g., Collins & Han, 2004) and practitioners (e.g., Cascio & Boudreau, 2008; http://www.staffing.org, 2005), although quality remains ill defined and likely differs according to firm objectives (e.g., diversity, cognitive ability).

Third, we have discussed the importance of using different metrics at different stages of the recruitment process. There is thus a need for better understanding of when a given recruitment metric is more or less optimal and why and to define success at each stage commensurate with the importance of the prevailing outcome. For example, at the stage of generating viable candidates, it seems vital to generate a large enough pool of applicants of acceptable quality. Yet many recruitment studies continue to rely on attitudinal outcomes such as attraction as the ultimate criterion at this phase, overlooking issues such as the number of candidates a company must reject. Beyond defining recruitment success differently at different stages, Barber, Wesson, Roberson, and Taylor (1999) also suggested that small and large firms tend to define recruitment success differently (e.g., longer- and shorter-term focuses, respectively). Several online (e.g., staffing.org) and print (Cascio & Boudreau, 2008) sources exist to enable companies to assess the value of their recruiting function and practitioners should avail themselves of these (see also, Carlson et al., 2002).

Finally, our review reveals that much more effort is needed to examine recruitment strategies and processes that occur after a job seeker applies for a position. We would be mistaken to assume that recruitment could end once a job seeker has submitted an application, yet the unbalanced state of the recruitment literature seems to reflect this logic. We hope that future literature reviews will show more progress in analyzing the stages that follow candidate generation.

Recruitment continues to be critical to organizational functioning, and much research is needed to inform practitioners in the throes of the talent war. Compared with prior work reflected in Exhibit 6.1, we are encouraged by the increased breadth of topics more recently being addressed as well as the increased depth of studies in areas such as firm reputation and the integration of marketing and recruitment principles. Yet, we still see a need for richer, more in-depth examinations of other crucial areas such as site visits, the labor market, and recruitment timing. Although we have provided a selective rather than exhaustive review, we once again encourage researchers to follow recommendations of other recent reviews and to embrace the unique challenges and opportunities we have attempted to illustrate in this chapter. It is an exciting time for advanced inquiry in an area greatly needing scholarly input. We look forward to future literature reviews that will undoubtedly be needed to classify and describe this pending work.

References

Adams, G., & Rau, B. (2004). Job seeking among retirees seeking bridge employment. *Personnel Psychology, 57,* 719–744.

Aiman-Smith, L., Bauer, T., & Cable, D. (2001). Are you attracted? Do you intend to pursue? A recruiting policy-capturing study. *Journal of Business and Psychology, 16,* 219–237.

Allen, D. G., Mahto, R. V., & Otondo, R. F. (2007). Web-based recruitment: Effects of information, organizational brand, and attitudes toward a web site on applicant attraction. *Journal of Applied Psychology, 92,* 1696–1708.

Armour, S. (2005, November 6). Generation Y: They've arrived at work with a new attitude. *USA Today,* p. B1.

Ashforth, B. E., Kreiner, G. E., Clark, M. A., & Fugate, M. (2007). Normalizing dirty work: Managerial tactics for countering occupational taint. *Academy of Management Journal, 50,* 149–174.

Ashforth, B. E., Kreiner, G. E., & Fugate, M. (2000). All in a day's work: Boundaries and micro role transitions. *Academy of Management Journal, 25,* 472–491.

Ashforth, B. E., & Mael, E. (1989). Social identity theory and the organization. *Academy of Management Review, 14,* 20–39.

Avery, D. R. (2003). Reactions to diversity in recruitment advertising—Are differences black and white? *Journal of Applied Psychology, 88,* 672–679.

Avery, D. R., Hernandez, M., & Hebl, M. R. (2004). Who's watching the race? Racial salience in recruitment advertising. *Journal of Applied Social Psychology, 34,* 146–161.

Avery, D. R., & McKay, P. F. (2006). Target practice: An organizational impression management approach to attracting minority and female job applicants. *Personnel Psychology, 59,* 157–187.

Avery, D. R., McKay, P. F., & Wilson, D. C. (2007). Engaging the aging workforce: The relationship between perceived age similarity, satisfaction with coworkers, and employee engagement. *Journal of Applied Psychology, 92,* 1542–1556.

Barber, A. E. (1998). *Recruiting employees: Individual and organizational perspectives.* Thousand Oaks, CA: Sage.

Barber, A. E., Wesson, M. J., Roberson, Q. M., & Taylor, M. S. (1999). A tale of two job markets: Organizational size and its effects on hiring practices and job search behavior. *Personnel Psychology, 52,* 841–868.

Barney, J. (1991). Firm resources and sustained competitive advantage. *Journal of Management, 18,* 99–120.

Billsberry, J. (2007). *Experiencing recruitment and selection.* Hoboken, NJ: Wiley.

Borman, W. C., Ilgen, D. R., & Klimoski, R. J. (Eds.). (2003). *Handbook of psychology: Industrial and organizational psychology* (Vol. 12). Hoboken, NJ: Wiley.

Boswell, W. R., Roehling, M. V., LePine, M. A., & Moynihan, L. M. (2003). Individual job-choice decisions and the impact of job attributes and recruitment practices: A longitudinal field study. *Human Resource Management, 42,* 23–37.

Breaugh, J. A. (2008). Employee recruitment: Current knowledge and important areas for future research. *Human Resource Management Review, 18,* 103–118.

Breaugh, J. A., Greising, L. A., Taggart, J. W., & Chen, H. (2003). The relationship of recruiting sources and pre-hire outcomes: Examination of yield ratios and applicant quality. *Journal of Applied Social Psychology, 33,* 2267–2287.

Breaugh, J. A., Macan, T. H., & Grambow, D. M. (2008). Employee recruitment: Current knowledge and directions for future research. In G. P. Hodgkinson & J. K. Ford (Eds.), *International review of industrial and organizational psychology* (Vol. 23, pp. 45–82). Hoboken, NJ: Wiley.

Breaugh, J. A., & Starke, M. (2000). Research on employee recruitment: So many studies, so many remaining questions. *Journal of Management, 26,* 405–434.

Bretz, R. D., & Judge, T. A. (1998). Realistic job previews: A test of the adverse self-selection hypothesis. *Journal of Applied Psychology, 83,* 330–337.

Brooks, M., Highhouse, S., Russell, S., & Mohr, D. (2003). Familiarity, ambivalence, and firm reputation: Is corporate fame a double-edged sword?. *Journal of Applied Psychology, 88,* 904–914.

Brown, D. J., Cober, R. T., Keeping, L. M., & Levy, P. E. (2006). Racial tolerance and reactions to diversity information in job advertisements. *Journal of Applied Social Psychology, 36,* 2048–2071.

Cable, D., Aiman-Smith, L., Mulvey, P., & Edwards, J. (2000). The sources and accuracy of job applicants' beliefs about organizational culture. *Academy of Management Journal, 43,* 1076–1085.

Cable, D., & Judge, T. (1996). Person–organization fit, job choice decisions, and organizational entry. *Organizational Behavior and Human Decision Processes, 67,* 294–311.

Cable, D., & Turban, D. (2001). Establishing the dimensions, sources, and value of job seekers' employer knowledge during recruitment. In G. Ferris (Ed.), *Research in personnel and human resource management* (Vol. 20, pp. 115–163). Greenwich, CT: JAI Press.

Cable, D., & Turban, D. (2003). The value of organizational reputation in the recruitment context: A brand equity perspective. *Journal of Applied Social Psychology, 33,* 2244–2266.

Cable, D., & Yu, K. (2006). Managing job seekers' organizational image beliefs: The role of media richness and media credibility. *Journal of Applied Psychology, 91,* 828–840.

Cappelli, P. (1999). *The new deal at work: Managing the market-driven workforce.* Boston: Harvard Business School Press.

Cappelli, P. (2001). Making the most of on-line recruiting. *Harvard Business Review, 79,* 139–146.

Cappelli, P. (2005). Will there really be a labor shortage? *Human Resource Management, 44,* 143–149.

Carless, S. A. (2005). Person–job fit versus person–organization fit as predictors of organizational attraction and job acceptance intentions: A longitudinal study. *Journal of Occupational and Organizational Psychology, 78,* 411–429.

Carlson, K. D., Connerley, M. L., & Mecham, R. L., III (2002). Recruitment evaluation: The case for assessing the quality of applicants attracted. *Personnel Psychology, 55,* 461–490.

Carless, S. A., & Wintle, J. (2007). Applicant attraction: The role of recruiter function, work–life balance policies and career salience. *International Journal of Selection and Assessment, 15,* 394–404.

Cascio, W. F., & Boudreau, J. W. (2008). *Investing in people.* Upper Saddle River, NJ: Pearson.

Casper, W. J., & Buffardi, L. C. (2004). Work–life benefits and job pursuit intentions: The role of anticipated organizational support. *Journal of Vocational Behavior, 65,* 391–410.

Chapman, D. S., Uggerslev, K. L., Carroll, S. A., Piasentin, K. A., & Jones, D. A. (2005). Applicant attraction to organizations and job choice: A meta-analytic review of the correlates of recruiting outcomes. *Journal of Applied Psychology, 90,* 928–944.

Chapman, D. S., & Webster, J. (2006). Toward an integrated model of applicant reactions and job choice. *International Journal of Human Resource Management, 17,* 1032–1057.

Cober, R. T., Brown, D. J., Keeping, L. M., & Levy, P. E. (2004). Recruitment on the net: How do organizational web site characteristics influence applicant attraction? *Journal of Management, 30,* 623–646.

Collins, C. J. (2007). The interactive effects of recruitment practices and product awareness in job seekers' employer knowledge and applicant behaviors. *Journal of Applied Psychology, 92,* 180–190.

Collins, C. J., & Han, J. (2004). Exploring applicant pool quantity and quality: The effects of early recruitment practices, corporate advertising, and firm reputation. *Personnel Psychology, 57,* 685–717.

Collins, C. J., & Stevens, C. K. (2002). The relationship between early recruitment-related activities and the application decisions of new labor-market entrants: A brand equity approach to recruitment. *Journal of Applied Psychology, 87,* 1121–1133.

Conlin, M. (2003, October 20). Unmarried America. *Business Week,* 106.

Cropanzano, R., Slaughter, J., & Bachiochi, P. (2005). Organizational justice and black applicants' reactions to affirmative action. *Journal of Applied Psychology, 90,* 1168–1184.

Davis, M. A. (2003). Factors related to bridge employment participation among private sector early retirees. *Journal of Vocational Behavior, 63,* 55–71.

Deal, J. (2007). *Retiring the generation gap.* San Francisco: Wiley.

Delaney, K. J. (2007, June 28). Start-ups make inroads with Google's work force. *Wall Street Journal,* B1.

Dineen, B. R., Ash, S. R., & Noe, R. A. (2002). A web of applicant attraction: Person–organization fit in the context of Web-based recruitment. *Journal of Applied Psychology, 87,* 723–734.

Dineen, B. R., Ling, J., Ash, S. R., & DelVecchio, D. (2007). Aesthetic properties and message customization: Navigating the dark side of web recruitment. *Journal of Applied Psychology, 92,* 356–372.

Dineen, B. R., & Noe, R. A. (2009). Effects of customization on application decisions and applicant pool characteristics in a Web-based recruitment context. *Journal of Applied Psychology, 94,* 224–234.

Dineen, B. R., & Williamson, I. O. (2008). Effects of environmental and organizational attributes on recruitment message orientation. Paper presented at the meeting of the Society for Industrial/Organizational Psychology, San Francisco.

Dunford, B., Boudreau, J., & Boswell, W. (2005). Out-of-the-money: The impact of underwater stock options on executive job search. *Personnel Psychology, 58,* 67–101.

Dunford, B., Oler, D., & Boudreau, J. (2008). Underwater stock options and voluntary executive turnover: A multidisciplinary perspective integrating behavioral and economic theories. *Personnel Psychology, 61,* 687–726.

Ehrhart, K. H., & Ziegert, J. C. (2005). Why are individuals attracted to organizations? *Journal of Management, 31,* 901–919.

Fisher, C. D., Ilgen, D. R., & Hoyer, W. D. (1979). Source credibility, information favorability, and job offer acceptance. *Academy of Management Journal, 22,* 94–103.

Flutie effect. (2008). Retrieved August 2008 from http://en.wikipedia.org/wiki/Flutie_effect

Frase-Blunt, M. (2003, August). Candidate glut. *HR Magazine,* 89–93.

Gardner, T. M. (2005). Interfirm competition for human resources: Evidence from the software industry. *Academy of Management Journal, 48,* 237–256.

Gong, Y. (2003a). Subsidiary staffing in multinational enterprises: Agency, resources, and performance. *Academy of Management Journal, 46,* 728–739.

Gong, Y. (2003b). Toward a dynamic process model of staffing composition and subsidiary outcomes in multinational enterprises. *Journal of Management, 29,* 259–280.

Granovetter, M. (1973). The strength of weak ties. *American Journal of Sociology, 78,* 1360–1380.

Heyman, F. (2008). How wage compression affects job turnover. *Journal of Labor Research, 29,* 11–26.

Hoffman, B. J., & Woehr, D. J. (2006). A quantitative review of the relationship between person–organization fit and behavioral outcomes. *Journal of Vocational Behavior, 68,* 389–399.

Horovitz, B. (2003, April 23). At P & G's historic reunion. *USA Today,* p. B1.

Horvath, M., & Millard, M. R. (2008). Recruitment stage, organizational attraction, and applicant intentions. Paper presented at the Society for Industrial and Organizational Psychology Meeting, San Francisco.

Internet misuse may contribute to long joblessness. (2003, February 18). *Silicon Valley/San Jose Business Journal.* Retrieved May 2005 from http://sanjose.bizjournals.com/sanjose/stories/2003/02/17/daily17.html

Jattuso, M. L., & Sinar, E. F. (2003). Source effects in Internet-based screening procedures. *International Journal of Selection and Assessment, 11,* 137–140.

Jones, D. A., Shultz, J. W., & Chapman, D. S. (2006). Recruiting through job advertisements: The effects of cognitive elaboration on decision making. *International Journal of Selection and Assessment, 11,* 167–179.

Kahneman, D., & Tversky, A. (1979). Prospect theory: An analysis of decision under risk. *Econometrica, 47,* 263–293.

Kanar, A. M., Collins, C., & Bell, B. (2006). *Can an organization overcome a negative image? A longitudinal experimental examination of the effect.* Paper presented at the meeting of the Academy of Management, Atlanta, GA.

Kanfer, R., Wanberg, C. R., & Kantrowitz, T. M. (2001). Job search and employment: A personality-motivational analysis and meta-analytic review. *Journal of Applied Psychology, 86,* 837–855.

Kilduff, M. (1990). The interpersonal structure of decision making: A social comparison approach to organizational choice. *Organizational Behavior and Human Decision Processes, 47,* 270–288.

Kim, S. S., & Gelfand, M. J. (2003). The influence of ethnic identity on perceptions of organizational recruitment. *Journal of Vocational Behavior, 63,* 396–416.

Kristof-Brown, A. L., Zimmerman, R. D., & Johnson, E. C. (2005). Consequences of individuals' fit at work: A meta-analysis of person–job, person–organization, person–group, and person–supervisor fit. *Personnel Psychology, 58,* 281–342.

Larsen, D. A., & Phillips, J. I. (2002). Effect of recruiter on attraction to the firm: Implications of the elaboration likelihood model. *Journal of Business and Psychology, 16,* 347–364.

Lavelle, L. (2003, September 29). After the jobless recovery, a war for talent. *BusinessWeek,* 3851, 92–92.

Leung, A. (2003). Different ties for different needs: Recruitment practices of entrepreneurial firms at different developmental phases. *Human Resource Management, 42,* 303–320.

Lievens, F., & Harris, M. M. (2003). Research on Internet recruitment and testing: Current status and future directions. In C. L. Cooper & I. T. Robertson (Eds.), *The international review of industrial and organizational psychology,* (Vol. 18, 131–165). Chichester, England: Wiley.

Lievens, F., & Highhouse, S. (2003). The relation of instrumental and symbolic attributes to a company's attractiveness as an employer. *Personnel Psychology, 56,* 75–102.

Ling, J., & Dineen, B. R. (2005). *Internal transfers: A tale of human capital, social capital, and the manager as agent or steward.* Paper presented at the meeting of the Southern Management Association, Charleston, SC.

Martins, L. L., & Parsons, C. K. (2007). Effects of gender diversity management on perceptions of organizational attractiveness: The role of individual differences in attitudes and beliefs. *Journal of Applied Psychology, 92,* 865–875.

Maurer, S., Howe, V., & Lee, T. (1992). Organizational recruiting as marketing management: An interdisciplinary study of engineering graduates. *Personnel Psychology, 45,* 807–833.

McConnon, A. (2007, September 10). Social networking is graduating—and hitting the job market: How do the online Rolodexes stack up? *Business Week, 4049,* 4.

McKay, P. F., & Avery, D. R. (2006). What has race got to do with it? Unraveling the role of racioethnicity in job seekers' reactions to site visits. *Personnel Psychology, 59,* 395–429.

Meglino, B. M., Ravlin, E. C., & DeNisi, A. S. (2000). A meta-analytic examination of realistic job preview effectiveness: A test of three counterintuitive propositions. *Human Resource Management Review, 10,* 407–434.

Milkovich, G. T., & Newman, J. M. (2008). *Compensation.* Boston: McGraw-Hill/Irwin.

Ordonez, L., Benson, L., III, & Beach, L. R. (1999). Testing the compatibility test: How instructions, accountability, and anticipated regret affect prechoice screening options. *Organizational Behavior and Human Decision Processes, 78,* 63–80.

Ostroff, C., & Clark, M. A. (2001). Maintaining an internal market: Antecedents of willingness to change jobs. *Journal of Vocational Behavior, 59,* 425–453.

Petty, R. E., & Cacioppo, J. T. (1986). *Communication and persuasion: Central and peripheral routes to attitude change.* New York: Springer-Verlag.

Phillips, J. M. (1998). Effects of realistic job previews on multiple organizational outcomes: A meta-analysis. *Academy of Management Journal, 41,* 673–690.

Ployhart, R. E. (2006). Staffing in the 21st century: New challenges and strategic opportunities. *Journal of Management, 32,* 868–897.

Rao, H., & Drazin, R. (2002). Overcoming resource constraints on product innovation by recruiting talent from rivals: A study of the mutual fund industry, 1986–94. *Academy of Management Journal, 45,* 491–507.

Rau, B. L., & Adams, G. A. (2005). Attracting retirees to apply: Desired organizational characteristics of bridge employment. *Journal of Organizational Behavior, 26,* 649–660.

Rau, B., & Hyland, M. (2002). Role conflict and flexible work arrangements: The effects on applicant attraction. *Personnel Psychology, 55,* 111–136.

Rindova, V., Pollock, T., & Hayward, M. (2006). Celebrity firms: The social construction of market popularity. *Academy of Management Review, 31,* 50–71.

Rindova, V. P., Williamson, I. O., Petkova, A. P., & Sever, J. M. (2005). Being good or being known: An empirical examination of the dimensions, antecedents, and consequences of organizational reputation. *Academy of Management Journal, 48,* 1033–1049.

Roberson, Q. M., Collins, C. J., & Oreg, S. (2005). The effects of recruitment message specificity on applicant attraction to organizations. *Journal of Business and Psychology, 19,* 319–339.

Rynes, S. (1991). Recruitment, job choice, and post-hire consequences: A call for new research directions. In M. Dunnette & L. Hough (Eds.), *Handbook of industrial and organizational psychology* (2nd ed., Vol. 2, pp. 399–444). Palo Alto, CA: Consulting Psychologists Press.

Rynes, S. L., & Barber, A. E. (1990). Applicant attraction strategies: An organizational perspective. *Academy of Management Review, 15,* 286–310.

Rynes, S. L., & Boudreau, J. W. (1986). College recruiting in large organizations: Practice, evaluation, and research implications. *Personnel Psychology, 39,* 729–757.

Rynes, S. L., Bretz, R. D., Jr., & Gerhart, B. (1991). The importance of recruitment in job choice: A different way of looking. *Personnel Psychology, 44,* 487–521.

Rynes, S. L., & Cable, D. M. (2003). Recruitment research in the 21st century. In W. C. Borman, D. R. Ilgen, & R. J. Klimoski (Eds.), *Handbook of psychology: Industrial and organizational psychology* (Vol. 12, pp. 55–76). Hoboken, NJ: Wiley.

Rynes, S. L., Orlitzky, M. O., & Bretz, R. D. (1997). Experienced hiring versus college recruiting: Practices and emerging trends. *Personnel Psychology, 50,* 487–521.

Schwab, D. P., Rynes, S. L., & Aldag, R. J. (1987). Theories and research on job search and choice. In K. M. Rowland & G. R. Ferris (Eds.), *Research in personnel and human resources management* (Vol. 5, pp. 129–166.) Greenwich, CT: JAI Press.

SHRM. (Producer). (2008). *Seeing forward: Succession planning at 3M* [DVD]. (Available from http://www.shrm.org/about/foundation/products/Pages/SeeingForwardDVD.aspx)

Slaughter, J. E., Zickar, M. J., Highhouse, S., & Mohr, D. C. (2004). Personality trait inferences about organizations: Development of a measure and assessment of construct validity. *Journal of Applied Psychology, 89,* 85–103.

Soelberg, P. (1967). Unprogrammed decision making. *Industrial Management Review, 8,* 19–29.

Somaya, D., Williamson, I. O., & Lorinkova, N. (2008). Gone but not lost: The different performance impacts of employee mobility between cooperators versus competitors. *Academy of Management Journal, 51,* 936–953.

Staffing.org. (2005, June 22). *How do you calculate the ROI of job boards?* Retrieved July 2005 from http://www.staffing.org/library_ViewArticle.asp?ArticleID=165

Taylor, M., & Bergmann, T. (1987). Organizational recruitment activities and applicants' reactions at different stages of the recruitment process. *Personnel Psychology, 40,* 261–285.

Taylor, M. S., & Collins, C. J. (2000). Organizational recruitment: Enhancing the intersection of theory and practice. In C. L. Cooper & E. A. Locke (Eds.), *Industrial and organizational psychology: Linking theory and practice* (pp. 304–334). Oxford, England: Basil Blackwell.

Turban, D. B. (2001). Organizational attractiveness as an employer on college campuses: An examination of the applicant population. *Journal of Vocational Behavior, 58,* 293–312.

Turban, D. B., & Cable, D. M. (2003). Firm reputation and applicant pool characteristics. *Journal of Organizational Behavior, 24,* 733–751.

Turban, D. B., Campion, J. E., & Eyring, A. R. (1995). Factors related to job acceptance decisions of college recruits. *Journal of Vocational Behavior, 47,* 193–213.

Van Hoye, G., & Lievens, F. (2007a). Investigating Web-based recruitment sources: Employee testimonials versus word-of-mouse. *International Journal of Selection and Assessment, 15,* 372–382.

Van Hoye, G., & Lievens, F. (2007b). Social influences on organizational attractiveness: Investigating if and when word of mouth matters. *Journal of Applied Social Psychology, 37,* 2024–2047.

Wanous, J. P. (1992). *Organizational entry: Recruitment, selection, orientation, and socialization of newcomers* (2nd ed.). Reading, MA: Addison Wesley.

Williams, M. L., & Dreher, G. F. (1992). Compensation system attributes and applicant pool characteristics. *Academy of Management Journal, 35,* 571–595.

Williamson, I. O., & Cable, D. M. (2003). Organizational hiring patterns, interfirm network ties, and interorganizational imitation. *Academy of Management Journal, 46,* 349–358.

Williamson, I. O., Cable, D. M., & Aldrich, H. (2002). Smaller but not necessarily weaker: How small businesses can overcome barriers to recruitment. In J. Katz & T. Welbourne (Eds.), *Advances in entrepreneurship, firm emergence, and firm growth* (Vol. 5, pp. 83–106). Greenwich, CT: JAI Press.

Williamson, I. O., Lepak, D. P., & King, J. (2003). The effect of company recruitment web site orientation on individuals' perceptions of organizational attractiveness. *Journal of Vocational Behavior, 63,* 242–263.

CHAPTER 3

CAREER ISSUES

Yehuda Baruch and Nikos Bozionelos

It has not been simple to arrive at a universally acceptable scientific definition of *career*. Nevertheless, definitions (e.g., Arnold, 1997; Arthur, Hall, & Lawrence, 1989; Greenhaus, Callanan, & Godshalk, 2000; Kram, 1985) revolve around the notion of sequential employment-related experiences through time and across space. Despite difficulties with its definition, career is a salient element in each person's working life and demands planning and management from both individuals and organizations. In this chapter, we focus on current career issues, with particular emphasis on the changing nature of careers and with a specific focus on the elements of time and space in their evolvement. We discuss new forms of employment and their impact on careers, the notion of career success and perspectives to approach it, as well as careers in the present era of globalization. We use the term *career actor* to denote the individual as an active accumulator of experiences that compose a career.

THE TIME ELEMENT IN CAREERS

Time is unidirectional and a common denominator for everyone. Hence, a substantial number of models conceptualize careers as sequences of distinct stages (see the seminal work of Levinson, 1978, and Super, 1957, as well as Baird & Kram, 1983; Dalton, Thompson, & Price, 1977; Evans, 1986; Form & Miller, 1949; Greenhaus, 1987; Hall & Nougaim, 1968; Schein, 1978). The principles and motives behind these models are not identical. For example, Levinson's intention was to describe individual development throughout life, a central aspect of which was career, whereas Super's intention was to specifically describe career development through the life course. Nevertheless, they all contain the notion of career progression through time from a nonstochastic point of view; that is, they legitimately posit that each stage is partly built on the previous ones. Transitions through the stages are not always smooth or painless (Smart & Peterson, 1997). For example, individuals may realize that they have to retrain or acquire additional formal education if they are to be competitive in the labor market.

There is some support for the notion of career stage. For example, as predicted, individuals in the early stages of their careers tend to report lower organizational commitment and job satisfaction and higher turnover intentions than individuals in more advanced career stages (Ornstein, Cron, & Slocum, 1989).

Baruch (2004) integrated and expanded extant career stage models into a single one that takes into account changes that have occurred since their inception. These include changes in the society, the economy, business practices, science, and technology. The model suggests the following stages in career progression:

1. *Foundation*, which starts from the early years of life and extends through childhood and adolescence. This part of life does not normally contain those systematic sequential work experiences that could be considered as career (though there are exceptions, such as in the case of performers and athletes). Nevertheless, for a substantial proportion of the population this stage does contain irregular, seasonal, and occasionally regular work

experiences (for a short review, see Hartung, Porfeli, & Vondracek, 2005, pp. 388–389). Furthermore, individuals appear to understand the concept of career and to think in terms of their own career development as early as in preadolescent years (Hartung et al., 2005). Most important, this period of life is associated with the accumulation of basic knowledge as well as with the development of fundamental values, attitudes, and aspirations that serve as anchors that guide, constrain, stabilize, and reinforce subsequent career direction and progress (Schein, 1978; Watson & McMahon, 2005). Indeed, attitudes toward work, occupational aspirations, and occupational expectations that are formed during that part of life are predictive of occupational aspirations, expectations, and career outcomes in adulthood (Helwig, 2008).

2. *Career entry,* which involves the acquisition of knowledge, skills, and qualifications (e.g., by means of tertiary education, apprenticeship, or on-the-job training) to enter a job or a profession. This can be either within an organization or independently (e.g., one's own business).
3. *Advancement,* which involves development of expertise in the job or profession as well as generally upward movements in the organizational hierarchy, or expansion of one's own business. This stage may be characterized by moves between functions and organizations, or by failures in one's own business endeavors. In some cases, and especially for those whose work lives evolve within organizations, this stage may be associated with reaching a *plateau,* that is, a level with no prospects, either objectively or subjectively evaluated, for further advancement (see Chao, 1990).
4. *Reevaluation,* which involves appraisal of the extent to which one's aspirations have been fulfilled. This may be triggered either by endogenous factors (e.g., lack of challenge in one's job) or by exogenous factors (e.g., plateauing, redundancy, or realization that one's skills or profession are facing obsolescence).
5. *Reinforcement,* which involves implementation of decisions that have been made in the previous stage. This may be revealed in a number of ways, ranging from refocusing on one's job or profession with reinvigorated enthusiasm to returning to formal education (e.g., training to qualify for a different job or working toward an advanced degree) for a career change.
6. *Decline,* a stage that is normally characterized by consideration of and preparation for withdrawal from working life. This withdrawal may be gradual. This is a stage in which the desire to pass on one's knowledge and experience tends to be strong in many individuals (Westermeyer, 2004).
7. *Retirement,* which involves disengagement from the labor market. This does not necessarily mean that the individual completely disengages from work or from one's job or profession. For example, one may continue to follow closely the developments in one's field, to conduct volunteer work, or to engage in *bridge employment,* that is, paid work of reduced amount and intensity (e.g., Griffin & Hesketh, 2008).

The model is general, in line with typical models that depict social processes. Therefore, the number and sequence of stages should be considered as a general indicator rather than as applying to every single individual. Furthermore, the model deliberately does not attach specific age boundaries to stages. As also acknowledged by later (e.g., Baird & Kram, 1983; Dalton et al., 1977) and, retrospectively, by early (Super, 1990) career models, the time of entry into and the timing of transitions between stages are not invariant. Indeed, empirical research indicates that the correspondence between chronological age and career stage is far from perfect. For example, Ornstein and her associates (Ornstein et al., 1989; Ornstein & Isabella, 1990) reported correlations of .32 and .26, for their predominantly male and female samples respectively, between age and Super's career stages. The following are some reasons for the lack of absolute correspondence:

1. Variance across jobs and professions in qualification requirements and the time needed to obtain these qualifications. Some jobs (e.g., manual work, some cases of service work) require only minimal training and no qualifications or accreditation, whereas many professions (e.g., medical, law specialists) require lengthy and rigorous education and training as well as professional accredi-

tation. Furthermore, there are differences across professions in the number of stages they involve (e.g., the military). These affect the point of entry into each career stage, as well as the duration of each stage.

2. Substantial variance among individuals in the way their lives evolve. As an illustration, volatile labor markets that require constant learning and flexibility, combined with state funding for support to the unemployed, have generated in recent times a new "breed" of individuals who live a significant proportion of their lives as unemployed or underemployed (e.g., Jensen & Slack, 2003; Marston & McDonald, 2008). This may happen, for example, when individuals are unable to find comparable jobs after redundancy and cannot adapt to an alternative career direction (see Feldman, 1996; Feldman & Leana, 2000; McQuaid & Lindsay, 2002).
3. A general, and ongoing, increase over time in educational qualifications that are required to enter the job market. Whereas in the early part of the 20th century people started working in their mid-teens and university education was reserved for the affluent or tiny minority of highly talented individuals, the 21st century witnesses a growing number of people attending university (i.e., up to 50% of the age group; e.g., Davis & Bauman, 2008), hence starting full-time work when they are about 10 years older than their counterparts in the relatively recent past.

Therefore, it is unrealistic and inappropriate to adopt the model under a "one-size-fits-all" mentality (Baruch, 2004; Sullivan, 1999); rather, it should be treated as a generic frame of reference. Nevertheless, age boundaries may be more precisely attached to career stages within certain professions. For instance, it is unlikely to find many full-time academics in their mid-20s, meaning that, for academics, the advancement stage does not normally start before the late 20s.

Minicycles Within Stages

It is important to view stages as involving minicycles that are composed of miniature stages themselves (Baruch, 2004; Hall, 2002; Hall & Mirvis, 1995; see also Smart & Peterson, 1997; Super, 1980, 1990; Super, Savickas, & Super, 1996, for empirical evidence). Career actors often need to evaluate their accomplishments and prospects and make decisions to reinvigorate or redirect their careers. For example, specialized workers may realize that their skills are becoming obsolete (e.g., Pang, Chua, & Chu, 2008) or professionals (e.g., engineer, physician) may attempt a switch to management to reenergize their careers (e.g., Linney, 2001). As a consequence, these individuals may decide to pursue retraining or additional education as a means to maintain their employability and reanimate their careers, respectively (e.g., Beutell & O'Hare, 2006). Naturally, the redirected career needs time to become established. However, competencies and experience gained in earlier cycles are likely to facilitate the advancement stage of subsequent cycles, hence accelerating the cyclical process (Baruch & Quick, 2007).

The frequency of minicycles has been increasing over the years. Continuous changes in the nature of work and skill requirements have been part of the cause. These changes have been effected by augmentation in competition and the accelerating pace of technological development (e.g., Iida & Morris, 2008; Landry, Mahesh, & Hartman, 2005), which has led to the decline or disappearance of industries with their attached jobs (e.g., the mining industry in the United Kingdom) along with the parallel creation of new industries. Another part of the cause has been the constant organizational transformation and the use of downsizing as part of the repertoire of organizational strategies (e.g., Tsai, Wu, Wang, & Huang, 2006); these factors have diminished the commitment to the employer (Baruch, 1998; Littler, Wiesner, & Dunford, 2003; Rubin & Brody, 2005). As a consequence, individuals are more likely to change jobs and work environments, either involuntarily (e.g., because of redundancy) or voluntarily (i.e., as a planned move for career enhancement; Farber, 2008). In either case, they have to reestablish themselves.

Key capacities for individuals in the process of minicycles are the ability to learn and the motivation to repeat the learning process (Hall & Mirvis, 1995). Though learning has always been an important factor in the way careers evolve, its importance has become even more critical in the contemporary era. Donohue (2007), for example, found that individuals pursuing career change are much more likely (odds ratio of 2.01) to engage in activities that involve learning, such as skills improvement by means of education.

A Contemporary Career Stage Model

Baruch's model, with some further modifications, has been incorporated into a comprehensive model of careers, depicted in Figure 3.1. The model aims to depict the current state of knowledge on career progression through stages, as discussed earlier. It attaches age intervals to stages, but this should serve only as a general indicator. The model considers foundation, career entry, and advancement as applicable to all individuals. Advancement is viewed as universal because the first years after career entry always contain advancements in experience, knowledge, and skills, hard and soft. Though these are not always translated into increases in status, they certainly advance the marketability of career actors. Reinforcement is included because it applies to the substantial numbers of individuals who still engage in traditional careers and to those who may abandon large organizations to pursue noncorporate careers (discussed later). However, it is by no means applicable to everyone (this is denoted by the faded script in the figure).

No reevaluation stage is included, unlike in earlier models, because this has been associated with the alleged midlife crisis of the early to mid 40s (Levinson, 1978), for which there is no support (Lachman, 2004). Instead, reevaluation may occur at any point in life that significant events, especially work-related ones, occur (Lachman, 2004). This fact was incorporated into the model by means of recurring cycles of evaluation, refoundation, and reestablishment, which are characterized by constant learning (also suggested by Hall, 1993, as cited in Hall & Chandler, 2005).

The last two stages have been labeled "gradual change of roles," instead of "decline," and "retirement(?)" The latter signifies that retirement is included only as a possibility, despite the fact that human lives are (still) finite, and their progression toward the end is associated with physical decline. This is an important theme for all parties involved—individuals, organizations, and societies; hence, it deserves some consideration.

Decline and retirement(?) There is no dispute that physical abilities, such as strength and agility, decline with age (e.g., Miyamoto et al., 2008; Over & Thomas, 1995). Yet, only a small proportion of jobs or occupations are highly physically demand-

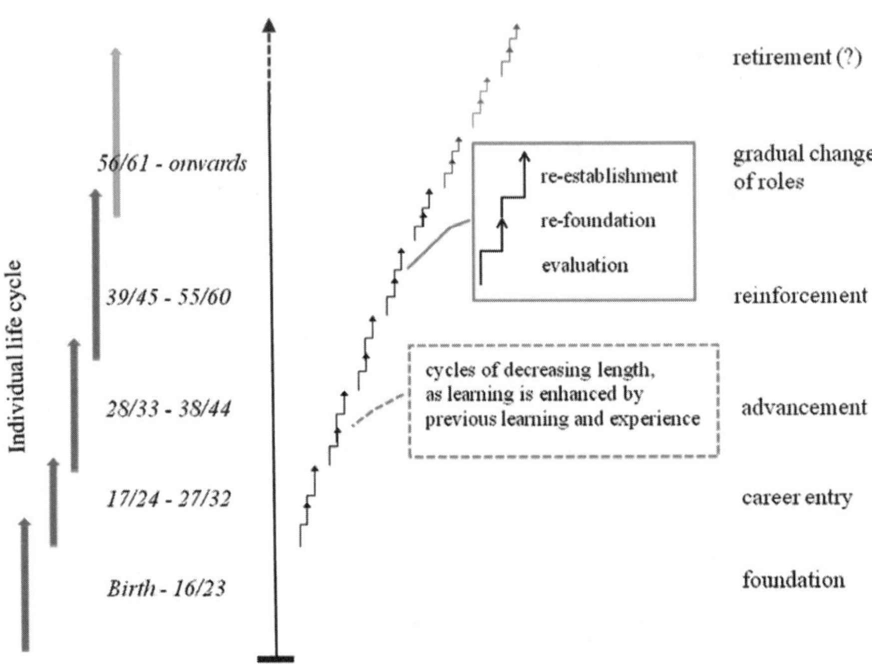

FIGURE 3.1. A contemporary model of career progression through time.

ing, especially in the contemporary era when technological advances and the change in the nature of the economy have shifted the great majority of the workforce away from manual work (Department of Professional Employees, 2008). Hence, the decline in physical strength and agility is an issue for only a small proportion of career actors.

When cognitive ability is considered, the picture becomes even more positive for aging career actors. From early adulthood until the age of 65, by which time most individuals in developed countries retire (e.g., Friedberg, 2007), there is a slight decline in general cognitive ability ($d = -.20$; Schaie, 2005; see also Schwartzman, Gold, Andres, Arbuckle, & Chaikelson, 1987).[1] However, this change is not uniform across all aspects of cognitive ability, with certain domains showing decline (i.e., those that pertain mostly to fluid intelligence, such as perceptual speed), other domains demonstrating improvement (i.e., those that pertain mostly to crystallized intelligence, such as verbal ability and mechanical tasks), and many other domains showing no alteration (Arbuckle, Maag, Pushkar, & Chaikelson, 1998; Schaie, 2005; Schwartzman et al., 1987). For example, in one of the most comprehensive longitudinal studies, Schaie (2005) found a decrease in scores on numerical ability ($d = -.29$) and perceptual speed ($d = -.26$) from age 25 to age 67 but also gains in scores on verbal ability ($d = .24$) and no significant changes in spatial orientation and inductive reasoning. Any decreases in cognitive ability that can be considered of substance (i.e., of magnitude of d in the order of .5 and beyond; Cohen, 1988) appear in the 7th and 8th decades of life (Schaie, 2005).[2] Importantly, however, that engagement in intellectual activities, such as reading and cognitive training (e.g., in the form of mentally stimulating activities), can prevent decline or can even improve cognitive ability in late adulthood (Arbuckle et al., 1998; Ball et al., 2002; Boron, Willis, & Schaie, 2007; Schaie, 2005). Furthermore, empirical research has reported no relationship between age and creativity, a quality that is in demand in today's economy, from the age of the early 20s until 60 (Binnewies, Ohly, & Niessen, 2008). Finally, older individuals can apparently be at least as comfortable in using new, sophisticated technology as their younger counterparts (Bozionelos, 2001).

Moreover, improvements in the way of life and medical advances have been dramatically increasing life expectancy and delaying the onset of physical decline (e.g., Kinsella, 2005). For example, life expectancy in the United States has increased from 47 years to nearly 77 years within the past century (e.g., Sonnega, 2006), and similar gains have been witnessed around the globe (Kinsella & Phillips, 2005). This means that individuals are able, and will be more so in the future, to continue working and developing themselves far beyond what traditional retirement schemes and career stage models assumed at the time of their inception.

In addition, increases and projected increases in life expectancy (United Nations, 2006) render the viability of pension programs highly problematic if people continue to retire at the ages that were the norm in previous generations (see Feldman & Ng, 2007). This is further exacerbated by the continuous decline in birth rates in most developed and fast developing economies (United Nations, 2008), which limits the numbers of younger individuals who enter the workforce. If people continue to retire by the "traditional" age of 65 and, even worse, at early retirement to avoid redundancies of younger employees, the workforce will be shrinking at levels that may not be able to sustain the economy (e.g., Kozhaya, 2007).

It appears, therefore, that for most people decline and retirement, although still relevant, would come at much older ages than might have been anticipated. This has implications for individuals (e.g., for targets set in personal career planning), organizations (e.g., reconsideration of their internal labor markets), and states, where legislators will have to confront these realities.

THE SPACE ELEMENT IN CAREERS

The space element encompasses both the job or profession (i.e., roles and tasks the individual performs) and the environment (social, organizational) in

[1] Effect sizes, d, in this section were calculated by the authors using relevant information provided by Schaie (2005).

[2] At this point it is worth noting that the peak in cognitive ability is not reached in early adulthood but in middle adulthood between the ages of 40 and 60, depending on the faculty; that is, the relationship between adult lifetime and cognitive ability is of inverted U-form (see Schaie, 2005).

which work takes place (Baruch, 2004; Baruch & Rosenstein, 1992). Hence, the space aspect of careers is multidimensional, because work environments differ substantially in their structures, cultures, sizes, and purposes. Before progressing further, the following points need to be made:

1. It is rather inappropriate to think of careers as always attached to particular jobs or professions or that they are composed of a natural evolution of roles within the same general occupational context (e.g., someone starts as an engineer in a corporation, and as he or she advances up the corporate ladder, he or she assumes managerial and executive responsibilities). That consideration had its roots in the economic and labor market structures that prevailed for a few decades before and after World War II (to be discussed later). The relative economic stability of that era meant that a substantial proportion of (e.g., Parkin, Powell, & Matthews, 2007), though by no means all, individuals were able to perform the same job or stay within the same profession for the totality of their working lives (e.g., Sullivan, 1999). However, as also implied earlier, this gradually changed in the last quarter of the previous century. The turbulent economic environment and the shift in the nature of western economies from manufacturing to services (Amsden, 2001; "The Great Jobs Switch," 2005; Shambaugh, 2006) forced many individuals to change jobs because the jobs they had been trained for were not available anymore. Hence, nowadays, individual careers should not be considered as progressing in parallel with a specific job or profession or even a series of related jobs.
2. Experiences that pertain to work roles and environments are the central, but not the only, aspect of careers. Personal life, and its related roles and experiences, is also part of them. Careers are shaped by both work and personal experiences between which there is a constant interplay (Greenhaus & Beutell, 1985; Greenhaus & Powell, 2006; Super, 1980).
3. The actual physical space where work takes place has been changing over the years. Traditionally, most individuals would fulfill their work-related tasks and roles within particular physical locations (e.g., office, desk, factory, till) where they would be physically placed. However, advances in technology (i.e., especially in telecommunications but also in transportation), societal changes (e.g., awareness of work–life balance; see, for example, Gregory & Milner, 2009), and changes in the ways business is conducted (e.g., globalization that places collaborators, clients, or suppliers within physical distance; see, for example, Moore et al., 2008) have led to changes in this respect. Hence, in the contemporary era, individuals may conduct their work-related activities at home (Baruch & Nicholson, 1997) or at multiple locations (i.e., teleworking; WorldatWork, 2009; Thatcher & Zhu, 2006) or may have physical bases that periodically change (e.g., individuals on expatriate missions).

Therefore, the pattern in which careers move through space has shifted over the years as a consequence of changes in business practices and in society, and this change is reflected in the notions of the traditional, the boundaryless, the protean, and the postcorporate career.

The Traditional Career

The notion of the *traditional career* reflects the view that careers are bound to single organizations or particular professions that individuals normally join at the entry stage of their careers. The consequent career stages evolve within that same organization or profession. Organizational and/or professional structures would support the advancement stage wherein individuals would gain promotions, moving up the organizational and/or professional ladder. These structures would provide help (e.g., by supporting acquisition of formal education, such as a graduate degree or additional professional accreditation), structures, and opportunities for the reinforcement stage so that individuals would be able to revamp their careers and assume more senior roles in the organization or in the profession. They would also assist in the final stages, offering, for example, retirement preparation programs (e.g., Peiperl & Baruch, 1997). Most career stage models discussed earlier made the implicit assumption that careers generally fit that pattern. An important aspect of the notion of the traditional career was that the career was managed by the organization (e.g., Arthur &

Rousseau, 1996; Gutteridge, Leibowitz, & Shore, 1993). The necessity or the pressure on individuals to actively manage their careers was limited.

The notion of the traditional career was shaped by the societal and work structures of the industrial and part of the postindustrial era and can be roughly placed as starting with the railroad and continuing until the 1970s. The growth of the economy during that era gave rise to organizational structures that abided by Weberian principles (i.e., large organizations with clearly delineated roles and hierarchies and clear prescriptions of rules for movement between roles and hierarchical layers). These structures supported the notion of the traditional career (Reitman & Schneer, 2008; Sullivan, 1999), especially for the white-collar workforce (Cappelli, 1999). Career systems were hierarchy-based (e.g., Whyte, 1956; Wilensky, 1961), and career progression was linear and mostly based on a series of contests or tournaments (Rosenbaum, 1979) the winners of which would progress in the hierarchy. Hughes (1937) considered that "a career consists, objectively, of a series of status and clearly defined offices . . . typical sequences of position, achievement, responsibility, and even adventure" (p. 409). It should be noted that the traditional notion of career does not exclude lateral moves, as far as these are part of a planned organizational career system and as far as employment within the organization is secure (Peiperl & Baruch, 1997).

Many considered the traditional career as the ideal type of career or career archetype (e.g., Reitman & Schneer, 2008). However, it is erroneous to assume that during the time period that gave rise to that notion of career organizational structures were entirely stable and careers devoid of unforeseen events or that there were not substantial numbers of individuals who were working outside organizational boundaries as self-employed (e.g., Blanchflower & Shadford, 2007). Therefore, the traditional career should be viewed as a metaphor that generally fits the mentality of careers in a particular era rather than as the norm in that era.

The Boundaryless Career

The notion of the *boundaryless career* was introduced in response to the changing conditions in the economy and in the corporate world that commenced in the 1970s and became evident in the 1980s. At that time, competition increased and the basis of the economy started shifting from process toward knowledge. In parallel, governments started weighing financial objectives, such as reduction in deficit and debt, more heavily; which meant reduced subsidies for problematic sectors (e.g., the manufacturing industry in the United Kingdom) and privatization (Baruch, 2004). As a reaction to these conditions, and to be financially efficient, organizations resorted to tactics that included restructuring and downsizing or moving operations abroad (e.g., Coucke, Pennings, & Sleuwaegen, 2007), which normally involved reshuffling and flattening of hierarchies as well as layoffs (e.g., Thornhill & Saunders, 1998). In addition, the partial shift in organizational priorities (e.g., toward maximization of shareholder value) motivated the acquisition of skills from outside rather than developing these internally (Cappelli, 1999, 2006). As a consequence, the stable internal labor markets that served as platform for the traditional career ceased to be the norm.

Another, though less powerful, force toward the change in career patterns was the shift in values of (Western) societies toward individualism as a result of the affluence of the post-World War II era and the liberal movements of the 1960s (for the connection between societal affluence and individualism, see Kashima & Kashima, 2003). Core values of individualism are personal choice and engagement in activities, including work tasks that are meaningful and interesting for the individual (e.g., Triandis, 1995). Hence, career actors were more likely to move between organizations on their own initiative in order to advance their careers or to find personally fulfilling roles (see Reitman & Schneer, 2008). Resiliency and self-efficacy, which pertain to the ability to sustain and rebound from adversary events, became a crucial career competence under these conditions (e.g., Betz, 2007; London, 1983; Rickwood, Roberts, Batten, Marshall, & Massie, 2004; Waterman, Waterman, & Collard, 1994). In parallel, as we have seen, the ability and especially the motivation for constant learning also became critical factors (e.g., Hall & Mirvis, 1996).

The idea of the boundaryless career, as initially understood, denotes the lack of being bound into a single organization and the lack of a single direction in career movement (Arthur et al., 1989; DeFillippi & Arthur, 1994). However, despite the broadness of its meaning (see Arthur & Rousseau, 1996), the connotation that had been typically assigned to the term was quite narrow (Briscoe & Hall, 2006; Sullivan & Arthur, 2006). Simply equating boundarylessness to physical mobility across organizational boundaries was a rather simplistic way to justify the attention that the concept enjoyed. Therefore, the meaning of the term has been recalibrated and refined over time. Authors (Baruch, 2006; Sullivan & Arthur, 2006) also considered boundarylessness in terms of the mental preparedness of career actors to be resilient in their choices and expectations so they are able to adapt to environmental contingencies. Preparedness to move even in cases when this is not personally convenient is not the same as actual movement. Indeed, empirical research has implied a distinction between mental preparedness for mobility and actual physical mobility of career actors (Briscoe, Hall, & DeMuth, 2006). Therefore, the current dominant thinking is that the notion of the boundaryless career encompasses both physical and psychological mobility (Lazarova & Taylor, 2009; Sullivan & Arthur, 2006) and that career actors can be classified according to their position into these two, apparently orthogonal, dimensions (though there is still some debate; see, for example, Greenhaus, Callanan, & DiRenzo, 2008, who conclude that it is more appropriate to view boundarylessness exclusively in terms of physical mobility).

The Protean Career

The protean idea (Hall, 1976) refers to careers as driven by the values of career actors (i.e., what individuals themselves consider important and worthy) and directed through personal choice rather than by external agents, such as the organization (Briscoe & Hall, 2006; Hall, 2004; Hall & Mirvis, 1996). (See also Vol. 3, chap. 4, this handbook.) Therefore, in a similar vein to the boundaryless career, the *protean career* can be conceived along two dimensions: the extent to which the career is driven by values and the extent to which it is self-directed. Briscoe et al. (2006) developed a scale measure of career propensity that assesses both values-drive (e.g., "In the past I have sided with my own values when the company has asked me to do something I don't agree with" and "What's most important to me is how I feel about my career success, not how other people feel") and self-directedness (e.g., "Ultimately, I depend on myself to move my career forward" and "I am responsible for my success or failure in my career"). Hence, career actors can be categorized according to their positions into these two dimensions (Briscoe & Hall, 2006). In a complementary manner, and to the extent that actors are able to conduct their careers according to their values and in the direction they wish, the protean career can also be viewed as a unidimensional attitude that reflects subjective career success (Baruch, Bell, & Gray, 2005; Baruch & Quick, 2007), a concept that will be reviewed later.

The notion of the protean career does appear to capture the demands that the contemporary era poses to career actors. For example, in a study of retired navy admirals who had pursued second careers, Baruch and Quick (2007) found that protean career orientation was associated with less stress, less emotional exhaustion, and greater satisfaction with the career transition process ($r = -.32$, $-.27$, and $.26$, respectively); shorter time in making the transition (i.e., to find the new job, $r = .13$); as well as higher overall career satisfaction ($\beta = .63$). And De Vos and Soens (2008) studied individuals who had received career counseling and found that protean orientation was strongly related to career insight, which reflects insight of the self, skills, and aspirations ($\beta = .87$), and to proactive career enhancement behaviors ($\beta = .76$).

At first glance, the notion of the protean career may appear to overlap with the notion of boundarylessness, and this is the view of certain authors (Granrose & Baccili, 2006). However, the two concepts are distinct. The concept of the protean career focuses on the orientation, both value-driven and behavioral, of the actor toward the career, whereas the boundarylessness concept is primarily concerned with the structure of the career itself. As an illustration, Briscoe and Hall (2006) described the "solid citizen" as the individual who is driven by personal values and who is in full control of his or her career, whilst at the same time choosing to pursue one's career within a single organization because the organizational culture is in line with his or her personal values. The career of that individual is protean in orientation but within organizational boundaries from a structural perspective. In line with the conceptual distinction between the protean and the boundaryless career, Briscoe et al. (2006) found average correlations of .28 and .38 (.21 and .28 for their executive sample alone) between scores on value-driven and self-directed career orientations and scores on the boundaryless career mindset, respectively.

The relationship between the boundaryless and the protean perspectives. The establishment of the conceptual distinction between the protean and the boundaryless career permits the contemplation to combine them. The combination of the two dimensions of boundaryless career, psychological and physical mobility, along with the two dimensions of protean career, value-drive and self-direction, yields 16 potential career profiles. Briscoe and Hall (2006) concluded that eight of these profiles are realistically likely to exist in contemporary career contexts, and they provided labels and descriptions of them. At the one extreme, there are individuals who score low on all four dimensions and who are described with the label *trapped/lost*. At the other extreme, there are those who score high on all four dimensions and who are labeled *protean career architects*. Exhibit 3.1 presents the 16 potential profiles along with the 8 profiles that were identified as realistic. Segers, Inceoglou, Vloeberghs, Bartram, and Henderickx (2008) were partly successful in identifying distinct relationships between some of these profiles and an array of motives. For instance, protean career architects were more likely to be motivated by personal principles (reflective of the value-drive dimension of the protean career), achievement and personal growth (reflective of the self-direction dimension of the protean career), autonomy and affiliation (reflective of the psychological mobility dimension of boundarylessness), and personal interests (pertinent to both the psychological and physical mobility dimensions of boundarylessness; Segers et al., 2008). Additional work is certainly needed to further solidify the foundation of the two concepts and their resulting career profiles. Furthermore, career scholars should be alert to identify career profiles that apparently do not exist in the present era but may emerge along with changes in the economic and social environment. Work on the further development and integration of these dominant perspectives will be of substantial benefit to the field of careers because it will provide the tools for a more accurate and precise understanding of the processes involved in career pathing of individuals and, hence, for a fine-grained diagnosis of career situations and guidance on career development.

The Postcorporate Career

The term *postcorporate career* (Peiperl & Baruch, 1997) refers to careers that take place outside large organizations, the actors being individuals who have left such organizations, voluntarily or involuntarily, or individuals who are unable or unwilling to pursue corporate careers because of the uncertainty that is inherent in them. The postcorporate notion was epitomized by the situation at the end of the previous century when many large organizations consistently resorted to layoffs and outsourcing their functions (e.g., Cascio, 1995; Insinga & Werle, 2000; Leanna & Feldman, 1992), hence creating the need for smaller and agile organizations to provide outsourcing services (e.g., computer network maintenance, specialized consultancy) and compelling many individuals to work either alone (e.g., independent vendors) or outside large corporations (e.g., small consultancy firms, partnerships).

The postcorporate career pattern cannot be easily located on the protean-boundaryless framework because it is difficult to identify with certainty the position of its actors on self-directedness, a protean dimension, and on the physical and psychological mobility dimensions of boundarylessness. That is, actors with different positions (i.e., high or low) on these dimensions could be equally likely to pursue postcorporate careers. Hence, it is considered separately.

Postcorporate careers do not normally provide hierarchical rewards; rather, they provide intrinsic (e.g., achievement) and financial rewards to their actors (e.g., Cascio, 1995; Feldman & Bolino, 2000). The notion of the postcorporate career is still highly contemporary, for example, with the major waves of redundancy following the credit-crunch crisis that

Exhibit 3.1
Combining the Protean With the Boundaryless Careers Orientation: Emerging Career Profiles

Protean orientation	***Values-driven***	No	Yes	No	Yes
	Self-directed	No	No	Yes	Yes
Boundarylessness					
Physical mobility	***Psychological mobility***				
No	No	***"Trapped/lost"*** Because of low proactiveness and inability to see possibilities across boundaries, career actors are restricted to very narrow career possibilities over which they can exercise limited control. Success is more a function of luck than of direct control.	***"Fortressed"*** These career actors are driven, without self-direction, solely by personal values, and they lack ability to recognize opportunities. Hence, sense of success is achieved only under conditions that both match their personal values and are stable (e.g., within a financially healthy organization with traditional structure whose culture matches the values of the career actor). Such conditions may be difficult to find in the contemporary era.	Not likely to encounter in contemporary career contexts.	Not likely to encounter in contemporary career contexts.
Yes	No	***"Wanderer"*** Because personal values are of limited importance to them, these career actors generally adapt easily. However, their careers are mostly controlled by circumstances because they lack the ability to identify, evaluate, and actively drive themselves to opportunities across boundaries.	Not likely to encounter in contemporary career contexts.	Not likely to encounter in contemporary career contexts.	Not likely to encounter in contemporary career contexts.

No	Yes	Not likely to encounter in contemporary career contexts.	***"Idealist"*** Career actors are able to identify opportunities across boundaries, but they generally lack the motive and ability to direct themselves towards these. Such individuals may thrive within environments that fit their values and allow and encourage information sharing.	***"Organization man/woman"*** Career actors generally tend to conduct their careers in ways that fit the needs of others (e.g., the employer) rather than their own needs. This is because their motivation to physically move is limited, though their preparedness to do so is high (hence, they may accept internal transfers); they are either unclear about or place low importance on their values and needs.	***"Solid citizen"*** Career actors are able to actively manage their careers according to their values. They have the ability to adopt a broad perspective across boundaries. Either because of values (e.g., belief that they should be committed to the employer) or because of circumstances (e.g., family or other constraints) there is limited ability to move.
Yes	Yes	Not likely to encounter in contemporary career contexts.	Not likely to encounter in contemporary career contexts.	***"Hired gun/hired hand"*** Career actors are able to identify opportunities across boundaries, are psychologically prepared to move, and are willing to physically move toward the directions they decide. Hence, these career actors are generally adaptive in their careers. However, the fact that their career decisions are not directed by values (either because they are unclear about these or because these are of a lower priority to them) may lower their probabilities of finding an environment where they fit perfectly. They may also lack loyalty.	***"Protean career architect"*** Driven by personal values, career actors self-direct their careers, being aware of possibilities across boundaries and willing to physically cross them. Presumably, few individuals fall into this category. A potential challenge for these career actors may be to find or maintain a balance (e.g., to temporarily resist their values in order to stay in a situation for as long as is required to establish themselves).

Note. Based on Briscoe and Hall (2006).

commenced in 2008 (e.g., Holman, 2009). However, postcorporate careers have not become the norm, as some had predicted (e.g., Gray, 2001). The traditional, corporate-bound, career has proved quite robust and has survived through the pressures of competition and rationalization.

Is the Traditional Career Still Alive?

As seen, the boundaryless and the postcorporate career notions were developed to describe changing career structures, and they were rather successful in their mission. However, has the traditional career vanished? The answer to that question is unequivocally negative, despite popular views (e.g., Hansen, 2009). This is what, for example, was demonstrated by a recent large-scale study (Moss, Salzman, & Tilly, 2008) that focused on call centers in the financial and retail industries and reconstructed the ways in which their organizational structures and internal labor markets have evolved since the early 1980s. Call centers epitomize the new economy; hence, they provided a most appropriate setting to investigate whether the traditional career has been inexorably disappearing. Findings suggested that the principles of the traditional career, with long-term employment and upward moves in the hierarchy being its trademarks, were clearly evident in the call center industry. Furthermore, far from disappearing, vertical career paths and additional hierarchical layers were often introduced to improve effectiveness and motivate and retain able employees, roles that simple monetary rewards were unable to fulfill (Moss et al., 2008).

Findings that are suggestive of the resilience of the traditional career have also been reported in more traditional industries, such as in the public sector (Koskina, 2008; McDonald, Brown, & Bradley, 2005) as well as in the Japanese private sector (Iida & Morris, 2008). Therefore, authors (Baruch, 2006; Lips-Wiersma & Hall, 2007) have called for balancing traditional and contemporary viewpoints: The traditional career is present, but the boundaryless and the postcorporate career also describe contemporary patterns, which, however, are not the norm.

It should be finally noted that the four notions of career described here are not mutually exclusive. They either represent career structures that are found in the contemporary environment (i.e., traditional, boundaryless, and postcorporate) or actors' mentalities (i.e., the protean and partly the boundaryless). As seen, there have been recent attempts to combine some of these concepts, and further systematic attempts in this direction will be of great benefit.

Holland's Theory: Struggling Through Time to Find the Ideal Space

Holland (1959, 1997) advanced the idea that individuals are inclined to enter work environments whose characteristics (e.g., demands, opportunities for cultivation and expression of talent, prestige) fit their personality and interests. He categorized individuals into six types: realistic, investigative, artistic, social, enterprising, and conventional. These types fall on a circumplex that is determined by two axes: working with things (e.g., materials, machines, tools) versus with people (e.g., care), and working with data (e.g., facts) versus with ideas (e.g., insights, concepts; Prediger & Vansickle, 1992). Each of Holland's types reflect particular interests and values and, hence, preferences for activities that are attached to particular jobs, professions, or occupations.

There is general support for the theory (Holland, 1996; Tracey & Rounds, 1993), which has enjoyed substantial popularity in practice (e.g., career counseling; Rayman & Atanasoff, 1999). More recently, cognitive abilities have been added as a parallel dimension to interest types; that is, individuals are more likely to pursue careers within those jobs or professions whose cognitive demands (e.g., task complexity) they have the ability to handle (see Armstrong, Day, McVay, & Rounds, 2008).

Holland's idea, therefore, implies that careers contain a "struggle" for career actors to find occupational environments that fit their interests and values and whose demands they can meet. This is relevant to the consideration of both the time and the space element of careers. For example, it can assist in the understanding of career-related decisions and mobility at the foundation and career entry stages because individuals are apparently more likely to choose educational subjects and move toward jobs that are in line with their interest types (see McLaughlin & Tiedeman, 1974). Furthermore, the theory appears compatible with the concepts of the protean and boundaryless career because the former emphasizes value-drive and self-directedness, and the latter emphasizes mobility across borders (until the individual finds an environment that fits his or her interests and values).

Nevertheless, the theory needs further development. For example, there is lack of clarity regarding what exactly the "types" represent. Holland apparently considered interests and values as functionally identical to personality, but these are distinct, though related, constructs (e.g., Hogan & Blake, 1999); current thinking about the theory considers personality, interests, and abilities as distinct dimensions (Armstrong et al., 2008; see also chap. 5, this volume). Furthermore, changes in the nature of the economy have caused the shrinkage of environments that fitted certain interest types. For example, realistic types (who tend to be attracted to specialist blue-collar jobs) flourished in the era in which the economy was based on manual work and manufacturing, but may have difficulties in finding appropriate work environments in today's service-driven and largely knowledge-based economy (see also Holland, 1996). In this respect, the theory may need to be developed to capture the influence of economic and social changes on occupational environments. This could be accompanied by work, which is lacking so far, to directly link Holland's theory with space notions of careers. For example, the degree of congruence between individuals' career interests and the characteristics of their work environment should be inversely related to their psychological boundarylessness (representing propensity to move to a different environment), with the relationship being moderated by the value-drive dimension of career proteity.

A SHORT INTERLUDE TO COMMENT ON THE UNIVERSALITY OF CAREER MODELS

Accounts of the development of the previously discussed notions of careers take the perspective of what we would refer to as the "Western developed world," which generally includes North America, Western Europe, Oceania (i.e., Australia and New Zealand), Japan, as well as some special areas (e.g., Hong Kong, Singapore). The perspective of this part of the world was adopted because its economy, albeit with some variance across regions, has been functioning according to the principles of capitalism for most of the 20th century (and especially after the second World War); political systems in this developed world generally allowed individuals to make choices according to their personal needs, attitudes, and values (though within norms influenced by the national cultures).

Whereas the rest of the world was functioning under different political and economic conditions, the previously discussed notions of careers are sufficient to describe career patterns around most parts of the globe. To illustrate, it appears that the notion of the traditional career captures well careers in the Soviet Union (which included Russia and nearby countries) and the countries that belonged to its sphere of direct control. Since the establishment of the communist regime in the early 1920s, and especially after the end of the second World War, unemployment was kept at zero levels and virtually everyone was directly or indirectly employed by the state. Employment was permanent and movement across enterprises was minimal, because it was strongly discouraged (Brand, 1991). Career ladders were rigid, financial compensation was tied to hierarchical position, and promotions were based on seniority and on connections with the communist party. Thus, the traditional career was both the archetype and the norm in the Soviet era (though apparently few there would consider their careers as "ideal"). A difference from the Western notion was that the largest proportion of the workforce (according to some estimates, up to two-thirds; Maslova, 1991) was employed in manual work, including agriculture. The economic and social conditions that gave rise to protean, boundaryless, and postcorporate careers were absent in the Soviet era.

Similar conditions to those in the Soviet Union were prevailing in China until the 1980s; with rigid state control over productivity targets, organizational structures, and hiring, as well as complete dissociation between individual performance and organizational rewards (e.g., Ding & Warner, 2001). The apparent difference in culture between the Soviet Union and China (with the Soviet Union being substantially more individualistic as a society than the collectivistic China; see Trompenaars, 1994) did not have much of an impact on the structure and ideology of careers because, in contrast to the West, the prevailing structures allowed minimal expression of thinking or individual choice. The notions of the protean and boundaryless career became especially relevant to China in the second period of economic reforms that commenced in 1993 and are still ongoing, because since that point in time the economy has been largely, though not entirely, operating according to capitalist principles (though to assume equality in the treatment of all employees in China in the preeconomic reform era is an erroneous oversimplification; see White, 1989). In the past 2 decades, the Chinese economy seems to have gone, albeit at much faster rate, through the same stages that gave rise to the notions of the protean, boundaryless, and postcorporate careers in Western economies. For example, the restructuring of the Chinese economy was accompanied by substantial layoffs in state-owned enterprises (e.g., Hassard, Morris, Sheehan, & Yuxin, 2006).

Back to the question of universality of career models, it should be noted that a large proportion of the world population (mostly in developing countries) might not have a cohesive set of work experiences that fits our idea of career and may not even have a concept of it. The lives, work and nonwork, of many people are still quite similar to the lives of human generations before the industrial revolution, the stage in history that gave rise to those sequential systematic work experiences we today conceive as career (Baruch, 2006).

CAREERS AND THE PSYCHOLOGICAL CONTRACT

The study of careers cannot be conducted in isolation from the psychological contract. (See also Vol. 3, chap. 5, this handbook.) As seen, careers are associated with particular mentalities that include expectations and obligations (e.g., the traditional career is accompanied by the expectation that the organization provides employment in exchange for fair effort). The *psychological contract* refers to perceptions regarding reciprocal obligations between the employee and the employer (Argyris, 1960; Rousseau, 1995). Recent meta-analytic work (Zhao, Wayne, Glibkowski, & Bravo, 2007) indicates that the extent to which employees perceive the psychological contract as honored or breached is related to key outcomes, which include work attitudes, such as job satisfaction, organizational commitment and turnover intentions (absolute $\rho = .54$, .38, and 42, respectively), and actual performance, such as in-role and extra-role behaviors (absolute $\rho = .24$ and .14, respectively).

The evolution in the nature of careers has been accompanied by changes in the nature of the career actor's psychological contract. Psychological contracts can be conceptualized as falling into a continuum, one end of which consists of relationships of a purely transactional nature and the other end of which consists of relationships that include transactional and relational elements (e.g., De Cuyper, Rigotti, De Witte, & Mohr, 2008). Contracts of a transactional nature are characterized by high reciprocity, normally based in exchange obligations of a monetary nature, such as pay-for-performance, and no expectations for long-term relationship. Relational psychological contracts do not contain limits regarding relationship duration and include emotional elements, such as commitment and loyalty (De Cuyper et al., 2008). Clearly, the notion of the traditional career is compatible with a psychological contract that includes relational elements.

Employment insecurity, unclear career paths, and involuntary employer changes have largely stripped the psychological contract from its relational elements (Baruch, 1998; Bozionelos, 2003a; Brown, 2005). For example, Allen, Freeman, Russell, Reizenstein, and Rentz (2001) found that reductions in downsizing survivors' feelings of employment security were associated with lowered organizational commitment ($\beta = .31$) and heightened turnover intentions ($\beta = -.18$), with the decrease in organizational commitment persisting 1 year after the downsizing. Krause, Stadil, and Bunke (2003) reported similar findings from a study with employees who simply witnessed layoffs in another organization rather than experiencing layoffs within their own organization.

This change in the psychological contract of career actors feeds back to career patterns: Career actors have low loyalty to their employers or are reluctant to commit to corporate careers, factors that reinforce modern forms of careers, such as the boundaryless and the postcorporate. This cycle may be difficult to break, especially considering the current economic climate and the fact that the new psychological contract may have been embedded in the mentality of the workforce.

Employability Instead of Security and Vertical Advancement?

The new psychological contract, which parallels the notions of boundaryless and postcorporate career, places emphasis on *employability* (Scholarios et al., 2008), which refers to work-centered adaptability that enhances individuals' ability to identify and seize career opportunities by means of facilitating intra- and interorganizational job movement (Fugate, Kinicki, & Ashforth, 2004; Van der Heijde & Van der Heijden, 2006). In the present era, employability is fundamental for most actors to maintain a career (Fugate et al., 2004) or at least an uninterrupted career. For example, employability has been found to relate strongly to intensity of job search ($\beta = .71$) and probabilities of reemployment ($\beta = .49$) in cases of job loss (McArdle, Waters, Briscoe, & Hall, 2007).

The fact that career actors may operate according to the new psychological contract, which places emphasis on employability instead of employment security and steady vertical advancement, does not necessarily mean that they welcome it (Baruch, 2004). For example, employees highly value promotions, a trademark of the traditional career and its attached psychological contract, because these represent increases in status and formal acknowledgement of service (e.g., Moss et al., 2008; Nicholson & De Waal-Andrews, 2005). Individuals also value highly employment security. For example, in a recent cross-generational study, Dries, Pepermans, and De Kerpel (2008) found that over 80% of participants attached prime importance to employment security, with no difference between those born in the years from 1925 to 1945, who presumably conducted their careers in an era dominated by the traditional career notion, and those born after 1981. Furthermore, it is rather questionable whether enhancement of employability is always feasible or counterbalances the lack of security and steady advancement (Baruch, 2001, 2004; De Cuyper, Bernhard-Oettel, Berntson, De Witte, & Alarco, 2008). To illustrate, Taylor, Audia, and Gupta (1996) found no evidence that increased job responsibility could offset the negative effects of reduced promotion opportunities on voluntary turnover. In addition, the new career with its quest for employability is associated with elevated stress levels and health risks for career actors (e.g., Cooper, 2006), whilst it does not appear advantageous in terms of monetary rewards or subjective feelings of success (e.g., Reitman & Schneer, 2003). Therefore, a stage may have been reached that is in the best interests of neither career actors nor organizations; as the new psychological contract with its emphasis on employability means reduced commitment on the part of the workforce (see, for example, D'Amato & Herzfeldt, 2008).

Some grounds for optimism? As a note of optimism, empirical work implies that career actors are able to appreciate those employers who offer them career environments that incorporate traditional career elements. Ng and Feldman (2008) found that employees who perceived that their employers provided them with better career deals (i.e., with respect to financial rewards, job security, advancement prospects, training opportunities) than the market expressed considerably greater affective and normative commitment ($\beta = .62$ and $.54$, respectively), which can be translated into a psychological contract with more relational elements. This may be an avenue for change. If a sufficient proportion of employers realize the benefits of offering good career deals to employees, even under conditions of pressure, the cycle may slow down or even reverse; with organizations trying to offer environments that simulate the traditional career and career actors adding relational elements to their mentalities.

CAREER SUCCESS

The notion of success or failure is inherent in the conceptualization of careers (e.g., Hall, 1976; see also Nicholson & De Waal-Andrews, 2005), and the identification of factors that govern the successful progression of individuals within the space element is a key issue in the study of careers. Major perspectives to career success include the structural, the human capital, and, more recently, the social capital view.

Objective and Subjective Career Success

Traditionally, career success was considered solely in terms of attainment of rewards that are valued by the society. This refers to the *objective* or *extrinsic* view, which judges careers via the prism of the external observer and uses objectively verifiable criteria to evaluate success (Heslin, 2005; Nicholson & De Waal-Andrews, 2005; see also Khapova & Korotov, 2007). Such criteria typically include status attained in the organization or the profession, the pace of vertical advancement in the corporate, professional or occupational hierarchy, occupational prestige, and financial attainment (e.g., Heslin). However, and in line with the notion of the protean career, career actors also conduct their own evaluations of their careers, using their personal values, beliefs, and aspirations in their judgments. In these judgments individuals use both self (e.g., levels of experienced satisfaction, perceived security, opportunities to be creative) and other (e.g., advancement and performance in comparison with others, recognition by others) reference points (Dries, Pepermans, & Carlier, 2008; Heslin) and consider past as well as prospective accomplishments (Gattiker & Larwood, 1986, 1988; Nicholson & De Waal-Andrews, 2005). This represents the *subjective* or *intrinsic* notion of career success (Gattiker & Larwood, 1986; Van Maanen, 1977).

In their meta-analysis, Ng, Eby, Sorensen, and Feldman (2005) found corrected correlations between measures of objective and subjective career success in the range of .18 to .30, a finding that indicates that these are related yet clearly distinct constructs. Subjective success acquires particular substantive importance when careers are characterized by deceleration or stagnation in objective terms, which appears more likely in the present era. For example, reduced likelihood for upwards promotion relates to poorer affective commitment and greater probability of voluntary turnover (Taylor et al., 1996). Furthermore, subjective evaluations of success can serve as compasses in career decisions and as motivators to reach career-related goals, hence eventually feeding back to objective career outcomes (see Hall & Chandler, 2005). Therefore, both perspectives need to be employed in the consideration of career success.

The Human Capital View of Career Success

The *human capital view* (Becker, 1964, 1975) suggests that societal or organizational rewards, such as hierarchical and income progression, are distributed according to relevant competencies which, de facto, contribute to organizational performance or to the functioning of the society. Such competencies can be acquired through a number of means, including education, training, general and job-specific work experience, and tenure with the organization. The human capital approach is in line with the contest mobility view of intraorganizational career progression, which advocates that individuals compete with each other for organizational rewards in open and fair contests where actors are judged solely on the basis of their credentials and contributions (Turner, 1960).

The concept of *know-how* that has been advanced by Arthur and associates (Arthur, Claman, & DeFillippi, 1995; DeFillippi & Arthur, 1994) bears substantial relevance to human capital. The idea of know-how, however, adopts specifically a career perspective because it refers to the total repertoire of knowledge, skills, and other talents that career actors have at their disposal in their quest for success.

Melamed (1996a) offered a comprehensive classification of human capital attributes into three categories: *General human capital,* which encompasses attributes that should facilitate performance in the vast majority of jobs. These include, for example, educational attainment, cognitive ability, and the personality traits of conscientiousness and emotional stability, all of which have been found to relate to job performance (Barrick, Mount, & Judge, 2001; Ng & Feldman, 2009; Salgado et al., 2003). *Job-specific human capital,* which refers to attributes that relate to performance only in certain jobs. For example, job-specific knowledge and skills or personality traits that facilitate performance in particular jobs, such as extraversion for managers (Barrick et al., 2001). Empirical evidence suggests that the distinction between general and job-specific human capital is valid and highly pertinent to the modern economy (Poletaev & Robinson, 2008). Finally, Melamed also identified *job-irrelevant human capital,* which is considered later.

Empirical research provides support for the human capital approach with respect to objective career success. Ng et al. (2005) found that an array of human capital variables was related to both number of promotions and financial attainment (average corrected correlations of .06 and .21, respectively). And in a longitudinal investigation, Judge, Higgins, Thoresen, and Barrick (1999) found that measures of cognitive ability, conscientiousness, and emotional stability obtained in the career foundation stage were related to occupational prestige in the reinforcement stage and to financial attainment on the edge of the retirement stage ($r = .53$, .41, and .34, respectively). Education, and its related attributes such as training, is probably the archetypical human capital factor. Indeed, human capital is frequently operationalized solely in terms of educational attainment (e.g., McArdle et al., 2007). This is partly justifiable because in Ng et al.'s meta-analysis, education, along with general work experience, demonstrated the strongest relationship (corrected $r = .29$ in both cases) of all human capital factors with financial attainment.

The pervasiveness of the idea of human capital is illustrated by the fact that it is considered a core aspect of employability (Fugate et al., 2004). And practices seem to espouse the approach: Employers normally hire for cognitive ability, conscientiousness, and other personality characteristics that they believe add value to their businesses (e.g., Tracey, Sturman, & Tews, 2007), and they invest in internal development or external acquisition of education, skills, and experience (e.g., Lepak & Snell, 1999). States also invest in the human capital of their citizens (e.g., by financing educational institutions and by providing training incentives to organizations; Lanzi, 2007). And, finally, individuals, as career actors, invest in their own human capital (e.g., undergraduate and graduate education, seeking international assignments for the acquisition of relevant experience).

Human capital generally fares less well in accounting for individual differences in subjective career success. For example, Ng et al. (2005) found very limited relationship of educational attainment, job, and organizational tenure with career satisfaction (corrected $r = .03$, −.02, and .02, respectively). However, stable human capital characteristics fare better. Ng et al. identified corrected correlations of .14 and .36 for conscientiousness and emotional stability with subjective career success. And in their lifelong longitudinal study, Judge et al. (1999) reported a correlation of .30 between cognitive ability and subjective career success. The route via which these stable human capital attributes relate to subjective evaluations of success, however, is not clear. As cognitive ability, conscientiousness, and emotional stability relate to job performance, which should in turn be translated to objective career achievements, the relationship may be spurious; taking into account that, as seen, objective success partly influences subjective evaluations. By the same token, however, education, which also relates to job performance, should also relate to subjective career success, but it essentially does not.

An alternative account invokes nature. Personality is to a substantial extent rooted in the genetic makeup (e.g., Bouchard & Loehlin, 2001; Jang et al., 2006) and is largely invariant during adulthood (e.g., Judge et al., 1999), and certain personality traits, including emotional stability and extraversion, are linked to the physiological mechanisms for emotion (see Eysenck, 1992; Hooker, Verosky, Miyakawa, Knight, & D'Esposito, 2008). This can account for the fact that certain personality traits appear to predispose individuals to consistently positive or negative outlooks of situations (Chien, Ko, & Wu, 2007; DeNeve & Cooper, 1998) and can also account for the relevant finding that subjective career success remains stable over substantial time intervals, whereas objective career success changes during those same intervals (Wolff & Moser, 2009). The implication is that certain individuals are predisposed to evaluate their careers favorably or unfavorably and, hence, that subjective career success is partly outside individual and organizational control. This means that availability of opportunities, such as education, training, and challenging assignments, to enhance human capital is not necessarily accompanied by improvements in employees' subjective feelings of success, at least not analogously to corresponding gains in objective success.

Career success and job performance. Readers may have noticed that in our discussion objective career success is not treated as tantamount to job performance. There are a number of reasons for this:

1. Objective career success is determined by the joint effect of multiple work-related outcomes, not all of which are under the control of career actors (e.g., a recession with its consequent contraction of the job market, as to be seen later). Furthermore, objective career outcomes are largely influenced by career decisions. These decisions range from the choice of employer at the career-entry stage to whether to contemplate an interorganizational move or to pursue additional education at a later stage. For example, a career actor who is an excellent performer may choose to stay with an employer instead of accepting a competitor's offer; however, the employer may subsequently restructure and downsize, which may restrict promotion opportunities or even leave the career actor temporary unemployed. In this case, the career success outcome may not be commensurate with job performance. Careers, and their attached success, have much deeper and broader determinants than how well career actors perform in particular work roles.
2. Consideration of the relationship between job performance and career success would be meaningful only within the same job or profession and within the same environment. Otherwise, comparability issues can seriously compromise the validity of any conclusions. To demonstrate, criteria for the allocation of organizational rewards, such as promotions and money, vary across sectors. For example, not-for-profit organizations are less likely to use job performance as a criterion for promotion (Devaro & Brookshire, 2007). Furthermore, criteria for career success vary widely across jobs and professions as well as across societal and organizational contexts, which means that objective evaluations may be conflicting depending on the criterion used. As an illustration, the success of a plateaued middle manager, a semiskilled worker who has always been able to find employment, and a heart surgeon with a poor survival record for his or her patients would be judged differently according to occupational prestige, employability, and monetary compensation.
3. Even in cases, however, in which the relationship has been tested with standardized instruments and with controls for structural factors, nonperfect associations have been identified. A recent study (Carmeli, Shalom, & Weisberg, 2007) of individuals pursuing corporate careers in both the service and the manufacturing sector found that an array of performance indices, including overall job performance, withdrawal behaviors (e.g., absenteeism), amount of overtime work, and organizational citizenship, accounted for 12% of the variance in objective career success; a significant but clearly not impressive amount. Similar findings were reported by Van Scotter, Motowidlo, and Cross (2000) in a study of air force mechanics, in which task and contextual performance combined together accounted for less than 10% of the variance in promotions. In fact, there is research that suggests an even more limited relationship. For example, Cannings and Montmarquette (1988) found no link between performance ratings and probabilities of promotion among male managers.

One potential explanation for the rather weak link between job performance and objective career success lies in the imperfections of organizational systems in evaluating employee performance (e.g., Latham & Mann, 2006) as well as in the error involved in the operationalization and measurement of job performance by researchers. Another explanation, however, involves the presence of factors that are not directly relevant to job performance but nevertheless affect career prospects. These include job-irrelevant human capital and social capital, which will be discussed next.

Job-irrelevant human capital. *Job-irrelevant human capital* refers to individual characteristics that logically should not bear a relationship to job performance but which nevertheless appear to influence career success (Melamed, 1996a). This category of human capital deserves some special attention because it has gained recognition only recently.

Physical characteristics of individuals, reflected by physical appearance, are most representative of job-irrelevant human capital. These include height and physical attractiveness. These features may indeed offer performance advantages in certain jobs (e.g., modeling, certain sports). However, in the majority of jobs or professions these characteristics should not present performance advantages or disadvantages, especially in the modern economy that relies heavily on cognitive rather than manual work. Hence, from a logical point of view these should bear no relationship to career success. However, Hosoda, Stone-Romero, and Coats's (2003) meta-analysis of 27 field and laboratory experiments indicated an advantage in promotion and hiring decisions for more physically attractive individuals (combined $d = .37$). Success in being hired may influence the timing of career entry, probabilities of upward interorganizational moves, or staying in employment in the case of lay-offs; hence, it is highly pertinent to career success. Furthermore, meta-analytic and field research conducted by Judge and Cable (2004) revealed a relationship of height with hierarchical status ($\rho = .24$) and financial attainment (average $\beta = .26$). Hence, empirical evidence suggests a clear link between observable physical characteristics and objective career success.

One account for the observed relationships invokes implicit personality theory (Bruner & Tagiuri, 1954) and posits that others form impressions of competence, social skill, and stature on the basis of individuals' appearance (e.g., Ashmore, 1981). These impressions, in turn, affect decisions on rewards (e.g., job offers, promotions; see Hosoda et al., 2003; Judge & Cable, 2004). According to this explanation, decision makers (e.g., line managers, promotion and hiring panels) advantage individuals with certain physical characteristics without being consciously aware of doing so. A second account, advanced herein, is that individuals with certain physical characteristics are consciously given an advantage (or disadvantage) by decision makers, who function under the belief that physical appearance has direct value adding properties for their units. This is especially the case in interactive service industries (e.g., hospitality) in which employers generally assume that physical attractiveness of service providers is related to customer satisfaction (Warhurst, Nickson, Witz, & Cullen, 2000). Both of these explanations imply passivity on the part of individual career actors whose physical characteristics simply evoke reactions that influence their careers.

Yet a third account implies that visible physical characteristics do not relate to career success simply because of how individuals "look" but because of what individuals "do." This account suggests that physical attributes, such as height, are directly linked to human personality (Judge & Cable, 2004) or cognitive ability (Case & Paxson, 2008), which in turn impact job performance and career success. However, Melamed and Bozionelos (1992) found that the significant relationship between height and promotion rate of British civil service managers remained virtually unchanged after imposing statistical control for personality. The corresponding finding of Judge and Cable (2004) for cognitive ability was analogous.

Systematic research on the mechanisms that link job-irrelevant human capital with career success is important because the magnitude of relationships is comparable with those of other forms of human capital. For example, the average correlation between physical height and financial attainment in Judge and Cable's (2004) studies was .29, whereas the corresponding correlations for education and conscientiousness, forms of general human capital, in Ng et al.'s (2005) meta-analysis were .29 and .07, respectively. States invest enormous amounts in educational programs, as do individuals for their personal education and development, and organizations invest considerable resources in training, development, and selection systems with the expectation of having educated and dependable individuals in their ranks. But, ironically, factors that are out of their control seem able to offset these investments. Identification of the mechanisms of the link should assist in the further development of hiring and award allocation procedures, including awareness and training of decision makers. This should reduce the likelihood of biased decisions, hence improving fairness and outcomes at individual, organizational, and societal level.

Fluid versus crystallized human capital. Using the analogy of fluid versus crystallized intelligence (e.g., Cattell, 1941; Horn & Cattell, 1966), it is proposed that human capital can be categorized in terms of attributes that can be developed or enhanced, such as skills and education, and attributes that are generally stable and cannot be easily modified or developed, such as personality traits, cognitive ability, and physical characteristics; the former labeled as *crystallized human capital* and the latter as *fluid human capital.*

This typology should be seen as orthogonal to Melamed's (1996a) typology. The combination of the two typologies yields six categories of human capital, according to relevance to job performance (ranging from general to job-irrelevant) and degree of modifiability. Such categorization can assist career decision making and planning. For example, specialists or career actors will be able to decide in favor of careers that fit best their crystallized human capital and avoid those directions that require fluid human capital in which they have serious deficiencies. Subsequently, they can identify which crystallized human capital characteristics they need to further cultivate to achieve success in their chosen career paths.

The Structural View of Career Success

The *structural view,* sometimes referred to as the *opportunistic approach,* places emphasis on the influence of structural factors on career progression (e.g., Spilerman, 1977). These can be of an organizational, environmental, or societal nature.

Organizational factors include organizational structure, size, type of ownership, criteria for allocation of organizational rewards, and characteristics of internal labor markets (e.g., Sonnenfeld, Peiperl, & Kotter, 1988). Gunz (1988) commented on the distinctive "career logic" of every organization, which denotes the fact that career paths and rules to navigate through these paths are determined by the unique structural and cultural features of each organization. Evidently, organizational factors concern only individuals who pursue traditional careers in the totality or part of their working lives. Environmental factors, or labor market forces, include the type of industry (e.g., service vs. manufacturing, degree of regulation, profit vs. non-profit) and the economic circumstances (e.g., period of war, recession) under which careers take place (e.g., Long & Link, 1983). Finally, societal factors refer to the structure of the society (e.g., Melamed, 1995a). These include, for example, the educational system and employment legislation, which can influence skill availability in the labor market and opportunities or constraints to career mobility, respectively.

There is empirical evidence for the veracity of the structural perspective. In a recent study of MBA graduates from elite schools, Oyer (2008) found that both the timing of their entry into investment banking careers and the financial success of these careers were related to the conditions in the stock market while they were in graduate school. MBAs were more likely to go directly into investment banking upon graduation ($\beta = .14$) if stock market returns were positive (i.e., the index increased) for the duration of the program, and probability of pursuing a career in investment banking was increased by 75% for those who went directly into the industry, in comparison with those who had an interest to do so but did not enter the industry directly upon graduation. And in a 20-year longitudinal study with a representative sample of the workforce with the United States in the career entry stage, Shin (2007) found that upward and downward intra- and interorganizational movements were affected by the industry's structural changes (e.g., contraction, expansion) and density of mergers.

The human capital and the structural approach account for the contribution of factors of different nature to career success; hence, they should be seen as complementary. To illustrate, in a study in a German engineering company, Bruderl, Preisendorfer, and Ziegler (1993) found that human capital affected probabilities of promotion, but the relationship was moderated by the opportunity structure of the organization, which was a function of the number of workers in each hierarchical level and of the number of promotions made at each level in a specific year. Number of promotions was affected by expansion or contraction of the company, which, in turn, was affected by the conditions in the industry and the economy in general.

At this point, it should be noted that it is erroneous to view career actors as passive followers of a script or as pawns for forces represented by, primarily, structural and, secondarily, human capital factors. Instead, it is more appropriate to view individuals as improvising actors who navigate within the space element of careers. The environment undoubtedly imposes constraints (see also Ozbilgin, Kusku, & Erdogmus, 2005, p. 2001), but individuals can optimize their career options within these constraints or even overcome them in some cases. For example, active job search behaviors, such as preparation and updating of one's resume, have been found to predict success in finding employment in the transition from university to the labor market ($\beta = .54$; Brown, Cober, Kane, Levy, & Shalhoop, 2006), as well as in the speed of the transition from the armed forces to the civilian labor market ($r = .23$; Baruch & Quick, 2007). And individual career choices account for career success over and above the contribution of structural and human capital factors (Melamed, 1996b).

Therefore, career progression and success should be regarded as the outcome of a constant interplay between extraneous forces, such as structural variables, and internal forces that are manifested in the actions of career actors. In fact, not only do individuals navigate through the structural element, but they may also shape it in an interactive manner; as the processes through which individual careers progress mold organizations and affect their probabilities of success (Feldman, 1985; Lazarova & Taylor, 2009).

The Social Capital View of Career Success

The *social capital* perspective has been consolidated rather recently (Seibert, Kramer, & Liden, 2001), though the principles behind it had been in place for a substantial amount of time. This approach asserts that factors going beyond structure and human capital should be taken into cognizance in order to develop an exhaustive description of what determines career success. The interest in social capital is evidenced by the fact that it is seen as a component of employability (Fugate et al., 2004).

The social capital view attests that informal interpersonal processes, which are captured by the concept of social capital, play an important role in career success. The term *social capital* was popularized by Coleman (1988),[3] though the notion, and the term itself, is found in earlier writings (see Portes, 1998), Bourdieu's (1980, 1986) being the most notable. Social capital can be considered at macro level (e.g., Inkpen & Tsang, 2005) or micro level. However, the present work exclusively focuses on the latter because this refers to the individual career actor.

Social capital signifies resources (i.e., information, influence, solidarity) that an individual has at one's disposal by means of his or her relationship ties with other individuals within a particular social structure, such as the work organization, the profession, or the society in general (Adler & Kwon, 2002; Bourdieu, 1986; Portes, 1998). These resources impact social outcomes, such as career success, by means of two properties: substitutability and appropriability (Adler & Kwon). *Substitutability* refers to the capacity to substitute for or complement qualities or resources that the individual may be lacking (e.g., credentials, performance, direct access to information, position power). *Appropriability* captures the fact that relationship ties of a certain type can be utilized for multiple purposes (e.g., friends in the workplace may offer emotional support, performance feedback, information on internal job openings, and access to organizational decision makers). Through these properties, social capital makes "possible the achievement of certain ends that in its absence would not be possible" (Coleman, 1988, p. S98). It should be noted that there are not only the relationship ties of which the individual is aware, and which compose his or her social capital, but also those ties of which the individual is not consciously aware (i.e., the ties of the ties) that influence outcomes (see Higgins & Kram, 2001). Elements of the social capital perspective are found in the *know-whom factor* of Arthur and associates' view of career enhancing strategies. The know-whom factor refers to the accumulation and mobilization of interpersonal ties in the pursuit of career success (Arthur et al., 1995; DeFillippi & Arthur, 1994).

Empirical literature provides support for the link between social capital and objective career success. Social capital appears to assist in the career entry and in later career stages. For example, Jokisaari and Nurmi (2005) found that the social capital of final year university students was related to the probability of having a full-time job commensurate with their educational credentials 6 months later (odds ratios

[3] The impact of Coleman's article becomes evident from a search of the Thompson Scientific database that covers the period from 1945 until present, using *social capital* as key word. Before 1988, when Coleman's article was published, there were 16 articles using the term, whereas after 1988 this number well exceeds 3,000.

1.89 and .65 for the two measures of social capital used, respectively). Similarly, Combes, Linnemer, and Visser (2008) found that social capital was able to overcompensate for deficiencies in number and quality of publications in the hiring of economics faculty in French academia: The combination of having one's doctoral advisor in the selection panel and having earned one's doctorate from a university with which another member of the panel was affiliated nearly tripled (i.e., increased from 17% to 47%) the probability of success from the baseline condition, whereas a shift from the 10th to the 90th percentile in quality of publications increased the probability of success over the baseline condition by only about half (i.e., from 14% to 21%; Combes et al., 2008). Finally, social capital has also been found to relate to subjective, along with objective, career success (Seibert et al., 2001).

Mentoring and network resources. An operationalization of social capital that facilitates the development of more fine-grained advice on tactics and strategies for individual career management can be expressed in terms of primary mentoring relationships and network ties (e.g., Bozionelos, 2003b; see also Seibert et al., 2001). *Mentoring* in its classical or traditional form refers to an intensive developmental relationship between two persons of unequal status or power, the mentor and the protégé, in which the former provides a variety of functions for the latter (e.g., Kram, 1985; see also chap. 17, this volume). These functions fall into two dimensions: career-instrumental (e.g., protection, assignment of challenging tasks, exposure and visibility) and socioemotional (e.g., acceptance and confirmation, role modeling; Kram, 1985; Tepper, Shaffer, & Tepper, 1996). The mentoring relationship develops over a long period of time and may transcend organizational boundaries (Baugh & Fagenson-Eland, 2005; Kram, 1985). The function of mentoring as a career-enhancing platform is in agreement with the sponsored mobility view, which asserts that certain individuals have an advantage in the allocation of organizational and societal rewards because they enjoy the sponsorship and support of powerful members of the organization or of the social system (Turner, 1960).

It should be borne in mind that mentoring relationships vary with respect to the number and quality of mentoring functions provided within them (Fletcher & Ragins, 2007; Ragins, Cotton, & Miller, 2000) and that individuals may be involved in none, one, or many mentoring relationships in their careers (for a mini-review of relevant evidence, see Kirchmeyer, 2005, p. 654).

Network ties encompass the totality of the individual's interpersonal ties, excluding any traditional mentoring relationships. Network ties vary in terms of strength, which encompasses longevity, intensity, intimacy, and reciprocity; range, which signifies the social distance that a particular tie can reach (see Marsden, 1990); diversity, which refers to the social domain (e.g., work, professional association, nonwork) of the tie's origin; and direction, as ties may be formed with individuals of lower, equal, or greater power or experience than the career actor (see Higgins & Kram, 2001). Mentoring relationships with peers (see McManus & Russell, 2007) fall into the category of network ties. In a direct analogy to the functions of mentoring, the functionality of network ties is also divided into career-instrumental and socioemotional (Fombrun, 1982; Ibarra, 1993; see also Saint-Charles & Mongeau, 2009), with most ties serving in varying proportions both instrumental and emotional functions (Brass, 1992; Kram & Isabella, 1985; Saint-Charles & Mongeau).

Meta-analyses (Allen, Eby, Poteet, Lentz, & Lima, 2004; Eby, Allen, Evans, Ng, & DuBois, 2008; Kammeyer-Mueller & Judge, 2008) of the abundant empirical research on the relationship between mentoring receipt and career success confirm the link between the two. Allen et al., for example, found relationships of mentoring received with monetary compensation and number of promotions (sample-weighted $r = .12$ and .31, respectively) as well as with career satisfaction and expectations for advancement (sample-weighted $r = .21$ and .26, respectively). Furthermore, empirical evidence is emerging that indicates that providing mentoring to others is linked with mentors' career success (Bozionelos, 2004; Eby, Durley, Evans, & Ragins, 2006). As a result, organizations have been implementing formal mentoring systems, which involve mentor–protégé relationships that are formally arranged, recognized, and supported; though the benefits of formal mentoring pertain mostly to subjective career outcomes (see Baugh & Fagenson-Eland, 2007).

A lesser amount of systematic empirical work has been dedicated exclusively to the relationship of network resources to career success, though relevant research is accumulating. Wolff and Moser (2009) investigated the relationship of six networking behaviors (i.e., building, maintaining, and using internal and external organizational contacts) to career success. Most of these behaviors were related, though only moderately at best, to current monetary compensation (mean partial $r = .10$, range of the four significant partial $rs = 11–.20$) and current subjective career success (mean partial $r = .17$, range of the four significant partial $rs = .16–.32$) over and above a range of human capital and structural factors. Two of these networking behaviors, maintaining and using internal contacts, were also related, albeit weakly (partial $r = .05$ and .03, respectively), to growth in monetary compensation over a 2-year period. And Higgins (2005), looking at the labor market as a wider system, described what she termed a "career ecosystem" by presenting the case of Baxter, a major company in the biochemical industry, and the way that their managers were indoctrinated into a network of relationships where entrepreneurship was a key factor to success. A substantial number of Baxter's former executives came to dominate the start-up bioindustry and a large proportion of its former managers became the CEOs of such start-ups. Their success can be attributed to their access to a common pool of knowledge, information, and solidarity that was available through their common links.

Mentoring or network ties? An issue that has implications for career tactics and strategies is whether mentors and network ties relate independently to career success or whether they can substitute for each other. For example, authors have suggested that in the present era career actors need multiple developmental relationships because professional and learning demands are greater and cannot be fulfilled by a single traditional mentoring relationship (de Janasz & Sullivan, 2004; Higgins & Kram, 2001) that best fits the demands of the traditional career.

Some research findings are suggestive of overlapping contributions of mentoring and network ties to career success, the implication being that network ties can substitute for mentoring and vice versa (Bozionelos, 2003b; 2008). However, Seibert et al.'s (2001) work appears to suggest that their effects are additive (i.e., independent), whereas yet other research suggests that the effects are additive only for subjective career success (Blickle, Witzki, & Schneider, 2009). Yet, and as a compromise, there is some evidence that the benefits of mentoring and network ties are realized at different career stages, with network ties being more beneficial in the long-term (Higgins & Thomas, 2001). However, to add to the complexity, recent empirical research (Blickle et al., 2009) implies that mentoring and network ties are linked in the sense that mentoring is partly responsible for the development of network ties (e.g., the protégé models the mentor's behaviors of ties acquisition), which in turn influences career success. Finally, perplexity is further augmented by the fact that the instrumental and the socio-emotional functions of mentoring and network ties appear to relate differentially to objective and subjective career outcomes. For example, Allen et al. (2004) found that socioemotional mentoring was substantially more strongly related to subjective (sample-weighted $r = .25$) than to objective career success (mean sample-weighted $r = .05$), a pattern that was partly repeated for career-instrumental mentoring (sample-weighted $r = .29$ and mean sample-weighted $r = .12$, respectively). On the other hand, Bozionelos (2003b) found that only the instrumental ($\beta = .12$), but not the socioemotional, network resources were associated with objective career success, whereas the pattern was more complicated with respect to subjective career success, with instrumental and socioemotional networking being related to different facets of it.

Additional research is necessary, taking into account that career actors' psychological resources (e.g., persistence, proactivity) and time are not limitless; hence, it is important to direct these correctly in their effort to build social capital.

The mechanism of the social capital effect: Politics or job performance? As we have seen, there is evidence that supports the social capital approach to career success. The mechanism for the link, however, remains to be unveiled. Potential explanations, not necessarily mutually exclusive, include job performance and political processes. The former posits that social capital enhances the performance of those who possess it, which, in turn, impacts career success (e.g., income attainment). For example, challenging assignments or role modeling that mentors provide increase protégés' job expertise and, subsequently, their performance, which is rewarded by means of organizational or societal rewards (e.g., more clients, hence, greater income). However, the political approach suggests that it is by means of political processes that social capital impacts career success. For example, a mentor or another powerful social tie may directly influence a promotion decision in favor of the career actor. This is in line with the political view of organizational life (e.g., Mintzberg, 1985), which posits that, on many occasions, decisions that influence careers (e.g., hiring, promotions, transfers, training) are based on political processes and motives rather than on transparent and merit-based processes and criteria (e.g., Bozionelos, 2005; Ferris & Judge, 1991; Ferris & King, 1991; Koskina, 2008; Pfeffer, 1989). Tharenou (1997), for example, posited that "promotion . . . is [also] determined by networks and politics" (p. 83) and that "politics influences who advances in management" (p. 83).

There is some evidence that social capital is linked with enhanced job performance. For example, Thompson (2005) found a relationship between network-building behaviors and supervisory performance ratings. However, Green and Bauer (1995) found no relationship between mentoring and objective measures of performance. Supervisory performance ratings may be influenced by the social capital of career actors (e.g., Bozionelos & Wang, 2007). Furthermore, in a study that deliberately compared the political and the performance approaches using objective performance criteria, Kirchmeyer (2005) found evidence that was more in support of the political rather than the performance view.

Additional research is crucial because the issue is of critical importance, especially for organizations that invest in formal mentoring systems or are advised to foster cultures that favor the development of informal mentoring relationships and social capital (e.g., Pastoriza, Arino, & Ricart, 2008; Singh, Bains, & Vinnicombe, 2002). Organizations' primary interest is the performance, rather than the career success, of their employees. If social capital operates mainly via the political route, which can be detrimental for both organizational performance and employee morale (e.g., Bozionelos, 2005; Vigoda, 2000; and for some points on the dangers of social capital, see Portes, 1998, pp. 15–18), organizational policies may need to be reconsidered or systems be developed that filter out the political elements of social capital.

DIVERSITY AND CAREERS

Diversity refers to heterogeneity among members of the workforce according to one or more salient characteristics (e.g., Bell, 2007; Milliken & Martins, 1996; see also Vol. 1, chap. 20, this handbook). Hence, a diverse workforce is composed of two or more subgroups. Diversity is pertinent to careers because it apparently relates to variance in employment patterns and opportunities. Individuals may pursue different career goals or be offered different career options, depending on the group they belong to.

Traditionally, diversity has been viewed in terms of *surface-level diversity* (Harrison, Price, & Bell, 1998), which signifies differences in overtly identifiable features that are usually rooted in biological or genetic differences. The most prominent of these features include sex, race, ethnicity, and age (Tsui, Egan, & O'Reilly, 1992). These characteristics are readily observable, are not susceptible to alteration, and are operationalizable in terms of demographic factors. Religion could also be added to these, as could sexual orientation (if revealed) and certain physical features, such as body weight and forms of disability. These features are either permanent or difficult to alter and are readily revealed in social contact. Finally, special types of family arrangements, such as being a single parent or a part of a dual-career couple, are other forms of surface-level diversity. Though not permanent, these conditions normally last for substantial portions of worklife and tend to manifest themselves early in the course of social interaction. Evidently, various forms of surface-level diversity may coexist (e.g., an overweight single mother), giving rise to hybrid diversity (Baruch, 2004). It should also be mentioned that some surface-level diversity characteristics, such as body weight, sex, and race, could also be seen under the prism of job-irrelevant human capital because these may influence career success independently of job performance.

Apart from the surface level, however, diversity also operates at "deep level." *Deep-level diversity* refers to heterogeneity or separation in attitudes, beliefs, values, or even skills, knowledge, and experiences (Harrison et al., 1998; Jackson, May, & Whitney, 1995; Milliken & Martins, 1996; see also Harrison & Klein, 2007). These characteristics are constructs; hence, they can only be inferred via substantial interpersonal interaction and long observation. Furthermore, unlike surface-level features, deep-level diversity characteristics are susceptible to change (Jackson et al., 1995).

Both surface- and deep-level diversity relate to outcomes in the work environment (Harrison et al., 1998; Harrison, Price, Gavin, & Florey, 2002). However, from a careers perspective, it is surface-level diversity that is of greatest relevance. Similarity at surface level leads to expectations for similarity at deep level (Philips & Loyd, 2006). And surface-level characteristics are more likely to evoke immediate reactions that pertain to bias and prejudice (Milliken & Martins, 1996), which give rise to discrimination. *Discrimination* refers to systematic disparity in opportunities and outcomes between groups with comparable potential (Dipboye & Halverson, 2004) and is linked to careers by its association with differentiation in career opportunities for diverse groups, such as probabilities of obtaining a job, being promoted, or offered a favorable transfer. The similarity-attraction paradigm (Byrne, 1971) and the self-categorization and social identity perspective (Tajfel & Turner, 1986) explain the link between diversity and discrimination: Individuals categorize themselves and others according to salient attributes, such as surface-level characteristics, and identify with those whom they perceive as belonging to the same categories as themselves, and to whom they are, in turn, attracted and with whom they prefer to associate.

Next, we focus on gender, the diversity form that has attracted most attention from the perspective of careers (Baruch, 2006). However, other forms of surface-level diversity are mentioned too, to the extent that these exhibit similarities with gender.

Gender and Careers

Women today comprise nearly half of the working population in developed countries (United Nations, 2007). It appears, however, that their careers lag behind those of men in terms of objective criteria for success. For example, Ng et al.'s (2005) meta-analysis indicated significant disadvantages for women in both number of promotions and financial attainment, with women lagging behind men one tenth and one fifth of a standard deviation, respectively (corresponding $d = .45$ and .18, respectively[4]). This finding concurs with the official statistics on earnings differences between women and men, which is in the ratio of 4 to 5, in the general population of the United States (U.S. Department of Labor, 2008). The term *glass ceiling* has been coined to describe the presence of an invisible barrier that prevents women and other groups from advancing into powerful positions (Morrison, White, & Van Velsor, 1987) in any environment where careers are pursued (e.g., Achkar, 2008). As to be seen below, there is some evidence of cracks in the glass ceiling, though this may not necessarily reflect elimination of disparity in career opportunities.

A number of accounts, which are not mutually exclusive, have been offered for the observed gender differences in objective career success:

1. Different expectations and priorities, rooted partly in socialization. Women, for example, are likely to be expected to prioritize family or their partner's careers over their own (e.g., by taking career breaks to look after their children, working less overtime, taking the burden of domestic labor, changing their jobs to trail their partners who relocate; Nieva, 1985; Russo, 1985). Indeed, in a study of women in dual-career couples, Valcour and Ladge (2008) found that prioritization of their partner's careers over their own was negatively related to their financial attainment ($\beta = -.32$). And in a study with university graduates in the United Kingdom, Chevalier (2007) found that women were substantially more likely than

[4] *d* values calculated by the authors.

their male counterparts to expect a career break for family reasons; which, in turn, accounted for 10% of the gender gap in financial attainment. Work–family conflict, the conflict between those work and family roles that are mutually incompatible (Greenhaus & Beutell, 1985), is also pertinent. Work–family conflict appears more detrimental for women than for men. For example, Mayrhofer, Meyer, Schiffinger, and Schmidt (2008) found that family responsibilities were negatively related to work centrality, which was, in turn, related to career success for women but not for men.

2. Human capital and career path differences. According to this view, women follow different educational paths and, hence, accumulate less or different crystallized human capital, which, in turn, handicaps their career attainment. Women, for example, are more likely to major in "soft" subjects whereas men tend to major in sciences, engineering, and business-related disciplines (e.g., Bradley, 2000; Dahlmann, Elsner, Jeschke, Natho, & Schroder, 2008) that are more likely to lead to corporate careers, line instead of staff positions, and higher earning occupations. Indeed, Penner (2008) found that occupational differences accounted for approximately three-quarters of the gender gap in earnings among newly hired employees in a large U.S. firm (for updated data on earnings gaps across occupations in the United States, see Bureau of Labor Statistics, 2007). Even nowadays, females with secondary education are less likely than their male counterparts to express intentions to follow a career in computer science or information technology (Anderson, Lankshear, Timms, & Courtney, 2008; Papastergiou, 2008). At this point, it should be mentioned that males tend to score higher in aspects of cognitive ability, such as mental rotation and mechanical reasoning (see Hyde, 2005), that facilitate entry into science- and engineering-related degree programs; whereas women tend to score higher in verbal ability (Hyde), which is associated with "softer" disciplines that are less likely to lead to careers with strong objective success prospects.

However, although these explanations have received empirical support, in many cases gender differences in objective career success persist even after controlling for the factors attached to these accounts. To illustrate, in a 10-year longitudinal study with a representative sample of university graduates, Bobbitt-Zeher (2007) found that around one-third of the gender difference in financial attainment remained unaccounted for after controlling for an array of background factors (e.g., socioeconomic background), personal values (e.g., importance attached to money), family situation, human capital (i.e., cognitive ability, undergraduate major, GPA), structural factors (i.e., profit vs. nonprofit sector, industry type, occupation) and work involvement (i.e., hours worked per week). This, therefore, provides an additional explanation for the gender gap in objective career success, which draws on social capital and direct discrimination. It is argued, for example, that women possess less social capital than men or use it suboptimally in the work environment, a fact that undermines their career advancement (e.g., Tharenou, 1997). Concurring with this view, a recent study with a representative sample of the U.K. adult population indicated that women have fewer network ties than their male counterparts (Li, Savage, & Warde, 2008). Explanations for women's deficit in social capital include the following:

1. Women's lower capacity, as relative newcomers in organizational life, to create career-instrumental social capital, as well as their alleged tendency to underestimate its importance for career advancement and to rely more on formal, merit-based, procedures and human capital in their quest for success. There is evidence to support this view. Van Emmerik (2006), in a study in academia, found that males were more able in creating career-instrumental network ties than were women. Ng et al.'s (2005) meta-analysis indicated that educational attainment and amount of working hours, two variables that are representative of human capital and work effort, respectively, were more strongly related to financial attainment for women than for men; and Forret and Dougherty (2004) found that networking behaviors accounted for greater variance in men's than in women's objective career success. In a qualitative study, Ozbilgin and Healy (2004) described how augmentation in the attention paid to human capital in hiring and promotion

increased the proportion of female representation in academic ranks in Turkey. Finally, in a study with women managers in Australian banks, Metz and Tharenou (2001) found that human capital accounted for seven and three times more variance than social capital in their objective career success at lower-middle and upper management levels, respectively.

2. High degree of homophily in women's social capital ties (Ibarra, 1993; Morrison & Von Glinow, 1990). This means that women tend to form mentoring and network ties primarily with other women and do not integrate into male networks, which carry most career-enhancing information and influence because of the traditional male dominance of organizational power structures. Indeed, Ibarra's (1992) findings on homophily differences between men and women's networks implied that that it was necessary for women to form career-instrumental ties with men, with similar findings reported by Stackman and Pinder (1999). And in a study that focused on career experiences of financial professionals in Wall Street firms, Roth (2004) found evidence for homophily in women's mentoring and network ties, which was, in turn, related to reduced likelihood to work in the most highly paid areas.

The theoretical underpinnings of women's deficit in social capital include the similarity-attraction paradigm, referred to earlier (Tsui & O'Reilly, 1989); the perception that formation of ties with women, and other career disadvantaged groups, are of lower value (Ibarra, 1993; Ragins & Sundstrom, 1989); and identity preservation, which suggests that women consciously choose not to integrate into male dominated networks in order to demonstrate loyalty to their gender (Ibarra; Kanter, 1977; Kram, 1985). Indeed, in line with the last point, Davey (2008) found that women in male-dominated professions detested the fact that they had to disguise their feminine values and characteristics, such as sensitivity, in order to acquire the social capital necessary to advance their careers.

A supplementary account invokes personality. For example, women score lower than men on the assertiveness aspect of extraversion ($d = .51$; Hyde, 2005), a personality trait that is associated with social capital (Okun, Pugliese, & Rook, 2007; Wolff & Moser, 2006). However, the role of personality should be secondary, taking into account that genders do not differ in the other aspects of extraversion (see Hyde, 2005).

Apart from being disadvantaged in the social capital arena, however, women may also face direct discrimination because of general beliefs held by key organizational players: that women are less committed to, less competent, and less suitable for tasks that pertain to organizational life (e.g., Adler, 1993; Eagly & Carli, 2007, p. 64). This view is partly represented by the status expectation theory (Berger, Fisek, Norman, & Zelditch, 1977), which suggests that those groups that have traditionally enjoyed higher status, such as men, are also implicitly assumed to be more competent than traditionally lower status groups, such as women. In line with this view, Greenhaus and Parasuraman (1993) found that women's successful performance was more likely than that of men's to be attributed to contingencies rather than abilities, a finding that was corroborated by those of Roth (2004). And Lyness and Heilman's (2006) finding that women managers who were promoted had substantially better performance ratings than their male counterparts ($\beta = .29$) implies that women may have to prove themselves more in terms of performance to receive organizational rewards.

These accounts, fully or in part, apply to a number of other diversity groups that are allegedly discriminated against, ranging from racial and ethnic minorities (see Ibarra, 1993) to overweight individuals (e.g., Rudolph, Wells, Weller, & Baltes, 2009). For example, Li et al. (2008) found that along with women, ethnic minorities were also disadvantaged in terms of social capital; and Penner (2008) found similar effects of occupational segregation on starting salaries of ethnic minorities as were found for women. Furthermore, any adverse effects of diversity on careers are likely to be exacerbated in cases of hybrid diversity (Baruch, 2004).

The Paradox of Subjective Career Success and the Kaleidoscope Career

Women's apparent disadvantage in objective career success is not reflected in their subjective career evaluations. Indeed, women do not lag behind their male counterparts in this dimension. In their meta-analysis, Ng et al. (2005) found no gender difference in subjective career success. And in a study with business owners that was conducted since the meta-analysis, Powell and Eddleston (2008) reported exactly analogous findings, with female business owners reporting the same levels of subjective success as their male counterparts despite the fact that their businesses were lagging behind in objective criteria.

This paradox can be accounted for in terms of differential career expectations for men and women (Powell & Eddleston, 2008) as well as in terms of alternative domains (e.g., family, work–family balance, social relations, contribution to the society) from which women can draw a sense of achievement and satisfaction; in contrast to men who appear to derive such sense mostly from work-related experiences that pertain to attainment of power and material rewards (Dyke & Murphy, 2006; see also Lirio et al., 2007). Therefore, it appears that women's careers have more protean elements than men's because women seem to use alternative criteria, apart from rigid definitions of success or failure, to guide and evaluate their work-related experiences (see Mainiero & Sullivan, 2005; Valcour & Ladge, 2008).

Mainiero and Sullivan's (2005, 2006) *kaleidoscope career model* builds on the subjective element of careers with the purpose of developing an explanation for the differential gender perspective. Using the kaleidoscope metaphor (see Inkson, 2007, for the use of metaphors in the study of careers), Mainiero and Sullivan (2005) suggested the following:

> Like a kaleidoscope that produces changing patterns when the tube is rotated and its glass chips fall into new arrangements, women shift the pattern of their careers by rotating different aspects of their lives to arrange roles and relationships in new ways. (p. 111)

Relationships are pivotal in women's careers, and the kaleidoscope contains three "glass chips" through which they evaluate and guide their careers: authenticity, or being true to oneself in the midst of the constant interplay of personal development with work and nonwork issues; balance, defined as making decisions in a way that work and nonwork aspects of life form a coherent whole; and challenge, or engagement in activities that demand responsibility and allow learning and growth. A problem and challenge, however, is that organizational structures and mentalities are not yet attuned to the female perspective and career needs, despite the fact that females comprise around half of the workforce (O'Neil, Hopkins, & Bilimoria, 2008).

A Final Note on Diversity and Careers

As seen, there is evidence that certain groups are disadvantaged in terms of objective career success, and there are theory-based accounts for these disadvantages. However, there is contrasting evidence as well. For example, using human resource records over a 9-year period from a large U.S. service sector company, Petersen and Saporta (2004) found no gender differences in promotion rates or salary attainment for administrative, professional, and managerial employees. In fact, at higher hierarchical levels, women had faster promotion rates than their male counterparts. Females were disadvantaged only in hierarchical level and salary on hiring, but this could be accounted for by a male superiority in previous work experience, that is, human capital (for a short review of literature with similar findings see Petersen & Saporta, 2004, p. 897).

Furthermore, there is some evidence that the female, and group minority, disadvantage in objective career outcomes is constantly falling as women and minorities are becoming established in the work environment. For example, in their meta-analysis, Ng et al. (2005) found that the strength of the relationship between gender and financial attainment was attenuated as a function of the publication year of the study, with more recent studies reporting weaker relationships. In line with this, in their narrative review, Altman and Shortland (2008) found some evidence that both organizational views of women's fitness for international assignments, which have traditionally been viewed as prestigious and sought after, and women's proportional representation in such assignments have been improving over the years. Finally, Beckman and Phillips (2005) found evidence that law firms were more likely to promote women to top positions when their clients also had women in such positions. This implies a "snowball" or "drag" effect: The more women advance into high positions, the more likely it is for women in general to break the glass ceiling.

Whether the apparent disadvantages of certain groups in objective career success will not be an issue in the future remains to be seen. However, it should also be kept in mind that ascendance to positions of power by individuals belonging to traditionally disadvantaged groups does not necessarily mean that the issue of differential opportunities has been resolved. This may simply reflect *window dressing* (e.g., appointing a token woman to the board, frequently in a "feminine" role, such as HR director), *conquering empty castles* (i.e., gaining positions that are not attractive for the dominant majority anymore; Hofbauer & Fischlmayr, 2004), or, even worse, cases of *glass cliff* (i.e., where minority members are deliberately appointed to senior positions that bear a greater risk of failure or criticism; Ryan & Haslam, 2007; Wilson-Kovacs, Ryan, Haslam, & Rabinovich, 2008). Therefore, the issue of diversity and careers probably goes beyond the achievement of statistical nonsignificance in financial or status attainment.

Legislation may assist in the striving for equality in opportunities for career success (e.g., Leck, 2002; Weichselbaumer & Winter-Ebmer, 2007). However, this may also be the cause of undesired side effects. For example, achievements and contributions of traditionally disadvantaged groups may be doubted because these may be attributed to legislation instead of merit (e.g., Heilman & Welle, 2006); and there may be majority (e.g., male) backlash (Leck, 2002). In addition, the partial move toward postcorporate careers and less rigid organizational structures with their attached work arrangements (e.g., temporary employment, freelancing) may in fact reduce career opportunities for disadvantaged groups (e.g., Holgate & McKay, 2009). Hence, abiding by legislation should not be the primary motivator for employers and key organizational players to work toward equality in career opportunities. The main motive should be enhancement of organizational performance (and of a harmonious society) rather than political correctness, an issue that has arguably plagued the struggle for equality. This is because perceptions of fairness in the allocation of career rewards are associated with organizational commitment and job performance (e.g., Parker & Kohlmeyer, 2005; Ramaswami & Singh, 2003). Furthermore, impartial allocation of career rewards (e.g., promoting the most able individuals) enables employers to exploit the talent of the totality of their workforce (Harel, Tzafrir, & Baruch, 2002) and enhance bottom-line performance, as empirical research attests (McKay, Avery, & Morris, 2008).

GLOBALIZATION AND CAREERS

Globalization has brought a flow of people, knowledge, information, ideas, and products across national borders and has added to the issues in the study of careers (Tams & Arthur, 2007). We now address the issue of careers across national cultures and the management of expatriation.

Careers Across Cultures

Our accumulated knowledge and models of careers have been primarily developed on the basis of work in North America and other highly economically developed parts of the Western world (as discussed earlier). The extent to which, and under what conditions, these are applicable across national cultural settings needs to be investigated because, for example, there is evidence that career orientations and priorities vary across cultures. To illustrate, in a study of MBA students from seven culturally distinct countries, Malach-Pines and Kaspi-Baruch (2008) found differences among participants from all countries in factors that included the meaning of work, protean and traditional career orientations, and expectations from careers in management. And Segers et al. (2008) identified relationships between dimensions of national culture and protean and boundaryless career orientations (e.g., $r = -.32$ between masculinity and the value-drive dimension of career proteity). Finally, in their meta-analysis, Tracey and Rounds (1993) found greater support for the structure of Holland's model in the United States than with research conducted outside the United States (mean correspondence indices of .69 and .46, respectively, $d = .81$,[5] calculated as the number of

[5] *d* value calculated by the authors.

model predictions that are in agreement with the data minus the number of model predictions that are not in agreement with the data divided by the total number of model predictions).

On the one hand, globalization has certainly increased the power and relevance of some already existing concepts, such as the boundaryless and the protean career (e.g., see Cappellen & Janssens, 2005; Hall, 2004; Thomas, Lazarova, & Inkson, 2005). The former can be viewed from the additional perspective of psychological preparedness of career actors to cross national boundaries and of actual movement across borders, and the latter can be viewed from the perspective of the extent to which career actors value cross-border work experiences and take initiatives in directing their careers toward such experiences.

On the other hand, concepts (and this may include the concept of career itself) that have been developed with economically developed societies as reference points may have limited or no applicability in certain areas or populations of the globe. For instance, the notion of the traditional career may be of limited relevance in many societies (e.g., see International Labour Organization, 2009) where the majority of the workforce is self-employed or employed only as temporary or seasonal workers (e.g., in farms) or in small businesses that have limited or no hierarchical structures. Ironically, in such societies, where work lives for the majority are similar to work lives before the industrial revolution, the notion of the postcorporate career may be most relevant as a career model, despite the fact that they have never experienced the traditional, corporate-bound career.

Another issue that emerged along with the movement of career actors across national boundaries is whether factors that are associated with career benefits within particular national contexts provide similar benefits in different contexts. As an illustration, as discussed earlier, mentoring has been established as an experience that relates to both objective and subjective career success. However, relevant empirical research has been conducted mainly in the Anglo-Saxon work environment. Research in non-Anglo-Saxon cultural environments yields results that are not always supportive of the career enhancing properties of mentoring. For example, Bozionelos (2006) found that informal mentoring was related to objective but not to subjective career success of protégés in Hellas (Greece) and subsequently developed a culture-dependent explanation, which suggests that receiving traditional mentoring may have detrimental effects on subjective evaluations and workplace adjustment in particular cultural environments (e.g., when there is no trust of authority and there is a clear separation between the ingroup and the outgroup). Furthermore, although mentoring appears to be a universal phenomenon (e.g., Gentry, Weber, & Sadri, 2008), there are some indications that its exact meaning, functions, and prevalence vary across cultures. For example, a study of information technology professionals from four European countries with distinct cultures indicated considerable variance in the prevalence of informal mentoring, with a range from 9.9% for Norway to 42.9% for Italy (Bozionelos, 2007). A complementary study reported a mentoring prevalence of 72.6% among white-collar workers in China (Bozionelos & Wang, 2006), suggesting that the national culture probably influences the meaning attached to developmental relationships, which, in turn, affects the prevalence of mentoring in the workplace.

In addition, careers that are pursued partly or thoroughly across national boundaries are likely to impose demands for new skills or qualities. For example, Ng et al. (2005) considered international experience as part of human capital, a view that is endorsed in the international management literature (e.g., Takeuchi, Tesluk, & Marinova, 2006). Other human capital attributes that may be essential in cross-border career movements include ability to learn languages, cultural empathy, cultural intelligence, and the personality trait of openness (e.g., Earley, 2002; Peltokorpi, 2008; Tarique & Schuler, 2008). We suggest using caution before adopting competencies or traits that are narrow and exclusive to cross-cultural adaptation (e.g., see Berry & Ward, 2006). There may be a need first to enrich or broaden the constructs we have developed for understanding careers to account for career progression and success in a globalized environment.

Finally, the movement of labor across national borders has increased the prevalence of another form of diversity, cultural diversity (e.g., Chope, 2008;

Sippola & Smale, 2007). Because culture represents beliefs, values, and assumptions, cultural diversity operates mostly at the deep level. This imposes additional challenges for organizations in terms of managing it with respect to their career systems, taking into account that, as seen, the effects of deep-level diversity tend to be realized in the longer term.

Expatriation

Expatriation refers to the pursuit and accumulation of work experiences outside the country in which an individual has been reared and whose cultural values the individual espouses. Expatriation and its natural consequence, repatriation, are becoming more common (e.g., Mercer Human Resource Consulting, 2008). This is due to the increasing numbers of organizations that cross national borders and the facilitation in labor movement across such borders (e.g., World Bank, 2009). Expatriation may be distinguished as either corporate-sponsored or self-initiated.

Corporate-sponsored expatriation. The term *corporate-sponsored expatriation* applies to individuals who are sponsored by a parent-country organization to go to a mission abroad. Traditionally, expatriation has been viewed from this perspective. Sponsoring employees in expatriate missions has necessitated the management of their careers during their stay in the host country and upon their return as repatriates (Baruch & Altman, 2002). Expatriate and repatriate career management imposes a number of challenges. For example, expatriates or their families may face cultural adaptation problems that may impact their performance (e.g., Harrison & Shaffer, 2005), which in turn may have repercussions for their careers. Furthermore, although expatriation is usually a choice made with the expectation of career enhancement (e.g., Doherty & Dickmann, 2009; Stahl, Miller, & Tung, 2002) it may fail to deliver its anticipated career benefits. In a recent matched-sample study within a single organization, Benson and Pattie (2008) found that repatriates had received fewer intraorganizational promotions than their counterparts who did not acquire expatriate experience and were not more likely to have been contacted by headhunters for potential interorganizational career moves. Kraimer, Shaffer, and Bolino (2009) found that the proportions of recent repatriates who reported that they had been demoted and promoted in their employing organizations were similar (15% and 17%, respectively). No career advantages of expatriation renders it not unusual for repatriates to express dissatisfaction with their intraorganizational career prospects and to express intentions to leave (Bossard & Peterson, 2005) or to actually leave the organization (e.g., Baruch, Steele, & Quantrill, 2002; Black & Gregersen, 1999); which makes intraorganizational career success on repatriation of interest to organizations. Indeed, repatriate turnover is apparently double the rate of the rest of the workforce (e.g., see GMAC Global Relocation Services, 2008). Organizations, nonetheless, can enhance career prospects for their expatriates upon their return if they use systems such as predeparture career planning, systematic career revision during the assignment, and allocation of a formal mentor based in the parent country (e.g., Bolino, 2007; Lazarova & Cerdin, 2007).

At this point, however, it should be noted that extant research has been methodologically constrained by the fact that, presumably because of accessibility issues, most samples are composed of individuals who are either still in their expatriate assignment or are repatriates and still employed with the parent organization; most samples do not include repatriates who have left the parent company. Hence, information on career success and motives for leaving of those expatriates who have actually left the parent organization are largely unaccounted for. Therefore, a complementary account for the effects of expatriation on career success, which draws on contemporary notions of careers as protean and boundaryless, has been developed (Lazarova & Cerdin, 2007; see also Suutari & Brewster, 2003). This explanation posits that expatriation has mostly positive effects on career success but not necessarily as this is viewed from the traditional corporate-bound career perspective. That is, career actors may, upon return, opt to "cash" the human capital gained by the expatriate experience by means of an interorganizational career move that is seen as providing greater career gains. Research provides some support for this view (Lazarova &

Cerdin; Stahl, Chua, Caligiuri, Cerdin, & Taniguchi, 2009; Suutari & Brewster, 2003). For example, Lazarova and Cerdin found that active engagement in tactics that should facilitate interorganizational career movement explained 19% of the variance in repatriate turnover intentions over and above the variance accounted for by their satisfaction with organizational support, whereas, the latter was not able to explain variance over and above the former. The implication is that organizations may not have full control over retaining their repatriates, regardless of the quality of their expatriation and repatriation management systems.

Whether pursuing intra- or interorganizational career success, a key aspect for successful career outcomes of expatriates upon repatriation appears to be proactivity. Activities that should enhance prospects for intraorganizational career success upon repatriation include the following (e.g., Bolino, 2007; Kraimer et al., 2009; O'Sullivan, 2002): seeking expatriate assignments with developmental value or in subsidiaries with strategic importance; actively maintaining and using one's social capital in the parent-country, which can provide information on developments back home and can prevent the "out of sight, out of mind" syndrome; and seeking a repatriate position that allows use and recognition of the skills and experience acquired while abroad. On the other hand, actively engaging one's social capital for career-related information and support and scanning the job market should enhance the prospects of interorganizational career moves (see Lazarova & Cerdin, 2007).

Finally, corporate-sponsored expatriation includes the cases of host country–origin individuals who are sent to the parent country (*inpatriates*) as well as cases of third-country origin individuals whom organizations use with increasing frequency (e.g., Kiessling & Harvey, 2006; Tarique, Schuler, & Gong, 2006). These individuals may encounter different or additional career issues than those faced by the traditional parent-country expatriates (e.g., an inpatriate may face the extra challenge of being treated as a minority member in the parent country; Harvey, Novicevic, Buckley, & Fung, 2005), which poses an additional challenge for organizations and for future research.

Self-initiated expatriation. *Self-initiated expatriation* involves cases of individuals who take on employment in a foreign country without sponsorship from a corporation in their home country. These individuals differ substantially from corporate-sponsored expatriates, as they cannot rely on the resources of a parent-country corporation in their endeavor (Bozionelos, 2009; see also Suutari & Brewster, 2000). It is surprising that this type of expatriation has received limited attention so far. Self-initiated expatriation is a phenomenon that has existed for a long time (e.g., Inkson, Arthur, Pringle, & Barry, 1997; Inkson & Myers, 2003) but is becoming more common for a number of partly interrelated reasons, including (a) increasing facilitation in the movement of labor across national borders (e.g., the European Union), (b) the development of technology (especially the World Wide Web) that provides information on job openings anywhere in the globe, and (c) dramatic shortages in skilled or unskilled labor that lead many countries to resort to hiring from abroad (e.g., Harry, 2007; Harvey, Hartnell, & Novicevic, 2004; Martin, 2003). The growing frequency of self-initiated expatriation is in line with the increasing tendency for individuals to take ownership of their own careers, as discussed earlier in the chapter.

The demographic synthesis of the population of self-initiated expatriates is apparently different from that of corporate-sponsored expatriates. The latter tend to be executives, managers, and high-profile professionals (e.g., scientists, engineers), whereas self-initiated expatriates come from every occupational and societal stratum. They can be high school or university graduates in the career exploration stage (e.g., Inkson & Myers, 2003), higher (Richardson & McKenna, 2002; Suutari & Brewster, 2000) or lower (e.g., Bozionelos, 2009) profile professionals or managers, or simply unskilled or semiskilled workers seeking employment. This last category is likely to be the largest. For example, in the United Kingdom alone, there are currently more than 2 million foreign nationals in employment, most of them unskilled or semiskilled workers, especially in the manufacturing, construction, and distribution sectors (Bowcott & Booth, 2009). Therefore, an additional reason for studying self-initiated expatriates is their difference in occupational terms from their corporate-sponsored counterparts.

Another distinguishing feature of self-initiated expatriation pertains to the motive behind the decision to expatriate. Corporate-sponsored expatriation is normally a conscious career enhancement move. In contrast, self-initiated expatriation is more likely to be either a spontaneous move at the career exploration stage without calculated career expectations (e.g., Inkson & Myers, 2003), or the only available move for survival (see Bozionelos, 2009), with career enhancement (e.g., increase in status, learning) not even remotely considered in the initial decision.

Self-initiated expatriation naturally has career instrumental value (e.g., Inkson & Myers, 2003; Jokinen, Brewster, & Suutari, 2008; Vance, 2005). However, the way it influences the career journey and career success may differ from corporate-sponsored expatriation. For example, objective career benefits may be realized in the longer term. Furthermore, in contrast to the majority of their corporate-sponsored counterparts, many self-initiated expatriates may never return to their home countries, staying abroad for the totality of their work lives instead and essentially becoming immigrants; though their initial plan may have been to return to their home countries after an interval abroad. There is still limited knowledge of the factors that contribute to the success of self-initiated expatriation and of the extent to which these factors overlap with the corresponding factors in corporate-sponsored expatriation. In addition, the notion of career success for self-initiated expatriates may differ. Traditional indexes of objective success (e.g., promotions) may not be applicable, and operationalizations of subjective success that are fully or partly anchored on conventional objective achievements (e.g., satisfaction with advancement and prospects for advancement) may equally be inappropriate. Instead, outcomes that pertain either to learning and accumulation of experience or to the assurance of a living for themselves and their offspring may be more pertinent to the concept of career success for the majority of self-initiated expatriates. Understanding the perspectives and needs of these expatriates is important because the extent to which these are met is likely to affect the performance of their host organizations or nations (e.g., Lee, 2005).

Virtual Global Careers—Nonphysical Crossing of Borders

Finally, the fact that information technology has enabled human interaction regardless of physical proximity has led to cases of individuals who regularly interact with colleagues or clients across borders without physically leaving their home countries (e.g., researchers collaborating in projects, employees in outsourced call center operations). This imposes additional challenges in the study of careers (Forret, 2007; Tams & Arthur, 2007). For example, these career actors are exposed to other cultures and may need to accommodate certain degrees of cultural adaptation (e.g., to adapt their behaviors to the styles of customers). However, it is uncertain whether, or to what extent, their careers can be characterized as global, considering that their experiences are probably different from those of expatriates in the traditional physical sense. What is also of importance is how their virtual cross-cultural experiences affect their own views of their work and personal lives. This is an issue of interest in the study of careers, taking into account that globalization has been boosted mostly by technology and that the latter is unlikely to reverse or come to a standstill; meaning that the cases of individuals who regularly engage in work-related interactions across borders without being physically mobile should be constantly increasing.

SUMMARY AND DIRECTIONS

In this chapter, we covered most major themes along with recent developments in the study of careers. Common axes in our consideration were the elements of time and space. These elements are common across individual careers, which are, however, highly differentiated by the timing and pace of movement through the space element, the content of that element, and the way career actors evaluate work-related experiences. Career progression and success is determined by both human capital and environmental factors, and are facilitated by processes that involve the social capital of career actors. The extent to which individuals actively direct their careers according to their values in a protean way, as well as their willingness and ability to learn, has acquired increasing importance over time; which has witnessed a shift from organizational toward individual or collaborative responsibility for career management.

The changing nature of careers has also been epitomized by the establishment of boundaryless and postcorporate careers. These, however, have not displaced the traditional career, and neither have they changed the fact that most individuals are still most comfortable with that archetypal career. The importance of diversity as a factor in career progression was also discussed, taking mainly the perspective of gender. The conclusion was that although there is an apparent reduction in career opportunities mismatch between diverse groups, actual equality may go beyond lack of significant results in pertinent studies. Finally, the impact of globalization on careers was considered, focusing on whether concepts and career-enhancing factors are applicable across geographical boundaries and on the movement, physical or virtual, of career actors across borders.

Despite the substantial knowledge accumulated, however, understanding is still far from complete, especially as careers are constantly evolving: The space element is embedded into societal structures and technology, which are interacting and constantly changing at an increasing pace. In addition, technology appears to influence the time element as well (i.e., extending the limits of work life). Hence, there is a requirement for continuous research that needs to focus on issues that include the following:

- The influence of the prolongation of life, and especially of the active part of life, on careers. Our models of the time element may need substantial updating.
- Further development and refinement of the notions of the protean and boundaryless careers, and their combination in order to understand individual career patterns and improve career advice. Extant notions should also be extended to the domain of cross-border work experiences. In addition, they could be integrated with theories of vocational choice such as Holland's.
- Documentation of new career patterns to which changes in the economic and social environment may give rise (i.e., in the same manner as it gave rise to the boundaryless and postcorporate notions).
- Further understanding of the relationship between organizational practices and the psychological contract of career actors and especially whether the conditions under which its relational elements can be cultivated.
- Enhancement of our knowledge of social capital and job-irrelevant human capital and the processes by which these influence careers.
- The monitoring of discrepancies in career progression among diverse groups and the development of understanding of the causes of any shifts in these discrepancies (e.g., apparent closure of differences in objective career success). Furthermore, attention may need to be directed at diversity dimensions (e.g., body weight) that have been neglected in the past.
- How globalization, and the familiarization of various cultures, races, and ethnicities with each other may be influencing the impact of surface-level diversity on careers.
- The meaning of work and life experiences for that substantial part of the world population for whom the concept of career as understood in the past 150 years does not seem to apply.
- The comprehension of how national culture influences careers and their related constructs (e.g., mentoring).
- The meaning of virtual global careers and their impact on career actors.

Careers are of critical importance to individuals, employers, society, and the economy, and we hope and believe that this chapter sheds light on the present state of the art in their study.

References

Achkar, E. (2008). Will women ever break the glass ceiling in medicine? *American Journal of Gastroenterology, 103,* 1587–1588.

Adler, N. J. (1993). An international perspective on the barriers to the advancement of women managers. *Applied Psychology: An International Review, 42,* 289–300.

Adler, P. S., & Kwon, S-W. (2002). Social capital: Prospects for a new concept. *Academy of Management Review, 27,* 17–40.

Allen, T. A., Freeman, D. M., Russell, J. E. A., Reizenstein, R. C., & Rentz, J. O. (2001). Survivor reactions to organizational downsizing: Does time ease the pain?

Journal of Occupational and Organizational Psychology, 74, 145–164.

Allen, T. D., Eby, L. T., Poteet, M. L., Lentz, E., & Lima, L. (2004). Career benefits associated with mentoring for protégés: A meta-analysis. *Journal of Applied Psychology, 89,* 127–136.

Altman, Y., & Shortland, S. (2008). Women and international assignments: Taking stock—A 25-year review. *Human Resource Management, 47,* 199–216.

Amsden, A. H. (2001). *The rise of "the rest": Challenges to the West from late-industrializating economies.* New York: Oxford University Press.

Anderson, N., Lankshear, C., Timms, C., & Courtney, L. (2008). "Because it's boring, irrelevant, and I don't like computers": Why high school girls avoid professionally oriented ICT subjects. *Computers and Education, 50,* 1304–1318.

Arbuckle, T. Y., Maag, U., Pushkar, D., & Chaikelson, J. S. (1998). Individual differences in trajectory of intellectual development. *Psychology and Aging, 13,* 663–675.

Argyris, C. (1960). *Understanding organizational behavior.* Homewood, IL: Dorsey.

Armstrong, P. I., Day, S. X., McVay, J. P., & Rounds, J. (2008). Holland's RIASEC model as an integrative framework for individual differences. *Journal of Counseling Psychology, 55,* 1–18.

Arnold, J. (1997). *Managing careers into the 21st century.* London: Chapman.

Arthur, M. B., Claman, P. H., & DeFillippi, R. J. (1995). Intelligent enterprise, intelligent careers. *Academy of Management Executive, 9*(4), 7–20.

Arthur, M. B., Hall, D. T., & Lawrence, B. S. (1989). Generating new directions in career theory: The case for a transdisciplinary approach. In M. B. Arthur, D. T. Hall, & B. S. Lawrence (Eds.), *Handbook of career theory* (pp. 7–25). Cambridge, England: Cambridge University Press.

Arthur, M. B., & Rousseau, D. M. (1996). The boundaryless career as a new employment principle. In M. G. Arthur & D. M. Rousseau (Eds.), *The boundaryless career* (pp. 3–20). New York: Oxford University Press.

Ashmore, R. D. (1981). Sex stereotypes and implicit personality theory. In D. L. Hamilton (Ed.), *Cognitive processes in stereotyping and intergroup behavior* (pp. 37–81). Hillsdale, NJ: Erlbaum.

Baird, L., & Kram, K. (1983). Career dynamics: Managing the supervisor/subordinate relationship. *Organizational Dynamics, 11*(4), 46–64.

Ball, K., Berch, D. B., Helmers, K. F., Jobe, J. B., Leveck, M. D., Marsiske, M., et al. (2002). Effects of cognitive training interventions with older adults: A randomized controlled trial. *JAMA, 288,* 2271–2281.

Barrick, M. R., Mount, M. K., & Judge, T. A. (2001). Personality and job performance at the beginning of the new millennium: What do we know and where do we go next. *International Journal of Selection and Assessment, 9,* 9–30.

Baruch, Y. (1998). The rise and fall of organizational commitment. *Human Systems Management, 17,* 135–143.

Baruch, Y. (2001). Employability: A substitute for loyalty? *Human Resource Development International, 4,* 543–566.

Baruch, Y. (2004). *Managing careers: Theory and practice.* London: Prentice Hall.

Baruch, Y. (2006). Career development in organizations and beyond: Balancing traditional and contemporary viewpoints. *Human Resource Management Review, 16,* 125–138.

Baruch, Y., & Altman, Y. (2002). Expatriation and repatriation in MNCs: A taxonomy. *Human Resource Management, 41,* 239–259.

Baruch, Y., Bell, M., & Gray, D. (2005). Generalist and specialist graduate business degrees: Tangible and intangible value. *Journal of Vocational Behavior, 67,* 51–68.

Baruch, Y., & Nicholson, N. (1997). Home, sweet work: Requirements for effective home working. *Journal of General Management, 23*(2), 15–30.

Baruch, Y., & Quick, J. C. (2007). Understanding second careers: Lessons from a study of U.S. Navy admirals. *Human Resource Management, 46,* 471–491.

Baruch, Y., & Rosenstein, E. (1992). Career planning and managing in high tech organizations. *International Journal of Human Resource Management, 3,* 477–496.

Baruch, Y., Steele, D. J., & Quantrill, G. A. (2002). Management of expatriation and repatriation for novice global player. *International Journal of Manpower, 23,* 659–671.

Baugh, S. G., & Fagenson-Eland, E. A. (2005). Boundaryless mentoring: An exploratory study of the functions provided by internal versus external organizational mentors. *Journal of Applied Social Psychology, 35,* 939–955.

Baugh, S. G., & Fagenson-Eland, E. A. (2007). Formal mentoring programs: A "poor cousin" to informal relationships? In B. R. Ragins & K. E. Kram (Eds.), *The handbook of mentoring at work* (pp. 249–271). Thousand Oaks, CA: Sage.

Becker, G. S. (1964). *Human capital.* New York: National Bureau of Economic Research.

Becker, G. S. (1975). *Human capital.* Chicago, IL: Chicago University Press.

Beckman, C. M., & Phillips, D. J. (2005). Interorganizational determinants of promotion: Client leadership and the attainment of women attorneys. *American Sociological Review, 70,* 678–701.

Bell, M. P. (2007). *Diversity in organizations*. Mason, OH: South-Western.

Benson, G. S., & Pattie, M. (2008). Is expatriation good for my career? The impact of expatriate assignments on perceived and actual career outcomes. *International Journal of Human Resource Management, 19*, 1636–1653.

Berger, J., Fisek, M. H., Norman, R. Z., & Zelditch, M., Jr. (1977). *Status characteristics and social interaction: An expectations-states approach*. New York: Elsevier.

Berry, J. W., & Ward, C. (2006). Commentary on "redefining interactions across cultures and organizations." *Group and Organization Management, 31*, 64–77.

Betz, N. E. (2007). Career self-efficacy: Exemplary recent research and emerging directions. *Journal of Career Assessment, 15*, 403–422.

Beutell, N. J., & O'Hare, M. M. (2006). Career pathfinders: A qualitative study on career development. *Psychological Reports, 98*, 517–528.

Binnewies, C., Ohly, S., & Niessen, C. (2008). Age and creativity at work: The interplay between job resources, age and idea creativity. *Journal of Managerial Psychology, 23*, 438–457.

Black, J. S., & Gregersen, H. B. (1999). The right way to manage expats. *Harvard Business Review, 77*(2), 52–63.

Blanchflower, D. G., & Shadforth, C. (2007). Entrepreneurship in the UK. *Foundations and Trends in Entrepreneurship, 3*, 257–364.

Blickle, G., Witzki, A. H., & Schneider, P. B. (2009). Mentoring support and power: A three-year predictive field study on protégé networking and career success. *Journal of Vocational Behavior, 74*, 181–189.

Bobbitt-Zeher, D. (2007). The gender income gap and the role of education. *Sociology of Education, 80*, 1–22.

Bolino, M. C. (2007). Expatriate assignments and intra-organizational career success: Implications for individuals and organizations. *Journal of International Business Studies, 38*, 819–835.

Boron, J. B., Willis, S. L., & Schaie, K. W. (2007). Cognitive training gain as a predictor of mental status. *Journal of Gerontology, 62B*, P45–P52.

Bossard, A. B., & Peterson, R. B. (2005). The repatriate experience as seen by American expatriates. *Journal of World Business, 40*, 9–28.

Bouchard, T. J., Jr., & Loehlin, J. C. (2001). Genes, evolution, and personality. *Behavior Genetics, 31*, 243–273.

Bourdieu, P. (1980). Le capital social: Notes provisoires [Social capital: Provisional notes]. *Actes de la Recherche en Sciences Sociales, 31*, 2–3.

Bourdieu, P. (1986). The forms of capital. In J. E. Richardson (Ed.), *Handbook of theory for research in the sociology of education* (pp. 241–258). New York: Greenwood Press.

Bowcott, O., & Booth, R. (2009, February 4). Increase in foreign workers over past three years. *The Guardian*. Retrieved March 23, 2009, from http://www.guardian.co.uk/uk/2009/feb/04/immigration-foreign-workers

Bozionelos, N. (2001). Computer anxiety: Relationship with computer experience and prevalence. *Computers in Human Behavior, 17*, 213–224.

Bozionelos, N. (2003a). Career perceptions and the psychological contract in organizational downsizing. In M. A. Rahim, R. T. Golembiewski, & K. D. Mackenzie (Eds.), *Current topics in management* (Vol. 8, pp. 295–312). New Brunswick, NJ: Transaction Publishers.

Bozionelos, N. (2003b). Intraorganizational network resources: Relation to career success and personality. *International Journal of Organizational Analysis, 11*, 41–66.

Bozionelos, N. (2004). Mentoring provided: Relation to mentor's career success, personality, and mentoring received. *Journal of Vocational Behavior, 64*, 24–46.

Bozionelos, N. (2005). When the inferior candidate is offered the job: The selection interview as a political and power game. *Human Relations, 58*, 1605–1631.

Bozionelos, N. (2006). Mentoring and expressive network resources: Their relationship with career success and emotional exhaustion among Hellenes employees involved in emotion work. *International Journal of Human Resource Management, 17*, 362–378.

Bozionelos, N. (2007, May). A comparative study on mentoring in four European countries. In L. T. Eby & S. C. Evans (Chairs), *Cross-cultural perspectives on mentoring research*. Symposium conducted at the meeting of the Society for Industrial and Organizational Psychology, New York.

Bozionelos, N. (2008). Intraorganizational network resources: How they relate to career success and organizational commitment. *Personnel Review, 37*, 349–363.

Bozionelos, N. (2009). Expatriation outside the boundaries of the multinational corporation: A study with expatriate nurses in Saudi Arabia. *Human Resource Management, 48*, 111–134.

Bozionelos, N., & Wang, L. (2006). The relationship of mentoring and network resources with career success in the Chinese organizational environment. *International Journal of Human Resource Management, 17*, 1531–1546.

Bozionelos, N., & Wang, L. (2007). An investigation on the attitudes of Chinese workers towards individually-based performance related reward systems. *International Journal of Human Resource Management, 18,* 284–302.

Bradley, K. (2000). The incorporation of women into higher education: Paradoxical outcomes. *Sociology of Education, 73,* 1–18.

Brand, H. (1991). Perestroika and its impact on the Soviet labor market. *Monthly Labor Review, 114*(12), 38–45.

Brass, D. J. (1992). Power in organizations: A social network perspective. In G. Moore & J. A. Whitt (Eds.), *Research in politics and society: The political consequences of social networks* (Vol. 4, pp. 295–323). Greenwich, CT: JAI Press.

Briscoe, J. P., & Hall, D. T. (2006). The interplay of boundaryless and protean careers: Combinations and implications. *Journal of Vocational Behavior, 69,* 4–18.

Briscoe, J. P., & Hall, D. T., & DeMuth, R. L. F. (2006). Protean and boundaryless careers: An empirical exploration. *Journal of Vocational Behavior, 69,* 30–47.

Brown, D. J., Cober, R. T., Kane, K., Levy, P. E., & Shalhoop, J. (2006). Proactive personality and the successful job search: A field investigation with college graduates. *Journal of Applied Psychology, 91,* 717–726.

Brown, W. S. (2005). The new employment contract and the "at risk" worker. *Journal of Business Ethics, 58,* 195–201.

Bruderl, J., Preisendorfer, P., & Ziegler, R. (1993). Upward mobility in organizations: The effects of hierarchy and opportunity structure. *European Sociological Review,* 9, 173–188.

Bruner, J. S., & Tagiuri, R. (1954). The perception of people. In G. Lindzey (Ed.), *Handbook of social psychology* (Vol. 2, pp. 634–654). Cambridge, MA: Addison-Wesley.

Bureau of Labor Statistics. (2007, May). May 2007 National occupational employment and wage estimates. Retrieved February 27, 2009, from http://www.bls.gov/oes/current/oes_nat.htm

Byrne, D. E. (1971). *The attraction paradigm.* New York: Academic Press.

Cannings, K., & Montmarquette, C. (1991). Managerial momentum: A simultaneous model of the career progress of male and female managers. *Industrial and Labor Relations Review, 44,* 212–228.

Cappellen, T., & Janssens, M. (2005). Career paths of global managers: Towards future research. *Journal of World Business, 40,* 348–360.

Cappelli, P. (1999). Career jobs are dead. *California Management Review, 42*(1), 146–167.

Cappelli, P. (2006). Churning of jobs. In J. H. Greenhaus & G. A. Callanan (Eds.), *Encyclopedia of Career Development: Vol. 1* (pp. 165–167). Thousand Oaks, CA: Sage.

Carmeli, A., Shalom, R., & Weisberg, J. (2007). Considerations in organizational career advancement: What really matters. *Personnel Review, 36,* 190–205.

Cascio, W. F. (1995). Whither industrial and organizational psychology in a changing world of work? *American Psychologist, 11,* 928–939.

Case, A., & Paxson, C. (2008). Stature and status: Height, ability, and labor market outcomes. *Journal of Political Economy, 116,* 499–532.

Cattell, R. B. (1941). Some theoretical issues in adult intelligence testing. *Psychological Bulletin, 38,* 592.

Chao, G. T. (1990). Exploration of the conceptualization and measurement of career plateau: A comparative analysis. *Journal of Management, 16,* 181–193.

Chevalier, A. (2007). Education, occupation, and career expectations: Determinants of the gender pay gap for UK graduates. *Oxford Bulletin of Economics and Statistics, 69,* 819–842.

Chien, L. L., Ko, H. C., & Wu, J. Y. W. (2007). The five-factor model of personality and depressive symptoms: One-year follow-up. *Personality and Individual Differences, 43,* 1013–1023.

Chope, R. C. (2008). Practice and research in career counseling and development—2007. *Career Development Quarterly, 57,* 98–173.

Cohen, J. (1988). *Statistical power analysis for the behavioral sciences* (2nd ed.). Hillsdale, NJ: Erlbaum.

Coleman, J. S. (1988). Social capital in the creation of human capital. *American Journal of Sociology, 94,* S95–S120.

Combes, P-P., Linnemer, L., & Visser, M. (2008). Publish or peer-ish? The role of skills and networks in hiring economics professors. *Labour Economics, 15,* 423–441.

Cooper, C. L. (2006). The changing nature of work: The new psychological contract and associated stressors. In A. M. Rossi, P. L. Perrewe, & S. L. Sauter (Eds.), *Stress and quality of working life: Current perspectives in occupational health* (pp. 1–7). Greenwich, CT: Information Age Publishing

Coucke, K., Pennings, E., & Sleuwaegen, L. (2007). Employee layoff under different modes of restructuring: Exit, downsizing or relocation. *Industrial and Corporate Change, 16,* 161–182.

Dahlmann, N., Elsner, M., Jeschke, S., Natho, N., & Schroder, C. (2008, June). *Gender gap in technological disciplines: Societal causes and consequences.* Paper presented at the IEEE International Symposium on Technology and Society, Fredericton, Canada.

Dalton, G., Thompson, M. P., & Price, P. (1977). The four stages of professional careers: A new look at performance by professionals. *Organizational Dynamics,* 6(1), 19–42.

D'Amato, A., & Herzfeldt, R. (2008). Learning orientation, organizational commitment, and talent retention across generations: A study of European managers. *Journal of Managerial Psychology, 23,* 929–953.

Davey, K. M. (2008). Women's accounts of organizational politics as a gendering process. *Gender, Work, and Organization, 15,* 650–671.

Davis, J. W., & Bauman, K. J. (2008). *School enrolment in the United States: 2006.* Washington, DC: U.S. Census Bureau.

De Cuyper, N., Bernhard-Oettel, C., Berntson, E., De Witte, H., & Alarco, B. (2008). Employability and employees' well-being: Mediation by job insecurity. *Applied Psychology: An International Review, 57,* 488–509.

De Cuyper, N., Rigotti, T., De Witte, H., & Mohr, G. (2008). Balancing psychological contracts: Validation of a typology. *International Journal of Human Resource Management, 19,* 543–561.

DeFillippi, R. J., & Arthur, M. B. (1994). The boundaryless career: A competency-based perspective. *Journal of Organizational Behavior, 15,* 307–324.

de Janasz, S. C., & Sullivan, S. E. (2004). Multiple mentoring in academe: Developing the professional network. *Journal of Vocational Behavior, 64,* 263–283.

DeNeve, K. M., & Cooper, H. (1998). The happy personality: A meta-analysis of 137 traits and subjective well-being. *Psychological Bulletin, 124,* 197–229.

Department of Professional Employees. (2008). *Vital workforce statistics: Fact sheet 2008.* Retrieved February 19, 2009, from http://www.dpeaflcio.org/programs/factsheets/fs_2008_workforce.pdf

Devaro, J., & Brookshire, D. (2007). Promotions and incentives in nonprofit and for-profit organizations. *Industrial and Labor Relations Review, 60,* 311–339.

De Vos, A., & Soens, N. (2008). Protean attitude and career success: The mediating role of self-management. *Journal of Vocational Behavior, 73,* 449–456.

Ding, D. Z., & Warner, M. (2001). China's labour-management system reforms: Breaking the "three old irons" (1978–1999). *Asia Pacific Journal of Management, 18,* 315–334.

Dipboye, R. L., & Halverson, S. K. (2004). Subtle (and not so subtle) discrimination in organizations. In R. W. Griffin & A. M. O'Leary-Kelly (Eds.), *The dark side of organizational behavior* (pp. 131–158). San Francisco: Jossey-Bass.

Doherty, N., & Dickmann, M. (2009). Exposing the symbolic capital of international assignments. *International Journal of Human Resource Management, 20,* 301–320.

Donohue, R. (2007). Examining career persistence and career change intent using the career attitudes and strategies inventory. *Journal of Vocational Behavior, 70,* 259–276.

Dries, N., Pepermans, R., & Carlier, O. (2008). Career success: Constructing a multidimensional model. *Journal of Vocational Behavior, 73,* 254–267.

Dries, N., Pepermans, R., & De Kerpel, E. (2008). Exploring four generations' beliefs about career. *Journal of Managerial Psychology, 23,* 907–928.

Dyke, L. S., & Murphy, S. A. (2006). How we define success: A quantitative study of what matters most to women and men. *Sex Roles, 55,* 357–371.

Eagly, A. H., & Carli, L. L. (2007). Women and the labyrinth of leadership. *Harvard Business Review, 85*(9), 62–71.

Earley, P. C. (2002). Redefining interactions across cultures and organizations: Moving forward with cultural intelligence. *Research in Organizational Behavior, 24,* 271–299.

Eby, L. T., Allen, T. D., Evans, S. C., Ng, T., & DuBois, D. L. (2008). Does mentoring matter? A multidisciplinary meta-analysis comparing mentored and non-mentored individuals. *Journal of Vocational Behavior, 72,* 254–267.

Eby, L. T., Durley, J. R., Evans, S. C., & Ragins, B. R. (2006). The relationship between short-term mentoring benefits and long-term mentor outcomes. *Journal of Vocational Behavior, 69,* 424–444.

Evans, P. (1986). New directions in career management. *Personnel Management, 18*(12), 26–30.

Eysenck, H. J. (1992). Four ways five factors are not basic. *Personality and Individual Differences, 13,* 667–673.

Farber, H. S. (2008). *Job loss and the decline in job security in the United States.* Manuscript in preparation.

Feldman, D. C. (1985). The new careerism: Origins, tenets, and consequences. *The Industrial Psychologist, 22,* 39–44.

Feldman, D. C. (1996). The nature, antecedents, and consequences of underemployment. *Journal of Management, 22,* 385–407.

Feldman, D. C., & Bolino, M. C. (2000). Career patterns of the self-employed: Career motivations and career outcomes. *Journal of Small Business Management, 38,* 53–67.

Feldman, D. C., & Leana, C. R. (2000). Whatever happened to laid-off executives: A study of reemployment challenges after downsizing. *Organizational Dynamics, 29*(1), 64–75.

Feldman, D. C., & Ng, T. W. H. (2007). Careers: Mobility, embeddedness, and success. *Journal of Management, 33,* 350–377.

Ferris, G., & Judge, T. (1991). Personnel/human resource management: A political influence perspective. *Journal of Management, 17,* 477–488.

Ferris, G. R., & King, T. R. (1991). Politics in human resources decisions: A walk on the dark side. *Organizational Dynamics, 20*(2), 59–71.

Fletcher, J. K., & Ragins, B. R. (2007). Stone center relational cultural theory: A window on relational mentoring. In B. R. Ragins & K. E. Kram (Eds.), *The handbook of mentoring at work* (pp. 373–399). Thousand Oaks, CA: Sage.

Fombrun, C. J. (1982). Strategies for network research in organizations. *Academy of Management Review, 7*, 280–291.

Form, W. H., & Miller, D. C. (1949). Occupational career patterns as a sociological instrument. *American Journal of Sociology, 54*, 317–329.

Forret, M. L. (2007, June). Verbal comment. In N. Bozionelos, M. Crocitto, & H. van Emmerik (Chairs), *Shaping the future: How to accommodate the global career of tomorrow?* Round Table Discussion conducted at the International Conference of the Eastern Academy of Management, Amsterdam, The Netherlands.

Forret, M. L., & Dougherty, T. W. (2004). Networking behaviors and career outcomes: Differences for men and women? *Journal of Organizational Behavior, 25*, 419–437.

Friedberg, L. (2007, March). The recent trend towards later retirement. *Work Opportunities for Older Americans, 9*, 1–7.

Fugate, M., Kinicki, A. J., & Ashforth, B. E. (2004). Employability: A psycho-social construct, its dimensions, and applications. *Journal of Vocational Behavior, 65*, 14–38.

Gattiker, U. E., & Larwood, L. (1986). Subjective career success: A study of managers and support personnel. *Journal of Business and Psychology, 1*, 78–94.

Gattiker, U. E., & Larwood, L. (1988). Predictors for managers' career mobility, success, and satisfaction. *Human Relations, 41*, 569–591.

Gentry, W. A., Weber, T. J., & Sadri, G. (2008). Examining career-related mentoring and managerial performance across cultures: A multilevel analysis. *Journal of Vocational Behavior, 72*, 241–253.

GMAC Global Relocation Services. (2008). *Global relocation trends: 2008 survey report.* Oak Brook, IL: GMAC Global Relocation Services.

Granrose, C. S., & Baccili, P. A. (2006). Do psychological contacts include boundaryless or protean careers? *Career Development International, 11*, 163–182.

Gray, J. (2001). The end of career. *Communications of the ACM, 44*(11), 65–69.

The great jobs switch. (2005, September 29). *The Economist.* Retrieved February 23, 2009, from http://www.economist.com/opinion/displaystory.cfm?story_id=4458528

Green, S. G., & Bauer, T. N. (1995). Supervisory mentoring by advisers: Relationship with doctoral student potential, productivity and commitment. *Personnel Psychology, 48*, 537–561.

Greenhaus, J. H. (1987). *Career management.* New York: Dryden Press.

Greenhaus, J. H., & Beutell, N. J. (1985). Sources of conflict between work and family roles. *Academy of Management Review, 10*, 76–88.

Greenhaus, J. H., Callanan, G. A., & DiRenzo, M. (2008). A boundaryless perspective on careers. In J. Barling & C. L. Cooper (Eds.), *The SAGE handbook of organizational behavior: Vol. 1. Micro approaches* (pp. 277–299). London: Sage.

Greenhaus, J. H., Callanan, G. A., & Godshalk, V. M. (2000). *Career management* (3rd ed.). Fort Worth, TX: Dryden Press.

Greenhaus, J., & Parasuraman, S. (1993). Job performance attributions and career advancement prospects: An examination of gender and race effects. *Organizational Behavior and Human Decision Processes, 55*, 273–297.

Greenhaus, J., & Powell, G. (2006). When work and family are allies: Theory of work-family enrichment. *Academy of Management Review, 31*, 77–92.

Gregory, A., & Milner, S. (2009). Editorial: Work–life balance: A matter of choice? *Gender, Work, and Organization, 16*, 1–13.

Griffin, B., & Hesketh, B. (2008). Post-retirement work: The individual determinants of paid and volunteer work. *Journal of Occupational and Organizational Psychology, 81*, 101–121.

Gunz, H. P. (1988). Organizational logics of managerial careers. *Organization Studies, 9*, 529–554.

Gutteridge, T. G., Leibowitz, Z. B., & Shore, J. E. (1993). *Organizational career development.* San Francisco: Jossey-Bass.

Hall, D. T. (1976). *Careers in organizations.* Pacific Palisades, CA: Goodyear.

Hall, D. T. (2002). *Careers in and out organizations.* Thousand Oaks, CA: Sage.

Hall, D. T. (2004). The protean career: A quarter-century journey. *Journal of Vocational Behavior, 65*, 1–13.

Hall, D. T., & Chandler, D. E. (2005). Psychological success: When the career is a calling. *Journal of Organizational Behavior, 26*, 155–176.

Hall, D. T., & Mirvis, P. H. (1995). The new career contract: Developing the whole person at midlife and beyond. *Journal of Vocational Behavior, 47*, 269–289.

Hall, D. T., & Mirvis, P. H. (1996). The new protean career: Psychological success and the path with a heart. In D. T. Hall (Ed.), *The career is dead—long live the career* (pp. 15–45). San Francisco: Jossey-Bass.

Hall, D. T., & Nougaim, K. (1968). An examination of Maslow's need hierarchy in an organizational setting. *Organizational Behavior and Human Performance, 3,* 12–35.

Hansen, R. S. (2009). Portfolio careers: Creating a career of multiple part-time jobs. *Quintessential Careers.* Retrieved February 22, 2009, from http://www.quintcareers.com/portfolio_careers.html

Harel, G. H., Tzafrir, S. S., & Baruch, Y. (2003). Achieving organizational effectiveness through promotion of women into managerial positions: HRM practice focus. *International Journal of Human Resource Management, 14,* 247–263.

Harrison, D. A., & Klein, K. J. (2007). What's the difference? Diversity constructs as separation, variety, or disparity in organizations. *Academy of Management Review, 32,* 1199–1228.

Harrison, D. A., Price, K. H., & Bell, M. P. (1998). Beyond relational demography: Time and the effects of surface- and deep-level diversity on work group cohesion. *Academy of Management Journal, 41,* 96–107.

Harrison, D. A., Price, K. H., Gavin, J. H., & Florey, A. T. (2002). Time, teams, and task performance: Changing effects of surface- and deep-level diversity on group functioning. *Academy of Management Journal, 45,* 1029–1045.

Harrison, D. A., & Shaffer, M. A. (2005). Mapping the criterion space for expatriate success: Task- and relationship-based performance, effort and adaptation. *International Journal of Human Resource Management, 16,* 1454–1474.

Harry, W. (2007). Employment creation and localization: The crucial human resource issues for the GCC. *International Journal of Human Resource Management, 18,* 132–146.

Hartung, P. J., Porfeli, E. J., & Vondracek, F. W. (2005). Child vocational development: A review and reconsideration. *Journal of Vocational Behavior, 66,* 385–419.

Harvey, M., Hartnell, C., & Novicevic, M. (2004). The inpatriation of foreign healthcare workers: A potential remedy for the chronic shortage of professional staff. *International Journal of Intercultural Relations, 28,* 127–150.

Harvey, M., Novicevic, M. M., Buckley, M. R., & Fung, H. (2005). Reducing inpatriate managers' "liability of foreignness" by addressing stigmatization and stereotype threats. *Journal of World Business, 40,* 267–280.

Hassard, J., Morris, J., Sheehan, J., & Yuxin, X. (2006). Downsizing the *danwei:* Chinese state-enterprise reform and the surplus labour question. *International Journal of Human Resource Management, 17,* 1441–1455.

Heilman, M. E., & Welle, B. (2006). Disadvantaged by diversity? The effects of diversity goals on competence perceptions. *Journal of Applied Social Psychology, 36,* 1291–1319.

Helwig, A. A. (2008). From childhood to adulthood: A 15-year longitudinal career development study. *The Career Development Quarterly, 57,* 38–50.

Heslin, P. A. (2005). Conceptualizing and evaluating career success. *Journal of Organizational Behavior, 26,* 113–136.

Higgins, M. (2005). *Career imprints: Creating leaders across an industry.* San Francisco: Jossey-Bass.

Higgins, M. C., & Kram, K. E. (2001). Reconceptualizing mentoring at work: A developmental network perspective. *Academy of Management Review, 26,* 264–288.

Higgins, M. C., & Thomas, D. A. (2001). Constellations and careers: Toward understanding the effects of multiple developmental relationships. *Journal of Organizational Behavior, 22,* 223–247.

Hofbauer, J., & Fischlmayr, I. C. (2004). Feminization of international assignments: Conquering empty castles? *International Studies of Management and Organization, 34*(3), 46–67.

Hogan, R., & Blake, R. (1999). John Holland's vocational typology and personality theory. *Journal of Vocational Behavior, 55,* 41–56.

Holgate, J., & McKay, S. (2009). Equal opportunities policies: How effective are they in increasing diversity in the audio-visual industries' freelance labour market? *Media, Culture and Society, 31,* 151–163.

Holland, J. L. (1959). A theory of occupational choice. *Journal of Counseling Psychology, 6,* 35–45.

Holland, J. L. (1996). Exploring careers with a typology: What we have learned and some new directions. *American Psychologist, 51,* 397–406.

Holland, J. L. (1997). Making vocational choices: A theory of vocational personalities and work environments (3rd ed.). Odessa, FL: Psychological Assessment Resources.

Holman, K. (2009). Downsized. *Mergers and Acquisitions: The Dealmaker's Journal, 44*(2), 30–31.

Hooker, C. I., Verosky, S. C., Miyakawa, A., Knight, R. T., & D'Esposito, M. (2008). The influence of personality on neural mechanisms of observational fear and reward learning. *Neuropsychologia, 46,* 2709–2724.

Horn, J. L., & Cattell, R. B. (1966). Refinement and test of the theory of fluid and crystallized general intelligences. *Journal of Educational Psychology, 57,* 253–270.

Hosoda, M., Stone-Romero, E. F., & Coats, G. (2003). The effects of physical attractiveness on job-related outcomes: A meta-analysis of experimental studies. *Personnel Psychology, 56,* 431–462.

Hughes, E. C. (1937). Institutional office and the person. *American Journal of Sociology, 43,* 404–413.

Hyde, J. S. (2005). The gender similarities hypothesis. *American Psychologist, 60,* 581–592.

Ibarra, H. (1992). Homophily and differential returns: Sex differences in network structure and access in an advertising firm. *Administrative Science Quarterly, 37,* 422–447.

Ibarra, H. (1993). Personal networks of women and minorities in management: A conceptual framework. *Academy of Management Review, 18,* 56–87.

Iida, T., & Morris, J. (2008). Farewell to the salaryman? The changing roles and work of middle managers in Japan. *International Journal of Human Resource Management, 19,* 1072–1087.

Inkpen, A. C., & Tsang, E. W. K. (2005). Social capital, networks, and knowledge transfer. *Academy of Management Review, 30,* 146–165.

Inkson, K. (2007). *Understanding careers: The metaphors of working lives.* Thousand Oaks, CA: Sage.

Inkson, K., Arthur, M. B., Pringle, J., & Barry, S. (1997). Expatriate assignment v. overseas experience: Contrasting models of international human resource development. *Journal of World Business, 32,* 351–368.

Inkson, K., & Myers, B. A. (2003). "The big OE": Self-directed travel and career development. *Career Development International, 8,* 170–181.

Insinga, R. C., & Werle, M. J. (2000). Linking outsourcing to business strategy. *Academy of Management Executive, 14*(4), 58–70.

International Labour Organization. (2009). *Laborsta: Database of labour statistics.* Retrieved March 10, 2009, from http://laborsta.ilo.org

Jackson, S. E., May, K. E., & Whitney, K. (1995). Understanding the dynamics of diversity in decision-making teams. In R. A. Guzzo & E. Salas (Eds.), *Team decision-making effectiveness in organizations* (pp. 204–261). San Francisco: Jossey-Bass.

Jang, K. L., Livesley, W. J., Ando, J., Yamagata, S., Suzuki, A., Angleitner, A., et al. (2006). Behavioral genetics of the higher-order factors of the Big Five. *Personality and Individual Differences, 41,* 261–272.

Jensen, L., & Slack, T. (2003). Underemployment in America: Measurement and evidence. *American Journal of Community Psychology, 32,* 21–31.

Jokinen, T., Brewster, C., & Suutari, V. (2008). Career capital during international work experiences: Contrasting self-initiated expatriate experiences and assigned expatriation. *The International Journal of Human Resource Management, 19,* 979–998.

Jokisaari, M., & Nurmi, J-E. (2005). Company matters: Goal-related social capital in the transition to working life. *Journal of Vocational Behavior, 67,* 413–428.

Judge, T. A., & Cable, D. M. (2004). The effect of physical height on workplace success and income: Preliminary test of a theoretical model. *Journal of Applied Psychology, 89,* 428–441.

Judge, T. A., Higgins, C. A., Thoresen, C. J., & Barrick, M. R. (1999). The big five personality traits, general mental ability, and career success across the life span. *Personnel Psychology, 52,* 621–652.

Kammeyer-Mueller, J. D., & Judge, T. A. (2008). A quantitative review of mentoring research: Test of a model. *Journal of Vocational Behavior, 72,* 269–283.

Kanter, R. M. (1977). *Men and women of the corporation.* New York: Basic Books.

Kashima, Y., & Kashima, E. S. (2003). Individualism, GNP, climate, and pronoun drop: Is individualism determined by affluence and climate, or does language use play a role? *Journal of Cross-Cultural Psychology, 34,* 125–134.

Khapova, S. N., & Korotov, K. (2007). Dynamics of western career attributes in the Russian context. *Career Development International, 12,* 68–85.

Kiessling, T., & Harvey, M. (2006). Global organizational control: A new role by inpatriates. *Multinational Business Review, 14*(2), 1–27.

Kinsella, K. G. (2005). Future longevity: Demographic concerns and consequences. *Journal of the American Geriatrics Society, 53,* S299–S303.

Kinsella, K., & Phillips, D. R. (2005). Global aging: The challenge of success. *Population Bulletin, 60*(1).

Kirchmeyer, C. (2005). The effects of mentoring on academic careers over time: Testing performance and political perspectives. *Human relations, 58,* 637–669.

Koskina, A. (2008). The "pros" and "cons" of career development in the Greek public sector. *Personnel Review, 37,* 264–279.

Kozhaya, N. (2007). *The retirement age in Quebec: A worrying situation.* Montreal, Canada: Montreal Economic Institute.

Kraimer, M. L., Shaffer, M. A., & Bolino, M. (2009). The influence of expatriate and repatriate experiences on career advancement and repatriate retention. *Human Resource Management, 48,* 27–47.

Kram, K. E. (1985). *Mentoring in the workplace: Development relationships in organizational life.* Glenview, IL: Scott, Foresman.

Kram, K. E., & Isabella, L. A. (1985). Mentoring alternatives: The role of peer relationships in career development. *Academy of Management Journal, 28,* 110–132.

Krause, A., Stadil, T., & Bunke, J. (2003). Auswirkungen von downsizing-maßnahmen auf das organisationale commitment der verbleibenden mitarbeiter: Ein vorher-nachher-vergleich [Impact of downsizing measures on the organizational commitment of remaining employees: Before-and-after-implementation]. *Gruppendynamik und Organisationsberatung, 34,* 355–372.

Lachman, M. E. (2004). Development in midlife. *Annual Review of Psychology, 55,* 305–331.

Landry, B. J. L., Mahesh, S., & Hartman, S. (2005). The changing nature of work in the age of e-business. *Journal of Organizational Change Management, 18,* 132–144.

Lanzi, D. (2007). Capabilities, human capital, and education. *The Journal of Socio-Economics, 36,* 424–435.

Latham, G. P., & Mann, S. (2006). Advances in the science of performance appraisal: Implications for practice. *International Review of Industrial and Organizational Psychology, 21,* 295–337.

Lazarova, M. B., & Cerdin, J-L. (2007). Revisiting repatriation concerns: Organizational support versus career and contextual influence. *Journal of International Business Studies, 38,* 404–429.

Lazarova, M., & Taylor, S. (2009). Boundaryless careers, social capital, and knowledge management: Implications for organizational performance. *Journal of Organizational Behavior, 30,* 119–139.

Leanna, C. R., & Feldman, D. C. (1992). *Coping with job loss: How individuals, organizations, and communities respond to layoffs.* New York: Lexington Books.

Leck, J. D. (2002). Making employment equity programs work for women. *Canadian Public Policy/Analyse de Politiques, 28,* S85–S100.

Lee, C. H. (2005). A study of underemployment among self-initiated expatriates. *Journal of World Business, 40,* 172–187.

Lepak, D. P., & Snell, S. A. (1999). The human capital resource architecture: Toward a theory of human capital allocation and development. *Academy of Management Review, 24,* 31–48.

Levinson, D. (1978). *Seasons of a man's life.* New York: Knopf.

Li, Y., Savage, M., & Warde, A. (2008). Social mobility and social capital in contemporary Britain. *British Journal of Sociology, 59,* 391–411.

Linney, G. (2001). Preparing for a career in medical management: 8 steps to help you evaluate your career path. *Physician Executive, 27*(4), 14–17.

Lips-Wiersma, M., & Hall, D. T. (2007). Organizational career development is not dead: A case study on managing the new career during organizational change. *Journal of Organizational Behavior, 28,* 771–792.

Lirio, P., Lituchy, T. R., Monserrat, S. I., Olivas-Lujan, M. R., Duffy, J. A., Fox, S., et al. (2007). Exploring career-life success and family social support of successful women in Canada, Argentina, and Mexico. *Career Development International, 12,* 28–50.

Littler, C. R., Wiesner, R., Dunford, R. (2003). The dynamics of delayering: Changing management structures in three countries. *Journal of Management Studies, 40,* 225–256.

London, M. (1983). Toward a theory of career motivation. *Academy of Management Review, 8,* 620–630.

Long, J. E., & Link, A. N. (1983). The impact of market structure on wages, fringe benefits, and turnover. *Industrial and Labor Relations Review, 36,* 239–250.

Lyness, K. S., & Heilman, M. E. (2006). When fit is fundamental: Performance evaluations and promotions of upper-level female and male managers. *Journal of Applied Psychology, 91,* 777–785.

Mainiero, L. A., & Sullivan, S. E. (2005). Kaleidoscope careers: An alternative explanation for the opt-out evolution. *Academy of Management Executive, 19*(1), 106–123.

Mainiero, L. A., & Sullivan, S. E. (2006). *The opt-out revolt: Why people are leaving companies to create kaleidoscope careers.* Palo Alto, CA: Davies-Black.

Malach-Pines, A., & Kaspi-Baruch, O. (2008). The role of culture and gender in the choice of a career in management. *Career Development International, 13,* 306–319.

Marsden, P. V. (1990). Network data and measurement. *Annual Review of Sociology, 16,* 435–463.

Marston, G., & McDonald, C. (2008). Feeling motivated yet? Long-term unemployed people's perspectives on the implementation of workfare in Australia. *Australian Journal of Social Issues, 43,* 255–269.

Martin, P. L. (2003). *Managing labor migration: Temporary worker programs for the 21st century.* Geneva: International Institute for Labour Studies.

Maslova, I. (1991). State employment programmes in the light of the new law of employment. In G. Standing (Ed.), *In search of flexibility: The new Soviet labour market* (pp. 121–144). Geneva: International Labour Organization.

Mayrhofer, W., Meyer, M., Schiffinger, M., & Schmidt, A. (2008). The influence of family responsibilities, career fields, and gender on career success. *Journal of Managerial Psychology, 23,* 292–323.

McArdle, S., Waters, L., Briscoe, J. P., & Hall D. T. (2007). Employability during unemployment: Adaptability, career identity, and human and social capital. *Journal of Vocational Behavior, 71,* 247–264.

McDonald, P., Brown, K., & Bradley, L. (2005). Have traditional career paths given way to protean ones? Evidence from senior managers in the Australian public sector. *Career Development International, 10,* 109–129.

McKay, P. F., Avery, D. R., & Morris, M. A. (2008). Mean racial-ethnic differences in employee sales performance: The moderating role of diversity climate. *Personnel Psychology, 61,* 349–374.

McLaughlin, D. H., & Tiedeman, D. V. (1974). Eleven-year career stability and changes as reflected in project talent data through the Flanagan, Holland, and Roe occupational classification systems. *Journal of Vocational Behavior, 5,* 177–196.

McManus, S. E., & Russell, J. E. A. (2007). Peer mentoring relationships. In B. R. Ragins & K. E. Kram (Eds.), *The Handbook of mentoring at work* (pp. 273–297). Thousand Oaks, CA: Sage.

McQuaid, R. W., & Lindsay, C. (2002). The "employability gap": Long-term unemployment and barriers to work in buoyant labour markets. *Environment and Planning C: Government and Policy, 20,* 613–628.

Melamed, T. (1995a). Career success: The moderating effect of gender. *Journal of Vocational Behavior, 47,* 35–60.

Melamed, T. (1996a). Career success: An assessment of a gender-specific model. *Journal of Occupational and Organisational Psychology, 69,* 217–242.

Melamed, T. (1996b). Validation of a stage model of career success. *Applied Psychology: An International Review, 45,* 35–65.

Melamed, T., & Bozionelos, N. (1992). Managerial promotion and height. *Psychological Reports, 71,* 587–593.

Mercer Human Resource Consulting. (2008). *Benefits survey for expatriates and globally mobile employees.* Geneva: Mercer LLC.

Metz, I., & Tharenou, P. (2001). Women's career advancement: The relative contribution of human and social capital. *Group and Organization Management, 26,* 312–342.

Milliken, F. J., & Martins, L. L. (1996). Searching for common threads: Understanding the multiple effects of diversity in organizational groups. *Academy of Management Review, 21,* 402–433.

Mintzberg, H. (1985). The organization as political arena. *Journal of Management Studies, 22,* 133–154.

Miyamoto, K., Takebayashi, H., Takimoto, K., Miyamoto, S., Morioka, S., & Yagi, F. (2008). A new simple performance test focused on agility in elderly people: The ten-step test. *Gerontology, 54,* 365–372.

Moore, P. R., Ng, A. H. C., Yeo, S. H., Sundberg, M., Wong, C. B., & De Vin, L. J. (2008). Advanced machine service support using internet-enabled three-dimensional-based virtual engineering. *International Journal of Production Research, 46,* 4215–4235.

Morrison, A. M., & Von Glinow, M. A. (1990). Women and minorities in management. *American Psychologist, 45,* 200–208.

Morrison, A. M., White, R. P., & Van Velsor, E. (1987). *Breaking the glass ceiling: Can women reach the top of America's largest corporations?* Reading, MA: Addison-Wesley.

Moss, P., Salzman, H., & Tilly, C. (2008). Under construction: The continuing evolution of job structures in call centers. *Industrial Relations, 47,* 173–208.

Ng, T. W. H., Eby, L. T., Sorensen, K. L., & Feldman, D. C. (2005). Predictors of objective and subjective career success: A meta-analysis. *Personnel Psychology, 58,* 367–408.

Ng, T. W. H., & Feldman, D. C. (2008). Can you get a better deal elsewhere? The effects of psychological contract replicability on organizational commitment over time. *Journal of Vocational Behavior, 73,* 268–277.

Ng, T. W. H., & Feldman, D. C. (2009). How broadly does education contribute to job performance? *Personnel Psychology, 62,* 89–134.

Nicholson, N., & De Waal-Andrews, W. (2005). Playing to win: Biological imperatives, self-regulation, and trade-offs in the game of career success. *Journal of Organizational Behavior, 26,* 137–154.

Nieva, V. F. (1985). Work and family linkages. In L. Larwood, A. H. Stromberg, & B. A. Gutek (Eds.), *Women and work* (Vol. 1, pp. 162–190). Beverly Hills, CA: Sage.

Okun, M. A., Pugliese, J., & Rook, K. S. (2007). Unpacking the relation between extraversion and volunteering in later life: The role of social capital. *Personality and Individual Differences, 42,* 1467–1477.

O'Neil, D. A., Hopkins, M. M., & Bilimoria, D. (2008). Women's careers at the start of the 21st century: Patterns and paradoxes. *Journal of Business Ethics, 80,* 727–743.

Ornstein, S., Cron, W. L., & Slocum, J. W. (1989). Life stage versus career stage: A comparative test of the theories of Levinson and Super. *Journal of Organizational Behavior, 10,* 117–133.

Ornstein, S., & Isabella, L. (1990). Age v. stage models of career attitudes of women: A partial replication and extension. *Journal of Vocational Behavior, 36,* 1–19.

O'Sullivan, S. L. (2002). The protean approach to managing repatriation transitions. *International Journal of Manpower, 23,* 597–616.

Over, R., & Thomas, P. (1995). Age and skilled psychomotor performance: A comparison of younger and older golfers. *International Journal of Aging and Human Development, 41,* 1–12.

Oyer, P. (2008). The making of an investment banker: Stock market shocks, career choice, and lifetime income. *The Journal of Finance, 63,* 2601–2628.

Ozbilgin, M., & Healy, G. (2004). The gendered nature of career development of university professors: The case of Turkey. *Journal of Vocational Behavior, 64,* 358–371.

Ozbilgin, M., Kusku, F., & Erdogmus, N. (2005). Explaining influences on career "choice": The case of MBA students in comparative perspective. *International Journal of Human Resource Management, 16,* 2000–2028.

Pang, M., Chua, B-L., & Chu, C. W. L. (2008). Learning to stay ahead in an uncertain environment. *International Journal of Human Resource Management, 19,* 1383–1394.

Papastergiou, M. (2008). Are computer science and information technology still masculine fields? High school students' perceptions and career choices. *Computers and Education, 51,* 594–608.

Parker, R. J., & Kohlmeyer, J. M. (2005). Organizational justice and turnover in public accounting firms: A research note. *Accounting, Organizations and Society, 30,* 357–369.

Parkin, M., Powell, M., & Matthews, K. (2007). *Economics* (7th ed.). Harlow, England: Pearson.

Pastoriza, D., Arino, M. A., & Ricart, J. E. (2008). Ethical managerial behaviour as an antecedent of organizational social capital. *Journal of Business Ethics, 78,* 329–341.

Peiperl, M., & Baruch, Y. (1997). Back to square zero: The postcorporate career. *Organizational Dynamics, 25*(4), 7–22.

Peltokorpi, V. (2008). Cross-cultural adjustment of expatriates in Japan. *International Journal of Human Resource Management, 19,* 1588–1606.

Penner, A. M. (2008). Race and gender differences in wages: The role of occupational sorting at the point of hire. *The Sociological Quarterly, 49,* 597–614.

Petersen, T., & Saporta, I. (2004). The opportunity structure for discrimination. *American Journal of Sociology, 109,* 852–901.

Pfeffer, J. (1989). A political perspective on careers: Interests, networks, and environments. In M. B. Arthur, D. T. Hall, & B. S. Lawrence (Eds.), *Handbook of career theory* (pp. 380–396). Cambridge, England: Cambridge University Press.

Phillips, K. W., & Loyd, D. L. (2006). When surface- and deep-level diversity collide: The effects on dissenting group members. *Organizational Behavior and Human Decision Processes, 99,* 143–160.

Poletaev, M., & Robinson, C. (2008). Human capital specificity: Evidence from the dictionary of occupational titles and displaced worker surveys, 1984–2000. *Journal of Labor Economics, 26,* 387–420.

Portes, A. (1998). Social capital: Its origins and applications in modern sociology. *Annual Review of Sociology, 24,* 1–24.

Powell, G. N., & Eddleston, K. A. (2008). The paradox of the contented female business owner. *Journal of Vocational Behavior, 73,* 24–36.

Prediger, D. J., & Vansickle, T. R. (1992). Locating occupations on Holland's hexagon: Beyond RIASEC. *Journal of Vocational Behavior, 40,* 111–128.

Ragins, B. R., Cotton, J. L., & Miller, J. S. (2000). Marginal mentoring: The effects of type of mentor, quality of relationship, and program design on work and career attitudes. *Academy of Management Journal, 43,* 1177–1194.

Ragins, B. R., & Sundstrom, E. (1989). Gender and power in organizations. *Psychological Bulletin, 105,* 51–88.

Ramaswami, S. N., & Singh, J. (2003). Antecedents and consequences of merit pay fairness for industrial salespeople. *Journal of Marketing, 67,* 46–66.

Rayman, J., & Atanasoff, L. (1999). Holland's theory and career intervention: The power of the hexagon. *Journal of Vocational Behavior, 55,* 114–116.

Reitman, F., & Schneer, J. A. (2003). The promised path: A longitudinal study of managerial careers. *Journal of Managerial Psychology, 18,* 60–75.

Reitman, F., & Schneer, J. A. (2008). Enabling the new careers of the 21st century. *Organization Management Journal, 5,* 17–28.

Richardson, J., & McKenna, S. (2002). Leaving and experiencing: Why academics expatriate and how they experience expatriation. *Career Development International, 7,* 67–78.

Rickwood, R. R., Roberts, J., Batten, S., Marshall, A., & Massie, K. (2004). Empowering high-risk clients to attain a better quality of life: A career resiliency framework. *Journal of Employment Counseling, 41,* 98–104.

Rosenbaum, J. L. (1979). Tournament mobility: Career patterns in a corporation. *Administrative Science Quarterly, 24,* 221–241.

Roth, L. M. (2004). The social psychology of tokenism: Status and homophily processes on Wall Street. *Sociological Perspectives, 47,* 189–214.

Rousseau, D. M. (1995). *Psychological contracts in organizations: Understanding written and unwritten agreements.* Thousand Oaks, CA: Sage.

Rubin, B. A., & Brody, C. J. (2005). Contradictions of commitment in the new economy: Insecurity, time, and technology. *Social Science Research, 34,* 843–861.

Rudolph, C. W., Wells, C. L., Weller, M. D., & Baltes, B. B. (2009). A meta-analysis of empirical studies of weight-based bias in the workplace. *Journal of Vocational Behavior, 74,* 1–10.

Russo, N. F. (1985). Sex-role stereotyping, socialization, and sexism. In A. G. Sargent (Ed.), *Beyond sex roles* (pp. 150–187). St. Paul, MN: West Publishing.

Ryan, M. K., & Haslam, S. A. (2007). The glass cliff: Exploring the dynamics surrounding the appointment of women to precarious leadership positions. *Academy of Management Review, 32,* 549–572.

Saint-Charles, J., Mongeau, P. (2009). Different relationships for coping with ambiguity and uncertainty in organizations. *Social Networks, 31,* 33–39.

Salgado, J. F., Anderson, N., Moscoso, S., Bertua, C., de Fruyt, F., & Rolland, J. P. (2003). A meta-analytic study of general mental ability validity for different occupations in the European Community. *Journal of Applied Psychology, 88,* 1068–1081.

Schaie, K. W. (2005). *Developmental influences on adult intelligence: The Seattle longitudinal study.* New York: Cambridge University Press.

Schein, E. H. (1978). *Career dynamics: Matching individual and organizational needs.* Reading, MA: Addison Wesley.

Scholarios, D., Van der Heijden, B. I. J. M., Van der Schoot, E., Bozionelos, N., Epitropaki, O., Jedrzejowicz, P., et al. (2008). Employability and the psychological contract in European ICT sector SMEs. *International Journal of Human Resource Management, 19,* 1035–1055.

Schwartzman, A. E., Gold, D., Andres, D., Arbuckle, T. Y., & Chaikelson, J. (1987). Stability of intelligence: A 40-year follow up. *Canadian Journal of Psychology, 41,* 244–256.

Segers, J., Inceoglou, I., Vloeberghs, D., Bartram, D., & Henderickx, E. (2008). Protean and boundaryless careers: A study on potential motivators. *Journal of Vocational Behavior, 73,* 212–230.

Seibert, S. E., Kraimer, M. L., & Liden, R. C. (2001). A social capital theory of career success. *Academy of Management Journal, 44,* 219–237.

Shambaugh, D. (Ed.). (2006). *Power shift: China and Asia's new dynamics.* Berkeley, CA: University of California Press.

Shin, T-J. (2007). The impact of structural dynamics on job mobility rates in the United States. *Social Science Research, 36,* 1301–1327.

Singh, V., Bains, D., & Vinnicombe, S. (2002). Informal mentoring as an organizational resource. *Long Range Planning, 35,* 389–405.

Sippola, A., & Smale, A. (2007). The global integration of diversity management: A longitudinal case study. *International Journal of Human Resource Management, 18,* 1895–1916.

Smart, R., & Peterson, C. (1997). Super's career stages and the decision to change careers. *Journal of Vocational Behavior, 51,* 358–374.

Sonnega, A. (2006, March). The future of human life expectancy: Have we reached the ceiling or is the sky the limit? *Research Highlights in the Demography and Economics of Aging, 8,* 1–4.

Sonnenfeld, J. A., Peiperl, M. A., & Kotter, J. P. (1988). Strategic determinants of managerial labor markets: A career systems view. *Human Resource Management, 27,* 369–388.

Spilerman, S. (1977). Careers, labor market structure, and socioeconomic achievement. *American Journal of Sociology, 83,* 551–593.

Stackman, R. W., & Pinder, C. C. (1999). Context and sex effects on personal work networks. *Journal of Social and Personal Relationships, 16,* 39–64.

Stahl, G. K., Chua, C. H., Caligiuri, P., Cerdin, J-L., & Taniguchi, M. (2009). Predictors of turnover intentions in learning-driven and demand-driven international assignments: The role of repatriation concerns, satisfaction with company support, and perceived career advancement opportunities. *Human Resource Management, 48,* 89–109.

Stahl, G. K., Miller, E. L., & Tung, R. L. (2002). Toward the boundaryless career: A closer look at the expatriate career concept and the perceived implications of an international assignment. *Journal of World Business, 37,* 216–227.

Sullivan, S. E. (1999). The changing nature of careers: A review and research agenda. *Journal of Management, 25,* 457–484.

Sullivan, S. E., & Arthur, M. B. (2006). The evolution of the boundaryless career concept: Examining physical and psychological mobility. *Journal of Vocational Behavior, 69,* 19–29.

Super, D. E. (1957). *The psychology of careers.* New York: Harper & Row.

Super, D. E. (1980). A life-span, life-space approach to career development. *Journal of Vocational Behavior, 16,* 282–298.

Super, D. E. (1990). A life-span, life-space approach to career development. In D. Brown & L. Brooks (Eds.), *Career choice and development* (2nd ed., pp. 197–261). San Francisco: Jossey-Bass.

Super, D. E., Savickas, M. L., & Super, C. M. (1996). The life-span, life-space approach to careers. In D. Brown & L. Brooks (Eds.), *Career choice and development* (3rd ed., pp. 121–178). San Francisco: Jossey-Bass.

Suutari, V., & Brewster, C. (2000). Making their own way: International experience through self-initiated foreign assignments. *Journal of World Business, 35,* 417–436.

Suutari, V., & Brewster, C. (2003). Repatriation: Empirical evidence from a longitudinal study of careers and expectations among Finnish expatriates. *International Journal of Human Resource Management, 14,* 1132–1151.

Tajfel, H., & Turner, J. C. (1986). The social identity theory of intergroup behavior. In S. Worchel &

W. G. Austin (Eds.), *Psychology of intergroup relations* (pp. 7–24). Chicago: Nelson-Hall.

Takeuchi, R., Tesluk, P. E., & Marinova, S. V. (2006). Role of international experiences in the development of cultural intelligence. In S. Dey & V. N. Posa (Eds.), *Cultural intelligence: An introduction* (pp. 56–91). Hyderabad, India: ICFAI University Press.

Tams, S., & Arthur, M. B. (2007). Studying careers across cultures: Distinguishing international, cross-cultural, and globalization perspectives. *Career Development International, 12,* 86–98.

Tarique, I., & Schuler, R. (2008). Emerging issues and challenges in global staffing: A North American perspective. *The International Journal of Human Resource Management, 19,* 1397–1415.

Tarique, I., Schuler, R., & Gong, Y. (2006). A model of multinational enterprise subsidiary staffing composition. *The International Journal of Human Resource Management, 17,* 207–224.

Taylor, M. S., Audia, G., & Gupta, A. K. (1996). The effect of lengthening job tenure on managers' organizational commitment and turnover. *Organization Science, 7,* 632–648.

Tepper, K., Shaffer, B. C., & Tepper, B. J. (1996). Latent structure of mentoring function scales. *Educational and Psychological Measurement, 56,* 848–857.

Tharenou, P. (1997). Managerial career advancement. In C. L. Cooper & I. T. Robertson (Eds.), *International review of industrial and organizational psychology* (Vol. 12, pp. 39–93). New York: Wiley.

Thatcher, S. M. B., & Zhu, X. M. (2006). Changing identities in a changing workplace: Identification, identity enactment, self-verification, and telecommuting. *Academy of Management Review, 31,* 1076–1088.

Thomas, D. C., Lazarova, M. B., Inkson, K. (2005). Global careers: New phenomenon or new perspectives? *Journal of World Business, 40,* 340–347.

Thompson, J. A. (2005). Proactive personality and job performance: A social capital perspective. *Journal of Applied Psychology, 90,* 1011–1017.

Thornhill, A., & Saunders, N. K. (1998). The meanings, consequences, and implications of the management of downsizing and redundancy: A review. *Personnel Review, 27,* 271–295.

Tracey, T. J., & Rounds, J. (1993). Evaluating Holland's and Gati's vocational-interest models: A structural meta-analysis. *Psychological Bulletin, 113,* 229–246.

Tracey, J. B., Sturman, M. C., & Tews, M. J. (2007). Ability versus personality. *Cornell Hotel and Restaurant Administration Quarterly, 48,* 313–322.

Triandis, H. C. (1995). *Individualism and collectivism.* Boulder, CO: Westview Press.

Trompenaars, F. (1994). *Riding the waves of culture.* New York: Irwin.

Tsai, C-F., Wu, S-L., Wang, H-K., & Huang, I-C. (2006). An empirical research on the institutional theory of downsizing: Evidence from MNC's subsidiary companies in Taiwan. *Total Quality Management, 17,* 633–654.

Tsui, A. S., Egan, T. D., & O'Reilly, C. A., III. (1992). Being different: Relational demography and organizational attachment. *Administrative Science Quarterly, 37,* 549–579.

Tsui, A. S., & O'Reilly, C. A., III. (1989). Beyond simple demographic effects: The importance of relational demography in superior-subordinate dyads. *Academy of Management Journal, 32,* 402–423.

Turner, R. J. (1960). Sponsored and contest mobility and the school system. *American Sociological Review, 25,* 855–867.

United Nations. (2006). *Life expectancy at birth, both sexes combined (years).* Retrieved January 23, 2009, from http://data.un.org/Data.aspx?d=PopDiv&f=variableID%3a68#PopDiv

United Nations. (2007). Women's share of labour force. Retrieved January 23, 2009, from http://data.un.org/Data.aspx?q=labour&d=GenderStat&f=inID%3a107

United Nations. (2008). *Average annual rate of reduction of total fertility rate.* Retrieved January 23, 2009, from http://data.un.org/Data.aspx?q=fertility+rate&d=SOWC&f=inID%3a80#SOWC

U.S. Department of Labor. (2008, October). *Highlights of women's earnings in 2007* (Report 1008). Retrieved February 27, 2009, from http://www.bls.gov/cps/cpswom2007.pdf

Valcour, M., & Ladge, J. J. (2008). Family and career path characteristics as predictors of women's objective and subjective career success: Integrating traditional and protean career explanations. *Journal of Vocational Behavior, 73,* 300–309.

Vance, C. M. (2005). The personal quest for building global competence: A taxonomy of self-initiating career path strategies for gaining business experience abroad. *Journal of World Business, 40,* 374–385.

Van der Heijde, C. M., & Van der Heijden, B. I. J. M. (2006). A competence-based and multidimensional operationalization and measurement of employability. *Human Resource Management, 45,* 449–476.

Van Emmerik, I. J. H. (2006). Gender differences in the creation of different types of social capital: A multilevel study. *Social Networks, 28,* 24–37.

Van Maanen, J. (1977) Towards a theory of career. In J. Van Maanen (Ed.), *Organizational careers: Some new perspectives* (pp. 161–179). New York: Wiley.

Van Scotter, J. R., Motowidlo, S. J., & Cross, T. C. (2000). Effects of task performance and contextual performance on systemic rewards. *Journal of Applied Psychology, 85,* 526–535.

Vigoda, E. (2000). The relationship between organizational politics, job attitudes, and work outcomes: Exploration and implications for the public sector, *Journal of Vocational Behavior, 57,* 326–47.

Warhurst, C., Nickson, D., Witz, A., & Cullen, A. M. (2000). Aesthetic labour in interactive service work: Some case study evidence from the "new" Glasgow. *The Service Industries Journal, 20*(3), 1–18.

Waterman, R. H., Jr., Waterman, J. A., & Collard, B. A. (1994). Toward a career-resilient workforce. *Harvard Business Review, 72*(4), 87–95.

Watson, M., & McMahon, M. (2005). Children's career development: A research review from a learning perspective. *Journal of Vocational Behavior, 67,* 119–132.

Weichselbaumer, D., & Winter-Ebmer, R. (2007). The effects of competition and equal treatment laws on gender wage differentials. *Economic Policy, 50,* 235–287.

Westermeyer, J. F. (2004). Predictors and characteristics of Erikson's life cycle among men: A 32-year longitudinal study. *International Journal of Aging and Human Development, 58,* 29–48.

White, L. T., III (1989). *Policies of chaos: The organizational causes of violence in China's cultural revolution.* Princeton, NJ: Princeton University Press.

Whyte, W. H. (1956). *The organization man.* New York: Simon & Shuster.

Wilensky, H. L. (1961). Careers, lifestyles, and social integration. *International Social Science Journal, 12,* 553–558.

Wilson-Kovacs, D., Ryan, M. K., Haslam, S. A., & Rabinovich, A. (2008). "Just because you can get a wheelchair in the building doesn't necessarily mean that you can still participate": Barriers to the career advancement of disabled professionals. *Disability and Society, 23,* 705–717.

Wolff, H-G., & Moser, K. (2006). Entwicklung und validierung einer networkingskala [Development and validation of a networking scale]. *Diagnostica, 52,* 161–180.

Wolff, H-G., & Moser, K. (2009). Effects of networking on career success: A longitudinal study. *Journal of Applied Psychology, 94,* 196–206.

WorldatWork. (2009, February 18). *Telework revs up as more employers offer work flexibility.* Retrieved February 19, 2009, from http://www.worldatwork.org/waw/adimComment?id=31331

World Bank. (2009). *World development report 2009: Reshaping economic geography.* Washington, DC: The World Bank.

Zhao, H., Wayne, S. J., Glibkowski, B. C., & Bravo, J. (2007). The impact of psychological contract breach on work-related outcomes: A meta-analysis. *Personnel Psychology, 60,* 647–680.

Part II

SPECIFIC SELECTION STRATEGIES AND ISSUES

Chapter 4

INDIVIDUAL DIFFERENCES: THEIR MEASUREMENT AND VALIDITY

Oleksandr S. Chernyshenko, Stephen Stark, and Fritz Drasgow

Individual differences can be defined broadly as the dimensions along which people vary. There are a great many individual difference dimensions, including how straight one can hit a golf ball, how much one likes to organize his or her work desk, or how fast one can read and comprehend a word passage. In domains of differential and industrial and organizational (I/O) psychology, however, the term *individual differences* is usually reserved to describe individuals' basic tendencies, capacities, and dispositions that influence the observed range and frequency of their behavior (Motowidlo, Borman, & Schmit, 1997). Traditionally, individual difference variables include cognitive and psychomotor abilities or skills, personality traits, motives, values, and interests. Although researchers may still debate the extent to which these tendencies are inherited and shaped by environmental factors early in life, the general consensus is that most individual difference variables are relatively stable throughout adulthood and, in the absence of strong situational constraints, play a significant role in guiding behavior.

Individual differences are an essential part of the person–situation interaction. Whereas the fields of experimental psychology and organizational behavior are devoted to the study of how situations influence behavior, differential psychology is devoted to the study of how individual differences influence behavior and performance. Mischel (1968) notwithstanding, both situations and individual differences are important and account for roughly equal amounts of variance (Funder & Ozer, 1983). In their widely cited article, Schmidt and Hunter (1998) provided estimates of correlations between job performance and various individual difference measures under optimal conditions (i.e., when job performance is measured without error and there is no restriction of range on the individual difference variable). Their Table 1 shows that cognitive ability can be expected to correlate in excess of .50 with performance and several other measures have correlations greater than .35. Importantly, in selection contexts, these criterion correlations are essentially effect size measures, because they directly indicate the expected performance improvement (in *z* score units) when the average applicants' scores on the predictor increase by one *z* score unit (or 1 *SD*). For example, a .50 correlation means that, on average, selection of applicants who are 1 *SD* higher on the predictor would result in a .50 *SD* improvement in performance. Clearly, individual differences are powerful predictors of behavior and performance in work organizations.

Interestingly, the person-by-situation interaction has been studied far less often and frequently accounts for much less variance than the main effects of people and situations. The relatively weak support for the person-by-situation interaction is one of the main reasons that I/O psychologists have shown an acute interest in using individual difference variables in theories of work behavior. To illustrate, consider Figure 4.1, in which we present a conceptual model for the role of individual differences in predicting job performance. Here, we have combined the ideas of Hunter (1983); Ackerman, Kanfer, and Goff (1995); Campbell (1990); McCrae

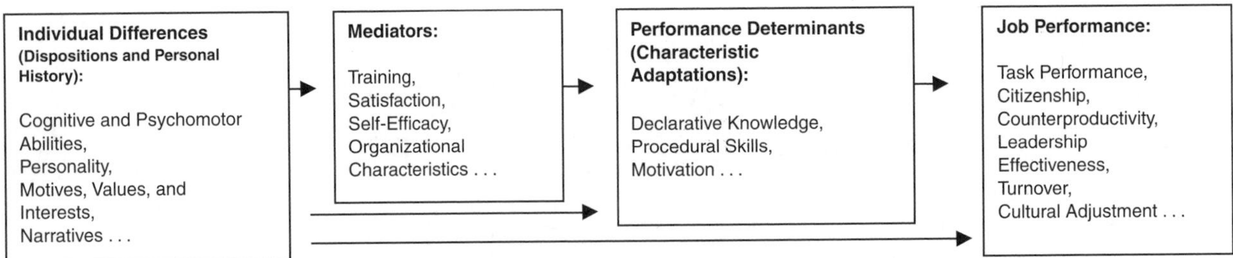

FIGURE 4.1. **Conceptual model of the role of individual differences in predicting job performance.**

and Costa (1996); Motowidlo et al. (1997); Chan and Drasgow (2001); Credé, Chernyshenko, Stark, Dalal, and Bashur (2007); and many others, to posit how the main classes of individual differences (i.e., abilities, personality, values) exert a direct or indirect influence on performance determinants (aka characteristic adaptations), which, in turn, directly influence employee performance. Of course, the strength of the path coefficients and the relevant mediators and outcomes will vary depending on whether one looks at cognitive ability, personality, or values, but the basic theoretical mechanisms are the same. For example, in the case of cognitive ability, researchers have shown that the relationship between general cognitive ability and task performance is partially or fully mediated by declarative knowledge, procedural skills, motivational factors, or all three (Ackerman et al., 1995; Hunter 1983; McCloy, Campbell, & Cudeck, 1994). Additionally, Ackerman et al. (1995) found that *ability self-concept* (aka self-efficacy) partially mediates the relationship between general cognitive ability and motivation. Chan and Drasgow (2001) showed that relationships between several personality variables and motivation to lead, a performance determinant in their model, were partially mediated by leadership experiences and self-efficacy, whereas motivation to lead variables predicted leadership potential ratings obtained from both assessment centers and 360-degree feedback. Arthur, Bell, Villado, and Doverspike (2006) also showed that the relationship between person–organization (P-O) fit variables and job performance were partially mediated by turnover intentions and organizational commitment, both of which can be seen as tapping motivational aspects of performance determinants. These and many other studies have illustrated how individual differences exert their influence on employee performance.

From the personnel selection perspective, these research findings are particularly useful because many mediator variables (training, experience, organizational characteristics) tend to be uniformly applied to all organizational members (i.e., every newcomer receives the same training course); so, in the absence of random work events or moderators, the rank order of individuals on many important performance dimensions is determined by their rank order on distal individual difference variables. The strength of direct effects may vary depending on which individual difference and performance variables are used, but many effects are appreciable enough to make a real difference to an organization's bottom line.

CHAPTER OUTLINE

In this chapter, we focus primarily on three broad domains of individual differences: (a) cognitive and psychomotor abilities, (b) personality, and (c) motives, values, and interests. This grouping follows B. W. Roberts's (2006) neosocioanalytic model of personality, which also includes *narratives* in the three classes of individual differences, a concept akin to what I/O psychologists call personal history or biographical data. Further, although narratives are clearly acquired throughout one's life, the endurance of personal histories and their role in influencing subsequent behavior places them within the individual differences domain, rather than within situational mediators or immediate performance determinants.

Recognizing that a detailed account of research in each of these domains is beyond the scope of this chapter, we only briefly review the predominant taxonomies and highlight the similarities and differences of various classification systems. We focus instead on approaches to measuring individual differences and using the test scores for selection and classification. Key findings related to validity, adverse impact, measurement bias, and faking are reviewed, as are emerging issues connected to Web-based testing and computerized adaptive testing (CAT), which is gradually propagating from large educational testing programs into I/O settings. The advantages and challenges of implementing and maintaining this new technology are discussed using examples from the noncognitive domain, in recognition of a broadened perspective on the performance criterion that now includes factors such as citizenship performance, counterproductivity, organizational adjustment, and adaptability. We address personality assessment, in particular, because there are so many unresolved psychometric and substantive questions and a growing body of evidence suggesting that personality factors predict performance and retention well beyond general cognitive ability and with far less adverse impact. (See also chap. 5, this volume.)

Because each individual difference domain can be seen as organized hierarchically from broad to narrow (B. W. Roberts, 2006), we begin each section with a brief overview of existing trait taxonomies, and we then discuss salient issues in measurement and scoring that may be domain specific. We begin with cognitive ability and then move to personality and vocational interests.

In the cognitive ability domain, the broadest construct is, of course, general cognitive ability, often referred to as *g*. The medium level of specificity includes fluid and crystallized intelligences, *Gf* and *Gc*, which subsume narrower domains such as word knowledge, reading comprehension, mathematical reasoning, inductive reasoning, and deductive reasoning. We start with Spearman's original (1904) model of intelligence, which hypothesized *g* and a specific ability for each domain. We then contrast Thurstone's (1938) findings of correlated primary abilities but no general ability. The resolution of the debate between these two camps is described via Schmid and Leiman's (1957) transformation and its modern alternative, the bifactor model. The most widely accepted current model of intelligence, Carroll's (1993) three-stratum theory, is then described. We conclude this section with a review of issues surrounding the use of cognitive ability test scores for job selection and licensure and certification.

In the personality domain, there is still considerable debate concerning the structure of personality at both the broad (global) factor and narrow (lower order) factor levels. We therefore review the most predominant higher order (global) factor trait taxonomy, the Big Five (Costa & McCrae, 1988; Goldberg, 1990, 1993) and then explore Ashton et al.'s (2004) HEXACO model, and the seven-factor models proposed by Almagor, Tellegen, and Waller (1995) and Saucier (2003). We then focus on lower order factors, which are sometimes referred to as *facets*, and discuss reasons why the measurement of facets is becoming more common in organizational research and practice. Finally, we draw attention to the numerous challenges associated with the use of personality measures in applied settings. Specifically, we discuss new psychometric models for scaling personality statements, formats designed to reduce response distortion, and how advances in measurement technology are being used to customize and increase the efficiency of personality assessment.

The third broad domain of individual differences is values. B. W. Roberts (2006) defined this construct as consisting of "all of the things that people feel are desirable—that is, what people want to do or would like to have in their life" (p. 7). As an illustration, we review Schwartz's (1992) model of human values and discuss how this and other models are used in the rapidly growing research area of P-O fit. We place vocational interests at the medium level of generality in the values domain and describe Holland's (1985) RIASEC model (realistic [R], investigative [I], artistic [A], social [S], enterprising [E], and conventional [C]). We then discuss some alternative ways of representing vocational interests (Tracey & Rounds, 1996) and the potential ramifications for using interest scores for vocational counseling, selection, and classification. (See also Vol. 3, chaps. 1 and 4, this handbook.)

The final trait category in the neo-socioanalytic model is narratives, that is, the stories people use to understand and explain themselves, their environments, and the actions of others. B. W. Roberts (2006) described narratives as helping people "create meaning and purpose in their lives and predictability in the events they observe and experience, and provide explanations of how people have come to be in their present circumstances" (p. 9). In a broad sense, information provided by narratives is already used in many selection systems. Information in personal statements, letters of recommendation, and unstructured interviews is often examined qualitatively and is used to make or support selection and promotion decisions. When this information is collected systematically using biodata forms or structured interviews, it is more readily quantified and has potentially higher validity. This section summarizes important research findings involving narrative data and highlights some unresolved questions about measurement and verification.

COGNITIVE ABILITY

The modern study of intelligence began with Spearman's seminal article in 1904 in which he introduced his "two-factor" theory of intelligence. Spearman labeled the first factor g, or general ability, which he assumed influenced performance in all domains. The second factor actually refers to a category, rather than a particular ability. Spearman hypothesized that performance in any domain was influenced by g as well as a specific factor that was unique to the domain. Thus, performance across domains was correlated because of the shared influence of g, but the correlation was less than perfect because each domain was influenced by an independent specific factor. Performance in physics, for example, is influenced by g and a specific ability in physics.

If data from a set of tests administered to a broad sample of individuals are factor analyzed, the first factor ordinarily provides a surprisingly good fit (see Drasgow, 2003, p. 110). Nonetheless, clear failures of the model can be seen in terms of large residuals unless the set of tests to be analyzed is carefully preselected. This led Spearman's students and junior colleagues to develop hierarchical models. These models have g at the apex as a single, broad trait that affects performance in all areas. Vernon (1950), for example, included two middle-level traits: *v:ed,* which refers to verbal–educational ability and was used to explain relations among reading comprehension, logical reasoning, and arithmetic reasoning, and *k:m,* which refers to spatial–mechanical ability. Hierarchical models with g influencing performance on all tests and midlevel traits affecting clusters of tests provide better fits to data than Spearman's original model.

Thurstone (1938) took a different approach to the study of human intelligence. In a landmark study, 218 University of Chicago students completed a battery of 56 tests. Thurstone extracted a dozen factors, and, after rotation, seven primary mental abilities were identified: spatial, perceptual, numerical, verbal relations, word fluency, memory, and inductive reasoning. To analyze his data, Thurstone had developed multiple factor analysis (Thurstone, 1947), with correlated factors defined by rotation to simple structure. Using his new methods, Thurstone did not find a general factor, only multiple correlated factors. This led to an acrimonious debate between Thurstone and the American group, on the one hand, and Spearman and the British group, on the other, concerning the existence of the general factor g.

This debate was resolved in 1957 when Schmid and Leiman showed the mathematical equivalence of models with correlated factors and higher order factor models with second-order general factors and orthogonal first-order factors. Conceptually, the Schmid and Leiman analysis can be seen as subjecting the factor correlation matrices obtained by Thurstone and others for batteries of ability tests to factor analysis. The resulting factor or factors are termed *second-order factors.* When the factor correlation matrix obtained from a battery of tests is subjected to this analysis, a single, strong second-order factor is often obtained.

Carroll (1993) described the results of a remarkably extensive literature review and reanalysis of factor analytic studies of cognitive ability. He identified 461 correlation matrices suitable for reanalysis (i.e., data from a broad sample were collected, at least three measures were included for each factor hypothesized, and a reasonably large number of factors were included). Carroll's findings were summarized in his three stratum model of intelligence, which is shown in Figure 4.2.

In the three-stratum model, as in Spearman's two-factor model and Vernon's hierarchical model, g sits at the apex and explains the most variance. Carroll found many second-level factors (Figure 4.2 contains eight of the most important), including fluid intelligence *Gf* and crystallized intelligence *Gc*. The length of the lines from g to each of the second stratum abilities is inversely related to the strength of the relationship, so that *Gf* and *Gc* are the most strongly related to g. Stratum I factors lie beneath the second stratum and refer to narrower traits. For example, deduction, induction, and quantitative reasoning are some examples of first stratum traits beneath *Gf* and verbal ability, reading comprehension, and lexical knowledge are examples of Stratum I traits beneath *Gc*.

Yung, Thissen, and McLeod (1999) explored the relation between Schmid and Leiman's (1957) higher order factor model and the increasingly popular hierarchical factor model, which includes the bifactor model as a special case. In the bifactor model, every test is allowed to load on a general factor and then sets of tests load on additional factors. Each test is allowed to load on exactly two factors (the general factor and one additional specific factor) and all factors are constrained to be uncorrelated. Yung et al. showed that the Schmid-Leiman higher order factor model is equivalent to the hierarchical factor model with additional constraints imposed. For example, they showed that the nonzero factor loadings of columns 1 and 2 of the factor loading matrix in their Table 1 have a 4:3 ratio. Here, Test 1 has a loading of .512 on Factor 1, so it has a loading of .384 (= .512 × ¾) on Factor 2 and Test 2 has a loading of .576 on Factor 1 and therefore a loading of .432 (= .576 × ¾) on Factor 2. There does not appear to be any substantive meaning to these proportionality constraints; they are simply a result of the "factor analyze a factor correlation matrix" strategy taken by Schmid and Leiman. Thus, with modern structural equations software, the more general hierarchical model seems preferable to higher order factor models. It has fewer constraints and therefore should fit even better than the models Carroll (1993) fit to find support for his three-stratum model.

Today, there appears to be a scientific consensus that human cognitive abilities are organized hierarchically. At the top of the hierarchy is the general factor; at the level below are fluid and crystallized intelligence factors (also sometimes represented as verbal, quantitative, and abstract reasoning factors) and several memory, perception, and cognitive speed

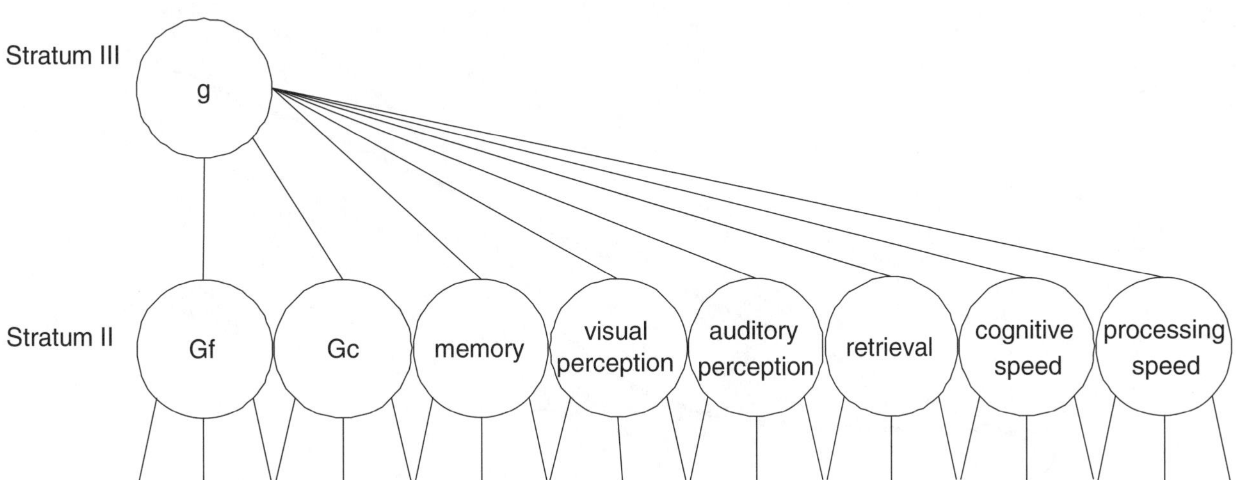

FIGURE 4.2. Carroll's three-stratum model. From *Handbook of Psychology: Industrial and Organizational Psychology* (p. 115), by W. C. Borman and D. R. Ilger (Eds.), 2003, New York: Wiley. Reprinted with permission.

factors; finally, at the third level are narrow factors representing fairly specific cognitive performances associated with higher order factors. This hierarchy is useful because it provides ways to account for variation among existing cognitive ability tests and performances and often serves as a basis for future test development efforts. It also allows researchers and practitioners to appreciate fully the strength of the general factor in terms of predicting both organizational and personal level outcomes. As many research studies have shown, unless the criterion being measured is very specific, there is usually little incremental validity beyond the general cognitive ability factor in predicting job performance (Ree, Earles, & Teachout, 1994) and training performance (Ree & Earles, 1991), and so a single score from a general intelligence measure is usually sufficient to make most selection decisions.

Assessment: Dominance Models: Classical Test Theory and Item Response Theory

Reliable and valid assessment of cognitive abilities and intellectual achievement is immensely important in many fields of psychology. Regardless of the psychometric framework within which one works, most models for cognitive ability data assume a dominance (Coombs, 1964) relationship between trait level and the probability of obtaining a correct response or a particular test score. Specifically, the more of the trait one possesses, the better the examinee's chance of answering the item correctly or earning a high test score. Classical test theory (CTT) and linear factor analysis assume the relationship between trait level and expected score is linear, whereas item response theory models typically allow for nonlinear but monotonically increasing relationships, making them particularly useful for binary data. If we were to plot the probability of observing a correct response as a function of examinee ability level for any item in a cognitive ability scale, the two psychometric frameworks would produce trace lines, known as *item response functions (IRFs)*, similar to those presented in Figure 4.3. The straight line curve represents CTT and linear factor analytic models. The monotonically increasing S-shaped curve is characteristic of item response theory (IRT) models such as the three-parameter logistic model (3PL; Birnbaum, 1968), which posits that each item has a discrimination parameter, a difficulty parameter, and lower asymptote (aka guessing) parameter (for details, see Hulin, Drasgow, & Parsons, 1983). Note that unlike the linear IRF, the 3PL IRF does not assume that the item is equally discriminating across all trait levels, as indicated by the flattening of the slope at the high and low ends of the trait continuum. In fact, the response probabilities show rapid change over the

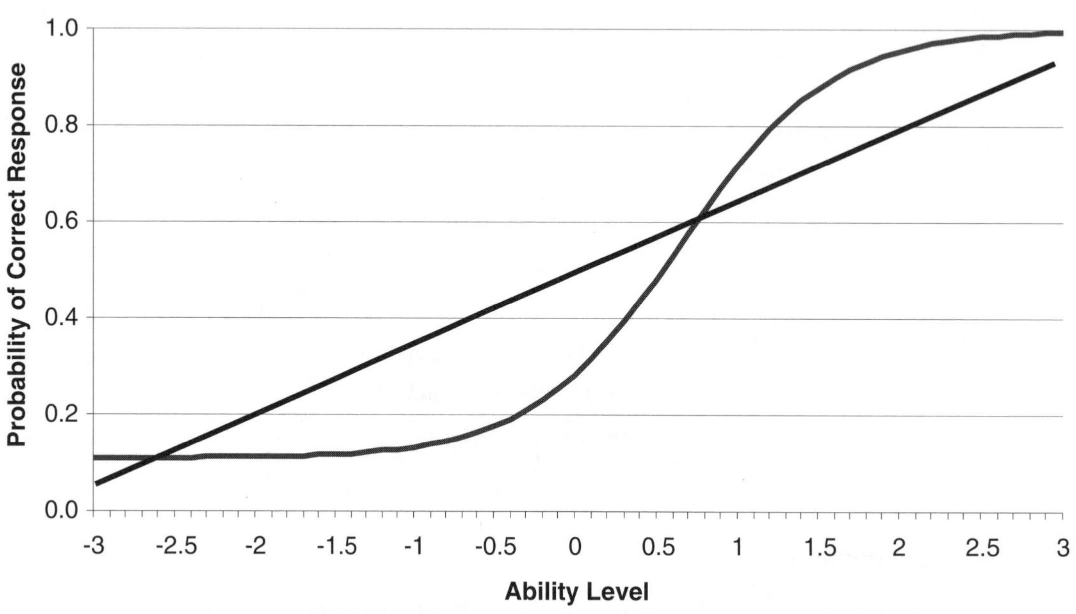

FIGURE 4.3. Example item response functions for linear and nonlinear dominance models.

interval +.20 to +1.20, which indicates that the item measures best for examinees located in that trait range and provides relatively little information about examinees located beyond. That nonlinear models can be used to examine how item information changes across the trait continuum makes them particularly suitable as the basis for CAT. In essence, CAT algorithms seek to identify and administer items or subsets of items that are most informative for each examinee, thus tailoring tests to increase score accuracy and reduce measurement error with the fewest number of items. The simplest example would be a test of mathematical achievement. In IRT, items involving simple algebraic operations are typically "easy" and would allow differentiation between examinees with very low or low ability scores (e.g., third graders vs. fifth graders), whereas items involving differential calculus are "difficult" and thus would be administered to differentiate among high-ability individuals. It would make little sense, however, to give calculus items to third graders or simple algebra items to examinees with degrees in statistics, because neither item group would differentiate within the inappropriate ability group.

Linear models would not make sense here because they assume that an item is equally informative for all examinees, so the same set of items would be seen as appropriate for all examinees. Classical test theory methods treat all items as equally important, and for that reason total score is often a simple sum of item responses; factor scores from linear factor analysis might weight items by their factor loadings, but the value of an item does not change across examinees with different standings on the latent trait.

A wide variety of cognitive ability measures are used in organizational settings. Because assessment time is often at a premium, most tests are relatively short and focus mainly on general cognitive ability. Perhaps the three best examples are the Wonderlic Personnel Test (WPT; Wonderlic Personnel Test, Inc., 1992), Raven's Progressive Matrices (Raven, Raven, & Court, 1998), and the Watson–Glaser Test of Critical Reasoning (Watson & Glaser, 1980). The WPT takes only 12 minutes to administer; contains a combination of vocabulary, arithmetic reasoning, and spatial reasoning items (Grubb, Whetzel, & McDaniel, 2004); and yields a single score that reflects an examinee's general cognitive ability. Several parallel forms of the WPT test are available to allow for retesting. The Raven's test, in contrast, consists exclusively of abstract reasoning items, which increase in difficulty as the test progresses. There are standard and advanced forms, both of which have multiple parallel versions and, like the Wonderlic, the Raven's yields a single score reflecting general cognitive ability, although arguably it assesses fluid intelligence. The Watson–Glaser Test contains 80 reading passages aimed at assessing several critical reasoning skills (i.e., drawing inferences, recognizing assumptions) that are mostly part of the crystallized intelligence factor. The test is designed to be fairly difficult and thus is used mainly to assess applicants' managerial potential. Parallel and shorter forms of the test are also available to allow retesting or to accommodate limited testing times. Manuals for these three tests, as well as others, usually provide extensive information with regard to their construct and predictive validity, availability of norms, and test administration procedures.

Tests such as these are usually constructed on the basis of CTT principles and are scored simply as "number correct." Most are available in both paper-and-pencil and computerized formats, although the latter are typically just electronic "page turners" (Drasgow & Olson-Buchanan, 1999) that present the same items in the same order as the paper-and-pencil forms. The continuing reliance on CTT does not necessarily mean that test developers are unaware of IRT and its benefits. Rather, it is a testament to the astounding success of such relatively straightforward measures for selecting the best performing employees. As long as a test contains a mix of easy, medium, and difficult items, the resulting CTT-based scores should provide a fairly good rank order of examinees in terms of their cognitive abilities, so any gains in precision that might be achieved by implementing more sophisticated and costly methods of item selection and scoring might be difficult to justify.

On the other side of the cognitive ability testing spectrum are standardized selection and classification tests. These measures take full advantage of the factor analytic research on the latent structure of cognitive ability and often use IRT techniques to evaluate and administer items and score examinees.

The most prominent example is the Armed Services Vocational Aptitude Battery (ASVAB), which is used to select and classify hundreds of thousands of recruits into hundreds of military occupational specialties (Campbell & Knapp, 2001). This is accomplished, in part, by using nine subtests (General Science, Arithmetic Reasoning, Word Knowledge, Paragraph Comprehension, Auto and Shop Information, Mathematics Knowledge, Mechanical Comprehension, Electronics Information, and Assembling Objects) to measure an array of specific skills, knowledge, and abilities rather than just one or a few broad dimensions.

The primary difference with respect to general cognitive ability tests, such as those just described, is that the ASVAB has a strong knowledge component (e.g., Electronics Information, Auto and Shop Information) that enhances its usefulness for predicting performance in technical jobs. The second difference is that rather than yielding only one ability score, the ASVAB yields nine subtest scores, which can be combined to form many composites for classification decisions. Today, the ASVAB is administered in both paper-and-pencil and computerized formats. The computerized version (i.e., CAT-ASVAB; Segall & Moreno, 1999) selects items adaptively and thus provides high measurement precision with fewer items. Scores on various "forms" are then equated using statistical methods commonly applied in large-scale educational testing programs (see Kolen & Brennan, 2004).

Using Cognitive Ability Measures in Selection: Validity, Effects of Range Restriction and Attenuation, and Adverse Impact

The meta-analytic estimate of the correlation between general cognitive ability and job performance is .51, and the estimate of the correlation with training performance is .53 (Schmidt & Hunter, 1998). Moreover, job complexity appears to moderate the relationship between ability and performance, with the relationship being even stronger than .51 for highly complex jobs (Hunter, 1980; Schmidt & Hunter, 2004). Such findings are not limited to studies conducted in U.S. work settings. Salgado et al. (2003), for example, reported similar validities for job and training performance in European Union Countries and also found that job complexity acted as a moderator.

It is important to note that these validity estimates are based on meta-analyses involving hundreds if not thousands of studies. In any particular organization, however, it is unlikely that one would observe validity coefficients of such magnitude. This is because measurement artifacts such as criterion unreliability and predictor range restriction can severely reduce the observed correlations between predictors and criteria. Range restriction is particularly problematic when assessing the usefulness of a test because almost any organizational sample has been subjected to direct or indirect range restriction, self-selection effects, or both, which reduce the variance of trait scores and thus the correlations with criterion measures. To say it differently, because performance data can only be collected from those already selected into the organization, one can never know what the true validity of a predictor is, unless selection is at random or every applicant has been selected. The best known example of how range restriction can reduce observed correlation coefficients was given by Thorndike (1949). Because of a severe shortage of pilots during World War II, the U.S. military had to take everyone in a group of 1,036 volunteers, even though only 136 of these men would have ordinarily qualified for pilot training (i.e., received a passing score on a cognitive ability composite). The observed correlation between the cognitive composite and pilot training performance was .64 for the full sample but would have been only .18 if the selection process had followed the normal procedure (i.e., if only the 136 men with passing cognitive composite scores were actually selected).

Unreliability of the criterion can also severely reduce (aka attenuate) observed predictor–criterion relationships because it is not uncommon for supervisor ratings to show reliabilities in only the .5 to .6 range (Viswesvaran, Ones, & Schmidt, 1996). This happens because unreliability increases the proportion of random variance contained in the criterion score, thus reducing the proportion of explainable variance. Consequently, correlation coefficients appear small, unless we remove or partial out the random variance component. For these reasons, various corrections for attenuation and range restriction have been developed (Gulliksen, 1950) and are used to gauge more accurately the usefulness of a test for a specific group of applicants.

The validity results just described notwithstanding, the use of cognitive ability tests for selection and promotion continue to raise concerns about fairness because of their impact on selection rates for members of protected groups, as defined by the Civil Rights Act of 1964. Criticisms of cognitive ability tests are fueled by differences in test score means across majority and minority groups, and the popular belief is that these differences result from measurement bias (i.e., a psychometric problem with the instruments). However, most studies suggest that these differences do not result from bias but rather from impact, which is defined as a difference in the underlying trait distributions at the time of testing (Stark, Chernyshenko, & Drasgow, 2004). Thus, a more fruitful path for future research might be to focus on the motivational and educational factors that influence test performance, rather than endlessly searching for fundamental flaws in current ability measures. Another avenue would be to augment selection batteries with measures of noncognitive constructs, such as personality or situational judgment tests, because they seem to provide incremental validity with minimal, if any, adverse impact (Lievens, Buyse, & Sackett, 2005; Olson-Buchanan et al., 1998).

Internet or computer-based delivery of selection tests has grown rapidly in recent years as advances in computer technology have rapidly expanded the options available for psychological assessment. In fact, computerized assessments have many distinct advantages over paper-and-pencil tests, such as the introduction of new item types (e.g., video-based scenarios, in-basket simulations), immediacy of scoring and feedback, and improved test security. When used in conjunction with adaptive testing algorithms, computerized assessments provide increased testing accuracy and efficiency because items are selected to match an examinee's skill level. Hence, adaptive tests do not contain items that are too easy or too difficult for a particular examinee. Proctored administration, such as provided by commercial computer-based testing organizations, can be obtained for a fairly hefty per hour of seat-time fee. Alternatively, many organizations have turned to unproctored Internet testing in which job applicants can take assessments at times and places of their choosing. Of course, with unproctored testing, there is no assurance that the job applicant is the person who actually answered the test items. This has led to controversy (Tippins et al., 2006) about the efficacy and ethicality of this form of assessment. One suggestion is to require individuals passing the unproctored Internet test to take a proctored confirmation test before receiving a job offer (Segall, 2001); another option is to use computer video technology to capture an applicant's image while he or she is taking the test for verification purposes. Research to date, however, has not found evidence of test compromise (Nye, Do, Drasgow, & Fine, 2008). Nonetheless, if applicants believe that the stakes are high enough, some will cheat. More work is needed to delineate the conditions under which applicants will, or will not, be tempted to increase their scores by seeking improper aid.

A Note About Physical and Psychomotor Abilities

Tests of physical and psychomotor abilities are often administered together with various cognitive ability measures to select police officers, firefighters, military personnel, clerical workers, or professional athletes. In fact, motor coordination and finger dexterity subtests have long been a part of many civil service exams administered in the U.S. Employment Service (e.g., the General Aptitude Test Battery). However, as Carroll (1993) pointed out, most physical and psychomotor tests have low correlations with cognitive ability tests, and thus should be considered as part of a distinct domain of individual differences. Most commonly measured factors in this domain are the following: static strength, body equilibrium, reaction time, speed and coordination of limb–wrist–finger movements, finger–manual dexterity, arm–hand steadiness, and aim (Caroll, 1993; Fleishman, 1964; see also Hogan's [1991] comprehensive review of the literature on physical abilities). In jobs in which excellent vision or hearings are required, various components of these sensory modes are also commonly measured.

Although many physical and psychomotor factors appear to be relevant and even necessary to perform certain jobs, the ways these factors have been measured and passing standards set have attracted substantial employment litigation (see Hogan & Quigley, 1986). For example, minimum height or weight requirements have often been arbitrarily set (perhaps as proxy measures of physical strength), resulting in a disproportional underselection of female applicants (*Medows v. Ford Motor Co.*) or Spanish Americans (*Guardians Association v. Civil Service Commission*). In the majority of such cases, the courts ruled in favor of the plaintiff and prohibited further use of such tests. Hence, organizations interested in using physical and psychomotor ability measures for selection and classification must ensure that these tests are nondiscriminatory or, if not possible, are job related and equally valid nondiscriminatory alternatives are unavailable.

PERSONALITY

Broad and Narrow Taxonomic Structures

The Big Five theory brought order to the somewhat chaotic research literature on the structure of personality. Before the Big Five, there was little agreement about the basic dimensions of normal personality, so many instruments and scales conceptualized the trait domain in their own unique ways (e.g., Gough, 1957). One consequence of this was that early reviews attempting to combine validities of various personality instruments found near zero correlations with important work outcomes (e.g., Guion & Gottier, 1965). These grim empirical findings were accompanied by the theoretical arguments of Mischel (1968, 1969, 1973) and his colleagues, who contended that the behavior of individuals was not sufficiently consistent across time and situations to allow valid predictions by means of personality measures (they cited the fact that observed validity coefficients for personality have rarely exceeded .30 and most are in the .10–.20 range). Fortunately, since the early 1990s, personality researchers have reached a consensus that the Big Five personality constructs, Extraversion, Agreeableness, Conscientiousness, Emotional Stability, and Openness to Experience, are sufficient to adequately describe the basic dimensions of normal personality (see Borkenau & Ostendorf, 1990; Costa & McCrae, 1988; Digman, 1990; Goldberg, 1990, 1993; McCrae & Costa, 1987). It is important that numerous studies have been conducted to map existing inventories onto the Big Five structure (e.g., Chernyshenko, Stark, & Chan, 2001; McCrae, Costa, & Piedmont, 1993), which facilitates integration of the vast empirical literature. Today, most personality test manuals include a section detailing how their scales and/or scale composites relate to the Big Five (e.g., Conn & Reike, 1994).

Of course, as with any taxonomic model, there is some debate whether the proposed factors are indeed sufficient to describe basic personality. In their HEXACO model, Ashton et al. (2004) argued for a six-factor solution. Almagor, Tellegen, and Waller (1995) and Saucier (2003), in contrast, have proposed even more elaborate seven-factor structures. All these authors have suggested that one or two extra evaluative dimensions (e.g., positive evaluation, negative evaluation, honesty) are needed in addition to the Big Five (B. W. Roberts, 2006). Similarly, although the Big Five model has been fairly well replicated in many countries and cultures, some cross-cultural researchers have suggested that additional dimensions may be beneficial (e.g., F. M. Cheung et al., 2001). These disagreements are not surprising given that the researchers are attempting to partition a large and heterogeneous set of behaviors, feelings, and thoughts using factor analytic methods. The number of factors extracted depends on what variables are included in the analyses, their psychometric properties, and the degree of heterogeneity researchers are willing to tolerate in their solutions. The hierarchical nature of the personality domain effectively ensures that one could continue extracting factors as long as desired, but each successive iteration would reconfigure the available factor space into increasingly narrow parts.

Although research into basic personality structures continues to be important, we want to draw attention to emerging research on narrower personality dimensions known as facets. Facets can be seen as more contextualized manifestations of broad personality factors (B. W. Roberts, 2006). For example, Conscientiousness can be seen as an overall tendency to exercise a certain degree of control over one's internal or external environment and thus includes a range of behavioral patterns and thoughts such as industriousness, responsibility, orderliness, self-control, virtue, and rule following (B. W. Roberts, Chernyshenko, Stark, & Goldberg, 2005). Order is particular to external features of one's immediate environment and reflects the extent to which one organizes and plans things, whereas Industriousness, which refers to one's drive to achieve goals and other outcomes, also reflects an attempt to control one's environment, but the emphasis is on more distal or far-reaching contextual features. One reason facets are important is that employee performance behaviors occur in specific organizational contexts, such as power relations (e.g., leadership), social exchanges (e.g., citizenship), or evaluations of one's costs and rewards (turnover). Hence, there is often a closer match between behaviors involved in a particular performance dimension and those pertaining to one or more narrow facets than with broad personality factors, which results in facets having higher predictive validities. Paunonen (1998) correlated several Big Five factor and facet measures with various behavioral criteria and concluded that "aggregating personality traits into their underlying personality factors could result in decreased predictive accuracy due to the loss of trait-specific but criterion-valid variance" (p. 538); other researchers have reached similar conclusions (e.g., Ashton, 1998; Mershon & Gorsuch, 1988). In the Ashton (1998) study, for example, the correlation between counterproductive work behaviors and scores on the Responsibility facet was −.40, but a correlation of only −.22 was obtained when a broad measure of Conscientiousness was used in place of the facet measure.

From a theory-building perspective, using facets translates into stronger theory because more precise hypotheses about employee behavior can be generated and tested. For example, Moon (2001) found that it is the Order facet of Conscientiousness that drives early job performance because organized employees are often more effective in dealing with the overwhelming amount of information that accompanies new jobs. In the long run, however, it is the Industriousness facet of Conscientiousness that drives performance because people who score high on this facet tend to set more difficult goals and work harder to achieve them.

Another important reason for studying facets is that it will help to clarify the conceptualization of broader factors (Briggs, 1989; Saucier & Ostendorf, 1999). Currently, there are inconsistencies in the way broad factors are defined. For example, in the widely popular NEO Personality Inventory (NEO-PI) model, Costa and McCrae (1994) place the Warmth facet, which includes emotionally supportive behaviors and displays of unconditional positive regard for others, within their Extraversion factor, whereas the abridged Big Five dimensional circumplex model (AB5C; Hofstee, De Raad, & Goldberg, 1992) locates it within Agreeableness. Better clarity in broad factor definitions is particularly important for meta-analyses of personality–performance relationships because the misplacement of facets could bias validity estimates or be a source of disagreement among various research groups. Finally, from an applied perspective, narrow traits offer much higher fidelity in terms of personality description and thus enhance the diagnostic value of assessment. This is especially beneficial for respondents who fall in the middle of the distribution on a measure of a broad factor, because such scores can be obtained in many ways. Unlike extreme scores on a broad factor, which suggest that an individual is generally high or low on all subcomponents, middle scores can be attained by being average on all lower order components or high on some and low on others.

A number of narrow trait taxonomies have been proposed to date. Among the most widely known are the 45-facet structure of the AB5C model (Hofstee, De Raad, & Goldberg, 1992) and the 30-facet structure of the NEO-PI (Costa, McCrae, & Dye, 1991). In both cases, the researchers used a combination of prior empirical studies, theoretical justifications, and intuitions to divide each Big Five factor into an equal number of facets. Another way to establish narrow trait taxonomies is to adopt a purely empirical stance and to conduct a series of factor analyses using examinees' responses to a diverse array of personality indicators (e.g., adjectives, behavioral statements, or scales). A good example of such an effort is the 22-facet narrow-order taxonomy of the Tailored Adaptive Personality Assessment System (TAPAS; Stark, Drasgow, & Chernyshenko, 2008), which is currently being tried for use with the ASVAB to facilitate military personnel selection and classification decisions. The TAPAS taxonomy, shown in Table 4.1, combines the results of Saucier

TABLE 4.1

Tailored Adaptive Personality Assessment System Facet Taxonomy Derived From Lexical and Questionnaire-Based Factor Analytic Studies

Lower order facets		Known facet markers	
Questionnaire-based studies	Lexical study	Adjectives	Existing scales
		Big Five factor: Conscientiousness	
Achievement	Industriousness	Ambitious, industrious, aimless,	NEO Competence, NEO Achievement Striving, AB5C Purposefulness
Order	Order	Organized, neat, disorganized, sloppy	AB5C Orderliness, NEO Order, 16PF Perfectionism, JPI Organization
Self-Control	Decisiveness	Decisive, firm, controlled, deliberate, inconsistent	AB5C Cautiousness, NEO Deliberation, MPQ Self-Control, HPI Impulse Control
Responsibility	Reliability	Dependable, responsible, prompt, unreliable	CPI Responsibility, CPI Achievement via Conformance, CPI Socialization, JPI Responsibility
Nondelinquency		Traditional, lawful, delinquent, law-abiding	MPQ Traditionalism, JPI Traditional, 16PF Rule Consciousness
Virtue		Honest, truthful, frank, honorable, deceitful,	CPI Good Impression, CPI Self-Control, HPI Virtuous
		Big Five factor: Openness to Experience	
Intellectual efficiency	Intellect	Intelligent, analytical, knowledgeable,	HPI Education, HPI Good Memory, CPI Intellectual Efficiency, AB5C Intellect
Ingenuity	Imagination	Creative, inventive, unimaginative	AB5C Ingenuity, HPI Generates Ideas, JPI Innovation
Curiosity	Perceptiveness	Curious, perceptive, insightful, unobservant,	16PF Sensitivity, HPI Curiosity, HPI Science Ability
Aesthetics		Aesthetic, artistic, musical, unsophisticated, unrefined	NEO Aesthetics, AB5C Reflection, MPQ Absorption, NEO Feelings, HPI Culture, AB5C Imagination, JPI Breadth
Tolerance		Tolerant, broadminded, biased	CPI Flexibility, NEO Values, JPI Tolerant
Depth		Introspective, reflective, philosophical, shallow	16PF Abstractness, AB5C Depth, AB5C Introspection, JPI Complexity
		Big Five factor: Extraversion	
Dominance	Assertiveness	Assertive, direct, bold, weak, submissive, feeble	CPI Dominance, HPI Leadership, NEO Assertiveness, MPQ Social Potency
Sociability	Sociability	Sociable, gregarious, talkative, withdrawn	CPI Sociability, CPI Social Presence, 16PF Social Boldness, HPI No Social Anxiety
Excitement seeking	Unrestraint	Loud, loquacious, entertaining, dull, unexciting, shy	16PF Liveliness, NEO Excitement Seeking, HPI Exhibitionistic, HPI Likes Crowds, HPI Entertaining
Physical condition	Adventurousness	Active, physical, adventurous, outdoorsy	JPI Energy, NEO Activity

TABLE 4.1 (*Continued*)

Lower order facets: Questionnaire-based studies	Lower order facets: Lexical study	Known facet markers: Adjectives	Known facet markers: Existing scales
		Big Five factor: Agreeableness	
Warmth	Warmth-Affectionate	Affectionate, compassionate, warm, cold, insensitive	AB5C Warmth,16PF Warmth, NEO Warmth, 16PF Self-Reliance, MPQ Social Closeness, NEO Positive Emotions
Generosity	Generosity	Charitable, helpful, generous, greedy, stingy, and selfish	CPI Femininity/Masculinity, 16PF Sensitivity, AB5C Sympathy, AB5C Tenderness, AB5C Understanding, AB5C Empathy
Cooperation	Gentleness	Agreeable, cordial, trusting, uncooperative, combative	AB5C Pleasantness, NEO Altruism, NEO Trust, HPI Easy to Live With
	Modesty	Modest, humble, conceited, snobbish, egocentric	
		Big Five factor: Emotional Stability	
No anxiety	Insecurity	Insecure, apprehensive, nervous, relaxed, certain	16PF Apprehensive, JPI anxiety, NEO Anxiety, HPI Not Anxious, MPQ Stress Reaction, JPI Cooperativeness,
Even temper	Irritability	Moody, hot-headed, calm, composed, temperamental	AB5C Calmness, AB5C Stability, AB5C Tranquility, NEO Hostility, HPI Even Tempered
Well-being	Emotionality	Happy, cheerful, optimistic, depressed, dejected	NEO Depression, AB5C Happiness, MPQ Well-Being, HPI No Guilt, 16PF Emotional Stability, CPI Well-Being

Note. Empty cells indicate that the dimensions do not appear in the lexical study or have equivalents. NEO = NEO Personality Inventory; AB5C = Big Five dimensional circumplex model; 16PF = Sixteen Personality Factor Questionnaire; JPI = Jackson Personality Inventory; MPQ = Multidimensional Personality Questionnaire; HPI = Hogan Personality Inventory; CPI = California Personality Inventory.

and Ostendorf's (1999) analyses of 312 vectors of responses to 500 temperament adjectives with a series of factor analyses of questionnaire data from several major personality inventories (see B. W. Roberts et al., 2005, for the Conscientiousness factor). Importantly, lexical and questionnaire-based studies produced remarkably similar facets structures, suggesting a reasonably good convergence across methods and different samples. Minor differences were observed in the Openness to Experience representation, which was most likely due to the lack of adjectives describing one's openness to non-intellectual stimuli (i.e., artistic, tolerant, or reflective) in the Saucier and Ostendorf (1999) study. There was also an Agreeableness facet, Modesty, produced by the lexical study, that failed to emerge in the questionnaire-based study. Interestingly, one of the main departures of Ashton and Lee's HEXACO model from the Big Five is the Honesty factor, which seems to be a combination of Modesty and Virtue and is a part of the Conscientiousness factor in the questionnaire-based study.

Table 4.1 presents the TAPAS narrow facet taxonomy derived from lexical and questionnaire-based studies, and, to facilitate interpretation of each facet, we list some adjectives and existing scale markers from such well-established inventories as the NEO-PI, the California Personality Inventory (CPI; Gough, 1957), the Sixteen Personality Factor Questionnaire (16PF; Conn & Rieke, 1994), the

Multidimensional Personality Questionnaire (MPQ; Tellegen,1982), the Jackson Personality Inventory (JPI; Jackson, 1994), the Hogan Personality Inventory (HPI; Hogan & Hogan, 1992), and the AB5C scales from the International Personality Item Pool (AB5C-IPIP; Goldberg, 1997). The table is organized around the Big Five factors, although this facet structure can be reconfigured to fit other broad factor taxonomies (i.e., the Virtue and Modesty facets can be combined into a separate Honesty factor). Alternatively, facets can be aggregated upward into somewhat broader dimensions, as was done by DeYoung, Quilty, and Peterson (2007).

Personality Assessment

There is no shortage of personality inventories measuring both broad and narrow Big Five traits. Among the most widely used for selection are the NEO PI, 16PF, HPI, and CPI. All these inventories were developed using classical test theory methods and comprise scales with 10 to 15 items that ask respondents about their typical behavior. The number of response categories varies for different inventories, but all require negatively worded items to be reversed scored before the total score computations. Further, although many of these measures have served well in research contexts, it is important to remember that they were not designed with high-stakes selection applications in mind (by "high stakes," we mean that personality scores are actually used to make decisions that carry significant monetary gains for an applicant). In a research context, the main goal is to examine patterns of covariation among variables, so a short scale with easy-to-understand item content and a straightforward response format is more than sufficient to provide a rough rank ordering of participants on the trait continua (as Drasgow & Kang, 1984, showed, correlations are robust). In a selection context, however, precision of measurement across a wide range of trait levels, test–retest capabilities, and at least some resistance to response distortions are needed. Recent research indicates that, to be useful in selection, not only considerable enhancements to current measures but, possibly, a change in the assessment approaches may be needed (White, Young, Hunter, & Rumsey, 2008). We discuss some of these assessment innovations in the next section.

Dominance versus ideal point models. The first issue is that CTT and Likert's (1932) approaches to scale construction may be inappropriate for personality items because they are based on dominance response process assumptions. Consider the following personality statement measuring Order: "When it comes to being clean and tidy, I am about average." Under the dominance model, respondents with increasingly higher scores on the Order facet should dominate this item and, thus, answer it *Agree* or *Strongly Agree.* Clearly, in the context of ability testing, dominance models make sense. For example, if respondents were asked to find an antonym to the word *dubious* among four alternatives, those with higher verbal aptitude would have higher probabilities of answering correctly.

However, research indicates that the process for the Order item above is different: Respondents with average orderliness tend to choose the *Agree* response, but those with either low or high orderliness tend to choose *Disagree* (Chernyshenko, Stark, Drasgow, & Roberts, 2007; Stark, Chernyshenko, Drasgow, & Williams, 2006). Coombs (1964) used the term *ideal point* to describe a response process in which individuals are more likely to endorse an item when it is close to them. The idea for ideal point models can be traced back to a series of remarkable papers by Louis Thurstone (1927, 1928, 1929) that developed theory and methods for measuring attitudes. However, Thurstone's methods for scaling attitude stimuli were laborious, and they were quickly replaced by Likert's techniques. Likert suggested identifying one end of the attitude continuum as positive, reverse-scoring items at the other end of the attitude continuum, and then computing a person's score as the sum of his or her item scores. He also suggested using item-total correlations to evaluate the quality of individual items. Interestingly, Likert (1932) found that items tending toward neutrality (aka intermediate items) had low item-total correlations, and thus he felt they should be eliminated. Thurstone, in contrast, deliberately included such items as he found them to be located in the middle of the scale, whereas items usually retained by Likert's approach were located either at the positive or the negative end of the scale.

How does this distinction between ideal point and dominance models affect personality assessment? First, the use of dominance models unnecessarily eliminates items located in the middle of the scale from consideration in the scale construction process. Items such as "My social skills are about average" or "I do a standard maintenance of my property and possessions, but rarely anything more" are not found in personality scales constructed under dominance process assumptions. That is because such items have IRF similar to the one shown in Figure 4.4. From the graph, it is clear that individuals having trait scores between −1 and +1 have a higher probability of endorsing the item than individuals at either extreme. Consequently, if one were to correlate the dichotomous item score with the total scale score, obtained by summing over the remaining items, the resulting item-total correlation would be small, thus suggesting that the item is virtually nondiscriminating and should be eliminated from consideration. However, the rapidly changing response probabilities between trait levels of −2 and −1 and between +1 and +2 indicate that the item discriminates well and provides high information for examinees located in those regions. Therefore, the commonly used yardsticks for judging the quality of items can be misleading if an ideal point response process applies.

Second, for sophisticated measurement applications, such as computerized adaptive testing and detection of differential item functioning across groups, it is important for one's psychometric model to provide a valid representation of the data. In such applications, a misspecified model can easily lead to incorrect results and conclusions. Third, this distinction becomes important for preferential choice items (i.e., pairwise preferences or tetrads or pentads), because one must explicitly specify how the choice for a given set of stimuli is made. Preferential choice items contain two or more personality statements from the same or different dimensions, and respondents are asked to choose statements that are most or least like them (or both). Will individuals select stimuli that are most descriptive of them (i.e., an ideal point process) or those that they most dominate (i.e., a dominance process)? Finally, important theoretical issues concerning the structure of personality hinge on psychometric analyses. For example, Ashton and Lee (2007) have argued for a six-dimensional model

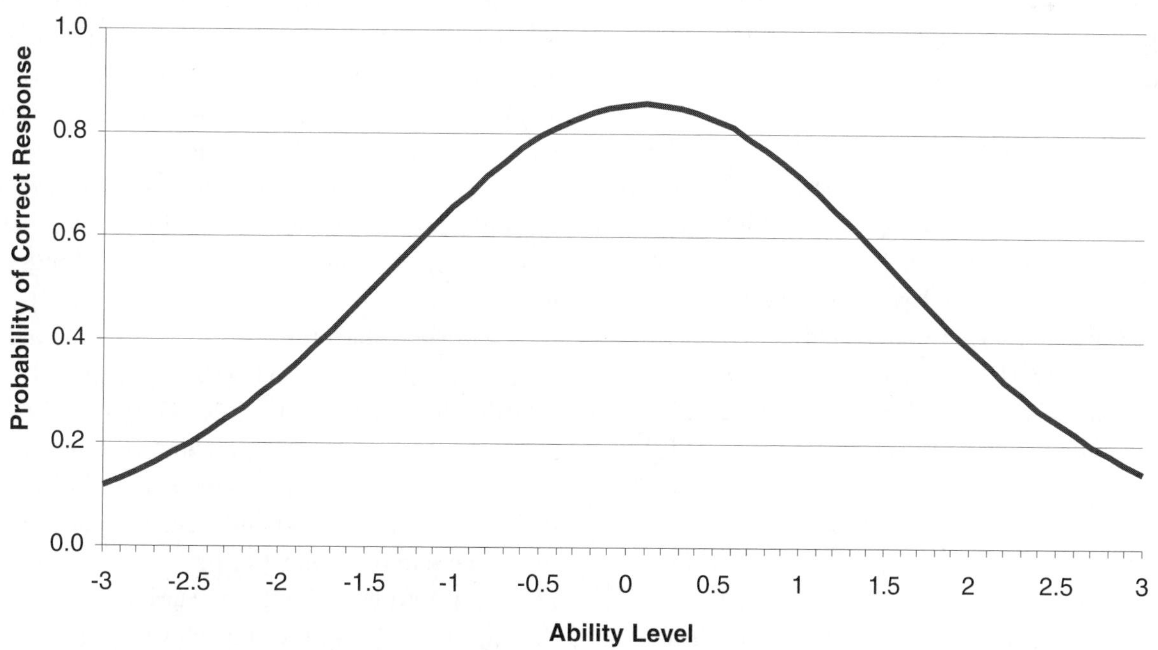

FIGURE 4.4. Example item response functions (IRF) for an intermediate item assuming an ideal point response process.

of personality on the basis of results from a dominance model analysis (i.e., factor analysis). If the model is misspecified, conclusions from such analyses should be drawn with less certainty.

Resistance to faking. Research comparing responses of applicants and nonapplicants on traditional personality measures clearly shows that applicants can increase their scores in socially desirable directions (Rosse, Stecher, Miller, & Levin, 1998; Stark, Chernyshenko, Chan, Lee, & Drasgow, 2001). Although there is some debate over the extent to which applicants actually do so, the experiences of military researchers show that the faking problem "has been one of the greatest challenges to the Army's ability to implement and sustain the operational, large-scale use of self-report personality measures, especially in high-stakes testing situations" (White et al., 2008, p. 291) and "High levels of faking . . . can lead to highly inflated test scores that have little or no criterion-related validity" (p. 292). Furthermore, approaches to detecting and correcting for faking that involve social desirability or impression management scales are only modestly effective because the scales misclassify too many honest individuals as fakers (Zickar & Drasgow, 1996). Because faking impairs the quality of hiring decisions by changing the rank order of applicants (Christiansen, Goffin, Johnston, & Rothstein, 1994), personality measures must be made more fake resistant before they can be successfully used in selection.

One of the promising avenues for making personality assessment more fake resistant is the multidimensional forced-choice (MFC) item format (Chernyshenko et al., 2009; Christiansen, Burns, & Montgomery, 2005; Heggestad, Morrison, Reeve, & McCloy, 2006; Jackson, Wrobleski, & Ashton, 2000; McCloy, Heggestad, & Reeve, 2005; Stark, 2002; Stark, Chernyshenko, & Drasgow, 2005; Vasilopoulos, Cucina, Dyomina, Morewitz, & Reilly, 2006; White & Young, 1998). In the MFC format, which actually dates back to the late 1940s and 1950s (Sisson, 1948), respondents are presented with a choice of two or more statements of similar desirability but different dimensions and asked to indicate which statement describes them more accurately. U.S. Army researchers recently implemented a variation of the forced-choice format in the Assessment of Individual Motivation (AIM; White & Young, 1998) inventory.

A prevalent MFC format has four statements (aka a tetrad) from which respondents are asked to select one statement that is "most like me" and another that is "least like me." By varying the number of statements representing each dimension and by assigning intermediate scores (1s) for statements that are not selected and 0s or 2s for selected statements, enough variation is introduced into the test scores to overcome the well-known problem of ipsativity and to recover normative information. Ipsative scores contain only information about the rank order of traits for a specific individual (i.e., trait profile) but do not indicate where an individual is actually located on those traits. Thus, ipsative scores can only be used for intraindividual comparisons (i.e., personal development feedback) but not selection or classification decisions requiring interindividual comparisons. Although several studies have shown criterion validity for such MFC measures and mixed results with respect to fakeability (Christiansen et al., 2005; Heggestad et al., 2006; Jackson et al, 2000; White & Young, 1998), formal measurement models for tetrad approaches have not been developed to date. Moreover, because of the complexity of the processes underlying respondents' judgments involving four dimensions simultaneously, we suspect that any measurement model would be quite complex. Thus, it appears that many measurement analyses and applications, such as determination of reliability, computer-adaptive testing, differential item and test functioning, and person fit analysis, would be difficult to devise and implement.

A more tractable MFC format is the pairwise preference judgment. Andrich (1989); Borman et al. (2001); Chernyshenko et al. (2009); Stark (2002); Stark and Drasgow (2002); and Stark et al. (2005) and proposed and evaluated several IRT models for both unidimensional and multidimensional pairwise preferences in the context of personality, performance, and attitude assessment. Stark's (2002) Multidimensional Pairwise Preference (MDPP) model, which was designed specifically for multidimensional pairwise preference data, seems to be particularly attractive for high-stakes personality assessment. The MDPP model assumes that respondents consider whether each statement in a two-alternative forced choice judgment accurately describes them. The generalized graded unfolding model (J. S. Roberts, Donoghue, & Laughlin, 2000) is used to characterize the process of evaluating the individual statements. Ultimately, the respondents pick the one statement in a pair that better describes them.

In the MDPP model, each statement in a pool of personality statements can be paired with many others to form pairwise preference items. If there are no "enemies" (i.e., pairs of statements that cannot be allowed together in an item), a set of 20 statements would generate $\binom{20}{2} = \frac{20 \cdot 19}{2} = 190$ items. A pool of 1,000 statements would generate close to a half a million unique pairs, so even if additional constraints were introduced for pairing statements (e.g., requiring similar social desirabilities), tens of thousands of items could still be formed. This is particularly attractive for CAT applications because job applicants could be allowed to retest without concerns that they would see the same items. Moreover, different applicants would see different items, and concerns about test compromise would be reduced.

In the new TAPAS inventory (Stark, Drasgow, & Chernyshenko, 2008), for example, which measures up to 22 personality facets using a pool of more than 1,400 statements, the MDPP model is used to dynamically create pairwise preference items and score responses using multidimensional Bayes modal estimation. The use of CAT principles allows for the construction of individualized tests having high measurement precision with far fewer items than traditional nonadaptive personality assessments. Although the algorithm and computations are complex, TAPAS, like any other adaptive test, tries to find the subset of items that are most informative for a particular examinee. Item information is computed at the examinee's trait location(s) using item response functions, but for items involving statements that represent different facets, the response functions are actually three-dimensional surfaces. An example item response surface involving personality statements representing Sociability ("My social skills are about average") and Order ("Usually, my notes are so jumbled, even I have a hard time reading them") is shown in Figure 4.5. In the figure, values along the vertical axis indicate the probability of preferring the Sociability statement (i.e., stimulus *s*) to the Order statement (i.e., stimulus *t*) given a

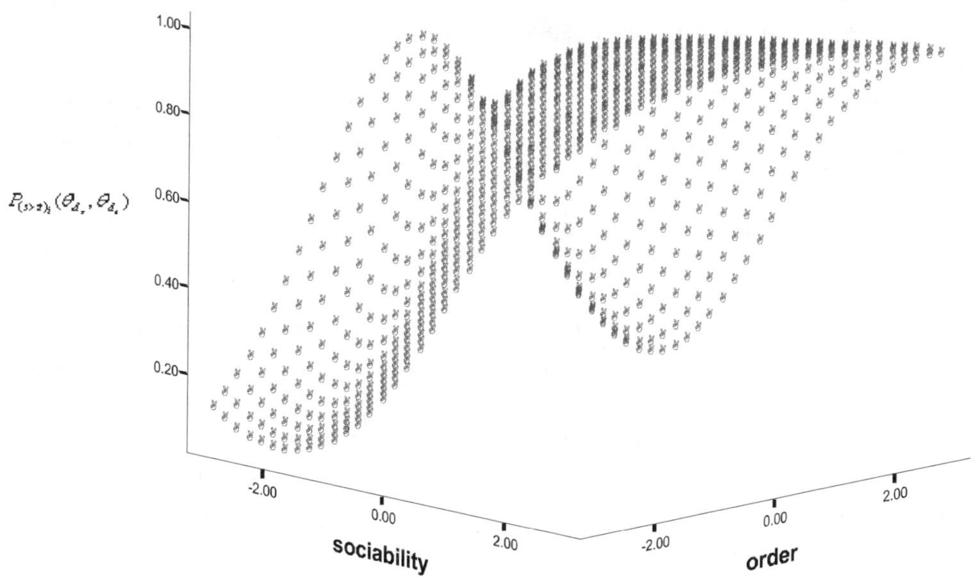

FIGURE 4.5. Item response surface for a MDPP item. From "Normative Scoring of Multidimensional Pairwise Preference Personality Scales Using IRT: Empirical Comparisons With Other Formats," by O. S. Chernyshenko, S. Stark, M. S. Prewett, A. A. Gray, F. R. Stilson, & M. D. Tuttle, 2009, *Human Performance, 22,* p. 113. Copyright 2009 by Taylor & Francis. Reprinted with permission.

respondent's standing on the respective dimensions and each statement's parameters (for more details, see Stark et al., 2005). As with the unidimensional item response function shown previously, MDPP information will be higher where the item response surface is steeper, or, in other words, where the probabilities change rapidly.

Validity and the Use of Personality Test Scores for Selection

On the basis of the Big Five framework, researchers have conducted several meta-analyses to examine which personality factors can be useful for predicting work performance (e.g., Hough, Eaton, Dunnette, Kamp, & McCloy, 1990; Ones, Viswesvaran, & Schmidt, 1993; Tett, Jackson, & Rothstein, 1991; see also chap. 5, this volume). Results have consistently shown that Conscientiousness is a valid predictor of job performance across nearly all occupations studied, whereas the other four broad factors predict success in specific occupations or relate to specific criteria. Barrick, Mount, and Judge (2001), for example, conducted a review of several meta-analyses involving personality dimensions and showed that the average corrected correlations between Conscientiousness and several performance criteria ranged between .19 and .26. In contrast, Openness to Experience had a .05 correlation with supervisory performance ratings but a .24 correlation with training performance.

More recently, a number of studies have suggested that measures of narrow factors or facets may further increase the predictive power of personality variables (e.g., Dudley, Orvis, Lebiecki, & Cortina, 2006; Paunonen 1998). As B. W. Roberts et al. (2005) pointed out, this can happen if facets of the same broad factor have differential relationships with a criterion; essentially, aggregation into a single, broad factor can result in the loss of valid trait specific variance and reduce observed validities. For example, in their study, the correlation between work dedication scores and conscientiousness was zero when facet scores were summed into a single composite, but a multiple correlation of .26 was obtained when facets were entered separately into a regression equation.

Further, although researchers continue to debate the actual magnitudes of personality-performance validities and whether certain meta-analytic corrections should or should not be performed (see Morgeson et al., 2007), it is clear that personality variables can add to the prediction of job performance and even more so to the prediction of many discretionary performance behaviors such as citizenship (Borman, Penner, Allen, & Motowidlo, 2001; Organ & Ryan, 1995), counterproductivity (Berry, Ones, & Sackett, 2007), and leadership emergence (Judge, Bono, Ilies, & Gerhardt, 2002). The within-person variance in behaviors emphasized by Mischel represents a limitation on the validity of any set of static personality predictors (i.e., the 0.3 "ceiling" on validity), but the consistency of behaviors allows valid predictions of various performance dimensions across situations.

In addition to predicting performance across a wide range of occupations, personality measures have shown little, if any, impact against protected groups. For example, Foldes, Duehr, and Ones (2008) conducted a large-scale meta-analysis of racial group differences on various personality scales and found only small mean differences that would be unlikely to cause an adverse impact in selection, particularly if aggregated to form composites, because the differences varied in directionality. Similar results have been found for gender groups. With the exceptions of Agreeableness, on which females generally score higher, and Dominance, a facet of Extraversion, on which males typically score higher, the extent of gender differences is small (Feingold, 1994). Thus, when personality measures are used in conjunction with cognitive ability measures in a compensatory selection system, adverse impact against protected groups will be reduced (Hough, Oswald, & Ployhart, 2001).

In summary, the outlook for personality measurement in selection contexts seems bright. Legal and societal concerns about adverse impact associated with the use of cognitive ability tests, as well as the increasing emphasis on citizenship performance, adaptability, and retention, should encourage organizations to use personality test scores for selection and classification decisions. As the predictive validity database for broad and narrow personality factors grows, organizations may want to tailor assessments to meet their specific needs in terms of the numbers of traits measured, the higher level composites formed from the primary trait scores, and how the scores can be used to enhance prediction across job families. To do that, future measures should have large pools of statements that can be used to measure broad and narrow factors, as well as the capability to assemble and administer multiple forms, in accordance with user specifications, and, if faking is likely, to present items in fake-resistant formats.

Compound Personality Variables and Their Use

Thus far, we have focused on broad and narrow personality traits consistent with the prevailing Big Five taxonomy. However, considerable research has been conducted on so-called compound personality variables, which are combinations of multiple personality traits. Examples of such traits include integrity (Ones et al., 1993), core self-evaluations (Erez & Judge, 2001), emotional intelligence (Goleman, 1995), and many others. The main advantage of these variables lies in their higher validities (which are obtained by virtue of combining several useful dimensions into an overall composite). The disadvantage is that they may carry a somewhat limited theoretical value because it is often unclear which part of the composite is driving validity. This situation seems analogous to the use of difference scores in the P-O fit literature. Edwards (2002) argued persuasively that much information is lost when the composite score (i.e., the difference) is created and that person and organization variables should be entered individually into regression equations to better understand fit. By entering the variables separately, their individual contributions can be clearly identified. Edwards noted that higher order relations can also be examined by entering quadratic and interaction terms. Similarly, with personality predictors of job performance, possible conjunctive and interactive effects could be better studied and tested with polynomial regression using unidimensional facet scores.

One example of a compound variable receiving substantial attention in organizational literature is Integrity. In the past 30 years, Paul Sackett and his colleagues have written several comprehensive reviews of the integrity testing literature (the latest being Berry, Sackett, & Wiemann, 2007). Whether "integrity" is measured with "overt" tests that explicitly ask respondents about their attitudes toward theft or with "covert" or personality-based tests that ask seemingly innocuous questions about the respondent's typical behaviors, the underlying construct being measured is, essentially, a personality composite consisting of responsibility, virtue, rule following, excitement seeking, angry hostility, self-control, and social conformity. Hence, a large proportion of the variance in integrity scale scores seems to be rooted in the Big Five factor of Conscientiousness, with some additional variance contributed by facets from Extraversion, Emotional Stability, and Agreeableness.

According to Ones et al.'s (1993) meta-analysis of 665 validity studies, integrity tests are valid predictors of job performance as well as counterproductive work behaviors (validity estimates range between .20 and .41), which is not surprising given the heterogeneity of this variable. Because most personality facets comprising integrity do not correlate with cognitive ability, integrity tests when used in conjunction with cognitive ability tests have the potential to significantly increase the validity of selection decisions. We deliberately use the word *potential* here because applicants can fairly easily fake integrity tests. As was shown by Hurtz and Alliger (2002), the difference between honest and fake-good conditions for both overt and covert integrity tests is about .70 SD, which is a sizable difference to ignore in the context of selection decisions.

Another frequently researched compound variable is Core Self Evaluations (CSE; Erez & Judge, 2001). In the development of the CSE scale, Judge, Erez, Bono, and Thoresen (2002) explicitly conceptualized the construct as a broad composite of self-esteem, generalized self-efficacy (Locke, McClear, & Knight, 1996); emotional stability, and locus of control (Rotter, 1966). In the Big Five nomenclature, this translates into a combination of Emotional Stability, Conscientiousness, and Extraversion (or, more specifically, well-being, industriousness, and dominance facets). In fact, in their latest study, Judge, Hurst, and Simon (2009) reported the 12-item CSE scale to correlate the highest with Emotional Stability (.43), Extraversion (.39), and Conscientiousness (.29). Although seemingly rooted in Big Five, CSE appears to be a useful construct from both theoretical and practical standpoints. Theoretically, it allows for a different factorial representation of the personality domain, in which achievement orientation, assertiveness, and optimistic tendencies are grouped into a single broad factor. Our own experience with many personality data sets supports such an alternative representation as well-being, achievement, and dominance facets tend to correlate more highly with each other than with any other Big Five facets, at least in samples of managers and U.S. military personnel. Practically, CSE has been shown to be related to a variety of outcomes including job and life satisfaction, job performance, and even better adjustment to foreign assignments with most validity coefficients ranging between .20 and .40 (for the latest review, see Judge, 2009).

Finally, we note that Emotional Intelligence (EI) is probably one of the most contentious compound individual difference variables in recent years. Initially popularized by Daniel Goleman (1995, 1998), emotional intelligence was defined as a set of conceptually related psychological skills involving processing of affective information and hailed as a panacea for modern businesses that neglected the "critical ingredient of success" (i.e., affect). More specifically, EI was said to comprise several related dimensions: the verbal and nonverbal appraisal and expression of emotion in oneself, appraisal and recognition of emotion in others, the regulation of emotion in oneself, and the use of emotion to facilitate thought and performance (Davies, Stankov, & Roberts, 1998). Unfortunately, from the onset, the EI field was hindered by ill-defined operationalizations of these dimensions and inflated validity claims, so it received skeptical scrutiny from personnel selection researchers (e.g., Landy, 2005, Matthews, Roberts, & Zeidner, 2004). Most initial EI studies espoused what was later called a *mixed model*—a blend of competencies and dispositions loosely related to emotion that could be measured using personality-like questionnaires (e.g., self-awareness, empathy, impulse control, assertiveness, stress tolerance, and social skills). To no surprise, measures based on mixed models showed little evidence of discriminant validity with respect to Emotional Stability, Extraversion, and Agreeableness (e.g., Davies et al., 1998), which is why we classify EI as a compound personality trait. We note, however, that more recent work on EI has focused on "mental ability models" (Mayer, Caruso, & Salovey, 1999) that explicitly define EI as an individual's aptitude for processing affective information and can be measured in ways similar to cognitive ability (i.e., identification of emotions in pictures). This area of research is promising, although not without its psychometric challenges (e.g., scoring is usually based on expert or consensus judgments, which tend to be unreliable). Moreover, it is not yet clear whether EI should be conceptualized as an ability or whether it would be more beneficial to treat it as a learned set of competencies (i.e., procedural skills). This latter approach is a route that has been taken by the emerging domain of Cultural Intelligence (Ang & Van Dyne, 2008; Oolders, Chernyshenko, & Stark, 2008).

VALUES AND VOCATIONAL INTERESTS

Value Taxonomies

Values and motives reflect stable individual differences in what people want to do or want to have in their lives. They influence how people interpret characteristics of their external environments and are linked to various affective and motivational systems. They play an important role in forming one's specific goals and, to some extent, define how those goals are pursued and with what intensity. Research on human values and their role in goal-oriented behavior is, of course, quite broad (see also Vol. 3, chap. 4, this handbook). Our focus here is on the structure and hierarchy of values and how that information can be used to predict employee behavior. Note that by hierarchy and structure, we do not imply priorities (e.g., Maslow, 1968) but rather how values can be aggregated into increasingly broader groupings.

In the domain of basic human values, Schwartz's (1992) taxonomy is one of the most widely researched. There are 10 motivationally distinct values groupings: power, achievement, hedonism, stimulation, self-direction, universalism, benevolence, tradition, conformity, and security. These values can be arranged into a circumplex having two orthogonal axes (openness–conservation and enhancement–transcendence) by using multidimensional scaling, as shown in Figure 4.6. Alternatively, the 10 value groupings can be organized hierarchically into four distinct higher order factors, because proximal values in Figure 4.6 tend to correlate higher with each other than with distal values (e.g., achievement and power would form the Self-Enhancement broad factor, whereas security, conformity, and tradition would form the Conservation broad factor). Schwartz and Boehnke (2004) recently showed that these structures replicate in numerous samples and countries.

A comparable taxonomy to Schwartz's, designed specifically for work settings, is the work value taxonomy from the Minnesota Importance Questionnaire (MIQ; Rounds, Henly, Dawis, Lofquist, & Weiss, 1981). Developed as part of the Theory of Work Adjustment, the MIQ taxonomy comprises 20 basic work values or needs that are aggregated into six broader factors: achievement, comfort, status, altruism, safety, and autonomy. Note that this is very similar to Schwartz's four-factor model, but Schwartz's Self-Enhancement factor is split into separate achievement and power factors, whereas the Conservation factor is split into a comfort factor, which is concerned specifically with one's working conditions, and a safety factor that deals primarily with company policies and employee relations. There are no hedonism themes in the MIQ taxonomy, probably because work is rarely perceived as something really fun or pleasurable.

One of the most interesting features of the MIQ taxonomy is that it was explicitly developed to help individuals make vocational choices. The Theory of Work Adjustment (Dawis & Lofquist, 1984) postulates that the correspondence between what an employee desires (basic needs and values) and what an organization actually provides (called *occupational reinforcers*) determines that employee's subsequent job satisfaction and, possibly, turnover decision. Hence, individuals should be advised about value profiles for various occupations to avoid poor vocational choices.

The importance of person–environment correspondence is now being recognized widely in the organizational behavior literature, and the term *P-O fit* has been coined to refer specifically to organizational contexts (Chatman, 1989). Many recent studies involving various value dimensions have shown that P-O fit predicts not only job satisfaction but also

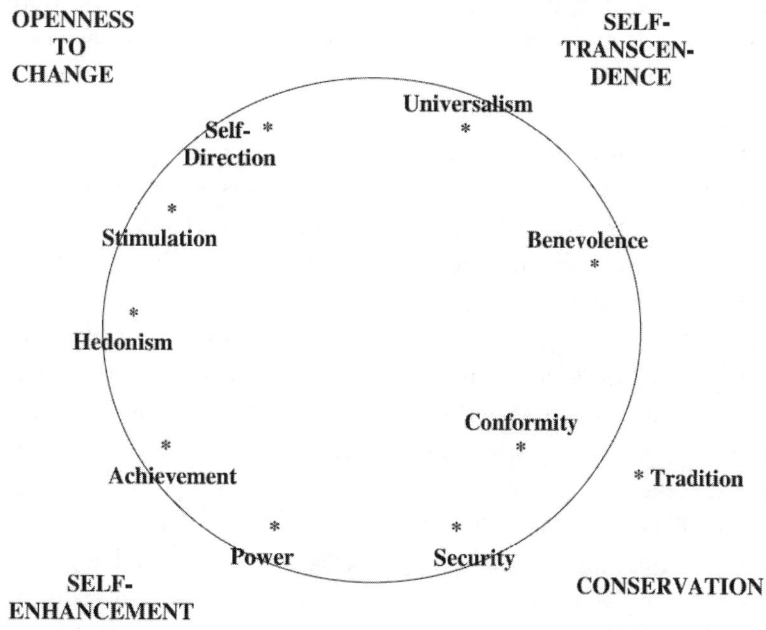

FIGURE 4.6. Schwartz's Value Taxonomy. From "Evaluating the Structure of Human Values With Confirmatory Factor Analysis," by S. H. Schwartz and K. Boehnke, 2004, *Journal of Research in Personality, 38,* p. 233. Copyright 2004 by Elsevier. Reprinted with permission.

contextual performance, organizational commitment, turnover intentions, and even overall performance (for a recent meta-analysis, see Kristof-Brown, Zimmerman, & Johnson, 2005). For example, Chatman (1991) found that, for newly hired employees, P-O fit scores predicted job satisfaction and intent to stay with an organization 1 year later, and actual turnover 2.5 years later. Given these and similar findings, many researchers have argued to use P-O fit when selecting employees for long-term commitments (Bowen, Ledford, & Nathan, 1991).

Measurement Challenges Involving Use of Values for Selection

Although research results concerning the use of values to enhance personnel decisions are compelling, there are many measurement and methodological challenges that must be overcome for operational use. First, traditional Likert-type measures just do not seem to work well. The problem is that most values, by definition, represent something desirable, so it is not uncommon to see uniformly high endorsement rates for nearly all values appearing in a questionnaire, even though Schwartz's model and others hypothesize that some values are in conflict with each other (i.e., they lie on opposite sides of the circumplex). Recognizing this limitation, many values measures use rankings or Q-sorts rather than ratings. For example, the Rokeach Value survey (RVS; Rokeach, 1973), the Organization Culture Profile (OCP; O'Reilly, Chatman, & Caldwell, 1991), the Comparative Emphasis Scale (CES; Ravlin & Meglino, 1987), and an earlier version of the Schwartz Value Survey require respondents to rank specific values or characteristics in order of their importance, thus generating a preference profile for each individual. Although this may help to overcome social desirability response biases, because one cannot like or dislike everything, the resulting ranks are ipsative and do not necessarily indicate value strength. For example, two people could exhibit the same pattern of scores for three values but differ dramatically in their levels of preference. An individual who is very high on Autonomy, high on Variety, and average on Status would have the same ranking profile as one who is average on Autonomy, low on Variety, and very low on Status. Hence, using ranking data to make normative comparisons or as components in a P-O fit equation is problematic. To be applicable to selection, value measurement approaches more akin to the MIQ, which uses a combination of pairwise preference and absolute judgment items to anchor the metric, might be needed (Rounds et al., 1981).

Another issue, which is specific to the use of values measures in the P-O fit context, involves the need to combine person and organization scores to form correspondence indices. One popular index is a difference score, which is simple to compute and shows both the direction and degree of correspondence. However, difference scores have been criticized widely in the P-O fit literature for reasons that include conceptual ambiguity and unreliability (Edwards, 1993). However, using both person and organization scores in a polynomial regression framework (Edwards & Parry, 1993) is quite complicated and may not be well suited for diagnostic feedback and selection purposes.

A second well-known correspondence index is the correlation between person and organization profiles. Such correlations reflect the rank-order similarity of person and organization values, but referring to them as measures of fit is somewhat misleading because they do not actually capture the distance between profiles. More important, it is unclear how this index can be used in selection, because an individual's value profile could be perfectly correlated with an organization's profile, but his or her value strengths could be extremely different. Conversely, one's value profile could have a near zero correlation with the organization's profile, yet the distances between his or her values and those of the organization could be very small, making the person a relatively good fit for a position. In addition, the reliability of the correspondence index is not known, and, as far as we know, no guidelines exist about what constitutes acceptable fit. These may be some of the reasons why values and congruence indices are not often used in selection contexts. Clearly, more research is needed in this area.

As things currently stand, direct fit approaches, which operationalize P-O fit as the perceived value match between person and environment, appear to hold more promise for organizational applications than indirect approaches relying on a combination of organizational and personal value scores. There are several kinds of direct fit measurement strategies (Edwards, Cable, Williamson, Lambert, & Shipp, 2006). Some approaches ask respondents to indicate explicitly the degree of fit (e.g., Posner, Kouzes, & Schmidt, 1985), whereas others use an implicit strategy and ask respondents to select statements that most closely describe their current situation with respect to a value being measured (Chernyshenko, Stark, & Williams, 2009). All direct fit measures are relatively easy to complete from a test taker's perspective, do not require organizational scores (and hence additional correspondence indices), and yield a single fit score that may withstand potential legal scrutiny (e.g., its psychometric properties can be readily examined). However, such direct fit scores may not be seen as strictly measures of individual differences, because they reflect a dynamic distance between one's current and desired states. Moreover, direct fit measures are not readily suitable for selection applications because they assume that individuals have been with an organization for some time period or are at least familiar with the job environment that they are likely to encounter.

Taxonomic Structures of Vocational Interests—RIASEC; People–Things, Data–Ideas, and Prestige

In the classification of vocational interests, Holland's (1959, 1985) theory of vocational personalities and work environments has been one of the most influential (see also chap. 3, this volume). Holland's theory states that vocational interests and work environments can be meaningfully classified into six types, as noted earlier: realistic (R), investigative (I), artistic (A), social (S), enterprising (E), and conventional (C; RIASEC). These types can be arranged into a hexagonal model, which graphically describes the relationship of each interest type to another (see Figure 4.7). The Vocational Preference Inventory (VPI, Holland, 1985), the Strong Interest Inventory (Harmon, Hansen, Borgen, & Hammer, 1994), and the O*NET Interest Profile (O*NET Resource Center, 2003) are just a few examples of measures currently using the RIASEC model for interest assessment and job matching.

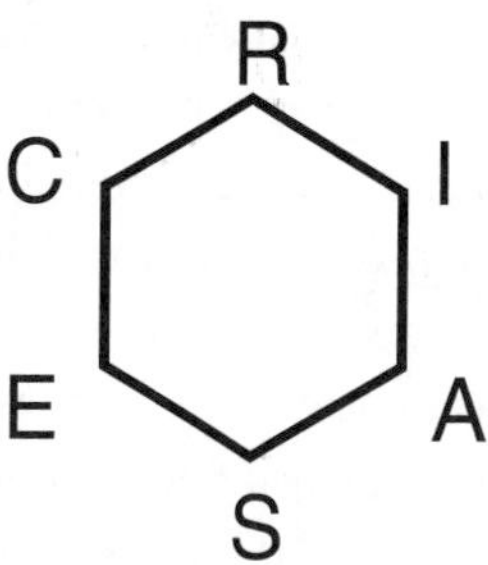

FIGURE 4.7. Holland's hexagonal model of vocational interests and occupations. R = realistic; I = investigative; A = artistic; S = social; E = enterprising; C = conventional.

The structural implication of the RIASEC model is that the adjacent interest types are more similar than those further apart. As with the values framework, it is proposed that the congruence between an individual's vocational interests and the work environment leads to higher satisfaction and performance. The other implication is that all individuals lie somewhere within the hexagon, and those lying closer to the periphery have more clearly defined interests. This assumption may be true to a limited extent. From a measurement perspective, vocational interest items that are near the perimeter would be the most informative, thereby providing reliable estimates of individual vocational interests. However, if there are vocational interest items that sit in the middle of the hexagon, measurement of individuals further from the periphery should be relatively stable as well.

Although there is substantial empirical support for the RIASEC structure, this evidence is found primarily with measures specifically designed to assess the six types (Tracey & Rounds, 1993). However, when Holland (1985) developed the VPI, only a small number of occupational titles were chosen to represent the six types. RIASEC codes for the remaining occupations have been generated under the implicit assumption that the model generalizes to the full range of U.S. occupations. Recognizing this shortcoming, Deng, Armstrong, and Rounds (2007) recently conducted a large empirical study involving ratings of interests in occupations representing approximately 85% of the U.S. labor market for which RIASEC codes were also available. Their multidimensional scaling (MDS) results showed that

RIASEC types and the associated hexagonal structure were not sufficient to represent the full range of occupations; instead a three-dimensional solution similar to the one proposed in the spherical model of job interests (Tracey & Rounds, 1996) was obtained with occupations located throughout the space, not just on the periphery (Deng et al., 2007). This suggests that current interest measures may present an overly restricted range of career choices because they are mainly limited to occupations showing the hexagonal structure in multidimensional scaling studies.

In light of the Deng et al. (2007) study, a new approach to vocational interest measurement is needed that allows vocational interests to be identified at one or more locations anywhere in the three-dimensional space. Moreover, the new approach should go beyond simply classifying interests by a vocational theme (e.g., R) because occupations with realistic characteristics may lie near the periphery of the three-dimensional space or near the center. The use of such an alternative model to represent occupational interest structures is likely to have profound consequences for how individuals are matched to jobs.

To locate individuals in a two or higher dimensional space, it may be necessary to use a set of reference axes such as the ones proposed by Hogan (1983) and Prediger (1982). Hogan (1983) postulated that there are two main factors: conformity (conventional–artistic items) and sociability. In contrast, Prediger (1982) had a different orientation to the axes and labeled them as *people–things* (realistic–social items) and *data–ideas*. Tracey and Rounds (1996) showed that these dimensions were not unique and could be generalizable across subject variables and RIASEC inventories. They also suggested adding a third dimension, prestige, to describe all jobs (see Sodano & Tracey, 2008). It is important to note that items falling close to these dimensional axes should be fairly unidimensional, a necessary assumption that allows one to use item response theory to measure individuals on the axes of interest.

From an item response theory perspective, the key issue is the underlying process by which individuals respond to RIASEC items. Tay, Drasgow, Rounds, and Williams (2009) recently presented evidence that an ideal point response process underlies answers to vocational interest items. Intuitively, when individuals indicate how much they would like a particular job, their judgment is based on how similar they are to the occupation on the underlying dimension, rather than how far they are above it. Thus, someone who has very high social interests would be just as unlikely to want a job offering only moderate social interaction as someone having very low social interests. Because many of the occupations studied by Deng et al. (2007) lie inside the hexagon, we should expect item response functions to exhibit folding (and this is what Tay et al., 2009, found), so the difference between ideal point models and dominance models in this context is large and, it appears, important.

Use of Vocational Interests in Selection and Classification

To date, the majority of interest measures have been used for classification rather than selection purposes. Essentially, after completing an interest inventory, an individual is assigned a three-letter RIASEC code (e.g., ASC) based on his or her highest interest scores. The individual's code is then compared with those for various occupations catalogued, for example, in the Dictionary of Occupational Titles (U.S. Department of Labor, 1991) or O*NET (O*NET Resource Center, 2003), and occupations matching the individual's interests are identified. Because not all codes have corresponding job types, congruence indices have been developed to assist with matching. One example is the Brown and Gore (1994) C-Index, which compares a person's three-letter RIASEC code with a set of occupations and yields a score between 0 and 18, with higher numbers indicating more congruence.

Validity studies involving interests can be divided into two general categories: those predicting occupational choice and those predicting the extent to which interest congruence influences job satisfaction and other outcomes in the person–environment fit frameworks. In general, studies find that interest scores predict people's future occupational choices reasonably well. For example, longitudinal studies by Zytowski (1974), Hansen and Swanson (1983), Hansen and Dik (2005) have found that approximately 50% to 60% of respondents subsequently worked in occupations consistent with their vocational interests. However, studies testing effects of congruence on job satisfaction have been less positive. Meta-analyses by Assouline and Meir (1987) and Tranberg, Slane, and Ekeberg (1993) found that the average correlation between interest congruence and job satisfaction was at best .20, which prompted concern about the "congruence problem." Tinsley (2000) even went as far as to conclude that Holland's theory is invalid. Arnold (2004), however, wrote an insightful commentary pointing out a number of measurement and methodological issues surrounding congruence studies that need to be resolved before the usefulness of interests is dismissed. He listed 14 potential problems for interest congruence studies and classified them as shortcomings of Holland's theory (e.g., Holland's framework may not provide an adequate characterization of the environment), as problems with research designs (e.g., using cross-sectional and between-subjects designs to test longitudinal hypotheses, overreliance on job satisfaction as an outcome), or as issues related to external validity (e.g., Holland's theory views a job's characteristics as fixed, but the requirements of many jobs change over time). Clearly, more research is needed to address these problems adequately.

In their widely cited article, Schmidt and Hunter (1998) stated that interests correlate .10 with job performance (see their Table 1) and .18 with performance in training. These correlations were originally obtained by Hunter and Hunter (1984) and bear some scrutiny. The validity estimate for job performance is based on just one inventory (the Strong Interest Inventory) and just three studies. The findings for training are again based on the Strong Interest Inventory, and just two studies with a total *N* of 383. Consequently, these relations should be interpreted cautiously. Certainly, more research is needed.

What type of relationship should be expected between vocational interest–job characteristics congruence and job performance? If the technical difficulties noted by Arnold (2004) and others can be resolved, it seems likely that a reasonably strong relation will be found between congruence and job satisfaction. Job satisfaction, however, has an interesting relationship with job performance. Judge, Thoresen, Bono, and Patton (2001) found that job satisfaction has a moderately strong relationship with performance for individuals in jobs of low to medium complexity, with an estimated mean validity of .29. However, for high-complexity jobs, a very strong relationship was found (mean validity of .52). Therefore, it seems reasonable to predict a modest relationship between vocational interest–job characteristic congruence and job performance for low- to medium-complexity jobs but a much stronger relationship for highly complex jobs.

BEHAVIORAL NARRATIVES

In his neo-socioanalytic model, B. W. Roberts (2006) placed narratives within the domain of individual differences, although personal history is clearly acquired throughout an individual's life. The reason is the endurance of personal histories, because they play an important role in forming one's identity and social reputation. Simply put, there are certain critical events in everyone's life requiring immediate actions, and the memories of how these events were handled shape how an individual perceives himself or herself, how he or she is perceived by others, and how he or she would likely respond to similar events in the future. Further, although I/O psychologists have some theories that take into account critical events and life histories (e.g., the developmental–integrative model by Owens and Schoenefeldt [1979] or affective events theory by Weiss and Cropanzano [1996]), this potentially fruitful research area appears to be well suited for incorporating ideas from other areas of psychology. For example, Mumford and colleagues drew from findings in developmental psychology to create their ecology model (Mumford & Stokes, 1992), and Mael (1991) also incorporated themes from social identity theory.

In a broad sense, information provided by narratives is already used in many selection systems, including personal statements, letters of recommendation, interviews, and biodata blanks. However, many of these measures also contain information about other domains of individual differences (i.e., abilities, personality, values, and interests), so the incremental validity of narrative measures largely depends on how much unique information is actually captured and whether it can be measured reliably. As noted by Mael (1991), in the discussion of biodata measures, the defining characteristic of narratives is that they are historical, so one's current intentions, views, or responses to hypothetical situations should not be considered part of that domain.

It is no surprise that there are conflicting accounts about the incremental validity of selection tools involving narrative information. Schmidt and Hunter (1998) noted, for example, that biodata measures provide little incremental validity beyond cognitive ability, whereas others have found significant incremental validities beyond both cognitive ability or personality tests (e.g., McManus & Kelly, 1999; Mount, Witt, & Barrick, 2002; Stokes, Toth, Searcy, Stroupe, & Carter, 1999). Furthermore, Bauer, McAdams, and Sakaeda (2005) found that narratives involving memories of personal growth events predict outcomes such as life satisfaction beyond the Big Five personality factors.

Setting aside the issue of incremental validity, many studies have shown that narratives provide useful information for selection. Typical empirically keyed biodata measures have validities ranging from .25 to .40. For example, Bobko, Roth, and Potosky (1999) reported a correlation of .28 between biodata and job performance, computed by taking a weighted average from four previous meta-analyses. Validities of interviews and letters of recommendations are typically a bit lower, however, perhaps due partly to difficulties associated with coding qualitative data.

Research on scoring biodata has mainly focused on methods for keying, rather than developing psychometric measurement models. For example, Stokes and Searcy (1999) discussed keying based on expert judgments, empirical keying based on correlations of the criterion with each option of each item, and internal consistency keying in which homogeneous clusters of items are identified by principal components or cluster analysis. There has been relatively little work on evaluating the fit of various IRT models to biodata or other measures of narratives, and we know of no research examining dominance versus ideal point models. Because narratives appear so important for understanding people's behavior, the development of formal measurement models for this domain should be a priority for future research. Findings from cognitive psychology, especially with regard to autobiographical memories, may hold particular promise in this endeavor.

CONCLUSIONS

In this chapter, we have reviewed several classes of individual differences that are important for understanding performance in organizational settings. Cognitive ability, personality, values, vocational interests, and narratives help us understand why some people find satisfaction in their jobs and perform well and others are dissatisfied and perform poorly.

By no means are we dismissive of the context in which people work. Certainly good leadership that fosters employee engagement, appropriate compensation, and a safe workplace enhance performance, satisfaction, and commitment. Nonetheless, it is individual differences that explain why one individual enjoys using differential equations to solve engineering problems whereas another person finds satisfaction in helping others address their personal problems.

Research on individual differences has progressed in different ways. For cognitive ability, there have been thousands of studies addressing a wide range of topics. We know that cognitive ability is a powerful predictor of performance in jobs that are complex, and the three-parameter logistic model provides an excellent fit to many tests. There has been much work on sophisticated measurement applications such as differential item functioning, computerized adaptive testing, and person fit. Carroll's three-stratum model provides a comprehensive framework for the structure of cognitive abilities. There has been so much work on cognitive ability that it is difficult to identify significant topics that need further research.

Barrick and Mount's (1991) seminal meta-analysis revivified research on personality in organizational settings. The role of personality in understanding organizational behavior seems intrinsically more complex than cognitive ability. With cognitive ability, "more is better" and, in unrestricted populations, different abilities are so highly correlated that it is difficult to show incremental validity (Ree, Earles, & Teachout, 1994). However, the effectiveness of personality dimensions seems much more context dependent: Extraversion is important for sales personnel but not for accountants. Moreover, it is not clear that the Big Five framework is optimal for predicting job performance. The facets underlying each Big Five dimension are not as highly correlated as cognitive abilities and may provide incremental validity (B. W. Roberts et al., 2005). Psychometric models for the measurement of personality have not received much attention, and instead researchers have simply borrowed from the cognitive domain. As we have noted, dominance models are not well suited for personality, whereas ideal point models fit better. Much more work on the psychometrics of personality measurement, especially with respect to resistance to faking, seems to be needed.

The burgeoning literature on P-O fit is a testament to the importance of values. As we noted, the measurement of values is a challenge because almost all values are socially desirable and consequently an agree–disagree format is unlikely to provide much information. Rankings and Q-sorts have been used, but these bring to bear another set of challenges related to ipsativity. More work on the measurement of values as well as on the ways of quantifying the congruence between people and organizations is needed (e.g., G. W. Cheung, 2009).

Vocational interests have been studied for more than a half century, but much remains to be examined. For example, psychometric theory for assessing vocational interests needs more development, as empirical keying and heuristic methods, such as multidimensional scaling, have been used primarily to date. Similarly, biodata has been criticized for its "dust-bowl empiricism," and thus framing biodata as an approach to studying life narratives may provide a useful theoretical conceptualization (e.g., Mael, 1991).

We have not discussed genetic testing or drug testing in this chapter. There are claims that attending to individual differences in job applicants' genes could improve their health and save lives by screening out people who are at risk from exposure to toxic substances. However, the Genetic Information Nondiscrimination Act of 2008 outlawed discrimination based on genetic information in employment and medical insurance, and consequently it is unlikely that employers will consider genetic testing. However, many employers (more than half according to Heneman & Judge, 2009) now use drug testing. The American Council for Drug Education (ACDE; 2007) claimed that substance abusers are 33% less productive and 10 times more likely to be absent from work. Although the ACDE asserted that one worker in four, ages 18 to 34, used drugs in the previous year, it is interesting that Quest Diagnostics (2008) found that only 3.8% of job applicants tested positive. In sum, the efficacy of drug testing for improving performance, broadly defined, in the workplace appears to be a topic that needs to be studied empirically.

In conclusion, we believe that individual difference variables will continue to be of vital importance for enhancing the effectiveness of selection, training, and performance management initiatives. Early research focused heavily on cognitive ability and its relationships with organizational criteria, but the past 20 years have shown a definite shift toward questions involving noncognitive predictors. In fact, many individual difference theories of job performance now explicitly incorporate one or more noncognitive variables (Chan & Drasgow, 2001; Motowidlo et al., 1997). Clearly, societal factors associated with test use have catalyzed this move toward broader assessments, but the benefits to both research and practice are unequivocal. The challenge now is to make noncognitive assessments work better in operational settings where testing time is a premium, response distortion is a serious concern, and the number of predictors that must be considered for decision making has increased dramatically.

References

Ackerman, P. L., Kanfer, R., & Goff, M. (1995). Cognitive and noncognitive determinants and consequences of complex skill acquisition. *Journal of Experimental Psychology: Applied, 1,* 270–304. doi:10.1037/1076-898X.1.4.270

Almagor, M., Tellegen, A., & Waller, N. (1995). The Big Seven model: A cross-cultural replication and further exploration of the basic dimensions of natural language of trait descriptions. *Journal of Personality and Social Psychology, 69,* 300–307. doi:10.1037/0022-3514.69.2.300

American Council for Drug Education. (2007). *Why worry about drugs and alcohol in the workplace?*

Retrieved July 10, 2009, from http://www.acde.org/employer/DAwork.htm

Andrich, D. (1989). A probabilistic IRT model for unfolding preference data. *Applied Psychological Measurement, 13,* 193–216. doi:10.1177/014662168901300211

Ang, S., & Van Dyne, L. (2008). Conceptualization of cultural intelligence: Definition, distinctiveness, and nomological network. In S. Ang & L. Van Dyne (Eds.), *Handbook of cultural intelligence: Theory, measurement, and applications* (pp. 3–15). New York: Sharpe.

Arnold, J. (2004). The congruence problem in John Holland's theory of vocational decisions. *Journal of Occupational and Organizational Psychology, 77,* 95–113. doi:10.1348/096317904322915937

Arthur, W., Jr., Bell, S. T., Villado, A. J., & Doverspike, D. (2006). The use of person-organization fit in employment decision making: An assessment of its criterion-related validity. *The Journal of Applied Psychology, 91,* 786–801. doi:10.1037/0021-9010.91.4.786

Ashton, M. C. (1998). Personality and job performance: The importance of narrow traits. *Journal of Organizational Behavior, 19,* 289–303. doi:10.1002/(SICI)1099-1379(199805)19:3<289::AID-JOB841>3.0.CO;2-C

Ashton, M. C., & Lee, K. (2007). Empirical, theoretical, and practical advantages of the HEXACO model of personality structure. *Personality and Social Psychology Review, 11,* 150–166. doi:10.1177/1088868306294907

Ashton, M. C., Lee, K., Perugini, M., Szarota, P., De Vries, R. E., DiBlas, L., et al. (2004). A six-factor structure of personality descriptive adjectives: Solutions from psycholexical studies in seven languages. *Journal of Personality and Social Psychology, 86,* 356–366. doi:10.1037/0022-3514.86.2.356

Assouline, M., & Meir, E. I. (1987). Meta-analysis of the relationship between congruence and well-being measures. *Journal of Vocational Behavior, 31,* 319–332. doi:10.1016/0001-8791(87)90046-7

Barrick, M. R., & Mount, M. K. (1991). The Big Five personality dimensions and job performance: A meta-analysis. *Personnel Psychology, 44,* 1–26. doi:10.1111/j.1744-6570.1991.tb00688.x

Barrick, M., Mount, M. K., & Judge, T. A. (2001). Personality and performance at the beginning of the new millennium: What do we know and where do we go next? *International Journal of Selection and Assessment, 9,* 9–30. doi:10.1111/1468-2389.00160

Bauer, J. J., McAdams, D. P., & Sakaeda, A. R. (2005). Interpreting the good life: Growth memories in the lives of mature, happy people. *Journal of Personality and Social Psychology, 88,* 203–217.

Berry, C. M., Ones, D. S., & Sackett, P. R. (2007). Interpersonal deviance, organizational deviance, and their common correlates: A review and meta-analysis. *Journal of Applied Psychology, 92,* 410–424. doi:10.1037/0021-9010.92.2.410

Berry, C. M., Sackett, P. R., & Wiemann, S. (2007). A review of recent developments in integrity test research. *Personnel Psychology, 60,* 271–301.

Birnbaum, A. (1968). Some latent trait models and their use in inferring an examinee's ability. In F. M. Lord & M. R. Novick (Eds.), *Statistical theories of mental test scores* (pp. 397–472). Reading, MA: Addison-Wesley.

Bobko, P., Roth, P. L., & Potosky, D. (1999). Derivation and implications of a meta-analytic matrix incorporating cognitive ability, alternative predictor and job performance. *Personnel Psychology, 52,* 561–589. doi:10.1111/j.1744-6570.1999.tb00172.x

Borkenau, P., & Ostendorf, F. (1990). Comparing exploratory and confirmatory factor analysis: A study on the 5-factor model of personality. *Personality and Individual Differences, 11,* 515–524. doi:10.1016/0191-8869(90)90065-Y

Borman, W. C., Buck, D. E., Hanson, M. A., Motowidlo, S. J., Stark, S., & Drasgow, F. (2001). An examination of the comparative reliability, validity, and accuracy of performance ratings made using computerized adaptive rating scales. *Journal of Applied Psychology, 86,* 965–973. doi:10.1037/0021-9010.86.5.965

Bowen, D. E., Ledford, G. E., & Nathan, B. R. (1991). Hiring for the organisation, not the job. *Academy of Management Executive, 4,* 35–51.

Briggs, S. R. (1989). The optimal level of measurement for personality constructs. In D. M. Buss & N. Cantor (Eds.), *Personality psychology: Recent trends and emerging directions* (pp. 246–260). New York: Springer.

Brown, S. D., & Gore, P. A., Jr. (1994). An evaluation of interest congruence indices: Distribution characteristics and measurement properties. *Journal of Vocational Behavior, 45,* 310–327. doi:10.1006/jvbe.1994.1038

Campbell, J. P. (1990). Modeling the performance prediction problem in industrial and organizational psychology. In M. Dunnette & L. M. Hough (Eds.), *Handbook of industrial and organizational psychology* (2nd ed., Vol. 1, pp. 687–731). Palo Alto, CA: Consulting Psychologists Press.

Campbell, J. P., & Knapp, D. J. (Eds.). (2001). *Exploring the limits in personnel selection and classification.* Mahwah, NJ: Erlbaum.

Carroll, J. B. (1993). *Human cognitive abilities: A survey of factor-analytic studies.* New York: Cambridge University Press.

Chan, K. Y., & Drasgow, F. (2001). Toward a theory of individual differences and leadership: Understanding the motivation to lead. *Journal of Applied Psychology, 86,* 481–498. doi:10.1037/0021-9010.86.3.481

Chatman, J. A. (1989). Improving interactional organizational research: A model of person–organization fit. *Academy of Management Review, 14,* 333–349. doi:10.2307/258171

Chatman, J. A. (1991). Matching people and organizations: Selection and socialization in public accounting firms. *Administrative Science Quarterly, 36,* 459–484. doi:10.2307/2393204

Chernyshenko, O. S., Stark, S., & Chan, K. (2001). Investigating the hierarchical factor structure of the Fifth Edition of the 16PF: An application of the Schmid–Leiman orthogonalization procedure. *Educational and Psychological Measurement, 61,* 290–302. doi:10.1177/00131640121971248

Chernyshenko, O. S., Stark, S., Drasgow, F., & Roberts, B. W. (2007). Constructing personality scales under the assumptions of an ideal point response process: Toward increasing the flexibility of personality measures. *Psychological Assessment, 19,* 88–106. doi:10.1037/1040-3590.19.1.88

Chernyshenko, O. S., Stark, S., Prewett, M. S., Gray, A. A., Stilson, F. R., & Tuttle, M. D. (2009). Normative scoring of multidimensional pairwise preference personality scales using IRT: Empirical comparisons with other formats. *Human Performance, 22,* 105–127.

Chernyshenko, O. S., & Stark, S., & Williams, A. (2009). Latent trait theory approach to measuring person–organization fit: Conceptual rationale and empirical evaluation. *International Journal of Testing, 9,* 358–380.

Cheung, F. M., Leung, K., Zhang, J., Sun, H., Gan, Y., Song, W., & Xie, D. Indigenous Chinese personality constructs: Is the Five-Factor model complete? *Journal of Cross-Cultural Psychology, 32,* 407–433.

Cheung, G. W. (2009). Introducing the latent congruence model for improving the assessment of similarity, agreement, and fit in organizational research. *Organizational Research Methods, 12,* 6–33. doi:10.1177/1094428107308914

Christiansen, N. D., Burns, G. N., & Montgomery, G. E. (2005). Reconsidering forced-choice item formats for applicant personality assessment. *Human Performance, 18,* 267–307. doi:10.1207/s15327043hup1803_4

Christiansen, N. D., Goffin, R. D., Johnston, N. G., & Rothstein, M. G. (1994). Correcting the 16PF for faking: Effects on criterion-related validity and individual hiring decisions. *Personnel Psychology, 47,* 847–860. doi:10.1111/j.1744-6570.1994.tb01581.x

Conn, S., & Reike, M. L. (Eds.). (1994). *The 16PF fifth edition technical manual.* Champaign, IL: Institute for Personality and Ability Testing.

Coombs, C. H. (1964). *A theory of data.* New York: Wiley.

Costa, P. T., Jr., & McCrae, R. R. (1988). From catalog to classification: Murray's needs and the five-factor model. *Journal of Personality and Social Psychology, 55,* 258–265. doi:10.1037/0022-3514.55.2.258

Costa, P. T., Jr., & McCrae, R. R. (1994). *Revised NEO Personality Inventory (NEO-PI-R) and NEO-Five-Factor Inventory (NEO-FFI) professional manual.* Odessa, FL: Psychological Assessment Resources.

Costa, P. T., Jr., McCrae, R. R., & Dye, D. A. (1991). Facet scales for agreeableness and conscientiousness: A revision of the NEO Personality Inventory. *Personality and Individual Differences, 12,* 887–898.

Credé, M., Chernyshenko, O. S., Stark, S., Bashshur, M., & Dalal, R. S. (2007). Job satisfaction as mediator: An assessment of job satisfaction's position within the nomological network. *Journal of Occupational and Organizational Psychology, 80,* 515–538. doi:10.1348/096317906X136180

Davies, M., Stankov, L., & Roberts, R. D. (1998). Emotional intelligence: In search of an elusive construct. *Journal of Personality and Social Psychology, 75,* 989–1015. doi:10.1037/0022-3514.75.4.989

Dawis, R. V., & Lofquist, L. H. (1984). *A psychological theory of work adjustment.* Minneapolis: University of Minnesota Press.

Deng, C.-P., Armstrong, P. I., & Rounds, J. (2007). The fit of Holland's RIASEC model to US occupations. *Journal of Vocational Behavior, 71,* 1–22. doi:10.1016/j.jvb.2007.04.002

DeYoung, C. G., Quilty, L. C., & Peterson, J. B. (2007). Between facets and domains: 10 aspects of the Big Five. *Journal of Personality and Social Psychology, 93,* 880–896. doi:10.1037/0022-3514.93.5.880

Digman, J. M. (1990). Personality structure: Emergence of the five-factor model. *Annual Review of Psychology, 41,* 417–440.

Drasgow, F. (2003). Intelligence and the workplace. In W. C. Borman & D. R. Ilgen (Eds.), *Handbook of psychology: Industrial and organizational psychology* (pp. 107–130). New York: Wiley.

Drasgow, F., & Kang, T. (1984). Statistical power of differential validity and differential prediction analyses for detecting measurement non-equivalence. *Journal of Applied Psychology, 69,* 498–508. doi:10.1037/0021-9010.69.3.498

Drasgow, F., & Olson-Buchanan, J. B. (Eds.). (1999). *Innovations in computerized assessment.* Mahwah, NJ: Erlbaum.

Dudley, N. M., Orvis, K. A., Lebiecki, J. E., & Cortina, J. M. (2006). A meta-analytic investigation of conscientiousness in the prediction of job performance: Examining the intercorrelations and the incremental validity of narrow traits. *Journal of Applied Psychology, 91,* 40–57. doi:10.1037/0021-9010.91.1.40

Edwards, J. R. (1993). Problems with these of profile similarity indices in the study of congruence in organizational research. *Personnel Psychology, 46,* 641–665. doi:10.1111/j.1744-6570.1993.tb00889.x

Edwards, J. R. (2002). Alternatives to difference scores: Polynomial regression analysis and response surface methodology. In F. Drasgow & N. Schmitt (Eds.), *Measuring and analyzing behavior in organizations* (pp. 350–400). San Francisco: Jossey-Bass.

Edwards, J. R., Cable, D. M., Williamson, I. O., Lambert, L. S., & Shipp, A. J. (2006). The phenomenology of fit: Linking the person and environment to the subjective experience of person-environment fit. *Journal of Applied Psychology, 91,* 802–827. doi:10.1037/0021-9010.91.4.802

Edwards, J. R., & Parry, M. E. (1993). On the use of polynomial regression equations as an alternative to difference scores in organizational research. *Academy of Management Journal, 36,* 1577–1613. doi:10.2307/256822

Erez, A., & Judge, A. (2001). Relationship of core self-evaluations to goal setting, motivation, and performance. *Journal of Applied Psychology, 86,* 1270–1279.

Feingold, A. (1994). Gender differences in personality: A meta-analysis. *Psychological Bulletin, 116,* 429–456. doi:10.1037/0033-2909.116.3.429

Fleishman, E. A. (1964). *Structure and measurement of physical fitness.* Englewood Cliffs, NJ: Prentice-Hall.

Foldes, H., Duehr, E. E., & Ones, D. S. (2008). Group difference in personality: Meta-analyses comparing five US racial groups. *Personnel Psychology, 61,* 579–616. doi:10.1111/j.1744-6570.2008.00123.x

Funder, D. C., & Ozer, D. J. (1983). Behavior as a function of the situation. *Journal of Personality and Social Psychology, 44,* 107–112. doi:10.1037/0022-3514.44.1.107

Goldberg, L. R. (1990). An alternative "description of personality: " The Big Five factor structure. *Journal of Personality and Social Psychology, 59,* 1216–1229. doi:10.1037/0022-3514.59.6.1216

Goldberg, L. R. (1993). The structure of phenotypic personality traits. *The American Psychologist, 48,* 26–34. doi:10.1037/0003-066X.48.1.26

Goldberg, L. R. (1997). A broad-bandwidth, public-domain, personality inventory measuring the lower-level facets of several five-factor models. In I. Mervielde, I. Deary, F. De Fruyt, & F. Ostendorf (Eds.), *Personality psychology in Europe* (Vol. 7, pp. 7–28). Tilburg, the Netherlands: Tilburg University Press.

Goleman, D. (1995). *Emotional intelligence.* New York: Bantam.

Goleman, D. (1998). *Working with emotional intelligence.* New York: Bantam.

Gough, H. G. (1957). *Manual for the California Psychological Inventory.* Palo Alto, CA: Consulting Psychologists Press.

Grubb, W., Whetzel, D. L., & McDaniel, M. A. (2004). General mental ability tests in industry. In J. Thomas (Ed.), *Comprehensive handbook of psychological assessment, Vol. 4: Industrial and organizational assessment* (pp. 7–20). Hoboken, NJ: Wiley.

Guion, R. M., & Gottier, R. F. (1965). Validity of personality measures in personnel selection. *Personnel Psychology, 18,* 135–164. doi:10.1111/j.1744-6570.1965.tb00273.x

Gulliksen, H. (1950). *Theory of mental tests.* New York: Wiley.

Hansen, J. C., & Dik, B. J. (2005). Evidence of 12-year predictive and concurrent validity for SII Occupational Scale scores. *Journal of Vocational Behavior, 67,* 365–378. doi:10.1016/j.jvb.2004.08.001

Hansen, J. C., & Swanson, J. L. (1983). Stability of interests and the predictive and concurrent validity of the 1981 Strong–Campbell Interest Inventory for college majors. *Journal of Counseling Psychology, 30,* 194–201. doi:10.1037/0022-0167.30.2.194

Harmon, L. W., Hansen, J. C., Borgen, F. H., & Hammer, A. L. (1994). *Strong Interest Inventory Applications and Technical Guide.* Stanford, CA: Stanford University Press.

Heggestad, E. D., Morrison, M., Reeve, C. L., & McCloy, R. A. (2006). Forced-choice assessments of personality for selection: Evaluating issues of normative assessment and faking resistance. *The Journal of Applied Psychology, 91,* 9–24. doi:10.1037/0021-9010.91.1.9

Heneman, H. G., III, & Judge, T. A. (2009). *Staffing organizations* (6th ed.). Middleton, WI: McGraw-Hill Irwin.

Hofstee, W. K., De Raad, B., & Goldberg, L. R. (1992). Integration of the Big Five and circumplex approaches to trait structure. *Journal of Personality and Social Psychology, 63,* 146–163. doi:10.1037/0022-3514.63.1.146

Hogan, J. C. (1991). Physical abilities. In M. D. Dunnette & L. M. Hough (Eds.), *Handbook of industrial and organizational psychology* (2nd ed., Vol. 2, pp. 753–831). Palo Alto, CA: Consulting Psychologists Press.

Hogan, J., & Quigley, A. M. (1986). Physical standards for employment and the courts. *American Psychologist, 41,* 1193–1217.

Hogan, R. (1983). A socioanalytic theory of personality. In *Nebraska Symposium on Motivation* (pp. 55–89). Lincoln: University of Nebraska Press.

Hogan, R., & Hogan, J. (1992). *Hogan Personality Inventory manual.* Tulsa, OK: Hogan Assessment Systems.

Holland, J. L. (1959). A theory of occupational choice. *Journal of Counseling Psychology, 6,* 35–45. doi:10.1037/h0040767

Holland, J. L. (1985). *Making vocational choices: A theory of vocational personalities and work environments.* Englewood Cliffs, NJ: Prentice Hall.

Hough, L. M., Eaton, N. K., Dunnette, M. D., Kamp, J. D., & McCloy, R. A. (1990). Criterion related validities of personality constructs and the effect of response distortion on those validities. *The Journal of Applied Psychology, 75,* 581–595. doi:10.1037/0021-9010.75.5.581

Hough, L. M., Oswald, F. L., & Ployhart, R. E. (2001). Determinants, detection and amelioration of adverse impact in personnel selection procedures: Issues, evidence, and lessons learned. *International Journal of Selection and Assessment, 9,* 152–194. doi:10.1111/1468-2389.00171

Hulin, C. L., Drasgow, F., & Parsons C. K. (1983). *Item response theory: Applications to psychological measurement.* Homewood, IL: Dow Jones-Irwin.

Hunter, J. E. (1980). *Test validation for 12,000 jobs: An application of synthetic validity and validity generalization to the General Aptitude Test Battery (GATB).* Washington. DC: U.S. Department of Labor.

Hunter, J. E. (1983). A causal analysis of cognitive ability, job knowledge, job performance, and supervisory ratings. In F. Landy, S. Zedeck, & J. Cleveland (Eds.), *Performance measurement and theory* (pp. 257–266). Hillsdale, NJ: Erlbaum.

Hunter, J. E., & Hunter, R. F. (1984). Validity and utility of alternative predictors of job performance. *Psychological Bulletin, 96,* 72–98. doi:10.1037/0033-2909.96.1.72

Hurtz, G. M., & Alliger, G. M. (2002). Influence of coaching on integrity test performance and unlikely virtue scale scores. *Human Performance, 15,* 255–273. doi:10.1207/S15327043HUP1503_02

Jackson, D. N. (1994). *Jackson Personality Inventory—revised manual.* Port Huron, MI: Sigma Assessment Systems.

Jackson, D. N., Wrobleski, V. R., & Ashton, M. C. (2000). The impact of faking on employment tests: Does forced-choice offer a solution? *Human Performance, 13,* 371–388. doi:10.1207/S15327043HUP1304_3

Judge, T. A. (2009). Core self-evaluations and work success. *Current Directions in Psychological Science, 18,* 58–62. doi:10.1111/j.1467-8721.2009.01606.x

Judge, T. A., Bono, J. E., Ilies, R., & Gerhardt, M. W. (2002). Personality and leadership: A qualitative and quantitative review. *Journal of Applied Psychology, 87,* 765–780. Medline doi:10.1037/0021-9010.87.4.765

Judge, T. A., Erez, A., Bono, J. E., & Thoresen, C. (2002). Are measures of self-esteem, neuroticism, locus of control, and generalized self-efficacy indicators of a common core construct? *Journal of Personality and Social Psychology, 83,* 693–710.

Judge, T. A., Hurst, C., & Simon, L. S. (2009). Does it pay to be smart, attractive, or confident (or all three)? Relationships among general mental ability, physical attractiveness, core self-evaluations, and income. *Journal of Applied Psychology, 94,* 742–755.

Judge, T. A., Thoresen, C. J., Bono, J. E., & Patton, G. K. (2001). The job satisfaction-job performance relationship: A qualitative and quantitative review. *Psychological Bulletin, 127,* 376–407. doi:10.1037/0033-2909.127.3.376

Kolen, M. J., & Brennan, R. L. (2004). *Test equating, scaling, and linking: Methods and practices* (2nd ed.). New York: Springer-Verlag.

Kristof-Brown, A. L., Zimmerman R. D., & Johnson, E. C. (2005). Consequences of an individual's fit at work: A meta-analysis of person-job, person-organization, person-group, and person-supervisor fit. *Personnel Psychology, 58,* 281–342. doi:10.1111/j.1744-6570.2005.00672.x

Landy, F. J. (2005). Some historical and scientific issues related to research on emotional intelligence. *Journal of Organizational Behavior, 26,* 411–424. doi:10.1002/job.317

Lievens, F., Buyse, T., & Sackett, P. R. (2005). The operational validity of a video-based situational judgment test for medical college admissions: illustrating the importance of matching predictor and criterion construct domains. *Journal of Applied Psychology, 90,* 442–452. doi:10.1037/0021-9010.90.3.442

Likert, R. (1932). A technique for the measurement of attitudes. *Archives of Psychology, 22*(140), 1–55.

Locke, E. A., McClear, K., & Knight, D. (1996). Self-esteem and work. *International Review of Industrial and Organizational Psychology, 11,* 1–32.

Mael, F. A. (1991). A conceptual rationale for the domain and attributes of bio-data items. *Personnel Psychology, 44,* 763–792.

Maslow, A. H. (1968). *Toward a psychology of being* (2nd ed.). Oxford, England: Van Nostrand.

Matthews, G., Roberts, R. D., & Zeidner, M. (2004). Seven myths about emotional intelligence. *Psychological Inquiry, 15,* 179–196. doi:10.1207/s15327965pli1503_01

Mayer, J. D., Caruso, D. R., & Salovey, P. (1999). Emotional intelligence meets traditional standards for an intelligence. *Intelligence, 27,* 267–298. doi:10.1016/S0160-2896(99)00016-1

McCloy, R. A., Campbell, J. P., & Cudeck, R. (1994). A confirmatory test of a model of performance determinants. *Journal of Applied Psychology, 79*, 493–505. doi:10.1037/0021-9010.79.4.493

McCloy, R. A., Heggestad, E. D., & Reeve, C. L. (2005). A silk purse from the sow's ear: Retrieving normative information from multidimensional forced-choice items. *Organizational Research Methods, 8*, 222–248. doi:10.1177/1094428105275374

McCrae, R. R., & Costa, P. T., Jr. (1987). Validation of the five-factor model of personality across instruments and observers. *Journal of Personality and Social Psychology, 57*, 17–40.

McCrae, R. R., & Costa, P. T. (1996). Toward a new generation of personality theories: Theoretical contexts for the five-factor model. In J. S. Wiggins (Ed.), *The five-factor model of personality* (pp. 51–87). New York: Guilford Press.

McCrae, R. R., Costa, P. T., Jr., & Piedmont, R. L. (1993). Folk concepts, natural language, and psychological constructs: The California Psychological Inventory and the five-factor model. *Journal of Personality, 61*, 1–26. doi:10.1111/j.1467-6494.1993.tb00276.x

McManus, M. A., & Kelly, M. L. (1999). Personality measures and bio-data: Evidence regarding their incremental predictive value in the life insurance industry. *Personnel Psychology, 52*, 137–148. doi:10.1111/j.1744-6570.1999.tb01817.x

Mershon, B., & Gorsuch, R. L. (1988). Number of factors in personality sphere: Does increase in factors increase predictability of real life criteria? *Journal of Personality and Social Psychology, 55*, 675–680. doi:10.1037/0022-3514.55.4.675

Mischel, W. (1968). *Personality and assessment.* New York: Wiley.

Mischel, W. (1969). Continuity and change in personality. *American Psychologist, 24*, 1012–1018. doi:10.1037/h0028886

Mischel, W. (1973). Toward a cognitive social learning reconceptualization of personality. *Psychological Review, 80*, 252–283. doi:10.1037/h0035002

Moon, H. (2001). The two faces of conscientiousness: Duty and achievement striving in escalation of commitment dilemmas. *Journal of Applied Psychology, 86*, 533–540. doi:10.1037/0021-9010.86.3.535

Morgeson, F. P., Campion, M. A., Dipboye, R. L., Hollenbeck, J. R., Murphy, K., & Schmitt, N. (2007). Are we getting fooled again? Coming to terms with limitations in the use of personality tests for personnel selection. *Personnel Psychology, 60*, 1029–1049. doi:10.1111/j.1744-6570.2007.00100.x

Motowidlo, S. J., Borman, W. C., & Schmit, M. J. (1997). A theory of individual differences in task and contextual performance. *Human Performance, 10*, 71–83. doi:10.1207/s15327043hup1002_1

Mount, M. K., Witt, L. A., & Barrick, M. R. (2000). Incremental validity of empirically keyed biodata scales over GMA and the five factor personality constructs. *Personnel Psychology, 53*, 299–323.

Mumford, M. D., & Stokes, G. S. (1992). Developmental determinants of individual action: Theory and practice in applying background measures. In M. D. Dunnette & L. M. Hough (Eds.), *Handbook of industrial and organizational psychology* (pp. 61–138). Palo Alto, CA: Consulting Psychologists Press.

Nye, C. D., Do, B.-R., Drasgow, F., & Fine, S. (2008). Two-step testing in employee selection: Is score inflation a problem? *International Journal of Selection and Assessment, 16*, 112–120. doi:10.1111/j.1468-2389.2008.00416.x

Olson-Buchanan, J. B., Drasgow, F., Moberg, P. J., Mead, A. D., Keenan, P. A., & Donovan, M. (1998). Interactive video assessment of conflict resolution skills. *Personnel Psychology, 51*, 1-24.

Ones, D. S., Viswesvaran, C., & Schmidt, F. L. (1993). Comprehensive meta-analysis of integrity test validities: Findings and implications for personnel selection and theories of job performance. *Journal of Applied Psychology, 78*, 679-703.

O*NET Resource Center. (2003). *The O*NET analyst database.* O*NET Consortium. Retrieved July 10, 2009, from http://www.onetcenter.org/database.html#archive

Oolders, T., Chernyshenko, O.S., & Stark, S. (2008). Cultural intelligence as a mediator of relationships between openness to experience and adaptive performance. In S. Ang & L. Van Dyne (Eds.), *Handbook of cultural intelligence: Theory, measurement, and applications* (pp. 145–158). New York: Sharpe.

O'Reilly, C. A., Chatman, J., & Caldwell, D. F. (1991). People and organizational culture: A profile comparison approach to assessing person-organization fit. *Academy of Management Journal, 34*, 487–516.

Organ, D. W., & Ryan, K. (1995). A meta-analytic review of attitudinal and dispositional predictors of organizational citizenship behavior. *Personnel Psychology, 48*, 775–802.

Owens, W. A., & Schoenfeldt, L. F. (1979). Toward a classification of persons. *Journal of Applied Psychology, 65*, 569–607.

Paunonen, S. V. (1998). Hierarchical organization of personality and prediction of behavior. *Journal of Personality and Social Psychology, 74*, 538–556.

Posner, B. Z., Kouzes, J. M., & Schmidt, W. H. (1985). Shared values make a difference: An empirical test of corporate culture. *Human Resource Management, 24*, 293–309.

Pratt, M. G. (2000). The good, the bad, and the ambivalent: Managing identification among Amway distributors. *Administrative Science Quarterly, 45,* 456–493.

Prediger, D. J. (1982). Dimensions underlying Holland's hexagon: Missing link between interests and occupations? *Journal of Vocational Behavior, 21,* 259–287.

Quest Diagnostics. (2008). *Drug testing index.* Retrieved July 10, 2009, from http://www.questdiagnostics.com/employersolutions/dti/2008_03/dti_index.html

Raven, J., Raven, J. C., & Court, J. H. (1998). *Raven Manual. 1998 edition.* Oxford, England: Oxford Psychologists Press.

Ravlin, E. C., & Meglino, B. M. (1987). Effect of values on perception and decision making: A study of alternative work values measures. *Journal of Applied Psychology, 72,* 666–673.

Ree, M. J., & Earles, J. A. (1991). Predicting training success: Not much more than *g. Personnel Psychology, 44,* 321–332.

Ree, M. J., Earles, J. A., & Teachout, M. (1994). Predicting job performance: Not much more than *g. Journal of Applied Psychology, 79,* 518–524.

Roberts, B. W. (2006). Personality development and organizational behavior. In B. M. Staw (Ed.), *Research on organizational behavior* (pp. 1–41). New York: Elsevier Science/JAI Press.

Roberts, B. W., Chernyshenko, O., Stark, S., & Goldberg, L. (2005). The structure of conscientiousness: An empirical investigation based on seven major personality questionnaires. *Personnel Psychology, 58,* 103–139.

Roberts, J. S., Donoghue, J. R., & Laughlin, J. E. (2000). A general model for unfolding unidimensional polytomous responses using item response theory. *Applied Psychological Measurement, 24,* 2–32.

Rokeach, M. (1973). *The nature of human values.* New York: Free Press.

Rosse, J. G., Stecher, M., Miller, J. L., & Levin, R. A. (1998). The impact of response distortion on preemployment personality testing and hiring decisions. *Journal of Applied Psychology, 83,* 634–644.

Rotter, J. B. (1966). Generalized expectancies for internal versus external control of reinforcement. *Psychological Monographs, 80* (1, Whole No. 609).

Rounds, J. B., Henly, G A., Dawis, R. V., Lofquist, L. H., & Weiss, D. J. (1981). *Manual for the Minnesota Importance Questionnaire.* Minneapolis: University of Minnesota at Minneapolis, Vocational Psychology Research.

Salgado, J. F., Anderson, N., Moscoso, S., Bertua, C., de Fruyt, F., & Rolland, J. P. (2003). A meta-analytic study of general mental ability validity for different occupations in the European Community. *Journal of Applied Psychology, 88,* 1068–1081.

Saucier, G. (2003). An alternative multi-language structure for personality attributes. *European Journal of Personality, 17,* 179–205.

Saucier, G., & Ostendorf, F. (1999). Hierarchical subcomponents of the Big Five personality factors: A cross-language replication. *Journal of Personality and Social Psychology, 76,* 613–627.

Schmid, J., & Leiman, J. M. (1957). The development of hierarchical factor solutions. *Psychometrika, 22,* 53–61.

Schmidt, F. L., & Hunter, J. E. (1998). The validity and utility of selection methods in personnel psychology: Practical and theoretical implications of 85 years of research findings. *Psychological Bulletin, 124,* 262–274.

Schmidt, F. L., & Hunter, J. E. (2004). General mental ability in the world of work: Occupational attainment and job performance. *Journal of Personality and Social Psychology, 86,* 162–173.

Schwartz, S. H. (1992). Universals in the content and structure of values: Theoretical advances and empirical tests in 20 countries. In M. P. Zanna (Ed.), *Advances in experimental social psychology* (Vol. 25, pp. 1–65). Orlando, FL: Academic Press.

Schwartz, S. H., & Boehnke, K. (2004). Evaluating the structure of human values with confirmatory factor analysis. *Journal of Research in Personality, 38,* 230–255.

Segall, D.O. (2001, April). *Detecting test compromise in high-stakes computerized adaptive testing: A verification testing approach.* Paper presented at the Annual Meeting of the National Council on Measurement in Education, Seattle, WA.

Segall, D. O., & Moreno, K. E. (1999). Development of the CAT-ASVAB. In F. Drasgow & J. B. Olson-Buchanan (Eds.), *Innovations in computerized assessment* (pp. 35–65). Hillsdale, NJ: Erlbaum.

Sisson, E. D. (1948). Forced choice—the new Army rating. *Personnel Psychology, 1,* 365–381.

Sodano, S. M., & Tracey, T. J. (2008). Prestige in interest activity assessment. *Journal of Vocational Behavior,* 73, 310–317.

Spearman, C. (1904). "General intelligence" objectively determined and measured. *American Journal of Psychology, 15,* 201–293.

Stark, S. (2002). *A new IRT approach to test construction and scoring designed to reduce the effects of faking in personality assessment.* Unpublished doctoral dissertation, University of Illinois at Urbana–Champaign.

Stark, S., Chernyshenko, O. S., Chan, K. Y., Lee, W. C., & Drasgow, F. (2001). Effects of the testing situation on item responding: Cause for concern. *Journal of Applied Psychology, 86,* 943–953.

Stark, S., Chernyshenko, O. S., & Drasgow, F. (2004). Examining the effects of differential item/test functioning (DIF/DTF) on selection decisions: When are statistically significant effects practically important? *Journal of Applied Psychology, 89,* 497–508.

Stark, S., Chernyshenko, O. S., & Drasgow, F. (2005). An IRT approach to constructing and scoring pairwise preference items involving stimuli on different dimensions: The multi-unidimensional pairwise preference model. *Applied Psychological Measurement, 29,* 184–201.

Stark, S., Chernyshenko, O. S., & Drasgow, F., & Williams, B. A. (2006). Examining assumptions about item responding in personality assessment: Should ideal point methods be considered for scale development and scoring? *Journal of Applied Psychology, 91,* 25–39.

Stark, S., & Drasgow, F. (2002). An EM approach to parameter estimation for the Zinnes and Griggs paired comparison IRT model. *Applied Psychological Measurement, 26,* 208–227.

Stark, S., Drasgow, F., & Chernyshenko, O. S. (2008, October). *Update on the Tailored Adaptive Personality Assessment System (TAPAS): The next generation of personality assessment systems to support personnel selection and classification decisions.* Paper presented at the 50th annual conference of the International Military Testing Association, Amsterdam, the Netherlands.

Stokes, G. S., & Searcy, C. A. (1999). Specification of scales in biodata form development: Rational vs. empirical and global vs. specific. *International Journal of Selection and Assessment, 7,* 72–85.

Stokes, G. S., Toth, C. S., Searcy, C. A., Stroupe, J. P., & Carter, G. W. (1999). Construct/rational bio-data dimensions to predict salesperson performance: Report on the U.S. Department of Labor sales study. *Human Resource Management Review, 9,* 185–219.

Tay, L., Drasgow, F., Rounds, J., & Williams, B. A. (2009). Fitting measurement models to vocational interest data: Are dominance models ideal? *Journal of Applied Psychology, 94,* 1287–1304.

Tellegen, A. (1982). *A brief manual for the Multidimensional Personality Questionnaire.* Unpublished manuscript, University of Minnesota, Minneapolis.

Tett, R. P., Jackson, D. N., & Rothstein, M. (1991). Personality measures as predictors of job performance: A meta-analytic review. *Personnel Psychology, 44,* 703–742.

Thorndike, R. L. (1949). *Personnel selection.* New York: Wiley.

Thurstone, L. L. (1927). A law of comparative judgment. *Psychological Review, 34,* 278–286.

Thurstone, L. L. (1928). Attitudes can be measured. *American Journal of Sociology, 33,* 529–554.

Thurstone, L. L. (1929). Theory of attitude measurement. *Psychological Review, 36,* 222–241.

Thurstone, L. L. (1938). Primary mental abilities. *Psychometric Monographs,* No. 1. Chicago: University of Chicago Press.

Thurstone, L. L. (1947). *Multiple factor analysis.* Chicago: University of Chicago Press.

Tinsley, H. E. (2000). The congruence myth: An analysis of the efficacy of the person–environment fit model. *Journal of Vocational Behavior, 56,* 147–179.

Tippins, N. T., Beaty, J., Drasgow, F., Gibson, W. M., Pearlman, K., Segall, D., & Shepherd, W. (2006). Unproctored Internet testing in employment settings. *Personnel Psychology, 59,* 189–225.

Tracey, T. J., & Rounds, J. (1993). Evaluating Holland's and Gati's vocational-interest models: A structural meta-analysis. *Psychological Bulletin, 113,* 229–246.

Tracey, T. J. G., & Rounds, J. (1996). The spherical representation of vocational interests. *Journal of Vocational Behavior, 48,* 3–41.

Tranberg, M., Slane, S., & Ekeberg, S. E. (1993). The relation between interest congruence and satisfaction: A meta-analysis. *Journal of Vocational Behavior, 42,* 253–264.

Vasilopoulos, N. L., Cucina, J. M., Dyomina, N. V., Morewitz, C. L., & Reilly, R. R. (2006). Forced-choice personality tests: A measure of personality and cognitive ability? *Human Performance, 19,* 175–199.

Vernon, P. E. (1950). *The structure of human abilities.* New York: Wiley.

Viswesvaran, C., Ones, D. S., & Schmidt, F. L. (1996). Comparative analysis of the reliability of job performance ratings. *Journal of Applied Psychology, 81,* 557–574.

U.S. Department of Labor. (1991). *Dictionary of occupational titles* (rev. 4th ed.). Washington DC: U.S. Government Printing Office.

Watson, G., & Glaser, E. M. (1980). *Watson–Glaser Critical Thinking Appraisal: Forms A and B.* San Antonio, TX: Psychological Corporation.

Weiss, H. M., & Cropanzano, R. 1996. An affective events approach to job satisfaction. In B. M. Staw & L. L. Cummings (Eds.), *Research in organizational behavior* (Vol. 18, pp. 1–74). Greenwich, CT: JAI Press.

White, L. A., & Young, M. C. (1998, May). *Development and validation of the Assessment of Individual Motivation (AIM).* Paper presented at the 106th Annual Convention of the American Psychological Association, San Francisco, CA.

White, L. A., Young, M. C., Hunter, A. E., & Rumsey, M. G. (2008). Lessons learned in transitioning personality measures from research to operational settings. *Industrial and Organizational Psychology: Perspectives on Science and Practice, 1,* 291–295.

Wonderlic Personnel Test. (1992). *User's manual for the Wonderlic Personnel Test and the Scholastic Level Exam.* Libertyville, IL: Author.

Yung, Y. F., Thissen, D., & McLeod, L. D. (1999). On the relationship between the higher-order factor model and the hierarchical factor model. *Psychometrika, 64,* 113–128.

Zickar, M. J., & Drasgow, F. (1996). Detecting faking on a personality instrument using appropriateness measurement. *Applied Psychological Measurement, 20,* 71–87.

Zytowski, D. G. (1974). Predictive validity of the Kuder Preference Record, Form B, over a 25-year span. *Measurement and Evaluation in Guidance, 7,* 122–129.

CHAPTER 5

PERSONALITY AND ITS ASSESSMENT IN ORGANIZATIONS: THEORETICAL AND EMPIRICAL DEVELOPMENTS

Frederick L. Oswald and Leaetta M. Hough

Whether a company is hiring customer sales representatives with an appropriate mix of friendliness and aggressiveness, or a space agency is training astronauts who require initiative, independent judgment, and team problem solving on long-duration space flights, individual personality traits are relevant to an organization's successful achievement of its goals. Personality traits relevant to organizations are those psychological characteristics that predict consistent work-related thoughts, motivations, behavior, and other outcomes across situations and over time.

Although laypeople take the influence of personality on individual and group outcomes for granted, the research evidence has not been as obvious. Indeed, the past 50 years have been tumultuous for researchers investigating the importance of personality variables to organizations and work outcomes. Critics in the mid-1960s challenged the power of personality traits to predict job performance. Today, the accumulated evidence has indicated that personality traits do predict variance in dependent variables of paramount importance to both organizations and their employees (e.g., career success, job performance, teamwork, job satisfaction, employee turnover). More important, this prediction is often incremental, meaning that personality measures often predict above and beyond the prediction afforded by cognitive ability measures, especially (and obviously) when the criteria rely more heavily on personality characteristics (e.g., police who must relate to members of the community to perform effectively). The magnitudes of the criterion-related validities for personality that we report weigh against classic critiques of the historical weakness of personality research (Guion & Gottier, 1965; Mischel, 1968). Those critiques had concluded that average validities were weak or highly variable at best when really they may have been a function of the state of personality research at the time.

Contemporary organizational researchers are taking on the challenge of continuing to refine the conceptualization, measurement, and modeling of personality and organizational outcomes. At the same time, they must grapple with the many practical realities that constrain any empirical research project that takes to the field. For instance, elaborate theories might specify more constructs than time allows for their appropriate measurement. In addition, although many personality measures designed for employment settings adhere to the standards required for appropriate psychological testing (e.g., American Educational Research Association, American Psychological Association, & National Council on Measurement in Education, 1999), they may lag behind the recommendations provided by current research. Finally, criterion-related validity may necessarily be based on administrative forms that reflect organizational goals such as promotion and compensation more than the outcome itself (e.g., job performance, turnover).

Our chapter first provides a brief history of personality assessment, especially as it pertains to organizational research and variables that form the structure of personality. Included in this section is a review of useful theoretical frameworks, namely, the five-factor personality model (FFM), the HEXACO (six-factor) model, and a nomological-web clustering model, all of which have been used to organize available personality measures and validity evidence.

Using these models to examine validity evidence, we learn that analyses focused at the facet (subfactor) level can improve both theoretical understanding and prediction of dependent variables of critical interest to the field. Second, we summarize important findings concerning the criterion-related validity of personality measures, often relying on meta-analytic evidence to summarize quantitative effects found within a particular research domain. Third, we move from a discussion of the structure and validity of personality factors and facets to an examination of mean ethnic–culture, gender, and age differences on personality measures and their implications for efforts to reduce adverse impact in personnel selection. Fourth, we review and provide a perspective on test-score faking, a phenomenon that pervades the personality testing literature. We argue that research investigating various proactive attempts to prevent faking may be more productive than the vast body of research that explores attempts to induce it in the lab or to detect and correct for it statistically. Fifth, we discuss several broad integrated psychological models involving the prediction of performance outcomes, pointing out the integral role that personality plays, often at a level more refined than the Big Five or HEXACO factors. Sixth, we review several innovative approaches to personality assessment, many of which attempt to thwart faking, reduce subgroup mean differences, and either improve or broaden the prediction of organizational criteria. Seventh, although we provide directions for future research throughout the chapter, we close with a discussion of areas of inquiry that appear especially productive and timely to pursue.

MODELS AND STRUCTURES OF PERSONALITY

Brief History and Background

The meta-analysis by Barrick and Mount (1991) is widely cited as a turning point in the decades-long saga of academic disputes concerning the usefulness of self-report measures of personality constructs for predicting job performance. The critical feature of this meta-analysis was in summarizing criterion-related validity coefficients by personality construct as well as by job or occupation. Specifically, they used the FFM, or the Big Five factors of Emotional Stability, Neuroticism, Extraversion, Agreeableness, Conscientiousness, and Openness (see Table 5.1 for the factors and their facets), to organize personality measures, summarizing the criterion-related validities for each personality construct within and across job types. In particular, they reported that conscientiousness was a valid predictor across most jobs, and extraversion was a predictor for those interpersonal jobs requiring it (e.g., sales, law enforcement). There has been a virtual explosion of personality research in industrial and organizational (I/O) psychology subsequent to this seminal work.

An important part of this history has been research examining the hierarchical nature of personality, in which facets are modeled as narrowly defined constructs whose covariances, in part, give rise to factors such as those of the Big Five (Costa & McCrae, 1995; Eysenck, 1947; J. Hogan & Roberts, 1996; Hough, 1992; John, Hampson, & Goldberg, 1991; Markon, Krueger, & Watson, 2005; Paunonen, 1998). Even the Big Five factors, broad as they are, have covariances that have been summarized by two even broader factors (labeled *alpha* and *beta* by Digman, 1997; *agency* and *communion* by Wiggins, 1991; or *getting ahead* and *getting along* by Hogan, 1983; although see Ashton, Lee, Goldberg, & de Vries, 2009, for a criticism).

A discussion of the merits of factors versus facets requires an awareness of a tension between personality theory and the use of personality variables in employment settings to which organizational research is intended to generalize. More specifically, practitioners often need to know whether a specific personality measure will be useful within the assessment system of a particular company, whereas researchers seek a broader and more theoretical understanding of the underlying nature, dimensionality, and relationships between latent personality constructs. Both sides of the research–practice coin are clearly necessary because a theoretical understanding of personality constructs informs the development and practical usefulness of measures. The present-day practice of applying meta-analysis to a wide array of personality measures in organizational research has been beneficial for interpreting our results in terms of theoretical constructs. The theoretical question of whether we

TABLE 5.1

Description and Alignment of Big Five (B5) and HEXACO (HX) Factors and Facets

Model	Factor	Facets
HX-H	Honesty–Humility	Sincerity, fairness, greed avoidance, modesty
B5	Emotional Stability (reversed)/Emotionality	Anxiety, anger, depression, self-consciousness, immoderation, vulnerability
HX-E		Fearfulness, anxiety, dependence, sentimentality
B5	Extraversion/Surgency	Friendliness, gregariousness, assertiveness, activity level, excitement seeking, cheerfulness
HX-X		Expressiveness, social boldness, sociability, liveliness
B5	Agreeableness	Trust, morality, altruism, cooperation, modesty, sympathy
HX-A		Forgiveness, gentleness, flexibility, patience
B5	Conscientiousness	Self-efficacy, orderliness, dutifulness, achievement striving, self-discipline, cautiousness
HX-C		Organization, diligence, perfectionism, prudence
B5	Openness to Experience	Imagination, artistic interests, emotionality, adventurousness, intellect, liberalism
HX-O		Aesthetic appreciation, inquisitiveness, creativity, unconventionality

Note. Facet descriptions are from the International Personality Item Pool (http://www.ipip.ori.org; Goldberg, 1999) for the Big Five and from K. Lee and Ashton (2004) for the HEXACO.

have identified—or ever will identify—fundamental constructs (*taxons*) that form the structure of human personality, however, may be less important than the extent to which we have consistent patterns of evidence for personality constructs predicting organizationally relevant constructs, thereby contributing meaningfully to practice and to our theoretical knowledge base.

In the next section, we discuss in greater depth the FFM and the HEXACO model; we also discuss the usefulness of personality facets that, both theoretically and empirically, are one level more refined than the factors contained in these models (see Table 5.1). We then describe a nomological-web clustering approach that incorporates facets in a more flexible bottom-up manner that increases our understanding of the structure of personality and patterns of criterion-related validity.

FFM: Past, Present, and Future

Regardless of whether the five personality constructs in the FFM are fundamental, it is obvious to anyone in I/O psychology that personality research has relied heavily on it since the 1990s. The FFM has influenced our theory building and our practice.

The FFM emerged from a factor analysis of ratings of personality-descriptive adjectives from the dictionary. The Big Five factors are thus natural-language constructs (Allport & Odbert, 1936; Goldberg, 1990, 1993; Tupes & Christal, 1992) and represent a shared or folk understanding of the structure of personality. In other words, the FFM's roots are in the English lexicon, not in psychological theory (Hough & Ones, 2001; Hough & Schneider, 1996; Tellegen, 1993; see Hough & Schneider, 1996, for a history of the FFM).

Strong proponents of the FFM have argued that it is a universal or nomothetic structure of personality variables that, like the very definition of a personality trait itself, is stable within individual across ethnic–cultural and gender groups and over time. Considerable research in the past 20 years has been devoted to examining the adequacy and universal nature of the FFM (e.g., Benet-Martínez & John, 1998;

Digman & Takemoto-Chock, 1981; Goldberg, 1990; Goldberg & Saucier, 1998; Katigbak, Church, & Akamine, 1996; McCrae & Costa, 1987, 1997; Norman, 1963; Ostendorf & Angleitner, 1994; Peabody & Goldberg, 1989; Somer & Goldberg, 1999). The FFM is often supported by the data, but there are trends showing that some parts of this model are more robust or replicable across studies than others. Extraversion and Emotional Stability are found in virtually all of the studies just cited, followed by Conscientiousness. Agreeableness is less robust; Openness to Experience tends to be the least replicable and thus the most controversial of the Big Five factors (Hough & Ones, 2001). Perhaps this latter construct is better understood at the level of its facets, which deal with openness to ideas and openness to art and culture. Openness to ideas correlates more strongly with intelligence measures, for instance (Zimprich, Allemand, & Dellenbach, 2009).

Two streams of research have investigated the universality of the FFM across culture and language. One stream takes the *lexical approach,* an approach similar to the development of the FFM itself, based on collecting and analyzing responses to single adjectives relevant to personality in the language of a particular culture. The other stream is the *person-descriptive approach,* based on responses to statements as might be found on a typical Likert-scale personality test (e.g., "I like parties"). The two approaches tend to produce different results and conclusions for reasons that have not been well understood; it may be the result of the content, the format, or both.

The lexical approach typically finds poor similarity of factors across culture and language (e.g., Di Blas & Forzi, 1999; De Raad, Perugini, & Szirmak, 1997), leading to the following conclusion: "A study of the various studies participating in the crusade for cross-lingual personality-descriptive universals makes it clear that researchers are unlikely to find one and only one canonical, cross-culturally valid trait structure" (De Raad, 1998, p. 122). By contrast, researchers using the person-descriptive sentences method have concluded that the FFM is a biologically based human universal (e.g., Eysenck & Eysenck, 1985; McCrae, Costa, Del Pilar, Rolland, & Parker, 1998), generalizing across culture, language, gender, type of assessment rating source, and type of factor extraction and rotation methods (e.g., McCrae & Costa, 1997). Continued research will surely qualify broad generalizations such as this one in important ways. For example, some factors appear to be more relevant in some cultures than in others (e.g., interpersonal relatedness in Chinese culture; F. M. Cheung et al., 2001), and measures that appear similar in content across cultures also need to have similar underlying psychometric properties and ensure that they are measuring the same constructs in a reliable manner (Church, 2000, 2001; van de Vijver & Leung, 2001).

Exploratory factor analysis is the typical approach to analyzing personality data (Goldberg & Velicer, 2006), and although it often yields interpretable and consistent patterns of factor loadings for the Big Five, the claims regarding the similarity of exploratory factor structures across groups (e.g., race, culture, gender) are often based on statistical indices that tend to be deceptively high (congruence indices; see Bijnen, van der Net, & Poortinga, 1986). Moreover, repeated attempts to fit the Big Five model of personality to empirical data using confirmatory factor analysis models have failed in accordance with standard model-fit criteria (Hopwood & Donnellan, 2009), and adequate fit within groups should be a prerequisite for appropriate comparisons between groups.

On the conceptual side of the coin, challenges to the FFM have resulted in a considerable body of research that questions the conclusion that the FFM is a comprehensive and universal taxonomy for predicting work behavior. Such a conclusion may very well be premature. Expanding personality constructs and content beyond the Big Five can lead to a more diverse set of personality constructs that might provide even greater insight into understanding and explaining work behavior, performance, and outcomes. Thus, although assuming a broad structure of personality such as the Big Five has the benefit of organizing a wide array of confusing and redundant constructs, treating broad factors as fundamental has the potential to stifle or misdirect the development of more sophisticated theory and research (Block, 1995).

In spite of continued controversies regarding the comprehensiveness and cross-cultural robustness of the FFM, I/O psychologists have generally embraced it as the model of choice for understanding direct and indirect relationships between personality and organizational outcomes, especially dimensions of job performance. Therefore, the FFM is the organizing structure for summarizing many of the criterion-related validities that we discuss. Models that incorporate FFM personality variables tend to explain more of the variability in work behavior than do cognitive ability measures alone (Borman, White, Pulakos, & Oppler, 1991; Pulakos, Schmitt, & Chan, 1996; Schmidt & Hunter, 1992).

Organizational researchers have begun to explore and refine the taxonomic structure of personality further. At the level of broad factors, the HEXACO is the major contender to the FFM in the organizational research literature.

HEXACO Model

The HEXACO model extends the FFM to include a sixth factor. The six factors that have been recovered from personality data are described in Table 5.1 and are termed *HEXACO,* simultaneously an acronym and a reference to the six factors (Ashton & Lee, 2001; Ashton, Lee, Perugini, et al., 2004). HEXACO contains analogs of all the Big Five factors and adds an Honesty–Humility factor, which increases the representativeness of the model over the FFM. This factor also enhances the prediction of criteria, demonstrating a 10% to 15% increase over the FFM in the prediction of workplace delinquency across four cross-cultural samples, for instance (K. Lee, Ashton, & deVries, 2005). This sixth factor also appears to be in line with a sixth factor called the ideal-employee factor, found in an analysis of job applicant data but not student data (Schmit & Ryan, 1993).

The HEXACO emerged from a critical reanalysis of a set of studies using the lexical approach across seven languages (Italian, French, German, Dutch, Hungarian, Polish, and Korean), yielding six major dimensions of personality, not just the Big Five (Ashton, Lee, Perugini, et al., 2004). One initial thought was that differences were based on the specificities of culture and language: Whereas five factors best described the data for research with English adjectives that describe personality, other languages and cultures required six factors. However, contrary to many previous lexical studies in English that have found support for the Big Five, a lexical study of the structure of 1,710 English adjectives also found a set of six factors (Ashton, Lee, & Goldberg, 2004). The argument for six factors in English is that researchers were more inclusive of the lexicon and used hundreds more adjectives than in research done previously, allowing for richer descriptions of people (K. Lee & Ashton, 2008). For example, Tupes and Christal (1992), who were credited with the discovery of the FFM, gathered self-ratings on only 35 adjectives. Computational limitations at that time made the factor analysis of large data sets virtually or literally impossible. Even studies conducted in the 1980s and 1990s that could have made use of greater computational resources may have been burdened by this history because they tended to restrict the number of adjectives as well. The more expansive analysis is what has led to the addition of this sixth factor of Honesty–Humility.

Using Personality Facets Instead of Factors

Although the HEXACO model might have greater conceptual breadth than the FFM, other data on criterion-related validity and mean score differences between ethnic–cultural and gender groups suggest that moving a level down the hierarchy of personality constructs to the facet level can yield even more useful information. Without a doubt, the FFM and HEXACO factors have been practically useful, but researchers and practitioners might incorrectly assume that they are in some sense comprehensive, fundamental, or the best that personality research can provide. We have long argued that FFM factors are too broad for advancing our understanding of personality traits and prediction of behavior in the workplace, and the HEXACO model, although adding a sixth factor, suffers from the same general problem. Research involving facets—more narrowly defined constructs that often define these superordinate factors—has provided a more substantive understanding of the relationships between personality and criterion variables of importance to organizations (Hough, 1989, 1992, 1997, 1998;

Hough & Oswald, 2000, 2005, 2008; Hough & Schneider, 1996; R. J. Schneider, Hough, & Dunnette, 1996).

Research that has empirically derived facet-level taxonomies for each Big Five domain is in its relative infancy, but at least one study or meta-analysis for facets underlying each of the Big Five domains has been reported (Extraversion: S. E. Davies, Connelly, Ones, & Birkland, 2008; Emotional Stability: Birkland & Ones, 2006; Conscientiousness: Connelly & Ones, 2007; Roberts, Bogg, Walton, Chernyshenko, & Stark, 2004; Roberts, Chernyshenko, Stark, & Goldberg, 2005; Agreeableness: Connelly, Davies, Ones, & Birkland, 2008a; Openness to Experience: Connelly, Davies, Ones, & Birkland, 2008b). Somewhat different facets are identified when the lexical approach versus person-descriptive approach is used to investigate the structure of Conscientiousness (see Roberts et al., 2003, 2005). Nonetheless, results of these studies hold the promise of facets as components for improved theory, model building, and validity.

Many other personality traits relevant to employee behavior appear to be either missing or not well represented in the FFM or HEXACO frameworks (Hough & Furnham, 2003, detailed 21 such variables). They include facets such as (a) rugged individualism (Hough, 1992) and masculinity–femininity (Costa, Zonderman, Williams, & McCrae, 1985); (b) social adroitness, social competence, and social insight (Ashton, Jackson, Helmes, & Paunonen, 1998; M. Davies, Stankov, & Roberts, 1998; Gough, 1968; Hogan, 1969; R. J. Schneider, Ackerman, & Kanfer, 1996); (c) self-regulation and ego resiliency (Baumeister, Gailliot, DeWall, & Oaten, 2006; Block & Block, 2006); (d) villainy (De Raad & Hoskens, 1990); (e) fairness (Goldberg & Saucier, 1998); (f) tolerance for contradiction (Chan, 2004); (g) humorousness (Paunonen & Jackson, 2000); (h) prowess or heroism (Saucier, Georgiades, Tsaousis, & Goldberg, 2005); (i) social independence (Dancer & Woods, 2006); (j) work pace (Sanz, Gil, Garcia-Vera, & Barrasa, 2008); and (k) ease in decision making (Sanz et al., 2008) as well as needs contextualized for the work setting such as (a) need for rules and supervision and (b) need to be supportive (Sanz et al., 2008). There are more facets such as these that are clearly relevant to organizational behavior. They may be subsumed by broader factors, conceptually and empirically, but treating the facets as if they are interchangeable or the same as a broader factor may lead to ignoring or obscuring important patterns of validity.

Facet-level constructs are promising building blocks for theory building. Figure 5.1 provides a simple illustration, breaking down the Conscientious construct into two facets, achievement and conformity, which are further broken down into six subfacets. At a conceptual level, one could see how some organizations may seek employees who are high on achievement and low on conformity (e.g., marketers for start-up companies) or, conversely, others may seek employees who are lower on achievement and high on conformity (e.g., security monitors). A conscientiousness composite that weights these two facets equally as part of a single compound construct will not be able to differentiate between these two different profiles of applicants and therefore would tend to select applicants who fit less well than if achieve-

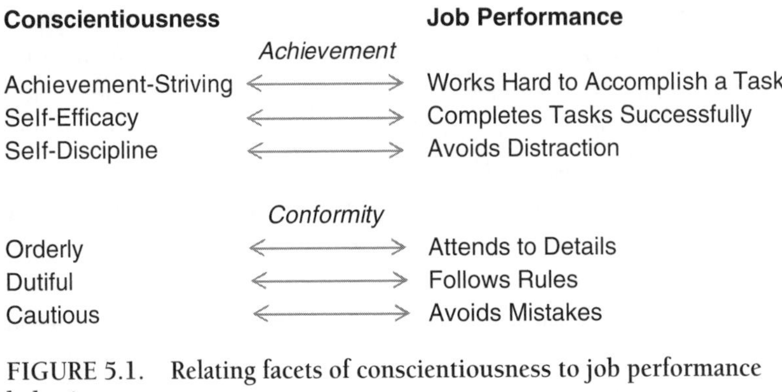

FIGURE 5.1. Relating facets of conscientiousness to job performance behaviors.

ment and conformity were measured and used as separate facets in a linear regression. Of course, this scenario assumes that empirically there are differential relationships to be found, but research has in fact supported this notion.

By now, there is a whole host of facet-level analyses that reveal different patterns of validity, and in many cases higher levels of validity, that were previously masked by analyses using broader factors. Here are several examples: In a newly hired sample of sales representatives, conformity was more predictive of obtaining new clients, whereas achievement was more predictive of the same criterion in later stages of employment (Stewart, 1999). Generally, achievement predicts performance more than conformity when it comes to overall performance, sales performance, and creativity (Hough, 1992). In a decision-making task, where performers had to discover that the rules were changing over time, those higher in conformity committed more errors, whereas achievement was unrelated to errors (LePine, Colquitt, Erez, 2000).

For those who continue to believe that "broader is better," we provide several more samples: Compared with Big Five scales, responsibility and risk taking demonstrated better prediction of self-reported delinquency such as unsafe workplace behavior and theft (Ashton, 1998); positive emotion and surgency, facets of Extraversion, predict citizenship behavior in opposite directions, obscuring any prediction by Extraversion itself (Moon, Hollenbeck, Marinova, & Humphrey, 2008); dependability, a facet of Conscientiousness, predicts counterproductive work behavior and job dedication better than does global conscientiousness (Dudley, Orvis, Lebiecki, & Cortina, 2006). Similarly, dependability and achievement, both facets of Conscientiousness, exhibit different patterns of criterion-related validity for job performance and law-abiding behaviors (Hough, 1992; Roberts et al., 2005), and dependability does not predict sales performance as strongly as achievement (Hough, 1992; Vinchur, Schippmann, Switzer, & Roth, 1998; Warr, Bartram, & Martin, 2005); harmony predicts interpersonal contextual behaviors but not personal contextual behaviors, and moral obligation and group loyalty predict personal contextual behaviors but not interpersonal ones (Kwong & Cheung, 2003); facets such as ambition and adjustment were most predictive of their criterion counterparts (Hogan & Holland, 2003; Tett, Steele, & Beauregard, 2003). Finally, in four large-sample data sets, 16 personality factors accounted for roughly twice the variance in organizational criteria compared with 6 factors, even after statistical adjustment for greater capitalization on chance as a result of including more facets than factors in the prediction equation (Mershon & Gorsuch, 1988; see also Paunonen & Nicol, 2001).

To be clear, however, we are not arguing for an infinite regress of increasingly narrow constructs, making distinctions that do not make a difference. We do not want to return to the "good old daze" (Hough, 1997) of our organizational research in personality, when each scale was considered a unique personality variable without any theoretical structure to organize it, making summaries of the literature unnecessarily difficult and subject to heavy criticism. Instead, we are suggesting that studies and meta-analyses of personality research in organizations should be conceptually and empirically examined at the facet level; they should use the FFM, HEXACO, or other broad factor models to organize facets, yet at the same time (a) acknowledge the existence of useful facets that do not fall conveniently under broad factors and (b) understand that facets may show criterion-related validities different from their parent factors. Regarding this latter point, when facets underlying a broader factor show similar correlations with criterion constructs, this indicates that the broader factor may account for more of the criterion variance—but only by researching facets can we know whether this is the case. In general, we are advocating more of a bottom-up approach, based on the accumulation and empirical examination of facet-level criterion-related validities, through meta-analysis, multilevel modeling, multigroups analysis, or other methods. Obviously, patterns of facet-level correlations that are revealed will depend on the criterion or criteria of interest (e.g., task performance, contextual performance, turnover).

Nomological-Web Clustering Approach

Hough and colleagues have long argued that nomological-web clustering should be the basis for forming clusters of homogeneous personality variables demonstrating high construct and criterion-related validity (e.g., Hough, 1992, 1997, 1998; Hough, Eaton, Dunnette, Kamp, & McCloy, 1990; Hough & Ones, 2001; Hough & Schneider, 1996; Schneider & Hough, 1995). More generally, this approach is aligned with the more stringent psychometric assumptions of convergent and discriminant validity in support of construct validity (Campbell & Fiske, 1959; Loevinger, 1957; McDonald, 1999). *Nomological-web clustering* is the general approach or philosophy that personality variables or facets that are grouped together (by factor analysis, expert-sorting methods, or some other method) should show similar patterns of correlation across an array of criterion variables. Its focus on both criterion-related validity and relationships between personality variables, and not either one in isolation, is what makes nomological-web clustering distinctive. It is an important way to test or extend the lexical hypothesis, which claims that analyzing personality content alone (without reference to criteria) yields a structure of personality that would be considered basic. An extensive and intensive nomological-web clustering of personality facets has been conducted through a rational sorting of facets based on criterion-related validity evidence, and further research should contribute to the taxonomy that resulted (for an extensive list of clusters, see the appendix of Hough & Ones, 2001).

At least two different studies to date have been conducted to this end. One study (Dudley et al., 2006) meta-analyzed criterion-related validities of Conscientiousness facets, concluding that the facets (a) have only low to moderate correlations with each other and are best conceived of as distinct rather than as parts of a single global factor; (b) have different patterns of correlations with criteria; and (c) depending on the criterion and occupation, have higher criterion-related validities than a global Conscientiousness factor that ignores facets (e.g., 24% more variance in overall job performance predicted in skilled and semiskilled jobs). Another study (Foldes, Duehr, & Ones, 2008) meta-analyzed mean score differences between Whites and different cultural–ethnic groups according to a nomological-web clustering taxonomy, reporting that the pattern of mean scores differed for the subgroups on the facets within the Big Five factors, even though subgroups scored similarly at the Big Five factor level.

Summary and Conclusion

Although the FFM has enjoyed significant support as a foundation of personality in I/O psychology, and in psychology as a whole, its base may be cracking. Support for the FFM relies primarily on factor analysis of self-reported personality descriptions (either person-descriptive sentences or adjectives); other methods suggest different models of personality. The FFM also is not comprehensive—important variables are missing. The HEXACO model is an improvement in its representativeness, but both the FFM and the HEXACO model combine facets into broad heterogeneous factors that, we argue, may not be as useful as the facets themselves for prediction and understanding. We are undoubtedly biased in favor of the nomological-web clustering approach that organizes personality facets into groups or factors, based on similar patterns of criterion-related validity and similar patterns of relationships with other personality variables. More important than our bias, the validity evidence for facet-based criterion-related validities that we have reviewed is generally supportive of nomological-web clustering as opposed to broader factor models of personality. Regardless of the taxonomic approach, the weight of additional criterion-related validity evidence at the personality facet level, based on more careful criterion measurement, should speak louder than anyone's theory-driven agendas.

As a general recommendation, we urge researchers to specify organizational criteria against which to pit different personality models against one another empirically, not just examining personality models on their own without respect to criteria. Creating a "fair fight" between competing models can be challenging. For example, measures of personality facets may contain fewer items than personality factors, and thus the predictive power of the former may be less than that of the latter. The comparison of non-nested models can pose an additional challenge because model fit can be confounded with model parsimony, although there are statistical methodologies that can contend with this issue (e.g., indices such as Bayes factors and root-mean-square error of approximation).

CRITERION-RELATED VALIDITY OF PERSONALITY TRAITS: BRIEF SUMMARY OF THE EVIDENCE

Measures of different personality traits first need to support the psychometric prerequisites of reliability (e.g., test–retest and internal consistency reliability) and convergent and discriminant validity (e.g., a multifactor model fit between personality factors and related factors) before one can begin to say that personality traits are being measured and meaningfully predict organizational outcomes via criterion-related validity or, in a broader multilevel sense, that personality measurement is useful for those organizations that implement it in their selection, training, or employee development systems (see Vol. 2, chap. 13, this handbook). We point out clear bottom-line trends based on cumulative research evidence indicating that personality measures do predict important work outcomes. We do not provide an exhaustive review of the evidence in this chapter; rather, we seek to summarize important findings that should encourage organizational researchers and practitioners to continue their pursuits in the personality domain. Although we have long known that higher levels of conscientiousness relates to occupational success (Barrick & Mount, 1991), recent meta-analytic work has shown it also relates to successful occupational attainment over the life span (Roberts, Kuncel, Shiner, Caspi, & Goldberg, 2007), and greater emotional stability is associated with the positive mental health required to function effectively in the workplace (Lahey, 2009). Exhibit 5.1 highlights other broad findings regarding the criterion-related validity of personality measures: Personality predicts leadership and career success, various dimensions of job performance, contextual performance, counterproductive work behaviors, team performance, and job satisfaction (see Vol. 1, chaps. 7 and 19, this handbook; chaps. 3, 9, 10, and 19, this volume; and Vol. 3, chaps. 4 and 17, this handbook). Many important mediators partially account for these relationships, such as goal setting, self-regulation, positive emotions, and motivation (Elliot & Church, 1997), as we later discuss.

In reporting criterion-related validity evidence, we tend to rely on meta-analytic correlations, each of which is a psychometrically corrected average validity across a set of studies. Although we do not consider these "true" validity coefficients that generalize across all samples, settings, and measures, these averages provide useful descriptive (if not inferential) summaries of various research domains. Meta-analysis invokes sampling error variance as a more parsimonious explanation of the variability across reported effect sizes; however, this explanation is always provisional until more data are available that allow one to conduct moderator analyses with appropriate statistical power (Oswald & McCloy, 2003). More powerful statistical tests may determine that at least some of the variance in criterion-related validities may be moderated by the type of occupations, samples, and settings under study.

The criterion-related validities we report are moderate in size, and—for a number of reasons—no apologies should be made for them not being larger: (a) Even moderate validities for personality prove to be highly valuable in practice, often incrementing the prediction afforded by ability measures and providing utility across an organizational workforce retained over time; (b) validities for personality in field settings are of similar magnitude to those found when examining the strength of main effects resulting from manipulating situations in social psychology research ($r \approx .2$ or $d \approx 0.4$ on average, see Richard, Bond, & Stokes-Zoota, 2003); (c) it is naive to think that all the variance of complex human behavior in the world of work can be fully predicted from a handful of personality scales and their bivariate relationships with criterion measures; (d) research findings often reflect the "criterion problem" of broad performance measures that were used for administrative purposes, and this cannot be corrected for psychometrically; and (e) the amount of variance predicted is not the same as the importance of variance predicted (e.g., no measure will predict much variance in low base-rate behaviors such as organizational theft, yet theft is a clearly important outcome). In addition, we are not unaware of the reality that validity coefficients are more trustworthy when the data are based on higher quality measurement, relevant and generalizable settings, and larger and more representative samples. No study achieves these ideals to the fullest. Thus, although meta-analytic validities corrected for psychometric artifacts may come closer to estimating

Exhibit 5.1
Criterion-Related Validity of Personality Measures: General Conclusions Across Occupational Groups

Leadership and career success

- Personality predicts occupational attainment and advancement ([.20 to .30]; Judge & Hurst, 2007; meta-analysis: Roberts, Kuncel, Shiner, Caspi, & Goldberg, 2007).
- Personality predicts overall managerial effectiveness, promotion, and managerial level (achievement orientation [.15 to .20], dominance and energy level [.20 to .25]; meta-analysis: Hough, Ones, & Viswesvaran, 1998).
- Personality predicts leadership, transformational leadership, and leadership emergence (sociability, dominance, achievement, and dependability [.30 to .35], conscientiousness [.10 to .30], extraversion [.20 to .30], emotional stability [.15 to .25], openness [.10 to .25]; meta-analyses: Bartram, 2005; Bono & Judge, 2004; Judge, Bono, Ilies, & Gerhardt, 2002).

Job performance outcomes

- Personality predicts overall job performance ratings, task performance, behavioral measures of performance, and career attainment (achievement and dependability [.15 to .25], conscientiousness [.15 to .30], agreeableness, emotional stability, extraversion [.10 to .20]; meta-analyses: Barrick, Mount, & Judge, 2001; Bartram, 2005; Dudley, Orvis, Lebiecki, & Cortina, 2006; Hurtz & Donovan, 2000).
- Personality predicts the performance of expatriates (cultural sensitivity and cultural flexibility [.25 to .30], conscientiousness and extraversion [.15 to .20], meta-analysis: Mol, Born, Willemsen, & Van Der Molen, 2005).
- Personality predicts goal setting, organizing, execution, and not procrastinating (self-efficacy [.45], depression [–.35], conscientiousness [.15 to .35], agreeableness [–.30], emotional stability [.30 to .35], extraversion [.15], openness [.20]; meta-analyses: Bartram, 2005; Judge & Ilies, 2002; Steel, 2007).
- Personality variables predict outcomes reflecting creativity and innovation (dominance and potency [.20], innovativeness [.30], conscientiousness [.35], openness [.15 to .40]; Grucza & Goldberg, 2007; Hough, 1992; Robertson & Kinder, 1993; meta-analyses: Bartram, 2005; Feist, 1998; Hough & Dilchert, 2007).
- Personality-based integrity tests predict overall job performance ([.30 to .45], meta-analysis: Ones, Viswesvaran, & Schmidt, 1993).

Contextual performance

- Personality predicts contextual performance, encompassing constructs such as organizational citizenship, altruism, job dedication, interpersonal facilitation, and generalized compliance (empathy, helpfulness, positive affectivity [.15 to .20], altruism [.25], dependability [.10 to .20], affective commitment [.25], conscientiousness [.15 to .20], agreeableness [.10 to .15], emotional stability [.15]; meta-analyses: Borman, Penner, Allen, & Motowidlo, 2001; Dudley et al., 2006; Hurtz & Donovan, 2000; LePine, Erez, & Johnson, 2002; Organ & Ryan, 1995).

Counterproductive work behaviors

- Personality variables predict counterproductive work behaviors (conscientiousness [–.20 to –.40], agreeableness [–.30 to –.45], emotional stability [–.25]; meta-analysis: Berry, Ones, & Sackett, 2007).
- Personality-based integrity tests predict counterproductive work behaviors ([.30]; meta-analysis: Ones et al., 1993).
- Personality-based integrity tests predict absenteeism ([.35]; meta-analysis: Ones, Viswesvaran, & Schmidt, 2003).

Training outcomes

- Personality predicts learning and skill acquisition during training (achievement motivation [.15 to .35], conscientiousness [.15 to .30], extraversion [.15 to .30], agreeableness [.15], openness [.25 to .35]; meta-analyses: Barrick & Mount, 1991; Barrick et al., 2001; Colquitt, LePine, & Noe, 2000).

Teamwork and team performance

- Personality variables predict team cohesion and teamwork (conscientiousness [.25], agreeableness [.35], emotional stability [.20], extraversion [.15], openness [.15]; meta-analyses: Barrick et al., 2001; Hogan & Holland, 2003).
- Personality variables predict team performance (conscientiousness [.25], agreeableness [.35], extraversion [.15], openness [.15]; meta-analysis: Peeters, Van Tuijl, Rutte, & Reymen, 2006).

Job satisfaction

- Personality predicts both job and career satisfaction (proactivity and locus of control [.40], conscientiousness [.25], agreeableness [.15], emotional stability [.30 to .35], openness [.15]; meta-analyses: Judge, Heller, & Mount, 2002; Ng, Eby, Sorensen, & Feldman, 2005).

Exhibit 5.1 (Continued)
Criterion-Related Validity of Personality Measures: General Conclusions Across Occupational Groups

- Personality variables are positively correlated with measures of subjective well-being (conscientiousness [.25 to .30], agreeableness [.15 to .35], emotional stability [.35 to .50], extraversion [.35 to .60]; meta-analysis: Steel, Schmidt, & Shultz, 2008).

Mediated models involving personality

- Conscientiousness predicts learning but is fully mediated by goal commitment (Klein & Lee, 2006).
- Relationships between personality variables and work-related criteria are influenced by motivational and self-regulatory mechanisms (Barrick, Mount, & Strauss, 1993; Erez & Judge, 2001; Kanfer & Heggestad, 1999; F. K. Lee, Sheldon, & Turban, 2003).
- Positive emotions help those high in psychological resilience recover from daily stress more effectively (Ong, Bergeman, Bisconti, &Wallace, 2006).
- Status striving mediates the relationship between extraversion and sales performance, such that those high in extraversion tend to be high-status strivers, who in turn are better performers (Barrick, Stewart, & Piotrowski, 2002).

Note. Brackets contain the approximate range of zero-order correlations, based on the most statistically stable estimates reported. Meta-analytic correlations were often corrected for statistical artifacts. Only practically significant correlations are reported (>.10).

both operational and latent relationships of interest, they should be taken with a grain of salt and a larger standard error (see discussions by Morgeson et al., 2007; Murphy & DeShon, 2000).

Researchers may appreciate the validity coefficients we report in their correlational metric, but it is also important to translate these values into other metrics that employees, managers, and other stakeholders can understand and appreciate, such as dollars, odds ratios, and expected average increases in performance (Cascio & Boudreau, 2008; Kuncel, Cooper, & Owens, 2009). For example, the binomial effect size display (Rosenthal, 1991) converts a correlation into the percentage increase in success rate, so, for instance, a validity coefficient of .20, although seemingly small, translates roughly into a 10% increase in hiring success, a value that many managers view as meaningful, in a metric that is more understandable than a correlation coefficient. As a more specific metric, validity coefficients combined with personality test cutoffs used in selection, training, or promotion contexts can be translated into sensitivity and specificity indices that describe the usefulness of a personality test, with *sensitivity* referring to the percentage of those who passed the test and were identified as successful performers and *specificity* referring to the converse, the percentage of those who failed the test and were identified as unsuccessful (Glaros & Kline, 1988). These percentages are themselves useful, but they can also be translated into the mean increase in performance of those selected, compared with either those not selected or with the total pool of test takers. Sensitivity and specificity metrics, however, assume that one has data- or model-based estimates for performance scores of those who fail the test. More generally, alternative metrics like these must either be corrected for the effects of direct and incidental range restriction, sampling error variance, and measurement unreliability or must be interpreted appropriately in the context of these known factors. Validity coefficients have the same problem; however, these alternative metrics may still provide managers, employees, and job applicants with a quicker appreciation for the usefulness of a valid personality measure than would a validity coefficient on its own.

SUBGROUP MEAN DIFFERENCES IN PERSONALITY SCALES: IMPLICATIONS FOR ADVERSE IMPACT

When personality assessment is used in personnel selection, the intent of personality theory and models is to produce measures that show improved prediction and a fairer selection process overall. The basic wisdom of providing fair selection procedures to all job applicants, the diversity in the global marketplace and labor pools, and the legal prohibitions that expressly affect employment decision making, taken together, strongly encourage employers to attend to a variety of factors that affect protected groups of applicants during the selection process. In the United States, fundamental pieces of legislation, such as the Civil Rights Acts of 1964 and 1991, the Americans With Disabilities Act of 1990, and the Age Discrimination in Employment Act of 1967 (amended in 1978), protect classes such as people with disabilities, minorities, women, and people age 40 and older. Adverse impact against protected groups is often a critical factor when evaluating the fairness of a selection process. For instance, if the percentage of Black applicants who are hired is close to the percentage of White applicants who are hired (e.g., the former being at least 80% of the latter by the "four-fifths rule"), then any adverse impact that exists is unlikely to generate a lawsuit (see Morris & Lobsenz, 2000).

Adverse impact in hiring is in part a function of the mean difference between applicant subgroups because larger mean differences will lead to disproportionate hiring of one group over another in top-down selection procedures. Therefore, it is important to be aware of subgroup mean differences for those personality constructs measured in personnel selection systems. Because we have argued for the usefulness of facet-level personality variables in future research and practice, this section not only provides mean score differences between various subgroups on the Big Five factors but also on its facets, as much as the data allow. We draw heavily on two meta-analyses in presenting summary results (Foldes et al., 2008; Hough, Oswald, & Ployhart, 2001), making use of conventional standards in the field for defining small, medium, and large standardized mean differences (i.e., *ds* = 0.2, 0.5, and 0.8, respectively; Cohen, 1988).

FFM: Mean Differences

Ethnic–cultural subgroup comparisons. These two meta-analyses summarized mean-score differences for ethnic–cultural subgroups (i.e., Blacks, Hispanics, Asians, and American Indians) according to the FFM of personality variables. At the broadly defined level of the Big Five, both meta-analyses found that Blacks, Hispanics, and Asians scored virtually the same when compared with Whites. One discrepancy was where in one meta-analysis (Hough et al., 2001), Blacks scored lower than Whites on average on Openness ($d \approx -0.2$), but in the other (Foldes et al., 2008), that difference was negligible ($d \approx -0.1$). Another discrepancy was for Asian–White mean differences on Openness to Experience; however, uniformly small sample sizes for Asians on this construct precluded accurate results. In both meta-analyses, mean scores for American Indians were also based on small sample sizes (even when accumulated across studies), making any mean differences too tenuous to report, in terms of both statistical power and appropriate representation of the subgroups. Compellingly large mean differences between Blacks and Asians were found in one of the meta-analyses (Foldes et al., 2008), with Blacks scoring higher on average on Emotional Stability ($d \approx 0.6$), Extraversion ($d \approx 0.4$), and Conscientiousness ($d \approx 0.4$). Future personality research comparing diverse subgroups is clearly warranted, particularly given the major demographic shifts occurring in today's global workforce.

In short, both meta-analyses reached the same general conclusion about Black, Hispanic, and Asian mean scores, namely, that mean scores on the broadly defined Big Five personality variables tend to be very similar when they are compared with scores of Whites as the majority group. To the extent this is true, the Big Five–level personality variables at this aggregate level do not tend to contribute to adverse impact against these protected classes. Instead, they have the potential to reduce adverse impact when used in combination with cognitive ability measures—although not as much as one would hope, as we discuss in more detail.

Gender comparisons. A meta-analysis averaged mean score differences between men and women across studies at the Big Five level (Hough et al., 2001), finding some noteworthy results: Women generally scored higher than men on Agreeableness ($d \approx 0.4$) and lower than men on Emotional Stability

($d \approx -0.2$). On the other three Big Five factors—Extraversion, Conscientiousness, and Openness to Experience—this meta-analysis found essentially no differences between men and women, consistent with more recent work exploring gender differences in two of these factors (Extraversion and Conscientiousness; Duehr, Jackson, & Ones, 2003).

Age group comparisons. A meta-analysis comparing older people (age 40 and older) and younger people (typically college age) on Big Five personality variables found similar scores across all Big Five factors (Hough et al., 2001). One exception was Agreeableness, on which older people scored somewhat higher on average than younger people ($d \approx 0.2$). A large, nationally representative Dutch sample supported a similar factor structure (measurement invariance) across age cohorts, which allows for a stronger substantive interpretation of the mean increases in Agreeableness and Conscientiousness that were found with age (Allemand, Zimprich, & Hendriks, 2008). A meta-analysis of cross-sectional age-cohort data, largely based on U.S. samples, reported similar increases, with Conscientiousness showing a more steady linear increase over time and Agreeableness showing a sharp increase when people are in their 50s. Emotional Stability increased steadily until people reached age 40 and then remained stable; social dominance increased until the mid-30s and then remained relatively stable (Roberts, Walton, & Viechtbauer, 2006). Unlike this meta-analysis, two studies have reported curvilinear relationships between conscientiousness and age: a cross-sectional two-nation study finding peak levels of conscientiousness in the mid-40s (Donnellan & Lucas, 2008), and a longitudinal study in which conscientiousness found its peak in the mid-60s (Terracciano, McCrae, Brant, & Costa, 2005).

Facet-Level Personality Variables: Mean Differences

Using facets identified through the aforementioned nomological-web clustering strategy (Hough & Ones, 2001), a meta-analysis summarized mean score differences between ethnic–cultural, gender, and age subgroups at the facet level of Big Five factors. Some interesting findings emerged that are not apparent at the broader Big Five level (Hough et al., 2001), with similar findings replicated in a subsequent meta-analysis (Foldes et al., 2008).

Ethnic–cultural subgroup comparisons. For achievement and dependability (two facets of Conscientiousness), Blacks scored about the same as Whites on achievement and only slightly lower than Whites on dependability ($d \approx -0.1$; only Hough et al., 2001, is reported because of its much larger sample size). For dominance and sociability (two facets of Extraversion), Blacks scored about the same as Whites on dominance but lower ($d \approx -0.4$) on sociability (Foldes et al., 2008; Hough et al., 2001). Hispanics scored on average higher ($d \approx 0.3$) than Whites on self-esteem, a facet of Emotional Stability (Foldes et al., 2008). Other minor differences occurred between some of the comparisons for other ethnic–cultural subgroups, but sample sizes are too small (even for meta-analysis) to have confidence in those results.

Gender comparisons. Small facet-level differences exist between men and women. For dependability (a facet of Conscientiousness), women tended to score somewhat higher than men ($d \approx 0.2$; Hough et al., 2001). For dominance and activity (two facets of Extraversion), men scored somewhat higher than women on both ($d \approx -0.2$; Duehr et al., 2003; Hough et al., 2001).

Age group comparisons. Small facet-level differences exist between older (age 40 and older) people and younger people on some facets. For dependability and achievement (both facets of Conscientiousness), older people generally score higher ($d \approx 0.5$) than younger people on dependability but somewhat lower than younger people on achievement ($d \approx -0.2$; Hough et al., 2001).

Overall conclusion. In general, differences between ethnic–cultural, gender, and age subgroups are small to moderate in size, but we have noted some sizable exceptions. Larger differences tend to be found at the level of narrowly defined facets that underlie Big Five–level personality constructs; in some cases, protected groups (e.g., Blacks or women) have higher average scores than traditional comparison groups (e.g., Whites or men). These findings are especially important because although an organization may focus its measurement efforts on personality facets exhibiting the highest levels of validity, it is the mean differences and correlations between all subtests in the selection battery that jointly determine adverse impact against a protected group (without the need for any criterion data or validity information).

The pattern of subgroup mean differences at the personality facet level between ethnic–cultural, gender, and age subgroups is complex and likely has meaningful moderator effects such as job complexity and requirements for engaging in teamwork on the job. We avoided a review of such effects because to our knowledge very little research evidence has spoken directly to this issue. However, both the attraction–selection–attrition model (Schneider, 1987) and theories of vocational interests (Holland, 1985) offer the general hypothesis that mean levels of personality traits should differ by both the type of jobs and the type of organizations in which employees are members (Schaubroeck, Ganster, & Jones, 1998); thus, it is reasonable to think that subgroup mean differences may vary as well, to the extent that occupations and organizations have varying personality requirements and members of different subgroups assort themselves differentially across occupations as a function of their personality (see chap. 3, this volume, and Vol. 3, chap. 1, this handbook). Future research may seek to explore this issue further to understand the extent to which mean differences in personality measures by particular subgroups (age, race, gender) lead to practically significant differences in hiring or promotion rates across different selection and assessment contexts. It is also an important practical issue to analyze large samples in terms of combinations of subgroup characteristics because examining race and gender differences independent of one another may not uncover more specific subgroup differences (e.g., Black women vs. White men).

Regarding the selection context, we remind the reader that even though many personality measures have shown little evidence for subgroup mean differences, adding them to a selection battery that already demonstrates large subgroup mean differences will not reduce adverse impact as much as one might anticipate. As a concrete example (see Sackett & Ellingson, 1997), when two group means differ on one measure by 1 standard deviation (e.g., the Black–White mean difference that has frequently been documented for cognitive ability measures), and there is no mean difference on a second uncorrelated measure (e.g., a measure of the trait of dominance), the resulting composite has a group mean difference of .71—not the difference of .50 that one might intuitively expect. As a result, minority rates of hiring will be improved, but the bad news is that adverse impact will not be reduced enough to satisfy the aforementioned four-fifths rule across a wide range of selection ratios and subgroup proportions in the applicant pool. This holds true even if it were legal to take a slight reduction in validity to reduce adverse impact (see the pareto-optimal tradeoff scenarios in DeCorte, Lievens, & Sackett, 2007). A more effective approach to reducing adverse impact would be to demonstrate that personality measures with low to no adverse impact predict noncognitive criteria that are highly relevant to the job (Sackett, Schmitt, Ellingson, & Kabin, 2001), although this approach is also not without its constraints, most notably because cognitive ability is a strong predictor of job performance criteria across almost every job and at the same time is accompanied by the persistence of large subgroup mean differences across racial–ethnic groups.

PERSONALITY TEST-SCORE FAKING

There has been an overwhelming concern in organizational research that people's responses to personality tests do not reflect their true standings on underlying traits of interest, particularly the responses of job applicants in high-stakes selection settings. One can easily imagine applicants inflating their self-report of the positive job-relevant traits they lack—whether on a personality test, in a face-to-face interview, or on a resume—especially in cases in which there is little perceived negative consequence along with the potential reward of being hired into a highly desired (if not desirable) job. Applicants who feel a greater incentive to present themselves in a more positive light and inflate personality scores would be more likely to be hired, without necessarily showing higher levels of performance on the job (Mueller-Hanson,

Heggestad, & Thornton, 2003). This has implications for establishing personality test norms as well: If applicant means are substantially higher than incumbent means (as in Weekley, Ployhart, & Harold, 2004), then cutoff scores based on the scores of the incumbent sample would clearly be inappropriate to apply to the applicant sample (Bott, O'Connell, Ramakrishnan, & Doverspike, 2007).

Research data have not unequivocally supported the commonsense notion of applicant score inflation. An early faking study found much higher means for people who were directly asked to fake a personality test like an ideal job applicant would versus those asked to respond honestly; however, the mean differences between applicant and incumbent scores in a military sample showed higher means for incumbents, meaning that effects of the entire selection process appear to have been stronger than any of the faking effects of applicants (Hough et al., 1990). Other evidence has also provided little reason to suspect score inflation in job applicants. Two recent large within-person studies found small differences in mean personality test scores when the first test was for selection purposes and the second was for developmental purposes or vice versa (Ellingson, Sackett, & Connelly, 2007), and they were near zero when job applicants took a personality test, were rejected on the basis of those scores, and then reapplied and were retested (J. Hogan, Barrett, & Hogan, 2007).

However, mean differences are more evident in other studies. For instance, a meta-analysis comparing incumbents and nonincumbents on Big Five measures found moderate standardized mean differences for Emotional Stability ($d = 0.45$) and Conscientiousness ($d = 0.45$); those effects were even larger for studies with scales explicitly intended to measure the Big Five (Birkeland, Manson, Kisamore, Brannick, & Smith, 2006). In general, within-subject designs appear to have smaller effects than between-subjects designs, but this conclusion must be qualified because between-subjects designs often compare applicants with incumbents, and within-subject designs do not compare these roles. Future research should continue to investigate differences between conditions of personality testing in a systematic manner, investigating lab versus field settings, role of the test taker, and strength of the motivational context.

Test-score faking can also be understood through Monte Carlo studies, in which the practical effects of known conditions can be investigated through simulated data. Two such studies have manipulated parameters relevant to personality test-score faking, such as the correlations between faking, personality, and performance outcomes; the selection ratio; and the prevalence and magnitude of faking. The simulations operationalized faking either as an inflated score on a personality measure (Komar, Brown, Komar, & Robie, 2008) or as a high score on a social desirability measure that serves as a flag to invalidate an applicant's score (Schmitt & Oswald, 2006). Together, the results suggested that under a wide array of realistic applicant scenarios, faking does not tend to affect the criterion-related validity of personality tests or the mean levels of performance in those selected in any material way.

Nonetheless, there are likely to be circumstances in which the effects of faking personality tests will alter the rank ordering of applicants in a top-down selection process. Although research has indicated that faking scales or lie scales do not reliably and sensitively determine who is prevaricating and who is not, a recent strategy using idiosyncratic patterns of item responses appears to show some promise (Kuncel & Borneman, 2007). Faking scores are developed from subsets of personality items that consistently show multimodal distributions under directed faking, thus creating large differences between faked and honest response distributions that are reflected in the scoring key. These scores show low correlations with cognitive ability; however, there is other evidence that cognitive ability may also improve people's faking ability on some personality tests (Christiansen, Burns, Montgomery, 2005; Vasilopoulos, Cucina, Dyomina, Morewitz, & Reilly, 2006), and some people can avoid detection on lie scales and social desirability scales through coaching (Hurtz & Alliger, 2002). However, people with higher ability and who are coachable may tend to be hired anyway on the basis of those characteristics, even if they can be coached to appear a more desirable candidate on a personality test. Further understanding of the effects of faking and coaching will require more thinking on multiple fronts: theory development, measurement issues, and ethical implications—and perhaps, above all, criterion-related validity.

Instead of attempting to detect faking after personality tests are administered, we recommend considering proactive approaches to preventing or reducing the likelihood of faking. Warnings may reduce the scores of those who would have inflated their scores—yet they also have the potential to reduce the scores of those who were responding honestly in the first place but were anxious about the warning. Perhaps the framing of a warning moderates this effect: a negative warning that dishonest responding will invalidate personality test scores, versus a positive warning providing encouragement that honest responding leads to usable scores, may have differential effects on mean scores and potentially on validity (Converse et al., 2008). Warning about response verification has also been shown to influence the measurement of conscientiousness such that it correlates more highly with cognitive ability (Vasilopoulos, Cucina, & McElreath, 2005), presumably because the thought required to respond carefully affects responses to the conscientiousness items. Warnings could also be provided during the test, so that test takers are alerted whenever their responses appear unusual (e.g., inconsistent with typical responders, randomly patterned, or too extreme).

An integrated psychological model of faking that includes warnings has received empirical support; it identifies attitudes toward faking, perceived behavioral control, and group norms for faking as variables that predict the intent to fake, which in turn predicts faking outcomes, with warnings and the ability to fake as important moderators (McFarland & Ryan, 2000, 2006). This model of faking could be productively extended into a broader model of factors that induce or reduce personality test scores, influence their psychometric reliability and factor structure, and ultimately affect criterion-related validities (see Hough & Oswald, 2008). Such a broad model could incorporate variables that may affect the extent to which job applicants would tend to inflate their scores, such as test-taker understanding of how the personality test is used within a larger personnel selection process; the test taker's own desire for person–job fit; the desirability of the job; the tightness or looseness of the job sector's labor market when applying; the test format (e.g., ipsative–normative, long form–short form, paper-and-pencil–Internet); test-taker individual differences (e.g., general and specific test experience [or test anxiety], reading ability, and impression management); and the strength of a perceived norm for faking. A recent model of faking incorporates many of the aforementioned individual differences and contextual factors that influence the ability and motivation to fake one's response to a personality item (Goffin & Boyd, 2009).

PROCESS MODELS: PUTTING IT ALL TOGETHER

It is clear from our review up to this point that contemporary organizational scholars have made meaningful advances in understanding how personality relates to important workplace behaviors and the practical issues associated with personality assessment. A critical and perennial challenge of personality research in I/O psychology is addressing or reconciling the dual purposes of practical prediction (developing personality measures that correlate with organizational outcomes of importance) and theoretical explanation (identifying personality constructs and testing psychological models that account for those predictive relationships). To address this challenge, we review important theoretical models found in the literature that we call *process models*. Generally speaking, process models are conceptualized such that (a) personality traits predict performance outcomes directly; (b) this relationship is mediated (partially explained) by narrower and more proximal variables (e.g., motivation; Judge & Ilies, 2002; Kanfer, 1990) and is moderated by organizational characteristics (e.g., team structure, leadership style); (c) the model is multilevel, with the impact of personality occurring at the individual, team, unit, and organizational levels (Tett & Burnett, 2003); and (d) the process of influence occurs over time.

Figure 5.2 is an example of a process model that integrates prediction and explanation. It incorporates goal setting, motivation (see Vol. 3, chap. 3, this handbook), goal orientation, episodic performance behaviors, and revisions of goals and behaviors over time. Relationships in this model may be enhanced or

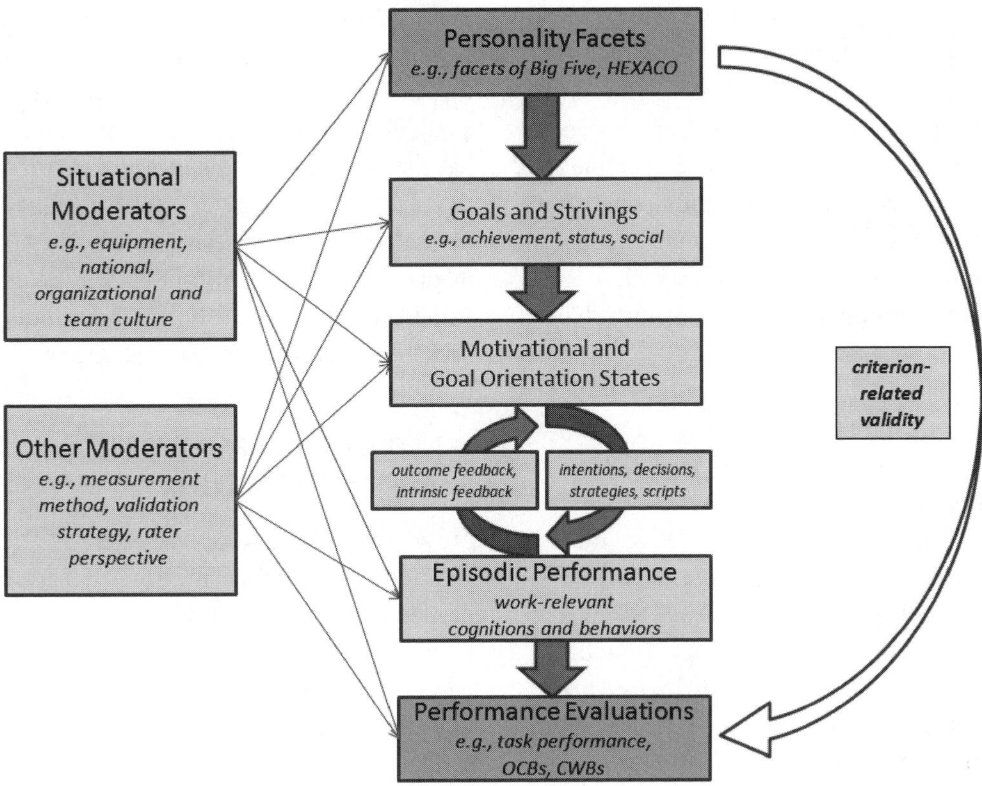

FIGURE 5.2. **Prediction and explanation: The "black box" of personality–performance validities.**

diminished in the presence of key features of the work situation, whether those are concrete features, such as the physical arrangement of the workplace or the equipment used, or psychological features, such as organizational and team climate and perceived norms. We provide this example for two major reasons. First, it illustrates the reality that criterion-related validities of personality variables, often relied on for personnel selection purposes, are necessarily removed from the "black box" of theory containing the more detailed psychological processes that employees undergo over time as they interact with supervisors, teams, and the organizational climate and culture. Data that describe these processes that are more proximal to performance outcomes simply are not available for an applicant at the point of selection. Instead, they often have to be inferred from measures of more distal constructs such as personality. Second, models such as this reinforce the reality that although organizational research on personality measures has largely focused on personnel selection settings with cross-sectional research designs, additional research efforts could investigate the longitudinal process of how employee personality and motivation predict individual and organizational outcomes over time. We discuss this latter point shortly.

There are many existing psychological models that fit our description of process models. One influential model reflects the influence of personality (achievement, anxiety, impulsivity) on motivation, which in turn affects cognitive task performance (Humphreys & Revelle, 1984). Another model of individual differences proposes that science–math, intellectual–cultural, clerical–conventional, and social "trait complexes" have their basis in personality, motivation, and interests and are a critical mediating or explanatory influence on the relationship between intellectual ability and occupational knowledge acquisition (process, personality, interests, and knowledge theory by Ackerman, 1996; see also investment theory by Cattell, 1971). A third integrated model proposes psychological relationships more specific to organizations, where personality, ability, experience, and organizational context are a collection of distal characteristics influencing constructs that are more proximal to work performance, such as stress, autonomy, self-efficacy, and goal setting (Johnson & Hezlett, 2008). A final example is a model and theory of training motivation, where personality and situational variables are exogenous predictors of motivation and knowledge, which in turn predict training performance and ultimately job performance (Colquitt, LePine, & Noe, 2000). These models are all important variations on the broader model we provide in Figure 5.2.

It may be impractical for empirical studies to test process models such as these in their entirety, or at least in as intensive or extensive a longitudinal manner as a researcher might find ideal, but research can provide empirical evidence (or lack thereof) for various parts of the model. A handful of examples is illustrative: One study investigated the conscientiousness–performance relationship in a sample of restaurant employees, finding that this relationship was dependent on high levels of work effort and a positive psychological climate; when either of these was low, the conscientiousness–performance relationship was not evident (Byrne, Stoner, Thompson, & Hochwarter, 2005). Another study found that personality traits influence performance through the types and levels of goals set, as well as through dedicated attention (called *mental focus;* F. K. Lee, Sheldon, & Turban, 2003). Meta-analyses can provide additional information about moderator effects that were not necessarily tested in the individual studies themselves because studies can be coded for the type of sample, the nature of the work setting, and other personal and situational factors.

These relatively detailed models need to stand up against the principles of scientific parsimony. Empirically, simpler models generally are preferred to more complex ones when they fit the data just as well (e.g., given a nonsignificant chi-square difference test between two nested models). Furthermore, researchers should report alternative models that are identical in terms of their overall statistical fit (MacCallum, Wegener, Uchino, & Fabrigar, 1993), particularly when they have different theoretical implications. Conceptually, parsimony also dictates that mediating variables should be psychologically distinct from the personality variables themselves if they are to be included as a meaningful component of a model. For instance, if a work motivation measure has the same content as a measure of conscientiousness except for the tag "at work" at the end of each item, then the finding that work motivation fully mediates the conscientiousness–performance relationship likely offers no meaningful contribution to our understanding of organizational settings.

INNOVATIVE PERSONALITY ASSESSMENT METHODS

New Forced-Choice Measures

Although forced-choice measures of personality have been in the literature for decades, they have resurfaced in the research literature and in real-world practice settings. The general notion prompting its use is that faking will tend to be reduced in a forced-choice format that requires test takers to endorse one of a pair of equally less desirable options (as suggested by Edwards, 1953). The Army's Assessment of Individual Motivation was a recent large and resource-intensive effort that led to reexamining the use of forced-choice personality measures in high-stakes selection testing as a predictor of attrition, with some promising validation results (Knapp, Heggestad, & Young, 2004). In a similar vein, the U.S. Navy has developed the Navy Computer Adaptive Personality System, a forced-choice computer adaptive measure (see Houston, Borman, Farmer, & Bearden, 2006). The Tailored Adaptive Personality Assessment System (Stark, Drasgow, & Chernyshenko, 2008) measures 23 narrow facets of personality that can be measured through unidimensional or multidimensional forced-choice formats (see chap. 4, this volume). An additional benefit of these three forced-choice measures for practice is their computerized adaptive nature. This means that tests can be shorter because items are only administered until the desired degree of trait precision is achieved (estimated using item response theory). This makes testing time more efficient, and it also reduces item exposure rates, which increases test security. These two advantages of adaptive testing are not limited to forced-choice measures, but they are evident in these new applications.

Forced-choice measures are psychometrically challenging because, regardless of the constructs being measured, they lead to negative intercorrelations because of the dependencies between item responses (Hicks, 1970). In other words, choosing one option in a forced-choice format necessarily means not choosing the other option. This dependency is reduced for larger numbers of scales, however (Baron, 1996); furthermore, modern statistical modeling and scoring tools are available to account for this interdependency, although large sample sizes (of at least 450 participants) are required for stable estimation (Stark & Drasgow, 2002; also see Cheung, 2004; Maydeu-Olivares & Böckenholt, 2005).

In general, forced-choice personality measures may retain higher levels of criterion-related validity in those high-stakes situations that tend to reduce validity for their Likert-scale counterparts, presumably because the format reduces faking. However, the jury is still out. Studies have demonstrated that forced-choice measures yield validities that are at least no worse than Likert-scale measures (lab samples: Chernyshenko et al., 2009; Converse, Oswald, Imus, Hedricks, Roy, & Butera, 2008), with initial evidence that they may be better (lab samples: Christiansen, Burns, & Montgomery, 2005, and Jackson, Wroblewski, & Ashton, 2000; U.S. Navy sample: Houston et al., 2006, showing some validities in the .40s in predicting supervisory ratings).

Conditional Reasoning Measures

Conditional reasoning measures (James, 1998) were developed as an innovative method for assessing personality traits in a manner that indirectly reveals motivational tendencies. A typical conditional reasoning item presents a scenario and then asks the test taker to select a response option that reflects a reasonable conclusion that would follow from it. The critical feature of conditional reasoning items lies in the response options, in that more than one response is logically correct, but the logically correct responses differ in terms of personality-relevant motives. For example, take the item "Why would a coworker comment on your interactions with a customer?" There may be two logical responses (among other distracters) that test takers usually endorse: "to provide developmental information to improve my sales performance" and "to criticize me while making him or her look better." If this were a conditional reasoning measure of aggression, then it is the latter response that gets scored, where test takers receive 1 point if they endorse it and 0 points otherwise.

In fact, conditional reasoning measures of aggression have been developed on the basis of an in-depth theoretical model (James, McIntyre, Glisson, Bowler, & Mitchell, 2004; James et al., 2005). Both self-report and conditional reasoning measures of aggression interact to predict counterproductive and prosocial behavior criteria (Bing et al., 2007) as well as aggressive physical behaviors in basketball (Frost, Ko, & James, 2007). One general issue with conditional reasoning measures is that once the nature of the measure is revealed to test takers, research has shown that they can easily identify items that reflect the construct of interest (at least for aggression). In this case, even if test takers knew about the nature of the test yet remained committed to responding logically, they may still respond differently, and there could be greater potential for faking (e.g., $d \approx 0.40$ in LeBreton, Barksdale, Robin, & James, 2007).

In line with the conditional reasoning approach to personality measurement, response options to situational judgment tests can also be designed so that personality traits are indirectly measured across hypothetical situations presented to test takers (e.g., Westring et al., 2009; see chap. 8, this volume), but once again, if test takers can identify which traits are being measured in the response options, that may alter their responses and thus the psychometric properties of the measure. Future research in this area should continue to address test-score faking issues and develop measures of other personality constructs that might be better measured indirectly or where indirect measures increment validity over that of their explicit counterparts.

Third-Party Ratings of Personality

Employees assume three simultaneous roles in their working lives, all of which are influenced by personality: actor (one who behaves), striver (one who plans his or her behavior), and narrator (one who self-reflects on his or her behavior and creates a self-identity; see McAdams & Olson, in press).

Personality-relevant information pertaining to all three roles can be gleaned from knowledgeable others (e.g., peers, supervisors, subordinates, customers), and some third-party ratings have been shown to yield higher validities in predicting work performance. A recent meta-analysis (Connelly, 2008) has shown that interrater reliability is generally high for the Big Five traits and highest for extraversion and conscientiousness, which is sensible given that these traits are often more visible than traits such as openness or emotional stability that may require observers to have more extensive contact or a deeper acquaintanceship to understand the person better. Perhaps the most practically important finding in this meta-analytic work is that "other" ratings of personality (e.g., ratings by coworkers, supervisors, and subordinates) also yielded significantly higher criterion-related validities than self-ratings for predicting job performance.

We strongly encourage continued research on the validity of third-party ratings of personality traits, examining facet-level ratings, and ensuring that higher correlations are because of personality–performance relationships and not because of raters and supervisors sharing a mental model that is not related to actual performance (e.g., shared liking or disliking the ratee independent of performance; Lefkowitz, 2000). Certainly, distorting effects of third-party ratings may arise just as much as they do in the self-report context, although perhaps for different reasons. But fundamentally, to have any hope of being accurate and valid, third-party ratings require that personality-relevant information about a person be available to the rater, that it be perceived, and that perception be accurate and translate into an accurate judgment (Funder, 1995). Given the promising findings for higher criterion-related validities than are typically found in self-report measures of personality, future research should work toward understanding third-party cognitive, affective, and relationship biases when judging personality traits, determining whether those biases are helpful or harmful to criterion-related validity, and investigating what situation manipulations or incentives will provide more veridical or valid personality ratings.

PROMISING RESEARCH DIRECTIONS IN PERSONALITY ASSESSMENT

Within-Person Structures of Personality

One avenue of promise in our understanding of personality constructs will come from research comparing intraindividual trends and covariances. Decades of organizational research on personality and criterion-related validity has focused primarily on correlations between typical characteristics of people, where scores reflect people's trait level (e.g., conscientiousness), both implicit and averaged, on a criterion (e.g., performance) over time. In addition to the average, people also show reliable and important levels of variability associated with their overall trait level (Fleeson, 2001); we reviewed, for example, longitudinal studies indicating mean age differences in personality over time. People also appear to show reliable differences in patterns of covariances as well. Repeated-measures personality data have demonstrated that intraindividual factor structures of personality can be very different from the factor structure found across individuals (Molenaar & Campbell, 2009). For example, the FFM or HEXACO factors may be represented in a set of personality items across people, and at the same time these items may support more factors for one person, yet fewer factors for another. Only under rigorous mathematical conditions that one generally would not expect from the data (measurement invariance across people and over time) would the within-person and between-persons structures be equivalent.

Therefore, organizational research and practice can benefit by extending traditional between-person analyses to within-person analyses that investigate which traits are more (or less) malleable over time given specific combinations of work situations and employees (Tett & Burnett, 2003). When they are reliable and take sampling error variance into account, within-person analyses can be a rich bottom-up approach to understanding people and situations more fully than assuming similar variable interrelationships and personality–situation interactions in the population as a whole (Cervone, 2005). Distinctions between dimensions of personality and personality types may emerge from such analyses (Ruscio & Ruscio, 2008), where types may be tied to advances in the biological underpinnings of personality and temperament (Cloninger, 2008). Historically, longitudinal research examining individual lives over time has yielded a wealth of useful within-person information in the general domains of human development (Block, 1971) and managerial work (Bray, Campbell, & Grant, 1974). Likewise, we hope that future researchers will invest their resources into well-planned intensive longitudinal projects that investigate the effects of personality on task and contextual performance over the spans of years, jobs, and careers.

Few within-person analyses of this sort have appeared in the organizational literature to date. However, several multilevel models have examined the within-person question of whether personality traits predict individuals' job performance level and rate of change over time (Ployhart, Weekley, & Baughman, 2006; Stewart & Nandkeolyar, 2006; Thoresen, Bradley, Bliese, & Thoresen, 2004; Wallace & Chen, 2006). Similar analyses have been conducted in the domain of skill acquisition and learning performance (Chen, Gully, Whiteman, & Kilcullen, 2000; Yeo & Neal, 2004) and could serve as models for examining whether personality predicts trajectories of learning outcomes in relatively autonomous settings such as self-paced Web-based training and active learning environments (Bell & Kozlowski, 2008; Ford & Oswald, 2003; Gully, Payne, Koles, & Whiteman, 2002).

Because longitudinal designs such as these operate on the traditional assumption that trait measures are enduring characteristics of people, it is important to determine the long-term reliability of trait measures. Reliance on Cronbach's alpha as an indicator of reliability has long been known to be generally problematic (see Sijtsma, 2009), but it is particularly problematic for trait measurement because alpha is only a rough indicator of how well scale items covary with one another; alpha does not indicate the stability of the scale score over time. Appropriate psychometric models of trait reliability distinguish between actual changes in the trait over time ("true change") and changes resulting from random error over time ("transient error"). Appropriate reliability estimates (i.e., coefficients of reliability and stability) tend to indicate meaningful amounts of variance resulting from transient error, and therefore Cronbach's alpha tends to be an overestimate of the reliability of personality traits (e.g., by 5%–13% for conscientiousness in F. L. Schmidt, Le, & Ilies, 2003; by 25% across traits in Chmielewski & Watson, 2009, with wide variation by trait).

Understanding the Situation

In addition to understanding the person through within-person factor analyses and multilevel models, we also need to have a greater understanding of the situations in which personality is more or less predictive of important work outcomes. This understanding has been only roughly described as *strong* and *weak* situational cues for behavior, with the notion that stronger cues (e.g., a micromanaging supervisor, peer pressure from teammates) will tend to dictate an employee's behavior, making personality less potent of a predictor than when cues are weak (e.g., an autonomous work environment; see Ackerman, Kanfer, & Goff, 1995; Beaty, Cleveland, & Murphy, 2001; Klehe & Anderson, 2007; Ployhart, Lim, & Chan, 2001). Strong situational cues may be real or perceived; when they are perceived, then maximally motivated performance may emerge, whereas when cues are perceived as weaker, typical performance results. A typical transition from maximal to typical performance is when new hires are in the initial "honeymoon" period of a job, motivated to perform at their maximum, but then transition into more typical performance, when personality is more likely to emerge as an influence on behavior (Helmreich, Sawin, & Carsrud, 1986).

Although evidence for the situational-strength hypothesis could benefit from more carefully conducted research (Cooper & Withey, 2009), situations might never be classified much further than strong versus weak because they are best defined by examining the complex goals (and constraints) within them. Employees in the same organization or on the same team likely have shared goals, but some of those goals are more clearly communicated, perceived, and shared than others; furthermore, there are personal goals held by each employee (Bagozzi, Bergami, & Leone, 2003), and still other goals are negotiated between organizations and teams or employees. Additionally, personal and organizational goals are dynamic; employees evaluate and revise the multiple goals they hold over the course of time, such as when feedback is obtained or a deadline is fast approaching (A. M. Schmidt, Dolis, & Tolli, 2009). Despite this real-world complexity, the hope is that variance in work behavior can be partially understood by examining how individual differences in personality interact with situational characteristics at the individual, team, and organizational levels that facilitate or constrain individual behavior and team performance (Pervin, 1989; Stewart, Fulmer, Barrick, 2005; Tett & Burnett, 2003). Studying important situations is likely to be more productive than developing an abstract theory of situations (Funder, 2009).

Personality traits likely have an influence on the selection, evaluation, revision, and pursuit of goals. For instance, leaders who define organizational goals clearly (a strong situation) may help conscientious workers direct their energies toward those goals (Colbert & Witt, 2009). Over a broader time scale, individuals may self-select their goals, in which case conscientiousness and emotional stability have been found to predict the goals of intrinsic career success (e.g., satisfaction) and extrinsic career success (e.g., job position, income), above and beyond general cognitive ability (Judge, Higgins, Thoresen, & Barrick, 1999). These latter findings may be more relevant in individualistic cultures such as that of the United States, where career success is highly valued. There are also personal goals (self-esteem) and interpersonal goals (affiliation; DeShon & Gillespie, 2005) that may likely be more important in other cultures. In general, cultural and multicultural factors need to have an increasing influence in models of personality and work behavior in today's global economy (Gelfand, Leslie, & Fehr, 2008). In addition to national culture, the culture of organizations may also create relatively strong or weak situations, and it may emphasize or facilitate some personality characteristics more than others (Schneider, 1987). One recent study identified how employees higher in extraversion are more influential in a team-driven organization and, by contrast, how conscientious individuals benefitted most in organizations in which the work was largely done alone (Anderson, Spataro, & Flynn, 2008).

CONCLUSION

Personality assessment has accumulated a noteworthy history in I/O psychology, yet researchers and practitioners alike continue to challenge and explore the core assumptions and boundary conditions related to the nature of personality and its measurement. Both personality theory and research that advances organizational practice tend to address time-honored questions such as the following: What is the most useful level of refinement for measuring personality from the perspectives of reliability and validity (how broad is too broad, and how narrow is too narrow)? Just how stable are personality traits over an employee's life span, and at what critical points in time are personality traits most (and least) predictive of employee behaviors? Can personality predict inter- and intraindividual changes in behavior over time? How do subgroups such as age, race, and culture and team composition moderate validities? These questions will never have definitive answers. Instead, it is the never-ending pursuit of those answers that contributes to the progress and promise of personality assessment in organizations.

References

Ackerman, P. L. (1996). A theory of adult intellectual development: Process, personality, interests and knowledge. *Intelligence, 22,* 227–257. doi:10.1016/S0160-2896(96)90016-1

Ackerman, P. L., Kanfer, R., & Goff, M. (1995). Cognitive and noncognitive determinants and consequences of complex skill acquisition. *Journal of Experimental Psychology: Applied, 1,* 270–304. doi:10.1037/1076-898X.1.4.270

Age Discrimination in Employment Act of 1967, Pub. L. 90-202, 81 Stat. 602 (29 U.S.C. 621 et seq.).

Allemand, M., Zimprich, D., & Hendriks, A. A. J. (2008). Age differences in five personality domains across the life span. *Developmental Psychology, 44,* 758–770.doi:10.1037/0012-1649.44.3.758

Allport, G. W., & Odbert, H. S. (1936). Trait names: A psycholexical study. *Psychological Monographs, 47,* 1–171.

American Educational Research Association, American Psychological Association, & National Council on Measurement in Education. (1999). *Standards for educational and psychological testing.* Washington, DC: American Educational Research Association.

Americans With Disabilities Act of 1990, Pub. L. 101–336, 42 U.S.C. § 12101.

Anderson, C., Spataro, S. E., & Flynn, F. J. (2008). Personality and organizational culture as determinants of influence. *Journal of Applied Psychology, 93,* 702–710.

Ashton, M. C. (1998). Personality and job performance: The importance of narrow traits. *Journal of Organizational Behavior, 19,* 289–303. doi:10.1002/(SICI)1099-1379(199805)19:3<289::AID-JOB841>3.0.CO;2-C

Ashton, M. C., Jackson, D. N., Helmes, E., & Paunonen, S. V. (1998). Joint factor analysis of the Personality Research Form and the Jackson Personality Inventory: Comparisons with the Big Five. *Journal of Research in Personality, 32,* 243–250. doi:10.1006/jrpe.1998.2214

Ashton, M. C., & Lee, K. (2001). A theoretical basis for the major dimensions of personality. *European Journal of Personality, 15,* 327–353. doi:10.1002/per.417

Ashton, M. C., Lee, K., & Goldberg, L. R. (2004). A hierarchical analysis of 1,710 English personality-descriptive adjectives. *Journal of Personality and Social Psychology, 87,* 707–721.doi:10.1037/0022-3514.87.5.707

Ashton, M. C., Lee, K., Goldberg, L. R., & de Vries, R. E. (2009). Higher order factors of personality: Do they exist? *Personality and Social Psychology Review, 13,* 79–91. doi:10.1177/1088868309338467

Ashton, M. C., Lee, K., Perugini, M., Szarota, P., De Vries, R. E., Di Blas, L., et al. (2004). A six-factor structure of personality-descriptive adjectives: Solutions from psycholexical studies in seven languages. *Journal of Personality and Social Psychology, 86,* 356–366. doi:10.1037/0022-3514.86.2.356

Ashton, M. C., Lee, K., & Son, C. (2000). Honesty as the sixth factor of personality: Correlations with Machiavellianism, psychopathy, and social adroitness. *European Journal of Personality, 14,* 359–368. doi:10.1002/1099-0984(200007/08)14:4<359::AID-PER382>3.0.CO;2-Y

Bagozzi, R. P., Bergami, M., & Leone, L. (2003). Hierarchical representation of motives in goal setting. *Journal of Applied Psychology, 88,* 915–943. doi:10.1037/0021-9010.88.5.915

Baron, H. (1996). Strengths and limitations of ipsative measurement. *Journal of Occupational and Organizational Psychology, 69,* 49–56.

Barrick, M. R., & Mount, M. K. (1991). The Big Five personality dimensions and job performance: A meta-analysis. *Personnel Psychology, 44,* 1–26. doi:10.1111/j.1744-6570.1991.tb00688.x

Barrick, M. R., Mount, M. K., & Judge, T. A. (2001). Personality and performance at the beginning of the new millennium: What do we know and where do we go next? *International Journal of Selection and Assessment, 9,* 9–30. doi:10.1111/1468-2389.00160

Barrick, M. R., Mount, M. K., & Strauss, J. P. (1993). Conscientiousness and performance of sales representatives: Test of the mediating effects of goal setting. *Journal of Applied Psychology, 78,* 715–722. doi:10.1037/0021-9010.78.5.715

Barrick, M. R., Stewart, G. L., & Piotrowski, M. (2002). Personality and job performance: Test of the mediating effects of motivation among sales representatives. *Journal of Applied Psychology, 87,* 43–51. doi:10.1037/0021-9010.87.1.43

Bartram, D. (2005). The Great Eight competencies: A criterion-centric approach to validation. *Journal of Applied Psychology, 90,* 1185–1203. doi:10.1037/0021-9010.90.6.1185

Baumeister, R. F., Gailliot, M., DeWall, C., & Oaten, M. (2006). Self-regulation and personality: How interventions increase regulatory success, and how depletion moderates the effects of traits on behavior. *Journal of Personality, 74,* 1773–1802. doi:10.1111/j.1467-6494.2006.00428.x

Beaty, J. C., Cleveland, J. N., & Murphy, K. R. (2001). The relationship between personality and contextual performance in "strong" versus "weak" situations. *Human Performance, 14,* 125–148. doi:10.1207/S15327043HUP1402_01

Bell, B. S., & Kozlowski, S. W. J. (2008). Active learning: Effects of core training design elements on self-regulatory processes, learning, and adaptability. *Journal of Applied Psychology, 93,* 296–316. doi:10.1037/0021-9010.93.2.296

Benet-Martínez, V., & John, O. P. (1998). Los Cinco Grandes across cultures and ethnic groups: Multitrait multimethod analyses of the big five in Spanish and English. *Journal of Personality and Social Psychology, 75,* 729–750. doi:10.1037/0022-3514.75.3.729

Berry, C. M., Ones, D. S., & Sackett, P. R. (2007). Interpersonal deviance, organizational deviance, and their common correlates: A review and meta-analysis. *Journal of Applied Psychology, 92,* 410–424. doi:10.1037/0021-9010.92.2.410

Bijnen, E. J., van der Net, T. Z., & Poortinga, Y. H. (1986). On cross-cultural comparative studies with the Eysenck Personality Questionnaire. *Journal of Cross-Cultural Psychology, 17,* 3–16. doi:10.1177/0022002186017001001

Bing, M. N., Stewart, S. M., Davison, H. K., Green, P. D., McIntyre, M. D., & James, L. R. (2007). Integrative typology of personality assessment for aggression: Implications for predicting counterproductive workplace behavior. *Journal of Applied Psychology, 92,* 722–744. doi:10.1037/0021-9010.92.3.722

Birkeland, S. A., Manson, T. M., Kisamore, J. L., Brannick, M. T., & Smith, M. A. (2006). A meta-analytic investigation of job applicant faking on personality measures. *International Journal of Selection and Assessment, 14,* 317–335.

Birkland, A. S., & Ones, D. S. (2006, July). *The structure of emotional stability: A meta-analytic investigation.* Paper presented at the International Congress of Applied Psychology, Athens, Greece.

Block, J. (1971). *Lives through time.* Berkeley, CA: Bancroft Books.

Block, J. (1995). Going beyond the five factors given: Rejoinder to Costa and McCrae (1995) and Goldberg and Saucier (1995). *Psychological Bulletin, 117,* 226–229. doi:10.1037/0033-2909.117.2.226

Block, J., & Block, J. H. (2006). Venturing a 30-year longitudinal study. *American Psychologist, 61,* 315–327. doi:10.1037/0003-066X.61.4.315

Bono, J. E., & Judge, T. A. (2004). Personality and transformational and transactional leadership: A meta-analysis. *Journal of Applied Psychology, 89,* 901–910. doi:10.1037/0021-9010.89.5.901

Borman, W. C., Penner, L. A., Allen, T. D., & Motowidlo, S. J. (2001). Personality predictors of citizenship performance. *International Journal of Selection and Assessment, 9,* 52–69. doi:10.1111/1468-2389.00163

Borman, W. C., White, L. A., Pulakos, E. D., & Oppler, S. H. (1991). Models of supervisory job performance ratings. *Journal of Applied Psychology, 76,* 863–872. doi:10.1037/0021-9010.76.6.863

Bott, J. P., O'Connell, M. S., Ramakrishnan, M., & Doverspike, D. (2007). Practical limitations in making decisions regarding the distribution of applicant personality test scores based on incumbent data. *Journal of Business and Psychology, 22,* 123–134. doi:10.1007/s10869-007-9053-x

Bray, D. W., Campbell, R. J., & Grant, D. L. (1974). *Formative years in business: A long-term AT&T study of managerial lives.* Malabar, FL: Krieger.

Byrne, Z. S., Stoner, J., Thompson, K. R., & Hochwarter, W. (2005). The interactive effects of conscientiousness, work effort, and psychological climate on work performance. *Journal of Vocational Behavior, 66,* 326–338. doi:10.1016/j.jvb.2004.08.005

Campbell, D. T., & Fiske, D. W. (1959). Convergent and discriminant validation by the multitrait–multimethod matrix. *Psychological Bulletin, 56,* 81–105. doi:10.1037/h0046016

Cascio, W., & Boudreau, J. (2008). *Investing in people: Financial impact of human resource initiatives.* Upper Saddle River, NJ: FT Press.

Cattell, R. B. (1971). *Abilities: Their structure, growth and action.* Amsterdam: North Holland.

Cervone, D. (2005). Personality architecture: Within-person structures and processes. *Annual Review of Psychology, 56,* 423–452. doi:10.1146/annurev.psych.56.091103.070133

Chan, D. (2004). Individual differences in tolerance for contradiction. *Human Performance, 17,* 297–324. doi:10.1207/s15327043hup1703_3

Chen, G., Gully, S. M., Whiteman, J. A., & Kilcullen, R. N. (2000). Examination of relationships among trait-like individual differences, state-like individual differences, and learning performance. *Journal of Applied Psychology, 85,* 835–847. doi:10.1037/0021-9010.85.6.835

Chernyshenko, O. S., Stark, S., Prewett, M. S., Gray, A. A., Stilson, F. R., & Tuttle, M. D. (2009). Normative scoring of multidimensional pairwise preference personality scales using IRT: Empirical comparison with other formats. *Human Performance, 22,* 105–127. doi:10.1080/08959280902743303

Cheung, F. M., Leung, K., Zhang, J.-X., Sun, H.-F., Gan, Y.-Q., Song, W.-Z., & Zie, D. (2001). Indigenous Chinese personality constructs: Is the five-factor model complete? *Journal of Cross-Cultural Psychology, 32,* 407–433. doi:10.1177/0022022101032004003

Cheung, M. W. L. (2004). A direct estimation method on analyzing ipsative data with Chan and Bentler's (1993) method. *Structural Equation Modeling, 11,* 217–243. doi:10.1207/s15328007sem1102_5

Chmielewski, M., & Watson, D. (2009). What is being assessed and why it matters: The impact of transient error on trait research. *Journal of Personality and Social Psychology, 97,* 186–202. doi:10.1037/a0015618

Christiansen, N. D., Burns, G. N., & Montgomery, G. E. (2005). Reconsidering forced-choice item formats for applicant personality assessment. *Human Performance, 18,* 267–307. doi:10.1207/s15327043hup1803_4

Church, A. T. (2000). Culture and personality: Toward an integrated cultural trait psychology. *Journal of Personality, 68,* 651–703. Medline doi:10.1111/1467-6494.00112

Church, A. T. (2001). Personality measurement in a cross-cultural perspective. *Journal of Personality, 69,* 979–1006. Medline doi:10.1111/1467-6494.696172

Civil Rights Act of 1964, Pub. L. 88–352, 42 U.S.C., Ch. 21 § 1981-2000.

Civil Rights Act of 1991, Pub. L. 102-166, Nov. 21, 1991, 105 Stat. 1071.

Cloninger, C. R. (2008). The psychobiological theory of temperament and character: Comment on Farmer and Goldberg (2008). *Psychological Assessment, 20,* 292–299. doi:10.1037/a0012933

Cohen, J. (1988). *Statistical power analysis for the behavioral sciences* (2nd ed.). Hillsdale, NJ: Erlbaum.

Colbert, A. E., & Witt, L. A. (2009). The role of goal-focused leadership in enabling the expression of conscientiousness. *Journal of Applied Psychology, 94,* 790–796. doi:10.1037/a0014187

Colquitt, J. A., LePine, J. A., & Noe, R. A. (2000). Toward an integrative theory of training motivation: A meta-analytic path analysis of 20 years of research. *Journal of Applied Psychology, 85,* 678–707. doi:10.1037/0021-9010.85.5.678

Connelly, B. S. (2008). *The reliability, convergence, and predictive validity of personality ratings: An other perspective.* Unpublished doctoral dissertation, University of Minnesota.

Connelly, B. S., & Ones, D. S. (2007, April). *Combining conscientiousness scales: Can't get enough of the trait, baby.* Poster session presented at the annual conference of the Society for Industrial and Organizational Psychology, New York.

Connelly, B. S., Davies, S. E., Ones, D. S., & Birkland, A. S. (2008a, April). Agreeableness: A meta-analytic review of structure, convergence, and predictive validity. In J. P. Thomas & C. Viswesvaran (Chairs), *Personality in the workplace: Advances in measurement and assessment.* Symposium conducted at the annual conference of the Society for Industrial and Organizational Psychology, San Francisco.

Connelly, B. S., Davies, S. E., Ones, D. S., & Birkland, A. S. (2008b, January). *Opening up openness: A meta-analytic review of measures of the personality construct.* Poster session presented at the annual conference of the Society for Personality and Social Psychology, Albuquerque, NM.

Converse, P. D., Oswald, F. L., Imus, A., Hedricks, C., Roy, R., & Butera, H. (2008). Comparing personality test formats and warnings: Effects on criterion-related validity and test-taker reactions. *International Journal of Selection and Assessment, 16,* 155–169. doi:10.1111/j.1468-2389.2008.00420.x

Cooper, W. H., & Withey, M. J. (2009). The strong situation hypothesis. *Personality and Social Psychology Review, 13,* 62–72. doi:10.1177/1088868308329378

Costa, P. T., & McCrae, R. R. (1995). Domains and facets: Hierarchical personality assessment using the Revised NEO Personality Inventory. *Journal of Personality Assessment, 64,* 21–50. doi:10.1207/s15327752jpa6401_2

Costa, P. T., Zonderman, A. B., Williams, R. B., & McCrae, R. R. (1985). Content and comprehensiveness in the MMPI: An item factor analysis in a normal adult sample. *Journal of Personality and Social Psychology, 48,* 925–933.

Dancer, L. J., & Woods, S. A. (2006). Higher-order factor structures and intercorrelations of the 16PF5 and FIRO-B. *International Journal of Selection and Assessment, 14,* 385–391.

Davies, M., Stankov, L., & Roberts, R. D. (1998). Emotional intelligence: In search of an elusive construct. *Journal of Personality and Social Psychology, 75,* 989–1015. doi:10.1037/0022-3514.75.4.989

Davies, S. E., Connelly, B. S., Ones, D. S., & Birkland, A. S. (2008, April). *Enhancing the role of extraversion for work related behaviors.* Poster session presented at the annual conference of the Society for Industrial and Organizational Psychology, San Francisco.

De Corte, W., Lievens, P., & Sackett, P. R. (2007). Combining predictors to achieve optimal trade-offs between selection quality and adverse impact. *Journal of Applied Psychology, 92,* 1380–1393.doi:10.1037/0021-9010.92.5.1380

De Raad, B. (1998). Five big, Big Five issues: Rationale, content, structure, status and cross-cultural assessment. *European Psychologist, 3,* 113–124.

De Raad, B., & Hoskens, M. (1990). Personality-descriptive nouns. *European Journal of Personality, 4,* 131–146. doi:10.1002/per.2410040206

De Raad, B., Perugini, M., & Szirmak, Z. (1997). In pursuit of a cross-lingual reference structure of personality traits: Comparisons among five languages. *European Journal of Personality, 11,* 167–185. doi:10.1002/(SICI)1099-0984(199709)11:3<167::AID-PER286>3.0.CO;2-B

DeShon, R. P., & Gillespie, J. Z. (2005). A motivated action theory account of goal orientation. *Journal of Applied Psychology, 90,* 1096–1127. doi:10.1037/0021-9010.90.6.1096

Di Blas, L., & Forzi, M. (1999). Refining a descriptive structure of personality attributes in the Italian language. *Journal of Personality and Social Psychology, 76,* 451–481. doi:10.1037/0022-3514.76.3.451

Digman, J. M., & Takemoto-Chock, M. K. (1981). Factors in the natural language of personality: Re-analysis and comparison of six major studies. *Multivariate Behavioral Research, 16,* 149–170. doi:10.1207/s15327906mbr1602_2

Digman, J. M. (1997). Higher-order factors of the Big Five. *Journal of Personality and Social Psychology, 73,* 1246–1256. doi:10.1037/0022-3514.73.6.1246

Donnellan, M. B., & Lucas, R. E. (2008). Age differences in the Big Five across the life span: Evidence from two national samples. *Psychology and Aging, 23,* 558–566.

Dudley, N. M., Orvis, K. A., Lebiecki, J. E., & Cortina, J. M. (2006). A meta-analytic investigation of Conscientiousness in the prediction of job performance: Examining the intercorrelations and the incremental validity of narrow traits. *Journal of Applied Psychology, 91,* 40–57. doi:10.1037/0021-9010.91.1.40

Duehr, E. E., Jackson, H. L., & Ones, D. S. (2003, April). *Gender differences in conscientiousness and extraversion: A multiple-culture, multiple-instrument meta-analysis.*

Poster presented at the annual conference of the Society for Industrial and Organizational Psychology, Orlando, FL.

Edwards, A. L. (1953). The relationship between the judged desirability of a trait and the probability that it will be endorsed. *Journal of Applied Psychology, 37,* 90–93. doi:10.1037/h0058073

Ellingson, J. E., Sackett, P. R., & Connelly, B. S. (2007). Personality assessment across selection and development contexts: Insights into response distortion. *Journal of Applied Psychology, 92,* 386–395. doi:10.1037/0021-9010.92.2.386

Elliot, A. J., & Church, M. A. (1997). A hierarchical model of approach and avoidance achievement motivation. *Journal of Personality and Social Psychology, 72,* 218–232. doi:10.1037/0022-3514.72.1.218

Erez, A., & Judge, T. A. (2001). Relationship of core self-evaluations to goal setting, motivation, and performance. *Journal of Applied Psychology, 86,* 1270–1279. doi:10.1037/0021-9010.86.6.1270

Eysenck, H. J. (1947). *Dimensions of personality.* London: Routledge & Kegan Paul.

Eysenck, H. J., & Eysenck, M. W. (1985). *Personality and individual differences: A natural science approach.* New York: Plenum Press.

Feist, G. J. (1998). A meta-analysis of personality in scientific and artistic creativity. *Personality and Social Psychology Review, 2,* 290–309. doi:10.1207/s15327957pspr0204_5

Fleeson, W. (2001). Toward a structure- and process-integrated view of personality: Traits as density distribution states. *Journal of Personality and Social Psychology, 80,* 1011–1027. doi:10.1037/0022-3514.80.6.1011

Foldes, H. J., Duehr, E. E., & Ones, D. S. (2008). Group differences in personality: Meta-analyses comparing five U.S. racial groups. *Personnel Psychology, 61,* 579–616. doi:10.1111/j.1744-6570.2008.00123.x

Ford, J. K., & Oswald, F. L. (2003). Understanding the dynamic learner: Linking personality traits, learning situations, and individual behavior. In M. R. Barrick & A. M. Ryan (Eds.), *Personality and work: Reconsidering the role of personality in organizations* (pp. 229–261). San Francisco: Jossey-Bass.

Frost, B. C., Ko, C.-H. E., & James, L. R. (2007). Implicit and explicit personality: A test of a channeling hypothesis for aggressive behavior. *Journal of Applied Psychology, 92,* 1299–1319.doi:10.1037/0021-9010.92.5.1299

Funder, D. C. (1995). On the accuracy of personality judgment: A realistic approach. *Psychological Review, 102,* 652–670.doi:10.1037/0033-295X.102.4.652

Funder, D. C. (2009). Naïve and obvious questions. *Perspectives on Psychological Science, 4,* 340–344. doi:10.1111/j.1745-6924.2009.01135.x

Gelfand, M. J., Leslie, L. M., & Fehr, R. (2008). To prosper, organizational psychology should . . . adopt a global perspective. *Journal of Organizational Behavior, 29,* 493–517. doi:10.1002/job.530

Glaros, A. G., & Kline, R. B. (1988). Understanding the accuracy of tests with cutting scores: The sensitivity, specificity, and predictive value model. *Journal of Clinical Psychology, 44,* 1013–1023.doi:10.1002/1097-4679(198811)44:6<1013::AID-JCLP2270440627>3.0.CO;2-Z

Goffin, R. D., & Boyd, A. C. (2009). Faking and personality assessment in personnel selection: Advancing models of faking. *Canadian Psychology, 50,* 151–160.

Goldberg, L. R. (1990). An alternative "description of personality:" The Big Five factor structure. *Journal of Personality and Social Psychology, 59,* 1216–1229. doi:10.1037/0022-3514.59.6.1216

Goldberg, L. R. (1993). The structure of phenotypic personality traits. *American Psychologist, 48,* 26–34. doi:10.1037/0003-066X.48.1.26

Goldberg, L. R. (1999). A broad-bandwidth, public domain, personality inventory measuring the lower-level facets of several five-factor models. In I. Mervielde, I. Deary, F. De Fruyt, & F. Ostendorf (Eds.), *Personality psychology in Europe* (Vol. 7, pp. 7–28). Tilburg, the Netherlands: Tilburg University Press.

Goldberg, L. R., & Saucier, G. (1998). What is beyond the Big Five? *Journal of Personality, 66,* 495–524. doi:10.1111/1467-6494.00022

Goldberg, L. R., & Velicer, W. F. (2006). Principles of exploratory factor analysis. In S. Strack (Ed.), *Differentiating normal and abnormal personality* (2nd ed., pp. 209–237). New York: Springer Publishing Company.

Gough, H. G. (1968). *The Chapin Social Insight Test manual.* Palo Alto, CA: Consulting Psychologists Press.

Grucza, R. A., & Goldberg, L. R. (2007). The comparative validity of 11 modern personality inventories: Prediction of behavioral acts, informant reports, and clinical indicators. *Journal of Personality Assessment, 89,* 167–187. doi:10.1002/pmh.3

Guion, R. M., & Gottier, R. F. (1965). Validity of personality measures in personnel selection. *Personnel Psychology, 18,* 135–164. doi:10.1111/j.1744-6570.1965.tb00273.x

Gully, S. M., Payne, S. C., Koles, K. L. K., & Whiteman, J. A. K. (2002). The impact of error training and individual differences on training outcomes: An attribute–treatment interaction perspective. *Journal of Applied Psychology, 87,* 143–155. doi:10.1037/0021-9010.87.1.143

Helmreich, R. L., Sawin, L. L., & Carsrud, A. L. (1986). The honeymoon effect in job performance: Temporal increases in the predictive power of achievement motivation. *Journal of Applied Psychology, 71,* 185–188. doi:10.1037/0021-9010.71.2.185

Hicks, L. E. (1970). Some properties of ipsative, normative, and forced-choice normative measures. *Psychological Bulletin, 74,* 167–184.

Hogan, J., Barrett, P., & Hogan, R. (2007). Personality measurement, faking, and employment selection. *Journal of Applied Psychology, 92,* 1270–1285. doi:10.1037/0021-9010.92.5.1270

Hogan, J., & Holland, B. (2003). Using theory to evaluate personality and job-performance relations: A socioanalytic perspective. *Journal of Applied Psychology, 88,* 100–112. doi:10.1037/0021-9010.88.1.100

Hogan, J., & Roberts, B. W. (1996). Issues and non-issues in the fidelity-bandwidth trade-off. *Journal of Organizational Behavior, 17,* 627–637.

Hogan, R. (1969). Development of an empathy scale. *Journal of Consulting and Clinical Psychology, 33,* 307–316. doi:10.1037/h0027580

Hogan, R. (1983). A socioanalytic theory of personality. In M. M. Page (Ed.), *Nebraska Symposium on Motivation: Vol. 30. Personality—Current theory and research* (pp. 336–355). Lincoln: University of Nebraska Press.

Holland, J. L. (1985). *Making vocational choices: A theory of careers.* Englewood Cliffs, NJ: Prentice-Hall.

Hopwood, C. J., & Donnellan, M. B. (2009). *Assessing the internal structure of personality inventories.* Unpublished manuscript.

Hough, L. M. (1989). Development of personality measures to supplement selection decisions. In B. J. Fallon, H. P. Pfister, & J. Brebner (Eds.), *Advances in industrial organizational psychology* (pp. 365–375). Holland: Elsevier Science.

Hough, L. M. (1992). The "Big Five" personality variables—Construct confusion: Description versus prediction. *Human Performance, 5,* 139–155. doi:10.1207/s15327043hup0501&2_8

Hough, L. M. (1997). The millennium for personality psychology: New horizons or good old daze. *Applied Psychology, 47,* 233–261.

Hough, L. M. (1998). Personality at work: Issues and evidence. In M. Hakel (Ed.), *Beyond multiple choice: Evaluating alternatives to traditional testing for selection* (pp. 131–166). Hillsdale, NJ: Erlbaum.

Hough, L., & Dilchert, S. (2007). *Inventors, innovators, and their leaders: Selecting for conscientiousness will keep you "inside the box"* (SIOP Leading Edge Consortium). Kansas City, MO: Society for Industrial and Organizational Psychology.

Hough, L. M., Eaton, N. K., Dunnette, M. D., Kamp, J. D., & McCloy, R. A. (1990). Criterion-related validities of personality constructs and the effects of response distortion on those validities. *Journal of Applied Psychology, 75,* 581–595. doi:10.1037/0021-9010.75.5.581

Hough, L. M., & Furnham, A. (2003). Importance and use of personality variables in work settings. In I. B. Weiner (Ed. in Chief) & W. Borman, D. Illgen, & R. Klimoski (Vol. Eds.), *Comprehensive handbook of psychology. Vol. 12: Industrial & organizational psychology* (pp. 131–169). New York: Wiley.

Hough, L. M., & Ones, D. S. (2001). The structure, measurement, validity, and use of personality variables in industrial, work, and organizational psychology. In N. Anderson, D. S. Ones, H. K. Sinangil, & C. Viswesvaran (Eds.), *International handbook of work and organizational psychology* (pp. 233–377). London: Sage.

Hough, L. M., Ones, D. S., & Viswesvaran, C. (1998, April). Personality correlates of managerial performance constructs. In R. Page (Chair), *Personality determinants of managerial potential, performance, progression and ascendancy.* Symposium conducted at the 13th Annual Conference of the Society for Industrial and Organizational Psychology, Dallas, TX.

Hough, L. M., & Oswald, F. L. (2000). Personnel selection: Looking toward the future—Remembering the past. *Annual Review of Psychology, 51,* 631–664. doi:10.1146/annurev.psych.51.1.631

Hough, L. M., & Oswald, F. L. (2005). They're right, well . . . mostly right: Research evidence and an agenda to rescue personality testing from 1960s insights. *Human Performance, 18,* 373–387. doi:10.1207/s15327043hup1804_4

Hough, L. M., & Oswald, F. L. (2008). Personality testing and industrial–organizational psychology: Reflections, progress, and prospects. *Industrial and Organizational Psychology: Perspectives on Science and Practice, 1,* 272–290. doi:10.1111/j.1754-9434.2008.00048.x

Hough, L. M., Oswald, F. L., & Ployhart, R. E. (2001). Determinants, detection, and amelioration of adverse impact in personnel selection procedures: Issues, evidence, and lessons learned. *International Journal of Selection and Assessment, 9,* 152–194. doi:10.1111/1468-2389.00171

Hough, L. M., & Schneider, R. J. (1996). Personality traits, taxonomies, and applications in organizations. In K. Murphy (Ed.), *Individual differences and behavior in organizations* (pp. 31–88). San Francisco: Jossey-Bass.

Houston, J. S., Borman, W. C., Farmer, W. F., & Bearden, R. M. (2006). *Development of the Navy Computer Adaptive Personality Scales (NCAPS)* (NPRST-TR-06-2). Millington, TN: Navy Personnel, Research, Studies, & Technology.

Humphreys, M. S., & Revelle, W. (1984). Personality, motivation, and performance: A theory of the relationship between individual differences and information processing. *Psychological Review, 91,* 153–184. doi:10.1037/0033-295X.91.2.153

Hurtz, G. M., & Alliger, G. M. (2002). Influence of coaching on integrity test performance and unlikely virtues scales. *Human Performance, 15,* 255–273. doi:10.1207/S15327043HUP1503_02

Hurtz, G. M., & Donovan, J. J. (2000). Personality and job performance: The Big Five revisited. *Journal of Applied Psychology, 85,* 869–879. doi:10.1037/0021-9010.85.6.869

Jackson, D. N., Wroblewski, V. R., & Ashton, M. C. (2000). The impact of faking on employment tests: Does forced-choice offer a solution? *Human Performance, 13,* 371–388. doi:10.1207/S15327043HUP1304_3

James, L. R. (1998). Measurement of personality via conditional reasoning. *Organizational Research Methods, 1,* 131–163. doi:10.1177/109442819812001

James, L. R., McIntyre, M. D., Glisson, C. A., Bowler, J. L., & Mitchell, T. R. (2004). The Conditional Reasoning Measurement System for aggression: An overview. *Human Performance, 17,* 271–295. doi:10.1207/s15327043hup1703_2

James, L. R., McIntyre, M. D., Glisson, C. A., Green, P. D., Patton, T. W., LeBreton, J. M., et al. (2005). A conditional reasoning measure for aggression. *Organizational Research Methods, 8,* 69–99. doi:10.1177/1094428104272182

John, O. P., Hampson, S. E., & Goldberg, L. R. (1991). The basic level in personality-trait hierarchies: Studies of trait use and accessibility in different contexts. *Journal of Personality and Social Psychology, 60,* 348–361. doi:10.1037/0022-3514.60.3.348

Johnson, J. W., & Hezlett, S. A. (2008). Modeling the influence of personality on individuals at work: A review and research agenda. In S. Cartwright & C. L. Cooper (Eds.), *Oxford handbook of personnel psychology* (pp. 59–92). Oxford, England: Oxford University Press.

Judge, T. A., Bono, J. E., Ilies, R., & Gerhardt, M. W. (2002). Personality and leadership: A qualitative and quantitative review. *Journal of Applied Psychology, 87,* 765–780. doi:10.1037/0021-9010.87.4.765

Judge, T. A., Heller, D., & Mount, M. K. (2002). Five-factor model of personality and job satisfaction: A meta-analysis. *Journal of Applied Psychology, 87,* 530–541. Medline doi:10.1037/0021-9010.87.3.530

Judge, T. A., Higgins, C. A., Thoresen, C. J., & Barrick, M. R. (1999). The Big Five personality traits, general mental ability, and career success across the life span. *Personnel Psychology, 52,* 621–652. doi:10.1111/j.1744-6570.1999.tb00174.x

Judge, T. A., & Hurst, C. (2007). Capitalizing on one's advantages: Role of core self-evaluations. *Journal of Applied Psychology, 92,* 1212–1227. doi:10.1037/0021-9010.92.5.1212

Judge, T. A., & Ilies, R. (2002). Relationship of personality to performance motivation: A meta-analytic review. *Journal of Applied Psychology, 87,* 797–807. doi:10.1037/0021-9010.87.4.797

Kanfer, R. (1990). Motivation theory and industrial/organizational psychology. In M. D. Dunnette & L. M. Hough (Eds.), *Handbook of industrial and organizational psychology. Volume 1: Theory in industrial and organizational psychology* (pp. 75–170). Palo Alto, CA: Consulting Psychologists Press.

Kanfer, R., & Heggestad, E. D. (1999). Individual differences in motivation: Traits and self-regulatory skills. In P. L. Ackerman & P. C. Kyllonen (Eds.), *Learning and individual differences: Process, trait, and content determinants* (pp. 293–313). Washington, DC: American Psychological Association.

Katigbak, M. S., Church, A. T., & Akamine, T. X. (1996). Cross-cultural generalizability of personality dimensions: Relating indigenous and imported dimensions in two cultures. *Journal of Personality and Social Psychology, 70,* 99–114. doi:10.1037/0022-3514.70.1.99

Klehe, U.-C., & Anderson, N. (2007). Working hard and working smart: Motivation and ability during typical and maximum performance. *Journal of Applied Psychology, 92,* 978–992. doi:10.1037/0021-9010.92.4.978

Klein, H. J., & Lee, S. (2006). The effects of personality on learning: The mediating role of goal setting. *Human Performance, 19,* 43–66. doi:10.1207/s15327043hup1901_3

Knapp, D. J., Heggestad, E. D., & Young, M. C. (Eds.). (2004). *Understanding and improving the Assessment of Individual Motivation (AIM) in the Army's GED Plus program* (ARI Study Note 2004–03). Alexandria, VA: U.S. Army Research Institute for the Behavioral and Social Sciences.

Komar, S., Brown, D. J., Komar, J. A., & Robie, C. (2008). Faking and the validity of conscientiousness: A Monte Carlo investigation. *Journal of Applied Psychology, 93,* 140–154. doi:10.1037/0021-9010.93.1.140

Kuncel, N. R., & Borneman, M. J. (2007). Toward a new method of detecting deliberately faked personality tests: The use of idiosyncratic item responses. *International Journal of Selection and Assessment, 15,* 220–231. doi:10.1111/j.1468-2389.2007.00383.x

Kuncel, N. R., Cooper, S. R., & Owens, K. (2009). *Communicating the predictive power of selection and admissions measures: Three alternatives to correlations.* Unpublished manuscript.

Kwong, J. Y. Y., & Cheung, F. M. (2003). Prediction of performance facets using specific personality traits in the Chinese context. *Journal of Vocational Behavior, 63,* 99–110. doi:10.1016/S0001-8791(02)00021-0

Lahey, B. B. (2009). Public health significance of neuroticism. *American Psychologist, 64,* 241–256. doi:10.1037/a0015309

LeBreton, J. M., Barksdale, C. D., Robin, J., & James, L. R. (2007). Measurement issues associated with conditional reasoning tests: Indirect measurement and test faking. *Journal of Applied Psychology, 92,* 1–16. doi:10.1037/0021-9010.92.1.1

Lee, F. K., Sheldon, K. M., & Turban, D. B. (2003). Personality and the goal-striving process: The influence of achievement goal patterns, goal level, and mental focus on performance and enjoyment. *Journal of Applied Psychology, 88,* 256–265. doi:10.1037/0021-9010.88.2.256

Lee, K., & Ashton, M. C. (2004). Psychometric properties of the HEXACO personality inventory. *Multivariate Behavioral Research, 39,* 329–358. doi:10.1207/s15327906mbr3902_8

Lee, K., & Ashton, M. C. (2008). The HEXACO personality factors in the indigenous personality lexicons of English and 11 other languages. *Journal of Personality, 76,* 1001–1053.

Lee, K., Ashton, M. C., & deVries, R. E. (2005). Predicting workplace delinquency and integrity with the HEXACO and five-factor models of personality structure. *Human Performance, 18,* 179–197. doi:10.1207/s15327043hup1802_4

Lefkowitz, J. (2000). The role of interpersonal affective regard in supervisory performance ratings: A literature review and proposed causal model. *Journal of Occupational and Organizational Psychology, 73,* 67–85. doi:10.1348/096317900166886

LePine, J. A., Colquitt, J. A., & Erez, A. (2000). Adaptability to changing task contexts: Effects of general cognitive ability, conscientiousness, and openness to experience. *Personnel Psychology, 53,* 563–593. doi:10.1111/j.1744-6570.2000.tb00214.x

LePine, J. A., Erez, A., & Johnson, D. E. (2002). The nature and dimensionality of organizational citizenship behavior: A critical review and meta-analysis. *Journal of Applied Psychology, 87,* 52–65. doi:10.1037/0021-9010.87.1.52

Loevinger, J. (1957). Objective tests as instruments of psychological theory. *Psychological Reports, 3,* 635–694. doi:10.2466/PR0.3.7.635-694

MacCallum, R. C., Wegener, D. T., Uchino, B. N., & Fabrigar, L. R. (1993). The problem of equivalent models in applications of covariance structure analysis. *Psychological Bulletin, 114,* 185–199. doi:10.1037/0033-2909.114.1.185

Markon, K. E., Krueger, R. F., & Watson, D. (2005). Delineating the structure of normal and abnormal personality: An integrative hierarchical approach. *Journal of Personality and Social Psychology, 88,* 139–157. doi:10.1037/0022-3514.88.1.139

Maydeu-Olivares, A., & Böckenholt, U. (2005). Structural equation modeling of paired comparison and ranking data. *Psychological Methods, 10,* 285–304. doi:10.1037/1082-989X.10.3.285

McAdams, D. P., & Olson, B. D. (in press). Personality development: Continuity and change over the life course. *Annual Review of Psychology.*

McCrae, R. R., & Costa, P. T., Jr. (1987). Validation of the five-factor model of personality across instruments and observers. *Journal of Personality and Social Psychology, 52,* 81–90. doi:10.1037/0022-3514.52.1.81

McCrae, R. R., & Costa, P. T., Jr. (1997). Personality trait structure as a human universal. *American Psychologist, 52,* 509–516. doi:10.1037/0003-066X.52.5.509

McCrae, R., Costa, P., Del Pilar, G., Rolland, J. P., & Parker, W. (1998). Cross-cultural assessment of the five-factor model: The revised NEO Personality Inventory. *Journal of Cross-Cultural Psychology, 29,* 171–188. doi:10.1177/0022022198291009

McDonald, R. P. (1999). *Test theory: A unified treatment.* Mahwah, NJ: Erlbaum.

McFarland, L. A., & Ryan, A. M. (2000). Variance in faking across noncognitive measures. *Journal of Applied Psychology, 85,* 812–821. doi:10.1037/0021-9010.85.5.812

McFarland, L. A., & Ryan, A. M. (2006). Toward an integrated model of applicant faking behavior. *Journal of Applied Social Psychology, 36,* 979–1016.

Mershon, B., & Gorsuch, R. L. (1988). Number of factors in personality sphere: Does increase in factors increase predictability of real life criteria? *Journal of Personality and Social Psychology, 55,* 675–680. doi:10.1037/0022-3514.55.4.675

Mischel, W. (1968). *Personality and assessment.* New York: Wiley.

Mol, S. T., Born, M. P. H., Willemsen, M. E., & Van Der Molen, H. T. (2005). Predicting expatriate job performance for selection purposes: A quantitative review. *Journal of Cross-Cultural Psychology, 36,* 590–620. doi:10.1177/0022022105278544

Molenaar, P. C. M., & Campbell, C. G. (2009). The new person-specific paradigm in psychology. *Current Directions in Psychological Science, 18,* 112–117. doi:10.1111/j.1467-8721.2009.01619.x

Moon, H., Hollenbeck, J. R., Marinova, S., & Humphrey, S. E. (2008). Beneath the surface: Uncovering the relationship between extraversion and organizational citizenship behavior through a facet approach.

International Journal of Selection and Assessment, 16, 143–154. doi:10.1111/j.1468-2389.2008.00419.x

Morgeson, F. P., Campion, M. A., Dipboye, R. L., Hollenbeck, J. R., Murphy, K., & Schmitt, N. (2007). Reconsidering the use of personality tests in personnel selection contexts. *Personnel Psychology, 60,* 683–729.

Morris, S. B., & Lobsenz, R. (2000). Significance tests and confidence intervals for the adverse impact ratio. *Personnel Psychology, 53,* 89–111. doi:10.1111/j.1744-6570.2000.tb00195.x

Mueller-Hanson, R., Heggestad, E. D., & Thornton, G. C., III. (2003). Faking and selection: Considering the use of personality from select-in and select-out perspectives. *Journal of Applied Psychology, 88,* 348–355. doi:10.1037/0021-9010.88.2.348

Murphy, K. R., & DeShon, R. D. (2000). Progress in psychometrics: Can industrial and organizational psychology catch up? *Personnel Psychology, 53,* 913–924. doi:10.1111/j.1744-6570.2000.tb02423.x

Ng, T. W. H., Eby, L. T., Sorensen, K. L., & Feldman, D. C. (2005). Predictors of objective and subjective career success. A meta-analysis. *Personnel Psychology, 58,* 367–408. doi:10.1111/j.1744-6570.2005.00515.x

Norman, W. T. (1963). Toward an adequate taxonomy of personality attributes: Replicated factor structure in peer nomination personality ratings. *Journal of Abnormal and Social Psychology, 66,* 574–583. doi:10.1037/h0040291

Ones, D. S., Viswesvaran, C., & Schmidt, F. L. (1993). Comprehensive meta-analysis of integrity test validities: Findings and implications for personnel selection and theories of job performance. *Journal of Applied Psychology, 78,* 679–703. doi:10.1037/0021-9010.78.4.679

Ones, D. S., Viswesvaran, C., & Schmidt, F. L. (2003). Personality and absenteeism: A meta-analysis of integrity tests. *European Journal of Personality, 17*(Suppl.), S19–S38. doi:10.1002/per.487

Ong, A. D., Bergeman, C. S., Bisconti, T. L., & Wallace, K. A. (2006). Psychological resilience, positive emotions, and successful adaptation to stress in later life. *Journal of Personality and Social Psychology, 91,* 730–749. doi:10.1037/0022-3514.91.4.730

Organ, D. W., & Ryan, K. (1995). A meta-analytic review of attitudinal and dispositional predictors of organizational citizenship behavior. *Personnel Psychology, 48,* 775–802. doi:10.1111/j.1744-6570.1995.tb01781.x

Ostendorf, F., & Angleitner, A. (1994). The five-factor taxonomy: Robust dimensions of personality description. *Psychologica Belgica, 34,* 175–194.

Oswald, F. L., & McCloy, R. A. (2003). Meta-analysis and the art of the average. In K. R. Murphy (Ed.), *Validity generalization: A critical review* (pp. 311–338). Mahwah, NJ: Erlbaum.

Paunonen, S. V. (1998). Hierarchical organization of personality and prediction of behavior. *Journal of Personality and Social Psychology, 74,* 538–556. doi:10.1037/0022-3514.74.2.538

Paunonen, S. V., & Jackson, D. N. (2000). What is beyond the Big Five? Plenty! *Journal of Personality, 68,* 821–835.

Paunonen, S. V., & Nicol, A. A. A. M. (2001). The personality hierarchy and the prediction of work behaviors. In B. W. Roberts & R. T. Hogan (Eds.), *Personality psychology in the workplace* (pp. 161–191). Washington, DC: American Psychological Association.

Peabody, D., & Goldberg, L. R. (1989). Some determinants of factor structures from personality-trait descriptors. *Journal of Personality and Social Psychology, 57,* 552–567. doi:10.1037/0022-3514.57.3.552

Peeters, M. A. G., Van Tuijl, H. F. J. M., Rutte, C. G., & Reymen, I. M. M. J. (2006). Personality and team performance: A meta-analysis. *European Journal of Personality, 20,* 377–396. doi:10.1002/per.588

Pervin, L. A. (1989). Persons, situations, interactions: The history of a controversy and a discussion of theoretical models. *Academy of Management Review, 14,* 350–360. doi:10.2307/258172

Ployhart, R. E., Lim, B.-C., & Chan, K.-Y. (2001). Exploring relations between typical and maximum performance ratings and the five factor model of personality. *Personnel Psychology, 54,* 809–843. doi:10.1111/j.1744-6570.2001.tb00233.x

Ployhart, R. E., Weekley, J. A., & Baughman, K. (2006). The structure and function of human capital emergence: A multilevel examination of the attraction–selection–attrition model. *Academy of Management Journal, 49,* 661–667.

Pulakos, E. D., Schmitt, N., & Chan, D. (1996). Models of job performance ratings: An examination of ratee race, ratee gender, and rater level effects. *Human Performance, 9,* 103–119. doi:10.1207/s15327043hup0902_1

Richard, F. D., Bond, C. F., Jr., & Stokes-Zoota, J. J. (2003). One hundred years of social psychology quantitatively described. *Review of General Psychology, 7,* 331–363. doi:10.1037/1089-2680.7.4.331

Roberts, B. W., Bogg, T., Walton, K., Chernyshenko, O. S., & Stark, S. (2004). A lexical investigation of the lower-order structure of conscientiousness. *Journal of Research in Personality, 38,* 164–178.

Roberts, B. W., Chernyshenko, O. S., Stark, S., & Goldberg, L. R. (2005). The structure of conscientiousness: An empirical investigation based on seven major personality questionnaires. *Personnel Psychology, 58,* 103–139. doi:10.1111/j.1744-6570.2005.00301.x

Roberts, B. W., Kuncel, N. R., Shiner, R., Caspi, A., & Goldberg, L. R. (2007). The power of personality:

The comparative validity of personality traits, socioeconomic status, and cognitive ability for predicting important life outcomes. *Perspectives on Psychological Science, 2,* 313–345. doi:10.1111/j.1745-6916.2007.00047.x

Roberts, B. W., Walton, K. E., & Viechtbauer, W. (2006). Patterns of mean-level change in personality traits across the life course: A meta-analysis of longitudinal studies. *Psychological Bulletin, 132,* 1–25. doi:10.1037/0033-2909.132.1.1

Robertson, I. T., & Kinder, A. (1993). Personality and job competencies: An examination of the criterion related validity of some personality variables. *Journal of Occupational and Organizational Psychology, 66,* 225–244.

Rosenthal, R. (1991). Effect sizes: Pearson's correlation, its display via the BESD, and alternative indices. *American Psychologist, 46,* 1086–1087. doi:10.1037/0003-066X.46.10.1086

Ruscio, J., & Ruscio, A. M. (2008). Categories and dimensions: Advancing psychological science through the study of latent structure. *Current Directions in Psychological Science, 17,* 203–207. doi:10.1111/j.1467-8721.2008.00575.x

Sackett, P. R., & Ellingson, J. E. (1997). The effects of forming multi-predictor composites on group differences and adverse impact. *Personnel Psychology, 50,* 707–721. doi:10.1111/j.1744-6570.1997.tb00711.x

Sackett, P. R., Schmitt, N., Ellingson, J. E., & Kabin, M. B. (2001). High-stakes testing in employment, credentialing, and higher education: Prospects in a post-affirmative-action world. *American Psychologist, 56,* 302–318. doi:10.1037/0003-066X.56.4.302

Sanz, J., Gil, F., Garcia-Vera, M. P., & Barrasa, A. (2008). Needs and cognition/behavior patterns at work and the Big Five: An assessment of the Personality and Preference Inventory-Normative (PAPI-N) from the perspective of the five-factor model. *International Journal of Selection and Assessment, 16,* 46–58. doi:10.1111/j.1468-2389.2008.00408.x

Saucier, G., Georgiades, S., Tsaousis, I., & Goldberg, L. R. (2005). The factor structure of Greek personality adjectives. *Journal of Personality and Social Psychology, 88,* 856–875. doi:10.1037/0022-3514.88.5.856

Schaubroeck, J., Ganster, D. C., & Jones, J. R. (1998). Organization and occupation influences in the attraction–selection–attrition process. *Journal of Applied Psychology, 83,* 869–891. doi:10.1037/0021-9010.83.6.869

Schmidt, A. M., Dolis, C. M., & Tolli, A. P. (2009). A matter of time: Individual differences, contextual dynamics, and goal progress effects on multiple-goal self-regulation. *Journal of Applied Psychology, 94,* 692–709. doi:10.1037/a0015012

Schmidt, F. L., & Hunter, J. E. (1992). Development of a causal model of processes determining job performance. *Current Directions in Psychological Science, 1,* 89–92. doi:10.1111/1467-8721.ep10768758

Schmidt, F. L., Le, H., & Ilies, R. (2003). Beyond alpha: An empirical examination of the effects of different sources of measurement error on reliability estimates for measures of individual differences constructs. *Psychological Methods, 8,* 206–224. doi:10.1037/1082-989X.8.2.206

Schmit, M. J., & Ryan, A. M. (1993). The Big Five in personnel selection: Factor structure in applicant and non-applicant populations. *Journal of Applied Psychology, 78,* 966–974. doi:10.1037/0021-9010.78.6.966

Schmitt, N., & Oswald, F. L. (2006). The impact of corrections for faking on the validity of noncognitive measures in selection settings. *Journal of Applied Psychology, 91,* 613–621. doi:10.1037/0021-9010.91.3.613

Schneider, B. (1987). The people make the place. *Personnel Psychology, 40,* 437–453. doi:10.1111/j.1744-6570.1987.tb00609.x

Schneider, R. J., Ackerman, P. L., & Kanfer, R. (1996). To "act wisely in human relations": Exploring the dimensions of social competence. *Personality and Individual Differences, 21,* 469–481. doi:10.1016/0191-8869(96)00084-0

Schneider, R. J., & Hough, L. M. (1995). Personality and industrial/organizational psychology. In C. L. Cooper & I. T. Robertson (Eds.), *International review of industrial and organizational psychology* (pp. 75–129). Chichester, England: Wiley.

Schneider, R. J., Hough, L. M., & Dunnette, M. D. (1996). Broadsided by broad traits: How to sink science in five dimensions or less. *Journal of Organizational Behavior, 17,* 639–655. doi:10.1002/(SICI)1099-1379(199611)17:6<639::AID-JOB3828>3.0.CO;2-9

Sijtsma, K. (2009). On the use, misuse, and the very limited usefulness of Cronbach's alpha. *Psychometrika, 74,* 107–120. doi:10.1007/s11336-008-9101-0

Somer, O., & Goldberg, L. R. (1999). The structure of Turkish trait-descriptive adjectives. *Journal of Personality and Social Psychology, 76,* 431–450.

Stark, S., & Drasgow, F. (2002). An EM approach to parameter estimation for the Zinnes and Griggs paired comparison IRT model. *Applied Psychological Measurement, 26,* 208–227. doi:10.1177/01421602026002007

Stark, S., Drasgow, F., & Chernyshenko, O. S. (2008, October). *Update on the Tailored Adaptive Personality Assessment System (TAPAS): The next generation of personality assessment systems to support personnel selection and classification decisions.* Paper presented at the 50th annual conference of the International Military Testing Association, Amsterdam.

Steel, P. (2007). The nature of procrastination: A meta-analytic and theoretical review of quintessential self-regulatory failure. *Psychological Bulletin, 133,* 65–94. doi:10.1037/0033-2909.133.1.65

Steel, P., Schmidt, J., & Shultz, J. (2008). Refining the relationship between personality and subjective well-being. *Psychological Bulletin, 134,* 138–161. doi:10.1037/0033-2909.134.1.138

Stewart, G. (1999). Trait bandwidth and stages of job performance: Assessing differential effects for conscientiousness and its subtraits. *Journal of Applied Psychology, 84,* 959–968. doi:10.1037/0021-9010.84.6.959

Stewart, G., Fulmer, I. S., & Barrick, M. R. (2005). An exploration of member roles as a multilevel linking mechanism for individual traits and team outcomes. *Personnel Psychology, 58,* 343–365. doi:10.1111/j.1744-6570.2005.00480.x

Stewart, G., & Nandkeolyar, A. K. (2006). Adaptation and intraindividual variation in sales outcomes: Exploring the interactive effects of personality and environmental opportunity. *Personnel Psychology, 59,* 307–322.

Tellegen, A. (1993). Folk concepts and psychological concepts of personality and personality disorder. *Psychological Inquiry, 4,* 122–130. doi:10.1207/s15327965pli0402_12

Terracciano, A., McCrae, R. R., Brant, L. J., & Costa, P., Jr. (2005). Hierarchical linear modeling analyses of the NEO-PI-R scales in the Baltimore Longitudinal Study of Aging. *Psychology and Aging, 20,* 493–506. doi:10.1037/0882-7974.20.3.493

Tett, R. P., & Burnett, D. D. (2003). A personality trait-based interactionist model of job performance. *Journal of Applied Psychology, 88,* 500–517. doi:10.1037/0021-9010.88.3.500

Tett, R. P., Steele, J. R., & Beauregard, R. S. (2003). Broad and narrow measures on both sides of the personality-job performance relationship. *Journal of Organizational Behavior, 24,* 335–356. doi:10.1002/job.191

Thoresen, C. J., Bradley, J. C., Bliese, P. D., & Thoresen, J. D. (2004). The Big Five personality traits and individual job performance growth trajectories in maintenance and transitional job stages. *Journal of Applied Psychology, 89,* 835–853. doi:10.1037/0021-9010.89.5.835

Tupes, E. C., & Christal, R. E. (1961). *Recurrent personality factors based on trait ratings* (USAF Tech. Rep. No. 61-97). Lackland Air Force Base, TX: U.S. Air Force.

Tupes, E. C., & Christal, R. E. (1992). Recurrent personality factors based on trait ratings. *Journal of Personality, 60,* 225–251. doi:10.1111/j.1467-6494.1992.tb00973.x

van de Vijver, F. J. R., & Leung, K. (2001). Personality in cultural context: Methodological issues. *Journal of Personality, 69,* 1007–1031. doi:10.1111/1467-6494.696173

Vasilopoulos, N. L., Cucina, J. M., Dyomina, N. V., Morewitz, C. L., & Reilly, R. R. (2006). Forced-choice personality tests: A measure of personality and cognitive ability? *Human Performance, 19,* 175–199. doi:10.1207/s15327043hup1903_1

Vasilopoulos, N. L., Cucina, J. M., & McElreath, J. M. (2005). Do warnings of response verification moderate the relationship between conscientiousness and cognitive ability? *Journal of Applied Psychology, 90,* 306–322. doi:10.1037/0021-9010.90.2.306

Vinchur, A. J., Schippmann, J. S., Switzer, F. S., & Roth, P. L. (1998). A meta-analytic review of predictors of job performance for salespeople. *Journal of Applied Psychology, 83,* 586–597. doi:10.1037/0021-9010.83.4.586

Wallace, C., & Chen, G. (2006). A multilevel integration of personality, climate, self-regulation, and performance. *Personnel Psychology, 59,* 529–557. doi:10.1111/j.1744-6570.2006.00046.x

Warr, P., Bartram, D., & Martin, T. (2005). Personality and sales performance: Situational variation and interactions between traits. *International Journal of Selection and Assessment, 13,* 87–91. doi:10.1111/j.0965-075X.2005.00302.x

Weekley, J. A., Ployhart, R. E., & Harold, C. M. (2004). Personality and situational judgment tests across applicant and incumbent settings: An examination of validity, measurement, and subgroup differences. *Human Performance, 17,* 433–461. doi:10.1207/s15327043hup1704_5

Westring, A. J. F., Oswald, F. L., Schmitt, N., Drzakowski, S., Imus, A., Kim, B., & Shivpuri, S. (2009). Estimating trait and situational variance in a situational judgment test. *Human Performance, 22,* 44–63. doi:10.1080/08959280802540999

Wiggins, J. S. (1991). Agency and communion as conceptual co-ordinates for the understanding and measurement of interpersonal behavior. In W. M. Grove & D. Cicchetti (Eds.), *Thinking clearly about psychology: Essays in honor of Paul E. Meehl* (Vol. 2, pp. 89–113). Minneapolis: University of Minnesota Press.

Yeo, G. B., & Neal, A. (2004). A multilevel analysis of effort, practice, and performance: Effects of ability, conscientiousness and goal orientation. *Journal of Applied Psychology, 89,* 231–247. doi:10.1037/0021-9010.89.2.231

Zimprich, D., Allemand, M., & Dellenbach, M. (2009). Openness to experience, fluid intelligence, and crystallized intelligence in middle-aged and old adults. *Journal of Research in Personality, 43,* 444–454. doi:10.1016/j.jrp.2009.01.018

CHAPTER 6

INTERVIEWS

Allen I. Huffcutt and Satoris S. Culbertson

The employment interview is something of an enigma. We know it predicts job performance, at least when properly designed (Campion, Palmer, & Campion, 1998; Huffcutt & Arthur, 1994; McDaniel, Whetzel, Schmidt, & Maurer, 1994), but we are not completely sure why. For instance, the degree to which it captures specific job-related knowledge, skills, abilities, and other characteristics (KSAOs; e.g., ability to soothe irate customers) versus general constructs such as mental ability or conscientiousness (Cortina, Goldstein, Payne, Davison, & Gilliland, 2000; Hunter & Hirsch, 1987) versus other things like general impressions (Sackett, 1982) is not perfectly clear. What adds further complexity is that the interview can be influenced by additional variables such as the applicant's impression management skills (Ellis, West, Ryan, & DeShon, 2002; Levashina & Campion, 2007), self-monitoring (Dipboye, 1992), or interview-specific self-efficacy (Tay, Ang, & Van Dyne, 2006). Arthur, Woehr, and Maldegen (2000) regarded the combination of assessment centers with criterion-related validity without clear construct validity as a *validity paradox,* a term that appears to apply equally well to the interview.

Despite the uncertainty, the interview continues to be used almost universally. It is rare, even unthinkable, for someone to be hired without some type of interview. When someone is hired without one, it is often because of extenuating circumstances, such as that the hiring organization is desperately short-handed (e.g., nursing). The interview is used far more frequently than any other selection technique (e.g., psychological testing, work samples, assessment centers; Nyfield & Baron, 2000; Sharf & Jones, 2000). The only other comparable component in the selection process (at least in terms of frequency of use) is the application form.

Of interest for several reasons is the question of why interviews are so popular despite uncertainty regarding what they measure and, for certain types (e.g., unstructured; Wiesner & Cronshaw, 1988), their reliability and validity. As a practical matter, the interview is not needed because critical KSAOs usually can be assessed by other means and often done so more accurately (Hunter & Hunter, 1984; Schmidt & Hunter, 1998). It would appear that there is a basic human need to want personal contact with others before placing them in a position of importance even if they have a proven track record, a tendency from which personnel managers and others involved in organizational selection do not appear to be exempt. It is almost as if a part of the human makeup does not trust objective information completely, even if it is accurate; mere facts do not supersede an underlying desire for personal verification.

The purpose of this chapter is to provide a comprehensive overview of the employment interview. We begin by tracing the history of its research, which provides a background of what issues have been addressed and where future research is headed. Then we go back and take a closer look at structure of the interview, arguably the single most important element of interview process and outcomes. Throughout this chapter, we discuss the substantive issues of why, when, and how interviews are the most reliable and valid. Finally, we close with a discussion of future research needs and directions.

HISTORY OF INTERVIEW RESEARCH

Thanks to a series of major narrative reviews (in chronological order: Wagner, 1949; Mayfield, 1964; Ulrich & Trumbo, 1965; Wright, 1969; Schmidt, 1976; Arvey & Campion, 1982; Harris, 1989; Posthuma, Morgeson, & Campion, 2002), it is possible to trace the history of interview research in some detail. When doing so, it becomes apparent that interview research has gone through a series of distinct phases or periods, five of which are outlined in this section. Two disclaimers are warranted. First, once a phase and its timeline are put forth, there is some tendency to assume that no other type of research was being conducted. That is clearly not the case, as research of many types tends to be scattered throughout all periods. Second, identifying the number of phases and the nature of these phases, choosing labels for them, and delineating their dates is an extremely subjective process, and there could be some noticeable differences if other researchers were to do the same thing (cf. Eder, Kacmar, & Ferris, 1989).

Introductory Period (Circa 1915–1950)

A key theme of this phase is the opening of the interview process to scientific inquiry and analysis. Rather than treating the interview as a given or as something that was not a proper topic for science, a host of issues were raised at once, tantamount to opening Pandora's box. The earliest reference to appear in modern journals describing a formal study was Scott (1915). In his study, six personnel managers individually interviewed and rank ordered 36 sales candidates as to their suitability for the position. Wide disagreement resulted. For instance, for 28 of the candidates the six managers could not agree whether they should be placed in the upper half or lower half of the group. Similar studies were conducted by Scott, Bingham, and Whipple (1916) and Hollingworth (1922), with similar results. Collectively, these studies called into question the reliability and general efficacy of the interview and established an early pessimism that influenced thinking for a number of decades.

Wagner (1949), the first major narrative review to appear in the literature, provided an excellent summary of the issues raised during this phase and the empirical studies that were conducted to address them. Concerns over basic reliability and validity not surprisingly were at the forefront, and the empirical data were too mixed to provide any real answers. There was considerable debate over the scope of the interview, including whether the interview should be used to evaluate a broad range of characteristics or used just to assess overall suitability. Those favoring the former raised the additional issues of what traits should be assessed (e.g., general versus job-specific) and whether the interviewers should integrate the ratings themselves or combine them mechanically. Yet others advocated a focus on a single or very select number of specific traits. For instance, Rundquist (1947) felt that social interaction skill was the only characteristic that should be assessed in the interview and that all other important job characteristics should be left to standardized testing. Another issue was whether interviewers should be allowed access to ancillary information (e.g., test scores), as that information appeared to increase the accuracy of the interview ratings. Lastly, a smattering of researchers were proponents of a standardized approach. Wonderlic (1942), for example, noted that without such an approach the interview "generally amounts to a disorganized conversation resulting in a series of impressions based upon impulsive reactions" (cited on p. 33, Wagner, 1949).

In summary of this phase, there were numerous questions raised and few answers developed. A number of these issues remain unresolved even today. For instance, many companies still use unstructured interviews that are not overtly designed around job requirements and which vary in scope from assessing specific job skills to overall suitability. In fairness, use of a standardized format has become much more common, so the trend is in the right direction. Per Rundquist (1947), social skill (discussed later in this chapter) appears to be getting more formal attention lately and could hold considerable promise. The method of combining ratings is also still an issue, as some interviewers continue to integrate the ratings and arrive at an overall evaluation subjectively.

Early Psychometrical Period (Circa 1950–1980)

The momentum created in the first phase that resulted from placing the interview under the lens of scientific scrutiny continued and expanded during this second phase, increasing not only in quantity but also in scope and sophistication. Three major narrative reviews emerged during this time frame: Mayfield (1964), Ulrich and Trumbo (1965), and Wright (1969). All three reviewers summarized reliability and validity data and again found mixed results, although they did note that the data appeared stronger for standardized interviews. The advent of meta-analysis was still years away, and researchers of this time did not have a full understanding that sampling error and other artifacts were a major source of variability among the findings.

These reviewers raised additional issues, which, while not being addressed strongly during this phase, planted some seeds that grew in subsequent ones or at least are starting to grow in current research. Mayfield (1964) questioned why the interview works, what is the effect of varying degrees of structure, and how we deal with the general lack of comparability across interviews (e.g., length, content, rating characteristics). Furthermore, he raised awareness of the importance of individual differences among interviewers, driven in part by data suggesting acceptable reliability across candidates by the same interviewer (intrarater) but poor consistency across interviews by different interviewers (interrater), and called for research into their decision-making processes. Ulrich and Trumbo (1965) called for analysis of how much variance in the ratings is attributable to ancillary data like test scores and how much is due to the interview itself and, in addition, raised the question of how accurate the information is that is obtained during an interview. Wright (1969) noted that the culture (e.g., ethnic group) of a candidate could affect both semantics and the rapport developed with the interviewer and the interviewer's ratings and/or decision and that interview research should expand and incorporate theories and concepts from other literatures such as communication. He also echoed Mayfield's concern that the influence of the interviewer on the applicant and the process had been overlooked far too much.

A line of research emerged during this phase that is unparalleled in terms of overall prominence and distinguishability: the McGill University studies led by E. C. Webster. In terms of timing, Mayfield (1964) noted that these studies had been conducted over the previous 10 years (i.e., since the early 1950s), whereas Wright (1969) noted that Webster's seminal 1964 report of work by him and his colleagues (e.g., dissertations by Springbett, 1958, and Anderson, 1960) covered 8 years of research. In the words of Wright, "It would be difficult to over-estimate the importance of the work done by Webster and his colleagues" (p. 394).

The defining nature of this line of research was its microanalytic nature, that is, that the interview was broken up into small segments and processes that were studied in isolation. Wright (1969) identified seven major principles from this work, as listed below.

1. Interviewers have a stereotype of a good candidate and match interviewees to that.
2. Interviewers establish biases early in the interview, which affect their subsequent decision.
3. Unfavorable information is more influential than favorable information.
4. Interviewers seek/focus on information that confirms their impressions.
5. Development and display of empathy varies by interviewer.
6. The decision interviewers make is different when given information is processed piece by piece rather than simultaneously in its totality.
7. Experienced interviewers tend to rank applicants in the same order although they differ in the number they would accept.

Schmitt (1976) and Arvey and Campion (1982), the next major reviews, highlighted the increase in research complexity. For instance, additional variables were being looked at (e.g., visual cues) and conceptual models of the interview process were being put forth (e.g., both of the narrative reviews cited contained such a conceptual model). The reviewers further noted that research designs appeared to be more realistic and generalizable (e.g., not as many "paper people" formats). Reliability and validity were still being questioned, although both continued to note stronger results for standardized formats. Arvey and Campion noted the influence of artifacts (from the early beginnings of meta-analysis) and that other literatures (e.g., person perception) were still not being utilized enough. They planted another seed by noting the importance of interviewees' preexisting motives and expectations.

One interesting but limited line of decision-making research was noted in the next major review by Harris (1989): use of the Brunswik lens model (Brunswik, 1955, 1956). This model proposed that interviewer perceptions and attributions of applicants are based in part on aspects of the physical or social environment, including qualities of the applicant, as well as on cues, such as applicant nonverbal behaviors. Several studies employed this technique, which included analysis of how interviewers arrive at an overall rating by looking at the correlation between it and the ratings for the individual dimensions (e.g., Dougherty, Ebert, & Callender, 1986; Gifford, Ng, & Wilkinson, 1985; Zedeck, Tziner, & Middlestadt, 1983). These studies showed considerable individual differences among interviewers, including with utilization of information, reliability, and validity. Harris also noted greater use of theories from other literatures, including attribution theory (Herriot, 1981), decision theory (Rowe, 1989), and confirmatory bias (Sackett, 1982), greater analysis of applicant characteristics (e.g., race), more focus on interviewer training, and more consideration of external validity (e.g., fewer paper-people studies).

Modern Structured Interviewing (Circa 1980–Present)

Few things have changed the field as much as the introduction of two specific structuring techniques: the situational interview (Latham, Saari, Purcell, & Campion, 1980) and the behavior description interview (Janz, 1982). Although there was a plethora of approaches and suggestions for how to structure an interview prior to this time, these two pioneering techniques provided an anchor for both researchers and practitioners. These techniques were not innovative in their standardization of questions, as a number of prior interviews had standardized questions. Moreover, use of these types of questions was not new, as we see earlier references to researchers posing questions regarding how candidates think they would react to a given problem situation (O'Rourke, 1932) and inquiring about past situations the candidates had that were relevant to the position (McMurry, 1947). Rather, what differentiated these two techniques from prior techniques was the exclusive use of a single type of question for the entire interview (hypothetical scenarios in the former, past behavior in the latter) coupled with a formal rating system, the combination of which made these techniques unique and powerful. The situational interview had two further distinctions in that the questions were completely standardized across candidates and responses were rated individually by question using a customized scale developed specifically for that question. These latter two practices helped move the interview closer to psychological tests that have standardized content and are scored at the item level (e.g., those for mental ability and personality).

In its original creation, the behavior description interview was introduced by Janz (1982) as the "patterned behavior description interview" because banks of questions were created for each job dimension (e.g., problem-solving, initiative) and interviewers could choose freely from among them. Then the interviewer made ratings by dimension afterward based on synthesis of whatever questions were asked. There is some advantage to banks of questions in that interviewers can adapt the interview to some degree to the unique background of each applicant, a format consistent with the modern idea of "adaptive testing" (see Belov & Armstrong, 2008; Lee, Ip, & Fuh, 2008). However, doing so loses consistency in "procedural variability" (Huffcutt & Arthur, 1994) across candidates. In more recent times, it has become common practice with behavior description interviews to standardize questions and rate responses individually by question using a benchmarked rating scale as is done in the situational interview (e.g., Campion, Campion, & Hudson, 1994; Pulakos & Schmitt, 1995).

Of course, this is not to say that question scoring is better than dimensional scoring for the interview, as which one is "better" likely depends on the purpose of the interview (e.g., selection vs. recruitment) and the specific dimensions captured by the interview. Nevertheless, what makes question-level scoring attractive is the large body of research in the cognitive area regarding the limitations of human information processing. Simply put, it appears that most people are limited in how much information they can process at one time, as exemplified by short-term memory being limited in capacity and easily interfered with (Baddely, 1986; Miller, 1956; Nairne, Neath, & Serra, 1997) and by the tendency to utilize mental shortcuts (heuristics) in the processing of that information (e.g., Kahneman & Tversky, 1973, 2000; Tversky & Kahneman, 1973, 1982). Furthermore, this research suggests that recall of information from long-term memory tends to be based on reconstruction of stored fragments (Loftus, 2007; Loftus & Cahill, 2007). Rating the response to each question individually using a carefully devised benchmarked rating scale should reduce the amount of information that must be processed at any one time considerably, help to prevent shortcuts in the processing of that information, and keep processing "immediate" rather than involving extensive memory recall.

Conceptually, both techniques are grounded in theory. Latham (1989) noted that the situational interview is grounded in goal setting, that is, that intentions are a precursor to actions. Janz (1982, 1989) noted that the behavior description interview is grounded in behavioral consistency, specifically, that past behavior is the best predictor of future behavior. While both premises are very reasonable, it might be possible to expand the theoretical basis behind these techniques further, which could generate some meaningful future research. To illustrate, the theory of planned behavior (Ajzen, 1991) from the social psychological literature lists three antecedents to behavioral intentions and behavior: attitudes, subjective norms (i.e., the perception that important others will approve of that behavior), and perceived behavioral control (i.e., the perception of how difficult it would be to perform that behavior). Each of these three components may in turn have its own antecedents, such as attitudes having both a learned (Bandura, 1986; Krosnick, Betz, Jussim, & Lynn, 1992) and a genetic (Bouchard, 2004; Olson, Vernon, Harris, & Jang, 2001) component. One avenue for future research is to examine these components and their antecedents specifically in relation to aspects of the interview process, such as the likelihood of applicants' faking answers (see Levashina & Campion, 2007). For example, what are their attitudes regarding deception, do they think others would approve of their deceptions, and how difficult would it be to falsify information in a convincing manner?

These two structured formats have remained at the forefront of interview research and practice, a span of almost 30 years. Moreover, they have remained largely unchanged, with the noted exception of complete standardization and question-level scoring with the behavior description interview. It would not be surprising to see the introduction of new structuring techniques in coming years, either modifications of these two techniques or entirely new approaches. For instance, rather than simply asking what an applicant would do in a specific situation, the underlying motivation for why they would that could be explored. Alternatively, there may be new types of questions that could be introduced.

Synthesis Era (Circa 1982–1996)

Four events stand out in the history of interview research as having changed the field in prominent, significant, and lasting ways. Two have already been mentioned: the microanalytic research program by Webster and his colleagues (1964) and the introduction of the situational and behavior description interview formats. The third is Title VII of the 1964 Civil Rights Act, which established legal considerations as a permanent fixture in the interview arena. Legal considerations are worthy of review as well but are beyond the scope of this chapter. The fourth is what we refer to as the *synthesis era*. It involves the introduction of meta-analysis, a technique that allows researchers to summarize data that have been collected over time, in different venues, and by different researchers. This era began formally with publication of the pioneering book by Hunter, Schmidt, and Jackson (1982; see Hunter & Schmidt, 2004, for the latest version).

Meta-analytic techniques have aided in the synthesis of interview information by providing much more precise estimates of criterion-related validity, overall and for specific levels of variables that moderate interview validity, such as structure. Prior to meta-analysis there was a tendency to take the results of a given study at face value, which helps explain among other things why most of the narrative reviewers noted a general lack of consistency across studies. The capability of meta-analysis to take into account the influence of artifacts such as sampling error, range restriction, and measurement error has led to a better understanding of the accuracy of interviews as a predictor of job performance and variables that moderate that prediction.

There have been three large-scale meta-analyses of the criterion-related validity of the interview: Wiesner and Cronshaw (1988), McDaniel et al. (1994), and Huffcutt and Arthur (1994). All three meta-analyses found greater validity for structured interviews (vs. unstructured ones), although the difference was smaller in McDaniel et al., most likely because of the way in which studies were coded (e.g., their unstructured category appeared to include studies with at least some degree of structure). There is also a large-scale meta-analysis of the reliability of the interview by Conway, Jako, and Goodman (1995), which found that the interview could achieve reasonable reliability, upward of .75 under the right design conditions (i.e., use of structure and a panel format).

The impact of the three validity meta-analyses cannot be understated. There was widespread pessimism about the interview prior to this time, resulting largely from the combination of psychometric effects that were not well understood (e.g., range restriction reducing magnitudes, sampling error inducing inconsistency) and failure to take the degree of structure into full consideration. After correction for artifacts, the results indicated that when properly designed (mainly structured and based on a job analysis), the employment interview appears to reach a level of criterion-related validity that is highly comparable with mental ability tests, job knowledge tests, work samples/simulations, and other top predictors (see Hunter & Hunter, 1984; Schmidt & Hunter, 1998). In short, meta-analytic techniques have not only helped to summarize and synthesize existing information but have also established the interview as a major validity component in the selection process, revitalized interest in it, and spurred new lines of research for it (which, as described later, continue today).

However, some caution in the interpretation of the result of interview meta-analyses is warranted. Like the assessment center, the interview is a method. As such, the constructs measured can vary from situation to situation and can impact resulting validity. As noted in the *Principles for the Validation and Use of Personnel Selection Procedures* (4th ed.; Society for Industrial and Organizational Psychology, 2003),

> Because methods such as the interview can be designed to assess widely varying constructs (from job knowledge to integrity), generalizing from cumulative findings is only possible if the features of the method that result in positive method-criterion relationships are clearly understood, if the content of the procedures and meaning of the scores are relevant for the intended purpose, and if generalization is limited to other applications of the method that include those features. (p. 30)

What this limitation emphasizes is the need for greater understanding of what constructs interviews measure and the factors that influence that measurement.

Large-scale validity analysis of the interview appears to have reached a saturation point during the mid 1990s. The meta-analyses cited earlier used hundreds of studies and tested most if not all of the major moderators (e.g., structure, job complexity). Meta-analytic research of varying types has continued to be conducted and published, of course, but its frequency clearly has dropped. Although there certainly is room for differing opinions, one can argue that its decline coincided to some degree with the emergence of the next phase. Although the issue of what interviews measure has always been of interest, a more concentrated effort to understand their constructs appears to be under way.

Interview Construct Research (Circa 1996–Present)

Throughout the history of interview research there has always been interest, speculation, and primary-study research (mainly correlating interview ratings to scores on one or more psychological tests) regarding what interviews measure. In 1996, Huffcutt, Roth, and McDaniel used meta-analysis to do a large-scale summary of the relationship between interview ratings and mental ability, which provided meaningful construct information and sharpened the focus on constructs.

Understanding what constructs interviews measure is a critical issue to its continued advancement as a formal selection technique. At a scientific level, even though an interview may provide comparable validity, the interview as a selection method cannot reach the same standing as cognitive ability tests unless a basic understanding of what it measures is obtained. At a more pragmatic level, issues such as incremental validity (Dipboye & Gaugler, 1993; Hakel, 1989; Harris, 1989) and ethnic group differences (Huffcutt & Roth, 1998) come into play. (Fortunately, the latter study suggests fairly low differences overall, certainly much lower than with ability tests.)

Unfortunately, identifying the constructs that interviews capture is difficult, first, because the dimensions they tend to assess are often complex and multifaceted (Roth, Van Iddekinge, Huffcutt, Eidson, & Schmit, 2005; Schmidt & Hunter, 1998) and, second, because of the variability in design, content, interviewees, and interviewers across settings. To illustrate the former point, a question about handling a difficult customer could include aspects of mental ability (e.g., thinking through options), conscientiousness (e.g., doing the right thing), and emotional stability (maintaining a calm composure). To illustrate the latter point, several studies involved careful matching of situational and behavior description questions to assess the same job dimensions, and they did not find a strong correspondence between the two parallel sets of questions. For instance, Huffcutt, Weekley, Weisner, DeGroot, and Jones (2001) found a mean correlation of .09 between matching situational and behavior description questions in their first study and a mean correlation of .05 in their second study.

There appear to be at least six types or lines of interview construct research. The first line consists of correlations between interview ratings and psychological measures and is illustrated by Huffcutt, Roth, and McDaniel's (1996) summary of the interview–mental ability association. They found a mean corrected correlation of .40 between interview ratings and mental ability, suggesting modest overall saturation and reasonable potential for incremental validity. Berry, Sackett, and Landers (2007) reanalyzed the relationship using a more modern approach for the range restriction correction (Le & Schmidt, 2006; Schmidt, Oh, & Le, 2006) and found a somewhat lower value. No large-scale meta-analyses have yet to be done for other psychological characteristics such as personality, mainly because those data tend to be scarce.

The second line revolves around applicant fit. Posthuma et al. (2002), the only major review of the employment interview literature since Harris (1989), noted the emergence of research on the fit between applicants and either the job or the company with which they are interviewing. This research has the potential to provide a better understanding of the dynamics of the interviewee–interviewer exchange, particularly for low- to medium-structure interviews. Research cited by Posthuma et al. suggested that fit is associated with characteristics such as interpersonal skills, goal orientation, values, attractiveness, and liking of the candidate (Adkins, Russell, & Werbel, 1994; Cable & Judge, 1997; Rynes & Gerhart, 1990).

The third line is analysis of the content of the dimensions rated in interviews, as illustrated by Huffcutt, Conway, Roth, and Stone's (2001) summary of the frequency at which various characteristics were rated across a sample of 47 interviews. Just over 60% of the dimensions rated in those studies pertained to personality and/or applied social skills, suggesting more effort to measure these types of characteristics than perhaps anticipated. A limitation of their work is that they were not able to verify the degree to which these characteristics were actually assessed, only the degree to which they were chosen as selection criteria.

The fourth line, which is particularly promising, pertains specifically to the dynamics of the interview process. Previous research tended to look at surface features such as structure, length, amount of applicant speaking time, and demographics (e.g., race, gender, age). A more concentrated effort has emerged that deals directly with the dynamics of the interviewee–interviewer exchange. The strongest venue appears to be with impression management tactics such as self-promotion, ingratiation, and even outright lying (Ellis et al., 2002; Higgins & Judge, 2004; Higgins, Judge, & Ferris, 2003; Levashina & Campion, 2007; McFarland, Ryan, & Kriska, 2003; Stevens & Kristof, 1995). Perhaps the most surprising find from this line is that candidates appear to engage in these behaviors frequently, even in tightly structured interviews (Ellis et al. 2002; Levashina & Campion, 2007). The related concept of social skills (Ferris, Witt, & Hochwarter, 2001) has been studied to a lesser extent (e.g., Schuler & Funke, 1989; see Salgado & Moscoso, 2002, for a meta-analysis of six correlations) but also holds considerable promise for understanding what interviews measure. Also less studied but potentially of importance are self-monitoring (e.g., Dipboye, 1992; Higgins & Judge, 2004) and relational control (e.g., Bateson, 1958; Engler-Parish & Millar, 1989; Tuller, 1989).

There are other aspects of the dynamics of the interview process that, although researched during and since the microanalytic era, continue to be assessed. Some of these aspects include attractiveness, verbal quality, and nonverbal behavior. Despite the abundant existing research in these particular areas, there are some differences in the more modern line regarding how they are being examined. For instance, more factors such as attractiveness (Burnett & Motowidlo, 1998) are being looked at in relation to specific types of interviews (e.g., structured interviews) rather than interviews in general. Utilizing concepts from the communication area, DeGroot and Motowidlo (1999, second study) analyzed voice quality by putting segments of videotaped structured interviews through a voice analyzer and found a moderate correlation ($r = .32$) between what they termed a *vocal cue index* and interview judgments.

The fifth line is barely beginning, but it answers the call by Arvey and Campion (1982) to look more at the applicants' state of mind coming into the interview. For example, applicants may have preexisting motives and expectations that they bring with them to the interview that could potentially influence their interview performance as well as their own perceptions of it. To further test these assertions, researchers have started to look more at factors such as interview-specific self-efficacy (Tay et al., 2006) and interview-specific motivation (Maurer, Solamon, Andrews, & Troxtel, 2001). As researchers continue to examine such issues, the role of applicants in the interview process will become better understood.

The last line is the most recent and is just beginning; it is model-based construct research. Previous models of the employment interview dealt with the process and/or the outcome (e.g., Arvey & Campion, 1982; Dipboye, 2005; Dipboye & Macan, 1988; Raza & Carpenter, 1987; Schmitt, 1976). A new model by Huffcutt, Van Iddekinge, and Roth (2007) focuses directly on the constructs captured by employment interviews. Their model, shown in Figure 6.1, has three main components. First, there are constructs related to job performance, which are proposed to carry over into the interview since their purpose is to assess potential to perform. Second, the model contains interviewee performance constructs, which are related to the notion that the interview is an interpersonal performance by the interviewees (e.g., use of impression management tactics), which can raise or lower ratings relative to actual qualifications. Finally, the model includes influences from interviewer rating tendencies (e.g., idiosyncrasies). Whereby research in the area of interview constructs appears to be in the very early stages of development, much like interview validity research a decade or two ago, this and other models yet to come should help to provide a solid foundation for the advancement of construct research. For instance, in an empirical summary of an updated (2009) version of their model, Huffcutt, Van Iddekinge, and Roth (unpublished manuscript) found that constructs relating to interviewee performance have a mean correlation with interview ratings that is twice as large as the mean correlation for constructs pertaining to job-related interview content.

What have we learned by viewing the history of interview research? One thing that is apparent is that interview research is very dynamic. It has evolved from its infancy with simplistic assessment of reliability into a major area of organizational study replete with rich and complex veins of research, and it should continue to evolve for the indefinite future, as there are a number of issues yet to be resolved (or for some issues, yet to be addressed). Table 6.1 summarizes what we see as 10 of the most major issues raised from this review of interview history (collectively across all five eras) and their current status.

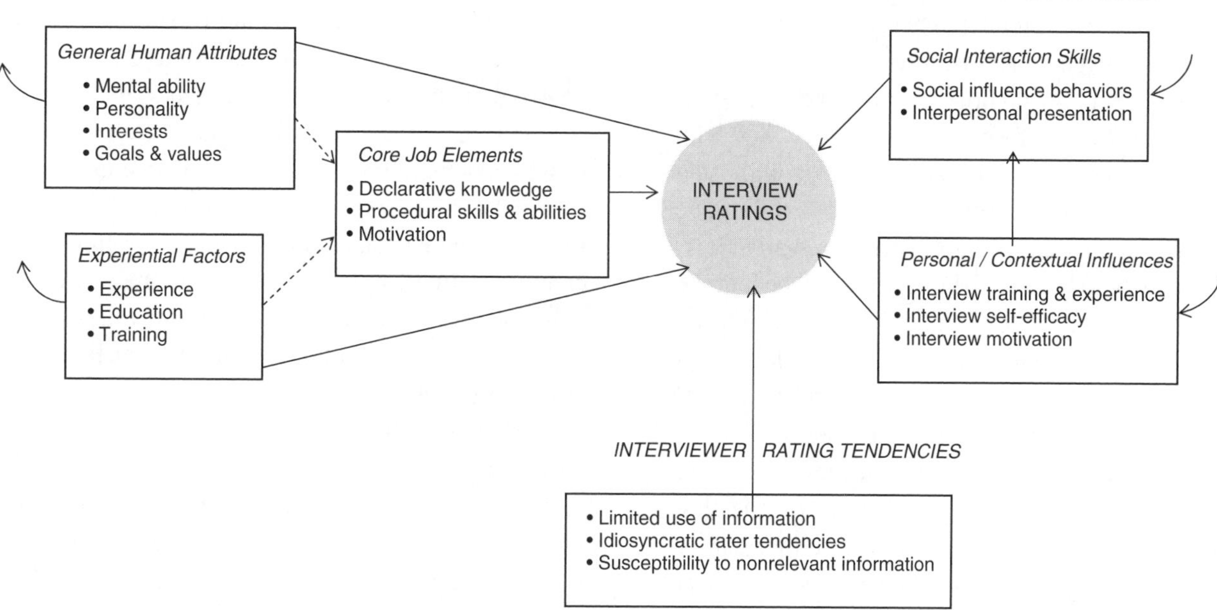

FIGURE 6.1. The Huffcutt, Van Iddekinge, and Roth (2007) model of the constructs that employment interviews capture. The curved arrows indicate that basic human attributes and experiential factors can influence both core job elements (declarative knowledge, procedural skills & abilities, motivation) and interviewee performance.

TABLE 6.1

Summary of Issues From the Historical Review

Issue	Status
1. Reliability validity/structure	Largely resolved because of large-scale meta-analyses such as Wiesner and Cronshaw's (1988).
2. Scope of the interview	Very much unresolved. To reach resolution, we need a much better understanding of the constructs interviews capture and the factors that influence their measurement.
3. Ancillary information	Resolved scientifically by Dipboye (1982, 1989) and others. Although extensive review of preinterview information is not advised, it is still done commonly in practice.
4. Combining ratings	Largely unresolved, although method of combining ratings is not as much of an issue since ratings are generally summed in modern structured interviews.
5. Constructs captured	Progress being made; perhaps the new frontier of interview research.
6. Interviewer influences	Unresolved, with a long history of being overlooked in interview research.
7. Use of other literatures	Slightly better but still vastly underutilized.
8. Applicant individual differences	Other than for mental ability and to a lesser extent personality, this aspect of interview research has for the most part been overlooked.
9. Interviewee–interviewer dynamics	Definite progress being made; perhaps another new frontier of interview research.
10. Interview to interview variability	Other than for structure and to a lesser extent purpose (selection versus recruitment), identification of interview variability factors and their influence on the interview process and the constructs assessed has been vastly overlooked and may be a particularly ripe area for future research.

We wish to highlight two issues in particular because they were raised decades ago but are still ongoing and relate to the fundamental nature or purpose of the interview. One is the scope. By default, interviews in our modern era seem to have gravitated toward being a broad measure of job-related characteristics, yet the potential remains for the interview to be more effective with a narrower scope. Resolving this issue will require obtaining a better understanding of constructs captured by interview ratings, one of the exciting directions of current research. It is entirely possible that the interview will be found to routinely assess at least some characteristics that could be better assessed through psychological testing, in which case the interview could be focused more selectively on characteristics not as easily assessed through psychological testing (e.g., social skills, per Rundquist, 1947). The other is the idea that there is no one "interview," but rather that the interview is a method that can vary widely from situation to situation depending on features such as the nature of the job, the type of questions, the interpersonal skills and personality of the interviewer, and the purpose of the interview (per Mayfield, 1964). In this line of thinking, what is measured by interview ratings is dependent on the specific combination of features for a given interview situation. Other than for level of structure and possibly interview purpose (selection vs. recruitment), this aspect of the interview has been largely overlooked.

THE PARAMOUNT ROLE OF STRUCTURE

If a sample of researchers and practitioners in the field were asked what has been the single most important influence on the interview process and its outcome, a majority would no doubt answer that it is structure. Structure has literally changed the way interviews are conducted, from being essentially a loosely constructed conversation to a uniform and carefully defined process, one that can approach standardized psychological tests psychometrically.

The Meaning of Structure

There are several operationalizations of the term *structure* as applied to the employment interview. In a classic definition, Huffcutt and Arthur (1994) defined structure in terms of reducing procedural variability across candidates. Such a definition has a somewhat psychometric flavor in that it positions the interview in potentially the same context as mental ability and personality tests. Put in terms of stimulus and response, interviews can be structured to such a degree that all candidates are exposed to the same stimuli (i.e., exactly worded questions with no probing) as is done in most of specifically psychometric tests (adaptive testing would be the exception), and responses are evaluated individually according to carefully defined and benchmarked rating scales. However, evaluation of responses in the interview can never match that of mental ability tests because the latter use absolute scoring (generally right or wrong), while rating of interview responses will always entail at least some degree of subjectivity. Still, interviews can be structured to the point where they come close to standardized tests, a point that is verified empirically by interview interrater reliabilities that can meet or even exceed test-retest reliabilities of some mental ability and personality tests (cf. Conway et al., 1995).

More practically, Huffcutt and Arthur (1994) identified four levels of question standardization and three levels of response standardization, which they combined into four overall levels of structure. In the first level, the lowest level, there are no formal constraints on the questions asked and a global evaluation of responses is used. The second level includes limited constraints on the questions and some degree of structure in how the responses are evaluated. Level 3 has some prespecified questions and responses that are evaluated along a specified set of job dimensions after the interview. Finally, Level 4, the highest level of structure, has completely prespecified questions, the responses to each of which are rated on a customized scale with benchmark answers. The corrected validities of these four levels (corrected for range restriction in the interview and unreliability in the performance criteria) are shown in Table 6.2 along with the mean corrected validity of other predictors. As is evident, the validity of Level 3 and Level 4 structure compares favorably with the corrected mean validity of .51 for mental ability tests, .54 for work sample tests, and .48 for job knowledge tests (Schmidt & Hunter, 1998). Not

TABLE 6.2

Corrected Validities for the Employment Interview and Other Selection Predictors

Predictor	Mean validity
All interviews	.37
Level 1 Structure	.20
Level 2 Structure	.35
Level 3 Structure	.56
Level 4 Structure	.57
Mental Ability Tests	.51
Work Sample Tests	.54
Integrity Tests	.41
Job Knowledge Tests	.48
Reference Checks	.26
Biographical Data Measures	.35
Assessment Centers	.37
Graphology	.02

Note. The validities for all interviews and for the four levels of interview structure are from Huffcutt and Arthur (1994) and are corrected for range restriction in the interview and unreliability in the performance criteria. All remaining validities, which are from Schmidt and Hunter (1998), are from various other meta-analyses and corrected for range restriction in the predictor and downward bias due to measurement error in job performance ratings.

surprisingly, increased structure has improved the utility of interview ratings as well, from very low to a level that is comparable to mental ability tests and other top predictors (Hunter & Hunter, 1984; Schmidt & Hunter, 1998).

An interesting aspect of the Huffcutt and Arthur (1994) definition of structure is that it focuses largely on operational consistency. In their scheme, structure is enhanced by reducing variability in how candidates are interviewed. It is conceptually possible to have an interview developed at the highest level of structure (Level 4 questions, Level 3 ratings) that contains totally irrelevant content. Fortunately, structure and job-relatedness tend to covary because professionals who take the time to create questions and relevant rating scales usually do so directly in relation to the requirements of the position.

Another seminal article that has provided an operationalization of interview structure is Campion, Palmer, and Campion (1997). They identified 15 ways in which an interview can be structured, separated into two categories: those that influence interview content and those that influence the evaluation process. The components of an interview that relate to content include (a) basing the questions on a job analysis, (b) asking the same questions of candidates, (c) limiting the extent to which the interviewer prompts the respondent, (d) using better types of questions (e.g., situational and past behavior questions rather than general background questions), (e) using longer interviews or a larger number of questions, (f) controlling ancillary information, and (g) not allowing questions from the candidate until after the interview. The interview components that relate to the evaluation process include (a) rating each answer or using multiple scales, (b) using detailed anchored rating scales, (c) taking detailed notes, (d) using multiple interviewers, (e) using the same interviewer for all candidates, (f) refraining from discussing candidates and their answers between interviews, (g) providing extensive interviewing training, and (h) using statistical rather than clinical prediction when combining data. Their operationalization of interview structure is quite helpful, particularly from a practical standpoint. As these authors noted, the reliability, validity, and user reactions of the interview can be easily enhanced by incorporating at least some of these 15 components. Although there is no magic number of components for making an ideal interview, and it is unclear which, if any, of the components could be considered more critical than others, it is presumed that the more components that can be taken into account, the better.

Building on Campion et al.'s (1997) conceptualization, Chapman and Zweig (2005) sought to identify the factor structure of interview structuring practices in order to develop a measure of interview structure. Using a field survey of 812 interviewees and 592 interviewers, they found four dimensions of interview structure: evaluation standardization, question consistency, question sophistication, and rapport building. In general, they noted that more structure is afforded to interviews in which evaluation is more standardized, questions are more consistent and sophisticated, and rapport building within the interview is lower.

The Importance of Structure

Why is structure so important? Several major meta-analyses have confirmed that structured interviews fare considerably better than unstructured interviews psychometrically. For instance, Wiesner and Cronshaw (1988) reported mean criterion-related validity coefficients of .31 for unstructured interviews versus .62 for structured interviews. Conway et al. (1995) reported mean interrater reliability coefficients of .37 for Level 1 interviews versus .66 for Level 4 interviews (when conducted individually).

But what is it about structured interviews that makes them superior? One obvious reason is greater consistency in content and process, which influences reliability and is important because reliability provides an upper limit for validity (Conway et al., 1995). Schmidt and Zimmerman (2004) found some evidence that the superiority of structured interviews can be traced largely to greater reliability. Put in a different way, unstructured interviews, by their very nature, provide more opportunity for random error in responses, more random error in what the responses represent, and more random error in evaluation. This random error throughout the interview process likely leads to lower reliability and validity for unstructured interviews. Another reason is that the standardization inherent in structured interviews serves to make the content more job-related. It is not surprising, therefore, that the first component on which to base interviews that Campion et al. (1997) identified for structuring interviews was a quality job analysis. Without this basis, unstructured interviews run the risk of tapping constructs that are unrelated to the job, and hence result in low validity.

Finally, the standardization and consistency found in structured interviews helps to reduce such troubling information-processing tendencies as contrast and similarity effects that often plague unstructured interviews (Latham, Wexley, & Pursell, 1975; Wexley, Sanders, & Yukl, 1973). For example, because the questions and scoring for structured interviews are the same across participants, there is less opportunity to compare applicants to each other rather than to the constructs and dimensions of interest. Along these lines, the cognitive complexity of response processing can be reduced through the increased structure (Tsai, Chen, & Chiu, 2005). Similarly, there is likely a reduction in interviewer susceptibility to influence tactics, which would thereby help keep the interview job-related and the ratings consequently more valid.

Creating Structure in Interviews

Given the clear advantages of increased structure in interviews, a logical transition is to discuss how structured interviews are developed. There are two general approaches for making a job-related structured interview. One approach is to create questions directly from the KSAOs. For example, Campion, Pursell, and Brown (1988) created a list of duties and requirements and wrote questions based on the KSAOs needed to perform them. The other approach, which is used more frequently, involves collecting critical incidents and turning them into questions. For example, Motowidlo et al. (1992) conducted critical incident workshops in which participants wrote critical incidents describing management performance and the researchers identified and defined various interpersonal and problem-solving dimensions based on them. Both approaches involve a fair degree of literary license, which could lead to differences in content and validity across interview developers.

Additionally, there is some evidence that formal interviewer training contributes to greater standardization, consistency, and formalization in the evaluation processes of interviews, as does having more of a selection (vs. recruitment) focus for the interview (Chapman & Zweig, 2005). Certainly, this is not altogether surprising, as Campion et al. (1997) noted that training is one of the components that influence the evaluation process. Nevertheless, if one is interested in creating more structure in interviews, proper interviewer training is clearly of importance.

Selecting the questions to use involves a variety of options. The two types of questions described earlier, situational and behavior description, have become very popular in recent decades. Several meta-analyses have demonstrated that both of these formats yield exceptional predictability overall, with mean corrected criterion-validity estimates ranging from .47 to .63 (e.g., Latham & Sue-Chan, 1999; Taylor & Small, 2002). The validity of these interviews may vary, however, depending on the type of job for which the interview is used. For example, several studies have shown that the validity of the situational interview is not as great as the behavioral description for higher-level jobs or those higher in complexity, such as managerial jobs (e.g., Huffcutt, Conway, Roth, & Klehe, 2004; Huffcutt, Weekley, et al., 2001; Krajewski, Goffin, McCarthy, Rothstein, & Johnston, 2006; Pulakos & Schmitt, 1995). Additionally, the specific question type used may actually influence the way in which candidates behave during an interview. For example, Ellis et al. (2002) found that situational questions led to applicants using more ingratiation techniques, while behavior description questions resulted in candidates using more self-promotion tactics.

There are also structured formats that utilized multiple types of questions. For example, Campion, Pursell, and Brown (1988) developed a comprehensive structured interview for entry-level employees at a pulp-and-paper mill that contained job knowledge questions assessing mechanical comprehension, simulation questions gauging reading ability, and worker characteristic or willingness questions determining fear of heights. Schuler (1989, 1992) devised a multimodal employment interview that included self-presentation, vocational, biographical, and situational questions.

Developers of interviews may also consider making the questions somewhat transparent, or clear as to what the question is trying to assess. A recent study conducted by Klehe, Konig, Richter, Kleinmann, and Melchers (2008) found that interviewees tended to perform better when interviews were transparent. Perhaps more important, although both nontransparent and transparent interviews were not significantly different in terms of their criterion-related validity, transparent interviews yielded greater construct validity than nontransparent interviews. Thus, although not directly related to the structure of interviews, it is definitely a consideration worthy of noting.

CONCLUDING SUMMARY AND DIRECTIONS FOR FUTURE RESEARCH

In this chapter, we have provided an overview of the history of employment interview research, tracing progress in this area from the early 1900s through to the present day. This overview makes it apparent that some key issues have largely been resolved (e.g., reliability, validity, structure), some have not been addressed in meaningful ways yet (e.g., scope), and some are being explored in new and exciting ways in current research (e.g., constructs, interviewee–interviewer dynamics). Given its paramount role in the interview process, we also took a closer look at structure, including how it has been conceptualized and operationalized, what makes it so critical to enhancing validity and reliability, and how to increase it. Of all the advances over almost a century of interview research, arguably the most clear and practically important finding is the superiority of structured interviews over unstructured interviews.

We now conclude with a brief discussion of future research needs and directions. The issues summarized in Table 6.1 that have not been fully resolved provide an excellent starting point, including scope, individual differences in interviewees and interviewers, and interviewee–interviewer dynamics. To illustrate, there may be differences in the effectiveness of interviews in different countries and across cultures. As organizations become more global and outsourcing becomes more prevalent, it is important to consider the effects of any selection technique in the context of the organization's business territory as well as the applicant's national and cultural background. Although studies have been conducted using samples from a variety of countries, most of the research in this area has studied samples from the United States. It is unclear, at this point, whether differences exist in interviews across countries, yet there is reason to believe they might (Moy, 2006). Similarly, the recent shift to a greater focus on constructs highlights a plethora of potential avenues. For example, there has been limited research to date that has examined the roles of social skills, self-monitoring, and relational control as key dynamics of the interview process. Further research could certainly aid in a better understanding not only of how these different activities influence the interview process and outcomes but also of how they might change what constructs the interview captures.

Returning to the use of meta-analysis to help summarize what we know about the validity and reliability of interviews while accounting for various artifacts, future researchers should revisit some lingering questions. As noted earlier, there have been recent and substantial advances in the ways to deal with the range restriction correction (Hunter, Schmidt, & Le, 2006; Le & Schmidt, 2006; Schmidt et al., 2006). Although researchers have already begun to reanalyze some relationships (e.g., Berry et al., 2007), more work is certainly called for in this area.

Another area worthy of research is the role of intentional response distortion within the employment interview. Although a plethora of research exists that examines the role of faking for such selection methods as personality testing, relatively little research has examined such issues for the employment interview (see Fletcher, 1990; Levashina & Campion, 2007, for exceptions). Although the research in this area has provided useful theoretical and practical insight (e.g., it appears questions that assess past behavior are more resistant to faking than are situational questions, and follow-up questions increase faking; Levashina & Campion, 2007), it remains unknown what the effect of faking (or outright lying) is on the reliability and validity of the employment interview. This is particularly important considering Levashina and Campion's finding that more than 90% of undergraduate job candidates engaged in faking during employment interviews.

Researchers have only begun to examine the impact of coaching as it relates to the employment interview, with the majority of work in this area coming from Maurer and colleagues (Maurer et al., 2001; Maurer, Solamon, & Troxtel, 1998; Maurer, Solamon, & Lippstreu, 2008). In general the research from this area has demonstrated that interviewees tend to perform better when they are coached, and the predictive validity and reliability of the interview is higher for those applicants who are coached than for those who are not coached. More work in the area of coaching and its effects on the various types of interviews, in terms of interviewee performance as well as the psychometric properties of the interviews, is still warranted.

Posthuma et al. (2002) raised the question of how the cognitive demands of the interview influence the process and outcomes, including in relation to cognitive capability of the interviewees and interviewer. For instance, are the correlations that have typically been found between interview ratings and mental ability (e.g., Berry et al., 2007; Huffcutt, Roth, et al., 1996) more a function of the cognitive demands of the interview or the cognitive capabilities of the candidates?

An examination of Huffcutt, Van Iddekinge, and Roth's (2007, 2009) model of interview constructs (the 2007 version is shown in Figure 6.1 and described earlier in this chapter) is also likely to provide ideas for years of research going forward. One could quite easily take any component of the model and find a multitude of questions awaiting research. For example, regarding job-related content, more research is needed to clarify the role of personality factors in the interview, as well as an examination of how different interview dimensions might relate to different kinds of mental ability (e.g., verbal ability vs. memory). Similarly, it is not clear to what extent other general human attributes (e.g., applicant goals, interests, and values), core job elements (e.g., KSAOs, motivation), or experiential factors (e.g., experience, training, education) may be assessed in both structured and unstructured interviews. These points, of course, are only for the job-related content portion of Huffcutt et al.'s (2007) model. Certainly, more research is justified for the interviewee performance and interviewer rating tendencies sections of their model.

Future research on employment interviews may also be influenced by technological advances. For example, as organizations have become more global, alternate mediums (other than face-to-face) have become more common. Researchers have examined the impact of such alternatives as telephone and videoconference interviews on applicant ratings and reactions (e.g., Chapman & Rowe, 2001; Chapman, Uggerslev, & Webster, 2003; Chapman & Webster, 2001; Silvester, Anderson, Haddleton, Cunningham-Snell, & Gibb, 2000; Straus, Miles, & Levesque, 2001). Certainly, as more and more technological advances occur and business adapts to capture these advances, it will be important to determine whether changes in the reliability, validity, and practicality of the interview will be hindered or enhanced.

Finally, there is the potential for incorporating some research from neuroscience into the research domain. For example, behavioral description interviews clearly require higher mental functions, such as memory searching and analyzing. Along these lines, there is evidence that these higher mental functions require large amounts of brain sugars (glucose, glycogen) to function optimally and that they tend to use up these sugars rather quickly (Gailliot, 2008; Gailliot & Baumeister, 2007). Furthermore, these sugars appear to be used up even more rapidly in situations involving high self-regulation (Masicampo & Baumeister, 2008), which again is characteristic of most interviews. When brain sugar levels drop, there is a tendency for individuals to rely more on mental shortcuts (heuristics) rather than doing full cognitive processing. This is just one example of how findings from neuroscience may shed light on interview processes. As such, this appears to be an area into which future researchers may want to delve.

In conclusion, it is clear that the interview has a long and rich history of research, almost a century at this point. Researchers have learned much over this time, including how to structure an interview and the psychometric benefits that result, and they have raised numerous questions that are being addressed currently and can continue to be addressed in future research. We look forward to many more exciting years of interview research, which should serve to both strengthen our understanding of this unique selection device and increase its efficacy in the organizational arena.

References

Adkins, C. L., Russell, C. J., & Werbel, J. D. (1994). Judgments of fit in the selection process: The role of work value congruence. *Personnel Psychology, 47,* 605–623.

Ajzen, I. (1991). The theory of planned behavior. *Organizational Behavior and Human Decision Processes, 50,* 179–204.

Anderson, C. W. (1960). The relation between speaking times and decision in the employment interview. *Journal of Applied Psychology, 44,* 267–268.

Arthur, W., Jr., Woehr, D. J., & Maldegen, R. (2000). Convergent and discriminant validity of assessment center dimensions: A conceptual and empirical reexamination of the assessment center construct-related validity paradox. *Journal of Management, 26,* 813–815.

Arvey, R. D., & Campion, J. E. (1982). The employment interview: A summary and review of recent research. *Personnel Psychology, 35,* 281–322.

Baddely (1986). *Working memory.* New York: Oxford University Press.

Bandura, A. (1986). Psychological mechanisms of aggression. In R. G. Green & E. I. Donnerstein (Eds.), *Aggression: Theoretical and empirical reviews* (Vol. 1, pp. 1–40). New York: Academic Press.

Bateson, G. (1958). *Naven.* Stanford, CA: Stanford University Press.

Belov, D. I., & Armstrong, R. D. (2008). A Monte Carlo approach to the design, assembly, and evaluation of multistage adaptive tests. *Applied Psychological Measurement, 32,* 119–137.

Berry, C. M., Sackett, P. R., & Landers, R. N. (2007). Revisiting interview–cognitive ability relationships: Attending to specific range restriction mechanisms in meta-analysis. *Personnel Psychology, 60,* 837–874.

Bouchard, T. J., Jr. (2004). Genetic influences on human psychological traits. *Current Directions in Psychological Science, 13,* 148–151.

Brunswik, E. (1955). Representative design and probabilistic theory. *Psychological Review, 62,* 236–242.

Brunswik, E. (1956). *Perception and the representative design of psychological experiments.* Berkeley: University of California Press.

Burnett, J. R., & Motowidlo, S. J. (1998). Relations between different sources of information in the structured selection interview. *Personnel Psychology, 51,* 963–983.

Cable, D. M., & Judge, T. A. (1997). Interviewers' perceptions of person–organization fit and organizational selection decisions. *Journal of Applied Psychology, 82,* 546–561.

Campion, M. A., Campion, J. E., & Hudson, J. P. (1994). Structured interviewing: A note on incremental validity and alternative question types. *Journal of Applied Psychology, 79,* 998–1102.

Campion, M. A., Palmer, D. K., & Campion, J. E. (1997). A review of structure in the selection interview. *Personnel Psychology, 50,* 655–702.

Campion, M. A., Palmer, D. K., & Campion, J. E. (1998). Structuring employment interviews to improve reliability, validity and users' reactions. *Current Directions in Psychological Science, 7,* 77–82.

Campion, M. A. Pursell, E. D., & Brown, B. K. (1988). Structured interviewing: Raising the psychometric properties of the employment interview. *Personnel Psychology, 41,* 25–42.

Chapman, D. S., & Rowe, P. M. (2001). The impact of videoconference technology, interview structure, and interviewer gender on interviewer evaluations in the employment interview: A field experiment. *Journal of Occupational and Organizational Psychology, 74,* 279–298.

Chapman, D. S., Uggerslev, K. L., & Webster, J. (2003). Applicant reactions to face-to-face and technology-mediated interviews: A field investigation. *Journal of Applied Psychology, 88,* 944–953.

Chapman, D. S., & Webster, J. (2001). Rater correction processes in applicant selection using videoconference technology: The role of attributions. *Journal of Applied Social Psychology, 31,* 2518–2537.

Chapman, D. S., & Zweig, D. I. (2005). Developing a nomological network for interview structure: Antecedents and consequences of the structured selection interview. *Personnel Psychology, 58,* 673–702.

Conway, J. M., Jako, R. A., & Goodman, D. F. (1995). A meta-analysis of interrater and internal consistency reliability of selection interviews. *Journal of Applied Psychology, 80,* 565–579.

Cortina, J. M., Goldstein, N. B., Payne, S. C., Davison, H. K., & Gilliland, S. W. (2000). The incremental validity of interview scores over and above g and conscientiousness scores. *Personnel Psychology, 53,* 325–351.

DeGroot, T., & Motowidlo, S. J. (1999). Why visual and vocal interview cues can affect interviewers' judgments and predict job performance. *Journal of Applied Psychology, 84,* 986–993.

Dipboye, R. L. (1982). Self-fulfilling prophecies in the selection/recruitment interview. *Academy of Management Review, 7,* 579–587.

Dipboye, R. L. (1989). Threats to the incremental validity of interviewer judgments In R. W. Eder & G. R. Ferris (Eds.), *The employment interview: Theory, research, and practice* (pp. 45–60). Newbury Park, CA: Sage.

Dipboye, R. L. (1992). *Selection interviews: Process perspectives.* Cincinnati, OH: South-Western.

Dipboye, R. L. (2005). The selection/recruitment interview: Core processes and contexts. In A. Evers, N. R. Anderson, & O. F. Smit-Voskuijl (Eds.), *The Blackwell handbook of personnel selection* (pp. 121–142). Malden, MA: Blackwell.

Dipboye, R. L., & Gaugler, B. B. (1993). Cognitive and behavioral processes in the selection interview. In N. Schmitt & W. Borman (Eds.), *Personnel selection in organizations* (pp. 135–170). San Francisco: Jossey-Bass.

Dipboye, R. L., & Macan, T. M. (1988). A process view of the selection-recruitment interview. In R. Schuler, V. Huber, & S. Youngblood (Eds.), *Readings in personnel and human resource management* (pp. 217–232). New York: West.

Dougherty, T. W., Ebert, R. J., & Callender, J. C. (1986). Policy capturing in the employment interview. *Journal of Applied Psychology, 71,* 9–15.

Eder, R. W., Kacmar, K. M., & Ferris, G. R. (1989). Employment interview research: History and synthesis. In R. W. Eder & G. R. Ferris (Eds.), *The employment interview: Theory, research, and practice* (pp. 17–31). Newbury Park, CA: Sage.

Ellis, A. P., West, B. J., Ryan, A. M., & DeShon, R. P. (2002). The use of impression management tactics in structured interviews: A function of question type? *Journal of Applied Psychology, 87,* 1200–1208.

Engler-Parish, P. G., & Millar, F. E. (1989). An exploratory relational control analysis of the employment screening interview. *Western Journal of Speech Communication, 53,* 30–51.

Ferris, G. R., Witt, L. A., & Hochwarter, W. A. (2001). Interaction of social skill and general mental ability on job performance and salary. *Journal of Applied Psychology, 86,* 1075–1082.

Fletcher, C. (1990). The relationships between candidate personality, self-presentation strategies, and interview assessments in selection interviews: An empirical study. *Human Relations, 43,* 739–749.

Gailliot, M. T. (2008). Unlocking the energy dynamics of executive functioning. *Perspectives on Psychological Science, 3,* 245–263.

Gailliot, M. T., & Baumeister, R. F. (2007). The physiology of willpower: Linking blood glucose to self-control. *Personality and Social Psychology Review, 11,* 303–327.

Gifford, R., Ng, C. F., & Wilkinson, M. (1985). Nonverbal cues in the employment interview: Links between applicant qualities and interviewer judgments. *Journal of Applied Psychology, 70,* 729–736.

Hakel, M. D. (1989). The state of employment interview theory and research. In R. W. Eder & G. R. Ferris (Eds.), *The employment interview: Theory, research, and practice* (pp. 285–293). Newbury Park, CA: Sage.

Harris, M. M. (1989). Reconsidering the employment interview: A review of recent literature and suggestions for future research. *Personnel Psychology, 42,* 691–726.

Herriot, P. (1981). Towards an attributional theory of the selection interview. *Journal of Occupational Psychology, 54,* 165–173.

Higgins, C. A., & Judge, T. A. (2004). The effect of applicant influence tactics on recruiter perceptions of fit and hiring recommendations: A field study. *Journal of Applied Psychology, 89,* 622–632.

Higgins, C. A., Judge, T. A., & Ferris, G. R. (2003). Influence tactics and work outcomes: A meta-analysis. *Journal of Organizational Behavior, 24,* 89–106.

Hollingworth, H. L. (1922). *Judging human character.* New York: Appleton.

Huffcutt, A. I., & Arthur, W., Jr. (1994). Hunter & Hunter (1984) revisited: Interview validity for entry-level jobs. *Journal of Applied Psychology, 79,* 184–190.

Huffcutt, A. I., Conway, J. M., Roth, P. L., & Klehe, U.-C. (2004). The impact of job complexity and study design on situational and behavior description interview validity. *International Journal of Selection and Assessment, 12,* 262–273.

Huffcutt, A. I., Conway, J. M., Roth, P. L., & Stone, N. J. (2001). Identification and meta-analytic assessment of psychological constructs measured in employment interviews. *Journal of Applied Psychology, 86,* 897–913.

Huffcutt, A. I., Roth, P. L., & McDaniel, M. A. (1996). A meta-analytic investigation of cognitive ability in employment interview evaluations: Moderating characteristics and implications for incremental validity. *Journal of Applied Psychology, 81,* 459–473.

Huffcutt, A. I., Van Iddekinge, C. H., & Roth, P. L. (2007, April). *A comprehensive review of the constructs captured by employment interview ratings.* Symposium held at the 22nd Annual Conference of the Society for Industrial and Organizational Psychology, New York.

Huffcutt, A. I., Van Iddekinge, C. H., & Roth, P. L. (2009). *An empirical review of the employment interview construct literature.* Manuscript submitted for publication.

Huffcutt, A. I., Weekley, J., Weisner, W. H., DeGroot, T., & Jones, C. (2001). Comparison of situational and behaviour description interview questions for higher-level positions. *Personnel Psychology, 54,* 619–644.

Hunter, J. E., & Hirsch, H. R. (1987). Applications of meta-analysis. In C. L. Cooper & I. T. Robertson (Eds.), *International review of industrial and organizational psychology* (Vol. 2, pp. 321–357). London: Wiley.

Hunter, J. E., & Hunter, R. F. (1984). Validity and utility of alternate predictors of job performance. *Psychological Bulletin, 96,* 72–98.

Hunter, J. E., & Schmidt, F. L. (2004). *Meta-analysis: Correcting errors and bias in research findings* (2nd ed.). Thousand Oaks, CA: Sage.

Hunter, J. E., Schmidt, F. L., & Jackson, G. B. (1982). *Meta-analysis: Cumulating research findings across studies.* Beverly Hills, CA: Sage.

Hunter, J. E., Schmidt, F. L., & Le, H. (2006). Implications of direct and indirect range restriction for meta-analysis methods and findings. *Journal of Applied Psychology, 91,* 594–612.

Janz, T. (1982). Initial comparison of patterned behavior description interviews versus unstructured interviews. *Journal of Applied Psychology, 67,* 577–580.

Janz, T. (1989). The patterned behavior description interview: The best prophet of the future is the past. In R. W. Eder & G. R. Ferris (Eds.), *The employment interview: Theory, research, and practice* (pp. 158–168). Thousand Oaks, CA: Sage.

Kahneman, D. & Tversky, A. (1973). On the psychology of prediction. *Psychological Review, 80,* 237–251.

Kahneman, D. & Tversky, A. (2000). *Choices, values, and frames.* New York: Cambridge University Press.

Klehe, U.-C., Konig, C. J., Richter, G. M., Kleinmann, M., & Melchers, K. G. (2008). Transparency in structured interviews: Consequences for construct and criterion-related validity. *Human Performance, 21,* 107–137.

Krajewski, H. T., Goffin, R. D., McCarthy, J. M., Rothstein, M. G., & Johnston, N. (2006). Comparing the validity of structured interviews for managerial-level employees: Should we look to the past or focus on the future? *Journal of Occupational and Organizational Psychology, 79,* 411–432.

Krosnick, J. A., Betz, A. L., Jussim, L. J., & Lynn, A. R. (1992). Subliminal conditioning of attitudes. *Personality and Social Psychology Bulletin, 18,* 152–152.

Latham, G. P. (1989), The reliability, validity and practicality of the situational interview. In R. W. Eder & G. R. Ferris (Eds.), *The employment interview* (pp. 162–182). Newbury Park, CA: Sage.

Latham, G. P., Saari, L. M., Pursell, E. D., & Campion, M. A. (1980). The situational interview. *Journal of Applied Psychology, 65,* 422–427.

Latham, G. P., & Sue-Chan, C. (1999). A meta-analysis of the situational interview: An enumerative review of the reasons for its validity. *Canadian Psychology,* 40, 56–67.

Latham, G. P., Wexley, K. N., & Pursell, E. D. (1975). Training managers to minimize rating errors in the observation of behavior. *Journal of Applied Psychology, 60,* 550–555.

Lee, Y.-H., Ip, E. H., & Fuh, C. D. (2008). A strategy for controlling item exposure in multidimensional computerized adaptive testing. *Educational and Psychological Measurement, 68,* 215–232.

Le, H., & Schmidt, F. L. (2006). Correcting for indirect range restriction in meta-analysis: Testing a new meta-analytic procedure. *Psychological Methods, 11,* 416–438.

Levashina, J., & Campion, M. A. (2007). Measuring faking in the employment interview: Development and validation of an interview faking behavior scale. *Journal of Applied Psychology, 92,* 1638–1656.

Loftus, E. (2007). Memory distortions: Problems solved and unsolved. In M. Garry & H. Hayne (Eds.), *Do justice and let the sky fall* (pp. 1–14). Mahwah, NJ: Erlbaum.

Loftus, E. & Cahill, L. (2007). Memory distortion: From misinformation to rich false memory. In J. S. Nairne (Ed.), *The foundation of remembering: Essays in honor of Henry L. Roediger, III* (pp. 413–425). New York: Psychology Press.

Masicampo, E. J., & Baumeister, R. F. (2008). Toward a physiology of dual-process reasoning and judgment: Lemonade, willpower, and expensive rule-based analysis. *Psychological Science, 19,* 255–260.

Maurer, T. J., Solamon, J. M., Andrews, K. D., & Troxtel, D. D. (2001). Interviewee coaching, preparation strategies, and response strategies in relation to performance in situational employment interviews: An extension of Maurer, Solamon, and Troxtel (1998). *Journal of Applied Psychology, 86,* 709–717.

Maurer, T. J., Solamon, J. M., & Lippstreu, M. (2008). How does coaching interviewees affect the validity of a structured interview? *Journal of Organizational Behavior, 29,* 355–371.

Maurer, T. J., Solamon, J. M., & Troxtel, D. D. (1998). Relationship of coaching with performance in situational employment interviews. *Journal of Applied Psychology, 83,* 128–136.

Mayfield, E. C. (1964). The selection interview: A re-evaluation of published research. *Personnel Psychology, 17,* 239–260.

McDaniel, M. A., Whetzel, D. L., Schmidt, F. L., & Maurer, S. (1994). The validity of employment interviews: A comprehensive review and meta-analysis. *Journal of Applied Psychology, 79,* 599–617.

McFarland, L. A., Ryan, A. M., & Kriska, S. D. (2003). Impression management use and effectiveness across measurement methods. *Journal of Management, 29,* 641–661.

McMurry, R. N. (1947). Validating the patterned interview. *Personnel, 23,* 263–272.

Miller, G. A. (1956). The magical number seven, plus or minus two: Some limits on our capacity for processing information. *Psychological Review, 63,* 81–97.

Motowidlo, S. J., Carter, G. W., Dunnette, M. D., Tippins, N., Werner, S., Burnett, J. R., & Vaughan, M. J. (1992). Studies of the structured behavioral interview. *Journal of Applied Psychology, 77,* 571–587.

Moy, J. M. (2006). Are employers assessing the right traits in hiring? Evidence from Hong Kong companies. *International Journal of Human Resource Management, 17,* 734–754.

Nairne, J. S., Neath, I., & Serra, M. (1997). Positional distinctiveness and ratio rule in free recall. *Journal of Memory and Language, 37,* 155–166.

Nyfield, G., & Baron, H. (2000). Cultural context in adapting selection practices across borders. In J. F. Kehoe (Ed.), *Managing selection in changing organizations* (pp. 242–270). San Francisco: Jossey-Bass.

Olson, J. M., Vernon, P. A., Harris, J. A., & Jang, K. L. (2001). The heritability of attitudes: A study of twins. *Journal of Personality and Social Psychology, 80,* 845–860.

O'Rourke, L. J. (1932). Measuring judgment and resourcefulness. *Personnel Journal, 7,* 427–440.

Posthuma, R. A., Morgeson, F. P., & Campion, M. A. (2002). Beyond employment interview validity: A comprehensive narrative of review of recent research and trends over time. *Personnel Psychology, 55,* 1–81.

Pulakos, E. D., & Schmitt, N. (1995). Experience-based and situational interview questions: Studies of validity. *Personnel Psychology, 48,* 289–308.

Raza, S. M., & Carpenter, B. N. (1987). A model of hiring decisions in real employment interviews. *Journal of Applied Psychology, 72,* 596–603.

Roth, P. L., Van Iddekinge, C. H., Huffcutt, A. I., Eidson, C. E. Jr., & Schmit, M. J. (2005). Personality saturation in structured interviews. *International Journal of Selection and Assessment, 13,* 261–273.

Rowe, P. M. (1989). Unfavorable information and interview decisions. In R. W. Eder & G. R. Ferris (Eds.), *The employment interview: Theory, research, and practice.* (pp. 77–89). Beverly Hills: Sage.

Rundquist, E. A. (1947). Development of an interview for selection purposes. In G. A. Kelly (Ed.), *New methods in applied psychology* (pp. 85–95). College Park: University of Maryland.

Rynes, S. L., & Gerhart, B. (1990). Interviewer assessments of applicant "fit": An exploratory investigation. *Personnel Psychology, 43,* 13–35.

Sackett, P. R. (1982). The interviewer as hypothesis tester: The effects of impressions of an applicant on interviewer questioning strategy. *Personnel Psychology, 35,* 789–803.

Salgado, J. F., & Moscoso, S. (2002). Comprehensive meta-analysis of the construct validity of the employment interview. *European Journal of Work and Organizational Psychology, 11,* 299–324.

Schmidt, F. L., & Hunter, J. E. (1998). The validity and utility of selection methods in personnel psychology: Practical and theoretical implications of 85 years of research findings. *Psychological Bulletin, 124,* 262–274.

Schmidt, F. L., Oh, I.-S., & Le, H. (2006). Increasing accuracy of corrections for range restriction: Implications for selection procedure validities and other research results. *Personnel Psychology, 59,* 281–305.

Schmidt, F. L., & Zimmerman, R. D. (2004). A counterintuitive hypothesis about employment interview validity and some supporting evidence. *Journal of Applied Psychology, 89,* 553–561.

Schmitt, N. (1976). Social and situational determinants of interview decisions: Implications for the employment interview. *Personnel Psychology, 29,* 79–101.

Schuler, H. (1989). Construct validity of a multi-model employment interview. In B. J. Fallon, H. P. Pfister, & J. Brebner (Eds.), *Advances in industrial and organizational psychology.* New York: North Holland.

Schuler, H. (1992). Das multimodale einstellungsinterview [The multimodal employment interview]. *Diagnostica, 38,* 281–300.

Schuler, H., & Funke, U. (1989). The interview as a multimodal procedure. In R. W. Eder & G. R. Ferris (Eds.),

The employment interview: Theory, research, and practice (pp. 183–192). Thousand Oaks, CA: Sage.

Scott, W. D. (1915, October). Scientific selection of salesmen. *Advertising and Selling Magazine,* pp. 5–6, 94–96.

Scott, W. D., Bingham, W. V., & Whipple, G. M. (1916). Scientific selection of salesmen. *Salesmanship, 4,* 106–108.

Sharf, J. C., & Jones, D. P. (2000). Employment risk management. In J. F. Kehoe (Ed.), *Managing selection in changing organizations* (pp. 271–318). San Francisco: Jossey-Bass.

Silvester, J., Anderson, N., Haddleton, E., Cunningham-Snell, N., & Gibb, A. (2000). A cross-modal comparison of telephone and face-to-face selection interviews in graduate recruitment. *International Journal of Selection and Assessment, 8,* 16–21.

Society for Industrial and Organizational Psychology, Inc. (2003). *Principles for the validation and use of personnel selection procedures* (4th ed.). College Park, MD: Author.

Springbett, B. M. (1958). Factors affecting the final decision in the employment interview. *Canadian Journal of Psychology, 12,* 13–22.

Stevens, C. K., & Kristof, A. L. (1995). Making the right impression: A field study of applicant impression management during job interviews. *Journal of Applied Psychology, 80,* 587–606.

Straus, S. G., Miles, J. A., & Levesque, L. L. (2001). The effects of videoconference, telephone, and face-to-face media on interviewer and applicant judgments in employment interviews. *Journal of Management, 27,* 363–381.

Tay, C., Ang, S., & Van Dyne, L. (2006). Personality, biographical characteristics, and job interview success: A longitudinal study of the mediating effects of interviewing self-efficacy and the moderating effects of internal locus of causality. *Journal of Applied Psychology, 91,* 446–454.

Taylor, P. J., & Small, B. (2002). Asking applicants what they would do versus what they did do: A meta-analytic comparison of situational and past behaviour employment interview questions, *Journal of Occupational and Organizational Psychology, 75,* 277–294.

Tsai, W.-C., Chen, C.-C., & Chiu, S.-F. (2005). Exploring boundaries of the effects of applicant impression management tactics in job interviews. *Journal of Management, 31,* 108–125.

Tuller, W. L. (1989). Relational control in the employment interview. *Journal of Applied Psychology, 74,* 971–977.

Tversky, A., & Kahneman, D. (1973). Availability: A heuristic for judging frequency and probability. *Cognitive Psychology, 5,* 207–232.

Tversky, A. & Kahneman, D. (1982). Judgment under uncertainty: Heuristics and biases. In D. Kahneman, P. Slovic, & A. Tversky (Eds.), *Judgment under uncertainty: Heuristics and biases* (pp. 251–258). New York: Cambridge University Press.

Ulrich, L., & Trumbo, D. (1965). The selection interview since 1949. *Psychological Bulletin, 63,* 110–116.

Wagner, R. (1949). The employment interview: A critical summary. *Personnel Psychology, 2,* 17–46.

Webster, E. C. (1964). *Decision-making in the employment interview.* Montreal: Industrial Relations Center, McGill University.

Wexley, K. N., Sanders, R. E., & Yukl, G. A. (1973). Training interviewers to eliminate contrast effects in employment interviews. *Journal of Applied Psychology, 57,* 233–236.

Wiesner, W. H., & Cronshaw, S. F. (1988). The moderating impact of interview format & degree of structure on interview validity. *Journal of Occupational Psychology, 61,* 275–290.

Wonderlic, E. F. (1942). Improving interview technique. *Personnel, 18,* 232–238.

Wright, O. R., Jr. (1969). Summary of research on the selection interview since 1964. *Personnel Psychology, 22,* 391–413.

Zedeck, S., Tziner, A., & Middlestadt, S. E. (1983). Interviewer validity and reliability: An individual analysis approach. *Personnel Psychology, 36,* 355–370.

CHAPTER 7

ASSESSMENT CENTERS

Winfred Arthur Jr. and Eric Anthony Day

The objective of this chapter is to provide the reader with an overview of the science and practice of assessment centers (ACs). To accomplish this objective, we present a broad summary overview of the pertinent issues in the extant AC literature. Thus, the chapter starts with a definition and description of ACs along with their historical background. This is followed with a description of the design, development, administration, and scoring of ACs. The next section pertains to the psychometric properties—namely, the reliability and validity of AC ratings—which is then followed by a discussion of costs and practical issues associated with the use of ACs. In the next two sections, we discuss the issue of subgroup differences and the potential for adverse impact as well as the international scope of AC research and practice. Finally, we conclude with a brief discussion of directions for future research and practice.

ASSESSMENT CENTERS: DEFINITION AND DESCRIPTION

In keeping with the predictor construct–predictor method distinction, Arthur and Villado (2008) described a *predictor* as a

> specific behavioral domain, information about which is sampled via a specific method. Thus, depending on one's focus, predictors can be represented in terms of what they measure [i.e., the constructs or content of the predictor] and how they measure what they are designed to measure [i.e., the method of assessment or measurement]. (p. 435)

AC science and practice specifies the behavioral domain of ACs in terms of *dimensions* (although in some of the recent practitioner literature the term *competencies* is being used; e.g., see International Task Force on Assessment Center Guidelines, 2000). Hence, as predictors, ACs are best conceptualized as a method by which information concerning multiple behavioral dimensions is collected.

The traditional use of ACs has been in managerial contexts for administrative purposes (e.g., selection and promotion), although the flexibility inherent in the AC methodology has led to its use in a wide variety of human resource settings and purposes. A general overview of the AC process is illustrated in Figure 7.1. In the AC method, participants work through a series of behavioral exercises (e.g., situational exercises and job simulations such as leaderless group discussions, in-baskets, and role plays). Multiple assessors observe and document participants' behavior in the exercises and then sort and organize their observations in terms of the focal dimensions of interest. After they have observed and documented participants' performance in all the exercises, the team of assessors meets and arrives at final dimension ratings for each participant. Finally, if warranted, such as in a developmental AC, assessors then meet with participants in one-on-one feedback interviews to review and discuss the participant's performance on the assessed behavioral dimensions and the strategies and activities for improvement. Participants receive a written feedback report at a later date.

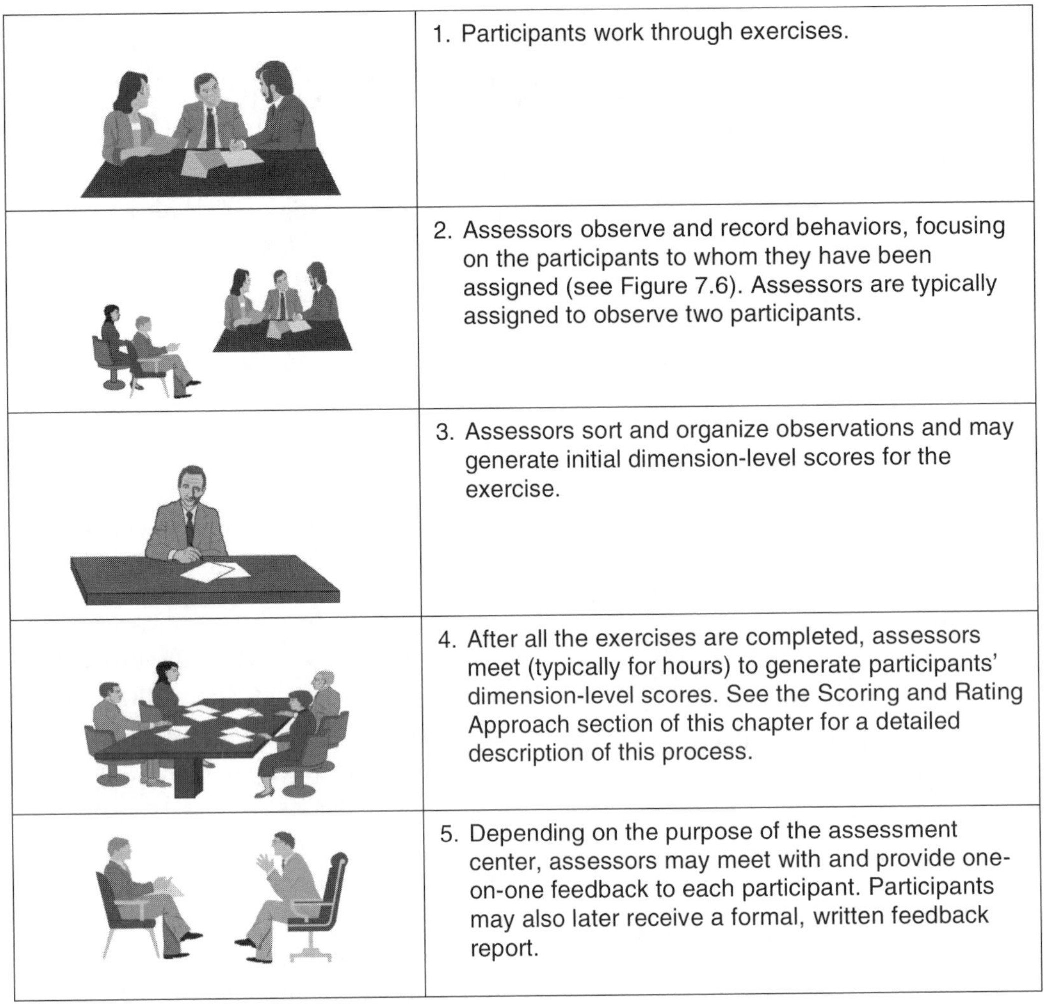

1. Participants work through exercises.
2. Assessors observe and record behaviors, focusing on the participants to whom they have been assigned (see Figure 7.6). Assessors are typically assigned to observe two participants.
3. Assessors sort and organize observations and may generate initial dimension-level scores for the exercise.
4. After all the exercises are completed, assessors meet (typically for hours) to generate participants' dimension-level scores. See the Scoring and Rating Approach section of this chapter for a detailed description of this process.
5. Depending on the purpose of the assessment center, assessors may meet with and provide one-on-one feedback to each participant. Participants may also later receive a formal, written feedback report.

FIGURE 7.1. A general overview of the assessment center process.

In summary, an AC is a comprehensive, standardized procedure that uses multiple techniques (exercises) and assessors to assess multiple behavioral dimensions of interest (International Task Force on Assessment Center Guidelines, 2000). A noteworthy distinguishing feature embedded in this definition is the use of multiple exercises (i.e., methods) to obtain multiple dimension scores. Figure 7.2 and Figure 7.3 present descriptions of some commonly used AC dimensions and exercises, respectively. Hence the standard design and use of ACs is to cross dimensions and exercises, and then collapse performance across exercises to obtain dimension scores from a "single" method; this feature is illustrated in Figure 7.4. It is important to note that dimension scores are also collapsed across multiple raters or assessors. So, the triangulation of dimensions through the use of multiple methods and multiple assessors is, in fact, the major defining characteristic of ACs. Therefore, because the set of specified multiple methods represents an AC, ACs are best conceptualized as a method instead of multiple methods.

HISTORICAL BACKGROUND

The origins of the AC can be traced to military and industrial efforts surrounding World War II, primarily first with the Germans, then the British War Office Selection Boards, and then the United States Office of Strategic Services (OSS; Thornton & Byham, 1982). With the massive human resources efforts needed to meet the demands of such a large-scale operation, military psychologists were faced with the critical task of developing procedures for identifying and

COMMUNICATION: The extent to which an individual conveys oral and written information and responds to questions and challenges.

CONSIDERATION/AWARENESS OF OTHERS: The extent to which an individual's actions reflect a consideration for the feelings and needs of others as well as an awareness of the impact and implications of decisions relevant to other components both inside and outside the organization.

DRIVE: The extent to which an individual originates and maintains a high activity level, sets performance standards and persists in his or her achievement, and expresses the desire to advance to higher job levels.

INFLUENCING OTHERS: The extent to which an individual persuades others to do something or adopt a point of view in order to produce desired results and takes action in which the dominant influence is his or her own convictions rather than the influence of others' opinions.

ORGANIZING AND PLANNING: The extent to which an individual systematically arranges his or her own work and resources as well as that of others for efficient task accomplishment, and the extent to which an individual anticipates and prepares for the future.

PROBLEM SOLVING: The extent to which an individual gathers information; understands relevant technical and professional information; effectively analyzes data and information; generates viable options, ideas, and solutions; selects supportable courses of action for problems and situations; uses available resources in new ways; and generates and recognizes imaginative solutions.

FIGURE 7.2. Some commonly used assessment center dimensions (see Arthur et al., 2003).

selecting military personnel, primarily officers and intelligence agents in the case of the OSS. On the basis of a behavioral consistency philosophy that "the best predictor of future performance is past performance" (Wernimont & Campbell, 1968, p. 372), psychologists were particularly interested in developing performance tests that presented officer candidates with complex stimuli requiring complex behavioral responses that translated well to actual performance situations. In other words, psychologists were interested in simulating the demands of real-world situations in the assessment of potential. Moreover, because no single simulation or test could fully represent all of the demands associated with serving as a military officer, psychologists placed great emphasis on the need for multiple simulations, both individual- and group-based, in conjunction with batteries of paper-and-pencil tests, projective tests, biographical inventories, and interviews. It was also thought that such complex simulations could not be feasibly scored in an objective manner; rather, scoring could be better accomplished by integrating the judgments of multiple psychologists who observe the behavior of the officer candidates during the performance simulations. Thus, the core distinguishing aspects of contemporary ACs—simulation and triangulation via methods and assessors—were born.

Commonalities and conspicuous differences among the German, the British War Office Selection Boards, and OSS efforts are evident when reading early accounts of their backgrounds, principles, and specific procedures (e.g., Ansbacher, 1941; Assessment Staff, 1948; Farago, 1942; Harris, 1949; Jennings, 1949; Morris, 1949). The overriding theoretical conceptualization of potential, and human nature in general, was very similar. Drawing on Freudian, neo-Freudian, and gestalt theories as well as Lewin's burgeoning group dynamics perspective, assessment had a holistic focus, involving a complex interplay between general intellectual ability, specific aptitudes, interests, personality, needs, and motives. This holistic approach emphasized the dynamic interplay among human characteristics (Bray, 1982),

IN-BASKET: The in-basket presents a high-volume of information to participants including letters, memos, informal correspondence, reports, and announcements that have accumulated in an in-box. The materials are designed to represent the full scope of contextual, procedural, and financial challenges of managerial work. Participants are given background information about the organization and key personnel as well as a calendar that may already show previously scheduled meetings and events. Participants are asked to take action on the materials in the in-box. These actions may take the form of drafting letters and memos, writing instructions, delegating responsibilities, and scheduling meetings. Responses may be handwritten or computer-mediated. Stimulus materials typically vary in urgency, job relevance, interrelatedness, complexity, and significance. The in-basket typically involves substantial time pressure. In many assessment centers (ACs), an assessor interviews the participant shortly after the in-basket is completed to provide better insight into the participant's priorities and rationale underlying the actions taken.

ORAL PRESENTATION: The oral presentation requires participants to formally present information and new ideas to one or more persons. Examples include meeting with a board of directors, managers from various organizational divisions, or members of the press. Participants may be given little or no background information on a topic, or they may be given some time to review more extensive background information and prepare for the presentation. The presentation is usually made to an assessor or group of assessors, and in many ACs the assessors also serve as role-players who have standardized scripted behaviors and questions intended to challenge the participant and simulate a more dynamic interpersonal interaction.

WRITTEN CASE ANALYSIS: The case analysis requires participants to review a set of background materials that describe a specific organizational problem or issue and then individually prepare a written report with a specific action plan. The problem or issue at hand may require a new set of policies or procedures, specific financial decisions, or a more systemwide strategy. In some ACs, an assessor interviews the participant afterward on the use of the information provided and the reasons for the recommendations made.

LEADERLESS GROUP DISCUSSION: The leaderless group discussion is designed to simulate the dynamics associated with decision making in small groups. Participants are given time to review background materials regarding a specific organizational problem or issue, and then they meet with three to seven other participants to discuss and resolve the matter. No one is designated as the leader or chairperson. In a competitive leaderless group discussion, various roles of equal status are assigned to the participants, and the participants are presented with a problem that involves the distribution of limited resources. Each participant is instructed to develop a solution that maximizes the payoff to them but also benefits the entire group. All participants in the group may be required to sign off on the final solution. In a cooperative leaderless group discussion, no specific roles are assigned and the discussion is similar to ad hoc committees formed to examine a specific organization problem. Participants are simply instructed to generate and integrate their ideas into a single course of action.

ONE-ON-ONE ROLE PLAY: The one-on-one role play requires participants to meet with another person to address a specific problem or issue. Examples include interviewing a job applicant, meeting with an employee who has performance problems, meeting with a potential new client or business partner, seeking information from a knowledgeable colleague, or dealing with a dissatisfied customer. The participant must talk with the role-player to gather new information and generate a solution or course of action. Role-players answer questions and they might also ask questions, make suggestions, or display specific emotions. Standardization of role-players is critical. Role-players typically receive general background information about their role and the general scenario along with a specific script for how to respond to potential participant behaviors and questions. In some ACs, the role-players also serve as assessors. Participants are typically given a brief period to review background materials prior to the role play. Afterward, participants may be asked to generate a brief report or plan of action.

FIGURE 7.3. Descriptions of some commonly used AC exercises.

	EXERCISES					ASSESSOR RATINGS	
DIMENSIONS	Competitive LGD (Resource Allocation)	In-Basket Exercise	In-Basket Interview	Cooperative LGD (Management Problem)	Written Analysis	Initial Rating	Final Rating
Consideration/ Awareness of Others							
Influencing Others							
Oral Communication							
Organizing and Planning							
Problem Solving							
Written Communication							

FIGURE 7.4. Dimension × Exercise matrix. LGD = leaderless group discussion. Shaded areas represent dimensions that are not observable in the specified exercise. The scores in the Dimension × Exercise cells will be filled in by the assigned assessor. The initial rating is generated independently by the assessor after incorporating all dimension-level information that has been shared by the assigned assessors, and so ratings will vary across assessors. The final rating is generated either mechanically or via consensus, and so these ratings will be the same across all assessors.

which required equally dynamic assessments in which individuals must face challenging and stressful circumstances. It was important for the simulations to focus on how individuals adjusted to frustrating social circumstances and failure.

This early period in the history of ACs can be described as a time of experimentation and inspiration. Because of their unfamiliarity with behavioral assessment, military psychologists had to experiment with new simulation techniques, much of the time by trial and error. Changing the assessment protocols and simulations midstream was common. Indeed, many of the chief scientists and authors of the early reports referred to these assessment efforts as experiments. The term *assessment center* was by no means in vogue at the time. The German assessment efforts inspired the British, and the British efforts during the war in turn inspired the first nonmilitary industrial application of this assessment approach used by the British Civil Service Selection Boards (Anstey, 1977). Although connections between the British War Office Selection Boards and OSS efforts are evident, Henry Murray and his associates at the Harvard Psychological Clinic (Murray, 1938), who used a similar assessment approach in a nonindustrial study of the normal human personality, also inspired the OSS effort. In turn, the OSS endeavor was the key source of inspiration for the AC methodology used in American Telephone and Telegraph's (AT&T's) seminal Management Progress Study (MPS).

The MPS began in 1956. It was originally conceived for purely research purposes as a longitudinal investigation of adult development in the context of managerial work (Howard & Bray, 1988). Douglas Bray introduced and directed the AC methodology applied to the MPS. The use of the AC methodology as a means of selecting and promoting managerial talent was a by-product of the extensive validation efforts showing how AC scores were predictive of salary and promotion progress (e.g., Bray & Grant, 1966). It is important to note that great care was taken to keep the AC data from AT&T executives to prevent later salary and promotion decisions from being contaminated by knowledge of the managers' AC performance.

The MPS established the use of multiple behavioral simulations with pooled assessor judgments as the hallmark of the AC methodology. Managerial potential was articulated via 26 dimensions derived from an extensive review of the management literature and interviews with behavioral scientists and personnel executives. The 26 dimensions reflected administrative and interpersonal skills, intellectual ability, and work, career, and social motives. Like its predecessors, the MPS approach combined behavioral simulations with a large battery of paper-and-pencil tests, projective tests, and unstructured interviews. However, in contrast to its predecessors, the explicit purpose of frustrating participants and examining adjustment in the face of failure was not part of the assessment process. Individual- and group-based simulations simply presented participants with the responsibility of addressing a wide range of managerial issues and problems.

The AT&T MPS quickly sparked the widespread development and adoption of the AC methodology throughout the public and private sectors in the United States (Bray, 1982; Dunnette, 1971; Mayes, 1997). By the end of the 1960s, organizations such as Standard Oil, IBM, Caterpillar Tractor, General Electric, Sears & Roebuck, J. C. Penney, the Peace Corps, and the U.S. Internal Revenue Service were using the AC model developed by AT&T. This period in AC history also witnessed the birth of consulting firms offering AC services to private and public organizations.

The 1970s to the present day can be characterized as a period of both proliferation and examination in AC history. Not only has the AC method remained popular as a means of selecting and promoting managerial talent, but it has also been extended to a wide variety of nonmanagerial employees, such as salespeople, teachers and principals, engineers, rehabilitation counselors, pilots, police officers, and firefighters. Advancements in video and computer technologies have opened doors to more streamlined and technologically based assessment and scoring procedures. Moreover, the use of ACs has been expanded to a variety of human resources purposes other than selection and promotion, such as training, development, recruitment, performance appraisal, human resource planning, layoffs, and organizational development (Joiner, 2002; Spychalski, Quiñones, Gaugler, & Pohley, 1997; Thornton & Rupp, 2006). Using ACs for developing talent rather than selecting and promoting talent is rather popular in today's business environment. In these instances, the AC may be labeled as a *development center* (Tillema, 1998). The scholarly literature is steadily becoming more populated with research and recommendations regarding the use of ACs for developmental purposes (e.g., Chen & Naquin, 2006; Jackson, Stillman, Burke, & Englert, 2007; Melancon & Williams, 2006; Rupp et al., 2006). ACs have also been used to assist high school and college students with career planning and the prediction of early career success (Arthur & Benjamin, 1999; Rowe & Mauer, 1991; Waldman & Korbar, 2004) and, even more interesting, to select political candidates (Silvester & Dykes, 2007). The number of companies in the United States using ACs is estimated in the thousands, with probably just as high a number outside the United States. It has also been noted that the vast majority of Fortune 500 companies use the AC methodology in some capacity (Mayes, 1997).

In spite of this growing popularity, the explanatory mechanisms underlying why ACs work have been greatly scrutinized over the past 3 decades. Despite ample evidence of criterion-related validity and assurances of content-related validity, scholars have hotly debated the extent to which AC scores actually represent the behavioral dimensions purported to be measured. The major impetus for this debate is that construct-related validity studies (e.g., factor analyses, multitrait–multimethod correlations) typically show that scores derived from ACs reflect exercise variance more so than dimension variance. Researchers (e.g., Klimoski & Brickner, 1987) have proposed multiple alternative explanations for why AC scores are predictive of performance-related job criteria such as ratings of performance, ratings of potential, performance in training, and career advancement (Gaugler, Rosenthal, Thornton, & Bentson, 1987). Scholars also continue to debate the construct-related validity evidence yielded by ACs. This debate is reviewed in more detail in the Reliability and Validity section of this chapter. In short, this debate can be summarized by two statements. On the one hand, scholars tend to agree that the overall assessment score derived from the entire AC process is a valid reflection of overall potential and thus, a valid predictor of future performance. On the other hand, scholars tend not to agree on the extent to which AC scores actually reflect the dimensions purported to be measured. Although this second statement may not be as critical a concern in the context of selection and promotion decisions, it does suggest that the use of ACs for developmental purposes may not be tenable. If the AC dimension scores are not valid reflections of the specific constructs purported to be assessed, then feedback concerning one's relative strengths and weaknesses vis-à-vis the dimension scores is unfounded and subsequent recommendations regarding developmental action steps are misguided. Regardless of this debate, the AC continues to be a popular tool for achieving a variety of human resource objectives.

DESIGN, DEVELOPMENT, ADMINISTRATION, AND SCORING

The steps involved in the design and development of ACs are, to a large extent, not any different from those involved in the development of other predictors in industrial and organizational (I/O) psychology. Figure 7.5 presents a general overview of the broad sequence of steps that one may follow in designing and developing an AC from a "best practices" perspective. However, because there is no such thing as the AC or a single AC, we acknowledge that there may be variations in the steps outlined in Figure 7.5 as a function of the specific situation. That is, there is no one way to structure an AC; the specific design, content, and administration will be a function of the objectives of the AC and the specific target group that is being assessed. Nevertheless, as illustrated in the Figure 7.5, the typical first step would be the implementation of a detailed job analysis using a variety of job analysis techniques. (See also chap. 1, this volume.) As the second step, this information would be used to generate a draft job description that will then be reviewed by incumbents and supervisors. On the basis of incumbent and supervisor feedback, the job description would be revised and finalized. Third, on the basis of the job description, critical knowledge, skills, abilities, and other characteristics

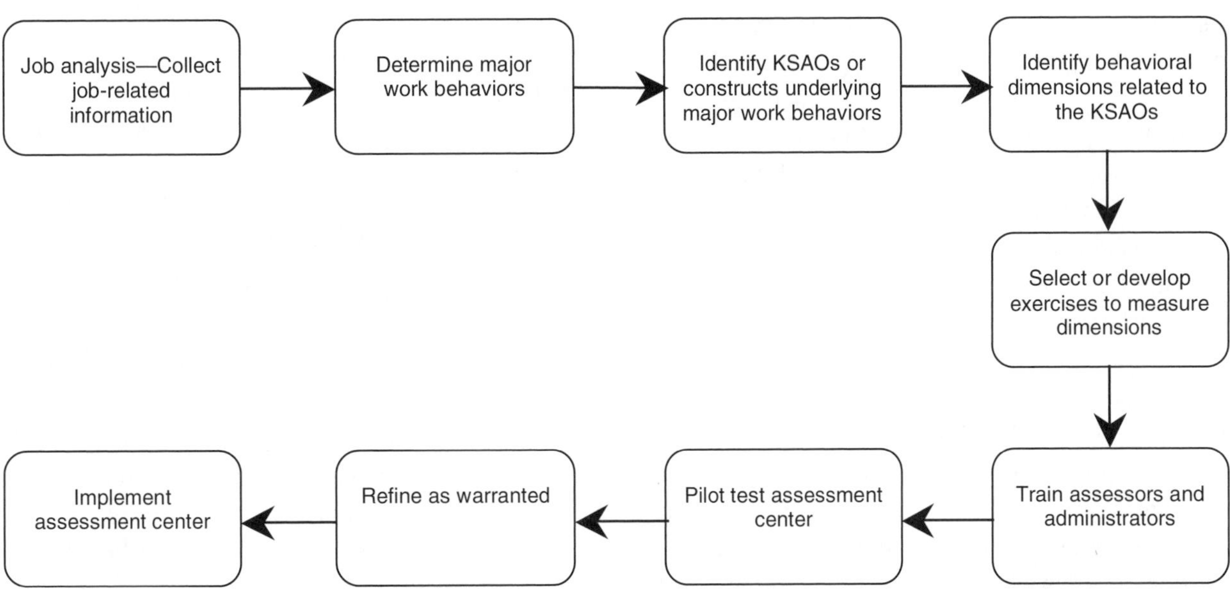

FIGURE 7.5. Assessment center design, development, and implementation sequence. KSAO = knowledge, skills, abilities, and other characteristics.

(KSAOs) necessary for successful job performance would be identified.

The fourth step calls for the identification of behavioral dimensions related to the identified KSAOs. For purposes of selection and promotion, dimensions should reflect abilities and traits that underlie potential, whereas knowledge- and skill-based dimensions are more applicable for training and development purposes. The implementation of this step (i.e., the identification, labeling, and definition of dimensions) is a particularly critical one in the development of the AC because it has been identified as a weak link in the common practice of AC design and development because of the proclivity to rely on espoused constructs (dimensions; Arthur, Day, & Woehr, 2008). In fact, the AC literature appears to be a domain in which assertions about the dimensions being measured are rarely, if ever, subjected to the psychometric standards that characterize test development in other domains (Arthur et al., 2008; Brannick, 2008). Merely labeling data as reflecting a particular dimension (espoused dimension or construct) does not mean that is the dimension being assessed (actual dimension or construct). Consequently, the overreliance on espoused dimensions or constructs has been highlighted as a threat to the construct-related validity of ACs. As noted by Arthur et al. (2008), the formulation and explication of construct definitions should not be approached casually, and support for the construct representation of the AC's content should be pellucidly demonstrated using multistage data collection and refinement efforts before the AC is put into operational or research use. Thus, it should be noted that contrary to common practice, efforts to establish the construct-related validity of the AC dimension ratings should be undertaken before the AC is put into operational or research use.

The fifth step entails the selection or development of exercises to measure the behavioral dimensions that were identified. Following the preceding developmental process is intended to ensure a high level of content-related validity. Finally, one would train the assessors and AC administrators, pilot test and refine the AC as warranted, and then, of course, operationally implement the AC. In contrast to construct-related validity evidence, if one were interested in demonstrating the criterion-related validity of the AC ratings, this validation effort would be undertaken after the implementation of the AC because the collection of predictor and criterion data is necessary for any criterion-related validation endeavor.

Still building on our illustrative example and assuming that the implementation of the first five steps resulted in the six dimensions and five exercises presented in Figure 7.4 (see also Figures 7.2 and 7.3), in the next section we present a description of a "typical" assessor training and an operational AC administration set of activities.

A Best-Practices Assessor Training and Assessment Center Administration Illustrative Example

The specific practices presented here were arrived at on the basis of a summation of the pertinent extant literature. Supporting research evidence for specified AC design and methodological choices summarized later is reviewed in the Important Methodological and Design-Related Characteristics and Features section of this chapter. With regard to the selection or choice of assessors, the research evidence indicates that it should be tilted in favor of I/O psychologists and similarly trained human resources management (HRM) professionals, and less so in favor of managers and supervisors (Gaugler et al., 1987; Lievens & Conway, 2001; Woehr & Arthur, 2003). After their selection, the next step is the training of the assessors, which will typically take the form of a full- or multiday frame-of-reference training program (Jackson, Atkins, Fletcher, & Stillman, 2005; Lievens, 2001; Schleicher, Day, Mayes, & Riggio, 2002; Woehr & Huffcutt, 1994) comprising the following steps:

1. Initial explanation of the AC method and the purpose of conducting the AC.
2. Definitions of the dimensions and descriptions of the exercises. Assessors are given examples of behaviors representing each dimension, and each set of behaviors (i.e., by dimension) is accompanied by an anchored rating scale (e.g., a 1- to 5-point scale) indicating the effectiveness levels of the specified dimension.
3. Once assessors are familiar with the dimensions and exercises, they then practice observing

behaviors elicited by the exercises. In our example, this is accomplished by having them view videotapes of past participant groups participating in the specified exercises, such as the resource allocation exercise (see Figure 7.4), and recording the behaviors of the participants. Prior to the practice observations, the trainers would emphasize the observing and recording of participant behaviors without trying to categorize the behaviors into dimensions while observing the participants.

4. Assessors categorize the behaviors into dimensions and provide ratings on each dimension.
5. Assessors discuss their observations and ratings, using this as an opportunity to build a common frame of reference.
6. Assessors practice another exercise, such as the in-basket. In this example, they are each given a completed in-basket and directed to record any information provided by the participant.
7. Assessors practice the in-basket interview. This is accomplished via a role-played in-basket interview during which assessors have the opportunity to clarify responses and seek explanations from the participant (e.g., why the participant took specific action[s]).
8. Assessors categorize the in-basket behaviors into dimensions and provide dimension ratings.
9. Again, assessors discuss behaviors and dimension ratings so that a common frame of reference can be developed.
10. Assessors train on and practice the remaining exercises using the general approach described earlier.

The next training segment has the objective of familiarizing assessors with the rating process. As discussed later, there are various approaches to generating assessment ratings and scores—specifically, the within- versus across-exercise (i.e., within-dimension) approach. The approach used in this example is the across-exercise approach. Hence assessors are trained to work across exercises and finish rating a dimension before moving on to the next one. If required, the final segment of training focuses on how to prepare feedback reports and conduct feedback interviews. Finally, as part of their training, new and inexperienced assessors shadow a more experienced assessor for at least one AC administration before they serve as a full assessor whose ratings are used operationally.

When the AC is administered, participants will participate in all the exercises and will be evaluated on the six dimensions (see Figure 7.4). Groups of three to four assessors—who serve as assessor groups—are assigned to observe and rate the materials of a group of four to six participants (a design feature that results in a 2:1 participant-to-assessor ratio [see Figure 7.6]; Woehr & Arthur, 2003). For the group exercises, assessors sit in the back of the room (to minimize their obtrusiveness) and record behaviors displayed by the participants (see Figure 7.1). It should be noted that behavioral checklists may be used as an aid in the recording of behaviors.

Because of the 2:1 participant-to-assessor ratio, for the group exercises (e.g., the leaderless group discussions), each assessor observes and records the behavior of one or two AC participants. However, all assessors in the group are present during each exercise, and each assessor observes different participants in each exercise using a rotation schedule that ensures that each assessor has the responsibility of being the primary observer for each participant in at least one exercise. Figure 7.6 presents an illustration of the rotation sequence. On the completion of each exercise, assessors categorize their recorded observations into dimensions using materials that describe each dimension in detail, along with a list of some representative behaviors. For the in-basket exercise (including the follow-up in-basket interview) and written exercise, assessors review and rate the materials for each participant to whom they are assigned.

Following the completion of all exercises, the assessors in each assessor group meet to rate the participants' performance. Each assessor provides independent ratings of each participant (in their participant group) on each dimension. For exercises in which an assessor was not assigned to record behaviors of a participant, ratings are based on a verbatim listing of observed behaviors recorded by the assigned assessor as well as the assessor's own observations. Consistent with the across-exercise (within-dimension) approach, the rating process proceeds as follows. Selecting a participant, the

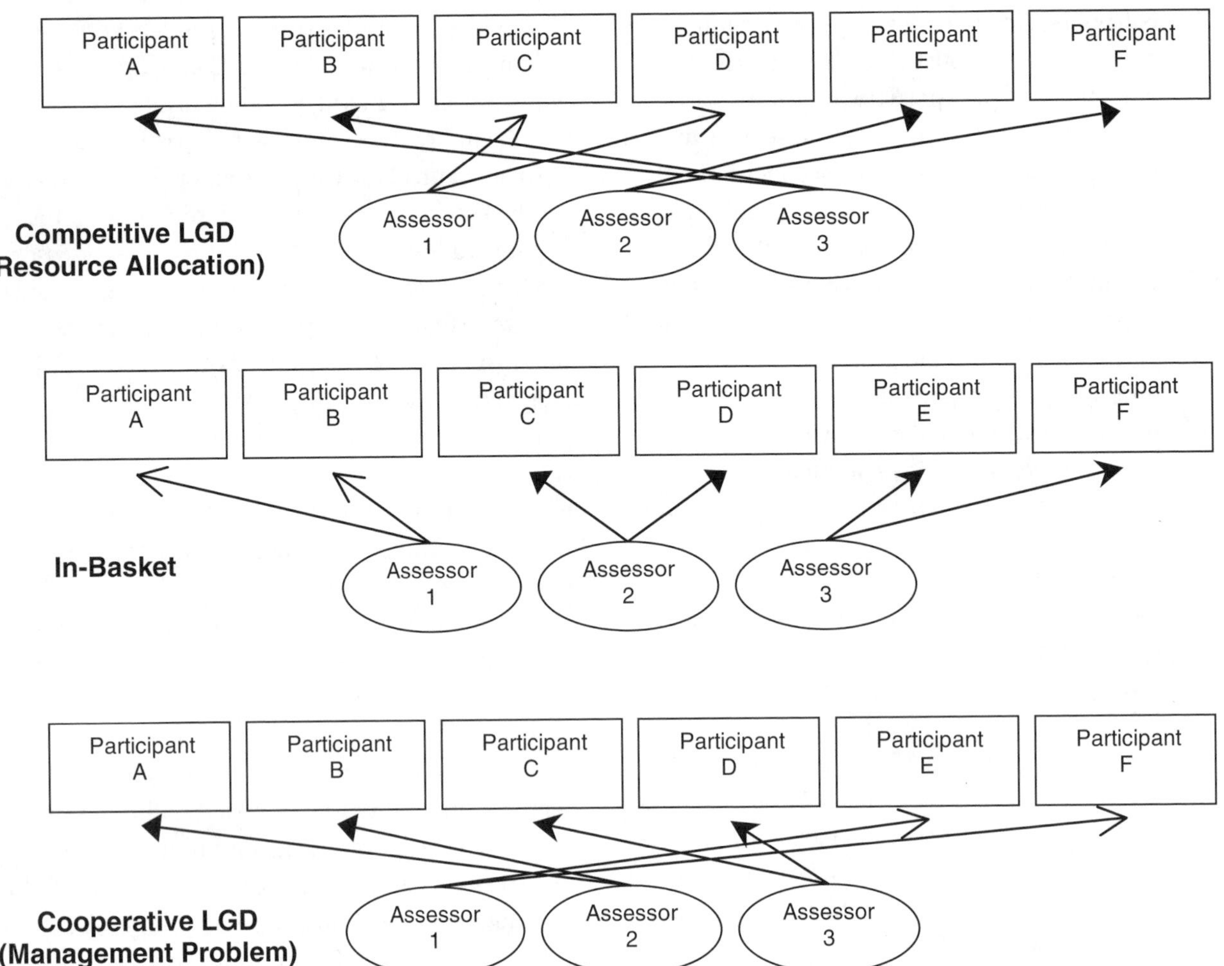

FIGURE 7.6. Assignments and rotation of assessors observing and recording participant behavior in a three-exercise assessment center. LGD = leaderless group discussion.

assessors start with a specified dimension (e.g., oral communication). A verbatim listing of observed behaviors for the first relevant exercise (e.g., resource allocation) for that dimension is presented by the assigned assessor. After the presentation of observed behaviors for the exercise, an independent rating is made on the dimension in question at the exercise level; this process is repeated for all the exercises (e.g., in-basket, management problem) relevant to the dimension in question. It is important to note that no group discussion or consensus process occurs prior to each assessor's ratings. Ratings are typically made on a Likert scale with descriptive anchors. After the assessors have completed their dimension rating for each exercise (i.e., cells in Figure 7.4), they then again make an independent initial dimension rating (see Figure 7.4). The members of the assessor group then share their initial ratings and discuss any differences before assigning a final dimension score (Roch, 2006; Schmitt, 1977). In this final step, assessors may be required to reach consensus; if that is the case, then they will have identical final dimension ratings. On the other hand, the AC designers may have opted to generate the final scores mechanically (e.g., average the assessors' ratings); if so, then assessors would obviously not be instructed to reach consensus. Regardless of whether they are instructed to reach consensus or not, the preceding sequence of steps would be repeated for the remaining (five) dimensions. The entire process would then be repeated for each participant assigned to the assessor group. It is also worth noting that it is common for AC designers to be interested in an overall assessment center rating (OAR) that is intended to represent the participant's overall future potential or overall performance in the AC collapsed across all the AC dimensions (cf. Arthur, Day, McNelly, & Edens, 2003).

The AC process does not end with the final determination of ratings. Once ratings have been finalized, feedback needs to be delivered to relevant constituents in a manner that is consistent with the purpose of the AC. Recognizing that federal and state privacy laws may also be applicable, ethical guidelines (American Educational Research Association, American Psychological Association, and National Council on Measurement in Education, 1999; American Psychological Association, 1992; International Task Force on Assessment Center Guidelines, 2000; Society for Industrial and Organizational Psychology, Inc., 2003) state that there should be policies for providing feedback to participants as well as for restricting access to AC ratings and reports to specific relevant persons within the organization. The nature of the feedback given to participants will likely vary depending on the purpose of the AC. General feedback regarding overall performance and resulting decisions (i.e., pass–fail, yes–no) is relevant in cases of selection and promotion, and more specific feedback regarding strengths and weaknesses is required in the case of training and development.

With regard to developmental ACs, the assessment itself is just the beginning of what should be a larger program that involves the delivery of accurate feedback from a credible source and the development and implementation of an action plan designed to remediate areas in need of improvement. At present there is very little empirical research examining the feedback and follow-up phases in developmental ACs (Thornton & Rupp, 2006). However, the limited research there is shows a positive relationship between AC ratings and feedback acceptance and feedback-seeking behavior. For instance, Bell and Arthur (2008) reported a correlation of .30 ($N = 141$) between OARs and feedback acceptance in a developmental AC used by a state auditing office and master's graduate program in public administration. In a case study of 20 call center workers, Dhanju (2007) reported that a majority of the participants who were promoted to center team leader as a result of their AC performance accepted their feedback whereas a majority of the participants who were not promoted did not accept their feedback. In a sample of 189 newly hired supervisors, Abraham, Morrison, and Burnett (2006) showed a standardized difference of 0.39 in OARs between participants who sought feedback after participating in a developmental AC versus those who did not seek feedback. Although other individual differences (e.g., agreeableness; Bell & Arthur, 2008) may also play roles in feedback acceptance and seeking behavior, this state of affairs is unfortunate given that those individuals most in need of development are the ones least likely to accept feedback and address their development needs. Without participation in follow-up developmental activities, it is unlikely that participation in the AC will benefit participants (Jones & Whitmore, 1995).

Important Methodological and Design-Related Characteristics and Features

As previously noted, because they are methods, there is not a single AC or *the* AC. Consequently, as with other methods such as the interview, ACs are only as good as their design and administration. However, there is a rich and reasonably large body of research that indicates what the desirable features of ACs are or should be (e.g., see International Task Force on Assessment Center Guidelines, 2000; Lievens, 1998; Woehr & Arthur, 2003) and subsequently provides some guidance on how to design and implement "good" ACs. This literature served as the basis for the practices described in the preceding section on best practices.

It is obvious that poor enactment and implementation of any of the steps in Figure 7.5—such as poor planning; inadequate job analysis; weakly defined, ambiguous, and poorly explicated dimensions; poor exercise selection or design; absence of pilot testing and evaluation; use of unqualified or inadequately trained assessors; and poor behavior documentation and scoring—is likely to have adverse effects on the effectiveness and validity of the resultant AC (Caldwell, Thornton, & Gruys, 2003; Chen, 2006). Furthermore, drawing from a relatively large body of research, one can identify specific AC methodological factors and design characteristics that have discernable hypothesized positive and negative effects on the effectiveness and validity of ACs as measurement tools (Lievens, 1998; Woehr & Arthur, 2003). These include (a) the number of dimensions assessors are asked to observe, record, and subsequently rate; (b) the conceptual distinctiveness of dimensions; (c) the transparency of dimensions; (d) the choice and design of exercises, and the type and number of exercises; (e) the participant-to-assessor ratio; (f) the scoring and rating approach; (g) the type of assessor used; and (h) assessor training.

Number of Dimensions

Primary studies (e.g., Bycio, Alvares, & Hahn, 1987; Gaugler & Thornton, 1989; Russell, 1985; Sackett & Hakel, 1979; Schmitt, 1977), qualitative reviews (e.g., Lievens, 1998), and meta-analytic studies (e.g., Arthur et al., 2003; Bowler & Woehr, 2006; Lievens & Conway, 2001; Meriac, Hoffman, Woehr, & Fleisher, 2008; Woehr & Arthur, 2003) have converged on the summary conclusion that all things being equal, a smaller number of dimensions is preferable to a larger number. This is primarily because of the high cognitive demands placed on assessors when they are asked to process a large number of dimensions. Thus, for instance, in a meta-analysis of 48 AC studies, Woehr and Arthur (2003) obtained partial support for the effect of the number of dimensions on the construct-related validity of ACs; fewer dimensions were associated with higher levels of convergent validity ($r = .37$) and more dimensions with a lower level ($r = .27$). In this meta-analysis, the mean number of dimensions was 10.60 ($SD = 5.11$, min = 3, max = 25)—a number that is a little higher than that recommended by the extant literature (Arthur et al., 2003; Gaugler & Thornton, 1989; Lievens, 1998; Russell, 1985; Sackett & Hakel, 1979; Schmitt, 1977).

Conceptual Distinctiveness of Dimensions

An issue related to the number of dimensions is the conceptual distinctiveness of the dimensions. One result of the reliance on espoused constructs is a lengthy, extensive list of dimensions purported to be measured by ACs such that recent meta-analyses (see Arthur et al., 2003; Bowler & Woehr, 2006; Woehr & Arthur, 2003) have extracted anywhere from 79 to 168 different dimension labels. Such large numbers of dimensions and the reliance on espoused constructs has perpetuated a lack of dimension distinctiveness within primary studies. Consequently, recent meta-analyses have generally obtained more favorable and supportive results for the construct validity of AC ratings after collapsing the myriad of dimensions in the extant literature into a smaller, conceptually distinct set of dimensions. Using Arthur et al.'s (2003) six-dimension taxonomy (communication, consideration and awareness of others, drive, influencing others, organizing and planning, and problem solving; see Figure 7.2), these meta-analyses provide evidence for the criterion-related validity of AC dimensions (Arthur et al., 2003) and the impact of dimension factors (Bowler & Woehr, 2006; Connelly, Ones, Ramesh, & Goff, 2008). For instance, using a regression-based composite consisting of four out of their six dimensions, Arthur et al. (2003) explained more variance in performance (20%) than Gaugler et al. (1987) were able to explain using the OAR (14%). In addition, Arthur et al.'s (2003) taxonomy has also been used to effectively demonstrate the differentiation from and incremental criterion-related validity of AC dimensions over cognitive ability and personality (Meriac et al., 2008).

Transparency of Dimensions

Lievens (1998) strongly recommended informing participants in developmental ACs of the dimensions to be assessed and suggested that this practice should be considered for ACs for selection purposes as well. This recommendation is based primarily on Kleinmann (1993) and Kleinmann, Kuptsch, and Köller (1996), who found that disclosing the dimensions to participants and informing them of which behaviors represented specified dimensions resulted in better validity evidence. Similar findings were obtained by Kolk, Born, and Van der Flier (2003), who found an increase in convergent validities from a nontransparent ($r = .22$) to a transparent condition ($r = .31$) with relatively similar discriminant validities ($r = .52$ and $.50$, respectively). The conceptual basis for this effect is that informed participants display higher levels of behavioral consistency which in turn enables assessors to differentiate the dimensions and also rate participants consistently across the AC exercises.

Choice and Design of Exercises and the Number and Type of Exercises

The choice and design of exercises are critical to the effectiveness of ACs, not just in terms of achieving face validity via replicating the job environment but, more important, also in terms of how well behaviors associated with the identified performance dimensions are elicited. All too often there is an overemphasis on replicating the job environment at the expense of the coupling between dimensions and exercises. For instance, over the past 2 decades practitioners have increasingly incorporated exercises in which stimulus materials and responses are computer-mediated (e.g., e-mails) in real time rather than the traditional approach of using printed and handwritten memos, letters, and reports. Although these higher fidelity formats may indeed reflect the nature of work today, the importance of dimensions in the assessment process should not be deemphasized. We were unable to locate any published research comparing the validity of such higher fidelity ACs to the more traditional paper-and-pencil approach.

It is crucial that the development of AC exercises includes an explicit blueprint for how the dimensions are represented in the exercises (Lievens, 1998; Thornton & Rupp, 2006). The use of standardized role-players can aid in the elicitation of dimension-relevant behaviors (Lievens, 1998). In light of the early history of ACs, it is important that a variety of exercises be used to better triangulate the assessment of dimensions. Indeed, Gaugler et al.'s (1987) meta-analysis showed that stronger predictive validities are associated with the use of a larger number of different types of exercises ($\rho = .25–.95$ depending on the criterion). Figure 7.3 provides a brief overview of commonly used AC exercises. For an instructive and detailed account of how to build AC exercises, the interested reader is referred to Thornton and Mueller-Hanson (2004).

With regard to the use of AC scores or ratings, if the AC is part of a larger assessment system that includes interviews, résumés, aptitude tests, and other forms of assessment, and one is interested in obtaining or focusing exclusively on performance on the AC, then it is recommended that information from the other tests be kept from the assessors during the administration of the AC to keep the AC ratings free from contamination. However, if the focus is on performance on the larger assessment system of which the AC is a component, then of course information from the other tests would be made available to the assessors who would in turn use them to arrive at the participants' scores. However, it should be emphasized that the performance scores in this latter instance reflect performance on the larger assessment system and not just the AC and indeed cannot be accurately described as being the AC score.

To facilitate clear communication and discussions of transportability of assessment, one must distinguish ACs from ostensibly similar types of assessment, including both low- and other high-fidelity simulations (Thornton & Rupp, 2006). Low-fidelity simulations such as situational judgment tests (video and paper-and-pencil administered), performance walk-throughs, and situational interviews should not be confused with AC exercises as they elicit behavioral intentions and not actual job-relevant behaviors. Likewise, there are meaningful distinctions that can be drawn between work samples (i.e., performance tests) and AC exercises. Work samples can be used as stand-alone tests or incorporated into ACs as one of several exercises. However, although work samples, like other AC exercises, also elicit job-relevant behaviors, in contrast to their use as stand-alone tests, when used as AC exercises, there is a deemphasis on current knowledge and skill in a specific domain and a strong focus on the assessment of future potential via multiple underlying performance dimensions. In fact, it is important to design AC exercises that do not closely resemble the specific demands of the job to prevent job knowledge and expertise from contaminating the assessment of broader underlying performance dimensions. In other words, work samples as stand-alone tests are designed to simulate actual job tasks, whereas AC exercises are designed to represent the general contexts surrounding the demands of the job. In the case of managerial work, such contexts include multitasking (in-basket exercises); interacting one-on-one with subordinates, clients, and other organizationally relevant constituents (role-play, interview, and fact-finding exercises); conducting meetings and working jointly with others to address organizational issues and problems (cooperative and competitive leaderless group discussion exercises and business games); developing action plans and proposals (case analysis exercise); and giving presentations (oral presentation exercise). Furthermore, work samples are frequently scored in terms of accuracy in accomplishing a given task, whereas ACs are scored in terms of the manner by which tasks are addressed.

As methods, work samples and ACs are both adaptable to a variety of purposes. Therefore, there are exceptions to the descriptions and distinctions made earlier. For example, it is thought that exercises that more closely resemble the actual job are appropriate for training and developmental ACs (Thornton & Rupp, 2006). In general, a single simulation is not an AC, and a system of work samples that separately assess different performance dimensions is also not an AC. Simulations in and of themselves do not define ACs; rather, ACs are defined by the use of simulations in an attempt to triangulate underlying performance components. For a comprehensive review of work samples, the interested reader is referred to Truxillo, Donahue, and Kuang (2004) and Roth, Bobko, and McFarland (2005) and the situational judgment test chapter by Ployhart and MacKenzie (see chap. 8, this volume).

Participant-to-Assessor Ratio

The arguments for using a small number of dimensions are similar to those for using a low participant-to-assessor ratio. As the number of participants that a given assessor is required to observe and evaluate in any given exercise increases, the cognitive demands placed on the assessor may make it more difficult for the assessor to process information at a dimension level. In addition, AC ratings are more likely to be susceptible to bias and information-processing errors under conditions of high cognitive demand. So for instance, depending on the criterion, Gaugler et al. (1987) reported rhos ranging from −.15 to −.29 for the relationship between AC ratings and specified criteria, indicating that higher ratios are associated with lower criterion-related validities. In Woehr and Arthur's (2003) meta-analysis, of the 26 studies that reported information on the participant-to-assessor ratio, the ratio ranged from 1 participant to 4 assessors to 4 participants for each assessor with a mean ratio of 1.71 (mode = 2) participants per assessor. The extant literature would recommend a participant-to-assessor ratio that does not exceed 2:1.

Scoring and Rating Approach

As previously noted, there are two primary rating approaches in the AC literature (Robie, Adams, Osburn, Morris, & Etchegaray, 2000; Sackett & Dreher, 1982; Woehr & Arthur, 2003): the within-exercise and across-exercise (i.e., within-dimension) approaches. In the within-exercise approach, participants are rated on each dimension after the completion of each exercise. Two variations of the within-exercise approach have been described: In one variation, the same assessors observe all exercises and provide dimension ratings after observing each exercise, and in the second variation, different sets of assessors observe each exercise and provide ratings for each dimension. In the across-exercise approach, evaluation occurs after all the exercises have been completed, and dimension ratings are based on performance in all of the exercises. Two variations of the across-exercise approach have also been described: In the first, assessors provide an overall rating for each dimension reflecting performance across all exercises, and in the second, assessors provide dimension ratings for each exercise, but only after all exercises are observed. In addition, as noted by Arthur et al. (2008), common to both of these rating approaches is the use of postconsensus dimension ratings to assess dimensions. Postconsensus dimension ratings represent the combination (either judgmentally or mechanically) of postexercise dimension ratings into a summary rating representing dimension-level performance information across multiple exercises and raters. From a traditional psychometric perspective, postexercise dimension ratings may be viewed as item-level information, whereas postconsensus dimension ratings represent scale-level information.

With regard to which is more appropriate and therefore the preferred practice, research examining the effect of the rating approach on the construct-related validity of AC ratings suggests that the across-exercise (within-dimension) approach is likely to result in higher levels of construct-related validity (Woehr & Arthur, 2003). Woehr and Arthur (2003) obtained a higher convergent validity for the across-exercise ($r = .43$) compared with the within-exercise approach ($r = .29$) and lower discriminant validity for the across-exercise ($r = .48$) compared with the within-exercise approach ($r = .58$). Thus, it would seem that the across-exercise approach results in dimension factors, whereas the within-exercise approach results in exercise factors.

Another aspect of the evaluation and scoring process is the use of behavioral checklists to record behaviors and even rate dimension performance. Behavioral checklists can reduce the assessors' load in terms of the amount of time spent taking notes and the number of judgments needed to be made, but assessors still need to match observed behaviors to listed behaviors, and they still have to make judgments about observed behaviors that do not appear on the checklists (Thornton & Rupp, 2006). An overreliance on behavioral checklists can also confine assessors to limited definitions of performance. An inspection of primary studies (e.g., Donahue, Truxillo, Cornwell, & Gerrity, 1997; Reilly, Henry, & Smither, 1990) reveals variability in the manner of use and efficacy of behavioral checklists. Overall, the influence that behavioral checklists have on validity appears to be modest (Lievens & Conway, 2001).

In the end, information from the multiple exercises and assessors must be integrated to derive final dimension ratings (as well as an OAR if one is desired). Information can be integrated either judgmentally (sometimes referred to as the clinical or consensus approach) or mechanically (sometimes referred to as the statistical or actuarial approach), or through some hybrid of the two. The judgmental approach is the traditionally advocated approach, and as previously described it involves assessors meeting to discuss their independent ratings (and observations) for each participant with the goal of arriving at a consensus about each participant for each dimension and then for the OAR. The mechanical approach removes discussion of participants' ratings from the integration process. At the dimension level, a mechanical approach would typically involve averaging assessor judgments. With respect to the OAR, dimension ratings can be unit-weighted, differentially weighted by importance to the job, or differentially weighted based on a cross-validated regression analysis. (See Bobko, Roth, & Buster, 2007, for a review of the use of unit weights in creating composite scores.)

A mechanical approach can streamline the rating process and dramatically reduce the cost of an AC. Consensus meetings can account for 25% to 33% of the AC time devoted to administering the AC (Gilbert, 1981). However, with a holistic perspective on understanding human nature, it is thought that a judgmental approach can provide deeper insights into each participant's potential by drawing on his or her unique combination of strengths and weaknesses (Thornton & Rupp, 2006). What does the research say? Numerous investigations from a wide variety of ACs have compared the two approaches. As a whole, these investigations show that mechanically derived ratings yield criterion-related validities that are as strong if not stronger than those derived through consensus (e.g., Feltham, 1988a; Pynes & Bernardin, 1992; Tziner, Meir, Dahan, & Birati, 1994; Wollowick & McNamara, 1969). Despite this body of research, it has been estimated that as many as 84% of operational ACs use the consensus approach (Spychalski et al., 1997). However, it must be noted that comparisons between the two approaches have always involved operational ACs using a within-subjects design. Recent research has shown that the anticipation of a discussion about ratings has a positive influence on the accuracy of assessors' observations, and that requiring assessors to reach consensus further improves accuracy (Roch, 2006, 2007). Thus, decisions to eliminate the consensus meeting from the AC to reduce costs should be made with caution.

Type of Assessor

The type of assessor, specifically the use of (I/O) psychologists (and similarly trained HRM professionals) versus managers and supervisors, has also been demonstrated to influence the validity of ACs. In an explanation of their meta-analytic results in which they obtained higher criterion-related validities for ACs that used psychologists as assessors compared with those that used managers and supervisors (ρ = .26–.39 depending on the criterion), Gaugler et al. (1987) posited that psychologists make better assessors because, as a result of their education and training, they are better equipped to observe, record, and rate behavior. Both Lievens and Conway (2001) and Woehr and Arthur (2003) provided additional support for this proposition by obtaining stronger construct-related validity evidence for ACs that used psychologists as assessors compared with those that used managers and supervisors. For instance, Woehr and Arthur obtained a higher convergent validity for psychologists ($r = .45$) compared with managers and supervisors ($r = .38$) and lower discriminate validity for the former ($r = .40$) compared with the latter ($r = .64$).

Assessor Training

The generation of AC ratings is inherently judgmental and subjective in nature. Hence, the training of assessors to observe, record, and categorize behaviors by dimension and subsequently rate performance is a very important element in the design, development, and administration of ACs. For instance, Woehr and Arthur (2003) obtained higher convergent validity when training was indicated in the description of the AC ($r = .36$) in contrast to when none was indicated ($r = .29$), and lower discriminant validity for the former ($r = .51$) compared with the latter ($r = .63$). In addition, the type and quality of training is also an important feature of ACs. For instance, there is consensus in the literature that the frame-of-reference approach, which imposes a common theory of performance on assessors enabling better judgment of behavior, is a highly effective approach to rater training (Lievens, 2001; Noonan & Sulsky, 2001; Schleicher & Day, 1998; Woehr & Huffcutt, 1994). Consistent with this, a conclusion that can be drawn from the extant AC literature is that the use of frame-of-reference training and also the extensiveness and quality of assessor training play an important role in establishing and enhancing the validity of AC ratings (Jackson et al., 2005; Lievens, 1998; Schleicher et al., 2002; Woehr & Arthur, 2003).

In summary, although empirical studies have demonstrated the role of each design factor (on its own) on the validity of AC ratings, we suspect that synergistic gains to validity will result by aligning all of these optimal features in one AC (Arthur, Woehr, & Maldegen, 2000). Consequently, in line with the results of multiple meta-analyses and the conceptual basis for their efficacy, we posit that a well-designed AC would be characterized by the following features: (a) the AC should be based on sound planning and an adequate job analysis; (b) the number of dimensions assessors are asked to observe, record, and subsequently rate is limited to a reasonable and manageable number (somewhere in the region of six to eight dimensions); (c) the dimensions are conceptually distinct, clearly defined, and unambiguously explicated; (d) the dimensions may be made transparent to the participants; (e) the choice and design of exercises are sound, multiple and different exercises are used, and each exercise elicits behaviors across multiple dimensions; (f) the marriage between dimensions and exercises should be strong; (g) the AC should be pilot tested and the exercises evaluated and refined accordingly; (h) the participant-to-assessor ratio is limited to about a 2:1 ratio; (i) an across-exercise (i.e., within-dimension) rating approach is used and, resources permitting, consensus meetings are incorporated into the generation of participants' scores; (j) the rating process generates postconsensus dimension-level scores (as well as an OAR if warranted); (k) I/O psychologists or other similarly trained HRM professionals are used as assessors or as part of assessor teams; and (l) assessors are extensively trained using methodologies such as frame-of-reference training.

RELIABILITY AND VALIDITY OF ASSESSMENT CENTER RATINGS

As with just about any test, the two psychometric properties of most interest in a discussion of AC ratings are the reliability and validity of said ratings. In reviewing the psychometric properties of ACs, it is important to keep in mind that because an AC is a method, there is a great deal of variability in operational ACs. Even if the purpose, exercises, dimensions, and assessor training are held constant, differences in the administration of an AC can dramatically influence validity conclusions (Schmitt, Schneider, & Cohen, 1990). So although we try to present an overall summary of the psychometric standing of the AC, one should keep in mind that the differences in psychometric quality from one AC to another can be substantial.

Reliability of AC Ratings

Within the context of ACs, reliability pertains to the consistency of assessor ratings and the extent to which they are free of measurement error. To this end, metrics of interrater reliability—the extent to which multiple raters assign the same dimension scores to the same participant—would seem to be the facets of most interest in the context of AC ratings. Although assessments of interrater reliability of dimension scores within exercises are not uncommon, a detailed search and reading of the extant literature would suggest that the reliability of dimension scores across exercises has rarely been examined. A similar observation was made by Schmitt (1977) and more recently by Brannick (2008). The paucity of interrater reliability data in the extant literature may be a result of the nature of AC design. That is, the use of postconsensus dimension ratings as the basis for dimension scores obviates the need to assess interrater reliability. However, what limited research there is suggests that assessors rate participants similarly. For instance, Schmitt (1977) found that postdiscussion interrater correlations were all between .74 and .91. In contrast, the prediscussion correlations were in the .60s and .70s.

To obtain additional summary information on the reliability of AC ratings, we turned to AC criterion-related validity meta-analyses to see how many had corrected for unreliability in the predictor scores and what the estimated levels of reliability were. We identified eight meta-analyses that had investigated the criterion-related validity of AC ratings. Some of these meta-analyses (i.e., Arthur et al., 2003; Meriac et al., 2008) corrected for predictor unreliability, but most did not (i.e., Aamodt, 2004; Gaugler et al., 1987; Hardison & Sackett, 2007; Hermelin, Lievens, & Robertson, 2007; Hunter & Hunter, 1984; Schmitt, Gooding, Noe, & Kirsch, 1984). Consistent with the previous point about the lack of data, the common reason for not reporting this information is best summarized by Gaugler et al. (1987), who stated that "the validities were not corrected for predictor unreliability because we were unable to obtain a reasonable estimate of the distribution of reliabilities for the overall assessment center ratings" (p. 495).

Of the two meta-analyses that provided information on the reliability of AC ratings, both used an artifact distribution correction approach. Hence, Arthur et al. (2003) reported a mean interrater reliability of .86 that was based on 37 data points obtained from six articles. In contrast, although they also used an artifact distribution approach, Meriac et al. (2008) used a different approach to estimate the reliability of the AC ratings:

> AC dimensions were corrected based on the mean dimension intercorrelations. For example, if two primary study dimensions (e.g., analysis and judgment) were both coded into one of Arthur et al.'s (2003) dimensions (e.g., problem solving), and the correlation between these two dimensions was provided, the square root of this value was used as input to form an artifact distribution for the AC dimensions. In essence, this represents a type of alternate form reliability in that alternate measures of the same construct (i.e., within each of the [6] AC dimensions) were used to assess reliability. (p. 1046)

Consequently, Meriac et al. reported the following dimension-level reliability estimates: consideration and awareness of others = .80, communication = .86, drive = .86, influencing others = .87, organizing and planning = .87, and problem solving = .91. So these data, in their totality, would suggest that AC ratings are fairly reliable.

Finally, if the AC is an ongoing one, with assessors participating in multiple temporally spaced ACs, then an important question is the extent to which the ratings made by individual assessors change over time. To address this question, Sackett and Hakel (1979) directly compared the correlation matrices generated from the ratings (of 719 participants) made by four assessor teams over 6 months. Their results indicated fairly high levels of consistency in assessors and assessor teams' rating patterns over time.

Validity of AC Ratings

In broad terms, construct validity pertains to an assessment of the extent to which a test is measuring what it purports to measure, how well it does so, and the appropriateness of inferences that are drawn from the test's scores (American Educational Research Association, American Psychological Association, and National Council on Measurement in Education, 1999; Society for Industrial and Organizational Psychology, 2003). Furthermore, there are several evidential bases for demonstrating the construct validity of a test or measure, some of which include but are not limited to the use of content-related, criterion-related, and construct-related validity evidence (Binning & Barrett, 1989; Messick, 1995; see also chap. 13, this volume). In fact, it is often noted that the continued popularity of ACs is due in large part to their strong criterion-related validity evidence and high content-related validity (and fidelity). In contrast, the adequacy of their construct-related validity evidence has been strongly debated and questioned. We review and discuss the research literature and evidence on these issues in the following sections.

Content-Related Validity Evidence

The content-related validity of ACs is commonly established by evidence pertaining to the links between (a) the underlying performance dimensions and job activities, (b) job activities and exercise content, and (c) exercise content and performance dimensions (Thornton & Mueller-Hanson, 2004; see also I. L. Goldstein, Zedeck, & Schneider, 1993). However, a careful reading of widely accepted definitions of content validation—demonstrating how and the extent to which the content of a test adequately represents the domain of interest (Anastasi & Urbina, 1997)—indicates that these three linkages do not fully address content-related validity. So in spite of the long-standing notion that job analysis is the primary mechanism by which the content-related validity of ACs is established, it is erroneous to assume that this is sufficient to establish or ensure the content-related validity of ACs (Sackett, 1987). The domain to be assessed in an AC is the set of dimensions. As such, demonstrations of representativeness pertain to how well the dimensions themselves are articulated and explicated (before linkages to exercises are made); job analysis by itself per se does not speak to the explication and articulation of dimensions.

Furthermore, although there are examples of comprehensive approaches taken to demonstrate all three linkages (e.g., I. L. Goldstein et al., 1993; Haymaker & Grant, 1982; Schmitt & Noe, 1983), the vast majority of published studies on ACs provide very little information that speaks to all of these linkages and none appear to speak to the dimension explication issues (Arthur et al., 2008; Sackett, 1987). At present, we believe that there are low expectations in the published literature for reporting how AC dimensions are explicated. It is common practice for authors to simply list the dimensions assessed and, in some cases, provide a single-sentence definition of each dimension. Without more complete descriptions of how dimensions were developed and what procedures were taken to ensure dimension representativeness, it is difficult to make strong conclusions regarding the content-related validity of ACs, even in the presence of job analysis (Arthur et al., 2008).

Criterion-Related Validity Evidence

In contrast to the paucity of published papers investigating the content-related validity of AC ratings, as previously noted, we identified eight meta-analyses investigating the criterion-related validity of ACs. However, of these, six (i.e., Aamodt, 2004; Gaugler et al., 1987; Hardison & Sackett, 2007; Hermelin et al., 2007; Hunter & Hunter, 1984; Schmitt et al., 1984) were based on the OAR, and two (i.e., Arthur et al., 2003; Meriac et al., 2008) focused on dimension-level ratings. Although using the OAR as the level of analysis is a fairly common practice, Arthur et al. (2003) and Arthur and Villado (2008) have noted problems with it. For example, collapsing dimension ratings to generate an OAR results in a loss of construct-level information. As a result, it is conceptually unclear exactly what an OAR represents, making it difficult if not impossible to interpret comparative validity statements because OARs represent method-level data. Contrary to this common practice, *Principles for the Validation and Use of Personnel Selection Procedures* (Society for Industrial and Organizational Psychology, Inc., 2003) clearly and explicitly states the need to consider constructs when conducting a meta-analysis of predictors. Furthermore, *Principles* also notes that "when studies are cumulated on the basis of common methods (e.g., interviews, biodata) instead of constructs, a different set of interpretational difficulties arise" (p. 30)—namely, to what extent do the predictor methods measure the same predictor construct? Because OARs are aggregates of dimensions, comparing ACs at the level of OARs is almost guaranteed to result in divergent findings because one is, after all, comparing amalgamations of different dimensions. In other words, no two OARs are necessarily going to be the same without holding the dimensions (that comprise the OARs) constant. So from this perspective, it is not surprising that meta-analytic estimates of the criterion-related validity of ACs, operationalized as OARs, have obtained a wide range of estimates, ranging from .43 (Hunter & Hunter, 1984) to .41 (Schmitt et al., 1984), to .37 (Gaugler et al., 1987), to .28 (Hardison & Sackett, 2007; Hermelin et al., 2007), to .22 (Aamodt, 2004). Although these differences could be due to differences in meta-analytic methodology, inclusion criteria, and historical changes in the quality of ACs, we submit that a major potential reason for the range and divergence in AC findings may be the pervasive focus on OARs.

Arthur et al. (2003), on the other hand, collapsed 168 AC dimension labels into an overriding set of six dimensions. Their meta-analysis of these six dimensions resulted in criterion-related validities that ranged from .25 (drive) to .39 (problem solving). In addition, as previously noted, a regression-based composite consisting of four out of the six dimensions accounted for the criterion-related validity of AC ratings and explained more variance in performance (20%) than Gaugler et al. (1987) were able to explain using the OAR (14%).

Another question pertaining to the criterion-related validity of ACs ratings (either dimension-level or OAR) has been the extent to which they contribute incremental validity over other predictor constructs and methods (e.g., see Collins et al., 2003). To this end, using Arthur et al.'s (2003) summary dimensions, Meriac et al. (2008) examined the degree of overlap between the six AC dimensions and cognitive ability and the five-factor model (FFM) personality dimensions. They also investigated the extent to which the AC dimensions explained incremental variance in job performance beyond these individual difference variables. Their results indicated that the six AC dimensions—communication, consideration and awareness of others, drive, influencing others, organizing and planning, and problem solving—are distinguishable from cognitive ability and the FFM personality dimensions. In addition, they also explained a sizable proportion of variance in job performance beyond these individual difference variables. Primary studies (e.g., Dayan, Kasten, & Fox, 2002; Goffin, Rothstein, & Johnston, 1996) that have compared the criterion-related validities of OARs and cognitive ability and conscientiousness have obtained similar results.

Construct-Related Validity Evidence

In sharp contrast to the consensus on the adequacy of AC content-related and criterion-related validity evidence, the status of the construct-related validity of AC ratings is controversial and has been strongly and actively debated. This debate originates from the fact that although ACs are designed to evaluate individuals on specific dimensions across multiple exercises, correlations among ostensibly different dimensions within exercises are typically larger than correlations among the same dimensions across exercises—a finding that is interpreted as a lack of construct-related validity. Furthermore, because ACs display relatively satisfactory levels of content-related and criterion-related validity evidence but allegedly not construct-related validity, this has been referred to as the AC construct-related validity paradox (Arthur et al., 2000; Woehr & Arthur, 2003). It is called a paradox because within the unitarian framework of validity, at a theoretical level, if a measurement tool demonstrates criterion-related and content-related validity evidence, as is widely accepted with ACs, then it should also be expected to demonstrate construct-related validity evidence (Binning & Barrett, 1989). Indeed, concerns with this issue have resulted in recent calls for the "redesign of ACs toward task- or role-based ACs and away from traditional dimension-based ACs"

(Lance, 2008a, p. 84) because AC participant behaviors are "inherently cross-situationally (i.e., cross-exercise) specific, not cross-situationally consistent as was once thought" (Lance, 2008a, p. 84).

Although there are contrarian opinions about their adequacy as explanations for the weak construct-related validity evidence observed for AC ratings (e.g., Lance, 2008a, 2008b), several explanations have been advanced to account for the weak evidence. These include (a) the aforementioned methodological and design-related factors (Arthur et al., 2000; Woehr & Arthur, 2003); (b) the use of espoused versus actual constructs (Arthur et al., 2008) and the misspecification of the target constructs; (c) issues with analytical approaches specifically, the use of post-exercise dimension ratings to represent AC scores, and the misapplication of the multitrait–multimethod design (Arthur et al., 2008; Bowler & Woehr, 2006; Howard, 2008; Lance, Woehr, & Meade, 2007); and (d) differential activation of traits depending on the demands of a particular exercise (Lievens, Chasteen, Day, & Christiansen, 2006).

Of course, a full treatment and resolution of construct-related validity debate is beyond the scope of the present chapter. The reader is, however, strongly encouraged to read the "Why Assessment Centers Do Not Work the Way They Are Supposed To" focal article and commentaries in *Industrial and Organizational Psychology: Perspectives on Science and Practice* (2008). Our interpretation of the gist and tone of the papers in this issue is that the critique of AC construct-related validity and the subsequent call to abandon a dimension-based approach to ACs for a task- or role-based one was not found to be particularly compelling by most of the commentary authors and that for theoretical, conceptual, and empirical reasons, a dimension-based approach will continue to be the primary focus in AC research and practice. Consistent with this, a process analysis of ACs might be an informative approach to investigating and understanding what ACs measure and the boundary conditions under which they may or may not do so effectively—a point that was made over 20 years ago by Zedeck (1986). Furthermore, a focus on dimensions has applied usefulness. As noted by Howard (1997),

> There are a number of practical reasons why assessment center users prefer dimensions based on human attributes rather than tasks. Lists of tasks can be long and generalize to fewer situations. Tasks are an unnatural way to describe people and are less meaningful than attributes for developmental feedback. . . . Task descriptions have little explanatory power . . . psychologists should be studying human qualities, not tasks. (p. 28)

Moreover, organizing ACs around exercises and evaluating participants against exercises rather than dimensions is challenging in applied practice (Mayes, 1997).

Response Distortion and Validity

Because participants in ACs know they are being assessed and that positive evaluations will result in favorable outcomes, issues pertaining to response distortion (i.e., faking) are germane. It is often thought that the realism and length of assessment involved in ACs make it difficult for participants to sustain disingenuous behavior. However, there is little empirical evidence to support or refute such a claim. To our knowledge, AC studies involving explicit instructions to "fake good" in comparison with control instructions have not been conducted.

The few studies examining relationships between self-monitoring and AC performance have yielded mostly weak and statistically nonsignificant correlations. For example, using data from five administrations of an operational assessment center ($n = 92$), Arthur and Tubré (1999) found that self-monitoring was related to 360° performance data collected after the implementation of the assessment center ($r = -.20$ [average of 360° dimension scores] and $-.29$ [single overall effectiveness item]) but was not related to assessment center scores ($r = .05$). Anderson and Thacker (1985) showed a statistically nonsignificant correlation of −.14 between self-monitoring and AC performance in a sample of 45 men applying for computer sales positions while also showing a statistically significant correlation of .45 in a sample of 15 women applying for the same positions. Heon (1989) showed a statistically nonsignificant correlation of .14 between self-monitoring and overall AC performance in a sample of 75 state police officers in a promotional AC, with dimension correlations ranging from .05 to a statistically significant .24 for oral communication (the only dimension yielding a statistically significant correlation) across eight dimensions. In a sample of 191 managers from a developmental AC in a large telecommunications organization, Warech, Smither, Reilly, Millsap, and Reilly (1998) showed statistically nonsignificant correlations between self-monitoring and dimensions related to business competence (−.07) and interpersonal skills (−.01) and between self-monitoring and dimensions related to business competence (−.08) but a statistically significant correlation between self-monitoring and dimensions related to interpersonal skills (.14). Rubin, Bartels, and Bommer (2002) reported a statistically significant correlation of .12 between self-monitoring and candidate peer nominations of leadership emergence in a budget meeting exercise (leaderless group exercise) with a sample of 346 undergraduate business students participating in a developmental AC.

In a similar vein, McFarland, Yun, Harold, Viera, and Moore (2005) showed predominantly weak relationships between impression management tactics and AC ratings in two samples of 30 firefighters participating in promotional ACs (Study 1 average r across 27 correlations = .07, SD = .15; Study 2 average r across 52 correlations = .11, SD = .24). However, their results also suggested relationships might depend on a complex interaction between type of tactic, AC exercise, and AC dimension. In contrast to the predominantly weak relationships for self-monitoring and impression management, König, Melchers, Kleinmann, Richter, and Klehe (2007) showed how the ability to identify the criteria for effective performance in AC exercises is positively related to AC performance (r = .39, N = 95). However, it is likely that such an extraneous influence of ability to identify criteria could be eliminated by making dimensions transparent to all participants (Kleinmann, 1993; Kleinmann et al., 1996). In general, the extent to which AC ratings are unduly influenced by intentional response distortion is an underresearched topic that warrants empirical attention.

COSTS AND PRACTICAL CONSIDERATIONS

The total costs associated with the design, development, and administration of ACs can be quite high. Although specific costs are likely to vary substantially, it is not uncommon for ACs to cost over $2,000 per participant (Spychalski et al., 1997), making them one of the most expensive human resources assessment tools. These costs result from expenses associated with conducting job analyses, identifying and defining dimensions, designing exercises, and training assessors, as well as the expenses associated with compensating the time for multiple assessors to observe, document, categorize, discuss, and rate the performance of participants (as well as generating written reports and conducting feedback sessions in the case of training or developmental ACs). However, these relatively high costs must be weighed against the benefits accrued from using ACs. Consequently, multiple utility analysis studies (e.g., Burke & Frederick, 1986; Cascio & Ramos, 1986; Feltham, 1988b; Goldsmith, 1990; Hoffman & Thornton, 1997; Hogan & Zenke, 1986; Thornton, Murphy, Everest, & Hoffman, 2000; Tziner et al., 1994) have consistently reported favorable utility gains from the use of ACs for a variety of purposes in a variety of domains. For instance, within the specified boundary conditions that they investigated, Burke and Frederick's (1986) utility estimates per selectee ranged from $998 to $5,306 per year (in 1986 dollars). Similarly, Cascio and Ramos's (1986) utility gains over the interview were $2,676 per selectee per year. Finally, Hogan and Zenke (1986) reported that using a pool of 115 applicants for seven school principal positions, the AC had utility gains in excess of $58,000 over the traditional interview.

There are additional nonfiscal benefits to using ACs that may also contribute to justifying their costs. For instance, applicants tend to view ACs as more face valid than (paper-and-pencil) cognitive ability tests and consequently have more favorable reactions to them and the selection process (Macan, Avedon, Paese, & Smith, 1994).

Finally, in light of the relative cost disparities between ACs and other predictors, the practical value of ACs is further enhanced to the extent that they demonstrate incremental validity over these predictors. To this end, although they have typically been at the level of OARs, the results of primary studies (e.g., Dayan et al., 2002; Goffin et al., 1996; H. W. Goldstein, Yusko, Braverman, Smith, & Chung, 1998; Krause, Kersting, Haggestad, & Thornton, 2006) generally indicate that ACs demonstrate incremental validity over commonly used predictor constructs such as cognitive ability and personality (cf. Arthur & Villado, 2008), an effect that was also replicated in Meriac et al.'s (2008) dimension-level meta-analysis.

SUBGROUP DIFFERENCES AND POTENTIAL FOR ADVERSE IMPACT

Efforts to reduce subgroup differences and adverse impact continue to be of interest to I/O psychologists and organizations. A test or other employment-related decision-making tool is said to display adverse impact when decisions made on the basis of the test's scores violate the 80% rule (i.e., the selection ratio in a subgroup of a protected class is less than 80% of the selection ratio of the other subgroup) or the differences between the scores of specified subgroups of the protected class (as per the Civil Rights Act of 1991) are statistically significant (Equal Employment Opportunity Commission, Civil Service Commission, Department of Labor, and Department of Justice, 1978). This definition characterizes *adverse impact* as a legal and administrative term or concept that arises from the psychological phenomena of subgroup differences on measures of psychological constructs or behavioral variables. Thus, at some specified selection ratio, adverse impact is primarily a function of the magnitude of the observed subgroup differences. Consequently, it is possible to have subgroup differences without adverse impact but less likely to have adverse impact without subgroup differences unless it is due to chance selection outcomes resulting from small sample sizes. Therefore, a focus on reducing subgroup differences would seem to be one direct approach to minimizing or eliminating adverse impact.

In the context of such a focus, one suggested approach to reducing subgroup differences (see Arthur and Doverspike, 2005, and also Ployhart and Holtz, 2008, for extensive reviews of various techniques and strategies) is the method-change approach. This approach to reducing subgroup differences focuses on changing the test method with the intention of altering test perceptions and attitudes and also reducing non-job-related reading demands. Thus, this approach posits that observed subgroup differences may partially arise from the mode of testing. Consequently, alternatives to traditional paper-and-pencil multiple-choice tests have included the use of ACs (H. W. Goldstein et al., 1998), performance tests (Chan & Schmitt, 1997), and situational judgment tests (Nguyen, McDaniel, & Whetzel, 2005). This stream of research has resulted in widely professed conclusions to the effect that adverse impact is less of a problem with ACs and work samples than it is for cognitive ability (Cascio & Aguinis, 2005, p. 372; Hoffman & Thornton, 1997; Thornton & Rupp, 2006; cf. Bobko, Roth, & Buster, 2005). However, the results of Dean, Roth, and Bobko's (2008) meta-analysis question this received doctrine. They found an overall Black–White d of −0.52 and a Hispanic–White d of −0.28. These results suggest that subgroup differences involving race, especially Black–White differences, may be larger than previously thought and, subsequently, that ACs may be associated with more adverse impact against Blacks than has typically been characterized in the extant literature.

Dean et al. (2008) also showed a small difference in favor of women over men ($d = 0.19$). Research has also shown negative relationships between age and AC scores (e.g., Burroughs, Rollins, & Hopkins, 1973), but it is thought such observed relationships have been primarily a function of sampling issues such as preassessment selection (Thornton & Byham, 1982). In addition, recent research also suggests that lower AC scores as a function of age do not occur for older workers who are high on certain personality variables such as exhibition and dominance (Krajewski, Goffin, Rothstein, & Johnston, 2007).

It is worth noting a pervasive problem with the method-change approach in general, and especially as it applies to ACs in particular. Because this approach, as practiced, fails to disaggregate predictor constructs and predictor methods, it is unclear whether the observed reductions in subgroup differences or lack thereof are due to changes in the constructs being measured or the methods of assessment (Anderson, Lievens, van Dam, & Born, 2006; H. W. Goldstein, Yusko, & Nicolopoulos, 2001). So, for example, in the case of ACs, because the methods and constructs are confounded, it is unclear whether the posited reduction in subgroup differences is due to the assessment method of ACs or the constructs measured by ACs (Arthur et al., 2003). With this in mind, research has shown that more cognitively loaded dimensions yield larger Black–White differences (H. W. Goldstein et al., 2001) and that interpersonally loaded dimensions yield larger female–male differences (Anderson et al., 2006). In short, any method of assessment can display high or low levels of subgroup differences; it depends on the construct(s) being measured. From a practical perspective, to clearly delineate which predictor will result in a lower level of subgroup differences, we need to know both the method of assessment (e.g., ACs) and the constructs (e.g., communication, consideration and awareness of others, drive, influencing others, organizing and planning, problem solving) assessed by said methods. Thus, although the results of a meta-analysis like that of Dean et al. (2008) are of some informational value, they are limited by the fact that they are conducted at the level of the OAR and are not disaggregated by dimensions. It is not unreasonable to posit that the presence and magnitude of subgroup differences is likely to be a function of the constructs assessed (e.g., see Foldes, Duehr, & Ones, 2008; Hough, Oswald, & Ployhart, 2001). However, we were unable to locate any empirical AC studies that investigated this issue. Any future studies investigating these issues will need to disaggregate the constructs (dimensions) assessed from the method of assessment to permit clear conclusions as to whether observed subgroup differences are dimension or method effects (Arthur & Villado, 2008).

In summary, in spite of (or maybe because of) its history and growing volume of case law (see Thornton and Rupp, 2006, for a list and review of cases), it would seem that there is no a priori favorable or unfavorable legal predisposition toward ACs, and rightfully so. The ability of an AC to withstand legal challenge is primarily a function of the demonstrable job-relatedness of that specific AC. This fact highlights the importance of recognizing the scientific versus legal demands and guidelines: that whereas they may on occasion be related and overlap, this is not always the case. Hence, whereas scientific endeavors stress validity generalization, legal challenges focus on situational specificity.

INTERNATIONAL SCOPE

From the historical account provided in the Historical Background section, it is evident that the science and practice of ACs is international in scope. The rapid growth of ACs in the public and private sectors in the United States sparked by the AT&T MPS was quickly followed by growth in AC use outside the United States. The first International Congress on Assessment Center Methods met in 1973. The Congress facilitates the sharing of knowledge on both research and practice through annual meetings, and it provides the guidelines and ethical considerations for AC operations emulated throughout the world. A clear sense for the international scope of ACs can be seen in the authorship of empirical journal articles appearing in the scholarly literature. As shown in Table 7.1, 75% of empirical journal articles on ACs over the past 10 years (identified via a PsycINFO

TABLE 7.1

Frequency Count of Empirical Journal Articles on Assessment Centers by Country of Lead Author Identified via a PsycINFO (January 1998–August 2008) Search

Country	No. of articles	% of articles
United States	20	25
Germany	14	18
Netherlands	11	14
Belgium	11	14
New Zealand	5	6
United Kingdom	5	6
China	3	4
Switzerland	3	4
Canada	2	3
Ireland	2	3
Israel	2	3
Australia	1	1
France	1	1

search) are from scholars outside the United States. For the most part, the vast majority of this empirical research focuses on issues pertaining to the criterion-related and construct-related validity of AC ratings.

Despite the international scope of AC practice, there is little published empirical research regarding the role cross-cultural factors play in AC use and practice. For instance, recent research has shown that compared with North Americans, Western Europeans are more likely to use presentation, group discussion, and case analysis exercises, and they are more likely to assess dimensions pertaining to drive and consideration of others (Krause & Thornton, 2009). So not only is there limited published research on differences in AC practice around the world, the empirical literature also has not adequately addressed the cross-cultural generalizability of AC scores. This is an especially important issue confronted by multinational companies that must balance applying universal standards for managing human resources and building a unifying organizational culture with sensitivity to local cultural differences. In light of the array of design elements to the AC methodology, although questions regarding cross-cultural generalizability can be targeted at a large number of specific issues, questions regarding the cross-cultural generalizability of exercises and dimensions are perhaps the most fundamental. For instance, it is conceivable that an exercise developed in one culture that effectively evokes behaviors for a specific set of dimensions may not evoke such behaviors in another culture. For example, competitive leaderless group discussions are frequently designed to spark contention among a group of peers; they are zero-sum exercises. Such an exercise may not be as effective in collectivistic cultures that value conformity and consensus seeking.

With regard to dimensions, again it is conceivable that they may be viewed differently across cultures. For example, the expectation in one culture could be that coaching (or leadership in general) involves a large degree of subordinate participation and empowerment, whereas a more autocratic and direct style may be expected in another culture. This is just a snippet of the challenging issues facing many AC practitioners. The notion that a given AC would be generalizable across varying cultures can easily be dismissed, but the manner by which ACs are to be designed, implemented, and evaluated vis-à-vis cross-cultural differences presents a great challenge that should not be ignored. As such, empirical research addressing international and cross-cultural issues surrounding ACs is sorely needed (Briscoe, 1997; Thornton & Rupp, 2006). Along these lines, empirical research presented at the 2008 International Congress on Assessment Center Methods showed significant cultural differences in AC performance across cultures with Anglo-Germanics generally achieving higher scores than Asians (Bernthal & Lanik, 2008). As with issues regarding examinations of adverse impact discussed earlier in this chapter, it is difficult to tease out the extent to which these culture-based performance differences reflect true differences in dimension performance or cultural bias in the exercises. With this in mind, empirical research examining the cross-cultural relevance of specific dimensions (i.e., constructs) is a strong starting point for a stream of research on cross-cultural differences in AC scores (e.g., Gibbons, Rupp, Kim, & Woo, 2006). This could then subsequently be followed by a focus on the cross-cultural generalizability of specific exercise formats, instructions, and the scenarios depicted in exercises.

CONCLUSIONS AND FUTURE DIRECTIONS

The AC has a rich history in the science and practice of identifying managerial talent. The simulation of job performance through behavioral exercises and the triangulation of performance dimensions through multiple exercises and multiple assessors distinguish the AC from other forms of assessment. Substantial meta-analytic criterion-related validity evidence supports the use of ACs for selection and promotion purposes. Utility analyses and evidence of favorable participant reactions also support the use of ACs. However, the AC approach has been criticized for weaknesses in how content-related validity is established and reported. In addition, the evidence surrounding construct-related validity has been strongly and actively debated.

The flexibility of the AC as a method is evident in its use by a wide range of public and private organizations around the world and application to a wide variety of jobs for a number of different purposes. Overall, it appears that the science and practice of ACs is quite vibrant. We hope to see more research in the near future concerning the use of ACs for purposes other than selection and promotion, especially training and development. More research is also warranted regarding the use of technology to improve AC fidelity as well as to streamline the scoring process. In light of the international scope of AC practice, future research needs to address the cross-cultural issues associated with the design, implementation, and evaluation of ACs. We also hope that the critiques concerning the evidence of content-related validity and the recent debates over the construct-related validity spark more research better targeted at understanding the constructs underlying work performance. Such efforts should include a better explication of dimensions and external validation approaches that examine the nomological network surrounding AC dimensions.

Finally, consonant with the centrality of constructs in the study and understanding of behavior, we call for a stronger focus and emphasis on dimension-level data and results. Thus, we recommend that OAR-only research should be discouraged and instead, whenever OAR results and data are reported, dimension-level data and results should be reported as well. This call is motivated by the fact that a focus on OARs makes it difficult if not impossible to meaningfully compare ACs with other predictor constructs such as cognitive ability and conscientiousness because the resultant comparison is one between a method and constructs (Arthur & Villado, 2008). Furthermore, with such comparisons, one is in effect comparing the validity of a single construct (e.g., cognitive ability or conscientiousness) to that of an aggregate of constructs (i.e., multiple AC dimensions). Finally, the use of OARs results in a loss of construct- (dimension-) level information and obscures the fact that some dimensions may be more predictive of performance than others (Arthur et al., 2003). We recognize and acknowledge that for selection and other administrative purposes, a composite score is required to aid in decision making. However, because AC dimensions represent different constructs, the procedures used to generate composite scores can be the same as those typically used to combine scores from multiple predictor batteries such as the use of multiple regression (e.g., see Arthur et al., 2003, Meriac et al., 2008) or other means of assigning weights to different dimensions (e.g., see Arthur, Doverspike, & Barrett, 1996; Bobko et al., 2007).

References

Aamodt, M. G. (2004). *Research in law enforcement selection.* Boca Raton, FL: Brown Walker.

Abraham, J. D., Morrison, J. D., Jr., & Burnett, D. D. (2006). Feedback seeking among developmental assessment center participants. *Journal of Business and Psychology, 20,* 383–394. doi:10.1007/s10869-005-9008-z

American Educational Research Association, American Psychological Association, & National Council on Measurement in Education. (1999). *Standards for educational and psychological testing.* Washington, DC: American Educational Research Association.

American Psychological Association. (1992). Ethical principles of psychologists and code of ethics. *American Psychologist, 47,* 1597–1611. doi:10.1037/0003-066X.47.12.1597

Anastasi, A., & Urbina, S. (1997). *Psychological testing* (7th ed.). Upper Saddle River, NY: Prentice-Hall.

Anderson, N., Lievens, F., van Dam, K., & Born, M. (2006). A construct-driven investigation of gender differences in a leadership-role assessment center. *Journal of Applied Psychology, 91,* 555–566. doi:10.1037/0021-9010.91.3.555

Anderson, L. R., & Thacker, J. (1985). Self-monitoring and sex as related to assessment center ratings and job performance. *Basic and Applied Social Psychology, 6,* 345–361. doi:10.1207/s15324834basp0604_5

Ansbacher, H. L. (1941). German military psychology. *Psychological Bulletin, 38,* 370–392. doi:10.1037/h0056263

Anstey, E. (1977). A 30-year follow-up of the CSSB procedure, with lessons for the future. *Journal of Occupational Psychology, 50,* 149–159.

Arthur, W., Jr., & Benjamin, L. T., Jr. (1999). Psychology applied to business. In A. M. Stec & D. A. Bernstein (Eds.), *Psychology: Fields application* (pp. 98–115). Boston: Houghton Mifflin.

Arthur, W., Jr., Day, E. A., McNelly, T. L., & Edens, P. S. (2003). Meta-analysis of the criterion-related validity of assessment center dimensions. *Personnel Psychology, 56,* 125–154. doi:10.1111/j.1744-6570.2003.tb00146.x

Arthur, W., Jr., Day, E. A., & Woehr, D. J. (2008). Mend it, don't end it: An alternate view of assessment center construct-related validity evidence. *Industrial and Organizational Psychology: Perspectives on Science and Practice, 1,* 105–111. doi:10.1111/j.1754-9434.2007.00019.x

Arthur, W., Jr., & Doverspike, D. (2005). Achieving diversity and reducing discrimination in the workplace through human resource management practices: Implications of research and theory for staffing, training, and rewarding performance. In R. L. Dipboye & A. Colella (Eds.), *Discrimination at work: The psychological and organizational bases* (pp. 305–327). San Francisco: Jossey-Bass.

Arthur, W., Jr., Doverspike, D., & Barrett, G. V. (1996). Development of a job analysis-based procedure for weighting and combining content-related tests into a single test battery score. *Personnel Psychology, 49,* 971–985. doi:10.1111/j.1744-6570.1996.tb02457.x

Arthur, W., Jr., & Tubré, T. C. (1999, April). The assessment center construct-related validity paradox: A case of construct misspecification? In M. A. Quiñones (Chair), *Assessment centers, 21st century: New issues and new answers to old problems.* Symposium presented at the 14th Annual Conference of the Society for Industrial and Organizational Psychology, Atlanta, GA.

Arthur, W., Jr., & Villado, A. J. (2008). The importance of distinguishing between constructs and methods when comparing predictors in personnel selection research and practice. *Journal of Applied Psychology, 93,* 435–442. doi:10.1037/0021-9010.93.2.435

Arthur, W., Jr., Woehr, D. J., & Maldegen, R. (2000). Convergent and discriminant validity of assessment center dimensions: An empirical re-examination of the assessment center construct-related validity paradox. *Journal of Management, 26,* 813–835. doi:10.1016/S0149-2063(00)00057-X

Assessment Staff, OSS. (1948). *Assessment of men.* New York: Rinehart.

Bell, S. T., & Arthur, W., Jr. (2008). Feedback acceptance in developmental assessment centers: The role of feedback message, participant personality, and affective response to the feedback session. *Journal of Organizational Behavior, 29,* 681–703. doi:10.1002/job.525

Bernthal, P., & Lanik, M. (2008, September). *Cross-cultural comparisons of assessment center performance.* Presentation at the 34th International Congress on the Assessment Center Method, Washington, DC.

Binning, J. F., & Barrett, G. V. (1989). Validity of personnel decisions: A conceptual analysis of the inferential and evidential bases. *Journal of Applied Psychology, 74,* 478–494. doi:10.1037/0021-9010.74.3.478

Bobko, P., Roth, P. L., & Buster, M. A. (2005). Work sample tests and expected reduction in adverse impact: A cautionary note. *International Journal of Selection and Assessment, 13,* 1–10. doi:10.1111/j.0965-075X.2005.00295.x

Bobko, P., Roth, P. L., & Buster, M. A. (2007). The usefulness of unit weights in creating composite scores: A literature review, application of content validity, and meta-analysis. *Organizational Research Methods, 10,* 689–709. doi:10.1177/1094428106294734

Bowler, M. C., & Woehr, D. J. (2006). A meta-analytic evaluation of the impact of dimension and exercise factors on assessment center ratings. *Journal of Applied Psychology, 91,* 1114–1124. doi:10.1037/0021-9010.91.5.1114

Brannick, M. T. (2008). Back to basics of test construction and scoring. *Industrial and Organizational Psychology: Perspectives on Science and Practice, 1,* 131–133. doi:10.1111/j.1754-9434.2007.00025.x

Bray, D. W. (1982). The assessment center and the study of lives. *American Psychologist, 37,* 180–189. doi:10.1037/0003-066X.37.2.180

Bray, D. W., & Grant, D. L. (1966). The assessment center in the measurement of potential for business management. *Psychological Monographs, 80* (17, Whole No. 625), 1–27.

Briscoe, D. (1997). Assessment centers: Cross-cultural and cross-national issues. *Journal of Social Behavior and Personality, 12,* 261–270.

Burke, M. J., & Frederick, J. T. (1986). A comparison of economic utility estimates for alternative SDy estimation procedures. *Journal of Applied Psychology, 71,* 334–339. doi:10.1037/0021-9010.71.2.334

Burroughs, W. A., Rollins, J. B., & Hopkins, J. J. (1973). The effect of age, departmental experience, and prior rater experience on performance in assessment center exercises. *Academy of Management Journal, 16,* 335–339. doi:10.2307/255335

Bycio, P., Alvares, K. M., & Hahn, J. (1987). Situation specificity in assessment center ratings: A confirmatory analysis. *Journal of Applied Psychology, 72,* 463–474. doi:10.1037/0021-9010.72.3.463

Caldwell, C., Thornton, G. C., III, & Gruys, M. L. (2003). Ten classic assessment center errors: Challenges to selection validity. *Public Personnel Management, 23,* 73–88.

Cascio, W. F., & Aguinis, H. (2005). *Applied psychology in human resource management* (6th ed.). Upper Saddle River, NJ: Prentice Hall.

Cascio, W. F., & Ramos, R. A. (1986). Development and application of a new method for assessing job performance in behavioral/economic terms. *Journal of Applied Psychology, 71,* 20–28. doi:10.1037/0021-9010.71.1.20

Chan, D., & Schmitt, N. (1997). Video-based versus paper-and-pencil method of assessment in situational judgment tests: Subgroup differences in test performance and face validity perceptions. *Journal of Applied Psychology, 82,* 143–159. doi:10.1037/0021-9010.82.1.143

Chen, H.-C. (2006). Assessment center: A critical mechanism for assessing HRD effectiveness and accountability. *Advances in Developing Human Resources, 8,* 247–264. doi:10.1177/1523422305286155

Chen, H.-C., & Naquin, S. S. (2006). An integrative model of competency development, training design, assessment center, and multi-rater assessment. *Advances in Developing Human Resources, 8,* 265–282. doi:10.1177/1523422305286156

Civil Rights Act of 1991, Pub. L. No. 102-166, 105 Stat. 1071 (1991).

Collins, J. M., Schmidt, F. L., Sanchez-Ku, M., Thomas, L., McDaniel, M. A., & Le, H. (2003). Can basic individual differences shed light on the construct meaning of assessment center evaluations? *International Journal of Selection and Assessment, 11,* 17–29. doi:10.1111/1468-2389.00223

Connelly, B. S., Ones, D. S., Ramesh, A., & Goff, M. (2008). A pragmatic view of assessment center exercises and dimensions. *Industrial and Organizational Psychology: Perspectives on Science and Practice, 1,* 121–124. doi:10.1111/j.1754-9434.2007.00022.x

Dayan, K., Kasten, R., & Fox, S. (2002). Entry-level police candidate assessment center: An efficient tool or a hammer to kill a fly? *Personnel Psychology, 55,* 827–849. doi:10.1111/j.1744-6570.2002.tb00131.x

Dean, M. A., Roth, P. L., & Bobko, P. (2008). Ethnic and gender subgroup differences in assessment center ratings: A meta-analysis. *Journal of Applied Psychology, 93,* 685–691. doi:10.1037/0021-9010.93.3.685

Dhanju, N. (2007). *The perceived effectiveness of assessment centers for successful and unsuccessful participants for the selection of team leaders in an Indian call center: A case study.* Unpublished doctoral dissertation, University of Minnesota, Minneapolis.

Donahue, L. M., Truxillo, D. M., Cornwell, J. M., & Gerrity, M. J. (1997). Assessment center construct validity and behavioral checklists: Some additional findings. *Journal of Social Behavior and Personality, 12,* 85–108.

Dunnette, M. D. (1971). The assessment of managerial talent. In P. McReynolds (Ed.), *Advances in psychological assessment* (Vol. 2, pp. 79–108). Palo Alto, CA: Science and Behavior Books.

Equal Employment Opportunity Commission, Civil Service Commission, Department of Labor, and Department of Justice. (1978). Uniform guidelines on employee selection procedures. *Federal Register, 43,* 38295–38309.

Farago, L. (1942). *German psychological warfare.* New York: G. P. Putnam's Sons.

Feltham, R. (1988a). Assessment centre decision making: Judgmental vs. mechanical. *Journal of Occupational Psychology, 61,* 237–241.

Feltham, R. (1988b). Validity of a police assessment centre: A 1-19-year follow-up. *Journal of Occupational Psychology, 61,* 129–144.

Foldes, H., Duehr, E. E., & Ones, D. S. (2008). Group differences in personality: Meta-analyses comparing five U.S. racial groups. *Personnel Psychology, 61,* 579–616. doi:10.1111/j.1744-6570.2008.00123.x

Gaugler, B. B., Rosenthal, D. B., Thornton, G. C., III, & Bentson, B. (1987). Meta-analysis of assessment center validity. *Journal of Applied Psychology, 72,* 493–511. doi:10.1037/0021-9010.72.3.493

Gaugler, B. B., & Thornton, G. C., III. (1989). Number of assessment center dimensions as a determinant of assessor generalizability of the assessment center ratings. *Journal of Applied Psychology, 74,* 611–618. doi:10.1037/0021-9010.74.4.611

Gibbons, A. M., Rupp, D. E., Kim, M., & Woo, S. E. (2006). Perceptions of managerial performance dimensions in Korea. *The Psychologist Manager Journal, 9,* 125–143. doi:10.1207/s15503461tpmj0902_5

Gilbert, P. J. (1981). An investigation of clinical and mechanical combination of assessment center data. *Journal of Assessment Center Technology, 4,* 1–10.

Goffin, R. D., Rothstein, M. G., & Johnston, N. G. (1996). Personality testing and the assessment center: Incremental validity for managerial selection. *Journal of Applied Psychology, 81,* 746–756. doi:10.1037/0021-9010.81.6.746

Goldsmith, R. F. (1990). Utility analysis and its application to the study of cost effectiveness of the assessment center method. In K. R. Murphy & F. E. Saal (Eds.), *Psychology in organizations: Integrating science and practice* (pp. 92–110). Hillsdale, NJ: LEA.

Goldstein, H. W., Yusko, K. P., Braverman, E. P., Smith, D. B., & Chung, B. (1998). The role of cognitive ability in the subgroup differences and incremental validity of assessment center exercises. *Personnel Psychology, 51,* 357–374. doi:10.1111/j.1744-6570.1998.tb00729.x

Goldstein, H. W., Yusko, K. P., & Nicolopoulos, V. (2001). Exploring Black-White subgroup differences of managerial competencies. *Personnel Psychology, 54,* 783–807. doi:10.1111/j.1744-6570.2001.tb00232.x

Goldstein, I. L., Zedeck, S., & Schneider, B. (1993). An exploration of the job analysis-content validity process. In N. Schmitt & W. C. Borman (Eds.), *Personnel selection in organizations* (pp. 3–34). San Francisco: Jossey-Bass.

Hardison, C. M., & Sackett, P. R. (2007). Kriterienbezogene Validität des Assessment Centers: Lebendig und wohlauf? [Assessment center criterion-related validity: Alive and well?]. In H. Schuler (Ed.), *Assessment Center zur Potenzialanalyse* (pp. 192–202). Göttingen, Germany: Hogrefe.

Harris, H. (1949). *The group approach to leadership testing.* London: Routledge and Paul.

Haymaker, J. C., & Grant, D. L. (1982). Development of a model for content validation of assessment centers. *Journal of Assessment Center Technology, 5,* 1–7.

Heon, S. M. (1989). *Self-monitoring and cognitive complexity as related to assessment center performance.* Unpublished doctoral dissertation, George Washington University, Washington, DC.

Hermelin, E., Lievens, F., & Robertson, I. T. (2007). The validity of assessment centres for the prediction of supervisory performance ratings: A meta-analysis. *International Journal of Selection and Assessment, 15,* 405–411. doi:10.1111/j.1468-2389.2007.00399.x

Hoffman, C. C., & Thornton, G. C., III. (1997). Examining selection utility where competing predictors differ in adverse impact. *Personnel Psychology, 50,* 455–470. doi:10.1111/j.1744-6570.1997.tb00916.x

Hogan, J., & Zenke, L. L. (1986). Dollar-value utility of alternative procedures for selecting school principals. *Educational and Psychological Measurement, 46,* 935–945. doi:10.1177/0013164486046000413

Hough, L. M., Oswald, F. L., & Ployhart, R. E. (2001). Determinants, detection and amelioration of adverse impact in personnel selection procedures: Issues, evidence and lessons learned. *International Journal of Selection and Assessment, 9,* 152–194. doi:10.1111/1468-2389.00171

Howard, A. (1997). A reassessment of assessment centers: Challenges for the 21st century. *Journal of Social Behavior and Personality, 12,* 13–52.

Howard, A. (2008). Making assessment centers work the way they are supposed to. *Industrial and Organizational Psychology: Perspectives on Science and Practice, 1,* 98–104. doi:10.1111/j.1754-9434.2007.00018.x

Howard, A., & Bray, D. W. (1988). *Managerial lives in transition: Advancing age and changing times.* New York: Guilford Press.

Hunter, J. E., & Hunter, R. F. (1984). Validity and utility of alternative predictors of job performance. *Psychological Bulletin, 96,* 72–98. doi:10.1037/0033-2909.96.1.72

Industrial and Organizational Psychology: Perspectives on Science and Practice. (2008). *1*(1).

International Task Force on Assessment Center Guidelines. (2000). Guidelines and ethical considerations for assessment center operations. *Public Personnel Management, 29,* 315–331.

Jackson, D. J. R., Atkins, S. G., Fletcher, R. B., & Stillman, J. A. (2005). Frame of reference training for assessment centers: Effects on interrater reliability when rating behaviors and ability traits. *Public Personnel Management, 34,* 17–30.

Jackson, D. J. R., Stillman, J. A., Burke, S., & Englert, P. (2007). Self versus assessor ratings and their classification in assessment centres: Profiling the self-rater. *New Zealand Journal of Psychology, 36,* 93–99.

Jennings, H. H. (1949). Military use of sociometric and situation tests in Great Britain, France, Germany, and the United States. *Sociometry, 12,* 191–201. doi:10.2307/2785386

Joiner, D. A. (2002). Assessment centers: What's new? *Public Personnel Management, 31,* 179–185.

Jones, R. G., & Whitmore, M. D. (1995). Evaluating developmental assessment centers as interventions. *Personnel Psychology, 48,* 377–388. doi:10.1111/j.1744-6570.1995.tb01762.x

Kleinmann, M. (1993). Are rating dimensions in assessment centers transparent to participants? Consequences for criterion and construct validity. *Journal of Applied Psychology, 78,* 988–993. doi:10.1037/0021-9010.78.6.988

Kleinmann, M., Kuptsch, C., & Köller, O. (1996). Transparency: A necessary requirement for the construct validity of assessment centres. *Applied Psychology: An International Review, 45,* 67–84. doi:10.1111/j.1464-0597.1996.tb00849.x

Klimoski, R., & Brickner, M. (1987). Why do assessment centers work? The puzzle of assessment center validity. *Personnel Psychology, 40,* 243–260. doi:10.1111/j.1744-6570.1987.tb00603.x

Kolk, N. J., Born, M. P., & Van der Flier, H. (2003). The transparent assessment center: The effect of revealing dimensions to applicants. *Applied Psychology: An International Review, 52,* 648–668. doi:10.1111/1464-0597.00156

König, C. J., Melchers, K. G., Kleinmann, M., Richter, G. M., & Klehe, U.-C. (2007). Candidates' ability to identify criteria in nontransparent selection procedures: Evidence from an assessment center and a structured interview. *International Journal of Selection and Assessment, 15,* 283–292. doi:10.1111/j.1468-2389.2007.00388.x

Krajewski, H. T., Goffin, R. D., Rothstein, M. G., & Johnston, N. G. (2007). Is personality related to assessment center performance? That depends on how old you are. *Journal of Business and Psychology, 22,* 21–33. doi:10.1007/s10869-007-9043-z

Krause, D. E., Kersting, M., Haggestad, E. D., & Thornton, G. C., III. (2006). Incremental validity of assessment center ratings over cognitive ability tests: A study at the executive management level. *International Journal of Selection and Assessment, 14,* 360–371.

Krause, D. E., & Thornton, G. C., III. (2009). A cross-cultural look at assessment center practices: Survey results from Western Europe and North America. *Applied Psychology: An International Review, 58,* 557–585.

Lance, C. E. (2008a). Why assessment centers do not work the way they are supposed to. *Industrial and Organiza-*

tional Psychology: Perspectives on Science and Practice, 1, 84–97. doi:10.1111/j.1754-9434.2007.00017.x

Lance, C. E. (2008b). Where have we been, how did we get there, and where shall we go? *Industrial and Organizational Psychology: Perspectives on Science and Practice, 1,* 140–146. doi:10.1111/j.1754-9434.2007.00028.x

Lance, C. E., Woehr, D. J., & Meade, A. W. (2007). Case study: A Monte Carlo investigation of assessment center construct validity models. *Organizational Research Methods, 10,* 430–448. doi:10.1177/1094428106289395

Lievens, F. (1998). Factors which improve the construct validity of assessment centers: A review. *International Journal of Selection and Assessment, 6,* 141–152. doi:10.1111/1468-2389.00085

Lievens, F. (2001). Assessor training strategies and their effects on accuracy, interrater reliability, and discriminant validity. *Journal of Applied Psychology, 86,* 255–264. doi:10.1037/0021-9010.86.2.255

Lievens, F., Chasteen, C. S., Day, E. A., & Christiansen, N. D. (2006). Large-scale investigation of the role of trait activation theory for understanding assessment center convergent and discriminant validity. *Journal of Applied Psychology, 91,* 247–258. doi:10.1037/0021-9010.91.2.247

Lievens, F., & Conway, J. M. (2001). Dimension and exercise variance in assessment center scores: A large-scale evaluation of multitrait-multimethod studies. *Journal of Applied Psychology, 86,* 1202–1222. doi:10.1037/0021-9010.86.6.1202

Macan, T. H., Avedon, M. J., Paese, M., & Smith, D. E. (1994). The effects of applicants' reactions to cognitive ability tests and an assessment center. *Personnel Psychology, 47,* 715–738. doi:10.1111/j.1744-6570.1994.tb01573.x

Mayes, B. T. (1997). Insights into the history and future of assessment centers: An interview with Dr. Douglas W. Bray and Dr. William Byham. *Journal of Social Behavior and Personality, 12,* 3–12.

McFarland, L. A., Yun, G., Harold, C. M., Viera, L., Jr., & Moore, L. G. (2005). An examination of impression management use and effectiveness across assessment center exercises: The role of competency demands. *Personnel Psychology, 58,* 949–980. doi:10.1111/j.1744-6570.2005.00374.x

Melancon, S. C., & Williams, M. S. (2006). Competency-based assessment center design: A case study. *Advances in Developing Human Resources, 8,* 283–314. doi:10.1177/1523422305286157

Meriac, J. P., Hoffman, B. J., Woehr, D. J., & Fleisher, M. S. (2008). Further evidence for the validity of assessment center dimensions: A meta-analysis of the incremental criterion-related validity of dimension ratings. *Journal of Applied Psychology, 93,* 1042–1052. doi:10.1037/0021-9010.93.5.1042

Messick, S. J. (1995). The validity of psychological assessment: Validation of inferences from persons' responses and performances as scientific inquiry into score meaning. *American Psychologist, 50,* 741–749. doi:10.1037/0003-066X.50.9.741

Morris, B. S. (1949). Officer selection in the British Army, 1942-1945. *Occupational Psychology, 23,* 219–234.

Murray, H. A. (1938). *Explorations in personality.* New York: Oxford University Press.

Nguyen, N. T., McDaniel, M. A., & Whetzel, D. (2005, April). *Subgroup differences in situational judgment test performance: A meta-analysis.* Paper presented at the 20th Annual Conference of the Society for Industrial and Organizational Psychology, Los Angeles, CA.

Noonan, L. E., & Sulsky, L. M. (2001). Impact of frame-of-reference and behavioral observation training on alternative training effectiveness criteria in a Canadian military sample. *Human Performance, 14,* 3–26. doi:10.1207/S15327043HUP1401_02

Ployhart, R. E., & Holtz, B. C. (2008). The diversity-validity dilemma: Strategies for reducing racioethnic and sex subgroup differences and adverse impact in selection. *Personnel Psychology, 61,* 153–172. doi:10.1111/j.1744-6570.2008.00109.x

Pynes, J. E., & Bernardin, J. H. (1992). Mechanical versus consensus-derived assessment center ratings: A comparison of job performance validities. *Public Personnel Management, 21,* 17–28.

Reilly, R. R., Henry, S., & Smither, J. W. (1990). An examination of the effects of using behavior checklists on the construct validity of assessment center dimensions. *Personnel Psychology, 43,* 71–84. doi:10.1111/j.1744-6570.1990.tb02006.x

Robie, C., Adams, K. A., Osburn, H. G., Morris, M. A., & Etchegaray, J. M. (2000). Effects of the rating process on the construct validity of assessment center dimension evaluations. *Human Performance, 13,* 355–370. doi:10.1207/S15327043HUP1304_2

Roch, S. G. (2006). Discussion and consensus in rater groups: Implications for behavioral and rating accuracy. *Human Performance, 19,* 91–115. doi:10.1207/s15327043hup1902_1

Roch, S. G. (2007). Why convene rater teams: An investigation of the benefits of anticipated discussion, consensus, and rater motivation. *Organizational Behavior and Human Decision Processes, 104,* 14–29. doi:10.1016/j.obhdp.2006.08.003

Roth, P. L., Bobko, P., & McFarland, L. A. (2005). A meta-analysis of work sample test validity: Updating and integrating some classic literature. *Personnel Psychology, 58,* 1009–1037. doi:10.1111/j.1744-6570.2005.00714.x

Rowe, F. A., & Mauer, K. A. (1991). Career guidance, career assessment, and consultancy. *Journal of Career Development, 17,* 223–233.

Rubin, R. S., Bartels, L. K., & Bommer, W. H. (2002). Are leaders smarter or do they just seem that way? Exploring perceived intellectual competence and leadership emergence. *Social Behavior and Personality, 30,* 105–118. doi:10.2224/sbp.2002.30.2.105

Rupp, D. E., Gibbons, A. M., Baldwin, A. M., Snyder, L. A., Spain, S. M., Woo, S. E., et al. (2006). An initial validation of developmental assessment centers as accurate assessments and effective training interventions. *The Psychologist Manager Journal, 9,* 171–200. doi:10.1207/s15503461tpmj0902_7

Russell, C. (1985). Individual decision processes in an assessment center. *Journal of Applied Psychology, 70,* 737–746. doi:10.1037/0021-9010.70.4.737

Sackett, P. R. (1987). Assessment centers and content validity: Some neglected issues. *Personnel Psychology, 40,* 13–25. doi:10.1111/j.1744-6570.1987.tb02374.x

Sackett, P. R., & Dreher, G. F. (1982). Constructs and assessment center dimensions: Some troubling empirical findings. *Journal of Applied Psychology, 67,* 401–410. doi:10.1037/0021-9010.67.4.401

Sackett, P. R., & Hakel, M. D. (1979). Temporal stability and individual differences in using assessment center information from overall ratings. *Organizational Behavior and Human Performance, 23,* 120–137. doi:10.1016/0030-5073(79)90051-5

Schleicher, D. J., & Day, D. V. (1998). A cognitive evaluation of frame-of-reference rater training: Content and process issues. *Organizational Behavior and Human Decision Processes, 73,* 76–101. doi:10.1006/obhd.1998.2751

Schleicher, D. J., Day, C. V., Mayes, B. T., & Riggio, R. E. (2002). A new frame for frame-of-reference training: Enhancing the construct validity of assessment centers. *Journal of Applied Psychology, 87,* 735–746. doi:10.1037/0021-9010.87.4.735

Schmitt, N. (1977). Interrater agreement in dimensionality and combination of assessment center judgments. *Journal of Applied Psychology, 62,* 171–176. doi:10.1037/0021-9010.62.2.171

Schmitt, N., Gooding, R. Z., Noe, R. A., & Kirsch, M. (1984). Meta-analysis of validity studies published between 1964 and 1982 and the investigation of study characteristics. *Personnel Psychology, 37,* 407–422. doi:10.1111/j.1744-6570.1984.tb00519.x

Schmitt, N., & Noe, R. A. (1983). Demonstration of content validity: Assessment center example. *Journal of Assessment Center Technology, 6,* 5–11.

Schmitt, N., Schneider, J. R., & Cohen, S. A. (1990). Factors affecting validity of a regionally administered assessment center. *Personnel Psychology, 43,* 1–12. doi:10.1111/j.1744-6570.1990.tb02003.x

Silvester, J., & Dykes, C. (2007). Selecting political candidates: A longitudinal study of assessment centre performance and political success in the 2005 UK General Election. *Journal of Occupational and Organizational Psychology, 80,* 11–25. doi:10.1348/096317906X156287

Society for Industrial and Organizational Psychology, Inc. (2003). *Principles for the validation and use of personnel selection procedures* (4th ed.). Bowling Green, OH: SIOP.

Spychalski, A. C., Quiñones, M. A., Gaugler, B. B., & Pohley, K. (1997). A survey of assessment center practices in organizations in the United States. *Personnel Psychology, 50,* 71–90. doi:10.1111/j.1744-6570.1997.tb00901.x

Thornton, G. C., III, & Byham, W. C. (1982). *Assessment centers and managerial performance.* San Diego, CA: Academic Press.

Thornton, G. C., III, & Mueller-Hanson, R. A. (2004). *Developing organizational simulations: A guide for practitioners and students.* Mahwah, NJ: Erlbaum.

Thornton, G. C., III, Murphy, K. R., Everest, T. M., & Hoffman, C. C. (2000). Higher cost, lower validity, and higher utility: Comparing utilities of two tests that differ in validity, costs, and selectivity. *International Journal of Assessment and Selection, 8,* 61–75. doi:10.1111/1468-2389.00134

Thornton, G. C., III, & Rupp, D. E. (2006). *Assessment centers in human resource management: Strategies for prediction, diagnosis, and development.* Mahwah, NJ: LEA.

Tillema, H. H. (1998). Assessment of potential from assessment centers to development centers. *International Journal of Selection and Assessment, 6,* 185–191. doi:10.1111/1468-2389.00088

Truxillo, L. M., Donahue, L. M., & Kuang, D. (2004). Work samples, performance tests, and competency testing. In J. C. Thomas & M. Hersen (Eds.), *Comprehensive handbook of psychological assessment: Vol. 4. Industrial and organizational assessment* (pp. 345–370). Hoboken, NJ: Wiley.

Tziner, A., Meir, E. I., Dahan, M., & Birati, A. (1994). An investigation of the predictive validity and economic utility of the assessment center for the high-management level. *Canadian Journal of Behavioural Science, 26,* 228–245. doi:10.1037/0008-400X.26.2.228

Waldman, D. A., & Korbar, T. (2004). Student assessment center performance in the prediction of early career success. *Academy of Management Learning & Education, 3,* 151–167.

Warech, M. A., Smither, J. W., Reilly, R. R., Millsap, R. E., & Reilly, S. P. (1998). Self-monitoring and 360-degree ratings. *The Leadership Quarterly, 9,* 449–473. doi:10.1016/S1048-9843(98)90011-X

Wernimont, P. F., & Campbell, J. P. (1968). Signs, samples, and criteria. *Journal of Applied Psychology, 52,* 372–376. doi:10.1037/h0026244

Woehr, D. J., & Arthur, W., Jr. (2003). The construct-related validity of assessment center ratings: A review and meta-analysis of the role of methodological factors. *Journal of Management, 29,* 231–258. doi:10.1177/014920630302900206

Woehr, D. J., & Huffcutt, A. I. (1994). Rater training for performance appraisal: A meta-analytic review. *Journal of Occupational and Organizational Psychology, 67,* 189–205.

Wollowick, H. B., & McNamara, W. J. (1969). Relationship of the components of an assessment center to management success. *Journal of Applied Psychology, 53,* 348–352. doi:10.1037/h0028102

Zedeck, S. (1986). A process analysis of the assessment center method. In B. Staw & L. Cummings (Eds.), *Research in organizational behavior* (Vol. 8, pp. 259–296). Greenwich, CT: JAI Press.

CHAPTER 8

SITUATIONAL JUDGMENT TESTS: A CRITICAL REVIEW AND AGENDA FOR THE FUTURE

Robert E. Ployhart and William I. MacKenzie Jr.

Situational judgment tests (SJTs) are measurement methods that present respondents with work-related situations and ask them how they would or should handle the situations. SJTs have become very popular among industrial and organizational (I/O) psychologists in the last 20 years. Much of their popularity has been attributed to the fact that SJTs exhibit moderately strong criterion-related validities but are more face valid and tend to exhibit smaller racial and sex subgroup differences. It is important to recognize that at least to date, they are generally considered to be measurement methods, which means they do not measure a homogeneous construct but rather can be developed to measure several different types of constructs (often simultaneously). In this sense, SJTs are very much multidimensional measurement methods.

The purpose of this chapter is to critically review and evaluate the theoretical basis of SJTs and their use in practice. We briefly review the historical antecedents of SJTs, offer a selective review of key scholarly research, and discuss practical issues. One important element of our review is an examination of SJT validity in terms of criterion-related, content, and construct validity. We conclude by emphasizing that SJT scholarship must move beyond criterion-related issues and meta-analytic methods if we are to understand this very useful, if not enigmatic, predictor.

HISTORICAL OVERVIEW AND SUMMARY OF SITUATIONAL JUDGMENT TESTS

SJTs have increased in popularity and use over the past 2 decades. According to McDaniel, Morgeson, Finnegan, Campion, and Braverman (2001), the origin of "modern" SJTs may be traced back to the 1920s, but tests designed to assess situational judgment have been around for quite some time. Early examples of United States Civil Service exams included items designed to assess situational judgment and date as far back as 1873 (DuBois, 1970). These early exams included open-ended questions that presented applicants with a situation and asked them to respond with how they would react in the described situation.

The George Washington Social Intelligence Test is considered one of the earliest known examples of a widely used SJT that provided subjects with closed-ended (multiple choice) response options (McDaniel et al., 2001; Moss, 1926). Subjects were given a situation and asked to choose a solution from a list of several possible alternatives. The use of SJTs continued through World War II, when Army psychologists administered SJTs to assess the judgment of soldiers (Northrop, 1989). The 1940s saw a surge in the use of SJTs to assess individual levels of supervisory potential (Cardall, 1942; File, 1945). SJTs were used in the late 1950s and through the 1960s to predict managerial potential

We thank Sheldon Zedeck for his helpful comments and suggestions on this chapter.

of employees for corporations (Bruce, 1965; Bruce & Learner, 1958; Greenberg, 1963; Kirkpatrick & Planty, 1960). Most of these early SJTs were criticized because of their high correlation with cognitive ability (e.g., File & Remmers, 1971; Millard, 1952; Taylor, 1949a; Taylor, 1949b; Thorndike, 1941; Thorndike & Stein, 1937), and they were viewed as being factorially complex (e.g., Northrop, 1989). The 1990s saw a reemergence of research on SJTs after Motowidlo, Dunnette, and Carter (1990) "reintroduced" SJTs as a low fidelity simulation.

Research increased geometrically after publication of the Motowidlo et al. (1990) article, with most research focusing on two core issues. The first was establishment of the criterion-related validity of SJTs and their incremental validity over other commonly used predictors (e.g., cognitive ability; Clevenger, Pereira, Wiechmann, Schmitt, & Harvey, 2001). The second was examination of how differences in response instructions could influence SJT criterion-related and construct validity (McDaniel & Nguyen, 2001). Only recently have there been theoretical attempts to understand *what* SJTs measure and *why* they may be related to job performance (Motowidlo, Hooper, & Jackson, 2006b). There have been several excellent review articles published on SJTs (Chan & Schmitt, 2005; Lievens, Peeters, & Schollaert, 2008; McDaniel & Nguyen, 2001; Schmitt & Chan, 2006), and an edited book tried to promote greater theoretical understanding (Weekley & Ployhart, 2006).

SJTs are generally considered to be multidimensional measurement methods (Chan & Schmitt, 1997). In some ways, it is difficult to define or operationalize SJTs because they share many key elements with other popular predictor methods such as interviews, certain assessment center exercises (e.g., role plays), and simulations (Ployhart, Schneider, & Schmitt, 2006). SJTs may be administered in a variety of formats that include paper, video, orally, and the Internet/computer. Therefore, we first describe the typical SJT structure, then compare/contrast this structure with other predictors, and conclude with identifying the unique features of SJTs.

The defining feature of an SJT is that it presents respondents with realistic work situations and then requires these respondents to pick the best/worst (or most/least likely) behavioral response to address the situation. Thus, SJTs are by definition context-bound, although these contexts may be described fairly generically to apply to different firms. The following is a sample SJT item that could be used to hire entry level managers:

> Imagine you are in charge of a project team with five members from different functional areas. The team members do not get along and several do not see the value in this project. The bickering and fighting are starting to jeopardize the quality of the project.
>
> a. Inform the team members that if they don't stop fighting, they will be kicked off the team.
> b. Try to instill greater commitment to the project by emphasizing the team's goals.
> c. Go to each of the team member's supervisors to inform him/her of the poor behavior.
> d. Wait just a bit longer and see if the fighting stops.
>
> Which is the most effective option?
> Which is the least effective option?

Notice that in this example there are multiple goals and competing goals that must be balanced. Several potentially plausible response options are provided, and these options reflect behaviors that may be effective or ineffective. The respondent must exercise his or her judgment and choose what he or she believes is the appropriate response.

At this point it may be apparent that SJTs have many similarities to other commonly used predictor methods. In particular, SJTs are very similar to situational interviews, with the main difference being that SJTs provide a more structured response format (i.e., multiple choice). SJTs can be similar to computer-based simulations. For example, the sample item shown here could be presented in a video-based format so that respondents watch a video of the team's interactions and then must indicate which options are most/least effective. Therefore, the SJT would be less interactive than the typical computer-based simulation. If the instructions ask about what one *should* do in a situation, the SJT functions very much like a maximum-performance test because it focuses on ability and knowledge; if the instructions ask about what one *would* do in a situation, the SJT functions more like a typical performance test (McDaniel, Hartman, Whetzel, & Grubb, 2007).

Thus, because the boundaries or defining features of SJTs are fairly amorphous, it has been somewhat difficult to define exactly what makes a predictor an SJT. This in turn has sometimes created confusion over fundamental issues with SJTs and how one goes about understanding them. For example, because SJTs are measurement methods, different SJT instructions or "structure" may affect SJT criterion-related validity. Likewise, SJTs with similar structure may be designed to measure different constructs, which may again affect SJT criterion-related validity. Therefore, when combining (e.g., meta-analysis) or contrasting SJTs, it is necessary to ensure that they are similar in terms of structure and constructs assessed (see Arthur & Villado, 2008, for a clear treatment of this issue). These are more than purely academic issues because being able to define an SJT has consequences for how validity should be established and how the SJT should be used in practice.

SJT DEVELOPMENT AND SCORING

Most of the variations around SJT measurement and scoring options are reviewed in Weekley, Ployhart, and Holtz (2006). Here we review the most common way to develop an SJT that involves a three-part process of situation generation, response option generation, and scoring.

Step 1: Situation Generation

The first step uses job incumbents (or supervisors) to identify critical incidents at work that are challenging, difficult, important, but reasonably common. A long list of potential situations is created to sample from the work environment domain. SJT item stems are most commonly generated using one of two sources: critical incidents or understanding of the job. The use of critical incidents is the most widely used of the two sources, even though it can be fairly expensive and time consuming. In general, job experts are asked to think of the context of a work situation, the behaviors that occurred in it, and the antecedents that lead up to it (e.g., Weekley & Jones, 1999). For example, a retail employee may discuss from personal experience a situation in which a customer wanted to return merchandise without a receipt (the antecedent), which created a situation (context) in which the employee was forced to choose between promoting customer satisfaction and following store policy stating no returns without receipts (behaviors). In addition to job experts, critical incidents may be generated using archival data sources.

The alternative approach to generating item stems is to use a theoretical basis. The first step to this approach is identifying theories related to the job of interest. Once the pertinent job-related theories have been identified, the researcher then generates items that capture the required underlying job-related constructs. For example, one might review the extensive psychological and marketing literatures on customer service provision to identify common types of service encounters (e.g., relational, long term, brief encounters) and challenges (e.g., balancing customer, peer, and supervisor demands) to comprise the basis of SJT stems. Lievens and Sackett (2007) discussed some variations on this approach. Although the various approaches for situation generation have certainly been useful, future research needs to identify how to best write or structure SJT items.

Step 2: Response Option Generation

The second step in SJT development involves another group of job experts identifying behavioral response options for each situation. Note that both effective and ineffective options are generated, and they are behavioral in nature. Use of both effective and ineffective options is done to increase variability in the item responses and help identify "good judgment." Response options, like item stems, may be generated by subject matter experts (SMEs) or SJT developers. As noted by Weekley et al. (2006), there has been little research exploring the differences between SJT response options generated by SMEs and those generated by test developers. However, experience has suggested that response options generated by job experts are likely to exceed those generated by developers in terms of both quality and quantity. A long list of possible response options for each situation will be developed and then reduced to approximately four to six options for each situation.

Step 3: Scoring

Finally, a third group of SMEs (usually supervisors) will indicate which options are effective/ineffective and hence create the scoring key. There are several different methods used to score SJTs, but in practice most methods follow one of two strategies: having respondents make a forced choice among response options or having respondents rate the effectiveness of each response option along a continuum.

Common applications of the forced-choice method involve having respondents choose the one best response (Hunter, 2003; O'Connell, Doverspike, Norris-Watts, & Hattrup, 2001; Sinar, Paquet, & Scott, 2002) or identifying both the best and worst (most/least effective) response to the situation (Motowidlo et al., 1990). Several methods are used to score both of these approaches. When respondents are asked to choose only the one best response, they may receive 1 point for each situation in which they identify the one best response and 0 points for incorrect responses. Because not all incorrect response options are equally wrong, another option is to rate the effectiveness of specific response options, which in essence allows for partial credit when respondents select a response option that falls between the best and worst option. The partial credit scoring method described by Motowidlo et al. (1990) has been particularly influential. Their approach asks respondents to identify both the best and worst options, so each item receives a score ranging from −2 to +2. Correctly identifying the best and worst option would each merit receiving 1 point, resulting in a score on the SJT item of +2. Identifying the best solution as the worst option, or vice versa, would result in losing 1 point, and incorrectly identifying both the best as the worst and the worst as the best would result in an SJT item score of −2. Incorrectly identifying any other response options (distracters) as the best or worst option would result in 0 points. This leads to respondents receiving a score of 1 when they correctly identify either the best or worst response option but incorrectly choosing a distracter as the correct response option for the other. A final method for forced-choice scoring is to have respondents rank order all response options and compare their rank with those of SMEs using Spearman's rank-order correlations. In a study conducted by Weekley, Harding, Creglow, and Ployhart (2004), respondents were asked to rank order all response options from best to worst. This method resulted in a small but significant improvement in validity over pick the best and pick the best/worst SJTs in two of the four samples.

The second strategy for scoring SJTs is to have respondents rate the effectiveness of each response option along a continuum using a Likert-type scale. For example, the options from the sample SJT item presented previously would appear as shown in Exhibit 8.1. In this example, respondents would evaluate the effectiveness of each option, so the number of scores would be the number of options times the number of items.

To score rating responses, job expert ratings are compared with respondent ratings. Common methods of calculating respondent scores for this strategy include assigning values depending on the percentage of agreement (Chan & Schmitt, 2002), taking the inverse of the absolute value of the difference between SME and respondent ratings (Sacco, Scheu, Ryan, & Schmitt, 2000; Sacco, Schmidt, & Rogg, 2000), and summing the squared deviations of respondent and SME ratings (Wagner, 1987). When compared with forced-choice strategies, there are some distinct advantages to having respondents rate each response option (McDaniel & Nguyen, 2001). Most notably, there is the potential for validity and reliability improvements because rating each response option provides more available items to score than with a forced-choice method.

When it comes to scoring SJTs, correct/incorrect responses are occasionally identified using empirical methods (e.g., correlating each response with the criterion) but more frequently on the basis of the consensus by a group of job experts—frequently supervisors. For those items for which consensus cannot be reached, the item is usually eliminated and will not be included in operational use. Consequently, scoring keys will often be organization specific. Clearly the organization's norms, cli-

Exhibit 8.1
Effectiveness Scale for Response Items in Sample Situational Judgment Test

Response option	Ineffective 1	2	3	4	Effective 5
a. Inform the team members that if they don't stop fighting, they will be kicked off the team.	1	2	3	4	5
b. Try to instill greater commitment to the project by emphasizing the team's goals.	1	2	3	4	5
c. Go to each of the team member's supervisors to inform him/her of the poor behavior.	1	2	3	4	5
d. Wait just a bit longer and see if the fighting stops.	1	2	3	4	5

mate, HR practices, and related contextual factors will affect the nature of the scoring key. Thus, it is quite common for a set of SJT items to be used in multiple organizations but the scoring of those items to be done separately within each firm.

Finally, please realize that at each stage, editing of the situations will be necessary, and the items should be written so that the language and jargon are not so specific that the targeted population will be unable to understand them. Additionally, item stems should take into account the content of the job, whereas response options should consider the desired construct to be measured.

Other SJT Development Issues

When developing the situations and response options, it is critical to consider their complexity and fidelity. *Stem complexity* refers to the level of detail that may be used in the item stem and response options. Simple stems are short and use simple language, for example, "Imagine you are trying to satisfy a difficult customer." Complex stems are longer, use more complex language, and will frequently require greater attentional resources. For example,

> A customer wishes to return some expensive clothing but does not have a receipt. Store policy is to never accept returns without a receipt. You state this to the customer, who quickly becomes so irate that he or she starts to make other customers leave the store. Unfortunately, the store manager is out to lunch and you have to do something fast.

Highly complex item stems may sometimes include subsituations (e.g., branching). The key feature of a branching SJT is that the choices you make "early" in the SJT influence the situations you are presented with as you proceed through the test. SJTs with branching questions, therefore, have multiple situations, but respondents will only complete a subset of the situations. As an extreme example of branching, the first author developed an SJT to assess leadership skills in U.S. Army captains. The SJT first presented all captains with a situation in which a town that should have been empty was in fact inhabited by civilians and insurgents. If captains charged into the town, they found themselves outnumbered and the situation becoming critical. On the other hand, if captains maneuvered around the town, they found themselves unable to achieve their objectives. Thus, the choices that captains made early in the assessment influenced the types of situations they subsequently entered and needed to respond to. The point is that just as in life, the judgments and decisions people make have implications for their future circumstances. Research has produced conflicting results on the ideal level of stem complexity (McDaniel et al., 2001; Reynolds, Winter, & Scott, 1999). However, it has been shown that complex item stems that require a higher reading level to comprehend tend to lead to racial subgroup differences in SJT performance (Sacco, Scheu, et al., 2000; Sacco, Schmidt, & Rogg, 2000).

The level of realism in the item, or its *fidelity*, must also be considered when developing item stems and response options. Whereas Motowidlo and colleagues (1990) referred to the SJT as a low-fidelity simulation, several more recent studies have used alternative formats of SJTs to increase their fidelity. Using richer formats, such as video, retains the basic attributes of an SJT (i.e., providing the subject with a situation and alternative response options) but provides a more vivid account of the situation (particularly nonverbal information). These multimedia situational judgment tests (MMSJTs) often use video clips as a means of presenting the SJT item stems. After watching each video clip (i.e., situation), respondents are then presented with multiple choice options as previously described. By administering the situations in a video-based format, the physical and potentially psychological fidelity of the SJT is enhanced (see Ployhart et al., 2006). Furthermore, MMSJTs typically exhibit higher levels of face validity (Chan & Schmitt, 1997; Richman-Hirsch, Olson-Buchanan, & Drasgow, 2000) and slightly reduced subgroup differences (Chan & Schmitt, 1997; Olson-Buchanan et al., 1998).

It is important for test developers to also give consideration to SJT response instructions. Response instructions have been shown to have a significant influence on SJT construct validity (McDaniel, Whetzel, Hartman, Nguyen, & Grubb, 2006; McDaniel et al., 2007). SJTs using "would do" instructions tend to correlate with different constructs than do SJTs using "should do" instructions. Specifically, SJTs that ask respondents which option they "would do" or "would most likely perform" tend to correlate more strongly with personality constructs, whereas SJTs that ask respondents what they "should do" or is the "best choice" tend to correlate more strongly with cognitive ability and knowledge constructs. As such, "would do" versions of SJTs are considered to be measures of behavioral tendencies or typical performance, and "should do" versions of SJTs are considered to be measures of cognitive ability, knowledge, or maximum performance (McDaniel et al., 2007).

In addition to moderating construct validity, prior research has examined the effects of response instructions on the criterion-related validity of SJTs (e.g., Ployhart & Ehrhart, 2003). However, a recent meta-analysis by McDaniel et al. (2007) suggested criterion-related validity may be unaffected by SJT response instructions. Using meta-analytic techniques to assess SJT construct and criterion-related validity poses certain challenges, chief among them is the variation of SJT content. In the few studies that held SJT content constant for both behavioral tendency and knowledge instructions, McDaniel et al. found knowledge SJT instructions exhibited higher levels of criterion-related validity than did behavioral tendency SJT instructions. In part this difference might be explained by differences in criterion construct, but unfortunately the meta-analysis did not code for or examine this question. Given the literature included in their analysis, our estimate is that the criteria were primarily ratings by supervisors or other individuals. As noted by McDaniel and colleagues, future research is needed to truly understand the moderating effect of response instructions on SJT criterion-related validity.

Although much research has been done on creating response options that target specific constructs, there has been only limited success (Motowidlo, Diesch, & Jackson, 2003; Ployhart & Ryan, 2000; Trippe & Foti, 2003). For example, Ployhart and Ryan (2000) tried to create a construct-oriented SJT that targeted traits most likely to be important in customer service (i.e., neuroticism, agreeableness, and conscientiousness). Further, and in contrast to the usual approach for developing SJT items, they tried to ensure that the options for each item represented a continuum of that trait's expression in that situation (the scaling of these options was derived from extensive pilot testing). Shown below is a sample item for agreeableness:

> You're working at the cash register on a very busy shift. There is a long line of customers waiting to check out, and you can see several individuals are getting impatient. What do you do?
> (a) Tell the waiting customers that you appreciate their patience.
> (b) Regularly look at those waiting so that they know you are aware of them.
> (c) Once in a while look at those waiting so that they know you are aware of them.
> (d) Focus on your job as a cashier and don't look at those waiting.

Despite the effort and care that went into developing this SJT, it still failed to reach high levels of convergent validity with the three personality traits, although it did correlate more strongly with the intended traits than a more "traditional" SJT. On the other hand, Motowidlo, Hooper, and Jackson (2006a) found that by building response options that expressed varying levels of specific traits, having individuals rate the effectiveness of each response option, and estimating the magnitude of a trait's influence on the effectiveness rating, they were able to measure the implicit trait policy for the traits of agreeableness and extraversion. Additionally, they were able to predict individual expressions of agreeableness in a work simulation using these implicit trait policy measures.

In practice, the number of items usually reflects the contextual nuances of the given occupation; for example, more complex managerial positions will frequently require more situations than will simpler jobs. Clearly the content of an SJT is highly affected by the work context of a given occupation. As a result, it is not difficult to adapt situations to different organizations so long as the critical job tasks are sufficiently similar. However, we have successfully adapted SJT items from very different domains (e.g., law enforcement to manufacturing) with surprisingly little difficulty. As noted earlier, it is usually the scoring key that is organization-specific.

SOURCES OF SJT VALIDITY EVIDENCE

In the following sections, we review the sources of SJT validity in terms of criterion-related, content, and construct.

Criterion-Related Validity

If one defines the magnitude of criterion-related validities (uncorrected correlations) in terms of low (.10), moderate (.20) and strong (.30; Ployhart et al., 2006), then SJTs have exhibited moderate criterion-related validity (McDaniel et al., 2001, 2007). A meta-analysis by McDaniel et al. (2007) estimated the population correlation between job performance and SJT scores to be .20 (uncorrected; corrected correlation = .26). Nearly all of this research has been conducted using concurrent validation designs with supervisor ratings of overall performance, and almost nothing is known about the criterion-related validity in predictive designs. For example, in an older meta-analysis, McDaniel et al. (2001) found only six predictive studies to analyze. They found that SJT scores obtained in concurrent samples demonstrated higher criterion-related validity (.27 uncorrected correlation, .35 corrected correlation) than predictive studies (.14 uncorrected correlation, .18 corrected correlation).

Several studies have shown that SJTs possess incremental validity over other predictors such as cognitive ability, personality, and experience. For example, Clevenger et al. (2001) used regression to demonstrate that SJT scores provided incremental validity over cognitive ability, conscientiousness, job experience, and job knowledge. In a similar study, Weekley and Ployhart (2005) used path analysis to examine relationships between an SJT, cognitive ability, GPA, personality, general work experience, and job tenure. They tested a series of path models that showed the SJT explained incremental variance after controlling for the other knowledge, skills, and abilities (KSAs). However, the best fitting model was one in which the SJT fully mediated the cognitive ability and experience relationships with performance, and partially mediated the performance relationships with personality. In the Clevenger et al. (2001) and Weekley and Ployhart (2005) studies, the SJTs explained an additional 2% to 3% of variance beyond other predictors. Although it has been suggested that SJTs capture a unique construct such as tacit knowledge (Sternberg, Wagner, Williams, & Horvath, 1995), this perspective has been questioned by others (McDaniel & Whetzel, 2005), and it is more widely held that they are multidimensional measurement methods that capture the influence of other constructs that are related to job performance (Chan & Schmitt, 1997).

Research has only begun to examine potential moderators of SJT criterion-related validity. Faking (i.e., intentionally providing a response that one believes will increase the chance of being hired, even though it is not what one would actually do) has been shown to reduce the criterion-related validity of SJTs and their incremental predictive validity over cognitive ability and personality tests, although one caveat is that respondents were instructed to fake and only on the SJT (Peeters & Lievens, 2005). On the other hand, response instructions do not appear to moderate the criterion-related validity of SJTs. A meta-analysis conducted by McDaniel et al. (2007) found the uncorrected mean correlation between SJT scores and job performance to be .20 (.26 corrected) for both behavioral tendency and knowledge SJT instructions.

Content Validity

McDaniel and Nguyen (2001) argued that content validity will usually comprise the key source of validity for SJTs. This is because of the critical incident nature of SJT development. That is, SJT content is usually based on critical incidents or an underlying model that captures a set of important determinants of effective performance (Weekley et al., 2006). Generating test content based on job-specific tasks may account for the validity of SJTs (Chan & Schmitt, 2002; Lievens, Buyse, & Sackett, 2005). Thus, by adopting the critical incident approach to SJT development, SJTs will usually have a high degree of content validity, although we are aware of no research that has tested this with various indices of content validity (e.g., Lawshe's, 1975, content validity ratio). Furthermore, by basing SJTs on a job analysis and developing items based on the opinions of job experts, the process of creating SJTs helps "build in" content validity.

Construct Validity

It is not possible to establish the construct validity of a method, but only whether the items used in the method are related to the constructs they are intended to measure (Arthur & Villado, 2008). Therefore, it is erroneous to talk about the construct validity of SJTs; rather, one must talk about whether a particular SJT has construct validity evidence given the construct it is intended to measure. This clarification is important because the extant SJT literature is vague on this point. Indeed, nearly every published study on SJTs discusses the SJT as a measure of some construct, but there is usually little or no construct validity evidence presented. For example, a study may claim that the SJT measures "interpersonal skills" or "managerial ability," but no correlations to existing measures of these constructs are offered. Instead, the field has proceeded as it has with interviews and assessment centers, using meta-analysis to determine the KSA correlates of SJTs irrespective of what the specific SJTs were intended to measure. We want to emphasize that even though we present this meta-analytic evidence, one must recognize that these estimates speak only to what SJTs tend to be correlated with and not whether a given SJT has construct validity or whether SJTs can be developed to specifically target these constructs.

Prior research has shown SJTs to be correlated with personality (McDaniel et al., 2007; McDaniel & Nguyen, 2001; O'Connell, Hartman, McDaniel, Grubb, & Lawrence, 2007; Weekley, Ployhart, & Harold, 2004), cognitive ability (McDaniel et al., 2001, 2007; O'Connell et al., 2007; Weekley & Jones, 1999), job knowledge (Clevenger et al., 2001), and job experience (Weekley & Jones, 1999). A meta-analysis conducted by McDaniel et al. (2007) reported moderately strong correlations between SJT scores and several personality dimensions. The observed mean correlations for each of these personality dimensions were .22 for agreeableness (corrected .25), .23 for conscientiousness (corrected .27), .13 for extraversion (corrected .14), and .11 for openness to experience (corrected .13). McDaniel and colleagues (2007) also reported a mean observed correlation between SJT scores and cognitive ability of .29 (corrected .32) and job knowledge of .20 (corrected .26). Thus, it would appear that SJTs do not strongly relate to any particular construct but are moderately related to many different constructs. Certainly these corrected correlations suggest SJTs are not redundant with cognitive ability and personality and raises the question of what SJTs measure. In a primary study that included measures of job tenure, general work experience, cognitive ability, and personality, Weekley and Ployhart (2005) concluded that the SJT was a measure of general work knowledge (vs. job-specific knowledge).

Response instructions are an important moderator of SJT construct relationships. SJTs that use behavioral tendency questions exhibit higher correlations with agreeableness, conscientiousness, and emotional stability, whereas SJTs that use knowledge instructions exhibit higher correlations with extraversion, openness to experience, and cognitive ability

(McDaniel et al., 2007). Specifically, the uncorrected correlation between SJT scores and agreeableness was .33 for behavioral tendency instructions compared with .17 for knowledge instructions, .30 compared with .21 for conscientiousness, .31 compared with .10 for emotional stability, .07 compared with .14 for extraversion, and .09 compared with .12 for openness to experience. Furthermore, McDaniel et al. (2007) found the uncorrected correlation between SJT scores and cognitive ability to be .32 for knowledge instructions compared with .17 for behavioral tendency instructions. These results suggest that response instructions moderate the relationship between both SJTs and cognitive ability as well as personality dimensions. However, it is not correct to simply note that behavioral tendency SJTs correlate more strongly with personality because this is only true for agreeableness, conscientiousness, and emotional stability.

Overall, one of the general conclusions from existing SJT research is that the SJT development method and response instructions can affect the construct relationships and criterion-related validity of SJTs. This is perhaps not surprising because SJTs are multidimensional measurement methods. However, systematic research on these issues has scarcely occurred with the exception of instruction format (would/should do). It should also be noted that the vast majority of SJT construct validity research has been conducted using incumbent samples (McDaniel & Nguyen, 2001). This may be rather limiting to the extent that different construct relationships may be found in applicant contexts due to differences in applicant motivation, socially desirable responding, experience, and job/occupational knowledge. We discuss these issues in more detail in the section concerning future research, but want to emphasize here that systematic research relating different aspects of SJT structure to construct relationships is long overdue but will greatly facilitate our understanding of enhancing SJT construct validity (see Weekley et al., 2006).

SUBGROUP DIFFERENCES

The majority of SJT research examining racial and sex subgroup differences has been conducted with incumbents. Ployhart and Holtz (2008) reviewed the literature on subgroup differences for various predictor constructs and methods and found that in general, SJTs show subgroup differences favoring Whites over Blacks ($d = .40$), Hispanics ($d = .37$), and Asians ($d = .47$). The SJT racial subgroup differences are about half as large as those obtained for general cognitive ability (White/Black, $d = .99$, White/Hispanic, $d = .58$ to .83; excluding Asians, who tend to score higher than Whites on cognitive ability, White/Asian, $d = -.20$), but approximately two to five times larger than those obtained with personality (White/Black, $d = -.04$ to .20; White/Hispanic, $d = -.01$ to .10; White/Asian, $d = .01$–.18). In terms of sex differences, women score higher than men by no more than .12 standard deviations. This is larger than sex differences found with cognitive ability ($d = .00$) but smaller than sex differences found with personality ($d = -.39$ to .24). The magnitude of subgroup differences also differ across applicant and incumbent settings. Weekley, Ployhart, and Harold (2004) found that racial and sex subgroup differences were higher in the incumbent sample, for both White–Black ($d_{applicant} = .40$, $d_{incumbent} = .49$) and sex ($d_{applicant} = .20$, $d_{incumbent} = .34$) differences.

Cumulatively, these findings suggest that SJTs may demonstrate smaller racial subgroup differences when compared with cognitively oriented predictors but larger subgroup differences when compared with noncognitive predictors. It has been known at least since Spearman (1927) that the cognitive loading of a test is a strong determinant of the subgroup difference likely to be manifested. Two lines of research offer preliminary support that Spearman's hypothesis holds for SJTs as well. First, some studies have found that there is a positive relationship between reading level and Black–White subgroup differences, such as the finding that as reading requirements increase, so do subgroup differences (Sacco, Scheu, et al., 2000; Sacco, Schmidt, & Rogg, 2000). Second, research has found that video-based SJTs show slightly lower ($d = .10$) Black–White subgroup differences than do written SJTs, attributable to the fact that video SJTs lower the relationship with verbal ability.

On the basis of these data, it is often claimed that SJTs exhibit lower subgroup differences than do cognitive ability tests. Although on the surface this appears to be true, one must interpret these findings with some caution because it must be remembered that internal consistency unreliability attenuates subgroup differences. Because they are multidimensional, SJTs usually manifest lower internal consistency reliability than do predictor constructs such as cognitive ability and personality, so SJT subgroup differences may be larger and hence more similar to other predictor constructs after correcting for internal consistency unreliability.

PRACTICE ISSUES

Although much of the research on SJTs goes hand in hand with practice, there are some issues unique to the implementation of SJTs that deserve special mention. We also offer a few of our own observations gained through several years of experience in working with SJTs in private industry and the public sector.

Cost

We rarely see predictor batteries composed only of an SJT. Instead, SJTs are usually used in conjunction with other cognitive and noncognitive predictors. In our experience with large-scale hiring, SJTs are administered early in a multihurdle process, in conjunction with personality tests and sometimes cognitive ability tests. Because SJTs often have higher criterion-related validity than personality tests and lower subgroup differences than cognitive tests, their inclusion in such a predictor battery helps balance diversity and validity. Other arguments for including SJTs in early hurdles are that they are more face valid and can offer a realistic preview of the job, thereby helping recruit the desired applicants.

Many major consulting firms and vendors have SJTs developed for different occupations, with the most common being the service industry, entry level management, and sales. Developing an SJT in-house can be more expensive, particularly given that job experts and supervisors will be required to leave work to help generate situations, response options, and the scoring key. On the other hand, the same tasks and materials required to develop an SJT may be leveraged into a variety of HR functions, including training and development, thereby creating more value from the SJT. Furthermore, given that job experts and managers help develop the SJT, they may be more committed to using it and accepting the results.

Time for Administration

Because the item stems are descriptions of situations and the response options represent different behaviors, it takes longer for a respondent to complete an SJT than it would the typical Likert-style personality test or cognitive ability test. In our experience, the time necessary to administer an SJT is similar to that of job knowledge tests. However, if a selection battery is going to include a large number of SJT items in addition to other predictors like personality, it is important to allow not only sufficient time but also breaks in the testing if at all feasible.

Reading Requirements

Earlier we noted how reading level influences the magnitude of racial subgroup differences on SJTs. It is consistent with professional standards to make the reading level as low as appropriate for the job. SJTs are not verbal ability tests, and the reading level should be no higher than the level minimally necessary for performing the job. Ensuring reading requirements are kept low also helps keep racial subgroup differences low, although perhaps only modestly. Of course, this issue is not as relevant for video-based or audio SJTs, although it may still have some relevance when the response options are presented in a written format.

Test Security and Alternative Forms

One of the key issues facing practitioners is that of test security. The high costs and resources needed to develop a predictor can be quickly compromised by the test items becoming copied, stolen, or distributed by test takers. One solution to this problem is to administer multiple forms of the test. However, given the multidimensional nature of SJTs, it can be difficult to create alternative forms. Lievens and Sackett (2007) recently presented a framework for addressing this issue. It is interesting that they found that randomly sampling items to create alternative forms produced correlations only in the .20s, even when those items came from the same content domain. Thus, a simple domain sampling approach with random assignment to a particular test form is unlikely to generate alternate forms that are highly related. Obviously, this finding will be affected by the internal consistency reliability of the SJT and the nature of the constructs and job in question, such that occupations or SJTs with more homogenous situations may have higher alternate form correlations. Regardless of such specific features, perhaps the key implication of Lievens and Sackett (2007) is that one must attend to specific item features (e.g., item's context, critical incidents used to generate the item) to create parallel forms. Overall, it is clear that developing alternative forms for SJTs presents a number of challenges. The framework presented by Lievens and Sackett (2007) offers a useful means of conceptualizing the various issues, but there is still much more to be learned.

SJTs as Tools of Change

Selection tests are often implemented because the firm wants to make a systematic change in terms of KSAs and values. Because SJT development is so heavily based on the opinions of SMEs who are current job experts and supervisors, the SJT may simply be a device that reinforces the status quo by selecting applicants with values and perspectives highly similar to incumbents. For example, SJTs might function as a form of realistic job previews, potentially turning away applicants whose values might not fit the company. This can be desirable in some instances or undesirable in other instances when it creates too much homogeneity within the firm. Although these issues are to varying degrees relevant for all predictors and selection systems, they are particularly salient with SJTs because they are so heavily influenced by incumbent opinions. Future research is sorely needed on the extent to which SJTs can serve as "tools of change."

A CRITICAL REVIEW OF SJT RESEARCH AND A LOOK TOWARD THE FUTURE

We conclude this chapter by taking stock of what is known about SJTs and contrasting this with what we need to know. Table 8.1 highlights these gaps in understanding, and Exhibit 8.2 presents several emerging directions for SJT research and practice.

TABLE 8.1

A Critical Review of What Is Known and Not Known About Situational Judgment Tests (SJTs)

What we know	What we do not know
▪ SJTs are moderately strong predictors of job performance.	▪ Which factors moderate SJT validity? ▪ Are SJTs more predictive of certain types of criteria? ▪ What is the "shelf-life" of SJT validity? ▪ Are SJTs seen as more job related by applicants and managers?
▪ SJTs have moderate to small racial and sex subgroup differences.	▪ Are these differences due to the lower internal consistency reliability of SJTs? ▪ Are subgroup differences explained by the cognitive loading of the SJT? ▪ What factors affect the size of subgroup differences? ▪ Can reading requirements be reduced without affecting criterion-related validity? ▪ Does culture affect SJT scores?
▪ The majority of SJT research is based on incumbent samples.	▪ Do these findings generalize to applicant settings? ▪ How does faking affect SJT validity? ▪ Can SJTs be developed to reduce the effects of faking? ▪ Does applicant/incumbent context affect construct validity? ▪ Do SJTs simply reinforce the firm's existing values and climate?
▪ An SJT methodology for assessing homogeneous constructs does not currently exist.	▪ Which SJT development methods and structures most impact construct validity? ▪ Do SJTs that measure more homogenous constructs have higher criterion-related validity? ▪ What is the best way to develop and score SJT items? ▪ Can meta-analysis adequately answer questions of SJT construct validity?

Exhibit 8.2
Neglected Situational Judgment Test (SJT) Issues Deserving Future Research

1. Where is the theory underlying SJT validity?
2. Where is the role of judgment in SJT research and practice?
3. Where is experimentation with SJTs?
4. Can SJTs be developed to isolate specific homogenous constructs?
5. Do SJT findings based on incumbents generalize to applicants?
6. Does culture and/or language affect the validity of SJTs?
7. How does faking affect the validity of SJTs?
8. Do SJTs reinforce the status quo; can they be tools of change?
9. Can SJTs be useful for development, training, and credentialing/certification?
10. What are the major similarities and differences between SJTs and situational interviews, simulations, and assessment centers exercises?

First, we know that SJTs are moderately strong predictors of supervisory ratings of job performance, but we know almost nothing of other factors that may affect criterion-related validity. For example, most of what we know about these factors is limited to instruction format (i.e., would/should do). We do not know whether SJTs are predictive of criteria such as organizational citizenship behavior, counterproductive work behavior, or objective criteria. In fact, nearly everything known about SJT criterion-related validity is based on incumbent samples with overall supervisory ratings. We also do not know how long an SJT will maintain its validity. And although there are many reasons to believe that SJTs are supposedly perceived as more job related (e.g., Bauer & Truxillo, 2006), we do not know if managers (and applicants) truly perceive them as such and hence are more likely to implement them.

Second, we know that SJTs have small to moderate racial and sex subgroup differences. It is unclear whether these smaller subgroup differences are simply due to lower internal consistency reliability, lower cognitive loadings, or some as yet unidentified factor. It would appear that lowering reading requirements can reduce racial subgroup differences, but does this in turn reduce the criterion-related validity? In general, we do not know why subgroup differences exist on SJTs, and understanding the causes of subgroup differences is likely to be complex because of the multidimensional nature of SJTs. To make things more complicated, there is almost no empirical research examining SJT responses and validity across cultures (see Lievens, 2006). There is within-culture research, but almost nothing that speaks to how culture and possibly language influence SJTs. For example, it is highly likely that the appropriate response to a situation is culturally bound, such as when those in collectivistic cultures endorse options that favor group harmony, whereas those in individualistic cultures endorse options that favor personal achievement. We do not even know whether situations are to a degree culturally bound, or whether it is possible to translate situations to new languages without losing some of the contextual meaning.

Third, our knowledge of SJTs is nearly entirely based on incumbent samples. Simply put, we have almost no data on whether SJT criterion-related and construct validity would generalize to applicant samples. On the one hand, we do not know the extent to which intentional response distortion (e.g., faking) may affect SJT responses and construct validity. For example, suppose an SJT is correlated .50 with agreeableness in an incumbent sample but only .25 with agreeableness in an applicant sample. Does this difference in the strength of relationships with agreeableness mean the SJT measures something different in each context, or does it mean that applicants so greatly fake the personality test and/or SJT that it distorts their relationship? On the other hand, there may be additional factors that create differences between applicant and incumbent contexts.

For example, age or experience differences favoring incumbents might result in their performing better than applicants. Similarly, SJTs may be susceptible to coaching influences or even repeated exposure through retesting. It may be possible to develop "rules" for deciphering SJT items just as there are with multiple choice testing (e.g., never pick an option with the word *always*). Researching these issues is important because McDaniel et al. (2001) found that the criterion-related validity of SJTs is nearly half in applicant samples relative to incumbent samples.

Finally, and perhaps most important, there is no existing methodology for creating homogenous SJTs. This is a problem only if the latent construct the SJT is designed to measure is itself homogenous, but the fact remains that nearly every study that examines KSA correlates of SJTs finds the convergent validities to be relatively small (e.g., in the .30s or less). There are some theoretical approaches that deserve examination (e.g., Motowidlo et al., 2006a), but simply put, we are aware of no SJT development method that can be used to create a homogenous SJT even when the intended latent construct is homogenous. For that matter, even though the profession refers to these predictors as measures of "situational judgment," there is almost no mention of judgment research or the processes of making judgments in the SJT literature (Brooks & Highhouse, 2006). This is troubling not only from a scientific point of view but also from a practical one, because professional standards indicate that it is important to understand what we are measuring (American Educational Research Association, American Psychological Association, & National Council on Measurement in Education, 1999; Society for Industrial and Organizational Psychology, 2003). Most of what we know about SJT construct validity has been created through the use of meta-analysis. We believe the meta-analytic research has been invaluable for providing initial guidance into SJT construct validity, but this research does not actually speak to whether a given SJT has construct validity or can have construct validity. We believe it is time to move beyond describing SJT construct relationships to testing SJT construct validity directly via experimentation and manipulation. We believe this experimentation must start by linking theory on the psychology of judgment with the structure and content of SJT items.

Toward this end, we offer two potential theoretical approaches for understanding the psychology of SJTs. The first approach is that presented by Motowidlo et al. (2006b) and is based on implicit trait policies (ITPs). According to ITPs, individuals value response options differently depending on the response option's level of trait expression and their own personality. Using their example, an individual high in agreeableness would be more drawn to the correct response option that is highly agreeable than an individual who is dispositionally low in agreeableness. Because of ITPs, an individual's perception of response option effectiveness will provide information regarding the test taker's dispositional traits. Although further research is needed, Motowidlo et al (2006a) demonstrated some support for this approach by successfully measuring the implicit trait policy for the traits of agreeableness and extraversion by having individuals rate SJT response option effectiveness.

The second approach also takes a fine-grained analysis of item responses. Ployhart (2006) proposed a model to study the SJT response process, the predictor response process model (PRPR; pronounced *proper*). The PRPR model is based on the survey response process literature (Krosnick, 1999; Ployhart, 2006; Tourangeau, Rips, & Rasinski, 2000) and may provide a useful guide for better understanding different sources of variance affecting predictor scores, including multidimensional predictors such as SJTs. The PRPR model proposes that an individual undergoes four latent processes when choosing a manifest response for an SJT item: comprehension, retrieval, judgment, and response. Comprehension is characterized by an individual engaging in cognitive processes to understand exactly what the question is asking of him or her. Retrieval takes place when an individual accesses information pertinent to the question from memory. Judgment takes place when an individual uses the information accessed during the retrieval stage to evaluate possible options. The final process takes place when an individual fits his or her selected response to the possible SJT response options.

Researchers could use the PRPR model to manipulate different features of items to determine their consequences on comprehension, retrieval, judgment, and response.

To conclude, research has scarcely scratched the surface of SJTs. Some questions, such as SJT criterion-related validity in incumbent samples, have been extensively examined, whereas SJT construct validity and operational issues such as faking and scoring alternatives have barely been touched. There are many important and fundamental questions about the nature and use of SJTs that need further study. As a profession, we cannot continue to rely on criterion-related evidence or meta-analysis to infer what SJTs measure. We need to also incorporate experimental designs to manipulate different features of SJT constructs, structure, and content. Given such needs, it is likely that research on SJTs will stay active for many years to come.

References

American Educational Research Association, American Psychological Association, & National Council on Measurement in Education. (1999). *Standards for educational and psychological testing.* Washington, DC: American Research Association.

Arthur, W., & Villado, A. J. (2008). The importance of distinguishing between constructs and methods when comparing predictors in personnel selection research and practice. *Journal of Applied Psychology, 93,* 435–442.

Bauer, T. N., & Truxillo, D. M. (2006). Applicant reaction to situational judgment tests: Research and related practical issues. In J. A. Weekley & R. E. Ployhart (Eds.), *Situational judgment tests: Theory, measurement and application* (pp. 233–252). Mahwah, NJ: Erlbaum.

Brooks, M. E., & Highhouse, S. (2006). Can good judgment be measured? In J. A. Weekley & R. E. Ployhart (Eds.), *Situational judgment tests: Theory, measurement and application* (pp. 39–56). Mahwah, NJ: Erlbaum.

Bruce, M. M. (1965). *Examiner's manual: Supervisory practices test* (Rev. ed.). Larchmont, NY: Author.

Bruce, M. M., & Learner, D. B. (1958). A supervisory practices test. *Personnel Psychology, 11,* 207–216.

Cardall, A. J. (1942). *Preliminary manual for the test of practical judgment.* Chicago: Science Research.

Chan, D., & Schmitt, N. (1997). Video-based versus paper-and-pencil method of assessment in situational judgment tests: Subgroup differences in test performance and face validity perceptions. *Journal of Applied Psychology, 82,* 143–159.

Chan, D., & Schmitt, N. (2002). Situational judgment and job performance. *Human Performance, 15,* 233–254.

Chan, D., & Schmitt, N. (2005). Situational judgment tests. In A. Evers, O. Smit-Voskuyl, & N. Anderson (Eds.), *The handbook of selection* (pp. 219–242). Oxford, England: Blackwell.

Clevenger, J., Pereira, G. M., Wiechmann, D., Schmitt, N., & Harvey, V. S. (2001). Incremental validity of situational judgment tests. *Journal of Applied Psychology, 86,* 410–417.

DuBois, P. H. (1970). *A history of psychological testing.* Boston: Allyn & Bacon.

File, Q. W. (1945). The measurement of supervisory quality in industry. *Journal of Applied Psychology, 29,* 381–387.

File, Q. W., & Remmers, H. H. (1971). *How supervise? Manual 1971 revision.* Cleveland, OH: Psychological Corporation.

Greenberg, S. H. (1963). *Supervisory judgment test manual.* Washington, DC: U.S. Civil Service Commission.

Hunter, D. R. (2003). Measuring general aviation pilot judgment using a situational judgment technique. *International Journal of Aviation Psychology, 13,* 373–386.

Kirkpatrick, D. L., & Planty, E. (1960). *Supervisory inventory on human relations.* Chicago: Science Research Associates.

Krosnick, J. A. (1999). Survey research. *Annual Review of Psychology, 50,* 537–567.

Lawshe, C. H. (1975). A quantitative approach to content validity. *Personnel Psychology, 28,* 563–575.

Lievens, F. (2006). International situational judgment tests. In J. A. Weekley & R. E. Ployhart (Eds.), *Situational judgment tests: Theory, measurement and application* (pp. 183–300). Mahwah, NJ: Erlbaum.

Lievens, F., Buyse, T., & Sackett, P. R. (2005). The operational validity of a video-based situational judgment test for medical college admissions: Illustrating the importance of matching predictor and criterion construct domains. *Journal of Applied Psychology, 90,* 442–452.

Lievens, F., Peeters, H., & Schollaert, E. (2008). Situational judgment tests: A review of recent research. *Personnel Review, 37,* 426–441.

Lievens, F., & Sackett, P. R. (2007). Situational judgment tests in high-stakes settings: Issues and strategies with generating alternate forms. *Journal of Applied Psychology, 92,* 1043–1055.

McDaniel, M. A., Hartman, N. S., Whetzel, D. L., & Grubb, W. L. (2007). Situational judgment tests, response instructions, and validity: A meta-analysis. *Personnel Psychology, 60,* 63–91.

McDaniel, M. A., Morgeson, F. P., Finnegan, E. B., Campion, M. A., & Braverman, E. P. (2001). Use of situational judgment tests to predict job performance: A clarification of the literature. *Journal of Applied Psychology, 86,* 730–740.

McDaniel, M. A., & Nguyen, N. T. (2001). Situational judgment tests: A review of practice and constructs assessed. *International Journal of Selection and Assessment, 9*(1–2), 103–113.

McDaniel, M. A., & Whetzel, D. L. (2005). Situational judgment test research: Informing the debate on practical intelligence theory. *Intelligence, 33,* 515–525.

McDaniel, M. A., Whetzel, D. L., Hartman, N. S., Nguyen, N. T., & Grubb, W. L., III. (2006). Situational judgment tests: Validity and an integrative model. In J. A. Weekley & R. E. Ployhart (Eds.), *Situational judgment tests: Theory, measurement and application* (pp. 183–204). Mahwah, NJ: Erlbaum.

Millard, K. A. (1952). Is How Supervise? an intelligence test? *Journal of Applied Psychology, 36,* 221–224.

Moss, F. A. (1926). Do you know how to get along with people? Why some people get ahead in the world while others do not. *Scientific American, 135,* 26–27.

Motowidlo, S. J., Diesch, A. C., & Jackson, H. L. (2003, April). *Using the situational judgment format to measure personality characteristics.* Paper presented at the 18th annual conference of the Society for Industrial and Organizational Psychology, Orlando, FL.

Motowidlo, S. J., Dunnette, M. D., & Carter, G. W. (1990). An alternative selection procedure: The low-fidelity simulation. *Journal of Applied Psychology, 75,* 640–647.

Motowidlo, S. J., Hooper, A. C., & Jackson, H. L. (2006a). Implicit policies about relations between personality traits and behavioral effectiveness in situational judgment items. *Journal of Applied Psychology, 91,* 749–761.

Motowidlo, S. J., Hooper, A. C., & Jackson, H. L. (2006b). A theoretical basis for situational judgment tests. In J. A. Weekley & R. E. Ployhart (Eds.), *Situational judgment tests: Theory, measurement and application* (pp. 57–81). Mahwah, NJ: Erlbaum.

Northrop, L. C. (1989). *The psychometric history of selected ability constructs.* Washington, DC: U.S. Office of Personnel Management.

O'Connell, M. S., Doverspike, D., Norris-Watts, C., & Hattrup, K. (2001). Predictors of organizational citizenship behavior among Mexican retail salespeople. *International Journal of Organizational Analysis, 9,* 272–280.

O'Connell, M. S., Hartman, N. S., McDaniel, M. A., Grubb, W. L., & Lawrence, A. (2007). Incremental validity of situational judgment tests for task and contextual job performance. *International Journal of Selection and Assessment, 15,* 19–29.

Olson-Buchanan, J. B., Drasgow, F., Moberg, P. J., Mead, A. D., Keenan, P. A., & Donovan, M. A. (1998). Interactive video assessment of conflict resolution skills. *Personnel Psychology, 51,* 1–24.

Peeters, H., & Lievens, F. (2005). Situational judgment tests and their predictiveness of college students' success: The influence of faking. *Educational and Psychological Measurement, 65,* 70–89.

Ployhart, R. E. (2006). The predictor response process model. In J. A. Weekley & R. E. Ployhart (Eds.), *Situational judgment tests: Theory, measurement and application* (pp. 83–106). Mahwah, NJ: Erlbaum.

Ployhart, R. E., & Ehrhart, M. G. (2003). Be careful what you ask for: Effects of response instructions on the construct validity and reliability of situational judgment tests. *International Journal of Selection and Assessment, 11,* 1–16.

Ployhart, R. E., & Holtz, B. C. (2008). The diversity–validity dilemma: Strategies for reducing racioethnic and sex subgroup differences and adverse impact in selection. *Personnel Psychology, 61,* 153–172.

Ployhart, R. E., & Ryan, A. M. (2000, April). *Integrating personality tests with situational judgment tests for the prediction of customer service performance.* Paper presented at the 15th annual conference of the Society for Industrial and Organizational Psychology, New Orleans, LA.

Ployhart, R. E., Schneider, B., & Schmitt, N. (2006). *Staffing organizations: Contemporary practice and theory* (3rd ed.). Mahwah, NJ: Erlbaum.

Reynolds, D. H., Winter, J. L., & Scott, D. R. (1999, May). *Development, validation, and translation of a professional-level situational judgment inventory.* Paper presented at the 14th annual convention of the Society for Industrial and Organizational Psychology, Atlanta, GA.

Richman-Hirsch, W. L., Olson-Buchanan, J. B., & Drasgow, F. (2000). Examining the impact of administration medium on examinee perceptions and attitudes. *Journal of Applied Psychology, 85,* 880–887.

Sacco, J. M., Scheu, C., Ryan, A. M., & Schmitt, N. W. (2000, April). *Understanding race differences on situational judgment tests using readability statistics.* Paper presented at the 15th annual convention of the Society for Industrial and Organizational Psychology, New Orleans, LA.

Sacco, J. M., Schmidt, D. B., & Rogg, K. L. (2000, April). *Using readability statistics and reading comprehension scores to predict situational judgment test performance, Black–White differences, and validity.* Paper presented at the 15th annual convention of the Society for

Industrial and Organizational Psychology, New Orleans, LA.

Schmitt, N., & Chan, D. (2006). Situational judgment tests: Method or construct? In J. A. Weekley & R. E. Ployhart (Eds.), *Situational judgment tests: Theory, measurement and application* (pp. 135–155). Mahwah, NJ: Erlbaum.

Sinar, E. F., Paquet, S. L., & Scott D. R. (2002, April). *Internet versus paper selection tests: Exploring comparability issues.* Paper presented at the 17th annual conference of the Society for Industrial and Organizational Psychology, Toronto, Ontario, Canada.

Society for Industrial and Organizational Psychology. (2003). *Principles for the validation and use of personnel selection procedures* (4th ed.). Bowling Green, OH: Author.

Spearman, C. (1927). *The abilities of man.* London: Macmillan.

Sternberg, R. J., Wagner, R. K., Williams, W. M., & Horvath, J. A. (1995). Testing common sense. *American Psychologist, 50,* 912–927.

Taylor, H. R. (1949a). Social Intelligence Test: George Washington University series. In O. K. Buros (Ed.), *The third mental measurements yearbook* (pp. 96–97). New Brunswick, NJ: Rutgers University Press.

Taylor, H. R. (1949b). Test of practical judgment. In O. K. Buros (Ed.), *The third mental measurements yearbook.* New Brunswick, NJ: Rutgers University Press.

Thorndike, R. L. (1941). Social Intelligence Test. In O. K. Buros (Ed.), *The 1940 mental measurements yearbook.* Highland Park, NJ: Mental Measurements Yearbook.

Thorndike, R. L., & Stein, S. (1937). An evaluation of attempts to measure social intelligence. *Psychological Bulletin, 34,* 275–285.

Tourangeau, R., Rips, L. J., & Rasinski, K. (2000). *The psychology of survey response.* Cambridge, UK: Cambridge University Press.

Trippe, M. D., & Foti, R. J. (2003, April). *An evaluation of the construct validity of situational judgment tests.* Paper presented at the 18th annual conference of the Society for Industrial and Organizational Psychology, Orlando, FL.

Wagner, R. K. (1987). Tacit knowledge in everyday intelligent behavior. *Journal of Personality and Social Psychology, 52,* 1236–1247.

Weekley, J. A., Harding, R., Creglow, A., & Ployhart, R. E. (2004). *Scoring situational judgment tests: Does the middle matter?* Paper presented at the 19th annual conference of the Society for Industrial and Organizational Psychology, Chicago, IL.

Weekley, J. A., & Jones, C. (1999). Further studies of situational tests. *Personnel Psychology, 52,* 679–700.

Weekley, J. A., & Ployhart, R. E. (2005). Situational judgment: Antecedents and relationships with performance. *Human Performance, 18,* 81–104.

Weekley, J. A., & Ployhart, R. E. (2006). *Situational judgment tests: Theory, measurement and application.* Mahwah, NJ: Erlbaum.

Weekley, J. A., Ployhart, R. E., & Harold, C. M. (2004). Personality and situational judgment tests across applicant and incumbent settings: An examination of validity, measurement, and subgroup differences. *Human Performance, 17,* 433–461.

Weekley, J. A., Ployhart, R. E., & Holtz, B. C. (2006). On the development of situational judgment tests: Issues in item development, scaling, and scoring. In J. A. Weekley & R. E. Ployhart (Eds.), *Situational judgment tests: Theory, measurement and application* (pp. 157–182). Mahwah, NJ: Erlbaum.

Part III

EVALUATING INDIVIDUALS AND PERFORMANCE

Chapter 9

THE APPRAISAL AND MANAGEMENT OF PERFORMANCE AT WORK

Angelo S. DeNisi and Shirley Sonesh

Most modern organizations engage in some form of performance appraisal in an effort to determine how well employees are performing their jobs. In the United States, these appraisals tend to be fairly formal and structured, in part because of potential legal liability when employment decisions are made on the basis of appraisals. Regardless of the system used, in the vast majority of cases, all of the parties involved are unhappy with the appraisal process. That is, employees often feel as though appraisal systems do not fairly assess their contributions, and many also believe that ratings are biased. The managers who typically conduct the appraisals often feel that they are not adequately trained in appraising performance, and they feel uncomfortable being put in the role of "judge." Managers at higher levels in the organization are often not convinced that there is a relationship between the appraisals and any measure of corporate performance. At all levels in the organization, there is often the feeling that appraisals are done because they have to be done but that nothing productive ever comes out of the process. These problems are well documented in both the academic literature (e.g., Murphy & Cleveland, 1995) and the practitioner literature (e.g., Pulakos, 2004). Yet, despite these problems and some calls for the abolishment of appraisals (cf. Coens & Jenkins, 2000), most organizations continue to conduct performance appraisals. Why?

Performance appraisal is the managerial evaluation of an employee's performance, often annually, in which an evaluator assesses the extent to which certain desired behaviors have been observed or achieved (note that our primary focus is on the performance of individual employees and not the performance of teams—that topic needs to be discussed in its own right). Organizations conduct appraisals for a number of reasons, such as providing documentation for decision making, providing performance feedback, and developing a basis for pay decisions (cf. Cleveland, Murphy, & Williams, 1989), but it is our view that the ultimate purpose for conducting appraisals is to improve organizational performance. In this chapter, however, we focus most of our attention on improving the performance of the individual because that is the area in which most of the attention in industrial and organizational psychology has been focused. We also make note of how organizational functioning can be enhanced by implementing performance management systems (PMSs) to complement performance appraisal systems. (See also Vol. 1, chap. 10, this handbook.)

More formal attempts to build the linkages between individual-level and organizational-level performance are beyond the scope of this chapter (see, e.g., the review in DeNisi, 2000), but we show how effective performance management can affect organizational-level performance by aligning individual performance goals with organizational performance goals. That is, we believe that in an ideal system employees are told about areas in which they need to improve, are given the tools they need to improve their performance, and then are shown how valued rewards, such as increased pay, will follow improved performance. Our view, then, is to combine the split goals of appraisals outlined by

H. H. Meyer, Kay, and French (1965) and argue that both feedback and decision-making functions serve the larger goal of performance improvement. Thus, we argue that performance management does not replace performance appraisals but complements appraisal, as both work in conjunction to yield greater performance improvements.

In addition to our call for performance management interventions to complement performance appraisal systems, we focus on a problem that we believe has slowed the development of more effective approaches to performance appraisals. Specifically, we discuss how many academicians and practitioners traditionally viewed the major issue in performance appraisals as one of measuring performance, emphasizing psychometric issues and rating accuracy. That is, the goal (whether explicit or implicit) was to develop more accurate measures of performance for appraisals. We do not believe that this is the right goal, and we believe that the pursuit of this goal, for its own sake, has led to many of the problems in the area of performance appraisal in the past. We review the roots of this traditional focus and also some of the efforts that were undertaken to improve rating accuracy. We conclude with more recent views on the issue, which have incorporated performance management ideas with performance measurement ideas, with the ultimate goal of performance improvement. We then discuss other types of research issues that are more germane to the problems of performance improvement, as part of a discussion of some ideas for future research.

Finally, we need to be clear that we believe that of course it is better to have accurate appraisals than inaccurate appraisals. The problem has been that by focusing on methods to improve rating accuracy, scholars and practitioners often introduced appraisal systems that were difficult to understand and were designed to reduce bias in appraisals by making it difficult for raters to know what they were really evaluating (e.g., mixed-standard ratings and forced-choice ratings, discussed later in the chapter). We believe that instead, perceived fairness is ultimately a more important goal to be satisfied in the appraisal process. Furthermore, we assume that accurate ratings are more likely to be perceived as accurate, and thus fair, by employees than inaccurate ratings and that more accurate ratings are more likely to be perceived as fairer, although we know of no direct evidence for either of these assumptions.

At this point, it is worth defining what we mean by *fairness*. We rely on the justice literature (see reviews by Brockner & Weisenfeld, 1997; Colquitt, Conlon, Wesson, Porter, & Ng, 2001; and Vol. 3, chap. 8, this handbook) to define two major types of justice or fairness: distributive justice and procedural justice. *Distributive justice* focuses on the actual allocation of rewards or outcomes and, in this context, would refer to an employee's perception that he or she received the rating he or she deserved. *Procedural justice* refers to the procedures followed to determine how outcomes were allocated. In this context, it would refer to the perception that the system for appraising performance was itself fair and transparent, which, in turn, depends on the extent to which the employee has some voice and can participate in the system and the extent to which the supervisor can provide a rational explanation for how ratings were derived. A third aspect of justice, *interactional justice* (cf. Bies & Moag, 1986), which refers to how an employee is treated by the supervisor and how the supervisor communicates the critical information to the subordinate during this process, is also likely to be relevant. The problem is that the exclusive focus on improved accuracy sometimes led to the development of appraisal systems that the parties involved in the process could not understand and could not explain, and thus, they were not as likely to be viewed as fair. We discuss the importance of perceived fairness in more detail later in the chapter.

SOME HISTORY

Industrial and organizational psychologists have certainly played a major role in focusing attention on rating accuracy. These psychologists have traditionally been concerned with issues of test validation, and in these cases, appraisals were viewed primarily as criterion measures. Along these lines, an article by Dunnette (1963) has been particularly important. Specifically, Dunnette argued that one reason for the relatively low validity coefficients that were often encountered was that performance criterion measures were unreliable, nonvalid, and inaccurate, which lowered the upper bounds of any correlations between predictors (e.g., test scores). If, somehow, psychologists could improve the quality of the criterion measures, however, they should be able to detect the true level of predictive validity of their tests.

However, although Dunnette's (1963) article was important, the tradition of trying to make ratings more accurate goes back much further. Since the early part of the 20th century, organizations relied primarily on some type of graphic rating scales for assessing performance. In 1920, Thorndike published an article about what he termed the *constant error* and discussed ways to eliminate this error from ratings. Rudd (1921) also wrote about these errors, and even though Bingham (1939) argued that not all of these "errors" were really errors, the field was well on its way. A great deal of the research in the 1950s and 1960s focused on ways to improve graphic rating scales (the traditional trait ratings using 5- to 7-point scales), such as by changing the number of scale points or even changing the way raters complete the rating form (e.g., Barrett, Taylor, Parker, & Martens, 1958; D. M. Johnson & Vidulich, 1956; Peters & McCormick, 1966). Other research focused on developing alternative types of rating scales—again with the goal of improving rating accuracy. Thus, suggestions were made for a critical-incidents approach to appraisal, in which raters describe specific events (a) that occurred in which the employee did something really well or something that needs improvement and (b) that are not associated with a rating or ranking method (e.g., Flanagan, 1949, 1954). Other types of rating scales included forced-choice methods in which raters are required to choose the most descriptive statement of an employee for each pair of statements (Sisson, 1948), various forced-distribution methods in which managers are required to distribute ratings for those being evaluated into a prespecified performance distribution ranking (e.g., Berkshire & Highland, 1953), and behaviorally anchored rating scales (BARSs) in which certain behaviors are benchmarked as a reference of comparison for behaviors of employees being appraised (P. C. Smith & Kendall, 1963).

Later, other suggestions were made for behavioral observation scales (BOSs), in which raters are taught to use aids such as diaries to standardize performance observation and recall (Latham & Wexley, 1977), and mixed-standard rating scales (Blanz & Ghiselli, 1972), in which statements representing good, average, and poor performance on various dimensions of performance (based on behavioral examples obtained from knowledgeable persons) are scattered randomly throughout the scale. As a result, the rater is meant to focus on a specific behavior rather than a dimension, and he or she really does not know what dimension is being tapped by a given behavior. The rater is then asked to indicate whether an employee fits the statement, is better than the statement, or is worse than the statement. The end result of all of these efforts was probably best summarized by Landy and Farr (1980), who concluded that the research on rating scale format failed to demonstrate that any one format was superior to others.

But, with few exceptions, rating scale formats were compared in terms of their ability to reduce rating errors. That is, for many years, rating accuracy was defined operationally as being "free from rating errors" such as the halo effect (i.e., allowing positive evaluation in one area to influence evaluations in all other areas; Jackson & Furnham, 2001), primacy–recency (i.e., allowing more recent incidents of performance to overshadow earlier incidents in forming an evaluation), and central tendency (i.e., clustering all evaluations near the center of the rating scale; see Landy & Farr, 1980, for a complete discussion of these rating errors). However, the relationship between rating errors and rating accuracy is not very clear, and interventions designed to reduce errors can also reduce rating accuracy. In fact, Murphy and Balzer (1989) reported that higher levels of rating error, in the form of the halo effect, were related to higher levels of rating accuracy (effect size, $d = 0.71$). Thus, even if a system could be designed that was free from rating errors, it would not ensure that the system was more accurate, and the system could, in fact, be reducing rating accuracy by reducing certain types of errors.

While a large body of research was being conducted to improve the rating scales used, some scholars began to argue that the true instruments in appraisals were the raters themselves and that the focus should be on making raters better judges, rather than on developing better rating scales. By the 1970s, this research focused on eliminating errors, similar to the work on rating scales (e.g., Latham, Wexley, & Pursell, 1975; Wexley, Sanders, & Yukl, 1973), but in the 1980s and 1990s, the focus shifted toward training raters to be more accurate in their ratings, through *frame-of-reference* (FOR) training (e.g., Bernardin & Buckley, 1981; Pulakos, 1984, 1986; Steiner, Dobbins, & Trahan, 1991). FOR training directs raters to various performance dimensions that they should be familiarized with to create a common frame of reference in observing and assessing behavioral performance. It provides behavioral anchors as operational definitions of various evaluations (e.g., what does "excellent" performance look like in a specific area?).

Landy and Farr's (1980) review, then, was truly a watershed event for appraisal research and practice, although it is important to note that Landy and Farr (1980) were still focusing on outcome measures such as elimination of rating errors and interrater reliability in their review. However, not only did their review summarize the disappointing results of many years of research in the area, it also ushered in a new era of research in performance appraisal. One of the suggestions of that review was that research should focus on the raters rather than on the rating scales. Although this was also the view of those scholars who focused on rater training, Landy and Farr (1980) suggested that researchers should focus, specifically, on the decision-making processes engaged in by the rater during performance appraisal, and thus, the *cognitive approach* to performance appraisal was born. Initially, this approach favored theoretical models rather than empirical research. For example, models proposed by Feldman (1981) and Ilgen and Feldman (1983) focused on the cognitive processes through which a rater formed an attribution of the causes for observed performance. DeNisi, Cafferty, and Meglino (1984) extended this approach by specifically considering how raters went about acquiring the information they then used for making decisions, and they gave a central role in the process to how raters stored information in memory and later retrieved it to make decisions. In fact, there had been some cognitively oriented models that had been published before Landy and Farr's review. Borman's (1978) model proposed that decision-making errors served as a limit to improving rater accuracy through training or the development of better scales. The model proposed by DeCotiis and Petit (1978) was the first to explicitly integrate rater affect into the process and discussed purposeful inaccuracy as opposed to the simple absence of information or a true error. Especially noteworthy was the model proposed by Wherry (1952; see also Wherry & Bartlett, 1982), which focused on rater schema as a source of rating inaccuracy and actually included many of the ideas that would be reinvented over the next decades.

These cognitive approaches tended to rely on direct measures of rating accuracy as the dependent variable of choice, rather than on the presence or absence of rating errors. These direct measures required a measure of "true score" (i.e., the true level of performance being observed and evaluated) and then calculated different types of deviation from that true score (see Cardy & Dobbins, 1994, for the most complete discussion of the various indices of accuracy that were used). As a result, most of the empirical research based on these models was done in laboratory settings (see DeNisi & Peters, 1996, and Varma, DeNisi, & Peters, 1996, for exceptions) and demonstrated that the ways in which raters searched for, stored, and later retrieved information influenced both recall and rating accuracy (see review in DeNisi, 1996; average effect sizes were 0.60 for recall accuracy and 0.30 for rating accuracy in the laboratory). This line of research also generated a great deal of interest in how accuracy was assessed, and some fairly complex methods were proposed (e.g., Sulsky & Balzer, 1988). Furthermore, interventions such as structured diary keeping (Bernardin & Walters, 1977; DeNisi, Robbins & Cafferty, 1989) and structured recall tasks (DeNisi & Peters, 1996) were proposed and tested (again, in laboratory settings). When DeNisi and Peters (1996) moved these tests to the field, they found that differences in diary-keeping conditions as well as in structured recall conditions were related to both discrimination among ratees (effect sizes ranged from

0.40 to 0.60) and discrimination within ratees (effect sizes ranged from 0.50 to 0.75). DeNisi, Robbins, and Summers (1997) even found that the nature of the rating scale (whether it focused on traits or behaviors) influenced the way in which raters organized information in memory and the accuracy of subsequent ratings (trait-based scales were found to produce the most accurate ratings, and differences in types of rating scales explained 42% of the variance in rating accuracy).

A New Emphasis

All of the aforementioned models were really little more than further extensions of ideas that had been around for almost a century. The focus was still on ways to make ratings better (i.e., more accurate) and performance appraisal rather than performance management. Thus, the field still ignored the ultimate goal of performance improvement, and (with the few exceptions noted earlier) there was little attention paid to the roles of rater affect and motivation—processes that might lead a rater to intentionally provide inaccurate ratings.

As noted earlier, the idea that rater motivation and rater affect might be important were first raised formally in the model of the appraisal process published by DeCotiis and Petit (1978). They focused primarily on affect and suggested that raters would simply give better ratings to employees they liked and lower ratings to employees they disliked. Although bias based on affect was also included in the Wherry (1952; Wherry & Bartlett, 1982) model of appraisals, the centrality of rater motivation was best stated by Murphy and Cleveland (1995). Whereas several researchers had examined rater decision making explicitly (e.g., Zedeck & Kafry, 1977), Murphy and Cleveland were the first to formally distinguish between a judgment and a rating. A *judgment* was the private evaluation formed by a rater after processing all the available performance information. A *rating* was the public statement of that evaluation, and it was not always consistent with the judgment that had been formed. In other words, a rater might know that someone was performing "well" but decide to give them a "poor" rating. Why would someone do this? Murphy and Cleveland outlined a number of reasons—some of which are positive (e.g., to maintain harmony within a work group) and some of which are not very positive (e.g., to deal with a threat from a competent subordinate). It was therefore critical not only that a rater be able to rate a subordinate accurately but also that the rater must want to rate the subordinate that way. Conscious distortion was never part of the more traditional approaches to performance appraisals, but it clearly is an important consideration.

Yet Another New Idea

The focus of appraisal research, even when researchers considered motivation and intentional bias, was still on rating accuracy; when ratings were inaccurate, it was either because the rater could not rate the person accurately or because the rater did not want to give the person the rating he or she deserved. Ilgen (1993) was one of the first scholars to actually go so far as to suggest that rating accuracy might be the wrong goal altogether. This idea was also stated and expanded in subsequent work (e.g., DeNisi & Gonzalez, 2004; DeNisi & Pritchard, 2006), and these scholars emphasized the importance of performance improvement as the ultimate goal in the appraisal process. Once the focus shifted to performance improvement, more attention had to be given to the process through which an employee might be motivated to improve his or her performance (or at least to try). Thus, concern grew over whether subordinates perceived appraisals as accurate and, even more critically, as fair. Although subordinates would (it was hoped) be more likely to perceive accurate ratings as being accurate, this is no guarantee that these ratings would be perceived as fair.

In fact, as mentioned earlier, it is entirely possible that attempts to achieve greater accuracy in performance ratings could actually result in lower perceptions of fairness and, as a result, less motivation to improve performance. For example, BARSs were designed to include exemplary behavioral dimensions, which are meant to better calibrate the performance evaluations of subordinates. However, Murphy and Constans (1987) found that when specific behaviors are explicitly deemed as "good," they become more salient in the minds of the raters, leading supervisors to become overly dependent on matching behaviors that may not be representative of the employee's overall performance, and so the resulting ratings are less accurate (the effect size for the nature of the anchor on mean ratings given was 1.147). Furthermore, for any type of rating instrument, standards and norms change over time in the dynamic business world, so that anchors must evolve and adapt to the business context. Otherwise, an anchor or standards of effective performance at one point in time may actually come to reflect ineffective performance at some later point in time. Not only may such changes result in less accurate appraisals, but they can also result in inconsistent messages being sent to employees about their expected performance. The recipients of such inconsistent messages may lose trust in the appraisal system, as the evaluations they received are mismatched with what they believed was expected of them (Pritchard & Diazgranados, 2008). This mismatch, then, is likely to reduce the employee's motivation to improve his or her performance on the basis of the feedback he or she received.

Consideration of all of these issues (as well as others) led a number of scholars to argue that regardless of the accuracy of ratings, if the procedures for generating those ratings were not clear, not understandable, or not seen as fair, then the ratings themselves would not be viewed as fair. In this case, employees would be less motivated to change their behavior following feedback based on these unfair ratings (see the review by Folger, Konovsky, & Cropanzano, 1992, and Vol. 3, chap. 8, this handbook, and the results from Taylor, Tracy, Renard, Harrison, & Carroll, 1995). Note that the implication here is that even if raters intended to be fair and accurate in their ratings, these ratings would not have the desired effect unless they were perceived as being fair by the employees. Otherwise, a major goal of the appraisal process (if not the major goal) would be defeated, as employee performance would not improve. These arguments also helped move the field from a focus purely on performance appraisal to a broader focus on performance management. Aguinis and Pierce (2008) suggested that this shift represents a move to include broader social processes and takes the research from a basis in industrial psychology to a basis in industrial and organizational psychology.

NEW MODELS OF PERFORMANCE APPRAISAL

In recent years, several authors have proposed models for managing employee performance that have combined ideas about the importance of employee perceptions of fairness with the realization that performance management must be part of any successful attempt to improve performance (cf. Aguinis, 2009; Aguinis & Pierce, 2008; DeNisi & Pritchard, 2006; Levy & Williams, 2004; Murphy & DeNisi, 2008). These authors have also moved beyond the more traditional views of feedback and feedback effectiveness (e.g., Ilgen Fisher, & Taylor, 1979), and even beyond the more recent views questioning the universal effectiveness of feedback for improving performance (Kluger & DeNisi, 1996). The research has moved on to integrate feedback acceptance into the larger discussion of the importance of subordinate perceptions in the process and the critical importance of performance improvement or behavioral change as the real goal in performance appraisal.

In addition, these newer models recognize that to attain the goal of improving performance or inciting behavioral change in employees, that goal must be aligned throughout the organization. The organization's goal to improve organizational performance may be achieved only to the extent that the managers foster the same goal of improving individual employee performance through the performance appraisal process. It is interesting to note that such an alignment was the stated goal of the FOR training interventions that were mentioned earlier. It has been suggested that FOR training creates a structured and easily identifiable prototype for a "good employee" (Bernardin & Buckley, 1981). Such prototypes could be useful for aligning goals at different levels of the organization and thereby coordinating performance management efforts, and Bernardin and Buckley (1981) have in fact suggested that FOR training is one way organizations can train raters to "think" like the organization. Unfortunately, the emphasis in FOR training has been on increasing rating accuracy rather than on performance improvement, but similar training interventions may have some potential to help goal alignment.

Examples of these new models can be found in DeNisi and Pritchard (2006), Levy and Williams (2004), Murphy and DeNisi (2008), and Aguinis (2009). Although we do not review the theoretical frameworks of each of these sources in the present chapter, there are a few features that are important to note. First, all of these authors emphasized the importance of employee reactions in the appraisal process. We discuss this issue in some detail later in the chapter, but this is an important departure from the more traditional concerns over measurement issues. Second, all of these works cast performance management interventions in a central role in the attempt to improve performance. DeNisi and Pritchard's (2006) article is more concerned with improving individual-level performance and emphasizes the key role of employee motivation to improve. It should be noted, however, that related work by Pritchard and his colleagues (e.g., Pritchard, Holling, Lammers, & Clark, 2002; Pritchard, Jones, Roth, Stuebing, & Ekeberg, 1989) has been more concerned with organizational productivity using a system known as ProMES (Productivity Measurement and Enhancement System).

The article by Levy and Williams (2004) and the book by Aguinis (2009) are more concerned with organizational performance, and both attempt to tie performance management processes with broader organizational strategic goals. Murphy and DeNisi (2008) emphasized the various distal and immediate factors that can influence the outcomes of the appraisal process, whereas Levy and Williams (2004) were also concerned with the way in which other contextual factors can influence the performance management process. Aguinis (2009) differed from the others by providing fairly detailed notions on exactly how one can improve individual, group, and organizational performance. Thus, these works differ in emphasis and specific focus, but they share a consideration of social processes and contextual factors that were not found in earlier models. These models also share a number of more specific concerns that we now discuss.

The Role of Employee Reactions

Newer approaches to studying appraisal and performance management focus on the importance of employee reactions to the success of the system. As discussed earlier, all parties involved in the performance appraisal process seem to be dissatisfied. It is important to note that performance appraisal satisfaction is different than job and employee satisfaction, although satisfaction with appraisals is surely a part of an employee's overall job satisfaction (e.g., Ellickson & Logsdon, 2002). A measure of employees' satisfaction with performance appraisal was developed based on prior work of J. P. Meyer and Smith (2000), with items assessing overall satisfaction with performance appraisal activities, the adequacy of feedback employees receive, and employees' perceptions of their organization's commitment to conducting developmental performance appraisal (J. P. Meyer & Smith, 2000).

Dissatisfaction with appraisals can result in anger and affect employee attitudes toward work and supervision (J. Johnson, 2005; W. J. Smith & Harrington, 2000), whereas satisfaction can lead to perceptions that the organization cares to invest in employee development and feelings that employees should "repay" the organization with increased effort (e.g., Kuvaas, 2006). Furthermore, Ellickson and Logsdon (2002) reported that appraisal satisfaction was also related to lower intentions to leave, greater work performance, and increased job commitment. However, to attain satisfaction from the employees, employers must meet several conditions. Employees must perceive justice and procedural equity, timeliness of appraisals, rating accuracy, and utility of ratings. Also, employees tend to be more satisfied with appraisals that foster future improvement, identify individual strengths and weaknesses, and are more encouraging than critical (Boswell & Boudreau, 2000). This satisfaction then leads to generalized positive affect toward the organization and increased commitment, which, in turn, can result in improved performance (Boswell & Boudreau, 2000).

Satisfaction with appraisals is also a function of how trusting and knowledgeable the employees are of the system (Horvath & Andrews, 2007; Williams & Levy, 2000). Silverman and Wexley (1984) reported that the more involved employees are in developing the rating scale, the more satisfied they are with the appraisal process (effect size, $d = 0.73$) because they believe the decision-making process has been fair and procedurally just (see also Dipboye & Pontbriand, 1981, and Roberts, 2002). Specifically, Roberts (2002) reported that when employees participated in the development of the rating scale, they had stronger motivation to improve their performance and, furthermore, that this motivation was highly correlated ($r = .57$) with actual performance improvements.

Moreover, appraisals are more likely to be perceived as fair and satisfaction is more likely to be high when the appraisal process includes two-way communications, when appraisals are frequent and consistently applied, and when employees perceive that the supervisor has sufficient knowledge of their performance to complete an appraisal (Dobbins, Cardy, & Platz-Vieno, 1990; Landy, Barnes, & Murphy, 1978). Finally, Horvath and Andrews (2007) reported that these positive reactions to appraisals are associated with higher intentions to remain with the organization, higher levels of organizational commitment, and higher levels of work performance (average effect size of $d = 0.15$). The major determinants of appraisal satisfaction are summarized as follows:

- perceived procedural justice,
- two-way communication,
- timeliness of appraisals,
- trust toward evaluator,
- perceptions that performance appraisal fosters future improvement,
- identification of individual strengths and weaknesses,
- perceived distributive justice,
- frequent and consistent feedback, and
- perceived interactional justice.

Before we leave the topic of employee reactions, however, it is important to note one other area in which employee reactions to appraisal are important. Employees' perceptions of inaccuracy and dissatisfaction in the appraisal process may also have implications when companies face lawsuits. When employees believe that irrelevant considerations contaminated evaluations, these evaluations can be perceived as being unfair (Aguinis, 2009). When appraisals are also used as the basis for making employment decisions such as pay raises, these perceptions of unfairness can lead to charges of discrimination. The increase in discrimination cases may not be indicative of actual unfair practices but simply the perception of unfairness; the increase illustrates that organizational practices that are seen as resulting in disparate treatment of protected groups are of great and salient concern to employees. If, in the view of the court, the appraisal decisions were, in fact, influenced by illegal factors such as race or gender, in a consistent pattern, the cost to the organization can be huge. Given the discussion that follows on rater motivation, it is clear that in many cases, the organization will not be able to defend its appraisal system as valid because there is ample evidence that raters are often intentionally inaccurate in their ratings (Harris, 1994). In fact, it is extremely difficult to validate appraisals systems in the usual sense of the term. Construct validation has often been suggested as the most promising method, but as noted by Murphy and Cleveland (1995), much of the evidence for construct validity is misleading because although "this evidence shows that raters *can* provide reasonably valid judgments . . . this does not mean that raters *will* provide valid ratings" (p. 274). Thus, it is even more important that employees perceive appraisals as fair and accurate so that they do not bring suit against the organization.

It is interesting to note that Werner and Bolino (1997) found that issues such as rater training and high interrater agreement (or triangulation) were important determinants of perceived fairness and the willingness to bring suit. It is also interesting to note that many of the requirements suggested for building a legally defensible appraisal system would also result in a system that was perceived as fair. For example, Cascio (1982) recommended that appraisal systems must be relevant, sensitive, reliable, acceptable, and practical to be defensible. So, systems that are more likely to be perceived as fair and reasonable by employees and result in positive attitudes are also more likely to keep the organization out of legal trouble.

Thus, in conclusion, the basic message in these models is that rating accuracy, per se, should not be the sole focus of research to improve ratings. Rating accuracy is important, but it is equally important that employees perceive the ratings as fair and accurate. Only when employees perceive the appraisal processes as fair, and are satisfied with them, will they be motivated to improve their performance (Kuvaas, 2006). Because this performance improvement is the ultimate goal of appraisal systems, we must broaden our focus to consider employee reactions and those factors that might influence those reactions. We turn to one such factor that may be important for employee reactions as well as the integrity of the process itself.

Rater Motivation

Another factor common to the appraisal models discussed earlier is the role of rater motivation. As noted earlier, Murphy and Cleveland (1995) first suggested the critical importance that rater motivation plays in the appraisal process. Specifically, Murphy and Cleveland (1991) outlined four possible goals that managers may adopt when conducting appraisals: (a) task performance goals that are purely motivated to increase performance levels and that are directly tied to the organization's goals in conducting appraisals; (b) interpersonal goals that focus on ways to maintain or improve positive climate of a work group and maintain feelings of equity or attempts of the manager to illustrate his or her power and influence over subordinates; (c) strategic goals in which the manager uses the appraisal to increase his or her standing in the organization by eliminating poor workers and rewarding and promoting good workers; and (d) internalized goals in which the manager tries to provide as accurate appraisals as possible. Thus, a manager may be trying to satisfy several of these goals when conducting an appraisal, and these goals may affect his or her motivation to be accurate.

The goal of maintaining harmony and fairness among the work group, for example, may influence the rater to reduce accuracy by elevating ratings and reducing variance among the ratings given to the employees in the group. This tactic might be seen as a way to avoid social comparison and jealousy among the work group and maintain harmony. For example, Wong and Kwong (2007) conducted a laboratory study in which they manipulated rater goals to focus on either fairness goals or harmony goals. Their results indicated that even when pursuing fairness goals, it is important to also pursue harmony goals in a work group if the members of the group are going to continue to interact with each other (effect size, $d = 0.53$).

Alternatively, a manager might want to encourage subordinates by giving higher ratings than are actually deserved. In fact, Buchner's (2007) PMS review used goal setting theory among others to demonstrate that elevated ratings may serve the function of increasing self-efficacy, which can ultimately result in increased job performance. As such, he illustrated that performance management may reorient employees attitudes to strengthen their beliefs of their own capabilities. Furthermore, managers might want to convey the impression that they are effective managers by giving their subordinates higher ratings than are deserved (Murphy & Cleveland, 1991).

These are only a few specific examples of how a rater might purposefully distort ratings to achieve some other goal. Notice that most of these goals are positive—that is, the rater's goal is beneficial to the employees and probably to the organization as well. Nonetheless, these goals result in less accurate ratings than are possible. However, the willingness of raters to provide accurate ratings affects performance above and beyond simply providing greater accuracy in ratings. It contributes to the effort expended by the rater, leading to employee reactions of perceived fairness and, thus, greater trust, satisfaction, and motivation, ultimately affecting employee behavior. It is also worth noting that when rater motivation is considered as part of the process, then some of the problems that were once thought of as appraisal errors are now seen not as errors but rather as the results of raters' intentions to achieve and fulfill certain goals.

Rater motivation might also be influenced by external forces such as accountability. As defined by Tetlock and Kim (1987), *accountability* refers to the amount of social pressure to justify one's judgments to others. Specifically, W. J. Smith and Harrington (2000) found that when raters believed ratings had important consequences, they were more likely to report discomfort with the appraisal process ($r = .26$) and to inflate their ratings. Horvath and Andrews (2007) proposed an interaction between the perceptions of fairness of a rating itself and accountability such that when ratings are perceived as unjust and the rater is accountable for that rating, the employee will react negatively. Specifically, they reported that when employees blamed their supervisor for low ratings, they indicated that they were less committed to the supervisor ($d = 0.23$), regardless of justice perceptions, but that when raters were held accountable, perceptions of justice were related to a willingness to exert effort to make the supervisor successful ($d = 1.21$).

Thus, raters might attempt to improve employee reactions to them, when they are accountable, by giving ratings they know to be higher than the employees deserve. On the other hand, when performance information is more ambiguous and accountability is high, raters will be more careful about their ratings and engage in deeper information processing so that ratings may be perceived as being more accurate (Tetlock & Kim, 1987). Although the outcomes are more fair, the effort that is involved in achieving distributive justice will be perceived by employees as procedurally just as well.

Trust may be another factor influencing rater motivation. Trust in the performance appraisal system includes the belief that the appraisal information and judgments will be used fairly and objectively (Bernardin & Beatty, 1984; Mayer & Davis, 1999). When raters making appraisals trust that their judgments will be used appropriately, their motivation to be accurate will be increased. Conversely, when this trust is low, the motivation to be accurate will decrease, and raters will tend to elevate ratings because accurate but low ratings would seem to serve no positive purpose and rather contribute to employee dissatisfaction. In the same vein, when subordinates do not trust the appraisal system characterized by inconsistent outcomes or if their expected and actual evaluations are discrepant, the perceptions of fairness will decrease, satisfaction will be reduced, and eventually lowered motivation will lead to lowered performance. Organizational culture and the importance placed on appraisals may also affect trust as well as the managerial motivation to conduct accurate performance appraisals.

Finally, behaviors other than role behavior or task performance of the employee can also influence rater motivation during the appraisal process. For example, when employees participate in organizational citizenship behaviors, voice, and organizational loyalty, raters are likely to feel the need to reciprocate with inaccurately high performance ratings (Whiting, Podsakoff, & Pierce, 2008). Specifically, Whiting et al. (2008) reported effect sizes for the relationship between helping behaviors and voice, on the one hand, and higher performance ratings, on the other, as 0.55 and 0.35, respectively. Borman (1991) also reported a relationship between citizenship behaviors and performance ratings, even though the appraisals used were intended to focus on task performance only.

Ingratiation is yet another type of behavior through which an employee can influence rater motivation to be accurate (or inaccurate). Ingratiation may increase a rater's perception of similarity, which could lead a rater to believe that he or she has a more positive leader–member exchange, when no such high-quality relationship exists. Such perceptions of similarity have been found to influence both ratings of applicant suitability for a job (Varma, Toh, & Pichler, 2006; effect size, $d = 0.32$) and inflated performance ratings (see review by Pichler, Varma, & Petty, 2008).

Thus, these newer appraisal models differ from more traditional models in the importance they place on ratee reactions and rater motivation. These models represent a move away from more traditional concerns with rating accuracy and toward recognizing the various factors than can influence a rater's willingness to provide the most accurate ratings he or she can. These factors can be either intentional or unintentional. *Intentional* factors include task performance goals, interpersonal goals, strategic goals, internalized goals, harmony goals, and the desire to increase self-efficacy. *Unintentional* factors include accountability, trust, and employee contextual behavior. Whether intentional or unintentional, these factors result in inaccurate ratings. These inaccuracies are then more likely to result in perceived inaccuracies, which lead to dissatisfaction and perceived unfairness, all of which are critical for an employee's decision to try to improve performance. Thus, these models recognize that performance improvement is ultimately an important outcome of the appraisal process, which leads to greater concern for performance management techniques, which is the focus of the next section.

PERFORMANCE MANAGEMENT

As noted earlier, more recent approaches to the study of performance appraisal recognize the critical role that performance management plays in the attempts to improve performance. Therefore, we turn to a discussion of PMSs and how they can be used to more effectively improve performance.

What Is Performance Management?

PMSs create an explicit link between individual performance and organizational strategic goals (Aguinis, 2009). For this link to be created, a shared understanding about what is to be achieved is necessary. Hence, the first step in the performance management cycle is that all employees must understand what is expected of them. By the organization articulating its standards to the employees, the raters themselves know what to be assessing and looking for, and thus everyone perceives the system to be fair, legitimate, and trustworthy. Performance management should provide feedback in a timely, frequent, and ongoing manner such that two-way communication exists, but as we have previously discussed, quality communication may depend on the strength of the relationship between supervisor and employee. By implementing a thorough and continuous feedback system, the final performance review or appraisal in which the judgments and evaluations are made will simply serve as a recapitulation of the developmental planning and discussions that have already occurred (Pulakos, Mueller-Hanson, & O'Leary, 2008).

Defensiveness toward negative appraisals will be reduced as they come as no surprise, thus increasing satisfaction with the system and ensuring that broad organizational goals can be delineated. In effect, PMSs have the ability to surpass the immediate short-term effects of once-a-year performance appraisals. Moreover, perceptions of fairness and accuracy will be heightened (Bernardin, & Beatty, 1984). Although we have reviewed that perceptions of procedural justice and fairness are important, they are only one aspect of the process. Employees must also perceive the system to be useful and valuable for behavioral change and motivation to be realized. We believe that PMSs can provide that utility by which employees will be motivated to improve, by demonstrating the existence of strong links between performance improvements and obtaining valuable outcomes (cf. DeNisi & Pritchard, 2006; Pritchard & Diazgranados, 2008).

Performance management, then, should be viewed as a complementary pathway to performance appraisal in improving organizational effectiveness. More specifically, performance appraisal is a critical component of the broader PMS. Organizational effectiveness is the criterion by which to judge performance management, but organizational effectiveness is a multilevel issue (Den Hartog, Boselie, & Pauewe, 2004). Organizational effectiveness can be thought of as being partly dependent on performance or effectiveness of individuals or teams at lower levels of analysis, but changing overall individual performance is not always sufficient for improving organizational performance. In fact, interview results suggest that most raters see very little constructive action or improvement, even at the individual level, as a result of their appraisals (H. H. Meyer et al., 1965).

Subsequent research has focused on the differences between the perceptions and attitudes of mangers (raters) and their subordinates (ratees) concerning the need for appraisals, how they are conducted, and how effective they are (Lawler, Mohrman, & Resnick, 1984). The results of this research indicate that subordinates' attitudes toward the need for and the actual conduct of appraisals is much more negative than those of their managers, whereas managers are much more positive about the effectiveness of appraisals than are their subordinates. Thus, it would seem that there is generally a great deal of dissatisfaction with various aspects of appraisal and even disagreement about which aspects of the appraisal process are more problematic.

We believe that effective performance management may be the key to dealing with these issues. Until now, performance appraisal has been discussed as a potential tool to improve performance at the individual level, but performance management can help move beyond that. An effective PMS can also help improve organizational performance by influencing employees' ability and motivation to achieve higher level organizational goals. Such systems involve ongoing processes that can aid in identifying the skills necessary to be trained and developed, in predicting future performance leading to succession decisions, in prompting discussions and agreements among managers and subordinates on performance planning, and in allocating resources on the basis of performance–rewards links. These benefits occur when there are specific organizational goals and continuous feedback, both of which are designed to emphasize strategic business considerations (Aguinis & Pierce, 2008; DeNisi, 2000). A road map for the development of such a PMS system is provided by Aguinis (2009); the road map begins with the explicit statement of organizational strategic initiatives and goals and includes coaching and feedback. Therefore, we turn next to a discussion of goal setting and feedback within the context of PMSs.

Goal Setting and Feedback

Locke and Latham (1990) summarized the research that clearly demonstrates how specific difficult goals are more effective than "do your best" goals. Thus, it is important that PMSs be thorough in describing and setting goals for improvement in specific domains and that they provide resources and advice as to how to achieve these specific goals. Locke and Latham (2002) subsequently presented data concerning moderators that affect goal-driven performance, arguing that goal importance and perceptions of self-efficacy moderate commitment to difficult goals and that providing performance feedback was critical to the effectiveness of any PMS.

In fact, the combination of goal setting and feedback has generally been found to be an effective way to improve motivation and performance (cf. Locke & Latham, 1990, 2002) and so should be a major part of any PMS. Specifically, *feedback interventions* (FIs), defined as actions taken by an external agent to provide information regarding some aspect of one's job performance (Kluger, & DeNisi, 1996), should be part of any performance management process (as opposed to naturally occurring feedback that might be available to the employee). More specifically, we argue that FIs are effective when used as a continuous and frequent tool for development purposes and when employee–supervisor participation exists to improve the process. In fact, Dipboye and Pontbriand (1981) found that employees reported being more satisfied with appraisal when they had the opportunity to express their sides ($d = 0.73$) and when employees reported that there had been a discussion of goals and objectives ($d = 0.36$). In other words, FIs are most likely to be effective when used as part of a larger PMS.

Otherwise, the evidence concerning the effectiveness of FIs is actually somewhat mixed (average effect size of 0.41; Kluger & DeNisi, 1996). In general, FIs are more effective at improving performance when they are able to promote elaborate versus shallow learning and the transfer of learning to similar tasks and when they do not result in deeper questions about self-worth and self-meaning that can actually interfere with task learning and performance improvement (cf. Kluger & DeNisi, 1996). In fact, the feedback intervention theory, proposed by Kluger and DeNisi (1996), suggests that people are demotivated when they receive feedback that may threaten their self-concept (they reported an average effect size of $d = 2.8$) and that people will have no motivation to continue performing the task if they believe they are too far away from achieving the performance standard or if they repeatedly receive negative feedback. In addition, if the feedback is perceived as unfair or inaccurate, it will not elicit expected positive effects. Feedback that threatens one's self-concept is likely to be attributed to external factors, as fundamental attribution error would predict, and thus would be perceived as inaccurate.

Thus, it is important to balance positive and negative feedback and to deliver negative feedback in a way that it is more likely to be accepted by employees. Unfortunately, some employees are simply not inclined to accept negative feedback and may question the data and information sources used, the criteria applied, and the value of the performance being measured. They may look for some way to discredit the feedback and become upset and angry about the process and at the appraiser himself or herself. Defensiveness resulting from negative appraisals leads to different coping strategies, which in turn may lead to lower satisfaction, motivation, and job performance (Buntrock & Reddy, 1992). Earlier models of the feedback process were especially concerned with ways to overcome this resistance (cf. Ilgen et al., 1979). However, it is truly important to balance positive and negative feedback, primarily because some negative feedback is usually necessary for improvement and because too much praise seems to have little effect on performance (H. H. Meyer et al., 1965).

When implemented effectively, FIs, then, can be important contributors to employee motivation and self-efficacy. In our discussion thus far, motivation has been viewed as the link between performance management and performance improvement. In other words, it is important for the employee to be motivated to improve his or her performance, and such motivation is enhanced when feedback is frequent. Ideally, positive feedback will reinforce effective behaviors and will motivate continued effort, whereas negative feedback will motivate improvement if communicated in a constructive manner. According to Pritchard and Diazgranados's (2008) motivation model, as long as the PMS's connections are strong, motivation will be maintained. Thus, any effective PMS must combine useful feedback with the clear statement of how improved performance can lead to desired outcomes for the employee.

One last aspect of feedback that is worth discussing relates to feedback from multiple sources. Multisource feedback is most frequently (but not exclusively) associated with 360-degree appraisal systems. These systems involve employee self-evaluation and evaluations by a superior, coworkers, and subordinates. Feedback from these systems usually involves showing the employee how she or he rated herself or himself and then contrasting these ratings with those received from all other evaluators. The potential benefit of receiving feedback from different sources is obvious, but evidence for the effectiveness of feedback from such systems has been mixed at best (see review by Smither, London, & Reilly, 2005; average effect size for multilevel feedback was 0.15). In fact, DeNisi and Kluger (2000), among others, argued that the conflicting feedback information often generated by 360-degree appraisal systems can actually make the feedback less useful and even problematic (see also Pfau & Kay, 2002, for a discussion of this issue). This finding has led many practitioners to become quite negative about these systems, even as they had been quite positive when they were first introduced. In fact, very little empirical data exist concerning the effectiveness of 360-degree appraisal systems (there is more about multisource feedback in general), and the data that are available suggest weak and inconsistent effects for this type of feedback. Roberson, Torkel, and Korsgaard (1993) found that employees who were not asked to provide self-ratings were more satisfied with the appraisal process than were those who were asked to provide self-ratings ($d = 0.27$). The reasoning is that those who self-rate and then receive discrepant appraisals are more likely to exhibit defensiveness, which will translate to lower satisfaction with the appraisal process as a whole.

Thus, in conclusion, goal setting and feedback should be an integral part of any PMS, but the feedback feature must be handled carefully. As demonstrated clearly by Kluger and DeNisi (1996), feedback is not the universally effective intervention it was traditionally believed to be (although the effect size was 0.41, one third of the effects were in the wrong direction; i.e., feedback hurt subsequent performance regardless of the sign of the feedback). Nonetheless, when frequent feedback is provided along with clear goals, it can be an important tool for improving performance.

Benefits of PMSs

The success of any PMS also depends on many factors such as the commitment of top management to the process (Pulakos et al., 2008), the clear articulation of expectations for what PMSs should be, and the training of supervisors to effectively implement PMSs. Aguinis (2009) went further in suggesting the need for strategic congruence, so that organizational initiatives can be clearly communicated to individual employees while clear and standardized methods of evaluations and practical considerations are communicated to the raters. Clear communication contributes to the perception of the relative merits of the PMS; without clear communication supervisors may come to believe that the PMS is detracting time from their real responsibilities because of its complexity, which may lead to a reduction in the supervisor's motivation to use the PMS properly. In addition, Aguinis (2009) cited the importance of the *meaningfulness* of the system, which refers to the links among performance, evaluations, and valued rewards discussed previously. Such clear links contribute to greater employee motivation to improve performance. The *specificity* of the system, which refers to the necessity for clear communication of detailed and concrete expectations and information on the areas in which an employee should improve; the *reliability* of the system, which refers to the notion that performance ratings should be consistent and free of error; and the *validity* of the system, which refers to the idea that only relevant performance dimensions will be evaluated, also affect motivation issues. Factors out of the control of the employee should not be considered because they "contaminate" the evaluation. It is also critical that the employees are provided the opportunity to have a voice in the process and that they be allowed input on the creation of the system as well as a means for appeal of any decisions that come from the system (e.g., Dipboye & Pontbriand, 1981).

If these recommendations are followed, several benefits should flow from PMSs. For example, the effective implementation of PMSs through participatory goal setting and continuous feedback functions as a vehicle for increasing employees' intrinsic motivation (Kuvaas, 2006). Performance management may also help to increase perceptions of organizational justice. Landy et al. (1978) demonstrated that perceptions of fairness and accuracy of a performance evaluation were significantly related to process variables. Specifically, they found that trust in the process was related to the frequency with which supervisors and subordinates met to discuss performance (effect size, $d = 1.661$). Such frequent discussions are ensured as part of any PMS, making it more likely that the employee will see this process not only as just but as useful and valuable and hence be more satisfied with the results, even if criticism is involved. At the same time, the PMS helps to shift the rater's role from one of judge to one of coach, which should make the rater more comfortable as well.

Of course, the most important potential benefit of performance management is that it can help align the interest and the efforts of all the forces in an organization. By aligning individual goals and efforts with organizational strategic goals, it is more likely that employee efforts will result in meaningful organizational outcomes. Even if the PMS does not directly lead to organizational improvement, it still serves as a means of communicating organizational goals to employees in such a way that they can direct their efforts in ways that benefit themselves as well as the larger organization. It is the appreciation of the importance of performance management to complement performance appraisal that represents such a point of departure for more recent models of performance appraisal as compared with more traditional models. This recognition, along with the recognition of the importance of employee perceptions and attitudes, makes it much more likely that these newer models can truly help organizations to improve performance. These newer models also have the potential to reduce the gap between research and practice that has been highlighted by Banks and Murphy (1985), Buchner (2007), and Harris (1994), among others. By focusing on performance improvement, feedback, and goal setting, rather than rating accuracy, research based on these new models is more likely to provide practitioners with the practical recommendations they need. Of course, these models are also useful for generating more academic research ideas, and we turn now to a discussion of future research directions (both academic and applied) suggested by these models and our discussion of them.

SOME DIRECTIONS FOR FUTURE RESEARCH

The discussion of the appraisal literature and the review of the newer developments and models in this area lead to a number of suggestions for new directions for research. The first, and the broadest, suggestion deals with the relationship between individual performance improvement and organizational performance improvement. As we have suggested, it is only recently that scholars interested in appraisals have turned their attention to the problem of performance improvement, but, in fact, psychologists have long had insights into ways to improve individual performance. The most obvious example of how appraisal research can be combined with more traditional research on motivation can be found in the model discussed by DeNisi and Pritchard (2006). There has been little research, however, devoted to understanding how to translate individual performance improvements to organizational performance improvements (see, e.g., the review in DeNisi, 2000).

There have been some good starts, such as the ProMES model mentioned earlier (Pritchard et al., 1989, 2002). This model is a systematic program developed to improve group- or firm-level productivity, which is one aspect of organizational performance. The program includes concepts from goal setting and relies heavily on feedback, but it also includes a system for tying individual and group performance to organizational productivity using a model similar to expectancy theory. Work group members attempt to literally map the relationship between specified outcomes and productivity, and a great deal of attention is paid to the connections between effort and performance, between performance and obtaining a desired outcome, and between desired outcomes and the satisfaction of needs. This system has been widely adopted and has been quite successful in linking individual effort to outcomes measured at the group or organizational levels. In fact, Pritchard, Jones, Roth, Stuebing, and Ekeberg (1988, 1989) reported effect sizes greater than 4.5, and similar effect sizes are reported for the various studies included in Pritchard et al. (2002). Finally, a recent meta-analysis reported effect sizes on productivity ranging as high as 5.37. (Pritchard, Harell, Diazgranados, & Guzman, 2008).

The study of organizational performance, or firm performance, has really been the purview of scholars in strategic management rather than in psychology. These scholars focus on measures such as profitability, stock price, or accounting and finance measures such as return on investment or return on equity (see DeNisi, Hitt, & Jackson, 2003, for a discussion of these indices and their role in research). These measures have rarely (if ever) served as dependent variables in studies of performance appraisal. These measures are used in studies of strategic human research management (e.g., Huselid, 1996), but these studies are concerned with *bundles* or human resource management practices (including performance appraisal) rather than with any specific aspect of one of those practices. Thus, it would be useful if we could determine whether there are any characteristics of performance appraisal or, more likely, of PMSs that can be shown to be related to organizational measures such as stock price or some other financial measure. Although it is ambitious to link microlevel practices to macrolevel organizational processes, not only would the demonstration of such links suggest that performance management can help improve performance, it would also provide a very useful practical link for management. At issue in any attempt to motivate individuals to improve organizational performance is that employees can rarely see how their own behavior can translate into higher stock prices (this is usually referred to as the *line of sight* problem; see Boswell & Boudreau, 2001). Therefore, if such a link could be established, it would aid scholarship, but it would also aid managers who could then show employees how their behavior influences indices of organizational performance, such as stock price. Furthermore, as we have stressed throughout the chapter, perceptions are as important as objective information. If one believes that he or she can manage the performance of a subordinate such that organizational performance will improve, he or she will be more likely to try to influence subordinate performance, thus setting up a virtuous cycle.

The shift to a more macrolevel of analysis also raises the notion of examining the role of leadership styles on the performance management process. For example, it has been suggested (e.g., Murphy & Cleveland, 1991) that leaders who believe that participation is important are more likely to devote time to providing feedback than is a more authoritarian leader and that a participative leadership style will also result in better organizational outcomes from appraisal. However, it would also seem reasonable to suggest that transformational leaders, who try to motivate followers to go beyond what is required and beyond immediate self-interest by setting transcendental goals, would be more likely (than transactional leaders) to provide more feedback than would more transactional leaders and that transformational leaders would be more likely to have integrated goals that will be considered during appraisals. In fact, Eagley, Johannesen-Schmidt, and Van Engen (2003) reported modest but meaningful effect sizes for transformational leadership on employee extra effort ($d = 0.09$), satisfaction ($d = 0.14$), and effectiveness ($d = 0.22$). Therefore, it is likely that the leadership style that is adopted will be related to the appraisal process, the performance management process, and even potentially, the overall effectiveness of any attempt to improve performance. Although certain types of leaders may be more motivated to engage in certain appraisal strategies, the ability to detect effective performance is also of importance. It may be that transformational leaders who are also experts in the domain in which they manage are more likely to appraise the critical behaviors that contribute to organizational functioning, more so than a transformational leader who manages engineers though has never had any training in relevant technology. Thus, there may be an Experience × Leader Style interaction. Clearly this is an area in which appraisal research needs to move as we consider the broader issues of performance management. Furthermore, because it has been suggested that coaching is an important tool for the effective use of 360-degree appraisals (e.g., DeNisi & Gonzalez, 2004), it seems likely that research on mentoring might also be integrated with performance management research to determine the best ways to improve performance.

A different direction for future research grows out of the fact that our field has become more aware of the global nature of work, and this has implications for performance appraisal and performance management (e.g., Varma, Budhwar, & DeNisi, 2008). As more and more organizations work internationally, collaboration and coordination of people located in different nations increase. Often this collaboration takes the form of global work teams. Performance management is problematic in such teams because members are likely to have widely differing viewpoints about appropriate ways to reward, recognize, evaluate, train, and develop team members (Kirkman & Den Hartog, 2004). Multinational organizations, whose managers often need to appraise employees from different cultures, must understand and tailor their performance management agendas appropriately. There has been almost no research examining whether PMSs developed in one culture can be effective in a different culture. There are surely reasons to believe that such systems would not transfer across cultures (e.g., because of a collectivist vs. individualistic culture or because of differential power relationships), but we have little empirical research concerning this issue. Research devoted to the relationship between cultural variables and the characteristics of effective appraisal and PMSs would not only help understand the limits of our proposed models but would also aid managers who must manage the performance of employees from different cultures. Can upward appraisals work in a society such as China's? Do peer evaluations work well in collectivist cultures? Is it necessary to have weaker or stronger links between performance and rewards in cultures that have different perspectives on time? These are the kinds of issues on which future research should focus.

More research is also needed concerning the reaction of employees to positive and negative feedback. The feedback intervention model proposed by Kluger and DeNisi (1996) is based largely on the work of Higgins (1987), but that model is based primarily on U.S. data. Would the same mechanisms apply in a different culture? For that matter, do employees from different cultures react the same way to positive and negative feedback? Although one might predict that employees in Asian cultures would react more negatively because of concerns over face saving, some research suggests that positive feedback may be more effective in Asian cultures than in Western cultures because Western self-views are so inflated that they expect only positive feedback and so praise has little effect relative to the effect for Asians (Lam, Yik, & Schaubroeck, 2002). Ratings for some elements of behavior are also affected by cultural differences of the observers (Li & Karakowsky, 2001). Specifically, Asian observers rated significantly higher on dimensions of behavior like provocativeness, egocentrism, and showing off ($d = 0.49$) and significantly lower on dimensions of submissive and obedient behavior ($d = 0.21$). There is also some preliminary research on cultural differences and self-evaluations (Farh, Dobbins, & Cheng, 1991) and even some data on increased bias toward elevating performance ratings when non-Western raters experience positive interpersonal affect with an employee (Briscoe & Claus, 2008). However, these studies are only a start. There is a clear need for studies examining the effectiveness of different performance appraisal and performance management techniques in different cultures.

The focus on rater motivation and the recognition that raters may intentionally distort their ratings suggest several additional areas for future research. For example, research on rater motivation needs to be integrated with research on gender bias in appraisals. Female stereotypes often result in evaluation asymmetry, such that appraisers often feel there is a lack of person–job fit. That is, the stereotyped attributes of women (kind, gentle, relationship oriented) are often not conducive to success in male-dominated job descriptions (Lyness & Heilman, 2006), and supervisors may attempt to confirm their expectations via upwardly biased evaluations.

Unfortunately, the nature, the timing, and even the intentionality of such bias have not been given much attention. For example, in a laboratory experiment, Robbins and DeNisi (1993) found that subjects processed information the same way for male and female subordinates but still rated female subordinates lower given the same level of actual performance. It is worthwhile to note that they found these differences in ratings only when more than one female ratee was being evaluated for a position that was incongruent with female stereotypes. They did not find these differences when there was only a single woman being evaluated for an "incongruent" job. One possible explanation is that when sex is distinctive, managers may be more aware that they are stereotyping, whereas it is more subtle and unconscious when sex is not so salient. Thus, we need to learn more about how stereotypes operate during the appraisal process and how they affect rater motivation to be accurate in actual field settings.

There is also some evidence that gender differences may occur on the side of the raters as well. Benedict and Levine (1988) found that female raters were more likely to delay providing negative feedback and were also more likely to positively distort ratings for low performers. We do not know much about gender differences in rater behavior, and this is an important area for future research. However, Benedict and Levine's (1988) results also suggest the possibility that employees may perceive their male managers to be more procedurally just in their appraisals and therefore more accurate and trustworthy. There is clearly a large body of research on the different types of justice perceptions in organizations (cf. Brockner & Weisenfeld, 1997; Colquitt et al., 2001). Specifically, perceptions of procedural justice are related to outcome satisfaction ($d = 0.48$), trust ($d = 0.52$), and evaluation of managers ($d = 0.56$). Thus, there is a need to apply more of this research to the appraisal setting, especially because those studies that have examined the role justice plays in determining the effectiveness of appraisal systems have found this to be an important factor for both employee and management reactions to appraisals (e.g., Taylor, Masterson, Renard, & Tracy, 1998; Taylor et al., 1995).

Other demographic issues that have recently been examined are age and ethnicity. A recent meta-analysis examining the age–performance relationship discovered four moderators: experience, physical demands, cognitive complexity, and frequency of training (Callahan, 1999). Note that the meta-analysis found that increases in performance due to experience are meaningful for only 5 years—after that performance begins to decline. On the other hand, bias in performance ratings may be a factor affecting the relationship, as it was found that the same correlations decreased and became negative when the employees were over 40 and their performance appraisals were subjective. Additionally, research has shown that older raters (above the median age of participants in the study) gave older secretaries significantly lower evaluations than younger secretaries, and conversely, younger raters gave older secretaries significantly higher evaluations than younger secretaries (Schwab & Heneman, 1978). Overall, there are certainly gaps in the research with regard to ageism that should be more thoroughly explored.

Regarding biases in performance ratings based on race and ethnicity, research shows that several different ethnic minority trainees were more than twice as likely to fail a compulsory training course for lawyers as White trainees. Although the potential effect of discrimination was investigated, no evidence was found even after controlling for variables that may be confounded with ethnicity (Dewberry, 2001). Specifically, the ratings of training performance, which represent maximum rather than typical performance, were lower for non-White trainees relative to White trainees, even when raters were blind to whose performance they were evaluating. Future research should broaden the focus of this work and examine the effects of culture and life experiences that may affect objective performance and subsequently performance appraisals, and these issues should be examined in a broad set of occupations.

Research examining how rater mood and affect can influence motivation is also needed. For example, Forgas (1992) found that when raters receive salient, positive evaluations, they tend to give others lenient and elevated evaluations, thus arguing that when people are elated, they tend to make decisions on a whim based on superficial information and fail to take relevant information into account. On the other hand, negative affect will prompt more thorough and integrated information processing. In fact, evidence suggests that depressed individuals often have the most realistic self-views (Moore & Fresco, 2007). Hence, it may be that negative affect leads to more careful information processing, resulting in more accurate judgments. It is interesting to note that Sinclair and Vealey (1989) found that slightly depressed raters were more accurate in their ratings than other raters. Thus, the mood of the rater can be important, so we need to know more about the determinants of rater mood in the appraisal context. In the studies described, mood was manipulated in a laboratory setting, but what factors might cause raters to become more elated or depressed during an appraisal? One factor might be the actual performance of the employees being rated (consistent with Forgas, 1992). Varma et al. (1996), in one of the few field studies on rater affect (not mood), found that ratee performance was an important determinant of rater affect toward the ratee ($r = .44$). Thus, rather than being a source of rating bias, affect might be the result of observed performance. Surely the same possibility exists relative to mood, and more research is needed that examines mood and affect as outcome variables rather than simply as sources of bias.

Moreover, research should examine the perceived fairness of ratings in situations in which the rater's mood is apparent. Employees may attribute their poor appraisals to the grouchy manager who has a reputation for being in a bad mood at work, and so they see no need for improvement. Over time, if these employees also received fewer organizational rewards, their perceptions of both distributive and procedural justice will decline, leading to lower levels of commitment ($d = 0.15$; Horvath & Andrews, 2007) and satisfaction (Andrews, Baker, & Hunt, 2008) and higher levels of withdrawal behaviors (Wang, Long, Zhou, & Zu, 2007).

In general, there is a need for more research on the reasons why a rater decides to provide ratings that are inaccurate. Not only is this important for a better understanding of the ratings process, but it is extremely important because we know that such inaccuracy may lead to perceptions that ratings are unfair and unjust. These perceptions, then, can lead to less effective performance management interventions. Tziner, Murphy, Cleveland, Yavo, and Hayoon (2008) proposed some explanations for this effect, which include contextual factors as variables that affect the performance appraisal process. Specifically, the personality characteristic of self-monitoring and general orientations toward performance appraisals were moderately related to performance appraisal measures, but there is very little empirical research examining intentional distortion of ratings and the reasons for such distortion. The purpose for which the appraisal is going to be used is surely a factor, but we need to know more about how contextual factors influence distortion. Does the cohesiveness of a work group lead to more distortion? Does the diversity (on almost any dimension) of the work group lead to distortion, and if so, in what direction? As noted earlier, the focus of this research should not just be the accuracy of the ratings but should focus instead on how employees react to the ratings.

This brings us to the other general area in which more research is needed: employee reactions to appraisals. We have suggested, as have others, that more accurate ratings would probably be viewed by employees as more accurate and therefore fairer, but we really do not have much evidence to support that position. Much earlier, we discussed how rating errors such as halo effects may not be errors at all and may be unrelated to rating accuracy. We do not know, however, whether any of these errors might be related to perceptions of rating accuracy and perceptions of fairness. For example, there is really no reason to believe that a set of ratings with more variance is more accurate than one with less variance (i.e., a set of ratings that conform to a normal distribution is not necessarily more accurate than another set of ratings), but it is possible that employees perceive ratings that conform to a normal distribution as more accurate. Perhaps employees are more likely to believe ratings that are uncorrelated with each other (i.e., exhibit less halo effect) and so react better to them. There are surely things we can learn from the research on organizational justice, but there may be some issues that are specific to appraisal and performance management that are important as well. In addition to the issues raised above, research on how employees react to ratings of task performance that are more or less influenced by contextual performance (cf. Rotundo & Sackett, 2002) behaviors is also needed.

There are many other areas in which research is still needed, and many areas in which appraisal research has not ventured in the past. We believe that the ideas presented here have the potential to increase our understanding of the processes involved in performance appraisal, performance management, and the decision, on the part of the employee, to try to improve performance. However, because these suggestions for future research address issues that are generally broader than those studied by appraisal researchers, we also think that research along these lines will help narrow the research–practice gap discussed earlier (e.g., Banks & Murphy, 1985; Harris, 1994).

This gap has created a discrepancy by which performance gains are compromised. The concerns of practitioners are often unmet with solutions from researchers, and this discrepancy may be a critical factor contributing to the low effectiveness of performance appraisals (Buchner, 2007). To solve any performance appraisal issues, a coordination of the concerns must be made between research and practice. We have posited that performance management is the solution to many of the effectiveness issues with which all parties are concerned. If research is to focus more broadly on ultimate performance appraisal goals and how to achieve them, practitioners would surely find a solution to their appraisal process issues.

Future research must also parallel the directions organizations are moving toward. With the emergence of globalization, technology, and improvement in long-distance communication, the workplace is becoming a flexible and dynamic environment in which managers must appraise employees with whom they rarely have direct contact, whether the employees are expatriates, traveling, or working from home. Motivation to intentionally distort may be less relevant in that there is less accountability because of the lack of face-to-face interaction. In the same way, motives to maintain harmony among workers would be irrelevant because there is less likelihood of appraisals being discussed among colleagues. In terms of the implementation of a PMS for individuals working from remote or virtual locations, regular and frequent communication, whether by phone, video chat, or e-mail, is necessary. Because observation is not applicable, a rater must seek out information on performance via daily updates, and thus, trust is a critical factor. Nonetheless, it would seem that appraising outcomes would be more salient than appraising the process because of the inability of the rater to see that process play out. Research should look into these issues, as organizations are headed toward virtual work at a rapid rate.

Moreover, team performance is emerging as an entity in itself that must be appraised. Performance management as it applies to teams differs depending on the time frame of a team's projects. If a team continues to work on subsequent projects together, performance management and feedback will be more important and useful than if the team disbands after a certain project is completed. A supervisor will be less motivated to provide developmental feedback and less likely to differentiate among team members. The issue of assessing relative individual contribution and differentiating between individual and team performance is an avenue for future research. Team appraisals are unique in that they have to be assessed in terms of individual performance, individual performance as it contributes to the team, and team performance as a whole. As Aguinis (2009) proposed, however, implementation of a team PMS can be successful if it follows basic principles that include determining the cohesiveness of a team, explicitly setting and defining common goals, measuring performance in terms of both outcomes and processes in multiple ways, and including long-term performance measures.

CONCLUSION

Our field has a long history of research on performance appraisal, and yet there is still frustration with appraisals and the appraisal process. We believe this is due, in part, to psychologists' focus primarily on measurement issues instead of on ways to improve performance. We have traced some reasons for this focus, leading up to recent models of the appraisals process that fully integrate performance management with performance appraisal. We believe this integration is crucial for making the process more effective and for clarifying that the central goal of the process is to help improve the performance of individuals and, perhaps, organizations.

We have also argued that although rating accuracy is important, it may not be as important as employee perceptions of appraisal accuracy and fairness. Satisfaction and the perception that the process and the ratings are fair are critical for employee motivation, and we must not lose sight of the importance of motivation in this process. If the goal is to improve performance, appraisals and feedback must be used to show the employee where there are weaknesses and areas for improvement. In addition, the employee must have the tools and training needed to improve performance. Finally, it is important to ensure that employees are motivated to improve their performance, which is why perceptions and satisfaction become important. Systems will maximize these attitudes and perceptions when they include some employee voice in the design, some form of appeal, frequent feedback, and high-quality relationships between supervisor and employee and when they are based on recognition that employee reactions and perceptions are as important for success as are accurate ratings. That is, a PMS cannot be effective unless objective accuracy is complemented by perceived accuracy.

The other aspect of the process that we have emphasized is the role of rater motivation. We should no longer assume that better appraisals require nothing more than more sophisticated appraisal instruments or even better rater training. The ultimate instrument in performance appraisal is the rater, and unless he or she wants to be fair and accurate, there is nothing an organization can do to develop a truly effective process. Furthermore, we believe that there are three important aspects of appraisal that separate the first 90 years of research from the past 10. First is the recognition that efforts to improve rating accuracy cannot guarantee success unless employees perceive that appraisals are fair and accurate. Second is the recognition that raters are not always motivated to be accurate in their ratings. Third, and finally, we must recognize that improving performance comes only when PMSs are integrated with performance appraisal systems. These three developments have the potential to generate research that is truly useful to practicing managers as well as interesting to scholars, thus narrowing the gap between research and practice. Of these, the recognition of the importance of performance management represents the single best chance to carry out appraisal-related research that is truly useful.

Effective performance management leads to the alignment of goals at all the levels of the organization—from individual-level goals to organizational goals. Through aligning individual performance criteria with organizational criteria for success and identifying and developing necessary skills, the PMS can achieve much more than what performance appraisal alone even strives to attain. Effective implementation and design of a PMS helps the allocation of resources in ways that matter most to the organization's strategy. But, more important, when performance management is implemented properly, it helps employees to understand what they must do to help the organization achieve its goals while achieving goals of their own.

References

Aguinis, H. (2009). *Performance management* (2nd ed.). Upper Saddle River, NJ: Pearson/Prentice Hall.

Aguinis, H., & Pierce, C. A. (2008). Enhancing the relevance of organizational behavior by embracing performance management research. *Journal of Organizational Behavior, 29,* 139–145.

Andrews, M., Baker, T., & Hunt, T. (2008). The interactive effects of centralization on the relationship between justice and satisfaction. *Journal of Leadership and Organizational Studies, 15,* 135–144.

Banks, C. G., & Murphy, K. R. (1985). Toward narrowing the research–practice gap in performance appraisal. *Personnel Psychology, 38,* 335–345.

Barrett, R. S., Taylor, E. K., Parker, J. W., & Martens, W. L. (1958). Rating scale content: I. Scale information and supervisory ratings. *Personnel Psychology, 11,* 519–533.

Benedict, M. E., & Levine E. L. (1988). Delay and distortion: Tacit influences on performance appraisal effectiveness. *Journal of Applied Psychology, 73,* 507–514.

Berkshire, J. R. & Highland, R. W. (1953). Forced-choice performance rating—A methodological study. *Personnel Psychology, 6,* 356–378.

Bernardin, H. J., & Beatty, R. W. (1984). *Performance appraisal: Assessing human behavior at work.* Boston: Kent Publishing.

Bernardin, H. J., & Buckley, M. R. (1981). A consideration of strategies in rater training. *Academy of Management Review,* 6, 205–212.

Bernardin, H. J., & Walters, C. S. (1977). Effects of rater training and diary keeping on psychometric error in ratings. *Journal of Applied Psychology, 62,* 64–69.

Bies, R. J., & Moag, J. F. (1986). Interactional justice: Communication criteria for fairness. In R. J. Lewicki, B. H. Sheppard, & M. H. Bazerman (Eds.), *Research on negotiations in organizations* (Vol. 1, pp. 43–55). Greenwich, CT: JAI Press.

Bingham, W. V. (1939). Halo, valid and invalid. *Journal of Applied Psychology, 23,* 221–228.

Blanz, F., & Ghiselli, E. E. (1972). The mixed standard scale: A new rating system. *Personnel Psychology, 25,* 185–200.

Borman, W. C. (1978). Exploring the upper limits of reliability and validity in job performance ratings. *Journal of Applied Psychology, 63,* 135–144.

Borman, W. C. (1991). Job behavior, performance and effectiveness. In M. Dunnette & L. Hough (Eds.), *Handbook of industrial and organizational psychology* (2nd ed., Vol. 1, pp. 271–326). Palo Alto, CA: Consulting Psychologists Press.

Boswell, W. R., & Boudreau, J. W. (2000). Employee satisfaction with performance appraisals and appraisers: The role of perceived appraisal use. *Human Resource Development Quarterly, 11,* 283–299.

Boswell, W. R., & Boudreau, J. W. (2001). How leading companies create, measure, and achieve strategic results through "line of sight." *Management Decisions, 39,* 851–859.

Briscoe, D., & Claus, L. M. (2008). Employee performance management: Policies and practices in multinational enterprises. In A. Varma, P. S. Budhwar, & A. S. DeNisi (Eds.), *Performance management systems: A global perspective* (pp. 15–39). London: Routledge.

Brockner, J., & Weisenfeld, B. M. (1997). An integrative framework for explaining reactions to decisions: Interactive effects of outcomes and procedures. *Psychological Bulletin, 120,* 189–208.

Buchner, T. W. (2007). Performance management theory: A look from the performer's perspective with implications for HRD. *Human Resource Development International, 10,* 59–73.

Buntrock, C., & Reddy, D. (1992). Coping dispositions and the stress appraisal process: The impact of defensiveness on emotional response to threat. *Personality and Individual Differences, 13,* 1223–1231.

Callahan, C. (1999). An examination of four occupational moderators of the age-job performance relationship. *Dissertation Abstracts International: Section B: The Sciences and Engineering, 59*(10-B), 5606. Retrieved December 23, 2008, from PsycINFO database.

Cardy, R. L., & Dobbins, G. H. (1994). *Performance appraisal: Alternative perspectives.* Cincinnati, OH: South-Western Publishing.

Cascio, W. F. (1982). Scientific, legal, and operational imperatives of workable performance appraisal systems. *Public Personnel Management, 11,* 367–375.

Cleveland, J. N., Murphy, K. R., & Williams, R. E. (1989). Multiple uses of performance appraisal: Prevalence and correlates. *Journal of Applied Psychology, 74,* 130–135.

Coens, T., & Jenkins, M. (2000). *Abolishing performance appraisals: Why they backfire and what to do instead.* San Francisco: Berrett-Koehler.

Colquitt, J., Conlon, D. E., Wesson, M. J., Porter, C. O. L. H., & Ng, K. Y. (2001). Justice at the millennium: A meta-analytic review of 25 years of organizational justice research. *Journal of Applied Psychology, 86,* 425–455.

DeCotiis, T. A., & Petit, A. (1978). The performance appraisal process: A model and some testable hypotheses. *Academy of Management Review, 21,* 635–646.

Den Hartog, D. N., Boselie, P., & Pauewe, R. (2004). Performance management: A model and research agenda. *Applied Psychology: An International Review, 53,* 556–569.

DeNisi, A. S. (1996). *A cognitive approach to performance appraisal: A program of research.* London: Routledge.

DeNisi, A. S. (2000). Performance appraisal and control systems: A multilevel approach. In K. Klein & S. Kozlowski (Eds.), *Multilevel theory, research, and methods in organizations: Foundations, extensions, and new directions* (pp. 121–156). San Francisco: Jossey-Bass.

DeNisi, A. S., Cafferty, T. P., & Meglino, B. M. (1984). A cognitive view of the performance appraisal process: A model and research propositions. *Organizational Behavior and Human Performance, 33,* 360–396.

DeNisi, A. S., & Gonzalez, J. A. (2004). Design performance appraisal to improve performance appraisal. In E. A. Locke (Ed.), *The Blackwell handbook of principles of organizational behavior* (pp. 60–72). London: Blackwell.

DeNisi, A. S., Hitt, M. A., & Jackson, S. E. (2003). Knowledge, human capital, and competitive advantage. In S. E. Jackson, M. A. Hitt, & A. S. DeNisi (Eds.), *Managing knowledge for sustained competitive advantage: Designing strategies for effective human resource management* (pp. 3–36). San Francisco: Jossey Bass.

DeNisi, A., & Kluger, A. N. (2000). Feedback effectiveness: Can 360-degree appraisals be improved? *Academy of Management Executive, 14*(1), 129–139.

DeNisi, A. S., & Peters, L. H. (1996). The organization of information in memory and the performance appraisal process: Evidence from the field. *Journal of Applied Psychology, 81,* 717–737.

DeNisi, A. S., & Pritchard, R. D. (2006). Improving individual performance: A motivational framework. *Management and Organization Review, 2,* 253–277.

DeNisi, A. S., Robbins, T., & Cafferty, T. P. (1989). The organization of information used for performance appraisals: The role of diary-keeping. *Journal of Applied Psychology, 74,* 124–129.

DeNisi, A. S., Robbins, T. L., & Summers, T. P. (1997). Organization, processing, and the use of performance information: A cognitive role for appraisal instruments. *Journal of Applied Social Psychology, 27,* 1884–1905.

Dewberry, C. (2001). Performance disparities between Whites and ethnic minorities: Real differences or assessment bias? *Journal of Occupational and Organizational Psychology, 74,* 659–673.

Dipboye, R. L., & Pontbriand, R. (1981). Correlates of employee reactions to performance appraisal and performance systems. *Journal of Applied Psychology, 66,* 248–251.

Dobbins, G. H., Cardy, R. L., & Platz-Vieno, S. J. (1990). A contingency approach to appraisal satisfaction: An initial investigation of the joint effects of organizational variables and appraisal characteristics. *Journal of Management, 16,* 619–632.

Dunnette, M. D. (1963). A note on the criterion. *Journal of Applied Psychology, 47,* 351–254.

Eagley, A. H., Johannesen-Schmidt, M. C., & Van Engen, M. L. (2003). Transformational, transactional, and laissez-faire leadership styles: A meta-analysis comparing women and men. *Psychological Bulletin, 129,* 569–591.

Ellickson, M. C., & Logsdon, K. (2002). Determinants of job satisfaction of municipal government employees. *Public Personnel Management, 31,* 343–358.

Farh, J. L., Dobbins G. H., & Cheng, B. S. (1991). Cultural relativity in action: A comparison of self-ratings made by Chinese and U.S. workers. *Personnel Psychology, 44,* 129–147.

Feldman, J. M. (1981). Beyond attribution theory: Cognitive processes in performance appraisal. *Journal of Applied Psychology, 66,* 127–148.

Flanagan, J. C. (1949). Critical requirements: A new approach to evaluation. *Personnel Psychology, 2,* 419–425.

Flanagan, J. C. (1954). The critical incident technique. *Psychological Bulletin, 51,* 327–358.

Folger, R., Konovsky, M. A., & Cropanzano, R. (1992). A due process metaphor for performance appraisal. In B. M. Staw & L. L. Cummings (Eds.), *Research in organizational behavior* (Vol. 14, pp. 129–177). Greenwich, CT: JAI Press.

Forgas, J. P. (1992). On mood and peculiar people: Affect and person typicality in impression formation. *Journal of Personality and Social Psychology, 62,* 863–875.

Harris, M. M. (1994). Rater motivation in the performance appraisal context: A theoretical framework. *Journal of Management, 20,* 737–756.

Higgins, E. T. (1987). Self-discrepancy: A theory relating self and affect. *Psychological Review, 94,* 319–340.

Horvath, M., & Andrews, S. B. (2007). The role of fairness perceptions and accountability attributions in predicting reactions to organizational events. *Journal of Psychology: Interdisciplinary and Applied, 141,* 203–222.

Huselid, M. A. (1996). The impact of human resource management practices on turnover, productivity and corporate financial reporting. *Academy of Management Journal, 39,* 779–801.

Ilgen, D. R. (1993). Performance appraisal accuracy: An illusive or sometimes misguided goal? In H. Schuler, J. Farr, & M. Smith (Eds.), *Personnel selection and assessment* (pp. 235–252). Hillsdale, NJ: Erlbaum.

Ilgen, D. R., & Feldman, J. M. (1983). Performance appraisals: A process focus. In L. Cummings & B. Staw (Eds.), *Research in organizational behavior* (Vol. 5, pp. 123–186). Greenwich, CT: JAI Press.

Ilgen, D. R., Fisher, C. D., & Taylor M. S. (1979). Consequences of individual feedback on behavior in organizations. *Journal of Applied Psychology, 64,* 349–371.

Jackson, C., & Furnham, A. (2001). Appraisal ratings, halo, and selection: A study using sales staff. *European Journal of Psychological Assessment, 17,* 17–24.

Johnson, D. M., & Vidulich, R. N. (1956). Experimental manipulation of the halo effect. *Journal of Applied Psychology, 40,* 130–134.

Johnson, J. (2005). Employees' justice perceptions of performance appraisal systems: Attitudinal, behavioral, and performance consequences. *Journal of Applied Psychology,* 79, 937–939.

Kirkman, B. L., & Den Hartog, D. N. (2004). Team performance management. In H. Lane, M. Maznevski, M. Mendenhall, & J. McNett (Eds.), *Handbook of cross-cultural management* (pp. 132–165). Maiden, MA: Blackwell.

Kluger, A. N., & DeNisi, A. S. (1996). The effects of feedback interventions on performance: Historical review, meta-analysis, a preliminary feedback intervention theory. *Psychological Bulletin, 119,* 254–284.

Kuvaas, B. (2006). Performance appraisal satisfaction and employee outcomes: Mediating and moderating roles of work motivation. *International Journal of Human Resource Management, 17,* 504–522.

Lam, S. S. K., Yik, M. S. M, & Schaubroeck, J. (2002). Responses to formal performance appraisal feedback: The role of negative affectivity. *Journal of Applied Psychology, 87,* 192–201.

Landy, F. J., Barnes, J. L., & Murphy, K. R. (1978). Correlates of perceived fairness and accuracy of performance evaluation. *Journal of Applied Psychology, 63,* 751–754.

Landy, F. J., & Farr J. L. (1980). Performance rating. *Psychological Bulletin, 87,* 72–107.

Latham, G. P., & Wexley, K. N. (1977). Behavioral observation scales for performance appraisal purposes. *Personnel Psychology, 30,* 255–268.

Latham, G. P., Wexley, K. N., & Pursell, E. P. (1975). Training managers to minimize rating errors in the observation of behavior. *Journal of Applied Psychology, 65,* 422–427.

Lawler, E., Mohrman, A., & Resnick, S. (1984). Performance appraisal revisited. *Organizational Dynamics, 13,* 20–35.

Levy, P. E., & Williams, J. R. (2004). The social context of performance appraisal: A review and framework for the future. *Journal of Management, 30,* 881–905.

Li, J., & Karakowsky, R. (2001). Do we see eye-to-eye? Implications of cultural differences for cross-cultural management research and practice. *Journal of Psychology: Interdisciplinary and Applied, 135,* 501–517.

Locke, E. A., & Latham, G. P. (1990). *A theory of goal setting and motivation.* Englewood Cliffs, NJ: Prentice Hall.

Locke, E. A., & Latham, G. P. (2002). Building a practically useful theory of goal setting and task motivation: A 35-year odyssey. *American Psychologist, 57,* 705–717.

Lyness, K. S., & Heilman M. E. (2006). When fit is fundamental: Performance evaluations and promotions of upper-level female and male managers. *Journal of Applied Psychology, 91,* 777–785.

Mayer, R. C., & Davis, J. H. (1999). The effect of the performance appraisal system on trust for management: A field quasi-experiment. *Journal of Applied Psychology, 84,* 123–136.

Meyer, H. H., Kay, E., & French, J. R. P. (1965). Split roles in performance appraisal. *Harvard Business Review, 43,* 123–129.

Meyer, J. P., & Smith, C. A. (2000). HRM practices and organizational commitment: Test of a mediation model. *Canadian Journal of Administrative Sciences, 17,* 319–331.

Moore, M. T., & Fresco, D. M. (2007). Depressive realism and attributional style: Implications for individuals at risk for depression. *Behavior Therapy, 38,* 144–154.

Murphy, K. R., & Balzer, W. K. (1989). Rating errors and rating accuracy. *Journal of Applied Psychology, 74,* 619–624.

Murphy, K. R., & Cleveland, J. N. (1991). *Performance appraisal: An organizational perspective.* Boston: Allyn & Bacon.

Murphy, K. R., & Cleveland, J. N. (1995). *Understanding performance appraisal: Social, organizational, and goal-based perspectives.* Thousand Oaks, CA: Sage.

Murphy, K. R., & Constans, J. I. (1987). Behavioral anchors as a source of bias in rating. *Journal of Applied Psychology, 72,* 573–577.

Murphy, K. R., & DeNisi, A. (2008). A model of the appraisal process. In A. Varma, P. S. Budhwar, & A. S. DeNisi (Eds.), *Performance management systems: A global perspective* (pp. 81–94). London: Routledge.

Peters, L. H., & McCormick, E. J. (1966). Comparative reliability of numerically versus job-task anchored rating scales. *Journal of Applied Psychology, 50,* 92–96.

Pfau, B., & Kay, I. (2002). Does 360-degree feedback negatively affect company performance? *HR Magazine, 47*(6), 54–59.

Pichler, S. M., Varma, A., & Petty, R. (2008). Rater-ratee relationships and performance management. In A. Varma, P. S. Budhwar, & A. S. DeNisi (Eds.),

Performance management systems: A global perspective (pp. 55–66). London: Routledge.

Pritchard, R. D., & Diazgranados, D. (2008). Motivation and performance management. In A. Varma, P. S. Budhwar, & A. S. DeNisi (Eds.), *Performance management systems: A global perspective* (pp. 40–54). London: Routledge.

Pritchard, R. D., Harell, M. M., Diazgranados, D., & Guzman, M. J. (2008). The productivity measurement and enhancement system: A meta-analysis. *Journal of Applied Psychology, 93,* 540–567.

Pritchard, R. D., Holling, H., Lammers, F., & Clark, B. D. (Eds.). (2002). *Improving organizational performance with the productivity measurement and enhancement system: An international collaboration.* Huntington, NY: Nova Science.

Pritchard, R. D., Jones, S. D., Roth, P. L., Stuebing, K. K., & Ekeberg, S. E. (1988). The effects of group feedback, goal setting, and incentives on organizational productivity. *Journal of Applied Psychology Monograph, 73,* 337–358.

Pritchard, R. D., Jones, S. D., Roth, P. L., Stuebing, K. K., & Ekeberg, S. E. (1989). The evaluation of an integrated approach to measuring organizational productivity. *Personnel Psychology, 42,* 69–115.

Pulakos, E. D. (1984). A comparison of rater training programs: Error training and accuracy training. *Journal of Applied Psychology, 69,* 581–588.

Pulakos, E. D. (1986). The development of training programs to increase accuracy in different rating tasks. *Organizational Behavior and Human Decision Processes, 38,* 76–91.

Pulakos, E. D. (2004). *A roadmap for developing, implementing, and evaluating performance management systems.* Alexandria, VA: SHRM Foundation.

Pulakos, E. D., Mueller-Hanson, R. A., & O'Leary, R. S. (2008) Performance management in the United States. In A. Varma, P. S. Budhwar, & A. DeNisi (Eds.), *Performance management systems: A global perspective* (pp. 97–114). New York: Routledge.

Robbins, T. L., & DeNisi, A. S. (1993). Moderators of sex bias in the performance appraisal process: A cognitive analysis. *Journal of Management, 19,* 113–126.

Roberson, L., Torkel, S., & Korsgaard, A. (1993). Self appraisals and perceptions of the appraisal discussion: A field experiment. *Journal of Organizational Behavior, 14,* 129–142.

Roberts, G. E. (2002). Employee performance appraisal system participation: A technique that works. *Public Personnel Management, 31,* 333–342.

Rotundo, M., & Sackett, P. R. (2002). The relative importance of task, citizenship, and counter-productive performance to global ratings of job performance: A policy-capturing approach. *Journal of Applied Psychology, 87,* 66–80.

Rudd, H. (1921). Is the rating of human character predictable? *Journal of Educational Psychology, 12,* 425–438.

Schwab, D. P., & Heneman, H. G. (1978). Age stereotyping in performance appraisal. *Journal of Applied Psychology, 63,* 573–578.

Silverman, S. B., & Wexley, K. N. (1984). Reaction of employees to performance appraisal interviews as a function of their participation in rating scale development. *Personnel Psychology, 37,* 703–710.

Sinclair, D. A., & Vealey, R. S. (1989). Effects of coaches' expectations and feedback on the self-perceptions of athletes. *Journal of Sport Behavior, 12,* 77–91.

Sisson, E. D. (1948). Forced choice: The new Army rating. *Personnel Psychology, 1,* 365–381.

Smith, P. C., & Kendall, L. M. (1963). Retranslation of expectations: An approach to the construction of unambiguous anchors for rating scales. *Journal of Applied Psychology, 47,* 149–155.

Smith, W. J., & Harrington, K. V. (2000). Predictors of performance appraisal discomfort: A preliminary examination. *Public Personnel Management, 29*(1), 21–32.

Smither, J. W., London, M., & Reilly, R. R. (2005). Does performance improve following multisource feedback? A theoretical model, meta-analysis, and review of empirical findings. *Personnel Psychology, 58,* 33–66.

Steiner, D. D., Dobbins, G. H., & Trahan, W. A. (1991). The trainer-trainee interaction: An attributional model of training. *Journal of Organizational Behavior, 12,* 271–286.

Sulsky, L. M., & Balzer, W. K. (1988). The meaning and measurement of performance accuracy: Some methodological concerns. *Journal of Applied Psychology, 73,* 497–506.

Taylor, M. S., Masterson, S. S., Renard, M. K., & Tracy, K. B. (1998). Managers' reactions to procedurally just performance appraisal systems. *Academy of Management Journal, 41,* 368–379.

Taylor, M. S., Tracy, K. B., Renard, M. K., Harrison, J. K., & Carroll, S. J. (1995). Due process in performance appraisal: A quasi-experiment in procedural justice. *Administrative Science Quarterly, 40,* 495–523.

Tetlock, P. E., & Kim, J. I. (1987). Accountability and judgment processes in a personality prediction task. *Journal of Personality and Social Psychology, 52,* 700–709.

Thorndike, E. L. (1920). A constant error in psychological ratings. *Journal of Applied Psychology, 4,* 469–477.

Tziner, A., Murphy, K., Cleveland, J., Yavo, A., & Hayoon, E. (2008). A new old question: Do contextual factors relate to rating behavior: An investigation with peer evaluations. *International Journal of Selection and Assessment, 16,* 59–67.

Varma, A., Budhwar, P. S., & DeNisi, A S. (2008). *Performance management systems: A global perspective.* London: Routledge.

Varma, A., DeNisi, A. S., & Peters, L. H. (1996). Interpersonal affect in performance appraisal: A field study. *Personnel Psychology, 49,* 341–360.

Varma, A., & Toh, S. M., & Pichler, S. (2006). Ingratiation in job applications: Impact on selection decisions. *Journal of Managerial Psychology, 21,* 200–210.

Wang, Y., Long, L., Zhou, H., & Zu, W. (2007). Withdrawal behaviors under distributive injustice: The influence of procedural justice and interactive justice. *Acta Psychologica Sinica, 39,* 335–342.

Werner, J. M., & Bolino, M. C. (1997). Explaining U.S. courts of appeals decisions involving performance appraisal: Accuracy, fairness, and validation. *Personnel Psychology, 50,* 1–24.

Wexley, K., Sanders, R., & Yukl, G. (1973). Training interviewers to eliminate contrast effects in employment interviews. *Journal of Applied Psychology, 57,* 233–236.

Wherry, R. J. (1952). The control of bias in ratings: A theory of ratings. Columbus, OH: The Ohio State Research Foundation.

Wherry, R. J., & Bartlett, C. J. (1982). The control of bias in ratings: A theory of ratings. *Personnel Psychology, 35,* 521–532.

Whiting, S. W., Podsakoff, P. M., & Pierce, P. (2008). Effects of task performance, helping, voice, and organizational loyalty on performance appraisal ratings. *Journal of Applied Psychology, 93,* 125–139.

Williams, J. R., & Levy, P. M. (2000). Investigating some neglected criteria: The influence of organizational level and perceived system knowledge on appraisal reactions. *Journal of Business and Psychology, 14,* 501–513.

Wong, K. F. E., & Kwong, J. Y. Y. (2007). Effects of rater goals on rating patterns: Evidence from an experimental field study. *Journal of Applied Psychology, 92,* 577–585.

Zedeck, S., & Kafry, D. (1977). Capturing rater policies for processing evaluation data. *Organizational Behavior and Human Performance, 18,* 269–294.

Chapter 10

EXPANDING THE CRITERION DOMAIN TO INCLUDE ORGANIZATIONAL CITIZENSHIP BEHAVIOR: IMPLICATIONS FOR EMPLOYEE SELECTION

Dennis W. Organ, Philip M. Podsakoff, and Nathan P. Podsakoff

Chester Barnard (1938) asserted that the "*willingness* of persons to contribute efforts to the cooperative system is indispensable" (p. 83). He did not offer a crisp definition of this *willingness* but did take some pains to differentiate it from *ability* or *effectiveness,* or what some might refer to as "productivity." Barnard seems to have been confident that readers would intuitively grasp what he was referring to, particularly if they, like he, had done much work as a manager.

Curiously, during most of the three fourths of a century that have elapsed since publication of Barnard's (1938) *The Functions of the Executive,* industrial and organizational (I/O) psychologists for the most part chose not to study or elaborate on the concept of "willingness to contribute to the cooperative system." Perhaps psychologists took Barnard's statement as an obvious truism, even a tautology, not amenable to further analysis. Maybe they interpreted task performance and productivity as largely capturing Barnard's concept or perhaps construed it as something otherwise known as *motivation.* Whatever the reason, social scientists until recently have not gone beyond task performance to explore dispositional and environmental predictors of "contributions to the cooperative system."

However, the past 2 decades have witnessed strenuous work on the measurement and conceptual development of Barnard's (1938) concept. Furthermore, researchers have learned something about the antecedents and consequences of the behaviors subsumed by that concept.

To briefly preview where we are headed in this chapter, we note here that, first of all, the *willingness to contribute,* as a construct, can be cast as a major variable in a comprehensive theory of organizations. Second, willingness to contribute can be operationally defined, measured, and distinguished from task performance, notwithstanding the usual finding of a substantial correlation between the two. Third, evidence suggests that managers themselves make such a distinction and include impressions about such willingness to contribute, as well as task productivity, in how they appraise people's performance. Finally, the empirical record indicates that there is substantial variance among individuals and groups in such willingness, as well as reliable attitudinal and dispositional predictors of it, and strongly suggestive evidence as to the organizational consequences.

The logical corollary to the above assertions is that researchers would do well to adapt or augment their expertise about work motivation, reward systems, performance appraisal, and selection methods, with due recognition of this "other kind of performance." Prescriptive inferences about the implications for leadership styles and fair procedures have not been lacking. However, little mention has been made with respect to selection methods.

ORGANIZATIONAL CITIZENSHIP BEHAVIOR AND CONTEXTUAL PERFORMANCE

Barnard (1938, p. 84) was impressed by the observation that willingness to contribute varied enormously from one individual to another. He also opined that something in the nature of "net satisfactions or dissatisfactions" causes willingness to contribute to vary over time within any given individual. It now seems ironic, albeit felicitous, that of the two streams of scholarly activity addressed to the articulation of willingness to contribute, one of them focused at the outset on situational influences and the other took an individual differences approach.

The two independent programs of theory development and research that have figured most prominently in the recent elaboration on Barnard's (1938) willingness to contribute are recognized by the labels they attached to his concept. The early studies of organizational citizenship behavior (OCB) emphasized contributions in the form of helping coworkers, making the job of supervisors easier, and following the spirit as well as letter of rules for conduct in the workplace. OCB researchers suggested that job satisfaction would have more to do with variance in these forms of contribution than with core task performance. Indeed, Organ (1977) suggested that when laypeople endorse the proposition that satisfaction causes performance, what they really mean is that satisfied people cooperate more with others. The rationale for this conceptual distinction is that variance in task performance is largely a function of ability, technology, and the design of the larger system in which individual or group performance takes place. OCB, on the other hand, is less a matter of ability or systemic variables and more a function of inclination, attitude, and discretion.

Meanwhile, research in contextual performance (CP) distinguished between productivity in core task responsibilities and contributions to the organizational, social, and psychological context that facilitate and sustain productivity and effectiveness. Task productivity depends on specific skills and aptitudes as applied to a relatively narrow range of work demands. CP, by contrast, has a more generalized applicability to a much broader range of work environments because it pertains to discipline, constructive interactions with coworkers and superiors, and manifestations of commitment to the organization's goals or mission. Although task-relevant skills and aptitudes, including many that are associated with general intelligence, had long since proved predictive of task performance, personality measures had not shown this power (Guion & Gottier, 1965). Recently, though, there does seem to be a good case to be made, theoretically and empirically, for a connection between certain dispositional traits and contributions in the form of CP (e.g., Hurtz & Donovan, 2000; Kamdar & Van Dyne, 2007).

What is interesting about both the attitudes–OCB and disposition–CP hypotheses is that contemporary social psychology sees both attitudes and traits as predictive of behavior, mainly in "weak situations" and only in consistent trends over days, weeks, or months (Epstein, 1980). Differences in measured attitudes and temperaments do not predict specific actions at a given time, nor do they correlate much with behaviors when the surrounding environment exerts strong pressures to do one thing rather than another. On the other hand, both attitudes and personality do have demonstrable power to predict differences in behavior profiles over time and across varied situations, particularly if the latter are not constrained by strong pressures for specific behaviors.

OCB was defined as "individual behavior that is discretionary, not directly or explicitly recognized by the formal reward system, and that in the aggregate promotes the effective functioning of the organization" (Organ, 1988, p. 4). *CP,* on the other hand, was defined by its more proximal effect, that is, enhancing or sustaining the social, psychological, and organizational context of the cooperative system (Borman & Motowidlo, 1993). The differences in definition are more apparent than real, more style than substance. The element of *discretion* in OCB mirrors the distinction in CP regarding core task or technical performance. And it is this discretionary component, the contributions that go beyond what is dictated by the core technical requirements of the work to which one is assigned, that seem to approximate what Barnard (1938) had in mind.

What makes a contribution discretionary? There is no simple answer to this query. Whatever is not in the employment contract or job description could be considered discretionary. On the other hand, something that is formally in that job description but only in the vaguest terms (e.g., "should strive to be a good team player," "should display initiative in responding to customer needs") could include elements of discretionary contributions, because nobody can foresee just which situations qualify as being team- or customer-relevant, nor the specific behaviors that would represent meaningful contributions in those situations. The level or frequency with which a contribution is rendered can also capture the sense of what is discretionary—for example, certain minimally acceptable levels of attendance and punctuality might either be specified in advance or established by historical precedent, such that rates recognizably above those levels are construed as discretionary. Finally, it is generally agreed that individuals vary in the extent to which they impute to their membership in an organization something along the lines of *moral obligation*—call it *work ethic, personal values,* or *job involvement*—to contribute whatever, whenever, and however they reasonably can, without overweening regard as to whether the form of contribution is part of the job description or who is watching or keeping score. Put differently, what is discretionary can be defined in part as the extent to which people go beyond explicit, specific requirements of the job to arrive at their own sense of the job (Morrison, 1994).

A more problematic issue arises when managers think of the effect of rewards on what is considered discretionary. It is instructive here to think in terms of what the economist Oliver Williamson (1975) referred to as *high-powered* versus *low-powered* incentives. The former refer to incentives that induce a high degree of confidence in a one-to-one correspondence between specific behaviors, their immediate consequences, or objectively measurable results, and assured payoffs for the individual. Low-powered incentives are distal (thus requiring some degree of faith or trust), uncertain of realization, imprecise, and likely to be more contingent on a general impression or reputation effected by a stream of behaviors over time. In sum, low-powered incentives are more tenuous, whereas high-powered incentives are more compelling.

One might well argue that a person has the discretion to forego even the most high-powered incentive. But a considerable empirical literature (as noted by Deci, 1975) indicates that the more salient the proffered incentive (or threat), the greater the tendency for the individual, as well as observers of that individual, to perceive the incentive as the "cause" of the person's behavior. Conversely, the less salient the incentive, the greater the extent to which the individual and others will infer some degree of internal causation, such as a psychological trait or characteristic. Furthermore, it can be surmised that organizations tend to use high-powered incentives to induce those contributions (e.g., sales, efficiency in manufacturing, service to clients) that can be objectively measured and that have the most direct relationship to generating new flows of inputs (e.g., revenues). On the other hand, managers simply "hope" that low-powered incentives will evoke the more subtle, qualitative, and discretionary forms of contribution. OCB, more or less by definition, and CP, by extension, pertain to low-powered, rather than high-powered, incentives.

Conceptually, the concept of OCB might be approached by thinking for a moment of its polar opposite: *working to rule.* This phrase signifies doing exactly as one is told (whether by a supervisor or written job manual) and nothing more. The term is usually associated with unions, that is, a method orchestrated by union leaders to "send a message" when the rank and file are not fully prepared for a strike (although some have argued that working to rule is itself, under the law, a form of work stoppage). The significance of the term, for the purposes here, is that at the extreme, doing exactly what the job description specifies has horrid consequences, else it would not be used as a weapon against management, nor would it be considered by law as a strike.

Of course, to the extent that union–management agreements set forth not only what tasks employees in various jobs must perform but also what to refrain from performing, the obvious effect is to limit somewhat the role of discretion in task behavior and, therefore, to rule out some forms of OCB. However, it seems unlikely that either job descriptions or explicit instructions could foresee in operational terms all forms of such qualities that would be associated with, for example, cooperation, "being a good team player," diligence, efficiency, and conscientiousness.

Both the OCB and CP camps have developed measures for quantifying (through self- or other ratings) the referents of their labels, and there is obvious similarity in the items that appear in their scales. Both instruments refer to such phenomena as helping a coworker, taking responsibility for some function not anticipated by the job description, taking the initiative to address a work-related problem, showing consideration for the work-related needs of both coworkers and supervisors, and generally showing evidence of subjectively interpreting their obligations broadly and implicitly, as opposed to minimally acceptable levels and the most explicit expectations. Furthermore, both streams of research (e.g., Borman & Motowidlo, 1997; Smith, Organ, & Near, 1983; L. J. Williams & Anderson, 1991) have consistently and robustly found that their measures yield two correlated but distinct factors, both of which are in turn empirically distinct from task performance or what is often referred to simply as *productivity*. OCB researchers refer to these factors as *individually targeted OCB* (*OCB-I*) in which the immediate focus of the OCB is a specific individual, such as a coworker or supervisor, and *organizationally targeted OCB* (*OCB-O*), referring to OCB that is more impersonal in tone, generally conceded to benefit the organization as a whole, but in the here and now cannot be said to provide tangible benefits for any particular individual. CP researchers use the terms *interpersonal facilitation* and *job dedication* to denote OCB-I and OCB-O.

The major difference between the OCB and CP communities is that the CP group has exhibited more consistency in taxonomy and measurement devices. OCB researchers have used instruments purporting to measure varied combinations of specific forms of OCB, such as Courtesy, Sportsmanship, Peacemaking, Civic Virtue (which in itself has varied content items, some versions of which emphasize passive participation, although others describe more challenging and assertive stances), Cheerleading, and Self-Development, along with the original factors of Helping and Conscientiousness (which, early on, were called Altruism and Generalized Compliance). It is fair to say that little consistency appears in the factorial structure of attempted measures of these myriad forms of OCB, other than—as noted previously—a reliable breakdown between OCB-I and OCB-O, which is consistent with the broad two-factor structure of CP.

It is far from clear at this point just what should be regarded as the most useful and parsimonious construal of what Barnard (1938) simply called *willingness to cooperate*. The specific forms in which an individual or group can manifest such willingness are undoubtedly more in number than those "dreamt of by all the philosophers." It is one thing to sample a goodly number of those specific forms in the development of measurement and research instruments; it is not necessary to give lofty theoretical status to the items themselves. Nor is it reasonable a priori to expect that all of the distinguishable forms by which OCB–CP are manifested will have much correlation with each other, particularly at the individual unit of analysis. It would hardly be shocking if some individuals, by temperament or training, are better suited for practicing some rather than other forms of OCB–CP. Finally, researchers would do well to anticipate that the most relevant forms of willingness to contribute would vary across organizations and especially from one societal culture to another (we note later some of the implications of cultural lenses for thinking about OCB).

Having noted that these two parallel but independent programs of research have converged in the essence of their reliable findings, from this point on and as a matter of convenience, we generally refer to just one of them, OCB, with the understanding that what we say of one could just easily be said of the other, particularly with respect to practices and applications within I/O psychology. Our impression is that the preponderance of the authors of published articles in this area have, to date, preferred the *OCB* label.

OCB AND ORGANIZATIONAL THEORY

Why is OCB essential to organizations? How does OCB make organizations viable and effective? To address such questions, we cannot avoid an excursion into organization theory. That is precisely the task in which Barnard (1938) was engaged. He raised questions about the very nature of organizations, such as why they exist at all and why a hierarchy of authority is inevitable if an organization is to survive.

Although Barnard (1938) recognized the importance of the willingness to cooperate and supposed it to be a function of both individual differences in character as well as the net gains of cooperative versus individual endeavors, he did not articulate the linkage of overt willingness to organizational viability. Rather, he made executive authority the linchpin of his theoretical scheme. Neither the executive nor anyone else can foresee all of the contingencies and exigencies that will arise in a cooperative endeavor. Put differently, the executive cannot draw up a contract that specifies in meaningful detail every action that an organizational participant will be called on to perform. Instead, an incentive is offered whereby the participants accept a brief list of the few most likely and frequent actions required of them. But in addition, the participants endorse a quantum of authority on the part of the executive, such that the latter can, when unforeseen exigencies arise, direct participants to perform actions not found in the original list. This quantum of authority is neither precise nor static. Just how far beyond the original list it extends is unclear. Experience, tradition, and perhaps some haggling will eventually lead to a degree of consensus as to the scope of that authority. Barnard suggested that participants will come to sense a "zone of indifference," such that they will be indifferent as to whether they perform or are instructed to perform an action that falls within that zone. They will resist instructions that go well beyond that zone. If executive orders lie at the boundary of the zone of indifference, there is likely to be some discussion, appeal to others' views, or perhaps a bit of spontaneous bargaining.

Much later, Williamson (1975) revisited the questions raised by Barnard, and, while paying his respects to the latter, Williamson came away with different answers. To Williamson, the organization exists because of market failures. When future states of nature cannot be foreseen, when buyer and seller are few in number for a specialized service or commodity, there can be no recourse to market price. Moreover, the process of setting a one-time negotiated price would entail such a high degree of transaction costs as to exceed the benefits either party would gain. Williamson saw this issue of transaction costs as particularly applicable to the unique tacit knowledge a participant develops from experience in a specific context. The buyer and seller of that context-specific knowledge both realize that there is no means of ascertaining its value in other contexts. So how will the executive (either the proprietor or the agent of such) and participant find agreement? In particular, how will the executive ascertain whether the participant uses that tacit knowledge to its full extent—in Williamson's terms, what conditions will enable the executive to be confident of *consummate cooperation* in the use of such knowledge? Williamson rejected *metering* (i.e., monitoring) not only because it essentially invented a different but equally tedious form of transaction costs but also because of unfortunate effects on the sentiments of those monitored. Williamson proposed instead the notion of the *internal labor market* (ILM).

The defining properties of the ILM, as a solution to excessive transaction costs are (a) wage rates attach to jobs, not persons, that is, the job exists as an entity independent of the particular person performing the duties associated with the job; (b) participants are recruited into the cooperative system at the entry level; (c) promotion to better jobs is from within the system, which sustains long-term tenure in that specific context; and (d) a form of governance exists by which disagreements, particularly contentious issues as to what is a fair basis of exchange, can meet with resolution. Long-term tenure would facilitate acquisition of site-specific knowledge and provide the basis for reputations as to comparative rates of consummate cooperation, which would be one important criterion for rate of promotion. Consummate cooperation would not be governed by high-powered incentives but by more tenuous anticipation that accumulated observations and impressions of cooperation would redound to the benefit of the conscientious worker.

The mapping of Williamson's (1975) terms into the framework of OCB should seem fairly straightforward. *Consummate cooperation* pertains to spontaneous contributions that go beyond the particular and specific foreseeable items detailed by the job description. Although many job descriptions mention such job specifications as "initiative," "cooperation," "teamwork," and "self-discipline," rarely if ever would the documents specify operational forms of such qualities, because no one can know precisely in what forms or contexts those qualities need to appear. In the ILM, transaction costs are minimized because not only do citizenship behaviors not require a priori specification or willful heeding of a manager's instruction but they also often do not even require the manager to notice that they are needed. The initiative and discretion are left to the participant. Those who take that initiative could well be said to practice consummate cooperation and thereby effect substantial savings in transaction costs.

In one respect, we might choose to modify Williamson's (1975) sketch of the ILM. In his scheme, the benefits for consummate cooperation come with promotion to a higher rank or a better paying position with more responsibility (i.e., of greater "worth," in job evaluation terms). However, promotions are sometimes a matter of years (particularly after the first one or two advancements) and thus probably strain the perceived credibility of the premise that OCB will be recognized, appreciated, and in some manner compensated. Second, long-term secular trends toward flatter, more decentralized, more entrepreneurial firms have probably diminished the scope of promotions for rewarding good citizens in the workplace. One would suspect that the device that now plays the larger role in recognizing and rewarding OCB is the performance appraisal (and therefore a compelling reason to revisit and reinterpret the role of performance appraisal systems). And indeed, research amply demonstrates (e.g., N. P. Podsakoff, Whiting, Podsakoff, & Blume, 2009; P. M. Podsakoff, MacKenzie, & Hui, 1993; P. M. Podsakoff, MacKenzie, Paine, & Bachrach, 2000) that supervisors do take OCB into account in appraisals, sometimes weighting it even heavier than more objective measures of task productivity. Moreover, the recommendations for pay increases, as well as ratings of fitness for promotion, correlate substantially with managerial estimates of subordinates' OCB–CP.

One area of concern in regard to the ILM is that it might prove to be a less viable organizational form in an era of increasingly global labor markets and the information technology that makes such markets possible. Such markets will bid up the going rate for those contributors with objective and universally recognized forms of expertise and training. Meeting this rate for human capital in specialized task knowledge would likely account for more variance in pay than locally, informally valued differences in OCB. Most likely, the recruitment and retention of such expertise would also limit the resources available to recompense more organization-specific tacit knowledge and subjective estimates of OCB (Organ & Lee, 2008). But it is also conceivable that the same information technology feeding global labor markets will make it possible for intricately linked networks to serve as media for many forms of OCB, as well as a means to create and sustain reputations about an individual's proclivity for OCB.

Katz and Kahn (1978) seemed to foresee this development when they referred to a "morale problem for years to come for organizations . . . one of equity" (p. 391) when they referred to the competing dynamics of steep incentive systems for attracting and holding excellence in talent versus flatter wage structures more likely to preserve one class of felt "citizenship." Earlier, Katz (1964) had raised a basic question: What kinds of behaviors do organizations require of participants? They suggested three broad and fundamentally different types of behavior: Organizations must attract and hold people within the system, elicit dependable role performance, and evoke "innovative and spontaneous" behaviors that go beyond routine role behaviors. It is not clear whether comparatively higher productivity or technical excellence in task performance would have fallen in the second or third category, or perhaps would have required a fourth class, but their further description of the third category leaves no doubt that it captures "spontaneous" and "intrinsically cooperative" behaviors "without which the system would break down . . . and few of them are included in the formal role prescriptions for any job" (Katz & Kahn, 1966, p. 339). The larger point emphasized is that different forms of system rewards motivate these qualitatively different classes of behavior. Thus, to pose the issue to our purposes here, the types of rewards that attract superior talent, reward technical excellence, or acknowledge high productivity are probably not the same as those that sustain an active orientation to OCB. In fact, even such a robustly tested motivational device as goal setting—particularly when the goals are difficult, accepted, and tied to pay—will encourage task productivity but will tend to inhibit much of what is associated with OCB (Wright, George, Farnsworth, & McMahan, 1993).

DETERMINANTS OF OCB

If OCB is to be considered as a kind of performance, one that is distinguishable from task productivity, one must ask the following questions: (a) What factors determine OCB? (b) How do the determinants of OCB differ from those governing task productivity? and (c) What methods allow organizations to enhance the determinants of OCB?

Satisfaction

As noted earlier, Barnard (1938) believed that "net satisfactions" of participants governed the "willingness" to contribute to cooperative systems. There is now a strong basis for thinking that Barnard was correct. Several meta-analytic studies confirm the proposition that job satisfaction correlates positively with OCB and that it does so to a somewhat greater extent than with measures of task performance (Hoffman, Blair, Meriac, & Woehr, 2007; Organ & Ryan, 1995). For example, Organ and Ryan (1995) found a mean uncorrected correlation of .38 between job satisfaction and a composite index of several OCB factors, as compared with Iaffaldano and Muchinsky's (1985) reported correlation of .15 from their meta-analysis of the relationship between satisfaction and task performance. Moreover, the results obtained by Organ and Ryan were based on data from varied formats and measures of satisfaction; some of the measures were general job satisfaction, and some were total measures based on varied combinations of several different facets or referents (e.g., pay, supervision, work itself, coworkers) of satisfaction. Their data showed no indication that any particular referent of satisfaction stood out as having a stronger or weaker relationship to OCB than did the others, including those intended to capture the notion of *general job satisfaction.*

However, *satisfaction* should be thought of in terms of a complex of various Morale factors. For example, Organ and Ryan (1995) found measures of perceived fairness also to correlate robustly with OCB, virtually to the same extent as did satisfaction; also, the correlations held up across varied measures and referents of the fairness construct (e.g., procedural justice, distributive justice, interactional justice). In addition, measures of affective commitment to the organization and perceptions of supportive leadership on the part of the supervisor yielded correlations with OCB that were actually slightly higher than those with satisfaction. Measures of these various indicators of Morale are associated with OCB at about the same level, and they are correlated with each other (often at .50 or higher).

We do not mean to suggest that satisfaction, perceived fairness, perceived supportiveness by one's boss, and affective attachment to the organization are all the same thing. Nor, for that matter, do we suggest that there is no use in differentiating satisfaction with pay from satisfaction with coworkers. Indeed, researchers might well find, as more data add to the empirical record, that different types of satisfaction, for example, might differ with respect to the specific forms of OCB that they predict. No single one of these attitudinal variables fully explains the effects of the others, although some evidence (Fassina, Jones, & Uggersly, 2008) suggests that the pattern of direct and indirect effects of fairness and satisfaction differs across OCB-I and OCB-O. Fassina et al. (2008), using estimated population correlation coefficients, found that job satisfaction and interactional fairness accounted for unique variance in the five dimensions of OCB that were studied, although distributive fairness explained unique variance only for the Civic Virtue aspect of OCB, and procedural fairness was uniquely linked only to Civic Virtue and Sportsmanship.

Nonetheless, sufficient evidence is at hand to think at some level of a broad Morale factor underlying various measures of how people perceive and evaluate their work environments. James and James (1989) characterized this broad factor as the extent to which the participant believes the work environment is beneficial to one's overall well-being. Just what factors weigh, positively or negatively, in establishing the level of that broad factor no doubt vary somewhat with context, perhaps also with the individual. However established, that underlying Morale (as reported by participants) appears to be associated with the degree to which their supervisors and coworkers describe those participants' OCB. In support of this assertion, Organ (1997), using estimated population correlations from the Organ and Ryan (1995) meta-analysis, reported that a model specifying latent constructs in the form of "Morale" (as a substratum of measures of satisfaction, fairness, affective commitment, and leader supportiveness) and OCB (reflective of both the Helping and

Conscientiousness forms) revealed those constructs to be highly related (with an estimated path coefficient of .69), with an overall goodness of fit of .94 of the model to the data.

The preponderance of research on OCB takes the form of cross-sectional field studies, an observation that might call into question our use of the term *determinant* (i.e., cause). However, Skarlicki and Latham (1996, 1997) conducted two separate field experiments that instituted formal programs for training union officers in applications of fair treatment and found in both instances that subsequent OCB by union members increased and did so to a greater extent than in control groups in which the training did not take place. Moreover, some cross-lagged panel studies, in which attitudes and OCB were assessed at two or more different times, indicate some causal connection of attitudes on OCB. One meta-analysis of such studies (Riketta, 2008) confirmed an overall effect of attitudes on performance, but the effect size was no different for OCB than for task performance. However, most of the longitudinal studies involved self-ratings of OCB, and it is well established that relationships between OCB and attitudes are more volatile for self-ratings of the behavior (Organ & Ryan, 1995).

Tentatively, to generalize, the evidence supports the general view that managers should strive to effect something like a "microcosm of a just world." That is, in matters pertaining to compensation, benefits, rule enforcement, disciplinary actions, and the interactions between managers and those who report to them, organization officials should exert efforts to adhere as much as is reasonably possible to broadly shared standards of distributive, procedural, and interactional fairness, because doing so would seem to go far to sustain the kind of morale that encourages OCB.

Such an admonition is easier to suggest than to follow. There are different and often conflicting standards for fairness, and doggedly following any one of them is virtually certain to leave some people feeling aggrieved. Such conflicts might be minimized to the extent that affected participants have some input into formulating the rules for workplace governance. But, to paraphrase Lincoln, "you can be fair to some people all of the time, you can be fair to all people some of the time, but you cannot be fair to all people all of the time." We could say the same about keeping people satisfied. Thus, we would hope that some other means is at hand to yoke with fair managerial treatment, toward the end of promoting OCB.

Dispositional Differences

Barnard (1938) thought individuals would vary in their natural inclination toward OCB. The program of research on CP was founded on the logic that personality factors, not notable for their success in predicting task performance, would come to the fore in explaining differences in contributions to the social, organizational, and psychological context of the workplace. (See also chap. 5, this volume.)

The empirical record to date on personality as a correlate of OCB is mixed. Individual studies and meta-analyses support the case for temperament having some measurable effects on OCB, but the absolute values of those effect sizes are generally lower in magnitude than is the case with job attitudes. For example, the Organ and Ryan (1995) meta-analytic study examined the empirical results from 10 studies including measures that either explicitly addressed dimensions of the Big Five framework (McCrae & Costa, 1987) or appeared on their face to be strongly suggestive of such dimensions (i.e., some studies used measures intended to measure Conscientiousness, one other study interpreted the so-called lie scale of the Eysenck Personality Inventory [Eysenck, 1958] as an alternative index of self-described Conscientiousness). Six studies had examined the relationship between OCB and the Big Five dimension Agreeableness, because one might well suspect a priori that those who get along well with others in both personal and work relationships would also represent those disposed to help coworkers. Five studies had included measures of Negative Affectivity, which is strongly suggestive of the Neuroticism (or its converse, Emotional Stability) factor of the Big Five. Seven studies looked at Positive Affectivity, which is somewhat suggestive of the characteristics imputed to Extraversion in the Big Five.

Of the four Big Five dimensions in the meta-analysis, only Conscientiousness revealed an estimated population coefficient exceeding .15. Conscientiousness was estimated to correlate .22

with the OCB dimension of Altruism (or Helping) and .30 with Generalized Compliance (the form of OCB interpreted as the more impersonal or organizational form of OCB, in contrast to the more directly personal form that targets specific individuals). Furthermore, when those studies using self-rating measures of OCB were excluded, only the relationship with Generalized Compliance remained significant.

A follow-up meta-analytic review (Borman, Penner, Allen, & Motowidlo, 2001), including studies conducted after the Organ and Ryan (1995) analysis, revealed somewhat consistent but still modest associations between OCB and personality. When self-report measures of OCB were excluded, none of the weighted mean correlations exceeded .20, the highest such estimate being .19 for Conscientiousness.

It appears that little if any scrutiny has been directed toward Openness to Experience (sometimes referred to as Intellectance) as a correlate of OCB. The paucity of such research can probably be chalked up to the difficulty of conceptualizing a plausible model or rationale by which this factor would be manifested in the form of OCB—which, in turn, might be explained by the difficulty in articulating the nature of this dimension. However, we should note that a meta-analytic review by Judge, Bono, Ilies, and Gerhardt (2002) indicated that Openness to Experience was one of three significant predictors (along with Conscientiousness and Extraversion) of leadership, and that Openness was equally significant in predicting leader emergence and leader effectiveness. To the extent that leaders emerge as a function of "doing more than is required" or "going the extra mile," and to the extent that they are effective in a general sense because of extra contributions, then perhaps there is a basis for surmising that this dimension of the Big Five has relevance to OCB.

If it seems at first glance that the generally accepted Big Five model has fared poorly in predicting OCB, one must remember that the same was once said about personality measures and job performance. There is now reason to believe that such an impression arose, at least in part, by studies that were done in essentially atheoretic fashion, failing to use explicit and coherent models that would selectively position dimensions of personality with relevant context reflected in job descriptions. J. Hogan and Holland (2003) demonstrated that aligning predictors and criteria on the basis of theory substantially improves the validity scorecard for Emotional Stability, Extraversion, Agreeableness, Conscientiousness, and Openness. Researchers might do well to think along those lines in future studies of personality and OCB. Not only might a specific personality factor better predict OCB in general in some contexts but it also might predict some dimensions of OCB better in some contexts, and different dimensions in different contexts. Researchers might also find that more specific facets of one or more of the Big Five factors, as opposed to any one of the Big Five, will serve them better in predicting specific forms of OCB in selective contexts.

Finally, a theoretically robust treatment of dispositional effects on OCB probably should consider forms of interaction or moderation as a function of Morale and/or job attitudes. A study by Kamdar and Van Dyne (2007) found that the relationship between personality and OCB was moderated by the perceived quality of interactions and relationships with the supervisor and coworkers. The quality of such interactions were indexed by subordinates' reports as to how much they liked their supervisor as a person, the belief that the supervisor would come to their support if they made honest mistakes, the extent to which they admired their boss, how strongly they believed their supervisor went the extra mile on their behalf, and similar such sentiments. Measures of quality relationships with coworkers were based on items capturing the degree to which participants believed they had reciprocal relationships in terms of helping each other finish work or understand each other's problems. When such relationships were of "high quality," neither Conscientiousness (from the Big Five taxonomy) nor Agreeableness (also a Big Five dimension) had reliable associations with any form of OCB (although both traits were related to task performance). Only when relationships with boss and coworkers were of lower perceived quality did Conscientiousness correlate significantly with helping the supervisor and Agreeableness predict helping coworkers. Thus, in a sense, it seems that dispositional differences affect OCB "when they are most needed," that is, when for whatever reasons the individual does not perceive requisite fairness or experience satisfaction in workplace relationships.

Cultural Variations on the Meaning and Causal Structure of OCB

The vast majority of the empirical work on OCB has occurred in the United States or Canada and other English-speaking countries. A modest amount of published work on this topic is based on studies in Mexico; Western Europe; and in Chinese-speaking settings, including the People's Republic of China (PRC). Very few articles have appeared reporting empirical analysis from studies in Eastern Europe, the Middle East, Africa, non–Chinese-speaking Asia, or South America. So far as we are aware, no meta-analytic reviews have looked at whether U.S. or non–U.S. work settings moderate the relationship between job satisfaction and OCB, perceived fairness and OCB, or established measures of personality (particularly the Big Five factors) and OCB (although published meta-analyses do include one or more studies based in non–U.S. work settings but either had too few such studies to scrutinize them separately or simply chose not to pursue the issue of culture as a moderator).

We can identify several respects in which societal culture conditions what we might have to say about OCB. First, the very idea of what fits the general definition of *OCB*—whether the definition is phrased as "spontaneous and nonrequired contributions to organizational effectiveness" or "contributions to the social and psychological context of task performance"—might well vary from one society to another. Thus, Farh, Earley, and Lin (1997) found that Taiwanese managers, when prompted to give examples of work behavior that fit the basic definition of OCB, matched three of the dimensions often studied in the United States but also consistently gave examples that reflected two dimensions not addressed in any studies in North American settings. Later, Farh, Zhong, and Organ (2004) found that managers in the PRC also seemed to think in terms of a structure of OCB different from that typically recognized in the United States. For example, helping coworkers away from the job was considered to fit the general definition of OCB. Furthermore, among managers in state-owned firms, volunteer work within the community and on behalf of the state figured prominently in the examples given of when they had observed (or heard of) behavior that fit the definition (which might also indicate that the meaning of *organizational effectiveness* itself can vary across contexts and thus would logically lead us to expect different guises of OCB).

Second, it would not be surprising if such predictors of OCB as found in U.S. studies are attenuated, or perhaps even reversed in direction, with certain variations in societal culture. Hofstede (1984) concluded that countries and regions vary immensely in terms of the steepness of the social hierarchy, the extent to which native inhabitants seek to avoid risk, and the degree to which resident people prioritize egoistic concerns versus those of the group or family. The relationship generally observed in the United States between measures of individual job satisfaction or perceived fairness to the individual and OCB might reflect the strongly individualistic orientation and flatter status hierarchy of the United States as compared with most other countries. In other cultures, to the extent that fairness is even contemplated, the issue might be fairness to the group, the local work organization, the family, class, or some other collective with which people most identify.

Culture might also figure in the general frequency or prevalence with which certain forms of OCB occur, thus attenuating any other effects. Anecdotal evidence abounds in the observation that first-generation Mexican and other Latin American immigrants in the United States will usually work very hard to do whatever the boss explicitly and precisely instructs but will refrain from doing anything that goes beyond those instructions. This observation—assuming its reliability—is understandable in terms of Hofstede's (1984) data that characterize Latin American culture as high in power distance and uncertainty avoidance. To go beyond the explicit orders of a powerful boss could be construed as disrespect, which might lead one to anticipate punishment for that reason alone, and if "taking initiative" turns out to be something that makes a situation worse, then such initiative becomes doubly risky.

We suggest caution in generalizing what we offer here, in terms of selection of people on the basis of predictors of OCB, to non–U.S. settings.

Nonetheless, we believe it reasonable to make the following observations:

1. *Culture* is not synonymous with *nation* or *country*. Even within so-called developing economies, one finds a mixture of the traditional culture (often in rural areas or villages) and the modern culture (usually in the large metropolitan areas and where large business and government organizations are found). Modern contexts do not utterly eliminate traditional values and mores, but global market forces arguably do condition and temper them in the direction of precepts and practices similar to those in the modern business world in other countries.
2. Wherever there is a high degree of modernity, it will probably be that the substance and causal structure of OCB have some similarity to what we have found in the United States, Canada, and much of Western Europe. Thus, for example, Farh et. al (1997) found that a measure of modernity (as an individual difference measure of values and self-identity) moderated the relationship between perceived fairness and OCB; the higher the score on modernity, the stronger the relationship between fairness and OCB. Also, a study conducted by Konovsky, Elliot, and Pugh (1995) in Mexico found that job satisfaction, fairness, and personality dimensions had very much the same level and direction of statistical relationships with different OCB factors as generally found in the United States. The study was done in Monterrey, near the U.S. border, where the business community has absorbed most of the mainstream managerial practices and values of its northern neighbor.
3. If valid predictors of OCB are to be found among measures of temperament and/or mental ability, there is reason to be optimistic that those predictors found in the United States will prove meaningful in other parts of the global economy. For example, the Big Five structure of personality has been replicated in Europe (Salgado, 1997) and in Chinese-speaking communities (Trull & Geary, 1997). This is not to suggest that the present Big Five factors will hold the answers to predicting OCB, or even that some specific facets of one of those factors will compose the best measure, but rather that structures and measures of personality have some similarity of meaning and relevance across many geographic and cultural borders. Salgado et al. (2003) also found that general mental ability had much the same relationship to job performance in Europe as that found in the U.S., including the observation that job complexity moderated the validity coefficients; indeed, Salgado et al. found that validities in Europe were somewhat stronger overall than in the United States.

WHAT IS THE JUSTIFICATION FOR INCORPORATING OCB INTO THE EMPLOYEE SELECTION PROCESS?

Quite some years ago, during a televised NBA game involving the Boston Celtics, the announcer noted to Bill Russell, former Celtic great and now color commentator, that then-current Boston center Dave Cowens was said by many pundits to be a great player, not because of his talent but rather because of his effort. Russell said, "Well, they're wrong, because effort *is* a talent, and it's the most important one you can have." Perhaps it is instructive to think of willingness to contribute as a kind of talent (even if we would not argue for now that "it is the most important" talent a person could have). If this willingness is indeed a talent in its own right and is distinguishable from task performance, then it is natural to ask, (a) Do managers recognize and value this talent (behavior) in their performance evaluations and reward allocation decisions? and (b) Do these forms of talent (behavior) actually influence an organization's effectiveness?

Effects of OCB on Job Performance Ratings and Reward Allocation Decisions

MacKenzie, Podsakoff, and Fetter (1991) were among the first to explore the potential effects that OCB might have on performance evaluations. For the purposes of their research, they examined the relationships between task performance and several dimensions of OCB (Altruism, Courtesy, Civic Virtue, and Sportsmanship) and job performance ratings among a primary sample composed of

259 insurance agents and a cross-validation sample that consisted of 113 agents. MacKenzie et al. (1991) reported that managers' subjective evaluations of their agents' job performance were determined as much by a salesperson's Altruism and Civic Virtue as they were by the agents' task performance and that the combination of objective task performance and OCB accounted for 44% of the variance in managerial evaluations in the primary sample and for 61% of the variance in this criterion variable in the cross-validation sample.

Since the publication of the MacKenzie et al. (1991) article, a number of additional studies have examined the relationships between task performance, OCB, and ratings of job performance in a wide variety of organizational settings (Ferris, Witt, & Hochwarter, 2001; Findley, Giles, & Mossholder, 2000; J. W. Johnson, 2001; Lovell et al., 1999; MacKenzie, Podsakoff, & Fetter, 1993; Motowidlo & Van Scotter, 1994; Van Scotter & Motowidlo, 1996; Wayne, Shore, & Liden, 1997). A meta-analytic summary of this research, which has been reported recently by N. P. Podsakoff et al. (2009), is reported in the top half of Table 10.1.

As indicated in this table, the average corrected correlation between OCB and performance evaluation ratings ($r_c = .60$) was somewhat higher than the corrected correlation between task performance and job performance ratings ($r_c = .52$). N. P. Podsakoff et al. (2009) also reported that when task performance, OCB-I, and OCB-O were included in a path analysis, they all had significant effects on job performance evaluations. Although the majority of studies reviewed by N. P. Podsakoff et al. (2009) were conducted in field settings, there are several experimental studies (Allen & Rush, 1998; Rotundo & Sackett, 2002; Werner, 1994; Whiting, Podsakoff, & Pierce, 2007) that have examined the effects of OCB on rater evaluations. Generally speaking, these studies showed that experimentally manipulated OCB are causally related to performance evaluation ratings.

Given that performance evaluations serve as the bases for the manner in which rewards are administered in organizations, one would also expect OCB to be related to the decisions managers make when allocating rewards. Indeed, the research that has been conducted to date supports this expectation. A summary of these relationships is reported in the

TABLE 10.1

Relationships Between Organizational Citizenship Behavior (OCB) and Individual-Level Outcomes

				90% CI			
Relationship	***k***	***N***	***r***	**Lower**	**Upper**	r_c	SDr_c
		Job performance ratings					
OCB–job performance ratings	72	21,881	.49	.48	.50	.60	.26
OCB-I–job performance ratings	43	15,860	.46	.45	.47	.55	.25
OCB-O–job performance ratings	38	12,745	.46	.45	.48	.63	.26
Task performance–job performance ratings	27	8,065	.46	.44	.47	.52	.23
		Reward allocation decisions					
OCB–reward recommendations	10	4,330	.58	.56	.60	.77	.00
OCB-I–reward recommendations	6	3,683	.59	.57	.61	.73	.00
OCB-O–reward recommendations	4	3,370	.52	.50	.54	.72	.00
OCB–actual rewards	8	2,631	.21	.18	.24	.26	.11
OCB-I–actual rewards	6	1,779	.14	.11	.18	.17	.00
OCB-O–actual rewards	5	1,527	.22	.18	.26	.28	.06

Note. CI = confidence interval; *k* = number of independent samples; SDr_c = standard deviation of corrected correlation coefficient; OCB-I = individually targeted OCB; OCB-O = organizationally targeted OCB. Subgroup *k* values may not add up to overall *k* because of the use of linear composites, which eliminated double-counting data from the same study. Adapted from "Individual- and Organizational-Level Consequences of Organizational Citizenship Behavior: A Meta-Analysis," by N. P. Podsakoff, S. W. Whiting, P. M. Podsakoff, and B. D. Blume, 2009, *Journal of Applied Psychology, 94,* p. 128. Copyright 2009 by the American Psychological Association.

bottom half of Table 10.1. As indicated in this part of the table, managers take both OCB-I and OCB-O into account when making their reward recommendations and when allocating actual rewards, although the relationships between the OCB and reward recommendations (r_c = .77) is substantially higher than the relationships between OCB and actual rewards allocated (r_c = .26). These findings suggest that even though managers' administrations of rewards do not correspond perfectly to their recommendations, OCBs have a significant impact on both of these criteria. Therefore, there is some fairly compelling evidence that managers include OCB in their performance evaluation and reward recommendation or allocation decisions.

Effects of Organizational Citizenship Behavior on Organizational Effectiveness

In addition to the fact that OCBs have been found to be related to managerial evaluations of employee performance and the rewards that managers recommend and administer to their employees, there is a growing body of evidence that OCBs are related to measures of organizational effectiveness. Indeed, OCBs have been found to be related to a variety of organizational effectiveness measures, including the quantity and quality of performance, operating efficiency, sales performance, customer satisfaction, and profitability. Table 10.2 reports a summary of these relationships, as reported by N. P. Podsakoff et al. (2009).

As indicated in this table, OCBs were positively related to measures of unit-level performance (r_c = .43) and were somewhat more strongly related to subjective measures of performance (r_c = .47) than to objective measures of this criterion (r_c = .37). A further breakdown of the objective measures of performance indicated relationships between OCB and unit-level performance measures were fairly consistent for measures of productivity, efficiency, and cost reductions but were somewhat less positive for profitability. However, this probably should not be too surprising, because profitability may be influenced by several factors (e.g., market influences, nature of industry, strategic planning) that are not under the employees' direct control. Therefore, profitability may have weaker relationships with OCB because this measure of performance is more distally related to these employee behaviors than are the other measures of performance included in this study.

N. P. Podsakoff et al. (2009) also examined the causal relationships between OCB and measures of

TABLE 10.2

Relationships Between Organizational Citizenship Behavior (OCB) and Organizational-Level Outcomes

				90% CI			
Relationship between unit OCB and . . .	***k***	***N***	***r***	**Lower**	**Upper**	r_c	SDr_c
Overall unit performance	33	2,750	.35	.32	.37	.43	.20
Overall unit performance, subjective measures	19	1,249	.41	.37	.45	.47	.28
Overall unit performance, objective measures	17	1,598	.29	.25	.33	.37	.11
Unit productivity	7	718	.34	.28	.39	.37	.03
Unit efficiency	3	102	.32	.17	.47	.40	.00
Unit costs	2	54	−.42	−.61	−.24	−.52	.00
Unit profitability	5	143	.13	.00	.27	.15	.27
Customer satisfaction	8	478	.19	.11	.26	.23	.00
Unit turnover	6	936	−.17	−.23	−.12	−.22	.11

Note. CI = confidence interval; *k* = number of independent samples; r_c = average correlation coefficient corrected for measurement and sampling error; SDr_c = standard deviation of corrected correlation coefficient. Subgroup *k* values may not add up to overall *k* because of the use of linear composites, which eliminated double-counting data from the same study. Adapted from "Individual- and Organizational-Level Consequences of Organizational Citizenship Behavior: A Meta-Analysis," by N. P. Podsakoff, S. W. Whiting, P. M. Podsakoff, and B. D. Blume, 2009, *Journal of Applied Psychology, 94,* p. 131. Copyright 2009 by the American Psychological Association.

organizational effectiveness. To do this, they conducted subgroup analyses comparing the results from studies using longitudinal or lagged designs with the results from studies using cross-sectional designs. They reported that the meta-analytic correlation ($r_c = .56$) for studies in which the organizational performance measures were lagged from the OCB measures was more positive than the correlation ($r_c = .37$) between these constructs when they were gathered at the same point in time. This led N. P. Podsakoff et al. (2009) to conclude that

> even though additional research needs to be conducted on the causal relationships before any definitive conclusions can be made, it does appear that OCBs either tend to lead to increases in . . . unit effectiveness, or that these variables may be reciprocally related. (p. 134)

WHAT ARE THE BEST PREDICTORS OF OCB?

Taken together, the results discussed above indicate that OCBs are related to performance evaluations and reward allocation decisions, as well as measures of organizational effectiveness and success. Therefore, it would appear worthwhile for organizations to select employees who demonstrate a predisposition to exhibit OCB at work. Unfortunately, little research has been conducted on techniques that can be used to predict OCB, and the research that has been reported has focused primarily on personality traits (Borman et al., 2001; Hurtz & Donovan, 2000; Organ & Ryan, 1995) and, to a lesser extent, interviews (Allen, Facteau, & Facteau, 2004; Klehe & Latham, 2005; Latham & Skarlicki, 1995). Nevertheless, in this section of the chapter, we broaden this focus to explore other selection techniques that may prove to be good predictors of OCB in the workplace, including cognitive ability (IQ), emotional intelligence (EQ), and situational judgment tests (SJTs). Note that we are shifting our focus from one in which ratings of a person's OCB serves as a predictor of that person's overall job performance to one in which we are treating OCB as a criterion variable in and of itself.

Personality Traits as Predictors of OCB

Although it was originally assumed that personality traits would be more predictive of OCB than task performance (Borman & Motowidlo, 1993, 1997; Van Scotter & Motowidlo, 1996), the meta-analytic evidence reported to date (e.g., Dalal, 2005; Hurtz & Donovan, 2000; Organ, Podsakoff, & MacKenzie, 2006; Organ & Ryan, 1995) has not been very supportive of this expectation. The findings from several meta-analyses are summarized in Table 10.3.

Taken together, the evidence reported in this table suggests that personality traits are not very good predictors of overall OCB, OCB-O, or OCB-I. Of the 11 traits included in Table 10.3, only a few have corrected validity coefficients that are close to or exceed .20. These include Conscientiousness (average corrected *r* for overall OCB = .22; average corrected *r* for OCB-O = .25) and Positive Affectivity (average corrected *r* for overall OCB =. 21), although the Hurtz and Donovan (2000) meta-analysis suggests that Agreeableness may also meet this standard. If one broadens the criteria to include studies that reported a mean weighted correlation of at least .17 (which would likely exceed .20 if corrected for unreliability), two other traits (empathy to others and helpfulness) may meet this relatively modest standard. However, the results also suggest that the source of the OCB ratings influence the nature of the relationships between personality variables and OCB. More specifically, when one excludes those studies in which self-reports of OCB were obtained from the same source as the personality variables, the correlations generally diminish.

One possible reason that personality traits have not been found to be good predictors of OCB may have to do with the fact that much of the research in the personality domain has been relatively indiscriminate in that it has not taken the job context or situation into account. This is consistent with arguments made by Tett and Christiansen (2007), who noted that although the average meta-analytic estimates for trait–performance relationships across jobs may be low, much of the previous research that has examined these relationships has not given enough consideration to the nature of the jobs that employees perform. More specifically, these authors argued that studies in which researchers focus on specific personality traits

TABLE 10.3

Summary of Meta-Analytic Relationships Between Personality Traits and Organizational Citizenship Behaviors (OCBs)

Personality trait	Meta-analytic study	Overall OCB				OCB-I				OCB-O			
		k	N	Mean r	r_c	k	N	Mean r	r_c	k	N	Mean r	r_c
Conscientiousness	Organ and Ryan (1995; includes self, other)					11	2,172	.16[a]	.22[a]	10	1,818	.21[b]	.30[b]
	Organ and Ryan (1995; excludes self)					7	1,231	.04[a]	.04[a]	7	1,231	.17[b]	.23[b]
	Hurtz and Donovan (2000; includes self, other)					23	4,301	.11[c]	.18[c]	17	3,197	.12[d]	.20[d]
	Borman et al. (2001; includes self, other)	12	2,378	.24	—								
	Borman et al. (2001; excludes self)	10	1,963	.19	—								
	LePine et al. (2002; includes self, other)	4	619	.11	.13	3	848	.18	.22	3	848	.20	.25
	Dalal (2005; includes self, other)	10	3,280	.23	.30								
Agreeableness	Organ and Ryan (1995; includes self, other)					6	916	.10[a]	.13[a]	6	916	.08[b]	.11[b]
	Hurtz and Donovan (2000; includes self, other)					23	4,301	.11[c]	.20[c]	17	3,197	.06[d]	.10[d]
	Borman et al. (2001; excludes self)	7	1,554	.13	—								
Extraversion	Hurtz and Donovan (2000; includes self, other)					21	4,155	.06[c]	.11[c]	16	3,130	.03[d]	.05[d]
	Borman et al. (2001; includes self, other)	8	1,832	.08	—								
	Borman et al. (2001; excludes self)	7	1,728	.06	—								
Emotional Stability	Hurtz and Donovan (2000; includes self, other)					21	3,685	.10[c]	.17[c]	15	2,581	.09[d]	.14[d]
Openness to Experience	Hurtz and Donovan (2000; includes self, other)					19	3,539	.03[c]	.05[c]	14	2,514	.01[d]	.01[d]
Positive Affectivity	Organ and Ryan (1995; includes self, other)					7	1,021	.12[a]	.15[a]	7	934	.06[b]	.07[b]
	Dalal (2005; includes self, other)	23	4,425	.28	.34								
	Borman et al. (2001; includes self, other)	5	985	.18	—								
	Borman et al. (2001; excludes self)	5	970	.16	—								

(continued)

TABLE 10.3 (*Continued*)

Personality trait	Meta-analytic study	Overall OCB				OCB-I				OCB-O			
		k	N	Mean r	r_c	k	N	Mean r	r_c	k	N	Mean r	r_c
Negative Affectivity	Organ and Ryan (1995; includes self, other)					6	1,201	−.05[a]	−.06[a]	5	847	−.09[b]	−.12[b]
	Dalal (2005; includes self, other)	23	4,101	−.08	−.10								
	Borman et al. (2001; includes self, other)	6	1,151	−.14	—								
	Borman et al. (2001; excludes self)	5	1,047	−.12	—								
Locus of Control	Borman et al. (2001; includes self, other)	3	559	.16	—								
	Borman et al. (2001; excludes self)	3	559	.12	—								
Collectivism	Borman et al. (2001; includes self, other)	4	857	.15	—								
	Borman et al. (2001; excludes self)	1	132	.04	—								
Empathy to Others	Borman et al. (2001; includes self, other)	7	1,343	.18	—								
	Borman et al. (2001; excludes self)	4	434	.17	—								
Helpfulness	Borman et al. (2001; includes self, other)	7	1,343	.22	—								
	Borman et al. (2001; excludes self)	4	434	.15	—								

Note. OCB-I = individually targeted OCB; OCB-O = organizationally targeted OCB; self = self-reports of OCB; other = other reports of OCB; k = number of independent samples; r_c = average correlation coefficient corrected for measurement and sampling error. A dash indicates that data were not reported.
[a]Employee Altruism represented OCB-I in this study.
[b]Generalized Compliance represented OCB-O in this study.
[c]Interpersonal facilitation represented OCB-I in this study.
[d]Job dedication represented OCB-I in this study.

that are matched with the characteristics required by a specific job report validities that are twice as large as those in studies that use exploratory designs, in which "all the (personality) subscales are administered in what amounts to a fishing expedition" (Tett & Christiansen, 2007, p. 973). This position is also consistent with trait-activation theory (Lievens, Chasteen, Day, & Christiansen, 2006), which argues that certain traits are activated by particular situational cues and that these traits are less likely to have an effect when these cues are not present.

If the arguments of Tett and Christiansen (2007) and Lievens et al. (2006) are accurate, they suggest two things. First, specific personality traits are likely to be associated with specific types of OCB. For example, employee Agreeableness or empathy might be expected to be more strongly related to Helping Behavior (or other forms of affiliation-oriented OCB) than they would be related to Voice (or other forms of challenge-oriented OCB). Second, OCBs are likely to be more strongly related to personality traits when those traits are made salient by the situation. This is consistent with Mount, Barrick, and Stewart (1998), who argued that individuals who possess higher levels of Agreeableness should perform jobs more effectively in contexts that require higher levels of interpersonal interactions (e.g., sales positions) or in situations that require consideration for the well-being or feelings of others (e.g., health care organizations). This also suggests that personality traits may be better predictors of OCB than they traditionally have been shown to be, if the specific situation is taken into account. Therefore, future research should explore this possibility.

Another possible reason that personality trait–OCB relationships have generally not been very strong may have to do with the fact that personality measures have traditionally been based on self-descriptions. There are two potential problems with this practice. The first problem is that many personality measures are not neutral with respect to what is valued in work settings. For example, most people probably perceive that expressing higher levels of Conscientiousness, Agreeableness, and Emotional Stability is better than expressing lower levels of these personality traits, either because these traits are personally desirable or because organizations are likely to value them. This may cause many respondents to feel the need to score themselves highly on these traits even if these ratings do not accurately reflect their personality. The second, related problem is that this practice reduces the variance in the personality measures, thereby attenuating the relationships between personality traits and OCB.

One possible way to address this problem is to obtain personality measures from other sources, such as spouses, coworkers, or supervisors. Of course, some researchers might argue that obtaining measures of personality from other people is not consistent with the notion of "personality traits." However, it is important to note that these traits may be conceptualized in two different ways (Barrick, Mount, & Judge, 2001; R. Hogan, Hogan, & Roberts, 1996; J. A. Johnson, 1997). On the one hand, personality traits may be defined *genotypically* as something that exists inside of a person that causes a distinctive pattern of behavior (over time and across situations). On the other hand, they could be defined *phenotypically* as the tendency to exhibit a particular distinctive pattern of behavior. Regardless of which of these conceptualizations is adopted, people who are high in the trait of Extraversion would be expected to exhibit a distinctively extraverted pattern of behavior.

However, the two different conceptualizations have different implications in a selection context. If personality is defined genotypically, then the job candidate is the best source of information about the extent to which the person possesses the trait producing the distinctive pattern of behavior. But, if personality is defined phenotypically, then other people who know the job candidate may be good sources of information about the extent to which the person exhibits the distinctive pattern of behavior. Mount, Barrick, and Strauss (1994) conducted a study consistent with the phenotypic definition of personality traits and found that the validity coefficients for trait–performance relationships were considerably higher than those traditionally reported in this literature. It is interesting that a substantial portion of the job performance measure used by Mount et al. in their study related to factors such as individual initiative, interpersonal skills, and commitment to the job. This suggests that elements of OCB were contained in the performance ratings made by coworkers and supervisors. Therefore, the results of this study indicate that when measures of personality traits are obtained from sources other than the job candidate, they may enhance the ability of these traits to predict OCB in organizational settings.

That being said, several issues need to be considered when obtaining ratings of personality from other sources in a selection context. First, we are not aware of many studies, other than the one reported by Mount et al. (1994), that have explicitly examined the predictive validity of personality measures obtained from other sources on employee OCB. Therefore, additional research will have to be conducted before the generalizability of their findings can be determined. Second, given that personality traits represent patterns of behavior across time and situations, the accuracy of these ratings will depend on the extent to which the rating source has an opportunity to observe the candidate's behavior in multiple settings over time. Generally speaking, the greater the opportunity for a potential rating source to observe candidate behavior, the more accurate the trait measure. However, it is important to note that even when a rater has had a substantial opportunity to observe the personality characteristics of the candidate (e.g., spouse, personal friend), he or she may still be unwilling to provide accurate assessments, for obvious reasons. Finally, it is important to consider the ability of organizations to gather measures of candidate personality from other sources. Obviously, if personality measures are to be obtained from sources other than the candidate in a selection context, the candidate will have to be an internal candidate, as opposed to an external one, because it is extremely unlikely that organizations will be able to obtain personality trait ratings from an external candidate's former coworkers or supervisors who work in other organizations. Therefore, these considerations may severely limit the usefulness of personality measures obtained from other sources in a selection context.

Using Interview Questions to Predict OCB

Several researchers have noted that interviews may be a particularly effective technique for identifying individuals with a propensity to exhibit OCB. (See also chap. 6, this volume.) For example, Gatewood and Feild (1998) argued that interviews are especially good for assessing "personal relations, such as sociability and verbal fluency, and good citizenship" (p. 482), and Werner (2000) noted that some of the traits that Gatewood and Feild identified as exemplars of good citizenship are similar to some forms of OCB. Therefore, it is somewhat surprising that little research has examined the ability of interview questions to predict OCB in organizational settings. Indeed, we were able to find only four studies that relate to this issue.

Latham and Skarlicki (1995) were the first to examine the criterion-related validity of interview questions with respect to OCB. These researchers examined the ability of situational interview (SI) questions and patterned behavior description interview (PBDI) questions to assess the propensity of business school faculty members to engage in OCB-O (e.g., taking part in fund-raising drives for the university, making connections with industry contacts to help students secure employment) and OCB-I (e.g., sharing expertise with colleagues who are less experienced, filling in for colleagues who are absent or sick). They found that although the PBDI questions were not related to either of these forms of OCB, SI questions significantly predicted colleagues' ratings of both OCB-O ($r = .50$) and OCB-I ($r = .30$).

Allen et al. (2004) conducted a follow-up study of the ability of SI and PBDI interview questions to predict OCB among 188 working students. For the purposes of this study, these researchers videotaped interviews designed to assess the participants' propensity to engage in OCB, and then OCB ratings were obtained from coworkers who were identified by the participants. Allen et al. (2004) reported that although the interview scores based on a composite of the SI and PBDI questions designed to assess *personal support* did not predict peer ratings of helping and cooperating with others, the composite interview scores for what they called *organizational support* significantly predicted ($r = .36$) peer ratings of the extent to which the students interviewed engaged in OCB aimed at supporting the organization (e.g., endorsing, supporting, and defending the organization) and the composite interview scores for *conscientious initiative* (e.g., successful task completion and organizational initiative) significantly predicted ($r = .50$) peer ratings of the extent to which those interviewed engaged in organizational initiative. In addition, these researchers also reported that the individual SI and PBDI scores did not predict as well as the composite SI and PBDI scores for any of the OCB dimensions, and the participants in their study were unable to improve their scores on the interview by faking their responses, even when they were instructed to approach the interview as if they were being interviewed for real and really wanted the job and/or they were told what the specific OCB dimensions that were being assessed. The latter finding is important, because it suggests that interview questions may be an effective way to assess the extent to which job candidates are likely to exhibit OCB on the job, even in the face of candidates who try to fake during the interview. However, Allen et al. (2004) also reported that the interview ratings for organizational support predicted conscientious initiative and personal support and that the interview ratings for personal support predicted conscientious initiative. Thus, this raises some questions about the discriminant validity of the interview scores.

Although not specifically intended to predict OCB, two other studies (Klehe & Latham, 2005; Sue-Chan & Latham, 2004) designed to examine the ability of interview questions to predict team-playing behavior would also appear to have some relevance to our discussion, because several of the items included in the team-playing measures in these studies (e.g., "Coordinates upcoming work with group members who are involved with the work," "Keeps group members accurately informed of progress on the project," "Asks questions, challenges, and/or improves ideas," "Acts as a mediator to resolve conflicts among group members") are similar to OCB measures. In the first of these studies, Sue-Chan and Latham (2004) examined the ability of SI questions and IQ tests to predict the academic performance and team-playing behavior of 75 managers and professionals enrolled in an executive MBA course. They found that although both the SI ($r = .29$) and IQ test ($r = .26$) predicted academic performance, only the SI questions predicted team-playing behavior as rated by peers ($r = .32$). In addition, these researchers reported that IQ and scores based on the SI questions were not related to each other, suggesting that these measures possessed discriminant validity.

In the second study, Klehe and Latham (2005) extended the work of Sue-Chan and Latham (2004) by examining the predictive validity of both the PBDI and the SI interview question formats on team-playing behavior among 79 students who had been accepted into the MBA program of a Canadian university. The results showed that both interview formats were significantly related to ratings of team-playing behavior (SI $r = .41$; PBDI $r = .34$). However, only the SI format accounted for incremental validity in this criterion variable when both the SI and the PBDI formats were entered into a regression equation.

Taken together, the results of the studies discussed above are encouraging in that they show that (a) responses to interview questions designed to tap OCB are correlated to other-source ratings of OCB; (b) responses to interview questions designed to tap student team-playing behaviors (which include OCB-like behaviors) are related to peer ratings of teamwork behaviors; and (c) interviewees given the opportunity to fake their responses to OCB questions are not rated significantly higher than interviewees who are asked to be as honest as possible in their responses. Thus, interviews may prove to be a worthwhile tool for organizations that want to select candidates with a propensity to exhibit OCB.

However, despite these encouraging findings, the OCB interview studies reported to date have several limitations. First, given the small number of studies that have been conducted, there is an obvious need to replicate these studies in additional samples to determine their generalizability. Second, it is important to note that it is not clear from the studies that have been reported whether raters can accurately distinguish between the various types of OCB. For example, although Latham and Skarlicki (1995) reported good evidence for the discriminant validity for the SI questions designed to tap OCB-O and OCB-I, these authors reported little evidence of the discriminant validity for the PBDI questions. In addition, Allen et al. (2004) reported that several of the OCB dimensions that they measured lacked adequate discriminant validity. One obvious difference between these two studies is that the Latham and Skarlicki study used two fairly broad dimensions of OCB (OCB-O and OCB-I), whereas Allen et al. used a much finer grained set of OCB dimensions in their study. Therefore, it is possible that the finer grained set of OCB made it more difficult for the raters to make these discriminations. However, LePine, Erez, and Johnson (2002) provided some evidence that OCB dimensions are fairly highly correlated with each other and that they have similar relationships with a variety of antecedents. This suggests that raters in organizational settings often do not make some of the finer distinctions that researchers make regarding OCB.

Related to the above discussion, another limitation of the studies reported to date is that none of them has included interview questions designed to assess task performance. This is important because excluding these questions from the interview does not allow researchers to assess the discriminant validity of OCB-related interview questions from task-related interview questions in predicting actual citizenship behavior on the job. In addition, excluding task-related questions also prevents researchers from determining whether interview questions tapping OCB possess incremental validity in predicting employee job performance, over and above that predicted by questions designed to capture task performance. Therefore, additional research should include interview questions aimed at task performance as well as OCB.

Finally, it is important to note that none of the studies reported in this domain have examined the influence of OCB-related interview questions within an actual selection context. Instead, all of these studies used employees (or students) who had already been selected into their organizations (or MBA program). Although this approach is beneficial for researchers because these samples are more readily available than actual job applicants, there are several potential problems associated with these kinds of studies. The first is that these designs may lead to range restriction in either the predictor or criterion variables because employees and/or students who did not meet organizational requirements generally are not selected into the organization. As a result, the relationships between responses to OCB interview questions and measures of employee OCB may have been attenuated. Second, it is important to note that although the objective of the studies that have been reported was to determine whether interviews could be used to predict employee OCB, none of them explicitly examined the weight that interviewer's assign to candidates' responses to OCB interview questions in their actual selection decisions. This is important because even though interview questions that tap OCB propensities may predict such behaviors, interviewers in organizational settings may or may not weight interview responses to these questions equally when making their employee selection decisions. Thus, although it is unlikely that interviewers would ignore information about candidate OCB in their selection decision-making process, we do not have direct evidence about how managers integrate this information into this process. Finally, the fact that none of the studies examined the hiring decisions of actual job candidates makes it impossible to determine whether OCB-related interview questions have adverse impact on protected classes of candidates.

Thus, even though the research on interviews conducted to date is encouraging, it is obvious that additional research is needed in this area before any definitive statements regarding the utility of interviews to predict citizenship behavior can be made. Such research should prove beneficial to the field.

Situational Judgment Tests as Predictors of OCB

Although SJTs have been used to identify managerial or supervisory potential since the 1940s, they have recently received renewed attention as potential predictors of job performance (Weekley & Ployhart, 2006; see also chap. 8, this volume). According to Gessner and Klimoski (2006), SJT items are designed to measure a job candidate's "preferences for appropriate behavior in a work situation" (p. 26). In a typical SJT, a job candidate is presented with a number of items describing situations that he or she is likely to encounter in the job for which he or she is being considered and then is asked to choose a course of action from a number of possible alternatives. The candidate's responses are then scored on a key that has been developed logically or empirically through the use of subject matter experts (SMEs).

The vast majority of research that has been conducted using SJT items has tended to focus on their ability to predict elements of task performance. However, Chan and Schmitt (2002) tested the ability of SJT items to predict employee OCB. In their study, they used job analysis and SMEs to develop items tapping an employee's ability to "adapt and respond to practical work-related situations that may arise in a variety of administrative and managerial jobs" (p. 240). Following this, effectiveness ratings obtained from another group of SMEs regarding possible employee responses to these situations were used to develop a scoring key. Next, they administered this test to a sample of 160 entry-level civil service administrators from Singapore, coded the responses, and obtained supervisor ratings of employees' core job proficiency (task performance), job dedication, and interpersonal facilitation. Chan and Schmitt reported that scores on the SJT items predicted both employee job dedication and interpersonal facilitation, even when controlling for employee IQ, the Big Five personality traits, and years of job experience. Therefore, this study provides preliminary evidence suggesting that SJTs may be valid predictors of employee OCB.

Although not explicitly designed to tap employee OCB, SJT-like items have been developed by Campion, Morgeson, and their colleagues (Morgeson, Rieder, & Campion, 2005; Mumford, Van Iddekinge, Morgeson, & Campion, 2008; Stevens & Campion, 1999) to predict a variety of team-related criteria, many of which are similar to citizenship behaviors. For example, Stevens and Campion (1999) developed SJT-like items tapping team-related knowledge, skills, and abilities that were designed to predict effective teamwork performance (e.g., collaboration, interpersonal communication, and conflict resolution) and taskwork performance (e.g., technical knowledge, learning orientation). These authors found support for their hypotheses that SJT items could predict teamwork behavior in two studies conducted in manufacturing plants. In Study 1, responses to the teamwork SJT by 70 employees of a paper pulp mill were positively related to supervisor ratings of employee teamwork, taskwork, and overall performance. In Study 2, responses to the teamwork SJT by 72 employees of a cardboard box factory were positively related to supervisor ratings of employee teamwork, taskwork, and overall performance. In addition, scores on the SJT items were found to be positively related to peer teamwork and overall performance nominations but not to peer taskwork nominations. However, these findings were qualified by the fact that scores on the items were found to be highly correlated with scores on traditional IQ tests and did not show significant incremental validity for any of the criterion variables when the ability tests were entered first into a stepwise regression analysis.

Morgeson et al. (2005) also provided evidence of the ability for SJT items to predict OCB-like behavior in team settings. These authors developed SJT items to measure employee social skills needed for successful team performance in a sample of 90 steel mill employees. These skills included coordinating actions with other employees, actively looking for ways to help coworkers, and displaying a cooperative attitude. Consistent with their hypotheses, Morgeson et al. reported that scores on the social skills SJT items were positively related to managerial measures of overall CP (a combination of interpersonal facilitation, interpersonal helping, job dedication, and individual initiative) but were not related to measures of task performance.

In a third study, Mumford et al. (2008) developed a situational test designed to assess three forms of team role knowledge: task, social, and boundary spanning. For the purpose of our review, we are primarily interested in the social roles identified by these authors because many of these roles include behaviors similar to OCB. For example, social roles include proactive, critical inquiry about decisions made by the group (i.e., Voice behavior); support for the team's decisions once they are made (i.e., good Sportsmanship); and responsibility for settling disputes between team members (i.e., Peacekeeping). After conducting a pilot study using undergraduates, Mumford et al. used a second sample of undergraduates to test the ability of a revised set of SJT items to predict the role performance of students in small groups responsible for completing a number of activities related to course grades. They found that even after controlling for student IQ and all the Big Five personality traits, student scores on the social role dimension of the SJTs were significantly related to social role performance (but not task or overall role performance).

Taken together, the findings discussed above suggest that SJT items may prove to be fairly good predictors of OCB-like behavior. However, the fact that Stevens and Campion (1999) found that scores on the teamwork SJT items were highly correlated with IQ test scores suggests that SJTs may contain a significant mental ability component. Therefore, additional research will need to be conducted to determine whether teamwork SJTs are distinguishable from IQ tests.

IQ as a Predictor of OCB

Although literally thousands of studies have reported on the relationship between cognitive abilities and job performance (Hunter & Schmidt, 1984), surprisingly little empirical research has examined the relationship between cognitive abilities and OCB. This is probably because some researchers (Borman & Motowidlo, 1993; Motowidlo & Van Scotter, 1994) in the OCB–CP domain have argued that IQ is more likely to be a determinant of task performance than it is of OCB. (See also chap. 4, this volume.)

Two of the earliest studies to examine the relationship between IQ and OCB-like behavior were reported by Motowidlo and Van Scotter (Motowidlo & Van Scotter, 1994; Van Scotter & Motowidlo, 1996). In the first study, Motowidlo and Van Scotter (1994) examined the relationships between ability, task performance, and CP in a sample of 421 U.S. Air Force mechanics. Contrary to their expectations, they reported that ability was not significantly related to task performance but was related to CP. However, IQ accounted for only about 2% of the variance in CP.

In a follow-up study, Van Scotter and Motowidlo (1996) examined the relationships between ability, task performance, and two dimensions of CP (i.e., interpersonal facilitation and job dedication) in a sample of 975 U.S. Air Force mechanics. These authors reported that ability was not related to task performance or either dimension of CP. Similar findings regarding the lack of relationships between scores on ability tests and interpersonal facilitation and job dedication have also been reported by Chan and Schmitt (2002); Ferris et al. (2001); and Mount, Oh, and Burns (2008).

In contrast, Côté and Miners (2006), using a sample of 175 full-time university employees, found that IQ was positively related to all three forms of job performance: task performance ($r = .35$), OCB-O ($r = .35$), and OCB-I ($r = .28$). Also, Stevens and Campion (1999) reported that a composite measure of IQ was correlated to supervisory ratings of teamwork behavior in both of their studies ($r = .33$ in Study 1; $r = .23$ in Study 2). However, ability was not found to be significantly related to either self-ratings of this criterion variable or to peer teamwork nominations.

Therefore, with a few exceptions, the pattern of relationships reported in the above studies suggests that cognitive abilities are generally not very good predictors of OCB. However, there are a few qualifications regarding the relationships between employee IQ and OCB that should be noted. First, all of the studies reported to date have been with workers who were already employed in their respective organizations. As a result, it is possible that there is a restriction in range in the predictor variable, the criterion variable, or both, in many of these studies. Therefore, additional research that does not have this limitation will have to be conducted before more definitive statements regarding the relationship between employee IQ and OCB can be made.

The second qualification regarding the relationships between IQ and OCB relates to the nature of the OCB that have been included in the studies. With the exception of the studies reported by Côté and Miners (2006) and Mount et al. (2008), the remainder of the studies used job dedication and interpersonal facilitation as measures of OCB–CP or as measures of teamwork behavior. Thus, the majority of the studies discussed above have focused on what Van Dyne, Cummins, and McLean-Parks (1995) referred to as *promotive* or *affiliative* forms of citizenship behaviors, rather than challenging forms of citizenship. Although both affiliative and challenging forms of OCB are proactive in that they "promote, encourage, or cause things to happen" (Van Dyne & LePine, 1998, p. 108), challenging behaviors differ from affiliative behaviors because they emphasize ideas and issues and may threaten the status quo, rather than developing and sustaining cooperative relationships.

This distinction may be important because the ability to challenge conventional wisdom and/or make suggestions about how to improve the organization's effectiveness may require more IQ than providing help to a coworker. For example, one would expect that employees who are better able to comprehend complex organization systems, develop potential solutions to problems, and select the right solution for the situation would be more likely to voice their recommendations than employees who lack these abilities. Therefore, even though IQ has generally not been shown to predict affiliative forms of OCB, it may predict challenging forms of these behaviors, and future research should explore this possibility.

EQ as a Predictor of OCB

In addition to the long-standing interest in the relationship between IQ and employee job performance, there is a growing interest in the relationship between EQ and this criterion variable. According to Salovey and Mayer (1990), EQ is defined as "the subset of social intelligence that involves the ability to monitor one's and others' feelings and emotions to discriminate among them and to use this information to guide one's thinking and actions" (p. 190). Several authors (e.g., Abraham, 1999; Côté & Miners, 2006; Lam & Kirby, 2002; Law, Wong, & Song, 2004; Sosik & Megerian, 1999) have argued that EQ should be related to measures of job performance. For example, Law et al. (2004) noted that

> theoretically, if we follow the social exchange framework (Blau, 1964), in which organizations use different types of exchanges to facilitate performance, and social exchange is one important type of exchange in organizations, then we know that factors that facilitate social exchanges improve employee performance. Social exchange involves interactions. As we argued above, emotional understanding, regulation, and utilization would help to cultivate positive social interactions and exchanges in an organization and, as a result, facilitate employee performance. (p. 486)

Although Law et al.'s (2004) discussion was directed at job performance in general, it is obviously also applicable to OCB. For example, individuals who understand the emotions of others should be more effective at detecting and offering help to them when they encounter problems at work. Moreover, individuals who are able to manage their own emotions and the emotions of others should be able to maintain their composure when small inconveniences occur in the workplace (Sportsmanship) and minimize their own interpersonal conflicts and those that occur between coworkers (Peacekeeping). Finally, individuals who are able to keep their emotions in check may be more effective in offering solutions to problems that occur in the workplace (Voice), rather than just becoming upset about the situation.

Consistent with these expectations, preliminary research has shown that employee EQ is positively related to OCB. Ferris et al. (2001) examined the relationships between employee social skills and measures of task and CP. Their social skills measure included items (e.g., "I find it easy to put myself in the position of others," "In social situations, it is always clear to me what to say and do") that are consistent with Salovey and Mayer's (1990) definition of EQ. This measure was positively related to task performance, interpersonal facilitation, and job dedication.

In a more explicit test of the relationships between employee EQ and job performance, Law et al. (2004) examined the ability of EQ to explain variance in task performance and CP in a sample of 181 Chinese factory workers. For the purposes of this study, these authors obtained self-, peer, and supervisory ratings of employee EQ and the performance constructs. They found that both peer- and self-report measures of employee EQ explained significant amounts of variance in supervisor ratings of employee task performance, job dedication, and interpersonal facilitation, even after controlling for a variety of employee demographic variables (i.e., age, education, gender), the Big Five personality traits, employee loyalty, and trust in and tenure with their supervisor.

Finally, using the sample of 175 full-time university employees discussed above, Côté and Miners (2006) also examined the relationships between employee EQ and task performance, OCB-O, and OCB-I. They reported that EQ was positively related to all three measures of performance, and that it interacted with IQ to influence OCB-O, such that the relationship between EQ and OCB-O was positive for employees of low IQ but was not significant for employees of high IQ.

In summary, the extant studies reported in the literature seem to suggest that EQ is positively related to OCBs, although the number of studies is quite small. Therefore, this may prove to be a worthwhile avenue for future research to explore. One particularly interesting avenue for this research might be to examine the moderating effects of occupational level on the relationship between EQ and OCB. Several researchers (Borman & Motowidlo, 1993; Organ, 1988) have argued that OCB may be more important in managerial positions than in lower level positions in an organization. Consistent with this, MacKenzie, Podsakoff, and Paine (1999) reported that OCBs accounted for a greater proportion of the appraisal of a sales manager's performance than they did for the appraisal of a sales representative's performance. In addition, Goleman (1998) has also argued that EQ is more important in managerial positions than in lower level positions because supervisors are required to effectively manage their own emotions and read and respond to the emotions of their subordinates and peers. Thus, taken together, these arguments suggest that EQ should be more strongly related to OCB in managerial positions than in nonmanagerial positions.

WHAT ARE THE LEGAL ISSUES INVOLVED IN EXPANDING THE CRITERION DOMAIN TO INCLUDE OCB?

In this section of the chapter, we turn our attention to some potential legal issues that may arise from expanding the criterion domain to include OCB. For the purposes of our discussion, we primarily focus our attention on three questions: (a) How do OCBs compare with other criteria measures? (b) Are OCB measures influenced by age, race, and gender? (c) Will the use of OCB as a criterion measure hold up in court? Because we are not aware of any actual court cases in which these issues have been addressed, we caution the reader in advance that this section of the chapter is, of necessity, somewhat speculative in nature.

Before beginning this section, it is perhaps important to note that a number of different citizenship behaviors have been identified in the literature. Indeed, reviews of the research in this domain (LePine et al., 2002; P. M. Podsakoff et al., 2000) have identified between 30 and 40 different types of OCB. Thus, it is probably not surprising that a number of scales have been developed to measure these types of behavior (e.g., Farh et al., 1997; P. M. Podsakoff & MacKenzie, 1994; P. M. Podsakoff, MacKenzie, Moorman, & Fetter, 1990; Smith et al., 1983; Van Dyne, Graham, & Dienesch, 1994; Van Scotter & Motowidlo, 1996; L. J. Williams & Anderson, 1991). However, closer examination of the literature indicates that the most widely used measures are those developed by Smith et al. (1983), P. M. Podsakoff et al. (1990), and L. J. Williams and Anderson (1991), or modifications of them.

The Smith et al. (1983) scales were designed to measure two dimensions (Altruism and Compliance). Previous research (Barksdale & Werner, 2001; Farh, Podsakoff, & Organ, 1990; Organ & Konovsky, 1989; P. M. Podsakoff, Niehoff, MacKenzie, & Williams, 1993) using these scales has generally provided substantial support for the Altruism factor, but the underlying structure of the Compliance factor is considerably less clear with this factor splitting into two and sometimes three factors in a variety of different ways across studies. For the purposes of their scale, L. J. Williams and Anderson (1991) measured two broad categories of citizenship behaviors: OCB-O (behaviors aimed at benefiting the organization) and OCB-I (behaviors aimed at benefiting specific individuals within the organization). In addition, these authors developed a third scale to assess in-role (or task) performance. Although only a few studies (Randall, Cropanzano, Borman, & Birjulin, 1999; Turnley, Bolino, Lester, & Bloodgood, 2003; L. J. Williams & Anderson, 1991) have tested the three-factor structure of these scales, the preliminary evidence suggests the items generally load on their intended factors, and the reliabilities of the three dimensions is acceptable. Finally, the P. M. Podsakoff et al. (1990) scales were designed to measure the five dimensions (Altruism, Courtesy, Conscientiousness, Sportsmanship, and Civic Virtue) identified by Organ (1988) in his original book. Although the initial studies (Moorman, 1991, 1993; Moorman, Niehoff, & Organ, 1993; Pillai, Schriesheim, & Williams, 1999; P. M. Podsakoff, MacKenzie, & Fetter, 1993) that used these measures provided support for the five-factor structure, more recent research (Bachrach, Bendoly, & Podsakoff, 2001; MacKenzie et al., 1999; P. M. Podsakoff & MacKenzie, 1994) that incorporates two additional aspects of citizenship behavior (peacekeeping and cheerleading) identified by Organ (1990) typically has shown that the Altruism, Courtesy, Peacekeeping, and Cheerleading dimensions are subdimensions of a higher order, more general construct called Helping Behavior, whereas Sportsmanship and Civic Virtue could be modeled as first-order constructs. In addition to the OCB scales briefly described previously, the more recent measures reported by Van Dyne and LePine (1998) are important because in addition to measuring Helping Behavior, these scales also measure Voice behavior, which is a form of citizenship behavior that has gained increased interest in recent years (Detert & Burris, 2007; LePine & Van Dyne, 1998; Tangirala & Ramanujam, 2008; Van Dyne, Ang, & Botero, 2003; Whiting et al., 2008). Although a comprehensive review of the various scales that have been developed to measure OCBs goes beyond the scope of this chapter, interested readers are directed to Organ et al. (2006; Appendix, pp. 243–316), which provides an extended discussion of the most popular measures of citizenship behavior, including their items, content validity, and general psychometric properties.

HOW DOES OCB COMPARE WITH OTHER CRITERION MEASURES?

Gatewood, Feild, and Barrick (2007) identified a number of characteristics that criteria should ideally possess to be considered valid measures of job performance. Seven of these characteristics directly relate to the use of OCB as performance measures in a selection context: (a) individualization, (b) controllability, (c) relevance, (d) measurability, (e) reliability, (f) variance, and (g) practicality. *Individualization* refers to the fact that valid job performance measures must assess an individual's performance and not that of the group in which he or she is a member. Thus, even though some studies have assessed employee OCB at the group level (e.g., Dunlop & Lee, 2004; Koys, 2001), it is important that these behaviors be measurable at the individual level if the goal of the selection system is to predict the individual's OCB.

Controllability refers to whether the measure of job performance can be influenced by the individual who performs the behavior. Given that OCBs are generally considered to be more discretionary than task performance (Organ, 1988, 1997), these behaviors are generally assumed to be under the control of the employees who perform them.

Job performance criteria should be designed to assess those aspects of the job that contribute to the productivity or effectiveness of the organization. This requirement was referred to as *relevance* by Gatewood et al. (2007). OCBs should be considered relevant performance criteria in that (a) they have been shown to be included in managerial evaluations of job performance (Organ et al., 2006) and (b) they are positively related with a variety of measures of organizational effectiveness, including productivity, efficiency, customer satisfaction, and to a lesser extent profitability, and are negatively related to unit-level costs and turnover (N. P. Podsakoff et al., 2009).

Measurability refers to the ability to effectively assess or quantify the job performance criterion. A criterion measure cannot be used to validate a selection procedure, unless the criterion itself can be measured in some meaningful way. Generally speaking, OCBs are assessed using subjective judgments provided by supervisors (or peers), rather than with objective measures. As a result, these measures are subject to all of the biases that come along with such ratings, including first impressions, implicit performance theories, halo effects, and so on (Dunning, Heath, & Suls, 2004; P. M. Podsakoff, MacKenzie, Lee, & Podsakoff, 2003). However, many performance appraisal systems gather measures of task performance through subjective assessment made by supervisors, peers, or subordinates. Therefore, the measurability of OCB as a performance criterion is not likely to differ much from subjective assessments of task performance typically gathered in organizations.

Reliability refers to the extent to which a measure is consistent, stable, and dependable and is generally determined by the "degree of consistency between two sets of scores on the measure" (Gatewood et al., 2007, p. 113). The most important types of reliability for job performance measures are internal consistency reliability, interrater reliability, and test–retest reliability. Internal consistency is important because all parts of a job performance measure should be measuring the same aspect of performance, unless the measure is multidimensional in nature. Interrater reliability, on the other hand, relates to the degree of consistency in the ratings of an individual's performance across raters. This form of reliability is particularly important when job performance measures are subjective in nature, because low interrater reliability may suggest that scores on the measure are determined more by the biases of the raters than by the behavior being rated. Finally, test–retest reliability relates to the extent to which a measure of a person's behavior is stable across two different points in time. This form of reliability is important because it shows whether measures of job performance are consistent over time. However, test–retest reliabilities may be low not only because of errors in measurement but also because of changes in actual job performance due to extraneous factors (e.g., volume of work).

Generally speaking, prior research has shown that most OCB measures possess adequate levels of internal consistency reliability (LePine et al., 2002; Organ et al., 2006). Unfortunately, there is substantially less information regarding either the test–retest reliability or the interrater reliability of these measures. Although the meta-analytic evidence that does exist for interrater reliability (e.g., Conway, 1999) suggests that relationships between self and other ratings of OCB-like behavior are not very strong (ranging from an uncorrected mean of .18 to .23), these values are similar to those reported for the average uncorrected correlations between self-ratings and other ratings of job performance (ranging from uncorrected means of .22 to .24) reported by Harris and Schaubroeck (1988). That being said, it is important to note that there at least two reasons that ratings of OCB obtained from different sources are not always in agreement. The first of these reasons has to do with the frequency with which OCBs are exhibited. Because OCBs are discretionary forms of behavior that are not required by the organization, it is possible that some employees do not exhibit them very frequently. The second reason why different raters may not see completely eye to eye in their ratings of OCB is that they may not have the same opportunities to observe the performance of these behaviors by a given employee. For example, when an employee helps a coworker by coming to his or her rescue when he or she needs help, the coworker will certainly observe the behavior, but the supervisor (and perhaps other peers) may not. Similarly, when an employee engages in Voice behavior by making a suggestion to his or her supervisor about how to improve a specific procedure or process at work, the supervisor will obviously observe the behavior but the employee's peers or coworkers may not. Thus, when obtaining ratings of OCB from different sources, it may be particularly important to try to get raters who interact with the employee regularly and have ample opportunity to observe his or her behavior.

Gatewood et al. (2007) also argued that measures of employee job performance should yield *variance* (i.e., variability across employees). Obviously, if everyone was rated very high (or very low) on a measure, then it does not discriminate very well between employees. Moreover, measures that suffer from a lack of variance (or a restriction in range) are unlikely to be related to other variables. Given that previous research on OCB has shown these behaviors to be related to a variety of antecedents, correlates, and consequences (Organ & Ryan, 1995; Organ et al., 2006; N. P. Podsakoff et al., 2009; P. M. Podsakoff et al., 2000), it appears that OCB measures do in fact yield appreciable variance.

Practicality generally refers to the costs and logistics of gathering employee performance data. In most organizations, these costs are major issues and limit the ability to gather some kinds of information (e.g., satisfaction ratings from all customers that interact with whom an employee interacts). Because OCBs are typically assessed using subjective ratings from supervisors or coworkers, they are similar to measures of employee task performance on this criterion. Indeed, there would probably be little additional time or costs involved with including measures of employee OCBs in previously existing employee performance appraisals from these sources. Therefore, gathering employee OCB as part of the validation of a selection system should not cause undue hardship on the employees, managers, or organizations.

In summary, the use of OCB as a performance criterion seems to compare favorably with subjective measures of task performance gathered in most organizations. Specifically, measures of OCB gathered from peers or supervisors seem to have similar levels of individualization, relevance, measurability, reliability, variance, and practicality as compared with measures of task performance from these sources. In addition, it is possible that measures of OCB reflect observations of contributions that are more likely to be under the control of the individual than is task performance. Thus, OCBs seem to exhibit the necessary characteristics to be considered elements of the employee job performance domain.

ARE ORGANIZATIONAL CITIZENSHIP BEHAVIOR MEASURES AGE, RACE, OR GENDER BIASED?

In addition to possessing the measurement properties discussed by Gatewood et al. (2007), it is also important to determine whether measures of OCB discriminate against protected classes of individuals. Although few studies have examined the relationships between OCB ratings and demographic factors specifically within the context of a selection decision-making study, a number of studies have reported on the relationships between age and gender and OCB ratings. Table 10.4 provides a meta-analytic summary of these relationships.

Age and OCB Relationships

The top part of Table 10.4 summarizes the meta-analytic relationships between OCB and age obtained by us and also presents a summary of these relationships reported recently by Ng and Feldman (2008). In addition to examining the relationships between undifferentiated forms of OCB, Ng and Feldman examined the relationships between age and OCB-I, OCB-O, and task-directed OCB. They indicated that this final category of OCB relates to (a) the extra effort and persistence that employees exhibit on the job and (b) trying hard to improve their personal and group performance. Finally, Ng and Feldman also examined the differences between the meta-analytic estimates of the relationships between age and self-rated OCB versus age and other-rated OCB. Therefore, we have also included this information in Table 10.4.

Although the relationships between age and OCB are generally significant (i.e., 95% confidence intervals exclude 0), the strength of these correlations is generally consistent with what J. Cohen (1988, 1992) would refer to as *small* effect sizes (less than .10), except for task-directed OCB. Even though it is not clear why age is more strongly related to task-directed OCB, these forms of OCB appear to include some elements of what Van Dyne et al. (1995) referred to as *challenging* forms of citizenship behaviors. These types of OCB challenge the status quo and may threaten those to whom they are directed. Perhaps younger employees are less willing to engage in these behaviors because they do not feel they have the requisite experience to do so, they do not feel that it is worth taking the chance on "rocking the boat," or because they do not feel committed enough to the organization to try to improve it. Whatever the reason, additional research aimed at this finding might prove worthwhile.

Finally, although not summarized in Table 10.4, Ng and Feldman (2008) reported that the relationship between age and OCB was more positive in samples in which (a) the job was less complex, (b) there was a smaller proportion of college degree holders, (c) there was a smaller proportion of managers, and (d) there was a smaller proportion of Caucasians. Of these findings, perhaps of greatest concern is that age was more positively related to OCB in samples with fewer Caucasians. Ng and Feldman suggested this finding may result from the fact that "older workers from racial minorities may feel that they have to work harder and display more citizenship behavior because of the 'double' minority status at work" (p. 407). If so, future research that examines the relationship between age and OCB ratings should take note of racial balance.

Future research should also be directed at the relationship between employee work experience and OCB ratings. As noted earlier, Williamson (1975) felt that one of the beneficial consequences of experience in a specific work context is that it leads to increases in tacit knowledge and the possibility of enhanced

TABLE 10.4

Meta-Analytic Relationships Between Organizational Citizenship Behavior (OCB) and Employee Age and Gender

Relationship	k	N	r	95% CI Lower	95% CI Upper	r_c	SDr_c
Age–OCB							
Employee age–OCB (present study)	52	16,988	.11	.07	.15	.12	.17
Employee age–OCB (undifferentiated target) (Ng & Feldman, 2008; other)	18	5,404	—	.05	.11	.06	.09
Employee age–OCB (undifferentiated target) (Ng & Feldman, 2008; self)	23	5,755	—	.05	.11	.08	.15
Employee age–OCB-I (present study)	51	13,480	.03	.00	.06	.03	.08
Employee age–OCB (directed at others) (Ng & Feldman, 2008; other)	42	10,565	—	.03	.07	.05	.08
Employee age–OCB (directed at others) (Ng & Feldman, 2008; self)	24	5,728	—	.04	.10	.07	.08
Employee age–OCB-O (present study)	43	16,321	.06	.03	.09	.07	.09
Employee age–OCB (directed at organization) (Ng & Feldman, 2008; other)	34	9,308	—	.04	.09	.06	.10
Employee age–OCB (directed at organization) (Ng & Feldman, 2008; self)	37	10,398	—	.12	.16	.14	.15
Employee age–OCB (directed at task) (Ng & Feldman, 2008; other)	3	1,205	—	.09	.33	.21	.07
Employee age–OCB (directed at task) (Ng & Feldman, 2008; self)	7	1,761	—	.07	.19	.13	.04
OCB–Gender relationships							
Employee gender[a]–OCB	45	16,621	−.03	−.06	.00	−.03	.10
Employee gender[a]–OCB-I	48	12,790	.02	.00	.05	.03	.09
Employee gender[a]–OCB-O	46	20,965	−.04	−.07	−.01	−.04	.10

Note. CI = confidence interval; k = number of independent samples; r_c = average correlation coefficient corrected for measurement and sampling error; SDr_c = standard deviation of corrected correlation coefficient; OCB-I = individually targeted OCB; OCB-O = organizationally targeted OCB; self = self-rated; other = other rated. A dash indicates that data were not reported.
[a]Female gender was high; therefore, negative correlation indicates that female employees (men) received lower (higher) ratings of OCB.

levels of consummate cooperation. This suggests that job experience should be positively related to measures of job performance, including OCB. Thus, additional evidence regarding the relationship between work experience and OCB might prove worthwhile.

OCB and Gender Relationships

The bottom part of Table 10.4 reports the relationships between employee gender and OCB. As indicated in this part of the table, no significant relationships were found between gender and overall OCB, OCB-O, or OCB-I. All of the correlation coefficients were small, and all of the confidence intervals included 0. Thus, it does not appear that gender has an appreciable effect on OCB ratings. These findings are generally consistent with studies that have shown that although gender does have a significant effect on evaluations of task performance for men and women, the average effect size is quite small (Pulakos & Wexley, 1983; Pulakos, White, Oppler, & Borman, 1989; Swim, Borgida, Maruyama, & Myers, 1989; Thompson & Thompson, 1985).

However, a few caveats are in order. First, several of the studies in our analysis did not report the percentage of women in their samples, so the low correlations could be because of low power of the statistical tests. Second, the results reported in Table 10.4 do not examine the possible effect that job type has on OCB ratings. This may be important, because Allen and Rush (2001) provided some evidence that gender interacts with job type to influence OCB ratings and that gender interacts with OCB to influence the accuracy of behavioral observations.

In their first study, Allen and Rush (2001) asked undergraduate students to (a) estimate the percentage of employees who typically exhibit 10 task performance behaviors and 10 OCB, (b) indicate the likelihood that employees exhibit each of the 20 behaviors, and (c) allocate the annual salary of the job in question to the 20 behaviors based on the perceived value of these behaviors, depending on whether the employees were men or women and whether the job was categorized as stereotypically male (automobile mechanic), female (secretary), or gender neutral (fast-food server). It is interesting to note that the results of their study showed that the participants generally expected women to exhibit OCB (but not task performance) more than men. In addition, they reported that ratee gender and job type interacted to influence participants' perceptions of the degree to which men and women engaged in OCB (but not task performance). More specifically, they reported that although the participants in their study perceived men and women to engage in OCB with similar frequency in the female-typed job, they perceived women to engage in OCB significantly more frequently than men in the neutral-gender–typed and male-typed jobs. This led Allen and Rush (2001) to conclude that the results of their study provided some initial evidence that

> assumptions regarding the occurrence of OCB are prone to gender stereotypes in that there are base-rate differences in the perceptions regarding the frequency with which men and women are expected to perform OCB. Specifically, when estimating the frequency of OCB, raters indicated that females were more likely than men to perform these behaviors, particularly when employed in gender-neutral and male-typed jobs. These results support the general supposition that women are more likely to be expected to be "good soldiers" than are men . . . in contrast, no gender differences were found with regard to the expected frequency of task-related behaviors. This suggests that different expectations for different types of behavior exist for females than for males. (p. 2570)

However, no differences were reported in the dollar values assigned to task performance or OCB behaviors based on either the job type or the interaction between the job type and the ratee's gender.

In their second study, Allen and Rush (2001) examined the possibility that the OCB of men might be noticed, encoded, and recalled from memory more readily than similar behaviors for women. Based on cognitive theories that suggest that raters search for distinctiveness information when making performance judgments (DeNisi, Cafferty, & Meglino, 1984), Allen and Rush (2001) hypothesized that the relationship between the occurrence of OCB and behavioral observation accuracy would vary as a function of ratee gender, such that behavioral observations would be more accurate for women who do not perform OCB and for men who do than for men who do not perform OCB and women who do. They also predicted that the relationship between OCB and, first, overall performance evaluations and, second, reward recommendations would vary as a function of ratee gender, such that the enhancing effect of OCB on performance evaluations and reward recommendations would be greater for men than for women. However, none of these interactive effects was expected in the case of task performance. Consistent with their expectations, Allen and Rush (2001) reported that OCB interacted with gender such that men were rated more accurately than women under the high-OCB condition, whereas women were rated more accurately than men under the low-OCB condition, and that no such interaction occurred in the case of task performance and gender. However, these researchers did not find the expected interactive effects between OCB and gender on either overall performance ratings or reward recommendations.

Taken together, the implications of the studies reported by Allen and Rush (2001) are somewhat unclear. On the one hand, the findings are troubling because they suggest that although women are observed more accurately when they do not engage in OCB, men are observed more accurately when they do engage in OCB. However, on a more positive note, the findings suggest that even though there were some differences in the perceived accuracy of the observations of OCB for men versus women, these differences did not have any appreciable effect on the overall evaluations or reward recommendations received by men and women in their studies. Thus, even though substantially more research needs to be done to determine the potential relationships between OCB ratings and the gender of the ratee, the preliminary evidence from the Allen and Rush (2001) study is somewhat encouraging.

OCB and Race or Ethnicity Relationships

Considerably fewer studies have been reported on the relationship between race or ethnicity and OCB ratings, and those that have been reported have tended not to use the same comparison groups. Therefore, it is difficult to review these results quantitatively. As a result, Table 10.5 summarizes the studies that we could find comparing two or more racial or ethnic groups. As indicated in this table, with the exception of two studies (Aquino & Bommer, 2003; A. Cohen, 2006), the majority of studies that have been conducted do not seem to show a decided bias for race or ethnicity in the case of OCB ratings. Thus, although considerably more research is needed in this area, the evidence reported to date suggests that OCB ratings are relatively free of age, gender, and race biases.

WILL THE USE OF ORGANIZATIONAL CITIZENSHIP BEHAVIOR AS A SELECTION CRITERION HOLD UP IN COURT?

One final question of interest is whether the use of OCB as a selection criterion will meet legal scrutiny. Although several researchers (Barrett & Kernan, 1987; Martin & Bartol, 1991; Martin, Bartol, & Levine, 1986) have provided narrative reviews of court decisions related to cases involving discrimination, for our purposes we focus on three studies (Feild & Holley, 1982; Feild & Thompson, 1984; Werner & Bolino, 1997) that have examined the factors that the courts have used in cases in which plaintiffs brought action against an organization for what they considered unfair practices in the company's performance appraisal system. The cases included in these studies do not relate specifically to the use of OCB as performance criteria. However, we believe that they do identify the types of factors that the courts consider important when determining whether a performance appraisal system is fair. In addition, we believe that the findings reported in these studies can be used to provide some recommendations to practitioners regarding the use of OCB as performance criteria in selection systems.

In the first study, Feild and Holley (1982) examined 66 state, federal, and Supreme Court cases related to alleged employee discrimination from performance evaluations. The authors searched the Fair Employment Practices series of the Bureau of National Affairs (1965–1980) publications and selected cases that included an employment discrimination charge based on protected classes, and in which performance appraisal results were used as the basis for making personnel decisions related to promotion, termination, or salary. After separating their sample into the 31 cases that ruled in favor of the plaintiff and the 35 cases that ruled in favor of the defendant, the authors used discriminant analysis to identify the factors that significantly influenced court decisions. They reported that courts were more likely to decide in favor of the organization when (a) job analysis was used to develop the performance appraisal system, (b) evaluators were given specific written instructions regarding how appraisals should be conducted, (c) performance appraisal results were reviewed with employees, (d) the performance evaluation system was behavior oriented as opposed to trait oriented, and (e) the organization was nonindustrial (e.g., a unit of government or a university) in nature. In contrast, court decisions tended to find in favor of the plaintiff when these criteria were not present in the performance appraisal systems. In addition, it should be noted that these authors did not find factors such as geographic region, whether information on validity or reliability was presented, evaluator training, or the purpose of the appraisal system to have an effect on the court's decisions. Therefore, the findings led Feild and Holley (1982) to conclude that "when an employment discrimination suit involving the use of performance appraisal data is brought against an employer, the characteristics of the appraisal system will help to determine the outcome of the litigation" (p. 399).

Similar findings were reported in a follow-up study by Feild and Thompson (1984), using a set of 31 federal district and court of appeals cases reported between 1980 and 1983. Consistent with the findings

TABLE 10.5

Summary of Studies Examining the Relationships Between Employee Race and Organizational Citizenship Behavior (OCB)

Study	Sample	Source and measure of OCB	Race comparison(s)	Summary of findings
Allen (2006)	440 employees in a variety of occupations from a utility company and a women's professional organization	Self-reports of OCB-O and OCB-I using the scale developed by L. J. Williams and Anderson (1991)	Whites vs. minorities	Race was not significantly correlated with either OCB-O ($r = -.02$; $p < .05$) and OCB-I ($r = -.02$; $p < .05$).
Aquino and Bommer (2003)	418 American manufacturing workers	Supervisors rated employees using 12-items taken from P. M. Podsakoff and MacKenzie (1989) included dimensions of Courtesy, Sportsmanship, and Altruism	Whites vs. African Americans	Race was significantly correlated with OCB ($r = .18$; $p < .05$); indicating that White employees received higher ratings of OCB than did African Americans.
Bowler and Brass (2006)	141 American manufacturing workers	Peers rated coworker interpersonal citizenship behavior	—	Race was not significantly correlated with OCB ($r = -.01$, $p > .05$).
Chattopadhyay (1999)	401 employees workers from four American organizations	Self-reports of employee Altruism using the scale reported by P. M. Podsakoff et al. (1990) plus six additional items	Whites vs. minorities	Race was not significantly correlated with Altruism ($r = -.08$, $p > .05$).
Chattopadhyay and George (2001)	326 manufacturing workers in two computer hardware companies	Self-reports of employee Altruism using the scale reported by P. M. Podsakoff et al. (1990) plus six additional items	Whites vs. minorities	Race was not significantly correlated with Altruism ($r = -.07$, $p > .05$).
A. Cohen (1999)	283 Israeli nurses	Self-reports of OCB using scale developed by Smith et al. (1983)	Arabs vs. Jews	Ethnicity was not significantly correlated with OCB ($r = .01$, $p > .05$).
A. Cohen (2006)	564 Israeli teachers	Principals rated teachers using 32 items taken from scales developed by L. J. Williams and Anderson (1991) and Organ and Konovsky (1989)	Arabs vs. Jews	Ethnicity was negatively related with OCB-O ($r = -.33$, $p < .05$) but was not significantly related to Altruism ($r = .03$, $p > .05$). This indicates that ratings of teacher OCB-O were higher for Jews than for Arabs, but that ratings of Altruism did not differ across these ethnic groups.
Detert and Burris (2007)	Sample 1: 3,149 restaurant employees; Sample 2: 223 restaurant managers	Self-reports of voice behavior to the general manager using three items reported by Van Dyne and LePine (1998)	African American, Hispanic, and Other	Dummy-coded ethnicity variables were not found to be significantly related to Voice behavior in either the employee or manger samples (all p values > .05).
Korsgaard et al. (2002)	115 American employees of three credit unions	Peers rated coworkers Helping Behavior using the scale reported by Van Dyne and LePine (1998)	Caucasian vs. non-Caucasian	Ethnicity was not significantly correlated with Helping Behavior ($r = .07$, $p > .05$).

(continued)

TABLE 10.5 (*Continued*)

Study	Sample	Source and measure of OCB	Race comparison(s)	Summary of findings
Van Dyne and LePine (1998)	441 American employees in a variety of jobs	Peers rated employee Voice behaviors using scales reported by Van Dyne and LePine (1998)	Whites vs. non-Whites	Ethnicity was positively related to voice behavior ($r = .10$, $p < .05$), indicating that White employees received higher evaluations of voice behaviors than did non-White employees.
Miceli and Mulvey (2000)	Sample 1: 250 American union members and manufacturing employees; Sample 2: 1,160 American citizens holding a variety of different jobs	Self-reports of OCB using scale developed by Smith et al. (1983)	Majority (non-Hispanic White) vs. Minority (African American, Hispanic, and any other race or ethnic group)	Race and OCB were uncorrelated in both studies (rs = .00, ps > .05).
Stamper and Van Dyne (2001)	257 American entry-level restaurant service employees	Supervisors rated employee helping and voice behaviors using the scales reported by P. M. Podsakoff et al. (1990) and Van Dyne et al. (1994), respectively	White vs. other	Race was not significantly related to either Helping ($r = .00$, $p > .05$) or Voice behavior ($r = -.03$, $p > .05$).
Treadway et al. (2007)	126 employees in two retail service organizations	Supervisors rated employee interpersonal facilitation with the scale reported by Motowidlo and Van Scotter (1994)	—	Race was not significantly related to Interpersonal Facilitation ($r = -.02$, $p > .05$).
Witt and Silver (1994)	366 American undergraduate students	Self-reports of extrarole behaviors were assessed using a modified version of the scale developed by O'Reilly and Chatman (1986)	—	Ethnicity was not significantly related to extrarole behaviors ($r = -.07$, $p > .05$).

Note. A dash indicates that data were not reported.

of Feild and Holley (1982), these authors found that courts were more likely to decide in favor of the defending organizations when (a) job analysis was used to develop the performance appraisal system, (b) evaluators received written instructions for conducting performance appraisals, (c) employees had the right to review their performance appraisal, and (d) the performance appraisal system was based on employee behaviors as opposed to traits. However, in contrast to the findings of Feild and Holley (1982), Feild and Thompson did not find the type of organization to be a significant determinant of court decisions in their sample of cases.

Finally, in a study conducted over a decade after those reported by Feild and his colleagues (Feild & Holley, 1982; Feild & Thompson, 1984), Werner and Bolino (1997) examined the factors that influenced court decisions using a larger, more recent sample of cases. These authors reviewed 295 U.S. circuit court decisions in cases of alleged discrimination in performance appraisal systems occurring between 1980 and 1995, and although they examined a larger set of predictors, they reported results that were generally consistent with those reported by Feild and his colleagues. Specifically, Werner and Bolino found that courts tended to decide in favor of the defending organization when (a) job analysis was used to help develop the performance appraisal system, (b) evaluators were given specific written instructions on how to perform appraisals, and (c) the results of appraisals were reviewed with employees. Also consistent with the findings of Feild and his colleagues, Werner and Bolino reported that evaluator training, the frequency of appraisal, the purpose of the appraisal system (i.e., layoff, discharge, transfer, or promotion), the basis for the discrimination charge (i.e., race, sex, age, or other or combinations), and the race and gender of the evaluator did not affect judicial decisions.

However, despite the generally supportive evidence reported by Werner and Bolino (1997), these authors also reported findings there were inconsistent with those reported by Feild and his colleagues (Feild & Holley, 1982; Feild & Thompson, 1984). For example, although Feild and his colleagues reported that using multiple performance evaluators did not significantly influence court decisions, Werner and Bolino found that courts were more likely to decide in favor of the defending organization when this factor was present, and although both Feild and Holley (1982) and Feild and Thompson (1984) reported that behaviorally based (as opposed to trait-based) appraisals were looked on more favorably by the courts, Werner and Bolino did not find this factor to be a significant predictor in their study.

In addition to the factors discussed above, Werner and Bolino (1997) also examined the influence of five other contextual factors on court decisions: (a) whether the case focused on disparate treatment versus disparate impact, (b) whether the case involved a class action versus individual plaintiff, (c) whether the decision was made before or after the 1991 Civil Rights Act was passed, (d) the district of the circuit court in which the case was decided, and (e) the type of organization (i.e., private vs. publicly owned) involved in the dispute. Although Roehling (1993) argued that environmental factors may influence disputes handled by courts, Werner and Bolino did not find that any of these contextual factors had a significant effect on court decisions. Thus, these findings led the authors to conclude that decisions were made on the basis of characteristics of the performance appraisal rather than on measurement issues or contextual factors that were not directly relevant to the case.

Taken together, the relative consistency of the findings across these studies suggests that some factors are likely to be important when considering whether OCBs are legally defensible performance criteria. First, citizenship behaviors may be legally defensible as criteria in employee performance appraisal systems if a job analysis indicates that they are important to the occupation. In other words, only OCBs that are identified by SMEs, job incumbents, or managers as important to a particular occupation should be incorporated into the appraisal criteria when selecting employees for that occupation. Although we are not aware of any job analysis techniques that have been explicitly designed to capture OCB, our own experiences suggest that these behaviors are often referred to when job incumbents or SMEs are asked to identify critical incidents (Flanagan, 1954) of successful job performance. This is particularly true in jobs for which interpersonal relationships, task interdependencies, and/or integrating one's work with other employees is considered an important aspect of the job. Therefore, future research that focuses on OCB identified through critical incidents of jobs with these characteristics should prove worthwhile. Second, those responsible for evaluating employee job performance (including elements of OCB) should have written instructions describing how the appraisal or interview should be conducted. This will help standardize the process and should increase employee (candidate) perceptions that the appraisal (selection) process is fair. Finally, in the case of performance appraisals, it is important to allow employees to review the feedback they receive from their supervisor.

Of course, the research findings regarding the factors that the courts have historically used in determining the fairness of performance appraisal systems must be tempered by the fact that the most recent summary of these judicial decisions that we could find (Werner & Bolino, 1997) was conducted over a decade ago. Therefore, it goes without saying that additional research should be directed at this issue. However, we doubt that the courts will lessen the importance they assign to job analysis, the training of those who evaluate employees, and providing employees with the ability to see their evaluations. Thus, we believe that these are important considerations for organizations that intend to use OCB to evaluate employees in the future.

CONCLUSION

Research on the topic of OCBs has indicated that managers include these behaviors in their evaluation of employee job performance and that they are related to a variety of bottom-line measures of organizational effectiveness. Therefore, it would make sense for organizations to try to identify and select those job candidates who have a propensity to exhibit these behaviors. In this chapter, we explored some of the techniques that may be useful in this selection process, as well as some of the legal issues that need to be considered when including OCB in the criterion domain in a selection context. Generally speaking, we think that this is an exciting area of research, and we are hopeful that this chapter will help to draw additional attention to several key areas that are in need of attention.

References

References used in the meta-analyses included in this chapter are indicated with an asterisk.

Abraham, R. (1999). Emotional intelligence in organizations: A conceptualization. *Social and General Psychology Monographs, 125,* 209–224.

*Allen, T. D. (2006). Rewarding good citizens: The relationship between citizenship behavior, gender, and organizational rewards. *Journal of Applied Social Psychology, 36,* 120–143.

Allen, T. D., Facteau, J. D., & Facteau, C.L. (2004). Structured interviewing for OCB: Construct validity, faking, and the effects of question type. *Human Performance,* 17, 1–24.

Allen, T. D., & Rush, M. C. (1998). The effects of organizational citizenship behavior on performance judgments: A field study and a laboratory experiment. *Journal of Applied Psychology, 83,* 247–260.

Allen, T. D., & Rush, M. C. (2001). The influence of ratee gender on ratings of organizational citizenship behavior. *Journal of Applied Social Psychology, 31,* 2561–2587.

*Alotaibi, A. G. (2001). Antecedents of organizational citizenship behavior: A study of public personnel in Kuwait. *Public Personnel Management, 30,* 363–376.

*Aquino, K., & Bommer, W. H. (2003). Preferential treatment: How victim status moderates the relationship between organizational citizenship behavior and workplace victimization. *Organization Science, 14,* 374–385.

*Aryee, S., & Chay, Y. W. (2001). Workplace justice, citizenship behavior, and turnover intentions in a union context: Examining the mediating role of perceived union support and union instrumentality. *Journal of Applied Psychology, 86,* 154–160.

*Aryee, S., Chen, Z. X., Sun, L. Y., & Debrah, Y. A. (2007). Antecedents and outcomes of abusive supervisor: Test of a trickle-down model. *Journal of Applied Psychology, 92,* 191–201.

Bachrach, D. G., Bendoly, E., & Podsakoff, P. M. (2001). Attributions of the "causes" of group performance as an alternative explanation of the relationship between organizational citizenship behavior and organizational performance. *Journal of Applied Psychology, 86,* 1285–1293.

Barksdale, K., & Werner, J. M. (2001). Managerial ratings of in-role behaviors, organizational citizenship behaviors, and overall performance: Testing different models of their relationship. *Journal of Business Research, 51,* 145–155.

Barnard, C. I. (1938). *The functions of the executive.* Cambridge, MA: Harvard University Press.

Barrett, G. V., & Kernan, M. C. (1987). Performance appraisal and termination: A review of court decisions since Brito v. Zia with implications for personnel practices. *Personnel Psychology, 40,* 489–503.

Barrick, M. R., Mount, M. K., & Judge, T. A. (2001). Personality and performance at the beginning of the new millennium: What do we know and where do we go? *International Journal of Selection and Assessment, 9,* 9–30.

*Begley, T. M., Lee, C., & Hui, C. (2006). Organizational level as a moderator of the relationship between justice perceptions and work-related reactions. *Journal of Organizational Behavior, 27,* 705–721.

Blau, P. M. (1964). *Exchange and power in social life.* New York: Wiley.

*Bolino, M. C., & Turnley, W. H. (2005). The personal costs of citizenship behavior: The relationship between individual initiative and role overload, job stress, and work–family conflict. *Journal of Applied Psychology, 90,* 740–748.

*Bommer, W. H., Dierdorff, E. C., & Rubin, R. S. (2007). Does prevalence mitigate relevance? The moderating effect of group-level OCB on employee performance. *Academy of Management Journal, 50,* 1481–1494.

Borman, W. C., & Motowidlo, S. J. (1993). Expanding the criterion domain to include elements of contextual performance. In N. Schmitt, W. C. Borman, and Associates (Eds.), *Personnel selection in organizations* (pp. 71–98). San Francisco, CA: Jossey-Bass.

Borman, W. C., & Motowidlo, S. J. (1997). Task performance and contextual performance: The meaning for personnel selection research. *Human Performance, 10,* 99–109.

Borman, W. C., Penner, L. A., Allen, T. D., & Motowidlo, S. J. (2001). Personality predictors of citizenship performance. *International Journal of Selection and Assessment, 9,* 52–69.

*Bowler, W. M., & Brass, D. J. (2006). Relational correlates of interpersonal citizenship behavior: A social network perspective. *Journal of Applied Psychology, 91,* 70–82.

*Byrne, Z. S., & Hochwarter, W. A. (2006). I get by with a little help from my friends: The interaction of chronic pain and organizational support on performance. *Journal of Occupational Health Psychology, 11,* 215–227.

*Carmeli, A., Shalom, R., & Weisberg, J. (2007). Considerations in organizational career advancement: What really matters. *Personnel Review, 36,* 190–205.

*Charbonneau, D., & Nicol, A. A. M. (2002). Emotional intelligence and prosocial behaviors in adolescents. *Psychological Reports, 90,* 361–370.

*Chambel, M. J., & Castanheira, F. (2007). They don't want to be temporaries: Similarities between temps and core workers. *Journal of Organizational Behavior, 28,* 943–959.

Chan, D., & Schmitt, N. (2002). Situational judgment and job performance. *Human Performance, 15,* 233–254.

*Chattopadhyay, P. (1999). Beyond direct and symmetrical effects: The influence of demographic dissimilarity on organizational citizenship behavior. *Academy of Management Journal, 42,* 273–287.

*Chattopadhyay, P., & George, E. (2001). Examining the effects of work externalization through the lens of social identity theory. *Journal of Applied Psychology, 86,* 781–788.

*Chen, X.-P. (2005). Organizational citizenship behavior: A predictor of employee voluntary turnover. In D. L. Turnipseed (Ed.), *Handbook of organizational citizenship behavior* (pp. 435–454). Hauppauge, NY: NOVA Science.

*Chen, X.-P., Hui, C., & Sego, D. J. (1998). The role of organizational citizenship behavior in turnover: Conceptualization and preliminary tests of key hypotheses. *Journal of Applied Psychology, 83,* 922–931.

*Chen, Z. X., & Francesco, A. M. (2003). The relationship between the three components of commitment and employee performance in China. *Journal of Vocational Behavior, 62,* 490–510.

*Chen, Z. X., Tsui, A. S., & Farh, J. L. (2002). Loyalty to supervisor vs. organizational commitment: Relationships to employee performance in China. *Journal of Occupational and Organizational Psychology, 75,* 339–356.

*Choi, J. N. (2007). Change-oriented organizational citizenship behavior: Effects of work environment characteristics and intervening psychological processes. *Journal of Organizational Behavior, 28,* 467–484.

Civil Rights Act of 1991, Pub. Law No. 102–166, 105 Stat. 1075 (1991).

*Cohen, A. (1999). The relation between commitment forms and work outcomes in Jewish and Arab culture. *Journal of Vocational Behavior, 54,* 371–391.

*Cohen, A. (2006). The relationship between multiple commitments and organizational citizenship behavior in Arab and Jewish culture. *Journal of Vocational Behavior, 69,* 105–118.

*Cohen, A., & Avrahami, A. (2006). The relationship between individualism, collectivism, the perception of justice, demographic characteristics, and organisational citizenship behavior. *Service Industries Journal, 26,* 889–901.

*Cohen, A., & Vigoda, E. (2000). Do good citizens make good organizational citizens? An empirical examination of the relationship between general citizenship and organizational citizenship behavior in Israel. *Administration & Society, 32,* 596–624.

Cohen, J. (1988). *Statistical power analysis for the behavioral sciences* (2nd ed.). Hillsdale, NJ: Erlbaum.

Cohen, J. (1992). A power primer. *Psychological Bulletin, 112,* 155–159.

Conway, J. M. (1999). Distinguishing contextual performance from task performance for managerial jobs. *Journal of Applied Psychology, 84,* 3–13.

*Côté, S., & Miners, C. T. H. (2006). Emotional intelligence, cognitive intelligence, and job performance. *Administrative Science Quarterly, 51,* 1–28.

*Coyle-Shapiro, J. A. M. (2002). A psychological contract perspective on organizational citizenship behavior. *Journal of Organizational Behavior, 23,* 927–946.

*Coyle-Shapiro, J. A. M., & Conway, N. (2005). Exchange relationships: Examining psychological contracts and perceived organizational support. *Journal of Applied Psychology, 90,* 774–781.

*Coyle-Shapiro, J., & Kessler, I. (2000). Consequences of the psychological contract for the employment relationship: A large-scale survey. *Journal of Management Studies, 37,* 903–930.

*Coyle-Shapiro, J. A. M., Kessler, I., & Purcell, J. (2004). Exploring organizationally directed citizenship behavior: Reciprocity or "It's my job"? *Organization Science, 41,* 85–106.

*Cropanzano, R., Rupp, D. E., & Byrne, Z. S. (2003). The relationship of emotional exhaustion to work attitudes, job performance, and organizational citizenship behaviors. *Journal of Applied Psychology, 88,* 160–169.

*Chiu, W. C. K., & Ng, C. W. (2001). The differential effects of work- and family-oriented woman-friendly HRM on OC and OCB: The case for single female employees in Hong Kong. *International Journal of Human Resource Management, 12,* 1347–1364.

Dalal, R. S. (2005). A meta-analysis of the relationship between organizational citizenships behavior and counterproductive work behavior. *Journal of Applied Psychology, 90,* 1241–1255.

*de Jong, S. B., Van de Vegt, G. S., & Molleman, E. (2007). The relationships among asymmetry in task dependence, perceived helping behavior, and trust. *Journal of Applied Psychology, 92,* 1625–1637.

Deci, E. L. (1975). *Intrinsic motivation.* New York: Plenum Press.

*Deckop, J. R., Mangel, R., & Cirka, C. C. (1999). Getting more than you pay for: Organizational citizenship behavior and pay-for-performance plans. *Academy of Management Journal, 42,* 420–428.

*Deckop, J. R., Merriman, K. K., & Blau, G. (2004). Impact of variable risk preferences on the effectiveness of control by pay. *Journal of Occupational and Organizational Psychology, 77,* 63–80.

*Den Hartog, D. N., & Belschak, F. D. (2007). Personal initiative, commitment, and affect at work. *Journal of Occupational and Organizational Psychology, 80,* 601–622.

DeNisi, A. S., Cafferty, T. P., & Meglino, B. M. (1984). A cognitive view of the performance appraisal process: A model and research propositions. *Organizational Behavior and Human Performance, 33,* 360–396.

*Detert, J. R., & Burris, E. R. (2007). Leadership behavior and employee voice: Is the door really open? *Academy of Management Journal, 50,* 869–884.

*Diefendorff, J. M., Brown, D. J., Kamin, A. M., & Lord, R. G. (2002). Examining the roles of job involvement and work centrality in predicting organizational citizenship behaviors and job performance. *Journal of Organizational Behavior, 23,* 93–108.

Dunlop, P. D., & Lee, K. (2004). Workplace deviance, organizational citizenship behavior, and business unit performance: The bad apples do spoil the whole barrel. *Journal of Organizational Behavior, 25,* 67–80.

Dunning, D., Heath, C., & Suls, J. M. (2004). Flawed self-assessment: Implications for health, education, and the workforce. *Psychological Science in the Public Interest, 5,* 69–106.

*Ellemers, N., de Gilder, D., & van den Heuvel, H. (1998). Career-oriented versus team-oriented commitment and behavior at work. *Journal of Applied Psychology, 83,* 717–730.

Epstein, S. (1980). The stability of behavior: II. Implications for psychological research. *American Psychologist, 35,* 790–806.

Eysenck, H. J. (1958). A short questionnaire for the measurement of two dimensions of personality. *Journal of Applied Psychology, 50,* 1211–1215.

*Farh, J. L., Earley, P. C., & Lin, S. C. (1997). Impetus for action: A cultural analysis of justice and organizational citizenships behavior in Chinese society. *Administrative Science Quarterly, 42,* 421–444.

*Farh, J. L., Hackett, R. D., & Liang, J. (2007). Individual-level cultural values as moderators of perceived organizational support-employee outcomes relationships in China: Comparing the effects of power distance and traditionality. *Academy of Management Journal, 50,* 715–729.

Farh, J. L., Podsakoff, P. M., & Organ, D. W. (1990). Accounting for organizational citizenship behavior—Leader fairness and task scope versus satisfaction. *Journal of Management, 16,* 705–721.

Farh, J. L., Zhong, C. B., & Organ, D. W. (2004). Organizational citizenship behavior in the People's Republic of China. *Organization Science, 15,* 241–253.

Fassina, M. E., Jones, D. A., & Uggersly, K. L. (2008). Relationship cleanup time: Using meta-analysis and path analysis to clarify relationships among job satisfaction, perceived fairness, and citizenship behaviors. *Journal of Management, 34,* 161–188.

*Feather, N. T., & Rauter, K. A. (2004). Organizational citizenship behaviors in relation to job status, job insecurity, organizational commitment and identification, job satisfaction, and work values. *Journal of Occupational and Organizational Psychology, 77,* 81–94.

Feild, H. S., & Holley, W. H. (1982). The relationship of performance appraisal system characteristics to verdicts in selected discrimination cases. *Academy of Management Journal, 25,* 392–406.

Feild, H. S., & Thompson, D. (1984, December 26). A study of court decisions in cases involving performance appraisal systems. *The Daily Labor Report,* pp. E1–E5.

*Ferris, G. R., Witt, L. A., & Hochwarter, W. A. (2001). Interaction of social skill and general mental ability on job performance and salary. *Journal of Applied Psychology, 86,* 1075–1082.

Findley, H. M., Giles, W. F., & Mossholder, K. W. (2000). Performance appraisal process and system facets: Relationships with contextual performance. *Journal of Applied Psychology, 85,* 634–640.

Flanagan, J. C. (1954). The critical incident technique. *Psychological Bulletin, 51,* 327–358.

*Francesco, A. M., & Chen, Z.-X. (2004). Collectivism in action: Its moderating effects on the relationship between organizational commitment and employees performance criteria. *Group & Organization Management, 29,* 425–441.

*Frenkel, S. J., & Sanders, K. (2007). Explaining variations in co-worker assistance in organizations. *Organization Studies, 28,* 797–823.

Gatewood, R. D., & Feild, H. S. (1998). *Human resource selection* (5th ed.). Mason, OH: Thompson.

Gatewood, R. D., Feild, H. S., & Barrick, M. (2007). *Human resource selection* (6th ed.). Mason, OH: South-Western.

Gessner, T. L., & Klimoski, R. J. (2006). Making sense of situations. In J. A. Weekley & R. E. Ployhart (Eds.). (2006). *Situational judgment tests: Theory, measurement, and application.* (pp. 13–38). Mahwah, NJ: Erlbaum.

Goleman, D. (1998). *Working with emotional intelligence.* New York: Bantam.

*Gregersen, H. B. (1993). (1993). Multiple commitments at work and extrarole behavior during 3 stages of organizational tenure. *Journal of Business Research, 26,* 31–47.

Guion, R. M., & Gottier, R. F. (1965). Validity of personality measures in personnel selection. *Personnel Psychology, 18,* 135–164.

*Halbesleben, J. R. B., & Bowler, W. M. (2007). Emotional exhaustion and job performance: The mediating role of motivation. *Journal of Applied Psychology, 92,* 93–106.

Harris, M. M., & Schaubroeck, J. (1988). A meta-analysis of self–supervisor, self–peer, and peer–supervisor ratings. *Personnel Psychology, 41,* 43–62.

Hoffman, B. J., Blair, C. A., Meriac, J. P., & Woehr, D. J. (2007). Expanding the criterion domain? A quantitative review of the OCB literature. *Journal of Applied Psychology, 92,* 555–566.

Hofstede, G. (1984). *Culture's consequences.* Newbury Park, CA: Sage.

Hogan, J., & Holland, B. (2003). Using theory to evaluate personality and job performance relations: A socioanalytic perspective. *Journal of Applied Psychology, 88,* 100–112.

Hogan, R., Hogan, J., & Roberts, B. W. (1996). Personality measurement and employment decisions. *American Psychologist, 51,* 469–477.

Howell, W. C., & Dipboye, R. L. (1982). *Essentials of industrial and organizational psychology.* Homewood, IL: Dorsey Press.

*Hui, C., Lam, S. S. K., & Law, K. K. S. (2000). Instrumental values of organizational citizenship behavior for promotion: A field quasi-experiment. *Journal of Applied Psychology, 85,* 822–828.

*Hui, C., Lee, C., & Rousseau, D. M. (2004). Employment relationships in China: Do workers relate to the organization or to people? *Organization Science, 15,* 232–240.

Hunter, J. E., & Schmidt, F. L. (1984). *Methods of meta-analysis: Correcting error and bias in research findings.* Newbury Park, CA: Sage.

Hurtz, G. M., & Donovan, J. J. (2000). Personality and job performance: The Big Five revisited. *Journal of Applied Psychology, 85,* 869–879.

Iaffaldano, M. T., & Muchinsky, P. M. (1985). Job satisfaction and job performance: A meta-analysis. *Psychological Bulletin, 97,* 251–273.

James, L. A., & James, L. R. (1989). Integrating work–environment perceptions—Explorations into the measurement of meaning. *Journal of Applied Psychology, 74,* 739–751.

*Jansen, K. J., & Kristof-Brown, A. L. (2005). Marching to the beat of a different drummer: Examining the impact of pacing congruence. *Organizational Behavior and Human Decision Processes, 97,* 93–105.

*Janssen, O. (2000). Job demands, perceptions of effort–reward fairness and innovative work behavior. *Journal of Occupational and Organizational Psychology, 73,* 287–302.

*Janssen, O. (2001). Fairness perceptions as a moderator in the curvilinear relationships between job demands, and job performance and job satisfaction. *Academy of Management Journal, 44,* 1039–1050.

*Janssen, O., & Huang, X. (2008). Us and me: Team identification and individual differentiation as complementary drivers of team members' citizenship and creative behaviors. *Journal of Management, 34,* 69–88.

Johnson, J. A. (1997). Units of analysis for the description and explanation of personality. In R. Hogan, J. Johnson, & S. Briggs (Eds.), *Handbook of personality psychology* (pp. 73–93). San Diego, CA: Academic Press.

Johnson, J. W. (2001). The relative importance of task and contextual performance dimensions to supervisor judgments or overall performance. *Journal of Applied Psychology, 86,* 984–996.

*Johnson, R. E., & Chang, C.-H. (2006). "I" is to continuance as "We" is to affective: The relevance of the self-concept for organizational commitment. *Journal of Organizational Behavior, 27,* 549–570.

Judge, T. A., Bono, J. E., Ilies, R., & Gerhardt, M. W. (2002). Personality and leadership: A qualitative and quantitative review. *Journal of Applied Psychology, 87,* 765–780.

*Kahya, E. (2007). The effects of job characteristics and working conditions on job performance. *International Journal of Industrial Ergonomics, 37,* 515–523.

Kamdar, D., & Van Dyne, L. (2007). The joint effects of personality and workplace social exchange relationships in predicting task performance and citizenship performance. *Journal of Applied Psychology, 92,* 1286–1298.

Katz, D. (1964). The motivational basis of organizational behavior. *Behavioral Science, 9,* 131–146.

Katz, D., & Kahn, R. L. (1966). *The social psychology of organizations* (1st ed.). New York: Wiley.

Katz, D., & Kahn, R. L. (1978). *The social psychology of organizations* (2nd ed.). New York: Wiley.

*Kickul, J., & Lester, S. W. (2001). Broken promises: Equity sensitivity as a moderator between psychological contract breach and employee attitudes and behavior. *Journal of Business and Psychology, 16,* 191–217.

*Kidder, D. L. (2002). The influence of gender on the performance of organizational citizenship behaviors. *Journal of Management, 28,* 629–648.

Klehe, U. C., & Latham, G. P. (2005). The predictive and incremental validity of the situational and patterned behavior description interviews for team-playing behavior. *International Journal of Selection and Assessment, 13,* 108–115.

Konovsky, M. A., Elliot, J., & Pugh, S. D. (1995, August). *Citizenship behavior and its determinants in Mexico.* Paper presented at the meeting of the National Academy of Management, Vancouver, British Columbia, Canada.

*Korsgaard, M. A., Brodt, S. E., & Whitener, E. M. (2002). Trust in the face of conflict: The role of managerial trustworthy behavior and organizational context. *Journal of Applied Psychology, 87,* 312–319.

Koys, D. J. (2001). The effects of employee satisfaction, organizational citizenships behavior, and turnover on organizational effectiveness: A unit-level, longitudinal study. *Personnel Psychology, 54,* 101–114.

*Kuehn, K. W., & Al-Busaidi, Y. (2002). Citizenship behavior in a non-Western context: An examination of the role of satisfaction, commitment, and job characteristics on self-reported OCB. *International Journal of Commerce and Management, 12,* 107–125.

Lam, L. T., & Kirby, S. L. (2002). Is emotional intelligence an advantage? An exploration of the impact of emotional and general intelligence on individual performance. *The Journal of Social Psychology, 142,* 133–143.

*Lambert, E. G., Hogan, N. L., & Griffin, M. L. (2008). Being the good soldier: Organizational citizenship behavior and commitment among correctional staff. *Criminal Justice and Behavior, 35,* 56–68.

Latham, G. P., & Skarlicki, D. P. (1995). Criterion-relation validity of the situational and patterned behavior description interviews with organizational citizenship behavior. *Human Performance,* 8, 67–80.

Law, K. S., Wong, C.-S., & Song, L. J. (2004). The construct and criterion validity of emotional intelligence and its potential utility for management studies. *Journal of Applied Psychology, 89,* 483–496.

*Lee, K., & Allen, N. J. (2002). Organizational citizenship behavior and workplace deviance: The role of affect and cognitions. *Journal of Applied Psychology, 87,* 131–142.

LePine, J. A., Erez, A., & Johnson, D. E. (2002). The nature and dimensionality of organizational citizenship behavior: A critical review and meta-analysis. *Journal of Applied Psychology, 87,* 52–65.

*LePine, J. A., & Van Dyne, L. (1998). Predicting voice behavior in work groups. *Journal of Applied Psychology, 83,* 853–868.

Lievens, F., Chasteen, C. S., Day, E. A., & Christiansen, N. D. (2006). Large-scale investigation of the role of trait activation theory for understanding assessment center convergent and discriminant validity. *Journal of Applied Psychology, 91,* 247–258.

Lovell, S. E., Kahn, A. S., Anton, J., Davidson, A., Dowling, E., Post, D., & Mason, C. (1999). Does gender affect the link between organizational citizenship behavior and performance evaluations? *Sex Roles, 41,* 469–478.

*Lynch, P. D., Eisenberger, R., & Armeli, S. (1999). Perceived organizational support: Inferior versus superior performance by wary employees. *Journal of Applied Psychology, 84,* 467–483.

MacKenzie, S. B., Podsakoff, P. M., & Fetter, R. (1991). Organizational citizenship behavior and objective productivity as determinants of managerial evaluations of salespersons performance. *Organizational Behavior and Human Decision Processes, 50,* 123–150.

MacKenzie, S. B., Podsakoff, P. M., & Fetter, R. (1993). The impact of organizational citizenship behavior on evaluations of salesperson performance. *Journal of Marketing, 57,* 70–80.

MacKenzie, S. B., Podsakoff, P. M., & Paine, J. E. (1999). Do citizenship behaviors matter more for managers than for salespeople? *Journal of the Academy of Marketing Science,* 27, 4, 396–410.

*Marler, J. H., Barringer, M. W., & Milkovich, G. T. (2002). Boundaryless and traditional contingent employees: Worlds apart. *Journal of Organizational Behavior, 23,* 425–453.

Martin, D. C., & Bartol, K. M. (1991). The legal ramifications of performance appraisal: An update. *Employee Relations Law Journal, 17,* 257–286.

Martin, D. C., Bartol, K. M., & Levine, M. J. (1996). The legal ramifications of performance appraisal: An update. *Employee Relations Law Journal, 12,* 370–396.

*Maslyn, J. M., & Fedor, D. B. (1998). Perceptions of politics: Does measuring different foci matter? *Journal of Applied Psychology, 83,* 645–653.

McCrae, R. R., & Costa, P. T., Jr. (1987). Validation of the five-factor model of personality across instruments and observers. *Journal of Personality and Social Psychology, 52,* 81–90.

*McKay, P. F., & McDaniel, M. A. (2006). A reexamination of Black–White mean differences in work performance: More data, more moderators. *Journal of Applied Psychology, 91,* 538–554.

*Miceli, M. P., & Mulvey, P. W. (2000). Consequences of satisfaction with pay systems: Two field studies. *Industrial Relations, 39,* 62–87.

*Moon, H., Kamdar, D., Mayer, D. M., & Takeuchi, R. (2008). Me or we? The role of personality and justice as other-centered antecedents to innovative citizenship behaviors within organizations. *Journal of Applied Psychology, 93,* 84–94.

Moorman, R. H. (1991). Relationship between organizational justice and organizational citizenship behaviors: Do fairness perceptions influence employee citizenship? *Journal of Applied Psychology, 76,* 845–855.

Moorman, R. H. (1993). The influence of cognitive and affective based job-satisfaction measures on the relationship between satisfaction and organizational citizenship behavior. *Human Relations, 46,* 759–776.

Moorman, R. H., Niehoff, B. P., & Organ, D. W. (1993). Treating employees fairly and organizational citizenship behavior: Sorting the effects of job satisfaction, organizational commitment, and procedural justice. *Employee Responsibilities and Rights Journal, 6,* 209–225.

Morgeson, F. P., Reider, M. H., & Campion, M. A. (2005). Selecting individuals in team settings: The importance of social skills, personality characteristics, and teamwork knowledge. *Personnel Psychology,* 58, 583–611.

*Morrison, E. W. (1994). Role definitions and organizational citizenships behavior: The importance of the employee's perspective. *Academy of Management Journal, 37,* 1543–1567.

*Mossholder, K. W., Settoon, R. P., & Henagan, S. C. (2005). A relational perspective on turnover: Examining structural, attitudinal, and behavioral predictors. *Academy of Management Journal, 48,* 607–618.

Motowidlo, S. J., & Van Scotter, J. R. (1994). Evidence that task performance should be distinguished from contextual performance. *Journal of Applied Psychology, 79,* 475–480.

Mount, M. K., Barrick, M. R., & Stewart, G. L. (1998). Five-factor model of personality and performance in jobs involving interpersonal relationships. *Human Performance, 11,* 145–165.

Mount, M. K., Barrick, M. R., & Strauss, J. P. (1994). Validity of observer ratings of the Big Five personality factors. *Journal of Applied Psychology, 79,* 272–280.

Mount, M. K., Oh, I.-S., & Burns, M. (2008). Incremental validity of perceptual speed and accuracy over general mental ability. *Personnel Psychology, 61,* 113–139.

Mumford, T. V., Van Iddekinge, C. H., Morgeson, F. P., & Campion, M. A. (2008). The team role test: Development and validation of a team role knowledge situational judgment test. *Journal of Applied Psychology, 93,* 250–267.

*Munene, J. C. (1995). The institutional environment and managerial innovations. A qualitative study of selected Nigerian firms. *Journal of Occupational and Organizational Psychology, 68,* 291–300.

Ng, T. W. H., & Feldman, D. C. (2008). The relationship of age to ten dimensions of job performance. *Journal of Applied Psychology, 93,* 392–423.

*O'Bannon, D. P., & Pearce, C. L. (1999). An exploratory examination of gainsharing in service organizations: Implications for organizational citizenship behavior and pay satisfaction. *Journal of Managerial Issues, 11,* 363–378.

*Ohly, S., & Fritz, C. (2007). Challenging the status quo: What motivates proactive behaviour? *Journal of Occupational and Organizational Psychology, 80,* 623–629.

O'Reilly, C., & Chatman, J. (1986). Organizational commitment and psychological attachment—The effects of compliance, identification, and internalization on pro-social behavior. *Journal of Applied Psychology, 71,* 492–299.

Organ, D. W. (1977). A reappraisal and reinterpretation of the satisfaction-causes-performance hypothesis. *Academy of Management Review, 2,* 46–53.

Organ, D. W. (1988). *Organizational citizenship behavior: The good soldier syndrome.* Lexington, MA: Lexington Books.

Organ, D. W. (1990). The motivational basis of organizational citizenship behavior. In B. M. Staw & L. L. Cummings (Eds.), *Research in organizational behavior* (Vol. 12, pp. 43–72). Greenwich, CT: JAI Press.

Organ, D. W. (1997). Toward an explication of "morale": In search of the *m* factor. In C. I. Cooper & S. E. Jackson (Eds.), *Creating tomorrow's organizations* (pp. 493–503). London: Wiley.

*Organ, D. W., & Konovsky, M. (1989). Cognitive versus affective determinants of organizational citizenship behavior. *Journal of Applied Psychology, 74,* 157–164.

Organ, D. W., & Lee, J. (2008). Organizational citizenship behavior, transaction cost economics, and the flat-world hypothesis. In R. J. Burke & C. L. Cooper (Eds.), *Building more effective organizations* (pp. 57–83). Cambridge, England: Cambridge University Press.

Organ, D. W., Podsakoff, P. M., & MacKenzie, S. B. (2006). *Organizational citizenship behavior: Its nature, antecedents, and consequences.* Thousand Oaks, CA: Sage.

Organ, D. W., & Ryan, K. (1995). A meta-analytic review of attitudinal and dispositional predictors of organizational citizenship behavior. *Personnel Psychology, 48,* 775–802.

*Pare, G., & Tremblay, M. (2007). The influence of high-involvement human resources practices, procedural justice, organizational commitment, and citizenships behaviors on information technology professionals' turnover intentions. *Group & Organization Management, 32,* 326–357.

*Parker, S. K., Williams, H. M., & Turner, N. (2006). Modeling the antecedents of proactive behavior at work. *Journal of Applied Psychology, 91,* 636–652.

Pillai, R., Schriesheim, C. A., & Williams, E. S. (1999). Fairness perceptions and trust as mediators for transformational and transactional leadership: A two-sample study. *Journal of Management, 25,* 897–933.

*Ployhart, R. E., Weichmann, D., Schmitt, N., Sacco, J. M., & Rogg, K. (2003). The cross-cultural equivalence of job performance ratings. *Human Performance, 16,* 49–79.

Podsakoff, N. P., Whiting, S. W., Podsakoff, P. M., & Blume, B. D. (2009). Individual- and organizational-level consequences of organizational citizenship behavior: A meta-analysis. *Journal of Applied Psychology, 94,* 122–141.

Podsakoff, P. M., & MacKenzie, S. B. (1994). Organizational citizenship behaviors and sales unit effectiveness. *Journal of Marketing Research, 31,* 351–363.

Podsakoff, P. M., & Mackenzie, S. B. (1989). *A second generation measure of organizational citizenship behavior.* Working paper, Indiana University.

Podsakoff, P. M., MacKenzie, S. B., & Fetter, R. (1993). Substitutes for leadership and the management of professionals. *Leadership Quarterly, 4,* 1–44.

Podsakoff, P. M., MacKenzie, S. B., & Hui, C. (1993). Organizational citizenship behaviors as determinants of managerial evaluations of employee performance: A review and suggestions for future research. In G. R. Ferris & K. M. Rowland (Eds.), *Research in personnel and human resources management* (Vol. 11, pp. 1–40). Greenwich, CT: JAI Press.

Podsakoff, P. M., MacKenzie, S. B., Lee, J.-L., & Podsakoff, N. P. (2003). Common method biases in behavioral research: A critical review of the literature and recommended remedies. *Journal of Applied Psychology, 88,* 879–903.

Podsakoff, P. M., MacKenzie, S. B., Moorman, R. H., & Fetter, R. (1990). Transformational leader behaviors and their effects on followers' trust in their leader, satisfaction, and organizational citizenship behaviors. *Leadership Quarterly, 1,* 107–142.

Podsakoff, P. M., MacKenzie, S. B., Paine, J. B., & Bachrach, D. G. (2000). Organizational citizenship behaviors: A critical review of the theoretical and empirical literature and suggestions for future research. *Journal of Management, 26,* 513–563.

Podsakoff, P. M., Niehoff, B. P., MacKenzie, S. B., & Williams, M. L. (1993). Do substitutes for leadership really substitute for leadership? An empirical examination of Kerr and Jermier's situational leadership model. *Organizational Behavior and Human Decision Processes, 54,* 1–44.

Pulakos, E. D., & Wexley, K. N. (1983). The relationship among perceptual similarity, sex, and performance ratings in manager–subordinate dyads. *Academy of Management Journal, 26,* 129–139.

Pulakos, E. D., White, L. A., Oppler, S. H., & Borman, W. C. (1989). Examination of race and sex effects in performance ratings. *Journal of Applied Psychology, 74,* 770–780.

Randall, M. L., Cropanzano, R., Borman, C. A., & Birjulin, A. (1999). Organizational politics and organizational support as predictors of work attitudes, job performance, and organizational citizenship behavior. *Journal of Organizational Behavior, 20,* 159–174.

*Redman, T., & Snape, E. (2005). Exchange ideology and member–union relationships: An evaluation of moderation effects. *Journal of Applied Psychology, 90,* 765–773.

Riketta, M. R. (2008). The causal relations between job attitudes and performance: A meta-analysis of panel studies. *Journal of Applied Psychology, 93,* 472–481.

Roehling, M. V. (1993). "Extracting" policy from judicial opinions: The dangers of policy capturing in a field setting. *Personnel Psychology, 46,* 477–502.

Rotundo, M., & Sackett, P. R. (2002). The relative importance of task, citizenship, and counterproductive performance to global ratings of job performance: A policy-capturing study. *Journal of Applied Psychology, 87,* 66–80.

Salgado, J. F. (1997). The five-factor model of personality and job performance in the European community. *Journal of Applied Psychology, 82,* 30–43.

Salgado, J. F., Anderson, N., Moscoso, S., Bertua, C., de Fruyt, F., & Rolland, J. P. (2003). A meta-analytic study of general mental ability for different occupations in the European community. *Journal of Applied Psychology, 88,* 1068–1081.

Salovey, P., & Mayer, J. D. (1990). Emotional intelligence. *Imagination, Cognition, and Personality, 9,* 185–211.

*Schappe, S. P. (1998). The influence of job satisfaction, organizational commitment, and fairness perceptions on organizational citizenship behavior. *Journal of Psychology, 132,* 277–290.

*Scott, S. B., & Colquitt, J. A. (2007). Are organizational justice effects bounded by individual differences? An examination of equity sensitivity, exchange ideology, and the Big Five. *Group & Organization Management, 32,* 290–325.

*Shore, L. M., Barksdale, K., & Shore, T. H. (1995). Managerial perceptions of employee commitment to the organization. *Academy of Management Journal, 38,* 1593–1615.

*Skarlicki, D. P., & Latham, G. (1996). Increasing citizenship behavior within a labor union: A test of organization justice theory. *Journal of Applied Psychology, 81,* 161–169.

*Skarlicki, D. P., & Latham, G. (1997). Leadership training in organizational justice to increase citizenship behavior within a labor union: A replication. *Personnel Psychology, 50,* 617–633.

*Smith, C. A., Organ, D. W., & Near, J. P. (1983). Organizational citizenship behavior: Its nature and antecedents. *Journal of Applied Psychology, 68,* 653–663.

*Snape, E., Chan, A. W., & Redman, T. (2006). Multiple commitments in the Chinese context: Testing compatibility, cultural, and moderating hypotheses. *Journal of Vocational Behavior, 69,* 302–314.

Sosik, J. J., & Megerian, L. E. (1999). Understanding leader emotional intelligence and performance: The role of self–other agreement on transformational leadership perceptions. *Group & Organization Management, 24,* 367–390.

*Stamper, C. L., & Van Dyne, L. (2001). Work status and organizational citizenship behavior: A field study of restaurant employees. *Journal of Organizational Behavior, 22,* 517–536.

Stevens, M. J., & Campion, M. A. (1999). Staffing work teams: Development and validation of a selection test for teamwork settings. *Journal of Management, 25,* 207–228.

Sue-Chan, C., & Latham, G. P. (2004). The situational interview as a predictor of academic and team performance: A study of the mediating effects of cognitive ability and emotional intelligence. *International Journal of Selection and Assessment, 12,* 312–320.

Swim, J., Borgida, E., Maruyama, G., & Myers, D. G. (1989). Joan McKay versus John McKay: Do gender stereotypes bias evaluations? *Psychological Bulletin, 105,* 409–429.

*Tang, T. L. P., & Ibrahim, A. H. S. (1998). Antecedents of organizational citizenship behavior revisited: Public personnel in the United States and in the Middle East. *Public Personnel Management, 27,* 529–550.

Tangirala, S., & Ramanujam, R. (2008). Exploring nonlinearity in employee voice: The effects of personal control and organizational identification. *Academy of Management Journal, 51,* 1189–1203.

*Tansky, J. W. (1993). Justice and organizational citizenship behavior: What is the relationship? *Employees Responsibilities and Rights Journal, 6,* 195–207.

Tett, R. P., & Christiansen, N. D. (2007). Personality tests at the crossroads: A response to Morgeson, Campion, Dipboye, Hollenbeck, Murphy, and Schmitt (2007). *Personnel Psychology, 60,* 967–993.

*Thau, S., Aquino, K., & Poortvliet, P. M. (2007). Self-defeating behaviors in organizations: The relationships between thwarted belonging and interpersonal work behavior. *Journal of Applied Psychology, 92,* 840–847.

Thompson, D. E., & Thompson, T. A. (1985). Task-based performance appraisal for blue-collar jobs: Evaluation of race and sex effects. *Journal of Applied Psychology, 70,* 747–753.

*Tierney, P., Bauer, T. N., & Potter, R. E. (2002). Extra-role behavior among Mexican employees: The impact of LMX, group acceptance, and job attitudes. *International Journal of Selection and Assessment, 10,* 292–303.

*Tjosvold, D., Hui, C., Ding, D. Z., & Hu, J. C. (2003). Conflict values and team relationships: conflict's contribution to team effectiveness and citizenship in China. *Journal of Organizational Behavior, 24,* 69–88.

*Tompson, H. B., & Werner, J. M. (1999). The impact of role conflict/facilitation on core and discretionary behaviors: Testing a mediated model. *Journal of Management, 23,* 583–601.

*Treadway, D. C., Ferris, G. R., Duke, A. B., Adams, G. L., & Thatcher, J. B. (2007). The moderating role of subordinate political skill on supervisors' impressions of subordinate ingratiation and ratings of subordinate interpersonal facilitation. *Journal of Applied Psychology, 92,* 848–855.

Trull, T. G., & Geary, D. C. (1997). Comparison of the Big Five factor structure across samples of Chinese and American adults. *Journal of Personality Assessment, 69,* 324–341.

*Tsai, W.-C., Chen, C.-C., & Lui, H. L. (2007). Test of model linking employee positive moods and task performance. *Journal of Applied Psychology, 92,* 1570–1583.

*Turnley, W. H., Bolino, M. C., & Lester, S. W., & Bloodgood, J. M. (2003). The impact of psychological contract fulfillment on the performance of in-role and organizational citizenship behaviors. *Journal of Management, 29,* 187–206.

*Turnley, W. H., & Feldman, D. C. (2000). Re-examining the effects of psychological contract violations: unmet expectations and job dissatisfaction as mediators. *Journal of Organizational Behavior, 21,* 25–42.

*Van der Vegt, G. S., Bunderson, J. S., & Oosterhof, A. (2006). Expertness diversity and interpersonal helping in teams: Why those who need the most help end up getting the least. *Academy of Management Journal, 49,* 877–893.

*Van der Vegt, G. S., & Van de Vliert, E. (2005). Effects of perceived skill dissimilarity and task interdependence on helping in work teams. *Journal of Management, 31,* 73–89.

*Van Dyne, L., & Ang, S. (1998). Organizational citizenship behavior of contingent workers in Singapore. *Academy of Management Journal, 41,* 692–703.

Van Dyne, L., Ang, S., & Botero, I. C. (2003). Conceptualizing employee silence and employee voice as multidimensional constructs. *Journal of Management Studies, 40,* 1359–1392.

Van Dyne, L., Cummings, L. L., & McLean-Parks, J. M. (1995). Extra-role behaviors: In pursuit of construct and definitional clarity (a bridge over muddied waters). In L. L. Cummings & B. M. Staw (Eds.), *Research in organizational behavior* (Vol. 17, pp. 215–285). Greenwich, CT: JAI Press.

*Van Dyne, L., Graham, J. W., & Dienesch, R. M. (1994). Organizational citizenships behavior: Construct redefinition, measurement, and validation. *Academy of Management Journal, 37,* 765–802.

Van Dyne, L., & LePine, J. A. (1998). Helping and voice extra-role behaviors: Evidence of construct and predictive validity. *Academy of Management Journal, 41,* 108–119.

*Van Dyne, L., & Pierce, J. L. (2004). Psychological ownership and feelings of possession: Three field studies predicting employee attitudes and organizational citizenships behavior. *Journal of Organizational Behavior, 25,* 439–459.

*Van Dyne, L., Vandewalle, D., Kostova, T., Latham, M. E., & Cummings, L. L. (2000). Collectivism, propensity to trust and self-esteem as predictors of organizational citizenship in a non-work setting. *Journal of Organizational Behavior, 21,* 3–23.

*Van Emmerik, I. H., Lambooy, M., & Sanders, K. (2002). Differential effects of individual-linked and team-level status allocation on professionals' job performance. *Small Group Research, 33,* 702–717.

Van Scotter, J. R., & Motowidlo, S. J. (1996). Interpersonal facilitation and job dedication as separate facets of contextual performance. *Journal of Applied Psychology, 81,* 525–531.

*Vandenberghe, C., Bentein, K., Michon, R., Chebat, J.-C., Tremblay, M., & Fils, J.-F. (2007). An examination of the role of perceived support and employee commitment in employee-customer encounters. *Journal of Applied Psychology, 92,* 1177–1187.

*Vandewalle, D., Van Dyne, L., & Kostova, T. (1995). Psychological ownership: An empirical examination of its consequences. *Group & Organization Management, 20,* 210–226.

*Venkataramani, V., & Dalal, R. S. (2007) Who helps and harms whom? Relational antecedents of interpersonal helping and harming in organizations. *Journal of Applied Psychology, 92,* 952–966.

*Wanxian, L., & Weiwu, W. (2007). A demographic study on citizenship behavior as in-role orientation *Personality and Individual Differences, 42,* 225–234.

*Wayne, S. J., Shore, L. M., Bommer, W. H., & Tetrick, L. E. (2002). The role of fair treatment and rewards in perceptions of organizational support and leader–member exchange. *Journal of Applied Psychology, 87,* 590–598.

*Wayne, S. J., Shore, L. M., & Liden, R. C. (1997). Perceived organizational support and leader–member exchange: A social exchange perspective. *Academy of Management Journal, 40,* 82–111.

Weekley, J. A., & Ployhart, R. E. (2005). Situational judgment: Antecedents and relationships with performance. *Human Performance, 18,* 81–104.

Weekley, J. A., & Ployhart, R. E. (Eds.). (2006). *Situational judgment tests: Theory, measurement, and application.* Mahwah, NJ: Erlbaum.

Werner, J. M. (1994). Dimensions that make a difference: Examining the impact of in-role and extrarole behaviors on supervisory ratings. *Journal of Applied Psychology, 79,* 98–107.

Werner, J. M. (2000). Implications of OCB and contextual performance for human resource management. *Human Resource Management Review, 10,* 3–24.

Werner, J. M., & Bolino, M. C. (1997). Explaining U.S. courts of appeals decisions involving performance appraisal: Accuracy, fairness, and validation. *Personnel Psychology, 50,* 1–25.

*Whitaker, B. G., Dahling, J. J., & Levy, P. (2007). The development of feedback environment and role clarity model of job performance. *Journal of Management, 33,* 570–591.

Whiting, S. W., Podsakoff, P. M., & Pierce, J. (2008). The effects of task performance, helping, voice, and organizational loyalty on performance appraisal ratings. *Journal of Applied Psychology, 93,* 125–139.

Williams, L. J., & Anderson, S. E. (1991). Job satisfaction and organizational commitment as predictors of organizational citizenships and in-role behaviors. *Journal of Management, 17,* 601–617.

*Williams, S., Pitre, R., & Zainuba, M. (2002). Justice and organizational citizenship behavior intentions: Fair rewards versus fair treatment. *Journal of Social Psychology, 142,* 33–44.

Williamson, O. E. (1975). *Markets and hierarchies.* New York: Free Press.

*Witt, L. A., Kacmar, K. M., Carlson, D. S., & Zivnuska, S. (2002). Interactive effects of personality and organizational politics on contextual performance. *Journal of Organizational Behavior, 23,* 911–926.

*Witt, L. A., & Silver, N. C. (1994). The effects of social responsibility and satisfaction on extra-role behaviors. *Basic and Applied Social Psychology, 15,* 329–338.

*Wong, C. S., & Law, K. S. (2002). The effects of leader and follower emotional intelligence on performance and attitude: An exploratory study. *Leadership Quarterly, 13,* 243–274.

Wright, P. M., George, J. M., Farnsworth, S. R., & McMahan, G. C. (1993). Productivity and extra-role behavior: The effects of goals and incentives on spontaneous helping. *Journal of Applied Psychology, 78,* 374–381.

*Yang, J., Mossholder, K. W., & Peng, T. K. (2007). Procedural justice climate and group power distance: An examination of cross-level interaction effects. *Journal of Applied Psychology, 92,* 681–692.

*Zellars, K. L., Tepper, B. J., & Duffy, M. K. (2002). Abusive supervision and subordinates' organizational citizenship behavior. *Journal of Applied Psychology, 87,* 1068–1076.

CHAPTER 11

ORGANIZATIONAL EXIT

Peter W. Hom

This chapter reviews prevailing themes in present-day research and perspectives on employee turnover. Generally speaking, scholars and practitioners define *turnover* as the voluntary separation of employees from employing institutions (Campion, 1991; Mobley, 1982; R. Smith, 1999). That is, employees decide to sever their employment ties, which differs from employer-initiated involuntary separations such as layoffs, dismissals, or retirements. Strictly speaking, turnover is the volitional act of departing a workplace permanently (though some firms rehire former employees), which can concurrently involve changing locales (migration), career fields (including workforce exits), or job functions. Expatriate assignments, promotions, lateral transfers, extended family leaves, or reduced work schedules (e.g., part-time work status) do not, however, technically qualify as turnover because employees remain with the same employer, though firms may reclassify employees whose status has changed. Viewed as individual choice behavior, turnover has long captivated academicians attempting to validate motivational models, as well as employers seeking to manage a costly behavior over which they have much less control (Campion, 1991).

Since the early 20th century (Price, 1977), organizational scientists have investigated turnover as symptomatic of fundamental motivational processes (e.g., expectancy theory) or as a phenomenon meriting separate scrutiny given March and Simon's (1958) early pronouncement that both the motivation to participate and the motivation to produce are essential for organizational functioning. Organizations sponsor and support turnover studies as they seek ways to avoid or reduce exorbitant turnover that is costly, hinders progress toward workforce diversity, and diminishes firm effectiveness (Hom & Griffeth, 1995). As awareness of its academic and practical significance spreads, turnover has became the subject of intense inquiry, generating a voluminous body of work during the past 40 years (Griffeth, Hom, & Gaertner, 2000; Maertz & Campion, 1998; Mobley, 1982). During this period of rising scholarship, turnover researchers followed a "standard" methodology, assessing employees' attributes (e.g., personnel data such as selection test scores, demographic traits, and work history) or self-reported workplace experiences (Appendix 11.1 shows common survey instruments). With multivariate statistics (e.g., regression), they then estimated how accurately these "predictors" forecast which employees later quit. To illustrate, Table 11.1 reports meta-analyses between demographic predictors and turnover derived from prevailing research (Griffeth et al., 2000). Rather than carrying out an intensive review (and repeat earlier reviews; Hom & Griffeth, 1995; Maertz & Campion, 1998), I highlight broad themes behind contemporary research streams in the next section, describing their theoretical and practical contributions and outlining future avenues of research to promote understanding of turnover.

TURNOVER MODELS

This section describes early schools of thought about the causes of turnover and then more complex formulations based on March and Simon's (1958) model that emerged in the 1970s and dominated empirical research for nearly 20 years. Finally, we consider a novel framework by Lee and Mitchell

TABLE 11.1

Meta-Analysis of Demographic Predictors

Predictors	Corrected predictive validity coefficients
Cognitive ability	.02
Education	.06
Training	−.08
Marital status	−.05
Kinship responsibilities	−.10
Children	−.16
Weighted application blank	.31
Race	−.02
Sex	−.03
Age	−.11
Firm tenure	−.23

Note. Correlations are corrected for measurement errors in predictors, sampling error, and suboptimal turnover base rates. Marital status is coded as high for married and low for single. Kinship responsibility is coded as high for employed spouse and low for no employed spouse. Race is coded as high for non-Whites and low for Whites. Sex is coded as high for women and low for men. From "A Meta-Analysis of Antecedents and Correlates of Employee Turnover: Update, Moderator Tests, and Research Implications for the Next Millennium," by R. Griffeth, P. Hom, and S. Gaertner, 2000, *Journal of Management, 26,* p. 465. Copyright 2000 by Sage Publications. Reprinted with permission.

(1994) that both refines and disputes standard views about why and how people quit.

Conventional Perspectives

Beginning 50 years ago (Wright, 1957, as cited in Price, 1977), early schools of thought maintained that job dissatisfaction is a prime—if not main—reason why employees vacate jobs (Hom, 2002). Emerging theories of work motivation, which later became dominant perspectives, reinforced this view, though specifying different mechanisms for employee disaffection. Specifically, motivational psychologists presume that unmet expectations (Porter & Steers, 1973), a job's low instrumentality for attaining valued outcomes (Vroom, 1964), or inequitable job rewards relative to inputs (J. S. Adams, 1965) occasion dissatisfaction as well as ensuing responses, such as organizational withdrawal. Empirical studies of these models affirmed that such motivational processes can instigate leaving (Dittrich & Carrell, 1979; Parker & Dyer, 1976; Wanous, 1973).

Explicitly theorizing about turnover, March and Simon's (1958) model of organizational equilibrium combined "ease of movement" (or "desirability of movement") with dissatisfaction as codetermining organizational participation. Labor economists have long known that unemployment rates lower quit rates (Burton & Parker, 1969; Price, 1977). Yet March and Simon (1958) most influenced present-day viewpoints on turnover to recognize that alternative employment prospects (e.g., "expected utility of alternatives," Mobley, Griffeth, Hand, & Meglino, 1979; "employment opportunity," Price & Mueller, 1981) play a crucial role in turnover decisions. That is, employees may not vacate dissatisfying jobs if they cannot secure employment elsewhere.

Unfortunately, few turnover scholars paid much attention to March and Simon's (1958) model until Price (1977) and Mobley (1977), who conceived models built on the notions of movement ease and desirability. Their seminal theories inspired causal model testing (beginning with their models) in the late 1970s (evaluating meditational mechanisms, not just predictive validity) as well as the more comprehensive formulations that followed (Hulin, Roznowski, & Hachiya, 1985; Lee & Mitchell, 1994; Mitchell, Holtom, Lee, Sablynski, & Erez, 2001; Mobley et al., 1979; Price & Mueller, 1981; Rusbult & Farrell, 1983; Steers & Mowday, 1981). A sociologist, Price (1977) proposed a structural model specifying various organizational (e.g., promotional opportunity, social integration) and environmental (e.g., opportunity) determinants of dissatisfaction and turnover. Price and Mueller (1981, 1986) later expanded this formulation by adding external antecedents, such as professionalism and kinship responsibility (i.e., family obligations in the community), and intervening constructs, such as organizational commitment and decisions to stay.

Focusing on *how* rather than *what* drives employees to quit, Mobley (1977) delineated intervening steps between dissatisfaction and turnover. His intermediate-linkages framework conceptualized that dissatisfied employees first think about leaving and then estimate the expected utility (costs and benefits) of a job search (e.g., chances of finding alternatives) and turnover costs. Optimistic expectations that a job search will yield attractive job offers and that turnover costs are not prohibitive in turn motivate an active search. After finding alternatives, prospective leavers compare them with their job. If any prove superior to the current job, they form quit decisions and quit. Refining this model, Mobley et al. (1979) attended to content (identifying turnover causes) more than process (describing how causes interrelate). This later view specified an array of distal influences on three proximal antecedents of leaving: job satisfaction, expected utility of the present role ("expectancies that the job will lead to the attainment of various positively or negative valued outcomes," p. 518), and expected utility of alternatives (expectancies that other jobs offer valued outcomes). Mobley and colleagues further distinguished between job satisfaction and current role expected utility by noting that employees dissatisfied with existing work conditions may stay if they foresee future job improvements or promotions (Mobley, 1982). Finally, they argued that nonwork values and roles can moderate the effects of satisfaction and role expected utilities on turnover, attenuating their effects when nonwork values or roles are central.

Since 1977, Mobley's and Price's frameworks have dominated empirical inquiry for 15 years (Hom, Caranikis-Walker, Prussia, & Griffeth, 1992; Price, 2001). Empirical research supported their basic tenets, though hypothesized structural relationships for some constructs have not always conformed to theoretical expectations (Gaertner, 1999; Hom et al., 1992; Hom & Kinicki, 2001; Price & Mueller, 1986). In particular, Hom and associates (Hom & Griffeth, 1991; Hom & Kinicki, 2001; see Figure 11.1) have substantiated an alternative configuration of intermediate stages, revising Mobley's (1977) causal sequence. Unlike any other scholar, Price (2001) systematically refined his theoretical formulation for decades. During his programmatic efforts, he has reconceptualized constructs and pathways, improved operationalizations, and added determinants (in light of new research findings; Price & Mueller, 1981, 1986). Moreover, researchers have generalized these two models to a variety of contexts, including the military, the part-time workforce, and other cultures (H. Miller, Katerberg, & Hulin, 1979; Price, 2001; Sager & Menon, 1994). Further, some authors have merged these models, as these sociological and psychological schools of thought (Hom & Griffeth, 1995; Price, 2001) emphasize different (though overlapping) constructs. The Price–Mueller models elaborate environmental antecedents of job attitudes, whereas intermediate-linkages perspectives specify the cognitions and (withdrawal) actions mediating attitudes and turnover.

All the same, literature reviews of prevailing research on traditional theories derived from March and Simon's (1958) formulation have widely criticized their predictive power (Maertz & Campion, 1998; Mitchell & Lee, 2001; O'Reilly, 1991). Despite greater scope, comprehensive models emerging in the late 20th century rarely explained more than 25% of the turnover variance (Maertz & Campion, 1998). Meta-analyses of turnover correlates reinforced such dismay (Mitchell & Lee, 2001), as they typically report modest predictive strength for most turnover antecedents (components often specified by standard theories). In a comprehensive meta-analysis, Griffeth et al. (2000) thus estimated the following effect sizes (correcting for predictor unreliability, sampling error, and suboptimal turnover base rates) for the strongest predictors: overall job satisfaction ($r = -.22$), leader–member exchange ($r = -.25$), role clarity ($r = -.24$), role conflict ($r = .22$), work satisfaction ($r = -.19$), comparison of alternatives with the job ($r = .19$), organizational commitment ($r = -.27$), search intentions ($r = .34$), job search methods ($r = .50$), and quit intentions ($r = .45$; see Tables 11.2 and 11.3). Such disappointing conclusions initiated the current generation of theory development and methodological advances to improve turnover prediction and understanding, which are next discussed.

Nontraditional Perspective: The Unfolding Model

Despite Mobley's and Price's profound impact on theory and research, Lee and Mitchell (1994) pinpointed several shortcomings with their theoretical (and other derivative) approaches. For one, they concluded that March and Simon's (1958) core constructs of movement desirability and ease, which Mobley and Price reconceptualized as job

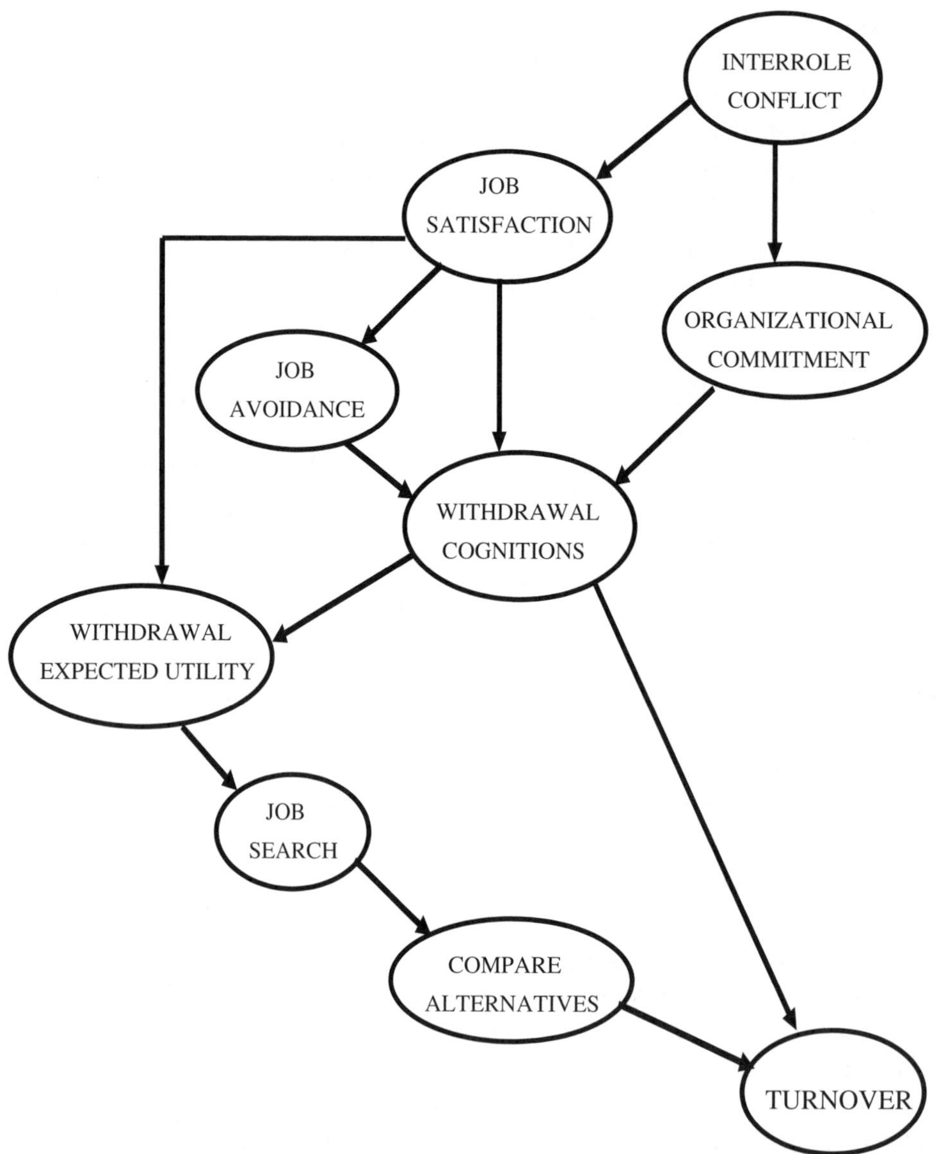

FIGURE 11.1. Hom–Griffeth–Kinicki model of intermediate linkages between job attitudes and turnover. From "Toward a greater understanding of how dissatisfaction drives employee turnover," by P. Hom and A. Kinicki, 2001, *Academy of Management Journal, 44,* p. 978. Copyright 2001 by the Academy of Management. Reprinted with permission.

satisfaction and perceived alternatives, inadequately explain turnover. Instead, they argued that external nonattitudinal factors, such as departures to follow relocating spouses or bear children, often prompt resignations. For these leavers, their feelings about the job or prospects for employment elsewhere have little to do with their decisions to leave. Moreover, they contended that prospective leavers do not always subject work alternatives to a rational calculation of their expected utilities as posited by Mobley et al. (1979). Instead, prospective leavers may screen jobs more quickly on a few valued criteria to determine their "fit." Indeed, Lee and Mitchell noted that many employees quit without first seeking or evaluating alternative jobs as they are abandoning the labor market to attend graduate school or care for children full time.

To acknowledge these unorthodox patterns of leaving, Lee and Mitchell (1994; see Figure 11.2) thus introduced the unfolding model, marking one of the

TABLE 11.2

Meta-Analysis of Job Attitudes, Job Aspects, and Alternative Employment

Predictors	Corrected predictive validity coefficients
Job attitudes	
Organizational commitment	−.27
Overall job satisfaction	−.22
Job content	
Job scope	−.14
Routinization	.11
Work satisfaction	−.19
Job involvement	−.12
Compensation	
Pay levels	−.11
Pay satisfaction	−.08
Distributive justice	−.11
Leadership	
Supervisory satisfaction	−.13
Leader–Member exchange	−.25
Coworkers	
Work group cohesion	−.13
Coworker satisfaction	−.13
Other job aspects	
Promotional chances	−.16
Participation	−.13
Instrumental communication	.14
Role stress	
Role clarity	−.24
Role overload	.12
Role conflict	.22
Overall stress	.16
Alternative employment	
Alternative job opportunities	.15
Comparison of alternatives with present job	.19

Note. Correlations are corrected for measurement errors in predictors, sampling error, and suboptimal turnover base rates. From "A Meta-Analysis of Antecedents and Correlates of Employee Turnover: Update, Moderator Tests, and Research Implications for the Next Millennium," by R. Griffeth, P. Hom, and S. Gaertner, 2000, *Journal of Management, 26,* pp. 466–468, 470. Copyright 2000 by Sage Publications. Reprinted with permission.

TABLE 11.3

Meta-Analysis of Withdrawal Cognitions and Actions

Predictors	Corrected predictive validity coefficients
Other withdrawal actions	
Lateness	.06
Absenteeism	.21
Job performance	−.17
Job search	
Search intentions	.34
General job search	.29
Job search behaviors	.31
Job search Methods	.50
Withdrawal cognitions	
Quit intentions	.45
Thinking of quitting	.29
Withdrawal cognitions	.36
Expected utility of withdrawal	.28

Note. Correlations are corrected for measurement errors in predictors, sampling error, and suboptimal turnover base rates. From "A Meta-Analysis of Antecedents and Correlates of Employee Turnover: Update, Moderator Tests, and Research Implications for the Next Millennium," by R. Griffeth, P. Hom, and S. Gaertner, 2000, *Journal of Management, 26,* pp. 469–470. Copyright 2000 by Sage Publications. Reprinted with permission.

most innovative theories in recent times. In particular, they pioneered the notion of *shocks*—experienced events prompting thoughts about quitting—that may induce even happy incumbents to vacate jobs (Mitchell & Lee, 2001). They also theorized four paths by which leavers abandon jobs. In Path 1 ("Following a Plan"), a shock—typically, a personal, nonwork event such as graduate-school admissions or pregnancy—activates a preexisting plan to quit (Holtom, Mitchell, Lee, & Inderrieden, 2005). For example, a nurse who becomes pregnant (the shock) may resign as she had planned to opt out of the workforce if she became a mother (Lee, Mitchell, Wise, & Fireman, 1996). Negative workplace shocks trigger another withdrawal path (Path 2, "I'm Outta Here"). These shocks violate employees' values or career goals. Employees determine whether the shock can be integrated (fit) into their values or goals. If judged a misfit, they depart without job offers in hand. To illustrate, Lee and associates (1996) described a nurse who left immediately when her hospital shifted from individualized patient care, her preferred nursing philosophy, to team-based nursing.

A third type of shock—unsolicited job offers or inquiries—prompts a third withdrawal path (Path 3,

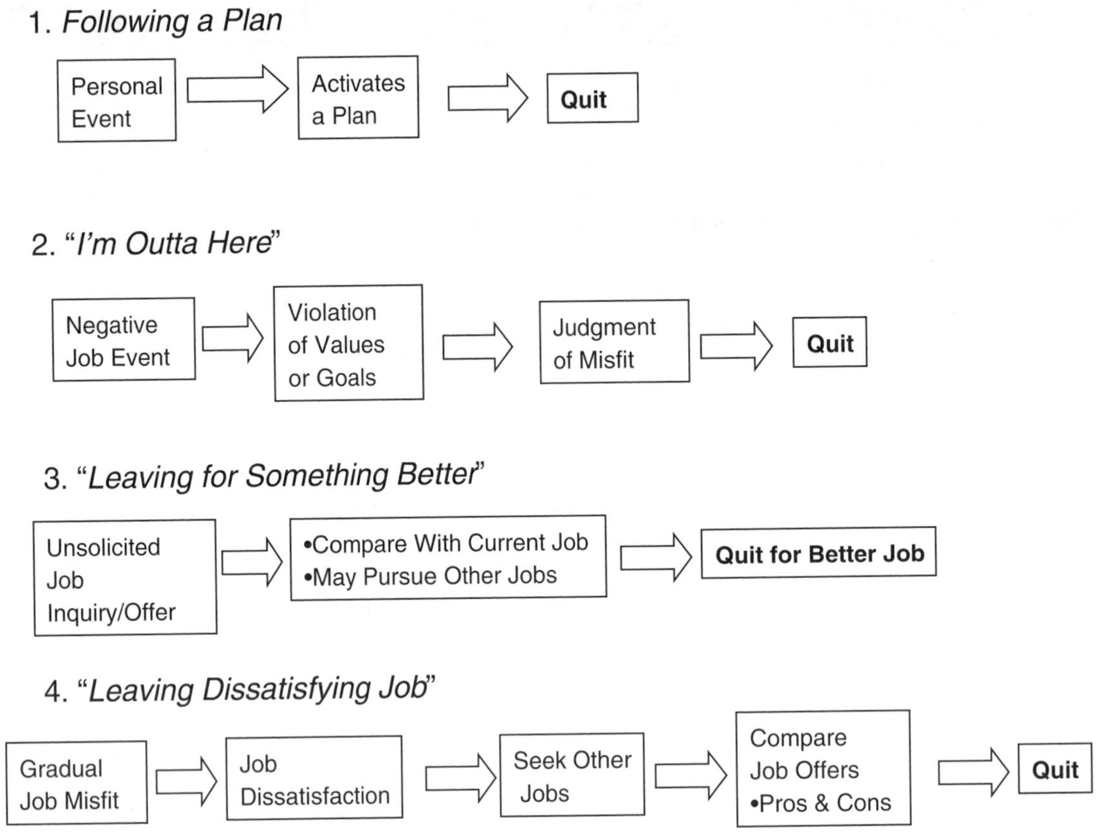

1. *Following a Plan*

Personal Event → Activates a Plan → **Quit**

2. "*I'm Outta Here*"

Negative Job Event → Violation of Values or Goals → Judgment of Misfit → **Quit**

3. "*Leaving for Something Better*"

Unsolicited Job Inquiry/Offer → •Compare With Current Job •May Pursue Other Jobs → **Quit for Better Job**

4. "*Leaving Dissatisfying Job*"

Gradual Job Misfit → Job Dissatisfaction → Seek Other Jobs → Compare Job Offers •Pros & Cons → **Quit**

FIGURE 11.2. Lee and Mitchell's (1994) unfolding model.

"Leaving for Something Better"). For example, Lee et al. (1996) observed that a nurse quit when a physician offered her a more enticing job. Such shocks lead incumbents to compare alternatives with the current job and may motivate them to pursue and evaluate still other jobs. Should an alternative deliver superior inducements to the present position, incumbents will choose this alternative. Those taking this route may like their current job but prefer an alternative. Finally, Lee and Mitchell (1994) designated Path 4 ("Leaving Dissatisfying Job") to depict the conventional withdrawal path envisioned by intermediate-linkages theorists (Hom & Griffeth, 1991; Mobley, 1977), in which disgruntled employees purse other jobs and exit when securing better ones.

The unfolding model has ignited considerable research and rethinking about how and why people leave (Holtom, Mitchell, Lee, & Eberly, 2008; Lee, Mitchell, Holtom, McDaniel, & Hill, 1999; Lee, Mitchell, Wise, & Fireman, 1996; Maertz & Campion, 2004). Lee et al. (1996) popularized qualitative methodology to verify this theory. They interviewed 44 formerly employed nurses, asking them about their reason and manner for departing their last position. Their questions assessed decision rules that capture essential features (e.g., experienced shocks, job pursuit) of each withdrawal route. Interviews were later transcribed and reviewed by other investigators who did not interview study participants. Following pattern matching, they independently classified 62.5% of the leavers into one of the four theorized withdrawal paths. In a follow-up, Lee et al. (1999) modified the unfolding model (e.g., adding nonwork alternatives and decoupling search and evaluation of alternatives) and surveyed 229 former accountants about their pattern of leaving. Analyzing leavers' survey responses, Lee and colleagues assigned 92.6% of leavers into one of the paths in the unfolding model using their revised classification protocol.

Accumulated qualitative evidence for the unfolding model yields new insight into how and why people sever employment ties. Summarizing research on

325 exiting nurses, accountants, and bank employees, Mitchell, Holtom, and Lee (2001) concluded that as much as 25% of leavers quit without first searching for another job and that shocks induce more quits than does job dissatisfaction. Indeed, Mitchell, Holtom, and Lee (2001) estimated that nearly half exit because of external shocks, such as pregnancies, unsolicited job offers, and spousal relocations. By contrast, only 37% of all leavers take the conventional affect-initiated turnover route conceptualized by Mobley (1977). Further, international studies corroborate the pervasiveness of these four withdrawal paths in other countries (e.g., Great Britain; Holtom et al., 2008). Finally, Maertz and Campion (2004) extended this framework by integrating how people quit (turnover process) with why they quit (turnover content). This integrated process-content theory identified different types of leavers on the basis of motives for leaving (e.g., affect driven, impulsive quits) and described how different types follow different withdrawal paths. For example, preplanned quitters likely follow Path 1 ("Following a Plan"), whereas impulsive quitters often take Path 2 ("I'm Outta Here").

The unfolding theory and research also suggest novel practical implications. For one, this model suggests that much turnover is unavoidable, such as that due to spousal relocations that firms cannot control (Campion, 1991; Hom & Griffeth, 1995). Employers, however, might remove such cases from estimates of overall (voluntary) quit rates to generate a more realistic picture of turnover severity. They can thus avoid misdirecting resources to improve morale or award greater inducements if external causes are behind such departures (though dissatisfied personnel may be more receptive to unsolicited job offers). Further, organizations can better manage turnover problems if they can estimate the extent of shock-induced turnover. If firms can anticipate that a certain segment of the workforce regularly leaves after childbirth, they might cope with predictable staffing shortages by recruiting an available supply of temp help for such occasions (Cappelli, 2000). Even so, family-friendly companies are trying to lessen unavoidable exits due to work–family conflicts by offering flexible or part-time work schedules and telecommuting (Griffeth & Hom, 2001; E. Johnson, Lowe, & Reckers, 2008).

Although the most groundbreaking conceptualization during the past 15 years, Lee and Mitchell's (1994) unfolding model warrants additional verification with predictive research designs that assess predictors on one occasion to forecast future quits. To date, its verification mainly rests on qualitative findings based on leavers' retrospective accounts of how they quit (cf. Holtom et al., 2008). Yet recall errors, postdecisional rationalization, and demand characteristics (socially desirable reasons for leaving) can bias qualitative data (Griffeth & Hom, 2001). Moreover, postdictive research generates causally ambiguous evidence, as the act of quitting may affect self-perceived motives for leaving. Leavers may exaggerate or invent justifications for their actions to preserve their self-esteem or reputation (Westaby, 2005). Further, qualitative tests fail to generate estimates of this model's predictive power, as they sample only leavers (and lack turnover variance), though conventional models' modest predictive validity was a main impetus for creating the unfolding model. Finally, existing tests possibly underestimated how job dissatisfaction impacts quit decisions. Lee and Mitchell (1994) presumed that job dissatisfaction only plays a role in withdrawal Path 4. Yet Maertz and Campion (2004) suggested that negative workplace shocks that trigger withdrawal Path 2 (and image violations) also elicit anger and dissatisfaction.

EXPLANATORY CONSTRUCTS AND PREDICTORS

Apart from conceiving and testing elaborate formulations, turnover scholars also focus on particular explanatory constructs and predictors because of their wide-ranging effects on behaviors other than attrition (e.g., organizational commitment) or because their effects have been overlooked by existing theories (despite the broader scope of modern models; Mitchell & Lee, 2001).

Organizational Commitment

Rather than comprehensive theory building, other scholars have developed multidimensional constructs that "incrementally" improve turnover prediction and explanation. Foremost among these antecedents is organizational commitment, pioneered by Porter and his colleagues and construed as employees' acceptance of an organization's goals and values and desire to maintain membership (Mowday, Porter, & Steers, 1982; Porter, Steers, Mowday, & Boulian, 1974; see also Vol. 3, chap. 4, this handbook). Though initially invoked to explain turnover (Porter, Crampon, & Smith, 1976), this construct has spawned a broader research stream, which elaborated its dimensionality and attested to its wider effects (Cohen, 2003; Mathieu & Zajac, 1990). Early studies determined whether commitment predicts turnover more accurately than does job satisfaction, the nature of the interrelationships between these job attitudes, and whether Porter et al.'s (1976) commitment scale has predictive power without items tapping quit decisions (Bozeman & Perrewé, 2001; Farkas & Tetrick, 1989; Hom & Griffeth, 1995; Tett & Meyer, 1993; Vandenberg & Scarpello, 1990). This line of inquiry established that commitment and satisfaction explained unique turnover variance, that these attitudes reciprocally interact, and that Porter et al.'s commitment scale continued to predict turnover after controlling quit propensity.

Since this early work, the most noteworthy theoretical developments are Meyer and Allen's (1997) multiform theory, Reicher's (1985) multiple-constituency commitment model, and Mael and Ashforth's (1995) organizational identification. Meyer and Allen (1997) identified three distinct forms of commitment: affective, continuance, and normative. In a nutshell, people commit to institutions because they want to (affective), need to (continuance), or ought to (normative). Factor analyses have upheld these forms (though splitting continuance into "lack of alternatives" and "costs of leaving"; Powell & Meyer, 2004), whereas other tests find that each form predicts quitting (Meyer, Stanley, Herscovitch, & Topolnytsky, 2002). Alternatively, Reicher (1985) conceptualized how organizational commitment depends on how employees commit to various organizational constituents (e.g., workgroup, supervisor). Hunt and Morgan (1994) later validated Reicher's formulation, showing that affinity for various constituents underpins corporate commitment. Going beyond common affect-based views, Mael and Ashforth (1995) proposed organizational identification, which represents a cognition rather than an affect like organizational commitment. They asserted that people identify themselves in terms of group affiliations (e.g., Arizona State faculty, Society for Industrial and Organizational Psychology member) and incorporate organizational membership as part of their core self-concept. Strong identification with an organization sustains membership, which has been observed with Army recruits and Japanese and British workers and university teachers (Abrams, Ando, & Hinkle, 1998; Mael & Ashforth, 1995).

Given ample evidence for its loyalty-sustaining influence, practitioners might track employees' levels of organizational commitment. Commitment assessments can gauge not only employees' quit propensities but also their engagement, as committed employees perform well (Mathieu & Zajac, 1990) and engage in organizational citizenship (Organ & Ryan, 1995). Moreover, Reicher's (1985) model suggests that employers can strengthen firm commitment by boosting employees' commitment to various workplace constituents, such as supervisors and teammates. Further, Mael and Ashforth's (1995) conceptualization suggests that businesses that promote organizational reputations by advertising products and services may also attract and retain employees through brand loyalty. Employees might thus form stronger organizational identification when they belong to prestigious or "cool" institutions.

Ease-of-Movement Constructs

Since March and Simon's (1958) seminal paper, scholars have widely assumed that the allure of alternative employment elsewhere can induce people to quit, even those who are satisfied with their current job. Testing March and Simon's (1958) notion about the ease of movement, much early work examined the abundance and quality of jobs in the external labor market. More recently, investigators have conceptualized this construct as a personal attribute, recognizing that certain types of individuals can more readily secure other positions (Trevor, 2001). We next consider the longstanding research stream on what facilitates interfirm mobility.

Job opportunities. Over the years, turnover investigators have discerned contrary findings from labor economics and organizational psychology about the extent to which alluring employment alternatives "pull" incumbents away from workplaces. Labor economic research typically finds stronger correlations between unemployment rates and quit rates (Hulin et al., 1985; Mobley, 1982; Price, 1977). For example, Hulin et al. (1985) reported a −.84 correlation between national unemployment and voluntary termination rates over a 31-year period, whereas Terborg and Lee (1984) estimated a −.24 correlation between sales personnel quit rates and joblessness rates in retail stores' locales. Despite robust macrolevel findings (aggregations across units, industries, or occasions) and theoretical prominence of ease of movement in prevailing turnover models (Mobley, 1977; Price & Mueller, 1981, 1986; Rusbult & Farrell, 1983), organizational psychologists, who study individual-level phenomena, usually detect much weaker correlations between employees' subjective impressions of job opportunities and their quit behaviors (Griffeth & Hom, 1988a; Steel & Griffeth, 1989).

To resolve these discrepancies, Hulin and associates (1985) theorized that organizational psychologists commit an ecological fallacy by assuming that aggregate- and individual-level relationships are alike. Rather, they argued that marginal workers—a significant but neglected proportion of the workforce consisting of temporary workers, part-timers, secondary wage earners, and drifters—do not base their quit decisions on job affect or expectations about alternative jobs. To illustrate, secondary wage earners often plan to resign even before starting work, especially after they have amassed sufficient savings to "pursue more pleasurable or less stressful avocations on a full-time basis" (Hulin et al., 1985, p. 240). More impulsive marginal workers may "quit their jobs on the basis of their experienced job dissatisfaction" (p. 246) without securing job offers before leaving (Hom, 2002). Hulin et al. (1985) noted that other peripheral workers "leave the regular work force temporarily, or permanently, to engage in other activities" (p. 246), whereas hobos "quit their jobs rather frequently, not because of any great dislike for work . . . but simply because they want to see what a different job with a different organization in a different location would have to offer" (p. 245).

Hulin and colleagues (1985) maintained that formulations by industrial psychologists poorly explain quits by marginal workers and drifters, whose nontrivial presence in empirical studies is responsible for weak correlations between perceived alternatives and individual-level quits ($r = .15$; see Table 11.2). Rather, they postulated a macrolevel selection mechanism to account for stronger aggregate-level associations between joblessness and quit statistics. The peripheral labor force expands and contracts with the business cycle. During expanding economies, employers raise wages or lower hiring standards, which attracts more drifters and casual laborers into the workforce. Given their tenuous or transient commitment to work, marginal workers and hobos readily quit once they amass sufficient funds or stay long enough on the job to become bored (and move on). During business downturns, companies avoid recruiting peripheral workers given a more ample labor supply. Quit rates are correspondingly lower during recessions because exit-prone marginal workers are missing from the payroll (having never been recruited). All told, the inflow and outflow of marginal workers into the workforce during rising and falling economic trends may underlie stronger (inverse) macrolevel correlations between unemployment and quit rates.

Alternatively, Steel and Griffeth (1989) asserted that methodological shortcomings are behind weak relationships between perceptual labor-market indices and individual-level quits. Most turnover studies sample employees from the same local or occupational labor markets (a single locale or occupation). As a result, survey respondents are describing the same referent (job availability in a community or occupational field), which constrains variance in perceptual measures and thereby undercuts their predictive utility. Besides this, common single-item unidimensional indicators, such as questions about perceived chances of finding acceptable alternatives (Mobley, Horner, & Hollingsworth, 1978; see Appendix 11.1), poorly reflect employment markets that are likely multifaceted and complex. In sum, narrow sampling of labor markets and deficient (and unreliable) measures may have attenuated the predictive power of labor-market perceptual indices.

Steel and Griffeth's (1989) methodological critique stimulated the development of more valid and multidimensional indicators of the job market. Steel (1996) thus collected a wide range of objective measures of job opportunities, such as volume of job advertising, historical retention rates in a job, and the Department of Labor projected job growth. Each index predicted Air Force enlistees' reenlistments. Moreover, he showed that objective measures of job availability explained unique variance in reenlistments (especially, a job's historical retention rate) beyond that explained by conventional measures of the perceived number of alternatives (see Appendix 11.1).

Griffeth, Steel, Allen, and Bryan (2005) next created the Employment Opportunity Index (EOI) to better capture employee perceptions of alternatives. After generating an item pool, their factor analyses verified five dimensions, such as ease of movement and crystallization of alternatives (see Figure 11.3). EOI scales showed discriminant validity as they were not highly correlated with each other or with theoretically dissimilar constructs (e.g., job satisfaction, role conflict). It is important that each EOI subscale explained unique variance in one or more withdrawal criteria (e.g., turnover, quit intentions, job search) after controlling other EOI subscales, job attitudes, and traditional indices of perceived alternatives. Collectively, the five EOI scales explained 10% of the turnover variance (according to the Nagelkerke index in logistic regression), outperforming existing perceptual indices (which correlate .15 with turnover on average; Griffeth et al., 2000; see Figure 11.3).

Employment Opportunity Index

- Ease of Movement
  - Accessibility and Quantity of Alternatives
- Desirability of Movement
  - Attractiveness of Available Alternatives
- Networking
  - Volume of Contacts Providing Job Leads
- Crystallization of Alternatives
  - Number of Discovered or Obtained Jobs
- Mobility
  - Impediments to Relocations Due to Dual Careers and Family Responsibilities

FIGURE 11.3. Employment Opportunity Index.

Improving instrumentation has thus reaffirmed received wisdom about employment opportunity. Although not disputing theoretical assertions that alternatives are immaterial for certain subpopulations or types of leavers (Hulin et al., 1985; Lee & Mitchell, 1994; Maertz & Campion, 2004), these methodological refinements have corroborated March and Simon's (1958) longstanding assumption that job incumbents truly contemplate the volume and quality of alternatives when deciding whether to resign. Objective indicators (e.g., projected job growth) and EOI scales may thus help employers monitor which occupational fields or local labor markets pose greater challenges to retaining and replacing incumbents with marketable skills. Many turnover researchers recommend tracking employee morale ("push" forces, or how dissatisfying conditions push people from jobs) but neglect "pull" forces (or how alternatives lure incumbents away; Griffeth & Hom, 2001). Inspecting morale scores alone can be insufficient as even satisfied employees are liable to quit when desired options exist (Lee & Mitchell, 1994; March & Simon, 1958; Salamin & Hom, 2005; Hulin et al. [1985] suggested that desirable alternatives can induce incumbents to derogate their jobs). Given Griffeth et al.'s (2005) finding that crystallized alternatives is a strong turnover predictor, firms might assess employees' attraction to specific employers—to whom they have submitted job applications or from whom they have received job offers—to better "compete" for them (Griffeth & Hom, 2001).

Job performance. Turnover researchers have long explored the nature of the relationship between job performance and voluntary terminations (Allen & Griffeth, 2001; McEvoy & Cascio, 1987; C. R. Williams & Livingstone, 1994). They pursued this inquiry because they suspected that overall quit rates are misleading indicators of turnover severity that neglect *who* quits. Dalton, Todor, and Krackhardt (1982) first pointed out that only some terminations, which they called *dysfunctional* *turnover*, are detrimental to employers' interests. Unwanted turnover occurs when high performers or those with difficult-to-replace skills leave. Using a 2 × 2 taxonomy based on whether turnover is voluntary and the employee's value, they defined *dysfunctional turnover* as "valuable" employees leaving (cell d in Figure 11.4) and *functional turnover* as low-performer quits (cell c), which benefits organizations. Jackofsky's (1984) provocative thesis of a curvilinear performance-turnover relationship further animated this research stream. Extrapolating from March and Simon's (1958) ease-of-movement idea, she argued that effective performers can easily quit because they have more job opportunities, whereas low performers readily quit to avoid dismissal.

In general, the research literature concludes that job performance is inversely related to voluntary terminations (Griffeth et al., 2000; C. R. Williams & Livingstone, 1994). In most organizations, high performers stay more than do low performers, and the former's loyalty is reinforced when they receive merit-based incentives (Harrison, Virick, & William, 1996). Yet some studies also lend credence to Jackofsky's (1984) original proposition, finding curvilinear associations in which high and low performers are more quit prone than moderate performers among American managers (Trevor, Gerhart, & Boudreau, 1997) and Swiss bankers (Salamin & Hom, 2005; see Figure 11.5). According to Hom and Griffeth (1995), such curvilinearity arises when the accomplishments of effective performers are visible or objective. In line with this conjecture, Allen and Griffeth (2001) showed that high performers most often quit when their achievements are externally visible to the marketplace (attracting other employers' attention). Besides visibility, other studies find that rapid promotion rates—especially when accompanying pay increases do offset such "market signals"—can accelerate leaving (among more promotable top performers). Presumably, promotions reveal worker productivity to outside employers, facilitating ease of movement (Salamin & Hom, 2005; Trevor et al., 1997).

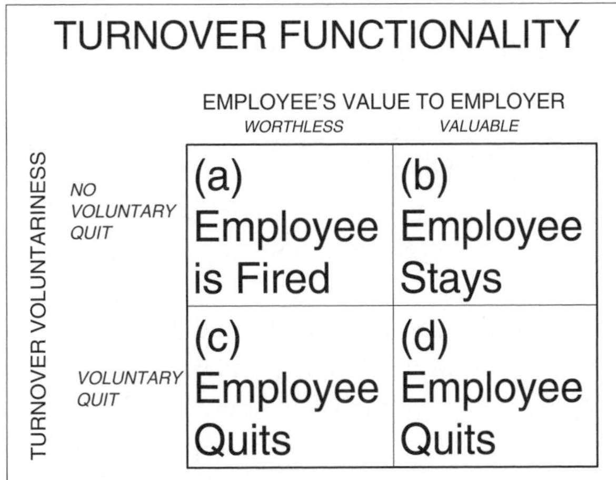

FIGURE 11.4. Turnover functionality. Based on Dalton, Krackhardt, and Porter (1981, Table 1, p. 717).

As for practical implications, this research suggests that employers interpret high turnover rates cautiously, as such statistics overstate turnover severity if they include low performer turnover. Rather, they might monitor rates of dysfunctional turnover, which they can reduce by distributing more rewards and recognition to high performers (and those having hard-to-replace skills; Griffeth et al., 2000). In some occupational fields, such as university scholars and professional athletes, employers must nevertheless attend to high quit rates, as their best performers are highly mobile by dint of their observable achievements. Greater enticements can help deter (some) superior performers from leaving (Harrison et al., 1996; Salamin & Hom, 2005). At the same time, organizations might avoid supplying top performers with credentials (e.g., degrees, promotions) that enhance their marketability. For example, they might reassign valued employees to challenging assignments (with pay hikes) rather than assigning them inflated job titles.

Further, industrial psychologists might develop prediction models to forecast turnover functionality (T_{func}), which Hollenbeck and Williams (1986) compute in the following way:

$$T_{func} = \text{Turnover} \times \text{Job Performance},$$

coding turnover as +1 for stayers and −1 for leavers and using a standardized performance index. This index is positive when high performers ($z = +1$) stay (+1) ($+1 = +1 \times +1$) or low performers ($z = -1$) quit (−1) ($+1 = -1 \times -1$). Turnover functionality is negative when superior performers leave ($-1 = +1 \times -1$)

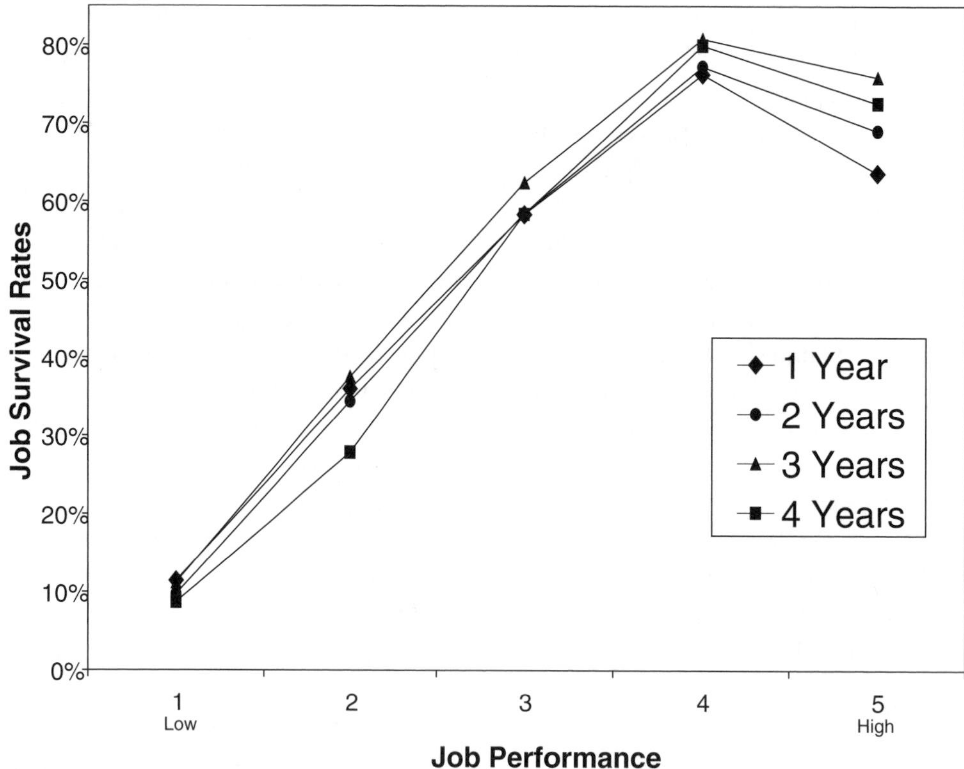

FIGURE 11.5. Job survival as a function of job performance and job tenure in Swiss bank. From "In Search of the Elusive U-Shaped Performance–Turnover Relationship: Are High Performing Swiss Bankers More Liable to Quit?" by A. Salamin and P. Hom, 2005, *Journal of Applied Psychology, 90,* p. 1212. Copyright 2005 by the American Psychological Association.

or poor performers stay (−1 = −1 × +1). Unlike a conventional turnover index, Hollenback and Williams' measure differentiates between functional and dysfunctional turnover. Using this index, they documented that job attitudes, which ordinarily predict turnover, did not predict turnover functionality. Similarly, J. Johnson, Griffeth, and Griffin (2000) found that high-performing leavers were more dissatisfied with promotions than were low-performing leavers, whereas the latter were more dissatisfied with their work. These demonstrations suggest that employers design selection instruments to optimally forecast turnover functionality rather than turnover per se. In this way, they can hire employees who stay as well as perform effectively, while avoiding low performers who stay. Besides conventional quit-rate statistics, organizations might also track this index, which explicitly captures low-performer retention rates. Otherwise, employers may neglect the "problem" of overly retaining marginal performers during business downturns when overall rates of turnover—especially among marginal performers (Trevor, 2001)—fall (Schiemann, 2009).

Movement capital. Espousing a labor-economic perspective, Trevor (2001) introduced the concept of movement capital, or human capital (e.g., training, education) that confers greater job mobility on employees. This construct departs from predominant schools of thought conceiving "ease of leaving" as an environmental factor representing labor market attributes (Steel, 1996; Steel & Griffeth, 1989). Using a national representative sample, Trevor (2001) developed a composite based on education, occupational-specific training, and cognitive ability to index movement capital and observed that job incumbents with high movement capital tend to quit when they feel dissatisfied. Unemployment conditions have little bearing on their quit decisions, though such considerations dominate quit decisions of those with less movement capital. The latter exit when job markets are strong.

Trevor's (2001) work has major practical implications, supporting long-held beliefs that highly skilled or highly talented incumbents can readily switch jobs, even during economic downturns (Jackofsky, 1984). Organizations thus face the dilemma of cultivating employees' human capital by way of developmental experiences, tuition assistance, and training that makes them productive without making them marketable. A historical solution has been to provide firm-specific rather than general training (Lazear, 1998). When employers furnish general training (e.g., tuition reimbursement for MBA degrees), they can mandate paybacks for premature quits (exiting right after degree completion). G. Benson, Finegold, and Mohrman (2004) noted that employees remain when they are completing graduate degrees but leave soon after graduating unless they are promoted to positions in which they can use newly acquired skills (better person–job match). Trevor's (2001) findings also imply vigilant monitoring of mobile incumbents' job attitudes; should their attitudes worsen, they will likely resign irrespective of labor market conditions.

Job Embeddedness

Mitchell, Holtom, Lee, Sablynski, and Erez (2001) first called attention to the pervasive neglect of the psychology of why people stay. Conventional views on why employees leave overlook the different emotional and psychological processes implicated in staying (vs. leaving). Mitchell and Lee (2001) thus introduced "job embeddedness," wherein "the more embedded one is, the less likely they are to leave their jobs" (p. 216). This construct comprises three dimensions: (a) links: formal or informal connections to others in an organization and community; (b) sacrifice: perceived costs of material and psychological benefits forfeited by exits; and (c) fit: compatibility or comfort with the work and external environments. Simply put, people remain if they have many links to colleagues and community members, would lose valuable perks or amenities if they quit and relocated (e.g., lose seniority benefits and safe neighborhoods), and fit their job and community (e.g., share workplace values). Though similar constructs have been advanced (e.g., continuance commitment; Yao, Lee, Mitchell, Burton, & Sablynski, 2004), this theoretical approach is more comprehensive (combining diverse forces for staying) and incorporates external influences on retention, such as neighbor ties (links), personal fit with community activities, and potential loss of community advantages (e.g., good weather and schools; see Figure 11.6).

Unlike traditional latent constructs that underlie empirical indicators, Mitchell and Lee (2001) formulated job embeddedness as a construct that is defined by its indicators, much like socioeconomic status. In other words, measures of fit, links, and sacrifice in combination "cause" job embeddedness (MacKenzie, Podsakoff, & Jarvis, 2005). By contrast, measurement operations for assessing most turnover antecedents presume that these constructs "cause" scores on scales. To illustrate, "being married or owning their house may cause people to be embedded in a job, whereas being embedded in their job does not cause people to get married or own a house" (Crossley, Bennett, Jex, & Burnfield, 2007, p. 1032). Mitchell and Lee (2001) further claimed that different forces for staying can produce the same level of embeddedness for different people. To illustrate, one person may stay because he or she enjoys recreational activities in the community, whereas another may stay to avoid surrendering long vacation time accumulated on a job. Internal-consistency reliability estimates are thus

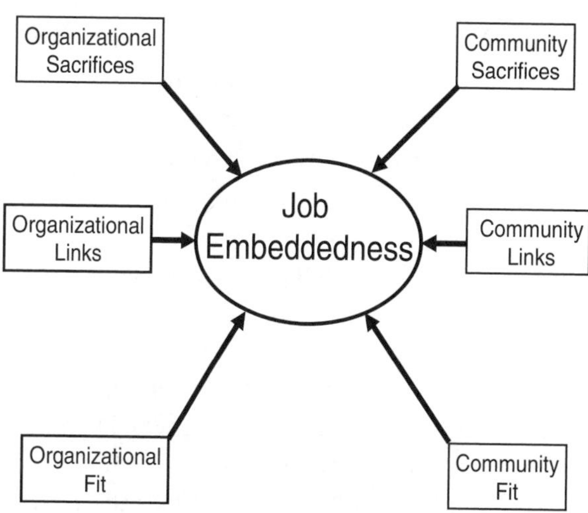

FIGURE 11.6. Job embeddedness theory of why employees stay.

inappropriate for embeddedness scales, as they comprise heterogeneous (and not necessarily positively correlated) items representing diverse embedding forces.

Numerous studies have shown that job embeddedness predicts turnover beyond that explained by standard antecedents, such as job attitudes (Holtom et al., 2008; Mitchell, Holtom, Lee, Sablynski, & Erez, 2001). Beyond this, Lee, Mitchell, Sablynski, Burton, and Holtom (2004) documented that embedded incumbents perform well and engage in organizational citizenship (supportive actions for organizations not explicitly mandated in job descriptions). Illustrating "turnover contagion," Felps et al. (2009) further established that employees whose coworkers are highly embedded at work remain, whereas those whose coworkers are less embedded leave. In addition, Hom, Tsui, Wu, Lee, Zhang, Fu, & Li (2009) found that embedded Chinese managers express stronger institutional commitment and intentions to stay. Further, college embeddedness can portend college persistence (Allen & Moffett, 2004; Murphy & Hom, 2008).

These scholarly explorations of institutional embeddedness generate practical implications that go beyond conventional approaches for boosting morale or person–job fit (via better recruiting and socialization; Griffeth & Hom, 2001). In particular, Holtom, Mitchell, and Lee (2006) suggested fostering community embeddedness by recruiting from areas near offices or factories and minimizing relocations. They also recommended promoting community links by supporting community service (so that employees can partner with community participants) and raising community sacrifice with home-buying assistance programs. Felps et al. (2009) also prescribed that employers proactively manage how employees surrounded by "unembedded" colleagues interpret coworker attrition, preventing such turnover from gaining social legitimacy.

Although job embeddedness theory is stimulating new explorations into the psychology of staying, direct evidence for Mitchell and Lee's (2001) premise that staying is the obverse of leaving is scant. This claim is reminiscent of Herzberg's (1958) thesis that job satisfaction and job dissatisfaction are different attitudes rather than anchor opposite ends of the same continuum, a view largely discredited (Locke, 1976). Indeed, some studies report that job embeddedness is inversely related to negative job affect, a prime stimulant for quitting (Hom et al., 2009). That is, why people remain (e.g., excellent management) may simply be due to the same causes (namely, their obverse) that induce them to resign (e.g., poor management). Conceivably, other psychological formulations can lend credence to Mitchell, Holtom, Lee, Sablynski, and Erez's (2001) claim that the psychology of staying differs from that of leaving. To illustrate, Westaby's (2005) behavioral choice model posits that both "reasons for" and "reasons against" enacting a behavior are needed to fully comprehend behavioral decisions. Regulatory focus theorists have also asserted that approaching desirable end states (e.g., employees stay in a good job for its intrinsic rewards) elicits different emotions and strategies than lessening avoidance from undesirable end states (e.g., incumbents remain in a bad job because they cannot afford to quit; Brockner & Higgins, 2001; Higgins, 1997).

Moreover, embeddedness scholars typically operationalize links as a volume of connections to workplace and community, but this procedure overlooks other ways relationships are embedding. Social network theory and methodology can enrich the links subdimension by identifying additional relational constraints on leaving as well as "de-embedding" links. In particular, network studies reveal that tie strength (Feeley & Barnett, 1997; Feeley, Hwang, & Barnett, 2008; Mossholder, Settoon, & Henagan, 2005) and third-party ties (Burt, 2005; Krackhardt, 1999) reinforce job incumbency, whereas social network approaches to career effectiveness (Ibarra, 1995; Siebert, Kramer, & Liden, 2001) and mentoring (Higgins, 2001; Morrison, 2002) suggest how relationships can improve newcomer socialization and career success (strengthening staying) by delivering social capital (resources embedded in relationships; Lin, 2001). Network studies further disclose how social contacts can undermine loyalty. In a classic study, Krackhardt and Porter (1986) showed that members exiting a network community (and workplace) prompt others to leave (or "turnover contagion"; Felps et al., 2009). Mentoring and occupational attainment literatures also reveal that external constituents encourage exits by advising employees to change careers, identifying job leads, or securing jobs for them (Granovetter, 1973; Higgins, 2001; Higgins & Kram, 2001; Lin, 2001).

Besides this, job embeddedness theory assumes that different embedding forces exert similar effects on staying, though some forces might work at cross-purposes. For example, Maertz and Griffeth (2004) noted that normative prescriptions (to stay or leave a job) from external constituents (e.g., family) may run counter to affective commitment to internal constituents. That is, employees may want to stay because they are emotionally attached to colleagues but their family may pressure them to leave (Hom & Hulin, 1981). Similarly, Murphy and Hom (2008) theorized that community and organizational fit may have opposing effects on employee attrition. Employees who are overly involved in external endeavors, such as family or schooling, may resign because of such extrawork interference with their job duties (Kelloway, Gottlieb, & Barham, 1999).

Dynamic Effects of Turnover Causes

Forty years ago, Hulin (1968) chronicled how temporal declines in job satisfaction foreshadow terminations, whereas Porter et al. (1976) discovered that falling organizational commitment over time translates into higher quits. Endorsing their pioneering efforts, Mobley (1982) prescribed more repeated measures designs to illuminate the temporal dynamics of the withdrawal process. His call inspired a stream of research assessing how changes in withdrawal antecedents over time portend subsequent terminations (Farrell, 1983; Hom & Griffeth, 1991; Rusbult & Youngblood, Mobley, & Meglino, 1983). Indeed, Rusbult and Farrell (1983) concluded that "It is the *process of change* . . . that distinguishes between those who stay and those who leave" (p. 437). Despite such provocative claims, growing awareness of the limitations of traditional approaches for gauging change (namely, change scores and repeated measures analysis of variance; Chan, 1998; Bergh, 1995; Hom & Haynes, 2007) basically curtailed dynamic inquiries for 2 decades.

Recent methodological innovations in panel-analytical techniques, such as hierarchical linear modeling (HLM; Raudenbush & Bryk, 2002) and latent growth modeling (LGM; Duncan, Duncan, Strycker, Li, & Alpert, 1999), are revitalizing scholarly interest in the dynamic effects of turnover causes. With three or more waves of predictor data, these approaches estimate a regression equation for each individual, regressing his or her "predictor" scores on their time of measurement. This equation computes an intercept, representing the person's Time-1 value for the predictor variable, and a slope—or (linear) rate of change in predictor score per unit time. Such approaches permit a "true" study of time by focusing on the slope (or velocity) rather than displacement—or overall amount of change (the focus of traditional methods), which masks the potential moment-to-moment changes in the rate of change (Hsee & Abelson, 1991; see Figure 11.7).

Using HLM, Kammeyer-Meuller, Wanberg, Glomb, and Ahlburg (2005) thus observed differential rates of change in several withdrawal antecedents between stayers and leavers. For example, leavers more rapidly seek alternatives over time (before exiting), compared with stayers. With LGM, Lance, Vandenberg, and Self (2000) and Bentein, Vandenberg, Vandenberghe, and Stinglhamber (2005) documented that precipitous declines in organizational commitment presage ascending quit intentions. What is more, these methodologies may reveal that determinants' temporal shifts can have unique effects on terminations beyond their static (intercept) values. Given more waves of predictor data, these approaches can also assess other (nonlinear) forms of

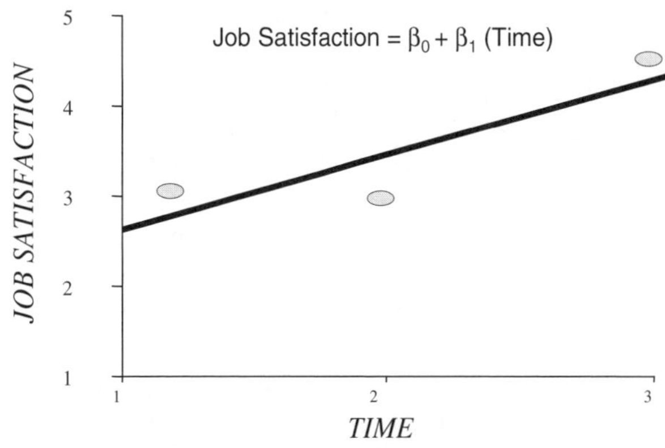

FIGURE 11.7. An individual's trajectory of change for a turnover cause.

change (Lance et al., 2000), such as velocity shifts (acceleration; Hsee, Salovey, & Abelson, 1995).

Second-order factor (SOF) LGM can adjust for fluctuating psychometric properties, which can yield artifactual evidence of change (Chan, 1998, 2002). Indeed, Chan (1998) and Lance et al. (2000) advocated longitudinal confirmatory factor analysis (CFA) to verify measurement invariance before examining change. Invariance tests require data from three or more waves of multiple-indicator assessments of a latent construct. CFA users would thus analyze a matrix comprising variances and covariances among indicators within and between occasions to test the stability of various psychometric attributes (Vandenberg & Lance, 2000). Specifically, CFA users evaluate a series of nested measurement models. Each measurement model designates occasions as factors and specifies same-period indicators to load on their respective occasion factor. An indicant's errors may be correlated over time to control autocorrelated errors, which often arise when indicants are repeated over brief time intervals (see Figure 11.8).

CFA researchers first assess a model specifying an identical pattern of factor loadings and number of factors across occasions. Evidence for configural invariance—the most essential form of measurement invariance—is forthcoming when this model fits data (Vandenberg & Lance, 2000). Given satisfactory fit, this model is next contrasted to a nested model constraining factor loadings to be equal over time (metric invariance). Should the latter model fit the data (and is not materially worse fitting than the first model), investigators then proceed to test a third model equating indicator intercepts over time (scalar invariance). If this third model fits as well as the second model, then all three forms of measurement invariance are satisfied. If measures lack invariance (especially configural invariance), further inquiry into change for the construct ends as instrumentation shifts would confound any evidence of apparent change (Lance et al., 2000).

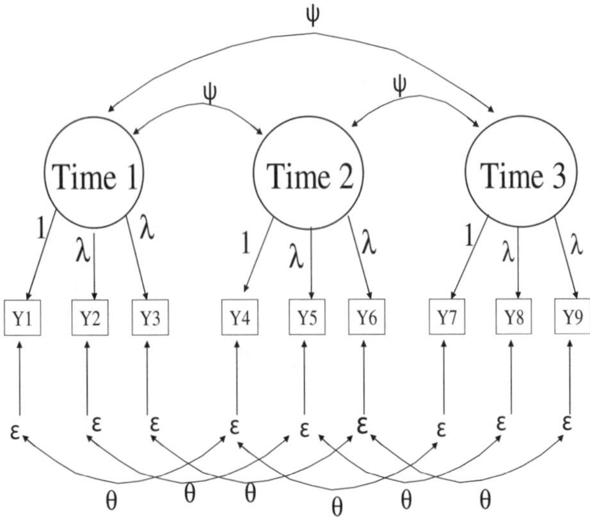

FIGURE 11.8. Longitudinal measurement model. From *Research Methodology in Strategy and Management* (Vol. 4, p. 239), by D. J. Ketchen & D. D. Bergh (Eds.), 2007, Amsterdam, the Netherlands: Elsevier. Copyright 2007 by Elsevier. Reprinted with permission.

After establishing that indicators have stable psychometric qualities, Lance and associates (2000) prescribed assessing change for a latent construct with SOF LGM. Essentially, this procedure "grafts" a structural model onto a focal variable's longitudinal measurement model. Figure 11.9 illustrates how SOF LGM represents temporal change in withdrawal cognitions (measured on three occasions with three indicators: thoughts of quitting [THINKQ], search intentions [BISEEK], and quit intentions [BIQUIT]) and how it relates to an antecedent (shocks) and consequent (turnover). As in longitudinal CFA, a SOF LGM model specifies that a variable's set of measures concurrently collected defines a first-order factor for an occasion (e.g., WCGTIME1). Unlike CFA, this model further introduces second-order (growth) factors to represent this variable's intercept and slope. In essence, SOF LGM presumes that each person has a distinct set of growth parameters (a different Time-1 value and rate of change) that describes his or her unique trajectory of change for withdrawal cognitions. This approach thus computes intercept and slope variances, representing amount of interindividual differences in growth parameters.

To identify the intercept factor (η_4), all first-order occasion factors have factor loadings of 1.0 on this second-order factor. To define the (linear) slope factor (η_6), the factor loading for the first occasion factor is fixed at 0, the loading for the second occasion factor is fixed at 1, and the loading for the third occasion factor is set at 2 (assuming time periods are identically spaced). Further, SOF LGM models can

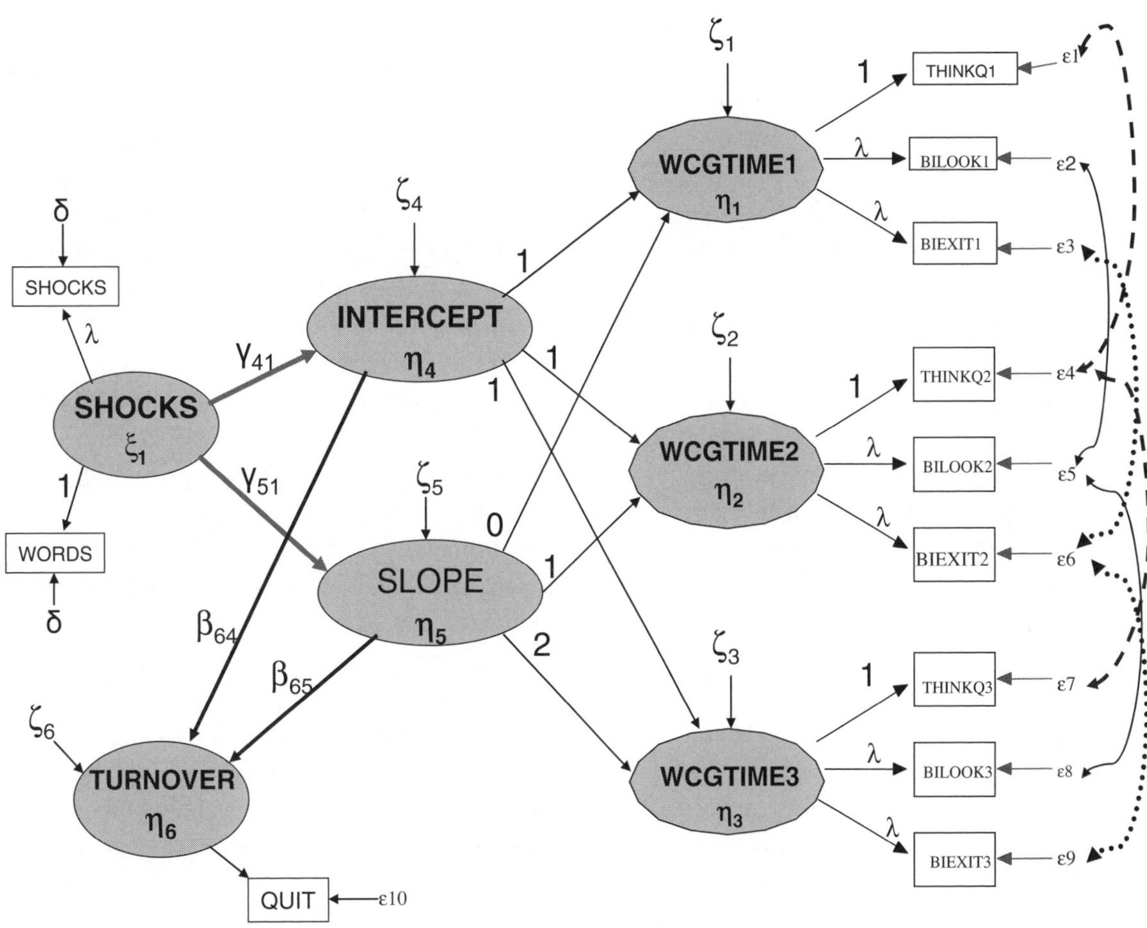

FIGURE 11.9. Trajectory model for withdrawal cognitions: An antecedent and consequent of its growth parameters. From *Research Methodology in Strategy and Management* (Vol. 4, p. 242), by D. J. Ketchen & D. D. Bergh (Eds.), 2007, Amsterdam, the Netherlands: Elsevier. Copyright 2007 by Elsevier. Reprinted with permission.

include antecedents and consequences of intercept and slope factors. To illustrate, the figure depicts shocks (ξ_1, experienced events that stimulate thoughts of quitting) as affecting withdrawal cognitions' initial status (γ_{41}) and rate of change (γ_{51}), both of which affect turnover (η_6). β_{65} estimates how much the velocity of change for withdrawal cognitions influence turnover, reflecting a dynamic effect.

In summary, LGM and HLM offer many advantages over conventional ways to assess change. First, they furnish stronger causal evidence by establishing that within-person changes in turnover antecedents can predict subsequent attrition, as most process-oriented formulations assume that "the causes and consequences change and interact over time" (Mobley, 1982, p. 135). Moreover, they can substantiate a theory's structural network of relationships by documenting that changes in distal antecedents are related to changes in proximal antecedents (capturing dynamic relationships; Chan & Schmitt, 2000), in accordance with theorized causal sequences. Using LGM, Bentein et al. (2005) thus demonstrated that changes in job attitudes predict changes in quit decisions. Further, these methods can improve turnover predictions by capturing predictors' dynamic effects, not simply their static values. For example, dynamic performance studies reveal that sharp declines in job performance over time can foreshadow subsequent exits independently of static performance levels (Harrison, Newman, & Roth, 2006; Sturman & Trevor, 2001).

SOF LGM has special advantages over HLM (Hom & Haynes, 2007). Unlike HLM, SOF LGM can control for temporal fluctuations in scale qualities to generate more valid estimates of mean change and how within-person change relates to other variables. Assuming unstable indicators are few in number (Lance et al., 2000), SOF LGM users can relax invariance constraints to allow for partial metric or scalar invariance (L. Williams, Edwards, & Vandenberg, 2003). SOF LGM can also adjust for the biasing effects of random measurement errors and more readily test complex structural models involving change trajectories.

Despite the promise of these advanced panel-analytical techniques, requisite data poses the greatest threat to their wider application as they require three or more waves of observations per individual (though HLM can analyze fewer observations for some respondents; Singer & Willett, 2003). SOF LGM also demands much larger samples to estimate the numerous structural and measurement parameters specified in multivariate dynamic models. If the goal is turnover prediction, HLM is preferable given its more flexible data requirements. In contrast to LGM, HLM does not require complete data on all individuals (as panel attrition often creates missing data) and time-structured observations (all persons are simultaneously assessed; Hom & Haynes, 2007). To lessen panel attrition, practitioners might monitor trends in changes in turnover antecedents using "pulse surveys" of business units (linking units rather than individuals over time) or archival personnel records (Harrison et al., 1996).

Demographic Correlates of Turnover

Scholars and practitioners are especially concerned about turnover among women and minorities in high-status, high-paying occupational fields, in which they have been historically, and for the foreseeable future, underrepresented (Helfat, Harris, & Wolfson, 2006; Hom, Roberson, & Ellis, 2008). Widespread reports by business consultants and journalists about a corporate exodus among women and people of color have fueled such interest. Notably, Schwartz (1989) concluded that "the rate of turnover in management positions is 2½ times higher among top-performing women than it is among men" (p. 65), whereas Daniels (2004) reported that "turnover rates are . . . 40% higher for black executives than for their counterparts" (p. 48). Such anecdotal evidence, if true, is alarming for employers seeking to diversify their workforces and executive ranks (Hewlett & Luce, 2005).

Unfortunately, empirical data on gender and racial differences in attrition in prestigious or influential occupations is mixed and sparse (Roberson, 2004). Previous work established that women professionals and managers face greater family responsibilities as well as more career obstacles (e.g., greater social isolation, fewer promotional opportunities; Brett & Stroh, 1999; Dalton, Hill, & Ramsay, 1997; Hewlett & Luce, 2005; Ibarra, 1995; Lyness & Heilman, 2006; Lyness & Thompson, 1997). Although revealing that women have more reasons to exit than men (work–family conflict, glass ceiling, sexual harassment; Glomb, Munson, Hulin, Bergman, & Drasgow, 1999), empirical studies rarely document higher voluntary female terminations (rather than quit intentions or a composite of voluntary and involuntary quits) in male-dominated fields and corporate settings, in which "there has been the most explicit concern about inequitable treatment and glass-ceiling effects" (Petersen & Saporta, 2004, p. 896; Lyness & Judiesch, 2001) rather than public sector and professional service firms (e.g., public accounting; Dalton et al., 1997). To furnish stronger evidence, Hom and associates (2008) recently collected turnover statistics from 16 corporations (collectively known as the Attrition and Retention Consortium [ARC]), sampling 404,052 professionals and managers (28.3% of whom are women). According to 2003 statistics, corporate women departed at higher rates than men, especially during early years of employment in which they predominate (see Figure 11.10).

Empirical corroboration for so-called "corporate flight" of minority managers and professionals (Cox & Blake, 1991; Daniels, 2004) is more uncertain and scant than that for corporate women (Roberson, 2004). Employment and economic discrimination toward racial minorities are well-documented (Brief, Butz, & Deitch, 2005; Brief, Umphress, et al., 2005; Dovidio & Hebl, 2005; McKay et al., 2007). Yet empirical—as opposed to anecdotal—evidence attesting to higher turnover among professionals and mangers of color is unavailable (Hom et al., 2008). Indeed, the common practice of combining

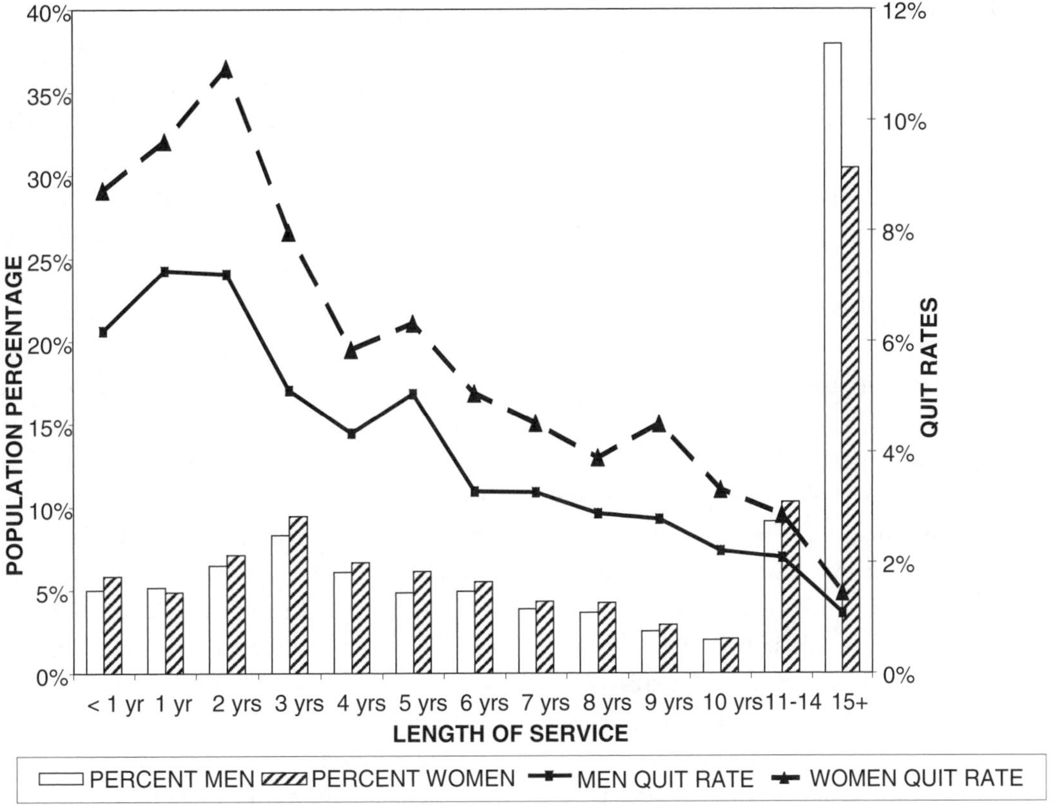

FIGURE 11.10. Gender differences in corporate exits by length of service.

various racial minorities together to contrast to Whites (because there are often too few of any minority group to consider separately) makes it difficult to gauge minority flight from corporate America (Griffeth et al., 2000). After all, racial minorities may exit at different rates, and grouping higher quitting minorities with lower quitting minorities may yield misleading estimates of minority–nonminority differences (Roberson, 2004).

Leveraging the large ARC data (comprising over 81,000 minorities), Hom and colleagues (2008) found that African Americans and Hispanics quit more than did White Americans (as well as Asian and Native Americans). Such findings accord with stereotyping research that African and Hispanic Americans face worse societal prejudice (Cottrell & Neuberg, 2005; Fiske, Cuddy, Glick, & Xu, 2002; Greenwald & Banaji, 1995). Racial differences, however, "vanished" once other variables, such as job tenure and occupation, were statistically controlled. Moreover, Hom et al. (2008) observed that African American and Hispanic women exit more than do men of their own race or Whites of either sex, though control variables (especially tenure) nullified evidence for minority women's corporate exodus. Such results seem consonant with the "double jeopardy" thesis, as women of color may face the dual disadvantages of racism and sexism (Berdahl & Moore, 2006).

Secondary analyses by Hom et al. (2008) further revealed that men and women of color are concentrated in "high-risk" short-tenure categories compared with Whites (perhaps because Corporate America is aggressively recruiting them). Given overrepresentation in the ranks of the newly hired, minorities may quit more than their White counterparts simply because more of them are adjusting to new workplaces and deciding if they are a good match for the job (Hom & Griffeth, 1995). It is not surprising that statistically controlling for racial differences in tenure thus shrank—if not erased—racial disparities in attrition. Such findings suggest that inadequate organizational assimilation is a prime impetus behind higher departures among minorities and women, though they may face greater (or different) socialization obstacles than do White men (Ibarra, 1995; Roberson, 2004). Hom and colleagues (2008) cautioned that "though the prevalence of 'rookies' among minorities and minority women may underlie this corporate exodus, their premature attrition constricts the pipeline of people of color available for future leadership" (p. 30).

Several practical implications derive from diversity research on turnover. For one, scholars have reported that women and people of color leave for disparate reasons, implying that organizations should customize different retention strategies for these populations. For example, greater work–family conflicts (Hewlett & Luce, 2005), sexual harassment (Wasti, Bergman, Glomb, & Drasgow, 2000), and glass ceilings (Stroh, Brett, & Reilly, 1996) may prompt women to exit, whereas slow career progress (Roberson, 2004) and poor diversity climates (McKay et al., 2007) may induce ethnic minorities to exit. As McKay et al. (2007) put it, "A 'one size fits all' approach to diversity management may not suffice" (p. 54). Still, Hom et al.'s (2008) work implies poor newcomer assimilation is responsible for excessive attrition among beginning employees regardless of their race or gender (though adjustment challenges may vary across groups). Effective efforts to socialize all entry incumbents would raise overall retention and thereby shrink racial and gender gaps in staying (Griffeth & Hom, 2001). Moreover, employers might track minority and female quit rates to gauge their progress toward a more diversified workforce. They might use such metrics to hold managers accountable for retaining minorities and women. Owing to their greater disadvantages (and underrepresentation in high-status, well-paid jobs), firms must take special steps to keep African and Hispanic American business professionals from leaving (Hom et al., 2008).

Further investigations might extend Hom et al.'s (2008) work by clarifying the underlying mechanisms mediating between diversity dimensions and turnover (cf. Stroh et al., 1996). To illustrate, Boudwin and Hom (2008) attempted to validate whether double jeopardy or work–family conflict can account for higher turnover among women of color by polling a regionally representative workforce sample about experienced discrimination and work–family interference. In this sample, minority women did not express stronger quit intentions nor did discrimination or work–family tension underpin their quit decisions. Moreover, turnover researchers might examine alternative explanations for why minorities and women flee corporate jobs, such as racial microaggression (Sue et al., 2007), stereotype threat (Roberson & Kulik, 2007), and affirmative action recruiting (Button & Rienzo, 2003). Overt discrimination may not be a main turnover cause. Rather, "benign" neglect or covert forms of prejudice, which are barely visible even to those mistreated (Sue et al., 2007), may create inhospitable environments that drive out the demographically different. Further, organizations might consider how well employees are embedded in local communities in which members of their race are numerically scarce. They might not fit such communities and forge fewer links with demographically dissimilar community members (Sacco & Schmitt, 2005). Such weaker community embeddedness may translate into higher quits (e.g., Hwang, 2005). Because organizations are experimenting with various solutions for retaining diverse groups, evaluations of which solutions actually reduce personnel losses are warranted. Finally, more inquiry into intergroup conflict among different racial minorities is warranted, as they are becoming a growing share of the workforce (Kinicki & Kreitner, 2008). Leonard and Levine (2006) thus report greater Black turnover when Asians (or Whites) predominate in a work setting.

International Differences in Turnover Predictors

American corporations increasingly employ foreign nationals to supply goods and services to domestic and overseas markets (Friedman, 2005; Hom & Griffeth, 1995; West, 2004). Tapping overseas labor markets in rising numbers, U.S. multinationals face intensifying labor competition from one another as well as from multinationals based in other countries (e.g., Japan). As a consequence, offshore attrition now plagues U.S. multinationals, especially in competitive labor markets, such as high-tech professions in India (Sheth, 2008) and managers in China (J. Benson & Zhu, 2002; Chow, Fung, &

Yue, 1999). Unfortunately, prevailing theory and research on turnover offer little guidance to U.S. multinationals on ways to retain host-country nationals as they are predominantly drawn from Anglo-American (North America, Britain, and Australia) studies (Maertz, Stevens, & Campion, 2003). After all, Hofstede (2001) had long forewarned that Anglo-American formulations and practices may not generalize to other cultures.

Because of its global ascendancy, turnover is increasingly explored in other cultures, especially those outside the Anglo-American culture (Hofstede, 2001). Following an etic orientation (that seeks cultural universals), preliminary international work has sought to generalize domestic theories or constructs, especially to Mexico (Linnehan & Blau, 2003; Maertz et al., 2003; J. Miller, Hom, & Gomez-Mejia, 2001; Posthuma, Joplin, & Maertz, 2005) or Asia (e.g., Korea: Kim, 1999; China: X.-P Chen, 2002; Z.-X Chen & Francesco, 2000; X.-P Chen, Hui, & Sego, 1998; Hom et al., 2009; Zhang & Li, 2004). Despite ubiquitous criticisms about ethnocentric Anglo-American perspectives (Boyacigiller, & Adler, 1991; Hofstede, 2001; Maertz et al., 2003), this inquiry uncovers findings that often resemble domestic findings (though some findings differ). In mainland China, Hsu, Hsu, Huang, Leong, and Li (2003) thus showed that supportive and participative leadership decreases quit intentions, whereas Hom et al. (2008) documented that job embeddedness reduces quit intentions. In Mexico, Tiano (1994) observed that dissatisfied factory workers formulate decisions to quit, whereas Linnehan and Blau (2003) reported that assemblers who actively pursue other jobs are more likely to later quit.

Though cultural universality is heartening, the dominant single-country etic research strategy may obscure cultural variability. Current efforts too freely apply standard formulations to probe turnover in other cultural milieus without regard for their suitability there. Exacerbating this ethnocentric bias, international researchers often use the same (domestic) measures (though carefully translated) to assess models (Kim, 1999) or constructs (Hsu et al., 2003). Although some researchers add culturally relevant or modify existing items for better cultural fit (and delete irrelevant ones; X.-P. Chen et al., 1998; Hom et al., 2009), the bulk of items assessing constructs are domestically derived. Such practices may omit indigenous expressions of theoretical constructs (Farh, Earley, & Lin, 1997; Wu et al., 2006). With rare exceptions (Posthuma et al., 2005), this research stream typically samples nationals from one culture, which precludes conclusive evidence for cultural stability (or instability). For example, active job searches boost quits in Mexico and America (G. Blau, 1993; Linnehan & Blau, 2003). Yet statistical tests between nationalities, if they had been done, might have disputed cross-national consistency.

To avoid being constrained a priori by Anglo-American viewpoints, some investigators adopt an "emic" approach (seeking culturally specific constructs) to develop culturally appropriate theories of turnover (Tsui, 2004). Using grounded theory building, Maertz and colleagues (2003) inductively deduced a withdrawal formulation for the maquiladoras, which are foreign-owned plants situated along the U.S.–Mexico border that employ Mexicans for assembly work, from semistructured interviews with assemblers. Their framework incorporates causal antecedents from Anglo-American models (such as perceived alternatives and constituent commitment) as well as culturally specific antecedents (e.g., "inertial resistance to job change" and "harmonious work environment"). Similarly, West (2004) drew from focus-group interviews with maquila managers and workers and the vast practitioner (Hecht & Morici, 1993; Salzinger, 2003; Teagarden, Butler, & Von Glinow, 1992; Tello & Greene, 1996) and ethnographic writings about maquila work (Cravey, 1998; Fernández-Kelly, 1983; Kopinak, 1996; Tiano, 1994) to "contextualize" domestic models and constructs. For her formulation about maquila turnover, West selected determinants that are salient for the maquila context (Tsui, 2004), such as continuance rather than organizational commitment (as Mexicans are loyal to people rather than faceless institutions) and fringe benefits (essential for subsistence in this poverty-stricken nation). Indigenous approaches can deepen insight into the withdrawal phenomenon in a culture, though their findings are more difficult to generalize across cultures.

Rather than adopt a strictly etic or emic orientation, capitalizing on both approaches may most enrich global knowledge about turnover, as they can be complementary (cf. qualitative and quantitative GLOBAL research; House, Hanges, Javidan, Dorfman, & Gupta, 2004). Although informed by prevailing (Anglo-American) thought and research (Holtom et al., 2008), scholars might identify (etic) constructs or processes that generalize across multiple cultural contexts by consulting cultural experts and scholarly (including historical, sociological, and psychological) writings about those cultures (Bond, 1996; House et al., 2004). Indeed, the few cross-national tests do find that some turnover influences are consistent across cultures (e.g., job attitudes, Posthuma et al., 2005; sexual harassment, Wasti et al., 2000), though their effect sizes may vary. Though rare, this etic strategy would sample multiple nationalities, especially from dissimilar cultural clusters (Hofstede, 2001), so that cross-cultural comparisons can be statistically tested. This research design would control key (noncultural) influences (e.g., occupational variability may outweigh cultural effects; Gomez-Mejia, 1984) and check measurement invariance (insuring configural and metric invariance before testing "relational equivalence," though scalar invariance is a precondition for validly comparing country means; Cheung & Rensvold, 1999; Wasti et al., 2000). Further, directly assessing purported cultural dimensions can best clarify how culture moderates the effects of withdrawal causes (Earley, 1989). To complement this etic strategy, emic explorations would seek indigenous explanatory constructs (Maertz et al., 2003) and indigenous manifestations of existing constructs (cf. Farh et al., 1997). In short, etic inquiries would identify which predictors and retention strategies are universally applicable, whereas emic inquiries would identify local predictors and retention practices that apply to particular societies.

MACROLEVEL CAUSES AND CONSEQUENCES OF ORGANIZATIONAL-LEVEL TURNOVER RATES

The preceding review clearly shows that scholarly inquiry has mainly focused on explaining and predicting individual-level turnover (and occasionally, individual-level consequences; Krackhardt, & Porter, 1986). The next section addresses a less common—but no less important—object of inquiry: the firm-level rate of attrition and its causes and consequences. Contemporary scholars are realizing that individual-level research findings may not generalize to the firm- or unit-level, where most interventions undertaken by management to control turnover are made (Hom & Griffeth, 1995; Hulin et al., 1985). To illustrate, demonstrations that wages are inversely related to individual-level quits (Griffeth et al., 2000) may not resemble firm-level relationships (J. Miller et al., 2001). To identify more effective turnover remedies as well as to further understanding of this neglected topic (Hom & Griffeth, 1995), more researchers are investigating the macrolevel causes and consequences of aggregate-level turnover. We thus consider this new avenue of research as follows.

High-Commitment Human Resources Management Systems

Departing from traditional preoccupation with individual-level quits, withdrawal researchers increasingly scrutinize how bundles of Human Resources Management (HRM) practices impact firm-wide quit rates (J. Miller et al., 2001; Shaw, Delery, Gupta & Jenkins, 1998). Specifically, a particular HRM system, known variously as "high involvement" (Gutherie, 2001; Lawler, 1990; Zatzick & Iverson, 2006), "mutual investment" employee-organization relationships (EOR; Tsui, Pearce, Porter, & Tripoli, 1997), or "people-centered management" (Pfeffer, 2005), has drawn much scholarly and practitioner attention. High-commitment HRM systems generally comprise employment security, empowered teams, collective incentives, flexible work designs, and egalitarian cultures, though different "flavors" exist (Baron & Kreps, 1999; Xiao & Björkman. 2006). Several perspectives maintain that these systems augment workforce commitment and loyalty via social exchange (P. Blau, 1964; Coyle-Shapiro & Conway, 2004; Takeuchi, Lepak, Wang, & Takeuchi, 2007). During social exchange, both employers and employees invest in their partnership and share socioemotional (and material) rewards, relying on mutual trust to meet open-ended, long-term obligations (P. Blau, 1964; Shore, Tetrick, Lynch, & Barksdale, 2006). To enact social exchange, high-commitment HRM systems offer enriched tasks, ample training, premium pay, and job security to employees (Huselid, 1995; Whitener, 2001), who reciprocate with greater allegiance (Shore & Barksdale, 1998; Tsui et al., 1997). By contrast, low-commitment HRM firms engage in economic exchange with personnel (Shore & Barksdale, 1998; Tsui et al., 1997). They treat them as "hired hands," expecting them to comply with formal employment contracts and releasing them when their services are no longer required (Tsui et al., 1997). Several studies affirm that high-commitment HRM practices diminish turnover in New Zealand (Gutherie, 2001) and America (Arthur, 1994; Huselid, 1995). Imposing demanding performance standards, these systems also initiate more turnover among ineffective performers (who face sanctions for failing to meet such standards) but less turnover among effective performers (who earn more rewards and recognition; Shaw, Dineen, Fang, & Vellella, 2009).

Most EOR inquiries assess firm-level relationships between HRM systems and aggregate quit rates, but several EOR scholars believe that such relationships are best conceived and examined as a multilevel phenomenon (Bowen & Ostroff, 2004; Shore et al., 2004). Following Tetrick's (2004) call for multilevel modeling (Heck & Thomas, 2000), Hom and associates (2009) thus studied the impact of mutual investment EOR, in which employers offer broad and ample inducements (e.g., training) in exchange for employees' broad and extensive contributions to the organization (e.g., citizenship; Tsui et al., 1997), on Chinese managers' commitment and quit propensity. Adding to the few mediation tests (Takeuchi et al., 2007), Hom et al. (2009) determined how mutual investment EOR (relative to other EOR forms) affects outcomes via social exchange and job embeddedness. Tsui and colleagues (1997) had long held that mutual investment EOR sustains workforce commitment and loyalty by invoking social exchange. Apart from this theoretical mechanism, Hom et al. (2009) also deduced that this EOR form embeds incumbents by way of greater sacrifice (because of generous inducements), fit (because of rigorous selection and socialization so that newcomers can fulfill exacting performance requirements), and links (because of employees' team contributions and service to others, which forge more colleague ties). Greater job embeddedness in turn promotes organizational commitment and retention decisions.

To test these EOR effects on both individual- and firm-level outcomes, Hom and associates (2009) deployed multilevel (ML) structural equation modeling (SEM), which preserves the original data structure by analyzing both levels of nested data simultaneously (Bauer, 2003). MLSEM models causal processes at individual and firm levels (testing two parallel models), adjusting for correlated errors inherent in nested data (as employees are nested within firms). By so doing, this procedure yields more efficient parameter estimates and more valid standard errors than conventional unilevel tests (Krull & MacKinnon, 2001). For this multilevel model, they recruited 171 top managers from 41 Chinese firms who described their firms' EOR toward middle managers (aggregating scores to represent the firm-level EOR attribute) and surveyed 535 middle managers about mediators and outcomes. With such data, the MLSEM simultaneously assessed a firm-level model, relating firm-level EOR to aggregated individual scores (i.e., top managers' EOR perceptions and middle managers' mediator and outcome reports), and an individual-level model, relating middle managers' mediator and outcome scores (this model omits firm-level EOR). Hom et al. (2009) verified this multilevel model, finding that social exchange and job embeddedness mediate how mutual investment EOR reinforces managerial loyalty and commitment (see Figure 11.11).

Future scholarship might generalize Hom et al.'s (2009) findings to other cultural settings (as Chinese nationals may especially abide by the reciprocal norm inherent in social exchange) as well as adopt multilevel analyses to test other EOR mediation models (cf. Takeuchi et al., 2007). To enrich multilevel frameworks, investigators might more fully elaborate the intervening variables translating the influence of firm-level EOR approaches onto personnel attrition, following Bowen and Ostroff's (2004) theoretical approach. Moreover, moderators of EOR effects on turnover merit greater attention. For

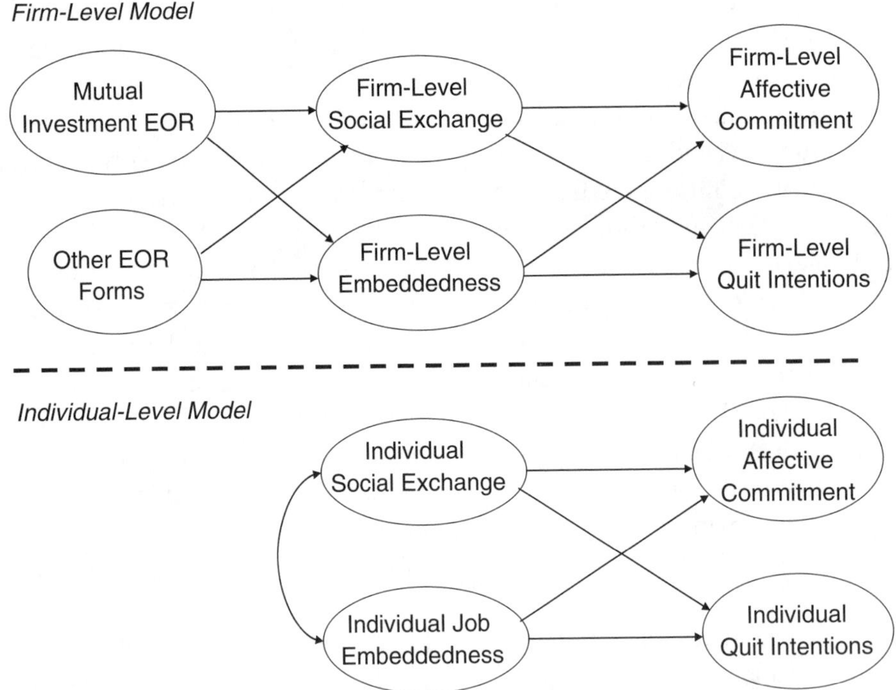

FIGURE 11.11. Multilevel model of the effects of employee–organization relationships (EOR).

example, Xiao and Tsui (2007) discerned that high-commitment HRM systems most strengthen organizational commitment among Chinese employees who belong to closed and dense colleague networks.

High-commitment HRM systems can thus sustain job incumbency (especially that of high performers; Shaw et al., 2009), but these systems are costly as employers must invest in extensive worker training and offer job guarantees (Godard & Delaney, 2000). Generous inducements are, however, difficult to sustain during recessions or intense industry competition (Baron & Kreps, 1999; Tsui, Pearce, Porter, & Hite, 1995). Indeed, Zatzick and Iverson (2006) noted that when high-commitment HRM systems must lay off staff during economic downturns, productivity declines are more pronounced for these systems. Members of such systems feel more betrayed because layoffs violate the "inflated" and trusting psychological contracts promulgated by their employers. During recessions, high-commitment firms must continue rather than discontinue their high investments in the workforce to forestall such counterproductive reactions.

Firm-Level Consequences of Quit Rates

Organizational scholars have long envisioned various consequences of high terminations, including firm-level and desirable effects (Mobley, 1982; Price, 1977; Staw, 1980). Price (1977) first specified how high firm-level turnover rates can impact organizational effectiveness and structure. Abelson and Baysinger (1984) later argued that an optimal level of firm-level turnover exists for each firm because the costs of turnover (e.g., costs of finding and training replacements) must be balanced by the costs of avoiding turnover (e.g., expensive inducements to keep staff). Attrition can thus be too low for businesses if they offer enticements to retain personnel at all costs that are not recouped by greater workforce productivity (see Figure 11.12).

Early work explored how coworker turnover affects the job attitudes of those staying (Krackhardt & Porter, 1985; Mowday et al., 1982). Yet research on turnover outcomes laid dormant for years until macrolevel tests began comparing aggregate turnover rates across multiple facilities or firms. Twenty years later, Glebbeek and Bax (2004) thus

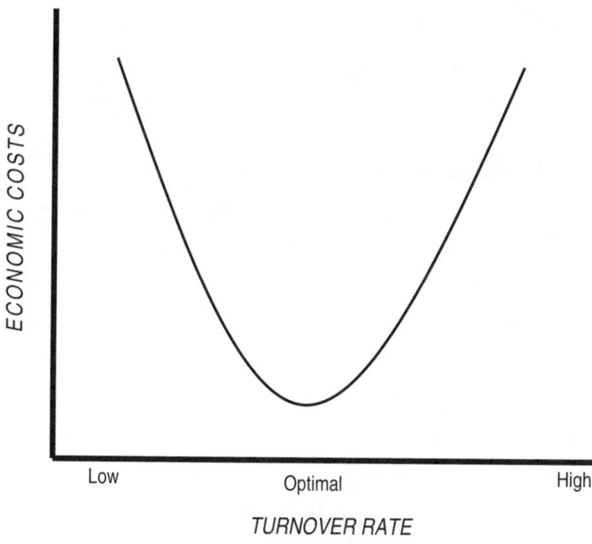

FIGURE 11.12. Optimal organizational turnover.

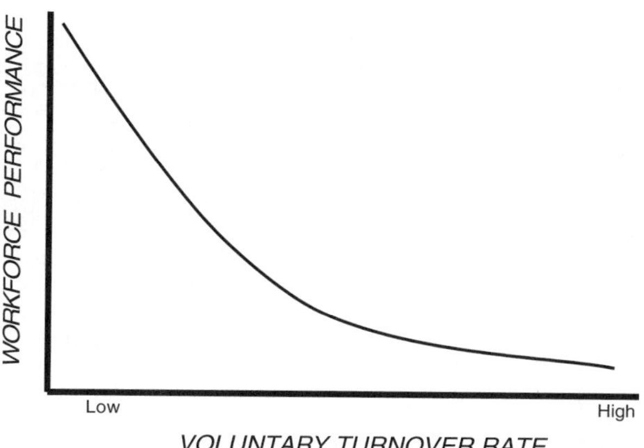

FIGURE 11.13. A negative attenuated relationship between workforce performance and voluntary organizational-level turnover rates. From "Alternative Conceptualizations of the Relationship Between Voluntary Turnover and Organizational Performance," by J. Shaw, N. Gupta, and J. Delery, 2005, *Academy of Management Journal, 48,* p. 54. Copyright 2005 by the Academy of Management. Adapted with permission.

confirmed Abelson and Baysinger's (1984) thesis, discovering an inverted U-shaped relationship between turnover rates (combining quits and discharges) and economic performance (sales revenue minus wage costs) among 110 offices of a Dutch temporary agency. In a partial replication, Shaw, Gupta, and Delery (2005) also documented curvilinear relationships between voluntary quit rates and firm performance in trucking and concrete-pipe industries. Firm effectiveness steadily fell as turnover rates grew, yet this decline decelerated when turnover rates were high. Presumably, companies install control mechanisms to handle exorbitant quits and their disruptive effects. Methodological differences may account for the discrepant results between these tests. Glebbeek and Bax measured overall turnover and used a single-organization design, whereas Shaw et al. measured voluntary turnover and used a cross-organization design (see Figure 11.13).

To elucidate how firm-level quits impact firm performance, Kacmar, Andrews, Rooy, Steilberg, and Cerrone (2006) demonstrated that high supervisory and crew turnover at 262 Burger King restaurants lengthen customer wait time, which in turn lowers store sales and profits. They concluded that a "stable workforce allowed units to be efficient, and that efficiency led to stronger performance" (p. 141). High crew turnover impairs customer service because new hires lack tacit knowledge for preparing meals and coordinating with teammates to serve meals quickly. Addressing less tangible costs, Shaw, Duffy, et al. (2005) studied how elevated quit rates can diminish a firm's social capital. They reasoned that turnover dissolves colleagues' relationships, which can disrupt communication networks that enable employees to share information and resources (destroying social capital). Surveying 38 locations of an upscale restaurant chain, they found that social capital losses decrease store productivity (sales per employee) when overall turnover (combining dismissals and quits) is low. Apparently, server attrition is most harmful when stable colleague relationships and social exchanges among colleagues exist (i.e., when restaurant turnover is low; see Figure 11.14).

Organizational-level research on turnover outcomes yields practical prescriptions. In particular, employers should not strive for zero quit rates as they would pay workers more than they are "worth" (exceeding the production or revenue they generate) to retain them. Rather, they might pursue nonzero quit rates that are optimal or common for their industry. Moreover, firms should regularly monitor turnover rates, which are leading indicators of firm effectiveness, especially in labor-intensive, service, or knowledge industries (Kacmar et al.,

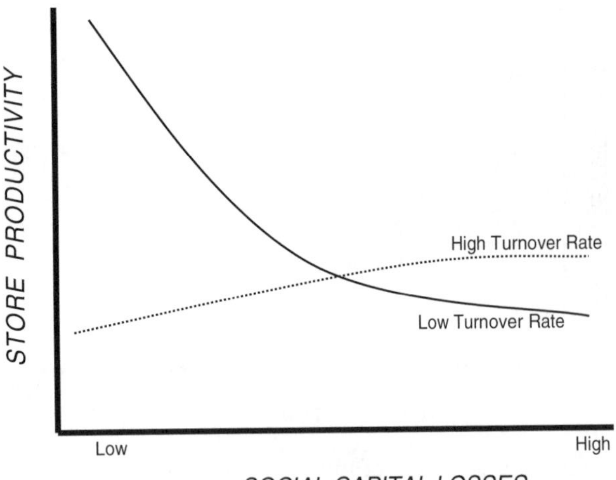

FIGURE 11.14. Store productivity based on the interaction between social capital losses and turnover rates in stores. From "Turnover, social capital losses, and performance," by J. Shaw, M. Duffy, J. Johnson, and D. Lockhart, 2005, *Academy of Management Journal, 48*, p. 602. Copyright 2005 by the Academy of Management. Adapted with permission.

2006; Shaw, Duffy, et al., 2005). Still, Shaw, Gupta, & Delery (2005) negative attenuated turnover-performance curve suggests that once quit rates exceed a (certain) high rate, high turnover minimally worsens firm effectiveness. Further, Shaw, Gupta, & Delery (2005) findings imply that managers should be mindful of the potential destruction of social capital due to personnel losses (especially incumbents bridging disconnected social networks; Burt, 2005). Some leavers may not necessarily be the most productive contributors, but their departure may upend communication flow and workgroup coordination, weakening collective performance.

PRACTICAL INTERVENTIONS

The previously mentioned review discloses that understanding why and how people quit is the dominant focus of scholarly publications (given that most researchers are university faculty). The following section examines the far fewer studies testing practical ways to manage attrition. Although many interventions have surely been tried in industry, these attempts rarely enter the annals of research, given corporate (or consultant) mandates to maintain proprietary secrets, failure to evaluate their effects, or omission of experimental (or quasi-experimental) controls. Nonetheless, some studies clearly validate certain techniques, which the next section addresses.

Realistic Job Previews

Compared with prevailing scholarly attention to explaining turnover, scientific explorations of interventions for decreasing turnover are scarce. The most voluminous work has evaluated realistic job previews (RJPs)—comprehensive previews about jobs featuring both their negative and positive aspects that are given to prospective or new employees (Wanous, 1992). In a comprehensive meta-analysis, Phillips (1998) estimated that previews modestly lower turnover (mean $r = -.09$). She further concluded that oral or written RJPs outperform audiovisual presentations, especially live presentations by job incumbents (Colarelli, 1984). Moreover, Wanous (1989, 1992) advised that previews should convey subjective reality—how incumbents experience jobs and what they like or dislike about their work—as new recruits are least informed about jobs' intrinsic content. He also prescribed delivering RJPs early, before newcomers enter organizations, so that they can make better informed job choices about whether the job is a good fit.

What is more, RJP investigations have tested explanations for why previews lessen newcomer attrition, notably the met expectations and self-selection mechanisms (Wanous, 1992). According to met expectations theory, beginning employees harbor inflated expectations about a job and encounter "reality shock" when they learn that the job fails to live up to their expectations. RJPs supposedly deter leaving by deflating initial expectations, aligning them with reality and preventing disillusionment (Wanous, 1992). Self-selection theory says that job applicants given previews can better decide if their needs can be fulfilled on a particular job (Wanous, 1992). Those who do not fit the job would decline a job offer and avoid ending up as future turnover "casualties." Without RJPs, job applicants may take a job for which they are ill-suited and later quit. Notwithstanding their enduring popularity (Wanous, 1992), these intervening mechanisms have not received conclusive support (Hom & Griffeth, 1995; Hom, Griffeth, Palich, & Bracker, 1998, 1999; Irving & Meyer, 1994, 1999).

Though effective, RJPs are costly to develop, as separate previews must be created for each job. Buckley, Fedor, Veres, Wiese, and Carraher (1998) thus pioneered an expectations lowering procedure (ELP) to alleviate reality shock without having to generate job-specific RJPs. During orientation, they instructed new hires about the benefits of having realistic job expectations, how common recruiting practices often inflate job expectations, and how initial expectations are often violated (inducing reality shock). They then asked newcomers to recall past situations in which their expectations were disconfirmed and share their experiences during the orientation session. Their field experiment demonstrated that this orientation lowered turnover as much as an RJP.

Selection Procedures

The other research stream devoted to turnover remedies considers employment tests to screen out prospective quit-prone employees. Weighted application blanks (WABs), employment interviews (especially, structured interviews; McDaniel, Whetzel, Schmidt, & Maurer, 1994; Schmidt & Rader, 1999), and personality measures (Hom & Griffeth, 1995) can identify such individuals. Traditional personnel studies demonstrated that WABs and biodata can forecast quits, but they have lost favor among scholars given their basis in dust-bowl empiricism (to locate valid items) and possible adverse impact (Hom & Griffeth, 1995). Drawing from theory and research for item selection, Barrick and Zimmerman (2005), however, considered tenure with immediate past jobs, employee referral, and number of family and friends employed at the firm as potential predictors. Collectively, these biodata items accounted for variance in voluntary, avoidable turnover beyond that explained by dispositional and attitudinal (e.g., prehire quit intentions) predictors and hardly diminished the hiring of minority, female, and older applicants.

Personality tests have historically been poor predictors of turnover (Griffeth & Hom, 1988b), but present-day research on the Big Five personality traits and person–job fit assessments are demonstrating higher predictive validity for such tests (Griffeth & Hom, 2001). To illustrate, Barrick and Mount's (1991) meta-analysis estimated a nontrivial and reliable correlation of .12 between conscientiousness and turnover. Abandoning the historical quest to discover leavers' personality profile (Griffeth & Hom, 1988b), Bernardin (1987; Villanova, Bernardin, Johnson, & Dahmus, 1994) sought to assess person–job fit with a forced-choice personality inventory. To control "faking," this inventory requires that job applicants choose descriptors from a set of descriptors matched on social desirability, only a few of which are "valid" answers. To design this selection test, employees and supervisors are interviewed to identify common discomforting events at work. Test items are then written describing these events (Griffeth & Hom, 2001). Test items about discomforting situations that are irrelevant to the job are also generated. The final inventory comprises sets of two relevant and two irrelevant statements matched for discomfort level (another group of job incumbents judge the items' discomfort levels; see Figure 11.15). For each item set, job candidates would select two situations most discomforting to them and would earn a "positive" score for each relevant item (correct descriptor) chosen. This inventory flags high-scoring applicants as job "misfits" (and potential leavers) for they would feel distressed by the actual discomforting events that occur on this job. They would be turned away. Impressively, this

Sample Force-Choice Question

A. Frequently Having to Interact with Senior Citizens (*valid*)
B. Frequently Having to Deal with Unintelligent People
C. Frequently Being Bored at the Work I Have to Do
D. Being Forced to Keep My Composure Around People Under Trying Circumstances (*valid*)

FIGURE 11.15. Force-Choice Personality Inventory for screening quit-prone job applicants. From "The Validity of a Measure of Job Compatibility in the Prediction of Job Performance and Turnover of Motion Picture Theater Personnel," by P. Villanova, J. Bernardin, D. Johnson, and S. Dahmus, 1994, *Personnel Psychology, 47*, p. 89. Copyright 1994 by Wiley. Reprinted with permission.

test moderately predicts turnover (correlations in the .30s) and produces no adverse impact (Bernardin & Russell, 1998).

Given the relative paucity of field experiments or quasi-experiments, the extant body of knowledge offers few evidence-based solutions for controlling turnover (Griffeth & Hom, 2001). Personnel studies nonetheless suggest valid tests or test-construction methodologies for identifying recruits who are liable to quit. Indeed, selection procedures, especially when multiple tests assessing varied attributes are combined, seem far more effective at curbing attrition than RJPs (or ELPs). In a rare comparative test, McEvoy and Cascio's (1985) meta-analytical review did, however, demonstrate that job enrichment is twice as effective as job previews. Despite practical and political impediments to their implementation, experimental evaluations of turnover-reduction interventions clearly warrant more attention by turnover researchers (Hom & Griffeth, 1995). When randomized field experiments are impractical, Pfeffer and Sutton (2006), however, have recommended that practitioners run trial programs, pilot studies, and small experiments. They reported that Harrah's lowered quits by almost 50% through experimentation testing various selection and retention efforts (i.e., RJPs, more training, and developing frontline supervisors).

HOW INDUSTRIAL AND ORGANIZATIONAL PSYCHOLOGISTS DIAGNOSE AND ADDRESS TURNOVER

This section describes how industrial and organizational (I/O) psychologists address turnover problems, greatly referencing state-of-the-art practices by ARC firms, Fortune 500 corporations that annually benchmark quit statistics for professionals and managers.

Estimating Turnover Severity

Although high-profile incidences of turnover frequently alarm managers, industrial psychologists often collect hard facts for a dispassionate analysis to estimate overall turnover severity. Generally speaking, the quit rate is calculated by dividing the number of voluntary quits (for a given period, such as a month or year) by the average number of employees on the payroll (during the period; Mobley, 1982):

$$\text{Quit Rate} = (\text{Number of Quits}) \\ / (\text{Number of Employed}) \times 100\%.$$

Alternatively, one can use the total workforce at the beginning or end of a period (R. Smith, 1999). Campion (1991) cautioned against overstating the distinction between voluntary and involuntary quits because employers may encourage some employees to resign before they are dismissed.

Some organizations refine this "gross" quit rate by omitting poor performer exits to focus on the dysfunctional quit rate (Dalton et al., 1982). Including functional turnover (those whom employers prefer to leave) in quit-rate calculations may exaggerate turnover severity. After making such adjustments, Northrup Grumman HRM specialists thus learned that "undesirables" comprised one third of all leavers when they asked supervisors to point out exiting engineers whom they would want to keep (Montoya, 2008). Concerned with dysfunctional quits, ARC companies also share quit statistics about top performers (employees rated in their employers' highest performance category) so that member firms can compare how well they retain superior performers. Indeed, several corporations, such as Cognos (Fulton, 2003) and Mutual of Omaha (Noon, 2004), include top-talent retention rates as metrics in their "balanced scorecards" (a method of gauging firm effectiveness holistically with financial indices and operational measures that drive future firm success [e.g., customer satisfaction indices]; Dess, Lumpkin, & Eisner, 2008), whereas United Airlines monitored the potential loss of their best contributors even during its bankruptcy (Lovato, 2002).

Some practitioners and scholars further recommend excluding unavoidable quits—employee separations that employers cannot control, such as exits due to pregnancy, family relocations, or medical disability (Griffeth & Hom, 2001). After omitting unavoidable (and functional) quits, Dalton et al. (1982) thus estimated that the voluntary quit rate of

30% in a company they had studied can be halved by such accounting. Specifically, only 7.5% of all leavers in this organization were both dysfunctional and preventable. Similarly, Griffeth and Hom (2001) calculated that the true extent of unwanted nursing turnover in a hospital was merely 1.3%—much lower than the 14.6% attrition rate that included involuntary, dysfunctional, and unavoidable quits.

All the same, ascertaining whether turnover is avoidable is challenging, for such determinations necessitate knowing leavers' true motives for exiting (Campion, 1991). Yet employers often rely on exit interviews with former employees (Branham, 2005), who likely distort their reasons (to avoid "burning their bridges") and overstate uncontrollable causes for quitting (Griffeth & Hom, 2001). Confidential interviews by HRM specialists or third-party consultants with employees some time after they have left workplaces can improve accuracy. Campion's (1991) confidential survey thus disclosed that former incumbents report more avoidable reasons for quitting than do supervisors, whereas the Saratoga Institute's surveys of nearly 20,000 workers in 18 industries revealed that 88% left for reasons related to the job, manager, culture, or work environment (though 89% of managers believed that they quit for higher pay). Similarly, the Gallup Organization carried out phone interviews with former Home Depot personnel and learned that 54% of salaried turnover was preventable (Lovato, 2004). Additionally, the types of turnover deemed unavoidable can change over time (and may vary across companies depending on resource constraints; Campion, 1991). To illustrate, pregnancies were historically considered unavoidable, but family-friendly corporations today try to preclude such quits by offering extended maternity leave and child-care assistance (Griffeth & Hom, 2001).

Finally, many employers interpret quit statistics in relation to prevailing industry rates (which vary widely across different industries; Steel, Griffeth, & Hom, 2002) to ascertain how they stand relative to other competitors (Baysinger & Mobley, 1983; Glebbeek & Bax, 2004). For example, Lovato, Davis, Schultz, and Comer (2007) noted that Home Depot quit rates compare favorably with retail-industry averages of 47%–53% for full-time and 90%–115% for part-time employees. Indeed, when a company's turnover rate is too low by industry standards, this business may be expending excessive payroll dollars to retain staff, which can worsen its competitiveness. To illustrate, Glebbeek and Bax (2004) estimated that the optimal turnover rates for Dutch temp agencies ranged from 6.3% to 9.9% with financial performance declining if turnover surpassed or fell below those rates. For this purpose, ARC thus provides its member firms information about (aggregated) quit statistics from other competitors belonging to the ARC consortium, whereas some maquiladora associations collect plant-level quit rates to share with their factory members (J. Miller et al., 2001). Finally, some corporations, such as the Ford Motor Company, Lockheed Martin, and Northrup Grumman (Henshaw & Rice, 2006; Montoya, 2008; R. Smith, 1999), track attrition rates among women and minorities (contrasting them to men and Whites, respectively) to monitor progress toward a diversified workforce (Hom et al., 2008). ARC firms even benchmark quit rates of these demographic subgroups against ARC population averages (Henshaw & Rice, 2006).

Diagnosing Turnover Causes

After measuring the extent of attrition severity (either firm-wide or specific to an occupational field or demographic subgroup), practitioners often seek to understand its root causes, relying on various means to ascertain motives for leaving. According to the Saratoga Institute, 95% of firms conduct exit interviews to learn why employees quit (Branham, 2005). Turnover researchers nonetheless report that interviews by employer representatives (e.g., in-house HRM specialists or supervisors) yield different findings than do third-party interviews or surveys (Branham, 2005; Campion, 1991; Griffeth & Hom, 2001). For instance, Zarandona and Camusco (1985) recounted how more departing employees cite "poor salaries and benefits" (38%) as reasons for resigning than "poor supervision" (4%) during exit interviews. Yet their follow-up survey 18 months later with these leavers finds them blaming poor supervision (24%) more than inferior compensation (12%) for why they left. In light of leavers' tendency to "sugar-coat" the truth during exit interviews (Steel et al., 2002), Ford Motor Company recruited Catalyst to interview minority and female leavers to understand their actual motives for quitting (Richard Smith, personal communication, April 2000), whereas Eli Lilly "validated" in-house exit interviews with postexit surveys by third-party vendors (Petersen, 2002). Because third-party interviews are not always available, exit interviews can be improved with interviewer training and structured interview formats (Griffeth & Hom, 2001).

I/O psychologists also administer surveys of supervisors, HRM specialists, and former and current employees to pinpoint turnover causes. For instance, the author collaborated with the Arizona Society of Certified Public Accountants to survey public accounting firms about what prompts exits among staff and senior accountants (Coolidge, 1986). This survey disclosed that long work hours and pay dissatisfaction are prime drivers of quitting among accountants (see Figure 11.16). Though informative, employers' views about why employees resign may not closely match leavers' own beliefs, as the author (and Anglo Kinicki) discovered when comparing managers' and former employees' perceptions about why the latter quit in a survey of a national retail chain. For some reasons, managers' perceptions of leavers' motives were sharply discrepant from leavers' self-reported motives. Specifically, store managers overestimated the influence of job alternatives and pay dissatisfaction over quit decisions compared with leavers themselves (see Figure 11.17), a finding consistent with Branham's (2005) research.

Assessing Strength of Turnover Drivers

To quantify impact of turnover causes, several corporations, such as the Home Depot (Lovato, 2004) and Microsoft (Bartlett & Wozny, 2001), survey current incumbents' satisfaction with job features (e.g., job content, supervision, pay) and statistically relate those ratings to other questions about their plans to quit (the best single turnover predictor; Griffeth et al., 2000) with causal modeling, regression, or correlation analyses. After pinpointing important causes, firms can identify which business units, occupational groups, or demographic subgroups score poorly on those crucial factors (e.g., low pay satisfaction) and which they must correct to avert personnel losses (Bartlett &

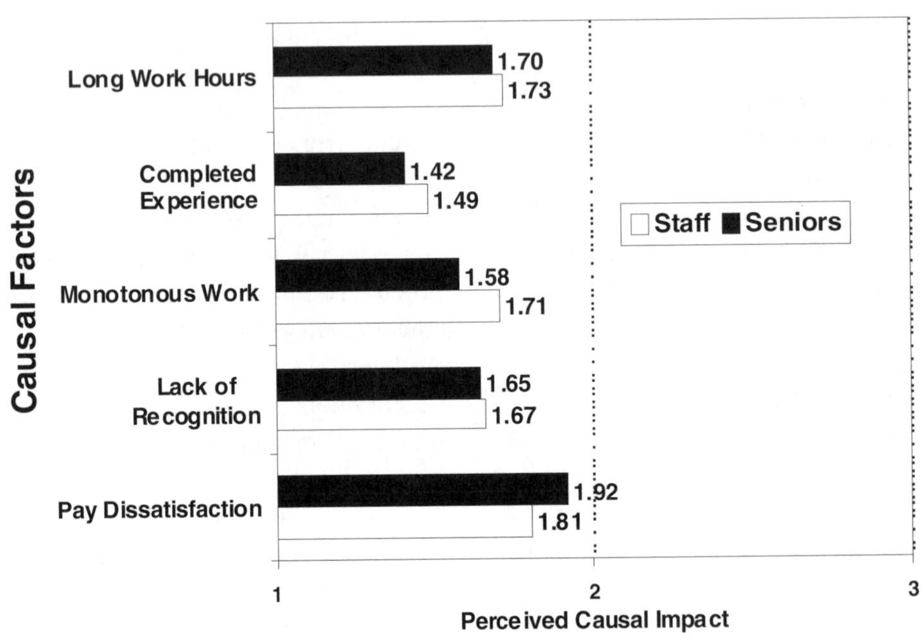

FIGURE 11.16. Employers' perceptions of why public accountants leave. CPA = certified public accountant.

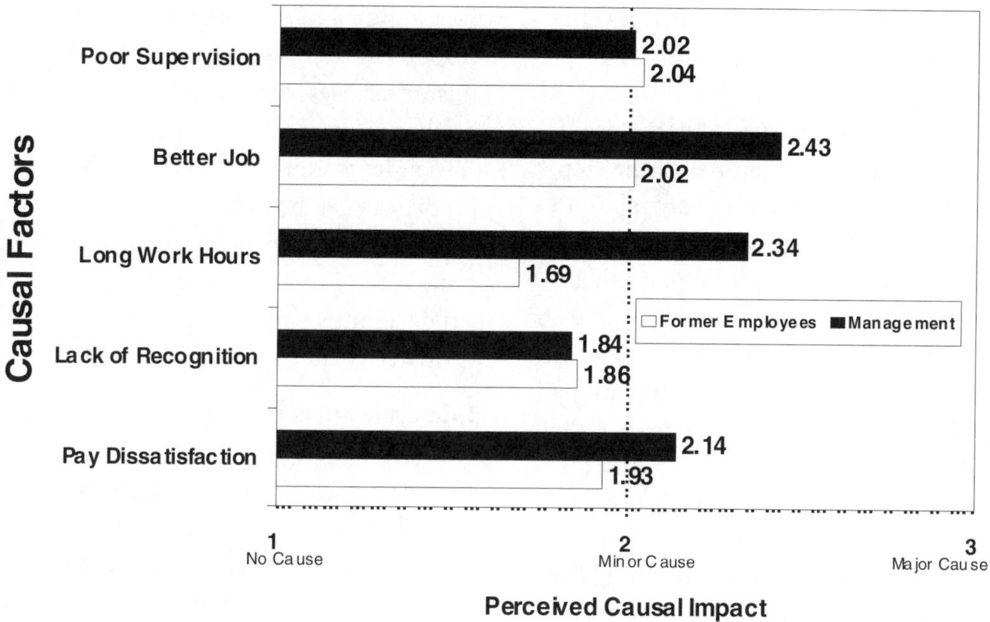

FIGURE 11.17. Managers' beliefs about turnover reasons versus former employees' self-reported reasons for leaving.

Wozny, 2001; Lovato, 2004). Using our running example, Hom and Kinicki (2001) surveyed a retail store workforce, assessing satisfaction with job facets and quit decisions. They then statistically compared mean satisfaction ratings between those intending to stay and those intending to quit, using *t* tests. Using significant findings, they concluded that prospective leavers are more unhappy with opportunities for recognition, training, wages, workload, work duties, and supervision than those planning to stay (see Figure 11.18). Their diagnosis thus identified

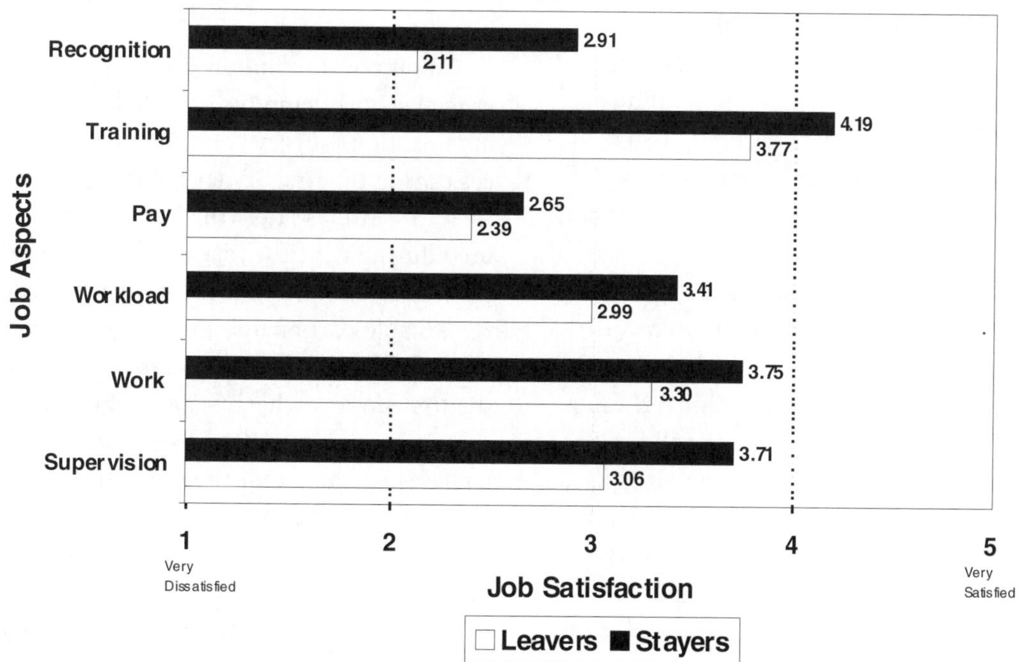

FIGURE 11.18. Attitudinal differences between intended stayers and intended leavers.

which dissatisfactions (i.e., turnover drivers) the retail store chain should ameliorate to lessen future quits.

For stronger causal evidence, some I/O psychologists take this statistical approach one step further by correlating survey data to actual turnover behavior rather than to intentions (as employees often do not follow through on their decisions to quit; Allen, Weeks, & Moffitt, 2005). Thus, I/O psychologists also survey leavers (with the same opinion survey filled out by incumbents), who describe dissatisfying features of their past job, and statistically compare their answers with those of incumbents. For example, the Gallop organization administered Home Depot's "employer of choice" survey to former associates and compared current and former employees' responses to estimate which disagreeable job features most drove attrition (Lovato, 2004). Similarly, Qualcomm contracted with Hay Associates to deliver its climate survey to leavers, though surveying only good performers who would be rehired (Maas, 2007). Statistical comparisons between leavers' and incumbents' survey answers ascertained retention drivers and their causal strength (Maas, 2007).

Predictive research designs. Longitudinal research designs can more rigorously verify causality for putative withdrawal determinants (or establish selection tests' predictive validity). To predict actual turnover, researchers assess antecedents on one occasion (using a survey, for example) and collect quit data on a later occasion. For a research project, Hom and Griffeth (1991) thus surveyed nurses from a hospital to gauge satisfaction with job facets, asking them to record their names so that their surveys could be matched with personnel data about future turnover. After matching surveys with turnover data collected 6 months later, Hom and Griffeth compared mean satisfaction ratings between nurses who remained employed with those who had quit since survey administration. Their analysis disclosed that leavers felt more dissatisfied with pay, workload and hours, and hospital location than did stayers (see Figure 11.19). Hospital administrators then responded to these findings, for example, by raising salaries. Most employers do not deploy predictive research designs, which require that respondents identify themselves on surveys so that predictors can be matched to turnover data. They suspect that requests for identification would reduce employees' willingness to participate (undermining sample representativeness) or furnish candid answers.

Life cycle surveys. Some corporations, such as Allstate (James, Berube, & Cassidy, 2007) and State Farm (Radefeld, Paul, Abrahams, & Mast, 2007), nevertheless are pioneering longitudinal research designs to monitor temporal changes in new hires' attitudes (job satisfaction, engagement) and person–job fit perceptions. To repeatedly survey the same newcomers, State Farm HRM analysts inform them that their survey responses are confidential (but not anonymous) and assigns identifiers that can link their surveys to other information (e.g., turnover) and future surveys (Paula Radefeld, personal communication, September 4, 2008). State Farm HRM analysts also do not solicit personal information and promise respondents that their individual answers are never shared (except in the form of aggregated statistics) or linked to personal information.

To pinpoint retention drivers during this crucial stage of employees' "life cycle," both organizations survey cohorts of beginning employees during the first 90 days of employment and then three times later (the last survey is distributed during the fifth year of tenure). Assuring confidentiality, these firms have achieved remarkable participation rates. For example, 59% of Allstate's 2005 new hires participated in the first survey, whereas 69% of State Farm newcomers participated. At Allstate, logistic regression analyses revealed that the predictive strength of determinants changes over time. For instance, newcomers' work satisfaction assessed on the 90th day of employment—but not work satisfaction assessed a year after joining Allstate—predicted turnover.

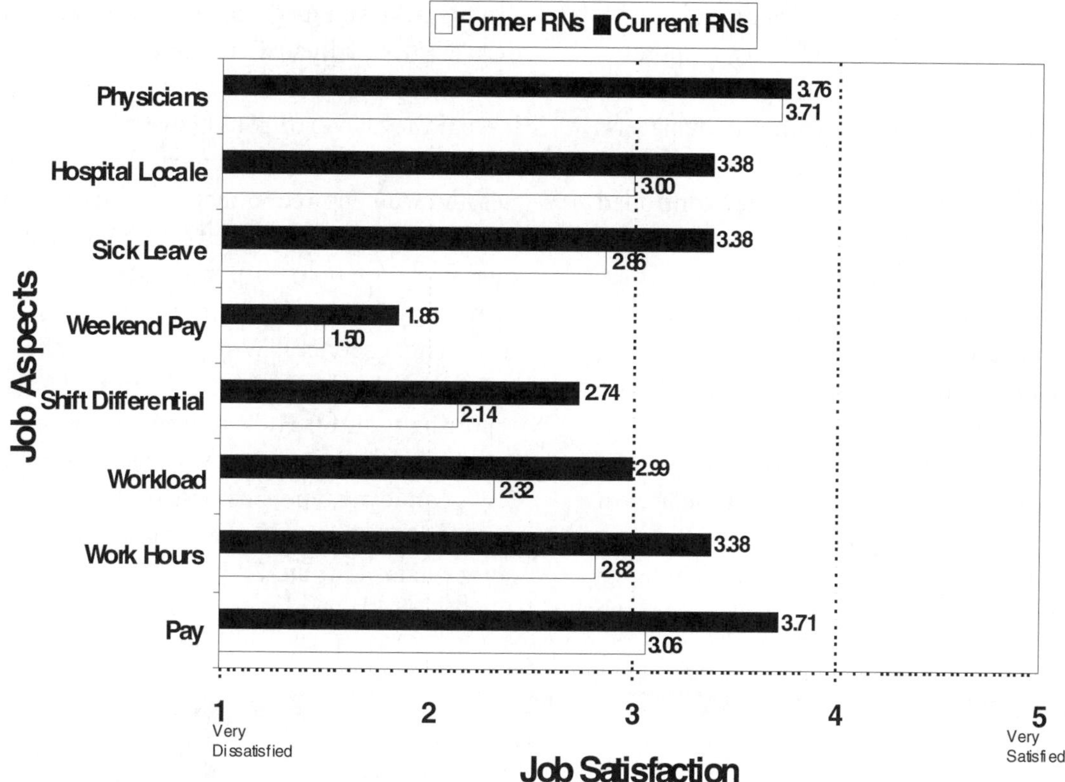

FIGURE 11.19. Differences in job satisfaction between current and former nurses. Data from Hom and Griffeth (1991).

Questionnaire content. Generally speaking, corporate psychologists use home-grown questionnaires rather than "standard" instruments used by academic researchers. Customized questionnaires more fully capture causes idiosyncratic to a particular work setting (e.g., dissatisfaction with a particular policy) than more generic measures used by scholars. To conform to space limits, they often use one-item rather than multi-item measures to cover a broader domain and focus more on actionable steps rather than "happiness" (Halamaj, 2004), such as "my manager and I have documented a relevant and challenging development plan for me" and "learning opportunities to advance my career have been made available" in Motorola's pulse survey (Dyson, 2002). Moreover, corporate instruments often assess familiar turnover antecedents, such as job satisfaction, organizational commitment (or "engagement"), quit intentions, person–job fit, and work–family balance, and are refined (via factor analysis) and validated (item correlations with quit intentions; James et al., 2007; Lovato, 2004; Maas, 2007; Radefeld et al., 2007; Tripp, 2002).

International work. Because foreign nationals represent a rising share of American multinationals' workforce, these corporations increasingly track attrition and its causes in offshore operations. For example, the ARC consortium is starting to benchmark quit statistics for member firms' foreign subsidiaries. Indeed, the Ford Motor company has surveyed its global workforce and investigated turnover causes across its overseas facilities (Tripp, 2002). In the course of his inquiry, Tripp (2002) found that some antecedents of quit intentions (e.g., job satisfaction) are common among different nationalities but others vary across nationalities. For instance, job satisfaction and organizational commitment decreased quit intentions in America, France, and Thailand. By contrast, empowerment diminished quit decisions in America but not in Thailand.

Reports and feedback. Besides careful and accurate data collection and analysis, corporate psychologists equally emphasize presenting results in a meaningful and timely manner to managers and executives (end users of turnover studies). To help managers comprehend how they controlled firm-tenure differences between demographic subgroups, Lockheed Martin HRM analysts thus use an intuitive epidemiological method instead of regression analysis to generate "valid" demographic comparisons (Henshaw & Rice, 2006). Applying this method (U.S. National Center for Health Statistics), they first compute the White (or male) quit rate and the proportion of the minority (or female) workforce employed in each tenure category. White quit rates are then multiplied by the corresponding minority proportions and the products are summed across tenure categories to derive a "risk-adjusted" minority (or female) quit rate, or the rate that minorities (or women) would leave if they have, or could have, the same tenure distribution as Whites (or men). Because minorities and women predominate "high-risk," low-tenure positions (Hom et al., 2008), raw quit rates overstate their corporate exodus relative to White men (whose lower quit rates partly reflect their longer service). With IT help, Raytheon HRM analysts also design sophisticated online reporting tools for HRM representatives who can easily "drill-down" to various levels of detail (e.g., employee type, business unit, location, survey date) to summarize (online) morale survey data (Motion, 2005; see Figures 11.20, 11.21, and 11.22).

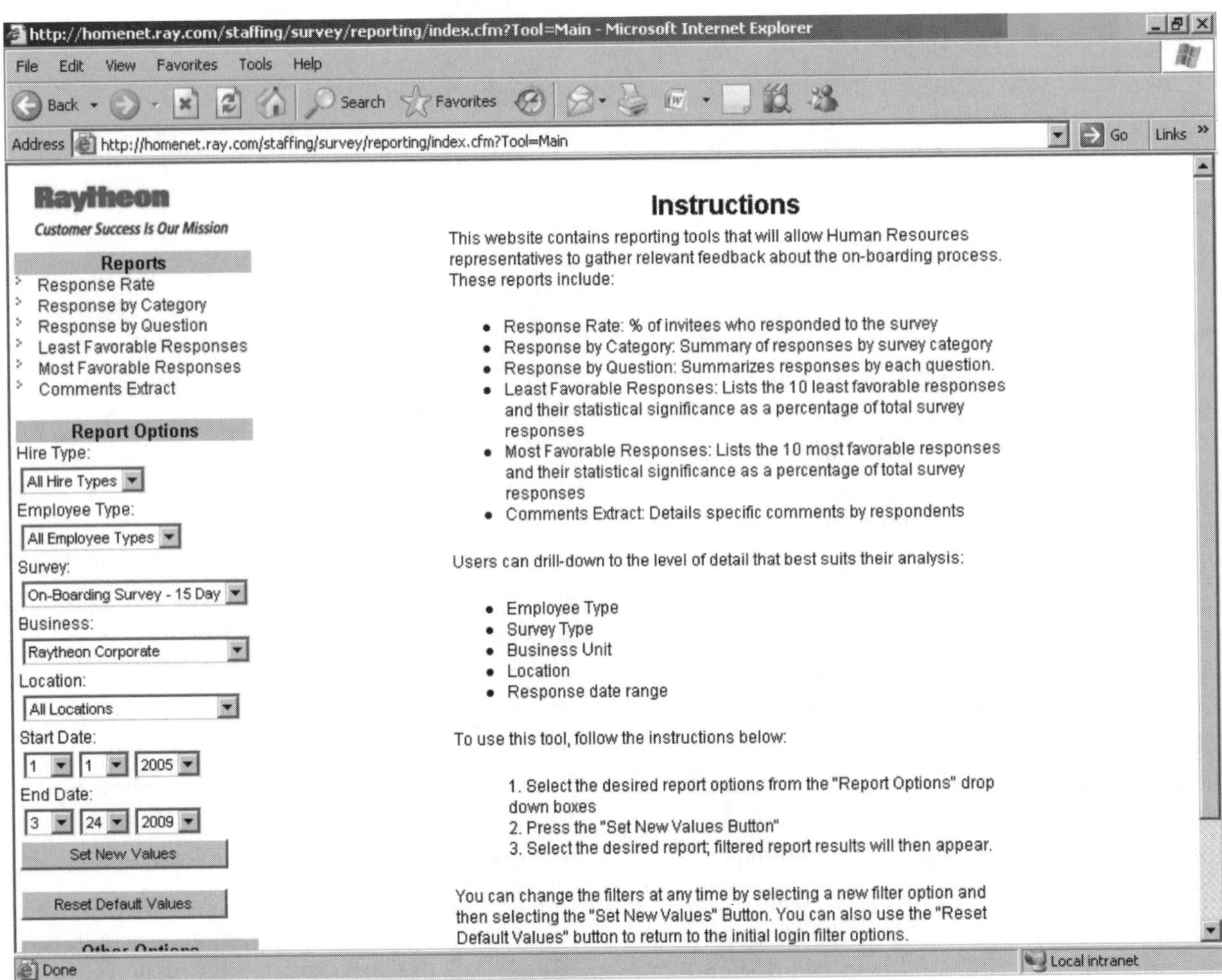

FIGURE 11.20. Raytheon Web site: Instructions for generating customized reports about workforce survey data. Used with permission of Raytheon.

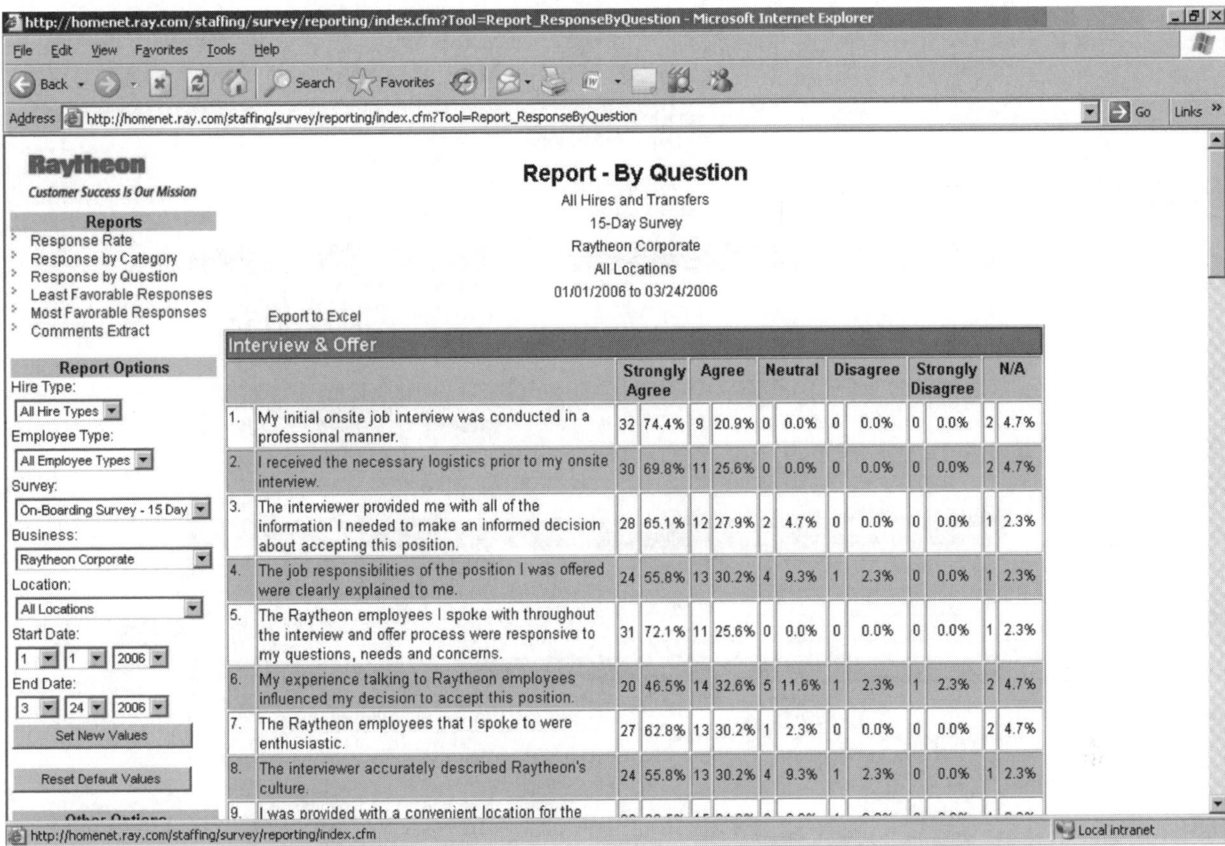
http://homenet.ray.com/staffing/survey/reporting/index.cfm?Tool=Report_ResponseByQuestion - Microsoft Internet Explorer

Raytheon
Customer Success Is Our Mission

Reports
- Response Rate
- Response by Category
- Response by Question
- Least Favorable Responses
- Most Favorable Responses
- Comments Extract

Report Options
Hire Type: All Hire Types
Employee Type: All Employee Types
Survey: On-Boarding Survey - 15 Day
Business: Raytheon Corporate
Location: All Locations
Start Date: 1 1 2006
End Date: 3 24 2006
Set New Values
Reset Default Values

Report - By Question
All Hires and Transfers
15-Day Survey
Raytheon Corporate
All Locations
01/01/2006 to 03/24/2006

Export to Excel

Interview & Offer

		Strongly Agree		Agree		Neutral		Disagree		Strongly Disagree		N/A	
1.	My initial onsite job interview was conducted in a professional manner.	32	74.4%	9	20.9%	0	0.0%	0	0.0%	0	0.0%	2	4.7%
2.	I received the necessary logistics prior to my onsite interview.	30	69.8%	11	25.6%	0	0.0%	0	0.0%	0	0.0%	2	4.7%
3.	The interviewer provided me with all of the information I needed to make an informed decision about accepting this position.	28	65.1%	12	27.9%	2	4.7%	0	0.0%	0	0.0%	1	2.3%
4.	The job responsibilities of the position I was offered were clearly explained to me.	24	55.8%	13	30.2%	4	9.3%	1	2.3%	0	0.0%	1	2.3%
5.	The Raytheon employees I spoke with throughout the interview and offer process were responsive to my questions, needs and concerns.	31	72.1%	11	25.6%	0	0.0%	0	0.0%	0	0.0%	1	2.3%
6.	My experience talking to Raytheon employees influenced my decision to accept this position.	20	46.5%	14	32.6%	5	11.6%	1	2.3%	1	2.3%	2	4.7%
7.	The Raytheon employees that I spoke to were enthusiastic.	27	62.8%	13	30.2%	1	2.3%	0	0.0%	0	0.0%	2	4.7%
8.	The interviewer accurately described Raytheon's culture.	24	55.8%	13	30.2%	4	9.3%	1	2.3%	0	0.0%	1	2.3%
9.	I was provided with a convenient location for the												

http://homenet.ray.com/staffing/survey/reporting/index.cfm

FIGURE 11.21. Raytheon Web site: Customized report about new hire on-boarding experiences (each question) for all locations. Used with permission of Raytheon.

Costing Turnover and Its Solutions

Once turnover is deemed a problem, business organizations can and do evaluate the economic costs of turnover to justify and compare prospective remedies (Cascio, 2000; Griffeth & Hom, 2001). Because turnover costs vary widely across jobs, employers must estimate for each job the costs associated with separation (e.g., removing leavers from payroll, overtime costs), replacement (e.g., advertising, testing, applicant interviews), and training (e.g., orientation, newcomers' productivity inefficiency; Cascio, 2000; Griffeth & Hom, 2001). Next, employers can calculate the "cost savings" of retention programs. To illustrate, Griffeth and Hom (2001) projected that job previews can realize cost savings of $72,216 for an accounting firm hiring 100 recruits, whereas Cascio (2000) calculated savings of $41,625 for 67 participants in an employee assistance program. Retention interventions are cost-justified when their cost savings exceed program costs. Aetna Life & Casualty thus recouped $1 million in annual savings by giving employees returning from family leave the option to work part time (which more than halved attrition; Griffeth & Hom, 2001). Home Depot improved newcomer orientation and furnished supervisors with a "retention tool kit," which helped lower annual turnover by 12% (Lovato et al., 2007). The cost savings of $21 million in averted attrition well surpassed program expenses.

FUTURE RESEARCH DIRECTIONS

Given this overview of contemporary research and practice, the following 11 areas merit further scholarly attention:

1. *Global research on turnover.* Despite its emergence for global corporations, personnel attrition

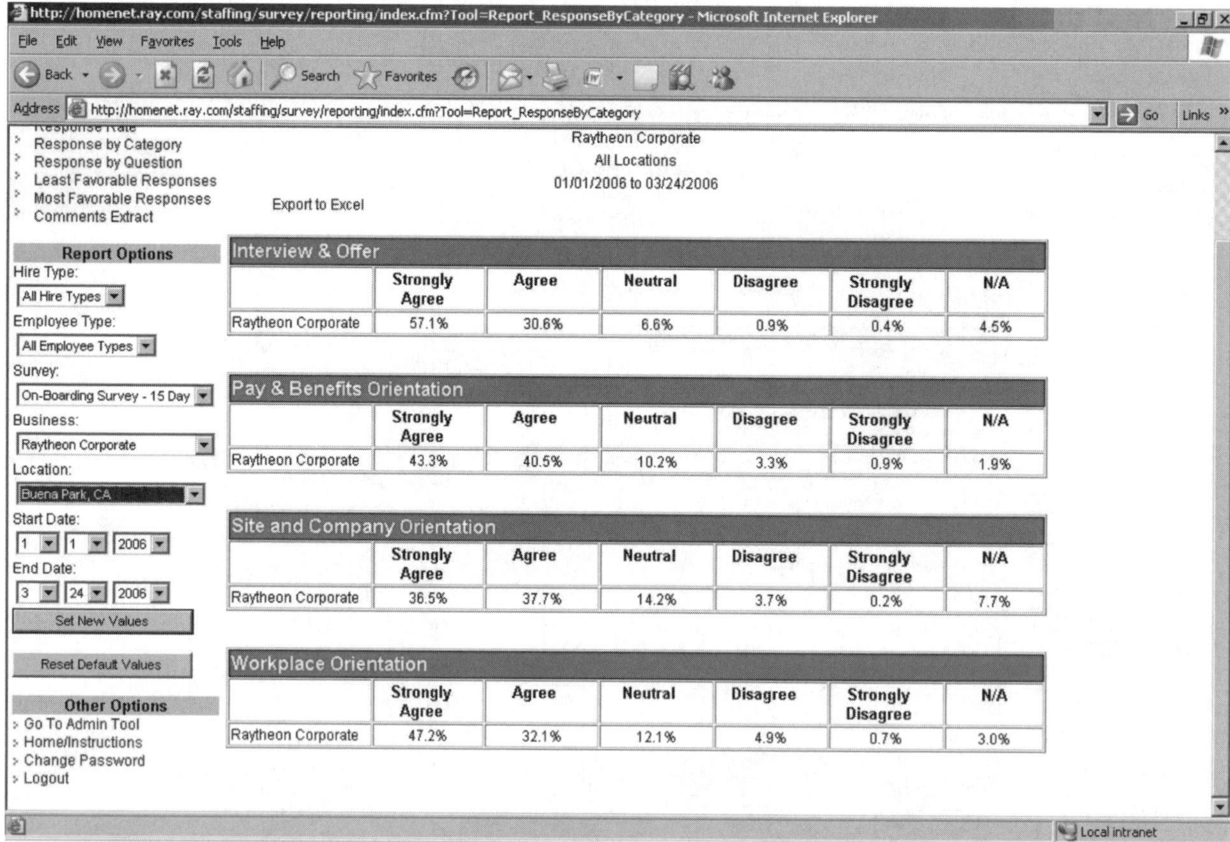

FIGURE 11.22. Raytheon Web site: Customized report about new hire attitudes (summated responses across multiple questions) for a particular locale. Used with permission of Raytheon.

abroad has been poorly studied by turnover researchers. This research has followed a pseudo etic research strategy by applying domestic models or constructs to different (usually single) foreign settings. Empirical generalization seems to be the implicit research goal, whereas cultural processes are rarely explicitly scrutinized. Advances in global understanding of turnover processes would come from genuine etic research that compares multiple (culturally diverse) nationalities (after establishing measurement invariance) and assesses cultural dimensions to test a priori hypotheses about cultural moderation. Heeding Tsui's (2004) call for high-quality indigenous work, turnover scholars should also explore emic explanatory constructs (or models) rather than slavishly adopt Anglo-American formulations. Indeed, constructs unearthed in other cultures may identify a theoretical void in Anglo-American perspectives (e.g., a study of Asian cultures first identified the cultural dimension of long- versus short-orientation; Hofstede, 2001), prompting their own theoretical revisions.

2. *Macrolevel models and research.* Organizational-level research has made remarkable progress identifying the consequences of firm-level turnover, though studied constructs and processes lack the breadth and complexity of individual-level models. This emerging research stream must go beyond comparing high- with low-commitment HRM systems and explore a greater variety of HRM systems, as different flavors of even high-commitment systems exist (Baron & Kreps, 1999). Moreover, additional multilevel modeling of causal antecedents can deepen insight into how organizational factors affect individual employees and how such effects in turn coalesce into aggregate quit rates (Bowen & Ostroff, 2004).

3. *Interventions for reducing turnover.* Potential solutions for managing turnover are abundant (Griffeth & Hom, 2001; Holtom et al., 2006). What is lacking is "high-caliber" evidence based on experimental or quasi-experimental research designs to validate solutions (Pfeffer & Sutton, 2006). More experimental evaluations are warranted, especially in other cultural settings.
4. *Additional validation for the unfolding and job embeddedness models.* These innovative theories have stimulated much reconceptualization about turnover causes and processes as well as considerable empirical scrutiny. As noted in this review, these models merit additional verification or elaboration, such as longitudinal predictive validation for the unfolding model and explorations of other forms of social embeddedness (e.g., social capital).
5. *Extend turnover formulations to retirement decisions.* Turnover theorists might extend their formulations to elucidate retirement decisions among the aging baby boomers, those born between 1946 and 1960. Corporate America frets over their impending mass retirement, especially in engineering and scientific fields whose thinning ranks will not be sufficiently filled by smaller cohorts of college graduates (Stevens, 2006). Some firms are thus actively enticing baby boomers to postpone retirement or participate in phased retirement ("Fewer firms set for boomer trend," 2006; "Phased retirement finds favor in survey," 2005). Turnover theories may help explain retirement decisions as some causal determinants (e.g., organizational commitment) underpin both turnover and retirement decisions (G. Adams & Beehr, 1998; Hanisch & Hulin, 1990). Indeed, turnover and retirement may converge in coming years as fewer organizations offer traditional defined-benefit pensions (Clements, 2007). Instead, employees receive defined-contribution plans and theoretically can retire according to their own timetable (when they have amassed ample pension funds) rather than wait until they have accumulated enough seniority or reach a certain retirement age. For them, retirement is tantamount to turnover.
6. *Synthesis with earlier turnover models.* Current turnover investigators treat constructs from earlier theoretical viewpoints as "control" variables, as they seek to demonstrate the incremental validity of new constructs (Mitchell, Holtom, Lee, Sablynski, & Erez, 2001). Owing to cumulative evidence for some traditional models (Gaertner, 1999; Hom et al., 1992; Price, 2001), future research might integrate well-established frameworks with recent perspectives for more comprehensive formulations. For example, Crossley et al. (2007) tested the interaction between job embeddedness and job satisfaction on search intentions. Lee and Mitchell (1994) incorporate the Mobley intermediate-linkages model within their unfolding model, but this integration has not been tested with predictive research designs. This "divorce" between old- and new-style thinking will stymie development of a cumulative science of organizational withdrawal.
7. *Studying dynamic processes.* Empirical studies lag conceptualization of process-oriented models of attrition (Hom & Kinicki, 2001; Lee & Mitchell, 1994; Sheridan & Abelson, 1983). Given the advent of more valid panel-analytical techniques (Hom & Haynes, 2007), scholars can apply these methodologies to validate such process-oriented formulations. Such work would better sustain causal assumptions and may identify new (and stronger) predictors of turnover (Harrison et al., 1996).
8. *Explaining dysfunctional turnover.* Because for-profit businesses are mostly concerned about losing high performing or difficult-to-replace personnel, turnover scholars should formulate more comprehensive predictive models to account for why and how they quit (J. Johnson et al., 2000). Different models may be necessary for different types of dysfunctional turnover, as employees contribute to organizations in various and distinct ways, such as being good citizens or "linking pins" (Shaw, Duffy, et al., 2005). Moreover, greater attention to how valuable contributors cultivate greater movement

capital is warranted to complement existing focus on their job attitudes (J. Johnson et al., 2000; Trevor, 2001). After all, valued contributors may most quit when they have both ease and desire to move (Allen & Griffeth, 2001).

9. *Exploring and explaining demographic diversity effects*. The evermore diverse American workforce is fueling interest in racial differences in attrition (Kreitner & Kinicki, 2008). Further inquiry should go beyond the traditional five EEO racial categories (White, African, Asian, Hispanic, and Native Americans) to explore turnover differences within these broad racial groupings. To illustrate, Asians are not homogenous and differ in nationality, nativity status, and Westernization. Such within-group differences can translate into different turnover patterns (Hom et al., 2008). Because theoretical mechanisms underlying race-turnover effects are underexplored, they warrant greater scrutiny.
10. *Nontraditional employment arrangements*. Turnover researchers should devote more attention to contingent and part-time workers, who have a significant presence in the workplace (Gakovic & Tetrick, 2003; Gallagher & Sverke, 2005) and provide firms with staffing flexibility to cope with fluctuating economic conditions (Tsui et al., 1995). Rather, conventional models have implicitly conceptualized explanations for regular, full-time employees who are committed to the workforce (Hulin et al., 1985; Peters, Jackofsky, & Salter, 1981). How do current theories account for attrition among the heterogeneous peripheral workforce (e.g., hobos, secondary wage earners; Hulin et al., 1985)? Does a part-time waiter completing a college degree quit this job differently (and for different reasons) than does a 70-year-old Wal-Mart greeter?
11. *Job-to-nonemployment turnover*. Over the years, turnover experts have recognized that some leavers—especially young, less-educated women and women in traditional female-dominated occupations—simultaneously exit both the job and labor market (Hulin et al., 1985; Lee et al., 1996; Royalty 1998). Though the unfolding model captures such exits (e.g., Path 1; Lee et al., 1999) and some theorists posit ad hoc explanatory constructs (e.g., work–family conflict; Hom & Kinicki, 2001), withdrawal scholars must develop fuller and more coherent explanations of what Royalty (1998) termed "job-to-nonemployment" turnover. These conceptualizations would take into account the expected duration of such employment hiatus, which can be abbreviated (e.g., motherhood) or prolonged (law school attendance), and which depend on leavers' financial resources (Steel, 2002). These frameworks would identify theoretical constructs underpinning such lifestyle or career plans and differentiate withdrawal processes for different types of job-to-nonemployment transitions. For example, do withdrawal paths differ between leavers attending college full time and those becoming full-time parents (though the unfolding model classifies them as Path 1; Lee & Mitchell, 1994)?

CLOSING REMARKS

In 1982, Mowday et al. concluded that well over 1,000 studies have investigated turnover. This chapter suggests that this field of inquiry remains vibrant today and for the foreseeable future. Present-day global, demographic, and technological developments are reshaping the meaning of turnover and will inspire new research streams. Workers in formerly socialistic and command economies are now "free" to change jobs. Foreign immigrants increasingly populate the American workplace, whereas American multinationals employ evermore foreign nationals. More Americans also work outside the office and belong to virtual teams (spanning members across the world) and workplaces. Despite the current meltdown in 401(k) plans (Maxey, 2009), younger generations of workers have the option to someday retire on their own timetable. Their retirement decisions will thus fall within the purview of turnover scholars. These current and impending changes bode well for continued scholarly explorations of turnover into the 21st century.

APPENDIX 11.1

Common Survey Instruments

Turnover predictors	Measurement	Sample item	Authors
Overall job satisfaction	Faces scale: Circle the face that best describes how you feel about your job in general; 18 items, 5-point Likert-type scale (1 = *strongly disagree;* 5 = *strongly agree*)	My job is like a hobby to me. I definitely dislike my work.	Kunin (1955); Brayfield and Rothe (1951)
Job facet satisfaction	Job Description Index: 72 items to assess satisfaction with work, pay, promotion, supervision, and coworkers; yes–no rating for various adjectival descriptions	Work on present job: Routine, Boring, Satisfying	P. Smith, Kendall, and Hulin (1969)[a]
	Minnesota Satisfaction Questionnaire: 20-item short-form assesses satisfaction with extrinsic (e.g., pay) and intrinsic (e.g., independence) rewards; rate satisfaction on 5-point rating scale (from 1 = *very dissatisfied* to 5 = *very satisfied*)	The chance to work alone on the job The way my boss handles his men The working conditions	Weiss, Dawis, England, and Lofquist (1967)[b]
Organizational commitment	Organization Commitment Questionnaire—Short Form; 7-point Likert-type agree–disagree scale	I really care about the fate of this organization.	Mowday, Steers, and Porter (1979)
	Meyer–Allen commitment forms: 7-point Likert-type scales	I find that my values and the organization's value are very similar. 8-item affective commitment scale: I do not feel "emotionally attached" to this organization. 6-item normative commitment scale: I owe a great deal to this organization. 12-item continuance commitment scale: ▪ It would be very hard for me to leave my organization right now, even if I wanted to. ▪ I feel that I have too few options to consider leaving this organization.	Meyer, Allen, and Smith (1993)

(*continued*)

APPENDIX 11.1 (*Continued*)

Common Survey Instruments

Turnover predictors	Measurement	Sample item	Authors
Job scope	Job Diagnostic Survey: 15 items rated by 7-point Likert scales assessing skill variety, task identity, task significance, autonomy, and job feedback	The job requires me to use a number of complex or high-level skills. This job is where a lot of other people can be affected by how well the work gets done.	Hackman and Oldham (1974)[c]
Role stress	Role ambiguity: 11-item 7-point Likert scale Role conflict	I don't know what is expected of me. I know what my responsibilities are. I often get myself involved in situations in which there are conflicting requirements. There are unreasonable pressures for better performance.	House, Schuler, and Levanoni (1983)
Work–family conflict	5-item 7-point Likert-type scale	The demands of my work interfere with my home family life. The amount of time my job takes up makes it difficult to fulfill family responsibilities.	Netermeyer, Boles, and McMurrian (1996)
Quit intentions	Staying/Leaving Index: 4 items rated with 7-point likelihood rating (1 = *terrible;* 7 = *excellent*)	How would you rate your chances of quitting in the next 3 months; quitting in the next 6 months (etc.)?	Bluedorn (1982)
Search intentions	Two items rated with 5-point rating scales	Within this year, I intend to search for an alternative role to my present job (5-point agree–disagree rating) What are the chances that you will search for an alternative role to your present job during this year? (5-point likelihood scale from 1 = *very unlikely* to 5 = *certain*)	Hom, Griffeth, and Sellaro (1984)
Thoughts of quitting	Two items rated with 5-point rating scales	How often do you think of quitting your job? (5-point frequency scale from 1 = *never;* 5 = *constantly*) I think often about quitting my job (5-point agree–disagree scale)	Hom et al. (1984)
Job involvement	10 items rated by 6-point Likert-type scale	I live, eat, and breathe my job. Usually I feel detached from my job.	Kanungo (1982)
Job search	Preparatory job search: 6 items rated by 5-point frequency scale Active job search—6 items rated by 5-point frequency scale	Prepared/revised your resume Talked with friends or relatives about possible job leads Sent out resumes to potential employers Had a job interview with a prospective employer	G. Blau (1994)

Perceived job alternatives	One-item 5-point likelihood scale (1 = *very unlikely;* 5 = *certain*)	What are the chances that you can find an acceptable alternative?	Mobley, Horner, and Hollingsworth (1978)
Job embeddedness	34 items rated with various rating formats	Community fit: I really love the place where I live. Job fit: I fit the company's culture Community links: Are you currently married? Job links: How long have you been in your present position? Community sacrifice: My neighborhood is safe. Job sacrifice: The perks on this job are outstanding.	Mitchell, Holtom, Lee, Sablynski, and Erez (2001)
Movement capital	Composite index of highest educational level, cognitive ability score, and occupation-specific training		Trevor (2001)
Leader–member exchange	11-item 7-point agree–disagree scale; assess four dimensions of affect, loyalty, contribution, and respect for supervisor	I like my supervisor very much as a person. My supervisor would come to my defense if I were "attacked" by others. I am impressed with my supervisor's knowledge of his/her job.	Liden and Maslyn (1998)[d]
Distributive justice	Three items assessing degree to which rewards and punishments are related to amount of input into organization	Compared to the effort that you put into your job, how do you feel about the pay you receive in the hospital? (on a scale of a = *very poor* to e = *very good*)	Price and Mueller (1981)
Kinship responsibility	Complex index based on self-reported family and extended family size	How many children under six years of age live either with you or with you and your husband or wife? (no children of this age to three or more) How many of your relatives live within 50 miles from where you live? (zero to four or more)	Blegen, Mueller, and Price (1988)

[a]Scales items from the Job Description Index (JDI). Copyright by Bowling Green State University. Used with permission of the Department of Psychology, Bowling Green State University. The JDI and related scales can be obtained from the Department of Psychology at Bowling Green State University, Bowling Green, OH 43403.
[b]Scale items from the Minnesota Satisfaction Questionnaire (MSQ) used with permission of Vocational Psychology Research, University of Minnesota. The MSQ is available from Vocational Psychology Research, University of Minnesota, Minneapolis, http://www.psych.umn.edu/psylabs/vpr/
[c]Scale items used with permission of Richard Hackman and Greg R. Oldham.
[d]Scale items from *Journal of Management, 24,* 42–72. Copyright 1998 by Sage Publications. Reprinted by permission of Sage Publications.

References

Abelson, M. A., & Baysinger, B. D. (1984). Optimal and dysfunctional turnover: Toward an organizational level model. *Academy of Management Review, 9,* 331–341.

Abrams, D., Ando, K., & Hinkle, S. (1998). Psychological attachment to the group: Cross-cultural differences in organizational identification and subjective norms as predictors of workers' turnover intentions. *Personality & Social Psychology Bulletin, 24,* 1027–1039.

Adams, G., & Beehr, T. (1998). Turnover and retirement: A comparison of their similarities and differences. *Personnel Psychology, 51,* 643–665.

Adams, J. S. (1965). Inequity of social exchange. In L. Berkowitz (Ed.), *Advances in experimental social psychology.* New York: Academic Press.

Allen, D., & Griffeth, R. (2001). Test of a mediated performance-turnover relationship highlighting the moderating roles of visibility and reward contingency. *Journal of Applied Psychology, 86,* 1014–1021.

Allen, D., & Moffitt, K. (2004). *Applying organizational retention theory and research methods to student retention* (Report to University Retention Committee). Memphis, TN: University of Memphis, Management Department, Fogelman College of Business and Economics.

Allen, D. G., Weeks, K. P., & Moffitt, K. R. (2005). Turnover intentions and voluntary turnover: The moderating roles of self-monitoring, locus of control, proactive personality, and risk aversion. *Journal of Applied Psychology, 90,* 980–990.

Arthur, J. B. (1994). Effects of human resource systems on manufacturing performance and turnover. *Academy of Management Journal, 37,* 670–687.

Baron, J., & Kreps, D. (1999). *Strategic human resources.* New York: Wiley.

Barrick, M., & Mount, M. (1991). The Big Five personality dimensions and job performance: A meta-analysis. *Personnel Psychology, 44,* 1–26.

Barrick, M., & Zimmerman, R. (2005). Reducing voluntary, avoidable turnover through selection. *Journal of Applied Psychology, 90,* 159–166.

Bartlett, C., & Wozny, M. (2001). *Microsoft: Competing on Talent (A)* (Harvard Business Case No. 9-300-001). Boston: Harvard Business School.

Bauer, D. (2003). Estimating multilevel linear models as structural equation models. *Journal of Educational and Behavioral Statistics, 28,* 135–167.

Baysinger, B., & Mobley, W. (1983). Employee turnover: Individual and organizational analysis. In K. Rowland & G. Ferris (Eds.), *Research in personnel and human resources management* (Vol. 1, pp. 269–319). Greenwich, CT: JAI Press.

Benson, G., Finegold, D., & Mohrman, S. (2004). You paid for the skills, now keep them: Tuition-reimbursement and voluntary turnover. *Academy of Management Journal, 47,* 315–331.

Benson, J., & Zhu, Y. (2002). The emerging external labor market and the impact on enterprise's human resource development in China. *Human Resource Development Quarterly, 13,* 449–466.

Bentein, K., Vandenberg, R., Vandenberghe, C., & Stinglhamber, F. (2005). The role of change in the relationship between commitment and turnover: A latent growth modeling approach. *Journal of Applied Psychology, 90,* 468–482.

Berdahl, J. L., & Moore, C. (2006). Workplace harassment: Double jeopardy for minority women. *Journal of Applied Psychology, 91,* 426–436.

Bergh, D. (1995). Problems with repeated measures analysis: Demonstration with a study of the diversification and performance relationship. *Academy of Management Journal, 38,* 1692–1708.

Bernardin, H. J. (1987). Development and validation of a forced choice scale to measure job-related discomfort among customer service representatives. *Academy of Management Journal, 30,* 162–173.

Bernardin, H. J., & Russell, J. (1998). *Human resource management: An experiential approach.* New York: McGraw-Hill.

Blau, G. (1993). Further exploring the relationship between job search and voluntary individual turnover. *Personnel Psychology, 46,* 313–330.

Blau, G. (1994). Testing a two-dimensional measure of job search behavior. *Organizational Behavior and Human Decision Processes, 59,* 288–312.

Blau, P. (1964). *Exchange and power in social life.* New York: Wiley.

Blegen, M., Mueller, C., & Price, J. (1988). Measurement of kinship responsibility for organizational research. *Journal of Applied Psychology, 73,* 402–409.

Bluedorn, A. (1982). The theories of turnover: Causes, effects, and meaning. In Samuel B. Bacharach (Ed.), *Research in the sociology of organizations* (pp. 75–128). Greenwich, CT: JAI Press.

Bond, M. (1996). *The handbook of Chinese psychology.* Oxford, England: Oxford University Press.

Bowen, D., & Ostroff, C. (2004). Understanding HRM-firm performance linkages: The role of the "strength" of the HRM system. *Academy of Management Review, 29,* 203–221.

Bozeman, D., & Perrewé, P. (2001). The effect of item content overlap on organizational commitment questionnaire-turnover cognitions relationships. *Journal of Applied Psychology, 86,* 161–173.

Branham, L. (2005). *The 7 hidden reasons employees leave.* New York: AMACOM.

Brayfield, A., & Rothe, H. (1951). An index of job satisfaction. *Journal of Applied Psychology, 35,* 307–311.

Brett, J., & Stroh, L. (1999). Women in management: How far have we come and what needs to be done as we approach 2000? *Journal of Management Inquiry, 8,* 392–398.

Brief, A., Butz, R., & Deitch, E. (2005). Organizations as reflections of their environments: The case of race composition. In R. Diboye & A. Colella (Eds.), *Discrimination at work: The psychological and organizational bases* (pp. 119–148). Mahwah, NJ: Erlbaum.

Brief, A. P., Umphress, E., Dietz, J., Burrows, J., Butz, R., & Scholten, L. (2005). Community matters: Realistic group conflict theory and the impact of diversity. *Academy of Management Journal, 48,* 830–844.

Brockner, J., & Higgins, E. (2001). Regulatory focus theory: Implications for the study of emotions at work. *Organizational Behavior and Human Decision Processes, 86,* 35–66.

Boudwin, K., & Hom, P. (2008, August). *A human resources "double whammy" or a myth: Are minority women really leaving?* Paper presented at the national conference of the Academy of Management, Anaheim, CA.

Boyacigiller, N., & Adler, N. (1991). The parochial dinosaur: Organizational science in a global context. *Academy of Management Review, 16,* 262–290.

Buckley, M. R., Fedor, D. B., Veres, J., Wiese, D., & Carraher, S. M. (1998). Investigating newcomer expectations and job-related outcomes. *Journal of Applied Psychology, 83,* 452–461.

Burt, R. (2005). *Brokerage and closure.* Oxford, England: Oxford University Press.

Burton, J., & Parker, J. (1969). Interindustry variations in voluntary labor mobility. *Industrial and Labor Relations Review, 22,* 199–216.

Button, J. W., & Rienzo, B. A. (2003). The impact of affirmative action: Black employment in six southern cities. *Social Science Quarterly, 84,* 1–14.

Campion, M. (1991). Meaning and measurement of turnover: Comparison of alternative measures and recommendations for research. *Journal of Applied Psychology, 76,* 199–212.

Cappelli, P. (2000, January–February). A market-driven approach to retaining talent. *Harvard Business Review, 78,* 103–111.

Cascio, W. (2000). *Costing human resources.* Boston: PWS-Kent.

Chan, D. (1998). The conceptualization and analysis of change over time: An integrative approach incorporating longitudinal mean and covariance structures analysis (LMACS) and multiple indicator latent growth modeling (MLGM). *Organizational Research Methods, 1,* 421–483.

Chan, D. (2002). Latent growth modeling. In F. Drasgow and N. Schmitt (Eds.), *Measuring and analyzing behavior in organizations* (pp. 302–349). San Francisco, CA: Jossey-Bass.

Chan, D., & Schmitt, N. (2000). Interindividual differences in intraindividual changes in proactivity during organizational entry: A latent growth modeling approach to understanding newcomer adaptation. *Journal of Applied Psychology, 85,* 190–210.

Chen, X.-P. (2002). Leader behaviors and employee turnover. In A. Tsui & C.-M. Lau (Eds.), *The management of enterprises in the People's Republic of China* (pp. 325–345). Norwell, MA: Kluwer Academic.

Chen, X.-P., Hui, C., & Sego, D. (1998). The role of organizational citizenship behavior in turnover: Conceptualization and preliminary tests of key hypotheses. *Journal of Applied Psychology, 83,* 992–931.

Chen, Z.-X., & Francesco, A. (2000). Employee demography, organizational commitment, and turnover intentions in China: Do cultural differences matter? *Human Relations, 53,* 869–887.

Cheung, G., & Rensvold, R. (1999). Testing factorial invariance across groups: A reconceptualization and proposed new method. *Journal of Management, 25,* 1–27.

Chow, C., Fung, M., & Yue, N. (1999). Job turnover in China: A case study of Shanghai's manufacturing enterprises. *Industrial Relations, 38,* 482–503.

Clements, J. (2007, September 9). Getting going: Six bad reasons not to save for retirement. *Wall Street Journal,* p. A3.

Cohen, A. (2003). *Multiple commitments in the workplace.* Mahwah, NJ: Erlbaum.

Colarelli, S. M. (1984). Methods of communication and mediating processes in realistic job previews. *Journal of Applied Psychology, 69,* 633–642.

Coolidge, P. (1986, January). Job turnover survey result. *Arizona Society of Certified Public Accountants Newsledger, 2,* 9–12.

Cottrell, C. A., & Neuberg, S. L. (2005). Different emotional reactions to different groups: A sociofunctional threat-based approach to "prejudice." *Journal of Personality and Social Psychology, 88,* 770–789.

Coyle-Shapiro, J., & Conway, N. (2004). The employment relationship through the lens of social exchange. In J. Coyle-Shapiro, L. Shore, M. S. Taylor, & L. Tetrick (Eds.), *The employment relationship: Examining psychological and contextual perspectives* (pp. 5–28). Oxford, England: Oxford University Press.

Cravey, A. (1998). *Women and work in Mexico's maquiladoras.* Lanham, MD: Rowman & Littlefield.

Crossley, C., Bennett, R., Jex, S., & Burnfield, J. (2007). Development of a global measure of job embeddedness and integration into a traditional model of voluntary turnover. *Journal of Applied Psychology, 92,* 1031–1042.

Dalton, D., Krackhardt, D., & Porter, L. (1981). Functional turnover: An empirical assessment. *Journal of Applied Psychology, 66,* 716–721.

Dalton, D. R., Hill, J. W., & Ramsay, R. J. (1997). Women as managers and partners: Context specific predictors of turnover in international public accounting firms. *Auditing: A Journal of Practice & Theory, 16,* 29–50.

Dalton, D., Todor, W., & Krackhardt, D. (1982). Turnover overstated: The functional taxonomy. *Academy of Management Review, 7,* 117–123.

Daniels, C. (2004, May 3). Young, gifted, Black—and out of here. *Fortune, 149.*

Dess, G., Lumpkin, G., & Eisner, A. (2008). *Strategic management.* New York: McGraw-Hill Irwin.

Dittrich, J., & Carrell, M. (1979). Organizational equity perceptions, employee job satisfaction and departmental absence and turnover rates. *Organizational Behavior and Human Performance, 24,* 29–40.

Dovidio, J. F., & Hebl, M. R. (2005). Discrimination at the level of the individual: Cognitive and affective factors. In R. L. Diboye & A. Colella (Eds.), *Discrimination at work: The psychological and organizational bases* (pp. 11–36). Mahwah, NJ: Erlbaum.

Dyson, P. (2002, November). *Retention strategy development at Motorola SPS.* Paper presented at the Attrition and Retention Consortium teleconference.

Duncan, T., Duncan, S., Strycker, L., Li, F., & Alpert, A. (1999). *An introduction to latent variable growth curve modeling.* Mahwah, NJ: Erlbaum.

Earley, C. (1989). Social loafing and collectivism: A comparison of the United States and the People's Republic of China. *Administrative Science Quarterly, 34,* 565–581.

Farh, L., Earley, C., & Lin, S.-C. (1997). Impetus for action: A cultural analysis of justice and organizational citizenship behavior in Chinese society. *Administrative Science Quarterly, 42,* 421–444.

Farkas, A., & Tetrick, L. (1989). A three-wave longitudinal analysis of the causal ordering of satisfaction and commitment on turnover decisions. *Journal of Applied Psychology, 74,* 855–868.

Feeley, T., & Barnett, G. (1997). Predicting employee turnover from communication networks. *Human Communication Research, 23,* 370–387.

Feeley, T., Hwang, J., & Barnett, G. (2008). Predicting employee turnover from friendship networks. *Journal of Applied Communication Research, 36,* 56–73.

Felps, W., Mitchell, T. R., Hekman, D., Lee, T. W., Harmon, W. S. & Holtom B. C. (2009). Turnover contagion: How coworkers' job embeddedness and coworkers' job search behaviors influence quitting. *Academy of Management Journal, 52,* 545–561.

Fernández-Kelly, M. (1983). *For we are sold, I and my people: Women in Mexico's frontier.* Albany: State University of New York Press.

Fewer firms set for boomer trend. (2006, May 23). *Wall Street Journal,* p. B7.

Fiske, S., Cuddy, A., Glick, P., & Xu, J. (2002). A model of (often mixed) stereotype content: Competence and warmth respectively follow from perceived status and competition. *Journal of Personality and Social Psychology, 82,* 878–902.

Friedman, T. (2005). *The world is flat.* New York: Farrar, Straus, & Giroux.

Fulton, C. (2003, May). *Talent retention strategy.* Paper presented at the conference of the Attrition and Retention Consortium, Austin, TX.

Gaertner, S. (1999). Structural determinants of job satisfaction and organizational commitment in turnover models. *Human Resource Management Review, 9,* 479–493.

Gakovic, A., & Tetrick, L. (2003). Perceived organizational support and work status: A comparison of the employment relationships of part-time and full-time employees attending university classes. *Journal of Organizational Behavior, 24,* 649–666.

Gallagher, D., & Sverke, M. (2005). Contingent employment contracts: Are existing employment theories still relevant. *Economic and Industrial Democracy, 26,* 181–203.

Glebbeek, A., & Bax, E. (2004). Is high employee turnover really harmful? An empirical test using company records. *Academy of Management Journal, 47,* 277–286.

Glomb, T., Munson, L., Hulin, C., Bergman, M., & Drasgow, F. (1999). Structural equation models of sexual harassment: Longitudinal explorations and cross-sectional generalizations. *Journal of Applied Psychology, 84,* 14–28.

Godard, J., & Delaney, J. (2000). Reflections on the "high performance" paradigm's implications for industrial relations as a field. *Industrial and Labor Relations Review, 53,* 482–502.

Gomez-Meijia, L. R. (1984). Effect of occupation on task related, contextual, and job involvement orientation: A cross-cultural perspective. *Academy of Management Journal, 27,* 706–720.

Granovetter, M. (1973). The strength of weak ties. *American Journal of Sociology, 78,* 1360–1380.

Greenwald, A. G., & Banaji, M. R. (1995). Implicit social cognition: Attitudes, self-esteem, and stereotypes. *Psychological Review, 102,* 4–27.

Griffeth, R., & Hom, P. (1988a). A comparison of different conceptualizations of perceived alternatives in turnover research. *Journal of Organizational Behavior, 9:* 103–111.

Griffeth, R., & Hom, P. (1988b). Locus of control and delay of gratification as moderators of employee turnover. *Journal of Applied Social Psychology, 18,* 1318–1333.

Griffeth, R., & Hom, P. (2001). *Retaining valued employees.* Thousand Oaks, CA: Sage.

Griffeth, R., Hom, P., & Gaertner, S. (2000). A meta-analysis of antecedents and correlates of employee turnover: Update, moderator tests, and research implications for the next millennium. *Journal of Management, 26,* 463–488.

Griffeth, R., Steel, R., Allen, D., & Bryan, N. (2005). The development of a multidimensional measure of job market cognitions: The employment opportunity index (EOI). *Journal of Applied Psychology, 90,* 335–349.

Gutherie, J. P. (2001). High involvement work practices, turnover and productivity: Evidence from New Zealand. *Academy of Management Journal, 44,* 180–190.

Hackman, J., & Oldham, G. (1974). *The job diagnostic survey: An instrument for the diagnosis of jobs and the evaluation of job redesign projects* (Tech. Rep. No. 4). New Haven, CT: Yale University, Department of Administrative Sciences.

Halamaj, J. (2004, May). *Utilizing employee surveys.* Paper presented at the annual conference of the Attrition and Retention Consortium, Lisle, IL.

Hanisch, K., & Hulin, C. (1990). Retirement as a voluntary organizational withdrawal behavior. *Journal of Vocational Behavior, 37,* 60–78.

Harrison, D., Newman, D., & Roth, P. (2006). How important are job attitudes? Meta-analytic comparisons of integrative behavioral outcomes and time sequences. *Academy of Management Journal, 49,* 305–326.

Harrison, D. A., Virick, M., & William, S. (1996). Working without a net: Time, performance, and turnover under maximally contingent rewards. *Journal of Applied Psychology, 81:* 331–345.

Hecht, L., & Morici, P. (1993). Managing risks in Mexico. *Harvard Business Review, 71*(4), 32–40.

Heck, R., & Thomas, H. (2000). *An introduction to multilevel modeling techniques.* Mahwah, NJ: Erlbaum.

Helfat, C., Harris, D., & Wolfson, P. (2006). The pipeline to the top: Women and men in the top executive ranks of U.S. corporations. *Academy of Management Perspective, 20,* 42–64.

Henshaw, T., & Rice, C. (2006, May). *How member companies use attrition/retention data and other metrics.* Paper presented at the conference of the Attrition and Retention Consortium, Atlanta, GA.

Hewlett, S. A., & Luce, C. B. (2005, March). Off-ramps and on-ramps. *Harvard Business Review,* 17–26.

Higgins, M. (2001). Changing careers: The effects of social context. *Journal of Organizational Behavior, 22,* 595–618.

Higgins, M., & Kram, K. (2001). Reconceptualizing mentoring at work: A developmental network perspective. *Academy of Management Review, 26,* 264–228.

Higgins, T. (1997). Beyond pleasure and pain. *American Psychologist, 52,* 1280–1300.

Hofstede, G. (2001). *Culture's consequences.* Thousand Oaks, CA: Sage.

Hollenbeck, J., & Williams, C. (1986). Turnover functionality versus turnover frequency: A note on work attitudes and organizational effectiveness. *Journal of Applied Psychology, 7,* 606–611.

Holtom, B., Mitchell, T., & Lee, T. (2006). Increasing human and social capital by applying job embeddedness theory. *Organizational Dynamics, 35,* 316–331.

Holtom, B., Mitchell, T., Lee, T., & Eberly, M. (2008). Turnover & retention research: A glance at the past, a closer review of the present, and a venture into the future. *The Academy of Management Annals, 2,* 231–274.

Holtom, B., Mitchell, T., Lee, T., & Inderrieden, E. (2005). Shocks as causes of turnover: What they are and how organizations can manage them. *Human Resource Management Journal, 44,* 337–352.

Hom, P. (2002). The legacy of Charles Hulin's work on turnover thinking and research. In J. Brett & F. Drasgow (Eds.), *The psychology of work* (169–187). Mahwah, NJ: Erlbaum.

Hom, P., Caranikis-Walker, F., Prussia, G., & Griffeth, R. (1992). A meta-analytical structural equations analysis of a model of employee turnover. *Journal of Applied Psychology, 77,* 890–909.

Hom, P., & Griffeth, R. (1991). Structural equations modeling test of a turnover theory: Cross-sectional and longitudinal analyses. *Journal of Applied Psychology, 76,* 350–366.

Hom, P., & Griffeth, R. W. (1995). *Employee turnover.* Cincinnati, OH: Southwestern.

Hom, P., Griffeth, R., Palich, L., & Bracker, J. (1998). An exploratory investigation into theoretical mechanisms underlying realistic job previews. *Personnel Psychology, 51,* 421–451.

Hom, P., Griffeth, R., Palich, L., & Bracker, J. (1999). Revisiting met expectations as a reason for why realistic job previews work. *Personnel Psychology, 52,* 97–112.

Hom, P., Griffeth, R., & Sellaro, L. (1984). The validity of Mobley's (1977) model of employee turnover. *Organizational Behavior and Human Performance, 34,* 141–174.

Hom, P., & Haynes, K. (2007). Advanced methods in panel data analysis. In D. J. Ketchen & D. D. Bergh (Eds.), *Research methodology in strategy and management* (Vol. 4, 193–272). Amsterdam, the Netherlands: Elsevier.

Hom, P. W., & Hulin, C. L. (1981). A competitive test of the prediction of reenlistment by several models. *Journal of Applied Psychology, 66,* 23–39.

Hom, P., & Kinicki, A. (2001). Toward a greater understanding of how dissatisfaction drives employee turnover. *Academy of Management Journal, 44,* 975–987.

Hom, P., Roberson, L., & Ellis, A. (2008). Challenging conventional wisdom about who quits: Revelations about employee turnover from corporate America. *Journal of Applied Psychology, 93,* 1–34.

Hom, P., Tsui, A., Wu, J., & Lee, T., Zhang, Y., Fu, P. P., & Li, L. (2009). Why do Chinese managers stay? A multilevel inquiry into the mediating role of social exchange and job embeddedness. *Journal of Applied Psychology, 94,* 277–297.

House, R., Hanges, P., Javidan, M., Dorfman, P., & Gupta, V. (2004). *Culture, leadership, and organizations.* Thousand Oaks, CA: Sage.

House, R. Schuler, R., & Levanoni, E. (1983). Role conflict and ambiguity scales: Reality or artifacts? *Journal of Applied Psychology, 68,* 334–337.

Hsee, C., & Abelson, R. (1991). Velocity relation: Satisfaction as a function of the first derivative of outcome over time. *Journal of Personality and Social Psychology, 60,* 341–347.

Hsee, C., Salovey, P., & Abelson, R. (1995). The quasi-acceleration relation: Satisfaction as a function of the change of velocity of outcome over time. *Journal of Experimental Social Psychology, 30,* 96–111.

Hsu, J., Hsu, J. C., Huang, S., Leong, L., & Li, A. (2003). Are leadership styles linked to turnover intention: An examination in Mainland China? *Journal of American Academy of Business,* 3, 37–43.

Hulin, C. (1968). Effects of changes in job satisfaction levels on employee turnover. *Journal of Applied Psychology, 52,* 122–126.

Hulin, C., Roznowski, M., & Hachiya, D. (1985). Alternative opportunities and withdrawal decisions: Empirical and theoretical discrepancies and an integration. *Psychological Bulletin, 97,* 233–250.

Huselid, M. (1995). The impact of human resource management practices on turnover, productivity, and corporate financial performance. *Academy of Management Journal, 38,* 635–672.

Hwang, S. (2005, November 19). The new white flight. *Wall Street Journal,* p. A1.

Ibarra, H. (1995). Race, opportunity, and diversity of social circles in managerial networks. *Academy of Management Journal, 38,* 673–703.

Irving, P., & Meyer, J. (1994). Reexamination of the met-expectations hypothesis: A longitudinal analysis. *Journal of Applied Psychology, 79,* 937–949.

Irving, P., & Meyer, J. (1999). On using residual and difference scores in the measurement of congruence: The case of met expectation research. *Personnel Psychology, 52,* 85–95.

Jackofsky, E. (1984). Turnover and job performance: An integrated process model. *Academy of Management Review, 9,* 74–83.

James, C., Berube, D., & Cassidy, J. (2007, April 27). *Making strategic personnel decisions through employee life cycle surveys.* Paper presented at the SIOP conference, New York.

Johnson, E., Lowe, D., & Reckers, P. (2008). Alternative work arrangements and perceived career success: Current evidence from the big four firms in the U.S. *Accounting, Organizations and Society, 33,* 48–72.

Johnson, J., Griffeth, R., & Griffin, M. (2000). Factors discriminating functional and dysfunctional salesforce turnover. *Journal of Business & Industrial Marketing, 15,* 399–415.

Kacmar, K., Andrews, M., Rooy, D., Steilberg, R., & Cerrone, S. (2006). Sure everyone can be replaced . . . but at what costs? Turnover as a predictor of unit-level performance. *Academy of Management Journal, 49,* 133–144.

Kammeyer-Mueller, J., Wanberg, C., Glomb, T., & Ahlburg, D. (2005). Turnover processes in a temporal context: It's about time. *Journal of Applied Psychology, 90,* 644–658.

Kanungo, R. (1982). Measurement of job and work involvement. *Journal of Applied Psychology, 67,* 341–349.

Kelloway, E., Gottlieb, B., & Barham, L. (1999). The source, nature, and direction of work and family conflict: A longitudinal investigation. *Journal of Applied Psychology, 4,* 337–346.

Ketchen, D. J., & Bergh, D. D. (Eds.). (2007). *Research methodology in strategy and management* (Vol. 4). Amsterdam, the Netherlands: Elsevier.

Kim, S. (1999). Behavioral commitment among the automobile workers in South Korea. *Human Resource Management Review, 9,* 419–451.

Kinicki, A., & Kreitner, R. (2008). *Organizational behavior.* New York: McGraw-Hill/Irwin.

Kopinak, K. (1996). *Desert capitalism.* Tucson: University of Arizona Press.

Krackhardt, D. (1999). The ties that torture: Simmelian tie analysis in organizations. *Research in the Sociology of Organizations, 16,* 183–210.

Krackhardt, D., & Porter, L. (1985). When friends leave: A structural analysis of the relationship between turnover and stayers' attitudes. *Administrative Science Quarterly, 30,* 242–261.

Krackhardt, D., & Porter, L. (1986). The snowball effect: Turnover embedded in communication networks. *Journal of Applied Psychology, 71,* 50–55.

Kreitner, R., & Kinicki, A. (2008). *Organizational behavior.* New York: McGraw-Hill Irwin.

Krull, J., & MacKinnon, D. (2001). Multilevel modeling of individual and group level mediated effects. *Multivariate Behavioral Research, 36,* 249–277.

Kunin, T. (1955). The construction of a new type of attitude measure. *Personnel Psychology, 8,* 65–77.

Lance, C., Vandenberg, R., & Self, R. (2000). Latent growth models of individual change: The case of newcomer adjustment. *Organizational Behavior and Human Decision Processes, 83,* 107–140.

Lawler, E. (1990). *Strategic pay: Aligning organizational strategies and pay systems.* San Francisco: Jossey-Bass.

Lazear, E. (1998). *Personnel economics for managers.* New York: Wiley.

Lee, T. W., & Mitchell, T. (1994). An alternative approach: The unfolding model of voluntary employee turnover. *Academy of Management Review, 19,* 51–89.

Lee, T. W., Mitchell, T., Holtom, B., McDaniel, L., & Hill, J. (1999). The unfolding model of voluntary turnover: A replication and extension. *Academy of Management Journal, 42,* 450–462.

Lee, T. W., Mitchell, T. R., Sablynski, C. J., Burton, J. P., & Holtom, B. C. (2004). The effects of job embeddedness on organizational citizenship, job performance, volitional absences and voluntary turnover. *Academy of Management Journal, 47,* 711–722.

Lee, T. W., Mitchell, T. R., Wise, L., & Fireman, S. 1996. An unfolding model of voluntary employee turnover. *Academy of Management Journal, 39:* 5–36.

Leonard, J., & Levine, D. (2006). The effect of diversity on turnover: A very large case study. *Industrial and Labor Relations Review, 59,* 547–572.

Liden, R., & Maslyn, J. (1998). Multidimensionality of leader–member exchange: An empirical assessment through scale development. *Journal of Management, 24,* 42–72.

Lin, N. (2001). *Social capital: A theory of social structure and action.* Cambridge, England: Cambridge University Press.

Linnehan, F., & Blau, G. (2003). Testing the impact of job search and recruitment source on new hire turnover in a maquiladora. *Applied Psychology: An International Review, 52,* 253–271.

Locke, E. (1976). The nature and causes of job satisfaction. In M. Dunnette (Ed.), *Handbook of industrial and organizational psychology* (pp. 1297–1349). Chicago: Rand McNally College.

Lovato, C. (2002, November). *Top talent retention in the midst of organizational crisis.* Paper presented at the Attrition and Retention Consortium midyear teleconference.

Lovato, C. (2004, December). *A broad approach to targeted talent retention.* Paper presented at the Attrition and Retention Consortium midyear teleconference.

Lovato, C., Davis, V., Schultz, M., & Comer, C. (2007, April). *Cultivating and sustaining a retention-oriented culture at the Home Depot.* Paper presented at the SIOP conference, New York.

Lyness, K. S., & Heilman, M. E. (2006). When fit is fundamental: Performance evaluations and promotions of upper-level female and male managers. *Journal of Applied Psychology, 91,* 777–785.

Lyness, K. S., & Judiesch, M. (2001). Are female managers quitters? The relationships of gender, promotions, and family leaves of absence to voluntary turnover. *Journal of Applied Psychology, 86,* 1167–1178.

Lyness, K. S., & Thompson, D. (1997). Above the glass ceiling? A comparison of matched samples of female and male executives. *Journal of Applied Psychology, 82,* 359–375.

Maas, J. (2007, November). *Engagement and retention at Qualcomm.* Paper presented at the Attrition and Retention Consortium teleconference.

MacKenzie, S. B., Podsakoff, P. M., & Javis, C. B. (2005). The problem of measurement model misspecification in behavioral and organizational research and some recommended solutions. *Journal of Applied Psychology, 90,* 710–730.

Mael, F., & Ashforth, B. (1995). Loyal from day one: Biodata, organizational identification, and turnover among newcomers. *Personnel Psychology, 48,* 309–333.

Maertz, C., & Campion, M. (1998). 25 years of voluntary turnover research: A review and critique. In C. L. Cooper and I. T. Robertson (Eds.), *International review of industrial and organizational psychology* (Vol. 13, pp. 49–86). Chichester, England: Wiley.

Maertz, C., & Campion, M. (2004). Profiles in quitting: Integrating process and content turnover theory. *Academy of Management Journal, 47,* 566–582.

Maertz, C., & Griffeth, R. (2004). Eight motivational forces and voluntary turnover: A theoretical synthesis with implications for research. *Journal of Management, 30,* 667–683.

Maertz, C., Stevens, M., & Campion, M. (2003). A turnover model for the Mexican maquiladoras. *Journal of Vocational Behavior, 63,* 111–135.

March, J., & Simon, H. (1958). *Organizations.* New York: Wiley.

Mathieu, J., & Zajac, D. (1990). A review and meta-analysis of the antecedents, correlates, and consequences of organizational commitment. *Psychological Bulletin, 108,* 171–194.

Maxey, D. (2009, March 2). Automatically enrolled into turmoil: Most workers continue funding 401(k)s despite losses; too heavy in stocks. *Wall Street Journal,* p. C9.

McDaniel, M., Whetzel, D., Schmidt, F., & Maurer, S. (1994). The validity of employment interviews: A comprehensive review and meta-analysis. *Journal of Applied Psychology, 79,* 599–616.

McEvoy, G., & Cascio, W. (1985). Strategies for reducing employee turnover: A meta-analysis. *Journal of Applied Psychology, 70,* 342–353.

McEvoy, G., & Cascio, W. (1987). Do good or poor performers leave? A meta-analysis of the relationship between performance and turnover. *Academy of Management Journal, 30,* 744–762.

McKay, P., Avery, D., Tonidandel, S., Morris, M., Hernandez, M., & Hebl, M. (2007). Racial differences in employee retention: Are diversity climate perceptions the key? *Personnel Psychology, 60,* 35–62.

Meyer, J., & Allen, N. (1997). *Commitment in the workplace.* Thousand Oaks, CA: Sage.

Meyer, J. P., Allen, N. J., & Smith, C. A. (1993). Commitment to organizations and occupations: Extension and test of a three-component conceptualization. *Journal of Applied Psychology, 78,* 538–551.

Meyer, J., Stanley, D., Herscovitch, L., & Topolnytsky, L. (2002). Affective, continuance, and normative commitment to the organization: A meta-analysis of antecedents, correlates, and consequences. *Journal of Vocational Behavior, 61,* 20–52.

Miller, H., Katerberg, R., & Hulin, C. (1979). Evaluation of the Mobley, Horner, and Hollingsworth model of employee turnover. *Journal of Applied Psychology, 64,* 509–517.

Miller, J., Hom, P., & Gomez-Mejia, L. (2001). The high costs of low wages: Do maquiladora compensation practices reduce turnover among Mexican production workers? *Journal of International Business Studies, 32,* 585–595.

Mitchell, T., Holtom, B., & Lee, T. (2001). How to keep your best employees: Developing an effective retention policy. *Academy of Management Executive, 15,* 96–108.

Mitchell, T. R., Holtom, B. C., Lee, T. W., Sablynski, C. J., & Erez, M. (2001). Why people stay: Using job embeddedness to predict voluntary turnover. *Academy of Management Journal, 44,* 1102–1121.

Mitchell, T. R., & Lee, T. W. (2001). The unfolding model of voluntary turnover and job embeddedness: Foundations for a comprehensive theory of attachment. In B. Staw (Ed.), *Research in organizational behavior* (Vol. 23, 189–246). Oxford, England: Elsevier Science.

Mobley, W. (1977). Intermediate linkages in the relationship between job satisfaction and employee turnover. *Journal of Applied Psychology, 62,* 237–240.

Mobley, W. (1982). *Employee turnover.* Reading, MA: Addison-Wesley.

Mobley, W., Griffeth, R., Hand, H., & Meglino, B. (1979). Review and conceptual analysis of the employee turnover process. *Psychological Bulletin, 86:* 493–522.

Mobley, W. H., Horner, S. O., & Hollingsworth, A. T. (1978). An evaluation of precursors of hospital employee turnover. *Journal of Applied Psychology, 63,* 408–414.

Montoya, K. (2008, April). *Northrop Grumman attrition and retention.* Paper presented at the conference of the Attrition and Retention Consortium, Seattle, WA.

Morrison, E. W. (2002). Newcomers' relationships: The role of social network ties during socialization. *Academy of Management Journal, 45,* 1149–1160.

Mossholder, K., Settoon, R., & Henagan, S. (2005). A relational perspective on turnover: Examining structural, attitudinal, and behavioral predictors. *Academy of Management Journal, 48,* 607–618.

Motion, R. (2005, May). *Employee on-boarding survey and reporting tool.* Paper presented at the annual conference of the Attrition and Retention Consortium, Van Buren, MI.

Mowday, R., Porter, L., & Steers, R. (1982). *Employee-organization linkages.* New York: Academic Press.

Mowday, R. Steers, R., & Porter, L. (1979). The measurement of organizational commitment. *Journal of Vocational Behavior, 14,* 224–247.

Murphy, K., & Hom, P. (2008, April). *College embeddedness: A network study of college freshmen persistence.* Paper presented at the Society of Industrial and Organizational Psychology conference, San Francisco.

Netermeyer, R., Boles, J., & McMurrian, R. (1996). Development and validation of work–family conflict and family–work conflict scales. *Journal of Applied Psychology, 81,* 400–410.

Noon, A. (2004, May). *New member presentation by Mutual of Omaha.* Paper presented at the annual conference of the Attrition and Retention Consortium, Lisle, IL.

O'Reilly, C. A. (1991). Organizational behavior: Where we've been, where we're going. *Annual Review of Psychology, 42,* 427–458.

Organ, D., & Ryan, K. (1995). A meta-analytic review of attitudinal and dispositional predictors of organizational citizenship behavior. *Personnel Psychology, 48,* 775–802.

Parker, D., & Dyer, L. (1976). Expectancy theory as a within-person behavioral choice model: An empirical test of some conceptual and methodological refinements. *Organizational Behavior and Human Performance, 17,* 97–117.

Peters, L., Jackofsky, E., & Salter, J. (1981). Predicting turnover: A comparison of part-time and full-time employees. *Journal of Occupational Behaviour, 2,* 89–98.

Petersen, M. (2002, December). *Retention initiatives at Eli Lilly and company.* Paper presented at the midyear conference of the Attrition and Retention Consortium.

Petersen, T., & Saporta, I. (2004). The opportunity structure for discrimination. *American Journal of Sociology, 109,* 852–901.

Pfeffer, J. (2005). Producing sustainable competitive advantage through the effective management of people. *Academy of Management Executive, 19,* 95–108.

Pfeffer, J., & Sutton, R. (2006, January). Evidence-based management. *Harvard Business Review,* 1–11.

Phased retirement finds favor in survey. (2005, March 14). *Wall Street Journal,* p. 1.

Phillips, J. M. (1998). Effects of realistic job previews on multiple organizational outcomes: A meta-analysis. *Academy of Management Journal, 41:* 673–690.

Porter, L., Crampon, W., & Smith, F. (1976). Organizational commitment and managerial turnover: A longitudinal study. *Organizational Behavior and Human Performance, 15,* 87–98.

Porter, L., & Steers, R. (1973). Organizational, work, and personal factors in employee turnover and absenteeism. *Psychological Bulletin, 80,* 151–176.

Porter, L., Steers, R., Mowday, R., & Boulian, P. (1974). Organizational commitment, job satisfaction, and turnover among psychiatric technicians. *Journal of Applied Psychology, 59,* 603–609.

Posthuma, R., Joplin, J., & Maertz, C. (2005). Comparing the validity of turnover predictors in the United States and Mexico. *International Journal of Cross Cultural Management, 5,* 165–180.

Powell, D., & Meyer, J. (2004). Side-bet theory and the three-component model of organizational behavior. *Journal of Vocational Behavior, 65,* 157–177.

Price, J. L. (1977). *The study of turnover.* Ames: Iowa State University Press.

Price, J. L. (2001). Reflections on the determinants of voluntary turnover. *International Journal of Manpower, 22,* 600–624.

Price, J. L., & Mueller, C. W. (1981). A causal model of turnover for nurses. *Academy of Management Journal 24,* 543–565.

Price, J. L., & Mueller, C. W. (1986). *Absenteeism and turnover of hospital employees.* Greenwich, CT.: JAI Press.

Radefeld, P., Paul, D., Abrahams, E., & Mast, A. (2007, April). *Retention research and initiatives at State Farm Insurance Company.* Paper presented at the SIOP conference, New York.

Raudenbush, S., & Bryk, A. (2002). *Hierarchical linear models.* Thousand Oaks, CA: Sage.

Reicher, A. (1985). A review and reconceptualization of organizational commitment. *Academy of Management Review, 10,* 465–476.

Roberson, L. (2004). On the relationship between race and turnover. In R. W. Griffeth & P. W. Hom (Eds.), *Innovative theory and empirical research on employee turnover* (pp. 211–229). Greenwich, CT: Information Age.

Roberson, L., & Kulik, C. (2007, May). Stereotype threat at work. *Academy of Management Perspectives,* 24–40.

Royalty, A. (1998). Job-to-job and job-to-nonemployment turnover by gender and education level. *Journal of Labor Economics, 16,* 392–443.

Rusbult, C., & Farrell, D. (1983). A longitudinal test of the investment model: The impact on job satisfaction, job commitment, and turnover of variations in rewards, costs, alternatives, and investment. *Journal of Applied Psychology, 68,* 429–438.

Sacco, J., & Schmitt, N. (2005). A dynamic multilevel model of demographic diversity and misfit effects. *Journal of Applied Psychology, 90,* 203–231.

Sager, J., & Menon, A. (1994). The role of behavioral intentions in turnover of salespeople. *Journal of Business Research, 29,* 179–188.

Salamin, A., & Hom, P. (2005). In search of the elusive U-shaped performance-turnover relationship: Are high performing Swiss bankers more liable to quit? *Journal of Applied Psychology, 90,* 1204–1216.

Salzinger, L. (2003). *Genders in production.* Berkeley, CA: University of California Press.

Schiemann, W. A. (2009). *Reinventing talent management: How to maximize performance in the new marketplace.* New York: Wiley.

Schmidt, F., & Rader, M. (1999). Exploring the boundary conditions for interview validity: Meta-analytic validity findings for a new interview type. *Personnel Psychology, 52,* 445–464.

Schwartz, F. (1989, January/February). Management women and the new facts of life. *Harvard Business Review,* 65–76.

Shaw, J., Delery, J., Jenkins, G., & Gupta, N. (1998). An organization-level analysis of voluntary and involuntary turnover. *Academy of Management Journal, 41,* 511–525.

Shaw, J., Dineen, B., Fang, R., & Vellella, R. (2009). Exchange relationships, HRM practices, and quit rates of good and poor performers. *Academy of Management Journal, 52,* 1016–1033.

Shaw, J., Duffy, M., Johnson, J., & Lockhart, D. (2005). Turnover, social capital losses, and performance. *Academy of Management Journal, 48,* 594–606.

Shaw, J., Gupta, N., & Delery, J. (2005). Alternative conceptualizations of the relationship between voluntary turnover and organizational performance. *Academy of Management Journal, 48,* 50–68.

Sheridan, J., & Abelson, M. (1983). Cusp catastrophe model of employee turnover. *Academy of Management Journal, 26,* 418–436.

Sheth, N. (2008, August 20). For India's tech titans, growth is waning. *Wall Street Journal,* pp. A1, A15.

Shore, L., & Barksdale, K. (1998). Examining degree of balance and level of obligation in the employment relationship: A social exchange approach. *Journal of Organizational Behavior, 19,* 731–744.

Shore, L., Tetrick, L., Lynch, P., & Barksdale, K. (2006). Social and economic exchanges: Construct development and validation. *Journal of Applied Social Psychology, 36,* 837–867.

Shore, L., Tetrick, L., Taylor, S., Coyle-Shapiro, J., Liden, R., McLean Parks, J., et al. (2004). The employment relationship. In J. Martocchio (Ed.), *Research in personnel and human resources management* (Vol. 23, pp. 291–370). Greenwich, CT: JAI Press.

Siebert, S., Kraimer, M., & Liden, R. (2001). A social capital theory of career success. *Academy of Management Journal, 44,* 219–237.

Smith, P., Kendall, L., & Hulin, C. (1969). *The measurement of satisfaction in work and retirement: A strategy for the study of attitudes.* Chicago: Rand McNally.

Smith, R. (1999, December). *Turnover: A workforce planner's perspective.* Paper presented at Chicago Society for Industrial/Organizational Psychology, Chicago.

Staw, B. (1980). The consequences of turnover. *Journal of Occupational Behavior, 1,* 253–273.

Steel, R. P. (1996). Labor market dimensions as predictors of the reenlistment decisions of military personnel. *Journal of Applied Psychology, 81,* 421–428.

Steel, R. (2002). Turnover theory at the empirical interface: Problems of fit and function. *Academy of Management Review, 27,* 346–360.

Steel, R., & Griffeth, R. (1989). The elusive relationship between perceived employment opportunity and turnover behavior: A methodological or conceptual artifact. *Journal of Applied Psychology, 74,* 846–854.

Steel, R., Griffeth, R., & Hom, P. (2002). Practical retention policy for the practical manager. *Academy of Management Executive, 16,* 148–162.

Steers, R. M., & Mowday, R. T. (1981). Employee turnover and postdecision accommodation processes. In L. Cummings & B. Staw (Eds.), *Research in Organizational Behavior, 3,* 235–281.

Stevens, R. (2006, April 19). Social engineering. *Wall Street Journal,* A12.

Stroh, L., Brett, J., & Reilly, A. (1996). Family structure, glass ceiling, and traditional explanations for the differential rate of turnover of female and male managers. *Journal of Vocational Behavior, 49,* 99–118.

Sturman, M., & Trevor, C. (2001). The implications of linking the dynamic performance and turnover literatures. *Journal of Applied Psychology, 86,* 684–696.

Sue, D., Capodilup, C., Torino, G., Bucceri, J., Holder, A., Nadal, K., & Esquilin, M. (2007). Racial microaggressions in everyday life. *American Psychologist, 62,* 271–286.

Takeuchi, R., Lepak, D., Wang, H., & Takeuchi, K. (2007). An empirical examination of the mechanisms mediating between high-performance work systems and the performance of Japanese organizations. *Journal of Applied Psychology, 92,* 1069–1083.

Teagarden, M., Butler, M., & Von Glinow, M. (1992, Winter). Mexico's maquiladora industry: Where strategic human resource management makes a difference. *Organizational Dynamics, 20,* 34–47.

Tello, M., & Greene, W. (1996). U.S. managerial strategies and applications for retaining personnel in Mexico. *International Journal of Management, 17,* 54–94.

Terborg, J., & Lee, T. (1984). A predictive study of organizational turnover rates. *Academy of Management Journal, 27,* 793–810.

Tetrick, L. (2004). Understanding the employment relationship: Implications for measurement and research design. In J. Coyle-Shapiro, L. Shore, M. S. Taylor, & L. Tetrick (Eds.), *The employment relationship: Examining psychological and contextual perspectives* (pp. 312–331). Oxford, England: Oxford University Press.

Tett, R. P., & Meyer, J. P. (1993). Job satisfaction, organizational commitment, turnover intention, and turnover: Path analyses based on meta-analytic findings. *Personnel Psychology, 46,* 259–293.

Tiano, S. (1994). *Patriarchy on the line: Labor gender and ideology in the Mexican maquila industry.* Philadelphia: Temple University Press.

Trevor, C. (2001). Interactions among actual ease-of-movement determinants and job satisfaction in the prediction of voluntary turnover. *Academy of Management Journal, 44,* 621–638.

Trevor, C. O., Gerhart, B., & Boudreau, J. W. (1997). Voluntary turnover and job performance: Curvilinearity and the moderating influences of salary growth, promotions, and labor demand. *Journal of Applied Psychology, 82,* 44–61.

Tripp, R. (2002, December). *Cross-culture attitude survey and turnover intent.* Paper presented at the Attrition and Retention Consortium midyear teleconference.

Tsui, A. (2004). Contributing to global management knowledge: A case for high quality indigenous research. *Asia Pacific Journal of Management, 21,* 491–512.

Tsui, A., Pearce, J., Porter, L., & Hite, J. (1995). Choice of employee-organization relationship: Influence of external and internal organizational factors. In G. Ferris (Ed.), *Research in personnel and human resources management* (pp. 117–151). Greenwich, CT: JAI Press.

Tsui, A., Pearce, J., Porter, L., & Tripoli, A. (1997). Alternative approaches to the employee-organization relationship: Does investment in employees pay off? *Academy of Management Journal, 40,* 1089–1121.

U.S. National Center for Health Statistics. (n.d.). *NCHS definitions.* Retrieved April 13, 2007, from http://www.cdc.gov/nchs/datawh/nchsdefs/ageadjustment.htm

Vandenberg, R., & Lance, C. (2000). A review and synthesis of the measurement invariance literature: Suggestions, practices, and recommendations for organizational research. *Organizational Research Methods, 3,* 4–69.

Vandenberg, R., & Scarpello, V. (1990). The matching model: An examination of the processes underlying realistic job previews. *Journal of Applied Psychology, 75,* 60–67.

Villanova, P., Bernardin, J., Johnson, D., & Dahmus, S. (1994). The validity of a measure of job compatibility in the prediction of job performance and turnover of motion picture theater personnel. *Personnel Psychology, 47,* 73–90.

Vroom, V. (1964). *Work and motivation.* New York: Wiley.

Wanous, J. P. (1973). Effects of a realistic job preview on job acceptance, job attitudes, and job survival. *Journal of Applied Psychology, 58,* 327–332.

Wanous, J. P. (1989). Installing a realistic job preview: Ten tough choices. *Personnel Psychology, 42,* 117–134.

Wanous, J. P. (1992). *Organizational entry* (2nd ed.). Reading, MA: Addison-Wesley.

Wasti, S., Bergman, M., Glomb, T., & Drasgow, F. (2000). Test of the cross-cultural generalizability of a model of sexual harassment. *Journal of Applied Psychology, 85,* 766–778.

Weiss, D., Dawis, R., England, G., & Lofquist, L. (1967). *Manual for the Minnesota Satisfaction Questionnaire.* Minneapolis: University of Minnesota, Industrial Relations Center.

West, M. (2004). Investigating turnover in the international context: A turnover model for the Mexican culture. In R. Griffeth & P. Hom (Eds.), *Innovative theory and empirical research on employee turnover* (pp. 211–230). Greenwich, CT: Information Age.

Westaby, J. (2005). Behavioral reasoning theory: Identifying new linkages underlying intentions and behavior. *Organizational Behavior and Human Decision Processes, 98,* 97–120.

Williams, C. R., & Livingstone, L. P. (1994). A second look at the relationship between performance and voluntary turnover. *Academy of Management Journal, 37,* 269–298.

Williams, L., Edwards, J., & Vandenberg, R. (2003). Recent advances in causal modeling methods for organizational and management research. *Journal of Management, 29,* 903–936.

Wu, J., Hom, P., Tetrick, L., Shore, L., Jia, L., Li, C., & Song, J. (2006). The norm of reciprocity: Scale development and validation in the Chinese context. *Management and Organization Review, 2,* 377–402.

Xiao, Z., & Björkman, I. (2006). High commitment work systems in Chinese organizations: A preliminary measure. *Management and Organization Review, 2,* 403–422.

Xiao, Z., & Tsui, A. (2007). When brokers do not work: Social capital in high-commitment organizations. *Administrative Science Quarterly, 52,* 1–31.

Yao, X., Lee, T., Mitchell, T., Burton, J., & Sablynski, C. (2004). Job embeddedness: Current research and future directions. In R. Griffeth & P. Hom (Eds.), *Innovative theory and empirical research on employee turnover* (pp. 153–187). Greenwich, CT: Information Age.

Youngblood, S., Mobley, W., & Meglino, B. 1983. A longitudinal analysis of the turnover process. *Journal of Applied Psychology, 68,* 507–516.

Zarandona, J., & Camusco, M. (1985). A study of exit interviews: Does the last word count? *Personnel, 62,* 47–48.

Zatzick, C., & Iverson, R. (2006). High-involvement management and workforce reduction: Competitive advantage or disadvantage. *Academy of Management Journal, 49,* 999–1015.

Zhang, M., & Li, S. Z. (2004, June). *An empirical study on a causal model of turnover intention among technical staff in 15 Chinese information and technology companies.* Paper presented at the International Association for Chinese Management Research conference, Beijing, China.

Part IV

EVALUATING SYSTEMS

CHAPTER 12

APPLICANT REACTIONS TO ORGANIZATIONS AND SELECTION SYSTEMS

Donald M. Truxillo and Talya N. Bauer

Historically, personnel selection research has focused on issues such as efficiency, validity, predictive power, and legal issues. In other words, selection research focused on the viewpoint of the employer, and the applicant viewpoint was given little consideration. However, in the past 2 decades, far more focus has been given to the viewpoint of applicants and test takers. For example, beginning in the 1980s, many European researchers began to develop models of personnel selection in which applicants were the centerpiece (Salgado, Anderson, & Hülsheger, in press), resulting in such concepts as social validity (e.g., whether applicants are provided with feedback; Schuler, 1993).

Early applicant reactions research was not usually based in a particular theoretical model but simply approached the issue from the standpoint of face validity. For example, Schmidt, Greenthal, Hunter, Berner, and Seaton (1977) compared reactions to a work sample test and a content-valid written test and found that applicants perceived the work sample as clearer and more fair, as well as being at the proper difficulty level. Cascio and Phillips (1979) found that employee complaints dropped after the introduction of performance tests at an organization that had used paper-and-pencil tests. Later research focused on direct comparisons between selection methods and generally found that applicants prefer face-valid methods such as simulations and work sample tests to methods such as multiple-choice tests (e.g., Macan, Avedon, Paese, & Smith, 1994; Rynes & Connerley, 1993; Smither, Reilly, Millsap, Pearlman, & Stoffey, 1993). However, with the development of theory-based models to explain applicant and test-taker reactions (e.g., Gilliland, 1993), research on applicant reactions began to hit its stride.

As a result, there have been several studies of applicant reactions and dispositions (e.g., test-taking self-efficacy, test-taking motivation) since the 1990s as well as review articles (e.g., Anderson, 2003; Ryan & Ployhart, 2000), meta-analyses (Hausknecht, Day, & Thomas, 2004), and special issues on the topic (e.g., Anderson, 2003; Morgeson & Ryan, in press). This proliferation of research has involved a major shift in focus from test validity to the applicant's perspective. A number of issues have motivated this shift in focus. Perhaps the central reason for interest in applicants' perceptions in North America is that reactions have been theorized to relate to legal challenges (e.g., Gilliland, 1993). Indeed, research in other arenas has found that fairness relates to self-reported claims of discrimination (e.g., with the U.S. Equal Employment Opportunity Commission or a court; Goldman, 2001), although this has yet to be examined among job applicants. Applicant reactions are also theorized to relate to a number of outcomes of interest to employers, such as perceptions of the organization, and the effects of reactions on certain outcomes has been empirically demonstrated (e.g., Bauer, Maertz, Dolen, & Campion, 1998; Macan et al., 1994). In addition, reactions were of interest because of their potential for addressing issues of importance to society. For example, although test-taking dispositions such as test-taking motivation were demonstrated to affect test validity (e.g., Schmit & Ryan, 1992), they were also theorized to explain ethnic differences in test performance (e.g., Ryan, 2001). Other researchers emphasized the importance of shifting the focus in personnel selection from the viewpoint of the employer to that of the individual (e.g., Schuler, 1993).

Although the field of applicant reactions has generated a great deal of research, there remains much to be understood about applicant reactions and dispositions. In addition, as noted by several researchers in this area, the importance of reactions and dispositions to many key organizational outcomes remains unclear, especially because some outcomes such as actual applicant litigation have not been examined (e.g., Ryan & Huth, 2008; Sackett & Lievens, 2008; Truxillo, Steiner, & Gilliland, 2004). Our goal in this chapter is to provide readers with an overview of applicant reactions and dispositions research, including a description of research design issues and ideas for the application of the research to organizations. We conclude by describing research streams we believe to be crucial.

APPLICANT REACTIONS MODELS AND THEORETICAL BASES

Research on applicant reactions was greatly enhanced by the infusion of theory and the development of applicant reactions models. In the 1980s, European researchers began taking into account the applicant's perspective in the selection process (e.g., Salgado et al., in press), developing the concept of social validity, which includes factors such as the transparency of the selection system and the provision of feedback (e.g., Schuler, 1993). Arvey and Sackett's (1993) model of applicant reactions specified a range of issues that could be important to applicants, such as job relatedness of selection methods and consistency of treatment of applicants during selection. However, the field needed a comprehensive, theoretically based model of applicant reactions to better organize and drive further research in the area.

This need was filled by Gilliland's (1993) model, which is based in organizational justice theory (e.g., Lind & Tyler, 1988; Greenberg, 1993; see Vol. 3, chap. 8, this handbook); it is the model that has driven much of the applicant reactions research. In addition to providing a proven theoretical basis for the study of applicant reactions, the model also comprehensively addressed issues of concern both to the employer (e.g., potentially taking legal action, ability of the employer to attract applicants) and to the individual (e.g., respectful treatment of applicants, effects on applicant self-perceptions). Gilliland's model describes 10 procedural justice rules (focused on the fairness of selection procedures themselves) and 3 distributive justice rules (focused on the fairness of outcomes).

Gilliland's (1993) 10 procedural justice rules relevant to the selection situation fall into three broad categories. The *formal characteristics* category includes job relatedness, chance to perform, reconsideration opportunity, and consistency. Under the *explanation* category is feedback, information known, and openness. Last, in the *interpersonal treatment* category are applicant (or candidate) treatment at the test site, two-way communication, and propriety of questions. According to the model, violation or compliance with these rules sums together to affect applicants' overall perceptions of fairness, which in turn affect a range of outcomes such as job acceptance decisions, litigation decisions, job satisfaction if hired, and self-perceptions (e.g., self-efficacy). Of the 10 rules, job relatedness is the most potent factor and has consistently been found to relate to important outcomes (Hausknecht et al., 2004). Opportunity to perform has also emerged as an important factor (Schleicher, Venkataramani, Morgeson, & Campion, 2006). Bauer et al. (2001) found that the rules from Gilliland's model factored into two broad higher order factors. They labeled these dimensions *structure fairness,* related to the actual selection process, such as the timing of feedback of results and the test itself, and *social fairness,* or communication with and treatment of job applicants. These structure and social fairness dimensions map onto Greenberg's social and structure dimensions of procedural justice (e.g., Greenberg, 1993). Thus, researchers interested in overall process fairness can create two factors, and researchers interested in details of each justice dimension can analyze them separately.

As a result of Gilliland's (1993) model, the majority of subsequent applicant reactions studies have been grounded in organizational justice theory, and as noted in greater detail later in this chapter, research has generally supported Gilliland's (1993) model (e.g., Bauer et al., 1998, 2001). The issues examined have included a wide range of selection issues, such as providing explanations to applicants (e.g., Horvath, Ryan, & Stierwalt, 2000; Ployhart, Ryan, & Bennett, 1999), the importance of job-related tests (e.g., Gilliland, 1994), newer selection methods such as video-based tests (e.g., Chan & Schmitt, 1997), and telephone and Internet screening (e.g., Bauer, Truxillo, Campion, Paronto, & Weekley, 2004; Bauer et al., 2006). Additionally, a meta-analysis by Hausknecht et al. (2004) used Gilliland's (1993) model as a starting point for examining the relationships among a number of applicant perceptions and applicants' preferences for a range of selection procedures.

APPLICANT PREFERENCES FOR SPECIFIC SELECTION PROCEDURES

Rynes (1993) noted that applicants tend to prefer methods that are perceived as job related. Subsequent research (Rynes & Connerley, 1993) has borne out this finding, and it has generally been shown to be robust across cultures. Steiner and Gilliland (1996) compared French and U.S. reactions to a range of selection procedures on a number of dimensions, developing a methodology that has been used to examine reactions across numerous countries and cultures (e.g., Anderson & Witvliet, 2008; Bertolino & Steiner, 2007; Nikolaou & Judge, 2007; Phillips & Gully, 2002; Steiner & Gilliland, 1996). For example, research has examined applicant reactions to specific selection procedures in Singapore (Phillips & Gully, 2002), Italy (Bertolino & Steiner, 2007), Greece (Nikolaou & Judge, 2007), Spain and Portugal (Moscoso & Salgado, 2004), and the Netherlands (Anderson & Witvliet, 2008). The results across these studies are generally similar: Interviews and work samples were perceived more positively than biodata, personality tests, and cognitive ability tests, which were perceived more favorably than honesty tests and graphology. Across these studies, face validity and opportunity to perform were the major determinants of reactions. Similarly, Ryan et al. (2008) recently found that perceptions of different selection tools were similar across countries regardless of cultural values. This is similar to the meta-analytic findings of Hausknecht et al. (2004), who found that interviews ($M = 3.84$) were rated most favorably by applicants, followed by work samples ($M = 3.63$), resumes ($M = 3.57$), and references ($M = 3.33$). Cognitive ability tests ($M = 3.14$), personality tests ($M = 2.88$), and biodata ($M = 2.81$) received moderate favorability ratings, and personal contacts ($M = 2.51$), honesty tests ($M = 2.47$), and graphology ($M = 1.76$) received the least favorable ratings. (Ratings reflect a 5-point scale.) The pattern of these findings clearly fits with Gilliland's (1993) rules of job relatedness, face validity, and opportunity to perform (e.g., work samples and interviews receiving the highest ratings, graphology receiving the lowest).

RESEARCH DESIGN ISSUES

The movement of applicant reactions research from a side topic to one of more central importance in the world of selection has much to do with changes in research design, which have occurred in tandem with theoretical advances. We place these research design issues that are particular to applicant reactions research under the umbrellas of longitudinal designs, control variables, complementary research in the lab and field, and new measurement instruments.

Longitudinal Designs

The earliest work on applicant reactions was cross-sectional and sought to answer fundamental questions such as which selection methods applicants prefer (e.g., Rynes & Connerley, 1993). Because the new research questions focused on changes in applicant attitudes across time and whether the effects of applicant attitudes on outcomes last over time, more longitudinal designs were used. This longitudinal research design approach has been used in a number of applicant reactions studies since the late 1990s (e.g., Bauer et al., 1998; Chan, Schmitt, DeShon, Clause, & Delbridge, 1997; Schleicher et al., 2006; Truxillo, Bauer, Campion, & Paronto, 2002; Van Vianen, Taris, Scholten, & Schinkel, 2004) and appears to be more of a norm in this research area today than an exception.

Control Variables

Researchers have argued that it is important to control for initial levels of perceptions if the research question involves understanding how applicant reactions change over time and what the lasting reactions might be. However intuitive this approach may seem, it has not historically been the norm. In fact, Ryan and Ployhart (2000) noted that at the time of their review of the literature, only 10% of the studies had gathered measures of applicants' initial perceptions before the selection process.

In addition, a key control variable to consider in the applicant reactions literature is outcome favorability. *Outcome favorability* refers to whether an applicant makes it to the next step in the selection process, passes or fails a test, gets offered a job, and so on. Researchers have consistently shown that this variable is a pivotal factor in applicant perceptions (e.g., Hausknecht et al., 2004; Ryan & Ployhart, 2000), and thus it is important to control for outcome favorability in examining applicant reactions and examining applicant attitudes after feedback.

Comparing Test Method and Test Content

One issue that is particularly vexing to applicant reactions research is the confound between test content and test method (e.g., Chan & Schmitt, 1997, 2004). That is, in making comparisons of selection procedures, the content of different procedures will also differ. Although this issue has generally not been overcome in the applicant reactions literature, Chan and Schmitt (2004) suggested that new study designs must be developed to address this issue head on.

Lab and Field Research

Studies of applicant reactions range from hypothetical hiring situations with students to field studies assessing the reaction of applicants in actual hiring contexts. To date, much of the empirical research on applicant reactions has been in laboratory settings (e.g., Chan & Schmitt, 1997; Ployhart & Ryan, 1998; Ployhart et al., 1999; Rynes & Connerley, 1993). This makes sense because many experimental manipulations such as using different selection procedures, providing different types of feedback, and giving different types of explanations would be difficult or impossible to carry out in the field because of legal and ethical issues. However, the ecological validity of laboratory studies (e.g., student samples) has been called into question (e.g., Anderson, 2003; Truxillo et al., 2004) because even highly motivated participants in lab studies may not react in the same way as actual job applicants. At the core of this dilemma is the difference between being an actual applicant in a selection situation and being a student participant in a simulation. Actual job applicants may have a lot at stake and are attuned to numerous issues in the selection situation other than the hiring processes (e.g., career implications, job market). To increase the fidelity of simulations, some researchers have taken the approach of giving incentives such as raffles or offering rewards for top performers in laboratory studies (e.g., Schmit & Ryan, 1992).

Although research has shown that laboratory and field studies often produce different results, their differences are inconsistent in both direction and magnitude. For example, laboratory studies have been found to lead to underestimates of some phenomena such as the relationship between explanations and fairness as expressed in mean correlations (simulation $r = .08$ vs. actual hiring context $r = .26$; student sample $r = .05$ vs. actual hiring context $r = .24$; Truxillo, Bodner, Bertolino, Bauer, & Yonce, in press). In contrast, Hausknecht et al.'s (2004) meta-analysis generally found larger effects in the laboratory when examining the relationship between fairness and future behavior outcomes (e.g., recommendation intentions). However, Hausknecht et al. also noted that there was no clearly consistent pattern regarding whether effect sizes were larger in hypothetical or authentic selection situations.

In sum, although laboratory studies provide a necessary methodology for examining a number of applicant reactions issues, field studies provide greater ecological validity. When determining whether to use a laboratory or a field design, the applicant reactions researcher should balance the practicality of studying the issue at hand in a field setting with whether ecological validity issues will call any findings into question. With only 38% of the research in applicant reactions occurring in authentic contexts with actual applicants (Hausknecht et al., 2004), there is certainly room for additional field research.

Measures of Applicant Reactions

In the past, the field of applicant reactions suffered from fragmented measurement, with researchers generating new scales to measure the same constructs, making for challenging comparisons. However, as Sackett and Lievens (2008) noted in their review of the personnel selection literature, the field of applicant reactions has been improved by the development of multidimensional, theory-driven measures. Over a series of studies, Bauer et al. (2001) developed a measure to tap Gilliland's (1993) 10 dimensions of procedural justice in selection. The initial pool of items was reduced through exploratory factor analysis, the factor structure confirmed through confirmatory factor analysis, and convergent and discriminant validity demonstrated using field samples. The scales were also shown to predict applicant reactions outcomes using two samples of employed students. The 10 dimensions fall under two second-order factors: structure fairness (e.g., "I could really show my skills and abilities through this test") and social fairness (e.g., "The test administrators were considerate during the test"). The factors can be used either as standalone measures or in their entirety to capture the full range of applicant fairness reactions.

Less focus has been given to measures of perceived distributive justice, which is often measured using a three-item measure by Smither et al. (1993), which includes items such as "The test results accurately reflected how well I performed on the examination." Similarly, outcome favorability is often captured by whether the applicant passed or failed the test, by whether a job offer was extended, or by simply assessing perceptions of how applicants believe they performed.

In terms of test-taking motivation, Arvey, Strickland, Drauden, and Martin (1990) developed and validated a test-taking motivation scale over a series of studies (a subscale of their large Test Attitude Scale). This scale has been well accepted in the literature and includes the sample item "I tried my best on this test." While developing a new scale, Sanchez et al. (2000) used two field studies of police applicants to demonstrate the factor structure and validity of their scale in terms of predicting test performance on the Valence, Instrumentality, Expectancy Motivation Scale. The Valence, Instrumentality, Expectancy Motivation Scale is a multifaceted, expectancy theory–based test-taking motivation scale (e.g., "How well you do on this test will affect whether you are hired"). Both of these carefully developed and validated measures of test-taking motivation have been used in subsequent research (e.g., Nguyen, O'Neal, & Ryan, 2003; Schmit & Ryan, 1992). For a comprehensive review and description of applicant reactions measures, see Bauer, Truxillo, and Paronto (2003).

Summary

These design issues are not new. I/O–organizational behavior researchers in many areas often grapple with trade-offs in terms of longitudinal designs, where to locate samples, and measurement. Going forward, researchers will need to continue to take into account how well the design of their study fits the questions being asked because this is the most appropriate way to understand which design will help to answer the questions in the most compelling way.

WHICH IMPORTANT OUTCOMES ARE AFFECTED BY APPLICANT REACTIONS?

As already noted, the "selection justice" approach to studying applicant reactions has provided the dominant framework (e.g., the Gilliland, 1993, model). By implication, perceived fairness of selection procedures has thus been seen as the dominant applicant reaction. That is, it is assumed that applicants' fairness perceptions are the necessary condition for other outcomes such as perceptions of the organization and self-perceptions to be affected. Despite the importance of outcome fairness to applicant perceptions (Ryan & Ployhart, 2000), perceptions of process fairness have been central to applicant reactions research. This is because organizations have relatively little control over the outcomes applicants receive. For example, applicant ability and test performance, not actions by the organization, largely affect whether applicants pass or fail. Large pools of applicants, again largely out of the control of the employer, are more likely to lead to large numbers of rejected applicants. But organizations do have some control over the selection processes they use. Thus, the selection process itself provides the leverage point for employers: They can choose more procedurally fair methods, provide explanations for procedures, provide feedback on performance, and so on.

In the following overview, we provide a summary of the empirical literature on the relationship between perceptions of selection process fairness and a number of outcomes. We refer interested readers to recent reviews for detailed descriptions of how applicants' fairness perceptions may affect key outcomes (Truxillo et al., 2004) and the interrelationship among reactions (Hausknecht et al., 2004).

Satisfaction With the Selection Process

Taken together, research on the relationship between perceived fairness of selection procedures and satisfaction with the selection process has suggested that fairness perceptions are related to perceptions of the selection process and that this relationship lasts over time (e.g., Macan et al., 1994; Truxillo, Bauer, & Sanchez, 2001). In their meta-analysis, Hausknecht et al. (2004) found that fairness dimensions and attitude toward selection were correlated .36 to .39.

Organizational Attractiveness

Research has suggested that there is a relationship between fairness and organizational attractiveness (Bauer et al., 2001; Cunningham-Snell, Anderson, & Fletcher, 1999; Macan et al., 1994) and that this effect also lasts over time (e.g., Bauer et al., 1998). This positive relationship between organizational attractiveness and process fairness ($r = .44$) and its subdimensions was generally supported by Hausknecht et al.'s (2004) meta-analysis. However, associations between process fairness and organizational attractiveness may not last over time (e.g., Cunningham-Snell et al., 1999), and fairness may not affect organizational attractiveness when applicants are already highly attracted to the organization (e.g., Truxillo et al., 2002).

Job Acceptance Intentions

The relationship between fairness and job acceptance intentions has received mixed support, with some individual studies finding a positive relationship (e.g., Macan et al., 1994) and others finding none (Ployhart & Ryan, 1997). Overall, however, meta-analytic results did find support for this relationship ($r = .28$; Hausknecht et al., 2004).

Recommendation Intentions

We define *recommendation intentions* as the applicant's intention to recommend the organization to others. Hausknecht et al. (2004) found support for the relationship between selection fairness and recommendation intentions ($r = .46$). However, note that some research has suggested that this relationship may weaken over time (e.g., Bauer et al., 1998; Gilliland, 1994).

Self-Efficacy

Hausknecht et al.'s (2004) meta-analysis suggests a weak, positive main effect relationship between fairness and self-efficacy ($r = .12$). However, Gilliland (1993) proposed that selection procedural fairness and outcomes would interact to affect self-efficacy, and research has found support for moderating effects of process fairness on self-efficacy (Bauer et al., 1998; Gilliland, 1994; Ployhart & Ryan, 1997; Truxillo et al., 2001).

Intentions to Pursue Legal Action

The possible relationship between the perceived fairness of hiring practices and the likelihood of applicants taking legal action is cited as a key factor that drives much of the interest in applicant reactions research (e.g., Gilliland, 1993; Truxillo & Bauer, 1999). Seymour (1988) made a compelling argument for this possibility, although no empirical test was conducted to bolster this claim. Empirical research has supported the relationship between selection fairness and litigation intentions in lab studies (e.g., Bauer et al., 2001; Ostberg, Truxillo, & Bauer, 2001). However, a few caveats are in order. First, because most organizations are unwilling to ask applicants about their legal intentions, the little research that has been done on this issue is in laboratory settings, which may not have captured the complex set of factors that affect actual legal action in the actual hiring context. Second, intentions to pursue litigation and actual legal action are very different and may have different antecedents (e.g., Goldman, 2001), including the fact that actually initiating a lawsuit requires a good bit of effort on the part of the applicant. Third, common method variance may be an issue in these cross-sectional studies.

Test-Taking Motivation

Gilliland (1993) proposed test-taking motivation as a potential outcome of fairness perceptions, and meta-analytic work has suggested a positive relationship between fairness and test-taking motivation ($r = .31$; Hausknecht et al., 2004).

Applicant Withdrawal

Hausknecht et al. (2004) were unable to include behavioral outcomes such as applicant withdrawal in their meta-analysis because of a lack of studies. A review of the few studies that do exist provides equivocal evidence. On the basis of interviews with applicants who withdrew from a police selection process, Schmit and Ryan (1997) noted that process fairness issues may influence withdrawal decisions of some applicants. However, in other studies of police applicants, Ryan, Sacco, McFarland, and Kriska (2000) and Truxillo et al. (2002) found no relationship between fairness and continuation in the selection process. Truxillo et al. also noted that because police applicants were highly attracted to the organization from the start, these null results may not generalize to other applicant pools.

Reapplication

In one of the few studies on reapplication behavior, Gilliland et al. (2001) found that applicants receiving an explanation that focused on fairness in a rejection letter were more likely to reapply for a future position than those who received a standard rejection letter.

Test Validity

Although there has been some research on the effects of test-taking motivation on test validity (e.g., Schmit & Ryan, 1992), research on whether selection fairness affects test validity is very limited. In a college student sample, Thorsteinson and Ryan (1997) found that fairness perceptions moderated the validity of a cognitive ability test for predicting GPA, such that validity was greater for those with more positive fairness perceptions. This effect was not found for a personality test. Thorsteinson and Ryan (1997) suggested that increased validity may result from increased motivation in participants who perceive selection processes as more fair. Consistent with this suggestion, Chan et al. (1997) showed that face-validity perceptions influenced test performance indirectly through their impact on test-taking motivation. Taken together, these findings suggest that increasing fairness perceptions may increase the validity (and hence the utility) of certain types of selection tests. However, as pointed out by previous authors (e.g., Chan & Schmitt, 2004), the effects of reactions and dispositions on the quality of scores on selection procedures needs far greater study.

Job Performance

The one published study (Gilliland, 1994) using job performance as an outcome found no relationship between test fairness perceptions and work performance. Thus, the relationship between applicant reactions and later job performance is inconclusive. However, we note that the likelihood of a relationship between fairness of selection procedures and later job performance is probably tenuous because there are a number of other variables that are more proximal to and thus more likely to affect on-the-job performance than applicants' initial reactions to the selection procedure. For example, cognitive ability, perceived fairness on the job, and job attitudes are all more proximal to on-the-job performance than recruitment events, as Rynes (1991) has noted. (See also chap. 4, this volume, and Vol. 3, chaps. 4 and 8, this handbook.) However, we believe that the effects of selection fairness on job performance outcome will become more clear with examinations of reactions in the promotion context (cf. Schaubroeck & Lam, 2004).

Organizational Commitment and Satisfaction

Despite the fact that organizational commitment and satisfaction are proposed as outcomes of applicant reactions (Gilliland, 1993), this topic has received scant attention. Cunningham-Snell et al. (1999) found no relationship between process fairness and organizational commitment and job satisfaction when measured 4 months after organizational entry. Bauer et al. (2001) found a relationship between fairness and organizational commitment in a sample of newly hired court officers, although these data were collected cross-sectionally. Perhaps the most compelling findings in this arena were from a field study by Ambrose and Cropanzano (2003), which found that the perceived fairness of a promotion procedure was related to job satisfaction and organizational commitment. In any case, the effects of applicant reactions on organizational commitment and job satisfaction have received little systematic study. Moreover, this too seems like an outcome best examined with applicants for promotion rather than entry-level applicants.

Turnover

One study (Truxillo et al., 2002) explored the effects of providing fairness information on later turnover among those hired. Although they found that information provided to applicants did not reduce later turnover, this finding may be because of the nature of police applicant samples, as noted earlier.

Legal Challenges

As mentioned earlier, the legal ramifications of applicant reactions may be the biggest reason that many organizations are interested in applicant perceptions. However, no research has explored the relationship between selection fairness and actual legal outcomes, perhaps because of base-rate issues regarding legal action among applicants. This gap remains perhaps the weakest link in applicant reactions research.

Summary

The literature has suggested that perceptions of process fairness relate to satisfaction with the selection process, organizational attractiveness, self-efficacy, legal intentions, and test-taking motivation. Although common method variance (i.e., the use of self-report questionnaires for both fairness perceptions and outcomes) may be an issue in interpreting the true magnitude of some of these effects, some of these relationships have also been found longitudinally (e.g., Bauer et al., 1998; Truxillo et al., 2001). Unfortunately, however, the effects of applicant reactions on behavioral outcomes remain unclear because few studies have been conducted on these outcomes. In fact, although the research has suggested that applicant reactions do affect litigation intentions, actual litigation has remained unexamined despite its interest to many selection practitioners. In short, although the effects of applicant reactions on many affective outcomes seem clear, these effects sometimes may not last over time, and more longitudinal research is necessary. In addition, the effects of reactions on applicant behavior have remained so understudied that meta-analytic reviews are not available. To that end, a number of authors (e.g., Hausknecht et al., 2004; Ryan & Huth, 2008; Truxillo et al., 2004) have pointed out that the effects on many outcomes have not been thoroughly examined, that other important outcomes (e.g., perceptions of HR) have not been examined at all, and that work still needs to be done in non-entry-level (promotional) samples.

TEST-TAKER DISPOSITIONS

One area of applicant reactions research has involved applicant dispositions. These dispositions include test-taking motivation (e.g., Arvey et al., 1990), test-taking self-efficacy (e.g., Gilliland, 1993), belief in tests (e.g., Arvey et al., 1990), and stereotype threat (e.g., Steele & Aronson, 1995). As we discussed earlier, these dispositions have been conceptualized as outcomes of the testing process (e.g., Sanchez et al., 2000). However, they have also been conceptualized as antecedent variables that affect later applicant behavior and reactions (e.g., Schmit & Ryan, 1992). Much of the dispositions research has focused on their role in test validity (e.g., Schmit & Ryan, 1992) and ethnic differences in test performance (e.g., Arvey et al., 1990; Chan et al., 1997; Sanchez et al., 2000).

Test-Taking Motivation

One of the more researched applicant dispositions is test-taking motivation (e.g., Arvey et al., 1990; Chan et al., 1997; Sanchez et al., 2000; Schmit & Ryan, 1992). Arvey et al.'s (1990) Test Attitude Scale stimulated much of the initial research on test-taking motivation. For example, Schmit and Ryan (1992) found that the validity of a cognitive ability test was higher for those who scored high on motivation, but lower for those who scored low on the Test Attitude Scale. The opposite was found for the personality test. Chan et al. (1997) found that test-taking motivation was related to test performance after controlling for ethnicity and previous test performance. Schmit and Ryan (1997) found small differences between African Americans and Whites on test-taking motivation. They also found that motivation predicted applicant withdrawal but that the effects were small. Later, Sanchez et al. (2000) found that the Valence, Instrumentality, Expectancy Motivation Scale (described earlier) explained variance in police applicants' test scores beyond that measured by the Arvey et al. (1990) scale and that the Expectancy subscale was related to actual test performance. There is also evidence that test-taking motivation mediates the relationship between explanations and test performance (Meckley & LaHuis, 2007; Truxillo et al., in press).

Stereotype Threat

A topic related to the concept of test-taking motivation is stereotype threat (e.g., Steele & Aronson, 1995), which has stimulated a large amount of research in the social psychology literature. In a typical stereotype threat study, participants are given information about a test (e.g., that people with their gender or ethnic background do poorly on the test), which leads to lower test scores under these conditions. Despite some support for a stereotype threat effect among students in laboratory settings, little evidence of stereotype threat in actual operational testing environments has been found, including within the personnel selection context (e.g., Cullen, Hardison, & Sackett, 2004; Cullen, Waters, & Sackett, 2006). As one example of stereotype threat in a simulated hiring situation, Nguyen et al. (2003) found that applicants' self-reported test-taking strategies (e.g., using time remaining after completion of the test to reconsider answers, using content information from other items) reduced the Black–White gap on a math test to a greater extent for those in a stereotype threat condition than in a control condition.

Test-Taking Self-Efficacy

Although Gilliland (1993) proposed that self-perceptions, including self-esteem and self-efficacy, could be a potential outcome of fairness reactions to selection methods, they also proposed that self-perceptions might affect later applicant behavior. Specifically, Gilliland proposed that process fairness and outcome fairness would interact to affect self-perceptions, such that the effects of outcome fairness would be greatest under unfair procedures. In other words, applicant self-perceptions would be most negatively affected when the test is seen as fair and when the applicant receives a negative outcome (e.g., fail). Subsequent research has generally, but not always, supported this interaction (e.g., Bauer et al., 1998; Ployhart & Ryan, 1997). This may be because test-taking self-efficacy is a fairly stable individual difference, as demonstrated in studies that have found test-taking self-efficacy measured at different time points to be highly correlated (e.g., Truxillo et al., 2002), or because outcome favorability has such strong effects on applicant self-perceptions that procedural justice can have little effect.

Belief in Tests

A number of researchers (e.g., Arvey et al., 1990; Chan, Schmitt, Sacco, & DeShon, 1998) have examined the concept of belief in tests, typically described as the degree to which applicants believe that tests are an appropriate way to select people for jobs. The rationale behind this construct is that applicants with lower belief in tests will score lower on a cognitive test and that belief in tests may to some extent explain Black–White differences. Hausknecht et al.'s (2004) meta-analysis provided support for a weak relationship between this construct and actual test performance ($r = .10$), although it was more strongly related to other variables such as self-efficacy ($r = .25$) and job offer acceptance intentions ($r = .27$). As noted by Ryan (2001), the evidence that belief in tests is linked to actual test performance is not strong.

Test Anxiety

Test anxiety has been linked to test performance (Hembree, 1988). Hausknecht et al. (2004) found that anxiety was negatively related to test performance ($r = -.28$). More recently, researchers have begun to consider the role of test anxiety in selection contexts in greater detail. For example, Carless and Imber (2007) found that interviewer characteristics (e.g., warmth, job knowledge) affected test anxiety. Proost, Derous, Schreurs, Hagtvet, and De Witte (2008) developed a measure of anxiety that included self-referenced anxiety (e.g., "I am afraid of a lower score on this test because then I cannot live up to my own expectations") and other-referenced anxiety (e.g., "I am afraid of a lower score on this test because then [significant other] may think I did not prepare hard enough for this test"). Interestingly, they found that self-referenced anxiety related positively to test performance, whereas other-referenced anxiety related negatively to test performance. Although some of this work on test anxiety of applicants is fairly recent, such examinations of the antecedents and outcomes of test anxiety hold promise for understanding how applicants view the selection process, the employer, and themselves.

Applicant Expectations

In his justice-based model of applicant reactions, Gilliland (1993) pointed out that applicants' expectations for the selection system might affect their subsequent reactions. For example, the expectations that applicants have for how they will be treated by HR staff and what types of selection procedures will be used should affect their reactions to the test procedures. Recently, applicant reactions researchers have begun to delve into these issues. Derous, Born, and De Witte (2004) developed a measure to assess applicant expectations, with factors that map onto many of the justice rules described by Gilliland. Bell, Wiechmann, and Ryan (2006) found that justice expectations moderate the relationship between justice perceptions and applicants' affective states such that applicants are more positive when they perceive that they have been treated fairly. Taken together, these studies suggest that the issue of applicants' expectations and their role as possible antecedents to applicant reactions and behavior deserve further examination.

Relationship Among Test-Taking Predispositions

Logically, there should be connections among motivation, self-efficacy, stereotype threat, and test anxiety. For example, Hausknecht et al. (2004) found that test-taking motivation was related to self-efficacy ($r = .29$). However, there have been few empirical examinations of the interrelationships among these variables. A key research issue, therefore, is to examine where these constructs overlap and the extent to which they account for unique variance in each other. Ryan (2001) discussed a range of test-taking dispositions and reactions in the context of reducing the Black–White gap in cognitive test performance, noting that these many dispositions are dynamic and likely change before, during, and after the testing process. We echo Ryan's (2001) recommendation that the complex interrelationship among dispositions be examined in greater detail.

WHAT CAN EMPLOYERS DO TO AFFECT REACTIONS?

Ryan and Ployhart (2000) noted that outcome favorability (i.e., whether applicants pass or get a job) is a key determinant of applicant reactions, and as noted earlier, outcome favorability should be taken into account when examining applicant reactions. However, given that most organizations must make decisions about whom to hire—that is, some applicants will, by definition, have negative outcomes—what aspects of the selection procedures can employers use to enhance applicant reactions? As noted earlier, applicants prefer certain selection procedures over others. All things being equal, employers should consider the use of these preferred methods.

In addition, research has uncovered a number of aspects of the selection system that may affect reactions, such as organizational attractiveness. First, clearly job-related and face-valid procedures appear to have positive effects on applicant reactions (e.g., Bauer et al., 1998; Hausknecht et al., 2004; Truxillo et al., 2001). Second, Schleicher et al. (2006) found that applicants' perceived opportunity to perform (i.e., ability to show what they knew) affected their reactions. Unfortunately, only a few studies have actually manipulated selection system characteristics to examine their effects on applicant reactions. For example, Ployhart and Ryan (1998) found that violations of administrative consistency, either detrimental to the applicant or in the applicant's favor, negatively affected perceptions of fairness, and Rolland and Steiner (2007) found that providing applicant voice negatively affected perceived face validity.

However, given that redesigning a valid selection program or only choosing selection methods preferred by applicants may be prohibitively expensive, employers should consider other alternatives. For example, in their meta-analytic review of providing explanations to applicants (e.g., that the procedure is valid, why the procedure is used, treating applicants with respect), Truxillo et al. (in press) found that simply providing an explanation may at least modestly improve applicant reactions. Specifically, expressed in terms of a mean correlation between explanations and applicant reactions across studies, explanations were related to fairness perceptions ($r = .12$), perceptions of the organization ($r = .06$), cognitive ability test performance ($r = .09$), and test-taking motivation ($r = .21$). In addition, some applicants may value detailed feedback about their test performance (e.g., Anseel & Lievens, in press), although the effects of specific types of feedback are still unclear. We suggest that employers considering these sorts of interventions approach them cautiously and tailor any such interventions to their own situation and applicant pool.

CRITICAL RESEARCH ISSUES

Several summaries of the applicant reactions literature have been published, citing unresolved questions (e.g., Chan & Schmitt, 2004; Ryan & Huth, 2008; Ryan & Ployhart, 2000; Truxillo et al., 2004). In this section, we provide an overview of some key areas of applicant reactions research. These are areas that are seeing some current research activity, as well as those that we believe show promise or are essential to the field. This list is not exhaustive.

Providing Explanations to Applicants

As noted earlier, Truxillo et al. (in press) found meta-analytic evidence that explanations to applicants affected fairness perceptions, perceptions of the hiring organization, test-taking motivation, and actual performance on cognitive ability tests. They also found that test-taking motivation mediated the relationship between explanations and test performance. However, the Truxillo et al. (in press) study also pointed out the substantial gaps that exist in this line of research. For example, most of the research on providing explanations to applicants has examined a very broad range of explanation types, presented in a number of ways (e.g., through different media, at different times in the selection process). Researchers need to carefully specify the type of explanation used in their research (e.g., focused on interpersonal sensitivity or test validity? justifications or excuses?) and how and when it is given to applicants. In addition, there are relatively few studies examining the effects of explanations on persistence in the selection process and actual work behavior. Moreover, as noted by Truxillo et al., a consistent theoretical framework has not been applied to the research on explanations to applicants, a serious limitation to understanding the effects of explanations on applicants.

Providing Feedback to Applicants About Their Performance

Related to the concept of explanations is the type of feedback given to applicants. Given that feedback is cited as a key organizational behavior variable (e.g., Ilgen, Fisher, & Taylor, 1979) and that professional standards recommend that feedback of some sort be given to applicants (Society for Industrial and Organizational Psychology, 2003), understanding how applicants react to different types of feedback is important because feedback could affect applicant attitudes and behavior relative to the employer as well as themselves. In addition, like explanations, applicant feedback could be one of the key "levers" available to employers to affect applicant reactions. Given that outcome favorability (pass/fail, hired/not hired) is one of the determinants of reactions (e.g., Ryan & Ployhart, 2000), it is important to know the best way to notify applicants about their performance.

Gilliland (1993) cited feedback as one of the key rules that will affect applicant reactions. Recently, researchers have begun to examine the complex nature of different types of feedback and their effects on different applicant outcomes. For example, Waung and Brice (2007) demonstrated that lack of feedback may lead to negative perceptions of the organization. Schinkel, van Dierendonck, and Anderson (2004) questioned the value of providing performance feedback with a rejection letter because such feedback appeared to lead to lower core self-evaluations and affective well-being. Anseel and Lievens (in press) found that informative feedback regarding performance on individual test components related to test attitudes and subsequent test performance, and they suggested that models of feedback from other domains, such as performance appraisal, be integrated into applicant reactions research. This research on applicant feedback seems like a potentially rich vein for applicant reactions researchers. Factors such as type of selection procedure, whether the selection process is entry level or promotional, applicant investment in the job, how well feedback can be tailored to individual applicants, the balance between providing feedback and risking test security, and cultural differences regarding feedback are relevant to this issue. We also note the importance of considering how feedback might have deleterious effects on applicants and how these negative outcomes can be avoided.

Additional Theoretical Approaches

As noted earlier, much of the applicant reactions research has been guided by Gilliland's (1993) model, which is based in organizational justice theory. Although we believe that fairness has been a productive approach to studying and understanding applicant reactions, we also see the value of using additional organizational justice models to further our understanding of applicant reactions. For example, fairness theory (e.g., Shaw, Wild, & Colquitt, 2003), with its focus on how individuals use counterfactuals to understand negative outcomes, has been applied to applicant reactions research on explanations (e.g., Gilliland et al., 2001). Similarly, fairness heuristic theory (e.g., Lind, 2001), with its focus on the development of the relationship between the organization and its members, seems particularly relevant to applicant reactions. Other authors have pointed out the need to examine unfairness (e.g., Gilliland & Chan, 2001) of selection procedures. Indeed, only a few authors (e.g., Ployhart & Ryan, 1998) have examined actual rule violations.

We also see the value of moving applicant reactions theory beyond organizational justice approaches. For example, Ployhart and Harold (2004) proposed a model integrating attribution theory into applicant reactions. The few empirical applications of the attributional framework to applicant reactions have demonstrated some promise (e.g., Ployhart, Ehrhart, & Hayes, 2005; Ployhart & Ryan, 1997). For example, Ployhart and Ryan (1997) found that causal attributions were related to self-perceptions, but only when selection procedures were perceived as fair. This approach has been used to some degree to explain the use of self-serving bias in applicants (e.g., Chan & Schmitt, 2004; Schleicher et al., 2006). It seems to be underused in the empirical literature, given its value to understanding beliefs about the organization and about the self. Moreover, as the literature expands into the realm of promotion procedures, social exchange theories such as leader–member exchange (e.g., Erdogan, Liden, & Kraimer, 2006) should provide further understanding of applicant reactions.

When Reactions Are Measured in the Selection Process

Another important consideration is the dynamic nature of applicant reactions. That is, applicant reactions and dispositions appear to change throughout the selection process (e.g., before tests, after feedback) and to show differential relationships with other variables over time. One exemplar of this issue is test-taking motivation: Some research has shown test-taking motivation to be qualitatively different if it is measured before versus after the test (e.g., Chan et al., 1998). These changes in applicant perceptions over time may partly be the result of a self-serving bias (e.g., Chan & Schmitt, 2004), such that test takers reassess their reactions as a result of how they performed or believed they performed on the test. Schleicher et al. (2006) demonstrated the dynamic nature of applicant perceptions, specifically that prefeedback and postfeedback opportunity to perform have a different relationship with justice perceptions for those receiving negative feedback. However, as of this writing, researchers have not examined changes in reactions and dispositions at more than two time points, an omission that likely hampers understanding the dynamics of applicant reactions. In summary, studying the dynamic nature of applicant reactions and dispositions seems key to understanding the selection process from the applicant's perspective.

Interrelationship Among Recruitment, Selection, and Socialization Processes

Recruitment and other selection functions play an essential role in finding the right employee and having good organization fit and can help to facilitate the socialization process (see Vol. 3, chap. 2, this handbook). Recruiting events can provide new employees with an important opportunity for information before formally starting a job. Selection-related activities can provide information about the job and organization and help newcomers form realistic expectations (Rynes, 1991). Given that it is essential for the potential newcomer to form realistic job expectations, organizations should relay realistic job previews so that the applicant does not have inflated expectations and, therefore, can socialize more rapidly and effectively, resulting in a more realistic and compatible organization fit.

Reaction to High-Tech Assessment

Some earlier concerns about how applicants would react to high-tech assessment have all but disappeared as online screening and other such technologically advanced alternatives have become commonplace. One key issue is that of timing. Individuals who apply for jobs and do not hear back tend to perceive no news as bad news (Rynes, Bretz, & Gerhart, 1991). An advantage of high-tech selection systems, however, is the potential for quick feedback to applicants (although it is unclear how often such feedback is provided in practice). Another major issue for high-tech assessments has been privacy concerns (Bauer et al., 2004, 2006; Harris, Van Hoye, & Lievens, 2003; Wiechmann & Ryan, 2003). Perhaps the greatest opportunity for future research in the area of high-tech assessments lies in understanding how to best manage privacy concerns and procedural justice using high-tech methods, and how this may differ across countries and cultures. For example, applicants from countries with stricter privacy laws may react more negatively to online selection systems requiring the disclosure of private information.

Individual Differences

One issue that has begun to be explored is that of individual differences in applicant reactions. In other words, applicant reactions may to an extent be predetermined; for example, some individuals may be more tolerant of unfairness than others. These inherent differences would suggest that there may be little that employers can do to improve reactions (e.g., Truxillo et al., 2006), but it could also mean that practitioners could consider the nature of their applicant pools when choosing selection procedures (e.g., Ryan & Huth, 2008). Although Hausknecht et al. (2004) found only weak relationships between personality and reactions, this was based on relatively few studies, and subsequent research has suggested such a relationship might exist. For example, Viswesvaran and Ones (2004) found weak relationships between some Big Five personality factors and the importance of certain selection system characteristics. For instance, people high on extraversion and emotional stability, which together make up optimism, placed importance on the process used in developing the selection system. Truxillo et al. (2006) found that neuroticism and agreeableness related to perceptions of the self and the organization and that personality accounted for variance in these outcomes after accounting for perceived fairness. In addition, we believe that research should examine other individual differences such as applicant privacy concerns (e.g., Bauer et al., 2006) and equity sensitivity (cf. Sauley & Bedeian, 2000). Research might also examine when individual differences matter, for example, in different hiring contexts, when receiving different outcomes, or in relation to different selection procedures.

Ethnicity and Gender

One source of interest in applicant reactions is studying their relationship with ethnicity and gender and whether this relationship could be used to explain test performance. In general, the results have been disappointing, with applicant perceptions such as fairness and motivation explaining relatively little in subgroup differences in test performance (e.g., Chan, 1997). Overall, the Hausknecht et al. (2004) meta-analysis found near-zero relationships between gender and ethnicity and applicant reactions. However, some recent studies have continued to examine this issue in hopes of more conclusive results. In terms of ethnicity, Viswesvaran and Ones (2004) found evidence that different ethnic groups placed differential value on different aspects of the selection system (e.g., Whites place greater importance than Asians on whether the selection process was developed by professionals; Whites place greater importance than Hispanics on whether the selection process allowed an opportunity to review scoring). However, Van Hooft, Born, Taris, and Van der Flier (2006) found no differences in reactions of Dutch majority and minority groups.

In terms of gender, although Viswesvaran and Ones (2004) found few differences between men and women on the importance placed on different selection system characteristics, Bernerth (2005) found that gender moderated the relationship between selection decision (pass–fail) and justice perceptions, such that the relationship was stronger for women than for men. The researchers explained the findings in terms of "justice expectations" of men and women (cf. Bell et al., 2006). Van Hooft et al. (2006) used the theory of reasoned action (Fishbein & Ajzen, 1975) to explain that gender differentially moderated the relationship among different perceptions. Taken together, because many of the findings regarding gender have been equivocal at best, future research on gender differences in applicant reactions should enlist theoretical models that could explain gender differences.

Reactions to Promotions

One issue that is particularly ripe for study is reactions to promotional procedures. Most of the applicant reactions literature has focused on external applicants' perceptions. However, internal applicants could arguably have a far greater impact on the organization: Rather than going away, internal applicants continue as organizational members. Moreover, examining how current employees view promotion procedures opens up a large number of outcomes such as morale, organizational commitment, organizational citizenship behaviors, turnover, and occupational health outcomes. Additionally, the inherent investment internal applicants have in the organization may lead to stronger reactions and greater impact on the organization.

The little empirical work in this area to date has shown promise. Truxillo and Bauer (1999) found that police applicants for promotion had stronger and more polarized reactions to test score banding (i.e., the grouping of test scores into ranges within which scores are considered statistically equal) than external applicant samples. Similarly, Ambrose and Cropanzano (2003) found that the reactions of candidates for promotion in academic jobs had longitudinal effects on job attitudes. Schaubroeck and Lam (2004) found that envy regarding coworkers was related to outcome fairness and even work performance, although this study did not examine reactions to selection procedures per se and focused primarily on envy. McCarthy, Hrabluik, and Jelley (in press) recently found that test motivation was related to test performance and that justice perceptions were related to recommendation intentions. Despite calls for additional research on reactions to promotional procedures (Ford, Truxillo, & Bauer, in press; Hausknecht et al., 2004), reactions to promotions still remains one area of applicant reactions research with some of the greatest research potential. Ford et al. (in press) recently illustrated the potential importance of job candidates' reactions to promotions and described the contextual issues (e.g., comparison with others in the job) that may drive such reactions, as well as a range of important affective and behavioral outcomes (e.g., stress). We also believe that social cues from others in the work environment (cf. Ambrose, Harland, & Kulik, 1991) could play a major role in reactions to promotions.

Faking and Response Distortion

One area that has received scant attention is whether the perceived or actual fakeability of tests will affect applicant reactions. The research has suggested that the practical effects of applicant faking on noncognitive tests in actual selection settings are unclear (Sackett & Lievens, 2008). Intuitively, the issue of faking seems to be closely linked with applicant reactions. For example, is there a general tendency to fake? How should applicants feel about fakeable tests? On the one hand, they may feel that fakeable or transparent tests increase their amount of control, but on the other hand, a test that is faked could lead to an unfair outcome. (Gilliland [1993] offered a detailed discussion of this issue.) However, how faking or response distortion relates to applicant reactions and predispositions has not been directly examined.

Recently, Marcus (in press) pointed out that considering the issue as one of faking or response distortion is employer focused and that an applicant-focused approach to this issue might lead to a greater understanding of the processes involved. Specifically, Marcus recommended that the issue be reframed as one in which the applicant is an actor in the process of self-presentation and in which self-presentation may be legitimate. We suggest that such applicant-focused approaches to faking may lead to greater understanding of the faking process and its operational effects in selection settings. Such links may be made with dispositions such as test-taking motivation and self-efficacy (cf. Arvey et al., 1990; Sanchez et al., 2000).

Applicant Reactions Across Jobs

Ryan and Ployhart (2000) noted that job type may moderate the effects of applicant reactions. In other words, applicant reactions may relate to important outcomes such as job acceptance for certain types of jobs than for others. For example, Truxillo et al. (2002) suggested that police applicants may score fairly high on organizational attractiveness because they really want to be police officers; in this case, they will endure whatever selection procedures might be involved. We believe that job type is an important contextual issue deserving of study.

Cross-Cultural Applicant Reactions Research

With the growth of multinational organizations, interest in how applicant perceptions may vary across countries and cultures has grown. For example, a recent conference session was designed as a research incubator to foster collaboration on projects across multiple countries on applicant reactions called *ARCOS* (applicant reactions cross-cultural studies; Bauer, 2008). As noted earlier, a number of studies have examined reactions to selection procedures across a number of countries and found that applicants generally prefer certain selection procedures (e.g., interviews) over others (e.g., graphology) across cultures (e.g., Anderson & Witvliet, 2008; Steiner & Gilliland, 1996). In perhaps the most ambitious cross-cultural study of applicant reactions to date, Ryan et al. (2008) examined applicant reactions to eight selection tools across 21 countries, finding greater convergence than divergence in perceptions of the tools across countries. Interestingly, a country's gross domestic product did appear to affect fairness perceptions, with applicants from countries with fewer economic opportunities reacting more positively to tests. Harris et al. (2003) also examined cross-cultural differences between the United States and Belgium regarding perceptions of online screening and found only a few differences between the two samples regarding privacy concerns, although these concerns were a bit stronger for U.S. participants.

In sum, research has established that applicants across a number of different cultures hold similar perceptions of a range of selection procedures. At the same time, research has begun to examine the factors (e.g., country gross domestic product, privacy issues) that may explain cross-cultural differences. Research that uncovers the factors that explain differences in applicants across countries and cultures will prove useful to implementing multinational selection systems. For example, a recent issue of *Industrial and Organizational Psychology* (e.g., Myors et al., 2008) provided a forum for discussing differences in the legal context across countries. A deeper examination of differences in the legal context across countries may yield differences in how applicants react to selection system characteristics such as invasiveness. More important, differences in the legal context may cause applicants to have very different behavioral responses to unfair treatment, such as taking legal action.

CONCLUSION

The study of applicant reactions and dispositions over the past 2 decades has moved well beyond concepts such as face validity. As a result, we now have a more complex understanding of the range of selection system features that may influence applicant reactions. We also know that these reactions affect a number of affective outcomes such as organizational attractiveness and self-perceptions. For practice, the research suggests that employers can take a number of steps to improve applicant reactions, such as using selection procedures preferred by applicants and providing explanations for selection procedure characteristics.

However, like others who have recently reviewed the literature on applicant reactions (Ryan & Huth, 2008; Sackett & Lievens, 2008), we observe that applicant reactions research has not yet lived up to its promise by showing the relationship between reactions and important behavioral outcomes such as litigation. This does not mean that applicant reactions to selection procedures do not affect these outcomes. Rather, this reflects that longitudinal studies with behavioral outcomes have not been sufficiently studied; that, in other words, applicant reactions researchers have focused on the "low-hanging fruit" in choosing outcomes for study. It is now time for applicant reactions researchers to reach higher.

Now that this field has begun to mature, the gaps in the literature have come into greater focus. At the same time, researchers have begun to identify the areas of great promise in the field. We have identified a number of these areas of promise in this chapter, and we hope that understanding of applicant reactions and dispositions will mature and deepen as a result.

References

Ambrose, M. L., & Cropanzano, R. (2003). A longitudinal analysis of organizational fairness: An examination of reactions to tenure and promotion decisions. *Journal of Applied Psychology, 88,* 266–275.

Ambrose, M. L., Harland, L. K., & Kulik, C. T. (1991). Influence of social comparisons on perceptions of organizational fairness. *Journal of Applied Psychology, 76,* 239–246.

Anderson, N. (2003). Applicant and recruiter reactions to new technology in selection: A review and agenda for future research. *International Journal of Selection and Assessment, 11,* 121–136.

Anderson, N., & Witvliet, C. (2008). Fairness reactions to personnel selection methods: An international comparison between the Netherlands, the United States, France, Spain, Portugal, and Singapore. *International Journal of Selection and Assessment, 16,* 1–13.

Anseel, F., & Lievens, F. (in press). The mediating role of feedback acceptance in the relationship between feedback and attitudinal and performance outcomes. *International Journal of Selection and Assessment.*

Arvey, R. D., & Sackett, P. R. (1993). Fairness in selection: Current developments and perspectives. In N. Schmitt & W. C. Borman (Eds.), *Personnel selection in organizations* (pp. 171–202). San Francisco: Jossey-Bass.

Arvey, R. D., Strickland, W., Drauden, G., & Martin, C. (1990). Motivational components of test-taking. *Personnel Psychology, 43,* 695–716.

Bauer, T. N. (2008, April). *ARCOS research incubator with hosts N. Anderson (Netherlands), T. N. Bauer (USA), C. Konig (Switzerland), & D. M. Truxillo (USA).* Interactive Session at the 23rd annual meeting of the Society for Industrial/Organizational Psychology, San Francisco.

Bauer, T. N., Maertz, C. P., Dolen, M. R., & Campion, M. A. (1998). Longitudinal assessment or applicant reactions to employment testing and test outcome feedback. *Journal of Applied Psychology, 83,* 892–903.

Bauer, T. N., Truxillo, D. M., Campion, M., Paronto, M., & Weekley, J. (2004). Fairness reactions: Does selection screening method matter? *International Journal of Selection and Assessment, 12,* 135–148.

Bauer, T. N., Truxillo, D. M., & Paronto, M. E. (2003). The measurement of applicant reactions to selection. In J. Thomas (Ed.), *Comprehensive handbook of psychological assessment. Vol. 4: Industrial/organizational psychology* (pp. 482–506). New York: Wiley.

Bauer, T. N., Truxillo, D. M., Sanchez, R. J., Craig, J., Ferrara, P., & Campion, M. A. (2001). Applicant reactions to selection: Development of the Selection Procedural Justice Scale (SPJS). *Personnel Psychology, 54,* 387–419.

Bauer, T. N., Truxillo, D. M., Tucker, J. S., Weathers, V., Bertolino, M., Erdogan, B., & Campion, M. A. (2006). Selection in the information age: The role of personal information privacy concerns and computer use in understanding applicant reactions. *Journal of Management, 32,* 601–621.

Bell, B. S., Wiechmann, D., & Ryan, A. M. (2006). Consequences of organizational justice expectations in a selection system. *Journal of Applied Psychology, 91,* 455–466.

Bernerth, J. B. (2005). Perceptions of justice in employment selection decisions: The role of applicant gender. *International Journal of Selection and Assessment, 13,* 206–212.

Bertolino, M., & Steiner, D. D. (2007). Fairness reactions to selection methods: An Italian study. *International Journal of Selection and Assessment, 15,* 197–205.

Carless, S. A., & Imber, A. (2007). The influence of perceived interviewer and job and organizational characteristics on applicant attraction and job choice intentions: The role of applicant anxiety. *International Journal of Selection and Assessment, 15,* 359–371.

Cascio, W. F., & Phillips, N. F. (1979). Performance testing: A rose among thorns? *Personnel Psychology, 32,* 751–766.

Chan, D. (1997). Racial subgroup differences in predictive validity perceptions on personality and cognitive ability tests. *Journal of Applied Psychology, 82,* 311–320.

Chan, D., & Schmitt, N. (1997). Video-based versus paper-and-pencil method of assessment in situational judgment tests: Subgroup differences in test performance and face validity perceptions. *Journal of Applied Psychology, 82,* 143–159.

Chan, D., & Schmitt, N. (2004). An agenda for future research on applicant reactions to selection procedures: A construct-oriented approach. *International Journal of Selection and Assessment, 12,* 9–23.

Chan, D., Schmitt, N., DeShon, R. P., Clause, C. S., & Delbridge, K. (1997). Reactions to cognitive ability tests: The relationships between race, test performance, face validity perceptions, and test-taking motivation. *Journal of Applied Psychology, 82,* 300–310.

Chan, D., Schmitt, N., Sacco, J. M., & DeShon, R. P. (1998). Understanding pretest and posttest reactions to cognitive ability and personality tests. *Journal of Applied Psychology, 83,* 471–485.

Cullen, M. J., Hardison, C. M., & Sackett, P. R. (2004). Using SAT-grade and ability job-performance relationships to test predictions derived from stereotype threat theory. *Journal of Applied Psychology, 89,* 220–230

Cullen, M. J., Waters, S. D., & Sackett, P R. (2006). Testing stereotype threat theory predictions for math-identified and nonmath-identified students by gender. *Human Performance, 19,* 421–440.

Cunningham-Snell, N., Anderson, N., & Fletcher, C. (1999, June). *A longitudinal analysis of procedural justice at an assessment centre: The immediate, intermediate and long-term impact.* Paper presented at the International Round Table: Innovations in Organizational Justice, Nice, France.

Derous, E., Born, M. P., & De Witte, K. (2004). How applicants want and expect to be treated: Applicants' selection treatment beliefs and the development of the social process questionnaire on selection. *International Journal of Selection and Assessment, 12,* 99–117.

Erdogan, B., Liden, R. C., & Kraimer, M. L. (2006). Justice and leader–member exchange: The moderating role of organizational culture. *Academy of Management Journal, 49,* 395–406.

Fishbein, M., & Ajzen, I. (1975). *Belief, attitude, intention, and behavior: An introduction to theory and research.* Reading, MA: Addison-Wesley.

Ford, D. K., Truxillo, D. M., & Bauer, T. N. (in press). Shifting the focus to the promotional context: A new path for applicant reactions research. *International Journal of Selection and Assessment.*

Gilliland, S. W. (1993). The perceived fairness of selection systems: An organizational justice perspective. *Academy of Management Review, 18,* 694–734.

Gilliland, S. W. (1994). Effects of procedural and distributive justice on reactions to a selection system. *Journal of Applied Psychology, 79,* 691–701.

Gilliland, S. W., & Chan, D. (2001). Justice in organizations: Theory, methods, and applications. In N. Anderson, D. S. Ones, H. K. Sinangil, & C. Viswesvaran (Eds.), *International handbook of work and organizational psychology* (pp. 143–165). Thousand Oaks, CA: Sage.

Gilliland, S. W., Groth, M., Baker, R. C., IV, Dew, A. F., Polly, L. M., & Langdon, J. C. (2001). Improving applicants' reactions to rejection letters: An application of fairness theory. *Personnel Psychology, 54,* 669–703.

Goldman, B. M. (2001). Toward an understanding of employment discrimination claiming: An integration of organizational justice and social information processing theories. *Personnel Psychology, 54,* 361–386.

Greenberg, J. (1993). The social side of fairness: Interpersonal and informational classes of organizational justice. In R. Cropanzano (Ed.), *Justice in the workplace* (pp. 79–106). Hillsdale, NJ: Erlbaum.

Harris, M. M., Van Hoye, G., & Lievens, F. (2003). Privacy attitudes toward Internet-based selection systems: A cross-cultural comparison. *International Journal of Selection and Assessment, 11,* 230–236.

Hausknecht, J. P, Day, D. V., & Thomas, S. C. (2004). Applicant reactions to selection procedures: An updated model and meta-analysis. *Personnel Psychology, 57,* 639–683.

Hembree, R. (1988). Correlates, causes, effects, and treatment of test anxiety. *Review of Educational Research, 58,* 47–77.

Horvath, M., Ryan, A. M., & Stierwalt, S. L. (2000). The influence of explanation for selection test use, outcome favorability, and self-efficacy on test-taker perceptions. *Organizational Behavior and Human Decision Processes, 83,* 310–330.

Ilgen, D. R., Fisher, C. D., & Taylor, M. S. (1979). Consequences of individual feedback on behavior in organizations. *Journal of Applied Psychology, 64,* 349–371.

Lind, E. A. (2001). Fairness heuristic theory: Justice judgments as pivotal cognitions in organizational relations. In J. Greenberg & R. Cropanzano (Eds.), *Advances in organizational justice* (pp. 56–88). Stanford, CA: Stanford University Press.

Lind, E. A., & Tyler, T. R. (1988). *The social psychology of procedural justice.* New York: Plenum Press.

Macan, T. H., Avedon, M. J., Paese, M., & Smith, D. E. (1994). The effects of applicants' reactions to cognitive ability tests and an assessment center. *Personnel Psychology, 47,* 715–738.

Marcus, B. (in press). "Faking" from the applicants' perspective: A theory of self-presentation in personnel selection settings. *International Journal of Selection and Assessment.*

McCarthy, J. M., Hrabluik, C., & Jelley, R. B. (in press). Progression through the ranks: Assessing employee reactions to high stakes employment testing. *Personnel Psychology.*

Meckley, K., & LaHuis, D. (2007, April). *Effects of explanations on applicants' test-taking motivation and test performance.* Paper presented at the 21st annual conference of the Society for Industrial and Organizational Psychology, New York, NY.

Morgeson, F. P., & Ryan, A. M. (in press). Reacting to applicant perspectives research: What's next? *International Journal of Selection and Assessment.*

Moscoso, S., & Salgado, J. S. F. (2004). Fairness reactions to personnel selection techniques in Spain and Portugal. *International Journal of Selection and Assessment, 12,* 187–196.

Myors, B., Lievens, F., Schollaert, E., Van Hoye, G., Cronshaw, S. F., Mladinic, A., et al. (2008). National perspectives on the legal environment for selection. *Industrial and Organizational Psychology: Perspectives on Science and Practice, 1,* 206–246.

Nguyen, H. D., O'Neal, A., & Ryan, A. M. (2003). Relating test-taking attitudes and skills and stereotype threat effects to the racial gap in cognitive ability test performance. *Human Performance, 16,* 261–293.

Nikolaou, I., & Judge, T. A. (2007). Fairness reactions to personnel selection techniques in Greece: The role of core self-evaluations. *International Journal of Selection and Assessment, 15,* 206–219.

Ostberg, D. E., Truxillo, D. M., & Bauer, T. N. (2001). Effects of pre-test information on applicants' perceptions of selection fairness. In R. E. Ployhart & D. M. Truxillo (Chairs), *Presenting selection information to applicants: Theoretical and practical implications.* Symposium conducted at the 16th annual meeting of the Society for Industrial and Organizational Psychology, San Diego, CA.

Phillips, J. M., & Gully, S. M. (2002). Fairness reactions to personnel selection techniques in Singapore and the United States. *International Journal of Human Resource Management, 13,* 1186–1205.

Ployhart, R. E., Ehrhart, K. H., & Hayes, S. C. (2005). Using attributions to understand the effects of explanations on applicant reactions: Are reactions consistent with the covariation principle? *Journal of Applied Social Psychology, 35,* 259–296.

Ployhart, R. E., & Harold, C. M. (2004). The applicant attribution-reaction theory (AART): An integrative theory of applicant attributional processing. *International Journal of Selection and Assessment, 12,* 84–98.

Ployhart, R. E., & Ryan, A. M. (1997). Toward an explanation of applicant reactions: An examination of organizational justice and attribution frameworks. *Organizational Behavior and Human Decision Processes, 72,* 308–335.

Ployhart, R. E., & Ryan, A. M. (1998). Applicants' reactions to the fairness of selection procedures: The effects of positive rule violations and time of measurement. *Journal of Applied Psychology, 83,* 3–16.

Ployhart, R. E., Ryan, A. M., & Bennett, M. (1999). Explanations for selection decisions: Applicants' reactions to informational and sensitivity features of explanations. *Journal of Applied Psychology, 84,* 87–106.

Proost, K., Derous, E., Schreurs, B., Hagtvet, K. A., & De Witte, K. (2008). Selection test anxiety: Investigating applicants' self- vs. other-referenced anxiety in a real selection setting. *International Journal of Selection and Assessment, 16,* 14–26.

Rolland, F., & Steiner, D. D. (2007). Test-taker reactions to the selection process: Effects of outcome favorability, explanations, and voice on fairness perceptions. *Journal of Applied Social Psychology, 37,* 2800–2826.

Ryan, A. M. (2001). Explaining the Black–White test score gap: The role of test perceptions. *Human Performance, 14,* 45–75.

Ryan, A. M., Boyce, A. S., Ghumman, S., Jundt, D., Schmidt, G., & Gibby, R. (2008). Going global: Cultural values and perceptions of selection procedures. *Applied Psychology: An International Review.* Advance online publication. doi: 10.1111/j.1464-0597.2008.00363.x

Ryan, A. M., & Huth, M. (2008). Not much more than platitudes? A critical look at the utility of applicant reactions research. *Human Resource Management Review, 18,* 119–132. doi: 10.1016/j.hrmr.2008.07.004

Ryan, A. M., & Ployhart, R. E. (2000). Applicants' perceptions of selection procedures and decisions: A critical review and agenda for the future. *Journal of Management, 26,* 565–606.

Ryan, A. M., Sacco, J. M., McFarland, L. A., & Kriska, S. D. (2000). Applicant self-selection: Correlates of withdrawal from a multiple hurdle process. *Journal of Applied Psychology, 85,* 163–179.

Rynes, S. L. (1991). Recruitment, job choice, and post-hire consequences: A call for new research. In M. D. Dunnette (Ed.), *Handbook of industrial and organizational psychology* (pp. 399–444). Palo Alto, CA: Consulting Psychologists Press.

Rynes, S. L. (1993). Who's selecting whom? Effects of selection practices on applicant attitudes and behavior. In N. Schmitt & W. C. Borman (Eds.), *Personnel selection in organizations* (pp. 240–274). San Francisco: Jossey-Bass.

Rynes, S. L., Bretz, R. D., & Gerhart, B. (1991). The importance of recruitment in job choice: A different way of looking. *Personnel Psychology, 44,* 487–521.

Rynes, S. L., & Connerley, M. L. (1993). Applicant reactions to alternative selection procedures. *Journal of Business and Psychology, 7,* 261–277.

Sackett, P. R., & Lievens, F. (2008). Personnel selection. *Annual Review of Psychology, 59,* 419–450.

Salgado, J., Anderson, N., & Hulsheger, U. R. (in press). Personnel selection in Europe: Psychotechnics and the forgotten history of modern scientific personnel selection. In J. L. Farr & N. T. Tippins (Eds.), *Handbook of personnel selection.* Mahwah, NJ: Erlbaum.

Sanchez, R. J., Truxillo, D. M., & Bauer, T. N. (2000). Development and examination of an expectancy-based measure of test-taking motivation. *Journal of Applied Psychology, 85,* 739–750.

Sauley, K. S., & Bedeian, A. G. (2000). Equity sensitivity: Construction of a measure and examination of its psychometric properties. *Journal of Management, 26,* 885–910.

Schaubroeck, J., & Lam, S. S. K. (2004). Comparing lots before and after: Promotion rejectees' invidious reactions to promotees. *Organizational Behavior and Human Decision Processes, 94,* 33–47.

Schinkel, S., van Dierendonck, D., & Anderson, N. (2004). The impact of selection encounters on applicants: An experimental study into feedback effects after a negative selection decision. *International Journal of Selection and Assessment, 12,* 197–205.

Schleicher, D. J., Venkataramani, V., Morgeson, F. P., & Campion, M A. (2006). So you didn't get the job . . . *now* what do you think? Examining opportunity-to-perform fairness perceptions. *Personnel Psychology, 59,* 559–590.

Schmidt, F. L., Greenthal, A. L., Hunter, J. E., Berner, J. G., & Seaton, F. W. (1977). Job sample vs. paper-and-pencil trades and technical tests: Adverse impact and examinee attitudes. *Personnel Psychology, 30,* 187–197.

Schmit, M. J., & Ryan, A. M. (1992). Test-taking dispositions: A missing link? *Journal of Applied Psychology, 77,* 629–637.

Schmit, M. J., & Ryan, A. M. (1997). Applicant withdrawal: The role of test-taking attitudes and racial differences. *Personnel Psychology, 50,* 855–876.

Schuler, H. (1993). Social validity of selection situations: A concept and some empirical results. In H. Schuler, J. L. Farr, & M. Smith (Eds.), *Personnel selection and assessment: Individual and organizational perspectives* (pp. 11–26). Hillsdale, NJ: Erlbaum.

Seymour, R. T. (1988). Why plaintiffs' counsel challenge tests, and how they can successfully challenge the theory of "validity generalization." *Journal of Vocational Behavior, 33,* 331–364.

Shaw, J. C., Wild, E., & Colquitt, J. A. (2003). To justify or excuse?: A meta-analytic review of the effects of explanations. *Journal of Applied Psychology, 88,* 444–458.

Smither, J. W., Reilly, R. R., Millsap, R. E., Pearlman, K., & Stoffey, R. W. (1993). Applicant reactions to selection procedures. *Personnel Psychology, 46,* 49–77.

Society for Industrial and Organizational Psychology. (2003). *Principles for the validation use of personnel selection procedures.* Bowling Green, OH: Author.

Steele, C. M., & Aronson, J. (1995). Stereotype threat and the intellectual test performance of African Americans. *Journal of Personality and Social Psychology, 69,* 797–811.

Steiner, D. D., & Gilliland, S. W. (1996). Fairness reactions to personnel selection techniques in France and the United States. *Journal of Applied Psychology, 81,* 134–141.

Thorsteinson, T. J., & Ryan, A. M. (1997). The effect of selection ratio on perceptions of the fairness of a selection test battery. *International Journal of Selection and Assessment, 5,* 159–168.

Truxillo, D. M., & Bauer, T. N. (1999). Applicant reactions to test score banding in entry-level and promotional contexts. *Journal of Applied Psychology, 84,* 322–339.

Truxillo, D. M., Bauer, T. N., Campion, M. A., & Paronto, M. E. (2002). Selection fairness information and applicant reactions: A longitudinal field study. *Journal of Applied Psychology, 87,* 1020–1031.

Truxillo, D. M., Bauer, T. N., Campion, M. A., & Paronto, M. E. (2006). A field study of the role of big five personality in applicant perceptions of selection fairness, self, and the hiring organization. *International Journal of Selection and Assessment, 14,* 269–277.

Truxillo, D. M., Bauer, T. N., & Sanchez, R. J. (2001). Multiple dimensions of procedural justice: Longitudinal effects on selection system fairness and test-taking self-efficacy. *International Journal of Selection and Assessment, 9,* 336–349.

Truxillo, D. M., Bodner, T., Bertolino, M., Bauer, T. N., & Yonce, C. A. (in press). Effects of explanations on applicant reactions: A meta-analytic review. *International Journal of Selection and Assessment.*

Truxillo, D. M., Steiner, D. D., & Gilliland, S. W. (2004). The importance of organizational justice in personnel selection: Defining when selection fairness really matters. *International Journal of Selection and Assessment, 12,* 39–53.

Van Hooft, E. A. J., Born, M. P., Taris, T. W., & Van der Flier, H. (2006). Ethnic and gender differences in applicants' decision-making processes: An application of the theory of reasoned action. *International Journal of Selection and Assessment, 14,* 156–166.

Van Vianen, A. E. M., Taris, R., Scholten, E., & Schinkel, S. (2004). Perceived fairness in personnel selection: Determinants and outcomes in different stages of the assessment procedure. *International Journal of Selection and Assessment, 12,* 149–159.

Viswesvaran, C., & Ones, D. S. (2004). Importance of perceived personnel selection system fairness determinants: Relations with demographic, personality, and job characteristics. *International Journal of Selection and Assessment, 12,* 172–186.

Waung, M., & Brice, T. (2007). The effects of acceptance/rejection status, status notification, and organizational obligation fulfillment on applicant intentions. *Journal of Applied Social Psychology, 37,* 2048–2071.

Wiechmann, D., & Ryan, A. M. (2003). Reactions to computerized testing in selection contexts. *International Journal of Selection and Assessment, 11,* 215–219.

Chapter 13

VALIDATION SUPPORT FOR SELECTION PROCEDURES

Neal Schmitt and Ruchi Sinha

Validity is defined as the degree to which the inferences researchers derive about job performance from some predictor measure are accurate. The term *predictor measure* in the selection context includes the usual paper-and-pencil test but also a wide variety of other methods of measurement, such as interviews, simulations, biographical data, situational judgment inventories, and letters of reference. (See also chaps. 4–8, this volume.) The methods by which researchers support these inferences are referred to as *validation designs* or *validation studies*. Validation is important for a number of reasons. First, from a scientific perspective validation can provide information as to what individual difference constructs underlie behavior; in industrial and organizational psychology, the behavior of interest is work behavior. From a practical perspective, organizations seek validation evidence to confirm that the procedures they use result in the selection of a competent and motivated workforce. In some Western societies, validation data are equally as important in the social and legal context in which organizations seek to thrive and prosper. These basic statements about validity have been repeated in many previous works (Guion, 1998; Landy, 1986; McPhail, 2007; Ployhart, Schneider, & Schmitt, 2006), and we assume they are widely accepted.

In this chapter, we begin with a discussion of the various types of evidence generally thought to support statements about the validity of measures. We summarize the database available and critique it. Then we provide a brief description of what we consider a model study and describe the research we believe would provide a stronger scientific basis on which to make statements about validity. It is important to note at the outset that we do not provide prescriptive or practical advice on how to conduct validation research. Such advice is provided in a number of good textbooks on the topic (e.g., Cascio & Aguinis, 2005; Guion, 1998; Ployhart et al., 2006).

More detailed expositions on validity are contained in these sources and also in professional guidelines (American Educational Research Association, American Psychological Association, & National Council on Measurement in Education, 1999; Society for Industrial and Organizational Psychology, 2003). Early versions of these guidelines (referred to in this chapter as the *Principles* and *Standards,* respectively) identified three aspects of validity or types of validation evidence. *Content validity* was generally based on a systematic sampling of content and tasks relevant to the performance of a particular domain of job tasks. This sampling was often supported by a variety of judgments made by subject matter experts that attest to the relevance and importance of test tasks and their linkage to targeted job performance. *Criterion-related validity* was evaluated by correlating scores on a selection device with current or future job performance measures. As its name implies, the relevance and appropriate measurement of the criterion in criterion-related studies were at least as important as predictor measurement. *Construct validity* was defined as the relationship between the underlying theoretical predictor and criterion variables. As such, there was concern with the degree to which researchers could defend the presumed theoretical meaning of the measured constructs, the degree to which they faithfully represented what they were called (e.g., empathy, spatial ability); that those labels were consistent with similar labels used in the scientific literature; and that the measures were not a function of the method of measurement or other extraneous influences.

This tripartite approach to validity has been replaced by the view that validity always concerns relationships between constructs and that there are various ways in which evidence can be marshaled to support construct validity. The most recent edition of the *Standards* (American Educational Research Association et al., 1999) identified eight different types of construct evidence. These include gathering information on what have traditionally been referred to as *content validity* (1) and *criterion-related validity* (2). In addition, the *Standards* suggested that validity can be assessed by investigating the processes engaged in when an examinee responds to a test item (3). For example, examination of eye movement or physiological activity while taking a test may reveal information consistent or inconsistent with the hypothesized attribution about the examinee's standing on a construct. These indices have been used to assess integrity of responses and the attention required to give an answer. Correlational and factor analyses (4) and item analyses (5) can be used to determine the nature of the dimensions underlying test performance, that is, the test's internal structure. Evidence based on relationships with other variables (6), including studies of convergent and discriminant validity (D. T. Campbell & Fiske, 1959) yields important information. These latter types of information would all have been included in earlier discussions of construct validity. Validity generalization (7) usually involves a summary of predictor–criterion relationships across multiple settings and can be considered a form of construct validity in that differences in situations, sample sizes, and artifacts are removed from the observed relationship to provide estimates of underlying predictor–criterion construct relationships. Finally, the *Standards* also viewed evidence about the consequences of decisions based on tests (8; e.g., differential rates of selection of demographic subgroups) as validity evidence.

A frequent application of test scores in industrial and organizational psychology is in personnel selection. The type of information most frequently used by personnel selection specialists to defend the use of their procedures (which include interviews, simulations, physical ability tests, etc.) is reflected in what have traditionally been called *content validity* and *criterion-related validity*.

CONTENT VALIDITY

As mentioned briefly in the preceding section, content validation involves a demonstration that test items are a representative sample of the behaviors to be exhibited in some performance domain. Content validation depends heavily on a job analysis that details the tasks performed on a job; the knowledge, skills, abilities, and other characteristics (KSAOs) required to do those tasks; and how those tasks (or very similar tasks) and KSAOs are reflected in the tests used to make employment decisions.

The content of a measure should be of concern whether or not other types of validity evidence are collected, but if a researcher is to rely only on careful specification of the content of a selection instrument to defend its use in making employment decisions, then several issues are paramount: (a) The job performance domain must be carefully specified, (b) the objectives of the test user must be clearly formulated, and (c) the method of sampling item content from the performance domain must be adequate.

There are no quantitative estimates of content validity outside of the Lawshe (1975) content validity ratio, which is a summary of the items in a test or set of KSAO statements judged to be relevant to the performance of some job task or tasks. Certainly one would hope that a very large majority of subject matter experts would agree that statements of job duties encompass all those that were relevant and important in some job. Most experts would also agree that KSAOs judged to be relevant to a majority of these performance domains should be represented in some way in the set of measures used to make selection decisions. Probably most important would be documentation and justification as to how decisions about the test content were made.

Obviously, a careful and reliable job analysis is important. (See also chap. 1, this volume.) The KSAOs or the tasks required for successful job performance and their relative necessity for successful performance must be identified. The content areas around which the selection measures are built must be derived from this job analysis. The format of written test items or the nature of test exercises must correspond as closely as possible to actual performance required on the job. An abstract paper-and-pencil personality test measuring empathy, for example, would ordinarily not be defensible as a sample of the work behavior required of a social worker, nor would the format of the testing instrument be consistent with the behavior required of social workers. The content of tests, based on careful job analyses, is also usually evaluated by subject matter experts who are asked to examine and often to rate each item on the degree to which it reflects some important job-related KSAO or task. The role of subject matter expert judgment in the construction of content valid measures is central. Goldstein, Zedeck, and Schneider (1993) provided a summary of the manner in which these linkages can be established using expert judgments.

Content validity evidence of predictor instruments has not frequently been published (for exceptions, see Robinson, 1981; Schmitt & Ostroff, 1986), although such evidence has frequently appeared in technical or in-house validation reports. However, this model of test validation has long been used in civil service jurisdictions (Mussio & Smith, 1973), and many personnel and educational psychologists have attested to its centrality in the whole process of predictor construction and validation (Ebel, 1977; Guion, 1978; Tenopyr, 1977). Furthermore, in many instances, no alternative method of validation is feasible or available. These include cases in which the sample size is small, there is a lack of previous published evidence on a predictor or performance in a given job, or the collection of performance data is infeasible. The lack of published evidence on the content validity of predictors may be the result of many factors, but one suspects it may have much to do with a lack of specific quantitative measures of the extent of a measure's content validity referred to earlier.

CRITERION-RELATED VALIDITY

The vast majority of the published evidence on the validity of tests in employee selection has been based on criterion-related validity. Criterion-related validity studies have followed a fairly similar sequence of steps, as outlined in Figure 13.1. Not necessarily obvious in this figure is the fact that the focus of this research has been almost solely on individual differences. Such differences in predictor measures are related to individual differences in performance. There has been little or no attention to the validity

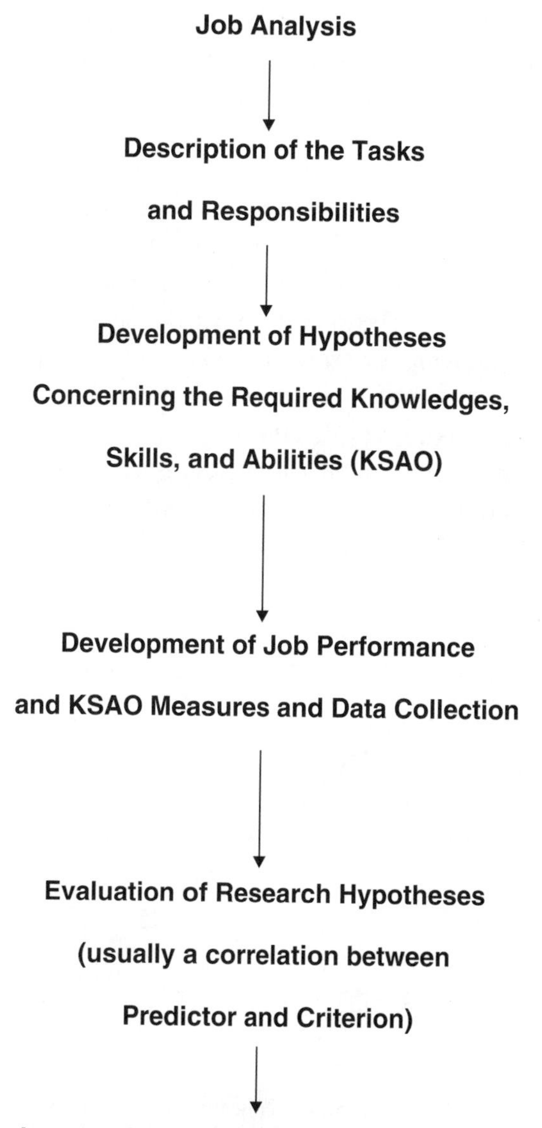

FIGURE 13.1. Steps in a traditional criterion-related validation study. KSAO = knowledge, skills, abilities, and other characteristics.

of these predictor–performance relationships at higher levels of aggregation such as the team or organization. This emphasis will undoubtedly change as the recognition of the importance of levels issues spreads from organizational psychology to selection research (Ployhart, 2004; Ployhart & Schmitt, 2007; Ployhart & Schneider, 2005). We return to this point later in this chapter in describing what we hope will be future research on job performance in organizations.

A test of the statistical significance of the correlation between a predictor and a job performance measure as well as the magnitude of that correlation is reported as the test validity. Binning and Barrett (1989) examined the inferences in applied personnel decision situations. Their model of this situation is depicted in Figure 13.2. In this figure, the relationship between the predictor and criterion measures is the observed correlation typically reported in the criterion-related validity study depicted in Figure 13.1. The relationship of interest, though, in applied situations is that between the predictor measure and the underlying performance domain or construct. We want to know how well our predictor measure relates to a theoretical performance construct when the unreliability and irrelevancies associated with the performance measure are eliminated or controlled. Scientifically, researchers would be interested in the relationships between the predictor construct or constructs and the criterion or performance construct or constructs. When dealing with constructs on either the predictor or criterion side of the equation, the researcher must defend the inference that the measures used represent the intended construct or constructs. The Binning and Barrett (1989) analysis underscores the important role of hypotheses in all validation research. Whether interested in scientific research or not, practitioners form a theory of job performance on the basis of their analysis of a job. They then draw on their understanding of the literature, or a formal review of the literature, to form hypotheses about what predictors might allow accurate inferences about the future performance of job applicants. The better informed by job analysis and the scientific literature those hypotheses are, the better the long-term results of selection.

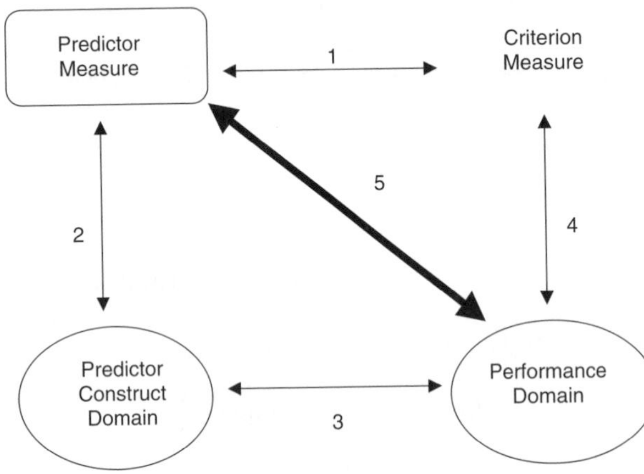

FIGURE 13.2. A common conception of the inferences for personnel selection. From "Validity of Personnel Decisions: A Conceptual Analysis of the Inferential and Evidential Bases," by J. F. Binning and G. V. Barrett, 1989, *Journal of Applied Psychology, 74*, p. 480. Copyright 1989 by the American Psychological Association.

The centrality of the criterion and its measurement is obvious in a criterion-related validation study. (See also chap. 9, this volume.) What criterion or aspect of job performance is measured and the quality of measurement dictates what predictors will display large predictor–criterion relationships. If a job performance measure is unreliable (i.e., performance measures taken at different points in time vary widely or informed observers of performance disagree on its quality), all observed predictor–criterion relationships will be diminished. If a job performance measure is biased or is irrelevant in some way to organizational goals (e.g., a function of race, gender, social desirability, or other factors not related to organizational goals), observed relationships may be inflated or deflated depending on the nature of the variance in the predictor measure. Organizational decision makers or experts, in concert with psychologists, should determine the importance of various aspects of performance; psychologists should be concerned with the adequate measurement of critical performance variables. There is a growing recognition that job performance is multidimensional (J. P. Campbell, Gasser, & Oswald, 1996); however, researchers are still required to combine information to come to single indices of performance to make selection decisions. This requires that decisions be made about the relative importance or weight applied to different aspects of performance. It may even be the case that an organization will choose to ignore some aspects of performance (give them a zero weight) in making decisions under unusual circumstances. In our view, it is better to make such decisions with full knowledge of what one is doing than to allow it to happen by default.

Criterion-related validity studies conducted in this manner produce estimates that appear to be highly variable across organizations and studies even when workers appear to be performing the same job. In the 1960s and 1970s, this was taken to mean that a test needed to be validated whenever it was used in a new situation. This belief became known as the *situational specificity hypothesis*. Schmidt and Hunter (1977) used meta-analysis to show that a large portion of this variability across studies could be attributed to the sampling error associated with the computation of the correlations between predictors and criteria. Moreover, examination of artifacts such as unreliability in the criterion measure used and the degree to which a restriction of range in test scores existed on the basis of the preselection of applicants before criteria were collected showed that validity variation was relatively less across studies. Artifacts often accounted for more than 75% of the variance in observed validity coefficients. In a series of studies, Schmidt, Hunter, and their colleagues (e.g., Schmidt & Hunter, 1998, 2003) convincingly demonstrated that test validity generalizes across a wide variety of situations. In fact, there appears to be few, if any, job situations in which one would not expect to find that a test of cognitive ability is related to job performance. This view of test–performance relationships is often referred to as *validity generalization*.

The thousands of primary validity studies conducted over the past century have been usefully summarized to provide estimates of various observed predictor–criterion relationships in many meta-analyses conducted over the past 3 decades. In addition, researchers have used corrections to estimate the population correlation (Inference 3 in Figure 13.2). Many of these meta-analyses were summarized in an article by Schmidt and Hunter (1998) and more recently in a book chapter by Schmitt and Fandre (2008). Both these efforts, and others, have indicated that many of the measures used in personnel selection can be used with great confidence that their validity in the prediction of job performance and training success will be nonzero and practically significant. This is especially true for measures of cognitive ability and for some personality constructs, such as conscientiousness and perhaps emotional stability.

Although the meta-analyses referred to established that validity for measures of these constructs is above zero, there are differences in the level of validity for a variety of reasons (e.g., job complexity in the case of cognitive ability; Hunter & Hunter, 1984). In the next section on meta-analyses, we will see that validity coefficients for different measures may range from less than .10 to as high as .60. This raises a question as to what constitutes a worthwhile level of validity or difference in validity when one has choices in the use of different measures. The answer to this question depends on a number of factors explored in the research on test utility, including the extent and value of differences in individual contributions to the organization (referred to as the *standard deviation of performance*), the level of validity or differences in validity across measures, and the degree to which an organization can be selective in its hiring decisions (i.e., selection ratio). Research on the utility of selection instruments (Boudreau & Ramstad, 2003; Cascio, 2000; Cascio & Boudreau, 2008) has indicated that relatively small validities (.10) can have a significant impact on organizations given some circumstances (low selection ratios and large individual differences in performance). These differences often have to be balanced against other organizational concerns such as the desirability of a diverse workforce (see Pulakos & Schmitt, 1996) or when different modes of test use are dictated by administrative decisions (Schmidt, Mack, & Hunter, 1984).

Schmitt and Fandre (2008), however, also pointed out that the primary database on which these meta-analyses are based is relatively old. Although we certainly do not maintain that the ability and personality correlates of performance have changed over the past 100 years, we do think the discipline has learned much about the nature and measurement of individual differences and job performance as well as research design in the past several decades.

In this chapter, we describe several ways in which industrial and organizational psychologists have developed evidence to support the inferences derived from selection procedures. We also make an effort to examine the nature of the research studies summarized in meta-analyses of test–performance relationships. We note how that database may be deficient in providing answers to important questions of relevance to scientists and to practitioners who are responsible for selecting today's workforce. We then describe characteristics of the U.S. Army's Project A that we believe should be the model for future validation work. Finally, we describe the features of an ideal validation project that will allow for a more modern, up-to-date database on which to defend the inferences described earlier and depicted in Figure 13.2.

META-ANALYSES AND VALIDITY GENERALIZATION EFFORTS

In an attempt to analyze the nature of validity studies that have been conducted over the past century, we coded 14 meta-analyses (marked with an asterisk in the References section) on certain important dimensions (see Table 13.1). We chose these dimensions to examine whether the current validity database provides information and data that can help scientists and practitioners support inferences about the use of tests to make selection decisions. We limited our review in several ways. First, we included only meta-analyses published in peer-reviewed outlets. Second, we included meta-analyses for two major domains: general cognitive ability and personality. The personality meta-analyses were limited to those focusing on the Big Five because that taxonomy is widely used in the literature on personality and it provides a means of summarizing a very diverse body of literature. We believe that meta-analyses on the Big Five are reasonably representative of the literature on personality test validity, although perhaps somewhat underestimating the validity of personality tests (Hough & Oswald, 2008).

The purpose of this review was to examine several influential meta-analyses in the area of cognitive ability and personality and to ascertain whether the information recorded and reported in these validation studies and the primary studies that were sum-

TABLE 13.1

Description of the Dimensions on Which the Validation Studies Were Coded

Dimension	Description
Predictive versus concurrent validation	Used to code whether the validation study was predictive or concurrent and whether the meta-analyses reported the time of predictor and criterion measurement.
Age of the primary studies	Used to code the age of the primary study database included in the validation study.
Sample demographics	Used to code whether the validation study recorded and reported sample demographics such as country of origin, ethnic status, gender, age, language preference, educational level, military versus civilian.
Contextual factors	Used to code whether the validation study recorded and reported organizational-level information such as geographical location of the organization, economy, industry, organization size, job(s) for which the candidate applying, and nature of selection practices (e.g., Western vs. other practices).
Model and measures of job performance	Used to code whether the validation study recorded and reported the conceptualization of job performance and the way in which the criterion was measured across studies.
Moderators	Used to code whether the validation study included moderators of the predictor–criterion relationship.
Assumptions behind artifact corrections	Used to code the process of correcting for artifacts; it entailed coding for amount of knowledge about range restriction and unreliability from the primary studies and assumptions behind developing validity distributions and the reported method of correction.

marized in the meta-analyses were sufficient to understand predictor–criterion relationships and to support the inferences usually drawn from these meta-analyses. To do so, we identified certain dimensions (coding categories) that would usually be considered desirable features of a validation study (Society for Industrial and Organizational Psychology, 2003), descriptors of the study conducted and the participants in the study, or both. These dimensions are described in Table 13.1.

Predictive Versus Concurrent Validation

Twelve of 14 meta-analyses did not report whether the primary studies involved concurrent or predictive criterion-related validation. Only one meta-analysis (Vinchur, Schippman, Switzer, & Roth, 1998) reported the percentage of concurrent validation samples, the percentage of predictive validation samples, and the percentage of primary studies that reported insufficient information to determine whether the research design was predictive or concurrent. Overall, there was a lack of information about the timing of predictor and criterion measurement.

Age and Sample Size of Primary Studies

One of the points we made about the validity generalization database was that the primary studies in that database were conducted many years ago. To determine whether that was the case, we reviewed the existing meta-analytic database for cognitive ability and personality. Only three (Bertua, Anderson, & Salgado, 2005; Salgado et al., 2003; Vinchur et al., 1998) of the eight cognitive ability meta-analyses we reviewed provided citations to the sources of their data that would allow us to ascertain when the primary studies were conducted. The dates at which studies in these meta-analyses were conducted are summarized in Table 13.2. The table indicates that around 60% of the primary studies included in these meta-analyses were conducted on or before 1970. Two of these meta-analyses were based on data collected in the European community, and the third (Vinchur et al., 1998) focused on clerical occupations. A meta-analysis by Schmitt, Gooding, Noe, and Kirsch (1984) reported on 53 published validity studies that involved a general mental ability test conducted between 1964 and 1982. Schmidt and Hunter (1977) used data on the validity of intelligence published in a book by Ghiselli (1966), so their studies would all have been conducted before that date. Hunter and Hunter (1984) used validity data collected by the U.S. Department of Labor on the General Aptitude Test Battery. Hartigan and Wigdor (1989) indicated that these data were collected between 1945 and 1980, with 90% of the data collected before 1970. The General Aptitude Test Battery data were also a major source of the data on cognitive ability summarized in a subsequent article by Schmidt and Hunter (1998). Hartigan and Wigdor provided analyses of an additional 264 studies conducted on the validity of the General Aptitude Test Battery in the 1980s. Kuncel, Hezlett, and Ones (2004) reported on the validity of the Miller Analogies Test for graduate school students and those in highly technical jobs, but they did not provide citations to the primary studies, and neither did Nathan and Alexander (1988) in their meta-analysis of clerical ability and performance.

TABLE 13.2

Publication Dates of Primary Studies in Meta-Analyses of Cognitive Ability and Personality Measures

Date	No. cognitive ability tests	No. personality tests
Before 1920	4	0
1920–1930	14	0
1931–1940	13	0
1941–1950	29	0
1951–1960	39	0
1961–1970	42	13
1971–1980	30	38
1981–1990	34	58
1991–2000	32	95
After 2000	0	5

Five out of six personality meta-analyses we coded provided citations to the sources of their data that would allow us to ascertain when the primary studies were conducted (Barrick, Mount & Judge, 2001; Dudley, Orvis, Lebiecki, & Cortina, 2006; Hurtz & Donovan, 2000; Salgado, 1997; Tett, Jackson, & Rothstein, 1991). Compared with the validation studies in the area of cognitive ability, the database of primary studies in personality meta-analyses were relatively newer. Of the primary studies, 52% were conducted between 1960 and 1990, and the remainder were conducted between 1991 and 2008. These data are also summarized in Table 13.2.

Sample Demographics

Half of the meta-analyses (7 of 14) did not code for demographics and potential cultural correlates of predictors such as personality and cognitive ability. Some validation studies (5 of 14) recorded demographic information such as gender, age, education, race, and employment status but did not include them in any analyses. Except for the Tett et al. (1991) work, which recorded and reported demographic information such as the applicant versus incumbent status of the study participants, tenure, and civilian versus military status, most of the other validation studies lacked any report of demographic information. Most studies coded for occupational type but lacked information about things such as ethnic status, age, gender, language preference, and educational level.

The fact that these meta-analyses did not include coding for demographic or cultural factors is not a deficiency attributable to the researchers conducting these meta-analyses but with the primary databases themselves. Reporting these variables is often neglected. Perhaps more fundamental is the fact that almost the entire available database in this area of psychology and others (Arnett, 2008) is American. Today, nearly all organizations and businesses are global; the role of work or even the availability of work varies greatly across the world, and the possibility that individual difference–performance relationships differ as a function of cultural factors is relatively unaddressed, although this may be changing (see Gelfand, Erez, & Aycan, 2007).

Contextual Factors

Of the 14 meta-analyses coded, 13 did not report information about the organization in which the participants worked or into which they were being selected. There was no information about the cultural or geographical profile of the organizations or institutions included in the sample. Some of the validation studies coded for occupational groups but did not code or report the industry type, the nature of the economy, and the country in which hiring was taking place. Neither the primary studies nor the meta-analyses coded whether the participants worked internationally, although it may be assumed that most did not, given the time period in which data were most often collected. The job or occupational category was recorded in all the meta-analyses we reviewed. The general nature of the performance measure (e.g., training success vs. job performance, supervisory ratings) was recorded in all but three of the meta-analyses. Only one meta-analysis (Pearlman, Schmidt, & Hunter, 1980) collected qualitative data (narratives) regarding the organizational context and firm type, but Pearlman et al. (1980) did not report or use the data in any analyses.

None of the meta-analyses reported the situational context of the jobs into which people were hired. For example, they lacked information about the organizational level of the job, nature and size of the work group to which an employee was assigned, the method of compensation, and other organizational-level variables that could conceivably influence the relationship between predictor and criterion or would allow for the analyses of relationships at multiple levels or cross-levels.

This tendency to minimize the description of the context of one's research may be the result of journalistic practices that often restrict the length of published articles and hence discourage the reporting of what is perceived to be extraneous detail. Johns (2006) noted this neglect in the broader area of organizational behavior research and felt that

> some quantitative researchers seem almost desperate to ensure that reviewers and readers see their results as generalizable. To facilitate this, they describe research as blandly as possible—dislocated from time, place, and space—and omit details of how access was negotiated. (p. 404).

Whatever the reasons, the end result is that archival research is often not as useful as it should be given the expense of conducting studies, particularly in organizational contexts. This lack of reporting makes it impossible to study the role of context in influencing the magnitude and type of relationships as well as the possibility of studying effects at different levels of analysis (e.g., Ployhart & Schneider, 2005).

Conceptualization of the Criterion

A large percentage of the validation studies (9 of 14) listed overall job performance and training success as the focus of the validation efforts reviewed. Of 14 meta-analyses, 3 reported use of a combination of supervisor ratings and objective performance (e.g., sales volume, production quantity, production quality). Of the 14 meta-analyses, 2 indicated that an overall job performance criterion was used in the studies reviewed. Neither these nor other validation studies provided details about the dimensional nature of the job performance measures used. They did not specify whether the overall job performance construct included only task performance or other dimensions such as organizational citizenship behavior or contextual performance.

Measurement of the Criterion

Of the 14 meta-analyses, 4 did not report how the performance criterion was measured—whether it was based on self-report or whether it was based on colleague or supervisor ratings. Seven included a combination of subjective and objective measures of the performance criterion. Most meta-analyses that used training success as their criterion did not report the kind of measure that was used to assess training success. None of the meta-analyses reported any data about the rater–ratee relationship, nor did they report the extent to which performance (criterion) measures differed from one study to another. There could be cultural and organizational differences in how performance is conceptualized across studies that may moderate the predictor–criterion relationships in those cases in which there is unexplained variability in validity coefficients. All of the personality meta-analyses reported that the primary studies reviewed included some form of subjective performance rating as well as objective data like sales or production quality.

Level of Analysis

None of the 14 validation studies we coded addressed relationships at other than the individual level of analysis.

Moderators

Of the 14 validation studies, 3 did not check for moderators of the predictor–criterion relationships. A few meta-analytic studies (3 of 14) assessed job complexity as a moderator. Five of 14 studies examined the type of criterion measurement (subjective ratings vs. objective data) as a moderator. Several meta-analyses (3 of 14) examined both occupation type and performance type as moderators. One meta-analysis in the personality area (Tett et al., 1991) included information on several relevant moderators like type of occupation, recruit versus incumbent, age, tenure, civilian versus military sample, confirmatory versus exploratory examination of personality–performance relationships, and whether the primary studies had used job analysis to select the trait measures. It should be noted that in some instances the meta-analysis revealed little or no variance in validity coefficients after correction for artifactual variance. In these instances, a search for moderators would have been meaningless.

The possible moderating effects of race and gender have generated a great deal of research in the selection area primarily because of the usual, relatively large minority–majority differences on cognitive ability measures. Using these tests to make employment decisions very often results in a smaller proportion of the lower scoring group being selected than is the case for the higher scoring group. In examining these and other demographic differences, the accepted practice is to regress performance on the predictor or predictors for the different subgroups and test for differential prediction. Evidence of differential prediction is usually taken as statistically significant differences in the slopes and intercepts of these two regressions and occasionally also the standard error of estimate (see *Principles,* Society for Industrial and Organizational Psychology, 2003, pp. 32–33). Moderated regression in which performance is regressed on the predictor, subgroup, and the product or interaction of the two is most often used (Bartlett, Bobko, Mosier, & Hannan, 1978).

For predictions based on cognitive ability, researchers have rarely found evidence of slope differences, although intercept differences are frequently reported (*Principles*, Society for Industrial and Organizational Psychology, 2003; *Standards*, American Educational Research Association et al., 1999). These intercept differences usually indicate that the performance of minority groups (at least that of African Americans and Hispanic Americans in the United States) is overpredicted (e.g., Schmidt, Pearlman, & Hunter, 1984). Research in the personality realm is not as abundant, but Saad and Sackett (2002) reported an absence of overprediction of female performance using personality tests. The astute reader, though, will recognize that the regression-based definition of predictive bias depends on the existence and use of an unbiased criterion measure.

It should also be pointed out that the probability of drawing a conclusion that no moderator effect exists when, in fact, there is a moderator of reasonable magnitude (a difference in correlations between groups of .2) is .30 and higher for a large number of realistic conditions (Aguinis, Sturman, & Pierce, 2008). Aguinis et al. (2008) found little difference in the error rates associated with three different approaches to testing for moderator effects.

Time

There was no examination of time between collection of predictor and criterion data in any of the validation studies. This issue has been examined in some meta-analyses not coded in this effort (e.g., Schmitt et al., 1984).

Correction for Statistical Artifacts

All meta-analysts corrected for sampling error in the validity coefficients, 12 of 14 corrected the mean and variance of the summed validity coefficients for unreliability in predictor measurement, 13 of 14 corrected for unreliability in criterion measurement, and 12 of 14 corrected for range restriction.

Knowledge About Range Restriction and Reliability of Measurement

All the validation studies reported having little or no information about the reliability of the predictor and criterion measures used in the primary studies. They also reported lack of information about the applicant pool being considered at the time of selection; thus, they had no information about the range restriction in the original sample. This led the meta-analysts to use assumed artifact distributions.

Assumed Artifact Distributions

All the validation studies developed a combination of sample-based and assumed artifact distributions for the sources of errors of interest. Meta-analysts usually cited other published articles for their estimated effects of range restriction and criterion unreliability. A check of these earlier sources usually revealed that the artifact distributions used were estimated rather than based on actual data regarding the extent of criterion unreliability or range restriction. Unreliability of the predictor was often estimated from test–retest and internal consistency coefficients published in the primary studies and from test manuals. Those validation studies that included both objective and subjective criteria developed assumed criterion reliability distributions separately for objective and subjective criteria. In some of the studies, perfect criterion reliability was assumed for objective data such as accidents, absenteeism, wages, and so forth.

The correlation or validity coefficients corrected for attenuation because of unreliability are theoretical values; practitioners must work with less than perfect measures in making decisions. Restriction of range corrections, however, does provide an accurate estimate of the operational validity among a group of applicants if one has data on the degree of selectivity (i.e., the actual standard deviations of applicants and those who are selected).

Other Sources of Error

None of the meta-analysts assessed the impact of various forms of social desirability or faking on self-report measures, perhaps because the original studies did not address these issues.

Summary of Meta-Analyses

Having provided a description of different shortcomings in the database underlying meta-analyses of KSAO–performance relationships, we do believe they still provide convincing evidence of the value of using cognitive and noncognitive measures when selecting employees. The average observed validities of cognitive ability measures across various meta-analyses are almost all in the .20s. Using measures with even these relatively low operational validities can certainly result in practically significant improvements in workforce productivity (Cascio, 2000). The lower bound of the credibility interval is always well above zero, meaning that we can expect the validity to generalize to other situations. The average validities of personality measures in predicting job performance ranges from .04 to .22 across dimensions and meta-analyses. We can be reasonably certain to find that measures of conscientiousness will have nonzero validity across jobs and that emotional stability will also prove valid in many instances. Results for other Big Five dimensions are not so positive, but they may have value in some instances for prediction of more specific criteria. Similar results apply when personality variables are used to predict alternate outcomes such as organizational citizenship behavior. So, we are not discounting the results of many decades of research (Schmidt & Hunter, 1998), but we do believe that we have made advancements in measure development; we know a great deal more about research design (Sussman & Robertson, 1986); the fallacies inherent in small-sample research are widely appreciated, as are the importance of artifacts; and we have made advancements in our theory of job performance (e.g., J. P. Campbell et al., 1996) and the nature of relationships and their context (e.g., Johns, 2006; Klein & Kozlowski, 2000) that dictate that this database be replenished and updated.

Although the primary studies in most of the meta-analyses reported in the peer-reviewed literature have various execution and reporting flaws, one large-scale study conducted in the 1980s (J. P. Campbell & Knapp, 2001) was noteworthy in avoiding, correcting, or estimating the impact of these potential flaws. We discuss this study for several reasons, including the fact that the researchers began with a careful consideration of the nature of job performance and the KSAOs required (see Linkages 2 and 4 in Figure 13.2). They paid careful attention to all aspects of data collection and provided both concurrent and predictive criterion-related validities. Different methods of measurement were used to assess various aspects of the performance and KSAO domains. Demographic descriptors of the sample were collected, allowing for subgroup analyses. In addition, they collected data that allowed them to make corrections for artifacts and estimate theoretical and operational validities. Because the researchers had considerable resources and the cooperation of the U.S. military, they were able to collect data from a large number of research participants. We turn next to a more detailed discussion of some of these aspects of that study.

PROJECT A RESEARCH

The most thorough and significant validation effort available is the effort by J. P. Campbell and colleagues referred to as *Project A*. The results of this effort were summarized in a book (J. P. Campbell & Knapp, 2001) and a special issue of *Personnel Psychology* (J. P. Campbell, 1990) and in numerous other publications. The major parts of this project, carried out over a 7-year period, reflect the questions and inferences depicted in Figure 15.2, the Binning and Barrett (1989) figure reproduced earlier.

To ensure that the predictor measures represented the domain of relevant knowledge, skills, abilities, and other characteristics (KSAOs; Inference 2 in Figure 13.2), Peterson et al. (1990) described a process that included an exhaustive literature review of reports, articles, books, computerized searches, and bibliographies. Each of these reports was summarized, using a taxonomy of the constructs discussed in a given domain, along with the validity of the measures against different types of performance criteria. Content analyses of these predictor measures yielded a potential set of 53 measures. The Army jobs were analyzed and used to identify 72 possible components of performance. An expert panel of 35 personnel psychologists then estimated the validities of each of the predictor variables for each of the criteria. A factor analysis of the predictor profiles across the criteria yielded eight factors that were then represented in preliminary test batteries. These factors were used as the basis for selection and test construction.

Project A researchers were equally as thorough in defining and measuring the performance domain

(Inference 4 in Figure 13.2). Their approach included extensive task and critical incidents analyses that were used to generate the major performance dimensions. Measures were constructed to index each dimension, and these were evaluated using expert judgments and field data. Specific measures included rating scales, job knowledge tests, hands-on job samples, and archival records (C. H. Campbell et al., 1990). Performance data for a sample of 9,430 job incumbents across 19 military jobs were analyzed using content analyses and principal-components analyses. A final model was fit to the data that included five performance dimensions (core technical proficiency, general soldiering proficiency, effort and leadership, personal discipline, and fitness or bearing) as well as rating and paper-and-pencil methods factors (J. P. Campbell, McHenry, & Wise, 1990).

Both concurrent and predictive criterion-related validation evidence (the first linkage in Figure 13.2) were collected (McHenry, Hough, Toquam, Hanson, & Ashworth, 1990). Responses to a predictor battery of cognitive ability, perceptual–psychomotor ability, temperament and personality, and interest measures were aggregated into 24 composites and correlated with the five performance components. Differential validity was observed across different jobs, but substantial observed validity was reported for all predictor composites and all performance domains (*r*s = .07–.47, *Mdn* = .15). Because both restricted and unrestricted standard deviations of predictor composites were available and reliability estimates for all criteria were computed, the observed validities could be corrected for range restriction and unreliability, providing estimates of both Inference 4 and Inference 5 in Figure 13.2. Corrected validities ranged from .37 to .70 for combined predictor composites against the five performance dimensions. It is clear from the Project A effort that a carefully conducted large-scale validation effort can clarify many of the issues that we raised earlier concerning inadequacies in the database underlying many of the published meta-analyses of predictor–criterion relationships. We turn next to alternative methods of providing validation evidence for employment practices.

ALTERNATIVE APPROACHES TO VALIDATION

Aside from the emphasis on content and criterion-related validity evidence in personnel selection, there are a number of alternative approaches that use validity evidence from existing research to support inferences about test–performance relationships in new or local situations. The meta-analytic evidence described provides support for a validity generalization defense when using cognitive ability tests and measures of conscientiousness to select workers for most jobs and when using other measures in a wide variety of other occupations. Validity generalization arguments involve using meta-analytic findings to support the conclusion that predictor–criterion validity evidence can be generalized across situations and that a new data collection effort is unnecessary. Meta-analytic findings provide researchers with outside evidence to support inferences in a local context, although this depends on evidence regarding the similarity of local job requirements to those represented by the studies in the meta-analytic database, which may often be lacking. The argument for validity generalization on the basis of meta-analyses is that some selection tests, such as cognitive ability tests (Ones, Viswesvaran, & Dilchert, 2005), are valid across selection contexts. Thus, the implication is that with validity generalization strategies, unlike transportability, discussed later, in-depth job analyses or qualitative studies of the local organizational context are unnecessary. Between-study variability in validity coefficients can largely be attributed to statistical artifacts, such as range restriction, unreliability, or sampling error (see Schmidt & Hunter, 2003). However, caution is warranted to the extent that meta-analyses have identified substantive moderators or in the presence of strong theory indicating that some variable may moderate the magnitude of validity. Moreover, with regard to generalization across contexts, inferences drawn from meta-analytic findings are limited to the situations represented in the studies included in the meta-analysis. As stated previously in this chapter, information about the context, and even the research participants, has not been reported in much of the primary research.

Meta-analytic findings should be referenced in test development and can be used to supplement evidence at the local level, either via theoretical or statistical means (Newman, Jacobs, & Bartram, 2007). In considering the use of validity generalization defenses in legal cases, Landy (2003) asserted that they have not been used frequently and, more important, that those considering validity generalization

> as the sole defense for a test or test type might want to seriously consider including additional defenses (e.g., transportability analyses) and would be well advised to know the essential duties of the job in question, and in its local manifestation, well. Persuasive expert testimony will be required to bridge the gap between [validity generalization] and a specific practice. (p. 189)

Transportability of validity evidence involves applying validity evidence from one selection situation to another, based on the notion that the two contexts are sufficiently similar. Specifically, the *Principles* (Society for Industrial and Organizational Psychology, 2003) noted that researchers should be concerned with assessing similarity in terms of job characteristics (e.g., the KSAOs needed to perform the job in each context), job tasks and content, applicant pool characteristics, or other factors that would limit transportability across two contexts (e.g., cultural differences). Assessing similarity in this manner usually requires that researchers conduct a job analysis or rely on existing job analysis materials combined with their own professional expertise and sound judgment.

One question that arises in those situations in which the examination of test content represents the primary means of supporting the use of selection procedures is the degree to which one can "transport" content validity evidence from one context to another in these instances. If a researcher wishes to transport content validity evidence from one context to another, it seems that a thorough and reliable job analysis indicating similar tasks requiring similar KSAOs would be sufficient evidence to support the use of the test in the new context. In addition, many selection systems derived on the basis of content validity arguments include job knowledge tests, training and experience inventories, and simulations or job samples. There is a large body of criterion-related evidence and meta-analyses of criterion-related research on all three of these methods of measurement that support their use (Schmidt & Hunter, 1998, 2003). It seems to us, though, that researchers interested in generalizing validity from these meta-analyses should also examine the degree to which similar constructs are targeted in the local study as were the basis of the selection procedures in the meta-analyses.

Support for a test battery can also be based on synthetic validity (*Principles,* Society for Industrial and Organizational Psychology, 2003), a process in which validity for a test battery is "synthesized" from evidence of multiple predictor–job component relationships (Peterson, Wise, Arabian, & Hoffman, 2001; Scherbaum, 2005). Job analysis would be used to identify the various components that make up a particular job, and then a review of the literature on predictor–job component relationships that are relevant to the target job is conducted for all available jobs with shared components. Synthetic validity may be a particularly useful strategy for organizations that have too few incumbents performing a focal job to reach adequate sample sizes for a traditional criterion-related study (Scherbaum, 2005). Validity is transported from other jobs that require performance on components similar to the focal job, but in different configurations. If a focal job requires the performance of mechanical and clerical tasks, the researcher might derive support for the use of a predictor from one set of studies to predict performance on the mechanical parts of the job and a predictor from a different set of studies to support inferences about the use of a second predictor and the clerical aspects of the job.

PROPOSAL FOR A MAJOR NEW VALIDATION EFFORT

The large body of criterion-related research along with the meta-analyses of this research support validity generalization in many instances in which tests are used, although we have argued that the primary database does have limitations, particularly in light of what we now know about the nature of job performance, research design, levels issues, the nature and role of artifacts in validation research, and more. The Project A effort represented a huge undertaking that was well conceived and executed, and it produced excellent results, documenting the potential role of selection in the production of high-performing individual soldiers. However, it is now 25 years since the project began and close to 20 years since the results of that effort were published. New issues have come to the fore (e.g., organizational-level analyses, multilevel analyses, applicant reactions to personnel selection issues). In addition, Project A participants and jobs were all military, and measures developed as part of this study were never implemented (the reasons for nonimplementation or abandonment of scientifically based human resource practices are beyond the scope of this chapter, but they clearly deserve more attention; Johns, 1993; Kehoe, Mol, & Anderson, in press). Much of this research should generalize to civilians and civilian occupations, but there are certainly differences between military and civilian organizations and jobs, and the nature of the U.S. military population itself has changed in the intervening years, at least in terms of gender composition. Our proposal is that the discipline as a whole initiate an effort to examine personnel selection procedures in a comprehensive way that would involve large samples of people, multiple institutions and organizations, and multiple countries organized as a research consortium. Moreover, this effort should be ongoing, allowing the collection and analysis of questions that can be answered more definitively with longitudinal data. This research effort should have the following characteristics and should collect the following data, although perhaps not all organizations would collect data on all measures at each data collection point.

First, as indicated earlier, this research effort should involve multiple organizations and units and be global in its scope. Of course, multiple jobs or major job families with presumed similar KSAO requirements should be included. The global economy is not futuristic; it is reality. Most large- and even medium-sized organizations have facilities, employees, contacts, suppliers, and customers in other parts of the world. We are only beginning to appreciate the cultural differences that organizations confront in managing these relationships and are only beginning to examine or be aware of the differences in personnel selection practices in the Western world (Salgado, Anderson, & Hulsheger, in press), much less in other parts of the globe. More broadly in organizational behavior, attention to cross-cultural issues also seems to be growing (see Gelfand et al., 2007), although psychology, and we suspect personnel selection and industrial and organizational psychology, remain very much American disciplines (Arnett, 2008). We are only beginning to appreciate the nuances of measurement equivalence in the presence of linguistic and cultural differences (Cascio & Aguinis, 2005; Schmitt & Kuljanin, 2008; Vandenberg & Lance, 2000). A modern understanding of individual differences in worker capacity, motivation, and performance must be multicultural in a very broad sense.

Second, there should be a careful conceptualization of common performance constructs and measures. The same or generic measures should be collected across organizations and cultures with provisions to measure and collect measures that may be of specific local interest. These measures surely ought to include a supervisory rating of overall job performance. In addition, measures that reflect current ideas about the multidimensionality of job performance (Borman & Motowidlo, 1997; J. P. Campbell, 1999) should be included. In all instances when ratings are used as performance measures, data regarding the rater–ratee relationship and the opportunity to observe performance should be recorded. There would likely be measures of organizational citizenship behavior or contextual performance, although those may need to be adapted to local situations. For those individuals who engage in training on a new or existing job, measures of training success with a description of the type of measure used should be recorded. Over time, measures of turnover and withdrawal, including absenteeism and tardiness (Hulin, Roznowski, & Hachiya, 1985), counterproductive work behaviors (Sackett, 2002), and safety behaviors (Hofmann & Stetzer, 1996) should be collected. Obviously, data should be collected to allow evaluation of the reliability of outcome measures.

On the predictor side, traditionally valid measures of cognitive ability and the Big Five personality constructs would be obvious candidates for inclusion. However, as suggested by Hough (1998), some of the personality measures may be too global, and more specific measures of personality targeting various outcomes will likely be more valid. Certainly different types of measures (e.g., interviews, biodata, situational judgment inventories, Web-based versions of tests) of these and other constructs should receive attention. Such hypotheses, or alternative methods of measurement, could be evaluated in small portions of the total population of applicants. The impact of various forms of social desirability or faking on self-report measures and their validity should be evaluated among applicants for positions rather than incumbents or college students. Interventions designed to minimize such effects should be evaluated. Cultural and demographic correlates of both personality and cognitive ability measures should be investigated. In the cognitive ability realm, computer technology that allows for presentation of stimuli in virtual reality may allow the novel exploration of the role of spatial ability when that seems relevant to job performance. Efforts at "cloning" test items (Embretson, 1999; Irvine & Kyllonen, 2002) based on cognitive theory may be helpful in furthering our understanding of the cognitive ability construct and provide the basis for generating new items while testing an examinee and minimizing item security concerns.

The research design should be longitudinal, with applicants as research participants. The data collection would be continuous, allowing for what some have called *data streaming*. Data on the performance and retention of participants would be collected across multiple points in time, perhaps every 2 or 3 years, and new participants would be added over time. Participants would be tracked after leaving an organization to allow for the collection of outcome data on these participants in new organizational contexts. Moreover, information on the applicant pool being considered at the time of selection will allow for corrections for restriction of range on real data as opposed to artifact distributions, as is now common practice (Schmidt, Oh, & Le, 2006).

Differential prediction (Cleary, 1968) and impact (Sackett, Schmitt, Ellingson, & Kabin, 2001; Sackett & Wilk, 1994) have been a central concern for scientists and practitioners in the United States and many other countries. Recently, the broader concern for the equivalence of measurement across various linguistic and cultural groups and the use of item response theory and confirmatory factor analytic examinations have taken central stage (see Schmitt & Kuljanin, 2008; Vandenberg & Lance, 2000). These studies obviously require that the demographic status of research participants be identified. At a minimum, gender, race, national origin, language background, educational level, and age of research participants should be collected. There may also be cultural subgroups in some countries that are of special interest, and the educational background and social economic status of one's parental family may also be of interest with some participants. Even these basic demographic data are often missing in the existing archival database.

The situational context of hiring decisions should be recorded. These variables would include the job(s) for which the applicant is being considered, the organization, the industry type, the nature of the economy, and the country in which hiring is taking place. It may also be desirable and possible to record the organizational level, nature and size of the work group to which an employee is assigned, the method of compensation, and other organizational-level variables that could conceivably influence the relationship between predictor and criterion or allow for the analyses of relationships at multiple levels or cross-levels (see later discussion). Analysis of these context variables and potential hypotheses about their impact can go well beyond the situational specificity hypothesis that has been largely discredited using the current database of mostly U.S. studies described earlier. The importance of the context of research was mentioned earlier in this chapter and has been underscored by other researchers as well (e.g., Cascio & Aguinis, 2008). The routine inclusion of these context variables would allow for multilevel analyses that would address hypotheses that we are only beginning to consider in personnel selection but that have become relatively routine in other areas of organizational science (see Bliese, Chan, & Ployhart, 2007; Ployhart, 2004; Ployhart & Schneider, 2005). Over time, the impact of interventions on organizational effectiveness could also be evaluated (e.g., Huselid, 1995).

The research design and long-term plans for this data collection should allow for ancillary studies. These studies would include provisions to collect more than the standard set of predictor and criterion variables and for the inclusion of more participants from special demographic or cultural groups. These studies would allow for the evaluation of novel hypotheses or developments in selection or the broader domain of industrial and organizational psychology and related disciplines or the social and cultural context in which people work. They might include studies that allow for testing or improving methods of data collection or measurement, such as efforts to address the potential problem of faking, response bias, or security issues. Proposals for such studies would need to be evaluated and supported by the members of the consortium that contribute to the larger project. One question might be what could be considered standard in this data collection, so as a starting point for discussion, we provide the list of variables in Table 13.3.

Collection of data on KSAO–performance relationships across jobs would also allow for the evaluation of classification models. In classification models, applicants may be evaluated and assigned to multiple different jobs. Each person is tentatively assigned to that job for which his or her predicted performance is highest. Classification efficiency is then expressed as the mean predicted performance of all applicants (Brogden, 1959; Scholarios,

TABLE 13.3

Suggested List of Standard Constructs

Type	Construct
I. Predictors	Cognitive ability (verbal and math components) Big Five (Conscientiousness, Agreeableness, Extraversion, Neuroticism, Openness) Interview measures of motivation and sociability Experience Social desirability, faking, and consistency
II. Outcomes	Overall performance rating Ratings of task and contextual performance (organizational citizenship behavior) Turnover intentions and turnover Counterproductive behavior Training success Absenteeism Safety behavior (or accidents)
III. Demographic	Country of origin Ethnic status Gender Age Language preference Educational level
IV. Contextual variables	Job(s) for which the candidate is applying Organization and organization size Country Industry Economy
V. Reactions: fairness, relevance, and procedures	

Johnson, & Zeidner, 1994). The major advantage of classification models of employment decision making is that the selection ratio is much lower when assignment of people to multiple jobs is possible. However, the utility of performance in the different jobs may vary, which means that jobs for which the variability (as well as the average) of performance utility is highest should take precedence when an organization assigns personnel. In most instances, too, there may be a fixed number of people required to fill each position, which constrains the ability to assign people to the jobs for which the mean predicted performance is highest. Finally, classification systems require that the set of predictors and criteria be multidimensional. If a general factor explains all the variance in predictor scores, then the mean predicted performance of all individuals will be highest for the same job and classification will provide no utility above selection. When there are multiple possible job assignments available, there are a set of predictors that are not highly correlated, and there are not overly restrictive quotas for each job (see Scholarios et al., 1994, for simulations evaluating the role of these factors), then classification can greatly increase the efficiency of selection procedures. For a more thorough and readable treatment of utility analyses, including utility in classification models, the reader should consult Cascio and Boudreau (2008).

The importance of classification and its use is most evident in military studies. J. P. Campbell and Knapp (2001) described the classification of 50,000 military recruits to 250 Army jobs. We have no other classification analysis of similar complexity, although Campbell and Knapp argued that similar systems can be devised in other large organizations. Especially when motivational and dispositional characteristics are added to the prediction equations in addition to ability measures, thereby producing a more multidimensional set of predictors, classification becomes possible and is likely to provide significant dividends in productivity. The collection of data across multiple jobs in multiple organizations would provide opportunities to evaluate classification strategies that have hitherto been proposed and used primarily in military contexts.

The type of study we are describing should also include the collection of reactions to selection procedures. Social validity (a concern with societal and examinee reactions) of selection procedures has long been of concern for European investigators (Schuler, 1993; Schuler & Stehle, 1985), but with the introduction of concerns for organizational justice, reactions of those who take selection instruments has become of central interest to researchers in various parts of the world (Anderson, 2004; Gilliland, 1993; Schmitt & Gilliland, 1992). Given that selection practices differ across the globe (Salgado et al., in press), we can expect differing reactions on the part of examinees when they evaluate the fairness and relevance of procedures, especially when those procedures are not commonly used in their culture. These reactions do have consequences for applicant intentions and appraisals of the organization (e.g., Truxillo, Bauer, Campion, & Paronto, 2002), and such reactions will likely have an impact on long-term use.

The existing database on the validity of selection procedures includes very few studies of selection for the purposes of constituting teams; this topic is not mentioned in any of the meta-analyses. Choosing people to form collaborative groups or to join existing groups or teams poses special problems, and the typical research study done at the individual level does not address them. Work assignments within a group may appear equal, but work may accumulate for one member while another has a temporary lull. Flexibility and the skill to undertake multiple roles may be needed in today's teams. The emphasis on teams also means that team performance must be measured, and it may not be a simple aggregation of individual team members' performance even when that is available. Likewise, a simple aggregation of team members' KSAOs may not be indicative of team performance or team capability. These issues may also be culturally determined, as has been suggested by research on the role of cultural values (Hofstede, 2001; Schwartz, 1994).

Finally, a study such as the one we are proposing would allow for the determination of the sustainability of selection projects over time. Those of us who have worked in the profession for any period of time are certainly able to identify procedures that we or someone else developed that were subsequently abandoned by the sponsoring organization. Kehoe et al. (in press) discussed the factors that make selection programs sustainable. Among the factors they mentioned is fit with the organizational culture; it would be hard to imagine that Microsoft would use paper-and-pencil measures, for example. Cultural fit may be even more serious in those cases in which an organization wants to use selection procedures globally. Issues of the trade-offs of quality of the data collection and time and speed of data collection are critical determinants of the use and utility of selection procedures. The perceived fairness and defensibility of the procedures certainly play a role in their continued use. Finally, the person in charge of a project inside the organization and his or her persuasiveness, credibility, and tenure are often determinants of the long-term viability of any human resource program, including those having to do with hiring personnel. These sustainability factors and their role in organizational effectiveness could be evaluated in a longitudinal, multiorganizational study. The full set of considerations that a major collaborative international study such as the one being proposed should address is provided in Exhibit 13.1.

Many issues need attention if a project such as this is ever to become reality. Among them are certainly the following:

- security and privacy issues for both individuals and organizations (see http://www.shrm.org, and search privacy regulations for various guidelines and regulations);
- provisions for data sharing with appropriate concern for security and privacy;
- need for continuity but also flexibility when necessary to evaluate new developments in the field; and
- accuracy and fidelity of translations.

Our review at the beginning of this chapter should provide human resources managers with a great deal of confidence in the validity of many of the commonly used selection procedures. However, it also suggests that we should be proactive in developing and evaluating procedures that will be defensible in the future. That project is the one we are proposing.

SUMMARY AND CONCLUSIONS

In sum, the large database available in meta-analyses of several individual difference—performance relationships should provide professionals with reasonable confidence to use these measures to select employees in a wide variety of situations, although legally (at least in the United States), it may be necessary to use more than a validity generalization defense of measures of these constructs. However,

Exhibit 13.1

Characteristics of Proposed Strategy for Continuous Data Collection and Analyses of the Role of Individual Differences in Job Performance

Longitudinal with applicant participants
Continuous data collection over time and including new cohorts
Multiple organizations with participants in multiple occupations and countries
Careful conceptualization and measurement of common performance constructs (multidimensional, longitudinal, and reliable)
Use of traditional predictors (Big Five and cognitive ability) and more specific measures when coupled with well-founded hypotheses about the nature of performance and predictor constructs
Collection of data that will allow for analysis of differential prediction analyses across cultural and linguistic groups
Collection of data on situational context to allow for analyses at multiple levels
Collection of data on team composition and effectiveness when relevant
Collection of data on organizational context and support that will allow investigation of sustainability
Collect data that will allow for classification studies
Provide for ancillary studies that investigate issues of new constructs, faking, response bias, reactions to selection procedures, and so forth.

the research on which the meta-analyses are based contains a large number of deficiencies, many of which we now know how to address. We have detailed many of these problems and given examples from the extant meta-analyses. We also proposed a large-scale multiorganizational and global study of a variety of jobs to address some of these issues and provided a better data-based scientific justification of selection procedures.

References

References marked with an asterisk indicate meta-analyses that were examined and coded.

Aguinis, H., Sturman, M. C., & Pierce, C. A. (2008). Comparison of three meta-analytic procedures for estimating moderating effects of categorical variables. *Organizational Research Methods, 11,* 9–34.

American Educational Research Association, American Psychological Association, & National Council on Measurement in Education. (1999). *Standards for educational and psychological testing.* Washington, DC: American Psychological Association.

Anderson, N. (Ed.). (2004). Applicant reactions and decision making in selection [Special issue]. *International Journal of Selection and Assessment, 12*(1–2).

Arnett, J. J. (2008). The neglected 95%: Why American psychology needs to become less American. *American Psychologist, 63,* 602–614.

*Barrick, M. R., & Mount, M. K. (1991). The Big Five personality dimensions and job performance: A meta-analysis. *Personnel Psychology, 44,* 1–26.

*Barrick, M. R., Mount, M. K., & Judge, T. A. (2001). Personality and performance at the beginning of the new millennium: What do we know and where do we go next? *International Journal of Selection and Assessment, 9,* 9–30.

Bartlett, C. J., Bobko, P., Mosier, S. B., & Hannan, R. (1978). Testing for fairness with a moderated regression strategy: An alternative to differential analysis. *Personnel Psychology, 31,* 233–242.

*Bertua, C., Anderson, N., & Salgado, J. F. (2005). The predictive validity of cognitive ability tests: A UK meta-analysis. *Journal of Occupational and Organizational Psychology, 78,* 387–409.

Binning, J. F., & Barrett, G. V. (1989). Validity of personnel decisions: A conceptual analysis of the inferential and evidential bases. *Journal of Applied Psychology, 74,* 478–494.

Bliese, P. D., Chan, D., & Ployhart, R. E. (2007). Multilevel methods: Future directions in measurement, longitudinal analyses, and nonnormal outcomes. *Organizational Research Methods, 10,* 551–563.

Borman, W. C., & Motowidlo, S. J. (1997). Task performance and contextual performance: The meaning for personnel selection research. *Human Performance, 10,* 99–109.

Boudreau, J. W., & Ramstad, P. M. (2003). Strategic industrial and organizational psychology and the role of utility analysis models. In W. C. Borman, D. R. Ilgen, & R. J. Klimoski (Eds.), *Handbook of psychology* (Vol. 12, pp. 193–224). Hoboken, NJ: Wiley.

Brogden, H. E. (1959). Efficiency of classification as a function of number of jobs, percent rejected, and the validity and intercorrelation of job performance estimates. *Educational and Psychological Measurement, 19,* 181–190.

Campbell, C. H., Ford, P., Rumsey, M. G., Pulakos, E. D., Borman, W. C., Felker, D. B., et al. (1990). Development of multiple job performance measures in a representative sample of jobs. *Personnel Psychology, 43,* 277–300.

Campbell, D. T., & Fiske, D. W. (1959). Convergent and discriminant validation by the multitrait–multimethod matrix. *Psychological Bulletin, 56,* 81–105.

Campbell, J. P. (1990). An overview of the Army selection and classification project (Project A). *Personnel Psychology, 43,* 231–239.

Campbell, J. P. (1999). The definition and measurement of performance in the new age. In D. R. Ilgen & E. D. Pulakos (Eds.), *The changing nature of performance* (pp. 399–429). San Francisco: Jossey-Bass.

Campbell, J. P., Gasser, M. B., & Oswald, F. L. (1996). The substantive nature of job performance variability. In K. R. Murphy (Ed.), *Individual differences and behavior in organizations* (pp. 258–299). San Francisco: Jossey-Bass.

Campbell, J. P., & Knapp, D. J. (Eds.). (2001). *Exploring the limits in personnel selection and classification.* Mahwah, NJ: Erlbaum.

Campbell, J. P., McHenry, J. J., & Wise, L. L. (1990). Modeling job performance in a population of jobs. *Personnel Psychology, 43,* 313–334.

Cascio, W. F. (2000). *Costing human resources: The financial impact of behavior in organizations.* Cincinnati, OH: Southwestern.

Cascio, W. F., & Aguinis, H. (2005). *Applied psychology in human resources management* (6th ed.). Englewood Cliffs, NJ: Prentice Hall.

Cascio, W. F., & Aguinis, H. (2008). Staffing 21st century organizations. *Academy of Management Annals, 2,* 133–165.

Cascio, W. F., & Boudreau, J. (2008). *Investing in people: The financial impact of human resource initiatives.* Upper Saddle River, NJ: Pearson Education.

Cleary, T. A. (1968). Test bias: Prediction of grades of Negro and White students in integrated colleges. *Journal of Educational Measurement, 5,* 115–124.

*Dudley, N. M., Orvis, K. A., Lebiecki, J. E., & Cortina, J. M. (2006). A meta-analytic investigation of conscientiousness in the prediction of job performance: Examining the intercorrelations and the incremental validity of narrow traits. *Journal of Applied Psychology, 91,* 40–57.

Ebel, R. L. (1977). Prediction? Validation? Construct validity? *Personnel Psychology, 30,* 55–63.

Embretson, S. E. (1999). Generating items during testing: Psychometric issues and models. *Psychometrika, 64,* 407–433.

Gelfand, M. J., Erez, M., & Aycan, Z. (2007). Cross-cultural organizational behavior. *Annual Review of Psychology, 58,* 479–514.

Ghiselli, E. E. (1966). *The validity of occupational aptitude tests.* New York: Wiley.

Gilliland, S. W. (1993). The perceived fairness of selection systems: An organizational justice perspective. *Academy of Management Review, 18,* 694–734.

Goldstein, I. L., Zedeck, S., & Schneider, B. (1993). An exploration of the job analysis–content validity process. In N. Schmitt & W. C. Borman (Eds.), *Personnel selection in organizations* (pp. 3–4). San Francisco: Jossey-Bass.

Guion, R. M. (1978). Content validity in moderation. *Personnel Psychology, 31,* 205–214.

Guion, R. M. (1998). *Assessment, measurement, and prediction for personnel decisions.* Mahwah, NJ: Erlbaum.

Hartigan, J. A., & Wigdor, A. K. (1989). *Fairness in employment testing.* Washington, DC: National Academies Press.

Hofmann, D. A., & Stetzer, A. (1996). A cross-level investigation of factors influencing unsafe behaviors and accidents. *Personnel Psychology, 49,* 307–339.

Hofstede, G. (2001). *Culture's consequences: Comparing values, behaviors, institutions, and organizations across nations.* Thousand Oaks, CA: Sage.

Hough, L. (1998). Personality at work: Issues and evidence. In M. D. Hakel (Ed.), *Beyond multiple choice: Evaluating alternatives to traditional testing for selection* (pp. 131–166). Mahwah, NJ: Erlbaum.

Hough, L. M., & Oswald, F. L. (2008). Personality testing and industrial-organizational psychology: Reflections, progress, and prospects. *Industrial and Organizational Psychology, 1,* 272–290.

Hulin, C. L., Roznowski, M., & Hachiya, D. (1985). Alternative opportunities and withdrawal decisions: Empirical and theoretical discrepancies and an integration. *Psychological Bulletin, 97,* 233–250.

*Hunter, J. E., & Hunter, R. F. (1984). Validity and utility of alternative predictors of job performance. *Psychological Bulletin, 96,* 72–88.

*Hurtz, G. M., & Donovan, J. J. (2000). Personality and job performance: The Big Five revisited. *Journal of Applied Psychology, 85,* 869–879.

Huselid, M. A. (1995). The impact of human resource management practices on turnover, productivity and corporate financial performance. *Academy of Management Journal, 38,* 635–672.

Irvine, S., & Kyllonen, P. (2002). *Generating items for cognitive tests: Theory and practice.* Mahwah, NJ: Erlbaum.

Johns, G. (1993). Constraints on the adoption of psychology-based personnel practices: Lessons from organizational innovation. *Personnel Psychology, 46,* 569–592.

Johns, G. (2006). The essential impact of context on organizational behavior. *Academy of Management Review, 31,* 386–408.

Kehoe, J. F., Mol, S. T., & Anderson, N. (in press). Managing sustainable selection programs. In J. L. Farr & N. T. Tippins (Eds.), *Handbook of employee selection.* New York: Taylor & Francis.

Klein, K. J., & Kozlowski, S. W. J. (Eds.). (2000). *Multilevel theory, research, and methods in organizations: Foundations, extensions, and new directions.* San Francisco: Jossey-Bass.

*Kuncel, N. R., Hezlett, S. A., & Ones, D. S. (2004). Academic performance, career potential, creativity, and job performance: Can one construct predict them all? *Journal of Personality and Social Psychology, 86,* 148–161.

Landy, F. J. (1986). Stamp collecting versus science: Validation as hypothesis testing. *American Psychologist, 41,* 1183–1192.

Landy, F. J. (2003). Validity generalization: Then and now. In K. R. Murphy (Ed.), *Validity generalization: A critical review* (pp. 155–196). Mahwah, NJ: Erlbaum.

Lawshe, C. H. (1975). A quantitative approach to content validity. *Personnel Psychology, 28,* 563–575.

McHenry, J. J., Hough, L. M., Toquam, J. L., Hanson, M. A., & Ashworth, S. (1990). Project A validity results: The relationship between predictor and criterion domains. *Personnel Psychology, 43,* 335–354.

McPhail, S. M. (Ed.). (2007). *Alternative validation strategies.* San Francisco: Jossey-Bass.

Mussio, S. J., & Smith, M. K. (1973). *Content validity: A procedural manual.* Minneapolis, MN: Civil Service Commission.

*Nathan, B. R., & Alexander, R. A. (1988). A comparison of criteria for test validation: A meta-analytic investigation. *Personnel Psychology, 41,* 517–535.

Newman, D. A., Jacobs, R. R., & Bartram, D. (2007). Choosing the best method for local validity estimation: Relative accuracy of meta-analysis versus a local study versus Bayes-analysis. *Journal of Applied Psychology, 92*(5), 1394–1413.

Ones, D. S., Viswesvaran, C., & Dilchert, S. (2005). Cognitive ability in selection decisions. In O. Wilhelm (Ed.), *Handbook of understanding and measuring intelligence* (pp. 431–468). Thousand Oaks, CA: Sage.

*Pearlman, K., Schmidt, F. L., & Hunter, J. E. (1980). Validity generalization results for tests used to predict job proficiency and training success in clerical occupations. *Journal of Applied Psychology, 65,* 373–406.

Peterson, N. G., Hough, L. M., Dunnette, M. D., Rosse, R. L., Houston, J. S., Toquam, J. L., & Wing, H. (1990). Project A: Specification of the predictor domain and development of new selection classification tests. *Personnel Psychology, 43,* 247–276.

Peterson, N. G., Wise, L. L., Arabian, J., & Hoffman, R. G. (2001). Synthetic validation and validity generalization: When empirical validation is not possible. In J. P. Campbell & D. J. Knapp (Eds.), *Exploring the limits in personnel selection and classification* (pp. 411–452). Mahwah, NJ: Erlbaum.

Ployhart, R. E. (2004). Organizational staffing: A multilevel review, synthesis, and model. In J. Martocchio (Ed.), *Research in personnel and human resource management* (Vol. 23, pp. 121–176). Oxford, England: Elsevier.

Ployhart, R. E., & Schmitt, N. (2007). The attraction-selection-attrition model and staffing: Some multilevel implications. In D. B. Smith (Ed.), *The people make the place: Exploring dynamic linkages between individuals and organizations* (pp. 89–102). Mahwah, NJ: Erlbaum.

Ployhart, R. E., & Schneider, B. (2005). Multilevel selection and prediction: Theories, methods and models. In A. Evers, O. Smit-Voskuyl, & N. R. Anderson (Eds.), *Handbook of personnel selection* (pp. 495–516). Chichester, England: Wiley.

Ployhart, R. E., Schneider, B., & Schmitt, N. (2006). *Staffing organizations.* Mahwah, NJ: Erlbaum.

Pulakos, E. D., & Schmitt, N. (1996). An evaluation of two strategies for reducing adverse impact and their effects on criterion-related validity. *Human Performance, 9,* 241–258.

Robinson, D. D. (1981). Content-oriented personnel selection in a small business setting. *Personnel Psychology, 34,* 77–87.

Saad, S., & Sackett, P. R. (2002). Examining differential prediction by gender in employment-oriented personality measures. *Journal of Applied Psychology, 87,* 667–674.

Sackett, P. R. (2002). The structure of counterproductive work behavior: Dimensionality and relationships with facets of job performance. *International Journal of Selection and Assessment, 10,* 5–11.

Sackett, P. R., Schmitt, N., Ellingson, J. E., & Kabin, M. B. (2001). High-stakes testing in employment, credentialing, and higher education: Prospects in a post-affirmative action world. *American Psychologist, 56,* 302–318.

Sackett, P. R., & Wilk, S. L. (1994). Within-group norming and other forms of score adjustment in preemployment testing. *American Psychologist, 49,* 929–954.

*Salgado, J. F. (1997). The five factor model of personality and job performance in the European Community. *Journal of Applied Psychology, 82,* 30–45.

Salgado, J. F., Anderson, N., & Hulsheger, U. R. (in press). Personnel selection in Europe: Psychotechnics and the forgotten history of modern scientific personnel selection. In J. L. Farr & N. T. Tippins (Eds.), *Handbook of personnel selection.* Mahwah, NJ: Erlbaum.

*Salgado, J. F., Anderson, N., Moscoso, S., Bertua, C., de Fruyt, F., & Rolland, J. P. (2003). A meta-analytic study of general mental ability validity for different occupations in the European community. *Journal of Applied Psychology, 88,* 1068–1081.

Scherbaum, C. A. (2005). Synthetic validity: Past, present, and future. *Personnel Psychology, 58,* 481–515.

*Schmidt, F. L., Gast-Rosenberg, I., & Hunter, J. E. (1980). Validity generalization results for computer programmers. *Journal of Applied Psychology, 62,* 529–540.

Schmidt, F. L., & Hunter, J. E. (1977). Development of a general solution to the problem of validity generalization. *Journal of Applied Psychology, 62,* 529–540.

Schmidt, F. L., & Hunter, J. E. (1998). The validity and utility of selection methods in personnel psychology: Practical and theoretical implications of 85 years of research findings. *Psychological Bulletin, 124,* 262–274.

Schmidt, F. L., & Hunter, J. E. (2003). History, development, evolution, and impact of validity generalization and meta-analysis methods, 1975–2001. In K. R. Murphy (Ed.), *Validity generalization: A critical review* (pp. 31–65). Mahwah, NJ: Erlbaum.

Schmidt, F. L., Mack, M. J., & Hunter, J. E. (1984). Selection utility in the occupation of U.S. park ranger for three modes of test use. *Journal of Applied Psychology, 69,* 490–497.

Schmidt, F. L., Oh, I., & Le, H. (2006). Increasing the accuracy of corrections for range restriction: Implications for selection procedure validities and other research results. *Personnel Psychology, 59,* 281–305.

Schmidt, F. L., Pearlman, K., & Hunter, J. E. (1980). The validity and fairness of employment and educational tests for Hispanic Americans: A review and analysis. *Personnel Psychology, 33,* 705–724.

Schmitt, N., & Fandre, J. (2008). Validity of selection procedures. In S. Cartwright & C. L. Cooper (Eds.), *Oxford handbook of personnel psychology* (pp. 163–193). Oxford, England: Oxford University Press.

Schmitt, N., & Gilliland, S. W. (1992). Beyond differential prediction: Fairness in selection. In D. M. Saunders (Eds.), *New approaches to employee management* (pp. 21–46). Greenwich, CT: JAI Press.

Schmitt, N., Gooding, R. Z., Noe, R. D., & Kirsch, M. (1984). Metanalyses of validity studies published between 1964 and 1982 and the investigation of study characteristics. *Personnel Psychology, 37,* 407–422.

Schmitt, N., & Kuljanin, G. (2008). Measurement invariance: Review of practice and implications. *Human Resource Management Review, 18,* 210–222.

Schmitt, N., & Ostroff, C. (1986). Operationalizing the "behavioral consistency" approach: Selection test development based on a content-oriented strategy. *Personnel Psychology, 39,* 91–108.

Scholarios, D. M., Johnson, C. D., & Zeidner, J. (1994). Selecting predictors for maximizing the classification efficiency of a battery. *Journal of Applied Psychology, 79,* 412–424.

Schuler, H. (1993). Social validity of selection situations: A concept and some empirical results. In H. Schuler, J. L. Farr, & M. Smith (Eds.), *Personnel selection and assessment: Individual and organizational perspectives* (pp. 11–26). Hillsdale, NJ: Erlbaum.

Schuler, H., & Stehle, W. (1985). Soziale validitat eignungsdiagnostischer verfahren: Anforderungen fur die zukunft [The social validity of assessment: Issues for the future]. In H. Schuler & W. Stehle (Eds.), *Organisationspsychologie und Unternehmenspraxis: Perspektiven der Kooperation* (pp. 133–138). Gottingen, Germany: Verlag fur Angewandte Psychologie/Hogrefe.

Schwartz, S. H. (1994). Beyond individualism and collectivism: New cultural dimensions of values. In U. Kim, H. C. Triandis, C. Kagitcibasi, S. C. Choi, & G. Yoon (Eds.), *Individualism and collectivism: Theory, method, and applications* (pp. 85–119). Thousand Oaks, CA: Sage.

Society for Industrial and Organizational Psychology. (2003). *Principles for the validation and use of personnel selection procedures.* Bowling Green, OH: Author.

Sussman, M., & Robertson, D. U. (1986). The validity of validity: An analysis of validation study designs. *Journal of Applied Psychology, 71,* 461–468.

Tenopyr, M. L. (1977). Content-construct confusion. *Personnel Psychology, 30,* 47–54.

*Tett, R. P., Jackson, D. N., & Rothstein, M. (1991). Personality measures as predictors of job performance: A meta-analytic review. *Personnel Psychology, 44,* 703–742.

Truxillo, D. M., Bauer, T. N., Campion, M. A., & Paronto, M. E. (2002). Selection fairness information and applicant reactions: A longitudinal field study. *Journal of Applied Psychology, 87,* 1020–1031.

Vandenberg, R. J., & Lance, C. E. (2000). A review and synthesis of the measurement invariance literature: Suggestions, practices, and recommendations for organizational research. *Organizational Research Methods, 3,* 4–69.

*Vinchur, A. J., Schippman, J. S., Switzer, F. A., III, & Roth, P. L. (1998). A meta-analytic review of predictors of job performance for salespeople. *Journal of Applied Psychology, 83,* 586–597.

CHAPTER 14

UTILITY OF SELECTION SYSTEMS: SUPPLY-CHAIN ANALYSIS APPLIED TO STAFFING DECISIONS

Wayne F. Cascio and John W. Boudreau

Traditionally, industrial and organizational (I/O) psychologists have focused on the economic payoffs of selection systems, either in terms of individual programs (predicted savings from the use of a particular method or selection system for a given number of selectees) or in terms of individuals (payoffs per selectee; Cascio & Boudreau, 2008; Schmidt & Hunter, 1983). Although the origins of utility analysis date back many decades (Brogden, 1946, 1949; Brogden & Taylor, 1950; Cronbach & Gleser, 1965), interest in it revived in the late 1970s (Cascio & Silbey, 1979; Schmidt, Hunter, McKenzie, & Muldrow, 1979). Since then, there have been many refinements to the basic utility-analysis approach (Sturman, 2000) and considerable published research on the various parameters of the model (see Boudreau, 1991; Boudreau & Ramstad, 2003; Cabrera & Raju, 2001; Cascio, 1993, 2000; Russell, Colella, & Bobko, 1993, for reviews).

By way of background, consider the basic utility equation that has been developed to estimate the payoffs from the use of valid selection procedures. If we assume that *n* workers are hired during a given year and that the average job tenure of those workers is *t* years, the dollar increase in productivity can be determined from Equation 1 below. Equation 1 is based on the principles of linear regression, although to save space, we do not derive it here (see, e.g., Bobko, 2001; Cascio & Boudreau, 2008).

$$\Delta U = ntr_{xy}SD_y\bar{Z}_x, \quad (1)$$

where ΔU = increase in productivity in dollars; n = number of persons hired; t = average job tenure in years of those hired; r_{xy} = the validity coefficient representing the correlation between the predictor and job performance in the applicant population; SD_y = the standard deviation of job performance in dollars (roughly 40% of annual wage; Schmidt & Hunter, 1983); and $\bar{Z}_x$ = the average predictor score of those selected in the applicant population, expressed in terms of standard scores.

When Equation 1 was used to estimate the dollar gains in productivity associated with use of the programmer aptitude test (PAT) to select computer programmers for federal-government jobs, given that an average of 618 programmers per year are selected, each with an average job tenure of 9.69 years, the payoff per selectee was $64,725 over his or her tenure on the job (roughly $210,000 in 2008 dollars). This represents a per-year productivity gain of $21,672 (in 2008 dollars) for each new programmer (Schmidt et al., 1979).

It is important to note, however, that Equation 1 is an "unadjusted" estimate of payoff. Subsequent research examined the effects of factors such as economic variables (corporate taxes, variable costs, and discounting future cash flows back to their present value), use of the selection process with multiple cohorts of employees ("employee flows" into and out of the workforce), probationary periods, multiple selection devices, and rejected job offers. A computer simulation of 10,000 scenarios, each of which comprised various values of the five factors just noted, found that economic variables had the largest effect, followed in rank order by multiple selection devices, departures from top-down hiring, probationary period, and employee flows (Sturman, 2000). The median effect size of the total set of adjustments was 91% lower than the unadjusted estimate, with a minimum total effect of 71% lower than the unadjusted estimate, and negative estimates 16% of the time. Although the majority of the utility estimates for the simulated scenarios remained positive, the five modifications had sizable and noteworthy practical effects.

These results suggest that although valid selection procedures may often lead to positive payoffs for the organization, actual payoffs depend significantly on organizational and situational factors that may moderate their effects. Utility analysis has been applied to a wide variety of employment activities, including recruitment (Boudreau & Rynes, 1985), staffing (Cascio & Ramos, 1986; Hunter & Hunter, 1984), performance measurement (Landy, Farr, & Jacobs, 1982), compensation (Sturman, Trevor, Boudreau, & Gerhart, 2003), separations and acquisitions (Boudreau & Berger, 1985), training and development (Schmidt, Hunter, & Pearlman, 1982), and downsizing (Mabon, 1996; Mabon & Westling, 1996).

Our purpose in writing this chapter is not to review this body of work. Rather, it is to propose a different way of looking at the outcomes of utility analysis—not from that of a technology but through the lens of decision systems, from an individual-level of analysis (individual programs, or cohorts of selectees) to an organizational-level of analysis. From that perspective, we will not emphasize the technical features of utility analysis (see Cascio & Boudreau, 2008). Rather, we argue for a change in orientation and present a framework and logic that might lead to new insights and applications of the approach—insights and applications that will lead to genuine impact on decisions at the level of the organization. This framework is already emerging in practice, which makes the practical value of research and the likelihood of available field data from organizational data systems even greater.

TOWARD AN INTEGRATIVE FRAMEWORK

In the conventional approach to staffing, activities like sourcing, recruitment, initial screening, selection, offers, onboarding of new hires, performance management, and retention tend to be viewed as independent activities, each separate from the others. A considerable body of theory and research findings are available in each of these areas (cf. Cascio & Aguinis, in press), even frameworks to calculate the costs and potential monetary benefits of each element described earlier. Such a microlevel or *silo* orientation has dominated the field almost from its inception, and within it, the objective has been to maximize payoffs for each element of the overall staffing process. Certainly much of our own research fits that orientation.

That said, we believe that there is an opportunity both for researchers and for practitioners to develop and apply an integrative framework whose objective is to optimize investments across the various elements of the staffing process, not simply to maximize payoffs within each element. To be sure, we are not the first to note this possibility. As Cascio (1978) wrote,

> By focusing only on selection, the classical validity approach neglects the implications of selection decisions for the rest of the personnel system. Such an observation is not new. Several authors (Dudek, 1963; Dunnette, 1962; Uhlaner, 1960; Wallace, 1965) have noted that an optimal selection strategy may not be optimal for other personnel functions such as recruiting and training. In addition, other factors, such as the cost of the selection procedure, the loss resulting from error, and the organization's ability to evaluate success must be considered. When attention is focused solely on selection, to the exclusion of other, related functions, the performance effectiveness of the overall personnel system may suffer considerably. In short, any selection procedure must be evaluated in terms of its total benefits to the organization. (p. 225)

SUPPLY-CHAIN ANALYSIS AND THE STAFFING PROCESS

When it comes to optimizing the overall results of a process, we believe that staffing researchers have much to learn from the field of supply-chain analysis. Supply-chain analysis pays careful attention to the ultimate quality of materials and components, and it analyzes inputs in terms of their effects on key organizational outcomes (e.g., reliability, failure rates). Supply-chain analysis seldom focuses solely on the volume or cost of what is acquired. Rather, it focuses on measurements that reflect the logic of the supply-chain process and provide diagnostic information to improve supply-chain decisions (Boudreau & Ramstad, 2001, 2004, 2007; Cappelli, 2008).

THE VALUE OF THE SUPPLY-CHAIN METAPHOR FOR STAFFING UTILITY

Reframing utility analysis research within the supply-chain framework makes optimization opportunities and related research directions more apparent. Perhaps more important, the supply-chain framework may help to solve one of the thorniest issues in utility analysis—the disturbingly stubborn difficulty in getting key decision makers to embrace it. As Boudreau and Ramstad (2003) observed, research has shown that utility-analysis models are seldom used by leaders, and when they are used, the effects are mixed, that is, sometimes they impact decision makers and sometimes they do not (Borman, Hanson, & Hedge, 1997; Florin-Thuma & Boudreau, 1987; Latham & Whyte, 1994; Macan & Highhouse 1994; Roth, Segars, & Wright, 2000; Whyte & Latham, 1997). Utility-analysis results seem to be more acceptable to operating executives when they are integrated with capital-budgeting considerations (Carson, Becker, & Henderson, 1998; Cascio & Morris, 1990; Hoffman, 1996; Mattson, 2003). Consistent with this approach, Boudreau (2008) proposed that progress might be more rapid if researchers and human resource (HR) leaders relate their analytical frameworks to the frameworks that decision makers outside of HR already use. This is consistent with a growing theme in disciplines such as management science, to encourage integrating behavioral insights into management-science frameworks and vice versa (Boudreau, 2004; Boudreau, Hopp, McClain & Thomas, 2003; Schultz, Juran, & Boudreau, 1999).

Boudreau (2008) specifically noted the potentially powerful metaphor of the supply chain applied to the issue of talent recruitment, selection, development and training:

> Your supply-chain model applies to talent-management decisions just as it does to raw materials, unfinished goods, or technology. Supply-chain analysis optimizes supply-chain elements to achieve desired outcomes with the minimum resources. If the quality of raw materials drops, supply-chain logic compares the value of things like switching suppliers, more careful screening of deliveries, or adjusting manufacturing processes to handle lower-quality materials. Supply-chain analysis isn't about one-size-fits-all, but about making the right decision.
>
> When a line leader complains that he or she is getting inferior talent, or not enough talent for a vital position, HR too often devises a solution without full insight into the broader supply chain. HR often responds by enhancing interviews or tests, and presenting evidence about the improved validity of the selection process. Yet a more effective solution might be to retain the original selection process with the same validity, but to recruit from sources where the average quality of talent is higher.
>
> Or, consider what happens when business leaders end up with too few candidates, and instruct HR to widen the recruitment search. HR is often too eager to respond with more recruiting activities, when in fact the number of candidates presented to business leaders is already sufficient. The problem is that some leaders are better at inducing candidates to accept offers. The more prudent response may be to improve the performance of the leaders who cause candidates to reject offers!
>
> Leaders are accustomed to a logical approach that optimizes all stages of the supply chain, when it comes to raw materials, unfinished goods, and tech-

nology. Why not adopt the same approach to talent? (paras. 4, 6–8)

SUPPLY-CHAIN LOGIC

Consider how organizations routinely consider the supply chain for resources, such as raw materials, components, technology, and consulting services. Figure 14.1 shows how the logic works for the acquisition process for such resources. The top row of boxes (numbered 1–7) shows the flow of resources through the decision process, and the bottom row of boxes (numbered 8–13) shows the processes themselves. In Box 1, exploration reveals potential sources of the resource, but not all of these may prove to be viable. In Box 2, the potential resources are winnowed down to those proven to be viable for the organization. As shown in Box 8, this might occur both through discovery (in which potential resources are vetted to prove their viability) or through building (in which formerly not-viable resources are made viable through vendor training, economic assistance, etc.). From this array of proven resources, a subset will become accessible to the organization (Box 3) by building connections (Box 9, using infrastructure, relationships, etc.). From among these accessible resources, the organization screens in (Box 10) those that meet minimum standards of quality, price, timeliness, and so forth, which become preferred resources (Box 4). These are then filtered further into a smaller set of resources that are selected (Box 11) to be solicited (Box 5) with offers made for acquisition, and so forth. The successful solicitations resulting from the contracting process (Box 12) produce resources (Box 6) that are under contract to be delivered at a specific quality, price, time, and so forth. Finally, the contract is executed (Box 13), and the resources are acquired, or an ongoing relationship with the supply source is created (Box 7). The bottom of Figure 14.1 (Box 14) shows the types of metrics used in supply-chain analysis to optimize outcomes.

Essentially, the decision process involves optimizing costs against price and time, to achieve levels of expected quality or quantity and risks associated with variations in quality or quantity. If the quality

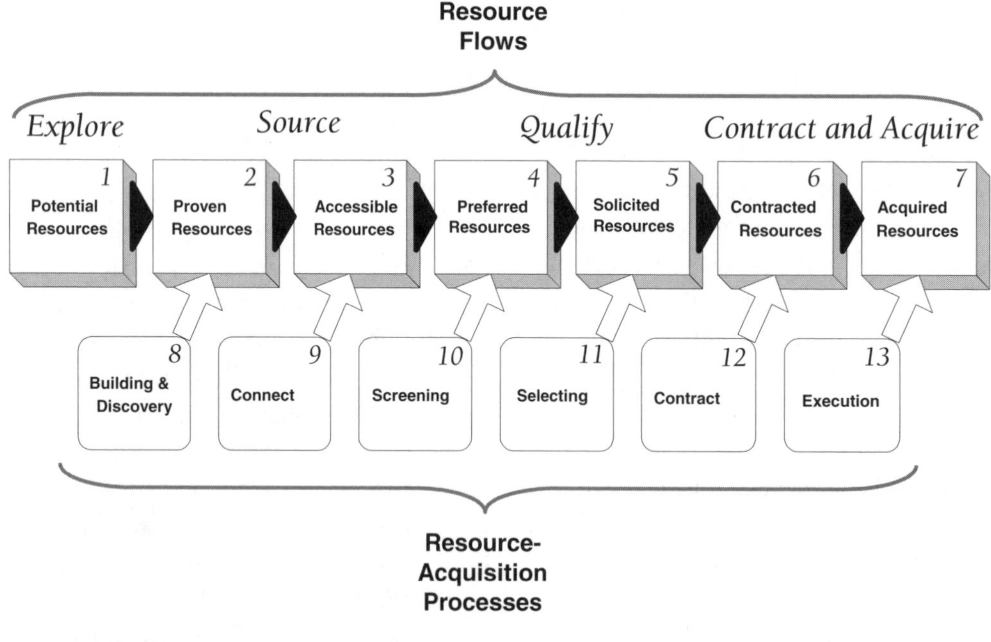

FIGURE 14.1. Resource-acquisition supply chain. Metrics: Cost, time, price, expected quality–quantity, variation in quality–quantity.

or quantity of acquired resources falls below standard or exhibits excessive variation, the organization can evaluate where investments in the process will make the biggest difference. One might enhance the contract process (Box 12) to hold existing suppliers to more stringent standards, or one might attempt to connect (Box 9) with new sources that promise greater uniformity or a more acceptable quantity and quality. In short, many combinations of investments to enhance the process elements in the supply chain are possible, and supply-chain analysis involves logical and mathematical modeling to find optimal combinations.

The mathematical modeling in this example might look like this: Suppose we build computer mice, and we observe that one of the components is showing a much greater percentage of unsatisfactory units, so we must discard more of those components (this is measured and observed in Box 7 of Figure 14.1). One solution might be to move one box to the left and change our execution (Box 13) to better assess the quality of incoming units, by assigning additional staff or technology to the last step of bringing the units into our production process. We could mathematically model how much variation we observe as the components arrive and estimate the cost tradeoffs to reduce that variation through better filtering or execution. We could also calculate a similar estimate based on the contract process (Box 12), by observing the variability in quality across the contractor candidates that we use and estimating what it would cost to switch to new providers and what that would do to variation, even if we kept our filtering processes (Boxes 10 and 11) the same. Similarly, we could examine if any other suppliers have emerged on the scene or if there are suppliers whom we solicit (Box 5) but that choose not to work with us (Box 6). If some of those suppliers seem to have lower variability, then we could consider the cost of engaging them (Box 12) with more attractive contracts, even if we keep our execution (Box 13) the same. This logical process of estimating the level of quality and its variation at each stage, and the cost of reducing that variation, can continue as we move left. The mathematical-optimization algorithm would be to examine each stage and the combinations of investments in several stages, to determine the most cost-effective combination of investments to make. For example, it might be a new supplier with a somewhat better contract or a new supplier with lower variability in quality and a slightly enhanced execution process on our part.

A powerful, fundamental concept is that at every stage the quality or variability of the resource flows can be enhanced at some cost, but the objective is not to maximize quality and reduce variation and cost at every stage. Rather, it is to achieve the appropriate quality, variability and cost standards in each one, for optimal balance between costs, returns, and risks. It may be quite appropriate to allow wide variability in the quality and quantity of accessible resources (Box 3) if the processes of screening and selecting (Boxes 10 and 11) can reduce variation sufficiently and establish sufficient quality standards in the solicited resources (Box 5). On the other hand, it does little good to stringently screen, select, and contract with resource suppliers (Boxes 10, 11, and 12) if the accessible resources (Box 3) are of such low quality that no amount of screening can yield enough satisfactory supply. Instead, the optimal answer may lie in expanding connections to new resources (Box 9) or even in enhancing technologies to build and discover other sources (Box 8).

THE SUPPLY CHAIN AND EXTERNAL STAFFING

Now, consider the similarities between the supply-chain metaphor and the external-staffing process. Figure 14.2 takes the earlier diagram and places the concepts into the domain of external staffing. This is what has been called the *supply-chain approach* to external staffing (Boudreau & Ramstad, 2001, 2004, 2007, Cascio & Boudreau, 2008).

Cascio and Boudreau (2008, p. 173) described this framework. Groups of individuals (talent pools) flow through the various stages of the staffing process, with each stage serving as a filter that eliminates a subset of the original talent pool. The top row shows the results of the filtering process, beginning with a potential labor pool (Box 1) that is developed into an available labor pool (Box 2), that organizations then winnow through recruitment and selection (Boxes 8, 9, and 10) down to a group

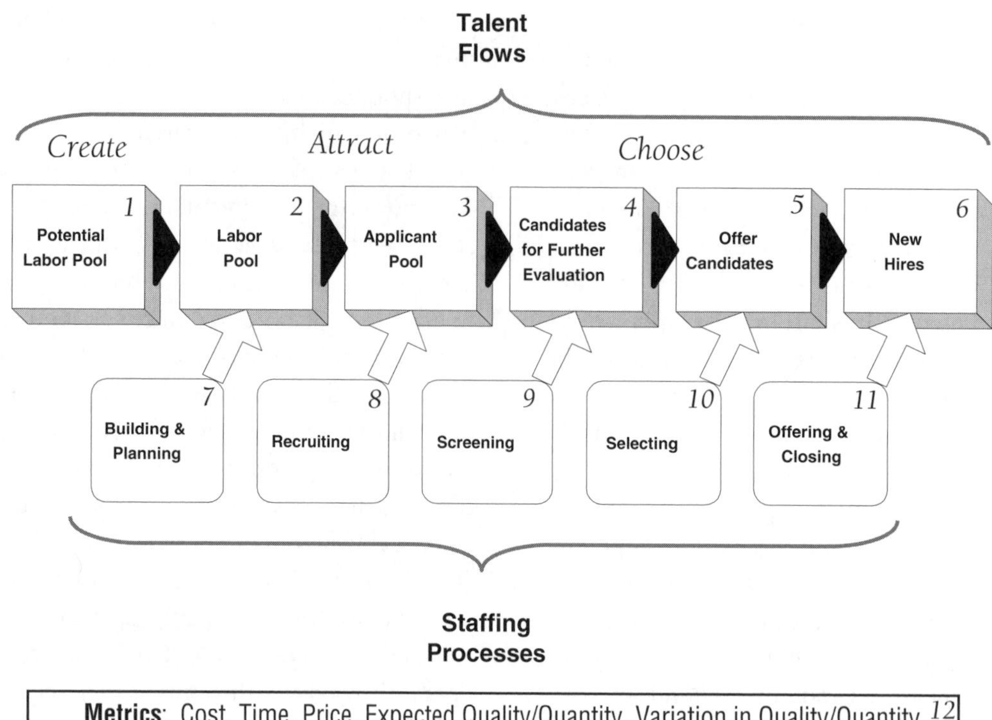

FIGURE 14.2. External staffing supply chain. Metrics: Cost, time, price, expected quality–quantity, variation in quality–quantity.

that receives offers (Box 5) and then is winnowed further as some accept offers (Box 11) and remain with the organization (Box 6).

The "staffing processes" in the lower row show the activities that accomplish the filtering sequence, beginning in Box 7 with *building and planning* (forecasting trends in external and internal labor markets, inducing potential applicants to develop qualifications to satisfy future talent demands), leading in Box 8 to *recruiting* (attracting applicants who wish to be considered), then in Box 9 to *screening* (identifying the clearly qualified and/or rejecting the clearly unqualified), moving in Box 10 to *selection* (rating those not screened in or out earlier) and ending in Box 11 with *offering and closing* (creating and presenting offers and getting candidates to accept).

Figure 14.3 shows a common selection utility-analysis formula, in which the parameters are categorized according to the common supply-chain metrics of quantity, quality, and cost. The derivation of the utility formula was described in detail in Cascio and Boudreau (2008).

In Figure 14.3, we chose one of many utility-analysis formulas, this one applying to selecting one cohort of new hires who remain with the organization for T years, on average. The same sort of logic can be applied to virtually all utility-analysis formulas, parsing them into these three elements: quantity, quality, and cost. We do not undertake a

$$\Delta U = \overbrace{(N_s)(T)}^{\text{Quantity}}\overbrace{(SD_y)(r_{x,y})(\bar{Z}_x)}^{\text{Quality}} - \overbrace{C(N_{app})}^{\text{Cost}}$$

FIGURE 14.3. Selection utility-analysis formula as quantity, quality, and cost. ΔU = dollar value of the improvement in hiring quality from using a selection device; N_s = no. of employees selected; T = average tenure of the employees selected; SD_y = dollar value of a one SD difference in yearly performance; $r_{x,y}$ = correlation between selection-device score (x) and job performance (y); $\bar{Z}_x$ = average selection-device score of those selected, in SD units; C = cost of selection device for one applicant; N_{app} = no. of applicants tested with the selection device.

comprehensive review of various utility-analysis equations here. Rather, our point is to demonstrate the close parallels between the logic of utility analysis and the logic of supply-chain analysis. Figure 14.3 depicts expected values of the three parameters, but several previous authors have demonstrated how simulation and sensitivity analysis can be used to incorporate variation in any or all of these parameters (see Cascio & Boudreau, 2008, for a summary).

Supply-chain analysis is also often concerned with delivery time, which does not appear explicitly in utility-analysis formulas. However, it is often implicitly included in the cost parameter, as the opportunity cost of the time of those involved in the staffing process. Thus, although traditional utility-analysis research has not connected explicitly to supply-chain parameters, much of the work on utility analysis is fully compatible with a supply-chain approach. This fact suggests that it may well be possible to increase the acceptability and use of utility analysis by connecting it more explicitly with the supply-chain framework familiar to most business leaders.

Boudreau and Ramstad (2007; see chap. 12, this volume) further refined the idea in Figure 14.2, with the following examples:

1. *Building and planning.* Building and planning influences the number and quality of individuals who might potentially become qualified candidates. It includes forecasting labor-force trends and talent demands, as well as direct intervention to increase the population qualified to meet the talent needs of the future. For example, The American Business Collaboration, a corporate partnership, produces middle school science and technology camps that serve 500 kids at 10 camps in five U.S. cities and overseas. The program is funded by IBM, Texas Instruments, and Exxon Mobil. Boeing is exploring possible expansion of a popular summer science camp for 1st through 12th graders near Huntington Beach, California. AT&T backs three science-and-math camps in Detroit and Chicago, and Intel sponsors three science camps in Colorado and Oregon. As the *Wall Street Journal* reported, year-round mentors for campers reinforce lessons learned the following:

   > With pink-streaked hair and body piercings, IBM software engineer Janel Barfield fit right in at the Austin, Texas, middle school cafeteria she visited last year to see the technology camper she was mentoring. When the girl confided that a relative had laughed at her dream of becoming an astronaut, Ms. Barfield said: "Girl, he doesn't know what he's talking about. . . . You'd make a great astronaut." (Shellenbarger, 2006, p. D1)

   There's no guarantee that every student in these camps will apply to one of the sponsoring organizations. At this stage of the pipeline, the goal is to increase the population of those that might.
2. *Recruiting.* Recruiting induces individuals in the labor pool to apply to the organization. Recruiting includes recruitment advertising, job fairs, online job posting, and so forth, and it increasingly encompasses less direct activities, such as company product or service advertisements that create an attractive image to job candidates. Recruiting should strive for "optimum" quantity and quality rather than "biggest and best" (Boudreau & Berger, 1985). The most effective applicant pools may be smaller (if a high percentage of them take the offers), and may even be less qualified than the maximum possible (if the organization can train them after they are hired). For example, one of the biggest challenges in online recruiting is that although online ads generate a large quantity of applicants, that can mean much higher costs of résumé screening ("The Pros and Cons of Online Recruiting," 2004). The key is to optimize the higher quantity against the organization's ability to exploit them with an array of other programs.
3. *Screening.* The purpose of screening is to help decision makers choose which applicants should be rejected or hired immediately. Often, screening is seen as weeding out the unqualified, but when labor is in short supply, screening can identify high-quality candidates who can bypass the selection process and receive immediate offers. Optimal screening therefore balances the benefits of quick hires and low cost against the long-term costs of making a poor hiring decision through

standards that are too low or missing "diamonds in the rough" with standards that are too high. These are subtle and important considerations, yet screening activities are often measured only in terms of the cost and time of their activities or in terms of the number of candidates who survive the initial screen. An interesting variant is to screen by using temporary work. In India, which is facing an increasingly acute shortage of professionals, "temping" becomes a means to screen candidates and, in effect, becomes a fast-track apprentice program (Dagar & Shukla, 2006).

4. *Selection.* The purpose of selection is to determine which of the prescreened applicants will receive offers. Is it always optimal to increase the *validity*, or degree of relationship between selection techniques and performance? When selection is viewed in the context of the talent-acquisition pipeline, high validity is a necessary condition only if there are enough applicants and if the applicant pool varies enough in quality to justify the effort to find the best ones. For example, consider the situation in which an organization recruits college graduates from regional campuses where the quality or fit between available candidates and available jobs varies a great deal, but applicants have strong regional ties, so they are likely to accept an offer of employment in the area. A highly valid test of management skills may be extremely valuable in identifying the stars. On the other hand, when recruiting at a top business program, there is little to be learned from a valid test of business skills, but increasing the hit rate of acceptances may be very pivotal.
5. *Offering and closing.* The purpose of offering and closing is to define and make offers. The focus is often only on whether a high proportion of offers are accepted, which is the *yield rate*. The pipeline approach described here suggests that a broader perspective would also examine whether the highest-quality applicants accept or reject offers and whether the organization is forced to make offers to candidates who are marginally qualified because of severe shortages. The offering-and-closing process often begins long before the final offer is actually presented. When striving for racial and ethnic diversity, for example, it is an interesting question whether the signals about organizational diversity that candidates encounter during their site visits affect their later willingness to accept offers of employment (McKay & Avery, 2006).

In Figure 14.2, we have included a box at the bottom that reflects the metrics from Figure 14.1. The idea is that at every stage of the staffing process, one could evaluate the cost and time invested in HR staffing processes against the price of the human resources that result from those processes, and the resulting average and variation in their quantity and quality.

For example, consider an organization that recruits technical professionals such as computer programmers or engineers. For this work, there might be many thousands of students in high school with potential (aptitude) for such work. Consider if we had data on a technical aptitude test (say the scores could range from zero to 1,000), first given in college to the 150,000 students that enter technical program majors. Then we continued to track those scores as students finished the program, decided to enter the profession and apply for jobs, as some of those applicants decided to apply to our organization, and then we winnowed down the candidates through successive screening, selection, and offers. The numbers might look something like this (where *no.* is the population of candidates, *average score* is the mean score on the technical aptitude test, and "*SD*" is the standard deviation of those scores), depicted in the framework of the numbered boxes of Figure 14.2:

Potential labor pool (Box 1): no. = 150,000, average score = 100, *SD* = 25;
Labor pool (Box 2): no. = 15,000, average score = 600, *SD* = 22;
Applicant pool (Box 3): no. = 500, average score = 400, *SD* = 20;
Candidates for further evaluation (Box 4): no. = 450, average score = 420, *SD* = 18;
Offer candidates (Box 5): no. = 50, average score = 500, *SD* = 10; and
New hires (Box 6): no. = 25, average score = 475, *SD* = 8.

Thus, we see that at the end of the process we are getting 25 technical professionals with an average score of 475 on the test and a standard deviation of 8. This is an increase in the quality compared with the applicant pool that came to our door (an increase of 75 points on the test) and a reduction in variation from a standard deviation of 20 for the applicant pool to a standard deviation of 8 for new hires. However, looking further back in the process, we see that the average score of the labor pool of technical professionals (average of 600 on the test) is actually higher than our new-hire average of 450. Why? Notice that lower scoring professionals tend to apply to our position (average score of 400), and although we manage to improve their quality through our screening and selection process (their scores increase to 500 at the offer stage), we lose some of the best because they refuse our offers (average of those accepting offers is only 475). Therefore, we are diligently using selection and screening to improve the quality of those who arrive at our door, but in the end we are doing worse than if we could just attract and hire candidates of even average quality in the labor pool.

Looking at the test scores alone, the most significant opportunity for improvement is not in enhanced selection or screening, but in getting better candidates to show up at our door. If we could attract an applicant pool with scores 200 points higher and equal our current improvement from that point, we would see a significant increase in candidate quality.

Now, imagine that we considered an array of process improvements at each stage of the sourcing pipeline in Figure 14.2. At the stage of enticing those in the labor pool to apply for our openings, we might include the cost of enhanced recruitment, enhancing the value proposition to be more attractive to the top candidates (are we the world-class destination for those who want to work with new technology, for example?), more aggressive recruiting at the "top schools," and so forth. This, in turn, might get the average quality of those applying above 400. However, an optimum system would also need to consider how to entice them to join, so we would consider the costs of various offer elements such as salary, benefits, development, and work–life balance. We would consider their costs and their likely effect both on the mean and on the standard deviation of qualifications.

Depending on costs and effects on the average and variability of quality, it might be better to enhance our job offers so that we keep more of the stars that we already recruited and selected. However, we might also discover that at a lower cost of more aggressive recruitment, we would be able to tap into a much higher quality group of applicants that didn't know about us, and they are as likely as our current applicants to accept our offers. With more complete data, one can imagine a very specific mathematical algorithm that would calculate the change in average and standard deviation of test score for a given investment at each stage or that would allow an organization to calculate break-even levels. For example, if we knew that investing a million dollars in better technology for these professionals to use would increase both the quality of applicants and their likelihood of accepting our offers, that might be superior to investing in better selection that must strive to find better candidates from a rather mediocre pool of applicants.

Integrating costs with the average and variation in quality has been the focus of a great deal of research in utility analysis, but too often such work has treated one element of the process in isolation. For example, most utility-analysis research can be characterized as focusing on the "screening" and "selecting" boxes in Figure 14.2, using statistical techniques to assess the relationships between dollars invested in improved selection and the change in average value between the applicant pool and those chosen to receive offers. Indeed, most utility-analysis research has also assumed that those receiving offers accept them (for an exception, see Murphy, 1986), thus combining the screening, selection, and offering and closing processes into one step.

This body of previous work has been immensely valuable in articulating the potential payoffs from improved selection, but Figure 14.2 reveals that such work also fails to account for a wide variety of factors that might affect the quality of new hires beyond the quality of selection per se. Boudreau and Rynes (1985) noted this limitation and showed how utility-analysis formulas and logic could be modified to encompass elements of the process shown on the left-hand side of Figure 14.2, by integrating recruitment into the mix. They also drew attention to the fact that most selection-utility analyses had focused on the effects of improved staffing for its effect on the difference in average value between those hired and those in the applicant pool. Boudreau and Rynes suggested that equally important effects of recruiting might be seen in the quantity of applicants and in their average value and variability. Yet, research on the variation in utility parameters across recruiting sources has been rare. Connerly, Carlson, and Mecham (2003) provided one notable exception, in a study that suggested such differences may be significant.

The supply-chain metaphor not only draws attention to this opportunity, it also articulates the relevant processes and paves the way to draw on established supply-chain-analysis techniques that are often not familiar to I/O psychologists and HR leaders. Thus far, we have focused on the segment of the talent-supply chain that involves external sourcing. The supply-chain metaphor allows us to connect these external staffing processes to what happens after applicants join the organization.

EXTENDING THE SUPPLY CHAIN TO INCLUDE RETENTION

Supply Chains and Inventory Loss

An important feature of supply-chain logic is that it integrates both the inflow and outflow of resources, using a consistent logic focused on the average and variation in quality and quantity, as well as the cost and time required to achieve those outcomes. For example, after a resource is acquired, it might be lost through spoilage, theft, or damage. If an organization wanted to prevent inventory spoilage completely, it might spend significant resources to install refrigeration or other systems that would drive spoilage to near zero. This could reduce the spoilage rate, and in doing so it might save a great deal of money. Managers who are constantly dealing with inventory spoilage would welcome the relief from this onerous task. Looking only at the cost of the refrigeration system compared with the managers' time and inventory loss saved, it might even be the case that the system covers its costs and produces a positive return.

Alternatively, it could still be the wrong investment. We have completely ignored the possibility that simply replacing the spoiled inventory might be inexpensive. The savings from not installing the refrigeration system may be greater than the cost of discarding the spoiled inventory and acquiring more. The organization may be able to tap suppliers with inventory that spoils less, perhaps at a much lower cost than installing the refrigeration system.

This may seem a bit confusing at first. How can it be that the refrigeration system can produce a payoff that achieves an acceptable rate of return and still be the wrong decision? The answer is that by looking only at the part of the system that deals directly with preventing spoilage after inventory is acquired, we have ignored other ways either to reduce spoilage, or to make the spoilage less costly by acquiring substitutes. The idea is that *the more of the process one can measure and analyze, the more likely the optimum solution will reveal itself.* This is not to say that installing refrigeration wouldn't produce a positive payoff, because it would. However, if one can simply replace the spoiled inventory at half the cost of the refrigeration system, that's an even better option. It may appear that these conclusions contradict each other, but in fact that is only true if they are seen in isolation. If we can compare them and examine their relative effects on the entire process and its outcomes (in this case, spoilage), the conflict disappears, and we can see that one alternative is simply a better way to achieve the goal.

In summary, the optimum solution is not apparent if the organization focuses only on the costs and benefits of a spoilage-reduction program, without considering its integration with the resource-acquisition process. The optimum solution does become apparent when one optimizes the value of the inventory against the costs and benefits of its acquisition as well as its depletion.

In the realm of utility analysis, we often see an analogy to this situation, in which organizations are quite attentive to the elements of the process that they have traditionally used to affect the quality, cost, and variability of the workforce, such as recruitment or selection. It may appear confusing when analysis shows that improved recruiting has a high payoff and so does improved selection, and so does landing better candidates. Looking at the entire process seems to offer lots of good ideas, but how does one choose? The answer is that by considering their individual effects on a specific set of process outcomes, and then by considering how they work in combination, one can arrive at an integrated solution. At the heart of utility analysis is the mathematical logic that shows how this might be possible. Figure 14.3 can capture the effects of integration across the staffing supply chain, because it contains parameters that reflect the level and variability in quality, as well as the costs of investments that affect them. To date, complete integration has not been described, but the logic of the utility formula makes it possible.

Application to Employee Separation and Retention

Figure 14.4 extends our utility-analysis framework to incorporate resource loss. In figure 16.4, the top row includes the supply-chain version of external sourcing, and the second row now adds a supply-chain metaphor to external retention. By *external retention,* we refer to the overall pattern of retention (and loss) that arises as employees move across the organization's boundary. It is often called *employee turnover,* but we focus on retention because of the lessons of the supply chain, that optimization requires focusing on the value of the resource that is available, not only on what is lost.

As Figure 14.4 shows, external retention can be thought of in parallel terms to external sourcing. The workforce is assessed in regard to its quality and quantity (e.g., through appraisals of past performance, future potential, skills inventories), and then existing employees are "rerecruited" through increased pay and benefits, enhanced career opportunities, and other approaches, so that the organization has a pool of existing employees who wish to remain with the organization. From that pool, the organization and the employees make retention choices, with some employees staying and others leaving. The result of this pattern determines the composition of the remaining workforce.

Thus, *spoilage* in terms of human resource analysis might be akin to the employee-turnover rate. The turnover rate alone is a very simplistic indicator of the full sourcing-retention process shown in

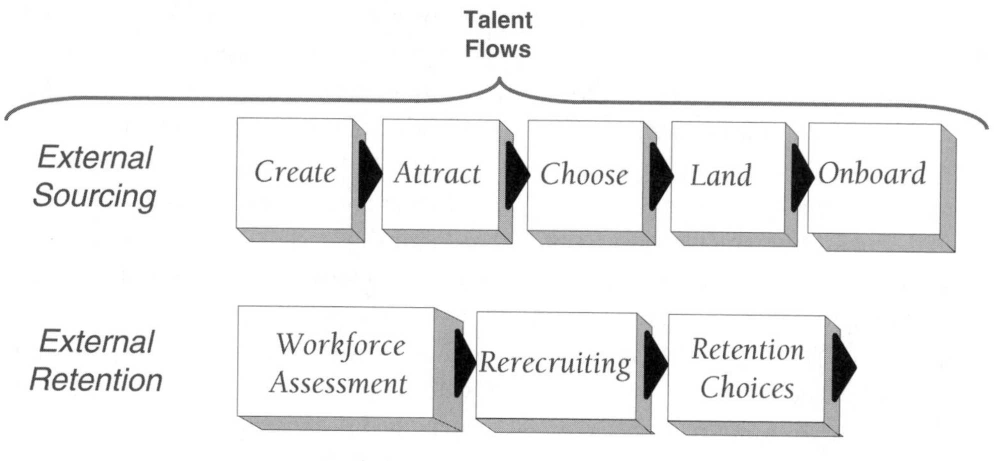

FIGURE 14.4. Supply chain and retention. Metrics: Cost, time, price, expected quality–quantity, variation in quality–quantity.

Figure 14.4, yet many organizations routinely set benchmark goals for turnover rates, or they hold leaders accountable for reducing turnover, without considering how it is integrated with the external-sourcing system. This is just as myopic as setting goals for spoilage reduction without considering how quickly and at what cost replacement inventory can be obtained (Cascio & Boudreau, 2008).

Boudreau and Berger's (1985) integration of employee selection and retention into the utility-analysis framework provided a basis for extending the connection between utility analysis and the resource-loss elements of the supply chain noted above. Boudreau and Berger noted that an extended utility framework would allow greater insights in regard to the payoff from human capital investments and more optimal staffing and retention decisions.

Boudreau and Berger showed that the parameters of employee retention utility are actually very similar to those for employee recruitment and selection, if one considers the existing workforce to be an internal pool of applicants and the retention pattern to be similar to the pattern of external selection. Existing employees make decisions to stay or leave, just as applicants make decisions to accept or reject offers. Employers make decisions about which employees to dismiss or lay off, just as they make decisions about which applicants to reject and which should receive employment offers. Boudreau and Berger noted that selection-utility frameworks had long recognized that the longer the expected tenure of selected applicants, the greater the time-frame of potential benefits from improved selection. Yet a deeper, fuller understanding of the utility of employee retention requires that an organization attend not simply to how long employees stay but also to the overall pattern of retention.

In supply-chain analysis, inventory spoilage is seamlessly integrated with inventory acquisition, and spoilage reduction simply becomes one of many parameters to be optimized. In many cases, it is better to allow spoilage or even to allow it to increase, rather than spend resources trying to reduce it. This is the case when inventory can be obtained quickly at low cost. Even when spoilage is costly, it may still be best to address the issue by enhancing the resource-acquisition system, than by investing in spoilage reduction after the resource has been acquired. This is the case when the same investment can create a greater reduction in acquisition cost, or the acquisition process can be used to acquire resources that are less likely to spoil.

In utility analysis, the implication is that a fixation on turnover reduction, or getting turnover rates to benchmark levels, may be misguided. It may be best to allow employee turnover to occur or even to increase, if replacement employees of equal or better quality are available quickly and at low cost. For example, in jobs in which employees with a wide array of qualifications can perform at satisfactory levels, and higher performance does not create significant organizational value (e.g., for some jobs at quick-service restaurants), it is logical not to spend a lot of time and energy reducing turnover but simply allow it to occur and to replace employees who leave. Replacements are very likely to be at least of equal quality to those leaving, and even if one of the best employees leaves, the job is such that higher performance may not make a great enough contribution to invest heavily in retention. The point is not simply that turnover can sometimes be functional but rather that the optimal analysis requires explicitly considering how the parameters shown in the bottom of Figures 14.2 and 14.4 will change under all circumstances, including high turnover.

An interesting application of these principles is the question of how the performance–pay relationship will affect the pattern of employee separation, and whether creating a very strong pay-for-performance relationship is actually worth the resulting potential increased separation of low and moderate performers who see smaller pay increases, to achieve the potential increased retention of high performers who are better rewarded. Sturman et al. (2003) simulated the effects of several alternative incentive-pay approaches, using parameters derived from an earlier empirical study by Trevor, Gerhart, and Boudreau (1997). Their results suggest that when a stronger pay-for-performance relationship increases the separations of low performers and increases the retention of high performers, the separation costs may well offset the benefits, depending on the economic value of the difference between high and low performance. Thus, a central utility parameter—the monetary value of performance variability—is an essential consideration to make to optimal pay-for-performance investments. Simply knowing the costs of the pay system and even knowing the retention and turnover pattern is not enough.

EXTENDING THE TALENT-SUPPLY CHAIN TO INCLUDE INTERNAL STAFFING

Utility analysis has seldom been applied to issues related to *internal staffing,* the movement of employees from one position or role to another, within the organization. Yet the number and significance of such decisions may well surpass those of external sourcing and retention. Again, the supply-chain metaphor is helpful. Internal staffing is very much like moving inventory from one location to another, to meet demand requirements. The location that loses the inventory experiences the same result as if that inventory had been lost or had spoiled, and the location receiving the inventory experiences the same result as if it had acquired the inventory from outside. In the case of the movement of internal resources, however, the organization bears the consequences of both sides of the transaction.

Similarly, internal staffing simultaneously creates separation from one position and acquisition into another. It is not uncommon for organizational units that are constantly being asked to give up their best performers to other units (e.g., through promotion, transfer) to complain that they are bearing a significant cost because of the constant need to acquire replacement talent and to process departures. Is there a guiding optimization principle that organizations might rely on to address the situation where certain units suffer from internal turnover for the greater good of the units that receive the talent? To date, empirical research in the fields of management and applied psychology has not addressed this question.

Similarly, units that receive talent may either be pleased or not so pleased with the quality or quantity of talent that they acquire from internal sources. On the one hand, internal sources may provide pools of employees with experiences that are uniquely gained within the organization, making them particularly well-suited for future positions. Such an approach optimizes the use of firm-specific human capital (Becker, 1965). On the other hand, internal sources may be tapped for other reasons than their ability to provide high-quality talent at low cost to the receiving units. For example, it is quite common for organizations to promote highly talented technical professionals to managerial positions, often systematically removing their highest-value technical talent from the technical roles, only to place them in managerial positions where they are, at best, average performers. In our experience in organizations, the receiving unit often believes that it could acquire leaders from outside of the organization that would be better performers than the technical professionals who were promoted internally or that the cost of developing technical professionals into high-quality leaders is much higher than obtaining leaders from outside sources. This is an example of the classic dilemma of *make* versus *buy.*

Figure 14.5 depicts these observations within our supply-chain framework. The top row shows how internal sourcing looks to the receiving unit. For the receiving unit, optimization requires considering the implications for cost, quality, quantity, and variability for several decisions. As examples, consider the following questions:

- How does the organization create a talent pool? For example, how does it prepare technical professionals for future management positions?
- How does the organization attract candidates for promotion? Do the most suitable technical professionals want to advance to management, or do they prefer to pursue technical work?
- How does the system choose candidates? Are promotion candidates chosen as a reward for good technical performance or for their leadership abilities?
- How does the organization make offers to land candidates? How successful is the organization in convincing technical professionals to move into leadership positions?
- How does the organization bring new employees onboard? How much support and training are technical professionals given after they assume their new positions, to help them become effective leaders?

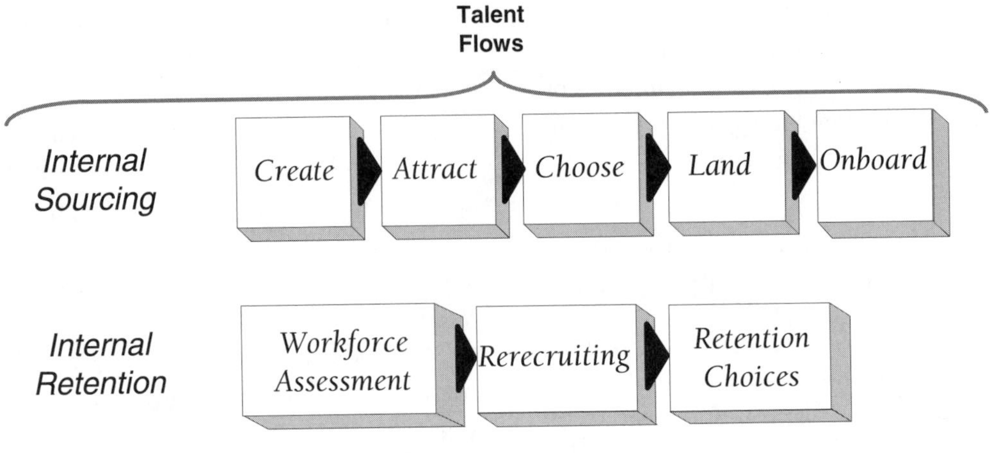

FIGURE 14.5. **Supply chain and internal staffing. Metrics: Cost, time, price, expected quality–quantity, variation in quality–quantity.**

The second row of Figure 14.5 shows the perspective of the unit that supplies (or loses) the internal talent. Optimization questions would include the three elements shown in Figure 14.5.

- How well does the workforce assessment reflect candidate value to the supplying unit?
- Are the best employees attracted to stay or leave? For example, if the only avenue to higher pay and status is to become a manager, it is difficult to rerecruit technical professionals to stay.
- What is the pattern of separation and retention choices by candidates and the organization? For example, if the decision rule is to promote the best technical performer to management, by definition that decision will create the greatest performance reduction in the unit that supplies the talent.

This is not to imply that units should avoid absorbing significant costs and losses for the greater good of the organization. However, analyses like those described above reveal the nuances of such decisions. The same utility-analysis parameters developed by Boudreau and Berger (1985) to integrate external sourcing and retention, discussed earlier, also provide a framework for considering the simultaneous selection and retention effects of internal employee movement. The utility-analysis framework provides the potential to develop an analytical approach that is akin to supply-chain analysis for internal movements of other organizational resources, such as materials, finished goods, and so forth.

SUPPLY-CHAIN PRINCIPLES FROM OPERATIONS RESEARCH APPLIED TO EXTERNAL STAFFING, RETENTION, AND INTERNAL STAFFING

The earlier sections of this chapter have shown how utility analysis, including staffing-utility analysis, has developed consistently with the general logic of supply-chain analysis. Our intention in this chapter is to show how utility analysis has evolved to a point where its logic and formulas can be interpreted through the supply-chain perspective.

In this section, we demonstrate the value of connecting these two disciplines in a different way. We present common supply-chain ideas and elements, and we show how those elements might apply to issues traditionally addressed by staffing-utility analysis. We are not attempting to present a comprehensive treatment of supply-chain analysis in this section but rather to demonstrate the value of future work that would explicitly draw on concepts from supply-chain analysis, to better inform utility-analysis application and development. Moreover, we believe that if those using utility analysis for staffing and other decisions become more facile with standard supply-chain concepts, they will be better equipped to find common ground with decision makers who are already using those concepts. That common ground may lead to opportunities for greater understanding and use of utility analysis in organizations.

Supply-chain optimization is often characterized as a series of steps required to take raw materials or unfinished goods, transport them to a manufacturing or processing facility, manufacture them into finished goods, transport them to a retailer's warehouse, organize them for retail distribution, distribute them to the final retail locations, and then sell them to customers at those locations. The analytical issues that underlie supply-chain optimization comprise four categories: (a) demand planning and forecasting, (b) production planning and scheduling, (c) distribution and logistics, and (d) inventory management. These elements come into play in different ways, depending on the nature of the particular supply chain or the element of the supply chain that is being considered, but they encompass many of the most vital and common supply-chain optimization issues.

Demand Planning and Forecasting

This is vital to supply-chain optimization, because signals about customer demand determine the level and timing of sales of the final product, which ultimately provides the revenue that supports the entire supply chain. A good deal of research and practical attention has been devoted to demand forecasting, including attention to the *bullwhip effect,* which occurs when wide inventory swings result if information about actual customer demand (often available at the point of sale) is not accurately and quickly conveyed through all the segments of the supply chain. When this occurs, then each actor in the supply chain must do his or her own forecasting based on the orders they receive from the next player in the process. This strategy may cause wasteful levels of inventory at each stage, to compensate for uncertainty (Cachon, Randall, & Schmidt, 2007; Caloiero, Strozzi, & Comenges, 2008; Ouyang & Daganzo, 2006).

A similar dilemma exists in the arena of selection-utility analysis, in that the number of available applicants depends on stages of applicant development and preparation that occur well before individuals actually apply for positions. As Figure 14.2 shows, the potential labor pool and the actual labor pool are both intermediate stages of applicant availability. Accurate demand forecasting influences the potential labor pool (e.g., public-sector projections of promising careers in sources such as the U.S. Department of Labor's *Occupational Outlook Handbook*). It also influences the actual labor pool (e.g., educational institutions; apprenticeship programs; and training grounds, like the military), and it directly affects the quality and quantity of available applicants. Moreover, wide swings in the quality and quantity of applicants can occur if organizations fail to convey their future needs accurately.

Demand planning and forecasting allows I/O and HR professionals to recast a common dilemma in selection and recruiting—open requisitions. It is often the case that managers articulate their talent demands in terms of a requested number of position requisitions, and then the recruitment organization sets out to fill those requisitions, often as quickly and at the lowest cost possible. Yet, a full accounting for the process would use a staffing-utility analysis approach, including the number of applicants, the selection ratio, the validity of the process of selecting applicants, and the costs involved. What is less well recognized is that these utility parameters can be used to analyze the impact of demand planning, just as in the supply chain. In some organizations, HR leaders have developed statistics that show the quality and quantity of applicants available as a function of the lead time provided by the hiring manager. With longer lead times, it is possible to alert the players that shape the potential labor pool and the actual labor pool earlier. That often means that longer lead times produce an applicant pool of higher quality and quantity.

In operations management, *demand management* refers to using things like discounts and incentives to alter the demand level and/or timing to fit production or inventory better (e.g., a clearance sale to reduce an unusually high inventory level). Emerging innovations in this area include dynamic pricing through internet auctions. The same kind of demand management might apply as HR leaders work with their clients to offer trade-offs. If the hiring manager is unable to provide much lead time, then the resulting applicant pool will be more expensive and possibly lower in quality or higher in variability. If the hiring manager can provide greater lead time, then these parameters can be changed. Another example from internal staffing is for units with a surplus of employees in certain areas to offer them on a cost-sharing basis to other units.

Utility-analysis logic and parameters (e.g., selection ratio, standard deviation of performance, anticipated compensation cost, validity) can be used to articulate more precisely the implications of longer lead times or more accurate or controllable demand forecasts. Moreover, there is a long history of research on demand forecasting in the fields of management science and operations research that might usefully be incorporated into the estimates of these parameters in utility analysis (Duc, Luong, & Kim, 2008; Erhun, Keskinocak, & Tayur, 2008; Ha & Tong, 2008).

Production Planning and Scheduling

To respond to the level, variability, and uncertainty in product demand, production systems can be designed and calibrated in a variety of ways. For example, operations research has long examined strategies to be used in manufacturing to maintain a particular level of inventory, manufacturing only when an order is placed, and so forth. Dell Computer revolutionized the PC industry with its insight that PCs could be assembled to order, thus removing inventory that traditionally had been required to build a stock of inventory waiting for orders. Supply-chain optimization provides analytical approaches and algorithms to determine when production should anticipate a flow of customer demand versus when to prepare for large spikes in demand. Techniques such as having flexible capacity, subcontracting, multiple-product manufacturing facilities and machines, and so forth, are all examples of this work.

When it comes to the staffing process and staffing utility, these concepts have significant potential to refine and make more practical utility-analysis approaches, and the parameters and logic of utility analysis provide a connection point to these ideas from production planning and scheduling. For example, the production process for employees can be conceived as including external sources, as depicted in Figure 14.2, and internal sources, as depicted in Figure 14.5. It can also include, in addition to internal staffing, internal training and development. There are utility-analysis frameworks for all of these production elements, as we have seen in earlier sections, and as depicted in detail elsewhere (Cascio & Boudreau, 2008). Using utility-analysis parameters, organizations could track the average and variation in applicant quantity and quality across various sources (e.g., universities, head hunters, employee referrals).

Thus, the utility parameters could be used to inform production arrangements. For example, if an organization is willing to guarantee to offer a large number of recruiting contracts to a search firm, then that firm can plan production differently than if it must guess about future demand. If an organization designs a job so that it can be performed by applicants with a very wide array of qualifications (e.g., by incorporating technology that offers guidance or automates key decisions), it can accommodate a larger number of suppliers of that labor, and thus perhaps it can increase the number of applicants and reduce variability in their likely performance levels (Boudreau & Ramstad, 2007).

Organizations routinely face decisions about whether and how to contract with external providers for applicants (a *buy* strategy), as well as decisions about whether to invest in the capacity to *make* future applicants through training or internal development. Yet, because these questions have not been couched within the utility-analysis framework, the opportunity to study them analytically has typically been missed. The combination of utility-analysis logic with production planning-and-scheduling frameworks is potentially a significant advance in such systematic analysis.

Distribution and Logistics

This aspect of supply-chain optimization focuses on the movement of materials and goods through physical space and time. It has produced algorithms for identifying the optimal placement of warehouses and their configuration, routing schemes for ground and air transport, and so forth. The Federal Express hub-and-spoke system of air and ground shipping is an example of a business model that revolutionized logistics systems. In essence, Federal Express realized that it could adopt the same system for packages that had been successful in passenger airlines. Bring many packages from lots of locations into one very large and central hub, process and sort them centrally to exploit economies of scale, and then move them by smaller planes or ground vehicles through spokes to their final destinations. It may seem rather incongruous that a package might actually travel farther as it moves through the hub and then on to its destination, than if it had been shipped directly from the starting point to the destination. However, if one considers the cost of processing packages through customs and the efficiencies of filled trucks on the ground, one can see the elegance of the Federal Express solution. Even though some packages move farther, the full system optimizes both cost and effectiveness.

The UPS approach to becoming an organization's complete inventory manager, with the technological capability to identify that customer's inventory at any stage of its movement, is another notable innovation. UPS chooses to compete by offering customers the security of being able to see their materials in transit at all stages. Thus, customers actually substitute UPS trucks and warehouses for building their own. This, however, requires very elegant optimization of information technology and logistics, ranging from hand-held devices for delivery personnel, to package tagging using radio-frequency technology, to a logistics system optimized to use all that information.

Again, these ideas have significant implications for the development of staffing processes and staffing-utility analysis, as well as implications for new uses for the staffing-utility frameworks that exist today. In the world of staffing, optimizing logistics and distribution would include decisions such as whether to recruit locally, regionally, nationally, or on a worldwide basis, and whether to locate workplaces where there are available and timely supplies of applicants. For example, many organizations now locate call centers in proximity to communities with large educational institutions, and they even offer attractive work schedules to attract student workers. Such decisions can be analyzed using the utility-analysis parameters, such as the quantity and quality of applicants, their variability, and the time and cost to obtain them.

Inventory Management

This element of supply-chain optimization works in concert with the others. At each stage of the process, some sort of inventory may exist, including raw materials being stored or in transit, finished goods being stored in warehouses or in the back rooms of retail outlets, and so forth. A great deal of research and analysis in operations research has examined how to optimize inventory levels against parameters such as the cost of inventory, the cost of being out of stock, the costs of holding goods at different stages of the supply chain, and the value of improving demand forecasts for reducing required inventory at many stages of the supply chain. *Just-in-time inventory* techniques, in which production and distribution are optimized to deliver goods just as they are needed, with virtually no in-process inventory, is one prominent example. Algorithms exist to optimize where inventory is held, the value of reducing or preventing loss and spoilage (discussed earlier with respect to employee turnover), and other decisions.

Applying these ideas to staffing and staffing utility reveals many potential arenas for integration and improvement. Establishing relationships with passive job seekers, well in advance of a need to recruit them, is now a common approach in organizations, often augmented and supported by the growing array of social-network facilities on the Web (e.g., LinkedIn, Facebook). This is analogous to creating a ready inventory of "unfinished goods" that could be refined further into finished goods. The passive job seekers may or may not eventually apply for positions, but by maintaining ongoing relationships with them, the organization knows where to contact them and increases the likelihood that if a position opens, they will consider it. Similarly, organizations might use their retired-employee communities as a source of available contractors for special projects, again analogous to holding inventory through open contracts for their skills and time.

With regard to internal staffing, one can envision situations in which it is optimum for an organization to continue the employment of vital human resources, even when economic conditions provide no current projects for them to work on (Boudreau & Ramstad, 2007). In many organizations, such an approach is often not even considered, because of the tangible costs of continued employment without offsetting projects to generate immediate revenue. Yet, retaining valued employees in a downturn is clearly consistent with the logic often used with inventory of highly valuable and rare goods, which are kept in inventory despite a temporary downturn in demand. Utility-analysis frameworks provide logical parameters to extend the decision debate beyond current costs to that of future value. For example, utility analysis could be used to compare the costs of holding on to the talent so that it is available in the future, to the costs, quantity, and quality of applicants and new hires that will be available once demand rises, and everyone else is also trying to attract these same individuals.

SUPPLY-CHAIN LOGIC IN ACTION: T-MOBILE AND VALERO ENERGY

In 2002, J. D. Power and Associates's customer-satisfaction surveys ranked T-Mobile dead last in its industry, trailing Verizon, Cingular, Nextel, and Sprint (Fisher, 2005). A pivotal talent pool in solving the problem was customer-service agents, and the supply-chain framework helps to understand T-Mobile's solution. The competencies for the customer-service-agent role were developed independently of any contact or input from customer-service or marketing representatives. That is actually symptomatic of a broader problem that cuts across many companies, according to one observer:

> We call the gap between HR and marketing the "white space" in organizations . . . The customer-contact people don't report to anyone in marketing or have any contact with them. Neither does anyone in HR, so HR isn't able to put customer-service people in place who can deliver on the marketers' message . . . We started studying this because people from 40-odd big companies like Honeywell, GE, and AT&T asked us how to fix it. (Schultz, quoted in Fisher, 2005, p. 272)

In terms of Figure 14.2, the recruiting, screening, and selection stages attracted and chose pools of applicants and selectees based on competencies that were not as informed as they might have been. At the same time, the article reported that the company instituted a set of incentives for customer-service representatives that failed to address the kinds of behaviors that managers responsible for employees in direct customer-contact positions believed were most important (e.g., problems resolved in a single phone call, problems resolved in a courteous manner). In terms of Figure 14.2, at the offering and closing stage, the incentives provided were not designed to produce the optimal pattern of job acceptance, as those highly motivated to do customer service would be less inclined to join and then to be motivated to perform well.

The first step toward improvement was to bring together T-Mobile's HR people, its customer-service managers, and its marketing managers to facilitate the understanding of each other's perspectives and situational constraints. The broad objective was to change the company's hiring practices to improve the quality of customer-service representatives who would be willing and able to follow through on the promises that marketing representatives made to customers.

As a result of the in-depth discussions among representatives from customer service, HR, and marketing, T-Mobile instituted a new set of hiring criteria that emphasized traits like empathy and quick thinking. It hypothesized that these traits would correlate more strongly with behaviors such as resolving customer problems fast, in one phone call, and in a courteous manner. Thus, the applicant pool and those screened and selected to receive offers now had signals to make it more likely the right traits would be available at the job-offer stage of the supply chain. In addition, T-Mobile made sure that all employees knew exactly how they would be evaluated. By ensuring that HR and marketing were well informed about hiring criteria as well as standards for assessing job performance, the company found that its employee-incentive plans also worked well, because hiring, performance management, and rewards all were linked to a common message and a common theme.

According to T-Mobile's senior vice president of customer service,

> the biggest mistake I've seen companies make is going after only one piece of the pie—trying to improve customer service by focusing on hiring alone or training alone or incentives alone. But it's an end-to-end process. It won't work unless you do the whole thing. (Nokes, in Fisher, 2005, p. 272)

Thus, when offers were made, the job description and reward criteria were more likely to be attractive to the right sort of applicant. Also, after hiring, the incentive system reinforced this pattern by creating retention among those motivated by these more optimal rewards (see Figure 14.4). This is an optimization strategy that had never existed before.

The broad-based effort paid off. By 2005 attrition and absenteeism each dropped 50%, relative to 2002, while productivity tripled. As for T-Mobile's formerly exasperated customers, by 2005 J. D. Power and Associates ranked T-Mobile number one in customer service for 2 years running. This was an external benchmark of the quality of employees in terms of the service they were providing to customers. At the same time, because true experimental controls were not feasible in this situation (manipulation of one or more independent variables, random assignment of people to groups, and random assignment of treatments to groups), we cannot say that the changes in selection, performance management, and incentives caused the changes noted above. Other unmeasured variables (exogenous or endogenous) may also account, to some extent, for the results observed at T-Mobile.

In terms of Figure 14.4, as a result of the assessment of existing employees and new hires (through the revised performance-management and incentive processes), both the organization and the employees were in a better position to be able to make "stay or leave" choices. Employees who were not well suited for jobs in customer service, as reflected in the new performance criteria and incentive scheme, tended to leave, whereas those who saw an excellent fit between their talents and the requirements of the customer-service job, became more engaged with their work. From a utility-analysis perspective, the quality, quantity, and cost of the flow of talent into and out of the organization could have been modeled by using the framework developed by Boudreau and Berger (1985) and the broader supply-chain framework presented here.

Valero Energy, the 20,000-employee, $70 billion energy-refining-and-marketing company, developed a new recruitment model out of human-capital metrics based on applying supply-chain logic to labor. According to Dan Hilbert, Valero's manager of employment services, "Once you run talent acquisition as a supply chain, it allows you to use certain metrics that you couldn't use in a staffing function . . . We measure every single source of labor by speed, cost, and efficiency" (Hilbert, in Schneider, 2006, p. 1). Computer-screen "dashboards" show how components in the labor supply chain, such as ads placed on online job boards, are performing according to those criteria. If the dashboard shows green, performance is fine. If it shows yellow or red, Valero staffing managers can intervene quickly to fix the problem (Valero Energy, 2006). By doing that, the company can identify where it can recruit the best talent at the most affordable price. From a strategic perspective, it also can identify whether it is better to recruit full-time, part-time, or contract workers, or to outsource the work entirely (Hilbert, in Schneider, 2006).

We do not have data showing precisely what elements are included in the Valero dashboard, nor how standards are set to determine what is "red," "green," or "yellow." On the basis of our earlier logic, we would speculate that the most appropriate indicators would reflect the average quantity and quality of talent moving through the different staffing stages, the variation in quality present at each stage, and the costs of the processes themselves, as well as the costs of the talent (e.g., salaries, benefits). In many such dashboards, the elements are treated in isolation when it comes to staffing, in contrast to the integration commonly accomplished when it comes to supply-chain analysis in more traditional areas. Nonetheless, the Valero example illustrates the power of the supply-chain metaphor for reframing the traditional approach to talent sourcing.

The supply-chain approach to labor and detailed analysis of metrics allow Valero to forecast the demand for talent by division and title 3 years in advance. To do that, the company (with the help of a contractor) analyzed 5 years' worth of employee data to develop equations to predict employee turnover by location, position, type, salary, tenure, and division. Then it forecast labor supply 3 years in advance and merged that data set with anticipated workforce needs (labor demand) for future capital projects, new systems, and services. As a result, the company established the capability to develop talent pipelines years in advance to meet specific talent needs, along with training programs and succession plans. This is employee movement (internal and external), and utility analysis can be used to assess the costs and benefits of the entire process over multiple time periods. Supply-chain logic facilitates the overall process, and it creates a significant opportunity to apply utility analysis by using the data from systems patterned after Valero's approach.

SUMMARY AND DIRECTIONS FOR FUTURE RESEARCH

This chapter is not a traditional review of developments in utility analysis—developments that often are described at a level of analysis that focuses on the individual. Rather, its purpose is to shift attention to decisions at the level of the organization. In terms of optimizing the overall results of the staffing process, we believe that I/O psychologists have much to learn from the field of supply-chain analysis. Supply-chain analysis pays careful attention to the ultimate quality of materials and components, and it analyzes inputs in terms of their effects on key organizational outcomes. With respect to staffing, such outcomes might include dependent variables like customer service or measures of innovation.

In the context of supply-chain modeling, if the staffing process is viewed as a series of resource flows, the objective is not to maximize the level of all of them but rather to achieve the appropriate quality standards in each one, for optimal balance between costs, returns, and risks. Groups of individuals (talent pools) flow through the various stages of the staffing process, with each stage serving as a filter that eliminates a subset of the original talent pool. We emphasized the close parallels between the logic of utility analysis and the logic of supply-chain analysis, and we examined applications of supply-chain logic to external staffing, retention, and internal staffing.

In terms of future research, the approach we have described here has many potential applications. One example is that of diversity and inclusiveness (D/I). Space constraints do not permit a fuller explanation, but the general framework is as follows. Both managers and scholars are calling for a broader view of diversity, beyond mere compliance with legal requirements for demographic representativeness. There is increasing recognition among managers that D/I has the potential to make a significant difference in the strategic success of their organizations, but to date there is almost no logic to suggest precisely how and under what conditions that might occur.

Using the concepts of pivotal talent and supply-chain analysis, we might reframe the question by asking, "In what talent pools does changing diversity (e.g., gender, age, race, functional expertise) provide the greatest potential change in strategic impact (key organizational processes and outcomes)?" This approach is completely opposite the traditional one, which often starts by identifying activities designed to enhance D/I or by identifying measures of diversity and then proceeding to search for possible areas of impact. That approach fails to focus on where D/I can make the most difference.

In the language of utility analysis, the concept of pivotal talent is related to SD_y. To appreciate this, consider that when scholars or managers write about mission-critical jobs or roles, they typically emphasize the average level of value (e.g., general importance, customer contact, uniqueness or power of certain jobs). Yet, as Cascio and Boudreau (2008) emphasized, variation interacts with average value to identify the talent where HR practices can have the greatest effect. Boudreau and Ramstad (2007) made a similar observation, emphasizing the distinction between pivotal roles versus important roles. Hence a key question for managers is not which talent has the greatest average value, but rather, in which talent pools does performance variation create the biggest strategic impact? Those are talent pivot points, and D/I can be cast into the same framework.

Framing the diversity question in terms of identifying where diversity is most pivotal reveals a connection between utility-analysis logic and a broader array of diversity research. Specifically, it clarifies the connection between what outcomes diversity may produce in the workforce, and where improving those outcomes make the biggest impact on business or strategic success. Roberson and Boudreau (2003) proposed a framework in which diversity-creating practices lead to workforce diversity (e.g., demographic, cultural, cognitive, technical), which leads to group-level outcomes (e.g., problem-solving, conflict, creativity) that may affect various organization processes (e.g., operations, R&D, sales), which in turn affect strategic capabilities, results, and outcomes. As an example, consider the logic of D/I and new-product development. Begin with the hypothesis that D/I leads to the expression and consideration of new viewpoints, and that those viewpoints produce greater creativity. Such creativity leads to product ideas that would not occur otherwise, which leads to enhanced variety and speed in new-product development. New products contribute to sales growth, especially sales to groups not reached previously.

When viewed from this perspective, it becomes much clearer precisely which talent pools are most likely to benefit from diversity. It is more important to note that the necessary alignment of HR processes and business processes also becomes clearer. For example, not only does the contribution of D/I to new-product-design teams become obvious, but also the pivotal importance of developing trusting relationships with commercial (outside) product-design groups who value and understand the perspective of key target markets.

Analyzed in this way, it becomes possible to connect diversity goals with market intelligence about customer segmentation and to identify more clearly where and why diversity is expected to make a difference. Such a rich conceptual framework should be useful in identifying connections between diversity-building HR activities and financial or market outcomes. Combining our conceptual framework with utility analysis of the net monetary benefits associated with increasing the D/I of pivotal talent pools will yield a richer, fuller understanding of the business impact of diversity.

This is just one application of the use of supply-chain logic combined with utility analysis. To be sure, this terrain is largely unexplored. To begin that process, scholars must adopt the scientist–practitioner model so that they understand deeply the concepts of talent flows, supply-chain logic, business processes, and the constraints that operating managers face. Then they can use the framework of utility analysis to model the financial effects of talent flows into and out of pivotal jobs. That kind of analysis will enable I/O psychologists to demonstrate genuine strategic impact.

The recent economic downturn offers additional insights on the potential value of a supply-chain approach to talent sourcing, and new potential applications of utility analysis. First, as Boudreau and Berger (1985) described, applying utility analysis logic to employee separation and retention can offer a useful perspective on employee downsizing. Specifically, the act of downsizing is, in many ways, similar in its effects to *reverse selection*. The organization begins with a starting workforce, and then it selects which employees from that population will stay. The larger the proportional workforce reduction, the greater the selection ratio, and thus the greater the potential change in the resulting retained group. The relationship between employee performance and long-term value to the probability of being retained is precisely analogous to the validity coefficient in selection. Like selection, employee retention through downsizing has effects that depend on the expected tenure of the retained workforce, its size, and economic factors such as variable costs, taxes, and the discount rate. One general principle, for example, is that where SD_y, the standard deviation of performance, is large, the degree to which the probability of retention is positively related to employee performance or future value will be far more impactful than where SD_y is small. Thus, an understanding of the patterns of performance variability across positions can usefully inform decisions about where organizations should be particularly vigilant to ensure that retention patterns reflect employee value.

As we noted earlier, the supply-chain logic also applies to decisions about organizational restructuring and survival. Organizations will want to consider the risks associated with reducing the workforce when ready replacements are unlikely to be available should economic conditions improve. On the other hand, reductions where ready replacements or substitutes are abundant may be more appropriate. Indeed, it may make sense to keep employees on the payroll even when they have little to do because of poor economic conditions, if that is less expensive or more risk mitigating than laying them off and rehiring them.

In sum, both diversity and economic restructuring demonstrate the fertile ground for future research that can be explored by using the logic and principles of utility analysis coupled with supply-chain logic, to extend the applicability of I/O psychology principles to issues of organizational performance and survival.

References

Bobko, P. (2001). *Correlation and regression: Applications for industrial and organizational psychology and management* (2nd ed.). Thousand Oaks, CA: Sage.

Borman, W., Hanson, M, & Hedge, J. (1997). Personnel selection. *Annual Review of Psychology, 48,* 299–337.

Boudreau, J. W. (1991). Utility analysis for decisions in human resource management. In M. D. Dunnette & L. M. Hough (Eds.), *Handbook of industrial and organizational psychology* (2nd ed., Vol. 2, pp. 621–745). Boston: Nicholas Brealey.

Boudreau, J. W. (2004). Organizational behavior, strategy, performance and design in *Management Science. Management Science, 50,* 1463–1476.

Boudreau, J. W. (2008). Guest column: Supply chain logic for evidence-based talent management. *Evidence-Based Management* [Blog]. Retrieved January 7, 2008, from http://www.evidence-basedmanagement.com/guests/boudreau_jan08.html

Boudreau, J. W., & Berger, C. J. (1985). Decision-theoretic utility analysis applied to employee separations and acquisitions. *Journal of Applied Psychology Monograph, 70,* 581–612.

Boudreau, J. W., Hopp, W., McClain, J. O., & Thomas, L. J. (2003). On the interface between operations and human resources management. *Manufacturing and Service Operations Management, 5,* 179–202.

Boudreau, J. W., & Ramstad, P. M. (2003). Strategic industrial and organizational psychology and the role of utility analysis models. In W. C. Borman, D. R. Ilgen, & R. J. Klimoski (Eds.), *Handbook of psychology: Vol. 12. Industrial and organizational psychology* (pp. 193–221). Hoboken, NJ: Wiley.

Boudreau, J. W., & Ramstad, P. M. (2001, May). *Beyond cost-per-hire and time-to-fill: Supply-chain measurement for staffing* (Working Paper 01–06). Ithaca, NY: Center for Advanced Human Resource Studies.

Boudreau, J. W., & Ramstad, P. M. (2004, September). *Beyond cost-per-hire and time-to-fill: Supply-chain measurement for staffing* (Publication G-04-16 [468]). Los Angeles, CA: Center for Effective Organizations.

Boudreau, J. W., & Ramstad, P. M. (2007). *Beyond HR: The new science of human capital.* Boston: Harvard Business School Publishing.

Boudreau, J. W., & Rynes, S. L. (1985). Role of recruitment in staffing utility analyses. *Journal of Applied Psychology, 70,* 354–366.

Brogden, H. E. (1946). On the interpretation of the correlation coefficient as a measure of predictive efficiency. *Journal of Educational Psychology, 37,* 64–76.

Brogden, H. E. (1949). When testing pays off. *Personnel Psychology, 2,* 171–185.

Brogden, H. E., & Taylor, E. K. (1950). The dollar criterion—Applying the cost accounting concept to criterion construction. *Personnel Psychology, 3,* 133–154.

Cabrera, E. F., & Raju, N. S. (2001). Utility analysis: Current trends and future directions. *International Journal of Selection and Assessment, 9,* 92–102.

Cachon, G. P., Randall, T., & Schmidt, G. M. (2007). In search of the bullwhip effect. *Manufacturing & Service Operations Management, 9,* 457–479.

Caloiero, G., Strozzi, F., & Comenges, J. Z. (2008). A supply chain as a series of filters or amplifiers of the bullwhip effect. *International Journal of Production Economics, 114,* 631–632.

Cappelli, P. (2008). *Talent on demand: Managing talent in an age of uncertainty.* Cambridge, MA: Harvard Business School Publishing.

Carson, K. P., Becker, J. S., & Henderson, J. A. (1998). Is utility really futile? A failure to replicate and an extension. *Journal of Applied Psychology, 83,* 84–96.

Cascio, W. F. (1978). *Applied psychology in personnel management.* Reston, VA: Reston Publishing.

Cascio, W. F. (1993). Assessing the utility of selection decisions: Theoretical and practical considerations. In N. Schmitt & W. C. Borman (Eds.), *Personnel selection in organizations* (pp. 310–340). San Francisco: Jossey-Bass.

Cascio, W. F. (2000). *Costing human resources: The financial impact of behavior in organizations* (4th ed.). Cincinnati, OH: Southwestern.

Cascio, W. F., & Aguinis, H. (in press). *Applied psychology in human resource management* (7th ed.). Upper Saddle River, NJ: Prentice-Hall.

Cascio, W. F., & Boudreau, J. W. (2008). *Investing people: financial impact of human resource initiatives.* Upper Saddle River, NJ: Pearson.

Cascio, W. F., & Morris, J. R. (1990). A critical re-analysis of Hunter, Schmidt, and Coggin's "Problems and pitfalls in using capital budgeting and financial accounting techniques in assessing the utility of personnel programs." *Journal of Applied Psychology, 75,* 410–417.

Cascio, W. F., & Ramos, R. A. (1986). Development and application of a new method for assessing job performance in behavioral/economic terms. *Journal of Applied Psychology, 71,* 20–28.

Cascio, W. F., & Silbey, V. (1979). Utility of the assessment center as a selection device. *Journal of Applied Psychology, 64,* 107–118.

Connerly, M. L., Carlson, K. D., & Mecham, R. L., III (2003). Evidence of differences in applicant pool quality. *Personnel Review, 32,* 22–39.

Cronbach, L. J., & Gleser, G. C. (1965). *Psychological tests and personnel decisions* (2nd ed.). Urbana, IL: University of Illinois Press.

Dagar, S. S., & Shukla, A. (2006, September). "Soaring salaries . . . vanishing workers." *Business Today, 24,* 66.

Duc, T. T. H., Luong, H. T., & Kim, Y. (2008). A measure of bullwhip effect in supply chains with a mixed autoregressive-moving average demand process. *European Journal of Operational Research, 187,* 243–253.

Dudek, E. E. (1963). Personnel selection. *Annual Review of Psychology,* 14, 261–284.

Dunnette, M. D. (1962). Personnel management. *Annual Review of Psychology, 13,* 285–314.

Erhun, F., Keskinocak, P., & Tayur, S. (2008). Dynamic procurement in a capacitated supply chain facing uncertain demand. *IIE Transactions, 40,* 733–735.

Fisher, A. (2005, November 28). *For happier customers, call HR.* Retrieved from http://money.cnn.com/magazines/fortune/fortune_archive/2005/11/28/8361923/index.htm

Florin-Thuma, B. C., & Boudreau, J. W. (1987). Performance feedback utility in a small organization: Effects on organizational outcomes and managerial decision processes. *Personnel Psychology, 40,* 693–713.

Ha, A. Y., & Tong, S. (2008). Contracting and information sharing under supply chain competition. *Management Science, 54,* 701–715.

Hunter, J. E., & Hunter, R. F. (1984). Validity and utility of alternative predictors of job performance. *Psychological Bulletin, 96,* 72–98.

Landy, F. J., Farr, J. L., & Jacobs, R. (1982). Utility concepts in performance measurement. *Organizational Behavior and Human Performance, 30,* 15–40.

Latham, G. P., & Whyte, G. (1994). The futility of utility analysis. *Personnel Psychology, 47,* 31–46.

Mattson, B. W. (2003). The effects of alternative reports of human resource development results on managerial support. *Human Resource Development Quarterly, 14,* 127–151.

Mabon, H. (1996). The cost of downsizing in an enterprise with job security. *Journal of Human Resource Costing and Accounting, 1,* 35–62.

Mabon, H., & Westling, G. (1996). Using utility analysis in downsizing decisions. *Journal of Human Resource Costing and Accounting, 1,* 43–72.

Macan, T. H., & Highhouse, S. (1994). Communicating the utility of HR activities: A survey of I/O and HR professionals. *Journal of Business and Psychology, 8,* 425–436.

McKay, P. F., & Avery, D. R. (2006). What has race got to do with it? *Personnel Psychology, 59,* 395–429.

Murphy, K. R. (1986). When your top choice turns you down: Effect of rejected offers on the utility of selection tests. *Psychological Bulletin, 99,* 133–138.

Ouyang, Y., & Daganzo, C. (2006). Characterization of the bullwhip effect in linear, time-invariant supply chains: Some formulae and tests. *Management Science, 52,* 1544–1556.

The pros and cons of online recruiting. (2004, April). *HR Focus, 81,* S2.

Roberson, Q. M., & Boudreau, J. W. (2003). *Value-based diversity: Understanding strategic impact by connecting talent diversity to the value chain.* Unpublished manuscript, Cornell University and University of Southern California.

Roth, P., Segars, A., & Wright, P. (2000, August). *The acceptance of utility analysis: Designing a model.* Paper presented at the Annual Meeting of the Academy of Management, Toronto, Ontario, Canada.

Russell, C. J., Colella, A., & Bobko, P. (1993). Expanding the context of utility: The strategic impact of personnel selection. *Personnel Psychology, 46,* 781–801.

Schmidt, F. L., & Hunter, J. E. (1983). Individual differences in productivity: An empirical test of estimates derived from studies of selection procedure utility. *Journal of Applied Psychology, 68,* 407–414.

Schmidt, F. L., Hunter, J. E., McKenzie, R., & Muldrow, T. (1979). The impact of valid selection procedures on workforce productivity. *Journal of Applied Psychology, 64,* 609–626.

Schmidt, F. L., Hunter, J. E., & Pearlman, K. (1982). Assessing the economic impact of personnel programs on work force productivity. *Personnel Psychology, 35,* 333–347.

Schneider, C. (2006, February 15). The new human-capital metrics. *CFO.com*. Retrieved August 5, 2008, from http://www.cfo.com

Schultz, K., Juran, D., & Boudreau, J. W. (1999) The effects of low-inventory on the development of productivity norms. *Management Science, 45,* 1664–1678.

Shellenbarger, S. (2006, February 23). In their search for workers, big employers go to summer camp. *The Wall Street Journal,* p. D1.

Sturman, M. C. (2000). Implications of utility analysis adjustments for estimates of human resource intervention value. *Journal of Management, 26,* 281–299.

Sturman, M. C., Trevor, C. O., Boudreau, J. W., & Gerhart, B. (2003). Is it worth it to win the talent war? Evaluating the utility of performance-based pay. *Personnel Psychology, 56,* 997–1035.

Trevor, C., Gerhart, B., & Boudreau, J. W. (1997). Voluntary turnover and job performance: Curvilinearity and the moderating influences of salary growth, and promotions. *Journal of Applied Psychology, 82,* 44–61.

Uhlaner, J. E. (1960, July). *Systems research—Opportunity and challenge for the measurement research psychologist* (Tech. Research Note 108). Washington, DC: U.S. Army Personnel Research Office.

Valero Energy, 2006 Optimas Awards. (2006, March 13). *Workforce Management,* p. 23.

Wallace, S. R. (1965). Criteria for what? *American Psychologist, 20,* 411–417.

Whyte, G., & Latham, G. P. (1997). The futility of utility analysis revisited: When even an expert fails. *Personnel Psychology, 50,* 601–611.

CHAPTER 15

THE UNIQUE ORIGINS OF ADVANCEMENTS IN SELECTION AND PERSONNEL PSYCHOLOGY

James L. Outtz

The purpose of this chapter is to explore significant advancements in the field of selection and personnel psychology over the past 4 decades. Identifying major advancements is admittedly arbitrary, but I will attempt to show, by focusing on one specific topic, selection, how forces external to scientific research in industrial and organizational (I/O) psychology have spurred advancements in our field. I believe that personnel selection practices are tied to personnel research—or at least they should be. Therefore, I will attempt to show the interdependence of I/O research, personnel selection practices, and concomitant social and legal developments over the past 40 years (e.g., Outtz, 2009). I will not attempt to provide an exact chronology of events external to I/O psychology that have influenced I/O research. I will, however, attempt to highlight examples of the interconnectedness of developments in social and legal areas and major scientific advances in the field of I/O psychology.

A useful beginning is to look back about 45 years. It is 1964, a year after Dr. Martin Luther King, Jr. delivered his "I have a dream" speech at the Lincoln Memorial in Washington, DC. The personnel selection practices of employers in the private sector were about to be subjected to increased scrutiny due to enactment of the Civil Rights Act of 1964 and, more specifically, Title VII of the act. Title VII applied primarily to private sector employers. In 1973, the Equal Employment Opportunity Act expanded coverage of Title VII to public sector employers, including state and local governments.

The 1964 Civil Rights Act took effect in 1965. The act prohibits employment discrimination on the basis of race, color, religion, sex, or national origin. There is a specific provision of the act, however, that was a catalyst for legal scrutiny of human resources practices usually considered the domain of I/O psychologists. That provision, subsection 703(h) of the act, states the following:

> Notwithstanding any other provision of this subchapter, it shall not be an unlawful employment practice for an employer to apply different standards of compensation, or different terms, conditions, or privileges of employment pursuant to a bona fide seniority or merit system, or a system which measures earnings by quantity or quality of production or to employees who work in different locations, provided that such differences are not the result of an intention to discriminate because of race, color, religion, sex, or national origin, *nor shall it be an unlawful employment practice for an employer to give and to act upon the results of any professionally developed ability test provided that such test, its administration or action upon the results is not designed, intended or used to discriminate because of race, color, religion, sex or national origin* [italics added].

The language regarding testing in this subsection was the focus of several major Supreme Court cases based on Title VII, and, as a result, I believe, has significantly impacted scientific research in I/O psychology for the past 40 years. I will focus on two

Supreme Court cases to support this point: *Griggs v. Duke Power Co.* (1971) and *Albemarle Paper Co. v. Moody* (1975). Although each of these cases has been mentioned frequently in the I/O literature over the years (e.g., Cascio, 1982; Gatewood & Field, 1994; Guion, 1998; Landy, 2005; Ledvinka & Shoenfeldt, 1978; Stockdale & Crosby, 2004), few, if any, attempts have been made to link specific aspects of the legal opinions to research in the field of I/O psychology.

GRIGGS V. DUKE POWER CO.

As noted earlier, the 1964 Civil Rights Act took effect in July of 1965. That same year, Duke Power Company instituted a policy at its Draper, North Carolina, facility requiring that (a) employees wishing to transfer from the Labor Department (a department to which African American employees had been restricted prior to that point) have a high school diploma, (b) incumbents without a high school diploma pass two aptitude tests in order to transfer, and (c) new employees who wished to work in any department other than Labor pass the same two aptitude tests. Thirteen African American employees filed suit in district court, alleging that the company's policies violated Title VII. The district court found in favor of Duke Power Company. Plaintiffs appealed the decision to the United States Court of Appeals for the Fourth Circuit. The court of appeals ruled there was no showing of intent to discriminate on the part of the company and, without a showing of intent, the company's new policies were permissible. The United States Supreme Court granted certiorari to address the issue of whether (a) intent was required to conclude that the company had engaged in discrimination and (b) the company had met its burden under Title VII of showing that there was a business necessity for the education and testing requirements. The Supreme Court reversed the decision of the lower court and, in laying out its reasoning, set off a firestorm within I/O psychology. The elements of the Supreme Court's decision that are most pertinent and the context and relevance of each are described as follows.

First, the Supreme Court concluded that African Americans had been harmed by the new policies put in place by Duke Power Company. The Court stated the following:

> The Court of Appeals' opinion, and the partial dissent, agreed that, on the record in the present case, "Whites register far better on the company's alternative requirements" than Negroes. This consequence would appear to be directly traceable to race. Basic intelligence must have the means of articulation to manifest itself fairly in a testing process. Because they are Negroes, petitioners have long received inferior education in segregated schools, and this Court expressly recognized these differences in *Gaston County v. United States,* 395 U.S. 285 (1969).

Note that the court did not appear to be saying that intelligence cannot be a legitimate requirement for employment. Rather, the court questioned the manner in which intelligence was being addressed within the context of this employment situation. The court expanded on this point by using one of Aesop's famous fables. As the fable goes, there was once a fox and a stork. The fox invited the stork to dinner. When the stork arrived, the fox served broth in a flat dish. Because of its long bill, the stork could not get any of the broth in its mouth. This caused the stork much distress and greatly amused the fox. However, the stork then invited to fox to dinner. The stork served milk in a pitcher with a long neck. Much to the stork's amusement, the fox was not able to partake of the warm milk because of its short snout. Making use of this fable to explain its reasoning, the Supreme Court stated the following:

> Congress has now provided that tests or criteria for employment or promotion may not provide equality of opportunity merely in the sense of the fabled offer of milk to the stork and the fox. In the contrary, Congress has now required that the posture and condition of the job seeker be taken into account. It has—to resort again to the fable—provided that the vessel in which the milk is proffered

> be one all seekers can use. The Act proscribes not only overt discrimination but also practices that are fair in form but discriminatory in operation.

Here the court laid down an interesting and, in some ways, prescient foundation for determining compliance with the act. The vessel in which an employment opportunity is offered must be equally usable by persons from groups that differ on the basis of demographics such as race, color, religion, sex, or national origin. This finding was prescient for at least two reasons. First, it implied that there may be different, equally useful methods (vessels) for assessing applicant qualifications. Second, the fact that a method may not be equally usable by different subgroups may make it appear to be fair in form but in actuality be discriminatory in impact. The dish that the fox presented to the stork was fair in form but was not usable by the stork because of the stork's makeup. Furthermore, it would be inappropriate to conclude that because of its makeup (i.e., because it possessed a bill instead of a snout), the stork was somehow deficient (i.e., less qualified in an employment sense) compared with the fox. Finally, the effect of serving dinner in a vessel that was not usable by both the fox and the stork put one or the other at an unfair advantage regardless of intent.

The court seemed to focus its assessment of the company's requirements on whether they served a legitimate purpose, given the way they were used. As an example, the court found that the high school diploma and testing requirements had not been shown by the company to be necessary. The court stated the following:

> On the record before us, neither the high school completion requirement nor the general intelligence test is shown to bear a demonstrable relationship to successful performance of the jobs for which it was used. Both were adopted, as the Court of Appeals noted, without meaningful study of their relationship to job performance ability. Rather, a vice-president of the Company testified, the requirements were instituted on the Company's judgment that they generally would improve the overall quality of the workforce.
>
> The evidence, however, shows that the employees who have not completed high school or taken the tests have continued to perform satisfactorily, and make progress in departments for which the high school and test criteria are now used. The promotion record of present employees who would not be able to meet the new criteria thus suggests the possibility that the requirements may not be needed even for the limited purpose of preserving the avowed policy of advancement within the company.

Critical standards were being established by this wording in the court's opinion. Employers were being asked to show that a requirement or test be related to or necessary for successful job performance. The origin or foundation for this standard can also be found in the court's opinion. Duke Power Company contended that general intelligence tests such as the ones it used were permitted under subsection 703(h) of the act. The tests used by the company were the Wonderlic Personnel Test (Wonderlic, Inc., 2003) and the Bennett Mechanical Comprehension Test (Bennett, 1970). Both measures are cognitively loaded and fairly abstract in that test items have little fidelity with the actual tasks carried out on the job. The court relied on guidelines promulgated by the Equal Employment Opportunity Commission (EEOC) in deciding this issue. It has often been reported in the literature that the court in the *Griggs* decision chose to give great deference to the EEOC's guidelines (Gatewood & Field, 1994). This is not completely accurate. The court considered the EEOC's guidelines to be the agency's interpretation of the act. The court reasoned that because the EEOC had enforcement responsibility for the act, the guidelines it issued constituted the appropriate interpretation of the act and, as such, were entitled to great deference. The court stated the following:

> The Equal Employment Commission, having enforcement responsibility, has

> issued guidelines interpreting § 703(h) to permit only the use of job-related tests. The administrative interpretation of the Act by the enforcing agency is entitled to great deference. See, e.g., *United States v. City of Chicago*, 400 U.S. 8 (1970); *Udall v. Tallman* 28-U.S. 1 (1965); *Power Reactor Co. v. Electricians*, 367 U.S. 396 (1961). Since the Act and its legislative history support the Commission's construction, this affords good reason to treat the guidelines as expressing the will of Congress.

The fact that the EEOC's interpretation of the act was given great deference proved critical because the EEOC interpreted section 703(h) as requiring that employment tests be "job-related."

The court elaborated on the job-relatedness standard as follows:

> The EEOC position has been elaborated in the new Guidelines on Employee Selection Procedures, 29 CFR §1607, 35 Fed. Reg. 12333 (Aug. 1, 1970). These guidelines demand that employers using tests have available data demonstrating that the test is predictive of or significantly correlated with important elements of work behavior which comprise or are relevant to the job or jobs for which candidates are being evaluated.

So the Supreme Court, in *Griggs*, identified a number of issues that, to some extent, were direct challenges to I/O psychology. Among those issues and challenges were the following:

- providing information (evidence) necessary to demonstrate validity,
- determining what it means for a test to have a manifest relationship to the employment in question or serve a legitimate business purpose,
- determining the standards to be used in establishing criterion-related validity, and
- determining whether an employer must consider different tests as well as different methods of use when establishing an employment requirement.

ALBEMARLE PAPER CO. V. MOODY

Although the plaintiffs in *Griggs* filed their action in 1965, the case was not argued before the Supreme Court until December of 1970. The Supreme Court rendered its decision on March 8, 1971. Four months later, in July of 1971, the case of *Albemarle Paper Co. v. Moody* came before a district court. In this case, plaintiffs sought relief from a number of employment practices put in place by Albemarle Paper Company, including its use of two employment tests that plaintiffs contended had disproportionate adverse impact on African Americans and were not shown to be related to job performance. The district court ruled that the tests at issue had undergone validation and, therefore, were not prohibited by Title VII. Plaintiffs appealed to the United States Court of Appeals for the Fourth Circuit. The appeals court reversed the district court's verdict. The court ruled specifically as follows:

> As is clear from *Griggs*, supra, and the Equal Employment Opportunity Commission's Guidelines for employers seeking to determine through professional validation studies whether employment tests are job-related, such tests are impermissible unless shown, by professionally acceptable methods, to be "predictive of or significantly correlated with important elements of work behavior which comprise or are relevant to the job or jobs for which candidates are being evaluated."
>
> Measured against that standard, Albemarle's validation study is materially defective in that (1) it would not, because of the odd patchwork of results from its application, have "validated" the two general ability tests used by Albemarle for all the skilled lines of progression for which the two tests are, apparently, now required; (2) it compared test scores with subjective supervisorial rankings, affording no means of knowing what job performance criteria the supervisors were considering; (3) it focused mostly on job groups near the

> top of various lines of progression, but the fact that the best of those employees working near the top of a line of progression score well on a test does not necessarily mean that the test permissibly measures the qualifications of new workers entering lower level jobs; and (4) it dealt only with job-experienced White workers, but the tests themselves are given to new job applicants, who are younger, largely inexperienced, and in many instances non-White.

The court of appeals also found the following:

> It was error to approve a validation study done without job analysis, to allow Albemarle to require tests for 6 lines of progression where there has been no validation study at all, and to allow Albemarle to require a person to pass two tests for entrance into 7 lines of progression when only one of those tests was validated for that line of progression.

The defendant, Albemarle, then appealed to the United States Supreme Court. The case was argued April 14, 1975, and decided June 25, 1975. In granting certiorari, the Supreme Court indicated that one of the important questions raised by the case was, "What must an employer show to establish that pre-employment tests, racially discriminatory in effect, though not in intent, are sufficiently job-related to survive challenge under Title VII?" The Supreme Court upheld the decision of the court of appeals and, in doing so, (a) clarified the burdens of proof for plaintiff and defendant and (b) provided further clarification as to the standards for demonstrating job relatedness.

As for the burden of proof, the court stated the following:

> In *Griggs v. Duke Power Co.*, 401 U.S. 424 (1971), this Court unanimously held that Title VII forbids the use of employment tests that are discriminatory in effect unless the employer meets "the burden of showing that any given requirement [has] . . . a manifest relationship to the employment in question. . . . If an employer does then meet the burden of proving that its tests are "job related," it remains open to the complaining party to show that other tests or selection devices, without similarly undesirable racial effect, would also serve the employer's legitimate interest in "efficient and trustworthy workmanship."

The Supreme Court agreed with the criticisms of the court of appeals as to the adequacy of Albemarle's validation study, stating the following:

> Four months before this case went to trial, Albemarle engaged an expert in industrial psychology to "validate" the job-relatedness of its testing program. He spent a half day at the plant and devised a "concurrent validation" study, which was conducted by plant officials, without his supervision. The expert then subjected the results to statistical analysis. The study dealt with 10 job groupings, selected from near the top of nine of the lines of progression. Jobs were grouped together solely by their proximity in the line of progression; no attempt was made to analyze jobs in terms of the particular skills they might require. All, or nearly all, employees in the selected groups participated in the study—105 employees in all, but only four Negroes. Within each job grouping, the study compared the test scores of each employee with an independent "ranking" of the employee, relative to each of his coworkers, made by two of the employee's supervisors. The supervisors, who did not know the test score, were asked to determine which ones they felt irrespective of the job that they were actually doing, but in their respective jobs, did a better job than the person they were rating against.

The court further stated the following:

> Measured against the guidelines, Albemarle's validation study is materially defective in several respects. Even if it

had been otherwise adequate, the study would not have "validated" the Beta and Wonderlic test battery for all of the skilled lines of progression for which the two tests are, apparently, now required. The study showed significant correlations for the Beta Exam in only three of the eight lines. Though the Wonderlic Test's Form A and Form B are in theory identical and interchangeable measures of verbal facility, significant correlations for one form but not the other were obtained in four job groupings. In two job groupings neither form showed a significant correlation. With some of the lines of progression, one form was found acceptable for some job groupings but not for others. Even if the study were otherwise reliable, this odd patchwork of results would not entitle Albemarle to impose its testing program under the Guidelines. A test may be used in jobs other than those for which it has been professionally validated only if there are attributes of, or the particular skills needed in, the studies job groups. There is accordingly no basis for concluding that "no significant differences" exist among the lines of progression, or among distinct job groupings within the studied lines of progression. Indeed, the study's checkered results appear to compel the opposite conclusion. There is no way of knowing precisely what criteria of job performance the supervisors were considering, whether each of the supervisors was considering the same criteria or whether, indeed, any of the supervisors actually applied a focused and stable body of criteria of any kind. There is, in short, simply no way to determine whether the criteria actually considered were sufficiently related to the company's legitimate interest in job-specific ability to justify a system with a racially discriminatory impact. . . . The APA Standards state that it is "essential" that "[t]he validity of a test should be determined on subjects who are at the age or in the same educational or vocational situation as the person for whom the test is recommended in practice." The EEOC Guidelines likewise provide that "data must be generated and results separately reported for minority and nonminority groups wherever technically feasible" 29 CFR § 1607.5(b)(5). In the present case, such "differential validation" as to racial groups was very likely not "feasible," because years of discrimination at the plant have insured that nearly all of the upper level employees are White. But there has been no clear showing that differential validation was not feasible for lower level jobs. More importantly, the Guidelines provide:

> If it is not technically feasible to include minority employees in validation studies conducted on the present workforce, the conduct of a validation study without minority candidates does not relieve any person of his subsequent obligation for validation when inclusion of minority candidates becomes technically feasible.

The Supreme Court's decision in *Albemarle* raised many issues and challenges for I/O psychology in addition to the ones already raised by *Griggs*. The more salient of these issues are exemplified by the following point in the Court's opinion:

> After the complaining party has made out a prima facie case showing a statistically significant difference in selection rates, the employer has the burden showing that any requirement (e.g., test or selection process) has a relationship to the job(s) in question.

The issue is what constitutes "a relationship." The court stated, "Even if the employer meets its burden of showing validity, the plaintiff has the opportunity to show that other tests or selection devices with similar adverse effects would serve the employer's interest just as well."

This point meant, by implication, that there may be several equally valid predictors for a given job or, more specifically, alternatives to cognitive tests with less adverse impact that would serve the employer's interest just as well. Albemarle's validation study was deemed deficient for several technical reasons, including the following:

- The tests were not significantly correlated with measures of job performance in every job for which the tests were used. This raised the question of the specificity of validity. It also raised the critical question of statistical power, given that Albemarle's validation sample included a total of 105 incumbents across 10 lines of progression. Obviously, this increased the likelihood of Type II error (i.e., the inability to detect significant validity when, in fact, it exists).
- There had been no job analysis. Did this mean that the validation study would not have passed muster even if significant validity coefficients had been found for all of the jobs at issue?
- The criterion measure was subjective in that one could not determine what standard each supervisor used in judging performance. This obviously raised the question of what standards must be met for a criterion to be appropriate.
- The validation sample used by Albemarle included only experienced incumbents. Therefore, the court reasoned, the study results were of limited relevance to hiring decisions involving applicants who had little or no experience. The court was saying, in essence, that a concurrent validation study was insufficient where selection decisions involve applicants.
- The company's validation study did not include a separate analysis of validity for African American and White employees (i.e., differential validation). This criticism was based on the assumption that differential validity occurred with sufficient frequency to warrant subgroup validation studies.

Clearly, the Supreme Court's decisions in *Griggs* and *Albemarle* marked the beginning of substantial governmental and legal involvement in personnel selection. Many thought this intrusion would be disastrous unless addressed directly. I/O psychology, guided by scientific research, played a leading role in this effort.

By 1975, governmental and legal involvement was beginning to have a profound effect on personnel selection practices as well as on personnel selection research. In 1976, Lewis Albright chaired a symposium at the 83rd Conference of the American Psychological Association. The title of the symposium was "Federal Government Intervention in Psychological Testing." The increasing involvement of the federal government in personnel selection issues is best exemplified by Albright's opening statement regarding the symposium. He stated, "Ten years ago, a symposium with this title would have been generally considered absurd." The point was that personnel practices, including selection, had been the purview of businesses and personnel managers with assistance from personnel psychologists. Federal guidelines and regulations and mushrooming litigation changed that.

FEDERAL REGULATION AND LEGAL INVOLVEMENT

Federal and legal involvement came primarily from guidelines issued initially by the EEOC. As the Supreme Court decisions in *Griggs* and *Albemarle* illustrate, these guidelines were to be given considerable deference. In 1978 a uniform set of guidelines was adopted by all of the agencies with direct responsibility for enforcement of Title VII. These new guidelines were the *Uniform Guidelines on Employee Selection Procedures* (1978).

The major provisions of these guidelines included the stipulation that they were applicable to an employer only in instances where adverse impact was demonstrated. The guidelines further stipulated that when adverse impact is shown, the employer can still justify the use of the selection procedure by producing evidence of its validity using a criterion-related, content, or construct validity strategy (see chap. 13, this volume). The guidelines also require, however, that even if validity is demonstrated, the employer may still be legally liable if there is an alternative procedure that is substantially equally valid and has less adverse impact.

External influences on personnel selection created a number of concerns that triggered debate, research associated with that debate, and, eventually, advances in I/O psychology that I believe would not otherwise have occurred, or at least not as rapidly. One major concern triggered by external social and legal influences was that employers would abandon valid, objective, merit-based selection practices in favor of highly subjective, arbitrary procedures designed to circumvent legal scrutiny.

Probably the greatest concern was that the practices struck down in *Albemarle* were widespread at that time. Ledvinka and Schoenfeldt (1978) estimated that only one fourth to one half of U.S. employers with up to 10,000 employees had conducted validation studies (Prentice-Hall, 1975).

THE RESPONSE FROM I/O PSYCHOLOGY

I/O research, in response to the social and legal forces described earlier, was quick in coming. More interesting than the speed of the response was the focus of the research. Given that many employers were using cognitive tests for selection without having conducted the kind of validation studies called for by the EEOC guidelines (or in some instances no validation studies at all), the question of whether criterion-related validation studies were necessary or even feasible for every job in an organization became paramount.

The Supreme Court issued the *Albemarle* decision in June of 1975. By August of 1976, the first of a number of groundbreaking articles was published on methodological considerations in conducting criterion-related validation studies (Schmidt, Hunter, & Urry, 1976). Schmidt et al. (1976) showed that sample sizes thought to be adequate for conducting criterion-related validity studies did not have the requisite statistical power to provide accurate evidence of validity. Schmidt et al. proposed, quite correctly, that in far more situations than previously thought, criterion-related validation simply was not feasible.

Schmidt et al. (1976) further hypothesized that the accepted view of the situational specificity of validity was possibly due to excessive faith in the small samples from which many of the coefficients were generated. The idea that validity coefficients are specific to the organization and/or job of interest had been widely accepted to that point (e.g., Ghiselli, 1966). This view was likely the source of the requirement in the EEOC guidelines that a criterion-related validity study must be conducted for each job of interest unless it could be shown, via job analysis or some other means, that validation results from other studies were applicable because the jobs in those studies were similar to the jobs of interest. Although questions of situational specificity and statistical power were, and still are, fascinating and tremendously important from a scientific perspective, there is little doubt that much greater attention was given to these issues because of the legal maelstrom created by Title VII and, more specifically, the Supreme Court's decisions in cases such as *Griggs* and *Albemarle*.

In raising questions about the feasibility of validation strategies, Schmidt and Hunter (1977) proposed a statistical model that would allow the generalization of validity across situations, organizations, or jobs. Validity generalization is a method of estimating validity using meta-analysis. Validity coefficients for a given predictor are identified from the research literature, and a single validity coefficient is estimated by combining the research findings using statistical methods to control for artifacts such as restriction of range, criterion unreliability, and the effects of small sample size. This technique results in a single estimate of the "true" validity coefficient. Schmidt and Hunter's validity generalization model only heightened the interest of the scientific community in validation research. Their research seemed to be aimed squarely at case law that was evolving with regard to validation. The initial work of Schmidt et al. (1976) was followed by a proliferation of research spanning 3 decades on validity generalizations and moderators of test validity (James, Demaree, & Mulaik, 1986; James, Demaree, Mulaik, & Ladd, 1992; James, Demaree, Malaik, & Mumford, 1988; Newman, Jacobs, & Bartram, 2007; Osburn & Callender, 1992; Rothstein, Schmidt, Erwin, Owens, & Sparks, 1990; Schmidt & Hunter, 1977, 1981; Schmidt, Hunter, & Pearlman, 1981; Schmidt et al., 1993).

Federal and legal influences on personnel selection affected not only professional opinion regarding personnel selection practices and validation methodology but also basic conceptualizations of validation itself. As an example, the *Uniform Guidelines on Employee Selection Procedures* (EEOC, 1978) defined three distinct forms of validity (i.e., content, criterion-related, and construct) based on the compendium of scientific thought at the time. However, in subsequent years, the collective thought has been that validity refers to the accuracy of inferences made on the basis of test scores. Validation is simply the process of gathering and presenting evidence that supports these inferences. This conceptualization of validity is in stark contrast to the notion that validity is a characteristic of a test; that is, the notion that a test is or is not "valid." The tripartite definition of validity embodied in the *Uniform Guidelines on Employee Selection Procedures* and in court decisions that have relied on those guidelines made it necessary for I/O psychology to be more precise in articulating what validity or validation means (see, e.g., *Principles for the Validation and Use of Personnel Selection Procedures,* Society for Industrial and Organizational Psychology, 1987).

ADVERSE IMPACT

The external influences that took hold in the mid 1970s resulted in a greater focus on subgroup outcomes or the adverse impact of selection procedures than had been the case prior to that time. *Adverse impact* is defined in the guidelines on the basis of a rule of thumb known as the *four fifths rule.* This rule states that the outcome(s) of a selection procedure or employment decision (e.g., hiring, promotion) should be similar for each demographic group participating in the procedure. "Similar" means the selection rate for one group is at least 80% of the selection rate for the group with the highest selection rate.

There was an increase in the number of research studies investigating not only the validity evidence associated with different selection devices but also the degree to which those devices produced adverse impact. Schmidt, Greenthal, Berner, Hunter, and Seaton (1977) compared job sample and paper-and-pencil tests with regard to validity and adverse impact. They reported that job sample tests had considerably less adverse impact. In addition, both minority and nonminority examinees saw the job sample tests as more fair. The Schmidt et al. study suggested greater exploration of the use of performance tests.

Field, Bayley, and Bayley (1977) compared minority and nonminority employees at a large paper company with regard to mean scores on four predictors and two job performance measures. They found that two of the four predictors did not produce a statistically significant difference in subgroup means. They found statistically significant subgroup differences on both criterion measures. All of the predictors produced statistically significant validity coefficients for both criterion measures. Findings such as these began to trigger more fundamental measurement questions. In other words, what were these tests really measuring and why would they produce different results in terms of subgroup differences, yet be correlated with job performance?

Kesselman and Lopez (1979) compared the validity and adverse impact of a written accounting job knowledge test with a commercially available mental ability test. They found that the job knowledge test produced validity evidence comparable with that produced by mental ability tests. However, the job knowledge test had less adverse impact.

I mention these studies as examples of the kinds of research conducted in the mid to late 1970s. There was a shift in emphasis toward examining the adverse impact of selection devices in addition to examining validity evidence. One finding that emerged from this sporadic research was that some valid predictors may have less adverse impact than others.

Four years after the *Uniform Guidelines on Employee Selection Procedures* (EEOC, 1978) were adopted, Reilly and Chao (1982) published a literature review assessing eight possible alternatives to cognitive ability tests. Each alternative was compared with cognitive ability tests in terms of validity and less adverse impact. Table 15.1 summarizes the results of their comparisons. The uncorrected validity coefficient for cognitive ability tests was estimated to be .35, based on the work of Ghiselli (1973). Reilly and Chao concluded that there was sufficient research evidence to recommend two alternatives: biodata and peer evaluations. Reilly and Chao made one of the first assessments of alternatives to cognitive ability tests. Reilly and Warech (1993) revisited this issue. Reilly and Warech made

TABLE 15.1

An Initial Evaluation of Alternatives to Cognitive Ability Tests

Alternative	Estimated validity	Adverse impact	Suitable as an alternative
Biodata	.36	Low	Yes
Interview	.19	Unknown	No
Peer evaluations	.37	Low (with rater training)	Yes
Self-assessment of an ability, knowledge skill, and so on	.15	Low	No
Reference checks	.18	Low	No
Academic performance (college or high school grade point average)	.14	Probable	No
Expert judgments	.17	Unknown	No
Projective techniques (Rorschach, Thematic Apperception Test, Worthington Personal History Test)	.28 (.18)[a]	Low	No

Note. Data from Reilly and Chao (1982).
[a]The authors note that the validity coefficient for this category was .18 when an outlier was excluded from the data.

one-to-one comparisons between several predictors and cognitive ability tests with regard to validity and adverse impact. Four predictors were found to be suitable alternatives: trainability tests, work samples, biodata, and assessment centers. An interesting aspect of the literature reviews of Reilly and Chao and Reilly and Warech is that they compared each potential alternative individually with cognitive ability tests. The implication was that each alternative standing alone might be a suitable alternative to cognitive ability measures in predicting job performance, while reducing adverse impact.

The research reported by Reilly and Chao (1982) and Reilly and Warech (1993) illustrates how the expansion of selection research, by virtue of social and legal influences, was evolving. A couple of additional examples further illustrate this evolution. The first example involves the personality inventory. For many years the personality inventory was considered to be useless as a tool for employee selection. After conducting a review of the literature, Guion and Gottier (1965) concluded, "There is no generalizable evidence that personality measures can be recommended as good or practical tools for employee selection" (p. 159). However, several studies conducted during the 1980s and 1990s indicated that the validity of personality inventories, particularly those based on the Big Five personality factors, may have been underestimated (e.g., Barrick & Mount, 1991; Hogan, Hogan, & Roberts, 1996; Schmitt, Gooding, Noe, & Kirsch, 1984; Tett, Jackson, & Rothstein, 1991). Many of these studies made use of the meta-analytic techniques first employed in validity generalization research to more accurately assess the validity of personality inventories.

There appears to have been a factor other than validity driving the sustained interest in personality inventories. That factor was low adverse impact. Reilly and Warech (1993), for example, reported that there appeared to be no evidence that personality inventories, in general, have adverse impact. Hough, Oswald, & Ployhart (2001) as well as Foldes, Duehr, & Ones (2008) reported similar findings. The search for alternative vessels in which to serve the milk of equal employment opportunity seems to have contributed to a better understanding of personality inventories as useful predictors.

Another example of the link between the evolution of selection research and social and legal influences is the employment interview. For many years, the research literature indicated the validity of the employment interview was quite low (Mayfield, 1964; Schmitt, 1976; Wagner, 1949). Despite this fact, use of the employment interview as a selection tool remained widespread and few believed that it would ever be completely abandoned (Arvey & Campion, 1982). However, the paucity of validity evidence made it vulnerable, in terms, to legal defensibility. Arvey (1979) predicted that there would be an increase in litigation involving the interview. His prediction proved accurate. Between 1972 and 1978, there were 32 cases brought in U.S. district courts directly involving use of the employment interview (Gollub-Williamson, Campion, Malos, Roehling, & Campion, 1997). There were 67 such cases between 1979 and 1995 (Gollub-Williamson et al.). The widespread use of the employment interview, together with a perceived lack of legal defensibility, generated, I think, more scientific research designed to determine why validity was so low and what might be done to improve it. This research began to bear fruit in the 1980s. Wright, Lichtenfels, and Pursell (1989) reported that a meta-analysis of structured interview validities resulted in an (estimated validity of .39). Opinion as to the validity of the interview was beginning to change (Harris, 1989).

Further research indicated that employment interview validities were moderated by a number of variables, including interview structure as well as the content and nature of the performance criteria (Huffcutt & Arthur, 1994; McDaniel, Whetzel, Schmidt, & Maurer, 1994). More important, research was beginning to indicate that not only was the employment interview more valid than previously thought but also that structured interviews could produce validities comparable with those of mental ability tests (Huffcutt & Arthur, 1994; Jelf, 1999). Even more interesting is the fact the researchers were beginning to discover that the employment interview had considerably less adverse impact than mental ability tests. The point is that social and legal influences served in part as the impetus for continued research on employment interviews, including how they should be implemented and their utility.

PROFESSIONAL STANDARDS AND FEDERAL REGULATION: FINDING COMMON GROUND

The *Uniform Guidelines on Employee Selection Procedures* (EEOC, 1978) were designed to be tied to professional standards in the field of testing. As an example, section 5c of the guidelines states the following:

> *Guidelines are consistent with professional standards.* The provisions of these guidelines relating to validation of selection procedures are intended to be consistent with generally accepted professional standards for evaluating standardized test and other selection procedures such as those described in the Standards for Educational and Psychological Tests prepared by a joint committee of the American Psychological Association, the American Educational Research Association, and the National Council on Measurement in Education (American Psychological Association, Washington, DC, 1974) . . . and standard textbooks and journals in the field of personnel selection.

Given that the guidelines have not been revised in over 30 years, there are many areas in which they are inconsistent with professional standards that have evolved via scientific research. As an example, the guidelines are not consistent with the extensive research evidence on validity generalization. That is, the validity generalization literature clearly demonstrates that it may not be necessary to conduct a validity study in each situation where a selection device is used. Moreover, accepted professional practice supports the notion that validation strategies need not be considered mutually exclusive in that validation evidence from consolidation of strategies may be more persuasive than evidence derived from any single strategy. There are some overarching areas, however, where the guidelines and professional standards seem to converge. Subgroup differences and adverse impact, for example, gained prominence as important testing outcomes.

Professional standards, such as the *Standards for Educational and Psychological Testing* (American Educational Research Association, American Psychological Association, & National Council on Measurement in Testing, 1999) as well as the Society for Industrial and Organizational Psychology's *Principles for the Validation and Use of Personnel Selection Procedures* (2003), also express concern regarding subgroup differences. The *Standards* and the *Principles* equate adverse impact with construct-irrelevant variance, or bias, a characteristic of the test itself. *Construct-irrelevant variance* is defined as excess, reliable variance that is irrelevant to the interpreted construct (Messick, 1989). Bias can also be defined as construct underrepresentation. Exhibit 15.1 provides a comparison of the *Standards*, the *Principles* and *Uniform Guidelines* as they relate to the concept of adverse impact.

Exhibit 15.1 shows that adverse impact is a concern to I/O psychologists both from a legal and professional perspective. Thus, I/O psychologists have accepted the difficult task of trying to adhere to the *Standards*, the *Principles*, and the *Uniform Guidelines* to the greatest extent possible. Exhibit 15.1 also shows that the *Uniform Guidelines* define adverse impact on the basis of outcomes, whereas the *Standards* and the *Principles* address it in terms of the characteristics of a test.

The *Uniform Guidelines* provide that if the employer can demonstrate validity, the selection procedure or the resulting employment decision may not be discriminatory. Put another way, subgroup differences constitute discrimination only to the extent that such differences are not reflected in legitimate business outcomes (e.g., job performance, turnover, absenteeism). The *Standards* and the *Principles* treat subgroup differences in a similar fashion. That is, subgroup differences are a concern if they are associated with variance that is irrelevant to the measurement and interpretation of the construct of interest. This approach assumes, of course, that the construct of interest is itself relevant to a legitimate business need. If the foregoing description of adverse impact makes the term appear to be relatively straightforward, that is not the case.

Exhibit 15.1
Adverse Impact: Different Perspectives

Guidelines[a] **Adverse impact**	***Standards***[b] **Measurement bias**	***Principles***[c] **Measurement bias**
A substantially different rate of selection in hiring, promotion, or other employment decision, which works to the disadvantage of members of a race, sex, or ethnic group (Definitions).	Evidence of mean test score differences between relevant subgroups of examinees should, when feasible, be examined . . . for construct-irrelevant variance (7.10). Construct irrelevance: The extent to which test scores are influenced by factors that are irrelevant to the construct that the test is intended to measure. Construct underrepresentation: The extent to which a test fails to capture the important aspects of the construct that the test is intended to measure (Definitions).	Sources of irrelevant variance that result in systematically higher or lower scores for members of particular groups, is a potential concern for all variables, both predictors and criteria (p. 33).

[a]From *Uniform Guidelines on Employee Selection Procedures* (Equal Employment Opportunity Commission, 1978). [b]From *Standards for Educational and Psychological Testing* (American Educational Research Association, 1999). [c]From *Principles for the Validation and Use of Personnel Selection Procedures* (4th ed.; Society for Industrial and Organizational Psychology, 2003).

The *Uniform Guidelines* further stipulate that even if the employer demonstrates that a selection procedure is valid, the procedure may nevertheless be discriminatory if there is an alternative procedure with similar validity and less adverse impact. The *Standards* also address this issue. Table 15.2 provides a comparison of the *Standards,* the *Principles,* and the *Uniform Guidelines* on the matter of alternatives.

It should be noted that the *Principles* do not address this issue directly but simply state that they are intended to be consistent with the *Standards.* The *Uniform Guidelines* provide that adverse impact is to be determined on the basis of the specific manner in which an organization uses a test or selection procedure. As an example, if an employer interprets test scores in rank order as opposed to pass/fail or establishing score bands, rank ordering must be validated. Similarly, if a noncompensatory model is used, that method of use must be validated. The *Uniform Guidelines* states the following:

> The evidence of both the validity and utility of a selection procedure should support the method the user chooses for operational use of the procedure, if that method of use has a greater adverse impact than another method of use. (Section 5G)

TABLE 15.2

Adverse Impact Ratios for Three Selection Strategies

Selection ratio	All four predictors	Interview, personality, and biodata	Cognitive ability alone
.90	.82 (.84)	.92 (.96)	.62 (.74)
.70	.71 (.66)	.82 (.91)	.51 (.51)
.50	.48 (.53)	.74 (.86)	.36 (.37)
.30	.37 (.41)	.64 (.80)	.24 (.25)
.10	.23 (.28)	.55 (.72)	.14 (.14)

Note. Data from Equal Employment Opportunity Commission (1978), American Educational Research Association et al. (1999), and Society for Industrial and Organizational Psychology (2003).

THE MELDING OF SCIENCE AND SOCIAL ISSUES

The debate over the issues discussed earlier revealed a more general controversy. There appeared to be a sense within the scientific community that employment tests, and similar selection procedures, were under attack by advocates of social change. Most within the scientific community believed the scientific questions in selection should be kept separate from social issues. I, for one, did not see how this would be possible. As long as selection practices had real consequences for everyday people, I did not see how issues regarding the type of selection procedures used, or the methods of use, could be resolved solely on the basis of science.

A number of significant scientific advances resulted from those early debates. We realized that concepts such as single-group and differential validity could not be studied adequately using small-sample data. That is, large-scale studies across samples were needed. Thus, we began to take note of sampling error as a possible explanation for some of these phenomena. It became apparent that validity may not be as situation-specific as once thought. Meta-analysis applied within the field of I/O resulted in a better understanding of the scope of validity evidence for specific predictors, particularly cognitive ability tests. Meta-analytic models came to the forefront and triggered new discoveries about a number of predictors.

BROADENING THE CONSTRUCTS USED IN PREDICTION

Spurred by a search for alternatives as required by the *Uniform Guidelines,* the range of predictors for which there is substantive validity evidence has grown rapidly. Biodata, cognitive ability tests, assessment centers, work samples, structured interviews, situational judgment tests, and personality inventories have all proven to be useful in increasing the accuracy of selection decisions (Hunter & Hunter, 1984; McDaniel et al., 1994; Meriac, Hoffman, Woehr, & Fleisher, 2008; Ones, Dilchert, Viswesvaran, & Judge, 2007; Rothstein et al., 1990; Salgado, 1997; Schmidt & Rader, 1999; see also chaps. 4–8, this volume, for discussion of predictors such as cognitive ability, biodata, personality, interviews, assessment centers, and situational judgment tests). Interest in expanding the types of selection devices available to employers has grown for a number of reasons, but I believe the primary reason is the following requirement of the *Uniform Guidelines:* "In conducting a validation study, the employer should consider available alternatives which will achieve its legitimate business purpose with lesser adverse impact" (p. 38291).

The search for alternatives has, in my opinion, been a tremendous impetus for validation research designed to broaden our understanding of ways to maintain and/or increase the accuracy of selection decisions while assisting employers in meeting an array of social, legal, and strategic objectives. We have also made considerable strides in broadening our understanding of the ways to use different selection procedures. Hunter and Hunter (1984) said that using other predictors in conjunction with cognitive ability tests might improve validity and reduce adverse impact, but there was at that time no database for studying this possibility. That database exists today, and it is growing. Considerable research has been conducted since 1984 on combining selection devices to improve validity. Since the mid 1990s, an increasing amount of research has been devoted to the investigation of various combinations of predictors designed to produce incremental validity and reduce adverse impact.

Researchers began exploring the effects of formulating composites consisting of cognitive ability tests and low adverse impact alternatives on subgroup differences and validity. The initial thinking was that combining a high impact predictor such as a cognitive ability test with a low impact predictor such as a personality measure could result in a composite with equal or higher validity (than either predictor alone) and substantially less adverse impact. It soon became apparent, however, that such composites might not reduce adverse impact but could actually result in adverse impact equal to or greater than that produced by either predictor alone (e.g., Ryan, Ployhart, & Friedel, 1998). A significant step toward unraveling this mystery came with the seminal work of Sackett and Ellingson (1997). They showed that the standardized mean difference between two groups (e.g., African Americans and Whites) on a composite consisting of high and low adverse impact predictors is a function of (a) the *d* value for each test in the composite, (b) the number of tests in the composite, and (c) the average intercorrelation among the tests. Counter to intuitive thought, Sackett and Ellingson showed that as the intercorrelation between predictors decreases, the effect size of their composite increases (where the summed *d* for the predictors is constant).

During the same time frame, a methodology was evolving for better estimating the likely affect on adverse impact and validity of forming composites with specific predictors. This methodology was a major scientific advance in that it was based on the use of meta-analytic techniques to determine the values for the three critical factors identified by Sackett and Ellingson (1997). The approach is to build a meta-analytic matrix composed of (a) the estimated effect size for each predictor to be included in a composite, (b) the intercorrelations among the predictors, and (c) the correlation between each predictor and job performance (i.e., validity). Once the meta-analytic matrix has been developed, estimates can be made regarding the difference in validity and adverse impact between alternative composites with or without cognitive ability tests and the cognitive ability tests alone.

A significant outcome of developing meta-analytic matrices has been a more scientifically rigorous method of estimating (a) the validity of various predictors and (b) the adverse impact of those predictors. Three alternative predictors have been studied extensively using this approach: the structured interview, the personality construct conscientiousness, and biodata. As a result of meta-analytic research conducted between 1995 and 2005, the validity and estimated adverse impact (based on African American and Whites standardized mean differences) for these predictors is fairly well established. For example, Table 15.3 shows meta-analytic matrices reported by Bobko, Roth, and Potosky (1999) and Schmitt, Rogers, Chan, Sheppard, and Jennings (1997). Values from Schmitt et al. are shown in parentheses. Bobko et al. and Schmitt et al. used the meta-analytic estimates in Table 15.3 to

TABLE 15.3

Meta-Analytic Matrix of Validity Coefficients and Effect Sizes for Several Predictors

Variable	Effect size	1	2	3	4
1. Cognitive ability	1.00 (1.00)				
2. Structured interviews	.23 (.09)	.24 (.17)			
3. Personality (conscientiousness)	.09 (.09)	.00 (.00)	.12 (.12)		
4. Biodata	.33 (.20)	.19 (.10)	.16 (.16)	.51 (.47)	
5. Criterion (job performance)	.45 (.45)	.30 (.29)	.30 (.30)	.18 (.12)	.28 (.24)

Note. Data from Bobko et al. (1999). Values in parentheses are from Schmitt et al. (1997).

determine the potential adverse impact of three selection strategies: (a) use of a composite consisting of the three alternative predictors and a cognitive ability test, (b) use of a composite consisting of the three alternative predictors without the cognitive ability test, and (c) use of the cognitive ability test alone. Table 15.4 shows the estimated adverse impact ratio of each strategy assuming five different selection ratios.

Bobko et al. (1999) and Schmitt et al. (1997) used the estimates from their meta-analytic matrices to determine (a) the multiple correlation between the four predictor composite and job performance, (b) the multiple correlation between the alternative three predictor composite and job performance, and (c) the effect size for each composite. The results are shown in Table 15.5.

TABLE 15.4

Adverse Impact Ratios for Three Selection Strategies

Selection ratio	All four predictors	Interview, personality, and biodata	Cognitive ability alone
.90	.82 (.84)	.92 (.96)	.62 (.74)
.70	.71 (.66)	.82 (.91)	.51 (.51)
.50	.48 (.53)	.74 (.86)	.36 (.37)
.30	.37 (.41)	.64 (.80)	.24 (.25)
.10	.23 (.28)	.55 (.72)	.14 (.14)

TABLE 15.5

Multiple Correlations and Effect Sizes for Two Predictor Composites

	Schmitt et al. (1997)		Bobko et al. (1999)	
Composite	*R*	*d*	*R*	*d*
Four predictors	.42	.67	.43	.76
Three predictor alternative	.36	.19	.38	.36
Cognitive ability test	.29	1.00	.30	1.00

Tables 15.3 through 15.5 are provided for the purpose of illustration. The information in these tables indicates the advances that have been made in I/O psychology with regard to adverse impact. Table 15.3 shows, for example, that cognitive ability tests, structured interviews, and biodata have similar validity but quite different levels of adverse impact. Table 15.4 shows that a predictor composite that includes a cognitive ability test will have substantially greater adverse impact than one that does not when selection ratios are .50 or lower. Table 15.4 also shows that an alternative selection battery of low adverse impact predictors can have substantially less adverse impact than a cognitive ability test alone regardless of the selection ratio. Table 15.5 shows that a predictor composite that does not include a cognitive ability test may result in a higher multiple *R* but substantially less of adverse impact. Tables 15.3 through 15.5 provide an example of how scientific research can be used to identify alternatives to cognitive ability tests and the value of such alternatives. That research is useful to practitioners because it provides a foundation for carrying out a search for alternative predictors as part of a validation study, as required by the *Uniform Guidelines*.

An interesting observation with regard to the data reported in Tables 15.3 through 15.5 is the difference in some of the meta-analytic estimates. For example, Table 15.3 shows differences in estimates of the effect sizes, validity (for the personality measure) and the intercorrelations between predictors. Differences between the meta-analytic matrices in turn produced differences in estimates of the adverse impact ratios shown in Table 15.4. For example, if one considers all but the highest selection ratio, the adverse impact ratio estimates for the alternative selection battery are substantially lower based on the Bobko et al. (1999) meta-analytic matrix. The significant point here is that many judgments have to be made in constructing a meta-analytic matrix. The accuracy of those judgments can significantly affect the values obtained (Bobko et al., 1999; Potosky, Bobko, & Roth, 2005). Examples of factors that can significantly affect matrix estimates include

- weighting of correlation coefficients and effect sizes by sample size,
- correcting validity coefficients for unreliability and restriction of range,
- combining predictors that measure different constructs (e.g., combining measures of specific aptitudes with measures of general mental ability),
- the type of criterion measure used (e.g., individual versus team performance ratings vs. other criteria such as turnover or pay),
- combining studies involving applicants with those involving incumbents, and
- estimating effect sizes based on incumbents, hence underestimating effect sizes for applicants.

Despite these difficulties, the use of meta-analytic approaches to provide estimates of the effect of forming predictor composites on adverse impact and validity has increased our knowledge substantially. Thus far, however, the discussion has been limited to selection strategies that treat the criterion as unidimensional. Our understanding of job performance has evolved to the point where the multidimensionality of job performance has become apparent. For example, job performance might consist of several dimensions including individual task performance or teamwork and contextual performance (e.g., Borman, Hanson, & Hedge, 1997; Borman & Motowidlo, 1993; see also Vol. 1, chap. 19, this handbook, and chaps. 9 and 10, this volume, for a discussion of these criteria). A number of researchers have proposed that the multidimensionality of job performance necessitates evaluation of the weights assigned to the predictors in a composite (De Corte, 1999; Doverspike, Winter, Healy, & Barrett, 1996; Hattrup, Rock, & Scalia, 1997; Murphy, 2009; Murphy & Shiarella, 1997).

Murphy and Shiarella (1997) proposed that weighting of predictors and criteria provides a better understanding of the relationship between selection and job performance. Using a Monte Carlo simulation, they showed that the validity of a predictor composite can vary substantially depending on the weight given to predictors and criterion measures. The 95% confidence interval for their validity coefficients was .20 to .78. Doverspike et al. (1996) used simulation methodology to show that when two of the three predictors in a composite have high adverse impact ($d = 1.08$ and $d = 1.06$, respectively), little reduction of adverse impact will result from differentially weighting the predictors.

Understanding the effect of weighting predictors in a composite is the next stage in the advancement of our knowledge of the relationship between selection strategies and adverse impact. The key question with regard to predictor weighting is how the weights should be determined. Some researchers propose that predictor weights should be determined by the importance of the facet of job performance with which the predictor correlates (Murphy & Shiarella, 1997). Thus, if an organization places substantial importance on a facet of performance such as teamwork or organizational citizenship, then predictors of those dimensions of performance should be given the most weight. Most, if not all, of the published research on weighting of predictors has dealt with the simple case of two applicant groups and how changes in weighting affect score differences for those groups. In reality, the selection situation is likely to be far more complex, involving two, three, or even four applicant groups based on race and ethnicity (e.g. Hispanic, Asian, Native American).

Another alternative that has been the subject of considerable discussion is banding. *Banding* is a procedure in which test scores are grouped within given ranges and treated as equivalent. It is based on the premise that small differences may not be meaningful for purposes of selection (Cascio, Outtz, Zedeck, & Goldstein, 1991). Banding can reduce adverse impact by providing more minorities who are "reachable" than would be the case with top-down selection. (See Campion et al., 2001, and Aguinis, 2004, for a comprehensive discussion treatment of banding including the advantages and disadvantages.) Although banding has proven to be controversial in some respects, it is considered useful in some selection situations, and it has been accepted as an appropriate alternative from a legal perspective (Campion et al., 2001).

Clearly, the issue of adverse impact and how to minimize it has become the focus of considerable scientific research over the past decade. Sackett, Schmitt, Ellingson, and Kabin (2001) and Sackett, De Corte, and Lievens (2009) provided a thorough discussion of the strategies for optimizing validity and minimizing adverse impact. They offered the caveat, however, that it is unreasonable to expect that one can maximize both the performance and ethnic diversity of selected individuals. Schmitt and Quinn (2009) assessed where we are terms of progress in developing valid alternatives that minimize adverse impact. It appears that by using the most optimistic estimates of the effect of various adverse impact reduction techniques, adverse impact can be reduced by about 50%. This, in my opinion, represents great progress. I/O psychology has made tremendous progress in broadening the range of predictors that can be used to improve the accuracy of selection decisions while significantly reducing adverse impact. The impetus for this progress has been social and legal influences, which were initially considered hindrances to our science.

THE IMPACT OF CHANGING WORKFORCE DEMOGRAPHICS

I have described a number of alternative selection procedures that have been the subject of research, particularly during the past decade. I have proposed that a significant factor underlying interest in these alternatives is the legal requirement that an employer search for them. A second and, I believe, more important factor has been the changing demographics of the U.S. workforce. In California alone, it is estimated that by 2010 Whites will make up only 48% of the population. Diversity programs that began as "affirmative action" a quarter century ago are now part of an organization's strategic planning. Competition for talent has never been higher. The changing workforce means that organizations must be able to manage diversity. Turnover among women and minorities is a significant and costly problem. The turnover rate for Blacks in the U.S. workforce is 40% higher than the rate for Whites (Robinson & Dechant, 1997). A major task for employers will be to attract and to keep talented employees, particularly members of minority groups.

Marketplace demands are shifting significantly. In 1988, the U.S. minority marketplace equaled the gross national product of Canada. Organizations must place themselves strategically within the marketplace to take advantage of changing market demands. For these reasons, employers need selection tools that will allow them to identify talented applicants from different demographic groups. This will require alternatives to traditional selection procedures.

SUMMARY

Earlier I described two concerns created by the external influences on personnel selection over the past 25 years. The first concern was that employers would abandon objective, merit-based selection procedures for which there was evidence of validity in favor of highly subjective, arbitrary procedures designed to comply with legal requirements. This concern has proven to be unwarranted. Traditional selection devices for which there is solid validity evidence are used as much, if not more, today than a quarter century ago. As an example, the abandonment of cognitive ability tests, which was widely feared in the early 1970s, has not taken place. Sackett et al. (2001) pointed out that cognitively loaded tests of knowledge, skill, and ability are commonly used to help make hiring, academic admissions, certification, and licensure decisions. Organizations have continued to be wary, however, of how these selection tools are used. Many organizations attempt to ensure that these tests are not overemphasized in the selection process.

A second concern was that scientific advances in selection would be overshadowed by programs and practices aimed at balancing selection outcomes on the basis of demographic characteristics rather than increasing the accuracy of selection decisions.

This concern also has proven to be unwarranted. Employers are eager to make use of the scientific knowledge we have gained over the past 25 years. Demographic changes in the applicant population, along with similar changes in the workforce, have increased rather than decreased the need for employers to find the most talented workers, workers who can adapt to and manage diversity. The evolution of personnel selection practices and research has been rocky at times. However, the external influences that began in the early 1970s have served as a stimulus for scientific advances we see today.

THE FUTURE

The signs regarding the future of personnel selection are mixed. On the one hand, we have made significant advances in our understanding of the range of predictors that can be used to improve selection decisions. We are discovering how to use these predictors, in combination, to identify talented workers in an increasingly diverse applicant population. On the other hand, we cling stubbornly to what I believe is a limited, if not myopic, view of the significance of selection in improving organizational effectiveness. The prevailing theory seems to be that there is a one-to-one correspondence between the measurement of individual differences and increased organizational effectiveness. This theory has not been adequately researched, let alone proven.

The use of cognitive ability tests in employment selection is a good example. Clearly, a threshold level of cognitive ability is necessary to successfully perform most jobs. That threshold differs by job. However, have we actually demonstrated that increasing the number of employees who are above that threshold results in greater organizational effectiveness? Is it possible that within certain "degrees of difference" or "ranges of tolerance," individual differences in cognitive ability are not as important as factors such as leadership or teamwork in improving organizational performance? This is one of the significant questions yet to be addressed in personnel selection research.

Finally, a look into the future of personnel selection would not be complete without mention of "e-technology," or Web technology. Job postings are sent out via the Internet. Job seekers send in their applications electronically via the Internet. The applications are processed almost instantaneously to identify and rank the most qualified candidates. Ranking is carried out via computer, based on prespecified criteria provided by the hiring organization. The process is touted as particularly useful for applying minimum qualifications and identifying the "right candidates."

Perhaps the novelty of this procedure is the speed with which information is processed. I really do not see much that is new in terms of the basic premise of selection, which is the accuracy of inferences made on the basis of scores. The criteria for screening applications must be demonstrated to be valid, whether the criteria are applied via computer or by some other means. The criteria used for screening still should be based on an analysis of work, regardless of the method of applicant screening. Perhaps, with computer-based processing, one would have to demonstrate that the key-word searches programmed into the computer accurately distinguish between applicants who meet the minimum requirements and those who do not. Perhaps one could establish validity evidence for the computer-screening process by comparing a sample of applications screened manually and via computer. In any event, the validation issues to be addressed are the same as those for any selection process. At this point, the appeal of the technology may be masking deficiencies in terms of validity evidence.

References

Aguinis, H. (Ed.). (2004). *Test-score banding in human resource selection: Technical, legal, and societal issues.* Westport, CT: Praeger.

Albemarle Paper Co. v. Moody, 422 U.S. 405 (1975).

Albright, L. (1976). Federal government intervention in psychological testing: Is it here? *Personnel Psychology, 29,* 519–520.

American Educational Research Association, American Psychological Association, & National Council on Measurement in Testing. (1999). *Standards for educational and psychological testing.* Washington, DC: Author.

Arvey, R. D. (1979). Unfair discrimination in the employment interview: Legal and psychological aspects. *Psychological Bulletin,* 86, 736–765.

Arvey, R. D., & Campion, J. E. (1982). The employment interview: A summary and review of recent research. *Personnel Psychology, 35,* 281–322.

Barrick, M. R., & Mount, M. K. (1991). The Big Five personality dimensions and job performance: A meta-analysis. *Personnel Psychology, 44,* 1–26.

Bennett, G. (1970). *Bennett Mechanical Comprehension Test.* New York: Psychological Corporation.

Bobko, P., Roth, P. L., & Potosky, D. (1999). Derivation and implications of a meta-analytic matrix incorporating cognitive ability, alternative predictors, and job performance. *Personnel Psychology, 52,* 561–589.

Borman, W. C., Hanson, M. A., & Hedge, J. W. (1997). Personnel selection. In J. T. Spence, J. M. Darley, & D. J. Foss (Eds.), *Annual review of psychology* (Vol. 48, pp. 299–337). Palo Alto, CA: Annual Review.

Borman, W. C., & Motowidlo, S. J. (1993). Expanding the criterion domain to include elements of contextual performance. *Personnel Selection in Organizations.* San Francisco: Jossey-Bass. [

Campion, M. A., Outtz, J. L., Zedeck, S., Schmidt, F. L., Kehoe, J. F., Murphy, K. R., & Guion, R. M. (2001). The controversy over score banding in personnel selection: Answers to 10 key questions. *Personnel Psychology, 54,* 149–185.

Cascio, W. F. (1982). *Applied psychology in personnel management* (2nd ed.). Reston, VA: Reston.

Cascio, W. F., Outtz, J., Zedeck, S., & Goldstein, I. L. (1991). The implications of six methods of score use in personnel selection. *Human Performance, 4C4,* 233–264.

Civil Rights Act, U.S.C. § 703h *et seq.* (1964).

Civil Rights Act, 42 U.S.C. § 2000e. (1964).

De Corte, W. (1999). Weighing job performance predictors to both maximize the quality of the selected workforce and control the level of adverse impact. *Journal of Applied Psychology, 84,* 695–702.

Doverspike, D., Winter, J. L., Healy, M. C., & Barrett, G. V. (1996). Simulations as a method of illustrating the impact of differential weights on personnel selection outcomes. *Human Performance, 9,* 259–273.

Equal Employment Opportunity Commission. (1978). *Uniform guidelines on employee selection procedures.* Washington, DC: Author.

Equal Employment Opportunity Commission, Civil Service Commission, Department of Labor, and Department of Justice, Adoption of Four Agencies of Uniform Guidelines on Employee Selection Procedures, 43 Federal Register 38, 290–38, 315 (1978).

Field, H., Bayley, G. A., & Bayley, S. (1977). Employment test validation for minority and nonminority production workers. *Personnel Psychology, 30,* 37–46.

Foldes, H. J., Duehr, E. E., & Ones, D. S. (2008). Group differences in personality: Meta- analyses comparing five U.S. racial groups. *Personnel Psychology, 61,* 579–616.

Gatewood, R. D., & Field, H. S. (1994). *Human resource selection* (3rd ed.). Fort Worth, TX: Dryden Press.

Ghiselli, E. E. (1966). *The validity of occupational tests.* New York: Wiley.

Ghiselli, E. E. (1973). The validity of aptitude tests in personnel selection. *Personnel Psychology, 26,* 461–477.

Gollub-Williamson, L., Campion, J. E., Malos, S. B., Roehling, M. V., & Campion, M. A. (1997). Employment interview on trial: Linking interview structure with litigation outcomes. *Journal of Applied Psychology, 82,* 900–912.

Griggs v. Duke Power Co., 401 U.S. 424 (1971).

Griggs et al. v. Duke Power Co., 420 F.2d 1225 (1970).

Guion, R. M. (1998). *Assessment, measurement, and prediction for personnel decisions.* Mahwah, NJ: Erlbaum.

Guion, R. M., & Gottier, R. F. (1965). Validity of personality measures in personnel selection. *Personnel Psychology, 18,* 135–164.

Harris, M. M. (1989). Reconsidering the employment interview: A review of recent literature and suggestions for future research. *Personnel Psychology, 42,* 691–726.

Hattrup, K., Rock, J., & Scalia, C. (1997). The effects of varying conceptualizations of job performance on adverse impact, minority hiring, and predicted performance. *Journal of Applied Psychology, 82,* 656–664.

Hogan, R., Hogan, J., & Roberts, B. W. (1996). Personality measurement and employment decisions: Questions and answers. *American Psychologist, 51,* 469–477.

Hough, L. M., Oswald, F. L., & Ployhart, R. E. (2001). Determinants, detection, and amelioration of adverse impact in personnel selection procedures: Issues, evidence, and lessons learned. *International Journal of Selection and Assessment, 9,* 152–194.

Huffcutt, A. I., & Arthur, W., Jr. (1994). Hunter and Hunter (1984) revisited: Interview validity for entry-level jobs. *Journal of Applied Psychology, 79,* 184–190.

Hunter, J. E., & Hunter, R. F. (1984). Validity and utility of alternative predictors of job performance. *Psychological Bulletin, 96,* 72–98.

James, L. R., Demaree, R. G., & Mulaik, S. A. (1986). A note on validity generalization procedures. *Journal of Applied Psychology, 71,* 440–450.

James, L. R., Demaree, R. G., Mulaik, S. A., & Ladd, R. T. (1992). Validity generalization in the context of situational models. *Journal of Applied Psychology, 77,* 3–14.

James, L. R., Demaree, R. G., Mulaik, S. A., & Mumford, M. D. (1988). Validity generalization: Rejoinder to Schmidt, Hunter, and Raju (1988). *Journal of Applied Psychology, 73,* 673–678.

Jelf, G. (1999). A narrative review of post-1989 employment interview research. *Journal of Business and Psychology, 14,* 25–58.

Kesselman, G. A., & Lopez, F. E. (1979). The impact of job analysis on employment test validation for minority and nonminority accounting personnel. *Personnel Psychology, 32,* 91–108.

Landy, F. (2005). *Employment discrimination litigation: Behavioral, quantitative, and legal perspectives.* San Francisco: Jossey-Bass.

Ledvinka, J., & Shoenfeldt, L. F. (1978). Legal developments in employment testing: Albemarle and beyond. *Personnel Psychology, 31,* 1–13.

Mayfield, E. C. (1964). The selection interview—A reevaluation of published research. *Personnel Psychology, 17,* 239–260.

McDaniel, M. A., Whetzel, D. L., Schmidt, F. L., & Maurer, S. (1994). The validity of employment interviews: A comprehensive review and meta-analysis. *Journal of Applied Psychology, 79,* 599–616.

Meriac, J. P., Hoffman, B. J., Woehr, D. J., & Fleisher, M. S. (2008). Further evidence for the validity of assessment center dimensions: A meta-analysis of the incremental criterion-related validity of dimension ratings. *Journal of Applied Psychology, 93,* 1042–1052.

Messick, S. (1989). Validity. In R. L. Linn (Ed.), *Educational measurement* (3rd ed., pp. 13–103). New York: Macmillan.

Moody et al. v. Albemarle Paper Company, 474 F .2d 134 (1973).

Murphy, K. (2009). How a broader definition of the criterion domain changes our thinking about adverse impact. In J. Outtz (Ed.), *Adverse impact implications for organizational staffing and high stakes selection* (pp. 137–160). New York: Routledge, Taylor & Francis Group.

Murphy, K. R., & Shiarella, H. A. (1997). Implications of the multidimensional nature of job performance for the validity of selection tests: Multivariate frameworks for studying test validity. *Personnel Psychology, 50,* 823–854.

Newman, D. A., Jacobs, R. R., & Bartram, D. (2007). Choosing the best method for local validity estimation: Relative accuracy of meta-analysis versus a local study versus Bayes-analysis. *Journal of Applied Psychology, 92,* 1394–1413.

Ones, D. S., Dilchert, S., Viswesvaran, C., & Judge, T. A. (2007). In support of personality assessment in organizational settings. *Personnel Psychology, 60,* 995–1027.

Osburn, H. G., & Callender, J. (1992). A note on the sampling variance of the mean uncorrected correlation in metal-analysis and validity generalization. *Journal of Applied Psychology, 77,* 115–122.

Outtz, J. (2009). *Adverse impact: Implications for organizational staffing and high stakes selection.* New York: Routledge, Taylor & Francis Group.

Potosky, D., Bobko, P., & Roth, P. (2005). Forming composites of cognitive ability and alternative measures to predict job performance and reduce adverse impact. *International Journal of Selection and Assessment, 13,* 304–315.

Prentice-Hall. (1975, April). P-H/ASPA survey: Employee testing procedures-where are they headed? In *Personnel Management: Policies and Practices.* Englewood Cliffs, NJ: Prentice-Hall.

Reilly, R. R., & Chao, G. R. (1982). Validity and fairness of some alternative employee selection procedures. *Personnel Psychology, 35,* 1–62.

Reilly, R. R., & Warech, M. A. (1993). The validity and fairness of alternatives to cognitive tests. In L. C. Wing & B. R. Gifford (Eds.), *Policy issues in employment testing* (pp. 131–224). Norwell, MA: Kluwer Academic.

Robinson, G., & Dechant, K. (1997). Building a business case for diversity. *Academy of Management Executive, 11,* 21–31.

Rothstein, H. R., Schmidt, F. L., Erwin, F. W., Owens, W. A., & Sparks C. P. (1990). Biographical data in employment selection: Can validities be made generalizable? *Journal of Applied Psychology, 75,* 175–184.

Ryan, A. M., Ployhart, R. E., & Friedel, L. (1998). Using personality testing to reduce adverse impact: A cautionary note. *Journal of Applied Psychology, 83,* 298–307

Sackett, P. R., De Corte, W., & Lievens, F. (2009). Decision aids for addressing the validity–adverse impact trade-off. In J. Outtz (Ed.), *Adverse impact implications for organizational staffing and high stakes selection* (pp. 453–472). New York: Routledge, Taylor & Francis Group.

Sackett, P. R., & Ellingson, J. E. (1997). The effects of forming multipredictor composites on group differences and adverse impact. *Personnel Psychology, 50,* 707–721.

Sackett, P. R., Schmitt, N., Ellingson, J. E., & Kabin, M. B. (2001). High-stakes testing in employment, credentialing, and higher education: Prospects in a postaffirmative-action world. *American Psychologist, 56,* 302–318.

Salgado, J. F. (1997). The Five Factor model of personality and job performance in the European Community. *Journal of Applied Psychology, 82,* 30–43.

Schmidt, F. L., Greenthal, A. L., Berner, J. G., Hunter, J. E., & Seaton, F. W. (1977). Job sample vs. paper-and-pencil trades and technical tests: Adverse impact and examinee attitudes. *Personnel Psychology, 30,* 187–197.

Schmidt, F. L., & Hunter, J. E. (1977). Development of a general solution to the problem of validity generalization. *Journal of Applied Psychology, 62,* 529–540.

Schmidt, F. L., & Hunter, J. E. (1981). Old theories and new research findings. *American Psychologist, 36,* 1128–1137.

Schmidt, F. L., Hunter, J. E., & Pearlman, K. (1981). Task differences as moderators of aptitude test validity in selection: A red herring. *Journal of Applied Psychology, 66,* 166–185.

Schmidt, F. L., Hunter, J. E., & Urry V. W. (1976). Statistical power in criterion-related validation studies. *Journal of Applied Psychology, 61,* 473–485.

Schmidt, F. L., Law, K., Hunter, J. E., Rothstein, H. R., Pearlman, K., & McDaniel, M. (1993). Refinements in validity generalization methods: Implications for the situation specificity hypothesis. *Journal of Applied Psychology, 78,* 3–12.

Schmidt, F. L., & Rader, M. (1999). Exploring the boundary conditions for interview validity: Meta-analytic validity findings for a new interview type. *Personnel Psychology, 52,* 445–464.

Schmitt, N. (1976). Social and situational determinants of interview decisions: Implications for the employment interview. *Personnel Psychology, 29,* 79–101.

Schmitt, N., Gooding, R. Z., Noe, R. A., & Kirsch, M. (1984). Meta-analyses of validity studies published between 1964 and 1982 and the investigation of study characteristics. *Personnel Psychology, 37,* 407–422.

Schmitt, N., & Quinn, A. (2009). Reductions in measured subgroup differences: What is possible. In J. Outtz (Ed.), *Adverse impact implications for organizational staffing and high stakes selection* (pp. 425–452). New York: Routledge, Taylor & Francis Group.

Schmitt, N., Rogers, W., Chan, D., Sheppard, L., & Jennings, D. (1997). Adverse impact and predictive efficiency using various predictor combinations. *Journal of Applied Psychology, 82,* 719–730.

Society for Industrial and Organizational Psychology. (2003). *Principles for the validation and use of personnel selection procedures* (4th ed.). Bowling Green, OH: Author.

Stockdale, M., & Crosby, F. (2004). *The psychology and management of workforce diversity.* Malden, MA: Blackwell.

Tett, R. P., Jackson, D. N., & Rothstein, M. (1991). Personality measures as predictors of job performance: A meta-analytic review. *Personnel Psychology, 44,* 703–742.

Title VII of the Civil Rights Act, as amended, 42 U.S.C. § 2000e. (1964).

Wagner, R. (1949). The employment interview: A critical summary. *Personnel Psychology, 2,* 17–46.

Wonderlic, Inc. (2003). *Wonderlic Personnel Test.* Libertyville, IL: Author.

Wright, P. M., Lichtenfels, P. A., & Pursell, E. D. (1989). The structured interview: Additional studies and a meta-analysis. *Journal of Occupational Psychology, 62,* 191–199.

Part V

DEVELOPING MEMBERS

Chapter 16

TRAINING AND EMPLOYEE DEVELOPMENT FOR IMPROVED PERFORMANCE

Kenneth G. Brown and Traci Sitzmann

Learning is fundamental to successfully navigating everyday life. Consequently, humans are quite adept at acquiring new knowledge and skills as demands arise. Most learning occurs in naturalistic settings, through unplanned and unguided activity. More specific to work settings, employees often learn to perform work-related tasks through activities ranging from experimentation (i.e., trial and error) to consultation (i.e., asking a colleague). The value of such learning, generally labeled *informal* (e.g., Tannenbaum, Beard, NcNall, & Salas, 2010) or *work based* (e.g., Raelin, 1997), is beyond question. After all, how well would organizations function without employees who learn on their own accord the new office building layout, software program, chain of command, copy machine codes, budgeting procedure, and so on?

Although the value of informal learning is beyond question, it is not always an efficient or effective option for individuals and the organizations that employ them. Informal learning works well when people can readily encounter high-quality information that will help them learn, such as by having access to accurate and up-to-date resources or colleagues (Cross, 2006). In addition, informal learning likely works best when people are aware of the need to learn something new and are willing to exert the effort to learn it. If the appropriate information is not readily available or if employees are unaware they need to learn it, then a planned and systematic process that helps employees learn may be required. Moreover, when the information to be learned is complex, formal methods are likely to be more effective and more efficient than informal methods (Bransford, Brown, & Cocking, 1999). The focus of this chapter is on formal programs that organizations use to help their employees learn. Such programs are collectively referred to as *training and development.*

Training is defined as a formal, planned effort to help employees gain job-relevant knowledge and skills (Goldstein & Ford, 2002; Noe, 2008). In contrast to training that is used to help employees with their current jobs, *development* activities help employees prepare for future jobs (London, 1989; Noe, Wilk, Mullen, & Wanek 1997). Consequently, development activities are typically more discretionary than training (Noe, 2008).

The potential usefulness of training and development in organizations cannot be overstated. These programs, when designed and delivered properly, improve employees' skills and job-related behaviors (Arthur, Bennett, Edens, & Bell, 2003), reduce accidents (Robinson & Robinson, 1989), increase innovation (Barber, 2004), enable trainees to perform consistently in stressful situations (Driskell, Johnston, & Salas, 2001), enhance organizational productivity (Zwick, 2006), and increase organizational profits

Kenneth G. Brown's time was funded in part by a fellowship from the Henry B. Tippie College of Business. Traci Sitzmann's time was funded by the Advanced Distributed Learning Initiative, Office of the Deputy Under Secretary of Defense for Readiness and Training, Policy and Programs. The views expressed here are those of the authors and do not necessarily reflect the views or policies of the Department of Defense. We thank Sheldon Zedeck, Herman Aguinis, and Lisa Burke for their insightful feedback. We also thank Katherine Ely and Shenan Hahn for their invaluable assistance.

(Montebello & Haga, 1994). Aguinis and Kraiger (2009), in a multidisciplinary review of the training literature, enumerated the benefits of training for individuals, teams, organizations, and society. Meta-analysis results also suggest training has positive effects. For example, Arthur et al. (2003) reported sample-weighted mean *d* values, comparing trained versus control groups, of 0.63 ($k = 234$, $N = 15{,}014$) for learning outcomes, 0.62 ($k = 122$, $N = 15{,}627$) for behavioral outcomes, and 0.62 ($k = 26$, $N = 1{,}748$) for results outcomes such as job performance. In a meta-analysis of organizational outcomes, Tharenou, Saks, and Moore (2007) found positive although substantially lower correlations between training and performance for objective measures (mean weighted $r = .14$, $k = 32$, $N = 2{,}882$) than for perceptual measures (mean weighted $r = .27$, $k = 18$, $N = 3{,}402$).

The positive effects of training are believed to occur through at least two mechanisms. First, training and development help employees learn to better perform their work. That is, training improves employees' job-related knowledge and skills and, by extension, their job performance. Second, training and development are perceived by many employees to be valuable benefits, and social exchange theory (Balkin & Richebe, 2007) suggests that employees who receive such benefits may reciprocate with increased effort and commitment. In support of this hypothesis, Lambooij, Flache, Sanders, and Siegers (2007) found that employees indicated they would be more willing to volunteer for overtime when their companies offered extensive training opportunities (see also Bartlett, 2002). In support of both skill and motivation mechanisms, Birdi et al. (2008) found that extensive training and development fosters organizational performance by improving employees' commitment as well as their skills.

Another mechanism that may explain positive benefits of training is its symbolic value. Training and development programs convey messages about what the organization values to its stakeholders, including customers, shareholders, and employees (Feldman, 1989; Moreland & Levine, 2001). Thus, training on safety, for example, may help legitimate claims that the organization is concerned about employees' welfare. In addition, in the case of litigation, past training efforts can be used to reduce the organization's liability (e.g., Willman, 2004).

Researchers and workforce learning and performance professionals often lament that training does little to change on-the-job behavior, and that they have minimal influence on broader decisions in their organizations (e.g., Kraiger, McLinden, & Casper, 2004; Maister, 2008). An underlying cause for these concerns is that some training is ineffective. If training is ill-conceived, poorly planned, or inadequately executed, then it is likely to waste organizations' and employees' limited resources. To avoid this outcome, training practitioners should use a deliberate and systematic process guided by the best available evidence for what works.

The focus of this chapter is maximizing the potential that training has to influence individual and organizational performance through changes in employees' knowledge, skills, attitudes, and motivation. Consequently, the symbolic and legal benefits of training, although interesting and important, are not reviewed in more detail. Instead, we focus our review on factors within the control of training designers, trainers, trainees, and managers that influence whether training fosters learning and, by extension, improve performance. Our review covers phases of the training process with an emphasis on research suggesting how to most effectively assess training needs, design training, and evaluate it. The chapter also includes sections on employee development activities and future research directions. To frame this material, we begin with descriptions of training practices today and with definitions of the concepts of learning and transfer of training.

TRAINING PRACTICES TODAY

What happens in organizations under the label of *training* is quite diverse. Organizations differ in how much training they offer, what content they include, and how they deliver it.

Incidence

Research in labor economics has provided some insight into which organizations offer training and why. Using a nationally representative sample of organizations in the United States, Lynch and Black

(1998) examined the percentage of employers who offered scheduled training events with predefined objectives. Most employers (81%) offered some type of training, and 57% reported that since 1991 the amount of formal training had increased. The researchers also found evidence that the incidence of training varied by establishment size, with virtually all of the largest establishments (more than 1,000 employees) offering training (see also Frazis, Herz, & Horrigan, 1995). There was also considerable variation by industry.

The cause for the observed relationship between organizational size and the incidence of training has been examined in more detail. Knoke and Kalleberg (1994) presented evidence that the relationships between training incidence and other factors such as size, unionization, and workforce composition are spurious. They demonstrated that employer-provided training is most likely to be offered in organizations with an elaborate internal structure, including those with formalized job positions and internal job markets, and in organizations that operate in complex markets, such as those with lots of competitors. They also suggested that less training is offered in industries with low unemployment (see also Majumdar, 2007). Thus, whether training is offered in an organization appears to be driven by both environmental variables and by the overall degree of formalization in that organization.

Content

According to the American Society for Training and Development (ASTD) Benchmarking Forum of large companies and public sector organizations (Paradise, 2008), the most common training programs focus on profession or industry-specific knowledge (average of 26% of learning content across 25 benchmark organizations). These programs are unlikely to be unique to the sponsoring organization. The fact that organizations offer training that is sufficiently general to be of value to many organizations contradicts a classic economic theory of workplace training. G. S. Becker (1964) theorized that employer-provided training could be classified into general and specific, with the former developing skills that are of equal value to many firms. Becker argued that employees receive the long-term returns of general skills training because they receive higher salaries as they are hired away by firms seeking their skills. Consequently, firms should rationally underinvest in general skills training and focus instead on specific skills training, such as processes unique to that company's work processes.

Research has called attention to labor-market imperfections that invalidate the basic premise of Becker's theory. These imperfections include the transaction costs of replacing workers and the lack of clear information on the quantity and content of workers' training experiences (Acemoglu & Pischke, 1999). Acemoglu and Pischke (1999) also reviewed studies that confirmed that many organizations pay for general as well as specific skills training. For example, temporary labor firms provide training, despite short-term contracts. Similarly, many firms reimburse employees for college courses, and others offer on-site literacy programs. In short, training in organizations today advances both general and specific skills.

Delivery

One trend over the past few years has been a general reduction in the use of instructor-led classroom training from 64% of available learning hours in 2003 to 58% in 2007 (Paradise, 2008). According to ASTD research, technology-based training has increased from 22% in 2001 to 35% in 2007. At least part of this growth can be attributed to technology convergence, which is a trend for different technological systems to evolve toward performing similar tasks. Most notable for training, Internet-enabled computers can now deliver printable books, audio clips, video clips, and computer simulations, reducing the need for nontechnology-based self-paced learning systems (e.g., workbooks) and independent technology-delivery systems (e.g., courses on CD-ROM). Although computer-delivery may not be appropriate in all training situations, computers are now a staple for training delivery. Nonetheless, the majority of training hours are still taken in traditional classroom settings.

LEARNING AND TRANSFER

In industrial and organizational (I/O) psychology, *learning* is typically defined as "a relatively permanent change in knowledge or skill produced by experience" (Weiss, 1990, p. 172). Learning can also be defined at higher levels of theory, such as with teams and organizations, both of which will be addressed briefly later in this section.

More in-depth analysis of the concept of learning can be found in the educational literature. In education, researchers argued that there are at least three distinct categories of learning theory that derive from different philosophical perspectives: behaviorist, cognitive, and situative (Greeno, Collins, & Resnick, 1996). These perspectives manifest in three different approaches to training design. Consistent with Greeno et al. (1996) and Ertmer and Newby (1993), we believe that all three perspectives offer useful insights into learning at work.

Behaviorist

The behaviorist perspective on learning focuses on changes in the form or frequency of observable behavior. Learning is said to occur when the appropriate response is given, following an environmental stimulus, such as a plumber selecting the proper tools given a particular problem. The primary focus of the behaviorist perspective is on the environment and the learning conditions it presents. For example, does the training offer opportunities for practice and feedback so that trainees learn the appropriate response?

The behaviorist model draws on theoretical work of Thorndike, Watson, Skinner, and others (Ertmer & Newby, 1993). A classic educational application of these theories was offered by Keller (1982), who developed and tested a Personalized System of Instruction (see also Bloom, 1976, Learning for Mastery). These systems require that courses be divided into units, and students must pass units with a minimum level of proficiency before moving on to the next unit. Meta-analytic research suggests that such instruction is effective, although the effects vary depending on the domain and type of test (C. C. Kulik, Kulik, & Bangert-Drowns, 1990). For example, the average effect size for the difference between control and individualized instruction was 0.52 ($k = 103$), but effect sizes were larger for social sciences courses evaluated with local (course specific) tests than for other types of courses evaluated with standardized tests.

Behavior modeling, drawn from Bandura's (1977) social learning theory, was a behavioral theory in its early formulations. Behavior modification efforts also fall under this perspective, and a stream of organizational research has emerged that uses this theory to alter employee behavior. The organizational behavior modification approach to increasing task performance involves a five-step process of identifying the change needed, measuring baseline frequency, analyzing consequences, contingently intervening, and evaluating. A meta-analysis of research in this area found large differences in task performance between employees who were undergoing organizational behavior modification and employees in a control condition (average variance-weighted $d = 0.95$, $k = 115$, $N = 2{,}818$; after removal of outliers $d = 0.51$; Stajkovic & Luthans, 1997). This particular area of research has not explicitly examined learning, but it is likely that both increased motivation and learning explain these findings.

Taken as a whole, prior research suggests that behaviorist approaches to training have value. Despite being somewhat displaced during the cognitive revolution in psychology, which emphasized the intervening cognitive mechanisms for learning (Greenwood, 1999), training based on behaviorism has been widely and successfully applied to facilitate learning and to improve job performance.

Cognitive

Cognitive learning theories stress the acquisition of knowledge, including both content and structure. These theories place considerable emphasis on learning as a form of mental activity, and they use perception, information processing, and memory as key explanatory mechanisms. From the cognitive perspective, environmental conditions are also important, but they are seen as antecedents to mental activities that influence learning (Ertmer & Newby, 1993).

Cognitive learning theories generally emphasize that learning a particular skill involves several interrelated changes in how people process information. Anderson's ACT* theory, for example, argues that learners initially acquire declarative knowledge (i.e., understanding of concepts and terms) and then acquire procedural knowledge (i.e., the application of knowledge to produce effective task performance; e.g., Anderson, 1985). A critical process involved in the acquisition of procedural knowledge is knowledge compilation, in which knowledge is reorganized to allow for more efficient and domain-appropriate skill. Other researchers have examined the concept of knowledge organization in more detail and argued that how knowledge is structured in memory is of equal or greater importance than the amount or type of knowledge (e.g., Johnson-Laird, 1983).

An example of research from this perspective was offered by Davis and Yi (2004). These researchers examined the influence of symbolic mental rehearsal on trainees' knowledge structures. Symbolic mental rehearsal is a technique drawn from Bandura's (1986) refinements to social learning theory, which emphasize how information is encoded and stored in memory. This technique asks trainees to (a) organize and reduce what they have seen from modeled performance into information that can be readily stored in and retrieved from memory, and (b) rehearse retrieving and applying that information through visualization. Davis and Yi tested this technique against basic behavior modeling where trainees watched an instructional video that included explanations of the task, a model performing the task, and practice. The researchers found that encouraging mental rehearsal increased the similarity of trainees' knowledge structures to the structures of experts (Study 1 and 2), and this increase mediated the relationship between the training technique and increases in declarative knowledge and task performance (Study 2). Thus, these studies and others demonstrate both the usefulness of training design from a cognitive perspective and the usefulness of knowledge structure measures for predicting posttraining performance (Cooke & Fiore, 2010; Goldsmith & Kraiger, 1997).

Situative

Behavioral and cognitive theories assume that knowledge is objective and learners should acquire it by learning the correct concepts and way to perform a task. Another philosophical perspective on knowledge asserts that there is no objective knowledge; all knowledge is limited to the individual's awareness and experiences. These situative models argue that learning is embedded in the context in which it occurs and results from each individual constructing meaning from his or her own experience (e.g., J. S. Brown, Collins, & Duguid, 1989; Greeno, 1998). Situative models are drawn from the work of Piaget and Bruner and emphasize engaging learners in an authentic social context through relationships (Ertmer & Newby, 1993). Many who study situative models are reluctant to use quantitative measures of learning because such measures require that knowledge be divorced, at least to some degree, from its use in context.

The dominant learning perspectives in I/O psychology have been the behaviorist and cognitive theories (Kraiger, 2008). At least to some degree, this has limited the training efforts studied and the outcomes used to evaluate them. From a situative perspective, we might study how training helps employees navigate their social roles and acquire new insights into their identity. We might also explore how employees make sense of and prioritize among different types of learning opportunities. Finally, we might place greater emphasis on learning through apprenticeships, coaching, and peer training: topics that have been understudied (for exceptions, see Chao, 1997; Sue-Chan & Latham, 2004) yet seem to be frequently used in organizations.

Transfer of Training

Transfer of training is commonly defined as the successful application of knowledge, skills, and attitudes gained in a training context to the job (Baldwin & Ford, 1988; Baldwin, Ford, & Blume, 2009). An often implicit assumption that underlies training is that what employees learn in training will transfer to work. If such transfer does not occur, then training investments may not be warranted. Some authors have offered dismal assessments of training transfer, specifically that only 10% of training transfers (e.g., Baldwin & Ford, 1988). However, precise estimates about the percentage of training that transfers are not based on research findings (Fitzpatrick, 2001). Research does suggest that the relationships among learning outcomes and transfer are neither simple nor uniformly strong. For example, Colquitt, LePine, and Noe (2000) used meta-analytic path analysis to estimate relationships between a variety of learning outcomes and transfer ($N = 173$). They found substantial differences across outcomes as follows: declarative knowledge ($\beta = -.03$), skill acquisition ($\beta = .59$), posttraining self-efficacy ($\beta = .27$), and reactions ($\beta = .03$). Considerable variability in the declarative knowledge and skill-acquisition effects across studies led the authors to suggest that moderators are present. Thus, transfer is predicted by at least some learning outcomes, but it should not be assumed to occur even if learning has occurred. Rather, transfer should be studied and managed directly.

Theories and research on training transfer often focus on two dimensions: (a) *maintenance*—remembering what was learned over time, and (b) *generalization*—applying what was learned to the job context (Baldwin & Ford, 1988). Another common distinction is between *near transfer* and *far transfer*. Near transfer refers to transfer to closely related contexts and tasks, whereas far transfer refers to different contexts and tasks (Royer, 1979). Although the distinction is not precise, it is useful for acknowledging that transfer is influenced by the degree of similarity between what trainees do in training and what they are asked to do on the job (Holton & Baldwin, 2003). Discussion of additional dimensions and complexities of transfer are useful but beyond the scope of this chapter (see Barnett & Ceci, 2002; Holton & Baldwin, 2003; Yelon & Ford, 1999).

The most frequently cited theory of training transfer is the Baldwin and Ford (1988) model. It suggests that transfer is determined first and foremost by the degree to which trainees have learned the material in the training context. According to the theory, features of the training design (e.g., sequencing of training material or extent of practice and feedback) influences transfer through its influence on learning. Other direct influences on transfer include trainee characteristics (i.e., trainee ability, personality, and motivation) and work environment characteristics (i.e., support and opportunity to use). Research supports trainee and work environment characteristics as direct predictors of transfer. In their meta-analytic path analysis of transfer ($N = 173$), which controlled for learning outcomes, Colquitt et al. (2000) found that trainees' locus of control ($\beta = .41$) and conscientiousness ($\beta = .52$) predicted transfer, as did the degree to which the work climate supports transfer ($\beta = .12$).

L. A. Burke and Hutchins (2008) surveyed training practitioners and developed categories of best practice for supporting transfer of training. These categories included the following: (a) supervisory support and reinforcement for using new knowledge and skills on the job, (b) coaching and opportunities to practice immediately on returning from training, (c) posttraining evaluation of transfer, (d) use of job-relevant content, and (e) use of interactive activities during training to encourage participation.

Prior research supports the idea that certain types of learning activities are more useful for stimulating transfer than others. Specifically, R. A. Schmidt and Bjork (1992) demonstrated the counterintuitive finding that preparing learners for transfer may require challenging trainees in ways that result in poor performance during training. For example, inducing variation in practice conditions during training enhances transfer but impairs performance during knowledge acquisition. Thus, the relationship between a learning measure collected in training and a learning measure collected following training is not always strong. It is also important to reiterate that learning is not fully captured with any one particular construct or measure. Measures of cognitive (e.g., declarative and structural knowledge) and affective (e.g., motivation and self-efficacy) outcomes offer incremental prediction of transfer beyond that of skill acquisition in training (Colquitt et al., 2000; Kozlowski et al., 2001).

Higher Levels of Theory

Learning and transfer can also be conceptualized at higher levels of theory, such as with teams and organizations. *Team learning* is "a relatively permanent change in the team's collective level of knowledge and skill produced by the shared experience of the team members" (Stagl, Salas, & Day, 2008, p. 822). Team learning is conceptualized as reliant on but distinct from individual learning. Research does suggest that team training, whether it is focused on the tasks that team members perform or on teamwork skills, helps teams improve their processes and performance. Salas et al. (2008) reported nearly equivalent effect sizes for teamwork ($\rho = .38$, $k = 17$,

$N = 374$) and taskwork ($\rho = .35$, $k = 6$, $N = 240$) training on team performance but stronger effects for teamwork ($\rho = .44$, $k = 13$, $N = 236$) than taskwork ($\rho = .28$, $k = 3$, $N = 145$) training on team-process outcomes. Thus, team training (particularly teamwork skills training) helps teams improve the processes they use to function and, by extension, their performance. However, the small numbers of studies suggest that further research on the effects of team training is needed.

Organizational learning is an organization-wide process of systematically and collectively interpreting new knowledge so the organization can respond to internal and external changes. Organizational learning is studied in a variety of disciplines, each offering distinct conceptualizations (Argote & Todorova, 2007; Easterby-Smith, 1997; Levitt & March, 1988). One particularly practical conceptualization emphasizes the structural mechanisms by which organizational learning can be facilitated. Lipshitz, Friedman, and Popper (2007) categorized such mechanisms according to who does them (i.e., people who are internal or external to the organization) and when they are completed (i.e., while conducting the work or after, labeled online or offline, respectively). Examples of internal online mechanisms include *active experimentation* and *online debriefing*, and examples of internal offline mechanisms include *afteraction reviews* and *communities of practice*. Research coverage of these mechanisms is uneven, but there is research on afteraction reviews by soldiers that suggests a positive effect on learning (Ellis & Davidi, 2005). There is also research on communities of practice, which are groups of people who work on shared concerns and deepen their knowledge through sustained interaction. This research suggests that such communities offer numerous benefits to individuals and organizations (Wegner, McDermott, & Snyder, 2007). However, in part because of its foundation in situative models of learning, research on communities of practice remains largely qualitative and anecdotal. Examples of external online mechanisms include coaching networks and peer assists; examples of external offline mechanisms include teams that engage in scenario planning and postproject assessment. Again, research coverage is uneven. Although there is research on executive coaching (see chap. 18, this volume), there is little research on peer coaching and assistance. Further research on these topics is encouraged.

The concept of transfer has also been extended to levels of theory and analysis beyond the individual. Knowledge transfer across organizational units has been defined as the process through which one unit is affected by the experience of another (Argote & Ingram, 2000). Research suggests that this process is impeded by a variety of forces (e.g., Szulanski, 1996). Reviews suggest that firms gain competitive advantage if they can develop knowledge-based resources (DeNisi, Hitt, & Jackson, 2003), facilitate knowledge transfer across units within their firm, and prevent its transfer to competitors (Argote & Ingram, 2000).

In another conceptualization, *vertical transfer* has been defined as transfer upward across levels of the organizational system (Kozlowski, Brown, Weissbein, Cannon-Bowers, & Salas, 2000; Kozlowski & Salas, 1997). This concept is concerned with how training outcomes combine across individuals and over time to influence team and organizational outcomes; it is distinguished from the traditional transfer concept of *horizontal transfer*, which is transfer within a level of analysis across contexts. Training evaluation, discussed later in this chapter, has often attempted to measure organizational level outcomes without sound theory on how those outcomes emerge as a result of training (i.e., Kirkpatrick, 1976). The concept of vertical transfer emphasizes that social processes underlying the organizational outcome in question must be understood to determine how training might have its influence. Empirical research on this concept is limited, and further research is encouraged.

TRAINING AS A HUMAN RESOURCE MANAGEMENT SUBSYSTEM

Training within an organization does not and should not occur within a vacuum. Organizational decision makers should seek to align training efforts with the strategy of the organization and with the other human resource management (HRM) practices. Failure to do so may limit transfer of training and, thus, the potential that training has to improve individual and organizational performance.

Sonnenfeld and Peiperl (1988) theorized that organizations adopt HRM systems that trade-off selection and training; organizations pursuing certain strategies, such as prospecting new business opportunities, emphasize recruiting and selection over training. Raghuram and Avery (1994) empirically demonstrated that firms with particular strategies adopt different training and staffing practices. Expanding on these ideas, Noe (2008) suggested that different types of training programs should be emphasized by firms that are pursuing concentration, internal growth, external growth, and disinvestment strategies (see also Blanchard & Thacker, 2007). Although these recommendations are logical, such as firms pursuing external growth offering training on how to execute mergers, research supporting these recommendations is needed.

Strategic HRM theorists have further argued that the portfolio of HRM practices, including recruiting, selection, compensation, rewards, performance management, and training, should be aligned to pursue the same outcomes (Delery, 1998; Wright, 1998). Consistent with this argument, research suggests that organizations display clusters of practices aimed toward particular outcomes (e.g., B. E. Becker & Huselid, 1996; Valle, Martin, Romero, & Dolan, 2000). Most recently, Toh, Morgeson, and Campion (2008) found that some organizations invested in training and other HRM practices in what appear to be efforts to maximize employee commitment; other organizations emphasized training to build internal resources. Still other organizations did not invest substantially in training because they appeared to be minimizing costs or because they emphasized contingent pay (rather than development) to encourage performance (Toh et al., 2008). Despite the progress in this area, research is needed to directly demonstrate the performance benefits of aligning training with strategy and aligning training with other HRM practices.

TRAINING AS A PROCESS

There is a substantial history to the development of a systematic process for designing training programs. The U.S. military, for example, developed a common process across all service branches (Branson et al., 1975). Drawing on this and other early process models, Goldstein (1986) proposed a system for the development of training that begins with a needs assessment. Needs assessment determines the instructional objectives, which in turn drives the training design and the development of criteria that will be used to evaluate training. The final phase is evaluating training, which helps to ascertain the effectiveness and efficiency of the program. This information then feeds back into the next cycle of training needs assessment, such that needs assessment, training, and evaluation are a continual process. Figure 16.1 depicts this process.

Over the past decade or so, the pressure to develop training more quickly has resulted in the development of alternative, more streamlined, models. One example of an alternative model, drawn from process models in the area of software development, is the rapid prototyping model (Tripp & Bichelmeyer, 1990). Although not commonly discussed in the I/O psychology literature, the rapid prototyping model offers an expedient alternative to the more traditional process. The first phase involves the assessment of needs and determination of training

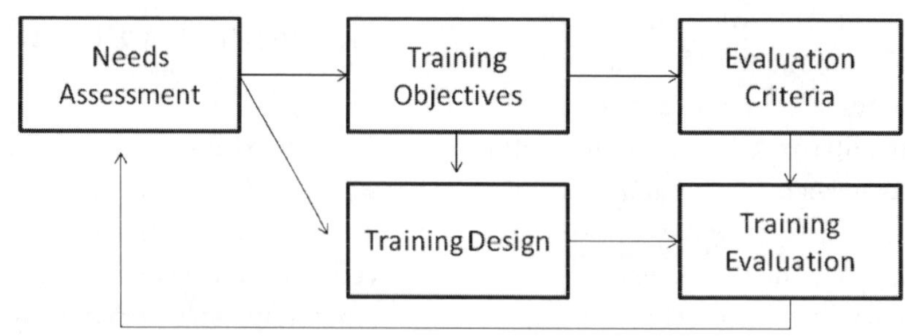

FIGURE 16.1. Traditional instructional design system.

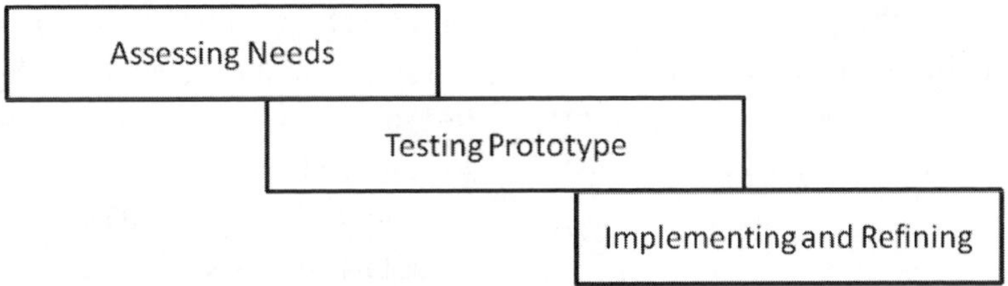

FIGURE 16.2. Rapid prototyping instructional design system.

objectives. The second phase involves constructing prototypes and testing them with users. The third and final stage involves implementing and refining the training. Figure 16.2 depicts this process. The model relies on the principles of parallel work effort, minimal commitments, and extensive user testing. Thus, designers are expected to create and test training before the needs assessment is complete and modify the training based on the results of user tests. This approach requires a setting in which instruction can be created, tested, and modified quickly. It would be impractical in settings where instruction is costly to develop or when user testing is infeasible.

NEEDS ASSESSMENT

Training needs assessment is a process used to determine where and when an organization should allocate resources toward training.[1] Compared with other related areas of training, this process has received little research attention (Salas & Cannon-Bowers, 2001). In addition, one meta-analysis of training effectiveness revealed that only 6% of 397 studies reported that a needs assessment was conducted (Arthur et al., 2003). Nevertheless, conducting a needs assessment is vitally important to ensure that training improves performance, and there is relevant research on work analysis that can inform both research and practice (Brannick, Levine, & Morgeson, 2007). The remainder of this section will cover the three components of a need assessment conducted for training-related purposes—organization, task, and person analysis. We also cover the closely related topics of human performance improvement and training objectives.

Organization Analysis

Organization analysis involves determining the appropriateness of training given the organization's strategic goals, environment, and characteristics. Different strategies demand different amounts and types of training (Blanchard & Thacker, 2007; Noe, 2008). Similarly, many facets of the environment, including technical and legal, influence the type of training that an organization should offer (Goldstein & Ford, 2002). The technical environment includes the current and forthcoming technologies that employees use to perform their work. The legal environment includes both legislation and regulatory mandates. Some industries are more affected by regulations than others (e.g., utilities more than services), and assessors should be aware of how training assists in compliance and reduces litigation risk (Johnson, 2004).

Organization analysis also measures work environment characteristics, such as *transfer of training climate*, which Rouiller and Goldstein (1993) defined as "those situations and consequences which either inhibit or help to facilitate the transfer of what has been learned in training into the job situation" (p. 379). Tracey, Tannenbaum, and Kavanagh (1995) found that transfer of training climate was a powerful predictor of transfer of training. Similarly, Smith-Crowe, Burke, and Landis (2003) found that the safety knowledge of hazardous waste workers had a stronger effect on safety performance in a supportive organizational climate. If trainees will be returning to a work environment that is not supportive of new skills, they should be prepared through training with strategies that help them to overcome barriers to transfer (Broad & Newstrom, 1992; L. A.

[1] In disciplines outside of I/O psychology, distinctions are often drawn between the terms *needs assessment* and *needs analysis* (e.g., Watkins & Kaufman, 1996). We generally use the umbrella term *needs assessment* to refer to determining needs and analyzing them to decide on priorities for future training-related activities.

Burke & Hutchins, 2007; Holton, 2003). Thus, data collected during the organization analysis helps to determine both what training programs are appropriate, if any, and how the training should be designed.

Task Analysis

Task analysis involves identifying the tasks performed by trainees and the knowledge and skills necessary to perform them effectively. Task analysis is a form of job analysis and involves different methods, depending on the desired data and the task being analyzed (Goldstein & Ford, 2002). Because job analysis is covered elsewhere (see chap. 1, this volume), we focus our discussion here on two increasingly important techniques relevant to training needs assessment: *cognitive task analysis* and *team task analysis.*

Cognitive task analysis examines the mental processes and skills required to perform a task. It is most appropriate for tasks that require an extensive knowledge base and involve complex judgments that take place in dynamic and uncertain environments (O'Hare, Wiggins, Williams, & Wong, 1998). Cognitive task analysis may be carried out by using a wide variety of techniques, including observations and interviews, process tracing, domain representation, and formal modeling (Wei & Salvendy, 2004). Observations and interviews involve the collection of qualitative data from participants by recording their behavior and asking about their thought processes. Process tracing refers to collecting verbal reports of thought processes while participants perform the tasks being analyzed. Domain representation involves collecting quantitative ratings from participants about the interrelations among task-related concepts and comparing participant ratings to expert ratings. Formal modeling moves beyond comparing to actually building a simulation of the participant performing the task and examining how the simulation performs relative to actual participant performance.

The most commonly used cognitive task analysis approach for developing training is interview and observation, in which the analyst watches participant activity in already functioning systems (O'Hare et al., 1998). This work is time consuming and labor intensive, but it is often necessary to develop training for jobs that are becoming increasingly complex and mentally challenging (Sackett & Laczo, 2003).

Team task analysis is a simultaneous examination of the task and coordination requirements of a group of individuals who are working together toward a common goal (Arthur, Edwards, Bell, Villado, & Bennett, 2005). A critical element of team task analysis is identifying the knowledge, skills, and abilities that team members must have to coordinate. Arthur et al. (2005) developed a teamwork task-analysis survey for students who were playing a computer simulation, and they found that participants generally agreed on the degree to which tasks required teamwork. However, this study did not examine participant ratings of required teamwork skills. In a study on teamwork skills, Bowers, Baker, and Salas (1994) found that aircraft pilots did not agree on the importance of various teamwork skills. The authors concluded that it is difficult for job incumbents to agree on the importance of various teamwork behaviors. Thus, additional research is needed to determine how to assess the importance of various teamwork behaviors.

Person Analysis

Person analysis involves determining (a) whether training or other solutions are necessary to improve performance; (b) who needs training, if in fact training is needed; and (c) whether trainees are ready for training (Noe, 2008).

First, person analysis should determine whether training is appropriate by assessing the underlying causes of the observed need or gap between the desired and actual state of affairs. If the need is preventing a repeat of an industrial accident, for example, and employees' lack of knowledge and skill was the cause of the original accident, then training is an appropriate intervention. There are, however, many other reasons why the accident may have occurred, including improper incentives and communication (Roberts & Bea, 2001). When these are the causes for poor performance, training may be unnecessary. Consequently, an effective person analysis identifies both training and nontraining needs, and it helps ascertain whether some intervention other than (or in addition to) training is required to improve performance.

Second, a number of different methods can be used to determine who needs training if it is deemed appropriate. Two of the most common are examining existing employee records and soliciting self-assessed needs, but each suffers from potential bias (Goldstein & Ford, 2002). Employee records may not be sufficiently detailed or may gloss over skill deficiencies because of legal concerns over keeping records of poor performance. Self-assessed needs may be inaccurate because they are influenced by person characteristics that are not always related to actual knowledge and skill levels (Ford & Noe, 1987; Ford, Smith, Sego, & Quiñones, 1993; Sitzmann, Ely, Brown, & Bauer, in press). Moreover, there is research indicating that people in the lower half of a distribution overestimate their performance relative to others (Dunning, Johnson, Ehrlinger, & Kruger, 2003). Another study demonstrated that, compared with an observer, those who perform a task for longer periods of time may be less able to accurately recall what they do (Richman & Quiñones, 1996).

Third, assessors must determine whether trainees are ready for training. The concept of trainee readiness is multifaceted (Noe, 2008). Research suggests that trainees are most likely to succeed if they have the basic skills and abilities required by the training and are motivated to learn the training content (Colquitt et al., 2000). Of course, this does not mean that training should only be offered to those who fit this profile. Training would, however, be more likely to improve an employees' performance if a person analysis identified who required remedial basic skills training, who required more time to learn the material, and who required supplemental interventions to boost motivation to learn. In general, methods for identifying trainees who are not ready for training and offering remediation or supplemental instruction are not well researched. We encourage creative efforts to propose and test new techniques.

Human Performance Improvement

The organization–task–person model is widely cited, but it is not without limitations. When a specific performance problem is the impetus for training, such as high turnover or poor sales, a thorough needs assessment may prove inefficient. In these situations, an alternative model that begins with problem definition and then moves to root cause identification and intervention design would be more efficient (e.g., Pershing, 2006). The key feature of this approach, often called *human performance improvement,* is that the nature of the problem and the appropriate solution are not assumed. Instead, it is assumed that the root causes of a performance problem are potentially numerous and unknown, and the analyst should identify those causes before selecting an intervention. Greater attention on this approach in published accounts of training by I/O psychologists may help to avoid the implementation of training when it is not warranted by the problem at hand.

Training Objectives

An important outcome of the assessment process is the creation of *training objectives.* Training objectives are the intended outcomes of training, and they should influence the selection of evaluation criteria and training design. Objectives can include learning objectives—which indicate what the learner should know and be capable of doing at the conclusion of training—and organizational objectives—which are the desired organizational outcomes. One often-cited book suggests that effective learning objectives should have three components: (a) behavior, or the observable behavior that trainees will exhibit following training; (b) conditions, or the conditions under which the behavior will occur, including tools and assistance available; and (c) standard, or the level of performance that is desirable (Mager, 1997). Objectives are useful to trainees, designers, trainers, and evaluators (Blanchard & Thacker, 2007), yet training studies do not always report the training objectives of the program being studied. Because ideally training objectives should influence training design and the selection of training evaluation criteria (see Figure 16.1), failing to report objectives leaves out potentially relevant contextual information. Providing such information would allow researchers to examine the types of objectives commonly used in training programs and whether objectives are, in practice, used to determine training design and evaluation criteria. This information would also be useful for future meta-analyses, as research could examine whether training is most effective when certain types of objectives are paired with certain types of training designs (for one start on this effort, see Day et al., 2006). Such research might also help to identify whether there are situations in which objectives are not useful, such as when designing a virtual learning environment for learners to share information and pursue their own learning objectives. Situative learning theories suggest that an instructor's predefined learning objectives may inhibit the design of an environment that meets learners' diverse needs.

TRAINING DESIGN

Training design refers to the process of planning events to facilitate learning (Gagné, Briggs, & Wager, 1992).[2] In this section, we cover research on design features that should be considered before, during, and after training. We also cover the topics of training media and instructor delivery. Research suggests that most organizations rely primarily on in-class activities to maximize learning and transfer (Saks & Belcourt, 2006). To maximize the possibility that training will improve performance, training should be more than a single isolated event; it should be designed to include interventions pretraining, during training, and posttraining (Burke & Hutchins, 2008; Broad & Newstrom, 1992; Machin, 2002).

Pretraining Interventions

Cannon-Bowers, Rhodenizer, Salas, and Bowers (1998) developed a conceptual framework of six interventions that make the time spent in skill-based practice both more efficient and more effective. These interventions include attentional advice, metacognitive strategies, advance organizers, goal orientations, preparatory information, and prepractice briefs. Each of these tactics may be used in training, but each also may be used as part of a coordinated effort to prepare trainees for training. For example, attentional advice and preparatory information could be provided as part of the description of training and as part of a preparation packet. Similarly, organizations might encourage pretraining briefs between supervisors and employees because research suggests that pretraining information influences the motivation and reactions of learners (Baldwin & Magjuka, 1997). Research in this area suggests that how information is conveyed to trainees can influence outcomes. For example, Martocchio (1992) found that labeling computer training as an opportunity, compared with a control condition, reduced computer anxiety and increased participants' computer self-efficacy and learning outcomes. Quiñones (1995) found that labeling training as *remedial* versus *advanced* interacted with trainee expectations to determine perceptions of training fairness and self-efficacy, both of which influenced subsequent motivation to learn. Baldwin et al. (2009) reviewed these and other studies in regard to the influence of pretraining influences on transfer of training.

As noted earlier, the work environment, particularly the transfer climate, also has a powerful influence on transfer. Although climates cannot be changed easily, it is possible to prepare the work environment to optimize the potential for transfer. For example, Taylor, Russ-Eft, and Chan (2005) reported that behavior-modeling training had stronger effects on learning and transfer if managers were also trained (mean $d = 0.53$, $k = 7$, $N = 302$) than if they were not trained (mean $d = 0.27$, $k = 59$, $N = 2{,}211$). Similarly, if rewards–sanctions were instituted to support the behavioral change, the effect of training was greater (mean $d = 0.51$, $k = 4$, $N = 223$) than if no mention was made of changes to rewards–sanctions (mean $d = 0.29$, $k = 59$, $N = 1{,}978$). Interventions during training and posttraining are discussed later in this section.

Instructional Methods

Instructional methods are the tactics used in the training environment to stimulate learning. Although there is no generally agreed on typology of methods, there are reviews that help to categorize them (see Day et al., 2006; Tennyson & Rasch, 1988). In this section, we review definitions and research on some of the most popular instructional methods in workplace training. It is unfortunate that training methods have not been systematically examined such that a research-based framework can be offered linking instructional methods to training objectives and desired learning outcomes (Goldstein & Ford, 2002).

[2] Some models of the instructional design process distinguish the steps of design (planning the events) and development (creating materials; e.g., Dick & Carey, 1990). In I/O psychology these are typically combined.

Lecture. *Lecture* involves an instructor explaining the content relevant to the learning objectives. Lectures can be presented in a variety of ways, including through computer conferencing, an audio or video recording, or a live lecture. The primary advantage of lecture is efficiency—it is the least time-consuming and least expensive way to deliver information to large groups of people (House, 1996). Arthur et al.'s (2003) meta-analysis revealed that the sample-weighted *d* for lecture (compared with the control condition) was 0.45 for learning ($k = 12$, $N =$ 1,176), which is a substantial effect even though it is lower than the average sample-weighted *d* of 0.63 for all methods ($k = 243$, $N = 15{,}014$). Clearly, lecture can be effective (see also M. J. Burke & Day, 1986), but there is a general consensus that lecture often allows learners to be passive, which can limit their learning (Noe, 2008). As a result, lectures are best suited to helping learners to gain knowledge rather than hands-on skill. In addition, lectures can be improved by combining them with other methods that require the learner to actively process information to be learned, such as methods explained below.

Discussion. *Discussion* involves two-way communication between instructors and trainees or among the trainees themselves. Discussion can take many forms, such as when trainees share answers to open-ended questions or when trainees debate the value of training materials. Although practical advice on guiding discussions is plentiful in the education literature, rigorous empirical research is scarce (for exceptions, see Arbaugh, 2000; Swan, 2001). Arbaugh (2000) found that learners may more readily participate in discussion online than in classroom instruction, but the increase in participation did not influence learning outcomes. It is possible that the benefits of discussion are greater for affective (e.g., motivation and satisfaction) than for cognitive outcomes, such as knowledge gain. However, it is also possible that carefully designed reflection and discussion activities may enhance knowledge, alter ways of thinking, and increase motivation and confidence (e.g., M. J. Burke, Scheuer, & Meredith, 2007).

Problem-based learning. *Problem-based learning* requires that learners solve real or simulated open-ended problems, often working in collaborative groups (Hmelo-Silver, 2004). In organizational training, a commonly used problem-based learning approach is action learning, which uses teams to solve ongoing organizational problems. This approach has been offered as a method that develops managers' analytical and problem-solving skills (Revans, 1980).

Case study. A *case study* is an approach to problem-based learning that asks learners to examine how employees or an organization dealt with a particular situation. Trainees analyze the situation and critique the actions taken, while suggesting other actions that should have been taken. Case studies are designed to develop analytical skills and are frequently used to train managers and other professionals who must render decisions (Noe, 2008).

Exploration. Another approach to training is to offer learning resources and allow learners to practice and *explore*. Exploration training can be guided or unguided, and research suggests that some form of guidance is necessary if learners are not already highly knowledgeable (Kirschner, Sweller, & Clark, 2006). In guided exploration, training is designed to ensure that trainees make progressive achievement. Debowski, Wood, and Bandura (2001) found a host of benefits for learners who received guidance, relative to those who did not receive guidance, as they explored an electronic search task.

Behavior modeling. *Behavior modeling* is a training technique that involves (a) describing a set of well-defined skills, (b) showing a model or models displaying the use of those skills, (c) practicing using those skills, and (d) providing feedback and reinforcement (Decker & Nathan, 1985). Taylor et al. (2005) reported large effects for knowledge outcomes—mean *d* ranged from 2.04 ($k = 4$, $N = 271$) for declarative knowledge of supervisory skill to 0.91 ($k = 4$, $N = 87$) for procedural knowledge of teamwork skills. They reported medium effects for attitudes and job behavior—mean *d* ranged from 0.35 ($k = 7$, $N = 310$) for job behavior related to teamwork skills to 0.19 ($k = 5$, $N = 597$) for attitudes related to technical skills.

Error management training. *Error management training* refers to a training design that encourages trainees to make errors. Trainees are explicitly told that errors are a natural part of the learning process and that they should use errors to help them understand the task. A meta-analytic summary of error management training studies suggests that this approach is generally effective overall and particularly effective for enhancing transfer ($d = 0.44$, $k = 24$, $N = 2{,}183$ overall; $d = 0.80$, $k = 11$, $N = 536$ for adaptive transfer; Keith & Frese, 2008). Many of these studies examined the development of computer skills; research using this method with other tasks and other learning outcomes would be beneficial.

Simulation and games. A *simulation* is a working representation of reality. Simulations can be live (i.e., people working face to face with real equipment but under artificial conditions), virtual (i.e., people working with simulated others and equipment), or a blend of the two. *Games* are activities that engage users and simultaneously entertain and instruct; they may or may not be a representation of a real environment (Cannon-Bowers & Bowers, 2010).

Bell, Kanar, and Kozlowski (2008) reviewed research suggesting that simulations are becoming increasingly prevalent in business schools and work organizations. Workplace training uses simulations most often when the actual performance of the task entails risk or access to limited resources. Pilots, for example, conduct many hours of simulator training to keep training costs low and to train for high-risk scenarios without endangering personnel and equipment.

The critical challenge for simulations is *psychological fidelity*. This term refers to a learning environment that faithfully reproduces the mental processes necessary for task performance (e.g., Cooke & Fiore, 2010). Psychological fidelity is at least theoretically distinct from physical fidelity, which refers to the reproduction of the physical characteristics of the transfer environment. Consistent with the concern regarding psychological fidelity, Cannon-Bowers and Bowers (2010) argued that the essential characteristics of simulations, games, and other virtual learning environments are that they provide deliberate, well-managed, and sufficiently realistic experiences. The challenge for future research is to define what constitutes "sufficiently realistic" for particular learners, objectives, tasks, and performance situations.

On-the-job training. *On-the-job training* involves one-on-one or small groups hands-on instruction conducted at the worksite. A new employee observes and interacts with an experienced employee to learn job-related knowledge and skills. Such training is very common (Jacobs & Osman-Gani, 1999) but frequently informal and ineffective (Goldstein & Ford, 2002). Jacobs, Jones, and Neil (1992) demonstrated that using a structured approach dramatically improved the efficiency of on-the-job training. Given the prevalence of this type of training, the dearth of research is surprising and additional work seems warranted.

Comparing methods. Experimental or quasi-experimental studies that compare different combinations of training methods would be invaluable for guiding practitioners in the selection of appropriate methods for particular training objectives, tasks, and situations. As noted earlier, research progress to date has been inconsistent in its coverage. Nevertheless, there have been excellent models to follow for this research. For example, Simon and Werner (1996) compared three approaches to computer training (behavior modeling, self-paced study, and lecture) against a control condition in which no training was offered. In a situation that involved employees with poor computer skills but high levels of motivation and support, behavior modeling offered the best learning outcomes both immediately after training and one month later. Studies like this one are useful because they offer strong evidence in support of a particular training method in a particular context.

Instructional Media

In addition to selecting a training method, instructional designers must select a training medium (or media), which is the means by which training content and methods are conveyed to learners. Many discussions of instructional methods confound method and media by, for example, discussing lecture and video as distinct methods. However, if an instructor lectures and that lecture is videotaped, then the nature of the lecture, including the content and the style, is conceptually independent from how the lecture is presented to the learner. That lecture may be delivered to the learner live face to face or live through technology such as television or streaming online video. The lecture could also be recorded and presented to a learner later through a videocassette, DVD, or an archived online video. Selecting among these options is a media choice.

Clark (1994) argued that media choices do not influence learning directly. That is, although media choices have cost and access implications, they do not directly influence trainees' learning processes and outcomes. Although there is not universal agreement on this hypothesis (see, e.g., Kozma, 1994), we believe it is useful to clearly distinguish between what is delivered (content and method) from how it is delivered (media).

Empirical support for this distinction was offered by Sitzmann, Kraiger, Stewart, and Wisher (2006), who conducted a meta-analysis to determine the relative effectiveness of online and classroom instruction. Results indicated that trainees learned the same amount from online and classroom instruction when the same instructional methods were used ($d = 0.04$, $k = 16$, $N = 2{,}032$). Accounting for instructional methods allowed the researchers to demonstrate that online instruction can be better or worse than classroom instruction. For example, in classes that optimized the advantages of the Internet (i.e., provided a high level of learner control and incorporated practice and feedback in training), online instruction was more effective than classroom instruction for teaching declarative knowledge ($d = 0.49$); in classes that failed to provide learner control, practice, and feedback, online training was less effective than classroom instruction ($d = -0.51$). This suggests that instructional methods, rather than delivery media, are the primary factor in determining how much trainees learn. Viewed from this perspective, media should be selected for the types of content and methods they can deliver and for their cost and accessibility benefits, rather than for some inherent characteristic hypothesized to benefit learning.

Instructor Delivery

Training effectiveness may be influenced by the instructors' delivery of the material as well as by the effectiveness of the instructional methods. Powers and Rothwell (2007) reviewed a variety of characteristics of effective instructors, such as energy, enthusiasm, commitment, and integrity, but they concluded that characteristics of effective instructors "depend on the nature of the course material and the nature of the organization" (p. 23). A framework that captures which characteristics are most important in different settings would be a useful addition to the literature.

Instructor *immediacy* is a relevant construct studied in great detail in the communication education field. Immediacy refers to the use of verbal and nonverbal instructional behaviors that reduce the perceived distance between the instructor and learners and thereby boost learners' motivation and learning efforts. Meta-analytic research suggests that instructor immediacy correlates with affective learning (i.e., a combined measure of reactions, attitudes toward the behaviors recommended, and behavioral intentions; $r = .50$, $k = 81$, $N = 24{,}474$), but has a smaller relationship with objectively assessed knowledge outcomes ($r = .13$, $k = 16$, $N = 5{,}437$; Allen, Witt, & Wheeless, 2006). Sitzmann, Brown, Casper, Ely, and Zimmerman (2008) found similar results in a meta-analysis of the nomological network of trainee reactions. Moreover, Towler and Dipboye (2001) found trainees' recall of key information was best after an expressive and organized lecture. Results for a transfer measure were more complex in that they interacted with trainees' mastery goal orientation. Thus, it may not be the case that a particular instructional delivery style is always necessary to facilitate learning. This supports the general conclusions by Snow (1986), explained below, regarding aptitude-by-treatment interactions. Overall, the topic of instructor characteristics relevant to effective training delivery has not been systematically studied in I/O psychology.

Enhancing Transfer During and After Training

There is evidence that particular training methods may increase transfer (Druckman & Bjork, 2001). Greater levels of practice and higher achievement during training, in general, are likely to increase maintenance of newly acquired knowledge and skills after training. In addition, certain training methods enhance the likelihood of generalization following training. For example, Gick and Holyoak (1983) found that generalization was more likely when a variety of examples were provided. R. A. Schmidt and Bjork (1992) found that transfer was enhanced when the frequency of feedback was reduced during training.

Transfer may also be enhanced with supervisor support (e.g., Lim & Johnson, 2002), peer support (e.g., Chiaburu & Marinova, 2005), and supplemental interventions (e.g., Tews & Tracey, 2008). One common supplemental method for encouraging transfer during and after training is to have trainees set transfer goals (Taylor et al., 2005). Goal-setting interventions are often studied in the context of relapse prevention programs. Relapse prevention is drawn from research on addictive behaviors and involves training self-management skills, including recognizing risky environments and understanding how to recover when a return to the prior undesired behavior occurs. Richman-Hirsch (2001) reported positive effects for a posttraining goal-setting intervention on transfer, particularly in supportive work environments. In contrast, Gaudine and Saks (2004) found little benefit for a relapse prevention module; they argued that transfer climate and support were likely more powerful determinants of transfer than posttraining interventions (see also L. A. Burke, 1997). Supporting this contention, L. A. Burke and Baldwin (1999) found that full relapse prevention programs had beneficial effects in less supportive work environments but harmful effects (relative to control) in more supportive environments. Thus, the effects of any particular transfer-enhancing intervention may depend on the transfer environment. More research is necessary if we are to fully understand how to intervene to boost transfer across different work environments.

INDIVIDUAL DIFFERENCES AND APTITUDE × TREATMENT INTERACTIONS

Aptitude × Treatment interaction (ATI) refers to the hypothesis that some types of instruction (treatments) are more or less effective for particular trainees, depending on their characteristics (aptitude; Cronbach & Snow, 1977). As a theoretical framework, ATI suggests that optimal learning occurs when the instructional method is matched to trainee characteristics.

The question of how to tailor instruction to different types of individuals is particularly relevant today. As organizations move toward technology-delivered instruction, one of the benefits is the ability to customize training programs (K. G. Brown & Ford, 2002; Kraiger & Jerden, 2007). For example, at the beginning of an online lesson, computer-based tests can be used to assess trainees' attributes and then tailor the instructional experience accordingly. The majority of research on ATIs has focused on a limited set of trainee characteristics, including *general mental ability* (GMA), *self-efficacy*, and *demographics*. The sections that follow include brief descriptions of the effects of these particular characteristics and ATI findings.

General Mental Ability

GMA determines both how much and how quickly a person learns (Hunter, 1986). Prior research suggested powerful main effects for GMA on learning outcomes (K. G. Brown, Le, & Schmidt, 2006; Ree & Earles, 1991). Snow (1986) further suggested that higher ability trainees benefit from relatively unstructured environments that provide room for autonomy, whereas lower ability trainees require more structure.

Recent research has examined whether GMA interacts with other types of training interventions, including error management training, prompting self-regulation, and goal setting. In error management training, Gully, Payne, Koles, and Whiteman (2002) found trainees with higher GMA were more capable of diagnosing and learning from errors, resulting in error management training being more effective for trainees with higher rather than lower GMA. Interventions designed to encourage self-regulation have generally found positive effects on learning (e.g., Kozlowski & Bell, 2006; A. M. Schmidt & Ford, 2003). Sitzmann, Bell, Kraiger, and Kanar (in press) conducted two studies where they prompted trainees to self-regulate by asking them to monitor and evaluate their learning behaviors and progress. Prompting self-regulation had a more positive effect on basic performance for higher ability trainees than for lower ability trainees, suggesting that trainees with higher levels of GMA may be better equipped to leverage self-regulation to aid learning. Similarly, higher ability trainees appear to benefit more from performance goals in training. In a series of studies, Kanfer and Ackerman (1989) demonstrated that performance goals had a positive effect on performance when the cognitive demands of training were low, but the effect was also influenced by the GMA of trainees. In training conditions with high cognitive demands, goal setting was detrimental for trainees with low GMA, relative to trainees with high GMA. Other research calls into question the underlying cause for these effects (DeShon, Brown, & Greenis, 1996) and suggests that learning goals may not have the same negative influence on skill acquisition as performance goals (Latham & Seijts, 2001). Nevertheless, the effectiveness of performance goals, error management training, and prompting self-regulation depends in part on trainees' GMA.

Self-Efficacy

Another trainee attribute that has been examined extensively in training research is self-efficacy (e.g., Saks, 1995). A parsimonious review of this literature is hindered by the fact that training research has studied self-efficacy as a pretraining characteristic, a process variable during training, and as a training outcome, and it has operationalized efficacy in a variety of forms, ranging from generalized, trait-like constructs to task-specific motivational states. In addition, there are ongoing debates about whether self-efficacy always has positive effects (Bandura & Locke, 2003; Vancouver, Thompson, Tischner, & Putka, 2002) and whether observed effects are spurious (Heggestad & Kanfer, 2005). Research generally suggests between-person effects of self-efficacy are positive, but because self-efficacy is correlated with GMA, skill, and prior performance, future research would benefit from controlling these variables to determine the true nature of observed effects.

In terms of ATIs, Gist, Stevens, and Bavetta (1991) found the effects of goal setting as a post-training intervention differed across levels of task self-efficacy—goal setting increased performance for trainees with high self-efficacy but was detrimental for trainees with low self-efficacy. Sitzmann et al. (in press) found self-efficacy also interacted with prompting self-regulating. Prompting had a stronger effect on strategic performance in training for trainees with high- rather than low-task self-efficacy. Similarly, Karl, O'Leary-Kelly, and Martocchio (1993) found performance feedback was more beneficial for trainees with higher self-efficacy. Finally, research suggests that self-efficacy may interact with individual differences to determine learning. One such interaction occurs with goal orientations (K. G. Brown, 2001; Fan, Meng, Billings, Litchfield, & Kaplan, 2008), an area of burgeoning research interest (Payne, Youngcourt, & Beaubien, 2007). Future research on the interaction of training methods and motivational constructs like self-efficacy and goal orientation are encouraged.

Demographics

The term *demographics* refers to observable characteristics, such as trainees' age, gender, and ethnicity. These characteristics are often correlated with nonobservable characteristics, such as values, interest, and beliefs, and have effects through these intervening mechanisms (Gully & Chen, 2009). However, demographics have important standing in society because of their importance for personal identity and the potential for legal violations that arise from treating individuals differently because of their demographics. Consequently, the relationship of demographics to training outcomes is of great concern.

Research in cognitive psychology suggests that as adults age, they are more knowledgeable but gain new knowledge more slowly (Hertzog, 1989). Colquitt et al.'s (2000) meta-analysis found a negative correlation between age and posttraining declarative knowledge ($\rho = -.19$, $k = 8$, $N = 1{,}774$). To assist older adults with learning, research suggests that it may be beneficial to allow older trainees to learn at their own pace (Callahan, Kiker, & Cross, 2003) and reduce their mental workload (Van Gerven, Pass, Van Merrienboer, & Schmidt, 2002). Specifically, Van Gerven et al. (2002) demonstrated that providing worked examples (rather than having learners work through the examples completely) reduced training times for older trainees without impairing learning.

Gender differences in learning outcomes have also been demonstrated. Kanfer and Heggestad (1997) proposed that gender might be related to motivational traits and skills and thus serve as a critical intervening mechanism. Stevens, Bavetta, and Gist (1993), as one example, found that gender differences in negotiation skills training disappeared when differences in negotiation goals were controlled—men performed better because they set higher goals, not because they learned more than women.

Research on the effects of race, nationality, and ethnicity in training is relatively scarce, except in the area of diversity training. A nonquantitative review of the diversity-training literature revealed mixed results for the effects of interventions on diversity attitudes and revealed little research on the effects of interventions on skills (C. T. Kulik & Roberson, 2008). One recent exception is a study of skill transfer that revealed that race–ethnicity mattered; non-White trainees were significantly more likely to attempt to use their training back on the job than White trainees ($\beta = .35$, $p < .01$; Roberson, Kulik, & Pepper, 2009). Further research on this topic is encouraged, as is research on how trainees' cultural backgrounds influence training outcomes. Given the increasing internationalization of the workforce, organizations will often be faced with diverse audiences drawn from many different cultures. Research should examine which training methods are more effective and efficient for trainees' from particular racial and cultural groups.

Future ATI Research

Meta-analytic evidence suggests that there is variability in the relationships between individual differences and learning outcomes (Colquitt et al., 2000; Payne et al., 2007), and ATIs are a plausible explanation for this unexplained variability. However, many studies that manipulated instructional methods and measured individual differences neither proposed ATI hypotheses nor reported ATI results (e.g., Bell & Kozlowski, 2002; Debowski et al., 2001). It is possible that researchers were simply not interested in ATIs or that interactions were not statistically significant and, thus, were omitted. However, Monte Carlo simulation research suggests that the power to detect interactions in the presence of small sample sizes and predictor range restriction is unacceptably low and may even approach chance levels (Aguinis & Stone-Romero, 1997). Thus, it is likely that ATIs are more prevalent than the current literature would suggest.

Although training research has increased dramatically in both volume and quality in recent years (Salas & Cannon-Bowers, 2001), we do not seem to know much more about ATIs than we did 30 years ago (Gully & Chen, 2010). Thus, we encourage further efforts to develop and test ATI hypotheses. Gully and Chen (2010) offered a promising start in this regard by suggesting four possible intervening mechanisms: (a) information-processing capacity, (b) attentional focus and metacognitive processing, (c) motivation and effort allocation, and (d) emotion regulation and control. Integrative research that tests multiple individual differences and intervening mechanisms is sorely needed.

TRAINING EVALUATION

Training evaluation is a process of collecting and using evidence to make decisions about training. Most commonly, evaluation is an effort to determine the *effectiveness, efficiency of a training program,* or both, to make decisions about whether to further invest in that program. This type of evaluation is often called *summative* or *impact* evaluation (Goldstein & Ford, 2002). Training effectiveness is defined as the extent to which trainees (and their organization) benefit as intended. Training efficiency is defined as the ratio of training-related benefits to training-related costs; thus, efficiency takes into account the resources used to design, develop, and deliver the training. Another potential purpose for evaluation is to collect information to improve the program in future administrations and increase the likelihood of learning and performance improvements. This type of evaluation is labeled *formative* (K. G. Brown & Gerhardt, 2002).

The evaluation process is driven by the training objectives and the situation under which the evaluation will take place. It typically involves the following steps, all of which have received at least some research attention: (a) determine the purpose, (b) decide on evaluation criteria, (c) develop outcome measures, and (d) choose an evaluation strategy (K. G. Brown, 2006).

Purpose

The distinction between summative and formative evaluation is useful but coarse. Kraiger (2002) offered a more detailed examination of the reasons to evaluate training. He suggested there are three primary purposes: (a) provide feedback to designers, trainers, and trainees; (b) provide input for decision making about training; and (c) provide information that can be used to market the training program. Kraiger's (2002) evaluation model further suggests three primary targets of evaluation: (a) training content and design, which can be assessed to provide feedback to designers and trainers; (b) changes in learners, which can be gauged to provide feedback to learners and to make decisions about training; and (c) organizational payoffs, which can be used for all three purposes. Each evaluation target offers multiple outcomes or criteria that can be assessed, and evaluators must decide both the criteria of interest and the methods by which the outcomes will be measured. In short, the purpose of the evaluation effort should drive all subsequent decisions about the evaluation effort.

Evaluation Criteria

The most widely cited model of training outcomes was developed by Kirkpatrick (1976), who outlined four levels at which training can be evaluated. Level 1 evaluation assesses reactions or how well trainees liked the training. Level 2 evaluation assesses learning or what knowledge was gained from the training. Level 3 evaluation assesses behavior or job-related behavior change that resulted from the training. Level 4 evaluation assesses results or tangible results of the training in terms of reduced cost, increased sales, and so on.

The Kirkpatrick model provides some useful guidelines for evaluation, but it has been criticized in the academic literature (Bates, 2004; Holton, 1996; Kraiger, Ford, & Salas, 1993). Consequently, at least four major refinements to our understanding of evaluation criteria have been offered.

The first refinement involves clarifying the nature of trainee reactions. Kirkpatrick's earliest work was unclear as to what reaction questions should be asked and how they should be used. Applications of the model have varied considerably in the number of dimensions or facets of reactions, from as few as one (overall satisfaction; Quiñones, 1995) to as many as six (satisfaction with instructor, overall satisfaction, satisfaction with testing, utility of training, satisfaction with materials, and satisfaction with course structure; Morgan & Casper, 2000). Phillips (1997) noted that there are as many at 15 different training-related issues on which participants could be asked to report. K. G. Brown (2005) suggested that a useful way to conceptualize reactions is hierarchically, with a global satisfaction construct underlying reactions to specific aspects of training (see also Sitzmann et al., 2008). Both facet reactions and the overall satisfaction measures may be useful, albeit for different reasons. Asking trainees about specific issues can be useful for diagnosing and reducing problems with specific elements of the training experience. Meanwhile, examining overall satisfaction may be useful for detecting more general or pervasive problems with training. Thus, depending on the evaluation purpose, overall or facet measures may be more or less useful.

The second refinement involves clarifying the multidimensional nature of learning. Kirkpatrick's treatment of learning was essentially unidimensional, proposing the use of knowledge tests to examine knowledge gained. In contrast, research suggests that learning is multidimensional and can be captured in different ways. Focusing first on theory and then on identifying relevant measures, Kraiger et al. (1993) suggested a tripartite model of learning: cognitive, skill-based, and affective. *Cognitive learning* refers to the acquisition of different types of knowledge, including declarative knowledge, structural knowledge, and cognitive strategies. In addition to traditional tests, these outcomes can be measured by asking trainees to draw out relationships among key concepts and testing whether trainees' beliefs about relationships are similar to experts' beliefs. *Skill-based learning* includes both compilation (i.e., the development of procedural knowledge that enables effective performance) and automaticity (i.e., performance without the need for conscious monitoring). Skill-based learning can be assessed with role-playing and simulations. *Affective learning* includes changes in attitudes, such as attitudes about learning or the training content, and motivation, such as self-efficacy and goals. This model expands on the Kirkpatrick perspective on learning and provides a wide array of options for evaluating learning outcomes. Ford, Kraiger, and Merritt (2010), in a recent review, suggested that this multidimensional perspective has taken root, and researchers are increasingly examining cognitive and affective outcomes.

The third refinement involves adding efficiency criteria as a fifth level to Kirkpatrick's model. According to Phillips and Phillips (2007), Level 5 evaluations focus on the *return on investment* (ROI) for training expenditures. ROI is an efficiency measure as it incorporates not only the benefits for the organization, as Level 4 evaluations require, but also the costs of training. A number of different approaches are now available to calculate results outcomes, including basic benefits analysis, utility analysis, ROI, and net present value. Each technique varies in the degree to which costs are carefully considered and the method by which training benefits and costs are assigned monetary value. The most common method used by I/O psychologists is utility analysis (Mathieu & Leonard, 1987). Using utility analysis, Morrow, Jarrett, and Rupinski (1997) found managerial training (mean ROI of 45%; $k = 11$, $N = 171$) often yielded lower economic returns than sales or technical training (with an outlier removed, mean ROI of 156%; $k = 6$, $N = 401$). For example, one management training program had total program costs of $73,200 with marginal utility of $91,500 (ROI = 125%). However, a team-building program had total program costs of $199,200 with marginal utility of −$171,000 (ROI = −86%). In contrast, sales and technical courses reported by Morrow et al. (1997) all yielded positive ROI, such as a written communication course that cost $30,700 with a marginal utility of $84,600 (ROI = 275%). Although ROI seems to be commonly reported in I/O psychology research, L. A. Burke and Hsieh (2006) reviewed various ROI calculations and suggested the need for further use of and research on net present value. Net present value is a useful approach because it takes into account the time value of money, which executives typically consider when making financial decisions about capital expenditures.

Whichever approach is used, organizational results evaluations can be resource intensive because they require estimates of the performance difference between trained and untrained groups and of the monetary value of this difference. Consequently, this outcome is measured much less often than other evaluation criteria. Moreover, there is reason to be cautious in the use of monetary figures in arguing for training investments. Some studies have demonstrated that many managers do not perceive utility analysis to be a useful tool for HRM decision making, and in fact, utility-analysis results can result in resistance (e.g., Whyte & Latham, 1997). Further research, however, has found more neutral reactions and suggests that how utility results are presented influences managers' reactions (Carson, Becker, & Henderson, 1998; Huint & Saks, 2003). Future research on how to present results to managers is encouraged, a topic addressed in more detail in chapter 14, this volume. In the study of training results, research on alternative approaches to convincing managers is encouraged, such as the Success Case Method described by Brinkerhoff (2005), which uses surveys and interviews to document cases of individuals or teams that benefited from training.

The fourth refinement is that basic assumptions of the Kirkpatrick model have been questioned, particularly the assumptions about causality across levels and about the relative value of evaluations at each level. Kirkpatrick's work has been interpreted to suggest a causal chain across levels (i.e., positive reactions lead to learning, which leads to behavioral change, etc.) and a bias toward higher level evaluations as providing the most information. Current thinking does not support these assumptions. Meta-analyses indicated that correlations among the levels are variable, suggesting that a simple causal chain is not the most accurate way to conceptualize the relationships among criteria (Alliger, Tannenbaum, Bennett, Traver, & Shotland, 1997; Colquitt et al., 2000; Sitzmann et al., 2008). Moreover, it has been argued that each level provides different information, not better information (Kraiger, 2002). Depending on the purpose of the evaluation effort, different outcomes will be more or less useful. It is also worth reiterating that criteria selection should be driven by the objectives of training, a point that should be considered in frameworks of training criteria.

Outcome Measures

Most evaluations consider trainees to be the primary data source. However, as suggested by Kraiger (2002), the possibilities are much broader, including trainees' managers, instructors, experts (e.g., subject matter, work group, instructional), and customers. In particular, when the purpose of the evaluation is to determine organizational payoffs, trainees' managers and customers are valuable sources of data. Ultimately, the decision of who provides data should be driven by the purpose of the evaluation, practical constraints, and the criteria of interest. Some criteria may require data from a particular source. Knowledge organization, for example, can generally only be measured by having learners complete an activity such as rating the similarity of concepts or organizing terms in a grid.

Other criteria can be measured in multiple ways. Reactions and behavior, for example, can be measured through paper surveys, computer surveys, interviews, or observations. Each method of data collection has strengths and weaknesses. Evaluators should consider these trade-offs when deciding which measures to adopt while ensuring the measures are reliable and valid indicators of the criteria being measured (Goldstein & Ford, 2002).

Evaluation Strategy

Drawing on the seminal work of Cook and Campbell (1979), training textbooks generally describe in detail the research designs that can be used to measure the impact of training on trainees. These include experimental, quasiexperimental, and preexperimental designs.

Experimental. *Experimental* designs, by definition, require random assignment of trainees to training conditions. This type of design allows for the greatest confidence in conclusions in regard to training effects; experimental designs control for common threats to the interpretation that training was the underlying cause for observed differences in outcomes. Within the subset of experimental designs, researchers can use a range of strategies, from posttest only to Solomon four-group designs. This last design is the most rigorous because it requires four training conditions: two treatment groups (one with pretest and one without) and two control groups (one with pretest and one without). This design allows the researcher to assess the effects of pretesting as well as the effects of training (for one example, see Bretz & Thompsett, 1992).

Quasiexperimental. *Quasiexperimental* designs allow for a comparison when participants have not been randomly assigned to conditions. Such comparisons may involve repeated observations of the same trainees (time series) or across naturally occurring groups given different training (nonequivalent control group). These designs are often required in field research and require ruling out alternative explanations for findings.

Preexperimental. The most commonly used designs in organizations are *posttest only* and *pre-posttest* designs, both of which are preexperimental designs. These designs are generally considered inadequate for controlling common threats to internal validity, including history, selection, and maturation (Cook & Campbell, 1979). Nevertheless, these designs may still be useful if the evaluator is primarily concerned that trainees reach a certain level of proficiency (Sackett & Mullen, 1993). For example, if training is intended to ensure that assembly line employees catch all products with a manufacturing defect, then improvement from pretest to posttest is less critical than having all trainees capable of identifying the defect.

Preexperimental designs may also be useful if the evaluator is familiar with the evaluation setting and critically examines competing explanations for the observed outcomes (Tannenbaum & Woods, 1992). An example of this type of critical examination is offered in the internal referencing strategy. This strategy requires testing trainees both on concepts that are relevant and irrelevant to the training objectives. If training causes improvement in trainees' knowledge, they should demonstrate improved understanding of relevant, but not irrelevant, concepts (see, e.g., Frese, Beimel, & Schoenborn, 2003). Thus, this strategy can rule out at least some threats to the conclusion that training caused changes in trainees' knowledge.

EMPLOYEE DEVELOPMENT

McCauley and Hezlett (2001) defined *individual development in the workplace* as "the expansion of an individual's capacity to function effectively in his or her present or future job and work organization" (p. 314). (See also chap. 18, this volume.) From this perspective, development is an intraindividual change that results in better work performance today or in the future. Organizations use four primary categories of interventions—work experiences, interpersonal relationships, education, and assessment and feedback (Noe et al., 1997).

In this section, we review research on participation in and outcomes of development generally, followed by research on each category of development. It is worth noting that some research on development, particularly as it relates to choices to participate, may also apply to the study of training programs.

Participation in Development

Research on participation in learning and development activities suggests that not all employees participate equally. The question of who participates is particularly relevant to the study of employee development because development programs are generally discretionary. Older adults, most notably, participate less frequently in voluntary development opportunities (Warr & Birdi, 1998). Maurer, Weiss, and Barbeite (2003) demonstrated that this trend is at least partially explained by confidence in learning abilities.

Birdi, Allan, and Warr (1997) examined the relationships between development activity participation, employee characteristics, and perceived outcomes in a large sample of manufacturing employees. They found that participation in most types of development is linked to employees' learning motivation (see also Major, Turner, & Fletcher, 2006) and management support. Tharenou (2001) found that employer support predicted participation in training and development more strongly for employees with higher rather than lower motivation. Thus, an interesting avenue for future research would be to examine how organizations could induce development of employees with lower motivation.

Work Experiences

Work experiences refer to the problems, demands, tasks, and other features of work that employees must handle as part of their role in their organization (Noe, 2008). Noe summarized how a variety of different experiences may challenge employees to learn, including promotions, job rotation, transfer, temporary assignments, job enlargement, and downward moves. Each of these changes in an employee's work experience presents a challenge to that employee to gain knowledge and skills that enable the adjustment necessary to succeed in the new role.

A series of studies conducted by the Center for Creative Leadership has helped to identify the characteristics of managerial jobs that contribute to personal development. McCauley, Ruderman, Ohlott, and Morrow (1994) studied midcareer managers and found that perceptions of greater learning occurred when their jobs included unfamiliar responsibilities, the challenge to prove oneself, developing new directions for the organization, high-level tasks, managing business diversity, and job overload. These results are useful for illustrating the point that not all work experiences will be beneficial as a form of development. To facilitate development, the work assignment should offer challenges and the opportunity for reflection and discussion (Noe, 2008). Follow-up research suggests that certain individuals may learn more from these experiences than others (Brutus, Ruderman, Ohlott, & McCauley, 2000). Future research in this area would benefit from adopting an ATI approach, examining potential interactions between the person and the work experience.

Interpersonal Relationships

Employees can learn knowledge and skills by interacting with more experienced organizational members. Mentoring and coaching are specific types of developmentally oriented relationships that are used by organizations. (See also chap. 17, this volume.) However, it is worth noting a few points about each type of relationship and emphasizing that managers and HRM professionals in organizations can serve in these particular roles. That is, it is not necessary to have a formal mentor or coach for employees to have these developmental relationships. First-line supervisors, for example, could be trained in coaching techniques and asked to perform this role as part of their job duties.

Mentoring refers to a one-to-one relationship between less (protégé) and more (mentor) experienced persons to assist in the personal and professional growth of the protégé. Kram (1983) suggested that mentors broadly provide a career function (i.e., aiding career advancement of protégé) and a psychosocial function (i.e., helping the protégé feel competent and included). Research suggested considerable value of mentoring for protégés (Allen, Eby, Poteet, Lentz, & Lima, 2004), although the outcome may depend on both the quality of the relationship between the protégé and mentor (Ragins, Cotton, & Miller, 2000) and characteristics of the program (Allen et al., 2004). Kammeyer-Mueller and Judge's (2008) meta-analysis suggested that ratings of mentor quality predict job satisfaction (meta-analytic path coefficient = .23, $p < .01$, $N = 2{,}485$) but not promotions (path coefficient = .04, $p > .05$, $N = 2{,}485$). Overall, these results suggest mentoring is valuable, particularly for protégés' affective work outcomes, and organizations should design mentoring programs to ensure that mentors and protégés develop a productive relationship (see also Wanberg, Welsh, & Hezlett, 2003). Recent theory also highlights the potential value for protégés of multiple relationships, whereby different mentors fulfill different functions (Higgins & Kram, 2001).

Coaching is a process whereby an individual helps another by motivating, encouraging, guiding, and providing reinforcement and feedback. Most research in this area has been conducted with coaches who work with senior managers to improve their management skills. One large sample study suggests that coaching can substantially improve managerial performance. Smither, London, Flautt, Vargas, and Kucine (2003) examined multisource feedback ratings of managers who did and did not work with an executive coach. Those working with a coach were more likely to set specific goals, solicit ideas for improvement, and showed greater gains on multisource feedback results. This suggests that coaching may add value above and beyond that provided by other development efforts, such as assessment and feedback. Additional research that combines coaching and other developmental efforts would be useful. Moreover, research on the specific dimensions of coaching behavior that are more or less useful for particular employees and learning objectives may provide insights into whether coaching must be tailored to some degree to the individual. Finally, it would be useful to see more research on the coaching of nonexecutive employees (e.g., Maurer, Solamon, & Lippstreu, 2008).

Education

Educational programs refer to onsite and offsite programs that improve employees' general knowledge and skills. Such programs may be designed specifically for employees, or they may be relatively generic and offered by consultants or universities (Noe, 2008). To help facilitate learning and transfer, instructors in educational programs can work with the organization's leaders to finalize the learning objectives and ensure that the instructional methods are appropriate for the employees. Similarly, learners may benefit from discussing their educational objectives with their managers or HR contact to establish a plan for applying course materials at work before the educational program begins. Although there is little published I/O psychology research demonstrating transfer from educational opportunities, what exists mirrors what has been demonstrated in and advocated for in all training programs: Transfer cannot be assumed but must be managed before, during, and after training (Broad & Newstrom, 1992).

Assessment and Feedback

Assessment involves collecting information and providing feedback to employees about their attitudes, behavior, or skills. Such feedback may include the results of tests or feedback from a particular individual or a range of individuals, including subordinates, peers, managers, and customers. This latter technique, often referred to as *multisource feedback,* is increasingly common as a form of management development.

Smither, London, and Reilly (2005) conducted a meta-analysis of the effectiveness of multisource feedback for managers. They found small effect sizes with wide confidence intervals (CIs; corrected mean $d = 0.12$, for measures by direct reports, 95% CI, –0.14–0.44; corrected mean $d = 0.15$, for measures by supervisors, 95% CI, 0.01–0.29). These results suggest that many employees do not change their behavior following feedback or exhibit relatively small changes in behavior. Smither et al. (2005) offered a theoretical model that highlights the importance of reactions to feedback, goal setting, and developmental action as essential mediators in the relationship between providing feedback and employee development. In addition, the model suggested that individual differences may influence each of the mediators. Future research on this model would be helpful for identifying the necessary conditions under which relatively expensive and time-consuming feedback systems lead to improved work performance.

A LOOK INTO THE FUTURE

Although it is impossible to accurately predict what the future holds, there are a few noteworthy trends in the design and delivery of workplace training. Five are discussed here to encourage research that is aligned with emerging training practices: (a) focus on outcomes of programs, particularly improved work performance; (b) shift toward online delivery; (c) use of intelligent agents and tutors; (d) integration of work and learning; and (e) increase in collaborative learning and peer production.

Focus on Outcomes

Organizations have been increasing their efforts to assess the value of training to reduce costs associated with learning. Although some organizations continue to train because their managers believe it works, many organizations are seeking evidence of a return on their investment (Phillips & Phillips, 2007). This effort is aided by the availability of technology to monitor performance as well as models for how to assign economic value to various levels of performance. However, as noted earlier, it should not be assumed that ROI figures will convince managers (Whyte & Latham, 1997). Thus, those who evaluate training are placed in the challenging role of collecting time-consuming data requested by managers even though such data may be insufficient (or even counterproductive) to actually convincing them of the value of training. Consequently, although research on the technical issues surrounding ROI are valuable (e.g., Wang, Dou, & Li, 2002), such research should be accompanied by an understanding of the decision-making processes around cancelling or expanding training and development programs. What types of evaluation outcomes, measures, and strategies are generally most persuasive, and do manager and organizational characteristics moderate their persuasiveness? A related set of studies could deal with the question of how managers select and evaluate training vendors. Research in this area is limited despite the frequency with which outside vendors provide training services (Gainey & Klaas, 2003).

Online Delivery

A second trend in training practice is a shift toward online delivery. Many organizations prefer online delivery to cut operational expenses by reducing travel and time away from work. However, it is worth noting that the trend to use computers for training delivery has not resulted in a dramatic decrease in the use of instructors. Face-to-face instruction is still widely used (Paradise, 2008) and at least some online courses are mediated by an instructor. Thus, the net effect on workplace learning professionals appears to be a broadening of their work to include both face-to-face and technology-based design and delivery.

Although there are practical benefits to online delivery of training, mentoring, and orientation programs, there are at least two potential drawbacks that should be considered. First, if the shift toward online programs results in dramatically shorter time spent learning, then learning outcomes may suffer. Although meta-analytic findings suggest that face-to-face and online training can result in similar learning outcomes (Sitzmann et al., 2006), many of these studies examined online training that was offered as part of a formal, structured program. Online learning that is made available through an organization's computer network with the expectation that learners participate on their own time may be less successful. Similarly, mentoring relationships forged through computer may be difficult to sustain, and the lack of ongoing contact may limit benefits of the mentoring relationship (Bierema & Hill, 2005). In studies of online training programs, K. G. Brown (2001, 2005) and Ely, Sitzmann, and Falkiewicz (2009) found large variability in time on task. Brown found the total amount of time had a positive effect on learning outcomes in a course with high learner control. Ely et al. required learners to meet a basic level of proficiency before advancing, which limited learner control. In their study, time spent in training was unrelated to learning. Thus, in situations in which remediation to certain proficiency levels is required, the relationship between time on task and learning may not be straightforward. What is clear is that learning does require time, and all things equal, more learning time is likely to increase learning outcomes. Therefore, efforts to push responsibility for learning completely to learners and asking them to learn on their own time may reduce the potential for training and development efforts to facilitate learning and boost performance.

A second potential drawback of shifting training online is that it may reduce the possibility that training and development events can benefit the organization in ways that relate to social processes and by extension organizational-level performance outcomes. For example, Wesson and Gogus (2005) found orientation programs conducted online were less effective at socializing employees. Drawing on these results, K. G. Brown and Van Buren (2007) argued that organizations that shift large amounts of face-to-face training to online media may damage the development of beneficial social networks. Research on this possibility would be helpful for determining whether this particular concern is warranted.

Of course, at least some downsides of online delivery can be offset by structuring time for learning and by deliberately incorporating face-to-face events or social activities into training, a practice labeled *blended learning*. Moreover, it is possible that advances in the sophistication of online experiences may increase the realism of social interaction and decrease negative side-effects of shifting to online delivery. Because technology is a moving target, the effects of various technologies on training practices and learning outcomes are hard to predict. Research will always be needed to examine the effects of new technologies. However, as noted by Welsh, Wanberg, Brown, and Simmering (2003), it would be useful for research on future technologies to focus on research questions beyond the simple, Does it work better than what we had before? Because research comparing technologies is fraught with potential confounds, it is neither theoretically nor practically useful. More interesting research on new technologies asks questions that include: For what objectives might this new technology or technique be useful? Under what conditions might this new technology boost job performance? For whom is this appropriate?

Intelligent Agents

The third trend involves the use of computer programs that model the learner's current state of knowledge and skill relative to an expert. Then, specific instructional tactics are selected to help the learner progress from novice to expert. This technology is often called *intelligent tutoring systems* (Salas & Rosen, 2010). These systems are not a recent development, but advances in computing power have made it more practical to develop and deploy them. With time, these systems can be embedded in a wide array of places, including computer software programs, Web sites, and other types of equipment. Research should explore ways to cost effectively build such agents as well as the ways that intelligent agents should interact with learners. For example, research suggests there is value in having computer-delivered materials presented in conversational style, using words like *I* and *you,* and speaking in a human voice if narration is involved (Mayer, 2010).

Integration of Work and Learning

As technology makes it easier to deliver training, training may begin to appear more readily as part of every computer program, Web site, and piece of office equipment. Such training might take the form of a job aid with simple directions or an interactive dialogue with an intelligent agent. As training becomes ubiquitous and workers can learn while they are engaged in economically valuable activity, the distinction between work and learning will blur. For example, if an employee can use troubleshooting software to repair a broken network connection, despite never having done it before, then the employee is learning and performing nearly simultaneously. The same principle applies to customers; organizations can use their Web sites to offer marketing of new products alongside training on how to use those products.

There may be long-term costs associated with the integration of work and learning, if taken to extremes. Heavy reliance on job aids may mean that the employee does little other than learn how to use those aids. Then, when situations arise that require performance without those aids or the situation is not addressed by the aids, employees may not have sufficient knowledge or skills to perform effectively. This concern has played out in arguments in regard to the proper time to introduce computers and calculators in elementary education. Introduction too early may result in failure to learn basic skills necessary to understand and subsequently acquire more complicated skills; introduction too late may be inefficient (e.g., Rittle-Johnson & Kmicikewycz, 2008). Organizations will increasingly have to struggle with which elements of employees' job performance should be learned so that they can be performed without technology support. It may be possible to adopt techniques such as cognitive task analysis to determine which tasks require memorization and which can be done with aids. Research in this area would benefit from integration with research on information systems, particularly work on knowledge management systems (e.g., Alavi & Leidner, 2001).

Collaborative Learning and Peer Production

The final trend discussed here deals with *communities of practice* and the possibility that they can engage in peer production of training content. A community of practice is a group of practitioners working on similar problems who share knowledge (e.g., Lave & Wenger, 1991). Drawing heavily on situative models of learning, this concept suggests that learning requires social participation, whereby an individual constructs his or her identity through engaging in and contributing to the practices of that community. Research on this idea is more common in the study of organizational development and knowledge management, but it clearly has implications for training and development.

An extension of the idea of communities of practice is peer production (Tapscott & Williams, 2006). Today's social computing capabilities, including file sharing (e.g., YouTube, Flickr), collaborative editing (e.g., Wikipedia, Wikihow), social networking (e.g., Facebook, MySpace, Twitter), and social tagging (e.g., Delicious, Connectbeam) allow for the possibility that communities can create their own learning and training materials without the assistance of workplace learning and development professionals. Although such materials are already being developed and distributed as informal learning, today's software has the potential to dramatically increase its quantity and quality. This, of course, raises questions in need of future research. For example, if peer production is encouraged and supported by an organization, then issues of quality control become increasingly important. How can organizations encourage the free flow of information and simultaneously ensure that the information exchanged is accurate and fosters the organization's best interests? There is little training research to guide such efforts, but research on digital monitoring of employees and information sharing suggests that organizations must be sensitive to issues of fairness and rewards when seeking to facilitate peer creation and distribution of content (e.g., Bartol & Srivastava, 2002). Another research question centers on how training professionals can balance peer and professional production to create high-quality learning spaces for employees, managers, and customers.

CONCLUSION

What happens under the label of *training and development* in organizations today is quite broad, and it is becoming even more so as technology increases the ways in which employees can create and access information. If training research is to keep pace with these changes, it will be increasingly necessary to bridge to other disciplines to tackle important questions. For example, as we study learning, it is helpful to draw on the work of educational researchers who have long philosophical and methodological traditions that can enrich our work. As we study the integration of work and learning, it would be beneficial to collaborate with management scholars who study ongoing challenges of motivation and control and information scientists who study the creation, collection, classification, and dissemination of information. These collaborations will help our field tackle important questions and ultimately improve the effectiveness and efficiency of our efforts to facilitate learning and improve work performance.

References

Acemoglu, D., & Pischke, J. S. (1999). The structure of wages and investment in general training. *Journal of Political Economy, 107,* 539–572.

Aguinis, H., & Kraiger, K. (2009). Benefits of training and development for individuals and teams, organizations, and society. *Annual Review of Psychology, 60,* 451–474.

Aguinis, H., & Stone-Romero, E. F. (1997). Methodological artifacts in moderated multiple regression and their effects on statistical power. *Journal of Applied Psychology, 82,* 192–206.

Alavi, M., & Leidner, D. E. (2001). Review: Knowledge management and knowledge management systems: Conceptual foundations and research issues. *MIS Quarterly, 25,* 107–136.

Allen, T. D., Eby, L. T., Poteet, M. L., Lentz, E., & Lima, L. (2004). Career benefits associated with mentoring for protégés: A meta-analytic review. *Journal of Applied Psychology, 89,* 127–136.

Allen, M., Witt, P. L., & Wheeless, L. (2006). The role of teacher immediacy as a motivational factor in student learning: Using meta-analysis to test a causal model. *Communication Education, 55,* 21–31.

Alliger, G. M., Tannenbaum, S. I., Bennett, W., Traver, H., & Shotland, A. (1997). A meta-analysis of the relations among training criteria. *Personnel Psychology, 50,* 341–358.

Anderson, J. R. (1985). *Cognitive psychology and its implications* (2nd ed.). New York: Freeman.

Arbaugh, J. B. (2000). Virtual classroom versus physical classroom: An exploratory study of class discussion patterns and student learning in an asynchronous internet-based MBA course. *Journal of Management Education, 24,* 213–233.

Argote, L., & Ingram, P. (2000). Knowledge transfer: A basis for competitive advantage in firms. *Organizational Behavior and Human Decision Processes, 82,* 150–169.

Argote, L., & Todorova, G. (2007). Organizational learning. In G. P. Hodgkinson & J. K. Ford (Eds.), *International review of industrial and organizational psychology* (Vol. 22, pp. 193–234). New York: Wiley.

Arthur, W., Jr., Bennett, W. Jr., Edens, P. S., & Bell, S. T. (2003). Effectiveness of training in organizations: A meta-analysis of design and evaluation features. *Journal of Applied Psychology, 88,* 234–245.

Arthur, W., Jr., Edwards, B. D., Bell, S. T., Villado, A. J., & Bennett, W., Jr. (2005). Team task analysis: Identifying tasks and jobs that are team based. *Human Factors, 47,* 654–669.

Baldwin, T. T., & Ford, J. K. (1988). Transfer of training: A review and directions for future research. *Personnel Psychology, 41,* 63–105.

Baldwin, T. T., Ford, J. K., & Blume, B. D. (2009). Transfer of training 1988–2008: An updated review and agenda for future research. In G. P. Hodgkinson & J. K. Ford (Eds.), *International review of industrial and organizational psychology* (Vol. 24, pp. 41–70). Hoboken, NJ: Wiley.

Baldwin, T. T., & Magjuka, R. J. (1997). Training as an organizational episode: Pretraining influences on trainee motivation. In J. K. Ford and Associates (Eds.), *Improving training effectiveness in work organizations* (pp. 99–127). Mahwah, NJ: Erlbaum.

Balkin, D., & Richebe, N. (2007). A gift exchange perspective on organizational training. *Human Resource Management Review, 7,* 52–62.

Bandura, A. (1986). *Social foundations of thought and action: A social cognitive theory.* Englewood Cliffs, NJ: Prentice-Hall.

Bandura, A. (1977). *Social learning theory.* Orville, OH: Prentice Hall.

Bandura, A., & Locke, E. A. (2003). Negative self-efficacy and goal effects revisited. *Journal of Applied Psychology, 88,* 87–99.

Barber, J. (2004). Skill upgrading within informal training: Lessons from the Indian auto mechanic. *International Journal of Training and Development, 8,* 128–139.

Barnett, S. M., & Ceci, S. J. (2002). When and where do we apply what we learn? A taxonomy for far transfer. *Psychological Bulletin, 28,* 612–637.

Bartlett, K. R. (2002). The relationship between training and organizational commitment: A study in the health care field. *Human Resource Development Quarterly, 12,* 335–352.

Bartol, K. M., & Srivastava, A. (2002). Encouraging knowledge sharing: The role of organizational reward systems. *Journal of Leadership and Organizational Studies, 9,* 64–76.

Bates, R. (2004). A critical analysis of evaluation practice: The Kirkpatrick model and the principles of beneficence. *Evaluation and Program Planning, 27,* 341–347.

Becker, B. E., & Huselid, M. A. (1996.) Methodological issues in cross-sectional and panel estimates of the human resource-firm performance link. *Industrial Relations, 35,* 400–422.

Becker, G. S. (1964). *Human capital: A theoretical and empirical analysis with special reference to education.* Chicago: University of Chicago Press.

Bell, B. S., Kanar, A. M., & Kozlowski, S. W. J. (2008). Current issues and future directions in simulation-based training in North America. *The International Journal of Human Resource Management, 19,* 1416–1434.

Bell, B. S., & Kozlowski, S. W. J. (2002). Goal orientation and ability: Interactive effects on self-efficacy, performance, and knowledge. *Journal of Applied Psychology, 87,* 497–505.

Bierema, L. L., & Hill, J. R. (2005). Virtual mentoring and HRD. *Advances in Developing Human Resources, 7,* 556–568.

Birdi, K., Allan, C., & Warr, P. (1997). Correlates and perceived outcomes of four types of employee development activity. *Journal of Applied Psychology, 82,* 845–857.

Birdi, K., Clegg, C., Patterson, M., Robinson, A., Stride, C. B., Wall, T. D., & Wood, S. J. (2008). The impact of human resource and operational management practices on company productivity: A longitudinal study. *Personnel Psychology, 61,* 467–501.

Blanchard, P. N., & Thacker, J. W. (2007). *Effective training: Systems, strategies, and practices* (3rd ed.). Upper Saddle River, NJ: Pearson Education.

Bloom, B. S. (1976). *Human characteristics and school learning.* New York: McGraw Hill.

Bowers, C., Baker, D., & Salas, E. (1994). Measuring the importance of teamwork: The reliability and validity of job/task analysis indices for team training design. *Military Psychology, 6,* 205–214.

Brannick, M. T., Levine, E. L., & Morgeson, F. P. (2007). *Job and work analysis: methods, research, and applications for human resource management.* Thousand Oaks, CA: Sage.

Bransford, J. D., Brown, A. L., & Cocking, R. R. (1999). *How people learn: Brain, mind, experience, and school.* Washington, DC: National Academy Press.

Branson, R. K., Rayner, G. T., Cox, J. L., Furman, J. P., King, F. J., & Hannum, W. H. (1975). *Interservice procedures for instructional systems development.* Ft. Monroe, VA: U.S. Army Training and Doctrine Command.

Bretz, R. D., & Thompsett, R. E. (1992). Comparing traditional and integrative learning methods in organizational training programs. *Journal of Applied Psychology, 77,* 941–951.

Brinkerhoff, R. O. (2005). The success case method: A strategic evaluation approach to increasing the value and effect of training. *Advances in Developing Human Resources, 7,* 86–101.

Broad, M., & Newstrom, J. (1992). *Transfer of training.* Cambridge, MA: Perseus.

Brown, J. S., Collins, A., & Duguid, P. (1989). Situated cognition and the culture of learning. *Educational Researcher, 18,* 42–42.

Brown, K. G. (2001). Using computers to deliver training: Which employees learn and why? *Personnel Psychology, 54,* 271–296.

Brown, K. G. (2005). Examining the structure and nomological network of trainee reactions: A closer look at "smile sheets." *Journal of Applied Psychology, 90,* 991–1001.

Brown, K. G. (2006). Training evaluation. In S. G. Rogelberg (Ed.), *Encyclopedia of industrial and organizational psychology* (Vol. 2, pp. 820–823). Thousand Oaks, CA: Sage.

Brown, K. G., & Ford, J. K. (2002). Using computer technology in training: Building an infrastructure for active learning. In K. Kraiger (Ed.), *Creating, implementing, and maintaining effective training and development: State-of-the-art lessons for practice* (pp. 192–233). San Francisco: Jossey-Bass.

Brown, K. G., & Gerhardt, M. W. (2002). Formative evaluation: An integrated practice model and case study. *Personnel Psychology, 55,* 951–983.

Brown, K. G., Le, H., & Schmidt, F. (2006). General versus specific abilities in the prediction of training performance. *International Journal of Selection and Assessment, 14,* 87–100.

Brown, K. G., & Van Buren, M. E. (2007). Applying a social capital perspective to the evaluation of distance training. In S. M. Fiore & E. Salas (Eds.), *Toward a science of distributed learning* (pp. 41–63). Washington, DC: American Psychological Association.

Brutus, S., Ruderman, M. N., Ohlott, P. J., & McCauley, C. D. (2000). Developing from job experiences: The role of organization-based self-esteem. *Human Resource Development Quarterly, 11,* 367–380.

Burke, L. A. (1997). Improving positive transfer: A test of relapse prevention training on transfer outcomes. *Human Resource Development Quarterly, 8,* 115–128.

Burke, L. A., & Baldwin, T. T. (1999). Workforce training transfer: A study of the effect of relapse prevention training and transfer climate. *Human Resource Management, 38,* 227–241.

Burke, L. A., & Hsieh, C. (2006). Operationalizing the strategic net benefit of HR. *Journal of Human Resource Costing and Accounting, 9,* 26–39.

Burke, L. A., & Hutchins, H. M. (2007). Training transfer: An integrative literature review and implications for future research. *Human Resource Development Review, 6,* 263–296.

Burke, L. A., & Hutchins, H. M. (2008). A study of best practices in training transfer and proposed model of transfer. *Human Resource Development Quarterly, 19,* 107–128.

Burke, M. J., & Day, R. R. (1986). A cumulative study of the effectiveness of managerial training. *Journal of Applied Psychology, 71,* 232–245.

Burke, M. J., Scheuer, M., & Meredith, R. (2007). A dialogical approach to skill development: The case of safety skills. *Human Resource Management Review, 17,* 235–250.

Callahan, J. S., Kiker, D. S., & Cross, T. (2003). Does method matter? A meta-analysis of the effects of training method on older learner training performance. *Journal of Management, 29,* 663–680.

Cannon-Bowers, J., & Bowers, C. (2010). Synthetic learning environments: On developing a science of simulation, games, and virtual worlds for training. In S. W. J. Kozlowski & E. Salas (Eds.), *Learning, training, and development in organizations* (pp. 229–261). New York: Routledge.

Cannon-Bowers, J., Rhodenizer, L., Salas, E., & Bowers, C. (1998). A framework for understanding prepractice conditions and their impact on learning. *Personnel Psychology, 51,* 291–320.

Carson, K. P., Becker, J. S., & Henderson, J. A. (1998). Is utility really futile? A failure to replicate and an extension. *Journal of Applied Psychology, 83,* 84–96.

Chao, G. T. (1997). Unstructured training and development: The role of organizational socialization. In J. K. Ford, S. W. J. Kozlowski, K. Kraiger, E. Salas, & M. S. Teachout (Eds.), *Improving training effectiveness in work organizations* (pp. 129–151). Mahwah, NJ: Erlbaum.

Chiaburu, D. S., & Marinova, S. V. (2005). What predicts skill transfer? An exploratory study of goal orientation, training self-efficacy and organizational supports. *International Journal of Training and Development, 9,* 110–123.

Clark, R. E. (1994). Media will never influence learning. *Educational Technology Research and Development, 42,* 21–29.

Colquitt, J. A., LePine, J. A., & Noe, R. A. (2000). Toward an integrative theory of training motivation: A meta-analytic path analysis of 20 years of research. *Journal of Applied Psychology, 85,* 678–707.

Cook, T. D., & Campbell, D. T. (1979). *Quasi-experimentation: Design and analysis for field settings.* Chicago: Rand McNally.

Cooke, N. J., & Fiore, S. M. (2010). Cognitive science-based principles for the design and delivery of training. In S. W. J. Kozlowski & E. Salas (Eds.), *Learning, training, and development in organizations* (pp. 169–201). New York: Routledge.

Cronbach, L. J., & Snow, R. E. (1977). *Aptitudes and instructional methods: A hand-book for research on aptitude-treatment interactions.* New York: Irvington.

Cross, J. (2006). *Informal learning: Rediscovering the natural pathways that inspire innovation and performance.* San Francisco: Pfeiffer.

Davis, F. D., & Yi, M. Y. (2004). Improving computer skills training: Behavior modeling, symbolic mental rehearsal, and the role of knowledge structures. *Journal of Applied Psychology, 89,* 509–523.

Day, E., Anthony, E., Blair, C., Daniels, S., Kligyte, V., & Mumford, M. D. (2006). Linking instructional objectives to the design of instructional environments: The integrative training design matrix. *Human Resource Management Review, 16,* 376–395.

Debowski, S. J., Wood, R. E., & Bandura, A. (2001). Impact of guided mastery and enactive exploration on self-regulatory mechanisms and knowledge construction through electronic inquiry. *Journal of Applied Psychology, 86,* 1129–1141.

Decker, P., & Nathan, B. (1985). *Behavior modeling training.* New York: Praeger.

Delery, J. E. (1998). Issues of fit in strategic human resource management: Implications for research. *Human Resource Management Review, 8,* 289–309.

DeNisi, A. S., Hitt, M. A., & Jackson, S. E. (2003). Knowledge-based approach to sustainable competitive advantage. In S. E. Jackson, M. A. Hitt, & A. S. DeNisi (Eds.), *Managing knowledge for sustained competitive advantage: Designing strategies for effective human resource management* (pp. 3–33). San Francisco: Jossey-Bass.

DeShon, R. P., Brown, K. G., & Greenis, J. L. (1996). Does self-regulation require cognitive resources? Evaluation of resource allocation models of goal setting. *Journal of Applied Psychology, 81,* 595–608.

Dick, W., & Cary, L. (1990). *The systematic design of instruction* (3rd ed.). New York: HarperCollins.

Driskell, J. E., Johnston, J., & Salas, E. (2001). Does stress training generalize to novel settings? *Human Factors, 42,* 99–110.

Druckman, D., & Bjork, R. A. (2001). *In the mind's eye: Enhancing human performance.* Washington, DC: National Academy Press.

Dunning, D., Johnson, K., Ehrlinger, J., & Kruger, J. (2003). Why people fail to recognize their own incompetence. *Current Directions in Psychological Science, 12,* 83–87.

Easterby-Smith, M. (1997). Disciplines of the learning organization: Contributions and critiques. *Human Relations, 50,* 1085–1113.

Ellis, S., & Davidi, I. (2005). After-event reviews: Drawing lessons from successful and failed experience. *Journal of Applied Psychology, 90,* 857–871.

Ely, K., Sitzmann, T., & Falkiewicz, C. (2009). The influence of goal orientation dimensions on time to train in a self-paced training environment. *Learning and Individual Differences, 19,* 146–150.

Ertmer, P. A., & Newby, T. J. (1993). Behaviorism, cognitivism, and constructivism: Comparing critical features from a design perspective. *Performance Improvement Quarterly, 6,* 50–72.

Fan, J., Meng, H., Billings, R. S., Litchfield, R. C., & Kaplan, I. (2008). On the role of goal orientation traits and self-efficacy in the goal-setting process: Distinctions that make a difference. *Human Performance, 21,* 354–382.

Feldman, D. C. (1989). Socialization, resocialization, and training: Reframing the research agenda. In I. L. Goldstein (Ed.), *Training and development in organizations* (pp. 376–416). San Francisco: Jossey-Bass.

Fitzpatrick, R. (2001). The strange case of the transfer of training estimate. *The Industrial–Organizational Psychologist, 39,* 18–19.

Ford, J. K., Kraiger, K., & Merritt, S. (2010). An updated review of the multidimensionality of training outcomes: New directions for training evaluation research. In S. W. J. Kozlowski & E. Salas (Eds.), *Learning, training, and development in organizations* (pp. 135–165). New York: Routledge.

Ford, J. K., & Noe, R. A. (1987). Self-assessed training needs: The effects of attitudes towards training, managerial level, and function. *Personnel Psychology, 40,* 39–53.

Ford, J. K., Smith, E., Sego, D., & Quiñones, M. A. (1993). The impact of individual and task experience factors on training needs assessment ratings. *Journal of Applied Psychology, 78,* 583–590.

Frazis, H. J., Herz, D. E., & Horrigan, M. (1995). Employer-provided training: Results from a new survey. *Monthly Labor Review, 118,* 3–18.

Frese, M., Beimel, S., & Schoenborn, S. (2003). Action training for charismatic leadership: Two evaluations of studies of a commercial training module on inspirational communication of a vision. *Personnel Psychology, 56,* 671–698.

Gagné, R., Briggs, L., & Wager, W. (1992). *Principles of instructional design* (4th ed.). Fort Worth, TX: HBJ College Publishers.

Gainey, T. W., & Klaas, B. S. (2003). The outsourcing of training and development: Factors impacting client satisfaction. *Journal of Management, 29,* 207–229.

Gaudine, A., & Saks, A. (2004). A longitudinal quasi-experiment of the effects of posttraining transfer interventions. *Human Resource Development Quarterly, 15,* 57–76.

Gick, M. L., & Holyoak, K. J. (1983). Schema induction and analogical transfer. *Cognitive Psychology, 15,* 1–38.

Gist, M. E., Stevens, C. K., & Bavetta, A. G. (1991). Effects of self-efficacy and post-training intervention on the acquisition and maintenance of complex interpersonal skills. *Personnel Psychology, 44,* 837–861.

Goldsmith, T., & Kraiger, K. (1997). Structural knowledge assessment and training evaluation. In J. K. Ford, S. Kozlowski, K. Kraiger, E. Salas, & M. Teachout (Eds.), *Improving training effectiveness in work organizations* (pp. 73–98). Mahwah, NJ: Erlbaum.

Goldstein, I. L. (1986). *Training in organizations: Needs assessment, development, and evaluation* (2nd ed.). Monterey, CA: Brooks/Cole.

Goldstein, I. L., & Ford, J. K. (2002). *Training in organizations: Needs assessment, development, and evaluation* (4th ed.). Toronto, Ontario, Canada: Wadsworth.

Greeno, J. G. (1998). The situativity of knowing, learning, and research. *American Psychologist, 53,* 5–26.

Greeno, J. G., Collins, A. M., & Resnick, L. B. (1996). Cognition and learning. In D. C. Berliner & R. C. Calfee (Eds.), *Handbook of educational psychology* (pp. 15–46). New York: Macmillan.

Greenwood, J. D. (1999). Understanding the "cognitive revolution" in psychology. *Journal of the History of the Behavioral Sciences, 35,* 1–22.

Gully, S. M., & Chen, G. (2010). Individual differences, attribute–treatment interactions, and training outcomes. In S. W. J. Kozlowski & E. Salas (Eds.), *Learning, training, and development in organizations* (pp. 1–64). New York: Routledge.

Gully, S. M., Payne, S. C., Koles, K. L. K., & Whiteman, J. A. K. (2002). The impact of error training and individual differences on training outcomes: An attribute-treatment interaction perspective. *Journal of Applied Psychology, 87,* 143–155.

Heggestad, E. D., & Kanfer, R. (2005). The predictive validity of self-efficacy in training performance: Little more than past performance. *Journal of Experimental Psychology: Applied, 11,* 84–97.

Hertzog, C. (1989). Influences of cognitive slowing on age differences in intelligence. *Developmental Psychology, 25,* 636–651.

Higgins, M. C., & Kram, K. E. (2001). Reconceptualizing mentoring at work: A developmental network perspective. *Academy of Management Review, 26,* 264–288.

Hmelo-Silver, C. E. (2004). Problem-based learning: What and how do students learn? *Educational Psychology Review, 16,* 235–266.

Holton, E. F., III (1996). The flawed four-level evaluation model. *Human Resource Development Quarterly, 7,* 5–21.

Holton, E. F., III (2003). What's really wrong: diagnosis for learning transfer system change. In E. F. Holton

III & T. T. Baldwin (Eds.), *Improving learning transfer in organizations* (pp. 59–79). San Francisco: Jossey-Bass.

Holton, E. F., III, & Baldwin, T. T. (2003). Making transfer happen: An action perspective on learning transfer systems. In E. F. Holton III & T. T. Baldwin (Eds.), *Improving learning transfer in organizations* (pp. 3–15). San Francisco: Jossey-Bass.

House, R. S. (1996). Classroom instruction. In R. L. Craig (Ed.), *The ASTD training and development handbook* (4th ed., pp. 437–452). New York: McGraw Hill.

Huint, P., & Saks, A. M. (2003). Translating training science into practice: A study of managers' reactions to posttraining transfer intentions. *Human Resource Development, 14,* 181–198.

Hunter, J. E. (1986). Cognitive ability, cognitive aptitudes, job knowledge, and job performance. *Journal of Vocational Behavior, 29,* 340–362.

Jacobs, R. L., Jones, M. J., & Neil, S. (1992). A case study in forecasting the financial benefits of unstructured and structured on-the-job training. *Human Resource Development Quarterly, 3,* 133–139.

Jacobs, R. L., & Osman-Gani, A. (1999). Status, impacts, and implementation issues of structured on-the-job training. *Human Resource Development International, 2,* 17.

Johnson, M. W. (2004). Harassment and discrimination prevention training: What the law requires. *Labor Law Journal, 55,* 119–129.

Johnson-Laird, P. N. (1983). *Mental models: Towards a cognitive science of language, inference, and consciousness.* Cambridge, MA: Harvard University Press.

Kammeyer-Mueller, J. D., & Judge, T. A. (2008). A quantitative review of mentoring research: Test of a model. *Journal of Vocational Behavior, 72,* 269–283.

Kanfer, R., & Ackerman, P. L. (1989). Motivation and cognitive abilities: An integrative aptitude-treatment interaction approach to skill acquisition [Monograph]. *Journal of Applied Psychology, 74,* 657–690.

Kanfer, R., & Heggestad, E. (1997). Motivational traits and skills: A person-centered approach to work motivation. *Research in Organizational Behavior, 19,* 1–57.

Karl, K. A., O'Leary-Kelly, A. M., & Martocchio, J. J. (1993). The impact of feedback and self-efficacy on performance in training. *Journal of Organizational Behavior, 14,* 379–394.

Keith, N., & Frese, M. (2008). Effectiveness of error management training: A meta-analysis. *Journal of Applied Psychology, 93,* 59–69.

Keller, F. S. (1982). The history of PSI. In F. S. Keller & J. G. Sherman (Eds.), *The PSI handbook: Essays on personalized instruction* (pp. 6–12). Lawrence, KS: TRI Publications.

Kirkpatrick, D. L. (1976). Evaluation of training. In R. L. Craig (Ed.), *Training and development handbook: A guide to human resource development.* New York: McGraw Hill.

Kirschner, P. A., Sweller, J., & Clark, R. E. (2006). Why minimal guidance during instruction does not work: An analysis of the failure of constructivist, discovery, problem-based, experiential, and inquiry-based teaching. *Educational Psychologist, 41,* 75–86.

Knoke, D., & Kalleberg, A. L. (1994). Job training in U.S. organizations. *American Sociological Review, 59,* 537–546.

Kozlowski, S. W. J., & Bell, B. S. (2006). Disentangling achievement orientation and goal setting: Effects on self-regulatory processes. *Journal of Applied Psychology, 91,* 900–916.

Kozlowski, S. W. J., Brown, K. G., Weissbein, D. A., Cannon-Bowers, J., & Salas, E. (2000). A multi-level perspective on training effectiveness: Enhancing horizontal and vertical transfer. In K. J. Klein & S. W. J. Kozlowski (Eds.), *Multilevel theory, research, and methods in organizations: Foundations extensions, and new directions* (pp. 157–210). San Francisco: Jossey-Bass.

Kozlowski, S. W. J., Gully, S. M., Brown, K. G., Salas, E., Smith, E. M., & Nason, E. R. (2001). Effects of training goals and goal orientation traits on multidimensional training outcomes and performance adaptability. *Organizational Behavior and Human Decision Processes, 85,* 1–31.

Kozlowski, S. W. J., & Salas, E. (1997). An organizational systems approach for the implementation and transfer of training. In J. K. Ford & Associates (Eds.), *Improving training effectiveness in work organizations* (pp. 247–290). Hillsdale, NJ: Erlbaum.

Kozma, R. B. (1994). Will media influence learning? Reframing the debate. *Educational Technology Research and Development, 42,* 7–19.

Kraiger, K. (2002). Decision-based evaluation. In K. Kraiger (Ed.), *Creating, implementing, and maintaining effective training and development: State-of-the-art lessons for practice* (pp. 331–375). Mahwah, NJ: Jossey-Bass.

Kraiger, K. (2008). Transforming our models of learning and development: Web-based instruction as enabler of third generation instruction. *Industrial and organizational psychology: Perspectives on science and practice* (Vol. 1, pp. 171–192). Hoboken, NJ: Wiley.

Kraiger, K., Ford, J. K., & Salas, E. (1993). Application of cognitive, skill-based, and affective theories of learning outcomes to new methods of training evaluation. *Journal of Applied Psychology, 78,* 311–328.

Kraiger, K., & Jerden, E. (2007). A meta-analytic investigation of learner control: Old findings and directions.

In S. M. Fiore & E. Salas (Eds.), *Toward a science of distributed learning* (pp. 65–90). Washington, DC: American Psychological Association.

Kraiger, K., McLinden, D., & Casper, W. J. (2004). Collaborative planning for training impact. *Human Resource Management, 43,* 337–351.

Kram, K. E. (1983). Phases of the mentoring relationship. *Academy of Management Journal, 26,* 608–625.

Kulik, C. C., Kulik, J. J., & Bangert-Drowns, R. (1990). Effectiveness of mastery learning programs: A meta-analysis. *Review of Educational Research, 60,* 265–306.

Kulik, C. T., & Roberson, L. (2008). Common goals and golden opportunities: Evaluations of diversity education in academic and organizational settings. *Academy of Management Learning & Education, 7,* 309–331.

Lambooij, M., Flache, A., Sanders, K., & Siegers, J. (2007). Encouraging employees to co-operate: The effects of sponsored training and promotion practices on employees' willingness to work overtime. *International Journal of Human Resource Management, 18,* 1748–1767.

Latham, G. P., & Seijts, G. H. (2001). The effect of learning, outcome, and proximal goals on a moderately complex task. *Journal of Organizational Behaviour, 22,* 291–307.

Lave, J., & Wenger, E. (1991). *Situated learning: Legitimate peripheral participation.* Cambridge, MA: Cambridge University Press.

Levitt, B., & March, J. G. (1988). Organizational learning. *Annual Review of Sociology, 14,* 319–340.

Lim, D. H., & Johnson, S. D. (2002). Trainee perceptions of factors that influence learning transfer. *International Journal of Training and Development, 6,* 36–48.

Lipshitz, R., Friedman, V. J., & Popper, M. (2007). *Demystifying organizational learning.* Thousand Oaks, CA: Sage.

London, M. (1989). *Managing the training enterprise.* San Francisco: Jossey-Bass.

Lynch, L. M., & Black, S. E. (1998). Beyond the incidence of employer-provided training. *Industrial & Labor Relations Review, 52,* 64–81.

Machin, M. A. (2002). Planning, managing, and optimizing transfer of training. In K. Kraiger (Ed.), *Creating, implementing, and managing effective training and development* (pp. 263–301). San Francisco: Jossey-Bass.

Mager, R. F. (1997). *Preparing instructional objectives.* Atlanta, GA. Center for Effective Performance.

Maister, D. H. (2008). Why (most) training is useless. *T+D, 62,* 53–58.

Major, D. A., Turner, J. E., & Fletcher, T. D. (2006). Personality predictors of motivation to learn: An examination of the Big Five and proactive personality. *Journal of Applied Psychology, 91,* 927–935.

Majumdar, S. (2007). Market conditions and worker training: How does it affect and whom? *Labour Economics, 14,* 1–23.

Martocchio, J. J. (1992). Microcomputer usage as an opportunity: The influence of context in employee training. *Personnel Psychology, 45,* 529–552.

Mathieu, J. E., & Leonard, R. L. (1987). Applying utility concepts to a training program in supervisory skills: A time-based approach. *Academy of Management Journal, 30,* 316–335.

Maurer, T. J., Solamon, J. M., & Lippstreu, M. (2008). How does coaching interviewees affect the validity of a structured interview? *Journal of Organizational Behavior, 29,* 355–371.

Maurer, T., Weiss, M., & Barbeite, F. (2003). A model of involvement in work-related learning and development activity: The effects of individual, situational, motivational and age variables. *Journal of Applied Psychology, 88,* 707–724.

Mayer, R. E. (2010). Research-based solutions to three problems in web-based training. In S. W. J. Kozlowski & E. Salas (Eds.), *Learning, training, and development in organizations* (203–227). New York: Routledge.

McCauley, C. D., & Hezlett, C. D. (2001). Individual development in the workplace. In N. Anderson, D. S. Ones, H. K. Sinangil, & C. Viswesvaran (Eds.), *Handbook of industrial, work, and organizational psychology* (pp. 311–335). Thousand Oaks, CA: Sage.

McCauley, C. D., Ruderman, M. N., Ohlott, P. J., & Morrow, J. E. (1994). Assessing the developmental components of managerial jobs. *Journal of Applied Psychology, 79,* 544–560.

Montebello, A. R., & Haga, M. (1994). To justify training, test again. *Personnel Journal, 73,* 83–87.

Moreland, R. L., & Levine, J. M. (2001). Socialization in organizations and work groups. In M. E. Turner (Ed.), *Groups at work: Theory and research* (pp. 69–112). Mahwah, NJ: Erlbaum.

Morgan, R. B., & Casper, W. J. (2000). Examining the factor structure of participant reactions to training: A multidimensional approach. *Human Resource Development Quarterly, 11,* 301–317.

Morrow, C. C., Jarrett, M. Q., & Rupinski, M. T. (1997). An investigation of the effect and economic utility of corporate-wide training. *Personnel Psychology, 50,* 91–119.

Noe, R. A. (2008). *Employee training and development* (4th ed.). Boston, MA: McGraw-Hill.

Noe, R. A., Wilk, S. L., Mullen, E. J., & Wanek, J. E. (1997). Employee development: Construct validation issues. In J. K. Ford (Ed.), *Improving training effectiveness in work organizations* (pp. 153–189). Mahwah, NJ: Erlbaum.

O'Hare, D., Wiggins, M., Williams, A., & Wong, W. (1998) Cognitive task analysis for decision centered design and training. *Ergonomics, 41,* 1698–1718.

Paradise, A. (2008). *ASTD State of the industry report 2008.* Alexandria, VA: American Society for Training & Development.

Payne, S. C., Youngcourt, S. S., & Beaubien, J. M. (2007). A meta-analytic examination of the goal orientation nomological net. *Journal of Applied Psychology, 92,* 128–150.

Pershing, J. A. (2006, Ed.). *Handbook of human performance technology: Principles practices potential.* San Francisco: Pfeiffer.

Phillips, J. J. (1997). *Handbook of training evaluation and measurement methods.* Houston, TX: Gulf.

Phillips, J. J., & Phillips, P. (2007). Measuring return on investment in leadership development. In K. M. Hannum, J. W. Martineau, & C. Reinalt (Eds.), *The handbook of leadership development evaluation* (pp. 137–166). Hoboken, NJ: Wiley.

Powers, B., & Rothwell, W. J. (2007). *Instructor excellence* (2nd ed.). San Francisco: Pfeiffer.

Quiñones, M. A. (1995). Pretraining context effects: Training assignment as feedback. *Journal of Applied Psychology, 80,* 226–238.

Raelin, J. A. (1997). A model of work-based learning. *Organization Science, 8,* 563–578.

Raghuram, S., & Avery, R. D. (1994). Business strategy links with staffing and training practices. *Human Resource Planning, 17,* 55–73.

Ragins, B. R., Cotton, J. L., & Miller, J. S. (2000). Marginal mentoring: The effects of type of mentor, quality of relationship, and program design on work and career attitudes. *Academy of Management Journal, 43,* 1177–1194.

Ree, M. J., & Earles, J. A. (1991). Predicting training success: Not much more than g. *Personnel Psychology, 44,* 321–332.

Revans, R. (1980). *Action learning: New techniques for management.* London: Blond & Briggs.

Richman, W. L., & Quiñones, M. A. (1996). Task frequency rating accuracy: The effects of task engagement and experience. *Journal of Applied Psychology, 81,* 512–524.

Richman-Hirsch, W. L. (2001). Post-training interventions to enhance transfer: The moderating effects of work environments. *Human Resource Development Quarterly, 12,* 105–120.

Rittle-Johnson, B., & Kmicikewycz, A. O. (2008). When generating answers benefits arithmetic skill: The importance of prior knowledge. *Journal of Experimental Child Psychology, 101,* 75–81.

Roberson, L., Kulik, C. T., & Pepper, M. B. (2009). Individual and environmental factors influencing the use of transfer strategies after diversity training. *Group & Organization Management, 34,* 67–89.

Roberts, K. H., & Bea, R. (2001). Must accidents happen? Lessons from high reliability organizations. *Academy of Management Executive, 15,* 70–78.

Rouiller, J. Z., & Goldstein, I. L. (1993). The relationship between organizational transfer climate and positive transfer of training. *Human Resource Development Quarterly, 4,* 377–390.

Royer, J. M. (1979). Theories of the transfer of learning. *Educational Psychologist, 14,* 53–69.

Sackett, P. R., & Mullen, E. J. (1993). Beyond formal experimental design: Toward an expanded view of the training evaluation process. *Personnel Psychology, 46,* 613–627.

Sackett, P. R., & Laczo, R. M. (2003). Job and work analysis. In W. C. Borman & D. R. Ilgen (Eds.), *Handbook of psychology: Industrial and organizational psychology* (Vol. 12, pp. 21–37). New York: Wiley.

Saks, A. M. (1995). Longitudinal field investigation of the moderating and mediating effects of self-efficacy on the relationship between training and newcomer adjustment. *Journal of Applied Psychology, 80,* 211–225.

Saks, A. M., & Belcourt, M. (2006). An investigation of training activities and transfer of training in organizations. *Human Resource Management, 45,* 629–648.

Salas, E., & Cannon-Bowers, J. A. (2001). The science of training: A decade of progress. *Annual Review of Psychology, 52,* 471–499.

Salas, E., DiazGranados, D., Klein, C., Burke, C. S., Stagl, K. C., Goodwin, G. F., et al. (2008). Does team training improve team performance? A meta-analysis. *Human Factors, 50,* 903–933.

Salas, E., & Rosen, M. A. (2010). Experts at work: Principles for developing expertise in organizations. In S. W. J. Kozlowski & E. Salas (Eds.), *Learning, training, and development in organizations* (pp. 99–134). New York: Routledge.

Schmidt, A. M., & Ford, J. K. (2003). Learning within a learner control training environment: The interactive effects of goal orientation and metacognitive instruction on learning outcomes. *Personnel Psychology, 56,* 405–429.

Schmidt, R. A., & Bjork, R. A. (1992). New conceptualizations of practice: Common principles in three paradigms suggest new concepts for training. *Psychological Science, 3,* 207–217.

Simon, S., & Werner, J. (1996). Computer training through behavior modeling, self-paced, and instructional approaches: A field experiment. *Journal of Applied Psychology, 81,* 648–659.

Sitzmann, T., Bell, B. S., Kraiger, K., & Kanar, A. M. (in press). A multilevel analysis of the effect of prompting self-regulation in technology-delivered instruction. *Personnel Psychology.*

Sitzmann, T., Brown, K. G., Casper, W., Ely, K., & Zimmerman, R. D. (2008). A review and meta-analysis of the nomological network of trainee reactions. *Journal of Applied Psychology, 93,* 280–295.

Sitzmann, T., Ely, K., Brown, K. G., & Bauer, K. N. (in press). Self-assessment of knowledge: A cognitive learning or affective measure? *Academy of Management Learning & Education.*

Sitzmann, T., Kraiger, K., Stewart, D., & Wisher, R. (2006). The comparative effectiveness of web-based and classroom instruction: A meta-analysis. *Personnel Psychology, 59,* 623–664.

Smith-Crowe, K., Burke, M. J., & Landis, R. S. (2003). Organizational climate as a moderator of safety knowledge-safety performance relationships. *Journal of Organizational Behavior, 24,* 861–876.

Smither, J. W., London, M., Flautt, R., Vargas, Y., & Kucine, I. (2003). Can working with an executive coach improve multisource feedback ratings over time? A quasi-experimental field study. *Personnel Psychology, 56,* 23–44.

Smither, J. W., London, M., & Reilly, R. R. (2005). Does performance improve following multisource feedback? A theoretical model, meta-analysis, and review of empirical findings. *Personnel Psychology, 58,* 33–66.

Snow, R. E. (1986). Individual differences and the design of educational programs. *American Psychologist, 41,* 1029–1039.

Sonnenfeld, J. A., & Peiperl, M. A. (1988). Staffing policy as a strategic response: A typology of career systems. *Academy of Management Review, 13,* 588–600.

Stagl, K. C., Salas, E., & Day, D. V. (2008). Assessing team learning outcomes: Improving team learning and performance. In V. Sessa & M. London (Eds.), *Work group learning: Understanding, improving, and assessing how groups learn in organizations* (pp. 367–390). New York: Erlbaum.

Stajkovic, A., & Luthans, F. (1997). A meta-analysis of the effects of organizational behavior modification on task performance, 1975–1995. *Academy of Management Journal, 40,* 1122–1149.

Stevens, C. K., Bavetta, A. G., & Gist, M. E. (1993). Gender differences in the acquisition of salary negotiation skills: The effects of goals, self-efficacy, and perceived control. *Journal of Applied Psychology, 78,* 723–735.

Sue-Chan, C., & Latham, G. P. (2004). The relative effectiveness of external, peer, and self-coaches. *Applied Psychology: An International Review, 53,* 260–278.

Swan, K. (2001). Virtual interaction: Design factors affecting student satisfaction and perceived learning in asynchronous online courses. *Distance Education, 22,* 306–331.

Szulanski, G. (1996). Exploring internal stickiness: Impediments to the transfer of best practice within the firm. *Strategic Management Journal, 17,* 27–43.

Tannenbaum, S. I., Beard, R., McNall, L. A., & Salas, E. (2010). Informal learning and development in organizations. In S. W. J. Kozlowski & E. Salas (Eds.), *Learning, training, and development in organizations* (pp. 303–331). New York: Routledge.

Tannenbaum, S. I., & Woods, S. B. (1992). Determining a strategy for evaluating training: Operating within organizational constraints. *Human Resource Planning, 15,* 63–81.

Tapscott, D., & Williams, A. D. (2006). *Wikinomics: How mass collaboration changes everything.* New York: Portfolio.

Taylor, P. J., Russ-Eft, D. F., & Chan, D. W. L. (2005). A meta-analytic review of behavior modeling training. *Journal of Applied Psychology, 90,* 692–709.

Tennyson, R. D., & Rasch, M. (1988). Linking cognitive learning theory to instructional prescriptions. *Instructional Science, 17,* 369–385.

Tews, M. J., & Tracey, J. B. (2008). An empirical examination of posttraining on-the-job supplements for enhancing the effectiveness of interpersonal skills training. *Personnel Psychology, 61,* 375–401.

Tharenou, P. (2001). The relationship of training motivation to participation in training and development. *Journal of Occupational & Organizational Psychology, 74,* 599–621.

Tharenou, P., Saks, A., & Moore, C. (2007). A review and critique of research on training and organizational-level outcomes. *Human Resource Management Review, 17,* 251–273.

Toh, S. M., Morgeson, F. P., & Campion, M. A. (2008). Human resource configurations: investigating fit with the organizational context. *Journal of Applied Psychology, 93,* 864–882.

Towler, A. J., & Dipboye, R. L. (2001). Effects of trainer expressiveness, organization, and trainee goal orientation on training outcomes. *Journal of Applied Psychology, 86,* 664–673.

Tracey, B. J., Tannenbaum, S. I., & Kavanagh, M. J. (1995). Applying trained skills on the job: The importance of the work environment. *Journal of Applied Psychology, 80,* 239–252.

Tripp, S. D., & Bichelmeyer, B. (1990). Rapid prototyping: An alternative instructional design strategy. *Educational Technology Research and Development, 38,* 31–44.

Valle, R., Martin, F., Romero, P. M., & Dolan, S. L. (2000). Business strategy, work processes and human resource training: Are they congruent? *Journal of Organizational Behavior, 21,* 283–297.

Vancouver, J. B., Thompson, C. M., Tischner, E. C., & Putka, D. J. (2002). Two studies examining the negative effect of self-efficacy on performance. *Journal of Applied Psychology, 87,* 506–516.

Van Gerven, P. W. M., Pass, F. G. W. C., Van Merrienboer, J. J. G., & Schmidt, H. G. (2002). Cognitive load theory and aging: Effects of worked examples on training efficiency. *Learning and Instruction, 12,* 87–105.

Wanberg, C. R., Welsh, E. T., & Hezlett, S. A. (2003). Mentoring research: A review and dynamic process model. In J. J. Martocchio & G. R. Ferris (Eds.), *Research in personnel and human resources management* (Vol. 22, pp. 39–124). Oxford, England: Elsevier Science.

Wang, G., Dou, X., & Li, N. (2002) A systems approach to measuring return on investment for HRD interventions. *Human Resource Development Quarterly, 13,* 203–224.

Warr, P., & Birdi, K. (1998). Employee age and voluntary development activity. *International Journal of Training and Development, 2,* 190–204.

Watkins, R., & Kaufman, R. (1996). An update on relating needs assessment and needs analysis. *Performance Improvement, 35,* 10–13.

Wegner, E., McDermott, R., & Snyder, W. M. (2007). *Cultivating communities of practice.* Cambridge, MA: Harvard Business School Press.

Wei, J., & Salvendy, G. (2004). The cognitive task analysis method for job and task design: Review and reappraisal. *Behaviour & Information Technology, 23,* 273–299.

Weiss, H. (1990). Learning theory and industrial and organizational psychology. In M. D. Dunnette & L. M. Hough (Eds.), *Handbook of industrial and organizational psychology* (2nd ed., Vol. 1, pp. 171–222). Palo Alto, CA: Consulting Psychologists Press.

Welsh, E. T., Wanberg, C. R., Brown, K. G., & Simmering, M. J. (2003). E-learning: Emerging uses, empirical results and future directions. *International Journal of Training and Development, 7,* 245–258.

Wesson, M. J., & Gogus, C. I. (2005). Shaking hands with a computer: An examination of two methods of organizational newcomer organization. *Journal of Applied Psychology, 90,* 1018–1026.

Whyte, G., & Latham, G. P. (1997). The futility of utility analysis revisited: When even an expert fails. *Personnel Psychology, 50,* 601–610.

Willman, S. K. (2004). The new law of training. *HR Magazine, 49,* 115–118.

Wright, P. M. (1998). Introduction: Strategic human resource management research in the 21st century. *Human Resource Management Review, 8,* 187–91.

Yelon, S., & Ford, J. K. (1999). Pursuing a multidimensional model of training transfer. *Performance Improvement Quarterly, 12,* 58–78.

Zwick, T. (2006). The impact of training intensity on establishment productivity. *Industrial Relations, 45,* 26–46.

CHAPTER 17

MENTORING

Lillian T. Eby

Mentoring refers to a developmentally oriented interpersonal relationship that is typically between a more experienced individual (i.e., the mentor) and a less experienced individual (i.e., the protégé; Kram, 1985). (See also Vol. 3, chap. 6, this handbook.) The appeal of mentoring is intuitive: When a wiser and more seasoned individual takes a novice organizational member under his or her wing, that individual should develop personally as well as professionally. Results of decades of research on mentoring have revealed that it is indeed related to a wide range of positive personal and career outcomes for protégés (Allen, Eby, Poteet, Lentz, & Lima, 2004; Eby, Allen, Evans, Ng, & DuBois, 2008; Underhill, 2006). Moreover, even though mentoring relationships develop with the expressed purpose of helping the protégé, there is growing recognition that the mentor (Allen, 2007; Eby, Durley, Evans, & Ragins, 2006) and the organization (Allen, Smith, Mael, O'Shea, & Eby, 2009) can also benefit from mentoring.

Although the construct of mentoring can be traced back to Greek mythology, two seminal works were the impetus for several decades of research on workplace mentoring and, correspondingly, the widespread use of mentoring as a career development tool in organizational settings. Levinson and colleagues' qualitative study of adult development provided an in-depth biographical account of the life experiences of 40 American-born adult men from childhood to adulthood (Levinson et al., 1978). Within Levinson and colleagues' resultant theory of adult development, having a mentor was suggested as the most important relational experience in adulthood. The importance of mentoring was elevated to that of parenting in childhood, as participants consistently discussed how having a mentor was essential to their development of a vision and purpose in life. Kram's (1985) groundbreaking research on workplace mentoring further piqued both scholarly and practitioner interest in mentoring. She provided the first comprehensive examination of mentoring at work, based on in-depth interviews with 18 mentor–protégé dyads. Kram's research delineated the major functions of mentoring, identified the phases of the mentoring relationship, discussed the complexities of cross-gender relationships, and outlined organizational factors that contribute to successful mentoring relationships.

In this early work on mentoring, both Levinson et al. (1978) and Kram (1985) discussed how mentoring is a unique type of work relationship. Levinson et al. (1978) conceptualized mentoring as a pivotal experience in the transition to adulthood, where one person (the mentor) acts as a teacher to help another person (the protégé) develop a sense of personal efficacy and professional identity. This type of highly personal, emotionally intense relationship was believed to be rare in work settings because organizational norms generally discourage the development of close, supportive relationships, and most individuals are limited in their capacity to provide such support to junior colleagues. Kram (1985) agreed that the classic type of mentoring relationship discussed by Levinson and colleagues was not often found in the workplace and opted to consider a fuller range of adult working relationships that could provide developmental support to individuals.

In so doing, she acknowledged that mentoring relationships could vary in effectiveness and change over time. Finally, both Levinson et al. (1978) and Kram (1985) acknowledged the mutuality associated with mentoring, noting that it is not just the protégé that stands to gain from the relationship but the mentor as well.

Over the years, there has been considerable discussion about the definition of mentoring and how the construct is similar to as well as distinct from other constructs. Through this work, researchers have clarified the distinction between mentoring and other types of relationships (e.g., teacher–student, adviser–advisee; see Eby, Rhodes, & Allen, 2007), conceptually similar organizational constructs (e.g., leader–member exchange, organizational citizenship behavior; see McManus & Russell, 1997), and other kinds of formal developmental experiences in the workplace (e.g., apprenticeships, action learning; Douglas & McCauley, 1999). The consensus is that mentoring is a distinct phenomenon. Although these efforts have been useful in helping to clarify the construct of mentoring, none have focused exclusively on distinguishing mentoring from other types of supportive experiences at work.

To further our understanding of what makes mentoring a unique type of supportive experience at work, Table 17.1 compares workplace mentoring with four conceptually similar supportive experiences in organizational settings: workplace friendships, social support at work, supervisory relationships, and coaching relationships. Comparisons are made on four specific dimensions: scope of support received, extent of reciprocity, whether the supportive behavior is prescribed by a formal organizational role, and whether the supportive interaction is time bound. The text in boldface type in Table 17.1 indicates areas where mentoring is similar to one or more of the other four types of supportive experiences at work.

As illustrated in Table 17.1, mentoring bears the greatest resemblance to a workplace friendship. Both mentoring relationships and friendships can provide a broad base of support and are characterized by moderate to high levels of reciprocity between relational partners. However, unlike friendships, which are never required by a formal organizational role, the support provided in a mentoring relationship may be role prescribed if the mentoring relationship is formally arranged by the organization (Ragins & Cotton, 1999). Mentoring also differs from workplace friendships in that it represents a time-bound series of interactions; typically mentoring relationships last around 1 year if they are formal and approximately 5 years if they are informal (Kram, 1985; Ragins & Cotton, 1999). In contrast, interactions associated with workplace friendships are not time dependent; friendships can grow in relational depth and continue indefinitely. Mentoring is less similar to social support at work, supervisory relationships, and coaching relationships, even though these three other types of supportive interactions at work are also

TABLE 17.1

Comparison of Workplace Mentoring to Other Types of Supportive Experiences at Work

	Dimensions for comparison			
Type of supportive experience	Scope of support received	Extent of reciprocity	Role prescribed behavior?	Time-bound interaction?
Workplace mentoring	**Task-related, professional, and personal**	**Moderate to high**	Sometimes	**Yes**
Workplace friendship	**Task-related, professional, and personal**	**Moderate to high**	No	No
Social support at Work	Task-related and personal	None required	No	**Yes**
Supervisory relationship	Task-related and professional	Low to moderate	Yes	**Yes**
Coaching relationship	Task-related and professional	None required	Yes	**Yes**

Note. Boldface type indicates where workplace mentoring is similar to other types of supportive experiences at work.

time bound. Although it can be delivered repeatedly, the receipt of social support at work is episodic. Supervisory relationships and coaching relationships are also time bound, as each lasts only as long as individuals occupy a formal role in the relationship. Examining how mentoring differs from other supportive interactions in the workplace sets the stage for a more detailed discussion of the prevalence and uses of mentoring in the workplace.

MENTORING IN ORGANIZATIONS

Approximately 71% of Fortune 500 companies report that they currently have one or more formal mentoring programs (Bridgeford, 2007). This includes organizations in a wide range of industries, including banking (e.g., Bank of America), hospitality (e.g., Marriott International, Inc.), consumer products (e.g., Proctor & Gamble), telecommunications (e.g., AT&T), and manufacturing (e.g., Lockheed Martin), among others. Moreover, a study of 246 for-profit organizations employing at least 500 employees found that 21% had at least one initiative in place that paired employees with others in the organization for the purpose of learning and development (Douglas & McCauley, 1999). Among organizations with such initiatives, an average of 178 employees had participated in, and subsequently completed, such a program (Douglas & McCauley, 1999). It is more difficult to gauge the overall percentage of employees who have experienced a mentoring relationship at work because convenience samples are typically used in organizational research and many mentoring relationships are informal in nature. Nonetheless, research suggests that somewhere between 45% (Chao, 1997) and 76% (e.g., Scandura & Ragins, 1993) of white-collar employees report experience as a protégé in the work setting.

Whereas all mentoring relationships share the overall goal of enhancing the personal and professional development of the protégé, mentoring can be used for many specific purposes in organizations. One way to appreciate the flexibility of mentoring as both an individual career management strategy and an organizational career development tool is to consider the many ways in which it can facilitate personal learning and individual career development. Figure 17.1 illustrates the role of mentoring across the career life cycle, starting at Stage 1 (exploration), when one is first learning about an occupational field, and ending at Stage 3 (establishment), when one is firmly entrenched in his or her occupation. In discussing the role of mentoring in each stage of the career life cycle, the focus is on an individual's "career age" (Hall, 1996, p. 9) rather than chronological age. This is an important distinction because a hallmark of contemporary careers is the recognition that individuals are likely to change jobs, occupations, and sometimes even careers several times during adulthood (Hall, 1996). Therefore, individuals may cycle through the three stages depicted in Figure 17.1 more than once.

In the *exploration* stage the focus is on career preparation. During this stage individuals obtain firsthand information about, or direct experience in, an occupational field. This may occur informally as individuals develop influential relationships with parents, nonparental relatives (e.g., aunts, cousins, older siblings), adult family friends, teachers, coaches, or community leaders (e.g., pastors, rabbis; Spencer, 2007). During the exploration stage mentoring can also be part of an organized educational experience, such as a cooperative education placement, internship, community volunteer experience, or a service learning opportunity (Hezlett, 2005; Lazovsky & Shimoni, 2006; Linnehan, 2001, 2003). Mentoring experiences during the exploration stage can provide protégés with a realistic occupational preview, which in turn may lead to better vocational decision-making and ultimately career success. At this stage mentoring can also facilitate the development of occupation-specific skills (e.g., learning how the judicial system works, learning basic counseling skills), general skills (e.g., teamwork, communication skills, task prioritization), and career-related self-efficacy.

The practical organizational implications of mentoring during the exploration phase are primarily related to formal mentoring experiences. Specifically, organizations might consider partnering with colleges and universities to develop structured learning experiences for students that include a mentoring component. This may benefit the organization not just in terms of acquiring relevant skills and expertise

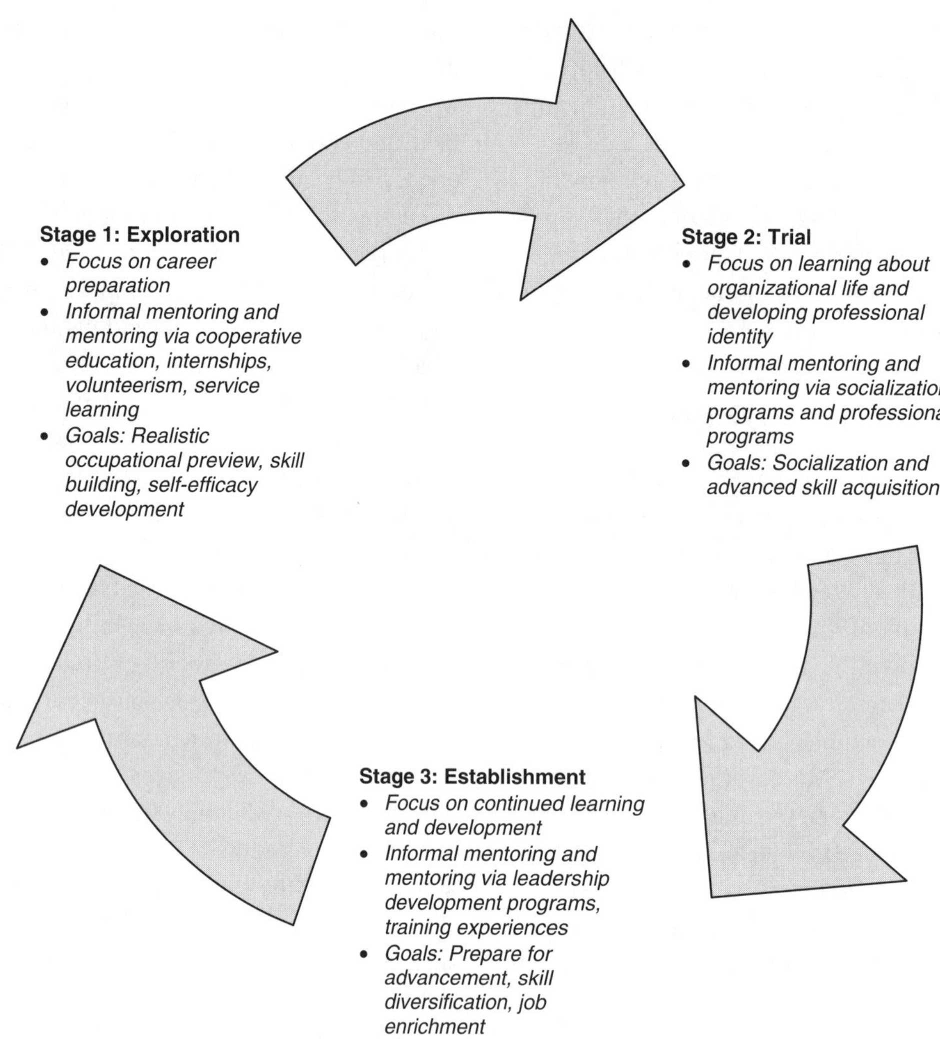

Stage 1: Exploration
Focus on career preparation
Informal mentoring and mentoring via cooperative education, internships, volunteerism, service learning
Goals: Realistic occupational preview, skill building, self-efficacy development
Stage 2: Trial
Focus on learning about organizational life and developing professional identity
Informal mentoring and mentoring via socialization programs and professional programs
Goals: Socialization and advanced skill acquisition
Stage 3: Establishment
Focus on continued learning and development
Informal mentoring and mentoring via leadership development programs, training experiences
Goals: Prepare for advancement, skill diversification, job enrichment

FIGURE 17.1. Mentoring across the career lifecycle.

but also by enhancing the organization's corporate image and providing a recruiting advantage. In terms of practical benefits of mentoring in the exploration phase for individuals, early mentoring experiences may be especially important because they provide protégés with a "mentoring schema" (Ragins & Verbos, 2007, p. 101). This is a cognitive map that guides protégé expectations in subsequent mentoring relationships and motivates future behavior. Consistent with this notion, previous experience as a protégé reliably predicts future willingness to assume the role of a mentor (Allen, 2003; Allen, Poteet, Russell, & Dobbins, 1997; Bozionelos, 2004; Eby, Lockwood, & Butts, 2006) and helps individuals develop specific skills that are important for assuming the role of mentor (Allen, Poteet, et al., 1997). Because mentoring cannot be sustained in organizations without individuals who are willing and able to serve as mentors, the availability of early, positive mentoring experiences to protégés is one strategy to increase an organization's mentoring bench strength.

Next is the *trial* stage. During this stage the individual must adapt to being a newcomer in an organization and his or her chosen occupation. The focus here is on learning about organizational life, gaining an appreciation of how a specific type of job fits into the broader occupational field, and developing a sense of professional identity. Mentoring relationships can develop informally during this stage or be part of a formal new employee socialization program (Allen, Day, & Lentz, 2001; Eddy, Tannenbaum, Alliger, D'Abate, & Givens, 2001; Kram, 1985; see also Vol. 3, chap. 2, this handbook). In some occupational fields, mentoring may also be used to facilitate the development of advanced technical skills. For example, mentoring is commonly used for new entrants into the fields of nursing, medicine (Jackson et al., 2003; Ramanan et al., 2006), education (Carter & Francis, 2001; Kaslow & Mascaro, 2007), and counseling (Powell & Brodsky, 2004). The goals of mentoring in the trial stage are socialization into the organization and profession as well as the development of advanced technical skills.

The mentoring literature has consistently demonstrated that individuals receive more mentoring support early in their careers (Finkelstein, Allen, & Rhoton, 2003; Scandura & Williams, 2001; Whitely, Dougherty, & Dreher, 1992) and when they have less overall experience in mentoring relationships (Ragins & McFarlin, 1990). As such, offering formal organizational mentoring programs as part of early training and socialization experiences is a way to help ensure that individuals receive maximum mentoring support early in their career. Another possibility is to incorporate mentoring into developmental experiences for individuals identified as "high potential" within the organization, as an important component of mentoring support is helping the protégé learn to navigate the political and strategic landscape of the organization. Actively seeking out mentoring relationships early in one's career is also recommended as an individual-level career development strategy, and there is some initial evidence that more proactive protégés do indeed reap greater mentoring benefits (Wanberg, Kammeyer-Mueller, & Marchese, 2006).

Once established in both an occupation and a specific organization, an individual moves to the *establishment* stage. Although individuals in this stage are seasoned professionals, learning and development can continue through horizontal and/or vertical skill development. They may become involved in mentoring relationships by seeking out an informal mentor, by participating in a management development program, or as part of an organizational training experience (Douglas & McCauley, 1999; Greenhaus, Callanan, & Godshalk, 2000). Because the experience of being a mentor can also provide new learning opportunities and help prevent career stagnation, individuals can build new skills and enrich their jobs by serving as mentors to others (Allen, 2007). Therefore, specific goals of mentoring during this stage include preparing the individual for advancement into high-level positions with the organization, skill diversification, and job enrichment.

In terms of practical implications, efforts to develop and sustain an organizational culture that places a high value on continued self-improvement and relationship building may increase the likelihood that individuals in the establishment phase continue to have opportunities to be mentored, and develop an interest in stepping up to the role of mentor themselves. Organizations might also consider more formal means of encouraging established individuals to become mentors, such as incorporating mentoring others into the performance management system or offering recognition to individuals for their mentoring efforts.

MENTORING TYPES, FORMS, AND FUNCTIONS

As noted previously, there are two distinct types of mentoring relationships. *Informal* mentoring relationships develop spontaneously through mutual attraction and shared interests. This type of mentoring relationship can be initiated by the mentor, the protégé, or both individuals (Scandura & Williams, 2001). What makes the relationship informal is that it is not part of an organizationally sanctioned program, and as such, individuals have freely entered into the relationship (Ragins & Cotton, 1999). *Formal* mentoring relationships occur as part of an organizationally sponsored program or initiative where a third party in the organization, such as a representative from human resources, facilitates the matching of mentors and protégés (Allen, et al., 2001; Eby et al., 2007). In a formal mentoring relationship there is often a mentoring contract that specifies mutually agreed-upon goals and sets expectations for the relationship (e.g., frequency of contact, meeting location, relationship length; Eby et al., 2007; Ragins & Cotton, 1999). Both formal and informal mentoring are related to positive protégé outcomes, although research tends to find that informal mentoring yields greater benefits than does formal mentoring (e.g., Chao, Walz, & Gardner, 1992; Ragins & Cotton, 1999).

Mentoring relationships can also take several different forms. The most commonly studied form of mentoring is hierarchical mentoring. This is a one-on-one relationship between a more experienced mentor and a less experienced protégé (Kram, 1985). A hierarchical mentor is usually several organizational levels above the protégé and is typically (but not always) outside the protégé's chain of command. This structural arrangement allows the mentor to provide the protégé with exposure and visibility to other parts of the company, as well as supplying an insider's perspective on the political structure of the organization. A variant of hierarchical mentoring is *supervisory* mentoring. In this type of mentoring relationship a supervisor takes a special interest in a subordinate and goes above and beyond his or her formal supervisory responsibilities to provide career and psychosocial support to a subordinate protégé (e.g., Scandura & Schriesheim, 1994). Potential benefits of supervisory mentoring include a better understanding of the protégé's specific skills and career goals, greater opportunity to develop a close relationship through daily interaction with the protégé, and the ability to easily provide challenging assignments and tangible resources to help the protégé reach his or her goals (Fagenson-Eland, Marks, & Amendola, 1997; Payne & Huffman, 2005; Ragins & McFarlin, 1990). The disadvantages of supervisory mentoring are perceptions of favoritism by others in the work group (Sias & Jablin, 1995) and potential role conflict in terms of being a sounding board for protégé work-related problems as well as the evaluator of the protégé's job performance (Le Maistre, Boudreau, & Paré, 2006). Though the literature is somewhat limited, supervisory mentoring relationships are generally associated with more mentoring received (Fagenson-Eland et al., 1997; Payne & Huffman, 2005; Ragins & McFarlin, 1990; Scandura & Viator, 1994). Another, third type of one-on-one mentoring is *peer* mentoring (Kram, 1985; McManus & Russell, 2007). This occurs between individuals of similar status and experience in the organization and fulfills some unique developmental functions for individuals, including career strategizing, information sharing, and emotional support (Kram & Isabella, 1985). Peer mentoring is also characterized by greater reciprocity and mutual learning than in hierarchical mentoring, making it a potentially valuable resource for personal and professional growth.

Mentoring relationships are defined in large part by the two primary types of support provided: career-related support and psychosocial support (Kram, 1985). *Career-related support* refers to mentor behaviors that are oriented toward helping the protégé understand how the organization works and preparing the protégé for advancement. Specific activities associated with career-related mentoring include sponsorship, exposure and visibility, coaching, providing challenging assignments, and protection. *Psychosocial support* focuses on building protégé self-efficacy, self-worth, and professional identity. Specific mentor behaviors associated with psychosocial support include offering unconditional acceptance and confirmation, providing counseling, offering friendship, and serving as a role model for the protégé. Career-related and psychosocial mentoring generally display similar relationships with protégé outcomes, although satisfaction with the mentor is more highly related to psychosocial support, and objective career success indicators (compensation, promotion) display a somewhat stronger relationship with career-related support (Allen et al., 2004).

BENEFITS OF MENTORING

Most research on the benefits of mentoring has focused on the protégé's perspective, and it is through the provision of career-related and psychosocial support that protégé benefits are realized. On the basis of Cohen's (1988) conventional standards for interpreting correlation-based effect sizes as small (absolute value of .10–.23), medium (absolute value of .24–.36), and large (absolute value of .37 or higher), the effect sizes associated with mentoring tend to be small to moderate in magnitude. For example, the receipt of mentoring is associated with higher salaries (meta-analytic $r = .12$), faster promotion rates (meta-analytic $r = .31$), and more positive attitudes toward one's work and career (meta-analytic $r = .06$ for intentions to stay to $r = .26$ for expectations for advancement; Allen et al., 2004). There is also evidence that mentoring is associated with higher performance (meta-analytic $r = .06$), less stress (meta-analytic $r = -.07$), more positive interpersonal relations (meta-analytic $r = .19$), higher motivation (meta-analytic $r = .12$), and an increased propensity to engage in helping behavior directed toward others (meta-analytic $r = .26$), although again the effect sizes tend to be small to moderate (Eby et al., 2008). Other protégé outcomes of mentoring include more rapid and effective organizational socialization (Chao, 1997) and lower turnover (Payne & Huffman, 2005). Again, the effect sizes here tend to be small in magnitude.

Although less extensive, some research has examined the benefits of mentoring for mentors. Experience as a mentor is related to perceptions of career success (Allen, Lentz, & Day, 2006; Bozionelos, 2004) as well as objective indicators of career success such as salary and promotion rates (Allen et al., 2006; Collins, 1994). Serving as a mentor is also related to feelings of personal satisfaction and generativity, more positive work attitudes, and recognition by others for one's mentoring efforts (Allen, Poteet, & Burroughs, 1997; Eby, Durley, et al., 2006). The effect sizes for mentors are generally small. It is particularly important to recognize that mentors can benefit from mentoring relationships because mentors rarely receive remuneration for their mentoring efforts.

Finally, some evidence suggests that organizations might also benefit from mentoring relationships. As discussed previously, some of the individual-level outcomes of mentoring, such as turnover, job performance, organizational commitment, and job satisfaction, can directly or indirectly influence important organizational outcomes (Wilson & Elman, 1990). Formal mentoring programs can also impact the ability to attract high-quality applicants (Allen & O'Brien, 2006). In addition, a recent study found that organizations with a greater proportion of employees who were mentored reported higher overall agency performance ($R^2 = .26$; Allen, Smith, et al., 2009), suggesting that there may be some bottom-line benefits of mentoring for organizations.

DRAWBACKS OF MENTORING

Although mentoring is typically viewed as a mutually enhancing relationship, research indicates that problems can arise between mentor and protégé. A series of studies by Eby and colleagues has cataloged the types of negative relational experiences reported by protégés as well as the correlates of these experiences. The most commonly reported problem by protégés is mismatched values, personalities, and work styles with their mentor. Mentor neglect is also a relatively common protégé concern. A more serious relational problem is mentor manipulation, which involves the mentor wielding his or her power inappropriately in the relationship (e.g., over-delegating work, taking undue credit, sabotage). Mentors may also lack technical and/or social skills necessary to develop an effective relationship with a particular protégé. Finally, some mentors may be struggling with personal problems or display cynical attitudes about the organization, which can influence the quality of relational exchanges with protégés (Eby, McManus, Simon, & Russell, 2000). Protégés' perceptions of relational problems are correlated with a wide range of outcomes, including reduced job satisfaction, negative reactions to the mentoring relationship, turnover intentions, and strain reactions (Eby & Allen, 2002; Eby, Butts, Lockwood, & Simon, 2004). Similar to research examining the benefits of mentoring, the effect sizes associated with protégé reports of relational problems and protégé outcomes tend to be small to moderate in magnitude. For instance, the correlation between protégé reports of relational problems and depressed mood at work ranges from $r = .30$ for mentor manipulation to $r = .20$ for mentor neglect.

Some mentors also report problems with protégés (Eby & Lockwood, 2005; Eby & McManus, 2004; Eby et al., 2008). Three general types of problems have been identified. The first is protégé performance problems and includes both the protégé failing to meet the mentor's performance expectations and the protégé being perceived as unwilling to learn. Interpersonal problems are also sometimes reported, which includes conflicts, disingenuousness on the part of the protégé, and other difficulties relating (e.g., protégé submissiveness). The third and most serious type of relational problem is destructive relational patterns. This includes behaviors that involve perceived breeches of mentor trust, relationship exploitation, sabotage, jealousy, and competitiveness. Similar to research from the protégé's perspective, mentors' negative experiences with protégés are related to unfavorable attitudinal, relational, and psychological outcomes for the mentor (Eby et al., 2008). For mentors, the effect sizes associated with relational problems are also small to moderate in magnitude.

DEVELOPING AND SUSTAINING MENTORING IN ORGANIZATIONS

As previously discussed, mentoring relationships can have positive effects on protégés, mentors, and the organization as a whole, but these relationships can have some negative aspects as well. Therefore, it is important to discuss the role that the organization can play in creating a culture that facilitates the development of high-quality mentoring relationships while simultaneously deterring the likelihood of negative mentor–protégé interactions. Strategies for encouraging high-quality mentoring relationships are discussed first, followed by specific suggestions for the design and delivery of formal mentoring programs. This section closes with a discussion of how organizations might deal with potential problems that arise in mentor–protégé relationships.

Facilitating High-Quality Mentoring

High-quality mentoring relationships refer to those partnerships in which both individuals are satisfied with and committed to the relationship, and both individuals are reaping some benefits from the exchange. These benefits can be proximal (e.g., career-related support for the protégé, sense of loyalty for the mentor) or distal (e.g., protégé promotion, mentor job satisfaction) in nature. Several protégé individual differences are associated with the receipt of greater mentoring support. This includes greater protégé ability, motivation, and commitment (Green & Bauer, 1995; Koberg et al., 1998; Noe, 1988; Whitely et al., 1992). Positive self-regard (Kalbfleisch & Davies, 1993; Koberg et al., 1998; Noe, 1988) and interpersonal skills (Eby, Lockwood, & Butts, 2006; Kalbfleisch & Davies, 1993) are also predictive of protégé reports of mentoring received. In addition, protégé achievement orientation predicts greater learning for both the mentor and the protégé alike (Hirschfeld, Thomas, & Lankau, 2006). In terms of mentor individual differences, there is initial evidence that greater proactivity (Wanberg et al., 2006) and openness to experience (Bozionelos, 2004) positively relate to protégé perceptions of mentoring support.

Surprisingly little empirical research has focused on the organizational factors that facilitate high-quality mentoring relationships. Nonetheless, some initial suggestions can be put forward on the basis of a few empirical studies on the topic. Mentors report that an organizational context that supports employee learning and development appears to be important in creating a positive climate for mentoring (Allen, Poteet, & Burroughs, 1997). Likewise, protégé reports of psychosocial-oriented peer mentoring received is positively related to the extent to which the organization is perceived as being open to new ideas and innovation, being tolerant of employee mistakes, providing learning opportunities, setting high performance expectations for employees, and employing managers and coworkers who support employee learning (Eddy, Tannenbaum, Lorenzet, & Smith-Jentsch, 2005). A comfortable and cooperative organizational environment has also been found to facilitate workplace mentoring, as do a more decentralized organizational structure and more team-oriented approaches to work (Allen, Poteet, & Burroughs, 1997; O'Neill, 2005). Employee perception of how much top management supports mentoring is also positively correlated with mentor reports of higher quality mentoring relationships and protégé reports of mentoring received (Eby, Lockwood, & Butts, 2006). Finally, an organization with a culture that supports individual development and provides ample opportunity for employees to interact with other organizational members is associated with the receipt of career-related mentoring (Aryee, Lo, & Kang, 1999). In addition to these empirical studies, Kram (1985) provided several other recommendations for supporting the development of mentoring relationships at work, including structuring work to maximize interaction among employees, rewarding mentors for providing mentoring support to protégés, and incorporating mentoring into performance management systems.

Designing High-Quality Formal Mentoring Programs

In terms of prescriptive advice regarding the design of formal mentoring programs, a wealth of anecdotal information is available on the topic (e.g., Murray, 1991). However, because it is dangerous to apply recommendations in practice that have not been substantiated by empirical research, the suggestions provided below are based on empirical research on formal mentoring programs. Three general topics are discussed: program design and training, participant selection, and how to most effectively match mentors and protégés.

Program design and training. Formal mentoring programs can be used for a wide range of purposes, including career advancement, employee socialization, diversity enhancement, and skill development (Eddy et al., 2001). Failure to clearly describe the goals and purpose of the program can lead to confusion about each individual's role in the relationship and may lead to unmet expectations for both mentors and protégés. In fact, a common complaint in formal mentoring programs is the lack of clear program goals or objectives (Eby & Lockwood, 2005). Ragins, Cotton, and Miller (2000) is the only published empirical study to examine how the stated program purpose relates to protégé outcomes. The only significant effect reported by Ragins and colleagues was that programs designed to promote a protégé's career were associated with greater protégé satisfaction with promotions.

In terms of training, evidence is starting to accumulate that both the receipt of training and the quality of training are associated with positive protégé (Allen et al., 2006a, 2006b) and mentor (Allen et al., 2006a, 2006b; Parise & Forret, 2008) outcomes of participating in formal mentoring programs. No research to date has examined the content of mentoring program training, although it is recommended that such preparation focus on a wide range of topics, including program goals and objectives, roles and responsibilities in the relationship, communication skills, and effective conflict management techniques (Allen, Finkelstein, & Poteet, 2009; Eby & Lockwood, 2005). It may also be useful to conduct additional training just for mentors. This is important because research indicates that those contemplating whether to assume the role of a mentor often report discomfort and ambiguity about how to interact with protégés and a lack confidence regarding whether they can help protégés develop professionally (Eby & Lockwood, 2005). In terms of program monitoring, Eby and Lockwood (2005) found that both mentors and protégés felt this was an area in need of improvement in formal mentoring programs. Eby, Lockwood, and Butts (2006) also found that when protégés perceived that there was greater accountability for their mentors' behavior, they were less likely to report problems in the relationship.

Participant selection. Research has found that most mentors voluntarily participate in mentoring programs (Allen et al., 2006a; Forret, Turban, & Dougherty, 1996). However, this is not always the case, and some mentors may feel subtly coerced into serving as a mentor. Since voluntary participation by mentors is associated with greater perceived rewards from mentoring and fewer costs (Parise & Forret, 2008), it seems safe to recommend that individuals should not be forced to participate as mentors in formal mentoring programs. Interestingly, voluntary participation on the part of protégés has not been associated with protégé outcomes (Allen et al., 2006a; Ragins et al., 2000). Another aspect of program participation involves the selection criteria used to identify potential mentors and protégés. Most of the research here is descriptive and highlights the personal attributes that are viewed as desirable in mentors (e.g., empathy, trust, communication skills, motivation to mentor; Cunningham, 1993; Eddy et al., 2001) and protégés (e.g., learning orientation, ability; Allen, 2004; Cunningham, 1993; Eddy et al., 2001). Perhaps more important than using universal screening criteria for selecting participants into formal mentoring programs is selecting participants who are a good fit to the goal of the program (Finkelstein & Poteet, 2007). For example, a formal mentoring program designed to identify talent should select protégés on the basis of performance criteria and use highly successful, established individuals as mentors. In contrast, if the goal of the program is diversity enhancement, it seems wise to recommend selecting mentors who are culturally competent and highly motivated to help further the talent of diverse individuals.

Matching mentors and protégés. A final issue in formal mentoring programs is deciding how to match potential mentors and protégés. In most formal programs some sort of systematic matching is used, rather than random assignment (Eddy et al., 2001). However, the matching criteria that are used vary considerably across formal mentoring programs. Lots of different personal characteristics are used to match mentors and protégés, including race, gender, technical background, personality, department, and geographic location (Eddy et al., 2001). Sometimes organizations intentionally match on similarity, whereas other times dissimilarity is desired (Eddy et al., 2001). Again, the appropriateness of the matching strategy may depend in large part on the purpose of the mentoring program. For example, in a formal mentoring program designed to provide protégés with a broad understanding of the company's business operations, it seems important to pair individuals from different business units and carefully consider what type of business exposure (e.g., finance, operations, human resources) will be most beneficial for a particular protégé. Alternatively, formal mentoring programs designed to help employees become socialized into the organization should consider pairing protégés with mentors from the same unit or work group, as this should increase interaction frequency and provide protégés with information that is particularly useful for their initial integration into the organization.

Empirical research on the effects of mentor–protégé matching is limited. However, several studies have found that *perceived* similarity predicts positive protégé outcomes (Ensher & Murphy, 1997; Matarazzo, Finkelstein, & Allen, 2008; Smith-Jentsch, Hudson, & Peuler, 2008; Wanberg et al., 2006) more consistently than does matching on specific criteria such as geographic proximity (Allen et al., 2006a; Eby & Lockwood, 2005; Donovan & Battista, 2008), rank (Allen et al., 2006a; Ragins et al., 2000), or departmental affiliation (Allen et al., 2006a; Ragins et al., 2000). Moreover, the extent to which individuals have input into the match has been found to predict satisfaction with the mentoring program (Allen et al., 2006b; Smith-Jentsch et al., 2008). Matching issues associated with race and gender are discussed in the next section.

Dealing with relational problems in mentoring. As discussed previously, both mentors and protégés can report problems in the relationship. Utilizing a formal mentoring program within an organization that has a learning and development culture should help deter the likelihood of relational problems, as should top management support for mentoring. However, even in a supportive organizational context relationship problems can occur. Because informal mentoring relationships are not officially sanctioned or monitored by the organization, the only real options for dealing with problems in informal relationships are discussing the issue with the mentor (or protégé) in hopes of clearing the air and moving on, or withdrawing from the relationship psychologically and/or behaviorally. Open discussion and resolution of the relational problem seems less likely if the protégé is experiencing difficulty with the mentor, given the status and power difference between the two individuals.

In formal mentoring relationships other options are available for dealing with relational problems. Developing jointly agreed-upon expectations for the relationship through contracting and goal setting is one strategy that may be used to head off relationship problems (Allen, Finkelstein, & Poteet, 2009). This can reduce the likelihood of unmet expectations and perceived boundary violations in the relationship (e.g., relationship is too intense or too superficial), both of which can be catalysts for relational problems. Closely monitoring and routinely evaluating formal mentoring programs may also deter relational problems. Monitoring by an organizational representative associated with the mentoring program can also help ensure that mentor and protégé are meeting regularly and that both individuals are gaining something from the relationship (Allen, Finkelstein, & Poteet, 2009; Eby & Lockwood, 2005). More frequent check-ins with mentoring dyads is probably important when the relationship is just beginning or if the program is new to the organization (Allen, Finkelstein, & Poteet, 2009). Program evaluation can also provide important information as to how the design and delivery of the program may be contributing to relational problems. For example, survey feedback by program participants may indicate that some of the formal relationships never got off the ground (which could be a sign of mentor neglect) or that program participants had difficulty "clicking" interpersonally (which would indicate a mentor–protégé mismatch).

DIVERSITY AND MENTORING

As organizations become increasingly diverse, it is important to consider the role of gender and race in mentoring relationships. (See also Vol. 1, chap. 20, this handbook.) Although individuals can differ on an infinite number of characteristics, gender and race are discussed here because individuals tend to use these attributes to make overall similarity judgments.[1] In addition, the gender and racial composition of the workforce is changing rapidly. The number of women obtaining a 4-year college degree has surpassed the number of men for the first time in history (http://www.census.gov/population/www/socdemo/educ-attn.html), and in 2006, 71.5% of women were in the labor force (U.S. Census Bureau, 2006). The number of racial minorities in the U.S. population is also increasing. The projected change in population size for 2000–2025 is merely 6% for non-Hispanic Whites, as compared with 27% for Blacks, 97% for Asians, and 112% for Hispanics (U.S. Census Bureau, 2008). Even though the numbers of women and racial minorities are increasing in the workplace, both groups still lag far behind men and Whites in terms of organizational rank, pay, and job prestige (Avery, 2006; Fouad, 2006; Ragins, Townsend, & Mattis, 1998). As such, many organizations use mentoring programs for the express purpose of enhancing the representation of women and racial minorities in management positions (Eddy et al., 2001).

As more powerful and senior organizational members, mentors are disproportionately likely to be White males (Blake-Beard, Murrell, & Thomas, 2007). Therefore, women and racial minorities are likely to be in cross-gender and cross-race mentoring relationships, respectively. Perhaps because of this, both women (Ragins, 1989; Ragins & Cotton, 1991) and racial minorities (Catalyst, 2001; Cox & Nkomo, 1991) perceive greater barriers to finding a mentor than do men and Whites, respectively. Women may be hesitant to initiate a mentoring relationship with a more senior male colleague owing to the fear of sexual innuendos or the concern that men cannot understand the unique issues facing working women (Ragins, 1989; Ragins & Cotton, 1991). Racial minorities may be uncertain about approaching a White mentor because of the concern that seeking help may be a sign of weakness or concerns about difficulties relating to and trusting someone of a different race (Blake, 1995; Blake-Beard et al., 2007; Dickens & Dickens, 1982; Thomas, 1989). If a cross-gender or cross-race relationship is forged, there is some evidence that it may be more superficial and less satisfying than mentoring relationships between individuals of the same gender (Burke, McKeen, & McKenna, 1990; Koberg, Boss, & Goodman, 1998) or same race (James, 2000; Thomas, 1990).

The dynamics associated with cross-race and cross-gender mentoring relationships create a dilemma for organizations in terms of how to support and facilitate workplace relationships for women and racial minorities (Blake-Beard et al., 2007; Murrell & James, 2001). On one hand, results of decades of research suggest that similarity in mentor–protégé pairings should increase interpersonal comfort and facilitate the development of strong relational bonds (Judge & Ferris, 1993; Tsui & O'Reilly, 1989). However, this may not be feasible for women and racial minorities owing to their numerical underrepresentation in higher level organizational positions. For those women and racial minorities who are able to secure a same-gender or same-race mentor, there may be some significant trade-offs. Although greater psychosocial support may be available in same-gender and same-race mentoring relationships, female and minority mentors may not be able to provide comparable career-related assistance owing to their lesser

[1] Cultural differences between mentor and protégé are increasingly common as organizations continue to expand their global operations. To date there is virtually no published research on cultural issues in mentoring.

power, influence, and access to resources within organizations (Ragins, 1997). In fact, research has found that protégés with White male mentors earn significantly more than those mentored by individuals with other demographic profiles (e.g., Black men, White women; Dreher & Cox, 1996). This suggests that for women and racial minorities in particular, it may be important to engage in multiple mentoring relationships to garner the full range of mentoring benefits (Ragins, 1997).

There are several strategies that organizations can adopt to help ensure that women and racial minorities receive value-added mentoring. First, although research has found few differences in the base rate of mentoring for men versus women (Dreher & Ash, 1990; Dreher & Cox, 1996; Viator & Scandura, 1991) or Whites versus non-Whites (Blake-Beard, 1999; Mobley, Jaret, Marsh, & Lim, 1994; Thomas, 1990), both women and non-Whites perceive more barriers to finding a mentor (Cox & Nkomo, 1991; Ragins & Cotton, 1991). Setting up mentoring programs with the stated purpose of providing mentoring opportunities for women and racial minorities should help reduce perceived barriers. Second, because many potential mentors are likely to be majority group members, it may also be important to provide training to mentors on how to deal with sensitive topics of gender and race in the mentoring relationship. In addition, training to enhance multicultural competence and knowledge of gender issues in the workplace may help prepare men and Whites for the mentor role. Third, organizations might discuss with diverse protégés the importance of obtaining multiple mentors, both formal and informal, as part of the organizational career development planning process. (See also Vol. 3, chap. 19, this handbook.) Doing so may help protégés take more proactive steps in managing their own career and seeking support from a wide range of individuals, within and outside their employing organization.

TECHNOLOGY AND MENTORING

Given the widespread effect of technology on organizational life, it is also important to consider how technology may influence workplace mentoring. The most profound effect of technology on mentoring is the widespread use of e-mentoring (Bierema & Merriam, 2002; Ensher & Murphy, 2007). E-mentoring involves the provision of career-related and psychosocial support primarily through e-mail or other electronic means (e.g., text messaging, teleconferencing; Ensher & Murphy, 2007). Electronic-mediated relationships between mentor and protégé can link individuals who would otherwise not have the opportunity to interact, owing to either scheduling constraints or geographic dispersion (Bierema & Merriam, 2002). E-mentoring can also substantially expand the network of potential contacts among individuals within professional associations, in computer-based social networking sites, and through intra-organizational referrals and connections (Single & Muller, 2001). Like traditional mentoring, e-mentoring can develop spontaneously or be part of a formal program within or outside the organization (Bierema & Hill, 2005).

Although e-mentoring represents a popular trend, limited research exists on its relative advantages and disadvantages. An exception is a study of peer mentoring that found lower levels of psychosocial and career-related mentoring in electronic compared with face-to-face mentoring (Smith-Jentsch, Scielzo, Yarbrough, & Rosopa, 2008). This suggests that virtual mentoring should be viewed cautiously until additional research documents its effectiveness. Other potential drawbacks of e-mentoring include greater potential for miscommunication, less commitment to the relationship by mentors or protégés, greater difficulty solidifying a close, trusting relationship without face-to-face contact, and concerns regarding confidentiality (Bierema & Hill, 2005; Ensher & Murphy, 2007; Kirk & Olinger, 2003). Unequal access to technology may also restrict access to virtual mentors for some potential protégés (Bierema & Hill, 2005). With these potential drawbacks in mind, it is important to identify several potential benefits of e-mentoring. Perhaps most important, e-mentoring is incredibly flexible and can happen at any time and in any place (Kirk & Olinger, 2003). The "just in time" nature of e-mentoring interactions may increase the utility of mentoring support for protégés (Guy, 2002). Other potential benefits of e-mentoring include strengthening one's writing skills, providing greater access to mentoring for protégés who might otherwise have difficulty securing a mentor, and delivering higher quality mentoring in diverse mentoring relationships because online technology may increase interpersonal comfort between individuals who are different from one another (Ensher & Murphy, 2007).

It is also important to realize that today most mentoring relationships are some hybrid of face-to-face and e-mentoring, based on the degree to which electronic communication is used (Ensher & Murphy, 2007). It seems difficult to imagine a mentoring relationship that does not incorporate phone calls, e-mail, or text messaging into relational interactions. Likewise, some mentoring relationships that are primarily Internet-based can be supplemented by face-to-face meetings or phone calls. For example, the Women's Technology Cluster in the San Francisco area connects high-tech entrepreneurial women with mentors via the Internet, although follow-up phone calls and face-to-face meetings also occur (Whiting & de Janasz, 2004).

PRACTICE TRENDS

As just discussed, because of its versatility and ability to easily connect individuals across vast geographic expanses, e-mentoring is currently the most widespread practice-based extension of traditional mentoring. E-mentoring is particularly common in organizations with global operations and among employees working in technology-oriented industries. A related practice trend is the use of chat rooms, newsgroups, interactive Web sites, and blogs to obtain professional advice and support (Parks & Roberts, 1998). Online mentoring that links less experienced and more experienced professionals for career development and mentoring is also a growing practice among professional associations, such as the Society for Human Resource Management, the Public Relations Society of America, and the Professional Association of Women in Technology.

Two other noteworthy practice-based trends are the use of reverse mentoring and group-based approaches to mentoring. With reverse mentoring the goal is typically learning and knowledge transfer from a younger, less experienced employee to an older, more experienced senior executive (Biss & DeFrene, 2006). The popularity of reverse mentoring began when Jack Welch, former CEO of General Electric, instituted this practice at GE. Other companies quickly followed suit, including Best Buy, Proctor & Gamble, Random House, 3M, and Philip Morris. The appeal of reverse mentoring is that it can provide top managers with the latest developments in the field, particularly in terms of technology (Stone, 2004). Reverse mentoring can also be used as a strategy to educate senior managers about issues facing younger, more diverse employees, including both women and racial minorities (Biss & DeFrene, 2006). A final practice trend is group-based approaches to mentoring. This includes mentoring within intact teams or business units and mentoring circles where one mentor works with a group of protégés (Ambrose, 2003). These approaches extend traditional one-on-one mentoring by capitalizing on the skills and expertise of multiple individuals and may be particularly useful in supporting a team-oriented and continuous learning organizational culture (Ambrose, 2003).

NEW DIRECTIONS FOR RESEARCH

Existing research has provided substantial knowledge about mentoring, particularly from the perspective of the protégé. However, there are several critical gaps in our understanding of mentoring in organizational settings. Several high-priority research areas are discussed in this section to provide a road map for future research. Because the scientific merit of research is judged in large part by the appropriateness and rigor of the methods used, the research design features of existing research on mentoring are also discussed in this section, along with methodological suggestions to push mentoring scholarship forward.

Although there has been increasing interest in the mentor's perspective on mentoring, the vast majority of research is from the protégé's perspective. This is somewhat puzzling because the mentor is a key player in successful (and unsuccessful) mentoring relationships and the mentor's behavior is clearly important to the success (or failure) of the relationship. Therefore, studying just one member of the relational dyad (the protégé) is insufficient. In addition to research designs that focus squarely on the mentor, a high-priority research area is the study of intact mentor–protégé dyads to understand how mentor and protégé influence one another. This could greatly enhance our understanding of the predictors and outcomes of high-quality relationships (Ragins & Verbos, 2007) as well as broaden our knowledge about how and why some mentoring relationships derail (Eby, 2007).

A related issue involves simultaneously considering both individual-level and dyadic-level effects. For example, path analysis with dyadic data could be used to examine the effect of protégé reports of mentoring on relationship quality while controlling for the correlation between protégé and mentor reports of mentoring, as well as the nonindependence between protégé and mentor reports of relational quality (Kenny, Kashy, & Cook, 2006). Examples of analytical strategies that allow for incorporation of effects at more than one level (i.e., individual–dyad, individual–group) simultaneously include hierarchical linear modeling (Raudenbush & Bryk, 2002) and multilevel structural equation modeling (Heck & Thomas, 2000). Finally, there are occasions where the primary research question focuses on how the similarity (or dissimilarity) between dyad members on the same construct affects other variables of interest. For instance, is the similarity in personality between mentor and protégé a stronger predictor of relational processes such as trust and disclosure than their dyadic mean-level personality? Two analytical techniques that provide the ability to examine such similarity, in addition to dyadic mean-level effects, include polynomial regression (Edwards, 2007) and the latent congruence model for structural equation modeling (Cheung, 2009).

Another suggestion for future research involves taking a more balanced view of mentoring relationships. Like any other type of close relationship, individuals in a mentoring relationship can experience positive, uplifting relational encounters as well as disappointments, betrayals, and conflicts (Eby, 2007). Future research on mentoring should examine the full range of relational experiences that mentors and protégés encounter in an effort to better understand the dynamics of mentoring relationships. Moreover, research on the negative aspects of mentoring is still in its infancy, and there is much to be learned about how these negative experiences influence the mentor, protégé, and organization. Several research design recommendations may be particularly useful here. Qualitative research examining relationship "turning points," events that fundamentally alter the mentoring relationship in a good or bad way, is essential in order to identify systematic patterns of relational change and take into consideration that such change may be nonlinear. In other words, a given mentoring relationship may be able to withstand a series of relational problems relatively well for a period of time. However, there may be a point in the relationship at which even a relatively minor relational event can be the proverbial straw that broke the camel's back, for either the mentor or the protégé. Alternatively, an otherwise high-quality mentoring relationship may be irrevocably damaged by a single instance of betrayal. Traditional statistical methods such as correlation and regression may be inadequate in capturing such systematic patterns of change. The use of rigorous empirical methods able to address causal processes unfolding over time (turning points) is critical to furthering the accumulation of scientific knowledge in this area (Cohen, 2008).

Several areas for future research hold particular relevance for the practice of mentoring in organizations. A high-priority area is expanding research on formal programs. Existing research has identified several aspects of effective formal mentoring programs such as participant input into the matching process and the provision of training for mentoring program participants. In contrast, less is known about the most effective way to match mentors and protégés or the circumstances best suited for mentor–protégé matching based on *dissimilarity* versus *similarity*. Quasi-experimental research designs are essential here to systematically manipulate various configurations of mentor–protégé similarity and examine the resultant effect on important outcomes such as satisfaction with the mentoring program, relationship quality, and mentoring provided or received. The role of contextual organizational variables such as a continuous learning culture and performance management systems that reward employee development also deserve careful attention in future research on formal mentoring programs. Making the business case for mentoring is also needed through research that links mentoring to organizational performance indicators such as customer service, return on investment, and profitability. Answers to these questions will require research designs that consider not just individual-level perceptions but also aggregate (shared) perceptions and organization-level performance indicators.

Additional research is needed on diversity issues in mentoring. Existing empirical research on diversified mentoring tends to focus on race and gender, typically comparing the experiences of individuals in same-gender (or same-race) relationships with those in cross-gender (or cross-race) relationships (see McKeen & Bujaki, 2007). Although this stream of research has yielded important insights into both the challenges and the potential benefits of diversified mentoring, research is generally silent with respect to other types of diversified mentoring relationships, such as the mentoring experiences of the physically or psychologically disabled; gays, lesbians, and bisexuals; or religious minorities. To what extent do individuals from these groups have less access to mentors? For those who obtain a mentor, is the quality and quantity of support received different from that reported by majority group members? Can mentoring experiences help diverse protégés overcome some of the unique social barriers and stigmas that they may encounter in the workplace? These represent some of the important yet unanswered questions regarding diversified mentoring.

NEW THEORETICAL PERSPECTIVES

From these practice trends and research suggestions come ideas for integrating new theories into mentoring scholarship. In terms of better understanding diversity issues in mentoring and how to create successful matches in formal mentoring programs, theory and research on close relationships holds promise. In particular, recent insights into the phenomena of assortative mating (i.e., whether there are systematic patterns in human mate selection; see Luo & Klohnen, 2005) could be creatively applied to examine which combinations of individual characteristics are important in terms of similarity (positive assortment) and dissimilarity (negative assortment) in predicting effective mentoring relationships.

Generally speaking, in relationships that develop informally partners tend to be more similar than different on a wide range of variables (e.g., age, education, religiousness, political affiliation, intelligence), and these differences are better explained by mate selection than by convergence among individuals over time (Watson, Klohnen, Casillas, Sims, & Berry, 2004). However, the effect of similarity on relational outcomes varies according to the specific variables examined. For example, Luo and Klohnen (2005) found that husband–wife profile similarity in personality as measured by the Big Five, attachment style, and trait-based affect reliably predicted marital quality. In contrast, profile similarity in political attitudes and religious views were generally unrelated to relationship quality. Likewise, Watson et al. (2004) found that similarity in age, education, intelligence, religiosity, and political attitudes were not predictive of marital satisfaction. Although mentoring relationships are clearly different from romantic partnerships, the literature on assortative mating may provide a fresh perspective for understanding what makes good mentor–protégé matches. Perhaps most important, current research on assortative mating brings into sharp relief the importance of taking a multifaceted view of similarity and recognizing that similarity may not always be a necessary condition for effective relational matches.

Theories of close relationships also have utility for understanding the full range of mentoring experiences—from relationships characterized by high-quality connections, deep emotional ties, and substantial personal growth (Ragins, 2007) to those characterized by destructive relational dynamics and personally damaging outcomes (Eby, 2007). The social psychological literature readily acknowledges that characterizing relationships as "good" or "bad" is a gross oversimplification (Wood & Duck, 1995). Some theories explicitly consider both relational costs and benefits in an effort to understand relationship outcomes. For example, one of the most widely studied and well-supported theories of close relationships is Rusbult's (1980a, 1980b, 1983) investment model. This model proposes that satisfaction and commitment in close relationships are a direct function of the relational costs versus benefits associated with the relationship. The investment model also predicts that individuals may stay in relationships where the costs actually outweigh the benefits because of sunk relationship costs (e.g., shared belongings, time and energy that cannot be recouped once the relationship dissolves) or the lack of alternative relational partners. This model may help us understand how positive and negative relational experiences jointly influence the course of a mentoring relationship. It may also provide insight into why some individuals may stay in mentoring relationships that are marked by negative relational experiences (for an example, see Eby & McManus, 2004).

On the positive side of the relational ledger, Ragins (Ragins, 2007; Ragins & Verbos, 2007) has argued that traditional approaches to mentoring treat it as a one-sided relationship that leads to instrumental gains for the protégé. As a consequence, most mentoring research has focused on a narrow range of outcomes associated with work and career-related gains. Notably missing from the literature is the discussion of how mentoring can be a generative, life-sustaining relationship for both mentor and protégé (Ragins & Verbos, 2007). Using theory and research from positive psychology (Seligman & Csikszentmihalyi, 2000) and the positive organizational behavior movement (Luthans, 2002) would allow us to examine a wider range of relational processes in mentoring relationships (e.g., disclosure, trust, mutuality) as well as examine additional individual-level outcomes indicative of psychological health (e.g., hope, optimism, resiliency, authenticity; Ragins & Verbos, 2007). It is interesting to note that the suggestion to examine a broader range of outcomes brings us full circle to the early work on mentoring by Levinson et al. (1978), who argued that mentoring relationships can be influential, positive, life-changing experiences for young adults. Likewise, Kram's (1985) seminal work on mentoring discusses how mentoring can influence overall well-being and positively contribute to personal growth, even though subsequent research has rarely examined such outcomes in relation to mentoring experiences at work.

CONCLUSION

After more than 20 years of research, mentoring has emerged as a legitimate field of scientific inquiry. In this chapter the literature on organizational mentoring was discussed, with a joint emphasis on what we know from existing empirical research and how we can most effectively use this knowledge to facilitate high-quality mentoring relationships in organizational settings. Practice and research trends were also outlined to provide the reader with a sense of where the science and practice of mentoring is headed and to spark additional research and practice innovations on the topic.

References

Allen, T. D. (2003). Mentoring others: A dispositional and motivational approach. *Journal of Vocational Behavior, 62,* 134–154. doi:10.1016/S0001-8791(02)00046-5

Allen, T. D. (2004). Protégé selection by mentors: Contributing individual and organizational factors. *Journal of Vocational Behavior, 65,* 469–483. doi:10.1016/j.jvb.2003.07.003

Allen, T. D. (2007). Mentoring relationships from the perspective of the mentor. In B. R. Ragins & K. E. Kram (Eds.), *The handbook of mentoring: Theory, research and practice* (pp. 123–147). Thousand Oaks, CA: Sage.

Allen, T. D., Day, R., & Lentz, E. (2001, April). *Formal mentoring programs: A review and survey of design features and recommendations.* Paper presented at the Annual Meeting of the Society for Industrial and Organizational Psychology, San Diego, CA.

Allen, T. D., Eby, L. T., & Lentz, E. (2006a). Mentorship behaviors and mentorship quality associated with mentoring programs: Closing the gap between research and practice. *Journal of Applied Psychology, 91,* 567–578. doi:10.1037/0021-9010.91.3.567

Allen, T. D., Eby, L. T., & Lentz, E. (2006b). The relationship between formal mentoring program characteristics and perceived program effectiveness. *Personnel Psychology, 59,* 125–153. doi:10.1111/j.1744-6570.2006.00747.x

Allen, T. D., Eby, L. T., Poteet, M. L., Lentz, E., & Lima, L. (2004). Outcomes associated with mentoring protégés: A meta-analysis. *Journal of Applied Psychology, 89,* 127–136. doi:10.1037/0021-9010.89.1.127

Allen, T. D., Finkelstein, L. M., & Poteet, M. L. (2009). *Designing workplace mentoring programs: An evidence-based approach.* Chichester, England: Wiley-Blackwell.

Allen, T. D., Lentz, E., & Day, R. (2006). Career success outcomes associated with mentoring others: A comparison of mentors and nonmentors. *Journal of Career Development, 32,* 272–285. doi:10.1177/0894845305282942

Allen, T. D., & O'Brien, K. E. (2006). Formal mentoring programs and organizational attraction. *Human Resource Development Quarterly, 17,* 43–58. doi:10.1002/hrdq.1160

Allen, T. D., Poteet, M. L., & Burroughs, S. M. (1997). The mentor's perspective: A qualitative inquiry and future research agenda. *Journal of Vocational Behavior, 51,* 70–89. doi:10.1006/jvbe.1997.1596

Allen, T. D., Poteet, M. L., Russell, J. E. A., & Dobbins, G. H. (1997). A field study of factors related to supervisors' willingness to mentor others. *Journal of Vocational Behavior, 50,* 1–22. doi:10.1006/jvbe.1995.1525

Allen, T. D., Smith, M. A., Mael, F. A., O'Shea, P. G., & Eby, L. T. (2009). Organization-level mentoring and organizational performance within substance abuse treatment centers. *Journal of Management, 35,* 1113–1128.

Ambrose, L. (2003, July/August). Multiple mentoring. *Healthcare Executive, 18,* 58–59.

Aryee, S., Lo, S., & Kang, I.-E. (1999). Antecedents of early career stage mentoring among Chinese employees. *Journal of Organizational Behavior, 20,* 563–576. doi:10.1002/(SICI)1099-1379(199909)20:5<563::AID-JOB890>3.0.CO;2-#

Avery, D. R. (2006). Racial discrimination. In J. H. Greenhaus & G. A. Callanan (Eds.), *Encyclopedia of career development* (pp. 667–671). Thousand Oaks, CA: Sage.

Bierema, L. L., & Hill, J. R. (2005). Virtual mentoring and HRD. *Advances in Developing Human Resources, 7,* 556–568. doi:10.1177/1523422305279688

Bierema, L. L., & Merriam, S. (2002). E-mentoring: Using computer mediated communication to enhance the mentoring process. *Innovative Higher Education, 26,* 211–227. doi:10.1023/A:1017921023103

Biss, J. L., & DeFrene, D. D. (2006). An examination of reverse mentoring in the workplace. *Business Education Digest, 15,* 30–41.

Blake, S. D. (1995. August). *At the crossroads of race and gender: Lessons from the mentoring experiences of professional Black women.* Paper presented at the Annual Meeting of the Academy of Management, Vancouver, British Columbia, Canada.

Blake-Beard, S. D. (1999). The costs of living as an outsider within: An analysis of the mentoring relationships and career success of black and white women in the corporate sector. *Journal of Career Development, 26,* 21–36. doi:10.1177/089484539902600103

Blake-Beard, S. D., Murrell, A., & Thomas, D. (2007). Unfinished business: The impact of race on understanding mentoring relationships. In B. R. Ragins & K. E. Kram (Eds.), *The handbook of mentoring at work* (pp. 223–247). Thousand Oaks, CA: Sage.

Bozionelos, N. (2004). Mentoring provided: Relation to mentor's career success, personality, and mentoring received. *Journal of Vocational Behavior, 64,* 24–46. doi:10.1016/S0001-8791(03)00033-2

Bridgeford, L. (2007, August 1). Mentoring programs still have a place in the 21st century. *Employee Benefit News,* p. 16.

Burke, R. J., McKeen, C. A., & McKenna, C. S. (1990). Sex differences and cross-sex effects on mentoring: Some preliminary data. *Psychological Reports, 67,* 1011–1023. doi:10.2466/PR0.67.7.1011-1023

Carter, M., & Francis, R. (2001). Mentoring and beginning teachers' workplace learning. *Asia-Pacific Journal of Teacher Education, 29,* 249–262.

Catalyst. (2001). *Women of color in corporate management: Opportunities and barriers.* New York: Author.

Chao, G. T. (1997). Mentoring phases and outcomes. *Journal of Vocational Behavior, 51,* 15–28. doi:10.1006/jvbe.1997.1591

Chao, G. T., Walz, P. M., & Gardner, P. D. (1992). Formal and informal mentorships: A comparison on mentoring functions and contrast with nonmentored counterparts. *Personnel Psychology, 45,* 619–636.

Cheung, G. W. H. (2009). Introducing the latent congruence model for improving the assessment of similarity, agreement, and fit in organizational research. *Organizational Research Methods, 12,* 6–33. doi:10.1177/1094428107308914

Cohen, J. (1988). *Statistical power for the behavioral sciences* (2nd ed.). Hillsdale, NJ: Erlbaum.

Cohen, P. (2008). *Applied data analytic techniques for turning points research.* New York: Routledge.

Collins, P. M. (1994). Does mentorship among social workers make a difference? An empirical investigation of career outcomes. *Social Work, 39,* 413–419.

Cox, T. H., & Nkomo, S. M. (1991). A race and gender-group analysis of the early career experience of MBAs. *Work and Occupations, 18,* 431–446. doi:10.1177/0730888491018004004

Cunningham, J. B. (1993). Facilitating a mentoring programme. *Leadership and Organization Development Journal, 14*(4), 15–20. doi:10.1108/01437739310039442

Dickens, F., & Dickens, L. (1982). *The Black manager.* New York: Amacom.

Donovan, C. B., & Battista, M. (2008, April). *Mentoring program relationship to mentor and protégé intent to remain.* Paper presented at the annual meeting of the Society for Industrial and Organizational Psychology, San Francisco, CA.

Douglas, C. A., & McCauley, C. D. (1999). Formal developmental relationships: A survey of organizational practices. *Human Resource Development Quarterly, 10,* 203–220. doi:10.1002/hrdq.3920100302

Dreher, G. F., & Ash, R. A. (1990). A comparative study of mentoring among men and women in managerial, professional, and technical positions. *Journal of Applied Psychology, 75,* 539–546. doi:10.1037/0021-9010.75.5.539

Dreher, G. F., & Cox, T. H. (1996). Race, gender, and opportunity: A study of compensation attainment and the establishment of mentoring relationships. *Journal of Applied Psychology, 81,* 297–308. doi:10.1037/0021-9010.81.3.297

Eby, L. T. (2007). Understanding problems in mentoring: A review and proposed investment model. In B. R. Ragins & K. E. Kram (Eds.), *Handbook of mentoring* (pp. 323–344). Thousand Oaks, CA: Sage.

Eby, L. T., & Allen, T. D. (2002). Further investigation of protégés' negative mentoring experiences: Patterns and outcomes. *Group & Organization Management, 27,* 456–479. doi:10.1177/1059601102238357

Eby, L. T., Allen, T. D., Evans, S. C., Ng, T., & DuBois, D. L. (2008). Does mentoring matter? A multidisciplinary meta-analysis comparing mentored and non-mentored individuals. *Journal of Vocational Behavior, 72,* 254–267. doi:10.1016/j.jvb.2007.04.005

Eby, L. T., Butts, M. M., Lockwood, A., & Simon, S. A. (2004). Protégés' negative mentoring experiences: Construct development and nomological validation. *Personnel Psychology, 57,* 411–447. doi:10.1111/j.1744-6570.2004.tb02496.x

Eby, L. T., Durley, J., Evans, S. C., & Ragins, B. R. (2006). The relationship between short-term mentoring benefits and long-term mentor outcomes. *Journal of Vocational Behavior, 69,* 424–444. doi:10.1016/j.jvb.2006.05.003

Eby, L. T., & Lockwood, A. (2005). Protégés' and mentors' reactions to participating in formal mentoring programs: A qualitative investigation. *Journal of Vocational Behavior, 67,* 441–458. doi:10.1016/j.jvb.2004.08.002

Eby, L. T., Lockwood, A., & Butts, M. M. (2006). Organizational support for mentoring: A multiple perspectives approach. *Journal of Vocational Behavior, 68,* 267–291. doi:10.1016/j.jvb.2005.07.003

Eby, L. T., & McManus, S. E. (2004). The protégé's role in negative mentoring experiences. *Journal of Vocational Behavior, 65,* 255–275. doi:10.1016/j.jvb.2003.07.001

Eby, L. T., McManus, S. E., Simon, S. A., & Russell, J. E. A. (2000). The protégé's perspective regarding negative mentoring experiences: The development of a taxonomy. *Journal of Vocational Behavior, 57,* 1–21. doi:10.1006/jvbe.1999.1726

Eby, L. T., Rhodes, J., & Allen, T. D. (2007). Definition and evolution of mentoring. In T. D. Allen & L. T. Eby (Eds.), *Blackwell handbook of mentoring* (pp. 7–20). Oxford, MA: Blackwell.

Eddy, E., Tannenbaum, S., Alliger, G., D'Abate, C., & Givens, S. (2001). *Mentoring in industry: The top 10 issues when building and supporting a mentoring program.* Technical report prepared for the Naval Air Warfare Training Systems Division (Contract No. N61339-99-D-0012). Orlando, FL: Naval Air Warfare Center Training Systems Division.

Eddy, E., Tannenbaum, S., Lorenzet, S. J., & Smith-Jentsch, K. A. (2005). The influence of a continuous learning environment on peer mentoring behaviors. *Journal of Managerial Issues, 17,* 383–395.

Edwards, J. R. (2007). Polynomial regression and response surface methodology. In C. Ostroff & T. A. Judge (Eds.), *Perspectives on organizational fit* (pp. 361–372). San Francisco: Jossey-Bass.

Ensher, E. A., & Murphy, S. E. (1997). Effects of race, gender, and perceived similarity, and contact on mentor relationships. *Journal of Vocational Behavior, 50,* 460–481. doi:10.1006/jvbe.1996.1547

Ensher, E. A., & Murphy, S. E. (2007). E-mentoring: Next-generation research strategies and suggestions. In B. R. Ragins & K. E. Kram (Eds.), *The handbook of mentoring at work* (pp. 299–322). Thousand Oaks, CA: Sage.

Fagenson-Eland, E. A., Marks, M. A., & Amendola, K. L. (1997). Perceptions of mentoring relationships. *Journal of Vocational Behavior, 51,* 29–42. doi:10.1006/jvbe.1997.1592

Finkelstein, L., Allen, T., & Rhoton, L. (2003). An examination of the role of age in mentoring relationships. *Group & Organization Management, 28,* 249–281. doi:10.1177/1059601103028002004

Finkelstein, L. M., & Poteet, M. L. (2007). Best practices in workplace formal mentoring programs. In T. D. Allen & L. T. Eby (Eds.), *Blackwell handbook of mentoring: A multiple perspectives approach* (pp. 345–367). Oxford, MA: Blackwell.

Forret, M. L., Turban, D. H., & Dougherty, T. W. (1996). Issues facing organizations when implementing formal mentoring programmes. *Leadership and Organization Development Journal, 17,* 27–30. doi:10.1108/01437739610116966

Fouad, N. A. (2006). Culture and careers. In J. H. Greenhaus & G. A. Callanan (Eds.), *Encyclopedia of career development* (pp. 214–220). Thousand Oaks, CA: Sage.

Green, S. G., & Bauer, T. N. (1995). Supervisory mentoring by advisers: Relationships with doctoral student potential, productivity, and commitment. *Personnel Psychology, 48,* 537–562. doi:10.1111/j.1744-6570.1995.tb01769.x

Greenhaus, J. H., Callanan, G. A., & Godshalk, V. M. (2000). *Career management.* Fort Worth, TX: Druden Press.

Guy, T. C. (2002). Telementoring: Sharing mentoring relationships in the 21st century. In C. A. Hansman (Ed.), *Critical perspectives on mentoring: Trends and issues* (pp. 27–37). Columbus, OH: ERIC.

Hall, D. T. (1996). Protean careers of the 21st century. *Academy of Management Executive, 10,* 8–16.

Heck, R. H., & Thomas, S. L. (2000). *An introduction to multilevel modeling techniques.* Mahwah, NJ: Erlbaum.

Hezlett, S. A. (2005). Protégés' learning in mentoring relationships: A review of the literature and an exploratory case study. *Advances in Developing Human Resources, 7,* 505–526. doi:10.1177/1523422305279686

Hirschfeld, R. R., Thomas, C. H., & Lankau, M. J. (2006). Achievement and avoidance motivational orientations in the domain of mentoring. *Journal of Vocational Behavior, 68,* 524–537. doi:10.1016/j.jvb.2005.11.004

Jackson, V. A., Palepu, A., Szalacha, L., Casell, C., Carr, P. L., & Inui, T. (2003). "Having the right chemistry": A qualitative study of mentoring in academic medicine. *Academic Medicine, 78,* 328–334.

James, E. H. (2000). Race-related differences in promotions and support: Underlying effects of human and social capital. *Organization Science, 11,* 493–508. doi:10.1287/orsc.11.5.493.15202

Judge, T. A., & Ferris, G. R. (1993). Social context of performance evaluation decisions. *Academy of Management Journal, 36,* 80–105. doi:10.2307/256513

Kalbfleisch, P. J., & Davies, A. B. (1993). An interpersonal model for participation in mentoring relationships. *Western Journal of Communication, 57,* 399–415.

Kaslow, N. J., & Mascaro, N. A. (2007). Mentoring interns and postdoctoral residents in academic health sciences center. *Journal of Clinical Psychology in Medical Settings, 14,* 191–196. doi:10.1007/s10880-007-9070-y

Kenny, D. A., Kashy, D. A., & Cook, W. L. (2006). *Dyadic data analysis.* New York: Guilford Press.

Kirk, J. J., & Olinger, J. (2003). *From traditional to virtual mentoring.* Washington, DC: ERIC.

Koberg, C. S., Boss, R. W., & Goodman, E. (1998). Factors and outcomes associated with mentoring among health-care professionals. *Journal of Vocational Behavior, 53,* 58–72. doi:10.1006/jvbe.1997.1607

Kram, K. E. (1985). *Mentoring at work.* Glenview, IL: Scott, Foresman.

Kram, K. E., & Isabella, L. A. (1985). Mentoring alternatives: The role of peer relationships in career development. *Academy of Management Journal, 28,* 110–132. doi:10.2307/256064

Lazovsky, R., & Shimoni, A. (2006). The components of on-site mentoring contracts: Perceptions of Israeli mentors and school counseling interns. *International Journal for the Advancement of Counseling, 28,* 343–357. doi:10.1007/s10447-006-9018-1

Le Maistre, C., Boudreau, S., & Paré, A. (2006). Mentor or evaluator? Assisting and assessing newcomers to the professions. *Journal of Workplace Learning, 18,* 344–354. doi:10.1108/13665620610682071

Levinson, D. J., Darrow, D., Levinson, M., Klein, E. B., & McKee, B. (1978). *Seasons of a man's life.* New York: Academic Press.

Linnehan, F. (2001). The relation of a work-based mentoring program to the academic performance and behavior of African American students. *Journal of Vocational Behavior, 59,* 310–325. doi:10.1006/jvbe.2001.1810

Linnehan, F. (2003). A longitudinal study of work-based adult-youth mentoring. *Journal of Vocational Behavior, 63,* 40–54. doi:10.1016/S0001-8791(02)00012-X

Luo, S., & Klohnen, E. C. (2005). Assortative mating and marital quality in newlyweds: A couple-centered approach. *Journal of Personality and Social Psychology, 88,* 304–326. doi:10.1037/0022-3514.88.2.304

Luthans, F. (2002). The need for and meaning of positive organizational behavior. *Journal of Organizational Behavior, 23,* 695–706. doi:10.1002/job.165

Matarazzo, K., Finkelstein, L. M., & Allen, T. D. (2008, April). *Making successful matches in formal mentoring relationships: An investigation of partner similarity.* Paper presented at the annual meeting of the Society for Industrial and Organizational Psychology, San Francisco, CA.

McManus, S. E., & Russell, J. E. A. (1997). New directions in mentoring research: An examination of related constructs. *Journal of Vocational Behavior, 51,* 145–161. doi:10.1006/jvbe.1997.1597

McManus, S. E., & Russell, J. E. A. (2007). Peer mentoring relationships. In B. R. Ragins & K. E. Kram (Eds.), *The handbook of mentoring at work* (pp. 299–322). Thousand Oaks, CA: Sage.

McKeen, C., & Bujaki, M. (2007). Gender and mentoring. In B. R. Ragins & K. E. Kram (Eds.), *Handbook of mentoring at work* (pp. 197–222). Thousand Oaks, CA: Sage.

Mobley, G. M., Jaret, C., Marsh, K., & Lim, Y. Y. (1994). Mentoring, job satisfaction, gender and the legal profession. *Sex Roles, 31,* 79–98. doi:10.1007/BF01560278

Murray, M. (1991). *Beyond the myths and magic of mentoring.* San Francisco: Jossey-Bass.

Murrell, A. J., & James, E. H. (2001). Gender and diversity within organizations. *Sex Roles, 45,* 243–257. doi:10.1023/A:1014393312588

Noe, R. A. (1988). An investigation of the determinants of successful assigned mentoring relationships. *Personnel Psychology, 41,* 457–479. doi:10.1111/j.1744-6570.1988.tb00638.x

O'Neill, R. M. (2005). An examination of organizational predictors of mentoring functions. *Journal of Managerial Issues, 17,* 439–460.

Parise, M. R., & Forret, M. L. (2008). Formal mentoring programs: The relationship of program design and support to mentors' perceptions of benefits and costs. *Journal of Vocational Behavior, 72,* 225–240. doi:10.1016/j.jvb.2007.10.011

Parks, M. R., & Roberts, L. D. (1998). "Making MOOsic": The development of personal relationships online and a comparison of their off-line counterparts. *Journal of Social and Personal Relationships, 15,* 517–537. doi:10.1177/0265407598154005

Payne, S. C., & Huffman, A. H. (2005). A longitudinal examination of the influence of mentoring on organizational commitment and turnover. *Academy of Management Journal, 48,* 158–168.

Powell, D. J., & Brodsky, A. (2004). *Clinical supervision in alcohol and drug abuse counseling.* San Francisco: Jossey-Bass.

Ragins, B. (1989). Barriers to mentoring: The female manager's dilemma. *Human Relations, 42,* 1–22. doi:10.1177/001872678904200101

Ragins, B. R. (1997). Diversified mentoring relationships: A power perspective. *Academy of Management Review, 22,* 482–521. doi:10.2307/259331

Ragins, B. R. (2007). Diversity and workplace mentoring relationships: A review and positive social capital approach. In T. D. Allen & L. T. Eby (Eds.), *Blackwell handbook of mentoring* (pp. 281–300). Oxford, MA: Blackwell.

Ragins, B. R., & Cotton, J. L. (1991). Easier said than done: Gender differences in perceived barriers to gaining a mentor. *Academy of Management Journal, 34,* 939–951. doi:10.2307/256398

Ragins, B. R., & Cotton, J. L. (1999). Mentor functions and outcomes: A comparison of men and women in formal and informal mentoring relationships. *Journal of Applied Psychology, 84,* 529–550. doi:10.1037/0021-9010.84.4.529

Ragins, B. R., Cotton, J. L., & Miller, J. S. (2000). Marginal mentoring: The effects of type of mentor, quality of relationship, and program design on work and career attitudes. *Academy of Management Journal, 43,* 1177–1194. doi:10.2307/1556344

Ragins, B. R., & McFarlin, D. B. (1990). Perceptions of mentor roles in cross-gender mentoring relationships. *Journal of Vocational Behavior, 37,* 321–339. doi:10.1016/0001-8791(90)90048-7

Ragins, B. R., Townsend, B., & Mattis, M. (1998). Gender gap in the executive suite: CEOs and female executives report on breaking the glass ceiling. *Academy of Management Executive, 12,* 28–42.

Ragins, B. R., & Verbos, A. K. (2007). Positive relationships in action: Relational mentoring and mentoring schemas in the workplace. In J. E. Dutton & B. R. Ragins (Eds.), *Exploring positive relationships at work: Building a theoretical and research foundation* (pp. 91–116). Mahwah, NJ: Erlbaum.

Ramanan, R. A., Taylor, M. C., Davis, R. B., & Phillips, R. S. (2006). Mentoring matters: Mentoring and career preparation in internal medicine residency training programs. *Journal of General Internal Medicine, 21,* 340–345. doi:10.1111/j.1525-1497.2006.00346.x

Raudenbush, S. W., & Bryk, A. S. (2002). *Hierarchical linear models: Applications and data analysis methods.* Thousand Oaks, CA: Sage.

Rusbult, C. E. (1980a). Commitment and satisfaction in romantic associations: A test of the investment model. *Journal of Experimental Social Psychology, 16,* 172–186. doi:10.1016/0022-1031(80)90007-4

Rusbult, C. E. (1980b). Satisfaction and commitment in friendships. *Representative Research in Social Psychology, 11,* 96–105.

Rusbult, C. E. (1983). A longitudinal test of the investment model: The development (and deterioration) of satisfaction and commitment in heterosexual involvements. *Journal of Personality and Social Psychology, 45,* 101–117. doi:10.1037/0022-3514.45.1.101

Scandura, T. A., & Ragins, B. R. (1993). The effects of sex and gender role orientation on mentorship in male-dominated occupations. *Journal of Vocational Behavior, 43,* 251–265. doi:10.1006/jvbe.1993.1046

Scandura, T. A., & Schriesheim, C. A. (1994). Leader-member exchange and supervisor career mentoring as complementary constructs in leadership research. *Academy of Management Journal, 37,* 1588–1602. doi:10.2307/256800

Scandura, T. A., & Viator, R. E. (1994). Mentoring in public accounting firms: An analysis of mentor-protégé relationships, mentorship functions, and protégé turnover intentions. *Accounting, Organizations and Society, 19,* 717–734. doi:10.1016/0361-3682(94)90031-0

Scandura, T. A., & Williams, E. A. (2001). An investigation of the moderating effects of gender on the relationships between mentorship initiation and protégé perceptions of mentoring functions. *Journal of Vocational Behavior, 59,* 342–363. doi:10.1006/jvbe.2001.1809

Seligman, M. E. P., & Csikszentmihalyi, M. (2000). Positive psychology: An introduction. *American Psychologist, 55,* 5–14. doi:10.1037/0003-066X.55.1.5

Sias, P. M., & Jablin, F. M. (1995). Differential superior-subordinate relations, perceptions of fairness, and coworker communication. *Human Communication Research, 22,* 5–38. doi:10.1111/j.1468-2958.1995.tb00360.x

Single, P. B., & Muller, C. B. (2001). When email and mentoring unite: The implementation of a nationwide mentoring program. In L. K. Stromei (Ed.), *Creating mentoring and coaching programs* (pp. 107–122). Alexandria, VA: American Society for Training and Development.

Smith-Jentsch, K., Hudson, N., & Peuler, M. (2008, April). *The impact of protégé choice on mentoring processes.* Paper presented at the annual meeting of the Society for Industrial and Organizational Psychology, San Francisco, CA.

Smith-Jentsch, K. A., Scielzo, S. A., Yarbrough, C. S., & Rosopa, P. J. (2008). A comparison of face-to-face and electronic peer-mentoring: Interactions with mentor gender. *Journal of Vocational Behavior, 72,* 193–206.

Spencer, R. (2007). Naturally occurring mentoring relationships involving youth. In T. D. Allen & L. T. Eby (Eds.), *Blackwell handbook of mentoring: A multiple perspectives approach* (pp. 99–117). Oxford, MA: Blackwell.

Stone, F. (2004). Leadership coach. *Executive Excellence, 21*(2), 5.

Thomas, D. A. (1989). Mentoring and irrationality: The role of racial taboos. *Human Resource Management, 28,* 279–290. doi:10.1002/hrm.3930280213

Thomas, D. A. (1990). The impact of race of managers' experiences of developmental relationships. *Journal of Organizational Behavior, 11,* 479–492. doi:10.1002/job.4030110608

Tsui, A. S., & O'Reilly, C. A. (1989). Beyond simple demographic effects: The importance of relational demography in superior-subordinate dyads. *Academy of Management Journal, 32,* 402–423. doi:10.2307/256368

Underhill, C. M. (2006). The effectiveness of mentoring programs in corporate settings: A meta-analytical review of the literature. *Journal of Vocational Behavior, 68,* 292–307. doi:10.1016/j.jvb.2005.05.003

U.S. Census Bureau. (2006). *American Community Survey: S2301. Employment status.* Retrieved from http://factfinder.census.gov/servlet/STTable?_bm=y& geo_id=01000US&-qr_name=ACS_2006_EST_G00_S2301&-ds_name=ACS_2006_EST_G00_

U.S. Census Bureau. (2008). *Projected change in population size by race and Hispanic origin for the United States: 2000 to 2050* (NP2008-T7). Retrieved from http://www.census.gov/population/www/projections/files/nation/summary/np2008-t7.xls.

Viator, R. E., & Scandura, T. A. (1991). A study of mentor-protégé relationships in large public accounting firms. *Accounting Horizons, 5,* 20–30.

Wanberg, C. R., Kammeyer-Mueller, J., & Marchese, M. (2006). Mentor and protégé predictors and outcomes of mentoring in a formal mentoring program. *Journal of Vocational Behavior, 69,* 410–423. doi:10.1016/j.jvb.2006.05.010

Watson, D., Klohnen, E. C., Casillas, A., Sims, E. N., & Berry, D. S. (2004). Match makers and deal breakers: Assortative mating in newlywed couples. *Journal of Personality, 72,* 1029–1068. doi:10.1111/j.0022-3506.2004.00289.x

Whitely, W., Dougherty, T. W., & Dreher, G. F. (1992). Correlates of career-oriented mentoring for early career managers and professionals. *Journal of Organizational Behavior, 13,* 141–154. doi:10.1002/job.4030130204

Whiting, V. R., & de Janasz, S. C. (2004). Mentoring in the 21st century: Using the Internet to build skills and networks. *Journal of Management Education, 28,* 275–293. doi:10.1177/1052562903252639

Wilson, J. A., & Elman, N. S. (1990). Organizational benefits of mentoring. *Academy of Management Executive, 4,* 88–94.

Wood, J. T., & Duck, S. (1995). Off the beaten track: New shores for relationship research. In J. T. Wood & S. Duck (Eds.), *Under-studied relationships: Off the beaten track* (pp. 1–21). Thousand Oaks, CA: Sage.

CHAPTER 18

EXECUTIVE COACHING: A CRITICAL REVIEW AND RECOMMENDATIONS FOR ADVANCING THE PRACTICE

David B. Peterson

Executive coaching has exploded in popularity over the past decade (Brock, 2008; Grant, 2009) and has many passionate advocates, including coaches, participants who have personally benefited from coaching, and their organizational sponsors who have seen the transformational power of coaching firsthand. Yet there is still considerable debate about such fundamental issues as the definition and effectiveness of coaching, the competencies and qualifications of effective coaches, and how to match coaches and participants.[1] This chapter examines these and other issues important to coaches, researchers, users of coaching services, and those who train coaches.

The field of executive coaching is still young and has been populated by practitioners from diverse backgrounds, including business, management consulting, organization development, training, human resources, linguistics, education, sports, and assorted psychological disciplines, including industrial and organizational (I/O), counseling, clinical, and social (Brock, 2008; Grant, 2007; Liljenstrand & Nebeker, 2008; Minahan, 2006; Walker, 2004). Two highly influential leaders in the field of life coaching, Thomas Leonard and Laura Whitworth, even began their careers as accountants and financial advisors (O'Connor & Lages, 2007). Given the varied backgrounds, experiences, and perspectives coaches bring, it is not surprising to see a lack of consensus about definitions, methods, and techniques. Executive coaching is also a field in which the practice is far ahead of relevant theory and research (Feldman & Lankau, 2005; Fillery-Travis & Lane, 2006; Joo, 2005). Whereas the amount of research on coaching has grown exponentially in the 2000s (Grant, 2009), the available theory on coaching is primarily adapted to coaching from other domains, often with only superficial modifications that do not necessarily address differences in audience, purpose, or context. As Tobias (1996) noted, many coaching models are "simply a repackaging of certain practices that were once subsumed under the more general terms consulting or counseling" (p. 87). The paucity of theory specific to coaching is reflected in the prevalence of published material based directly on therapeutic models (e.g., behavioral, cognitive, psychodynamic, person-centered, humanistic, gestalt) found in broad overviews such as Palmer and Whybrow (2007), Peltier (2009), and Stober and Grant (2006) or in models based on principles from social psychology and learning theory (e.g., Law, Ireland, & Hussain, 2007), positive

This work has benefited greatly from the contributions and ideas of Mary Dee Hicks, Carol Kauffman, Bob Lee, Susan Mecca, John Muros, Alexis Shoemate, Marc Sokol, Elyse Sutherland, and Rebecca Turner. Special thanks to Sheldon Zedeck for his insightful and extremely useful feedback, comments, and suggestions. I also express my appreciation to PDI Ninth House's senior leadership, especially Cindy Marsh and R. J. Heckman, for their ongoing support.

[1]This chapter refers to coaching *participants* rather than *coachees,* a commonly used term that characterizes executives as passive recipients of the coach's actions rather than as active learners and fully engaged partners in a collaborative working relationship.

psychology (e.g., Biswas-Diener & Dean, 2007; Kauffman, 2006), and even schools of philosophy such as existentialism and phenomenology (e.g., Flaherty, 2005). Because many of the ideas presented in the coaching literature, including this chapter, need further validation and research, the closing section of this chapter addresses fundamental research questions and methodological issues for the study of coaching.

DEFINITIONS OF EXECUTIVE COACHING

There are many definitions of *coaching* (Ives, 2008) and *executive coaching* (Hamlin, Ellinger, & Beattie, 2008; Joo, 2005). Several authorities have even modified their definitions over time as their perspectives have evolved (Palmer & Whybrow, 2007). The challenges of attempting to define such a broad, diverse practice include delimiting the boundaries relative to other fields (e.g., therapy or consulting) and producing a definition that is specific enough to be of practical use and yet broad enough to be inclusive and representative of the diversity in the field (D'Abate, Eddy, & Tannenbaum, 2003; Hamlin et al., 2008; Ives, 2008; Jackson, 2005; Olson, 2008; Stern, 2004; Stewart, O'Riordan, & Palmer, 2008; Thach & Heinselman, 1999; Walker, 2004). Two of the simplest, most straightforward definitions of executive coaching are presented by Ely et al. (in press), "a relationship in which a client engages with a coach in order to facilitate his or her becoming a more effective leader" and Bluckert (2006), "the facilitation of learning and development with the purpose of improving performance and enhancing effective action, goals achievement, and personal satisfaction" (p. 3). Compare those to Kampa and White's (2002) elaborate definition:

> a formal, ongoing relationship between an individual or team having managerial authority and responsibility in an organization and a consultant who possesses knowledge of behavior change and organizational functioning. This relationship has the goal of creating measurable behavior change in the individual or collection of individuals (the team) that results in increased individual and organizational performance and where the relationship between individual or team and consultant facilitates this change by or through giving direct behaviorally based feedback, creating opportunities for change, and demanding accountability. (p. 141)

Although the former definitions may be seen as too broad, the latter is so overspecified that many would disagree with key points, noting that the term *executive coaching* is occasionally used for those without managerial authority, such as highly valued individual contributors and professionals (e.g., lawyers, physicians) and that there are experienced executive coaches who do not necessarily have knowledge of behavior change or organizational functioning, do not necessarily have the goal of creating measurable change, would not include "direct behaviorally based feedback" as a necessary part of coaching, and who do not consider it appropriate to demand accountability. Thus, a definitive, widely agreed-on definition of executive coaching has been elusive. Nonetheless, it is essential to have some type of definition to guide research, training of coaches, and evaluation of coaching effectiveness.

Executive Coaching: Defining Criteria

Given the lack of definitional consensus in the field, the following criteria are used to define executive coaching for this chapter. Executive coaching is:

1. *One-on-one,* as opposed to group or team coaching. Although team coaching is a useful development tool (Diedrich, 2001; Dunlop, 2006) and some view individual and group coaching as roughly equivalent (e.g., Kampa & White, 2002), the processes and outcomes of individual and group coaching are significantly different and worth studying separately (cf. Bloom, 1984). Furthermore, it is not entirely clear how group coaching differs from related practices such as team building, group facilitation, action learning, process consultation, and just-in-time training.
2. *Relationship-based,* assuming a certain level of trust, understanding, and rapport as opposed to primarily content-based development processes (e.g., training, tutoring, self-guided learning).

3. *Methodology-based,* drawing on specific tools and techniques as part of a relatively structured overall process, as opposed to conversations with a trusted advisor or simple feedback and advice-giving.
4. *Provided by a professional coach,* as opposed to coaching provided by a manager, peer, or human resources (HR) professional for whom coaching is not a primary role. In recent years, several organizations have hired professional coaches to work internally (Hunt & Weintraub, 2007), so distinctions between internal and external coaches have become more ambiguous over time.
5. *Scheduled in multiple sessions over time,* which allows for follow-through and accountability, as opposed to one or two conversations as might be seen in multirater survey-based development planning or brief coaching delivered as follow-up to a leadership development program. There is solid evidence that even short-term, focused coaching can be effective (Luthans & Peterson, 2003; Smither, London, Flautt, Vargas, & Kucine, 2003; Smither, London, & Reilly, 2005; Thach, 2002), but it is not the primary focus of this chapter.
6. *Goal-oriented for both organizational and individual benefit.* Executive coaching involves important stakeholders beyond the coach and participant. The goals, values, and expectations of both the participant and the organization are central to the process.
7. *Customized to the person.* Although this criterion may appear obvious, there are instances in which organizations have overreacted to what they perceive to be chaotic and out-of-control coaching activities (Sherman & Freas, 2004) by overregulating and homogenizing their coaching process. By doing so, they lose efficiency and personalization and thus sacrifice some of the unique value that coaching offers (Agarwal, Angst, & Magni, 2006; Witherspoon & White, 1996). Customization may include aspects of the content, style, goals, and scheduling, as well as the mix of tools and techniques that are used.
8. *Intended to enhance the person's ability to learn and develop independently* (Gray, 2006; Peterson, 1996). Although this criterion is less frequently mentioned in the literature than most of the other criteria listed here, its inclusion emphasizes the developmental focus of executive coaching and excludes approaches that foster dependence or long-term reliance on the coach.

Executive Coaching: A Taxonomy of Four Types of Coaches

A second way to clarify the construct of executive coaching is to differentiate the types of coaches on the basis of the primary ways they add value. One approach uses a framework such as the Development Pipeline (Hicks & Peterson, 1999), which outlines the following five necessary and sufficient conditions for learning:

1. *Insight:* The extent to which the person understands which areas he or she needs to develop to be more effective.
2. *Motivation:* The extent to which the person is willing to invest the time and energy it takes to develop specified capabilities.
3. *Capabilities:* The extent to which the person has the necessary skills and knowledge.
4. *Real-world practice:* The extent to which the person applies his or her skills and knowledge at work.
5. *Accountability:* The extent to which the person pays attention to and experiences meaningful consequences for his or her development.

Using this framework, there appear to be four major categories of people who call themselves executive coaches, each of which adds value by focusing on different aspects of the Development Pipeline.

1. *Feedback coaches* focus chiefly on Insight, providing third-party feedback (e.g., interviews with boss, peers, and direct reports; multirater surveys) or instrument-based assessment information (e.g., cognitive abilities tests, personality, interest, values inventories) and helping the person interpret and evaluate the information to identify development themes. Typically feedback coaches meet with participants for only one or two sessions with the ultimate goal of generating a development plan with concrete action steps.

This category includes HR professionals who serve as multirater feedback coaches and some psychologists who provide assessment and consultative development planning services. For example, White and Shullman (2002) described an intensive feedback process involving a multirater survey, four to eight personality inventories (e.g., Myers-Briggs Type Indicator, Myers, McCaulley, Quenk, & Hammer, 1998; California Psychological Inventory, Gough & Bradley, 1996), and a minimum of 14 hour-long interviews with the person's boss, peers, and direct reports, plus friends and family members. The results are presented and reviewed over a 2-day session, from which a development plan is generated.

2. *Insight+Accountability coaches* help the person clarify goals, values, and desires, and then generate specific action steps to accomplish those goals. Accountability is provided when the coach follows up on progress in each subsequent meeting. Many life coaches operate in this style, and the preferred mode of weekly conversations is an excellent way to help people make progress by setting clear short-term goals and then following up to debrief what is working and what is getting in the way of progress (Creane, 2006). Whitmore (2002) described the GROW model (GROW is an acronym for Goal setting, Reality checking, Options for action, and What is to be done; Alexander, 2006; Passmore, 2007b; Whitmore, 2002), a popular tool of many life coaches, as focused on increasing the participant's awareness and responsibility (i.e., Insight and Accountability). Coaches who provide follow-up coaching for leadership development and training programs fit this category as well by helping people solidify the lessons they learned, define action steps, and then stay on track by reviewing their progress periodically over the subsequent few months (Hernez-Broome, 2005).
3. *Content coaches* are experts in particular skills and knowledge areas that executives often need to know. They focus on the Capabilities segment of the Development Pipeline. Examples include presentation and communication coaches, academics and authors who are experts in a particular topic, and former executives who have significant business experience. Zeus and Skiffington (2000) used the term *business coaching* for this category as a way to differentiate content-oriented coaching from process-oriented executive coaching. By most definitions, mentoring fits into this category of content coaching (e.g., "a more experienced individual willing to share their knowledge with someone less experienced," Clutterbuck, 1991, reported in Passmore, 2007c, p. 12). Similarly, consultants and professionals who serve as trusted advisors because of their expertise in business or management issues (Maister, Green, & Galford, 2001; Nadler, 2005; Sheth & Sobel, 2000) would also be content coaches. Although content coaches may use a variety of techniques, such as teaching, skill building, behavioral rehearsal, role-plays, consultative problem solving, and offering feedback and advice, they are all primarily focused on increasing the person's skills and knowledge.
4. *Development-process coaches* are experts in the process of learning and the psychology of human behavior (e.g., interpersonal and group dynamics, personality, adult development, motivation, organizational behavior). Their coaching is oriented to helping people enhance any and all aspects of the Development Pipeline. Coaches in this category often have backgrounds in psychology or other behavioral sciences, extensive consulting experience, and significant life experience dealing with people and their development. Some coaches in the other categories move toward this type of coaching as they gain experience in handling a wider and wider range of client issues. Development-process coaches may follow a relatively consistent, sequential process that systematically addresses each element of the Pipeline (e.g., starting with feedback or assessment to enhance insight, followed by development planning and contracting to tap into motivation, problem-solving discussions and skill building to build capabilities, action planning and transfer techniques to facilitate real-world practice, and concluding with specific follow-up review and debrief to activate accountability), or they may take a constraint-based approach (Goldratt & Cox, 1992) that begins where the person has the

greatest immediate need, then moves to the next greatest constraint, then the next, and so on (Peterson, 2006). For example, the coach may work briefly on insight, move to capabilities, then back to insight, then to accountability as each in turn is identified as the chief barrier to progress.

Executive Coaching: Comparison to Mentoring, Consulting, and Therapy

A third way to clarify the construct of executive coaching is to differentiate it from related practices, such as mentoring, consulting, and therapy. However, similar to the challenges in defining coaching, these fields overlap, and no clear consensus has emerged on the distinctive differentiators. For example, some authors differentiate coaching from therapy by stating that coaching focuses on the present and future and that therapy focuses on the past and present (Hart, Blattner, & Leipsic, 2001; Kauffman & Coutu, 2009). Yet brief therapy (Miller, Hubble, & Duncan, 1996) and cognitive–behavioral methods (Dobson, 1988; Hollon & Beck, 2004) focus just as much on the future as coaching does, and some psychodynamically oriented coaches (e.g., Kilburg, 2000, 2004b) may focus on the person's history as well as the present and future. The lines are still blurred on this dimension.

Coaching and mentoring. The classic distinction is that mentors are people "older, wiser, more experienced, higher in status and formal position" (Bokeno, 2009, p. 6) who share their knowledge and perspective with a less experienced person, whereas coaches play a more facilitative and less of an expert role (Renard, 2005). However, there are clearly coaches who bring a great deal of expertise and share that with clients (e.g., content coaches), just as there are mentors who take a more Socratic approach. Although the discussion continues in an attempt to differentiate mentoring and coaching (Bokeno, 2009; D'Abate et al., 2003), several authors have suggested that mentoring has changed significantly in the past decade (Clutterbuck, 2008) or that there is so much overlap, it is difficult to clearly differentiate the two (Passmore, 2007c; Zeus & Skiffington, 2000). Given that there are counterexamples for virtually every distinction that has been drawn—for example, senior executives in some organizations are being mentored on new uses of technology by much younger employees—the solution may be to cease trying to differentiate the two terms and instead to define clearly an appropriate solution based on the development need and then refer to the intervention by whichever term is preferred (see also chap. 17, this volume).

Coaching and consulting. There are many parallels between the techniques of coaching and consulting, especially in regard to Schein's process consultation (Lambrechts, Grieten, Bouwen, & Corthouts, 2009; Schein, 1999, 2000). Schein (2003) talked about the critical importance of beginning with the relationship rather than with an assessment or technique and then working in partnership to equip the person to be more effective in addressing his or her own needs. From his perspective, an executive coach is essentially a process consultant to an individual. Although it is common to say that consultants provide answers, solutions, and expert advice and coaches do not (e.g., Kauffman & Coutu, 2009), both coaches and consultants seem to cover the entire spectrum of content versus process. Schein's distinction between expertise-based consultation and process consultation parallels the distinction between content coaches and development-process coaches. Thus, it may be difficult to differentiate clearly executive coaching and consultation at an individual level (Tobias, 1996). The major distinction appears to be that coaches are primarily concerned with helping people increase their capabilities and change their own behavior to enhance performance and that consultants focus on helping people solve a specific problem, which may not necessarily require learning new skills or changing one's own behavior.

Coaching and therapy. Of all the comparisons examined in this section, isolating the differences between therapy and coaching is the most important because of the ethical, legal, and professional obligations of therapists and counselors and the largely unregulated arena of coaching. One complication in this comparison is that many coaches have backgrounds in counseling, clinical psychology, and psychodynamic or other therapeutic traditions and have brought their models with them into coaching. Therapists have also contributed a great deal to the professional literature on coaching and frequently suggest that the majority of principles, models, tools, and research findings from therapy are applicable to executive coaching. Nonetheless, the substantial differences in audience, purpose, context, and provider need to be systematically examined to see what might realistically transfer and what might be inappropriate or irrelevant (Thomas, 2006). So it is also important to compare and contrast coaching and therapy to increase our understanding of when and how theories and research might transfer between the two fields and when and how they need to be adapted or disregarded.

Similarities between coaching and therapy include such elements as the importance of the relationship and the active engagement of the client, many of the core skills involved (e.g., listening, questioning, clarifying, feedback, goal setting), and the overarching purpose of assisting the people's development and enhancing their well-being (Bachkirova, 2007). Any comparison of coaching and therapy must acknowledge that each field is quite diverse in itself (Bono, Purvanova, Towler, & Peterson, 2009; Kiesler, 1966) and that there is clearly some degree of overlap between the two (Bachkirova & Cox, 2005; Jopling, 2007). Similarities between coaching and therapy include the importance of the relationship and the active engagement of the client, many of the core skills involved (e.g., listening, questioning, clarifying, feedback, goal setting), and the overarching purpose of assisting the person's development and enhancing his or her well-being (Bachkirova, 2007). Key differences between the two are described in the following paragraphs.

The *purpose* of coaching is to increase work performance, enhance leadership potential, and accelerate development of successful performers. The purpose of therapy is to address a goal that is typically stated as a problem, often related to mood, affect, or personal relationships, that are rarely presenting issues in coaching. Regardless of the coach's approach, there is almost always an expectation of behavioral change to enhance performance at work, whereas in some cases, a therapist is likely to accept a change in affect as sufficient. Meinke, Friedman, Krapu, Kramer, and Salinger (2004) illustrated some of the differences in the types of issues addressed by recommending that coaches refer their clients to a mental health professional when they notice symptoms including feelings of helplessness, hopelessness, or despair; significant changes in appetite; inability to sleep; strong feelings of guilt; increased irritability or outbursts of anger; substance abuse; and thoughts of death or suicide.

The *participants* for executive coaching are drawn from managerial populations and tend to score higher on measures of intelligence, assertiveness, extraversion, adjustment, and well-being than the general population (S. L. Davis & Barnett, 2009; Hughes, Ginnett, & Curphy, 2008). The client base in therapy is much broader, drawing from the entire general population. There is some debate on whether leaders are actually more well adjusted than members of the general population. Some authors argue that many therapy clients are in fact well adjusted—merely seeking help for coping with loss or other types of short-term needs—and that some leaders and coaching clients are not (Bluckert, 2006; Hogan & Hogan, 2001; Nelson & Hogan, 2009). Berglas (2002) took the relatively extreme position that all coaching clients should be assessed before beginning coaching to identify when there are significant psychological problems requiring treatment.

The *providers* in coaching are relatively diverse. They come from backgrounds including management, consulting, training, teaching, sales, psychology, and other helping professions (Grant, 2007), and they may or may not have any formal training in relevant areas such coaching, psychology, or ethics. Although therapists also come from diverse backgrounds and disciplines, they tend to have some formal education in psychology, ethics, and specific therapeutic techniques and skills.

The *stakeholders* in coaching include the coach, participant, and the organization (which is generally paying for the coaching), the latter often represented by the person's boss and HR professional. Thus, there is essentially a dual accountability (Spinelli, 2008). In therapy, there are rarely more than two explicit stakeholders, the therapist and the client, although others may care deeply about the outcome, and the therapist has a relatively clear single accountability to the individual.[2] The nature of

[2] To some extent even this distinction is changing because many therapists no longer work in the private practice model. They work in medical institutions or primary care settings in which their organization monitors costs, customer satisfaction, and patient outcomes, thus becoming an important stakeholder.

the various stakeholder roles and expectations leads to significantly different boundaries for confidentiality as well (Hart et al., 2001).

The *relationship* between the coach and participant is characterized as more egalitarian, whereas the therapist–client relationship is more hierarchical, and the patient may be more vulnerable (Hart et al., 2001; Spinelli, 2008). Therapists in general have greater training and experience in identifying and working in the moment with relationship-related issues such as transference and countertransference, which many executive coaches are not aware of (Frisch & Lee, 2009; Spinelli, 2008).

COACHING COMPETENCIES

The challenges in defining coaching extend to identifying the competencies of an effective coach (Ferrar, 2004). Quite a few authors have offered their perspectives on coaching competencies (e.g., Ahern, 2003; Auerbach, 2006; Bluckert, 2006; Brotman, Liberi, & Wasylyshyn, 1998; Hawkins & Smith, 2006; Homan & Miller, 2008; Poteet & Kudisch, 2007), but there is virtually no empirical validation of any specific competencies. This section discusses two competency models.

A Comparison of Two Models

The two competency models discussed here were chosen because they are among the few developed by established coaching organizations through extensive reviews of the literature and in close consultation with coaching experts and because the contrast between the two highlights some of the challenges in such a task.

Executive Coaching Forum model. The Executive Coaching Forum (ECF, 2008) model begins with a summary of the value of competency models for four important stakeholders:

- organizations that hire coaches to provide coaching services to their employees,
- executives who are choosing a coach,
- coaches planning their own development, and
- designers of training programs and curricula for executive coaches.

It is important to include a fifth audience—coaching researchers—because none of the currently available competency models have been empirically validated. In fact, although there is significant convergence among experts on a core set of coaching competencies (e.g., active listening and communication skills, assessment and feedback skills, integrity, empathy), there is no research demonstrating that these competencies actually differentiate effective and ineffective performance in coaches. The authors of the ECF model are well aware of this and explicitly note the tentative and preliminary nature of their model, a rarity in this arena.

The ECF competency model is organized into three major sections, each with lists and descriptions of both basic and advanced competencies. The first section, coaching competencies, provides one of the most comprehensive descriptions of the various types of knowledge critical to successful coaching:

- psychological knowledge, including an understanding of personality, motivation, learning and behavior change, adult developmental theories, stress management, emotional intelligence, and social psychology;
- business acumen, including an understanding of basic business practices and financial concepts, management principles and processes, and HR management;
- organizational knowledge, including an understanding of organizational structures and functions, organizational design, organizational culture, team effectiveness, leadership models, systems theory, consulting theory and practices, business ethics, and leadership development; and
- coaching knowledge, including an understanding of executive coaching models and theories, coaching competencies, specific coaching practices (e.g., managing confidentiality, assessment, goal setting), various roles of a coach, coaching research, and developing oneself as a coach.

The ECF's second section surveys in considerable detail the specific tasks and skills required for six phases of the coaching process (i.e., building and maintaining relationships, contracting, assessment, development planning, facilitating development and change, ending formal coaching and transitioning to long-term development). Finally, it lists nine categories of general attributes and abilities: mature self-confidence, positive energy, assertiveness, interpersonal sensitivity, openness and flexibility, goal orientation, partnering and influence, continuous learning and development, integrity.

Worldwide Association of Business Coaching model. The Worldwide Association of Business Coaching's (WABC, 2007) competency model is divided into three sections:

- self-management: knowing oneself and self-mastery, including self-regulation, integrity, adaptability, emphasizing excellence, initiative, and creativity and innovation;
- core coaching skill base, including contracting, developing the relationship, communicating and promoting client understanding, facilitating the personal transformation, and professional development; and
- business and leadership coaching capabilities, including systems thinking, understanding organizational behavior, aligning coaching with business needs, assessment, respecting diversity and multicultural issues, being a role model, and managing one's own coaching business.

Compared with the ECF model, the WABC model is less detailed regarding the specific types of knowledge required. However, it places much greater emphasis on the coach's self-awareness and self-management and, in general, reflects a more humanistic, constructivist philosophical bent. Although research is needed to validate the elements included, both models may still serve as educational guides for those seeking to understand the vast domain of potentially important coaching skills and knowledge.

Competence in Coaching: Easy to Be Good, Hard to Be Great?

Given the large number of new coaches entering the field (Grant & Cavanagh, 2004; Hamlin et al., 2008; Liljenstrand & Nebeker, 2008) and that there are virtually no barriers to entry, there are significant reasons to be concerned about coaches' qualifications and the quality of coaching that is being delivered (Grant & Cavanagh, 2007; Platt, 2008; Sherman & Freas, 2004; Thomas, 2006). In fact, it is not difficult to find people with barely more than a weekend's study who have launched their own coaching business. Some organizations have responded by seeking only certified coaches. Unfortunately, there are no generally accepted standards for certification, and coaches can receive certification simply on the basis of attending a 2-day program. As Wellner (2006) noted, "Anyone, with any amount of experience, can crown himself coach and start offering advice. Hairstylists face more stringent licensing procedures" (p. 88).

However, for a surprisingly large number of reasons, it is fairly easy to become a reasonably effective coach, especially for anyone with a solid base of intelligence, maturity, emotional intelligence, and basic social and communication skills (Bluckert, 2006; Peterson, 2009). People from a variety of backgrounds, such as HR, training, consulting, management, and education, have often already acquired skills and knowledge that readily transfer to coaching. Consider the following activities, all of which potentially contribute to the effectiveness of coaching, and yet require virtually no coaching experience or training:

- offering an external, independent, objective perspective;
- creating space and time for reflection (Burke & Linley, 2007);
- identifying development goals and preparing an action plan;
- sharing ideas, tips, tools, and models;
- facilitating an accepting, positive, supportive, encouraging relationship (O'Broin & Palmer, 2007; Uhl-Bien, 2003; in the therapeutic literature, the relationship is often seen as one of the primary factors contributing to positive outcomes; Bachelor & Horvath, 1999; Horvath & Bedi, 2002; Lambert & Barley, 2002);
- providing follow-up conversations that foster a sense of accountability, especially if the person makes a commitment to the coach to pursue a specific action (Goldsmith & Morgan, 2004); and
- simply asking the person what would be helpful and responding accordingly.

Add to this set of activities the following, which require minimal experience or training and are also likely to contribute to positive outcomes in coaching:

- asking questions that challenge assumptions and help reframe issues;
- offering feedback and advice, including third-party feedback from interviews or multirater surveys (Levenson, 2009);
- spaced practice and repetition; and
- using simple coaching formulas such as the GROW model, a basic and popular framework for coaching conversations.

Finally, one of the most significant reasons that it is relatively easy to be a good coach—and yet one that is virtually never mentioned in the literature—is that coaches get multiple tries. That is, if their first attempt to be helpful on a particular issue is not effective, they can offer a second and even a third option. Coaches have the advantage of being able to gauge the person's reaction through verbal and non-verbal cues and respond in real time with a more suitable effort. The coach's ability to read the person's reactions and respond with new alternatives affords a significant opportunity to produce powerful results.

Although it appears to be relatively easy to be a reasonably competent coach, for a number of reasons it is extremely difficult to become an expert at coaching, not the least of which is the diverse range of skills and knowledge evident in the extensive lists of coaching competencies just summarized. The distinction here between reasonably competent and expert coaching parallels the work on what is required to develop expertise and world-class performance (Colvin, 2008; Ericsson, 2006).

One of the major reasons that it is difficult to become a great coach is that the coaching process unfolds over a relatively long period of time, and feedback on outcomes is slow and distal. Any immediate feedback is likely to be related to satisfaction or specific substeps in the process, not to the ultimate objectives of coaching. Because coaching is a complex, elaborate process, it is difficult to identify causal connections between specific actions and the final outcome, especially given all the other things that might take place concurrently in a coaching participant's life. Thus, it is difficult for coaches to discover whether what they are doing is truly effective, which makes it easy to maintain their belief system about what works and simply to continue doing what they have always done. In fact, when coaching is not successful, it is often easy for coaches to place responsibility for the failure on the participant or external circumstances—especially because they see that their approach has generally been successful in the past—rather than examine what they could have done differently.

The research on developing great expertise for complex tasks such as chess, musical performance, and medical diagnosis suggests that at least 10,000 hours of practice are required (Colvin, 2008). The term *practice* refers here to either engaging in the actual task with the specific intention of improving one's performance or to rehearsing specific, isolated elements of the activity in a different setting. Both types of practice require feedback of some kind to evaluate success. The two can be combined, such as when a coach practices various ways to deliver a difficult feedback message in advance of a coaching session, reflecting on which might best accomplish the desired effect, and then tries out the selected message in an actual coaching session, observing the person's response and directly asking the participant for feedback on his or her reactions to that message.

In addition to the sheer number of hours, Ericsson (2006) pointed out the need for specific, deliberate practice. Deliberate practice is significantly different from merely engaging in an activity (Colvin, 2008). Deliberate practice requires conscious attention to improving performance, continuous feedback, and frequent repetition with the opportunity to self-correct and try alternate variations (Colvin, 2008; Ericsson, 2006). Colvin further pointed out that deliberate practice requires significant effort and "isn't much fun" (2008, p. 71). Given that coaching is a complex activity with a long cycle time to evaluate final outcomes, it is plausible that it would take more than 10,000 hours to develop world-class expertise.

Finally, certain parts of the coaching process are easier and more seductive than others, and some coaches never develop their capabilities beyond those facets. For example, asking powerful questions, generating insight, and sharing advice are relatively easy, quick, and tangible activities. When they are perceived as useful, the coach gets credit immediately. In contrast, facilitating real-world practice and ensuring on-the-job application of new behaviors is relatively slow, tedious, and difficult. The participant has to do the majority of the work, and success is rarely directly attributable to the coach. Yet it is absolutely necessary for real change and results. So coaches may gravitate toward the relatively easy, more rewarding aspects of coaching in which they are seen as directly adding value rather than persist in the more difficult and less immediately rewarding tasks of ensuring that people stick with their learning and make progress when it is slow and tedious.

THE COACHING PROCESS

Many authors describe a sequence of steps or stages in the coaching process. Bluckert's (2006) six-stage process is representative: (a) engagement and contracting, (b) assessment and feedback, (c) creating the coaching agenda, (d) structuring the coaching intervention, (e) delivering the coaching, and (f) review and evaluation. Although recognizing the value of this type of depiction in providing structure and clarity to coaches and participants, stepwise descriptions of the coaching process generally fail to capture important elements. First, building a relationship of trust and understanding is essential to the entire coaching engagement. Although it is not made explicit in his coaching process, Bluckert (2006) elsewhere emphasized the fundamental importance of the relationship and offered useful insights into establishing and maintaining the working alliance. Ghods (2009) noted that despite the prevalence in the coaching literature of discussions regarding the importance of the relationship, few models specify it clearly. Second, step models generally leave the actual delivery of coaching (Step 5 in Bluckert's model) unspecified. Because this is where the majority of the time is spent and the real learning occurs, it leaves the impression that coaching is a black box and raises questions about what is really taking place. Third, such models portray coaching as relatively mechanical and linear, with little tailoring to the individual. In reality, coaching is fluid, constantly evolving, and different for each person. Finally, the broader context is often absent from step models. Although it may be assumed, there is no mention of helping participants apply what they learn in the coaching conversation back in the workplace environment. Step models overemphasize the clear, tactical aspects of the engagement and coaching sessions, leave the less tangible elements unspecified, and ignore the wide variability in what coaching actually looks like in practice.

The Society for Organizational Learning's (n.d.) process offers a distinctly different perspective, especially in terms of referencing the coaching relationship and the broader context: (a) Enter the coaching relationship, (b) establish and commit to or renew the coaching relationship, (c) clarify aspirations and current reality, (d) set goals for development in a systems context, (e) support learning in action, (f) coach to full potential, (g) create sustainable results, and (h) exit the coaching relationship. In addition to expanding the description of the actual coaching, the Society includes three activities labeled *recursive elements* because they occur throughout the coaching process: partnered reflection for learning and results (debriefing what has been learned and action steps), generative conversations (raising awareness, exploring assumptions), and community of practice (sharing learning with other coaches and with the organization about what has been learned about coaching and about the organization).

Kilburg's (2000) process model references five components of coaching interventions, thus avoiding the notion of discrete steps. His components are (a) developing an intervention agreement, (b) building a coaching relationship, (c) creating and managing expectations of coaching success, (d) providing an experience of behavioral mastery or cognitive control over the problems and issues, and (e) evaluating and attributing coaching success or failure in each session. His description of the fourth component illuminates the delivery of coaching, and he included a detailed list of specific coaching techniques in his framework. It should be noted as well that Kilburg's (2000, 2001, 2002) work is perhaps the best example of addressing the complexities at every level of the coaching process—the psychodynamics of the participant, the psychology of the learning process, the dynamics of the coaching relationship, and the intricate realities of the organizational context.

Another approach to the coaching process addresses constraints and challenges to the participant's learning as they are identified rather than following a predetermined set of steps. Such constraint-based approaches lead to a customized and differentiated coaching process for each participant. Peterson and Hicks (1996; Peterson, 2006), for example, specified six critical issues for the coach to address as needed: the coaching relationship, insight, motivation, capabilities, real-world practice, and accountability. Participants who enter coaching with a clear sense of their learning objectives may require minimal or no assessment. Conversely, participants who wish to accelerate their career progress but are uncertain exactly what they need to do so might engage in a comprehensive leadership assessment. This conceptual framework and customized approach has the advantage of efficiency, allowing coaches to focus their attention on what will make the biggest impact and helping participants learn more in a shorter time. It is not, however, a procedural outline and thus can be more difficult to learn and more challenging to explain to participants and their sponsors.

It is evident from the variety of approaches outlined here that there is no simple answer to how to define the coaching process. Each framework along this spectrum, from relatively linear step models to customized, contextual models, has strengths and weaknesses, and coaches are encouraged to explore multiple models and borrow from them to develop their own perspective.

SIX DIMENSIONS FOR EXAMINING EXECUTIVE COACHING

As a framework for an in-depth examination of executive coaching, this chapter considers six dimensions that are core to the coaching process: the coaching relationship plus the five necessary and sufficient conditions for systematic development—insight, motivation, capabilities, real-world practice, and accountability—proposed by Hicks and Peterson (1999; Peterson, 2006).

The Coaching Relationship

The *coaching relationship* refers to the extent to which the working alliance or partnership between the coach and participant is characterized by trust, acceptance, understanding, open, honest communication, and other interpersonal factors that support learning and development. To date there has been little research on the coaching relationship (O'Broin & Palmer, 2007), although a great deal has been written by practitioners based on their experience and extrapolation from research on the working alliance in therapeutic relationships (e.g., Bachelor & Horvath, 1999; Lambert & Barley, 2002). The majority of research actually conducted on the relationship in executive coaching is based on interviews or surveys of participants, who consistently report that trust and a positive working relationship are among the most important, if not the single most important, elements of effective coaching (Baron & Morin, 2009; Bush, 2005; Creane, 2006; Dembkowski, Eldridge, & Hunter, 2006; Gyllensten & Palmer, 2007; Hall et al., 1999; Luebbe, 2005; Wales, 2003; Wasylyshyn, 2003). Trudeau (2004), using a modified Delphi technique, including an extensive review of the coaching literature and interviews with subject matter experts, identified establishing a coaching relationship as the first phase of eight critical components of coaching. Alvey and Barclay (2007) found that clear expectations about confidentiality and a nonjudgmental attitude from the coach enhance trust and therefore strengthen the coaching relationship. Additional evidence for the importance of the relationship is provided by analysis of the causes of premature termination or other breakdowns of the coaching process, which include inadequate trust and lack of chemistry (Dembkowski et al., 2006; Marshall, 2006; Noer, 2000). Thompson et al. (2008) reported that, in their survey of users of coaching, the number one reason that coaching engagements fail (81% of the time) is a mismatch between coach and participant. They do not specify the exact nature of the mismatch, but the other items on their list (e.g., coach's lack of expertise) imply that it is due to a mismatch on elements of the relationship, such as lack of chemistry or poor personality fit.

There are at least three ways in which the coaching relationship is important in coaching. First, having a relationship of trust and open communication in a safe, supportive environment in which the person feels accepted and understood is a prerequisite for most types of coaching. Participants must trust coaches sufficiently to engage with them; openly share their development needs, personal weaknesses, and concerns; and take risks and try new things (Wales, 2003). The coach needs to listen attentively and demonstrate understanding and acceptance of what matters to the person. These two aspects of the relationship—trust and understanding—need to be established quickly (Gyllensten & Palmer, 2007) and will then tend to deepen over time as the two work together. However, coaches need to be sensitive to maintaining the level of trust because it can still be disrupted through negligence or a careless act. Therefore, coaches need to monitor and assess the quality of the working relationship throughout the engagement. It is possible that the nature of the relationship may evolve over time in other ways. Prochaska and Norcross (2001) suggested that the working relationship needs to adapt to the person's needs at each of the six stages of change outlined in the transtheoretical model of change: precontemplation, contemplation, preparation, action, maintenance, and termination (Prochaska & DiClemente, 1984). Similarly, Grant (2006) discussed the greater need for the coach to focus on support, encouragement, and motivation early in the process, to engage the person fully and increase the likelihood of sustaining commitment to achieving the desired outcomes. Although a basic level of trust and rapport is necessary for all coaching, it is likely that greater levels of trust and a stronger working relationship are necessary, for example, when the person has had negative experiences with past coaches, does not trust his or her manager, is skeptical of the coaching process, does not see the need for coaching, is working in a politically charged organizational environment, or the boundaries of confidentiality and communication are not clear.

The second way the coaching relationship is important is that it may serve as a tool that the coach uses to facilitate certain aspects of the change process. For example, the coach may intentionally act more challenging and skeptical or more warm and supportive at times, or he or she may use self-disclosure as an explicit way to illustrate an important principle. Depending on the development needs of the participant, the coach might use aspects of the relationship to role model appropriate behaviors for the person, such as conveying empathy, listening nonjudgmentally, or expressing appreciation.

Third, the coaching relationship itself may be a vehicle of change for at least some participants. A number of coaches have argued that the relationship is actually the most significant factor in effective coaching (e.g., Kemp 2008a, 2008b; McKenna & Davis, 2009), largely on the basis of analogy to therapeutic findings. The therapy research on the working relationship was nicely summed up by Highlen and Hill (1984), who concluded that "clients have always consistently attributed success in therapy to relationship factors, whereas therapists have associated outcome success with their techniques and skill" (p. 360). This perception is not surprising but may be misleading. At a minimum, the relationship is the most tangible and significant thing that participants experience. They may in fact interpret the coach's techniques as aspects of the relationship itself. For example, a coach who offers carefully timed, well-structured feedback or a provocative question might be perceived as either supportive and helpful or as challenging and confrontational, which the participant perceives as a direct aspect of their relationship and its degree of trust, openness, honesty, and acceptance.

McKenna and Davis (2009) argued that coaches should expect to find the same balance of active ingredients in coaching as Asay and Lambert (1999) summarized for therapy: 40% of therapeutic change is attributable to factors in the client or outside the therapeutic setting; 30% to the relationship itself; 15% results from expectancy, hope, and placebo effects; and only 15% appears to result from the techniques and actions of the therapist. However, McKenna and Davis, along with others who take this position, did little to justify that the audience, needs, and conditions of coaching are similar enough to warrant this conclusion. In contrast, it might be argued that the research on training outcomes (e.g., Lawton-Smith & Cox, 2007; MacKie, 2007) or action learning (e.g., Carson & Marquardt, 2004)—in which the audience and purpose and many of the techniques are quite similar to coaching—are a more appropriate comparison than therapy, which appears similar to coaching on the surface but differs more fundamentally on audience and purpose. At best, one might reasonably conclude that the coaching relationship itself might be a more relevant factor in coaching contexts that resemble therapy (e.g., addressing anger management, aggression, or personal values) and less of a factor in contexts that resemble training (e.g., addressing strategic thinking or learning other management skills). Palmer (2007) also argued against the primacy of the relationship as the causal mechanism of coaching's effectiveness, pointing out that many of the techniques used in coaching are effective even when a coach is not involved. Using a randomized experimental design, Grbcic and Palmer (2006) found statistically significant improvement in the group using self-coaching with specific cognitive–behavioral techniques and no improvement in the control group.

As necessary as the relationship is as a condition for doing the work of coaching, it is unlikely that it is a sufficient condition for effecting significant leadership development. This does not necessarily conflict with client reports that the relationship is the most important element of the coaching process. It is quite possible that participants would not recognize the specific techniques or methodology that a coach is using and may in fact experience and interpret certain techniques as aspects of the relationship. For example, coaches who thoughtfully explore participants' motivations, goals, and values might be perceived as simply being interested in them, caring about them, and helping them.

Overall, it seems clear that there is a minimum threshold of trust and rapport for a lasting and effective working relationship in coaching (MacKie, 2007). When the relationship does not surpass that threshold, participants are likely to drop out of coaching (Thompson et al., 2008). As a result, research on the role of the relationship in coaching is likely to show greater effects in examining persistence or duration in coaching, and it would be helpful to understand what relationship related behaviors and attitudes are related to drop out versus completion of coaching. The relationship may also be a more significant factor in short-term coaching, in which the ability of a coach to establish rapport and trust quickly could conceivably have a large impact. There may be other settings, such as distance coaching, in which the quality of the relationship makes a difference. Berry (2005) examined the relationship in distance coaching compared with face-to-face coaching and found a significant relationship between the coach-reported quality of the relationship and coaching outcomes in distance coaching but not in the face-to-face condition.

A wealth of practical advice is available on building trust and effective working relationships in coaching (e.g., Auerbach, 2001; Bacon & Spear, 2003; O'Connor & Lages, 2007; Peterson & Hicks, 1996; Stober 2006; Whitworth, Kimsey-House, & Sandahl, 1998). Some useful and interesting advice is also emerging from the relatively new fields of positive psychology (e.g., Biswas-Diener & Dean, 2007; Kauffman, 2006) and social neuroscience (e.g., Rock & Page, 2009; Waring, 2008). Rock's (2008; Rock & Page, 2009) SCARF model outlines five domains of human social experience—Status, Certainty, Autonomy, Relatedness, and Fairness—that he viewed as biologically wired to activate a reward or threat response in social environments. Several of these domains have direct implications for the coaching relationship, although research support for their actual impact in coaching is lacking. For example, he suggested that the human brain often responds automatically to advice and feedback as a possible threat to one's status. Coaches who position themselves as experts, side with the participant's boss, and launch immediately into feedback are thus more likely to activate this type of defensive limbic system response, which inhibits learning. Coaches who are accepting, positive, supportive, curious, and actively engage the person in defining his or her own goals are more likely to activate positive brain responses, such as increased dopamine levels, which are conducive to activities related to learning such as reflection, cognitive processing, taking risks, and persisting in challenging situations (Fredrickson, 2009). Autonomy, the sense of having choices and control over one's environment, can be threatened when people feel that they are being forced to participate in coaching or forced to make changes they dislike. Coaches can reduce the threat and enhance the relationship by offering choices, enhancing self-efficacy, and showing people where they can increase their sense of control over their involvement in coaching and at work. Relatedness—the sense of being included or excluded from a group—can be positively activated by behaving in accord with the traditional Rogerian values of unconditional positive regard, acceptance, and warmth (Rogers, 1957). Relatedness can be negatively activated simply by being around strangers, especially strangers who belong to different groups (such as psychologists) and who use unfamiliar jargon.

Insight

Insight refers to the extent to which people understand what areas they need to develop to be more effective. In many coaching models, there is a strong emphasis on feedback as the primary tool for insight, with some authors viewing feedback as a defining aspect of coaching itself (e.g., Feldman & Lankau, 2005; Kampa & White, 2002). Such a major focus on feedback, which is really the means to the end, obscures the end goal itself, which is insight—clarity about the person's most important development objectives. Insight about development priorities can be obtained through a variety of methods, including feedback from others (whether gathered firsthand, through the coach, or a multirater survey), reflection and self-assessment, self-monitoring and behavioral recording, and inventories and surveys on personality, abilities, values, or leadership style. However, optimal insight into one's development needs requires an understanding and analysis of four types of information (Peterson & Hicks, 1996): (a) knowledge of the person's own goals, values, and motivations; (b) how the person perceives his or her own abilities, style, and performance; (c) how others perceive the person (i.e., feedback from others); and (d) the success factors for a given role, including what others expect from the person. Respectively, these four elements are labeled Goals and Values, Abilities, Perceptions, and Success Factors (GAPS; Peterson, 2006).

It is common for many coaching engagements to begin with feedback, or perceptions data, when in fact the most productive place to start is by gaining an understanding of what matters to the person—his or her goals, values, and motivations. Although how to work with and enhance motivation is addressed in the next section of this chapter, finding out what matters to people is an essential component of insight, as well as a way to build the coaching relationship. So, for a variety of reasons, coaches often begin a coaching engagement by attending to participants' goals and values at several levels—what they would like to accomplish in coaching and how they would like to work together with the coach, as well as life and career goals, personal aspirations, values, and motivations. With this foundation, coaches can connect the data from other people—Success Factors and Perceptions—to what matters to the person. If there is no perceived connection between external data and the person's Goals and Values, the participant will tend to dismiss it either passively by ignoring it or actively through debate or defensiveness. Coaches can enhance the person's insight into his or her Goals and Values by asking questions that encourage the person to reflect on what matters to them and by discussing the person's choices and what values seem to be guiding them. They can also use tools, such as interest and values inventories or card sorts, designed to clarify motivations.

Next, it is most helpful to examine Success Factors data. This can begin by asking participants what they think it takes to be successful in their roles. Ultimately, however, Success Factors data must come from the other key stakeholders, which might include the boss, the boss's boss, and other senior executives, as well as peers, direct reports, customers, and others. Participants can talk with them directly, observe what they pay attention to, and talk with others to assess what contributes to success or failure in those roles. Other information may also be helpful, such as what is addressed in performance reviews, competency models, and organizational vision, mission, and values statements. As important as Success Factors information is, it is surprising how often managers do not regularly communicate to their employees what matters in the job. The Gallup survey of more than 80,000 employees found that responses to the question "Do I know what is expected of me at work?" are the most predictive correlates of productivity and performance (Buckingham & Coffman, 1999). Success Factors data are by nature multidimensional, representing a variety of different perspectives (e.g., boss, peer, direct reports) and domains (e.g., behavior, results, values, relationships, attitude). Coaches can often add real value by helping people sort through the data to determine what they think is most important and what they wish to focus on, given their own goals and values.

Next, coaches can help people evaluate their own portfolio of strengths and weaknesses (i.e., Abilities data) relative to the Success Factors. Finally, coaches can make sure the person has an accurate view of how others view the person (i.e., Perceptions). As noted earlier, Perceptions data can come from a variety of sources. The coach can facilitate gathering feedback through interviews and multirater instruments, as well as incorporating appropriate tests and inventories to provide additional perspectives on abilities, personality, and style. However, one of the main values of coaching is to teach people how to develop themselves, including how to gather and interpret feedback from others (Peterson & Hicks, 1995).

Note that multirater feedback surveys, which are frequently used in executive coaching (Kauffman & Coutu, 2009), incorporate three aspects of GAPS information. The individual survey items and dimensions represent behaviors and competencies that are viewed as Success Factors in a management role. Ratings by self and others are Abilities and Perceptions data, respectively. However, the multirater literature seems to assume that the observer ratings are somehow more accurate than the self-ratings, concluding that individuals overrate themselves (Eichinger & Lombardo, 2003). Coaches generally find that accepting both views as providing useful information from the perspective of the rater is a helpful way to frame the information. After the different perspectives are clearly understood, the coach and participant can discuss possible reasons for any significant differences and then decide together how the participant might wish to respond.

In addition to multirater surveys, executive coaches use a variety of methods to gather information for enhancing insight, including interviews with the participant, supervisor, and peers; ability or aptitude tests; interest and personality inventories; objective performance data from the organization; and role-plays and simulations (Bono et al., 2009). However, coaches from different philosophical perspectives may use distinctly different tools and approaches. Advocates of positive psychology, for example, gravitate toward assessments of strengths, optimism, courage, and positive emotions (Lopez & Snyder, 2003; O'Connor & Lages, 2007). Organizational consultants often emphasize multirater surveys, organizational input, and standardized assessment instruments. Developmental coaches tend to assess the participant's developmental level (Berger & Fitzgerald, 2002; Laske 1999). Humanistic and phenomenologically oriented coaches generally place greater emphasis on exploring the person's own goals and values and processing the meaning of real-time behavior. W. G. Lawrence (2006) even advocated that coaches explore the client's dreams and unconscious as a means to enhancing insight.

Like many practices within coaching, the use of assessments and feedback methods in coaching seems to be driven by the coach's philosophical perspective and familiarity with specific instruments. Little information is available on how and when to use various methods and their relative contribution to coaching process and outcome. Passmore's (2008) volume is a useful step in this direction, discussing a number of psychometric instruments and how they may be best used in coaching. Barner (2006) took a similar step forward by proposing three approaches to tailor the coaching interview to gather the information most relevant to remedial, developmental, or transition coaching.

As a final note, a rarely questioned assumption of coaching is that assessment is only done at the beginning of coaching and perhaps at the conclusion as an outcome evaluation. This is explicitly defined in almost every model of the coaching process (e.g., Bluckert, 2006). However, from a constraint-based perspective on coaching, assessment, and feedback may occur at any point in the coaching process, whenever low levels of insight prevent further development. For example, relatively insightful and motivated clients might have a clear sense of what they wish to work on at the outset of coaching. Additional assessment and feedback might be helpful to some degree, but in most cases, it merely confirms what is already known and simply slows their momentum. As participants make significant progress on their objectives, they may decide with their coach that additional insight would be helpful, and they can consider together the advantages of gathering feedback or using other methods such as personality and leadership style inventories. Often, participants are more receptive and even hungry for additional insight after they have experienced significant gains and see how a clearer picture of Success Factors or Perceptions might be useful.

Although most coaches would agree that the participant's level of insight tends to increase throughout the entire coaching process, few seem manage the process to actively and strategically to facilitate insight at those times when the participant is most likely to benefit, rather than simply offering an assessment of needs at a single point in time.

Motivation

Motivation in coaching and development activities can be analyzed from three perspectives (see also Vol. 3, chap. 3, this handbook). First is the person's overall motivational makeup in terms of drives, such as need for achievement, power, and affiliation (Latham & Pinder, 2005). Ultimately, coaching is a means to an end, and the participant's fundamental motivation to engage in coaching and development is contingent on their perception that it will lead to fulfilling some desired goal or need. Typically, the more the coach knows about the person's core values and motivational makeup, the better the coach can tailor the coaching and the working relationship itself to the person's needs and personality. A person with a high need for status, for example, might value examples and illustrations from other highly regarded leaders and organizations, whereas a person with a high achievement drive would be more concerned about finding a technique that he or she could use successfully, regardless of who else might be using it. Understanding the participant's motivational profile can also help the coach understand potential strengths and weaknesses that might be addressed in coaching (e.g., Spreier, Fontaine, & Malloy, 2006).

The second aspect of motivation in coaching is the person's drive and approach to learning and development in general. This includes constructs such as learning or performance orientation (Dweck, 1986, 2000), locus of control (Colquitt, LePine, & Noe, 2000), self-efficacy (Bandura, 1997), proactivity (Major, Turner, & Fletcher, 2006), and trait anxiety (low levels being better for learning; Bell & Kozlowski, 2008). In contrast to the first set of motivational factors, which are relatively enduring, these constructs appear to be more malleable, and coaches who work to enhance them are likely to achieve greater, more long-lasting results (Biswas-Diener & Dean, 2007). Many situational aspects of the work environment, including supervisor support, organizational climate, and the perceived consequences of behavior change, also affect motivation (Colquitt et al., 2000).

The third consideration is the participant's motivation to work on specific development needs or learning objectives. If needed, a coach can influence this type of motivation in a number of ways, including connecting development objectives to the person's intrinsic motivations, increasing the person's sense of autonomy and control over their choices and related outcomes (Heatherton & Nichols, 1994; Ryan & Deci, 2008), breaking down learning tasks into small, manageable steps, and identifying and addressing perceived barriers.

Three frameworks are particularly useful for addressing motivation in coaching. First, motivational interviewing (Miller & Rollnick, 2002; Passmore, 2007a) is designed specifically to address ambivalent motivations, where a person's long-term goal requires discipline and sustained effort (e.g., working on one's personal development) but the short-term behavioral alternative (e.g., checking e-mail) is easier and often more immediately reinforcing. Second is the transtheoretical model of change (Prochaska & DiClemente, 1984; Prochaska & Norcross, 2001), in which the first three stages—precontemplation, contemplation, and preparation—are primarily related to insight and motivation. The referenced works include many helpful suggestions that can be applied to coaching.

Finally, the goal-setting literature (Locke & Latham, 1990, 2002) is rich with advice on how to set goals to enhance motivation and performance. However, goal-setting techniques that lead to the best performance (e.g., set specific, difficult goals) do not always lead to the best learning. When the task is complex and novel, learning goals generally result in higher performance than specific outcome goals and "do your best" goals (Latham, Seijts, & Crim, 2008). There is also a growing literature on conflicts and choices between multiple goals (Beck, Gregory, & Carr, 2009) that is extremely useful for coaches to understand. When faced with multiple goals and insufficient time, people are more likely to work on goals for which they perceive greater urgency (Ashford & Northcraft, 2003), in which they are receiving more feedback, and goals that they feel are more likely to be achieved (Schmidt & Dolis, 2009).

Capabilities

Coaches can help participants gain new skills and knowledge through a wide variety of techniques, including sharing advice, ideas, and best practices; helping people find appropriate resources and opportunities to learn; exploring alternative ways to handle difficult situations; and practicing new skills and behaviors in realistic situations.

Druckman and Bjork (1991) reviewed the extant literature to identify the training and development principles most associated with effective skill learning, transfer, and retention. By its very nature, coaching tends to incorporate several of the principles they identified, such as using spaced practice; actively engaging the learner in the process through conversation, reflection, and goal-setting; and integrating new knowledge with existing knowledge.

However, Druckman and Bjork (1991) described a trade-off between the most effective methods for acquiring skills (i.e., building capabilities) and for helping people transfer and apply their skills in real-world practice. For example, massed practice is often the quickest way to learn a skill, but spaced practice leads to greater retention. Working on one simple skill in isolation, such as active listening, leads to rapid learning but tends to inhibit transfer to situations that demand use of multiple skills simultaneously. Techniques that enhance transfer and generalization, such as practicing complex, difficult situations with significant interference and distractions, tend to inhibit rapid learning and are often less enjoyable for the participant (Druckman & Bjork, 1991). This dynamic tension between short-term learning and longer-term retention highlights an implicit choice that coaches make between focusing on the learning experience within the coaching conversation and what participants do to apply their learning when they leave. As noted previously, there is often a greater seductive appeal for the coach to get positive feedback on having a great coaching session where participants feel that they really learned something than there is in having them leave with a sense that they really struggled and are not exactly comfortable with their new skills. Yet the latter may be more valuable in the long run.

Two of the Druckman and Bjork (1991) principles, in fact, are likely to be relatively difficult for some coaches to incorporate into their work. Increasing the cognitive and affective demands on the participant by raising the level of challenge, interference, and emotional intensity requires many coaches to step out of their comfort zone and may stress the working relationship between the two. Diminishing feedback over time is also difficult for some coaches because it takes the focus off of them. However, it is very important to ensuring lasting results because participants need to learn to generate independently their own feedback and evaluate the effectiveness of their behaviors.

Another aspect of building capabilities is equipping people to be effective self-directed learners. Teaching and encouraging participants to seek feedback for themselves, reflect on their learning and progress, self-monitor behavior, adapt and plan new actions, engage others to support their learning, and so on (Peterson & Hicks, 1995, 1996) enhances learning, intensifies the effects of coaching, and ensures that progress will be maintained. Furthermore, it reduces the risk of creating overdependence on the coach (Berglas, 2002; Noer, 2000).

Many coaches believe that giving advice is inappropriate in coaching (O'Connor & Lages, 2007), claiming the focus should be on asking questions to help people generate their own insights and ideas. Many clients also value this approach (Bacon & Spear, 2003). Research from neuroscience (Rock & Page, 2009) and social psychology (Ryan & Deci,

2008) shows that people are more likely to value and act on self-generated ideas and choices. Yet advice giving is common, even among coaches who claim they disagree with the practice (Stein, 2008). Therefore, it is important for coaches to understand when it is actually useful or appropriate (Carr, 2009; Cunningham, 2008) and when participants are most likely to heed it (Gino, 2008; Gino & Schweitzer, 2008). Participants experiencing negative affect (e.g., defensiveness, anger) are less receptive to advice and suggestions, and those experiencing positive affect (e.g., gratitude) are more receptive. Advice is better accepted from those perceived to be experts, when the problem is complex and unfamiliar, and when a high price has been paid for the advice (Gino & Schweitzer, 2008). Content coaches (i.e., experts) working with motivated participants on challenging capabilities may thus find their advice is welcomed, whereas coaches working with defensive participants on what are perceived to be simple topics such as listening and relationship-building may find their advice repeatedly spurned.

In summary, capability building is a more complex and artful aspect of coaching than many perceive. Coaches who use a wide range of techniques and understand when and where to use them appropriately are likely to be more effective than those who either reject an approach out of hand or universally apply their favorite tool to all cases (Cunningham, 2008; Peterson, 2006).

Because this discussion only scratches the surface of capability building, readers are encouraged to explore other useful information that can be found in many domains, including training (A. P. Goldstein, 1996; I. L. Goldstein & Ford, 2002; see also chap. 16, this volume), the lessons of experience (McCall, Lombardo, & Morrison, 1988), and leadership development (Avolio & Chan, 2008; London, 2002; see also Vol. 1, chap. 7, this handbook).

Real-World Practice

Real-world practice (RWP), the extent to which people apply their skills and knowledge at work, is similar to the notions of generalization and transfer of training (Holton & Baldwin, 2003a), conscious competence (Dembkowski et al., 2006), relapse prevention (Marx, 1986), homework compliance in therapy (Scheel, Hanson, & Razzhavaikina, 2004), and implementation intentions (Gollwitzer, 1999).

Peterson and Hicks (1996) identified two major challenges to RWP. First, trying new behaviors is not always successful at first. Participants who are reluctant to make mistakes or appear incompetent will benefit from practicing new behaviors in safe environments (e.g., with their coach); making changes in small, incremental steps; positive self-talk; and having strategies for explaining to others what they are trying to do. The second challenge is that changing old habits and implementing new behavior requires conscious effort and cognitive attention (Rock & Page, 2009). Coaches can help reduce the cognitive load and enhance transfer by making sure participants do some of that work in the coaching session, such as preparing action plans specifying exactly when, where, and how new behaviors will be implemented (what Gollwitzer, 1999, referred to as *intention plans*); anticipating obstacles and identifying appropriate responses ahead of time; identifying specific signals ahead of time that will cue the new behavior or response; and practicing new responses repeatedly using diverse and challenging scenarios to enhance automaticity (Peterson & Muros, 2008). Coaches can also make sure participants develop skills for self-reflection and self-monitoring, to ensure they review their progress regularly and plan adjustments in real time or in anticipation of the next relevant event (Tziner, Haccoun, & Kadish, 1991).

Accountability

The two components of accountability—monitoring and ensuring logical consequences for progress—can be established either internally to the person or externally through the environment (Cummings & Anton, 1990; London, Smither, & Adsit, 1997; Peterson & Muros, 2008). When the participant's motivation is high, the development task is straightforward, and the environment is supportive, simple internal accountability mechanisms, such as self-evaluation of progress and regular discussions with the coach, are sufficient. The lower the person's motivation, the more difficult the learning task, and the less supportive the environment, the greater the importance of establishing clear accountability mechanisms. Additional techniques that address the monitoring aspect of accountability include having the participant seek regular feedback, ensuring ongoing feedback from the boss, setting up periodic progress reviews with the boss and other organizational stakeholders (including meetings that also include the coach), and daily documentation of behavior through journaling or recording specific behaviors. Consequences can be as informal and simple as participants' own satisfaction or dissatisfaction with their progress or the coach's asking questions to assess the seriousness of participants' commitments to follow-through on their development plans and to make the expectations of others and possible consequences more salient. Feedback from others can be explicitly connected to praise and positive recognition (or disappointment and negative comments) regarding progress as well as to the likelihood of obtaining more distal rewards, such as bonuses, promotions, or other opportunities.

HOW CAN ORGANIZATIONS GET THE GREATEST VALUE FROM EXECUTIVE COACHING?

Surveys indicate that relatively few organizations believe they are deriving the full benefits of executive coaching (Earley & Masarech, 2009; Jarvis et al., 2006; McDermott et al., 2007). Concerns include the lack of clarity and consistency in how coaching is used in the organization, lack of cumulative organizational learning about how to manage coaching, inconsistent quality, and the lack of systematic goal setting and outcome evaluation. Typically, as organizations strive to increase the value they obtain from coaching, they move through four stages along a continuum from relatively ad hoc and unstructured uses of coaching toward more systemic and strategic applications (Peterson & Little, 2008; Sokol, 2000).

Stage 1: Ad hoc coaching—driven by individuals. Most organizations begin using executive coaching when one individual, such as a boss, HR person, or potential coaching participant, decides he or she would like to find a coach. Others in the organization may also begin to seek coaching, although not in any coordinated or organized fashion. Coaching at this stage is reactive rather than proactive, typically in response to a specific situation, such as a new executive who needs assistance in on-boarding into a critical or challenging role. Organizations in the ad hoc stage of coaching have little idea regarding who is receiving coaching, who is providing it, what the process looks like, what the real value is, and how much is being spent. This stage exemplifies the ungoverned and chaotic image depicted by Sherman and Freas (2004) in "The Wild West of Executive Coaching."

Stage 2: Managed coaching—driven by a champion or sponsor. Organizations tend to move toward managed coaching when they recognize either that they are spending significant amounts of money on coaching or that coaching has great potential value that they wish to harness in a more structured way. They typically appoint someone to establish a more consistent way to manage all the coaches working in the organization. These managers establish coach selection criteria, screen and keep track of coaches, define the coaching process, and often begin to measure participant reactions to the coaching they receive (Hunt & Weintraub, 2007). Rarely at this stage do organizations define formal criteria for who receives coaching or even attempt to measure overall organizational outcomes.

Stage 3: Proactive coaching—driven by a business need. Organizations move to the next stage of the continuum when they begin to use coaching for groups of people to address a specific business or organizational need, such as on-boarding new executives or accelerating the development of high-potential leaders. The key shift in this stage is focusing on developing talent pools to generate clear organizational value in addition to the value received by individual participants. Organizations at this stage often start to think more strategically about who provides coaching (e.g., calling on managers and HR professionals or setting up a network of internal coaches; Frisch, 2001) and who receives coaching (e.g., setting up specific criteria and an approval process). Some organizations attempt to create a coaching culture (Clutterbuck & Megginson, 2005; Earley & Masarech, 2009) by enhancing their internal coaching capabilities and limiting the use of external coaches to very selective needs to reduce costs. Similarly, some organizations define coaching roles for specific needs, such as providing internal coaches for new hires from outside the organization and providing external coaches for promotions from within or using internal coaching for middle managers and primarily external coaches for senior executives (Holstein, 2005; McDermott et al., 2007).

Stage 4: Strategic coaching—driven by organizational talent strategy. Although at present there appear to be few organizations operating at Stage 4, where coaching is used strategically and systematically in alignment with the overall talent management strategy, a clearer picture is beginning to emerge as to what is required to get there (e.g., Clutterbuck & Megginson, 2005; Hunt & Weintraub, 2007; Peterson & Little, 2008; Thompson et al., 2008; Underhill, McAnally, & Koriath, 2007). At this stage, organizations have identified their most critical talent and prioritized where development will make the biggest difference. On the basis of their needs, these pivotal talent pools (Boudreau & Ramstad, 2007) are then provided the optimal development program, which may or may not involve executive coaching. One of the defining characteristics of Stage 4 organizations is they have a clear understanding of their talent and their development needs, the array of development tools that may be used, and a method for matching the talent need with the appropriate solution, based on factors such as cost, effectiveness of the method, convenience, and criticality or potential business impact of the need.

Finding the Best Match Between Participants and Coaches

Finding the right match between participant and coach is viewed as a critical decision in the coaching process (Hall et al., 1999), and yet there is little clarity on the criteria to be used. Some advice is even contradictory, with those who say the coach should be similar in background to the participant so he or she can relate well and others who claim the coach should be different so he or she can challenge and stretch the participant (Underhill et al., 2007), or that coaches and participants should be matched on sex or countermatched on sex (Wycherly & Cox, 2008). This type of advice focuses on superficial characteristics such as similarity, rather than on seeking a coach who meets more meaningful criteria, such as having demonstrated both the ability to relate well and to challenge and stretch participants. In their review of the research on matching in coaching and mentoring, Wycherly and Cox (2008) concluded that trying to match coaches and participants "based on the right 'chemistry' and other surface diversity factors may be neither necessary nor effective" (p. 48). The primary consideration for matching on superficial characteristics such as sex, race, or personality seems to be the extent to which the participant's biases and expectations will create difficulties in accepting their coach and building trust and rapport quickly (Wycherly & Cox, 2008).

One of the more contentious issues in selecting coaches is whether they should have actual business experience in a role similar to the person to be coached. In their thoughtful discussion of this issue, Jarvis et al. (2006) concluded that "executive coaches do need a strong understanding of organisational dynamics and the business world to be effective. However, direct experience of a particular industry or role is unlikely to be necessary for a person to be an effective coach—their real contribution is their ability to help individuals learn and develop" (p. 91). Also problematic is the often-mentioned issue of matching on "chemistry." Given the importance of the coaching relationship, it seems reasonable to let participants choose their own coach from two or three qualified options. Yet, as McDermott et al. (2007) pointed out, "most executives do not understand coaching provider differentiators or how they should use a coach; they simply want to complete the coaching process" (p. 35). Because they are not familiar with how to evaluate coaches, they may simply choose the person they like best. There is nothing inherently wrong with providing executives a choice among competent coaches; however, it often takes additional time and delays the beginning of coaching, with little additional value. One of the qualifications for being accepted into an organization's pool of coaches should be the ability to establish trust, credibility, and an effective working relationship with a specific audience. If a coach has a dominant personal style, such as being direct, forceful, and assertive or open-ended, unstructured, and free-flowing, which they are unable to moderate to meet the needs of a given client, then matching on personal style may also matter for some participants (Hunt & Weintraub, 2007). Given all this, having a knowledgeable person recommend a specific coach is advised. If the participant is not comfortable with the match, he or she should have the option to ask for another coach.

Coachability

Some coaches take a position that some people are uncoachable and cannot benefit from coaching. Naficy and Isabella (2008) described the following as characteristics of "uncoachable" people: having a fixed mind-set, being forced into coaching, lacking trust and openness, and feeling manipulated by performance management in the guise of coaching. Goldsmith (2009) claimed that all people who do not think they have a problem, are in the wrong job, are pursuing the wrong strategy for the organization, or who blame others for their problems are uncoachable. Bacon and Spear (2003) proposed seven levels of coachability:

- C0, not coachable; psychologically or medically impaired and require clinical help;
- C1, extremely low coachability; narcissistic types who are arrogant and impatient;
- C2, very low coachability; resistant to feedback, defensive, lacking self-insight;
- C3, fair coachability; complacent and unmotivated to change;
- C4, good coachability; accepts some feedback and sees some reason to change;
- C5, very good coachability; desire to improve but may be too busy to work on it; and
- C6, excellent coachability; self-directed, lifelong learners with an intrinsic need to grow.

There are two major problems with this notion of coachability. First, it labels people as globally uncoachable when the reality is that they may not want coaching on a given topic because they do not currently see the need to change. It may be more reasonable to assume that virtually all people are able to learn new things and change their behavior, and will accept coaching eagerly, when they see how it can help them accomplish goals that they value. When people are labeled as uncoachable, it is often simply because they do not want to be forced to change in the ways that others want them to change. Conversely, intrinsically motivated, enthusiastic learners who fit the C6 category of excellent coachability might be completely unreceptive to coaching on a topic such as strategic thinking if they do not see how enhancing that skill serves their needs in current or future roles. The second problem is that the types of people labeled as uncoachable are the very people who need coaching the most. Leaders with an intrinsic desire to grow, who accept feedback willingly, and are self-directed learners may not need much coaching. Those who are stubborn, arrogant, closed-minded, and defensive seem to most need the help of a professional coach. Given that leaders with narcissistic qualities, for example, typically demonstrate many positive leadership qualities and often rise to senior positions (Brunell et al., 2008; Maccoby, 2000; Rosenthal & Pittinsky, 2006), it is important to find coaches who are able to work with them.

The real consideration is that not all coaches are qualified to work with difficult or complex coaching situations. It is more accurate to label the situation as complex or difficult and thus requiring a specific expertise from the coach, rather than labeling the person as uncoachable (Ludeman & Erlandson, 2004; Mansi, 2009; Peterson & Sutherland, 2003). The majority of the coachability issues have to do with motivation. Of the four types of coaches defined earlier, the development-process coaches are best qualified to explicitly address resistance, defensiveness, and other motivation-related issues.

Skills and Issues Best Suited to Coaching

Just as some coaching participants may appear to be more challenging than others, some capabilities appear to be easier to learn than others (Hogan & Warrenfeltz, 2003; Lombardo & Eichinger, 2002; Tessmann-Keys & Wellins, 2007). Using a framework that clusters management competencies into four domains, Hogan and Warrenfeltz (2003) proposed that intrapersonal competencies such as self-control, integrity, and attitude toward authority are relatively difficult to change. Next most difficult are interpersonal skills, such as empathy and relationship building. Leadership skills, such as building and maintaining a team, build on intrapersonal and interpersonal skills but are easier to learn. Finally, the easiest to learn competencies are business skills, such as planning, running meetings, and evaluating performance. From their perspective, the skills that are more difficult to learn are closely linked to relatively hardwired personality variables and the easiest to learn are primarily cognitive in nature (although cognitive ability per se is difficult to change). Although there are discrepancies between this framework and other lists of easy- and difficult-to-learn capabilities (e.g., Lombardo & Eichinger, 2002; Tessmann-Keys & Wellins, 2007), this notion is potentially a useful factor in considering when to use coaching. Specifically, because coaching is a relatively powerful intervention, it may be most useful for the more difficult-to-learn skills. Training and other less costly interventions might be sufficient for the easier to learn competencies, especially as a first step.

A second way to identify skills for which coaching is well suited considers a continuum ranging from relatively fact- or data-based skills and knowledge (e.g., finance, law, geography, mathematics) to more principle-based and contextual competencies (e.g., leadership, coaching, influence). Coaching seems most appropriate for the latter. In fact, the more the competency is content-based with relatively clear right-or-wrong answers, the more it can be delivered efficiently through training, books, and self-study materials. Coaching on such fact-based topics would resemble one-on-one tutoring. However, the greater the requirement for situational judgment, the more helpful coaching can be to help people figure out how to analyze the situation and then, on the basis of their goals, skills, and other factors, decide how they would like to approach it. Lazar and Bergquist (2003) made a similar point by differentiating puzzles, problems, and mysteries and then comparing the types of coaching best suited to each. In their framework, *puzzles* have relatively clear answers and reasonable criteria for evaluating whether something was done correctly. They use the label performance coaching for these primarily behavioral issues such as delivering presentations, giving feedback, or managing the agenda for a meeting. This category is similar to content coaching. *Problems* refer to complex, multidimensional situations in which judgment involving cognitive and affective components is critical, and choices must be made without explicit criteria for correctness. Lazar and Bergquist labeled this executive coaching, which seems to parallel development-process coaching. Examples include choosing a leadership approach to handle a particular challenge and determining whether to give feedback in a specific instance. They defined alignment coaching as the approach to working with *mysteries,* the unfathomable, unpredictable areas of life related to spiritual and philosophical issues, to values and ethics, and to the deeper meaning and purpose of life and career.

RESEARCH ON COACHING

Virtually every author who seriously examines coaching has declared that there is a paucity of research evaluating the effectiveness of coaching (Kilburg, 2001; Sherman & Freas, 2004). Yet substantial evidence indicates that coaching can be an effective development tool that leads to significant improvements in performance and results (Jarvis et al., 2006; Peterson & Kraiger, 2004; Wise & Voss, 2002). In terms of participant satisfaction, most studies report that participants have favorable or highly favorable views toward coaching (e.g., Gegner, 1997; Hall, Otazo, & Hollenbeck, 1999; Olivero, Bane, & Kopelman, 1997). De Meuse, Dai, and Lee's (2009) summary of the empirical research on this topic reports that 75% to 95% of coaching participants are positive about their coaching experience. In addition, a number of coaching research studies report tangible improvements in outcomes such as learning, performance, and business results.

Bersin (2007) analyzed 62 talent management practices in 760 organizations and concluded that having formal or well-established coaching programs had the highest impact of all practices they examined.

Evers et al.'s (2006) quasi-experimental study found statistically significant improvements of approximately 0.5 standard deviation units in two of six areas of self-efficacy beliefs and outcome expectancies. No significant changes were found in their control group. This study reports little information about the coaching process or the qualifications of the coaches themselves, so it is difficult to generalize from their findings.

Finn (2007) reported the following statistically significant pre–post effect sizes for his coaching group for improvements in: self-efficacy ($d = 0.31$), positive affect ($d = 0.23$), openness to new behaviors ($d = 0.41$), and developmental planning ($d = 1.05$). Much larger effect sizes were obtained for most of these variables in the comparison between the coaching group and the control group at Time 2, although this was reported to be primarily a function of decreases in the control groups scores at time 2: self-efficacy ($d = 1.05$), positive affect ($d = 0.18$, not significant), openness to new behaviors ($d = 1.26$), and developmental planning ($d = 2.24$).

Gegner (1997) interviewed 25 executives and found that 84% were positive about their experience in coaching. Although all reported learning more about themselves and gaining new skills, only 32% reported improvements in actual job performance.

Kombarakaran et al. (2008) found that 81% of 114 coaching participants reported meeting their expectations in coaching, and 73% saw it as providing a good return on investment. A principal components analysis revealed five areas of improvement: people management (with at least 90% of participants reporting increases in insight into others, managing direct reports, influencing, conflict management, giving feedback, and leadership style), relationships with managers (79% of participants reported improvement), goal setting and prioritization (88% reported improvement in their ability to define performance goals, 76% reported increased insight into the business drivers of decisions), productivity and personal engagement with work (e.g., 78% reported improvements in personal productivity), and communications (68% reported improved communications with their colleagues).

McDermott et al. (2007) surveyed organizational sponsors of external coaching initiatives from 55 organizations. Their respondents reported the most significant benefits of coaching, as rated on a scale of 1 to 5 (1 = *not at all effective*, 3 = *moderate*, 5 = *highly effective*), to be development of future leaders (3.8), reinforcing the notion that development is important (3.7), getting senior managers to use appropriate leadership behaviors (3.6), and improving individual performance (3.5).

McGovern et al.'s (2001) study reported that 86% of 100 coaching participants surveyed were very or extremely satisfied with their coaching. Participants reported improvements in a wide variety of tangible and intangible business variables, including relationships with direct reports (77%), peers (63%), and other stakeholders (71%); teamwork (67%); job satisfaction (61%); productivity (53%); and quality (48%).

Peterson's (1993b) research on 370 executives found an average effect size (Cohen's d) of just over 1.5 on specific coaching objectives across a wide range of leadership, communication, interpersonal, and intrapersonal skills as rated by both participants and their bosses. The average improvement in overall performance was greater than .5 standard deviations, again from both rater perspectives. For comparison, participant and boss ratings on control group items (Peterson, 1993a) showed no significant change. Follow-up ratings an average of one full year later showed all results to be stable.

Schlosser and colleagues (Schlosser & Steinbrenner, 2008; Schlosser et al., 2006) launched a major study of coaching impact and value in 2004. Highlights from their results to date include the following. On a 10-point scale (1 = *very little;* 10 = *very much*), participant, manager, and coach, respectively, reported that coaching had a positive impact on the participant's overall effectiveness (8.0, 6.5, 8.0), that coaching was worth the participant's time (8.9, 7.8, 8.7), and worth the amount invested (8.7, 7.4, 8.7). Participant, manager, and coach also report the following degrees of improvement due to coaching: 36%, 26%, and 47%, attributing substantial portions of this improvement directly to the coaching: 47%, 39%, and 57%. When asked to estimate the financial value of the improvements in the specific capabilities and behaviors worked on, coaches report a mean of $371,000, participants $276,000, and managers $268,000. As a side note, capabilities with the highest average estimated value to the business are partnering across boundaries and silos ($515,000), strategic thinking ($475,000), and delegating and empowering others ($433,000).

In terms of comparing research on skill improvement with improvements in job performance and business results, Feldman and Lankau (2005) sounded a cautionary note, suggesting that coaching may be too many causal linkages removed from financial and business results to demonstrate consistently a direct relationship. Similarly, on the basis of their survey of users of coaching in large organizations, McDermott et al. (2007) concluded that coaching has a greater impact on proximal learning outcomes, such as improving leadership behaviors and individual performance, than it does on relatively distal organization-level outcomes, such as strategy execution and change management. Levenson (2009) concurred and pointed out that even when objective measures of organizational impact are chosen, they may be chosen because they are readily available and not because they measure the variables most critical to organizational success. More important, Levenson noted that coaching objectives are frequently chosen on the basis of low ratings on multirater surveys based on generic competency models and not necessarily because an improvement in the skills is clearly linked to objective business impact (see also Kaiser et al., 2008, for an insightful discussion on the importance of differentiating leadership perceptions from leadership effectiveness).

Return on Investment: ROI of Coaching

At least four studies report an average return on investment (ROI) in the range of 5 to 7 times the cost of coaching (Anderson, 2001; International Coach Federation, 2009; McGovern et al., 2001; Parker-Wilkins, 2006). The Corporate Leadership Council (2004) reported that additional studies have obtained similar ROI results. Phillips (2007) reports an ROI of 221%, using a fairly rigorous approach (Phillips & Phillips, 2007), involving detailed analysis of fully loaded costs (including both direct and indirect costs, such as the value of the executives time), the specific area affected (e.g., an 11% reduction in turnover due to the coaching), rater estimates of the degree to which the impact could be attributed to coaching (including asking raters to list other factors that might have contributed to the result), and specific cost bases for estimating financial value. In addition, they asked raters to estimate their level of confidence in the overall analysis, resulting in estimates ranging from 50% to 90%. Such an approach has greater credibility than studies based solely on direct financial costs, which underestimate the total costs, thus inflating ROI, and retrospective self-report, which suffers from methodological problems such as potential hindsight bias, self-serving bias (on the part of both the participants and in some cases the consulting firms conducting the studies), and cognitive dissonance (De Meuse et al., 2009; MacKie, 2007).

Future attempts to calculate ROI would benefit from careful consideration of the challenges, among them determining the fully loaded costs of the coaching, including the value of the time spent by the participant and other organizational stakeholders. Another rarely noted challenge is trying to estimate the future value of any capabilities acquired through coaching. It is always possible that the strategic insights or enhanced leadership capabilities gained might contribute to a success long after the coaching has ended. In that regard, carefully designed ROI analyses may potentially underestimate the long-term ROI of coaching.

It is important to keep in mind that ROI is inherently context dependent, and no numerical calculation in isolation can provide an estimate of the value of coaching (Levenson, 2009; Peterson & Kraiger, 2004). For example, the ROI of coaching on strategic thinking is likely to be significantly greater for a person with little background or experience in that topic who is moving into a leadership role in a highly competitive business setting than it is for either a person of comparable abilities who is operating in a stable, profitable environment (who would have a difficult time putting the new skills to use) or a leader who is already a highly skilled strategist and thus would likely show little incremental gain. Schlosser et al. (2006) cited such issues for why, even though they are gathering detailed financial information, they do not calculate ROI outside of a specific organizational context.

The ROI of coaching, or any other development intervention, is best understood as a function of three factors: impact, effectiveness, and efficiency (Boudreau & Ramstad, 2007). *Impact* refers to the business value resulting from the change in leadership behavior. In practice, it is preferable to obtain an estimate of the business impact before an intervention takes place—even before one is chosen—because it is less subject to the biases evident in after-the-fact surveys. *Effectiveness* is the degree to which the coaching or other intervention can actually produce the desired results. Coaching appears to have a relatively high level of effectiveness compared with less potent development options such as books or multirater feedback in isolation. Finally, *efficiency* refers to the cost of the coaching.

ROI blends these three factors, but much can be learned by keeping them separate. In principle, it is relatively easy to estimate impact and efficiency—we can obtain estimates of both the value of the enhanced capabilities or desired changes in performance and of the cost of various interventions. Specifically, obtaining an estimate of the business value of a given improvement in skill or performance (i.e., the impact as defined in Boudreau and Ramstad's, 2007, framework) from the coaching participant's boss, or, preferably, even an average of estimates from several relatively objective stakeholders in advance of the coaching reduces the typical biases that may affect retrospective ratings.

What is missing in our understanding of the ROI of coaching, and where research on coaching and other leadership development interventions is sorely needed, is on how effective coaching is in achieving the stated objectives, factoring in such variables as type of coach (e.g., content or process coach, experience level), participant variables (e.g., motivation, current skill level, intelligence), purpose (e.g., remedial or developmental coaching), organizational context (e.g., boss support, opportunities to apply new skills), type of coaching program (e.g., length, intensity), and other elements, such as those found in the research taxonomies proposed by Bennett (2006), Joo (2005), and MacKie (2007).

Such research could guide the choice of interventions to best meet individual circumstances and organizational needs. As a hypothetical example, suppose that coaching method A (long-term, delivered by a development-process coach) consistently produces two units of change and method B (short-term content coaching) produces one unit of change. Also assume that method A costs twice as much as B. Given that the ratio of cost to amount of change is the same in both, it would be easy to conclude that the ROI of the two methods is equivalent. However, if the organization requires two units of change for a person to be successful in the job, then the ROI of method B is actually negative. The organization made a moderate investment but did not accomplish its goals. If the organization only requires one unit of change for a person to be successful, then the ROI of method B would actually be higher than method A, because the additional returns from method A produce little incremental difference in the outcome.

Other Support for the Effectiveness of Coaching

In addition to the studies summarized in this section, there is a significant body of what might be considered relatively weak data in support of coaching, given the considerable variations in quality and rigor of the methods used. However, it is noted here because of the relatively consistent findings that across such a variety of methods, purposes, and measures, researchers are reporting positive findings. Each of the references noted here describes some tangible positive outcomes from coaching:

- research based on self-report from participants and their managers using diverse samples and data-collection methodologies (e.g., Bush, 2005; B. L. Davis & Petchenik, 1998; Kombarakaran, Yang, Baker, & Fernandes, 2008; Leedham, 2005; Seamons, 2006; Thompson, 1986; Wasylyshyn, 2003; Wasylyshyn, Gronsky, & Haas, 2006);
- individual case studies (e.g., Blattner, 2005; Diedrich, 1996; Hunt, 2003; Kiel, Rimmer, Williams, & Doyle, 1996; Kralj, 2001; Libri & Kemp, 2006; Natale & Diamante, 2005; Orenstein, 2006; Peterson, 1996; Peterson & Millier, 2005; Schnell, 2005; Tobias, 1996; Wasylyshyn, 2005; Winum, 2005);
- organizational case studies, dozens of which are described in books by Clutterbuck and Megginson (2005), Hunt and Weintraub (2007), and Jarvis et al. (2006);
- surveys of organizational purchasers of coaching (Dagley, 2006; Leedham, 2005; McDermott, Levenson, & Newton, 2007);

- evaluations of ROI (e.g., Anderson, 2001; Corporate Leadership Council, 2004; Holt & Peterson, 2006; McGovern et al., 2001; Parker-Wilkins, 2006; Phillips, 2007; Schlosser, Steinbrenner, Kumata, & Hunt, 2006);
- a small but growing number of quasi-experimental and other carefully designed research studies (e.g., Evers, Brouwers, & Tomic, 2006; Finn, 2007; Finn, Mason, & Griffin, 2006; Grant, Curtayne, & Burton, 2009; Offermanns, 2004 [as reported in Greif, 2007]; Peterson, 1993b; Smither et al., 2003; Steinmetz, 2005 [as reported in Greif, 2007]; Sue-Chan & Latham, 2004); and
- literature reviews that critically examine the available research and conclude that the evidence supports the effectiveness of coaching (e.g., De Meuse et al., 2009; Ely et al., in press; Feldman & Lankau, 2005; Fillery-Travis & Lane, 2006, 2007; Jarvis et al., 2006; Joo, 2005; Kampa-Kokesch & Anderson, 2001; Kampa & White, 2002; Levenson, 2009; MacKie, 2007; Passmore & Gibbes, 2007).

In addition to this evidence, there is the simple but compelling logic that executive coaching incorporates multiple techniques already shown to be effective in facilitating learning (Jarvis et al., 2006; Latham, 2007), including goal setting (Locke & Latham, 1990; 2002), feedback (Kluger & DeNisi, 1996; London, 1997), accountability (Holton & Baldwin, 2003b), behavioral practice (Druckman & Bjork, 1991), communicating performance expectations (Buckingham & Clifton, 2001; Buckingham & Coffman, 1999), enhancing self-efficacy (Bandura, 1997), reflection (Seibert & Daudelin, 1999), and establishing a trusting, supportive relationship (Lambert & Barley, 2002; Mahoney, 1991).

Although it is easy to conclude from the aggregate evidence that coaching produces generally positive outcomes, well-designed research on any specific aspect of coaching is virtually unavailable. For example, there is scant evidence to suggest that any given approach is more effective than another (Kilburg, 2004a; Olson, 2008), despite the fact that advocates of various approaches claim superiority and criticize other approaches (e.g., Berglas, 2002; Peel, 2005). Some proprietary approaches to coaching make extravagant claims that appear to be motivated by self-marketing rather than science, a practice that continues to make coaching resemble a business more than a profession (Bennett, 2006; Grant & Cavanagh, 2004). For example, consider Corbett and Coleman's statement that "the Sherpa process is the only credible standard for executive coaching" (2006, p. xiv). Rock and Donde (2008) claimed an ROI of 17 times the cost of the investment for training internal coaches in their proprietary approach to replace external coaches, but they did not provide sufficient details to understand how that claim is calculated. Garman, Whiston, and Zlatoper (2000) noted that there are even questions as to whether psychological training is helpful or harmful for executive coaches. Although only 31% of the articles they surveyed even mentioned psychological training for coaches, 18% of those articles presented it as potentially harmful, 36% were mixed on the perceived value, and only 45% were positive.

In addition, reviewers of coaching research often note several methodological problems. The majority of studies are based on relatively small sample sizes and rely on retrospective self-report from participants (Feldman & Lankau, 2005; MacKie, 2007) in which hindsight bias or cognitive dissonance could be factors. A number of studies have been conducted by practitioners who are essentially evaluating and reporting on their own work. Many other studies have been conducted by graduate students unfamiliar with the actual practice of coaching. There is little consistency in how findings are reported, with results often presented in vague qualitative terms and frequently incomplete. De Meuse et al. (2009) reported that for their meta-analysis they found only six studies for which effect sizes were available or could be calculated from the data. Some of these problems are perhaps due to the nature of coaching; it is a relatively long-term process, and the participants are busy executives who are reluctant to spend their time on detailed research protocols. It is difficult to conduct control group studies with this population as well (De Meuse et al., 2009).[3]

In summary, the cumulative evidence from multiple sources and methods supports the efficacy of executive coaching (De Meuse et al., 2009; Ely et al., in press). However, as Fillery-Travis and Lane (2006) pointed out, the research to date primarily enables us to answer yes to the question, Does coaching work? It is time for researchers to address more substantive questions regarding how coaching works, what aspects of coaching are most effective, which types of coaching work best for which purposes, and which criteria can be used to define when coaching is most appropriate (Grant & Cavanagh, 2007). Furthermore, it is by no means clear that all coaches and all coaching approaches are effective. It is therefore reasonable for consumers of coaching to be skeptical in evaluating outcome and ROI claims (Coutu & Kauffman, 2009).

COACHING RESEARCH: FUNDAMENTAL QUESTIONS AND CHALLENGES

Calls for more research on executive coaching are pervasive in the literature. On the basis of Grant's (2009) summary of dissertations and peer-reviewed publications on coaching, it appears that researchers are responding enthusiastically. Grant's report shows that 61 dissertations on coaching were completed in the nearly 10-year period between 2000 and May 2009, compared with 10 dissertations in the decade before that and only 6 in the decade earlier. There were 117 empirical studies published in the most recent 4.5 years of his summary (2005–May 2009), almost triple the 40 that were completed in the preceding 5-year period (2000–2004), and vastly more than the 29 published the entire 20 years before that (1980–1999). In addition to these research-based publications, more than 60% of all other coaching articles published in peer-reviewed journals since 1937 have appeared in just the 5 years 2005 to 2009, as this chapter went to press.

Compared with the dramatic increases in quantity, it is more difficult to assess the increases in quality of research and theory and how that has enhanced our understanding of coaching. Rather than trying to address all of the potential methodological and design issues with coaching research (De Meuse et al., 2009; Ely et al., in press; Feldman & Lankau, 2005; Greif, 2007; Joo, 2005; MacKie, 2007; Passmore & Gibbes, 2007), this final section is intended to highlight a few topics that have not received adequate attention elsewhere. Similarly, rather than attempting to summarize all of the important questions to be answered through research (Joo, 2005), this section tries to provide a fresh perspective on selected topics of value to the field.

Measuring Groups Versus Individuals

Executive coaching is a diverse and highly individualized activity, yet much of the research looks at group-level effects rather than individual-level effects, using the same measures for all participants regardless of differences in coaching objectives and initial skill level. Even for two people ostensibly working on the same objective, such as strategic thinking, there may be significant differences in each person's degree of insight, motivation, capabilities, opportunities for real-world practice, and accountability, variables that could lead to significantly different outcomes or at least to widely different experiences in coaching. Similarly, the same coach working with two different people may take a distinctly different approach with each. With so much variability between coaching engagements, it is impossible to determine what is really going on when results are averaged across individuals. As an example of how critical this is, consider that 77% of coaching participants in the McGovern et al. (2001) study reported improved relationships with direct reports. Such a finding might be an exemplary result if only 50% of the participants had that as an objective of the coaching or a tremendous disappointment if 100% of the participants had that as a goal.

[3] Although the most common control group designs are difficult to use in organizational settings, researchers may consider other quasi-experimental methods, such as the nonequivalent dependent variable design (Shadish, Cook, & Campbell, 2002). Peterson (1993b), for example, used this approach by having participants, their coaches, and their managers rate participants on their current effectiveness on specific coaching objectives as well as a set of unrelated control items drawn from a management multirater survey.

There is also no indication of the degree to which those 77% who showed improvement actually reached a satisfactory level of performance. It is conceivable that all 77% showed some improvement, yet only a small percentage achieved their desired level of performance on improved relationships. In fact, when asked to rate their success, participants said they achieved 73% of their stated goals *very effectively* or *extremely effectively,* although 12% of participants reported not achieving a single one of their development objectives. Ratings from organizational stakeholders were even lower in terms of degree of success on attaining specified coaching objectives.

What is often missing from outcome research on coaching, surprisingly so, is an answer to the simple question, Did the participants achieve their objectives? Researchers need to incorporate measures of what specific goals each individual is working on, the extent to which they achieve their goals, and how much they change in the process (see Peterson, 1993a, for a discussion of issues in measuring change in coaching). With these types of data, comparisons can be made between subgroups based on specific features (e.g., comparing groups working on different types of goals or participants who met their goals vs. those who did not). In addition, researchers could ask both coaches and participants to list the specific actions and techniques that they thought contributed most to the perceived outcome. Goal-attainment scaling (GAS; Kiresuk, Smith, & Cardillo, 1994; Spence, 2007) is one way to measure accomplishment of specific objectives directly. Simply put, GAS is a process for defining individually tailored coaching objectives and then measuring outcomes in terms of the degree of successful goal attainment. A difficulty factor can also be calculated, which facilitates comparison across different goals and individuals. In addition to evaluating progress on stated goals, it is also useful to ask about other benefits of coaching, which would make it clear to what extent coaching is likely to deliver both direct and secondary benefits.

Another consideration in measuring groups versus individuals is to consider single-subject research design methodologies used in counseling and therapeutic research (Barlow & Hersen, 1984; Galassi & Gersh, 1993). Although not common in I/O psychology, such designs have long been accepted as the equivalent of group-based experiments for establishing cause and effect (Thomas, 2006). Part of the power of repeated single-subject designs is showing that the same treatment (i.e., coaching), delivered to different people at different times and for different reasons, produces the same pattern of results. The cumulative evidence increases the confidence that the treatment is causing the effect. A simple design, which occurs informally all the time, is to get multiple baseline measures of a person's behavior before coaching. Many organizations have performance reviews or multirater data that show a certain skill level or behavior over several years. Then the question is, after coaching, do those same measures show a change. No single instance is conclusive, but repeated across many individuals, this AAAB design—showing no change, no change, no change, coaching,—is compelling. Another design, which might be described as ABCDE—where each letter represents a different treatment, such as performance review, multirater feedback, training program, new manager, executive coaching—is also relatively common. It is represented well in the statement, "We've tried everything else, and nothing seems to work." In such a case, if coaching is introduced and results in change, it can be concluded that coaching was the causal factor. Again, although it is difficult to rule out other causal factors in any individual circumstance, repeatedly finding that coaching works when other treatments have not is a powerful indicator of causality.

Designing Research Suited to the Dynamics of Coaching

Much of the research on coaching to date has been broad and exploratory rather than aimed at testing specific hypotheses. With the complexity and variability of coaching and the small sample sizes typical of each study, meaningful results are difficult to find. Even when specific hypotheses are tested, they are often derived without reference to theoretical frameworks of individual learning and development and with minimal regard to the unique nature of the coaching process itself. As one illustration of how research questions need to be tailored, consider that because an effective coach customizes his or her approach to a participant's specific needs and context rather than treating all participants all the same, the variance due to personal and contextual variables is diminished. Working with a participant who demonstrates low motivation and a lack of boss support, an effective coach will naturally focus on specific methods to address those issues. Peterson (1993b), for example, began his research with specific hypotheses about the relationship between coaching outcomes and individual differences such as motivation, intelligence, and neuroticism. However, none of the hypothesized correlations, nor in fact any of the dozens of unhypothesized relationships between personality scale scores and outcomes, were statistically significant. Similarly, Dawdy (2004) also found no relationship between participant personality variables and outcome. So it is quite likely that individual differences such as participant motivation (Colquitt et al., 2000) or learning orientation (Dweck, 1986), which might have significant predictive value in training and other standardized group programs in which everyone receives the same treatment, are uncorrelated to outcomes in many executive coaching programs.

However, it is quite likely that personal and contextual variables may matter in certain situations. Participant motivation is more likely to have an impact on participation and dropout rates in coaching, time required to achieve development objectives, and in the specific processes, techniques, and assignments their coaches use in their coaching engagement. Individual difference variables are also likely to be more predictive of outcomes in short-term and highly standardized approaches to coaching, where the parallels to predictors of training outcomes (e.g., Naquin & Baldwin, 2003; Noe, 1986) are more direct. These are empirical questions that remain to be answered, but the important principle is to formulate hypotheses based on a solid understanding of the unique dynamics of coaching.

Exploring Research on Coaching From Multiple Levels

There are a multitude of important questions to be answered about coaching (Bennett, 2006; Joo, 2005; MacKie, 2007). Paradoxically perhaps, one flaw in much of the coaching research is its exclusive focus on coaching. Both broadening and narrowing the scope of research questions might increase our understanding of coaching faster than some of the questions currently being examined. From a broader perspective, it would be helpful to compare coaching with other skill building, behavior change, and leadership development interventions. Where is each intervention most effective relative to cost? Who benefits the most from each approach? What are the advantages and disadvantages of coaching relative to other options?

From a narrower perspective, we might learn more as a field if we studied the component elements of development (e.g., the five Development Pipeline conditions) and how they contribute to coaching. For example, a significant contribution to coaching as well as leadership development in general could be made by comparing different methods for facilitating insight, such as having the coach deliver feedback based on interviews with key stakeholders versus teaching the participant how to get their own feedback and having them interview key stakeholders themselves. A feasible research design for a slightly different comparison might be as simple as giving half the coaching participants personality inventory feedback in Session 1 and multirater feedback in Session 2, with the other participant group receiving the same sources of feedback but in the opposite order. Participants and coaches could be interviewed after each session to ask how much their insight increased, in what ways, what contributed to that increase, and what they plan to do on the basis of that information. Ideally, a follow-up conversation several months later would ask about the longer term impact, including actual action taken. Understanding the best ways to accomplish specific subgoals in coaching, such as increasing insight, enhancing motivation and accountability, and ensuring real-world practice, would allow coaches to design optimal programs for specific people and needs.

CONCLUSION

As popular as it has become, executive coaching is still an emerging discipline. As Coutu and Kauffman (2009) pointed out in their survey of 140 leading executive coaches, "The coaching field is filled with contradictions. Coaches themselves disagree over why they're hired, what they do, and how to measure success" (p. 91). Yet despite the many questions about exactly how it works, coaching appears to be one of the most potent, versatile, and efficient leadership development tools available. In fact, its adaptability and versatility probably explain in some part why it is so difficult to quantify and define. Nonetheless, as long as coaches continue to seek better ways to help leaders accelerate their learning and improve performance, coaching itself is likely to continue to flourish long into the future.

References

Agarwal, R., Angst, C. M., & Magni, M. (2006, February). *The performance effects of coaching: A multilevel analysis using hierarchical linear modeling* (University of Maryland Robert H. Smith School Research Paper No. RHS 06-031). Retrieved October 26, 2008, from http://ssrn.com/abstract=918810.

Ahern, G. (2003). Designing and implementing coaching/mentoring competencies: A case study. *Counselling Psychology Quarterly, 16,* 373–383. doi:10.1080/0951507032000156871

Alexander, G. (2006). Behavioral coaching: The GROW model. In J. Passmore (Ed.), *Excellence in coaching: The industry guide* (pp. 61–72). Philadelphia: Kogan Page.

Alvey, S., & Barclay, K. (2007). The characteristics of dyadic trust in executive coaching. *Journal of Leadership Studies, 1*(1), 18–27.

Anderson, M. C. (2001). *Executive briefing: Case study on the return on investment of executive coaching.* Retrieved March 12, 2008, from http://www.coachfederation.org/NR/rdonlyres/16C73602-871A-43B8-9703-2C4D4D79BDAB/7720/053metrixglobal_coaching_roi_briefing.pdf

Asay, T. P., & Lambert, M. J. (1999). The empirical case for the common factors in therapy: Quantitative findings. In M. A. Hubble, B. L. Duncan, & S. D. Miller (Eds.), *The heart & soul of change: What works in therapy* (pp. 33–55). Washington, DC: American Psychological Association. doi:10.1037/11132-001

Ashford, S. J., & Northcraft, G. (2003). Robbing Peter to pay Paul: Feedback environments and enacted priorities in response to competing task demands. *Human Resource Management Review, 13,* 537–559. doi:10.1016/j.hrmr.2003.11.002

Auerbach, J. E. (2001). *Personal and executive coaching: The complete guide for mental health professionals.* Ventura, CA: Executive College Press.

Auerbach, J. E. (2006). Inviting a dialogue about core coaching competencies. In F. Campone & J. L. Bennett (Eds.), *Proceedings of the third International Coach Federation research symposium* (pp. 55–70). Lexington, KY: International Coach Federation.

Avolio, B. J., & Chan, A. (2008). The dawning of a new era for genuine leadership development. In G. P. Hodgkinson & J. K. Ford (Eds.), *International review of industrial and organizational psychology* (Vol. 23, pp. 197–238). New York: Wiley. doi:10.1002/9780470773277.ch6

Bachelor, A., & Horvath, A. (1999). The therapeutic relationship. In M. A. Hubble, B. L. Duncan, & S. D. Miller (Eds.), *The heart & soul of change: What works in therapy* (pp. 133–178). Washington, DC: American Psychological Association. doi:10.1037/11132-004

Bachkirova, T. (2007). Role of coaching psychology in defining boundaries between counselling and coaching. In S. Palmer & A. Whybrow (Eds.), *Handbook of coaching psychology* (pp. 351–366). New York: Routledge.

Bachkirova, T., & Cox, E. (2005). A bridge over troubled water: Bringing together coaching and counselling. *Counselling at Work, 48,* 2–9.

Bacon, T., & Spear, K. (2003). *Adaptive coaching: The art and practice of a client-centered approach to performance improvement.* Mountain View, CA: Davies-Black.

Bandura, A. (1997). *Self-efficacy: The exercise of control.* New York: Freeman.

Barlow, D., & Hersen, M. (1984). *Single case experimental designs: Strategies for studying behavior change* (2nd ed.). Elmsford, NY: Pergamon.

Barner, R. (2006). The targeted assessment coaching interview: Adapting the assessment process to different coaching requirements. *Career Development International, 11,* 96–107. doi:10.1108/13620430610651868

Baron, L., & Morin, L. (2009). The coach–coachee relationship in executive coaching: A field study. *Human Resource Development Quarterly, 20,* 85–106. doi:10.1002/hrdq.20009

Beck, J. W., Gregory, J. B., & Carr, A. E. (2009). Balancing development with day-to-day task demands: A multiple-goal approach to executive coaching. *Industrial and Organizational Psychology: Perspectives on Science and Practice, 2,* 293–296. doi:10.1111/j.1754-9434.2009.01152.x

Bell, B. S., & Kozlowski, S. W. J. (2008). Active learning: Effects of core training design elements on self-regulatory processes, learning, and adaptability. *Journal of Applied Psychology, 93,* 296–316. doi:10.1037/0021-9010.93.2.296

Bennett, J. (2006). An agenda for coaching-related research: A challenge for researchers. *Consulting Psychology Journal: Practice and Research, 58,* 240–248. doi:10.1037/1065-9293.58.4.240

Berger, J. G., & Fitzgerald, C. (2002). Leadership and complexity of mind: The role of executive coaching. In C. Fitzgerald & J. G. Berger (Eds.), *Executive coaching: Practices and perspectives* (pp. 27–58). Palo Alto, CA: Davies-Black.

Berglas, S. (2002). The very real dangers of executive coaching. *Harvard Business Review, 80*(6), 86–92.

Berry, R. M. (2005). *A comparison of face-to-face and distance coaching practices: The role of the working alliance in problem resolution.* Unpublished doctoral dissertation, Georgia State University, Atlanta.

Bersin, J. (2007). *High-impact talent management: Trends, best practices and industry solutions.* Oakland, CA: Bersin & Associates.

Biswas-Diener, R., & Dean, B. (2007). *Positive psychology coaching: Putting the science of happiness to work for your clients.* Hoboken, NJ: Wiley.

Blattner, J. (2005). Coaching: The successful adventure of a downwardly mobile executive. *Consulting Psychology Journal: Practice and Research, 57,* 3–13. doi:10.1037/1065-9293.57.1.3

Bloom, B. S. (1984). The search for methods of group instruction as effective as one-to-one tutoring. *Educational Researcher, 13,* 4–16.

Bluckert, P. (2006). *Psychological dimensions of executive coaching.* New York: Open University Press.

Bokeno, R. M. (2009). Genus of learning relationships: Mentoring and coaching as communicative interaction. *Development and Learning in Organizations,* 23(1), 5–8. doi:10.1108/14777280910924045

Bono, J. E., Purvanova, R. K., Towler, A. J., & Peterson, D. B. (2009). A survey of executive coaching practices. *Personnel Psychology, 62,* 361–404. doi:10.1111/j.1744-6570.2009.01142.x

Boudreau, J. W., & Ramstad, P. M. (2007). *Beyond HR: The new science of human capital.* Cambridge, MA: Harvard Business School Press.

Brock, V. G. (2008). *Grounded theory of the roots and emergence of coaching.* Unpublished doctoral dissertation, International University of Professional Studies, Maui, HI.

Brotman, L. E., Liberi, W. P., & Wasylyshyn, K. M. (1998). Executive coaching: The need for standards of competence. *Consulting Psychology Journal: Practice and Research, 50,* 40–46. doi:10.1037/1061-4087.50.1.40

Brunell, A. B., Gentry, W. A., Campbell, W. K., Hoffman, B. J., Kuhnert, K. W., & DeMarree, K. G. (2008). Leader emergence: The case of the narcissistic leader. *Personality and Social Psychology Bulletin, 34,* 1663–1676. doi:10.1177/0146167208324101

Buckingham, M., & Clifton, D. O. (2001). *Now, discover your strengths.* New York: Free Press.

Buckingham, M., & Coffman, C. (1999). *First, break all the rules: What the world's greatest managers do differently.* New York: Simon & Schuster.

Burke, D., & Linley, P. A. (2007). Enhancing goal self-concordance through coaching. *International Coaching Psychology Review, 2,* 62–69.

Bush, M. (2005). *Client perceptions of effectiveness in executive coaching.* Unpublished doctoral dissertation, Pepperdine University, Malibu, CA.

Carr, R. (2009). Advice-giving: The forbidden fruit of mentoring, coaching and peer assistance. *Peer Bulletin,* No. 176, not paginated.

Carson, B., & Marquardt, M. J. (2004). Coaching via action learning. *OD/Leadership Network News, 2*(3), not paginated.

Clutterbuck, D. (1991). *Everyone needs a mentor.* London: Chartered Institute of Personnel and Development.

Clutterbuck, D. (2008). What's happening in coaching and mentoring? And what is the difference between them? *Development and Learning in Organizations,* 22(4), 8–10. doi:10.1108/14777280810886364

Clutterbuck, D., & Megginson, D. (2005). *Making coaching work: Creating a coaching culture.* London: Chartered Institute of Personnel and Development.

Colquitt, J. A., LePine, J. A., & Noe, R. A. (2000). Toward an integrative theory of training motivation: A meta-analytic path analysis of 20 years of research. *Journal of Applied Psychology, 85,* 678–707. doi:10.1037/0021-9010.85.5.678

Colvin, G. (2008). *Talent is overrated: What really separates world-class performers from everybody else.* New York: Portfolio.

Corbett, B., & Colemon, J. (2006). *The Sherpa guide: Process-driven executive coaching.* Mason, OH: Texere.

Corporate Leadership Council. (2004). *ROI of executive coaching.* Washington, DC: Corporate Executive Board.

Coutu, D., & Kauffman, C. (2009). What can coaches do for you? *Harvard Business Review, 87*(1), 91–97.

Creane, V. E. (2006). Personal coaching from the client's perspective. In F. Campone & J. L. Bennett (Eds.), *Proceedings of the third International Coach Federation coaching research symposium* (pp. 112-122). Lexington, KY: International Coach Federation.

Cummings, L. L., & Anton, R. J. (1990). The logical and appreciative dimensions of accountability. In S. Srivastva & D. L. Cooperrider (Eds.), *Appreciative management and leadership: The power of positive thought and action in organizations* (pp. 257–286). San Francisco: Jossey-Bass.

Cunningham, I. (2008). Coaching shouldn't be non-directive—or even directive: Really responding to needs. *Development and Learning in Organizations,* 22(4), 5–7. doi:10.1108/14777280810886355

D'Abate, C. P., Eddy, E. R., & Tannenbaum, S. I. (2003). What's in a name? A literature-based approach to understanding mentoring, coaching, and other constructs that describe developmental interactions. *Human Resource Development Review, 2,* 360–384. doi:10.1177/1534484303255033

Dagley, G. (2006). Human resources professionals' perceptions of executive coaching: Efficacy, benefits and return on investment. *International Coaching Psychology Review, 1*(2), 34–44.

Davis, B. L., & Petchenik, L. (1998). *Measuring the value of coaching at Amoco.* Presented at The Coaching and Mentoring Conference, Washington, DC: Linkage.

Davis, S. L., & Barnett, R. C. (2009). Changing behavior one leader at a time. In R. Silzer & B. E. Dowell (Eds.), *Strategy-driven talent management: A leadership imperative* (349–398). San Francisco: Jossey-Bass.

Dawdy, G. N. (2004). *Executive coaching: A comparative design exploring the perceived effectiveness of coaching and methods.* Unpublished doctoral dissertation, Capella University, Minneapolis, MN.

De Meuse, K. P., Dai, G., & Lee, R. J. (2009). Evaluating the effectiveness of executive coaching: Beyond ROI? *Coaching: An International Journal of Theory, Research, and Practice, 2,* 117–134.

Dembkowski, S., Eldridge, F., & Hunter, I. (2006). *The seven steps of effective executive coaching.* London: Thorogood.

Diedrich, R. C. (1996). An iterative approach to executive coaching. *Consulting Psychology Journal: Practice and Research, 48,* 61–66. doi:10.1037/1061-4087.48.2.61

Diedrich, R. C. (2001). Lessons learned in—and guidelines for—coaching executive teams. *Consulting Psychology Journal: Practice and Research, 53,* 238–239. doi:10.1037/1061-4087.53.4.238

Dobson, K. S. (Ed.). (1988). *Handbook of cognitive-behavioral therapies.* New York: Guilford Press.

Druckman, D., & Bjork, R. A. (1991). *In the mind's eye: Enhancing human performance.* Washington, DC: National Academy Press.

Dunlop, H. (2006). An exploratory investigation into the perceived effects of team coaching in the construction sector. *International Journal of Mentoring and Coaching, 4*(2), 24–44.

Dweck, C. S. (1986). Motivational processes affecting learning. *American Psychologist, 41,* 1040–1048. doi:10.1037/0003-066X.41.10.1040

Dweck, C. S. (2000). *Self-theories: Their role in motivation, personality, and development.* Philadelphia: Psychology Press.

Earley, C., & Masarech, M. A. (2009). *The coaching conundrum 2009: Building a coaching culture that drives organizational success.* Princeton, NJ: BlessingWhite.

Eichinger, R. W., & Lombardo, M. M. (2003). Knowledge summary series: 360-degree assessment. *Human Resource Planning, 26*(4), 34–44.

Ely, K., Boyce, L. A., Nelson, J. K., Zaccaro, S. J., Hernez-Broome, G., & Whyman, W. (in press). Evaluating leadership coaching: A review and integrative framework. *The Leadership Quarterly.*

Ericsson, K. A. (2006). The influence of experience and deliberate practice on the development of superior expert performance. In K. A. Ericsson, N. Charness, R. R. Hoffman, & P. J. Feltovich (Eds.), *The Cambridge handbook of expertise and expert performance* (pp. 683–703). New York: Cambridge University Press.

Evers, W. J. G., Brouwers, A., & Tomic, W. (2006). A quasi-experimental study on management coaching effectiveness. *Consulting Psychology Journal: Practice and Research, 58,* 174–182. doi:10.1037/1065-9293.58.3.174

Executive Coaching Forum. (2008). *The executive coaching handbook: Principles and guidelines for a successful coaching partnership* (4th ed.). Retrieved December 1, 2008, from http://www.executivecoachingforum.com

Feldman, D. C., & Lankau, M. J. (2005). Executive coaching: A review and agenda for future research. *Journal of Management, 31,* 829–848. doi:10.1177/0149206305279599

Ferrar, P. (2004). Defying definition: Competences in coaching and mentoring. *International Journal of Evidence Based Coaching and Mentoring, 2*(2), 53–60.

Fillery-Travis, A., & Lane, D. (2006). Does coaching work or are we asking the wrong question? *International Coaching Psychology Review, 1,* 23–36.

Fillery-Travis, A., & Lane, D. (2007). Research: Does coaching work? In S. Palmer & A. Whybrow (Eds.), *Handbook of coaching psychology* (pp. 57–70). New York: Routledge.

Finn, F. A. (2007). *Leadership development through executive coaching: The effects on leaders' psychological states and transformational leadership behaviour.* Unpublished doctoral dissertation, Queensland University of Technology, Brisbane, Australia.

Finn, F. A., Mason, C. M., & Griffin, M. (2006, July). Investigating change over time—the effects of executive coaching on leaders' psychological states and behaviour. Presented at the 26th International Congress of Applied Psychology, Athens, Greece.

Flaherty, J. (2005). *Coaching: Evoking excellence in others* (2nd ed.). Boston: Butterworth-Heinmann.

Fredrickson, B. L. (2009). *Positivity.* New York: Crown.

Frisch, M. H. (2001). The emerging role of the internal coach. *Consulting Psychology Journal: Practice and Research, 53,* 240–250. doi:10.1037/1061-4087.53.4.240

Frisch, M. H., & Lee, R. J. (2009). More hidden but more useful than we realize. *Industrial and Organizational Psychology, 2,* 261–265. doi:10.1111/j.1754-9434.2009.01144.x

Galassi, J. P., & Gersh, T. L. (1993). Myths, misconceptions, and missed opportunity: Single-case designs and counseling psychology. *Journal of Counseling Psychology, 40,* 525–531. doi:10.1037/0022-0167.40.4.525

Garman, A., Whiston, D., & Zlatoper, K. (2000). Media perceptions of executive coaching and the formal preparation of coaches. *Consulting Psychology Journal: Practice and Research, 52,* 201–205. doi:10.1037/1061-4087.52.3.201

Gegner, C. (1997). *Coaching: Theory and practice.* Unpublished master's thesis. University of San Francisco, CA.

Ghods, N. (2009). *Distance coaching: The relationship between the coach–client relationship, client satisfaction, and coaching outcomes.* Unpublished doctoral dissertation, Alliant International University, San Diego, CA.

Gino, F. (2008). Do we listen to advice just because we paid for it? The impact of advice cost on its use. *Organizational Behavior and Human Decision Processes, 107,* 234–245. doi:10.1016/j.obhdp.2008.03.001

Gino, F., & Schweitzer, M. E. (2008). Blinded by anger or feeling the love: How emotions influence advice taking. *Journal of Applied Psychology, 93,* 1165–1173. doi:10.1037/0021-9010.93.5.1165

Goldratt, E. M., & Cox, J. (1992). *The goal: A process of ongoing improvement* (2nd rev. ed.). Great Barrington, MA: North River.

Goldsmith, M. (2009). *How to spot the "uncoachables."* Retrieved March 25, 2009, from http://blogs.harvardbusiness.org/goldsmith/2009/03/how_to_spot_the_uncoachables.html?cm_mmc=npv-_-LISTSERV-_-MAR_2009-_-LEADERSHIP2

Goldsmith, M., & Morgan, H. (2004, fall). Leadership is a contact sport: The "follow-up factor" in management development. *Strategy + Business,* Fall. Retrieved June 23, 2005, from http://www.strategy-business.com/press/article/04307?pg=0

Goldstein, A. P. (1996). Coordinated multitargeted skills training: The promotion of generalization-enhancement. In W. O'Donahue & L. Kranser (Eds.), *Handbook of psychological skills training* (pp. 383–399). Boston: Allyn & Bacon.

Goldstein, I. L., & Ford, J. K. (2002). *Training in organizations: Needs assessment, development, and evaluation* (4th ed.). Boston: Wadsworth.

Gollwitzer, P. M. (1999). Implementation intentions: Strong effects of simple plans. *American Psychologist, 54,* 493–503. doi:10.1037/0003-066X.54.7.493

Gough, H. G., & Bradley, P. (1996). *CPI manual* (3rd ed.). Mountain View, CA: CPP.

Grant, A. M. (2006). An integrative goal-focused approach to executive coaching. In D. R. Stober & A. M. Grant (Eds.), *Evidence based coaching handbook* (pp. 153–192). Hoboken, NJ: Wiley.

Grant, A. M. (2007). Past, present and future: The evolution of professional coaching and coaching psychology. In S. Palmer & A. Whybrow (Eds.), *Handbook of coaching psychology* (pp. 23–39). New York: Routledge.

Grant, A. M. (2009, May). *Workplace, executive and life coaching: An annotated bibliography from the behavioural science and business literature.* Unpublished manuscript, Coaching Psychology Unit, University of Sydney, Australia.

Grant, A. M., & Cavanagh, M. J. (2004). Toward a profession of coaching: Sixty-five years of progress and challenges for the future. *International Journal of Evidence Based Coaching and Mentoring,* 2(1), 1–16.

Grant, A. M., & Cavanagh, M. J. (2007). Evidence-based coaching: Flourishing or languishing? *Australian Psychologist, 42,* 239–254. doi:10.1080/00050060701648175

Grant, A. M., Curtayne, L., & Burton, G. (2009). Executive coaching enhances goal attainment, resilience and workplace well-being: A randomized controlled study. *Journal of Positive Psychology, 4,* 396–407.

Gray, D. E. (2006). Executive coaching: Toward a dynamic alliance of psychotherapy and transformative learning processes. *Management Learning, 37,* 475–497. doi:10.1177/1350507606070221

Grbcic, S., & Palmer, S. (2006, November). *A cognitive–behavioral self-help approach to stress management and prevention at work: A randomised controlled trial.* Paper presented at the Joint Association for Rational Emotive Behavior therapy and the Association for Multimodal Psychology National Conference, London.

Greif, S. (2007). Advances in research on coaching outcomes. *International Coaching Psychology Review, 3,* 222–247.

Gyllensten, K., & Palmer, S. (2007). The coaching relationship: An interpretive phenomenological analysis. *International Coaching Psychology Review, 2,* 168–177.

Hall, D. T., Otazo, K. L., & Hollenbeck, G. P. (1999). Behind closed doors: What really happens in executive coaching. *Organizational Dynamics,* 27(3), 39–53. doi:10.1016/S0090-2616(99)90020-7

Hamlin, R. G., Ellinger, A. D., & Beattie, R. S. (2008). The emergent "coaching industry": A wake-up call for HRD professionals. *Human Resource Development International, 11,* 287–305. doi:10.1080/13678860802102534

Hart, V., Blattner, J., & Leipsic, S. (2001). Coaching versus therapy: A perspective. *Consulting Psychology Journal: Practice and Research, 53,* 229–237. doi:10.1037/1061-4087.53.4.229

Hawkins, P., & Smith, N. (2006). *Coaching, mentoring and organizational consultancy: Supervision and development.* New York: Open University Press.

Heatherton, T., & Nichols, A. (1994). Personal accounts of successful versus failed attempts at life change. *Personality and Social Psychology Bulletin, 20,* 664–675. doi:10.1177/0146167294206005

Hernez-Broome, G. (2005). Impact of coaching following a leadership development program: Coaching is key to continued development. In I. F. Stein, F. Campone, & L. J. Page (Eds.), *Proceedings of the Second ICF Coaching Research Symposium* (pp. 88–94). Washington, DC: International Coach Federation.

Hicks, M. D., & Peterson, D. B. (1999). The Development Pipeline: How people really learn. *Knowledge Management Review, 9,* 30–33.

Highlen, P. S., & Hill, C. E. (1984). Factors affecting client change in individual counseling: Current status and theoretical speculations. In S. D. Brown & R. W. Lent (Eds.), *The handbook of counseling psychology* (pp. 334–396). New York: Wiley.

Hogan, R., & Hogan, J. (2001). Assessing leadership: A view from the dark side. *International Journal of Selection and Assessment, 9*(1–2), 40–51. doi:10.1111/1468-2389.00162

Hogan, R., & Warrenfeltz, R. (2003). Educating the modern manager. *Academy of Management Learning & Education, 2*(1), 74–84.

Hollon, S. D., & Beck, A. T. (2004). Cognitive and cognitive behavioral therapies. In M. J. Lambert (Ed.), *Bergin and Garfield's handbook of psychotherapy and behavior change* (5th ed., pp. 447–492). New York: Wiley.

Holstein, W. J. (2005, November). Best companies for leaders. *Chief Executive, 213,* 24–30.

Holt, K., & Peterson, D. B. (2006, May). *Measuring and maximizing the ROI of executive coaching.* Master tutorial presented at the annual conference of the Society for Industrial and Organizational Psychology, Dallas, TX.

Holton, E. F., III, & Baldwin, T. T. (Eds.). (2003a). *Improving learning transfer in organizations.* San Francisco: Jossey-Bass.

Holton, E. F., III, & Baldwin, T. T. (2003b). Making transfer happen: An action perspective on learning transfer systems. In E. F. Holton, III, & T. T. Baldwin (Eds.), *Improving learning transfer in organizations* (pp. 3–15). San Francisco: Jossey-Bass.

Homan, M., & Miller, L. J. (2008). *Coaching in organizations.* Hoboken, NJ: Wiley.

Horvath, A. O., & Bedi, R. P. (2002). The alliance. In J. C. Norcross (Ed.), *Psychotherapy relationships that work: Therapist contributions and responsiveness to patients* (pp. 37–70). New York: Oxford University.

Hughes, R. L., Ginnett, R. C., & Curphy, G. J. (2008). *Leadership: Enhancing the lessons of experience* (6th ed.). Boston: McGraw-Hill Irwin.

Hunt, J. M. (2003, April). *Successful executive coaching experiences: Report on a case study research program.* Paper presented at the annual conference of the Society for Industrial and Organizational Psychology, Orlando, FL.

Hunt, J. M., & Weintraub, J. R. (2007). *The coaching organization: A strategy for developing leaders.* Thousand Oaks, CA: Sage.

International Coach Federation. (2009). *ICF global coaching client study: Executive summary.* Lexington, KY: Author. Retrieved July 10, 2009, from http://www.coachfederation.org

Ives, Y. (2008). What is "coaching"?: An exploration of conflicting paradigms. *International Journal of Evidence Based Coaching and Mentoring, 6,* 100–113.

Jackson, P. (2005). How do we describe coaching? An exploratory development of a typology of coaching based on the accounts of UK-based practitioners. *International Journal of Evidence Based Coaching and Mentoring, 3*(2), 45–60.

Jarvis, J., Lane, D. A., & Fillery-Travis, A. (2006). *The case for coaching: Making evidence-based decisions.* London: Chartered Institute of Personnel and Development.

Joo, B. K. (2005). Executive coaching: A conceptual framework from an integrative review of practice and research. *Human Resource Development Review, 4,* 462–488. doi:10.1177/1534484305280866

Jopling, A. (2007). *The fuzzy space: Exploring the experience of the space between psychotherapy and executive coaching.* Unpublished master's thesis, New School of Psychotherapy and Counselling, London.

Kaiser, R. B., Hogan, R., & Craig, S. B. (2008). Leadership and the fate of organizations. *American Psychologist, 63,* 96–110. doi:10.1037/0003-066X.63.2.96

Kampa, S., & White, R. P. (2002). The effectiveness of executive coaching: What we know and what we still need to know. In R. L. Lowman (Ed.), *Handbook of organizational consulting psychology* (pp. 139–158). San Francisco: Jossey-Bass.

Kampa-Kokesch, S., & Anderson, M. Z. (2001). Executive coaching: A comprehensive review of the literature. *Consulting Psychology Journal: Practice and Research, 53,* 205–228. doi:10.1037/1061-4087.53.4.205

Kauffman, C. (2006). Positive psychology: The science at the heart of coaching. In D. R. Stober & A. M. Grant (Eds.), *Evidence-based coaching handbook: Putting best practices to work for your clients* (pp. 219–253). Hoboken, NJ: Wiley.

Kauffman, C., & Coutu, D. (2009). *HBR research report: The realities of executive coaching.* Cambridge, MA: Harvard Business Review. Retrieved January 12, 2009, from http://www.coachingreport.hbr.org

Kemp, T. J. (2008a). Coach self-management: The foundation of coaching effectiveness. In D. B. Drake, D. Brennan, & K. Gørtz (Eds.), *The philosophy and practice of coaching* (pp. 27–50). San Francisco: Jossey-Bass.

Kemp, T. J. (2008b). Self-management and the coaching relationship: Exploring coaching impact beyond models and methods. *International Coaching Psychology Review, 3,* 32–42.

Kiel, F., Rimmer, E., Williams, K., & Doyle, M. (1996). Coaching at the top. *Consulting Psychology Journal: Practice and Research, 48,* 67–77. doi:10.1037/1061-4087.48.2.67

Kiesler, D. J. (1966). Some myths of psychotherapy research and the search for a paradigm. *Psychological Bulletin, 65,* 110–136. doi:10.1037/h0022911

Kilburg, R. R. (2000). *Executive coaching: Developing managerial wisdom in a world of chaos.* Washington, DC: American Psychological Association. doi:10.1037/10355-000

Kilburg, R. R. (2001). Facilitating intervention adherence in executive coaching: A model and methods. *Consulting Psychology Journal: Practice and Research, 53,* 251–267. doi:10.1037/1061-4087.53.4.251

Kilburg, R. R. (2002, February). *Postmodern approaches to executive coaching.* Preconference workshop presented at the annual conference of the Society for Consulting Psychology, San Antonio, TX.

Kilburg, R. R. (2004a). Trudging toward Dodoville: Conceptual approaches and case studies in executive coaching. *Consulting Psychology Journal: Practice and Research, 56,* 203–213. doi:10.1037/1065-9293.56.4.203

Kilburg, R. R. (2004b). When shadows fall: Using psychodynamic approaches in executive coaching. *Consulting Psychology Journal: Practice and Research, 56,* 246–268. doi:10.1037/1065-9293.56.4.246

Kiresuk, T. J., Smith, A., & Cardillo, J. E. (Eds.). (1994). *Goal attainment scaling: Applications, theory, and measurement.* Hillsdale, NJ: Erlbaum.

Kluger, A. N., & DeNisi, A. (1996). The effects of feedback interventions on performance: A historical review, a meta-analysis and a preliminary feedback intervention theory. *Psychological Bulletin, 119,* 254–284. doi:10.1037/0033-2909.119.2.254

Kombarakaran, F. A., Yang, J. A., Baker, M. N., & Fernandes, P. B. (2008). Executive coaching: It works! *Consulting Psychology Journal: Practice and Research, 60,* 78–90. doi:10.1037/1065-9293.60.1.78

Kralj, M. M. (2001). Coaching at the top: Assisting a chief executive and his team. *Consulting Psychology Journal: Practice and Research, 53,* 108–116. doi:10.1037/1061-4087.53.2.108

Lambert, M. J., & Barley, D. E. (2002). Research summary on the therapeutic relationship and psychotherapy outcome. In J. C. Norcross (Ed.), *Psychotherapy relationships that work: Therapist contributions and responsiveness of patients* (17–35). New York: Oxford University Press.

Lambrechts, F., Grieten, S., Bouwen, R., & Corthouts, F. (2009). Process consultation revisited: Taking a relational practice perspective. *Journal of Applied Behavioral Science, 45*(1), 39–58. doi:10.1177/0021886308326563

Laske, O. E. (1999). An integrated model of developmental coaching. *Consulting Psychology Journal: Practice and Research, 51,* 139–159. doi:10.1037/1061-4087.51.3.139

Latham, G. P. (2007). Theory and research on coaching practices. *Australian Psychologist, 42,* 268–270. doi:10.1080/00050060701648209

Latham, G. P., & Pinder, C. C. (2005). Work motivation theory and research at the dawn of the twenty-first century. *Annual Review of Psychology, 56,* 485–516. doi:10.1146/annurev.psych.55.090902.142105

Latham, G. P., Seijts, G., & Crim, D. (2008). The effects of learning goal difficulty level and cognitive ability on performance. *Canadian Journal of Behavioural Science, 40,* 220–229. doi:10.1037/a0013114

Law, H., Ireland, S., & Hussain, Z. (2007). *The psychology of coaching, mentoring and learning.* West Sussex, England: Wiley.

Lawrence, W. G. (2006). Executive coaching, unconscious thinking, and infinity. In H. Brunning (Ed.), *Executive coaching: A systems-psychodynamic approach* (pp. 97–111). London: Karnac.

Lawton-Smith, C., & Cox, E. (2007, Summer). Coaching: Is it just a new name for training? *International Journal of Evidence Based Coaching and Mentoring,* 1–9.

Lazar, J., & Bergquist, W. (2003). Alignment coaching: The missing element of business coaching. *International Journal of Coaching in Organizations, 1*(1), 14–27.

Leedham, M. (2005). The coaching scorecard: A holistic approach to evaluating the benefits of business coaching. *International Journal of Evidence Based Coaching and Mentoring, 3*(2), 30–44.

Levenson, A. (2009). Measuring and maximizing the business impact of executive coaching. *Consulting Psychology Journal: Practice and Research, 61,* 103–121. doi:10.1037/a0015438

Libri, V., & Kemp, T. (2006). Assessing the efficacy of a cognitive behavioural executive coaching programme. *International Coaching Psychology Review, 1*(2), 9–20.

Liljenstrand, A. M., & Nebeker, D. M. (2008). Coaching services: A look at coaches, clients, and practices. *Consulting Psychology Journal: Practice and Research, 60,* 57–77. doi:10.1037/1065-9293.60.1.57

Locke, E. A., & Latham, G. P. (1990). *A theory of goal setting and task performance.* Englewood Cliffs, NJ: Prentice-Hall.

Locke, E. A., & Latham, G. P. (2002). Building a practically useful theory of goal setting and task motivation: A 35-year odyssey. *American Psychologist, 57,* 705–717. doi:10.1037/0003-066X.57.9.705

Lombardo, M. M., & Eichinger, R. W. (2002). *The leadership machine: Architecture to develop leaders for any future.* Minneapolis, MN: Lominger.

London, M. (1997). *Job feedback: Giving, seeking, and using feedback for performance improvement.* Mahwah, NJ: Erlbaum.

London, M. (2002). *Leadership development: Paths to self-insight and professional growth.* Mahwah, NJ: Erlbaum.

London, M., Smither, J. W., & Adsit, D. J. (1997). Accountability: The Achilles' heel of multisource feedback. *Group & Organization Management, 22,* 162–184. doi:10.1177/1059601197222003

Lopez, S. J., & Snyder, C. R. (2003). *Positive psychological assessment: A handbook of models and measures.* Washington, DC: American Psychological Association. doi:10.1037/10612-000

Ludeman, K., & Erlandson, E. (2004). Coaching the alpha male. *Harvard Business Review, 82*(5), 58–67.

Luebbe, D. M. (2005). *The three-way mirror of executive coaching.* Unpublished doctoral dissertation, Union Institute & University, Cincinnati, OH.

Luthans, F., & Peterson, S. J. (2003). 360-degree feedback with systematic coaching: Empirical analysis suggests a winning combination. *Human Resource Management, 42,* 243–256. doi:10.1002/hrm.10083

Maccoby, M. (2000). Narcissistic leaders: The incredible pros, the inevitable cons. *Harvard Business Review, 78*(1), 68–77.

MacKie, D. (2007). Evaluating the effectiveness of executive coaching: Where are we now and where do we need to be? *Australian Psychologist, 42,* 310–318. doi:10.1080/00050060701648217

Mahoney, M. J. (1991). *Human change processes: The scientific foundations of psychotherapy.* New York: Basic Books.

Maister, D. H., Green, C. H., & Galford, R. M. (2001). *The trusted advisor.* New York: Free Press.

Major, D. A., Turner, J. E., & Fletcher, T. D. (2006). Linking proactive personality and the Big Five to motivation to learn and development activity. *Journal of Applied Psychology, 91,* 927–935. doi:10.1037/0021-9010.91.4.927

Mansi, A. (2009). Coaching the narcissist: How difficult can it be? Challenges for coaching psychologists. *The Coaching Psychologist, 5,* 22–25.

Marshall, M. K. (2006). *The critical factors of coaching practice leading to successful coaching outcomes.* Unpublished doctoral dissertation, Antioch University, Yellow Springs, OH.

Marx, R. (1986). Improving management development through relapse prevention strategies. *Journal of Management Development, 5*(2), 27–40. doi:10.1108/eb051607

McCall, M. W., Lombardo, M. M., & Morrison, A. M. (1988). *The lessons of experience: How successful executives develop on the job.* New York: Free Press.

McDermott, M., Levenson, A., & Newton, S. (2007). What coaching can and cannot do for your organization. *Human Resource Planning, 30*(2), 30–37.

McGovern, J., Lindemann, M., Vergara, M., Murphy, S., Barker, L., & Warrenfeltz, R. (2001). Maximizing the impact of executive coaching: Behavioral change, organizational outcomes, and return on investment. *Manchester Review, 6*(1), 1–9.

McKenna, D. D., & Davis, S. L. (2009). Hidden in plain sight: The active ingredients of executive coaching. *Industrial and Organizational Psychology: Perspectives on Science and Practice, 2,* 244–260. doi:10.1111/j.1754-9434.2009.01143.x

Meinke, L., Friedman, R., Krapu, T., Kramer, L., & Salinger, H. (2004, November). *Squirrels in your attic: Maintaining integrity and presence when facing clinical Issues in the coaching process.* Paper presented at the annual conference of the International Coach Federation, Quebec City, Quebec, Canada.

Miller, S. D., Hubble, M. A., & Duncan, B. L. (Eds.). (1996). *Handbook of solution-focused brief therapy.* San Francisco: Jossey-Bass.

Miller, W. R., & Rollnick, S. (2002). *Motivational interviewing: Preparing people for change* (2nd ed.). New York: Guilford Press.

Minahan, M. (2006). The foundations of coaching: Roots in OD. *OD Practitioner, 38*(3), 4–7.

Myers, I. B., McCaulley, M. H., Quenk, N. L., & Hammer, A. L. (1998). *MBTI manual: A guide to the development and use of the Myers-Briggs Type Indicator* (3rd ed.). Gainesville, FL: Center for Applications of Psychological Type.

Nadler, D. A. (2005). Confessions of a trusted counselor. *Harvard Business Review, 83*(9), 68–77.

Naficy, K., & Isabella, L. (2008). How executive coaching can fuel professional and personal growth. *OD Practitioner, 40*(1), 40–46.

Naquin, S. S., & Baldwin, T. T. (2003). Managing transfer before learning begins: The transfer-ready learner. In

E. F. Holton, III, & T. T. Baldwin (Eds.), *Improving learning transfer in organizations* (pp. 80–96). San Francisco: Jossey-Bass.

Natale, S. M., & Diamante, T. (2005). The five stages of executive coaching: Better process makes better practice. *Journal of Business Ethics, 59,* 361–374. doi:10.1007/s10551-005-0382-2

Nelson, E., & Hogan, R. (2009). Coaching on the dark side. *International Coaching Psychology Review, 4,* 9–21.

Noe, R. A. (1986). Trainee's attributes and attitudes: Neglected influences on training effectiveness. *Academy of Management Review, 11,* 736–749. doi:10.2307/258393

Noer, D. (2000). The big three derailment factors in a coaching relationship. In M. Goldsmith, L. Lyons, & A. Freas (Eds.), *Coaching for leadership* (pp. 317–323). San Francisco: Jossey-Bass.

O'Broin, A., & Palmer, S. (2007). Reappraising the coach–client relationship: The unassuming change agent in coaching. In S. Palmer & A. Whybrow (Eds.), *Handbook of coaching psychology* (pp. 295–324). New York: Routledge.

O'Connor, J., & Lages, A. (2007). *How coaching works: The essential guide to the history and practice of effective coaching.* London: A & C Black.

Offermanns, M. (2004). *Braucht Coaching einen Coach? Eine evaluative Pilotstudie* [Does coaching need a coach? An evaluative pilot study]. Stuttgart: Ibidem Verlag.

Olivero, G., Bane, K. D., & Kopelman, R. E. (1997). Executive coaching as a transfer of training tool: Effects on productivity in a public agency. *Public Personnel Management, 26,* 461–469.

Olson, P. O. (2008). A review of assumptions in executive coaching. *The Coaching Psychologist, 4,* 151–159.

Orenstein, R. L. (2006). Measuring executive coaching efficacy? The answer was right here all the time. *Consulting Psychology Journal: Practice and Research, 58,* 106–116. doi:10.1037/1065-9293.58.2.106

Palmer, S. (2007). Foreword. In H. Law, S. Ireland, & Z. Hussain (Eds.), *The psychology of coaching, mentoring and learning* (pp. ix–xi). West Sussex, England: Wiley.

Palmer, S., & Whybrow, A. (2007). Coaching psychology: An introduction. In S. Palmer & A. Whybrow (Eds.), *Handbook of coaching psychology* (pp. 1–20). New York: Routledge.

Parker-Wilkins, V. (2006). Business impact of executive coaching: Demonstrating monetary value. *Industrial and Commercial Training, 38*(3), 122–127. doi:10.1108/00197850610659373

Passmore, J. (2007a). Addressing deficit performance through coaching—using motivational interviewing for performance improvement at work. *International Coaching Psychology Review, 2,* 265–279.

Passmore, J. (2007b). Behavioural coaching. In S. Palmer & A. Whybrow (Eds.), *The handbook of coaching psychology* (pp. 73–85). New York: Routledge.

Passmore, J. (2007c, Summer). Coaching and mentoring: The role of experience and sector knowledge [Special issue]. *International Journal of Evidence Based Coaching and Mentoring,* 10–16.

Passmore, J. (Ed.). (2008). *Psychometrics in coaching, Using psychological and psychometric tools for development.* Philadelphia: Kogan Page.

Passmore, J., & Gibbes, C. (2007). The state of executive coaching research: What does the current literature tell us and what's next for coaching research? *International Coaching Psychology Review, 2,* 116–128.

Peel, D. (2005). The significance of behavioral learning theory to the development of effective coaching practice. *International Journal of Evidence Based Coaching and Mentoring, 3*(1), 18–28.

Peltier, B. (2009). *The psychology of executive coaching: Theory and application* (2nd ed.). New York: Routledge.

Peterson, D. B. (1993a, March). *Measuring change: A psychometric approach to evaluating individual coaching outcomes.* Presented at the annual conference of the Society for Industrial and Organizational Psychology, San Francisco.

Peterson, D. B. (1993b). *Skill learning and behavior change in an individually tailored management coaching program.* Unpublished doctoral dissertation, University of Minnesota, Minneapolis.

Peterson, D. B. (1996). Executive coaching at work: The art of one-on-one change. *Consulting Psychology Journal: Practice and Research, 48,* 78–86. doi:10.1037/1061-4087.48.2.78

Peterson, D. B. (2006). People are complex and the world is messy: A behavior-based approach to executive coaching. In D. R. Stober & A. M. Grant (Eds.), *Evidence-based coaching handbook: Putting best practices to work for your clients* (pp. 51–76). Hoboken, NJ: Wiley.

Peterson, D. B. (2009). Coaching and performance management: How can organizations get the greatest value? In J. W. Smither & M. London (Eds.), *Performance management: Putting research into action* (pp. 115–156). San Francisco: Jossey-Bass.

Peterson, D. B., & Hicks, M. D. (1995). *Development FIRST: Strategies for self-development.* Minneapolis, MN: Personnel Decisions International.

Peterson, D. B., & Hicks, M. D. (1996). *Leader as coach: Strategies for coaching and developing others.* Minneapolis, MN: Personnel Decisions.

Peterson, D. B., & Kraiger, K. (2004). A practical guide to evaluating coaching: Translating state-of-the-art techniques to the real world. In J. E. Edwards, J. C. Scott, & N. S. Raju (Eds.), *The human resources program evaluation handbook* (pp. 262–282). Thousand Oaks, CA: Sage.

Peterson, D. B., & Little, B. (2008, January–February). Growth market: The rise of systemic coaching. *Coaching at Work, 3*(1), 44–47.

Peterson, D. B., & Millier, J. (2005). The alchemy of coaching: "You're good, Jennifer, but you could be really good." *Consulting Psychology Journal: Practice and Research, 57,* 14–40. doi:10.1037/1065-9293.57.1.14

Peterson, D. B., & Muros, J. (2008, August). *Accountability and transfer of learning in executive coaching.* Invited address, American Psychological Association, Boston.

Peterson, D. B., & Sutherland, E. (2003, April). *Advanced coaching: Accelerating the transition from good to great.* Preconference workshop at the annual conference of the Society for Industrial and Organizational Psychology, Orlando, FL.

Phillips, J. J. (2007). Measuring the ROI of a coaching intervention, part 2. *Performance Improvement, 46*(10), 10–23. doi:10.1002/pfi.167

Phillips, J. J., & Phillips, P. P. (2007). Show me the money: The use of ROI in performance improvement, part 1. *Performance Improvement, 46*(9), 8–22. doi:10.1002/pfi.160

Platt, G. (2008). *Coaching: A faster way to lose money than burning it.* Retrieved February 1, 2009, from http://www.trainingzone.co.uk/cgi-bin/item.cgi?id=179384

Poteet, M. L., & Kudisch, J. D. (2007, April). The voice of the coachee: What makes for an effective coaching relationship? In J. E. A. Russell (Chair), *Enhancing the effectiveness of executive coaching through research with clients.* Paper presented at the 22nd annual conference of the Society for Industrial and Organizational Psychology, New York.

Prochaska, J. O., & DiClemente, C. C. (1984). *The transtheoretical approach: Crossing the traditional boundaries of therapy.* Homewood, IL: Dow-Jones.

Prochaska, J. O., & Norcross, J. C. (2001). Stages of change. *Psychotherapy (Chicago), 38,* 443–448. doi:10.1037/0033-3204.38.4.443

Renard, L. (2005). *Executive coaching for professional organisations.* Unpublished doctoral dissertation, American University of London, London.

Rock, D. (2008). SCARF: A brain-based model for collaborating with and influencing others. *NeuroLeadership Journal, 1,* 44–52.

Rock, D., & Donde, R. (2008). Driving organisational change with internal coaching programmes: Part two. *Industrial and Commercial Training, 40*(2), 75–80. doi:10.1108/00197850810858901

Rock, D., & Page, L. J. (2009). *Coaching with the brain in mind: Foundations for practice.* Hoboken, NJ: Wiley.

Rogers, C. R. (1957). The necessary and sufficient conditions of therapeutic personality change. *Journal of Consulting Psychology, 21,* 95–103. doi:10.1037/h0045357

Rosenthal, S. A., & Pittinsky, T. L. (2006). Narcissistic leadership. *The Leadership Quarterly, 17,* 617–633. doi:10.1016/j.leaqua.2006.10.005

Ryan, R. M., & Deci, E. L. (2008). A self-determination theory approach to psychotherapy: The motivational basis for effective change. *Canadian Psychology, 49,* 186–193. doi:10.1037/a0012753

Scheel, M. J., Hanson, W. E., & Razzhavaikina, T. I. (2004). The process of recommending homework in psychotherapy: A review of therapist delivery methods, client acceptability, and factors that affect compliance. *Psychotherapy: Theory, Research, Practice. Training (New York), 41*(1), 38–55.

Schein, E. H. (1999). *Process consultation revisited: Building the helping relationship.* Reading, MA: Addison-Wesley/Longman.

Schein, E. H. (2000). Coaching and consultation: Are they the same? In M. Goldsmith, L. Lyons, & A. Freas (Eds.), *Coaching for leadership: How the world's greatest coaches help leaders learn* (pp. 65–73). San Francisco: Jossey-Bass/Pfeiffer.

Schein, E. H. (2003). Five traps for consulting psychologists: Or, how I learned to take culture seriously. *Consulting Psychology Journal: Practice and Research, 55,* 75–83.

Schlosser, B., & Steinbrenner, D. (2008, October). *The coaching impact study: Understanding the value of executive coaching.* Presented at the Society for Industrial and Organizational Psychology Leading Edge Consortium, Cincinnati, OH.

Schlosser, B., Steinbrenner, D., Kumata, E., & Hunt, J. (2006). The coaching impact study: Measuring the value of executive coaching. *International Journal of Coaching in Organizations, 4*(3), 8–26.

Schmidt, A. M., & Dolis, C. M. (2009). Something's got to give: The effects of dual-goal difficulty, goal progress, and expectancies on resource allocation. *Journal of Applied Psychology, 94,* 678–691. doi:10.1037/a0014945

Schnell, E. R. (2005). A case study of executive coaching as a support mechanism during organizational growth and evolution. *Consulting Psychology Journal: Practice and Research, 57,* 41–56. doi:10.1037/1065-9293.57.1.41

Seamons, B. L. (2006). *The most effective factors in executive coaching engagements according to the coach, the client, and the client's boss.* Unpublished doctoral dissertation, Saybrook Graduate School and Research Center, San Francisco.

Seibert, K. W., & Daudelin, M. W. (1999). *The role of reflection in managerial learning: Theory, research, and practice.* Westport, CT: Quorum.

Shadish, W. R., Cook, T. D., & Campbell, D. T. (2002). *Experimental and quasi-experimental designs for generalized causal inference.* Boston: Houghton Mifflin.

Sherman, S., & Freas, A. (2004). The wild west of executive coaching. *Harvard Business Review, 82*(11), 82–90.

Sheth, J. N., & Sobel, A. (2000). *Clients for life: How great professionals develop breakthrough relationships.* New York: Simon & Schuster.

Smither, J. W., London, M., & Reilly, R. R. (2005). Does performance improve following multisource feedback? A theoretical model, meta-analysis, and review of empirical findings. *Personnel Psychology, 58,* 33–66. doi:10.1111/j.1744-6570.2005.514_1.x

Smither, J. W., London, M., Flautt, R., Vargas, Y., & Kucine, I. (2003). Can working with an executive coach improve multisource feedback ratings over time? A quasi-experimental field study. *Personnel Psychology, 56,* 23–44. doi:10.1111/j.1744-6570.2003.tb00142.x

Society for Organizational Learning. (n.d.). *Executive coaching: Partnered reflection for learning and results.* Cambridge, MA: Author. Retrieved January 20, 2009, from http://www.solonline.org/repository/download/SoL_coaching.pdf?item_id=9028045

Sokol, M. (2000, July). *Demystifying coaching: Executive development in the context of organisational change.* Keynote presentation at the Linkage Coaching and Mentoring Conference, London.

Spence, G. B. (2007). GAS powered coaching: Goal attainment scaling and its use in coaching research and practice. *International Coaching Psychology Review, 2,* 155–167.

Spinelli, E. (2008). Coaching and therapy: Similarities and divergences. *International Coaching Psychology Review, 3,* 241–249.

Spreier, S. W., Fontaine, M. H., & Malloy, R. L. (2006). Leadership run amok: The destructive potential of overachievers. *Harvard Business Review, 84*(6), 72–82.

Stein, I. F. (2008). *Enacting the role of coach: Discursive identities in professional coaching discourse.* Unpublished doctoral dissertation, Fielding Graduate University, Santa Barbara, CA.

Steinmetz, B. (2005). *Stressmanagement fuer Fuehrungskraefte* [Stress management for executives]. Hamburg, Germany: Kova.

Stern, L. R. (2004). Executive coaching: A working definition. *Consulting Psychology Journal: Practice and Research, 56,* 154–162. doi:10.1037/1065-9293.56.3.154

Stewart, L. J., O'Riordan, S., & Palmer, S. (2008). Before we know how we've done, we need to know what we're doing: Operationalising coaching to provide a foundation for coaching evaluation. *The Coaching Psychologist, 4,* 127–133.

Stober, D. R. (2006). Coaching from the humanistic perspective. In D. R. Stober & A. M. Grant (Eds.), *Evidence-based coaching handbook: Putting best practices to work for your clients* (pp. 17–50). Hoboken, NJ: Wiley.

Sue-Chan, C., & Latham, G. P. (2004). The relative effectiveness of external, peer, and self-coaches. *Applied Psychology: An International Review, 53,* 260–278. doi:10.1111/j.1464-0597.2004.00171.x

Tessmann-Keys, D., & Wellins, R. S. (2007). *The CEO's guide to preparing future global leaders.* Pittsburgh, PA: Development Dimensions International.

Thach, E. C. (2002). The impact of executive coaching and 360 feedback on leadership effectiveness. *Leadership and Organization Development Journal, 23,* 205–214. doi:10.1108/01437730210429070

Thach, L., & Heinselman, T. (1999). Executive coaching defined. *Training & Development, 53*(3), 35–39.

Thomas, J. C. (2006, December 6). Does coaching work? Who knows? [Review of the book *Evidence based coaching handbook: Putting best practices to work with your clients*]. *PsycCRITIQUES: Contemporary Psychology—APA Review of Books, 51*(49), Article 6. Retrieved December 14, 2006, from the PsycCRITIQUES database.

Thompson, A. D., Jr. (1986). *A formative evaluation of an individualized coaching program for business managers and professionals.* Unpublished doctoral dissertation, University of Minnesota, Minneapolis.

Thompson, H. B., Bear, D. J., Dennis, D. J., Vickers, M., London, J., & Morrison, C. L. (2008). *Coaching: A global study of successful practices: Current trends and future possibilities 2008-2018.* New York: American Management Association.

Tobias, L. L. (1996). Coaching executives. *Consulting Psychology Journal: Practice and Research, 48,* 87–95. doi:10.1037/1061-4087.48.2.87

Trudeau, D. A. (2004). *Toward a conceptual model of executive coaching practices in organizations in the United States: A modified Delphi forecasting technique.* Unpublished doctoral dissertation, University of Nebraska, Lincoln.

Tziner, A., Haccoun, R., & Kadish, A. (1991). Personal and situational characteristics influencing the effectiveness of transfer of training improvement strategies. *Journal of Occupational Psychology, 64,* 167–177.

Uhl-Bien, M. (2003). Relationship development as a key ingredient of leadership development. In S. E. Murphy & R. Riggio (Eds.), *The future of leadership development* (pp. 129–148). Mahwah, NJ: Erlbaum.

Underhill, B. O., McAnally, K., & Koriath, J. J. (2007). *Executive coaching for results.* San Francisco: Berrett-Koehler.

Wales, S. (2003). Why coaching? *Journal of Change Management, 3,* 275–282. doi:10.1080/714042542

Walker, S. (2004). The evolution of coaching; patterns, icons and freedom. *International Journal of Evidence Based Coaching and Mentoring, 2*(2), 16–28.

Waring, P. A. (2008). Coaching the brain. *The Coaching Psychologist, 4,* 63–70.

Wasylyshyn, K. M. (2003). Executive coaching: An outcome study. *Consulting Psychology Journal: Practice and Research, 55,* 94–106. doi:10.1037/1061-4087.55.2.94

Wasylyshyn, K. M. (2005). The reluctant president. *Consulting Psychology Journal: Practice and Research, 57,* 57–70. doi:10.1037/1065-9293.57.1.57

Wasylyshyn, K. M., Gronsky, B., & Haas, W. (2006). Tigers, stripes, and behavior change: Survey results of a commissioned coaching program. *Consulting Psychology Journal: Practice and Research, 58,* 65–81. doi:10.1037/1065-9293.58.2.65

Wellner, A. S. (2006). Do you need a coach? *Inc., 28*(4), 86–92.

White, R. P., & Shullman, S. L. (2002, August). *Executive coaching: Models, context and practice.* Workshop presented at the 110th Annual Convention of the American Psychological Association, Chicago.

Whitmore, J. (2002). *Coaching for performance* (3rd ed.). London: Nicholas Brealey.

Whitworth, L., Kimsey-House, H., & Sandahl, P. (1998). *Co-active coaching: New skills for coaching people toward success in work and life.* Palo Alto, CA: Davies-Black.

Winum, P. C. (2005). Effectiveness of a high-potential African American executive: The anatomy of a coaching engagement. *Consulting Psychology Journal: Practice and Research, 57,* 71–89. doi:10.1037/1065-9293.57.1.71

Wise, P. S., & Voss, E. S. (2002). *Research report: The case for executive coaching.* Durango, CO: Lore International Institute.

Witherspoon, R., & White, R. P. (1996). Executive coaching: A continuum of roles. *Consulting Psychology Journal: Practice and Research, 48,* 124–133. doi:10.1037/1061-4087.48.2.124

Worldwide Association of Business Coaches. (2007). *Business coaching definition and competencies.* Retrieved March 12, 2008, from http://www.wabccoaches.com/includes/popups/definition_and_competencies.html

Wycherly, I. M., & Cox, E. (2008). Factors in the selection and matching of executive coaches in organisations. *Coaching: An International Journal of Theory. Research and Practice, 1*(1), 39–53.

Zeus, P., & Skiffington, S. (2000). *The complete guide to coaching at work.* North Ryde, Australia: McGraw-Hill.

CHAPTER 19

PROACTIVE WORK BEHAVIOR: FORWARD-THINKING AND CHANGE-ORIENTED ACTION IN ORGANIZATIONS

Uta K. Bindl and Sharon K. Parker

> On a few occasions if there's something that's not working or is causing a duplication of work then I've challenged it. One particular incident is that there was a process not so long back where we'd send out a letter to a customer, then also leave a message on their phone. So what we did—we evaluated that—so to leave a message first then, if there's no response, send a letter rather than doing both at the same time. I know it's only a little thing, but it saves a lot of time.

The preceding quotation is from a call center agent whose job it is to sell energy. The behavior reported by the agent aptly illustrates individual proactivity, or self-starting, future-oriented behavior that aims to bring about change in one's self or the situation (Grant & Ashford, 2008; Jones, 1986; Parker, Williams, & Turner, 2006). This particular comment is an example of proactive behavior that is aimed at improving work processes or changing the situation. Several studies have found that employees who are proactive in this way also perform their job more effectively (Ashford & Black, 1996; Morrison, 1993a, 1993b; Thompson, 2005). Proactivity also applies in other domains; for example, individuals can be more or less proactive in managing their careers (Seibert, Kraimer, & Crant, 2001), shaping their work environment (Wrzesniewski & Dutton, 2001), and coping with stress (Aspinwall & Taylor, 1997).

In recent times, there has been a surge of interest in proactivity at work, partly reflecting academic developments and partly reflecting the increasing importance of this type of behavior in today's organizations. Academically, there has been a flurry of proactive concepts, albeit varying in whether proactivity is seen as a stable disposition (Crant, 2000), a pattern of behaviors (Frese & Fay, 2001), or—as we do in this chapter—a way of behaving at work (Grant & Ashford, 2008; Parker, Williams, & Turner, 2006). As Frese (2008) noted in a recent article entitled "The Word Is Out: We Need an Active Performance Concept for Modern Work Places," the current interest in proactivity is warranted given the inadequacy of traditional models that "assume that employees ought to follow instructions, task descriptions, and orders" (p. 67). Practically, organizations are increasingly decentralized, change is fast paced, there is a demand for innovation, and operational uncertainty is greater than ever, all trends that mean employees need to use their initiative and be proactive (e.g., Campbell, 2000; Wall & Jackson, 1995). Moreover, careers are increasingly boundaryless and not confined to one organization, requiring individuals to take charge of their own careers (Mirvis & Hall, 1994). Thus, for both theoretical and practical reasons, a review on proactivity is timely.

We consider definitions and different types of proactivity in the first part of our review. We then propose an integrating framework of proactive behavior that includes antecedents, motivational processes, outcomes, and moderators (see Figure 19.1). We discuss how proactive behavior is in part a function of individual attributes but is also influenced, shaped, and constrained by the work context (e.g., the degree

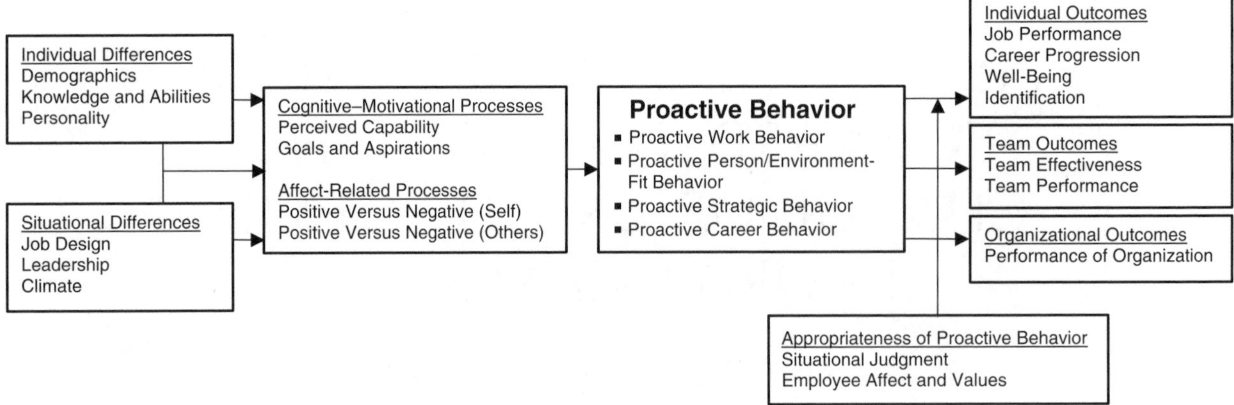

FIGURE 19.1. **Model of individual-level proactive behavior.**

of job autonomy provided). We conclude by offering future research directions. We focus primarily on individual-level proactivity, although we also briefly discuss research on team and organization-level proactivity.

WHAT IS PROACTIVE BEHAVIOR?

Traditionally, work psychology has focused on work characteristics to which employees adjust to perform their job (e.g., Hackman & Oldham, 1976), on employees' commitment to goals that are provided by the organization (Locke, Shaw, Saari, & Latham, 1981), and on social structures and cultures at work to which new employees need to adapt (Van Maanen, 1976). In contrast, research on *active* behavior focuses on how employees change the characteristics of their job and situation (Frese, Garst, & Fay, 2007). For example, employees sometimes redefine the goals they are provided with by the organization to come up with more challenging goals (Hacker, 1985) and actively influence socialization processes to improve the quality of their experiences at work (Ashford & Black, 1996; Saks & Ashforth, 1996). These active behaviors have increasingly come to be referred to as examples of proactivity.

What does it mean to be proactive? In line with previous research (Grant & Ashford, 2008; Parker, Williams, & Turner, 2006), we define proactive behavior as self-directed and future-focused action in an organization in which the individual aims to bring about change, including change to the situation (e.g., introducing new work methods, influencing organizational strategy) and/or change within him- or herself (e.g., learning new skills to cope with future demands). This definition concurs with lay definitions, which highlight both a future focus (anticipation) and a change focus (taking control). Thus, the *Oxford English Dictionary* (Simpson et al., 2008) defines being proactive as "creating or controlling a situation by taking the initiative and anticipating events or problems, rather than just reacting to them after they have occurred; (hence, more generally) innovative, tending to make things happen."

As an example, personal initiative is a form of proactive behavior that involves going beyond assigned tasks, developing one's own goals, and attempting to solve problems that have not yet occurred (Frese & Fay, 2001). Taking charge is also an example of proactive behavior, referring to active efforts to bring about change on work methods (Morrison & Phelps, 1999). Further examples include individuals proactively shaping their work environment as a newcomer (Ashford & Black, 1996), actively building networks (Morrison, 2002), and persuading leaders to take notice of important strategic issues (Dutton & Ashford, 1993). All of these behaviors have in common an emphasis on taking control of a situation by looking ahead and initiating change. They are also all behaviors that are partially determined by disposition and partially influenced by situational forces such as job design and leadership.

Similarities and Differences in Proactive Behavior

Although the concepts of proactive behavior have in common an emphasis on taking control of a situation in a self-directed and future-focused way, they also vary from each other. In response to criticism that the field is not sufficiently integrated (Crant, 2000), Grant and Ashford (2008) proposed that proactive behaviors vary in terms of their form (the type of behavior), their intended target of impact (self, others, and/or the organization), their frequency (how often), their place and timing (where and when), and their tactics (how). For example, employees can engage in either feedback seeking or social network building (form). The intended target of impact of this behavior can be the self (e.g., to improve one's own performance), or others (e.g., to improve how one manages others). Employees can seek feedback more or less often (frequency), and they can choose certain times for seeking feedback, such as when project work is completed (timing). Employees can also use different tactics when engaging in feedback seeking; for example, an employee might ask another person directly for feedback or rather concentrate on monitoring and interpreting the other person's reactions.

Adopting an empirical approach, Parker and Collins (2008) investigated a higher order factor structure of proactive behavior at work. Factor analyses of multiple forms of proactive behavior suggested at least three higher order categories, each with a different target of impact. First, proactive work behavior includes those behaviors aimed at taking control of and bringing about change in the internal organization environment. Examples include taking charge (Morrison & Phelps, 1999), voice (Van Dyne & LePine, 1998), the implementation items of individual innovation (Scott & Bruce, 1994), and problem prevention (Frese & Fay, 2001; Parker & Collins, 2008). Second, proactive strategic behavior includes those behaviors aimed at taking control of and causing change in the broader unit's strategy and its fit with the external environment. For example, individuals can sell important issues to the leader and thereby influence strategy (Ashford, Rothbard, Piderit, & Dutton, 1998), and they can scan the environment to anticipate new products and services the organization might introduce to better achieve competitive advantage (Parker & Collins, 2008). Third, proactive person–environment fit behavior includes those self-initiated behaviors that aim to achieve greater compatibility between one's own attributes (skills, knowledge, values, preferences) and the organizational environment. An example is actively seeking feedback about performance such as through inquiry or monitoring (Ashford, Blatt, & VandeWalle, 2003). Through such action, the individual aims to improve his or her performance within the organization. Proactive person–environment fit behaviors also include those aimed at ensuring the environment supplies the attributes desired or valued by an individual (supplies-values fit), such as job-change negotiation (Ashford & Black, 1996) and ex post i-deals and job crafting. Ex post i-deals (Rousseau, Ho, & Greenberg, 2006) are arrangements that are negotiated by a new person in the job to accommodate personal needs for the joint benefit of the individual and the organization. Job crafting (Wrzesniewski & Dutton, 2001) involves individuals' changing tasks, roles, and relationships to derive meaning and satisfaction from the work.

Grant and Parker (2009) identified a further higher order dimension—proactive career behavior. In contrast to the other types of proactivity that occur within the context of a designated job, this dimension refers to proactivity beyond a specific job, such as actions to secure a job or to get a new job (career initiative; Tharenou & Terry, 1998) or actions to negotiate a better deal prior to accepting a job (ex ante i-deals; Rousseau et al., 2006).

One of the advantages of identifying these higher order categories of proactive behaviors is that the approach can help to identify common processes across the related behaviors within each category. For example, the Parker and Collins (2008) study highlighted commonalities among voice, individual innovation, and taking charge—all types of proactive work behavior—even though these tend to be distinct areas of inquiry. At the same time, the study also identified differences across the categories of proactivity. For example, whereas conscientiousness was an important predictor of proactive person–environment fit behaviors, as expected given the desire of conscientious individuals to be dependable and fit well with the organization, it did not predict proactive work behaviors or proactive strategic behaviors. The findings, therefore, also serve to highlight how motivating forces for proactivity vary across different domains and targets of impact.

Other scholars too have differentiated types of proactive behavior. Thus, Griffin, Neal, and Parker (2007) identified individual proactivity, team member proactivity, and organization member proactivity. These are effectively all types of proactive work behavior (Parker & Collins's higher order category) in that they aim to take control of and bring about change within the internal organization environment. However, individual proactivity is directed toward one's individual job (e.g., improving one's work procedures); team proactivity is directed toward helping the team and other team members (e.g., making improvements to the way the team works); and organization member proactivity is directed toward changing wider organization systems or practices (e.g., improving systems for knowledge management across the organization). Similarly, Belschak and Den Hartog (in press) identified three types of proactivity: self-oriented, social, and organizational proactive behaviors, which are targeted at personal goals such as individual career progression, at coworkers, and at the broader organization, respectively.

Issues Around the Conceptualization of Proactivity

In this chapter, we have defined proactivity as a way of behaving, and we therefore acknowledge the role of both individual-differences variables (e.g., personality) and situational forces (job design) in shaping this type of action. (See also chap. 5, this volume, and Vol. 1, chap. 13, this handbook.) Early research on the topic of proactivity, however, conceived of it as a stable dispositional variable. From this view point, *proactive personality* refers to an individual who is relatively unconstrained by situational forces and who effects environmental change (Bateman & Crant, 1993). This concept assumes proactive individuals are proactive across multiple contexts and over time, regardless of the contingencies of a situation. Although this personality approach is valid, we prefer to focus on proactive actions within a particular context, recognizing that proactive behavior is shaped not only by one's overarching personality but also by one's motivation in a particular context.

A further perspective is to consider proactivity as a special type of citizenship or extrarole behavior. (See also chap. 10, this volume.) Some have argued that proactive behavior is by definition extrarole because in-role activities are nondiscretionary and hence not self-directed (Van Dyne & LePine, 1998). However, classifications of in-role and extrarole behavior are unclear and depend on how employees construe the boundary of their role (Morrison, 1994). Proactive individuals are likely to construe their roles more broadly (Parker, Wall, & Jackson, 1997) and to redefine their roles to encapsulate new tasks and goals (Frese & Fay, 2001). These issues have led researchers to suggest that a more useful way of understanding proactivity is in terms of a dimension that is distinct from in-role and extrarole behavior (and the related dimension of task contextual performance). Thus, all types of performance—whether they are defined as task, conceptual, citizenship, or extrarole—can be carried out more or less proactively (Crant, 2000; Grant & Ashford, 2008; Griffin et al., 2007). From this perspective, there is no need to confine proactive behavior to be citizenship or extrarole behavior, and not all extrarole or citizenship behavior is proactive.

Proactive behavior can also be distinguished from related behaviors such as innovation and adaptivity. (See also Vol. 1, chap. 9, this handbook.) Innovation is by definition *novel,* whereas being proactive does not necessarily imply novelty. Employees might, for example, speak out on issues that affect their work group or they might take charge to resolve a preexisting problem. Such behavior can be classified as proactive, yet not as innovative (Unsworth & Parker, 2002). Nevertheless, proactivity and innovation are related in that future and change-oriented behaviors are important for the implementation aspect of innovation. For example, Parker and Collins (2008) found high correlations between two proactive behaviors (taking charge and voice) with the implementation items of Scott and Bruce's (1994) individual innovation measure ($r = .58$, $r = .45$, both $ps < .01$, for taking charge and voice, respectively).

Thus, in line with Rank, Pace, and Frese (2004), we recommend that research in these two distinct research fields would benefit if findings were better integrated. In a similar vein, adaptivity and proactivity have some parallels in that both behaviors are especially important in uncertain, unpredictable contexts (Griffin et al., 2007). However, adaptivity is about adjusting to and responding to change, whereas proactivity is about initiating change.

A further perspective on proactivity, which coincides with our understanding of proactivity as a way of behaving, is that it is not just a single act but rather a process involving distinct phases. Grant and Ashford (2008) suggested that proactive action involves several phases (anticipation, planning, action toward impact). Frese and Fay (2001) similarly identified the redefinition of tasks, information collection and prognosis, plan and execution, monitoring and feedback as key phases of proactivity. Thus far, there is little empirical research from this perspective, as we elaborate later in the chapter.

Summary

In sum, although there are many ways of thinking about proactivity as well as many relevant concepts across different domains, a useful approach is to consider proactivity as a self-directed way of behaving (or process) that involves thinking ahead to take charge of a situation and to bring about change in that situation or in one's self. Most fundamentally, it is about behavior that "makes things happen," whether that be to change the work place, the broader organization and its strategy, one's fit within the organization, or one's personal career. We turn now to the core of the chapter: understanding the antecedents, processes, and outcomes relevant to proactivity.

ANTECEDENTS, PROCESSES, AND OUTCOMES OF PROACTIVE BEHAVIOR

Figure 19.1 shows a model that integrates existing research on the antecedents, outcomes, and underpinning processes of proactive behavior. Individual differences (personality, demographics, knowledge, and abilities) as well as situational differences (job design, leadership, and climate-related constructs) have been identified as predictors of proactive behavior, both independently from each other as well as in interaction with one another. These individual and situational differences form distal antecedents of proactive behavior. They appear to, at least in part, have their effects through more proximal cognitive–motivational and affect-related processes that influence proactivity. In turn, proactive behavior has been shown to influence individual outcomes (e.g., job performance, well-being, identification). It has further been linked to outcomes on the team level (e.g., team effectiveness) and to the organizational level (performance of the organization). The link between proactive behavior and different individual outcomes has been shown to be partially dependent on individual and situational moderators, labeled in our model *appropriateness of proactive behavior*. Our proposed model extends Crant's (2000) earlier model that also showed antecedents and outcomes of proactive behavior. In contrast to Crant, in our model, we indicate interactions between individual and situational antecedents, differentiate proximal motivational processes from more distal antecedents of proactive behavior, identify broad categories of proactive behavior, and consider moderators of the outcomes of proactive behaviors.

Motivational Processes (Proximal Antecedents)

We start our discussion of the model with the motivational processes that underpin proactive behavior because it is these processes that are the most direct in their influence. (See also Vol. 3, chap. 3, this handbook.) Specifically, we report evidence suggesting the importance for proactivity of what Mitchell and Daniels (2003) refer to as "cold" (or cognitive–motivational) processes as well as "hot" (or affect-related) processes.

Cognitively oriented motivational processes. From a motivational perspective, most attention has been given to two cognitive–motivational processes that underpin proactivity (Parker, Williams, & Turner, 2006): first, one's perceived capability of being proactive and second, one's wish to or interest in performing proactive behaviors.

Regarding the first of these, engaging in proactive behaviors is likely to involve a deliberate decision process in which the individual assesses the likely outcomes of these behaviors (see Vroom, 1964). A belief that one can be successful (perceived capability) is important because being proactive entails quite a high potential psychological risk to the individual. Consistent with this idea, there is good evidence of the importance for proactivity of self-efficacy, or people's judgments with regard to their capability to perform particular tasks (Bandura, 1986). In a sample of part-time master of business administration (MBA) students, self-efficacy beliefs were linked with higher levels of taking charge behaviors as rated by coworkers ($\beta = .20$, $p < .001$; Morrison & Phelps, 1999). Similarly, in a highly sophisticated, longitudinal design over four time points, Frese and colleagues (2007) showed that employees with higher levels of self-efficacy (operationalized in a combined measure with control aspirations and perceived opportunity for control) were also more likely to be rated as higher in self-initiative at the corresponding time point. In addition to general self-efficacy beliefs, specific domains of self-efficacy have been tested in proactivity research. For example, in a meta-analysis over 59 studies and across 19,957 individuals, Kanfer, Wanberg, and Kantrowitz (2001) found a significantly positive mean-corrected sample-weighted correlation between job-search-related self-efficacy and proactive job search ($r_c = .27$, $p < .05$). Another example is role breadth self-efficacy, or one's perceived capability of carrying out a range of proactive, interpersonal, and integrative activities beyond the prescribed technical core (Parker, 1998). Role breadth self-efficacy has been shown to promote the suggesting of improvements ($\beta = .31$, $p < .001$; Axtell, Holman, Unsworth, Wall, & Waterson, 2000), a combined measure of problem solving and idea implementation ($\beta = .24$, $p < .01$; Parker, Williams, & Turner, 2006); personal initiative ($\beta = .27$, $p < .05$; Ohly & Fritz, 2007); voice, taking charge, and strategic scanning ($\beta = .23$, $\beta = .15$, $\beta = .16$, respectively; all *ps* < .01; Parker & Collins, 2008); as well as individual, team member, and organization member proactivity across two different organizations ($\beta = .35$–.37, $\beta = .33$–.41, $\beta = .33$–.34, respectively; all *ps* < .001; Griffin et al., 2007), to name but a few. In sum, there is consistent and collectively strong evidence that perceived capability is positively related with proactivity at work.

However, it is not enough for individuals to believe that they can achieve an outcome; they also need to want to: "Even if people are certain they can do a task, they may have no compelling reason to do it" (Eccles & Wigfield, 2002, p. 112). In other words, there is a need to focus on the *why* of proactive behavior. Relevant to this, a second motivational process underpinning proactive behavior is that one sees this behavior as important for fulfilling one's goals or aspirations. This theme fits with broader motivational theories such as goal-setting theory (Locke & Latham, 1990), action theory (Hacker, 1985), and social cognitive theory (Bandura, 1986) and relates to Crant's (2000) recommendation to consider the role of goals in proactive behavior. At the simplest level, the outcome individuals are aiming for needs to be important to them. For example, meta-analytic evidence suggests a positive relationship between a strong financial need for employment as well as high levels of employee commitment with proactive job search ($r_c = .21$, $r_c = .29$, respectively; both *ps* < .05; Kanfer et al., 2001).

What individuals aspire for is also important. For example, Tuckey, Brewer, and Williamson (2002) in a sample of civil service employees found that the desire for useful information positively predicted feedback seeking ($\beta = .23$, $p < .05$). Fay and Frese (2001) investigated the antecedents of personal initiative for employees in East Germany over the duration of 6 years, starting at the time of the unification of East and West Germany. The researchers found that those individuals who indicated high aspirations for control, who wished to be "on top of things," were more likely to show high levels of personal initiative. In a very similar vein, Ashford and Black (1996) found that individuals' desire for control was positively linked with engagement in proactive socialization tactics: Employees who indicated high levels of desire for control were more likely to engage in information seeking ($\beta = .30$, $p < .01$), socializing ($\beta = .24$, $p < .05$), networking ($\beta = .29$, $p < .01$), job-change negotiation ($\beta = .24$, $p < .05$), and positive framing ($\beta = .22$, $p < .05$). Similarly, an individual's belief that he or she is personally obligated to bring about environmental change has been repeatedly positively linked with proactive behaviors such as taking charge ($\beta = .28$, $p < .001$, in Morrison & Phelps, 1999; $\beta = .42$, $p < .01$, in Parker & Collins, 2008), voice ($\beta = .31$, $p < .05$, in Fuller, Marler, & Hester, 2006; $\beta = .24$, $p < .01$, in Parker &

Collins, 2008), individual innovation and problem prevention ($\beta = .18$, $\beta = .22$, respectively; both *ps* < .01; Parker & Collins, 2008), and continuous improvement ($\beta = .38$, $p < .05$; Fuller et al., 2006). Likewise, employees' high levels of prosocial motives are positively related with the display of initiative at work ($\beta = .22$, $p < .01$; Grant & Mayer, 2009).

The employees' attitude toward their organization seems to take on an influencing role in determining levels of proactivity at work. For example, employees who intend to leave the organization are less likely to voice concerns about organizational improvements ($\beta = -.14$, $p < .001$; Burris, Detert, & Chiaburu, 2008). Organizational commitment, on the other hand, may set the frame for employees' goals to engage in proactive behaviors at work. For example, among employees working in the financial services sector, affective commitment was positively related with employees' engagement in proactive service performance ($\beta = .24$, $p < .01$; Rank, Carsten, Unger, & Spector, 2007). In a study across two organizations, Griffin and colleagues (2007) found positive relationships between affective organizational commitment with proactive behaviors directed at improving the effectiveness of the organization ($\beta = .17$, $p < .001$; $\beta = .23$, $p < .001$, for Organizations 1 and 2, respectively). The relationships between organizational affective commitment with proactive behaviors directed at the individual or the team were comparatively smaller or nonsignificant altogether, thus indicating a match between the focus of commitment with the type of proactive action taken. Similarly, Den Hartog and Belschak (2007) showed that different foci of commitment (career, supervisor, team, or organization) related in differential ways with self-ratings and supervisor ratings of personal initiative. Controlling for work-related affect, the researchers found that team commitment was most consistently positively related with self-rated personal initiative ($\beta = .16$, $p < .01$; $\beta = .30$, $p < .01$, for two independent samples), whereas organizational commitment emerged as a strong positive predictor of supervisor-rated self-initiative ($\beta = .43$, $p < .01$). An explanation for these findings could be that different types of commitment might shape different types of self-initiative. For example, self-initiated actions that are motivated by the employees' goal to benefit the organization might be more salient to supervisors (hence the significant relationship), than are career- or team-commitment-driven actions.

A final theorized driving force of proactivity is employees' having a flexible role orientation (Parker et al., 1997). Flexible role orientation refers to individuals' defining their job broadly, such as to include feeling ownership for customer satisfaction, rather than possessing a narrow and passive "that's not my job" mentality. As Gagné and Deci (2005) argued, the concept of flexible role orientation might reflect the process of internalization by which external structures (e.g., the organization's goals) are internalized. Parker, Williams, and Turner (2006) found flexible role orientation worked together with role breadth self-efficacy to predict self-rated proactive behavior, with both of these aspects being significant and unique predictors, whereas affective commitment became unimportant once these beliefs were controlled for. Likewise, Dorenbosch, van Engen, and Verhagen (2005) showed that ownership of work issues beyond one's immediate job (an indicator of flexible role orientation) predicted three types of self-reported innovative work behavior among Dutch administrative employees ($\beta = .29$–$.44$).

Affect-related processes. There is good evidence that affect influences behavior (e.g., Ashforth & Humphrey, 1995; Brief & Weiss, 2002; Isen & Baron, 1991). In regard to proactivity more specifically, drawing on Fredrickson (1998), Parker (2007) proposed a model that identified two pathways by which positive affect might shape proactive behavior: a "broaden" mechanism in which positive affect broadens momentary motivational and cognitive processes and a "build" mechanism in which accumulated positive affect has an effect on more enduring cognitive–motivational states (e.g., self-efficacy, role orientation) and ultimately affects individuals' capabilities (e.g., their resilience and coping ability). In regard to the broaden mechanism, Parker argued that proactive behavior requires that individuals choose to allocate their effort toward challenging, longer term, and often rather risky goals. Positive affect is likely to influence the selection of such goals because it broadens thinking and results in more flexible cognitive processes (Fredrickson, 1998,

2001; Isen, 1999). Positive affect also promotes more responsible behavior that is consistent with a long-term focus (Isen & Reeve, 2005). Consistent with these ideas, positive affect has been linked with the setting of higher and more challenging goals (Ilies & Judge, 2005) as well as with engagement with a more problematic future (Oettingen, Mayer, Thorpe, Janetzke, & Lorenz, 2005). Moreover, proactive behavior, with its focus on change, requires regulating one's effort, staying on task, and not being derailed by negative events. Evidence suggests that positive mood can create an upward spiral of self-regulatory advantage that will help individuals sustain their proactive action (Martin, Ward, Achee, & Wyer, 1993). Parker therefore proposed that positive affect also promotes the goal striving that is necessary for proactivity.

In regard to the build mechanism, Parker argued that these processes over time accumulate to build more enduring aspects of individuals, such as self-efficacy, resilience, and cognitive complexity. This building thesis is consistent with Weiss and Cropanzano (1996) who proposed that as well as affective states leading to affect-driven behaviors, affect can also cumulatively shape overall job attitudes and judgments and hence influence judgment-driven behaviors.

A further feature of the model developed by Parker (2007) is that it identifies individual and contextual contingencies that affect the key relationships. For example, prior evidence shows that the broadening effect of positive mood on cognitive processes only occurs if the task is judged to be important (see Isen, 1999). Positive affect might therefore promote proactivity only when the goals or tasks are considered important and significant. Parker also proposed that high-arousal positive affect (e.g., enthusiasm) will be more important in driving proactive behavior than low-arousal positive affect (e.g., contentment). Contentment, for example, has been linked with inactivity (Frijda, 1986) and appears to facilitate reflection rather than forward thinking. Enthusiasm, in contrast, is likely to enhance individuals' energy for behaving proactively.

Recent research supports some of Parker's (2007) propositions. In a cross-sectional study conducted in a health care sector environment (Den Hartog & Belschak, 2007), employees who indicated positive high-arousal work-related affect also reported higher levels of personal initiative at work ($\beta = .26$, $p < .01$; $\beta = .29$, $p < .05$, for two independent samples). Interestingly, the researchers did not find any relationship between positive affect and supervisor-rated self-initiative. This could indicate that relationships between self-reported affect and proactive behavior at work merely reflect respondents' tendencies to view their behavior in a more positive light when in a good mood, thus stressing the importance of using multiple sources for measuring the relationship between affect and proactivity. Fritz and Sonnentag (2009) investigated day-level variations of affect and proactivity at work. The researchers distributed daily questionnaires over the period of 4 consecutive work days to a sample of civil service employees. High-arousal positive affect was positively related with taking charge behaviors both on the same day ($\gamma = .33$, $p < .01$) as well as on the following day ($\gamma = .27$, $p < .05$). Fritz and Sonnentag's study relied on self-reports of taking charge, but the lagged effect of affect on behavior over time helped to establish that affect causes behavioral change rather than the association being a methodological artifact.

In a study of MBA students that used other reports of proactivity, Parker, Collins, and Grant (2008) showed that high-arousal positive affect predicted taking charge ($\beta = .20$, $p < .01$) and strategic scanning ($\beta = .30$, $p < .01$). Positive affect was, however, only associated with individual innovation and issue selling when individuals did not possess a high performance orientation. When performance orientation was high, the negative association of a strong desire to prove one's competency on proactivity appeared to overwhelm any value of positive affect. The authors interpreted these findings as suggesting that positive affect has a direct influence on some types of proactive behaviors, whereas for others—perhaps those that are perceived as more risky such as innovation and issue selling—other motivational dynamics might play a suppressing role.

Several studies investigated the influence of concepts on proactivity at work that are rather close to, albeit not identical with, positive work-related affect. Job engagement, for example, was measured by investigating respondents' feelings of work-related vigor, dedication, and absorption. Employees who feel engaged should be more likely to engage in effortful behaviors that are related with changing the situation or themselves than employees who feel less engaged. In support of this argument, Salanova and Schaufeli (2008) found for a Spanish and a Dutch sample positive relationships between work engagement and self-reported personal initiative ($\beta = .56$, $\beta = .64$, respectively; both *ps* $< .001$). There has been evidence that this relationship also holds for a 3-year time frame: In a sample of dentists, those individuals who indicated higher levels of work engagement at Time Point 1 also indicated higher levels of personal initiative 3 years later, while controlling for previous levels of personal initiative ($\beta = .13$, $p < .001$; Hakanen, Perhoniemi, & Toppinen-Tanner, 2008). Interestingly, the authors further found a weakly positive association between personal initiative and subsequent higher levels of work engagement for the same time frame ($\beta = .09$, $p < .001$), indicating a reciprocal effect between work engagement and personal initiative.

Regarding the possible influence of work engagement on personal initiative, further support stems from longitudinal frames of investigations conducted through diary studies. Sonnentag (2003) found positive relationships between day-level work engagement and day-level self-initiative ($\gamma = .77$, $p < .001$) as well as the pursuit of learning ($\gamma = .78$, $p < .001$) over the period of 5 consecutive days. In a similar string of research, but showing even more powerful lagged effects, Binnewies, Sonnentag, and Mojza (2009a) showed that the feeling of being recovered in the morning predicted higher levels of self-initiative during the same workday ($\gamma = .21$, $p < .001$), and Binnewies, Sonnentag, and Mojza (in press) showed that employees who recover well from work over the weekend are likely to engage in higher levels of personal initiative during the following workweek ($\gamma = .15$, $p < .001$). Further, Binnewies, Sonnentag, and Mojza (2009b) found that positive reflection about work during nonwork time may contribute to subsequent higher levels of personal initiative at work ($\beta = .10$, $p < .05$), thus indicating a positive spillover effect from nonwork to work. Altogether, there is good evidence of the beneficial role of positive affect and affect-related concepts, such as feeling recovered and vigorous, for proactive behavior, although the contingencies that affect this relationship need further investigation.

Even though it might be expected that negative affect would suppress proactivity, under some situations negative affect might signal a discrepancy between an actual situation and a desired situation, thereby stimulating individuals to engage in self-initiated and change-oriented behaviors to reduce the perceived discrepancy (Carver & Scheier, 1982). In support of this argument, Den Hartog and Belschak (2007) across two cross-sectional studies found some evidence that high-arousal work-related negative affect positively related to personal initiative, although the effect was not consistent across different samples and only applied to self-ratings of initiative. Further calling into question the relationship between negative affect and proactivity, Fritz and Sonnentag (2009) in their diary study found that high-arousal negative affect was not related with proactivity, although the same measure for affect was used, and a similar type of proactivity at work was investigated. Altogether, more research is needed. Perhaps, to signal action to remove an unpleasant situation, more constant feelings of negative affect are needed as opposed to daily feelings of negative affect over the course of 1 single week.

Finally, in her model of affect, Parker (2007) proposed contagion and signaling as two processes by which individuals' affect can affect others' affect and thereby their proactive behavior. In this vein, Ang, Cummings, Straub, and Earley (1993) in a series of laboratory studies showed that individuals were more likely to engage in feedback seeking when they perceived that the person they were to seek feedback from was in a good mood. Similarly, Morrison and Bies (1991) in their literature review argued that employees are more likely to engage in feedback seeking if the person to seek feedback from is in a positive mood because employees feel their act of feedback seeking will be seen more favorably. Additionally, Rafaeli (2008) proposed that colleagues' negative affect may deplete an individual's own resources. A depletion of resources, in turn, could result in decreased levels of proactivity at work.

Overall, there is reasonably good evidence that affect can promote or inhibit proactive behaviors.

However, future research needs to disentangle the role of different types of affect as well as dynamic intra- and interpersonally affective processes in more detail. For example, Russell and Feldman Barrett (1999; Russell, 2003) suggested differentiating affect into the dimensions of pleasure versus displeasure and activation versus deactivation. Research that accounts for these dimensions will yield further insights into the role of affective experiences on proactivity at work. Moreover, how affect relates to judgments of efficacy and individuals' proactive goals has yet to be investigated as have the build mechanisms proposed by Parker (2007).

Individual and Situational Antecedents of Proactive Behavior

Whereas in the preceding section we focused on the proximal motivational processes, in this section we look at more distal influences, including individual antecedents (demographics, knowledge and abilities, as well as personality), situational antecedents (job design, leadership, and climate), and the interaction between individuals and their situations (see Figure 19.1). We also describe evidence suggesting that the various individual and situational factors can have their influence through the motivational processes described previously.

Individual antecedents. Most research to date has focused on individual antecedents of proactive behaviors. In the following paragraphs we review pertinent findings on the role of demographics, knowledge and abilities, as well as personality for proactivity at work.

Demographics. Several studies have investigated the relationship between demographical factors and proactive behavior at work. Age appears to be negatively related to several proactive person–environment fit and career behaviors. For example, Kanfer and colleagues (2001) in their meta-analysis found a very small, albeit significantly negative, mean-corrected sample-weighted correlation ($r_c = -.06$, $p < .05$) between age and proactive job search behaviors. This finding coincides with previous research that showed that older individuals typically tend to show lower levels of training motivation (e.g., Maurer, Weiss, & Barbeite, 2003; Warr & Birdi, 1998). Warr and Fay (2001) in a longitudinal interview-based study found that age related negatively to person–environment fit proactivity (measured by education initiative) over the two time points of investigation, each 14 months apart ($\beta = -.16$, $p < .05$; $\beta = -.27$, $p < .01$).

In relation to work improvement types of proactivity, results are inconsistent. Some studies show no relationships with age (Morrison & Phelps, 1999; Warr & Fay, 2001, for male respondents), whereas others suggest less proactivity for older workers (Axtell et al., 2000; Jannsen & Van Yperen, 2004), and one study shows greater proactivity with age, at least for women (Warr & Fay, 2001). Altogether, although younger employees might not have arrived at their final career position and are therefore likely to engage in career behaviors, employees of all ages could be equally concerned with improving the effectiveness of work processes and methods. Further studies are needed, including studies that carefully distinguish age from tenure.

Research findings also suggest a mixed picture with regard to the influence of gender on proactive behaviors: Men were found to be more proactive then women both in terms of their willingness to engage in proactive job search ($r_c = .05$, $p < .05$; Kanfer et al., 2001) and, as a finding of a multinational study in several industrialized countries, in networking behaviors ($\beta = .09$, $p < .05$; Claes & Ruiz-Quintanilla, 1998). Men have also been found to be more likely to voice concerns about issues in the workplace ($\beta = .15$, $p < .01$; LePine & Van Dyne, 1998). However, all of these effects are small, and Griffin et al.'s (2007) study showed inconsistent results with regard to the relationship between gender and proactivity depending on the sample. An issue here is that gender often confounds with occupational type and level, and these aspects need to be controlled to understand the role of gender and proactivity at work. An interesting insight into the relationship between personal initiative and age was provided by Warr and Fay (2001). When the researchers controlled for hierarchical level, job control, and complexity, there was no relationship between age and personal initiative for men. However, with regard to women, mixed results were found: Interestingly, for women, age and interview-measured self-initiative at the first time point were negatively related ($\beta = -.15$, $p < .05$), whereas age and self-reported self-initiative measured at the second time point were positively related ($\beta = .29$, $p < .001$). The authors argued that the female respondents who lived in East Germany possibly felt alienated from work out of feelings of age discrimination after the reunification of Germany, and this resulted in lower interview-based self-initiative. The positive relationship between age and self-rated personal initiative was argued to have resulted out of higher levels of self-esteem in older women. Further research could take into account possible aspects related to gender-specific social norms on the development of work proactivity.

Ethnicity could also play a role in influencing individuals' engagement in proactive behaviors. Proactive behavior is a risky behavior that is facilitated if individuals feel they belong to an in-group (Dutton, Ashford, Lawrence, & Miner-Rubino, 2002), possibly discouraging ethnic minorities from engaging in proactive behaviors. To date, U.S.-based research that included ethnicity as an antecedent for proactive behaviors at work did not reveal clear insights into these possible relationships. LePine and Van Dyne (1998) found that White employees were more likely to engage in voice ($\beta = .09$, $p < .05$); Kanfer and colleagues (2001), on the other hand, found that White employees were less likely to engage in proactive job search than were their non-White colleagues ($r_c = -.05$, $p < .05$). However, these results are overall small in size, and third variables could explain the results. In this vein, in the study by LePine and Van Dyne (1998), ethnicity correlated more strongly with education than it did with proactivity ($r = .15$, $p > .01$, for education, compared with $r = .10$, $p > .05$, for proactivity) in that non-White employees typically also possessed lower educational qualifications. These qualifications in their own right might explain the relationship between ethnicity and the level of engagement in proactive behaviors.

To our knowledge there is only one study so far that has explicitly investigated the role of culture on proactive behavior at work. In a study across six countries, including Flanders, England, Israel, Italy, the Netherlands, and Spain, Claes and Ruiz-Quintanilla (1998) investigated the influence of cultural dimensions (Hofstede, 1991) on different types of proactive career behaviors. The researchers followed young workers for 3 years after their first job entry. Culture significantly related to all proactive behaviors investigated. For example, if individuals within a country generally tended to feel less comfortable with uncertain or unknown situations, they were also less likely to engage in skill development ($\beta = -.12$, $p < .05$) or in networking behaviors ($\beta = -.29$, $p < .001$) when at work. These findings make sense in the light of proactive behavior being a risky behavior that "rocks the boat" and may yield uncertain outcomes as a result of its change-oriented motivation (Frese & Fay, 2001). Similarly, individuals in more collectivist countries, where the in-group protects and cares for an individual, showed less engagement in career-planning behaviors than did their more individualistic counterparts ($\beta = -.13$, $p < .01$). Related research found that in U.S. companies, Asian American employees, who are typically high in collectivism, tend to progress more slowly in their careers than do their individualist European American colleagues (Xin, 2004), probably because they feel more uncomfortable directing too much attention to their own person (Heine, Markus, Lehman, & Kitayana, 1999)—an effect that is likely to be prevalent when engaging in proactive behaviors. These findings raise interesting future research questions as to, for example, how far proactivity varies in Asian companies compared with in U.S. or European companies where most research on proactivity has been conducted so far.

In sum, little research has explicitly investigated the relationship between demographical factors and proactivity at work. So far, research on proactivity has almost exclusively looked at the antecedents of proactivity at work for white-collar employees in industrialized Western countries and has investigated relationships with demographic factors more to statistically control for their effects than to understand them.

Knowledge and abilities. Knowledge and abilities have been suggested to influence individuals' proactive behavior at work. Fay and Frese (2001, p. 104) argued: "To be able to take initiative, one needs a good and thorough understanding of what one's work is, that is, one needs job-relevant knowledge, skills, and cognitive ability." There has been some empirical support for this argument. For example, for employees in East and West Germany, Fay and Frese (2001) found moderately positive relationships between job qualification and both self-rated and other-rated personal initiative ($r = .24–.48$, $p < .01$). In a study with just employees from East Germany, the authors found additional support for a stable positive correlation between cognitive ability and personal initiative ($r = .27–.46$ across five time points, all $ps < .01$). Kanfer and colleagues (2001) found meta-analytical evidence of a positive relationship ($r_c = .12$, $p < .05$) between educational background and the degree of proactive job search. In the same vein, in their research on voicing behavior in groups, LePine and Van Dyne (1998) found that individuals with a higher educational background were also more likely to speak out with suggestions for improvements ($\beta = .13$, $p < .05$). Likewise, job-specific expertise has been found to be a promoting factor for proactivity at work. In their qualitative study with employees from different hierarchical levels, Dutton, Ashford, O'Neill, and Lawrence (2001) identified three facets of knowledge that facilitated individuals' proactive issue-selling attempts to the top management: relational knowledge (e.g., insights into questions such as, who will be affected by the issue?), normative knowledge (e.g., insights into the question, what kinds of meetings or social gatherings are considered legitimate decision forums?), and strategic knowledge (e.g., insights into the question, what are the organization's goals?). Building on Dutton et al.'s (2001) work in a further qualitative study, Howell and Boies (2004) compared 19 pairs of innovation champions and nonchampions across 15 organizations. Results for coded content analyses indicated that contextual knowledge positively related to individuals' packaging ideas for promotion ($\lambda = .53$, $p < .01$). In a related vein, Ohly, Sonnentag, and Pluntke (2006) found that routinization, the automaticity with which employees carry out their tasks, was as a tendency positively related with the engagement in personal initiative ($\beta = .09$, $p < .10$). Routinization likely reflects deep-level knowledge of the task.

In sum, most of the existing studies indicate a consistently significant and positive relationship between cognitive ability and job-specific expertise with proactive behaviors. However further longitudinal research is needed to provide more secure insight into these relationships.

Personality. A considerable amount of research has investigated personal trait characteristics as antecedents for proactive behavior, particularly using the concept of proactive personality, or the tendency of an individual to influence his or her environment and to bring about change across multiple contexts and times. (See also chap. 5, this volume.) Bateman and Crant (1993) developed and validated a 17-item proactive personality scale, which investigates respondents' agreement to items such as "If I see something I don't like, I fix it." The change-oriented and self-initiated focus of the proactive personality scale makes it highly relevant as an antecedent to specific proactive behaviors. Indeed, a vast number of findings confirm a consistently positive relationship between proactive personality and distinct proactive behaviors. To name a few exemplary findings, proactive personality has been positively linked with network building ($\beta = .18$, $p < .05$, in Lambert, Eby, & Reeves, 2006; $\beta = .37$, $p < .05$, in Thompson, 2005); proactive socialization into the organization ($\gamma = .13$, $p < .01$; Kammeyer-Mueller & Wanberg, 2003); career initiative ($\beta = .32$, $p < .01$; Seibert et al., 2001); and various proactive work behaviors such as taking charge, individual innovation, problem prevention, and voice ($\beta = .15$, $\beta = .23$, $\beta = .17$, $\beta = .20$, respectively; all $ps < .01$; Parker & Collins, 2008).

Apart from a direct relationship with proactive behavior, evidence suggests that proactive personality has its effects through several cognitive–motivational states (role breadth self-efficacy as well as flexible role orientation in Parker, Williams, & Turner, 2006; job search self-efficacy in Brown, Cober, Kane, Levy, & Shalhoop, 2006; motivation to learn in Major, Turner, & Fletcher, 2006). Several of these studies include longitudinal designs, and the use of other reports of proactivity at work provides rather good evidence that proactive personality drives a range of specific proactive behaviors.

Another potentially relevant personality dimension is conscientiousness, reflecting tendencies and behaviors related to dependability, conformity, and perseverance (Costa & McCrae, 1992). Unlike other Big Five personality dimensions, conscientiousness has been rather consistently linked to proactive behaviors such as proactive job search (meta-analytic evidence of $r_c = .38$, $p > .05$; Kanfer et al., 2001), proactive performance and task information seeking ($r = .18$, $r = .18$, both $ps < .01$; Tidwell & Sias, 2005), as well as career-planning behaviors ($r = .32$, $p < .05$; Carless & Bernath, 2007). Consistent with these studies, Parker and Collins (2008) showed that conscientiousness predicted proactive person–environment fit behaviors such as feedback inquiry both directly as well as indirectly through the influence of role breadth self-efficacy and felt responsibility for change. However, Parker and Collins found conscientiousness unimportant for proactive work behaviors such as taking charge and individual innovation. The researchers argued that conscientious individuals tend to be rather cautious and appreciative of rules, which stands in contrast to the change-oriented nature of proactive work and strategic behaviors. In contrast, conscientious individuals have a special desire to be dependable and therefore strive to fit in well with the organization and are thereby more likely to engage in proactive person–environment fit behaviors.

Several further character traits that are linked to employees' willingness to look ahead and to learn new things also influence proactive behavior: For example, employees who are high in intellectual curiosity were found to be more likely to engage in environmental scanning, specifically in gathering useful information from outside and inside the organization, than were intellectually less curious employees (Howell & Shea, 2001). Employees who are high in consideration of future consequences, the extent to which one considers distant versus immediate consequences, were also found to be more proactive over a wide range of domains (Parker & Collins, 2008). On the contrary, employees who tend to have a reluctant attitude toward change, also tend to show less proactivity at work. Fay and Frese (2000) showed that psychologically conservative individuals, measured as the degree to which individuals favored an authoritarian way of upbringing and were politically conservative, scored lower on personal initiative, probably because they were conservative about change ($\beta = -.23$, $p < .05$). Similarly, Fay and Frese (2001) in longitudinal analyses of the same sample reported consistently positive relationships between individuals' tendency of readiness to change and their current and future levels of personal initiative ($r = .25$–$.45$, all $ps < .01$).

Likewise, individuals who are high in learning goal orientation (a preference to understand or master new aspects) as opposed to in performance goal orientation (a preference to gain favorable and avoid negative judgments of their competence; Dweck, 1986) have been found to be more likely to engage in feedback seeking ($\beta = .16$, $p < .05$, in Parker & Collins, 2008; $\beta = .30$, $p < .001$, for a student sample in Tuckey et al., 2002; $\beta = .13$, $p < .05$, in VandeWalle, Ganesan, Challagalla, & Brown, 2000). One explanation for the favorable role of learning goal orientation is that individuals who emphasize learning processes rather than demonstrating capability might find it less risky and more valuable to engage in feedback seeking and therefore engage more frequently in this type of behavior (VandeWalle, 2003; VandeWalle & Cummings, 1997). Finally, consistent with the importance of perceived capability for the choice to engage in proactive behaviors as outlined earlier in this chapter, traits that tap into individuals' perception of control and self-worth have been positively linked to proactive behaviors at work ($r_c = .25$, $p > .05$, for self-esteem in Kanfer et al., 2001; see, e.g., Wrzesniewski & Dutton, 2001, for a theoretical elaboration on the relationship between control-related needs and job crafting).

In sum, plenty of research to date has focused on dispositional antecedents of proactivity at work and has provided multifaceted insights into the role of different types of predispositions for proactive behaviors. Interestingly, some dispositions seem to promote a wide range of proactive behaviors (e.g., proactive personality), whereas others seem to be helpful in promoting only very specific types of proactivity at work (e.g., learning goal orientation). Systematic meta-analyses could reveal more insight into the overall strengths of relationships while taking into account nonsignificant results in published as well as unpublished studies.

Situational antecedents. Being proactive is certainly about the type of person one is: Demographics and personality factors all play a role. However the situation also makes a big difference. Individuals in psychologically unsafe, demotivating work teams, for example, are unlikely to take the risk to be proactive. In recent times, there has been a growing focus on work and organizational differences in predicting proactive behavior at work. We summarize findings concerning job design, leadership, and climate-related variables.

Job design. A long history of job design research has shown that work structures influence the motivation, behavior, and well-being of employees (for reviews, see, e.g., Latham & Pinder, 2005; Morgeson & Campion, 2003; Parker & Ohly, 2008; see also Vol. 1, chap. 13, this handbook). As elaborated earlier, proactive behavior at work is a special type of motivated behavior that goes hand in hand with perceptions of control and capability. Work design aspects that promote these perceptions should therefore be linked with higher levels of proactivity. In this vein, the concepts of job autonomy, complexity, and control, all concerned with the degree to which employees can choose how to proceed with their work, have been very consistently shown to be positively related with proactive behaviors (e.g., Frese et al., 2007; Morrison, 2006). For example, job autonomy has been positively linked with proactive behaviors such as personal initiative ($\beta = .38$, $p < .05$, for a longitudinal investigation; Hornung & Rousseau, 2007) and idea implementation and problem solving ($\beta = .27$, $p < .01$; Parker, Williams, & Turner, 2006). Frese, Kring, Soose, and Zempel (1996) recommended as a result of their longitudinal study that it would be wise to increase job control and complexity to enhance personal initiative at work rather than to focus solely on selecting dispositionally proactive employees into the organization.

Different pathways through which job design has its influence on proactivity at work are possible. Recently, Salanova and Schaufeli (2008) found that job engagement (feelings of vigor and dedication) mediated the relationship between job resources (job control, feedback, and variety) and personal initiative. Several longitudinal studies have shown that job enrichment predicts self-efficacy and flexible role orientations (Axtell & Parker, 2003; Parker, 1998; Parker et al., 1997), which in turn have been shown to predict proactivity (Parker, Williams, & Turner, 2006). In a study based on nurses, Tangirala and Ramanujam (2008) found a U-shaped relationship between personal control and voice such that high levels of personal control were most highly positively related with voice; medium levels of job control showed a negative relationship with voice; and low levels of personal controls again showed a positive relationship with voice, albeit not as strong as the high personal control and voice combination. The researchers interpreted their findings thus:

> At low levels of control, employees engage in voice owing to a particularly strong motivation arising from personal dissatisfaction with the status quo. At high levels of control, employees engage in voice owing to a particularly strong motivation arising from enhanced expectancy of successfully influencing organizational outcomes. At intermediate levels of control, neither motivation is strong. (Tangirala & Ramanujam, p. 1192)

These findings relate to our earlier review of the influence of affect-related motivational processes on proactivity. One could speculate that low control evokes high-arousal negative affect and thereby promotes voice through a discrepancy-reduction motivation; high control is likely associated with high-arousal positive affect, thus encouraging voice out of a broadening mechanism; and medium levels of control might be related with low-arousal affective states, which thus promote inactivity.

In line with Tangirala and Ramanujam's (2008) findings, other negative work characteristics have been positively linked with proactive behavior. There have been both conceptual consideration (Frese & Fay, 2001) as well as empirical support (e.g., Fay & Sonnentag, 2002; Ohly et al., 2006) the positive role of job stressors like time pressure and situational constraints in motivating employees to engage in proactive behavior at work. For example, Ohly and Fritz (in press) in an experience-sampling approach found support for the assumption that employees perceive time pressure as challenging and that challenge appraisal in turn promotes proactivity at work. A theory that researchers repeatedly drew on is control theory (Carver & Scheier, 1982). Stressors can thus be perceived as a deviation between a desired and an actual situation, thereby motivating employees to take an active approach to decrease the difference between the desired and actual states. Research on proactive coping similarly highlights this active approach to decreasing an unpleasant situation (Aspinwall & Taylor, 1997).

In sum, research on job design and proactivity suggests that proactivity may be shaped by job features, both positive and negative ones. More research is now needed to reveal how these influences develop over time. For example, time pressure might be helpful as a motivator for proactive behavior in the short run, but conservation of resources theory (Hobfoll, 1989, 2001) suggests that repeated exposure could deplete individuals' resources in the long run, thus not only decreasing well-being (e.g., Zapf, Dormann, & Frese, 1996) but also decreasing long-term proactivity. Other work characteristics have also been suggested (Grant & Ashford, 2008) to be important for proactivity (e.g., accountability; see also Anseel, Lievens, & Levy, 2007, for future avenues of research in feedback seeking) but have thus far not had much empirical attention.

Leadership. Leaders, through their impact on motivation as well as their direct effect on the work environment, likely have a role to play in shaping proactive action. (See also Vol. 1, chap. 7, this handbook.) Participative leadership, which emphasizes the value of subordinates' contributions as well as involvement in decision making, predicted higher levels of proactive service performance beyond several individual antecedents ($\beta = .30$, $p < .01$; Rank et al., 2007). Transformational leadership, leading toward motivating employees to go beyond standard expectations, was positively linked with supervisor-rated individual innovation behaviors ($\beta = .33$, $p < .01$; Rank, Nelson, Allen, & Xu, 2009). In a more fine-grained investigation, Strauss, Griffin and Rafferty (2008) showed that it is not only the type of leadership approach that is important but also the level of the leader. Team leaders' transformational leadership predicted role breadth self-efficacy and in turn team member proactivity (proactivity directed at changing a team situation and methods), whereas organizational leaders' transformational leadership predicted enhanced affective commitment, which in turn predicted organization member proactivity (e.g., making suggestions to improve the organization). In a study that considered different types of proactivity, Belschak and Den Hartog (in press) reported positive relationships between transformational leadership and proactive behavior with an organizational focus ($\beta = .29$, $p < .01$) as well as with an interpersonal focus ($\beta = .32$, $p < .01$). Self-focused proactivity (e.g., career initiative), however, was not predicted by transformational leadership.

A high-quality exchange between leader and employee should promote a climate of trust in which employees dare to engage in change-oriented, self-initiated behaviors. In support of this, leader–member exchange has been positively related to individual innovation behaviors ($r = .34$, $p < .01$; Janssen & Van Yperen, 2004) as well as to supervisor-rated voice ($r = .25$, $p < .01$; Burris et al., 2008).

It is surprising that findings regarding the relationship between supportive leadership with proactive behaviors have been found to be inconsistent across studies. Although some research has found that supervisor support predicts higher levels of personal initiative ($\beta = .15$, $p < .05$; Ohly et al., 2006) and the implementation of ideas ($\beta = .18$, $p < .05$; Axtell et al., 2000), other research has found nonsignificant relationships between supportive leadership and the implementation of ideas (Frese, Teng, & Wijnen, 1999; Parker, Williams, & Turner, 2006). Similarly, although Axtell and colleagues (2000) found no significant relationship between supervisor support and employees' suggestions of ideas, Ohly et al. (2006) reported a significant negative relationship between the two constructs (parameter estimate = −2.05, $p = .04$). Parker, Williams, and Turner (2006) suggested that supervisors might experience an "initiative paradox" (see Campbell, 2000) in which they feel threatened by their employees' proactive behavior, which might explain why supportive leadership is not necessarily beneficial.

In light of the preceding, it might be important for employees to perceive not only support from their immediate supervisors but also from more powerful individuals in the organization at higher hierarchical levels to risk the engagement in proactive behaviors. In this vein, top management's appreciative attitude toward proactive behaviors seems to be helpful: Axtell et al. (2000) found that management support facilitated the implementation of ideas over and above the positive influence of supervisor support ($\beta = .23$, $p < .01$). Further, Morrison and Phelps (1999) found that top management's openness to change was positively related with employees' willingness to engage in taking charge behaviors ($\beta = .15$, $p < .01$). Similarly, Dutton, Ashford, O'Neill, Hayes, and Wierba (1997) in a qualitative research approach based on grounded theory explored that top management's willingness to listen to employees as well as a supportive organizational culture were positively related to employees' perception that it was favorable to engage in issue-selling behaviors.

Climate. Proactive behavior is an interpersonal behavior in that it is likely to affect and provoke reactions from other individuals in the work environment because of its change-oriented nature. The way individuals perceive their work climate, such as others' receptiveness of their proactive actions, is therefore likely to be relevant. (See also Vol. 1, chap. 12, this handbook.) Empirically, those individuals who report being satisfied with their work group (LePine & Van Dyne, 1998) and who have a good relationship with the individuals who would be affected by their proactive action (Ashford et al., 1998) are more likely to engage in proactive behaviors. Similarly, the perception of being supported by coworkers (Griffin et al., 2007; Kanfer et al., 2001) or by the organization (Ashford et al., 1998; Dutton et al., 1997) positively relates to proactive behaviors at work. It would be interesting to see research that links climate at work with motivational processes such as self-efficacy or positive affect and to track changes in proactive behavior over time in such a research design. Parker, Williams, and Turner (2006) provided a first insight into these links: For a sample of wire makers, the researchers showed that trust in coworkers may increase levels of self-reported proactivity at work through broadening employees' perception of their role. Future longitudinal research may help to further disentangle the relationship underlying organizational climate and proactivity at work.

Interactions between individual and situational antecedents. Individual and situational factors likely interact with each other. Mischel and Shoda (1995) argued that a strong situation (e.g., low autonomy) can overwhelm the role of individual differences, whereas a weak situation (e.g., high autonomy) can mean more scope for individual factors to play a role. Consistent with this, in a study measuring the daily performance at work, Binnewies and colleagues (2009a) showed that for employees with a high level of job control, the positive relationship between feeling recovered in the morning with personal initiative during the working day was stronger. Job control seemingly allows employees to be proactive when they feel recovered at work and equally to engage in less proactive behavior if they do not feel recovered. Those employees with low job control may not be in the position to vary their behavior at work regardless of how recovered they feel. Similarly, Grant and Sumanth (2009) investigated proactivity among a sample of professional fundraisers working for a U.S.-based university. The researchers found that disposition can compensate for a weak situation: Those individuals who were high in dispositional trust propensity and were also prosocially motivated showed high levels of job-related initiative even if they indicated their managers were not trustworthy.

Sometimes there is a positive synergy between the work situation and individuals. For example, Kim and Wang (2008) showed that individuals who are high in proactive personality are more likely to seek feedback from their supervisors if the overall climate in the organization is perceived to be fair and if the supervisor usually engages in positive feedback than are employees who are less dispositionally proactive. Similarly, McAllister, Kamdar, Morrison, and Turban (2007) found that employees who perceive their organization as high in procedural justice and who simultaneously hold high role breadth self-efficacy beliefs were rated highest as taking charge at work by their supervisors (interaction effect of $\beta = .20$, $p < .001$). Recently, Griffin, Parker, and Mason (in press) found that leader vision in combination with high levels of role breadth self-efficacy led to significant increases in proactivity 1 year later. Parker and Sprigg (1999) showed that job control mitigated the stressful effects of high job demands for employees who were high in proactive personality but not for those who were more passive (interaction effect of $\beta = -.12$, $p < .01$). The researchers argued that proactive employees take advantage of high levels of job control to manage their job demands more effectively, whereas passive employees do not make good use of autonomy, and so high levels of job demands lead to higher levels of strain irrespective of the level of job control.

Sometimes the situation and individual differences seem to substitute for each other. For example, Speier and Frese (1997) showed that the relationship between job control and initiative is higher for those individuals who have low levels of self-efficacy beliefs. The favorable work situation thus seemed to substitute low individual predispositions to act proactively. In a similar vein, LePine and Van Dyne (1998), drawing on behavior plasticity theory (Brockner, 1988), showed that individuals with low self-esteem were more receptive to favorable situational characteristics promoting voice behaviors in a group (e.g., high levels of overall group autonomy) than were individuals with high levels of self-esteem. Similarly, Rank and colleagues (2009), also drawing on behavioral plasticity theory, found that leadership may substitute for a lack of individual self-esteem. The researchers investigated the influence of leadership styles and individual differences (organization-based self-esteem) on individual innovation behavior. Transformational leadership was more strongly positively related with individual innovation for individuals with lower levels of organization-based self-esteem than for individuals with high levels in organization-based self-esteem, indicating a compensatory effect of leadership on individual differences.

There are of course many other potential interactions between the situation and the individual that might influence proactivity. Grant and Ashford (2008) proposed that three situational antecedents (accountability, ambiguity, and autonomy) are moderated by several dispositional moderators (self-monitoring and conscientiousness, neuroticism and openness, as well as core self-evaluations and maximizing or satisficing) to predict proactive behavior. For example, the authors hypothesized that individuals who are low in conscientiousness will be likely to display more proactive behavior under situations of high accountability, whereas highly conscientious individuals may be willing to engage in proactive behavior irrespective of the prevalence of accountability. These ideas, although theoretically promising, still await empirical support.

In sum, the focus of research on antecedents of proactive behavior at work to date has been on individual differences, such as proactive personality. In recent times, researchers have begun to investigate the influences of situational characteristics on proactive behavior at work as well as interactions between personality factors and situational characteristics. The nature of work, leadership, and work climate can clearly shape employee proactivity. Future research that focuses on a theory-driven, integrated, and thoroughly longitudinal approach to studying the field of interest will be needed to gain further insights into the complex and possibly reciprocal influences of disposition and situation on proactive behaviors at work.

Outcomes of Proactive Behavior

Although most of the research on employee proactivity focused on antecedents, some research has investigated outcomes of proactive behaviors. Here we focus on individual, team, and organizational-level outcomes. (See also Vol. 1, chap. 10, this handbook.)

Individual-level outcomes of proactivity. Proactive behavior has both conceptually as well as empirically been linked to superior performance. Particularly in uncertain contexts, taking charge of the situation rather than passively waiting to be instructed should have performance benefits (Griffin et al., 2007). Grant, Parker, and Collins (2009) found that proactive individuals were rated more positively in their overall job performance by supervisors, especially if the employees were low in negative affect and high in prosocial motivation. Likewise, employees who engaged in network building and personal initiative were evaluated more favorably by their supervisors ($\beta = .46$, $\beta = .15$, respectively; both $ps < .05$; Thompson, 2005), and employees who engaged in voice were rated higher in individual performance by their supervisors 6 months later ($\beta = .15$, $p < .001$; Van Dyne & LePine, 1998). Individuals who seek feedback should overall perform more highly (Ashford, 1986; Ashford et al., 2003). Consistent with this, in a series of studies, Morrison (1993a, 1993b) found a positive influence of proactive information seeking on individual performance. Specifically, in a sample of accountants who were new to their jobs, higher levels of feedback seeking predicted increased levels of task mastery 3 months later ($\beta = .18$, $p < .05$; Morrison, 1993a). Similarly, in a further sample of accountants, Morrison (1993b) found that information seeking with regard to technical aspects of the job was related with higher levels of job performance as rated by supervisors 3 months later ($r = .18$, $p < .05$). Likewise, in a study of real estate agents, Crant (1995) showed that proactive agents are likely to sell more houses, obtain more listings, and to gain higher commission incomes ($\beta = .31$, $p < .01$).

If supervisor performance is used as the dependent variable, it is important to understand what this relationship actually means. It might be that proactive employees do indeed perform more effectively (and this would certainly make sense). But other processes might play a role as well. For example, proactive employees might be better at managing the supervisory relationship, thereby resulting in higher performance evaluations. For example, in a study of newcomers, Ashford and Black (1996) found that proactive relationship building with the supervisor had a strong relationship with self-rated performance 6 months later ($\beta = .56$, $p < .001$). Similarly, early career employees who actively sought possibilities to be mentored and get into contact with senior colleagues at the beginning of their career were more likely to have a higher income and a higher hierarchical position 2 years later ($\beta = .20$, $p < .05$, for both income and hierarchical position; Blickle, Witzki, & Schneider, 2009). In a related vein, Singh, Ragins, and Tharenou (2009) showed that employees who engaged in career initiative and in skill development were more likely to have acquired a personal mentor at work 1 year later ($\beta = .25$, $p < .05$, for both career initiative and skill development); these findings are again stressing the importance of proactive career behaviors for shaping interpersonal relations to progress within a company.

By being proactive, individuals seem to be able to craft better jobs for themselves and to achieve jobs that represent advances in their career and/or jobs that are satisfying. For example, higher levels of career initiative and individual innovation predicted substantial increases in career satisfaction ($\beta = .36$, $\beta = .37$, respectively; both *ps* $< .01$) and in actual promotions at work ($\beta = .20$, $\beta = .36$, respectively; both *ps* $< .01$) 2 years later (Seibert et al., 2001). Career-oriented proactive behaviors such as seeking several types of information proactively (Morrison, 1993b), feedback seeking, relationship building, and positive framing (Wanberg & Kammeyer-Mueller, 2000) have all been linked to higher levels of job satisfaction. For example, in a study of organizational newcomers, greater employee engagement in different types of information seeking (e.g., technical information) was positively related with a lower intention to leave the organization 3 months later ($r = -.15$, $p < .10$; $r = -.20$, $p < .05$; Morrison, 1993b). Similarly, employees who engaged in proactive coping at work were more likely to report higher levels of positive affect ($\beta = .37$, $p < .001$), which in turn was associated with lower levels of absenteeism ($\beta = -.13$, $p < .05$; Greenglass & Fiksenbaum, 2009).

Some research suggests mechanisms by which these effects occur. Proactive behaviors might lead to a better fit between the job and the individual. Both feedback inquiry and monitoring have been suggested to lead to increased individual adaptation (Ashford, 1986). Job crafting, another form of proactive behavior, has been suggested to be able to alter employees' meaning of work as well as work identity (Wrzesniewski & Dutton, 2001). Empirically, proactive normative information seeking has been positively linked with social integration ($\beta = .20$, $p < .01$; Morrison, 1993a), and the engagement in feedback seeking has been negatively linked with actual turnover 3 months later ($\beta = -.19$, $p < .05$; Wanberg & Kammeyer-Mueller, 2000). Likewise, employees who show personal initiative at work have been found to be also more likely to negotiate more flexible working conditions ($\beta = .10$, $p < .01$) with better development opportunities ($\beta = .13$, $p < .01$; Hornung, Rousseau, & Glaser, 2008). In sum, there is good evidence that engaging in proactive behaviors is related to favorable individual outcomes.

Team-level outcomes of proactivity. Although the vast majority of proactivity research has been conducted at the individual level of analysis, there are some studies that have focused on the team level of analysis. These studies suggest that proactivity is a relevant team-level concept. For example, in a study of 111 work teams across four organizations, Kirkman and Rosen (1999) found that supervisor-rated team proactive behavior was positively related to supervisors' assessments of team customer service ($r = .61$, $p < .001$) and team productivity ($r = .70$, $p < .001$) as well as to team members' aggregated individual assessments of job satisfaction ($r = .23$, $p < .05$), organizational commitment ($r = .40$, $p < .001$), and team commitment ($r = .33$, $p < .01$). The very high correlations of supervisor ratings of team proactivity with team productivity could indicate a halo effect from a supervisor's perspective in that high-performing teams might be automatically viewed as being rather proactive. Given that the results of this study are correlational only, further longitudinal investigations are needed to obtain insights into the causality of the relationships investigated.

In a similar string of research, Hyatt and Ruddy (1997) investigated the relationship between team-level proactivity and team performance in the field of customer service. Team members were asked to report on proactivity on the team level. Team effectiveness was determined by supervisor ratings on the team as well as by objective performance measures over the previous 6 months. Although this partially temporally backward-oriented approach does not warrant causal conclusions, correlational analyses do indicate a relevant positive relationship between team-level proactivity and team effectiveness measured by records of the typical response time to service requests ($r = .24$, $p < .05$) as well as by supervisor ratings of overall team effectiveness ($r = .45$, $p < .05$). In a further study with a team focus, Druskat and Kayes (2000) asked MBA students in short-term, part-time project groups after the completion of their group work to indicate the extent to which their group had engaged in proactive problem solving. Aggregated scores indicated that team-level proactivity positively related to team learning ($\beta = .50$, $p < .01$) as well as to team performance measured by the final mark received on the project as well as by instructor ratings ($\beta = .42$, $p < .05$). In their research on long-term, full-time groups, Tesluk and Mathieu (1999) investigated how road crews manage performance barriers. The researchers used focus groups and interviews to identify ways that crews manage performance barriers, and many of these strategies were highly proactive (e.g., our crew "takes advantage of low-workload times to try to invent new and better ways to do our work" and "tries to experiment with new ways of doing jobs within project specifications"). Crews that used these strategies, as rated by their supervisors, simultaneously indicated lesser situational constraints that interfered with their performance as a team ($r = -.22$, $p < .05$) as well as higher levels of team cohesion ($\beta = .31$, $p < .001$).

In sum, team-level research on proactivity, although adding validity to analyses by drawing on multiple data sources such as self-, supervisor, and peer reports as well as organizational figures, has been conducted using mostly correlational designs. Longitudinal designs will be necessary to draw more secure conclusions. Future research could also usefully investigate how proactivity at the individual level relates to team-level proactivity. For example, in order for a team to act proactively, does it require all team members to be individually proactive or only a certain number of team members? Such processes have not yet been examined.

Organizational-level outcomes of proactivity. Frese and Fay (2001), in their seminal article, suggested that personal initiative, a special type of proactivity at work, predicts performance not only at the individual or the team level but also at the organizational level. They argued that personal initiative "means dealing actively with organizational and individual problems and applying active goals, plans, and feedback. This furthers individual self-development and contributes to organizational success" (p. 165). Consistent with this proposition, studies have shown that small enterprise owners' proactivity is positively related with firm success in Uganda and in East Germany (Koop, de Reu, & Frese, 2000; Zempel, 1999; both cited in Frese & Fay, 2001). In a further study, Frese, Van Gelderen, and Ombach (2000) conducted structured interviews with small-scale firm owners ($N = 80$), investigating their proactive strategies. Responses were numerically coded to reflect different degrees of proactivity. Although proactive business strategies were not necessarily linked with business success, reactive business strategies, the opposite dimension of proactivity, related negatively with the success of the firm measured on the basis of objective profit data ($r = -.26$, $p < .05$) as well as with the business owners' subjective impression on how well their business had developed ($r = -.41$, $p < .01$).

Some studies have focused on organizations' environmentally oriented proactivity. In this vein, research led by Aragón-Correa (1998) found organizational proactivity to predict greater engagement in more modern environmental activities as well as more positive financial performance (Aragón-Correa, Hurtado-Torres, Sharma, & García-Morales, 2008). With a similar focus of investigation, Ramus and Steger (2000) investigated the consequences of organization-level proactivity directed at environmental activities in a sample of mid- to low-level employees working for large European companies. The researchers proposed and found partial support for a relationship between organization-level proactivity, as measured by the extent to which employees indicated their company provided a published environmental policy supporting sustainable actions, and higher individual engagement in environment-related initiatives ($\beta = .37$, $p < .05$). The causality of this relationship awaits further longitudinal support. Moreover, further research could aim to investigate organizational-level proactivity by surveying different organizational stakeholders to capture differing point of views on the proactivity of the corporation in question.

Moderators of outcomes. Proactive behavior might not always lead to positive individual outcomes. Seibert and colleagues (2001) found that employees who voiced many concerns at work were less likely to progress with their salary and to be promoted 2 years later than were their colleagues who voiced fewer concerns. Given that other studies have found proactivity to enhance career outcomes, this study suggests the role of moderators. For example, it might be that voice is not always displayed in an appropriate way, thereby being perceived negatively by supervisors, or perhaps in some situations, voicing concerns might be rather passive behavior, representing complaining with little effort to take charge of the problems or issues oneself.

Most attention in disentangling the contingencies under which proactivity unfolds positive outcomes has been given to psychological moderators. For example, the role of situational judgment, which reflects the degree to which individuals obtain the general ability to make effective judgments or responses to situations, was highlighted by Chan (2006): Individuals who were both highly proactive and high in situational judgment reported significantly higher levels of job satisfaction and organizational commitment and were rated more favorably by their supervisor in terms of job performance. Individuals who were proactive but low in situational judgment, on the other hand, were rated less favorably by their supervisors.

In a similar vein, Grant and colleagues (2009) found values and affect to play an important role in determining whether employees' proactive behaviors are rewarded by supervisors. The authors investigated in two samples of managers versus firefighters the relationship between employee voice, issue selling, taking charge, and anticipatory helping with supervisors' ratings of performance. Employees' proactive behaviors were more likely to lead to favorable performance ratings by supervisors when employees had high levels of prosocial values or low levels of negative affect. Drawing on attribution theory, the authors reasoned that employees' values and affect signal to supervisors the appropriateness to make positive attributions for proactivity. For example, the proactivity of employees with prosocial values is likely to be directed toward benefiting others—coworkers, supervisors, the wider team, and/or the organization—behaviors of interest to supervisors who are responsible for facilitating collective goal achievement. In support of this, Grant and Mayer (2009) found that employees who are both high in prosocial as well as impression management motives were rated highest in terms of their initiative at work by supervisors and colleagues. The researchers concluded that "employees who are both good soldiers *and* good actors are most likely to emerge as good citizens in promoting the status quo" (p. 900).

Moderating effects of proactive behaviors have also been found within the context of socialization into the organization. Erdogan and Bauer (2005) investigated the relationship between dispositional proactivity and career satisfaction as well as job satisfaction. The authors found that the degree of fit between employees with their organization and their job can predict whether proactivity leads to higher satisfaction. For example, among teachers, proactivity led to higher job satisfaction only when these teachers also reported a high fit between themselves and their schools.

Together, these findings suggest the perils of assuming that proactivity will always lead to positive outcomes. As well as situational judgment, prosocial values, and affect, other individual differences might be important moderators on the effects of proactive behavior. Situational influences as well as temporal aspects also need to be considered. For example, Šverko, Galić, Seršić, and Galešić (2008) in their longitudinal study over 27 months suggested that demographical variables such as educational background take on a more dominant role in subsequent employment success among job searchers ($\beta = .27$, $p < .01$) than do proactive job search behaviors ($\beta = .07$, $p < .01$). Finally, Parker, Williams, and Turner (2006) proposed that proactive behavior might be more important in highly uncertain operational environments where it is not possible to prespecify all desired responses (see also Griffin et al., 2007), but this hypothesis has not been examined.

METHODOLOGICAL ISSUES

In this section, we focus on questions that are related to the assessment of proactive behavior at work as well as on questions related to the research design involved in the assessment.

Assessment of Proactive Behavior

Most proactive research to date has focused on self-report, Likert-type measures of proactive behavior at work (e.g., Bateman & Crant, 1993; Parker & Collins, 2008). As with all behaviors, there are the usual challenges associated with asking individuals to self-rate their proactivity, such as social desirability bias. Nevertheless, gauging employee proactivity from other sources such as supervisors or colleagues has its own disadvantages, including egocentric bias as a means of impression management (e.g., supervisors reporting that "of course, their subordinates are proactive") and observational bias (e.g., employees might behave more proactively when they are being observed). A more specific problem is that because proactive behavior can involve questioning directions and challenging accepted practices, it is not always welcomed by supervisors or colleagues and can be assessed negatively by them (Frese, Fay, Hilburger, Leng, & Tag, 1997).

Several solutions have been employed to overcome these challenges of assessing proactive behavior. Frese and colleagues (1997) used a complex interview procedure based on the situational interview technique (Latham & Saari, 1984). The researchers presented the interviewees with hypothetical problems at work and asked them to explain how they would solve these problems. Interviewees' responses were then coded in terms of activeness and the degree of overcoming of barriers, both core parts of the definition of self-initiative at work. The researchers further probed for past examples of self-initiative at work and rated the quantitative and qualitative degree of these instances to arrive at an overall measure for interview-rated self-initiative. These interview ratings were complemented by additional quantitative self-report measures of the employees as well as by spouse ratings of proactivity. Another interview and survey combination was employed by Parker, Williams, and Turner (2006). On the one hand, the researchers investigated two proactive behaviors (proactive idea implementation as well as proactive problem-solving behaviors) by means of a survey. Proactive idea implementation was investigated by asking respondents about the quantity of new ideas related to improvement at work that they had had over the last year, such as saving money or cutting down costs. Answers were scored on the number of ideas mentioned, in conjunction with the criteria on whether they had put this idea forward and whether it was implemented. Proactive problem solving was measured by using context-specific problem scenarios (e.g., dealing with tangled wire). Respondents were asked how they would usually act in these situations and could choose from a list of preset possible answers that varied in their degree of proactivity as previously rated by a group of managers and researchers. The researchers then correlated these survey measures with ratings based on in-depth interviews with a subsample of employees. For example, in interviews, proactive problem prevention was investigated by asking participants about barriers for effectiveness at work and then probing them on how they dealt with this problem while confronting them with several barriers to a solution of the problem. The resulting, significantly positive, correlations between the survey-based measures and the ratings from interviews suggested the former was a valid approach.

A scenario-based approach to measuring proactive behavior was recently introduced by Bledow and Frese (2009). In the Situational Judgment Test of Personal Initiative (SJT-PI), respondents are asked to reveal their most as well as least likely preferences of acting in simulated situations. The actions provided in the survey reflect typical self-initiative-related behaviors across different professions. The SJT-PI was found to be valid, and the results obtained correlated positively with supervisors' ratings of personal initiative ($r = .48$, $p < .01$). This approach, however, aims to assess personal initiative as a dispositional variable—one's stable level of proactivity across lots of situations—rather than Parker, Williams, and Turner's (2006) focus on proactivity within a specific context.

In sum, the assessment of proactive behavior at work so far has varied in terms of approaches that choose self- versus other-report measures of proactive behavior and context-free or context-specific measures. Regarding the former, self-report measures have been found valid (Parker, Williams, & Turner, 2006), so this appears to be a legitimate approach to measuring this type of behavior. Nevertheless, if the study design permits it, a combination of different sources for assessment seems the optimal solution. Regarding the question of whether proactive behavior should be measured in a rather context-specific or context-free way, this depends on whether the focus is proactivity in a particular situation or general proactive personality. One advantage of context-specific approaches is that general statements for proactive behavior such as "I make things happen" might result in less valid answers as a result of social desirability relative to context-specific questions for which socially desirable answers are less obvious (Parker, Williams, & Turner, 2006). On the other hand, context-specific measures are less applicable to other contexts, therefore inhibiting generalized inferences across samples. Highly context-specific measures also require more resources than generalized measures in that they need to be specifically developed prior to the investigation. We recommend a careful choice according to the specific objectives that underlie each investigation.

A further issue regarding the assessment of proactive behavior is the choice of the concrete measure. Sometimes, even though researchers speak of proactive behavior, in fact the construct measured resembles rather a stable disposition or attribute. For example, some studies (e.g., Chiaburu, Marinova, & Lim, 2007; Kirkman & Rosen, 1999) have used the proactive personality scale (Bateman & Crant, 1993) as a proxy for assessing proactive behavior as an outcome. The problem with measuring a stable disposition as an indicator for situation-specific behavior is that differences across situations might not be captured. Similarly, at the team and organizational level, proactivity has been measured either as the aggregation of individual-level behavior or as an attribute rather than as team or organizational behavior. An approach to conceptualizing proactivity at the organizational level was formulated by Shepard, Betz, and O'Connel (1997). The researchers argued that proactive organizations are characterized by engaging in cooperation, participation, and negotiation with stakeholders as well as by directly anticipating potential harm to stakeholders. This approach awaits empirical assessment.

Methodological Approaches

Much research on proactive behavior at work to date has focused on cross-sectional, interindividual approaches to measurement (e.g., Den Hartog & Belschak, 2007; Parker, Williams, & Turner, 2006). Several studies tried to overcome the limitations of such designs by employing rigorous longitudinal designs (e.g., Frese et al., 2007; Parker, 1998). However, one challenge with longitudinal studies is choosing the appropriate time frame. At the moment, little is known about the temporal linkages between antecedents and proactive behavior, such as how long it takes work characteristics to promote or prevent proactive behavior or the time it takes for proactive behavior to unfold and influence well-being or performance. For example, Parker and Ohly (2008) proposed that

> work design can impact on positive affect, which might have a relatively immediate (although perhaps short-lived) effect on job crafting consistent with the broaden-and-build theory (Fredrickson, 2001). However, work design might also affect employees' level of self-esteem or their aspiration . . . , which will likely have longer-term and more enduring consequences on role innovation and job crafting. (p. 266)

A further problem related with some longitudinal studies carried out is that the independent and dependent variables were sometimes not consistently measured and controlled for at all time points (e.g., LePine & Van Dyne, 1998; Seibert et al., 2001). It is important to control for both independent and dependent variables at all measurement time points to be able to partial out the amount of variance caused by the measure of interest over time (see Zapf et al., 1996).

Another challenge when measuring proactive behavior over time lies in its dynamic nature. Proactive behaviors by definition influence the situation. At the same time, situations influence proactive behaviors. For example, employees might engage in job-change negotiation to better fit the job, which might result in higher autonomy that then promotes further proactive behaviors. Methods that allow in-depth investigation of processes, such as intraindividual techniques like diary studies (Fritz & Sonnentag, 2009; Sonnentag, 2003) and laboratory studies (LePine & Van Dyne, 2001; Morrison, 2006; Staw & Boettger, 1990), are fruitful. Qualitative methods that involve a more exploratory approach could also be useful for understanding the processes that underpin proactivity (Dutton et al., 1997, 2001; Howell & Boies, 2004).

We also recommend intervention studies as an especially powerful way to demonstrate causal processes (Parker, Johnson, & Collins, 2006; Raabe, Frese, & Beehr, 2007; Searle, 2008; Yu, Collins, White, Fairbrother, & Cavanagh, 2008). For example, Raabe and colleagues introduced career self-management training. In a four-wave study design, the authors showed that the intervention led to higher levels of active career self-management behaviors through influences in goal commitment ($\beta = .34$, $p < .001$), planning quality ($\beta = .48$, $p < .001$), and knowledge of personal strengths and weaknesses ($\beta = .43$, $p < .001$). Parker, Johnson, and Collins (2006) showed that the introduction of an advanced nursing role during overtime shifts led to more proactive care and taking charge and voice behaviors among junior doctors. Several mechanisms underpinned this finding, such as the presence of an advanced nurse, and increased the self-efficacy of trainee doctors.

A further useful way of reaching more generalizable insights about proactivity is by conducting meta-analyses. Meta-analytic evidence exists for specific types of proactivity at work. For example, Kanfer and colleagues (2001) conducted a meta-analysis on antecedents of proactive job search behaviors comprising 68 independent samples with overall 19,957 participants. However, what is now needed is meta-analytic work on the antecedents of proactive behaviors more generally, for example, by drawing on systematic frameworks summarized earlier in this chapter (e.g., Belschak & Den Hartog, in press; Griffin et al., 2007; Parker & Collins, 2008). Researchers have recently started to engage in this type of more integrated meta-analytic work on proactive behaviors (e.g., Tornau & Kunze, 2008), but such work is currently unpublished. The use of more integrative approaches to proactive research, as discussed in this section of our review, we hope will generate a more complete insight into the nature of proactivity at work.

AN AGENDA FOR FUTURE RESEARCH

We complete our chapter on proactive behavior at work by suggesting some key directions for research in this area, including some of the methodological challenges.

A Process Perspective

Proactivity research has focused on a rather static view on proactive behavior, assuming that being proactive is a single event. The dynamic processes involved in being proactive have thus largely been neglected. Building on earlier conceptual work (Frese & Fay, 2001; Grant & Ashford, 2008), Bindl and Parker (2009) proposed and found initial empirical support for a process model of proactivity. The authors proposed four phases that derived from consideration of action theory (Frese & Zapf, 1994; Hacker, 1985). In the first phase, *envisioning*, individuals set and decide on proactivity-related goals. For example, in the envisioning phase an employee would realize that the way a task is completed is inefficient and identify ways to improve the process of completing this task. The second phase, *planning*, constitutes the preparation aimed at engaging in proactive behavior. For example, employees might go through different scenarios in their mind of how to bring about the desired change. The third phase, *enacting*, is the actual engagement in proactive behavior, as previously investigated in proactivity research, and the fourth phase, *reflecting*, consists of the individuals' efforts to retrospectively think about the success, failure, consequences, or implications of their proactive behavior. Whereas the third phase, enacting, is outward focused and observable, the other three phases are likely to be mostly, even though not necessarily fully, internalized. Bindl and Parker (2009) suggested that the four phases, although logically sequential, will not always be sequential in an applied context. For example, employees might think about ways of improving their tasks, prepare for and engage in behaviors to improve their tasks, and then if the behavior does not appear satisfactory, go back and rethink alternative ways to improve their tasks.

Although Bindl and Parker (2009) showed that different phases of proactive behavior at work can be empirically meaningfully distinguished, future research is needed to investigate the process of employees engaging in these different phases of proactive behavior, including how the process varies for different forms of proactive behavior (see, e.g., Belschak & Den Hartog, in press; Parker & Collins, 2008). Voicing an issue that affects the workplace might represent a more momentary act, whereas the engagement in individual innovation might involve a phase of planning with intense information processes or liaising with experts. How these processes evolve over time is also unclear. For example, Grant and Ashford (2008) proposed that the repeated display of proactive behavior results in more automated processes, with employees then displaying proactive behavior regardless of expected feedback or consequences.

Situational Antecedents

As noted earlier, although researchers have begun to investigate situational variables as predictors of proactive behavior, several issues remain unsolved. For example, there have been contrasting findings on the effects of leadership on proactive behavior, with findings that transformational leadership promotes proactive behavior at work (Belschak & Den Hartog, in press; Rank et al., 2009; Strauss et al., 2008), whereas the effects of supportive supervision are mixed (Axtell et al., 2000; Frese et al., 1999; Ohly et al., 2006; Parker, Williams, & Turner, 2006). Similarly, stressors at work have been found to have either promoting (Fay & Sonnentag, 2002) or inhibiting (Sonnentag, 2003) effects on proactive behavior. Research is needed to further identify under which circumstances situational influences may promote or inhibit proactive behaviors at work. Moreover, because proactive behaviors are both rather interpersonal as well as risky in character, issues such as trust in the supervisor and/or colleagues (e.g., McAllister, 1995), organizational climate (e.g., Baer & Frese, 2003) as well as leader–membership exchange (e.g., Graen & Uhl-Bien, 1995) are likely more important determinants of proactive behavior than hitherto considered.

Benefits Versus Costs

As we noted earlier, the boundary conditions around the outcomes of proactivity have not been fully explored. Grant and Ashford (2008) concluded,

> Insofar as proactive behavior involves expending additional effort, challenging the status quo, and disrupting or deviating from assigned tasks, prescribed roles, reified norms, accepted practices, and existing routines, researchers should expect to find mixed effects and unintended consequences for groups, organizations, and employees themselves. (p. 24)

We advocate more studies of the effects of proactive behavior on employee well-being. For example, Chan (2006) showed that employees who are proactive but lack situational judgment may encounter negative evaluations from supervisors. Such negative evaluations might lower employee well-being. Proactive behaviors may be regarded as an attempt to rock the boat, resulting in negative responses from colleagues and supervisors (Frese & Fay, 2001). How employees cope with negative reactions from their environment related to proactive behaviors and whether proactive behavior might, in certain constellations, decrease rather than increase individual well-being are important avenues of further study.

Synergies and Theoretical Development

As should be clear from our review thus far, proactivity research has emerged from different streams of interest. Theoretically, efforts to understand proactivity have mostly drawn on motivation theory (e.g., Bandura, 1986; Hacker, 1985; Hackman & Oldham, 1976). We join with the call made by prior reviews on proactive behavior (Crant, 2000; Grant & Ashford, 2008) for theoretical advancement on the topic. Theories pertaining to self-identity (e.g., Markus & Nurius, 1986) and social processes (e.g., Tajfel & Turner, 1986), for example, could usefully be applied to the topic of proactive behavior. Additionally, further integration of proactivity research with advances in related fields of research, such as entrepreneurship (e.g., Baron, 2008), innovation (e.g., Scott & Bruce, 1994), and stress management (e.g., proactive coping, Aspinwall & Taylor, 1997) will also help to synthesize and develop knowledge.

CONCLUSION

Proactive behavior at work is a timely and relevant topic for today's work places. With greater decentralization and fast-paced change, it is increasingly important that employees take charge of their careers and their work environments. Such behavior will not always be positive, as our review suggests. But the price of passivity might be even greater than occasional misdirected proactivity. Most importantly, our review suggests that one can shape employee proactivity through designing work structures, leader behaviors, and work climates that foster employees' confidence, activate challenging goals, and promote positive affect. We hope our review will guide researchers and practitioners to gain further insight into proactive behavior at work.

References

Ang, S., Cummings, L. L., Straub, D. W., & Earley, P. C. (1993). The effects of information technology and the perceived mood of the feedback giver on feedback seeking. *Information Systems Research, 4*, 240–261.

Anseel, F., Lievens, F., & Levy, P. E. (2007). A self-motives perspective on feedback-seeking behavior: Linking organizational behavior and social psychology research. *International Journal of Management Reviews, 9*, 211–236.

Aragón-Correa, J. A. (1998). Strategic proactivity and firm approach to the natural environment. *Academy of Management Journal, 41*, 556–567.

Aragón-Correa, J. A., Hurtado-Torres, N., Sharma, S., & García-Morales, V. J. (2008). Environmental strategy and performance in small firms: A resource-based perspective. *Journal of Environmental Management, 86*(1), 88–103.

Ashford, S. J. (1986). Feedback-seeking in individual adaptation: A resource perspective. *Academy of Management Journal, 29*, 465–487.

Ashford, S. J., & Black, J. S. (1996). Proactivity during organizational entry: The role of desire for control. *Journal of Applied Psychology, 81*, 199–214.

Ashford, S. J., Blatt, R., & VandeWalle, D. (2003). Reflections on the looking glass: A review of research on feedback-seeking behavior in organizations. *Journal of Management, 29*, 773–799.

Ashford, S. J., Rothbard, N. P., Piderit, S. K., & Dutton, J. E. (1998). Out on a limb: The role of context and impression management in selling gender-equity issues. *Administrative Science Quarterly, 43*(1), 23–57.

Ashforth, B. E., & Humphrey, R. H. (1995). Emotion in the workplace: A reappraisal. *Human Relations, 48*(2), 97–125.

Aspinwall, L. G., & Taylor, S. E. (1997). A stitch in time: Self-regulation and proactive coping. *Psychological Bulletin, 121*, 417–436.

Axtell, C. M., Holman, D. J., Unsworth, K. L., Wall, T. D., & Waterson, P. E. (2000). Shopfloor innovation: Facilitating the suggestion and implementation of ideas. *Journal of Occupational and Organizational Psychology, 73*, 265–285.

Axtell, C. M., & Parker, S. K. (2003). Promoting role breadth self-efficacy through involvement, work redesign and training. *Human Relations, 56*(1), 113–131.

Baer, M., & Frese, M. (2003). Innovation is not enough: Climates for initiative and psychological safety, process innovations, and firm performance. *Journal of Organizational Behavior, 24,* 45–68.

Bandura, A. (1986). *Social foundations of thought and action: A social cognitive theory.* Englewood Cliffs, NJ: Prentice Hall.

Baron, R. A. (2008). The role of affect in the entrepreneurial process. *Academy of Management Review, 33,* 328–340.

Bateman, T. S., & Crant, J. M. (1993). The proactive component of organizational behavior: A measure and correlates. *Journal of Organizational Behavior, 14,* 103–118.

Belschak, F. D., & Den Hartog, D. N. (in press). Pro-self, pro-social, and pro-organizational foci of proactive behavior: Differential antecedents and consequences. *Journal of Occupational and Organizational Psychology.* Retrieved July 31, 2009, from http://masetto.ingentaselect.co.uk/fstemp/570837d6f3d282161b550d8d953828e9.pdf

Bindl, U. K., & Parker, S. K. (2009, May). *Phases of proactivity: How do we actually go the extra mile?* Paper presented at the European Congress of Work and Organizational Psychology, Santiago de Compostela, Spain.

Binnewies, C., Sonnentag, S., & Mojza, E. J. (2009a). Daily performance at work: Feeling recovered in the morning as a predictor of day-level job performance. *Journal of Organizational Behavior, 30,* 67–93.

Binnewies, C., Sonnentag, S., & Mojza, E. J. (2009b). Feeling recovered and thinking about the good sides of one's work. A longitudinal study on the benefits of non-work experiences for job performance. *Journal of Occupational Health Psychology, 14,* 243–256. Retrieved July 31, 2009, from http://www.phwa.org/resources/research/detail/2269

Binnewies, C., Sonnentag, S., & Mojza, E. J. (in press). Recovery during the weekend and fluctuations in weekly job performance: A week-level study examining intra-individual relations. *Journal of Occupational and Organizational Psychology.*

Bledow, R., & Frese, M. (2009). A situational judgment test of personal initiative and its relationship to performance. *Personnel Psychology, 62,* 229–258.

Blickle, G., Witzki, A., & Schneider, P. B. (2009). Self-initiated mentoring and career success: A predictive field study. *Journal of Vocational Behavior, 74,* 94–101.

Brief, A. P., & Weiss, H. M. (2002). Organizational behavior: Affect in the workplace. *Annual Review of Psychology, 53,* 279–307.

Brockner, J. (1988). *Self-esteem at work: Research, theory, and practice.* Lexington, MA: Lexington Books.

Brown, D. J., Cober, R. T., Kane, K., Levy, P. E., & Shalhoop, J. (2006). Proactive personality and the successful job search: A field investigation with college graduates. *Journal of Applied Psychology, 91,* 717–726.

Burris, E. R., Detert, J. R., & Chiaburu, D. S. (2008). Quitting before leaving: The mediating effects of psychological attachment and detachment on voice. *Journal of Applied Psychology, 93,* 912–922.

Campbell, D. J. (2000). The proactive employee: Managing workplace initiative. *Academy of Management Executive, 14*(3), 52–66.

Carless, S. A., & Bernath, L. (2007). Antecedents of intent to change careers among psychologists. *Journal of Career Development, 33,* 183–200.

Carver, C. S., & Scheier, M. F. (1982). Control theory: A useful conceptual framework for personality-social, clinical, and health psychology. *Psychological Bulletin, 92,* 111–135.

Chan, D. (2006). Interactive effects of situational judgment effectiveness and proactive personality on work perceptions and work outcomes. *Journal of Applied Psychology, 91,* 475–481.

Chiaburu, D. S., Marinova, S. V., & Lim, A. S. (2007). Helping and proactive extra-role behaviors: The influence of motives, goal orientation, and social context. *Personality and Individual Differences, 43,* 2282–2293.

Claes, R., & Ruiz-Quintanilla, S. A. (1998). Influences of early career experiences, occupational group, and national culture on proactive career behavior. *Journal of Vocational Behavior, 52,* 357–378.

Costa, P. T., & McCrae, R. R. (1992). *Revised NEO personality inventory (NEO PI-R) and NEO five factor inventory: Professional manual.* Odessa, FL: Psychological Assessment Resources.

Crant, J. M. (1995). The proactive personality scale and objective job performance among real estate agents. *Journal of Applied Psychology, 80,* 532–537.

Crant, J. M. (2000). Proactive behavior in organizations. *Journal of Management, 26,* 435–462.

Den Hartog, D. N., & Belschak, F. D. (2007). Personal initiative, commitment and affect at work. *Journal of Occupational and Organizational Psychology, 80,* 601–622.

Dorenbosch, L., Van Engen, M. L., & Verhagen, M. (2005). On-the-job innovation: The impact of job design and human resource management through production ownership. *Creativity and Innovation Management, 14*(2), 129–141.

Druskat, V. U., & Kayes, D. C. (2000). Learning versus performance in short-term project teams. *Small Group Research, 31,* 328–353.

Dutton, J. E., & Ashford, S. J. (1993). Selling issues to top management. *Academy of Management Review, 18,* 397–428.

Dutton, J. E., Ashford, S. J., Lawrence, K. A., & Miner-Rubino, K. (2002). Red light, green light: Making sense of the organizational context for issue selling. *Organization Science, 13,* 353–369.

Dutton, J. E., Ashford, S. J., O'Neill, R. M., Hayes, E., & Wierba, E. E. (1997). Reading the wind: How middle managers assess the context for selling issues to top managers. *Strategic Management Journal, 18,* 407–425.

Dutton, J. E., Ashford, S. J., O'Neill, R. M., & Lawrence, K. A. (2001). Moves that matter: Issue selling and organizational change. *Academy of Management Journal, 44,* 716–736.

Dweck, C. S. (1986). Motivational processes affecting learning. *American Psychologist, 41,* 1040–1048.

Eccles, J. S., & Wigfield, A. (2002). Motivational beliefs, values, and goals. *Annual Review of Psychology, 53,* 109–132.

Erdogan, B., & Bauer, T. N. (2005). Enhancing career benefits of employee proactive personality: The role of fit with jobs and organizations. *Personnel Psychology, 58,* 859–891.

Fay, D., & Frese, M. (2000). Conservatives' approach to work: Less prepared for future work demands? *Journal of Applied Social Psychology, 30*(1), 171–195.

Fay, D., & Frese, M. (2001). The concept of personal initiative: An overview of validity studies. *Human Performance, 14,* 97–124.

Fay, D., & Sonnentag, S. (2002). Rethinking the effects of stressors: A longitudinal study on personal initiative. *Journal of Occupational Health Psychology, 7,* 221–234.

Fredrickson, B. L. (1998). What good are positive emotions? *Review of General Psychology, 2,* 300–319.

Fredrickson, B. L. (2001). The role of positive emotions in positive psychology: The broaden-and-build theory of positive emotions. *American Psychologist, 56,* 218–226.

Frese, M. (2008). The word is out: We need an active performance concept for modern workplaces. *Industrial and Organizational Psychology: Perspectives on Science and Practice, 1*(1), 67–69.

Frese, M., & Fay, D. (2001). Personal initiative (PI): An active performance concept for work in the 21st century. *Research in Organizational Behavior, 23,* 133–187.

Frese, M., Fay, D., Hilburger, T., Leng, K., & Tag, A. (1997). The concept of personal initiative: Operationalization, reliability and validity in two German samples. *Journal of Occupational and Organizational Psychology, 70,* 139–161.

Frese, M., Garst, H., & Fay, D. (2007). Making things happen: Reciprocal relationships between work characteristics and personal initiative in a four-wave longitudinal structural equation model. *Journal of Applied Psychology, 92,* 1084–1102.

Frese, M., Kring, W., Soose, A., & Zempel, J. (1996). Personal initiative at work: Differences between East and West Germany. *Academy of Management Journal, 39,* 37–63.

Frese, M., Teng, E., & Wijnen, C. J. D. (1999). Helping to improve suggestion systems: Predictors of making suggestions in companies. *Journal of Organizational Behavior, 20,* 1139–1155.

Frese, M., Van Gelderen, M., & Ombach, M. (2000). How to plan as a small scale business owner: Psychological process characteristics of action strategies and success. *Journal of Small Business Management, 38*(2), 1–18.

Frese, M., & Zapf, D. (1994). Action as the core of work psychology: A German approach. In H. C. Triandis, M. D. Dunnette, & L. M. Hough (Eds.), *Handbook of industrial and organizational psychology* (2nd ed., Vol. 4, pp. 271–340). Palo Alto, CA: Consulting Psychologists Press.

Frijda, N. H. (1986). *The emotions.* Cambridge, England: Cambridge University Press.

Fritz, C., & Sonnentag, S. (2009). Antecedents of day-level proactive behavior: A look at job stressors and positive affect during the workday. *Journal of Management, 35,* 94–111.

Fuller, J. B., Marler, L. E., & Hester, K. (2006). Promoting felt responsibility for constructive change and proactive behavior: Exploring aspects of an elaborated model of work design. *Journal of Organizational Behavior, 27,* 1089–1120.

Gagné, M., & Deci, E. L. (2005). Self-determination theory and work motivation. *Journal of Organizational Behavior, 26,* 331–362.

Graen, G. B., & Uhl-Bien, M. (1995). Relationship-based approach to leadership: Development of leader-member exchange (LMX) theory of leadership over 25 years: Applying a multi-level multi-domain perspective. *Leadership Quarterly, 6,* 219–247.

Grant, A. M., & Ashford, S. J. (2008). The dynamics of proactivity at work. *Research in Organizational Behavior, 28,* 3–34.

Grant, A. M., & Mayer, D. M. (2009). Good soldiers *and* good actors: Prosocial and impression management motives as interactive predictors of affiliative citizenship behaviors. *Journal of Applied Psychology, 94,* 900–912.

Grant, A. M., & Parker, S. K. (2009). Redesigning work design theories: The rise of relational and proactive perspectives. *Academy of Management Annals, 3,* 317–375.

Grant, A. M., Parker, S. K., & Collins, C. G. (2009). Getting credit for proactive behavior: supervisor reactions depend on what you value and how you feel. *Personnel Psychology, 62,* 31–55.

Grant, A. M., & Sumanth, J. J. (2009). Mission possible? The performance of prosocially motivated employees depends on manager trustworthiness. *Journal of Applied Psychology, 94,* 927–944.

Greenglass, E. R., & Fiksenbaum, L. (2009). Proactive coping, positive affect, and well-being. Testing for mediation using path analysis. *European Psychologist, 14*(1), 29–39.

Griffin, M. A., Neal, A., & Parker, S. K. (2007). A new model of work role performance: Positive behavior in uncertain and interdependent contexts. *Academy of Management Journal, 50,* 327–347.

Griffin, M. A., Parker, S. K., & Mason, C. M. (in press). Leader vision and the development of adaptive and proactive performance: A longitudinal study. *Journal of Applied Psychology.*

Hacker, W. (1985). Activity: A fruitful concept in industrial psychology. In M. Frese & J. Sabini (Eds.), *Goal directed behavior: The concept of action in psychology* (pp. 262–283). Hillsdale, NJ: Erlbaum.

Hackman, J. R., & Oldham, G. R. (1976). Motivation through the design of work: Test of a theory. *Organizational Behavior and Human Performance, 16,* 250–279.

Hakanen, J. J., Perhoniemi, R., & Toppinen-Tanner, S. (2008). Positive gain spirals at work: From job resources to work engagement, personal initiative and work-unit innovativeness. *Journal of Vocational Behavior, 73,* 78–91.

Heine, S. J., Markus, H. R., Lehman, D. R., & Kitayana, S. (1999). Is there a universal need for positive self-regard? *Psychological Review, 106,* 766–794.

Hobfoll, S. E. (1989). Conservation of resources: A new attempt at conceptualizing stress. *American Psychologist, 44,* 513–524.

Hobfoll, S. E. (2001). The influence of culture, community, and the nested-self in the stress process: Advancing conservation of resources theory. *Applied Psychology: An International Review 50,* 337–421.

Hofstede, G. (1991). *Cultures and organizations: Software of the mind.* London: McGraw-Hill.

Hornung, S., & Rousseau, D. M. (2007). Active on the job-proactive in change: How autonomy at work contributes to employee support for organizational change. *Journal of Applied Behavioral Science, 43,* 401–426.

Hornung, S., Rousseau, D. M., & Glaser, J. (2008). Creating flexible work arrangements through idiosyncratic deals. *Journal of Applied Psychology, 93,* 655–664.

Howell, J. M., & Boies, K. (2004). Champions of technological innovation: The influence of contextual knowledge, role orientation, idea generation, and idea promotion on champion emergence. *Leadership Quarterly, 15,* 123–143.

Howell, J. M., & Shea, C. M. (2001). Individual differences, environmental scanning, innovation framing, and champion behavior: Key predictors of project performance. *Journal of Product Innovation Management, 18*(1), 15–27.

Hyatt, D. E., & Ruddy, T. M. (1997). An examination of the relationship between work group characteristics and performance: Once more into the breech. *Personnel Psychology, 50,* 553–585.

Ilies, R., & Judge, T. A. (2005). Goal regulation across time: The effects of feedback and affect. *Journal of Applied Psychology, 90,* 453–467.

Isen, A. M. (1999). On the relationship between affect and creative problem solving. In S. W. Russ (Ed.), *Affect, creative experience, and psychological adjustment* (pp. 3–17). Philadelphia: Taylor & Francis.

Isen, A. M., & Baron, R. A. (1991). Positive affect as a factor in organizational behavior. *Research in Organizational Behavior, 13,* 1–53.

Isen, A. M., & Reeve, J. (2005). The influence of positive affect on intrinsic and extrinsic motivation: Facilitating enjoyment of play, responsible work behavior, and self control. *Motivation and Emotion, 29,* 297–325.

Jannsen, O., & Van Yperen, N. W. (2004). Employees' goal orientations, the quality of leader–member exchange, and the outcomes of job performance and job satisfaction. *Academy of Management Journal 47,* 368–384.

Jones, G. R. (1986). Socialization tactics, self-efficacy, and newcomers' adjustments to organizations. *Academy of Management Journal 29,* 262–279.

Kammeyer-Mueller, J. D., & Wanberg, C. R. (2003). Unwrapping the organizational entry process: Disentangling multiple antecedents and their pathways to adjustment. *Journal of Applied Psychology, 88,* 779–794.

Kanfer, R., Wanberg, C. R., & Kantrowitz, T. M. (2001). Job search and employment: A personality-motivational analysis and meta-analytic review. *Journal of Applied Psychology, 86,* 837–855.

Kim, T. Y., & Wang, J. (2008). Proactive personality and newcomer feedback seeking: The moderating roles of supervisor feedback and organizational justice. In M. A. Rahim (Ed.), *Current Topics in Management* (Vol. 13, pp. 91–108). London: Transaction Publishers.

Kirkman, B. L., & Rosen, B. (1999). Beyond self-management: Antecedents and consequences of team empowerment. *Academy of Management Journal, 42,* 58–74.

Koop, S., de Reu, T., & Frese, M. (2000). Sociodemographic factors, entrepreneurial orientation, personal initiative, and environmental problems in Uganda. In M. Frese (Ed.), *Success and failure of microbusiness owners in Africa: A psychological approach* (pp. 55–76). Westport, CT: Quorum Books, with Greenwood Press.

Lambert, T. A., Eby, L. T., & Reeves, M. P. (2006). Predictors of networking intensity and network quality among white-collar job seekers. *Journal of Career Development, 32,* 351–365.

Latham, G. P., & Pinder, C. C. (2005). Work motivation theory and research at the dawn of the twenty-first century. *Annual Review of Psychology, 56,* 485–516.

Latham, G. P., & Saari, I. M. (1984). Do people do what they say? Further studies on the situational interview. *Journal of Applied Psychology, 69,* 569–573.

LePine, J. A., & Van Dyne, L. (1998). Predicting voice behavior in work groups. *Journal of Applied Psychology, 83,* 853–868.

LePine, J. A., & Van Dyne, L. (2001). Voice and cooperative behavior as contrasting forms of contextual performance: Evidence of differential relationships with big five personality characteristics and cognitive ability. *Journal of Applied Psychology, 86,* 326–336.

Locke, E. A., & Latham, G. P. (1990). *A theory of goal setting and task performance.* Englewood Cliffs, NJ: Prentice-Hall.

Locke, E. A., Shaw, K. N., Saari, L. M., & Latham, G. P. (1981). Goal setting and task performance: 1969–1980. *Psychological Bulletin, 90,* 125–152.

Major, D. A., Turner, J. E., & Fletcher, T. D. (2006). Linking proactive personality and the big five to motivation to learn and development activity. *Journal of Applied Psychology, 91,* 927–935.

Markus, H., & Nurius, P. (1986). Possible selves. *American Psychologist, 41,* 954–969.

Martin, L. L., Ward, D. W., Achee, J. W., & Wyer, R. S. (1993). Mood as input: People have to interpret the motivational implications of their moods. *Journal of Personality and Social Psychology, 64,* 317–326.

Maurer, T. J., Weiss, E. M., & Barbeite, F. G. (2003). A model of involvement in work-related learning and development activity: The effects of individual, situational, motivational, and age variables. *Journal of Applied Psychology, 88,* 707–724.

McAllister, D. J. (1995). Affect- and cognition-based trust as foundations for interpersonal cooperation in organizations. *Academy of Management Journal, 38,* 24–59.

McAllister, D. J., Kamdar, D., Morrison, E. W., & Turban, D. B. (2007). Disentangling role perceptions: How perceived role breadth, discretion, instrumentality, and efficacy relate to helping and taking charge. *Journal of Applied Psychology, 92,* 1200–1211.

Mirvis, P. H., & Hall, D. T. (1994). Psychological success and the boundaryless career. *Journal of Organizational Behavior, 15,* 365–380.

Mischel, W., & Shoda, Y. (1995). A cognitive–affective system theory of personality: Reconceptualizing situations, dispositions, dynamics, and invariance in personality structure. *Psychological Review, 102,* 246–268.

Mitchell, T. R., & Daniels, D. (2003). Motivation. In W. C. Borman, D. R. Ilgen, & R. J. Klimoski (Eds.), *Handbook of psychology: Industrial and organizational psychology* (Vol. 12, pp. 225–254). Hoboken, NJ: Wiley.

Morgeson, F. P., & Campion, M., A. (2003). Work design. In W. C. Borman, D. R. Ilgen, & R. J. Klimoski (Eds.), *Handbook of psychology: Industrial and organizational psychology* (Vol. 12, pp. 423–452). Hoboken, NJ: Wiley.

Morrison, E. W. (1993a). Longitudinal study of the effects of information seeking on newcomer socialization. *Journal of Applied Psychology, 78,* 173–183.

Morrison, E. W. (1993b). Newcomer information seeking: Exploring types, modes, sources, and outcomes. *Academy of Management Journal, 36,* 557–589.

Morrison, E. W. (1994). Role definitions and organizational citizenship behavior: The importance of the employee's perspective. *Academy of Management Journal, 37,* 1543–1567.

Morrison, E. W. (2002). Newcomers' relationships: The role of social network ties during socialization. *Academy of Management Journal, 45,* 1149–1160.

Morrison, E. W. (2006). Doing the job well: An investigation of pro-social rule breaking. *Journal of Management, 32,* 5–28.

Morrison, E. W., & Bies, R. J. (1991). Impression management in the feedback-seeking process: A literature review and research agenda. *Academy of Management Review, 16,* 522–541.

Morrison, E. W., & Phelps, C. C. (1999). Taking charge at work: Extrarole efforts to initiate workplace change. *Academy of Management Journal, 42,* 403–419.

Oettingen, G., Mayer, D., Thorpe, J. S., Janetzke, H., & Lorenz, S. (2005). Turning fantasies about positive and negative futures into self-improvement goals. *Motivation and Emotion, 29,* 237–267.

Ohly, S., & Fritz, C. (2007). Challenging the status quo: What motivates proactive behavior? *Journal of Occupational and Organizational Psychology, 80,* 623–629.

Ohly, S., & Fritz, C. (in press). Work characteristics, challenge appraisal, creativity and proactive behavior: A multi-level study. *Journal of Organizational Behavior.*

Ohly, S., Sonnentag, S., & Pluntke, F. (2006). Routinization, work characteristics and their relationships with creative and proactive behaviors. *Journal of Organizational Behavior, 27,* 257–279.

Parker, S. K. (1998). Enhancing role breadth self-efficacy: The roles of job enrichment and other organizational interventions. *Journal of Applied Psychology, 83,* 835–852.

Parker, S. K. (2007, August). *How positive affect can facilitate proactive behavior in the work place.* Paper presented at the annual meeting of the Academy of Management, Philadelphia, PA.

Parker, S. K., & Collins, C. G. (2008). Taking stock: Integrating and differentiating multiple proactive behaviors. *Journal of Management.* Retrieved August 1, 2009, from http://jom.sagepub.com/cgi/content/abstract/0149206308321554v1

Parker, S. K., Collins, C. G., & Grant, A. (2008, April). *The role of positive affect in making things happen.* Paper presented at the Society for Industrial and Organizational Psychology Annual Conference, San Francisco, CA.

Parker, S. K., Johnson, A., & Collins, C. G. (2006, August). *Enhancing proactive patient care: An intervention study.* Paper presented at the annual meeting of the Academy of Management, Atlanta, GA.

Parker, S. K., & Ohly, S. (2008). Designing motivating work. In R. Kanfer, G. Chen, & R. D. Pritchard (Eds.), *Work motivation: Past, present, and future* (pp. 233–384). New York: Routledge.

Parker, S. K., & Sprigg, C. A. (1999). Minimizing strain and maximizing learning: The role of job demands, job control, and proactive personality. *Journal of Applied Psychology, 84,* 925–939.

Parker, S. K., Wall, T. D., & Jackson, P. R. (1997). "That's not my job": Developing flexible employee work orientations. *Academy of Management Journal, 40,* 899–929.

Parker, S. K., Williams, H. M., & Turner, N. (2006). Modeling the antecedents of proactive behavior at work. *Journal of Applied Psychology, 91,* 636–652.

Raabe, B., Frese, M., & Beehr, T. A. (2007). Action regulation theory and career self-management. *Journal of Vocational Behavior, 70,* 297–311.

Rafaeli, A. (2008, June). *Anger in the workplace.* Paper presented at the Institute of Work Psychology International Conference, Sheffield, England.

Ramus, C. A., & Steger, U. (2000). The roles of supervisory support behaviors and environmental policy in employee "ecoinitiatives" at leading-edge European companies. *Academy of Management Journal, 43,* 605–626.

Rank, J., Carsten, J. M., Unger, J. M., & Spector, P. E. (2007). Proactive customer service performance: Relationships with individual, task, and leadership variables. *Human Performance, 20,* 363–390.

Rank, J., Nelson, N. E., Allen, T. D., & Xu, X. (2009). Leadership predictors of innovation and task performance: Subordinates' self-esteem and self-presentation as moderators. *Journal of Occupational and Organizational Psychology, 82,* 465–489.

Rank, J., Pace, V. L., & Frese, M. (2004). Three avenues for future research on creativity, innovation, and initiative. *Applied Psychology: An International Review, 53,* 518–528.

Rousseau, D. M., Ho, V. T., & Greenberg, J. (2006). I-deals: Idiosyncratic terms in employment relationships. *Academy of Management Review, 31,* 977–994.

Russell, J. A. (2003). Core affect and the psychological construction of emotion. *Psychological Review, 110,* 145–172.

Russell, J. A., & Feldman Barrett, L. (1999). Core affect, prototypical emotional episodes, and other things called emotion: Dissecting the elephant. *Journal of Personality and Social Psychology, 76,* 805–819.

Saks, A. M., & Ashforth, B. E. (1996). Proactive socialization and behavioral self-management. *Journal of Vocational Behavior, 48,* 301–323.

Salanova, M., & Schaufeli, W. B. (2008). A cross-national study of work engagement as a mediator between job resources and proactive behaviour. *International Journal of Human Resource Management, 19*(1), 116–131.

Scott, S. G., & Bruce, R. A. (1994). Determinants of innovative behavior: A path model of individual innovation in the workplace. *Academy of Management Journal, 37,* 580–607.

Searle, B. J. (2008). Does personal initiative training work as a stress management intervention? *Journal of Occupational Health Psychology, 13,* 259–270.

Seibert, S. E., Kraimer, M. L., & Crant, J. M. (2001). What do proactive people do? A longitudinal model linking proactive personality and career success. *Personnel Psychology, 54,* 845–874.

Shepard, J. M., Betz, M., & O'Connel, L. (1997). The proactive corporation: Its nature and causes. *Journal of Business Ethics, 16,* 1001–1010.

Simpson, J., et al. (Eds.). (2008). *Oxford English dictionary* (2nd ed.). Retrieved September 24, 2008, from http://www.oed.com/

Singh, R., Ragins, B. R., & Tharenou, P. (2009). Who gets a mentor? A longitudinal assessment of the rising star hypothesis. *Journal of Vocational Behavior, 74,* 11–17.

Sonnentag, S. (2003). Recovery, work engagement, and proactive behavior: A new look at the interface between nonwork and work. *Journal of Applied Psychology, 88,* 518–528.

Speier, C., & Frese, M. (1997). Generalized self-efficacy as a mediator and moderator between control and complexity at work and personal initiative: A longitudinal field study in East Germany. *Human Performance, 10,* 171–192.

Staw, B. M., & Boettger, R. D. (1990). Task revision: A neglected form of work performance. *Academy of Management Journal, 33,* 534–559.

Strauss, K., Griffin, M. A., & Rafferty, A. E. (2008). Proactivity directed toward the team and organization: The role of leadership, commitment and role-breadth self-efficacy. *British Journal of Management.* Retrieved August 1, 2009, from http://www3.interscience.wiley.com/journal/120736723/abstract

Šverko, B., Galić, Z., Seršić, D. M., & Galešić, M. (2008). Unemployed people in search of a job: Reconsidering the role of search behavior. *Journal of Vocational Behavior, 72,* 415–428.

Tajfel, H., & Turner, J. C. (1986). The social identity theory of intergroup behavior. In S. Worchel & W. G. Austin (Eds.), *Psychology of intergroup relations* (2nd ed., pp. 7–24). Chicago: Nelson-Hall.

Tangirala, S., & Ramanujam, R. (2008). Exploring nonlinearity in employee voice: The effects of personal control and organizational identification. *Academy of Management Journal, 51,* 1189–1203.

Tesluk, P. E., & Mathieu, J. E. (1999). Overcoming roadblocks to effectiveness: Incorporating management of performance barriers into models of work group effectiveness. *Journal of Applied Psychology, 84,* 200–217.

Tharenou, P., & Terry, D. J. (1998). Reliability and validity of scores on scales to measure managerial aspirations. *Educational and Psychological Measurement, 58,* 475–492.

Thompson, J. A. (2005). Proactive personality and job performance: A social capital perspective. *Journal of Applied Psychology, 90,* 1011–1017.

Tidwell, M., & Sias, P. (2005). Personality and information seeking: Understanding how traits influence information-seeking behaviors. *Journal of Business Communication, 42*(1), 51–77.

Tornau, K., & Kunze, N. (2008, June). *The nomological network of proactivity: A meta-analytic investigation.* Paper presented at the Institute of Work Psychology International Conference, Sheffield, England.

Tuckey, M., Brewer, N., & Williamson, P. (2002). The influence of motives and goal orientation on feedback seeking. *Journal of Occupational and Organizational Psychology, 75,* 195–216.

Unsworth, K., & Parker, S. K. (2002). Proactivity, creativity, and innovation: Promoting a new workforce for the new workplace. In D. Holman, T. D. Wall, C. W. Clegg, P. Sparrow, & A. Howard (Eds.), *The new workplace: A handbook and guide to the human impact of modern working practices* (pp. 175–196). Chichester, England: Wiley.

VandeWalle, D. (2003). A goal orientation model of feedback-seeking behavior. *Human Resource Management Review, 13,* 581–604.

VandeWalle, D., & Cummings, L. L. (1997). A test of the influence of goal orientation on the feedback-seeking process. *Journal of Applied Psychology, 82,* 390–400.

VandeWalle, D., Ganesan, S., Challagalla, G. N., & Brown, S. P. (2000). An integrated model of feedback-seeking behavior: Disposition, context, and cognition. *Journal of Applied Psychology, 85,* 996–1003.

Van Dyne, L., & LePine, J. A. (1998). Helping and voice extra-role behaviors: Evidence of construct and predictive validity. *Academy of Management Journal, 41,* 108–119.

Van Maanen, J. (1976). Breaking in: Socialization to work. In R. Dubin (Ed.), *Handbook of work, organization and society* (pp. 67–130). Chicago: Rand McNally.

Vroom, V. H. (1964). *Work and motivation.* New York: Wiley.

Wall, T. D., & Jackson, P. R. (1995). New manufacturing initiatives and shopfloor work design. In A. Howard (Ed.), *The changing nature of work* (pp. 139–174). San Francisco: Jossey-Bass.

Wanberg, C. R., & Kammeyer-Mueller, J. D. (2000). Predictors and outcomes of proactivity in the socialization process. *Journal of Applied Psychology, 85,* 373–385.

Warr, P., & Birdi, K. (1998). Employee age and voluntary development activity. *International Journal of Training and Development, 2*(3), 190–204.

Warr, P., & Fay, D. (2001). Short report: Age and personal initiative at work. *European Journal of Work and Organizational Psychology, 10,* 343–353.

Weiss, H. M., & Cropanzano, R. (1996). Affective events theory: A theoretical discussion of the structure, causes and consequences of affective experiences at work. *Research in Organizational Behavior, 18,* 1–74.

Wrzesniewski, A., & Dutton, J. E. (2001). Crafting a job: Revisioning employees as active crafters of their work. *Academy of Management Review, 26,* 179–201.

Xin, K. R. (2004). Asian American managers: An impression gap? An investigation of impression management and supervisor–subordinate relationships. *The Journal of Applied Behavioral Science, 40,* 160–181.

Yu, N., Collins, C. G., White, K., Fairbrother, G., & Cavanagh, M. (2008). Positive coaching with front-line managers: Enhancing their effectiveness and understanding why. *International Coaching Psychology Review, 3*(2), 30–42.

Zapf, D., Dormann, C., & Frese, M. (1996). Longitudinal studies in organizational stress research: A review of the literature with reference to methodological issues. *Journal of Occupational Health Psychology, 1,* 145–169.

Zempel, J. (1999). Selbstaendigkeit in den neuen Bundeslaendern: Praediktoren, Erfolgsfaktoren und Folgen—Ergebnisse einer Laengsschnittuntersuchung [Self-employment in East Germany: Predictors, success factors, and outcomes—Results of a longitudinal study]. In K. Moser, B. Batinic, & J. Zempel (Eds.), *Unternehmerisch erfolgreiches Handeln* (pp. 69–91). Goettingen, Germany: Verlag fuer Angewandte Psychologie.